American Studies

American Studies

An Anthology

Edited by Janice A. Radway, Kevin K. Gaines,
Barry Shank and Penny Von Eschen

A John Wiley & Sons, Ltd., Publication

This edition first published 2009

© 2009 Blackwell Publishing Ltd except for editorial material and organization © 2009 Janice A. Radway, Kevin K. Gaines, Barry Shank and Penny Von Eschen.

Blackwell Publishing was acquired by John Wiley & Sons in February 2007. Blackwell's publishing program has been merged with Wiley's global Scientific, Technical, and Medical business to form Wiley-Blackwell.

Registered Office

John Wiley & Sons Ltd, The Atrium, Southern Gate, Chichester, West Sussex, PO19 8SQ, United Kingdom

Editorial Offices

350 Main Street, Malden, MA 02148-5020, USA

9600 Garsington Road, Oxford, OX4 2DQ, UK

The Atrium, Southern Gate, Chichester, West Sussex, PO19 8SQ, UK

For details of our global editorial offices, for customer services, and for information about how to apply for permission to reuse the copyright material in this book please see our website at www.wiley.com/wiley-blackwell.

The right of Janice A. Radway, Kevin K. Gaines, Barry Shank and Penny Von Eschen to be identified as the authors of the editorial material in this work has been asserted in accordance with the Copyright, Designs and Patents Act 1988.

Wiley also publishes its books in a variety of electronic formats. Some content that appears in print may not be available in electronic books.

Designations used by companies to distinguish their products are often claimed as trademarks. All brand names and product names used in this book are trade names, service marks, trademarks or registered trademarks of their respective owners. The publisher is not associated with any product or vendor mentioned in this book. This publication is designed to provide accurate and authoritative information in regard to the subject matter covered. It is sold on the understanding that the publisher is not engaged in rendering professional services. If professional advice or other expert assistance is required, the services of a competent professional should be sought.

Library of Congress Cataloging-in-Publication Data is available for this title.

9781405113519 (hbk) / 9781405113526 (pbk)

A catalogue record for this book is available from the British Library.

Set in 9.5/11.5pt Minion by Graphicraft Limited, Hong Kong

001   2009

Contents

Notes on the Editors

Kevin Gaines is Director of the Center for Afroamerican and African Studies and Professor of History at the University of Michigan. He is author of *Uplifting the Race: Black Leadership, Politics and Culture During the Twentieth Century* (1996), winner of the John Hope Franklin Book Prize of the American Studies Association, and *American Africans in Ghana: Black Expatriates and the Civil Rights Era* (2006). He was elected president of the American Studies Association in 2008.

Janice Radway is the Walter Dill Scott Professor of Communication and Professor of American Studies and Gender Studies at Northwestern University. She received her PhD in English and American Studies from Michigan State University and is past President of the American Studies Association and former editor of *American Quarterly*. She is the author of *Reading the Romance: Women, Patriarchy, and Popular Literature* (1991) and *A Feeling for Books: The Book-of-the-Month Club, Literary Taste and Middle Class Desire* (1999). She is co-editor (with Carl Kaestle) of Volume 4 of *A History of the Book in America, Print in Motion: The Expansion of Publishing and Reading in the United States, 1880–1940* (2008), and is currently working on a book about girl zines, subjectivity, and the future of feminism in the twenty-first century.

Barry Shank teaches in the Department of Comparative Studies at Ohio State University. He is the author of *Dissonant Identities: The Rock'n'Roll Scene in Austin, Texas* (1994) and *A Token of My Affection: Greeting Cards and American Business Culture* (2004) as well as numerous articles on music, culture, and cultural theory. His current project, "Silence, Noise, Beauty: The Political Agency of Music," features analyses of the music of the Velvet Underground, Yoko Ono, Bob Dylan, Prince, Moby, and Eric Dolphy as it interrogates the specific role that music plays in the shaping of the political.

Penny Von Eschen is Professor of History and American Culture at the University of Michigan. She is the author of *Satchmo Blows Up the World: Jazz Ambassadors Play the Cold War* (2004) and *Race against Empire: Black Americans and Anticolonialism, 1937–1957* (1997). She is co-editor, along with Manisha Sinha, *of Contested Democracy: Freedom, Race, and Power in American History* (2007). She was awarded the Dave Brubeck Institute 2008 Distinguished Achievement Award and co-curated the photography exhibition, "Jam Sessions: America's Jazz Ambassadors Embrace the World" with Curtis Sandberg, Vice-President for the Arts at Meridian International Foundation in Washington, DC. She is currently working on a transnational history of Cold War nostalgia.

Acknowledgments to Sources

Chapter 1: Nikhil Pal Singh, "Rethinking Race and Nation," pp. 20–32, 37–8, 232–6 from *Black is a Country: Race and the Unfinished Struggle for Democracy* (Cambridge MA: Harvard University Press, 2004). © 2004 by the President and Fellows of Harvard College. Reprinted with permission from Harvard University Press.

Chapter 2: Amy Kaplan, "Manifest Domesticity," pp. 26, 28–42, 220–2 from *The Anarchy of Empire in the Making of US Culture* (Cambridge, MA: Harvard University Press, 2002). © 2002 by the President and Fellows of Harvard College. Reprinted with permission from Harvard University Press.

Chapter 3: José David Saldívar, "Nuestra América's Borders: Remapping American Cultural Studies," from Jeffrey Belnap and Raúl Fernández (eds.), *José Martí's "Our America": From National to Hemispheric Cultural Studies* (Durham, NC: Duke University Press, 1998), pp. 145–54, 170–3, 175. © 1998 by Duke University Press. All rights reserved. Used by permission of the publisher.

Chapter 4: Brent Hayes Edwards, "Prologue", pp. 1–9, 11–15, 321–5 from *The Practice of Diaspora: Literature, Translation, and the Rise of Black Internationalism* (Cambridge, MA: Harvard University Press, 2003). © 2003 by the President and Fellows of Harvard College. Reprinted with permission from Harvard University Press.

Chapter 5: Tiya Miles, "Removal," pp. 149–61, 254–6 from *Ties that Bind: The Story of an Afro-Cherokee Family in Slavery and Freedom* (Berkeley, CA: University of

California Press, 2005). © 2005 by the Regents of the University of California. Reprinted by permission of the author and University of California Press.

Chapter 6: Yoko Fukumura and Martha Matsuoka, "Redefining Security: Okinawa Women's Resistance to U.S. Militarism," pp. 239–41, 246–9, 251–4, 257–61, 287, 292–3, 297–9, 302, 307, 310, 312, 316, 318 from Nancy Naples and Manisha Desai (eds.), *Women's Activism and Globalism: Linking Local Struggles and Transnational Politics* (New York: Routledge, 2002). © 2002 by Taylor & Francis Group LLC – Books. Reproduced with permission of Taylor & Francis Group LLC – Books, in the format Textbook via Copyright Clearance Center.

Chapter 7: Laura Doyle, "Introduction," pp. 1–5, 6–17 from *Freedom's Empire: Race and the Rise of the Novel in Atlantic Modernity* (Durham, NC: Duke University Press, 2008). © 2008 by Duke University Press. All rights reserved. Used by permission of the publisher.

Chapter 8: Mae M. Ngai, "The Johnson-Reed Act of 1924 and the Reconstruction of Race in Immigration Law," pp. 21–7, 29–37, 282–5 from *Impossible Subjects: Illegal Aliens and the Making of Modern America* (Princeton, NJ: Princeton University Press, 2004). © 2004 by Princeton University Press. Reprinted with permission from Princeton University Press.

Chapter 9: Leti Volpp, "The Citizen and the Terrorist," pp. 1575–82, 1584–99 from *UCLA Law Review* 49 (June

2002). © 2002 by Leti Volpp. Reprinted with permission from the author.

Chapter 10: Peggy Pascoe, "Race, Gender, and the Privileges of Property," pp. 215–30 from Valerie Matsuomota and Blake Allmendinger (eds.), *Over the Edge: Remapping the American West* (Berkeley, CA: University of California Press, 1999. © 1999 by the Regents of the University of California. Reprinted by permission of the author and University of California Press.

Chapter 11: Moustafa Bayoumi, "Racing Religion," pp. 267–93 from *The New Centennial Review* 6:2 (Fall 2006). © 2006 by New Centennial Review. Reprinted with permission from Michigan State University Press.

Chapter 12: Lauren Berlant, "Introduction: The Intimate Public Sphere," pp. 1–10, 15–20, 262–4, 266, 289–302 from *The Queen of America Goes to Washington City: Essays on Sex and Citizenship* (Durham, NC: Duke University Press, 1997). © 1997 by Duke University Press. All rights reserved. Used by permission of the publisher.

Chapter 13: Christopher Newfield, "Democratic Passions: Reconstructing Individual Agency," pp. 314–25, 329–44 from Russ Castronovo and Dana Nelson (eds.), *Materializing Democracy: Towards a Revitalized Cultural Politics* (Durham NC: Duke University Press, 2002). © 2002 by Duke University Press. All rights reserved. Used by permission of the publisher.

Chapter 14: Susan Lee Johnson, "Domestic Life in the Diggings," pp. 99–113, 118–19, 121–3, 125–8, 138–9, 368–75 from *Roaring Camp: The Social World of the California Gold Rush* (New York: Norton, 2000). © 2000 by Susan Lee Johnson. Reprinted by permission of W. W. Norton & Company, Inc.

Chapter 15: Jennifer L. Morgan, " 'Women's Sweat': Gender and Agricultural Labor in the Atlantic World," pp. 144–54, 156–8, 161–5, 237–42 from *Laboring Women: Reproduction and Gender in New World Slavery* (Philadelphia, PA: University of Pennsylvania Press, 2004). © 2004 by University of Pennsylvania Press. Reprinted with permission from the University of Pennsylvania Press.

Chapter 16: Nan Enstad, "Fashioning Political Subjectivities: The 1909 Shirtwaist Strike and the 'Rational Girl Striker'," pp. 84–6, 88–101, 103–9, 111–12, 116, 118, 227–33 from *Ladies of Labor, Girls of Adventure: Working Women, Popular Culture and Labor Politics at the Turn of the Twentieth Century* (New York: Columbia University Press, 1999).

Chapter 17: Michael Denning, "The Age of the CIO," pp. 21–38, 479–82 from *The Cultural Front: The Laboring of American Culture in the Twentieth Century* (London and New York: Verso Books, 1996). © 1996 by Verso Books. Reprinted with permission of Verso.

Chapter 18: Lisa Lowe, "Work, Immigration, Gender: New Subjects of Cultural Politics," pp. 354–74 from Lisa Lowe and David Lloyd (eds.), *The Politics of Culture in the Shadow of Capital* (Durham, NC: Duke University Press, 1997). © 1997 by Duke University Press. All rights reserved. Used by permission of the publisher.

Chapter 19: Saskia Sassen, "Global Cities and Survival Circuits," pp. 255–6, 260–74, 310–16 from Barbara Ehrenreich and Arlie Russell Hochschild (eds.), *Global Woman: Nannies, Maids, and Sex Workers in the New Economy* (New York: Metropolitan Books, 2003). © 2002 by Saskia Sassen. Reprinted with permission from the author.

Chapter 20: Robert A. Orsi, "Snakes Alive: Religious Studies between Heaven and Earth," pp. 177–84, 186–9, 191–204, 237–9 from *Between Heaven and Earth: The Religious Worlds People Make and the Scholars Who Study Them* (Princeton, NJ: Princeton University Press, 2005). © 2005 by Princeton University Press. Reprinted with permission from Princeton University Press.

Chapter 21: Leigh Eric Schmidt, "From Demon Possession to Magic Show: Ventriloquism, Religion, and the Enlightenment," pp. 274–90, 292–8, 301–4 from *Church History* 67:2 (June 1998). © 1998 by the American Society of Church History. Reprinted with permission from the American Society of Church History.

Chapter 22: Evelyn Brooks Higginbotham, "Rethinking Vernacular Culture: Black Religion and Race Records in the 1920s and 1930s," pp. 157–77 from Wahneema Lubiano (ed.), *The House that Race Built* (New York: Vintage 1997). © 1997 by Wahneema Lubiano. Used by permission of Pantheon Books, a division of Random House, Inc.

Chapter 23: Elizabeth McAlister, "The Madonna of 115th Street Revisited: Vodou and Haitian Catholicism in the Age of Transnationalism," pp. 123–40, 145–52, 154–60 from R. Stephen Warner and Judith G. Wittner (eds.), *Gatherings in Diaspora: Religious Communities and the New Immigration* (Philadelphia, PA: Temple University Press, 1998). © 1998 by Temple University. All rights reserved. Reprinted with permission from Temple University Press.

Chapter 24: Melani McAlister, "The Good Fight: Israel after Vietnam, 1972–1980," pp. 155–9, 165–70, 175–87, 192–7, 303–9, 363, 365–6, 368, 370–2, 375–86 from *Epic Encounters: Culture, Media, and US Interests in the Middle East, 1945–2000* (Berkeley, CA: University of California Press, 2001). © 2005 by the Regents of the University of California. Reprinted by permission of the author and University of California Press.

Chapter 25: Janet R. Jakobsen and Ann Pellegrini, "Getting Religion," pp. 101–14 from Marjorie Garber and Rebecca Walkowitz (eds.), *One Nation Under God?: Religion and American Culture* (New York: Routledge, 1999). © 1999 by Taylor & Francis Group LLC – Books. Reproduced with permission of Taylor & Francis Group LLC – Books, in the format Textbook via Copyright Clearance Center.

Chapter 26: Richard M. Ohmann, "The Origins of Mass Culture," pp. 12–14, 16, 18–29, 366–7 from *Selling Culture: Magazines, Markets and Class at the Turn of the Century* (London and New York: Verso, 1996). © 1996 by Verso Books. Reprinted with permission from Verso.

Chapter 27: Robin D. G. Kelley, "The Riddle of the Zoot: Malcolm Little and Black Cultural Politics during World War II," pp. 163–81, 281–7 from *Race Rebels: Culture, Politics and the Black Working Class* (New York: Free Press, 1994). Revised version of original essay published in Joe Wood (ed.), *Malcolm X: In Our Own Image* (New York: St. Martin's Press, 1992). © 1994 by Robin D. G. Kelley. Reprinted with the permission of the author and The Free Press, a Division of Simon & Schuster, Inc.

Chapter 28: George Lipsitz, "Mardi Gras Indians: Carnival and Counter-Narrative in Black New Orleans," pp. 99–121 from *Cultural Critique* 10 (Fall 1988). Republished in *Time Passages: Collective Memory and American Popular Culture* (Minneapolis, MN: University of Minnesota Press, 1990), pp. 233–43, 245–50, 252–3, 288–90. © 1988 by the Regents of the University of Minnesota. Reprinted with permission from University of Minnesota Press.

Chapter 29: Sunaina Marr Maira, "To Be Young, Brown, and Hip: Race, Gender, and Sexuality in Indian American Youth Culture," pp. 29–30, 34–5, 39, 42, 44–6, 48–50, 57–9, 65–6, 69–70, 72, 74–5, 217–23, 226–31, 233–7 from *Desis in the House: Indian American Youth Culture in New York City* (Philadelphia, PA: Temple University Press, 2002). © 2002 by Temple University. All rights reserved. Reprinted with permission from Temple University Press.

Chapter 30: David Román, "Teatro Viva! Latino Performance and the Politics of AIDS in Los Angeles," pp. 184–201, 305–7 from Emile Bergmann and Paul Julian Smith (eds.), *Entiendes? Queer Readings/Hispanic Writings* (Durham, NC: Duke University Press, 1995). © 1995 by Duke University Press. All rights reserved. Used by permission of the publisher.

Chapter 31: Takayuki Tatsumi, "Waiting for Godzilla: Toward a Globalist Theme Park," pp. 176–84, 221, 223–9, 231, 233 from *Full Metal Apache: Transactions between Cyberpunk Japan and Avant-Pop America* (Durham, NC: Duke University Press, 2006). © 2006 by Duke University Press. All rights reserved. Used by permission of the publisher.

Chapter 32: Eva Cherniavsky, "Hollywood's Hot Voodoo," pp. 71–90, 96–9, 169–171, 174–7 from *Incorporations: Race, Nation, and the Body Politics of Capital* (Minneapolis, MN: University of Minnesota Press, 2006). © 2006 by the Regents of the University of Minnesota. Reprinted with permission from University of Minnesota Press.

Chapter 33: Walter Johnson, "Turning People into Products," pp. 117–34, 249–54 from *Soul by Soul: Life inside the Antebellum Slave Market* (Cambridge, MA: Harvard University Press, 1999). © 1999 by the President and Fellows of Harvard College. Reprinted with permission from Harvard University Press.

Chapter 34: Saidiya V. Hartman, "Redressing the Pained Body: Toward a Theory of Practice," pp. 49–59, 61, 64–5, 215–19 from *Scenes of Subjection: Terror, Slavery and Self-Making in Nineteenth Century America* (New York: Oxford University Press, 1997). © 1997 by Oxford University Press, Inc. Reprinted with permission from Oxford University Press, Inc.

Chapter 35: Nayan Shah, "Between 'Oriental Depravity' and 'Natural Degenerates': Spatial Borderlands and the Making of Ordinary Americans," pp. 703–14, 717–25 from *American Quarterly* 57:3 (October 2005). © 2005 by The American Studies Association. Reprinted with permission from The Johns Hopkins University Press.

Chapter 36: Lennard J. Davis, "The Rule of Normalcy: Politics and Disability in the USA [United States of Ability]," pp. 102–18, 181–3 from *Bending Over Backwards: Disability, Dismodernism and Other Difficult Positions* (New York: New York University Press, 2002). Originally published as "The Rule of Normalcy: Politics and Disability in the USA [United States of Disability]," in M. Jones and Lee Ann Marks (eds.), *Disability, Diversability, and Legal Change* (London: Kluwer, 1999), pp. 35–47. © 1999 by Lennard J. Davis. Reprinted by permission of the author.

Chapter 37: Virginia L. Blum, "The Patient's Body," pp. 11–26 from *Flesh Wounds: The Culture of Cosmetic Surgery* (Berkeley, CA: University of California Press, 2003). © 2003 by the Regents of the University of California. Reprinted by permission of the author and University of California Press.

Chapter 38: Mimi Nguyen, "Queer Cyborgs and New Mutants: Race, Sexuality, and Prosthetic Sociality in Digital Space," pp. 281–95, 300–5 from Rachel C. Lee and Sau-ling Cynthia Wong (eds.), *Asian America. Net: Ethnicity, Nationalism, and Cyberspace* (New York: Routledge, 2003). © 2003 by Taylor & Francis Group LLC – Books. Reproduced with permission of Taylor & Francis Group LLC – Books, in the format Textbook via Copyright Clearance Center.

Chapter 39: Laurel Thatcher Ulrich, "Two Spinning Wheels in an Old Log House," pp. 76–9, 83–93, 95–105, 433–9 from *The Age of Homespun* (New York: Alfred A. Knopf Books, 2001). © 2001 by Laurel Thatcher Ulrich. Used by permission of Alfred A. Knopf, a division of Random House, Inc.

Chapter 40: Michael Warner, "The Cultural Mediation of the Print Medium," pp. 1–5, 19–26, 30–3 and notes from *Letters of the Republic: Publication and the Public Sphere in Eighteenth-century America* (Cambridge, MA: Harvard University Press, 1990). © 1990 by the President and Fellows of Harvard College. Reprinted with permission from Harvard University Press.

Chapter 41: Alan Trachtenberg, "Likeness as Identity: Reflections on the Daguerrean Mystique," pp. 173, 178–92, 219–20 from Graham Clarke (ed.), *The Portrait in Photography* (London: Reaktion Books, 1992). © 1992 by Reaktion Books. Reprinted with permission from Reaktion Books.

Chapter 42: Philip Deloria, "Technology: 'I Want to Ride in Geronimo's Cadillac'," pp. 136, 138–41, 143–56, 163–8, 266–73 from *Indians in Unexpected Places* (Lawrence: University Press of Kansas, 2004). © 2004 by the University Press of Kansas. Reprinted with permission of the University Press of Kansas.

Chapter 43: Sarah E. Chinn, "Reading the 'Book of Life': DNA and the Meanings of Identity," pp. 141–8, 150–2, 162–7, 212–16, 218–19, 221, 223–5 from *Technology and the Logic of American Racism: A Cultural History of the Body as Evidence* (New York: Continuum, 2000). © 2000 by Sarah E. Chinn. By kind permission of Continuum.

Chapter 44: Herman S. Gray, "Television and the Politics of Difference," pp. 89, 96–113, 207–12 from *Cultural Moves: African Americans and the Politics of Representation* (Berkeley, CA: University of California Press, 2005). © 2005 by the Regents of the University of California. Reprinted by permission of the author and University of California Press.

Chapter 45: Amy Kaplan, "Where is Guantánamo?," pp. 831–45, 851–8 from *American Quarterly* 57:3 (October 2005). © 2005 by The American Studies Association. Reprinted with permission from The Johns Hopkins University Press.

Chapter 46: Richard White, "Knowing Nature through Labor: Energy, Salmon Society on the Columbia," pp. 3–9, 12–16, 22–4 from *The Organic Machine: The Remaking of the Columbia River* (New York: Hill and Wang, 1995). © 1995 by Richard White. Reprinted with permission from the author.

Chapter 47: Laura Pulido, "Rethinking Environmental Racism: White Privilege and Urban Development in Southern California," pp. 12–20, 34–40 from *Annals of the Association of American Geographers* 90:1 (March 2000). © 2000 by Association of American Geographers. Reprinted with permission from Blackwell Publishing.

Chapter 48: Lizabeth Cohen, "Commerce: Reconfiguring Community Marketplaces," pp. 257–9, 261–7, 274–8,

282–3, 484–8, 490–2, 494 from *A Consumers' Republic: The Politics of Mass Consumption in Postwar America* (New York: Knopf, 2003). © 2003 by Lizabeth Cohen. Used by permission of Alfred A. Knopf, a division of Random House, Inc.

Chapter 49: Ruth Wilson Gilmore, "The Prison Fix," pp. 88–102 and references from *Golden Gulag: Prisons, Surplus, Crisis, and Opposition in Globalizing California* (Berkeley: University of California Press, 2007). © 2007 by the Regents of the University of California. Reprinted by permission of the author and University of California Press.

Chapter 50: George Yúdice, "The Globalization of Latin America: Miami," pp. 192–7, 198–213 and references from *The Expediency of Culture: Uses of Culture in the Global Era* (Durham, NC: Duke University Press, 2003). © 2003 by Duke University Press. All rights reserved. Used by permission of the publisher.

Chapter 51: Clyde Woods, "Do You Know What it Means to Miss New Orleans?: Katrina, Trap Economics, and the Rebirth of the Blues," pp. 1005–18 from *American Quarterly* 57:4 (December 2005). © 2005 by The American Studies Association. Reprinted with permission from The Johns Hopkins University Press.

Chapter 52: Avery Gordon, "Not Only the Footprints But the Water Too and What is Down There," pp. 143–51, 169–79, 183–4, 226, 228–34, 237, 239–41 from *Ghostly Matters: Haunting and the Sociological Imagination* (Minneapolis, MN: University of Minnesota Press, 1997). © 1997 by the Regents of the University of Minnesota. Reprinted with permission from University of Minnesota Press.

Chapter 53: David Blight, "The Lost Cause and Causes Not Lost," pp. 258–64, 272–9, 281–4, 451–8 from *Race and Reunion: The Civil War in American Memory* (Cambridge, MA: Harvard University Press, 2001). © 2001 by the President and Fellows of Harvard College. Reprinted with permission from Harvard University Press.

Chapter 54: Marita Sturken, "The Wall and the Screen Memory," pp. 44–8, 50–1, 58–63, 72–81, 268, 271–2, 275–7 from *Tangled Memories: The Vietnam War, the AIDS Epidemic, and the Politics of Remembering* (Berkeley, CA: University of California Press, 1997). © 1997 by the Regents of the University of California. Reprinted by permission of the University of California Press.

Chapter 55: Donald E. Pease, "The Patriot Acts," pp. 29–43 from *Boundary 2* 29:2 (2002). © 2002 by Duke University Press. All rights reserved. Used by permission of the publisher.

Chapter 56: Michel-Rolph Trouillot, pp. 19–20, 22–30, 75–8, 80–3, 87–9, 95–105 from *Silencing the Past: Power and the Production of History* (Boston, MA: Beacon Press, 1995). © 1995 by Michel-Rolph Trouillot. Reprinted with permission from Beacon Press, Boston.

Chapter 57: Liam Kennedy, "Spectres of Comparison: American Studies and the United States of the West," pp. 135–49 from *Comparative American Studies* 4:2 (2006). © 2006 Sage Publications (London, Thousand Oaks, CA and New Delhi). Reprinted with permission from Sage Publications Ltd.

Chapter 58: Robyn Wiegman, "Romancing the Future: Internationalization as Symptom and Wish," unpublished manuscript pp. 1–30.

Chapter 59: Donatella Izzo, "Outside Where? Comparing Notes on Comparative American Studies and American Comparative Studies," unpublished manuscript pp. 1–25.

Introduction

Although the field of American Studies is still a relatively young one, it has expanded and changed rapidly since the late 1970s in response to a range of social, cultural, and intellectual developments. The extent of the field's expansion can be seen in the increasing size of the US-based American Studies Association's membership list and in the growth of the program for its annual conference. In addition, a number of international associations for American Studies have increased their memberships and expanded the already significant role they play in the publication of research about the United States, the Americas, and the relationship of both to the rest of the world.

As the field of American Studies has expanded, so has it changed. Indeed the change has been so extensive that lively debates are now carried out among scholars about the character, sources, and consequences of that change. There is even debate about when the field began its reconfiguration and whether that reconfiguration has done enough to affect the dominance of what is now sometimes called *American* American Studies. As a consequence, it is a distinct challenge to summarize succinctly the nature of the intellectual reformulations that began to alter American Studies at least as far back as the mid-1970s. Still, there is some sense that the field has been substantially affected by the growth of race-based scholarship and ethnic studies; by the development of feminist intellectual inquiry and research on sexuality; by efforts to understand the United States as part of an international, global system; and by burgeoning interest in previously neglected cultural forms, everyday life and the incompletely explored archives in which their history rests.

As a consequence of these changes, a number of initiatives, projects, conferences, and symposia have been designed in recent years to take stock of the field and to chart its likely future. These include such things as the annual symposium held at Dartmouth College called "Futures of American Studies" and its accompanying volumes; *The Encyclopedia of American Studies* edited by Miles Orville, Johnella Butler, and Jay Mechling; conferences organized by the International American Studies Association; the journal *Comparative American Studies*; and the semi-annual Maple Leaf and Eagle conference in Finland. These events are, in effect, a slightly more institutionalized version of the broad-based intellectual ferment that has led to the proliferation and transformation of courses in American Studies at many different sites around the globe. These developments suggest that, however extensive the nature of the ferment, scholars in the field are looking for ways to make sense of the field's recent history and to understand how that history relates to earlier periods in its past. At the same time, American Studies scholars are eager to map the ongoing processes of reconfiguration.

We want to highlight the importance of the fact that this reconfiguration is ongoing and being actively pursued from many different quarters even as we go to press with this volume. It is important to acknowledge as well that our own efforts to map this changing field ought to be approached as contingent and fluid. We have selected the essays collected here because we believe they represent key intellectual trends and research practices in the field as it has evolved in recent years. At the same time, we have organized them and grouped them categorically in a way that we hope helps to make sense of the myriad theoretical, historical, political, and methodological questions that have animated research in the field and altered the way its critical concerns are regularly articulated. We will explain our organizational scheme more fully below, but here we want to urge our readers and all who might make use of this book in and outside of the classroom to remember that any effort to organize, summarize, or map a field through the process of anthologization, however self-consciously its schemas are offered, cannot avoid appearing to fix what is in fact a complex social process with a long history, a contested and ever-changing present, and an as yet unsecured future. We offer this volume of essays, then, as another intervention in the history of our field's formation in the hope that the extraordinary work collected here will be further discussed, debated, and assessed for the ways in which it engages the past history of American Studies anew and demands of it an altered future.

Although we cannot specify, as Virginia Woolf once did, that on or about a certain date the world changed irrevocably, we suggest in *American Studies: An Anthology* that the field of American Studies has been substantially altered by a concatenation of political, economic, and cultural changes that have taken place around the world since the end of World War II. While it is often said that American Studies first developed institutionally as a manifestation of Cold War politics, we want to note that this history has been contested in recent years and that the Cold War itself was not the only political formation to emerge in the post-war world. Other developments, including the independence movements that emerged in Africa, South and Southeast Asia, and Latin America, substantially affected global political relations. These developments, whose combined effects first emerged with notable force in the 1960s and 1970s, substantially challenged the hegemony of the United States both within and beyond its borders and in a manner that was at once political and intellectual. As these relatively autonomous developments, each with its own history and trajectory, interacted and played out, it became more and more difficult for students of the United States to understand its history with the conceptual tools and analytic frameworks born of earlier moments. Chief among these changes, we believe, were the anticolonial independence projects of the immediate postwar period; the new social and political movements of the 1960s that oftentimes drew their inspiration from those projects; and a fundamental economic restructuring that transformed the global economy and produced extensive migration of peoples from place to place. Not only did these changes substantially alter economic, political, and cultural relations around the globe; they also transformed basic political and intellectual vocabularies for making sense of those relations. Most significantly, the assumption of American exceptionalism – the claim that the American experiment was an unprecedented model for social and political relations – that had supported a significant portion of early American studies scholarship no longer seemed tenable.

American Studies: An Anthology pays significant attention to the impact of the changing global economy on the perceived legitimacy of the United States and concomitantly on the intellectual project known as American Studies. However, the volume also foregrounds our strong sense that the impact of changed and changing economic relations was registered initially and most intensely within the field of American Studies when alternative knowledge projects were generated by anticolonial independence movements and by the new social movements of the 1960s. Although we believe that these were related in complex ways to the generation of what is now often called the post-Fordist economy, we also believe that these political and social movements were generated by complex, multi-focal aims and that they exhibited a certain autonomy from the economic arrangements within which they were embedded. In other words, while we attend here to recent theoretical accounts attempting to link what has variously been called late capitalism, postmodern capitalism, post-Fordism, transnational capitalism, and neocolonial capitalism to changing political movements and intellectual frameworks around the globe, we do not wish to provide a monocausal explanation for the recent intellectual ferment in American Studies. Rather, we register the complex ways in which American Studies as a field has been reconfigured and reshaped by these shifting economic relations and, *equally and autonomously*, by contestatory knowledge projects originating in social and political movements that conceived themselves in part in opposition to older understandings of the American nation. We showcase here the myriad ways in which the American nation has been debated, reformulated, and reconceived in recent years in response to these intersecting economic, social, and political developments.

Since the late 1990s, presidential addresses to the US-based American Studies Association membership have acknowledged the impact of the social and political movements of the 1960s on the field of American Studies. Often grouping these movements and the intellectual projects that they generated under the rubric of multiculturalism, the Association's presidents have collectively given voice to the widespread sense that it was the Civil Rights movement, the women's movement, the American Indian movement, the Chicano movement, the gay rights movement and a number of other movements that first began to alter scholarship in the field. They did so because these movements were never simply political movements alone. In their desire to contest familiar power arrangements that worked to disadvantage particular groups of people, these movements began to generate alternative knowledge that did not repeat traditional stereotypes and assumptions. Intellectuals in the various movements worked to provide a contestatory account of the beliefs and ideologies that justified the exploitation, subordination, demonization, incarceration, and even exclusion of specific populations. In addition, they sought to demonstrate who benefited from these practices of subordination and how they did so. Finally, they sought to generate counter-hegemonic accounts of the history of minority populations, in part to lay claim to their central role in democratic struggles over the meaning of the American nation. Initially, this produced an historically oriented recovery effort seeking to unearth the forgotten, lost, repressed, and discounted efforts of those who, despite their labor, had been officially defined by a range of national practices, and institutional forms as lesser Americans.

This collection of intellectual desires generated a raft of early work in the disciplines that traditionally constituted American Studies, that is, within history and literary studies as well as in folklore, art history, cinema studies, communication studies, sociology, and anthropology. Much of this work sought to enlarge our understanding of the American population and to challenge the semi-official narratives familiarly inscribed in high-school and college history textbooks. Influential books explored the world the slaves and freed people made, detailed the particulars of women's separate sphere, recovered the histories of millworkers, railroad laborers, and steelworkers, and searched dusty attics and archives as well as dimly lit libraries and secondhand bookstores for the literary and artistic efforts of those with only limited access to the traditional means of intellectual production. As these recovery efforts succeeded over time, they produced new sets of questions, preoccupations, and research agendas. Intellectuals associated with or inspired by the political movements of the 1960s began to ask how the individuals whose work they unearthed had conceptualized their situation. They wondered how they had maintained a sense of self and a vigorous

community in the face of discrimination and degradation. They asked how these people told their own histories differently and they wondered how they related to a nation whose very borders and boundaries were often predicated on their exclusion and exploitation.

In response to such questions, a body of scholarship emerged through the 1970s, 1980s, and 1990s that explored alternative ways of making sense of American history, including the history of American Studies itself. In effect, this body of writing articulated new grids of intelligibility for making sense of the American experiment by focusing on different principal actors, different signal events, and different chronologies from those that had dominated traditional Americanist narratives. The familiar American pantheon that included people like Jefferson, Adams, Lincoln, Hawthorne, Melville, and James was enlarged and transformed by the addition of intellectuals like Margaret Fuller, Frederick Douglass, W. E. B. Du Bois, Jose Martí, Marcus Garvey, Anzia Yezierska, and Abraham Cahan. Soon, it could be argued that American Studies as an intellectual pursuit had emerged much earlier than the Cold War and that its early history was bound up with left cultural critique in the United States. Equally as important, however, new historical narratives focused not only on the writings of insurgent elites but sought as well to uncover popular logics and modes of thought as they were expressed in vernacular forms and everyday life. Advertising, the shotgun house, vaudeville, jazz, women's clubs, Hollywood cinema, country music, parades, and zoot suits, to name only a few, became as important to the exploration of American history as written documents like the Constitution, the lectures of William James, or the poetry of Ezra Pound.

Even as these transformations in American Studies research practice and modes of thought were burgeoning, new forces for change were incubating. Corporations internationalized in new ways. They expanded and extended their reach into virtually all the interstices of everyday life around the globe and, in the process, substantially transformed the nature of capitalism. As we have already noted, there is substantial disagreement over what constituted the critical characteristics of the new, transnational forms of capitalism that emerged in the 1980s and 1990s. Despite disagreements, however, it has seemed clear to many that the world's economy is increasingly being integrated ever more tightly not only through the extension and dispersal of production but also through increased geographical mobility and flexible responses to labor markets, labor processes, and consumer markets. This has augmented the flow of people, commodities, and information around the globe, thereby challenging national capacities for control and regulation and the very efficacy of borders themselves. With respect to American Studies, what these flows and altered economic and political relations have produced is an increased tendency to reexamine the very concept of American nationalism itself, as well as the complex conditions of possibility necessary for its past emergence and for its future perpetuation. Questions about borders and borderlands, about empire and neocolonialism, about migrations of all sorts, and the hybrid histories and subjects they have produced have moved to center stage in the field.

These new questions have almost always been posed with a keen eye to the contributing and intersecting effects of raced, gendered, and sex-based differentiations produced by a capitalism that will take advantage of virtually anything it can to increase profitability. As a result, some of the newest work in American Studies focuses on the ways racialization and gender and sex discrimination have been fundamental to the construction of the American national subject. At the same time, however, this work also asks what political possibilities have emerged from the differentiating process that concomitantly gives people reason to find common cause with each other and thereby to produce dissident ways of understanding the "American." As much as the new research is attentive to the macro and micro processes through which American national power has been exercised, so too is it interested in the contradictions produced by that power, that is, in the counter-forces that have emerged both in critique of American forms of domination and in utopian yearning for social arrangements that might be more democratic still.

As new perspectives have emerged from the effort to comprehend the rapidly changing world situation and the place of the United States in it, they have tended to focus on the historical connections between peoples and nations as well as on the forms of movement that have stitched them together, sometimes in affiliation, sometimes in relations of structured dominance, often in both. Within American Studies, this trend has produced an increased interest in reviewing past American history through a perspective attentive to the working out of colonial economic and political relations. At the same time a keen interest has developed in the various migrations and flows of people that have developed in the context of those relations. New Americanists of various sorts have consequently attended to the sorts of hybridities that

have been produced as a consequence, that is, to the mixed identities, memories, cultural practices, and forms of knowledge that have emerged out of the complex social experiment that has been called the United States. These new ways of understanding the complexities of identity could not have been possible without the previous work of recovery that brought back to awareness alternative histories produced at the margins of American culture.

It is essential to acknowledge here that the basic transformations in research orientation and practice in American Studies that we have just described did not lead to the wholesale abandonment of the themes and topics that had previously dominated Americanist scholarship. Nor have younger researchers completely eschewed familiar methods or totally rejected older frameworks for analysis. Rather, previous topics and modes of analysis have been decentered, that is, placed in relation to new objects, changed theoretical frameworks, altered concerns, and new forms of evidence. Equally significantly, familiar events, trends, and ideas from the American past have been shown to have quite other genealogies than we had been led to believe. Familiar themes like American nationalism, the nature of citizenship and democracy, the role of utopian social experiment, the centrality of religious practice in American history, and the question of what constitutes "American" culture reappear in this new scholarship but in transfigured form. They have been read differently in the light of a heightened awareness that the supposed benefits and goods of the American nation have continuously been denied to some even as those benefits and goods were themselves produced through the indispensable efforts of those repudiated groups. Contradictions, it seems to us, and the myriad, complex ways they have played out in American history, have emerged at the heart of the new American Studies scholarship. These contradictions have wheeled into view at the intersection between new frameworks for analysis and older ways of narrating the American past. And they have been occasioned, we believe, by the ongoing tensions in American life between a relentlessly differentiating capitalism, a residual, persistent, shape-shifting liberalism, and an ongoing attraction to utopian social experiment.

It is from the transformative alchemies produced by these tensions that new frameworks of analysis have emanated. We call these frameworks *analytics* as a way of suggesting that they are something more than mere themes or topics and something other than simple perspectives or points of view. Rather, they are emergent, loosely clustered modes of analysis that tend to bring together certain theoretical assumptions, research questions, and bodies of evidence with particular perspectives on the American past and a transformed sense of what will be significant in the future. These analytics have reconfigured the set of problems considered worthy of investigation just as they have altered the questions that must be asked. They have looked at older forms with new eyes and directed our attention to unfamiliar archives. They have sparked creative recovery efforts and required re-tellings of the past. They have inspired the construction of new genealogies and asked us to read older writers in new contexts. Though these analytics sometimes treat the same events, cultural forms, and social relations as previous scholarship, those forms appear quite differently as research subjects when they emerge at the center of these altered analytics.

It is our sense that these new analytics have emerged slowly and at somewhat different rates since the late 1970s in response to changes in the social and political climate more generally, to changes in the university environment more specifically, and in dialogue with earlier research agendas and frameworks for analysis within American Studies itself. Although these analytics have not erased entirely some of the earlier ways of organizing research or mapping the field, they have challenged older tendencies to divide the field by disciplinary method, chronological period, or according to the more recent trinity of race, class, and gender-based scholarship. Indeed it is our sense that it is increasingly rare at American Studies conferences to find panels organized by discipline, by self-contained chronological period, or by a singular focus on class, race, sex, or gender issues. Rather, recent American Studies scholarship has tended to be organized thematically and to draw on multiple disciplines and bodies of evidence. Equally significantly, it has tended to assume that the categories of race, class, gender, and sexuality should be treated simultaneously as intersecting, mutually penetrating, and therefore as mutually constitutive. What has emerged, as a consequence, is a set of frameworks for research and analysis that tend to take off from older preoccupations in American Studies but in transfigured form. Responding at once to the economic, social, and political changes in the contemporary environment discussed above and to altered theoretical assumptions and commitments, American Studies scholarship has clustered around a number of newly relevant questions, issues, and preoccupations.

Our volume is organized into ten analytics: (I) Empire, Nation, Diaspora; (II) States, Citizenship, Rights; (III) Reproduction of Work; (IV) Religion, Spirituality, and Alternate Ways of Being in the United States; (V) Performances and Practices; (VI) Body Talk; (VII) Mediating Technologies; (VIII) Sites, Space, and Land; (IX) Memory and Re-Memory; and (X) Internationalization and Knowledge Production about American Studies. These analytics are not independent autonomous generators of knowledge, but emergent and overlapping modes of intellectual production, ways of generating thought about the past, present, and future of the United States as it has engaged with the rest of the world. They are the products of transformations in the understanding of knowledge production: the specific and irreducible difference in understanding that results from taking into account the position of the knowing subject, the primacy of structuring and structured relationships over free-standing objects of investigation, the recognition of the fundamental materiality of symbolic culture, and the generative as well as the disciplinary effects of power. Equally, they are the consequence of the new histories that result from global changes and that have spawned, supported, and legitimated new ways of knowing.

Our analytics insist on the fluidity of "objects" of study and their mutability in relation to changing social, political, and technological contexts. Indeed it is our sense that recent work in American Studies is characterized more generally by an attention to social processes and practices and the complex relations that obtain among them (including those that produce our own research questions and objects of study) than it is by attention to discrete, self-contained objects as such. Events, institutions, organizations, and even objects themselves such as books, films, paintings, and different technological forms more generally tend to be treated as the contingent, only temporarily fixed result of a complex and always contested set of social practices. Seeking resolutely even if sometimes unconsciously to escape the effects of reification, this new scholarship treats the United States and its many constituent components as thoroughly historical social productions and therefore as contingent in nature. What has emerged over time might have developed otherwise and, in fact, might look different in the future when seen from different eyes and from a newly emergent perspective. Contemporary research practice in American Studies thus foregrounds in a particularly intense way the generative relation between the past and the present and thereby calls attention to itself as also always a practice, an act, an intervention. It is important, therefore, that our analytics not be reified as, simply, content areas. Nor should they be associated with or imply singular distinct methodologies. Rather these analytics are themselves social practices, ways of conceptualizing, investigating, and generating knowledge about the United States, its constituent histories, peoples, political, social, and cultural relations.

A final note should be added here about the inevitably difficult process of selection that troubles any anthology project from the very beginning. Ours has been no different in that regard. We began by compiling long lists of books both scholarly and popular, articles, essays, museum installations, music, conferences, and even events that we believed had changed American Studies scholarship since the late 1970s. As we read this material anew and discussed it among ourselves, we began to sort much of it into loose categories that seemed to emerge from our conversations. It was in that way that we identified, critiqued, developed, and refined our analytics. We were assisted in this process by our Advisory Editorial Board, whose members questioned us closely about the nature of our proposed categories, about why we called them analytics, about how we saw their histories, and about what material we would include within them. Once we settled on the ten analytics that organize our volume, we began the halting and even more difficult process of deciding what to include and what to exclude. Inevitably, length considerations and assumptions about the volume's intended audience affected our decisions. Our ideal volume, of course, would be at least twice as long as what we are able to offer here and it would include not only recently published academic material but writings from the long history of thought about the United States, including popular writings, as well as images and music. We hope that the material we have been able to include here at least gestures toward the altered and expanded archive of thought, whether embedded in words, images, performances, and or even music that we believe has altered thinking about the United States and its relations with the rest of the world.

Additionally, although we selected the essays principally for the ways in which they articulated the analytics, we also attempted to include material that covered roughly four centuries of US history and sought to represent work from a range of disciplines. We also attempted to include writings both from within and without the U. S. and by scholars trained at different moments in the field's recent past. We note here that our final analytic, Internationalization and Knowledge Production about American Studies, is significantly shorter than the rest. This has resulted from our sense that this analytic is still quite unsettled, despite the fact that conversations about American Studies in an international frame have been going on for some time. These older conversations have been augmented recently and rendered more intense by the events of 9/11 and the responses to those events by the US government and other agents. Because we felt uncertain about our abilities to map this especially dynamic conversational field – in part because a good deal of it is being carried out in languages other than English – we opted to include three essays that we believe summarize the nature of these extended debates and point to the key points in contention. Our hope is that in the near future a new team of editors and publishers will undertake the challenging task of producing a multilingual American Studies Reader that will foreground the complex politics of language and translation and the structural inequalities that make genuine international discussion both difficult and necessary.

In conclusion, we would like to observe that the primary goals of this reader are (1) to enable students of American culture to understand the new American Studies in its continuity with traditional approaches to questions of American identity and the narration of American history; and (2) to provide an organized accounting for the decentering of those traditional approaches as a result of the global transformations that we have outlined above. We believe that this reader will help students of American culture to recognize the ongoing revisioning of the field that is a result of the necessary self-reflection and commitment to politically engaged scholarship that has always characterized the best thinking in American Studies.

Editors' Note

We chose to maintain the variety of citation styles appropriate to the disciplinary origins of many of these pieces for two reasons. First, to maintain the integrity of the different scholarly traditions from which they came, and secondly to emphasize the value and rigor of a truly interdisciplinary approach that encourages engagement with a variety of scholarly practices. It is the nature of a volume like this to present edited selections of the original work. Students who are interested in the more complete version of the argument or who wish to seek out more complete citations are encouraged to turn to the original version of the articles.

Part I

Empire, Nation, Diaspora

We group the terms empire, nation, and diaspora because the articulation of each as recent fields of study has often been explicitly or implicitly constituted in relation to the other terms. During the 1980s and 1990s, long-standing critical perspectives on the use of US power around the globe converged with new social movements that opposed the reinvigoration of empire under the Reagan administration. This convergence produced a remarkable range of new work foregrounding US empire globally as well as questions of how the nation was figured as an imperial space through the overlapping dynamics of conquest, slavery, Indian removals, and immigration. Theoretically, these developments have been marked by debates over the multifaceted nature of power relationships, the relationship between power and culture, and the character of the globalization of capitalism. As forced and voluntary migrations were driven by the imperatives of mercantile, industrial, and multinational capital, they have often collided with the dictates of nationalisms. Much of this scholarship has called into question the meaning, viability, and political and cultural efficacy of the nation. Contingencies wrought by multinational capitalism, American imperial expansion, and immigration, along with the salience of race and gender ideologies in constituting nationalist discourse and in the making of the modern American nation, have undermined the very coherence and stability of the category of nation. Many of the articles that we have included in this analytic could also be productively read through our second analytic, "State, Citizenship, Rights," yet we note a productive tension in methodologies, as much of the work that is included in this first

analytic takes the subjectivities of displaced and/or non-elite people as its entry point, whereas post-Foucauldian understandings of the state have tended to focus on the relationship between law and society and technologies of discipline.

Scholars have probed the reshaping of gender and race in the imperial arena with the emergence of the United States as a global power, as well as the myriad ways in which the politics of US continental and overseas expansion, conflict, and resistance have shaped American culture. The relational study of empire, nation, and diasporas has fundamentally altered our conversations organized through older analytics such as race and gender. These areas of inquiry have also effected the displacement of an older Americanist paradigm that was bound up with civic republicanism. Nikhil Singh, for instance, examines the ways in which race is articulated within a critique of nation, and offers an understanding of racial formation as rethought through the formation of empire and through diaspora. Singh exemplifies the displacement of an older American paradigm that was bound up with civic republicanism. In his critique of the traditional debate between liberalism and republicanism, and in his analysis of the performative effects of representation, Singh examines the ways in which the "idea of American universalism, and the moral and political primacy it attributes to individual freedom and civic egalitarianism," is implicated in creating and sustaining racial division, Singh argues that "liberalism as a theory of market society and democratic–republicanism as a theory of political society" both deny their own limitations and collude in the perpetuation of racial inequality by locating the problem in the other paradigm. Amy Kaplan explores the spatial and political interdependence of home and empire and considers rhetorically how the meaning of the domestic relies structurally on its intimate opposition to the notion of the foreign. Examining the ways in which race and gender were integral to nineteenth-century projects of manifest destiny/imperialism and how the sentimental ethos was underwritten by and abetted imperial expansion, Kaplan revises older (and predominantly) feminist accounts of the ideology of domesticity, contesting the idea of separate spheres by showing that the boundary was both ideological and functional for the state/nation. Kaplan uses the feminist analytic to rethink older categorical distinctions and, in the process, unsettles the first set of feminist optics. Thus, in Singh and Kaplan, race and gender are reread through new analytics.

Challenging older distinctions between continental and extra-continental expansion, scholars have increasingly highlighted location and displacement in a new mapping of American cultural studies. José Saldívar explores "frontier modernism" and the irrevocably global *and* local character of US imperialism. He outlines a beginning genealogy of US–Mexico border studies and stresses the need to put such comparative work in a global context. Focusing on imperialism as a subject-constituting practice, as well as the imaginative work of transnational identity as a response to empire, Saldívar poses the critical question: what happens if US imperialism is displaced from its location in a national imaginary to its proto-imperial role in the Americas and the rest of the world? Brent Edwards reads a complex black diaspora as shaped by cultural practices of translation across national, linguistic, and political boundaries. Drawing on Stuart Hall's theoretical elaboration of the concept-metaphor of articulation, and insisting on a focus on the ways in which discourses of internationalism travel – are translated and debated – in transnational contexts marked by difference, for Edwards the discourse of diaspora articulates difference. Diaspora does not imply identity but calls for the examination of specific and strategically joined structures, the non-naturalizable linkages between disparate societal elements. Edwards shows the importance of aesthetic/cultural production in producing intellectual and political change; the cultures of black internationalism can only be seen in translation. In drawing our attention to internal empires and diasporas in the tragic intersections of Indian removal and the western expansion of slavery, Tiya Miles challenges older categories of ethnic studies by showing the profoundly relational and intersectional histories of Native Americans and African Americans. Racial formation within the Americas was constituted through these intertwined histories and cannot be grasped by attempting to bring together discrete building blocks of what have often been presumed to be distinct ethnic identities.

Exploring the collaborations between Okinawan women activists and East Asian–US international women's networks of anti-base activists, Yoko Fukumura and Martha Matsuoka argue for the inefficacy of national understandings and responses to globalized projects of empire. For these activists, a cohesive resistance against the US military entails a global redefinition of national security. As military violence is systemic, wreaking havoc in ostensibly civilian spaces, the story of the military is a story of sexual violence, environmental degradation, and the violent creation of multiple diasporas in the wake of profound social and economic disruptions. The broader problem of the military points to methodological challenges faced by Americanists: how to take on the scope and hubris of US hegemonic projects without reproducing the hubris and/or totalizing logics. The transnational responses to US empire of anti-base activists suggest ways of responding to this challenge through participation in collaborative transnational modes of knowledge production and critique.

1

Rethinking Race and Nation

Nikhil Pal Singh

[...]

American Race/American Racism

No single argument could possibly condense the full scope of American "multiracism" over centuries of continental expansion, racial slavery, imperial conquest, and international labor migration.[1] It is crucial to begin with the recognition, however, of the extent to which a normalizing claim to whiteness preceded the assertion that US nationality and citizenship transcend allegedly prior differences of kinship, ethnicity, race, or nationality. Beginning in the early republic, whiteness was invested both literally and symbolically with the attributes of property. If property rights were the foundation of liberal theories of political order, property-in-oneself was the basis for conceptualizing republican government and political democracy. One owned oneself insofar as one was white and male. Self-ownership, in turn, was a cornerstone of both the market contract and the social contract. It signified at least a potential, if not actual, access to Indian lands and African slaves. And it underwrote the most dramatic feature of the American Revolution, a "universal" right to participation in politics.[2]

In this founding liberal-republican schema, the development of an order of difference with respect to phenotype, affect, intelligence, and what W. E. B. Du Bois called "gross morphology" was codified as racial difference and legally constituted as an obstacle to both market activity and the exercise of citizenship rights for those marked as "other" by their color. Here, the incipient scientific racism of

Thomas Jefferson's *Notes on the State of Virginia* (1785) emerges as at least as important as the nonracial, revolutionary lines he authored in 1776 [...] The two Jeffersons suggest a complicated history of interdependence between race and nation, racism and nationalism, as ways of imagining kinship, community, economic activity, and political society. This is not to say that the American civic-nation had a racial basis at its inception. Rather, racial definitions enabled the very process of thinking about US national belonging as both a normative and a universal condition.

In the US context, the ideal national subject has actually been a highly specific person whose universality has been fashioned from a succession of those who have designated his antithesis, those irreducibly *non-national* subjects who appeared in the different guises of slave, Indian, and, at times, immigrant.[3] The capaciousness of American nationalism was due not to its inclusiveness, but to its ability to accommodate significant national, class, and religious diversity among its settler populations. Here, the forging of national subjectivity, famously described by Hector St. John Crevecoeur as the "melting" of men of all nations and ranks into a "new race of men ...an American race," was derived from a carefully delimited heterogeneity, or what Crevecoeur qualified as that "mixture of English, Scotch, Irish, French, Dutch, Germans and Swedes."[4]

Of course, it's not enough to stop here. The power of American nationalism, for its defenders, is that it has enabled the "widening of the circle of we."[5] The contours of the national "we" have been constantly recomposed as those previously excluded have asserted their own claims to be a nothing-in-particular American, or true national subject. This is where things get interesting, because the process of reshaping the boundaries of nation has also involved rearticulations of race. This process allowed for the incorporation of not-quite-white, but not-quite-not-white Irish, Jewish, and southern and eastern European immigrants into the canons of whiteness through the nineteenth and early twentieth centuries, making them Americans first in a legal and then in a cultural sense.[6] The question remains, how does this process work – or does it – for groups that have been more durably caught within the world-system of racial marks, particularly peoples of African descent?

If whiteness became the privileged grounding and metaphor for the empty abstraction of US citizenship, blackness presented an apparent contradiction and a fixed limit against which it was enacted and staged, beginning with the consolidation of a slave regime based on African origins and the codification of racial rules of descent. While other racialized groups have since been similarly subordinated, and in the case of American Indians violently expelled from the nation's borders, blacks presented the anomaly of an exclusion that was at once foundational to and located within the polity. Despite the wish of iconic US presidents like Jefferson and Lincoln that black slaves be emancipated and then removed ("beyond the reach of mixture," as Jefferson put it), an enduring black presence within the nation-state has led to an extraordinary cultural and political dynamic.[7] In this dynamic, African – and later Negro, black, and African American – struggles against civil death, economic marginalization, and political disenfranchisement accrued the paradoxical power to code all normative (and putatively universal) *redefinitions* of US national subjectivity and citizenship. Lurking within the original conceptions of American freedom, providing the underlying logic of the brutal civil war of national unification, unsettling the fragile legitimacy of the US defense of the free world after World War II, and inhabiting contemporary justifications for dismantling the welfare-state is the question of the status of black existence: the problem of race in the United States.

From this standpoint, then, comes another reading of America's universalism: it is built around an exception, leading to torturous but creative efforts to accommodate the racism internal to the nation-state's constitution. For most of US history this problem was simply resolved by defining black people apart from any representation of the national interest. At the delicate intersection of public opinion formation and public policy formulation

– national sovereignty and state institution building – was a broad racial consensus based on black exclusion. This may be the most succinct definition of racism as a social and institutional fact: the construction of black people as subjects proscribed from participating in the social state in which they live, and that part of the public whose relation to the public is always in radical doubt.

Prior to slave emancipation and political enfranchisement that culminated in the constitutional revisions of the Reconstruction era, the vast majority of blacks in the United States were excluded from the nation-state as a guarantor of natural rights and political participation. The slave was not merely the other of the republican citizen, but was the symbol of what was incommensurable with political society, a representative of a boundary to national belonging, a zone where the radical Enlightenment ideal of "the rights of man and citizen" was irrelevant. This was evident in the evasions of the Constitution, which refused to refer directly to slavery even while including the "three-fifths" clause that rendered slaves as part persons, part property.[8] Senator Henry Clay was more straightforward in 1850, pronouncing, in response to rising sectional tensions, that slavery was "an exception (resulting from stern but inexorable necessity) to the general liberty in the U.S."[9] The paradox of a parenthetical black presence – never absent but never fully present – was best captured by the antebellum blackface minstrel show, a popular form that underlined the creation of a national popular culture whose basic grammar and content was predicated on what was excluded from that culture.[10]

By making ex-slaves into citizens and enfranchising black men, the Civil War and Reconstruction era established a new cultural and political trajectory. Of paramount import was the augmentation of a universalizing nationalist imperative in which the masses of black people – no longer located outside the US nation-state, its imagined community, public sphere, and political society – entered America's shared, if fiercely contested symbolic, social, and political space. At the same time, freeing the slaves also freed racism as a constituent element of national popular politics.[11] In the South the attack on Reconstruction was swift and immediate after the northern armies withdrew in 1877. It led to the organization of new segregated institutions, white supremacist ideologies, legal rationalizations, extralegal violence, and everyday racial terror, which elaborated black racial difference as the basis of a new order of unequal social relations. While the severe policing of racial boundaries was already a fact of life in many northern states where free blacks lived, the end of Reconstruction led to the nationalization of a new racial regime in which blacks were reconstructed as "anti-citizens . . . enemies rather than members of the social compact."

There's a difference between being socially unintelligible and being society's enemy.[12] As enemies of a newly emerging liberal-nationalist order, blacks virtually had no room to maneuver politically, but their collective situation could at least be grasped as one subject to politics and to their collective influence as political subjects. Nothing can better explain the intensification of white supremacist activity during this period – lynching, segregation, "scientific" racism, the white riot, and pogrom – than the real possibility of black participation in the common social and institutional life of the nation-state. As Senator William Windon of Minnesota put it in a telling admission in 1879: "the black man does not excite antagonism because he is black but because he is a *citizen*."[13]

Periods of democratic upheaval, in which an activated citizenry threatened to overturn or radically reorder governmental powers in the name of civic-egalitarian principles, such as Jacksonian democracy, the Populist movement of the 1890s, or the labor movement of the early twentieth century, not only failed to challenge racial hierarchies, but often heightened them, succumbing to explicit "master race" appeals that helped to shape the future course of democratic expansion. At the same time, it was often the guardians of established property relations who paternalistically presented themselves as the true champions of defenseless blacks and Indians, in the context of an overall defense of social order and as a counterweight to socially disruptive political challenges from below. The political divide between northern and southern elites that led to the Civil War complicates this argument, but the compromises that led to a segregationist South after the Civil War reverted to the pattern. Once the radically democratic hopes of interracial populism were undermined, segregation was advanced by both northern industrialists and rising New South boosters as a more moderate form of white supremacy, a check on the "democratic" excesses of the white rabble and a political solution that would guarantee the orderly succession of property relations in the South that liberals believed would be the true source of social progress.[14]

It might seem puzzling or contradictory that proposals to ameliorate racial subordination have been tied to the reinforcement of hierarchies of property, and democratic social movements tied to the reproduction of hierarchies of race. The destruction of the fleeting experiments with interracial politics during Reconstruction

and the end of interracial populism and trade union organization during the 1880s and 1890s led to the wholesale exclusion of blacks from participation in the egalitarian struggles that were beginning to reshape the republic at the end of the nineteenth century. The attitude of American Federation of Labor (AFL) founder Samuel Gompers was typical when he said that blacks did not need to be afforded trade union protection because they had "no understanding of the philosophy of human rights." At the 1901 convention of the National American Women's Suffrage Association (NAWSA), President Carrie Chapman Catt divorced the suffrage movement of white women from the "hasty and ill-advised" enfranchisement of black men, which, she said, had led to "inertia in the growth of democracy" and "the introduction into the body politic of vast numbers of irresponsible citizens." One time populist-egalitarians like Tom Watson were irresistibly drawn to herrenvolk ideas. Even the incipient socialist movement had little interest in racial inequality. As Eugene Debs, otherwise one of the most radical political thinkers of his generation, put it, "we have nothing special to offer the Negro."[15]

What historians and theorists have represented as a deep-seated conflict between liberalism and civic-republicanism in American political life has actually been mediated through a series of negotiated compromises around racial boundaries. That these have been forged at the expense of black equality is ignored by partisans on both sides of the debate.[16] To understand this more fully we need to unpack a series of oppositions inscribed in the wider debate surrounding liberalism and republicanism in US political thought: the market versus the state, the private and the public, the defense of liberty and the goal of equality. If the ideal inhabitants of the nation-state are citizen-subjects, abstract, homogeneous, and formally equivalent participants in a common civic enterprise, then the ideal inhabitants of the market are private individuals endowed with an unknowable range of different attributes and engaged in competition and personal advancement. The principles that apply to the market and those that apply to the nation-state, in other words, are in direct conflict much of the time. While the market presumes the atomistic freedom of individual competition and advantage, the state presumes equality with respect to nationality and the forging of a common communal life through politics. The market derives its theories from eighteenth-century liberalism, while the modern political state is an achievement of democratic revolutions and republican theories of good government. Both the state and the market posit an abstract individual subject, but within the market that abstraction opens the way for the play of differences, while the political state is organized around the principle of sameness.

While these two realms are imagined as separable, they are deeply intertwined. The political state not only literally underwrites social faith in the market (in the form of money), it creates the basis of accumulation, stabilizing market exchange in a sphere of civic order and preventing the war of all against all. What needs to be grasped is how in the United States the market and state combinatory (i.e., the capitalist state) constitutes and maintains racial inequality. This is most easily perceived in relation to the operations of the state, in which racial exclusion has taken the force of juridical sanction. In this case, alleged sensuous particularities of black embodiment (odor, unsightliness, sexual excess) have provided a variety of rationales for denying abstract equality and political participation within the national community. But antiblack racism has also operated at the level of market activity and so-called private life, where blacks have been prevented both formally and informally from acting as proprietors of their own capacities, sellers of their labor-power, and sensuous participants within exchange relations. In these cases, racial stigma has been applied to blacks as a group, preventing them from being perceived as qualitatively differentiated individuals.

Indeed, what makes racial ascription and antiblack racism so powerful and so difficult to undo is that it has possessed this double optic, working its pernicious effects, both as an inscription of embodied particularity and as an abstract universality. In the process, it has helped to suture the otherwise problematic split between the public and the private that characterizes the development of modern bourgeois society. Thus, on the one hand, racial differentiation has underwritten the abstract egalitarianism that animates the idea of the democratic public, providing the latter with a particular, putatively "real" sensuous precedent, the idea of different skin and physical embodiment. On the other hand, racial differentiation is itself a form of abstraction, providing what is imagined to be an infinitely differentiated realm of private individuality and sensuous embodiment with a normative framework (that is, whiteness).

Liberalism as a theory of market society and democratic-republicanism as a theory of political society collude in the perpetuation of racial inequalities by denying their own theoretical limitations and by locating the cause of racial division in the other theory. Thus, liberalism would understand racial inequality to be the result of state interference with otherwise neutral market principles, suggesting that such discrimination would disappear if the market were only allowed to operate according to those principles. The liberal's answer to racism, in other words, is to remove the barriers to market freedoms and private individuality. On the other hand, democratic-republican, civic-nationalist, and communitarian arguments understand racial inequality as a subset of the inequalities generated by the market itself, which has engendered competition and distinction among a range of excluded groups and prevented their unified political pursuit of the common good. The answer for the republican theorist is removing the barriers to democratic politics and public power.

In each instance, to combat racial ascription, it is merely necessary to affirm the universality and rightness of the original theory and to bring it into line with practice, just as in both cases, the specific fate of racially aggrieved populations causes no special alarm within the terms of the theory. Since these frameworks of theory, social action, and institutional development are in practice interdependent rather than oppositional, each provides the other with a kind of plausible deniability around the historical persistence of racism and the problems it poses for producing the good society. The irony is that even when liberals and civic republicans take racism into account, it does not contradict their own fundamental premises, but instead reconfirms their universal validity. In each case, racism winds up being little more than an aberration of, or deviation from, what is otherwise a fundamentally sound liberal or civic-nationalist project, rather than something that has shaped and animated US society at every turn.[17]

Racism and the reproduction of racial hierarchy are blind spots for the forms of liberal and democratic political theory and practice that are said to constitute American nationhood. What needs to be recognized is that white supremacy is neither the essence of US nationality nor its antithesis, but an ever-active ideological formation that has structured market behavior and social movements within the constitution and governance of the US nation-state. More precisely, racial classification has provided what Evelyn Brooks Higginbotham terms a "metalanguage" of American culture and politics. As such, it has operated as a durable medium of symbolic constitution, cutting across conventional boundaries between the economic and the political, the private and the public, with the power to shape both the dispensation of value and the formation of groups.[18]

To put this a different way, racism (here, more specifically antiblack racism) and conceptions of racial hierarchy have provided decisive symbolic and cultural elements for creating hegemonic political and economic arrangements throughout US history. The liberal-republican antithesis in American politics, in this sense, converges around a two-pronged acceptance of racial exclusion – the uses of blackness as a market differential (for example, housing markets, labor markets, capital investment), and as an index of political community (for example, residential segregation, civic participation, public investment). Just as the question of black employment (including the deployment of black strikebreakers, practices of "lily-white" trade unionism, the protection of occupational sinecures) has been integral to more than a century of conflicts between labor and capital, the question of black social and political participation has been a flashpoint in struggles over the proper scope of government authority (including debates about federalism, state's rights, and private entitlements to discrimination).

This approach can help explain the steady reproduction of racial ascription in US political culture across time. Often this has been understood too simply as a function of an invariant need to constitute a compelling collective identity for the nation. In other words, racism is often conceived as a distortion arising from the symbolic identity requirements of civic-egalitarian dynamics and democratic sovereignty. Racism, in this view, provides specific cultural content to an otherwise empty democratic universalism, enabling the forms of boundary-drawing and fusions of past and present crucial to fashioning the story of a particular national "we."[19] But this is not the whole picture. Racism has also been central to the constitution and defense of material investments and market inequalities (in the United States and globally). This begins with the world trade in black skin and includes imperialist land grabs, quests for markets and raw materials, use of racist ideologies and practices to drive down the price of labor at home and abroad, and phenomena of property devaluation and residential segregation tied to concentrations and population movements of peoples of color. Just as racism fills the empty universalism of democratic theory, it provides an otherwise abstract capitalist market with one of its most reliable mechanisms of value-differentiation.

Insofar as liberalism insists on divorcing universal questions of individual rights from a historical context of unequal property relations and what Karl Marx termed primitive capital accumulation, it is not only ill-equipped to combat white supremacist constructions of peoplehood, but invested in their reproduction. Recent scholars have taken this further, suggesting that it is not

possible to separate the core ideas of liberalism from the milieu of imperial expansion in which they were fashioned. Uday Singh Mehta thus argues that a politically exclusionary impulse can be found *within* the "theoretical framework of liberalism" itself. This is not, he suggests, because liberal ideals (i.e., universal suffrage, individual freedom, self-determination, etc.) are themselves fictitious or hypocritical, or even because they are practically difficult to implement. Rather, liberal universalism has been based upon a distinction between "anthropological capacities and the conditions for their political actualization." Behind the liberal notion of universal human capacity has been a thicket of delimiting "social credentials" – cultural, historical, material, biological, and psychological "preconditions" – for which race (and gender) have proved to be highly durable shorthand and broadly disseminating rubrics.[20]

[...]

Americans have largely lived in denial about the centrality of their racial-imperial project to national self-conceptions. One of the main bulwarks against admission has been the typical argument of US exceptionalism: the United States it is said, has never pursued the kind of territorial colonialism of European nation-states. The turn-of-the-century acquisitions of Hawaii, Cuba (for practical purposes), the Philippines, and Puerto Rico forces some qualification of this claim. Yet, even this might be considered a minor episode in US history. What can hardly be disputed, however, is that relative absence of territorial conquest abroad was enabled by an unprecedented expansion of the contiguous national territory, from the revolution and westward expansion to Indian wars and removal policies to the seizure of northern Mexico from the Southwest to the Pacific Coast.[21]

A major psychic motivation for denying the role and scope of American empire is that so much of this activity proceeded under the terms of a now-discredited, overt, and extreme racism. Here, in fact it is less easy to differentiate the United States from Europe. Both viewed themselves as carrying a superior civilization to subject peoples, through conquest, forced labor, and extermination of indigenous populations. Even when engaged in so-called great power rivalry, each advanced a transnational racial vision of the historical progress of European-derived, or in the case of the great US imperialist Teddy Roosevelt, "Anglo-Teuton" peoples. The boundaries of the civilizing process were secured by a remarkably simple axiom: the uncivilized (that is, racialized) subject was a person who could be killed with impunity. They were, in the words of the great British imperialist poet Rudyard Kipling "lesser breeds without the law."

The racism of imperialism presents a significant problem for its latter-day defenders. This is one reason that no matter how much historians may now claim that statist liberalism triumphed over republicanism in the twentieth century, when it comes to imperialism, America is still cast as a republic, not an empire. Here we see similar tactics of bait-and-switch, in which a domestically racist republicanism can, from another vantage point, become the source of aggressive claims for US anti-imperialism (just as a globally expansionist liberalism is often heralded as the intellectual harbinger of a more benign racial order at home). Once we recognize that racist commitments have routinely transcended such oppositions, however, a different picture can emerge. Rather than canceling out the other's racism, racist practice has been more likely to demonstrate a cumulative logic. In this sense, rather than seeing domestic racism simply fueling empire, we can recognize how imperial expansion at the turn of the century and Jim Crow had reciprocal effects. Both gave new life to racist schemas of thought already deposited in the American past.

The flowering of US liberal internationalism in the twentieth century, encapsulated by Woodrow Wilson's "Fourteen Points," was nominally anti-imperialist, offering general support to the principle of national self-determination in international affairs. This should not mislead us, however. Wilson's views were partially born of strategic considerations, particularly of the threat posed by the radical, left-wing anticolonialism of the Bolshevik revolution under V. I. Lenin, which quickly gained adherents among intellectuals and insurgents of the colonial peripheries. Defeated by the more robust vision of imperialist rivalry favored by Senator Henry Cabot Lodge, Wilson failed to transform US foreign policy and public opinion, which returned to isolationism within a hemispheric dominion after World War I. Indeed, even in its most enlightened form, Wilsonian internationalism failed to address colonial and minority questions, as both the United States and European powers remained notoriously hostile to the grievances of colonial subjects and rising nonwhite powers such as Japan. A Southerner, Wilson's own racial antipathies were well known. He enforced rigid segregation on the capitol during his years in the White House and he regarded US black soldiers as an especially dangerous group, a fertile

conduit, he said, for the spread of Bolshevism in the United States. This viewpoint gained a wider purchase through popular period works depicting western civilization imperiled by the twinned threats of international revolutionary politics and white racial degeneration. Following World War I, the combination of Red scares and race riots fueled a counter-subversive imagination that would inextricably link antiblack racism and anti-radicalism for years to come.[22]

From the turn of the century until the New Deal era, black political actors faced a world defined by competing versions of capitalist imperialism (in which the entitlements of national belonging had little or no relevance or value for non-national subjects) and a nation-state organized around herrenvolk republicanism (in which civil, legal, and political institutions were effectively established as a white monopoly and institutional preserve).[23] In fact, whiteness was arguably solidified as a structure of privilege during this period, as immigration restriction and virulent Americanization campaigns hastened the assimilation of previously stigmatized European immigrants and the intensification of the legal and cultural codes of US biracialism at the national level. Even though whiteness and Americanness were never perfect synonyms, during the imperial scramble for territories they increasingly operated in concert as signs of universality, humanity, and civilization as the nation entered the globalizing epoch. The power of whiteness was enhanced by its mutability in a context of national and global expansion, even as the idea of blackness was more powerfully fixed as its antithesis.[24]

Thus, just as the state and the market have converged around practices of racial ascription and hierarchy, so have the realms of the domestic and the transnational. Indeed, the great power of modern racism as a mode of symbolic action – a way of organizing ideas in relation to practice – is that its purview has been at once so great and so varied. No amount of qualifying American nationalism with the terms "liberal" or "democratic" can mitigate how the accumulated history of racial inequality has weighed on the movements of US history into the present day. The long centrality and normativity of whiteness in US political culture has not been inconsistent with the history of American liberal-democracy, but integral to it.[25]

[. . .]

We will not understand the historical functioning and durability of race (and its cognate terms) until we recognize that it is at once larger and smaller than the nation-state. We might think of race, racism, and fictive ethnicity as mysteries lodged within the "hyphen" joining the nation and the state, society and the market, liberalism and democracy. For what is the hyphen but the place of what is occluded from view, or ancillary to politics, and yet also what allows us to assemble these unstable conjunctions? On the one hand, the hyphen allows us to imagine that the universalizing value of national sovereignty can be separated from the racial depredations of modern imperialism. On the other hand, it suggests that the global expansion of Enlightenment universals and capitalist markets progressively overcomes parochialism and ethnocentrism, rather than unendingly renewing them.

Despite living in a democratic age, we remain haunted by a legacy of white men of property who adjudicated the "fitness" for self-government of their social inferiors. The racism that has shaped the world's "core" nation-states has in this sense not only helped to limit the most profound social injuries of the market to those cast outside the sphere of democratic sovereignty, it has also helped to ensure that rising democratic demands for social protection have never been commensurate with market expansion. Racialized peoples in turn are those who have been defined by a status that is never individuated enough to grant rights, nor collective enough to justify sovereignty. In the US context, this has entailed the production of a host of "exceptional" figures and legal fictions exorbitant to liberal-democracy: the three-fifths person (African slave), the "domestic dependent nation" (American Indians), "separate but equal," (black citizen), "foreign in a domestic sense" (Puerto Ricans), the "immigrant ineligible for naturalization" (Asians), and of course the "free white person."

It may not be possible to fully disaggregate racist commitments and histories from the liberal-democratic components of US national identity. Rather than being definitively separated from Europe, the United States emerged as a major tributary of the modern European stream of racist projections of an idealized humanity against an abject prehumanity or subhumanity. American universalism then, in both its liberal and democratic articulations, has degenerated into racism not because it has failed to be "true" to itself, but because racial demarcation has historically been a central measure of the inner constitution of modern, civic identity. As a consequence, when considering the historical and political status of racial exclusion and inequality perpetuated under the auspices of US liberal-nationalism, the reasser-

tion of American universalism provides few answers; it only begs more questions.

[...]

Notes

1 "Multiracism" . . . is a term I borrow from Vijay Prasad, "Bruce Lee and the Anti-Imperialism of Kung-Fu: A Polycultural Adventure," *Positions* 11(1) (2003): 51–90.

2 Edmund Morgan, *American Slavery, American Freedom* (New York: W. W. Norton, 1975); Francis Jennings, *The Invasion of America: Indians, Colonialism and the Cant of Conquest* (New York: W. W. Norton, 1975); Matthew Frye Jacobson, *Whiteness of a Different Color: Immigrants and the Alchemy of Race* (Cambridge, Mass.: Harvard University Press, 1998), p. 25; Cheryl I. Harris, "Whiteness as Property," in Kimberle Crenshaw et al., eds., *Critical Race Theory* (New York: New Press, 1995), pp. 276–92.

3 Eric Foner, *The Story of American Freedom* (New York: W. W. Norton, 1998), p. 39. Also see Jacobson, *Whiteness of a Different Color*, p. 22.

4 J. Hector St. John Crevecoeur, *Letters from an American Farmer*, ed. Albert E. Stone (London: Penguin, 1986), p. 68. Also see Ned Landsman, "Pluralism, Protestantism and Prosperity: Crevecoeur's American Farmer and the Foundations of American Pluralism," in Ned Landsman et al., eds., *Beyond Pluralism: The Conception of Groups and Group Identities in America* (Chicago: University of Illinois Press, 1998), p. 114.

5 David Hollinger, "How Wide the Circle of 'We,' American Intellectuals and the Problem of the Ethnos since World War II," *American Historical Review* 57 (Spring 1993): 318.

6 The fullest account of this is Jacobson, *Whiteness of a Different Color*.

7 Thomas Jefferson, *Notes on the State of Virginia* (New York: Harper and Row, 1964), p. 134.

8 Rogers M. Smith, *Civic Ideals: Conflicting Visions of Citizenship in U.S. History* (New Haven, Conn.: Yale University Press, 1997), p. 133.

9 Jacob Lawrence, *Harriet Tubman* series, panel #2 [paintings 1938–40]. . . . Jacobson, *Whiteness of a Different Color*, p. 27.

10 Eric Lott, *Love and Theft: Blackface Minstrelsy and the American Working-Class* (New York: Oxford, 1993); Alexander Saxton, *The Rise and Fall of the White Republic* (New York: Verso, 1990).

11 Saxton, *The Rise and Fall of the White Republic*, p. 259; Barbara Fields, "Racism in America," *New Left Review* 181 (1990): 95–118. See Leon Litwack, *North of Slavery: The Negro in the Free States, 1790–1860* (Chicago: University of Chicago Press, 1961), p. vii.

12 Chantal Mouffe, *The Democratic Paradox* (New York: Verso, 2000), p. 12.

13 Quoted in Rayford Logan, *The Negro in American Life and Thought, 1877–1901: The Nadir* (New York: Collier, 1965), p. 7.

14 John Cell, *The Highest Stage of White Supremacy: The Origins of Segregation in South Africa and the U.S. South* (New York: Oxford University Press, 1982), p. 47; Stanley Greenberg, *Race and the State in Capitalist Development* (New Haven, Conn.: Yale University Press, 1980); C. Vann Woodward, *The Origins of the New South* (Baton Rouge: Louisiana State University Press, 1951).

15 Gompers quoted in Woodward, *Origins of the New South*, p. 361; Catt quoted in Angela Davis, *Women, Race and Class* (New York: Random House, 1978), p. 122; Debs quoted in Harvard Sitkoff, *A New Deal for Blacks: The Emergence of Civil Rights as a National Issue in the Depression Decade* (New York: Oxford University Press, 1978), p. 20. Also see C. Vann Woodward, *Tom Watson: Agrarian Rebel* (New York: Macmillan, 1938); Michael Dawson, "A Black Counter-Public?: Economic Agendas, Racial Earthquakes and Black Politics," in *The Black Public Sphere* (Chicago: University of Chicago Press, 1995), pp. 199–229.

16 Smith, *Civic Ideals*, pp. 13–40. Also see Harris, "Whiteness as Property," pp. 276–92; Michael Sandel, *Liberalism and the Limits of Justice* (Cambridge: Cambridge University Press, 1982); and Michael Sandel, *Democracy's Discontent: America in Search of a Public Philosophy* (Cambridge: Cambridge University Press, 1996).

17 See Derek Bell, *Faces at the Bottom of the Well: The Permanence of Racism* (New York: Basic Books, 1992). Here I am paraphrasing from Derek Bell, *Race, Racism and American Law* (Boston: Little, Brown, 1988), p. 60.

18 Evelyn Brooks Higginbotham, "African American Women's History and the Metalanguage of Race," *Signs* (Winter 1992): 251–74. Pierre Bourdieu, "Social Space and Symbolic Power," in *In Other Words* (Stanford, Calif.: Stanford University Press, 1990), p. 138.

19 Smith, *Civic Ideals*, pp. 6–10; Etienne Balibar and Emmanuel Wallerstein, *Race, Nation, Class: Ambiguous Identities* (New York, Verso, 1991), p. 95.

20 Uday Singh Mehta, "Liberal Strategies of Exclusion," in Ann Laura Stoler and Frederick Cooper, eds., *Tensions of Empire* (Berkeley: University of California Press, 1997), p. 60. Also see Uday Singh Mehta, *Liberalism and Empire* (Chicago: University of Chicago Press, 1999). Karl Marx, *Capital*, vol. 1 (New York: Vintage, 1977), p. 915, see Alys Eve Weinbaum, *Wayward Reproductions: Genealogies of Race and Nation in Trans-Atlantic Modern Thought* (Durham, N.C.: Duke University Press, 2004).

21 See Gareth Stedman Jones, "The Specificity of U.S. Imperialism," *New Left Review* 60 (1972): 59–86. Also see Amy Kaplan, *The Anarchy of Empire in the Making of U.S. Culture* (Cambridge, Mass.: Harvard University Press, 2002).

22 Perry Anderson, "Internationalism – A Breviary," *New Left Review* 14 (March/April 2002): 5–26; Bill Mullen, "Du Bois, Dark Princess and the Afro-Asian International," *Positions* 11(1) (Spring 2003): 217–40. Also see Oswald Spengler, *Decline of the West* (New York: Knopf, 1926); Madison Grant, *The Passing of the Great Race* (New York: Scribner's, 1916); Lothrop Stoddard, *The Rising Tide of Color against White World Supremacy* (New York: Scribner's, 1920).

23 Neil Gotanda, "A Critique of 'Our Constitution Is Color-Blind,'" in *Critical Race Theory*, p. 263.

24 Matthew Guterl, *The Color of Race in America, 1900–1940* (Cambridge, Mass.: Harvard University Press, 2001).

25 Jacobson, *Whiteness of a Different Color*, p. 12.

2

Manifest Domesticity

Amy Kaplan

Empire of the Home

Domesticity dominated middle-class women's writing and culture from the 1830s through the 1850s, at a time when national boundaries were in violent flux. During this period the United States increased its national domain by seventy percent, engaged in a bloody campaign of Indian removal, fought its first prolonged foreign war, wrested the Spanish borderlands from Mexico, and annexed Texas, Oregon, California, and New Mexico.

[. . .]

One of the major contradictions of imperialist expansion is that while the United States strove to nationalize and domesticate foreign territories and peoples, annexation threatened to incorporate non-white foreign subjects into the republic in a way that was perceived to undermine the nation as a domestic space. The discourse of domesticity was deployed to negotiate the borders of an expanding empire and divided nation. Rather than stabilize the representation of the nation as home, this rhetoric heightened the fraught and contingent nature of the boundary between the domestic and the foreign, a boundary that broke down around questions of the racial identity of the nation as home. Domestic discourse, I argue, both redressed and reenacted the anarchic qualities of empire through its own double movement: to expand female influence beyond the home and the nation, and simultaneously to contract woman's sphere to that of policing domestic boundaries against the threat of foreignness.

At this time of heightened imperial expansion, proponents of "woman's sphere" applied the language of empire to the home and even to women's emotional lives. "Hers is the empire of the affections," wrote Sarah Josepha Hale, influential editor of *Godey's Lady's Book*, who opposed the women's rights movement as "the attempt to take woman away from her empire of home."[1] To educational reformer Horace Mann, "the empire of the Home" was "the most important of all empires, the pivot of all empires and emperors."[2] Writers who counseled women to renounce politics and economics, "to leave the rude commerce of camps and the soul hardening struggling of political power to the harsher spirit of men," urged them in highly political rhetoric to take up a more spiritual calling, "the domain of the moral affections and the empire of the heart."[3] Catharine Beecher gave this calling a nationalist cast in *A Treatise on Domestic Economy*, when, for example, she used Queen Victoria as a foil to elevate the American "mother and housekeeper in a large family" who is "the sovereign of an empire demanding as varied cares, and involving more difficult duties, than are exacted of her, who wears the crown and professedly regulates the interests of the greatest nation on earth, [yet] finds abundant leisure for theaters, balls, horse races, and every gay leisure."[4] This imperial trope might be interpreted as a compensatory and defensive effort to glorify the shrunken realm of female agency, in a paradox of what Mary Ryan calls "imperial isolation," whereby the mother gains her symbolic sovereignty at the cost of withdrawal from the outside world.[5] For these writers, however, metaphor has a material efficacy in the world.

The representation of the home as an empire exists in tension with the notion of woman's sphere as a contracted space, because it is in the nature of empires to extend their rule over new domains while fortifying their borders against external invasion and internal insurrection. If, on the one hand, domesticity drew strict boundaries between the private home and the public world of men, on the other, it became the engine of national expansion, the site from which the nation reaches beyond itself through the emanation of woman's moral influence.

The paradox of what might be called "imperial domesticity" is that, by withdrawing from direct agency in the male arena of commerce and politics, woman's sphere can be represented by both women and men as a more potent agent for national expansion. The outward reach of domesticity in turn enables the interior functioning of the home. In her introduction to *A Treatise on Domestic Economy*, Beecher inextricably links women's work to the unfolding of America's global mission of "exhibiting to the world the beneficent influences of Christianity, when carried into every social, civil, and political institution" (12). Women's maternal responsibility of molding the character of men and children has global repercussions: "to American women, more than to any others on earth, is committed the exalted privilege of extending over the world those blessed influences, that are to renovate degraded man, and 'clothe all climes with beauty'" (14). Beecher ends her introduction with an extended architectural metaphor in which women's agency at home is predicated on the global expansion of the nation:

> The builders of a temple are of equal importance, whether they labor on the foundations, or toil upon the dome. Thus also with those labors that are to be made effectual in the regeneration of the Earth. The woman who is rearing a family of children; the woman who labors in the schoolroom, the woman who, in her retired chamber, earns with her needle the mite to contribute for the intellectual and moral elevation of her country; even the humble domestic, whose example and influence may be molding and forming young minds, while her faithful services sustain a prosperous domestic state; – each and all may be cheered by the consciousness that they are agents in accomplishing the greatest work that ever was committed to human responsibility. It is the building of a glorious temple, whose base shall be coextensive with the bounds of the earth, whose summit shall pierce the skies, whose splendor shall beam on all lands, and those who hew the lowliest stone, as much as those who carve the highest capital, will be equally honored when its

> top-stone shall be laid, with new rejoicing of the morning stars, and shoutings of the sons of God. (14)

The political charge of this metaphor is contradictory: it unifies women of different social classes in a shared project of construction while sustaining class hierarchy among women.[6] This image of social unity depends upon and underwrites a vision of national expansion, as women's varied labors come together to embrace the entire world. As the author moves down the social scale, from mother to teacher to spinster, her geographic reach extends outward from home to schoolroom to country, until the "humble domestic" returns back to the "prosperous domestic state," an ambiguous phrase whose double meaning refers at once outward to the nation and inward to the home. Woman's work here performs two interdependent forms of national labor; it forges the bonds of internal unity and pushes the nation outward to encompass the globe. This outward expansion in turn enables the internal cohesiveness of woman's separate sphere by making women agents in erecting an infinitely expanding edifice.

Beecher thus introduces her detailed manual on the regulation of the home as a highly ordered space by fusing the boundedness of the home with the boundlessness of the nation. Her 1841 introduction bears a remarkable resemblance to the rhetoric of Manifest Destiny, particularly to this passage by one of its foremost proponents, O'Sullivan, in his "The Great Nation of Futurity" of 1839:

> The far-reaching, the boundless future will be the era of American greatness. In its magnificent domain of space and time, the nation of many nations is destined to manifest to mankind the excellence of divine principles; to establish on earth the noblest temple ever dedicated to the worship of the most high – the Sacred and the True. Its floor shall be a hemisphere – its roof the firmament of the star-studded heavens, and its congregation an Union of many Republics, comprising hundreds of happy millions, calling, owning no man master, but governed by God's natural and moral law of equality.[7]

While these passages exemplify the stereotype of separate spheres (one describes work in the home and the other the work of nation building), both use a common architectural metaphor, a biblical temple coextensive with the globe. O'Sullivan's grammatical subject is the American nation, which, while it remains unnamed in Beecher's passage, is the medium for channeling women's work at home to a Christianized world. The construction of an edifice ordinarily entails walling off the inside from the outside, but in these two cases there is a paradoxical effect whereby the distinction between inside and outside is obliterated by the expansion of the home/nation/temple to encompass the globe. The rhetoric of Manifest Destiny and that of domesticity share a vocabulary that turns imperial conquest into spiritual regeneration in order to efface internal conflict or external resistance in visions of geopolitical domination as global harmony.

Although in the reaches of imperial domesticity a home is ultimately coextensive with the entire world, the concept also continually projects a map of unregenerate outlying foreign terrain that gives coherence to its boundaries and justifies its domesticating mission. When in 1869 Catharine Beecher revised her *Treatise* with her sister, Harriet Beecher Stowe, as *The American Women's Home*, they downplayed the earlier role of domesticity in harmonizing class differences and enhanced domesticity's outward reach. The book ends by advocating the establishment of Christian neighborhoods settled primarily by women as a way of putting into practice domesticity's expansive potential to Christianize and Americanize immigrants in Northeastern cities and "all over the West and South, while along the Pacific coast, China and Japan are sending their pagan millions to share our favored soil, climate, and government." No longer a leveling factor among classes within America, domesticity could be extended to those perceived as foreign within and beyond American national borders: "Ere long colonies from these prosperous and Christian communities would go forth to shine as 'lights of the world' in all the now darkened nations. Thus the Christian family and Christian neighborhood would become the grand ministry as they were designed to be, in training our whole race for heaven."[8] Though Beecher and Stowe emphasize domesticity's service to "darkened nations," the existence of "pagans" as potential converts performs a reciprocal service in the extension of domesticity to single American women. Such Christian neighborhoods would allow unmarried women without children to leave their work in "factories, offices and shops," or reject their idleness in "refined leisure," to live domestic lives on their own, in some cases adopting native children. Domesticity's imperial reach allows the woman's sphere to include not only the heathen but also the unmarried Euro-American woman, who can be freed from biological reproduction to rule her own maternal empire.

If writers about domesticity encouraged the extension of female influence outward to civilize the foreign, their writings also evoked anxiety about the opposing trajectory that brings foreignness into the home. Analyzing the widespread colonial trope that compares colonized people to children, Ann Stoler and Karen Sánchez-Eppler have each shown how this metaphor can work not only to infantilize the colonized but also to portray white children as young savages in need of civilizing.[9] This metaphor at once extends domesticity outward to the tutelage of heathens and inward to regulate the threat of foreignness within the boundaries of the home. For Beecher, this internal savagery appeared to endanger the physical health of the mother. Throughout her *Treatise*, the vision of the sovereign mother with imperial power is countered by the description of the ailing invalid mother. This contrast can be seen in the titles of the first two chapters, "Peculiar Responsibilities of American Women" and "Difficulties Peculiar to American Women." The latter focuses on the pervasive invalidism that makes American women physically and emotionally unequal to their global responsibilities. In contrast to the ebullient temple building of the first chapter, Beecher ends the second with a quotation from Tocqueville describing a fragile frontier home centered on a lethargic and vulnerable mother, whose

> children cluster about her, full of health, turbulence and energy; they are true children of the wilderness; their mother watches them from time to time, with mingled melancholy and joy. To look at their strength, and her languor one might imagine that the life she had given them exhausted her own; and still she regrets not what they cost her. The house, inhabited by these emigrants, has no internal partition or loft. In the one chamber of which it consists, the whole family is gathered for the night. The dwelling itself is a little world; an ark of civilization amid an ocean of foliage. A hundred steps beyond it, the primeval forest spreads its shade and solitude resumes its sway. (24)

The mother's health appears drained less by the external hardships inflicted by the environment than by her own "children of the wilderness," who violate the border between home and primeval forest. This boundary is partially reinforced by the image of the home as an "ark of civilization" whose internal order should protect its inhabitants from the "ocean of foliage" that surrounds them. Yet the undifferentiated inner space, which lacks "internal partition," replicates rather than defends against the boundlessness of the wilderness around it. The rest of Beecher's *Treatise*, with its detailed attention to the systematic organization of the household, works to "partition" the home in a way that distinguishes it from an external wilderness.[10]

Although the infirmity of American mothers is a pervasive concern throughout *Treatise*, its physical cause is difficult to locate. Poor health afflicts middle-class women in Northeastern cities as much as women on the frontier, according to Beecher, and she sees the cause in geographic and social mobility: "everything is moving and changing" (16). This movement affects women's health most directly, claims Beecher, by depriving them of reliable domestic servants. With "trained" servants constantly moving up and out, middle-class women must resort to hiring "ignorant" and "poverty-stricken foreigners," with whom they are said in *American Woman's Home* to have a "missionary" relationship (332). Though Beecher does not label these foreigners as the direct cause of illness, their presence disrupts the orderly "system and regularity" of housekeeping, leading American women to be "disheartened, discouraged, and ruined in health" (18). Throughout her *Treatise* Beecher turns the lack of good servants – at first a cause of infirmity – into a remedy; their absence gives middle-class women the opportunity to perform regular domestic labor that will revive their health. By implication, their self-regulated work at home will also keep "poverty-stricken foreigners" out of their homes. Curiously, then, the mother's ill health stems from the unruly subjects of her domestic empire – children and servants – who bring uncivilized wilderness and undomesticated foreignness into the home. The fear of disease and of invalidism that characterizes the American woman also serves as a metaphor for anxiety about foreignness within. The mother's domestic empire is at risk of contagion from the very subjects she must domesticate and civilize, who ultimately infest both the home and the maternal body.[11]

Beecher's concept of the domestic thus generates and is constituted by images of the foreign. On the one hand, domesticity's "habits of system and order" appear to anchor the home as an enclosed stable center against a fluctuating alien world of expanding national borders; on the other, domesticity must be spatially and conceptually mobile to travel to the nation's far-flung frontiers. Beecher's use of Tocqueville's ark metaphor suggests the rootlessness and the self-enclosed mobility necessary for the efficacy of middle-class domesticity to redefine the meaning of habitation, to make Euro-Americans feel at home in a place where *they* are initially the foreign ones. Domesticity inverts this relationship to create a home by rendering prior inhabitants alien and undomesticated and by implicitly nativizing newcomers. The empire of

the mother thus embodies the anarchy at the heart of the American empire; the two empires follow a double compulsion to conquer and domesticate – to control and incorporate – the foreign within the borders of the home and the nation.

Domesticating the Empire

The imperial scope of domesticity was central to the work of Sarah Josepha Hale, throughout her half-century editorship of the influential *Godey's Lady's Book* and in her fiction and history writing. Hale has been viewed by some scholars as advocating a woman's sphere more thoroughly separate from male political concerns than the one Beecher promoted.[12] This withdrawal seems confirmed by the refusal of *Godey's* even to mention the Civil War throughout its duration, much less take sides. Yet when Hale conflates the progress of women with the nation's Manifest Destiny in her history writing, other scholars have judged her as inconsistently moving out of the woman's sphere into a conventional male political realm.[13] Hale's conception of separate spheres, I argue, is predicated on the imperial expansion of the nation. Although her writing as editor, essayist, and novelist focused on the interior spaces of the home, with ample advice on housekeeping, clothing, manners, and emotions, she gave equal and related attention to the expansion of female influence through her advocacy of female medical missionaries abroad and the colonization of Africa by former black slaves. Even though Hale seemed to avoid the issue of slavery and race relations in her silence about the Civil War, in the 1850s her conception of domesticity took on a decidedly racial cast, exposing the intimate link between the separateness of gendered spheres and the effort to keep the races apart in separate national spheres.

In 1847, in the middle of the Mexican-American War, Hale launched a campaign on the pages of *Godey's Lady's Book* to declare Thanksgiving Day a national holiday, a campaign she avidly pursued until Lincoln made the holiday official in 1863.[14] This effort typified the way in which Hale's map of woman's sphere overlaid national and domestic spaces; *Godey's* published detailed instructions and recipes for preparing the Thanksgiving feast, while it encouraged women readers to agitate for a nationwide holiday as a ritual of national expansion and unification. The power of Thanksgiving Day stemmed from its center in the domestic sphere; Hale imagined millions of families seated around the table on the same day; thereby unifying the vast and shifting space of the national domain through simultaneity. This domestic ritual would "unite our great nation, by its states and families" from "St. John's to the Rio Grande, from the Atlantic to the Pacific border," and it should therefore become an official holiday "as long as the Union endures."[15] If the celebration of Thanksgiving unites individual families across regions and brings them together in an imagined collective space, Thanksgiving's continental scope endows each individual family gathering with national meaning. Furthermore, the Thanksgiving story commemorating the founding of New England – which in Hale's version makes no mention of Indians – could create a common history by nationalizing a regional myth of origins and transposing it to the territories most recently wrested away from Indians and Mexicans. Hale's campaign to transform Thanksgiving from a regional to a national holiday grew even fiercer with the approach of the Civil War. In 1859 she wrote, "If every state would join in Union Thanksgiving on the 24th of this month, would it not be a renewed pledge of love and loyalty to the Constitution of the United States?"[16] Thanksgiving Day, she hoped, could avert the coming Civil War. As a national holiday celebrated primarily in the home, the cross-country Thanksgiving celebration serves to write a national history of origins, to colonize newly acquired Western territories, and to unite North and South.

The domestic ritual of Thanksgiving could expand and unify the nation, provided its borders were fortified against foreignness; for Hale, the nation's boundaries not only defined its geographical limits but also set apart nonwhites within the national domain. In Hale's fiction of the 1850s, Thanksgiving polices the domestic sphere by making black people, whether free or enslaved, foreign to the domestic nation and homeless within America's expanding borders. In 1852 Hale reissued *Northwood*, the novel which had launched her career in 1827 with a highly publicized chapter about a New Hampshire Thanksgiving dinner, showcasing the values of the American republic to a skeptical British visitor. For the 1852 version Hale changed the subtitle from "A Tale of New England" to "Life North and South," to highlight the new material she added on slavery.[17] Pro-union yet against abolition, Hale advocated sending all black people to settle in Africa and Christianize its inhabitants. Colonization in the 1850s had a two-pronged ideology: to expel blacks to a separate national sphere, and to expand US power through the civilizing process; black Christian settlers would become both outcasts from and agents for the American empire.[18]

Hale's 1852 *Northwood* ends with an appeal to use Thanksgiving Day as an occasion to collect money at all American churches "for the purpose of educating and colonizing free people of color and emancipated slaves" (408). This annual collection would contribute to "peaceful emancipation" as "every obstacle to the real freedom of America would be melted before the gushing streams of sympathy and charity" (408). While "sympathy," a sentiment associated with woman's sphere, seems to extend to black slaves, the goal of sympathy in this passage is not to free them but to emancipate white America from their presence. Thanksgiving for Hale thus celebrates national cohesiveness around the domestic sphere by simultaneously rendering blacks within America foreign to the nation.

For Hale, colonization would also transform American slavery into a civilizing and domesticating mission. One of her Northern characters explains to the British visitor that "the destiny of America is to instruct the world, which we shall do, with the aid of our Anglo-Saxon brothers over the water. . . . Great Britain has enough to do at home and in the East Indies to last her another century. We have this country and Africa to settle and civilize" (167). When his listener is puzzled by the reference to Africa, the American explains "that is the greatest mission of our Republic, to train here the black man for his duties as a Christian, then free him and send him to Africa, there to plant Free States and organize Christian civilization" (168). The colonization of Africa becomes the goal of slavery by making it part of the civilizing mission of global imperialism. Colonization thus not only banishes blacks from the domestic union, but, as the final sentence of *Northwood* proclaims, it proves that "the mission of American slavery is to Christianize Africa" (408).

In 1853 Hale published the novel *Liberia*, which begins where *Northwood* ends, with the settlement of Liberia by freed black slaves.[19] Seen by scholars as a retort to *Uncle Tom's Cabin*, it can also be read as the untold story of Stowe's novel, starting where she concludes, with former black slaves migrating to Africa.[20] Although the subtitle, "Mr. Peyton's Experiment," places colonization under the aegis of a white man, the narrative turns colonization into a project emanating from woman's sphere in at least two directions. In its outward trajectory, the settlement of Liberia appears as an expansion of feminized domestic values. Yet domesticity is not only exported to civilize native Africans; the framing of the novel also makes African colonization necessary to the establishment of domesticity within the United States as exclusively white. While Hale writes that the purpose of the novel is to "show the advantages Liberia offers to the African," in so doing it construes all black people as foreign to American nationality by asserting that they must remain homeless within the United States. At the same time, Hale paints a picture of American imperialism as the embodiment of the feminine values of domesticity: "What other nation can point to a colony planted from such pure motives of charity; nurtured by the counsels and exertions of its most noble and self-denying statesmen and philanthropists; and sustained, from its feeble commencement up to a period of self-reliance and independence, from pure love of justice and humanity?" (iv). In this passage America is figured as a mother raising her baby, Africa, to maturity; the vocabulary of "purity," "charity," "self-denial" represents colonization as an extension of the values of woman's separate sphere.

The narrative opens with a scene fraught with danger to American domesticity. The last male of a distinguished Virginia family is on his deathbed, helpless to defend his plantation from a rumored slave insurrection. The women of the family, led by his wife, Virginia, rally with the loyal slaves to defend their home from the insurrection that never occurs. Thus the novel's separate spheres have gone awry, with the man of the family abed at home, while white women and black slaves act as protectors and soldiers. The ensuing plot to settle Liberia overtly rewards those slaves for their loyalty by giving them freedom and a homeland; it also serves to reinstate separate spheres and reestablish American domesticity as white.

When the narrative shifts to Africa, the black colonizers, now deprived of American nationhood, have the task of Americanizing that continent through domesticity. A key figure in the settlement is the slave Keziah, who has nursed the white plantation owners. She is the one most responsive to Peyton's proposal for colonization, because of her desire to be free and to Christianize the natives. Her future husband, Polydore, more recently arrived in the United States as a slave and thus less "civilized," is afraid to return to Africa because of his memory of native brutality and superstition. This couple represents two faces of enslaved Africans central to the white imagination of colonization: the degenerate heathen represented by the man, and the redeemed Christian represented by the woman. Keziah, however, can only become a fully domesticated woman at a geographic remove from American domesticity. When Keziah protects the plantation in Virginia, her maternal impulse is described as that of a wild animal – a "fierce lioness." Only in Africa can she become the domestic center of the new settlement, where she establishes a home that

resembles Beecher's Christian neighborhood. Keziah builds a private home with fence and garden, and civilizes her husband while she expands her domestic sphere to adopt native children and open a Christian school.

Keziah's domestication of herself and her surroundings in Africa can be seen as part of the movement in the novel (noted by Susan Ryan) in which the freed black characters are represented as recognizably American only at the safe distance of Africa.[21] Once banished from the domestic sphere of US nationality, they can be resurrected as American in a foreign terrain. The novel narrates the founding of Liberia as a story of colonization, but Hale's storytelling also colonizes Liberia as an imitation of America, replete with images of the frontier, the *Mayflower*, and the planting of the American flag. A double narrative movement at once contracts US borders to exclude blacks from domestic space and simultaneously expands those borders by re-creating that domestic space in Africa. Thus the novel ends with a passage that compares the Liberian settlers to the Pilgrims and represents them as part of a global expansion of the American nation:

> I do not doubt but that the whole continent of Africa will be regenerated, and I believe the Republic of Liberia will be the great instrument, in the hands of God, in working out this regeneration. The colony of Liberia has succeeded better than the colony of Plymouth did for the same period of time. And yet, in that little company which was wafted across the mighty ocean in the *May Flower*, we see the germs of this already colossal nation, whose feet are in the tropics, while her head reposes upon the snows of Canada. Her right hand she stretches over the Atlantic, feeding the millions of the Old World, and beckoning them to her shores, as a refuge from famine and oppression; and, at the same time, she stretches forth her left hand to the islands of the Pacific, and to the old empires of the East. (303)

In Hale's view, both slavery and domesticity are necessary to the imperial mission; African slaves are brought to America to become Christianized and domesticated, but they cannot complete this potential transformation until they "return" to Africa.

Hale's writing makes race central to woman's sphere. Nonwhites are excluded from domestic nationalism; moreover, the capacity for domesticity becomes an innate defining characteristic of the Anglo-Saxon race. Reginald Horsman has shown how in political thought by the 1840s the meaning of Anglo-Saxonism had shifted from a historical understanding of the development of republican institutions to an essentialist definition of a single race that possesses an innate and unique capacity for self-government.[22] His analysis, however, limits this racial formation to the traditionally male sphere of politics. Hale's *Woman's Record* (1853), a massive compendium of the history of women from Eve to the present, establishes woman's sphere as central to the racial discourse of Anglo-Saxonism. To Hale the empire of the mother spawns the Anglo-Saxon nation and propels its natural inclination toward global power. In her introduction to the fourth part of her volume on the present era, Hale represents America as manifesting the universal progress of women that culminates in the Anglo-Saxon race. To explain the Anglo-Saxon "mastery of the mind over Europe and Asia," she argues that

if we trace out the causes of this superiority, they would center in the moral influence, which true religion confers on the female sex.... There is still a more wonderful example of this uplifting power of the educated female mind. It is only seventy-five years since the Anglo-Saxons in the New World became a nation, then numbering about three million souls. Now this people form the great American republic, with a population of twenty-three millions; and the destiny of the world will soon be in their keeping! Religion is free; and the soul which woman always influences where God is worshipped in spirit and truth, is untrammeled by code, or creed, or caste.... The result before the world – a miracle of advancement, American mothers train their sons to be men.[23]

Hale here articulates the imperial logic of what has been called "republican motherhood," which ultimately posits the outward expansion of maternal influence beyond the home and the nation's borders.[24] The Manifest Destiny of the nation unfolds logically from the imperial reach of woman's influence emanating from her separate domestic sphere. Domesticity makes manifest the destiny of the Anglo-Saxon race, while Manifest Destiny becomes in turn the condition for Anglo-Saxon domesticity. For Hale domesticity influences national expansion in a double manner: it casts the image of the nation as a home delimited by race, and the image of the nation as propelled outward through imperial female agency.

Advocating domesticity's expansive mode, *Woman's Record* includes only those nonwhite women who contributed to the spread of Christianity to colonized peoples. In the third volume, Hale designates Ann Judson, a white American missionary to Burma, as the most distinguished woman to 1830 (152). The fourth volume of *Woman's Record* focuses predominantly on

American women as the apex of historical development. In contrast to the aristocratic accomplishment of English women, "in all that contributes to popular education and pure religious sentiment among the masses, the women of America are in advance of all others on the globe. To prove this we need only examine the list of American female missionaries, teachers, editors and authors of works instructive and educational, contained in this 'Record'" (564). While Anglo-Saxon men marched to conquer new lands, female influence had a complementary outward reach from within the domestic sphere.

The argument for African colonization can be seen as part of the broader global expansion of woman's sphere. In 1853 Hale printed in *Godey's Lady's Book* "An Appeal to the American Christians on Behalf of the Ladies' Medical Missionary Society," in which she argued for the special need for women physicians abroad because they would have unique access to foreign women's bodies and souls.[25] Her argument for training female medical missionaries both enlarged the field of white women's agency and feminized the force of imperial power. She saw female medical missionaries as not only curing disease but also raising the status of women abroad: "All heathen people have a high reverence for medical knowledge. Should they find Christian ladies accomplished in this science, would it not greatly raise the sex in the estimation of those nations, where one of the most serious impediments to moral improvement is the degradation and ignorance to which their females have been for centuries consigned?" (185). Though superior to heathen women in status, American women would accomplish their goal by taking gender as a common ground, which would give them special access to women abroad. As women they could be more effective imperialists, penetrating those interior colonial spaces, symbolized by the harem, that remain inaccessible to male missionaries:

Vaccination is difficult of introduction among the people of the east, though suffering dreadfully from the ravages of small-pox. The American mission at Siam writes that thousands of children were, last year, swept away by this disease in the country around him. Female physicians could win their way among these poor children much easier than doctors of the other sex. Surely the ability of American women to learn and practice vaccination will not be questioned, when the more difficult art of inoculation was discovered by the women of Turkey, and introduced into Europe by an English woman! Inoculation is one of the greatest triumphs of remedial skill over a sure loathsome and deadly disease which the annals of Medical Art record. Its discovery belongs to women. I name it here to show that they are gifted with genius for the profession, and only need to be educated to excel in the preventive department.

Let pious, intelligent women be fitly prepared, and what a mission-field for doing good would be opened! In India, China, Turkey, and all over the heathen world, they would, in their character of physicians, find access to the homes and harems where women dwell, and where the good seed sown would bear an hundredfold, because it would take root in the bosom of the sufferer, and in the heart of childhood. (185)

In this passage the connections among women branch out in many directions, but Hale charts a kind of evolutionary narrative that places American women at the apex of development. Though inoculation was discovered by Turkish women, it can only return to Turkey to save Turkish children through the agency of English women transporting knowledge to Americans, who can then go to Turkey as missionaries and save women who could not save themselves or their children. The needs of heathen women allow American female missionaries to conquer their own domestic empire without reproducing biologically. Instead, American women are metaphorically cast as men in a cross-racial union, as they sow seeds in the bodies of heathen women who will bear Christian children. Through female influence, women physicians will transform heathen harems into Christian homes.

Thus the concept of female influence in Hale's writing, so central to domestic discourse and at the heart of the sentimental ethos, was underwritten by and abetted the imperial expansion of the nation. While the empire of the mother advocated retreat from the world-conquering enterprises of men, this renunciation promised a more thorough kind of world conquest. Both the empire of the mother and the American Empire sought to encompass the entire world outside their borders, yet this same outward movement contributed to and relied on the contraction of the domestic sphere to exclude persons conceived of as racially foreign within those expanding national boundaries.

[...]

Notes

1   Sarah Josepha Hale, "Editor's Table," *Godey's Lady's Book*, 44 (January 1852): 88.

2   Quoted in Mary P. Ryan, *The Empire of the Mother: American Writing about Domesticity, 1830–1860* (Binghamton, N.Y.: Harrington Park Press, 1982); p. 112.

3   From "The Social Condition of Woman," *North American Review*, 42 (1836): 513, quoted in Annette Kolodny, *The Land Before Her: Fantasy and Experience of the American Frontiers, 1630–1860* (Chapel Hill: University of North Carolina Press, 1984), p. 166.

4   Catharine Beecher, *A Treatise on Domestic Economy* (Boston: Marsh, Capen, Lyon and Webb, 1841), p. 144. Subsequent page references are cited parenthetically in the text.

5   Ryan, *Empire of the Mother*, pp. 97–114.

6   Katherine Sklar, *Catharine Beecher: A Study in American Domesticity* (New Haven, Conn.: Yale University Press, 1973); Jenine Abboushi Dallal, "The Beauty of Imperialism: Emerson, Melville, Flaubert, and Al-Shidyac" (Ph.D. diss., Harvard University, 1996), ch. 2.

7   John L. O'Sullivan, "The Great Nation of Futurity," in Paterson, *Major Problems in American Foreign Policy*, vol. 1, p. 241.

8   Catharine Beecher and Harriet Beecher Stowe, *American Woman's Home* (Hartford, Conn.: J. B. Ford, 1869), pp. 458–59.

9   Karen Sánchez-Eppler, "Raising Empires like Children: Race, Nation and Religious Education," *American Literary History*, 8 (Fall 1996): 399–425; Ann L. Stoler, *Race and the Education of Desire: Foucault's History of Sexuality and the Colonial Order of Things* (Durham, N.C.: Duke University Press, 1995), pp. 137–64.

10   Although the cleanliness and orderliness of the home promises to make American women healthier, Beecher also blames the lack of outdoor exercise for American women's frailty, as though the problematic space outside the home, the foreign, can both cause and cure those "difficulties peculiar to American women."

11   This generalized anxiety about contamination of the domestic sphere by children may stem from the circulation of stories by missionaries, who expressed fear of their children being raised by native servants or too closely identified with native culture. These stories would have circulated in popular mission tracts and in middle-class women's magazines, such as *Godey's* and *Mother's Magazine*. See, for example, Stoler, and Patricia Grimshaw, *Paths of Duty: American Missionary Wives in Nineteenth-Century Hawaii* (Honolulu: University of Hawaii Press, 1989), pp. 154–78. The licentiousness of men was also seen as a threat to women's health within the home. In general, domesticity is usually seen as an ideology that develops in middle-class urban centers (and, as Sklar shows, in contrast to European values) and then is exported outward to the frontier and empire, where it meets challenges and adaptations. It remains to be studied how domestic discourse might develop out of the confrontation with colonized cultures in what has been called the "contact zone" of frontier and empire.

12 Sklar, *Catharine Beecher*, p. 163; Ann Douglas, *The Feminization of American Culture* (New York: Farras, Straus and Giroux, 1998), pp. 51–4.

13 Nina Baym, "Onward Christian Women: Sarah J. Hale's History of the World," *New England Quarterly*, 63 (1990): 249–70.

14 Sarah J. Hale, "Editor's Table," *Godey's Lady's Book*, 34 (January 1847): 53.

15 *Godey's*, 45 (November 1852): 303; *Godey's*, 34 (January 1847): 52.

16 Ruth E. Finley, *The Lady of Godey's, Sarah Josepha Hale* (Philadelphia: Lippincott, 1931), p. 199.

17 Sarah J. Hale, *Northwood, or, Life North and South* (New York: H. Long and Brother, 1852). See her 1852 preface, "A Word with the Reader," on revisions of the 1827 edition.

18 On the white ideological framework of African colonization, see George Fredrickson, *The Black Imago in the White Mind: The Debate on Afro-American Character and Destiny, 1817–1914* (New York: Harper and Row, 1971), pp. 6–22, 110–17; Susan M. Ryan, "Errand into Africa: Colonization and Nation Building in Sarah J. Hale's Liberia," *New England Quarterly*, 68 (1995): 558–83; Bruce Dorsey, "A Gendered History of African Colonization in the Antebellum United States," *Journal of Social History* (Fall 2000): 77–103; Timothy B. Powell, "Harriet Beecher Stowe: *Uncle Tom's Cabin* and the Question of the American Colonization Society," in *Ruthless Democracy: A Multicultural Interpretation of the American Renaissance* (Princeton: Princeton University Press, 2000), pp. 108–30.

19 Sarah J. Hale, *Liberia; or Mr. Peyton's Experiments* (1853: reprint, Upper Saddle River, N.J.: Gregg Press, 1968).

20 On Liberia as a conservative rebuff to Stowe, see Thomas F. Gossett, *Uncle Tom's Cabin and American Culture* (Dallas: Southern Methodist University Press, 1985), pp. 235–36.

21 Ryan, "Errand into Africa," p. 572.

22 Reginald Horsman, *Race and Manifest Destiny: The Origins of American Racial Anglo-Saxonism* (Cambridge, Mass.: Harvard University Press, 1981), pp. 62–81.

23 Sarah J. Hale, *Woman's Record* (New York: Harper, 1853), p. 564.

24 Linda Kerber, *Women of the Republic: Intellect and Ideology in Revolutionary America* (Chapel Hill: University of North Carolina Press, 1980).

25 Sarah J. Hale, "An Appeal to the American Christians on Behalf of the Ladies' Medical Missionary Society," *Godey's Lady's Book*, 54 (March 1852): 185–88.

Nuestra América's Borders: Remapping American Cultural Studies

José David Saldívar

In the United States . . . the real [José] Martí is almost forgotten. . . . It is odd that there is no single book that explores Martí's ties with the United States. . . . And it is all the more surprising because, except for short intervals, the 15 years of his prime (1880–1895) were spent in exile in the United States, whose inner life he came to know profoundly. – Roberto Fernández Retamar, "Jose Martí: A Cuban for all Seasons"[1]

In the following pages, we shall consider how US–Mexican border paradigms strive for comparative theoretical reach while remaining grounded in specific histories of what José Martí in 1891 called "Nuestra América" [Our America]. We shall also ask what such projects tell us about the cultures of US imperialism and the cultures of displacement? Finally, we shall turn our attention to a late nineteenth-century articulation of an uneven and contradictory frontier modernism,[2] one situated along the banks of the Rio Grande in South Texas [. . .] late *fin de siglo* quests for empire, politics, and subaltern difference.

Culturally, I write these days as a teacher and avid reader and consumer of US–Mexico border texts, soundings, and visual cultural performances. Like many US Latino/a intellectuals, I have lived both in the North and in the South, and the South in the North, as Rubén Martínez once dizzyingly and aptly put it.[3] While I now find myself located in what some hundred and fifty years ago was called the northern frontier of Alta California, I spent the first half of my life at the mouth of the Rio Grande in South Texas. My quest for a new mapping of American Cultural Studies necessarily worries about the politics of location.

When I first went to Yale to study American literature in 1973, I knew hardly anything about America. I had been nurtured in the rhetoric of the US–Mexico Borderlands, what Américo Paredes called the liminal spaces of "Greater Mexico."[4] I was absorbed, moreover, in South Texas attitudes toward "El Norte" – a subalternity deepened by the pressures of economic, military, and cultural displacements. This interpretation of America, however, was not given to me in my provincial public school education in South Texas, where history began and ended with the master periodizing narratives of the Alamo. So I learned on my own all the hard facts about regional hegemony and global colonialism's cultures; for culture, my teachers believed, always lived somewhere else – never in our own backyard. I learned all the hard facts which were, of course, pejorative. But the symbology of the two Americas that José Martí mapped out for us in "Nuestra América" remained largely hidden from me.

Nothing in my background prepared me for my encounter with the Other America – a secular nation living like a dream on back of a tiger. With the sound tracks of my adolescence recirculating in me (hybrid *corrido* and *conjunto* soundings), I left South Texas to walk down the mean streets of New Haven to discover the rather different musics of America – from Walt Whitman's "I Hear America Singing" to the Funkadelics' "One Nation under a Groove" and Rubén Blades's *salsa* national anthem, "Buscando América." Quickly I was immersed in the foundational myths of the Puritan Ur-fathers, evident everywhere all around me at the Old Campus, from its neo-Gothic buildings named after dissenters like Jonathan Edwards to the mainline American and British literature taught me in undergraduate seminars and tutorials. Beyond the walled-in panopticon of the Old Campus was something called the New England Way. To see this New England America as a phantasmatics was to historicize my identifications.[5]

The purpose of these brief personal remarks is not to demonstrate a Manichaean clash of identities and affiliations, but rather to begin mapping out the phantasmatics of Nuestra América's borders at our own complex *fin de siglo*. So what began in New England America with mainline American Studies became, years later, at an "Alta" California private university (founded by a prominent robber baron and member of the Gilded Age's "Big Four"), a trail into the intricate symbologies of American Cultural Studies.[6] Both in New England America and in California I encountered an imperial literary and cultural history: Perry Miller's garden variety errand into the wilderness; R. W. B. Lewis's constructions of the American Adam; Harold Bloom's Western canon based on elite European and Euro-American isolatoes. Likewise, in California, I encountered Yvor Winters's and Wallace Stegner's constructions of the Western American literary frontier passages. The America they discovered (East Coast and West) seemingly (as Sacvan Bercovitch suggests) appeared out of nowhere, out of some Hegelian telos, respectively labeled Nature, the New England Mind, the Jeffersonian Way, and the American Frontier thesis, culminating in Newt Gingrich's all too familiar and tired "Contract with America."

American literary and cultural studies had developed, as Amy Kaplan suggests in "Left Alone with America," with a method designed *not* to explore its subject of empire, for "the study of American culture had traditionally been cut off from the study of foreign relations."[7] This was a simple lesson for someone like myself steeped in the US–Mexico "contact zone," but it required (as they say) time, comparative study, and observation to absorb. My own view of American Studies fully formed (when I studied with Sacvan Bercovitch at the School of Criticism and Theory at Dartmouth College in 1987) was that mainline America was an "artifact" made foundational text by academics, Americanists, soldiers,

anthropologists, and emergent traveling theorists. Occasionally, as in the work of a Gilded Age, frontier Americanist-ethnologist like Captain John Gregory Bourke – commissioned a first lieutenant at West Point in 1869, an Indian and Mexican hunter, and later a friend and colleague of the Smithsonian's Major John Wesley Powell and a follower of Franz Boas and Hubert Howe Bancroft – all of these force fields were embodied simultaneously.[8] Bourke's American Studies in the 1890s, I want to suggest, allow us to begin asking to what extent such disciplines as anthropology, ethnography, and travel writing legitimated the imperializing project of the U.S. government. [...]

John Gregory Bourke's eminent career as a frontier "Americanist" requires a more precise exploration, which I will elaborate below, but even in modest outline form his project as a soldier-ethnologist is a rich and intricate thematization of the United States' famous frontier field-imaginary. As his biographer Joseph Porter put it, Bourke's "fascination with the land, the history and the peoples of the Southwest" not only "compelled [him] to keep extensive diaries"[9] but also obliged him to reproduce in the writing of his cultural poetics the paradoxes of Gilded Age imperialist formation.

After graduating from West Point, Bourke was ordered by the War Department to Fort Craig, New Mexico, where he began his military and ethnographic espionage, observation, and destruction of Pueblo Indian cultures. From March 1870 to August 1871, Bourke was continually in battle with the Apaches. It was "after hours" that he wrote his prodigious diary entries, "studied up" the Native American Indians of the region, and mastered the Spanish vernacular language of the Nuevo Mexicanos. According to Porter, a pattern developed in New Mexico: after Native American (and later Mexican) hunting, Bourke "stoically worked on his diary, recording incidents and details of that day's march, noting the natural scenery, and making cartographic and geological notes" (16).

Throughout much of the 1870s, Bourke was in battle against the Native American tribes of the Southwestern United States, and he was primarily responsible for what his biographer called "the only successful campaign against the Apaches since the acquisition of the Gadsden Purchase" (20). Now a fully developed "hero of the American frontier," as Porter characteristically phrased it, Bourke traveled from New Mexico to Omaha in 1875, where he was ordered to escort the US Geological Expedition to the Black Hills. The soldier-ethnologist as well as a newly self-made "engineer officer" thus turned his attention to the Lakota and Cheyenne peoples and their native cultures. Typical of his diary entries during this period of ethnographic writing and military conquest is the following: "the sooner the manifest destiny of the race shall be accomplished and the Indian as an Indian cease to exist, the better" (quoted in Porter, 49).

Curiously enough, Bourke's destruction of "the Indian as Indian" occurred at the very same time that he was busy collecting notes, plants, animals, and pictographic artifacts of Native American and Mexican American cultures, items that he preserved by sending them off to the Smithsonian Institution in Washington, DC. In other words, Bourke, together with Major John Wesley Powell, who in 1879 became the director of the Bureau of Ethnology at the Smithsonian, displayed almost *avant la lettre* what the ethnohistorian Renato Rosaldo calls "imperialist nostalgia," nostalgia "for the very forms of life they intentionally altered and destroyed."[10]

In 1881, Lieutenant General Philip Sheridan readily agreed to Bourke's personal request to be reassigned as an "ethnologist" with the Third United Cavalry, for he concurred with Bourke's assessment that there was institutional value in documenting what we now call the cultural poetics of, in Bourke's words, "the people whom we so often had to fight and always to manage" (quoted in Porter, 280). From Chicago, Bourke embarked on a late *fin de siglo* traveling tour that took him to Idaho, Texas, and New Mexico. In Santa Fe, he began his fieldwork at the Pine Ridge Agency, observing and writing an account in his diary of the sacred Oglala Sun Dance. As Porter writes, Bourke was "amazed, moved, and impressed by what he saw" (93). These and other extended military and ethnographic search-and-destroy missions allowed Bourke to write up his first ethnographic study of Native American peoples, *The Dance of the Moquis of Arizona* (1884). Later, after he crossed the present-day US–Mexico border near Guaymas in pursuit of the Chiricahuas, he completed *An Apache Campaign in the Sierra Madre* (1886), a book largely chronicling his military travails and travels in the Western American frontier. For the remainder of his career as a soldier-ethnologist, Bourke traveled to and from Arizona, Texas, and Washington, DC. Although many of his friends in Washington attempted to secure for him various positions in the War Department offices, Bourke eventually was ordered in 1891 to rejoin the Third Cavalry unit in South Texas.[11]

The dissident Chicano folklorist and cultural anthropologist José E. Limón offers us in his cogent and provocative *Dancing with the Devil* (1994) the first detailed metacommentary on Bourke's ethnographic writings about the South Texas–Mexico border. For

Limón, Bourke's interests and his fascination with Mexicano border culture and folklore stem largely out of a "not too unconscious projection of [his] own uneasy and ambivalent ethnic identity onto the mexicanos."[12] In other words, Limón suggests, Bourke's double career as a "literal warrior turned anthropologist" (17) is not completely an example of colonialist desire; for, as a Catholic Irish-American, Bourke possessed the same ethnoracial contradictions of domination as his objects of study.

Some of Bourke's most engaging ethnographic writing about the US–Mexico borderlands, Limón asserts, unconsciously represented the Mexicanos of South Texas as suffering from the very same hegemonic forces that his own Celtic forebears had earlier experienced at the hands of the Saxon and Danish invaders of Ireland. In thus "constructing [the cultural poetics of] mexicanos," Limón claims, "Bourke was also coping with his own repudiated and projected self-ambivalences" (33). Be that as it may, my own view of Bourke's writing US–Mexico border culture, elaborated below, focuses more specifically on the molecular and molar dialectics of the cultures of US imperialism.

If US imperialism was also a cultural process, imagined and energized through recognizable signs, metaphors, tropes, and master narratives, Bourke's project of US empire was expressive and (to use Raymond Williams's term) "constitutive" of imperial relations in themselves. Through his official military reportage and documents relating to the uneven modernizing process of governing well from Fort Ringold, Rio Grande City, Texas, Bourke situated hemispheric and global colonialism's cultures and narratives in terms of what he embodied – a military captain and agent of US empire, a travel writer, and an ethnographer of South Texas border culture. Here in Bourke's frontier – not *frontera* – cultural work, my coordinates of travel, nativist modernity, anthropology, and cultures of US imperialism can be seen as constitutive of one another.

Tracking the US–Mexico Borderlands in the Gilded Age

Just three years after José Martí warned us in his magisterial "Nuestra América" of the profound gap between the two Américas, [John Gregory] Bourke collected, gathered, and published his first so-called empirical studies of the US–Mexico Borderlands. Part travel writer, and part participant-observer of the Rio Grande

Valley from "Point Isabel to Roma," Texas, Bourke wanted his travel writing/ethnographic work to shed light (as he put it in his 1894 essay "Popular Medicine, Customs, and Superstitions of the Rio Grande") "upon the character of the Mexican population of our extreme southern border."[13] Like a latter-day Perry Miller in the African wilderness, Captain Bourke traveled up and down the Rio Grande into what must have been for him and his readers the American heart of darkness. This river project leads Bourke not to Perry Miller's displaced discovery of American studies, which Amy Kaplan has shown brilliantly,[14] but to the discoveries and trespasses of an imperial American border studies, a project overwhelmingly grounded in a rhetoric of "turbulence" and "ignorance," debasement and negation. Like many ethnographers, Bourke begins his project by traveling and looking: "As the Rio Grande is the main line of communication, a trip along its waters will be necessary for anyone who desires to become even fairly well acquainted with the general character of the country and that of the people living in it."[15]

Bourke's 1894 *Scribner's Magazine* essay, symptomatically entitled "The American Congo," demonstrates how US culture in the Gilded Age was always already a global phenomenon, or at least already an extralocal and transregional project. While a good part of Bourke's essay is structured around the "being there" of travel writing and ethnographic thick description, it is also entirely underpinned with the theories of Franz Boas's anthropological project. Anthropology for Boas and his generation was, as Nicholas Thomas puts it, "a modern discourse that ha[d] subsumed humanity to the grand narratives and analogies of natural history."[16] Not surprisingly, "The American Congo" represents the US–Mexico border zone exclusively in terms of its exoticized landscape, its unceasing *mesquites*, its noisy *urracas*, and its fantastic *javelinas* and *armadillos* – what the Cuban novelist and theorist Alejo Carpentier calls "lo barroco americano" [the American baroque].[17] A sympathetic reading of "The American Congo" might therefore stress how Bourke was merely following Boas's famous dictum that "cultures differ like so many species, perhaps genera, of animals" (quoted in Thomas, 89) and so on. In other words, in "The American Congo" there is not a simple, smoothed-over colonial discourse, but instead a highly ambiguous and ethnically fraught study of Mexican *pelados* and *peones* who are represented by a Catholic, Irish American gunfighter as if they were newly discovered species, as the bearers of particular characters, physiques, dispositions, political organizations, and juridical practices.

My own reading of Bourke's "The American Congo" is less idealist, though I hope not uncharitable. Bourke is to be congratulated for showing how two imperializing hemispheric events made the Rio Grande Borderlands and its local population what he called "a sealed book" (592). Two "ethnic storms," he writes, had erased for the rest of the United States the Greater Mexican population from the national imaginary. The first was Zachary Taylor's "march from Point Isabel, near the mouth of the Rio Grande to Camargo" and then to Saltillo (592); the second was "our own Civil War, when the needs of the Confederacy suggested the transportation of all available cotton . . . across the Rio Grande to the Mexican side, and then down to Matamoros, there to be placed on steamers to Nassau and Liverpool" (592). To his great credit Bourke shows, in decidedly spatial terms, how US imperial culture is irrevocably local and global, for what makes the US–Mexico Borderlands and its inhabitants "a sealed book" are the competing mappings of global capital, the multiple roots and routes of the Black Atlantic, and the submarine discourses of what Glissant calls Antillean discourses.[18] More locally, Fort Ringold, Fort McIntosh, and Fort Brown in South Texas were part and parcel of Zachary Taylor's military campaigns in the service of US empire that resulted in what José Limón calls "the American incorporation of the Southwest" (22).

If the force field of American Border Studies in the United States was conceived by John Bourke, soldier-ethnographer, on the swirling, countercurrents of the Rio Grande in the 1890s, Chicano/a Cultural Studies – from Américo Paredes in the 1930s to John Rechy and Helena Viramontes in the 1990s – has had to challenge and undo Bourke's plethora of imperializing crude acts constituted in classic American frontier chronicles like "The American Congo," "Popular Medicine, Customs, and Superstitions of the Rio Grande" (both 1894), and "The Miracle Play of the Rio Grande" (1893). Bourke's title "The American Congo" immediately allows us metonymically and synecdochically to associate his brand of "American studies" with immediate acts such as conquest, underdevelopment, intervention, intrusion, and domination of the local *mestizo/a* Mexican inhabitants.

At the beginning of the essay, for example, Bourke recalls how a few years earlier from his military post at Fort Ringold, he had written about the Borderlands of Nuestra América to the War Department in Washington, DC: "I compared the Rio Grande to the Nile in the facts that, like its African prototype, the fierce River of the North had its legends as weird and improbable to be found in the pages of . . . Herodotus" (592). Almost in the very next sentence, however, Bourke corrects his rather baroque tropic comparison of the Rio Grande to the Nile by writing that the border zones between the United States and Mexico can be better "compared to the Congo than [to] the Nile the moment that the degraded, turbulent, ignorant, and superstitious character of its populations comes under examination" (594). One of the first constructions of the US–Mexico Borderlands of Nuestra América is therefore cast in a literalized episode of rhetorical and anthropological war between the two shifting Américas, built upon what Jacques Derrida called "the violence of the letter"[19] by one culture upon the other. Culture in this light is the nimbus perceived by one group when it comes into contact with and observes another one. It is the objectification of everything alien and weird and exotic about the contact group.

Everything about "The American Congo" from this point on draws attention to Bourke's nativist, modernist, and politically unconscious representations and to the gross imperial inequities in the dominance of Nuestra América and Africa by the United States and by Europe's cultures of imperialism. While Bourke painstakingly surveys the landscape, flora, fauna, and zoology, from "the unvarying succession of the mesquite," the "nopal," "the chappro prieto," to the fabulous "jabalin," the "rasping noise of the urraca," and the "clumsy looking armadillos" (596, 597, 598), he remains oblivious to his project of imperial gazing – surveying, collecting, organizing, and aestheticizing the landscape, flora, and fauna. His work as a travel writer–ethnographer of the US–Mexico Borderlands enabled and informed the imperial cultures of the United States to see the Mexicans of the Borderlands as ill-bred *pelados*, as lawless ("The Rio Grande Mexican has never known what law is") [606]), and as culturally inferior fatalists who indiscriminately practice what he calls a "weird pharmacy" and therapeutics of *curanderismo* (folk-healing medicine).

Bourke's "The American Congo" gives us a common-sense understanding of the emergent cultures of US imperialism. His mirroring of the African jungle and the *frontera* of Nuestra América all but effaces the local inhabitants of both continents. The geopolitical border-contact zone, moreover, is all too like the under-developed continent of Africa for Bourke. The site-specific Borderland of the Rio Grande Valley is at once a "Dark Belt" grounded in "chocolate soils," marked by the unspoken signs of melancholy, the *agachado* (stooping)

mestizo, white man's burden, and the nativist, modernist dialectics of barbarism and savagery. "The American Congo," seen in this light, founds and enacts a paradigmatic "American Studies travel tale": the construction of an ethnoracial and male soldier–culture collector in the wilderness *frontera*, surrounded by exotic animals, plants, and human cultural practices of everyday life. Moreover, we can see Bourke embodying the desire for what Richard Slotkin calls "regeneration through violence."[20] The captain of Fort Ringold, after all, is in South Texas specifically to hunt down border-crossing revolutionaries like the journalist Catarino Garza, who, as José Limón writes, "attempted to bring down the US-supported autocratic dictatorship of Mexico's Porfirio Díaz in 1891" (29) – coincidentally the very same year José Martí published his incisive critique of the Díaz regime, among others, in "Nuestra América." As Martí sharply put it, "some of the sleeping republics are still beneath the sleeping octopus." Others, he angrily criticized, are "forgetting that [Benito] Juárez went about in a carriage drawn by mules, hitched their carriages to the wind, their coachmen to soap bubbles."[21]

By exploring John Bourke's "The American Congo," I have been attempting to supplement my provisional 1991 reading of José Martí's "Nuestra América" by now bringing Bourke and Martí [. . .] spatially together in order to begin reconceptualizing American Cultural Studies. Here I am fully in agreement with Gayatri Chakravorty Spivak's challenge that "transnational Cultural Studies must put [transactions between the Americas] into an international frame."[22] The difficulties of such a project are almost insurmountable. How can we begin displacing what Donald Pease calls the old "field-Imaginary"[23] of American cultural and literary studies? How are we to begin remapping a field that is clearly no longer mappable by any of the traditional force fields I have touched on above? "If we are to benefit," as Carolyn Porter suggests in her splendid review of the emergent inter-American studies, from "trying to construct a new field imaginary, it seems crucial to pursue the logic"[24] of this comparative model.

[. . .]

What is the point in juxtaposing Bourke's imperialist and Martí's [. . .] anti-imperialist chronicles of the Borderlands of Nuestra América? In the dispersed archives of "The American Congo," . . . , and "Nuestra América," we can track the almost forgotten histories of the cultures of US imperialism. These narratives shed light on the late nineteenth-century world, on everyday life in advanced capitalism and how *letrado* and anti-*letrado* intellectuals write for and against the uneven development of modernization and modernity. These chronicles help us remember the world systems that catalyzed the rise of what Edward Said has described as the United States' truncated century of empire.[25] [...] These chronicles, too, express a great hope for an alternative chronicle of the Gilded Age – what José Martí proposed as a total rejection of the monumentalist European university for the American: "The European university must yield to the American. ... The history of America, from the Incas to the present, must be taught letter perfect, even if the Argonauts of Greece are never taught."[26] These alternative archives are indispensable for perusing crucial political visions: worlds after "The American Congo" and American empire, after Contracts with America, after nativist Proposition 187s and so-called illegal aliens.

Notes

1 *Washington Post Book World* (May 14, 1995): 8.
2 Of relevance here are the following works: Jürgen Habermas, *The Philosophical Discourse of Modernity: Twelve Lectures*, trans. Frederick G. Lawrence (Cambridge: MIT Press, 1987); Zygmunt Bauman, *Modernity and the Holocaust* (Ithaca: Cornell University Press, 1989); Julio Ramos, *Desencuentros de la modernidad en América Latina: Literatura y política en el siglo XIX* (Mexico City: Fondo de Cultura Económica, 1989); Roberto Fernández Retamar, *"Nuestra América": Cien años y otros acercamientos a Martí* (Havana: Editorial Si-Mar, 1995); and Fernando Coronil, *The Magical State: Nature, Money, and Modernity in Venezuela* (Chicago: University of Chicago Press, 1997).
3 See Rubén Martínez's *The Other Side: Fault Lines, Guerrilla Saints, and the True Heart of Rock'n'Roll* (New York: Verso, 1992), p. 1.
4 Américo Paredes, *Folklore and Culture on the Texas-Mexican Border* (Austin: CMAS and University of Texas Press, 1993), p. 84.
5 For more on phantasmatic identification, see Judith Butler's *Bodies That Matter: On the Discursive Limits of "Sex"* (New York: Routledge, 1993), esp. pp. 93–120.
6 José David Saldívar, "Chicano Border Narratives as Cultural Critique," in *Criticism in the Borderlands: Studies in Chicano Literature, Culture, and Ideology*, ed. Héctor Calderón and José David Saldívar (Durham: Duke University Press, 1991), pp. 167–80.

7 Amy Kaplan, "Left Alone with America: The Absence of Empire in the Study of American Culture," in *Cultures of U.S. Imperialism*, ed. Donald Pease and Amy Kaplan (Durham: Duke University Press, 1993), p. 11.
8 My discussion here makes use of Joseph C. Porter's *Paper Medicine: John Gregory Bourke and His American West* (Norman: University of Oklahoma Press, 1986) and José E. Limón's *Dancing with the Devil: Society and Cultural Poetics in Mexican-American South Texas* (Madison: University of Wisconsin Press, 1994).
9 Porter, *Paper Medicine*, p. 4. All subsequent references to this book will be cited parenthetically in the text.
10 Renato Rosaldo, *Culture and Truth: The Remaking of Social Analysis* (Boston: Beacon Press, 1989), p. 69.
11 Between 1886 and 1891, Bourke wrote the following books: *On the Border with Crook* (New York: Charles Scribner's Sons, 1891); *Scatologic Rites of All Nations: A Dissertation upon the Employment of Excretious Remedial Agents in Religion, Therapeutics, Divination, Witchcraft, Love Philters, etc., in All Parts of the Globe* (Washington, D.C.: W. H. Lowermilk, 1891); and *The Medicine Men of the Apache: Ninth Annual Report of the Bureau of Ethnology, 1887–1888* (Washington, D.C.: Government Printing Office, 1892).
12 Limón, *Dancing with the Devil*, p. 4. All subsequent references to this book will be cited parenthetically in the text.
13 John Gregory Bourke, "Popular Medicine, Customs, and Superstitions of the Rio Grande," *Journal of American Folk-lore* 7 (April–June 1894): 119.
14 See Kaplan, "Left Alone with America," pp. 3–21.
15 John Gregory Bourke, "The American Congo," *Scribner's Magazine* 15 (May 1894): 590–610. All subsequent references to this essay will be cited parenthetically in the text.
16 See Nicholas Thomas's *Colonialism's Culture: Anthropology, Travel, and Government* (Princeton: Princeton University Press, 1994), p. 89. All subsequent references to this book will be cited parenthetically in the text.
17 Alejo Carpentier, "The (American) Baroque and the Marvelous Real," in *Magical Realism: Theory, History, Community*, ed. Wendy Faris and Lois P. Zamora (Durham: Duke University Press, 1995), pp. 89–108.
18 See Paul Gilroy's *The Black Atlantic: Modernity and Double Consciousness* (Cambridge: Harvard University Press, 1993) and Edouard Glissant's *Caribbean Discourses: Selected Essays*, trans. and intro. J. Michael Dash (Charlottesville: University Press of Virginia, 1992).
19 Jacques Derrida, *Of Grammatology*, trans. Gayatri Chakravorty Spivak (Baltimore: Johns Hopkins University Press, 1976), p. 107.
20 Richard Slotkin, *Regeneration through Violence: The Mythology of the American Frontier, 1600–1860* (Middletown, Conn.: Wesleyan University Press, 1973).

21 José Martí, "Our America," in *The Heath Anthology of American Literature*, ed. Paul Lauter (Lexington, Mass.: D. C. Heath & Co., 1994), p. 826.

22 Gayatri Chakravorty Spivak, *Outside in the Teaching Machine* (New York: Routledge, 1993), p. 262.

23 See Donald Pease's "New Americanists: Revisionist Interventions into the Canon," in a special issue of *boundary* 2 17 (Spring 1990): 1–37.

24 Carolyn Porter, "What We Know That We Don't Know," *American Literary History* 2, no. 4 (1994): 507.

25 Edward W. Said, *Culture and Imperialism* (New York: Knopf, 1993).

26 Martí, "Our America," p. 823.

4

The Practice of Diaspora

Brent Hayes Edwards

At the dawn of the last century, W. E. B. Du Bois coined a phrase that was at once a prophecy and a preface. In July 1900, he came to London from France, where he had helped install the American Negro exhibit at the grandiose *bilan du siècle* of the Paris Universal Exposition on the banks of the Seine. Du Bois crossed the Channel to join such figures as African American feminist Anna Julia Cooper, Haitian politician Benito Sylvain, black British composer Samuel Coleridge-Taylor, and well-known former slave Henry "Box" Brown at the Pan-African Conference organized by Trinidadian lawyer Henry Sylvester Williams. In the final sessions of the conference in Westminster Town Hall, Du Bois gave a speech titled "To the Nations of the World" that opened with a stunning paragraph:

> In the metropolis of the modern world, in this closing year of the nineteenth century there has been assembled a congress of men and women of African blood, to deliberate solemnly upon the present situation and outlook of the darker races of mankind. The problem of the twentieth century is the problem of the colour line, the question as to how far differences of race . . . are going to be made, hereafter, the basis of denying to over half the world the right of sharing to their utmost ability the opportunities and privileges of modern civilisation.[1]

The second sentence ("the problem of the twentieth century is the problem of the colour line") would reverberate three years later in the famous "Forethought" to Du Bois's masterwork, *The Souls of Black Folk*, in a formulation that is often considered an inauguration for

thinking about the significance of race in the modern world.[2]

Reading *The Souls of Black Folk* as an echo of the prior usage at the Pan-African Conference necessitates coming to terms with the ways that the phrase emphatically frames the "color line" not in the US debates and civil rights struggles that are commonly taken to be its arena, but in the much broader sphere of "modern civilization" as a whole. This preface addresses "the nations of the world," but from the setting and in the name of a transnational gathering of men and women. Although the conference gathered intellectuals of African descent, it aimed to "deliberate" on and even speak for a larger population of the colonized and oppressed, the "darker races of the world." Or as Du Bois would underline again and again in the next few years, the "Negro problem" in the United States is only a "local phase" of a much greater problem: "the color line belts the world."[3]

If the Pan-African Conference was an ephemeral organization with little lasting impact, still Du Bois's phrase set the tone for the eruption of black expressive culture and political initiatives in the 1920s. As he put it later, a "world view" on the color line was all the more indispensable in the wake of a series of earthshaking events in the second decade of the century, most of all "that great event of these great years, the World War."[4] What Nathan Huggins terms the "post-war effort to thrust Negro social thought into an international arena" is a constant thread in the work of black intellectuals of the period no matter what their ideological outlook, whether Du Bois or Marcus Garvey, whether Jessie Fauset or W. A. Domingo, whether Claude McKay or

Lamine Senghor.[5] The cosmopolite Howard University philosophy professor Alain Locke claimed in the introduction to his 1925 anthology *The New Negro* that his title was partly an allusion to the Negro's "new internationalism," which represented one of the few "constructive channels" for black cultural institution building beyond the "cramped horizons" of postwar US racism and segregation.[6] With very different aims, the brilliant black socialist orator Hubert Harrison picked up the internationalist implications of Du Bois's "color line" right after the war, calling for attention to the self-determination struggles of the peoples of Egypt, India, China, and Africa, and prescribing that "before the Negroes of the Western world can play any effective part they must first acquaint themselves with what is taking place in that larger world whose millions are in motion. . . . If our problem here is really a part of a great world-wide problem, we must make our attempts to solve our part link up with the attempts being made elsewhere to solve the other parts."[7]

[. . .]

One approach to the stirrings of the cultures of black internationalism is to consider the ways that during and after the war, metropolitan France was one of the key places where African Americans, Antilleans, and Africans were able to "link up." During World War I, about 370,000 African Americans served in the segregated American Expeditionary Force in France, in both service and combat units. Along with a warm reception from French civilians, African American soldiers encountered the tangible presence of soldiers of color from throughout the French Empire. During the war, the French conscripted nearly 620,000 soldiers from the colonies, including approximately 250,000 from Senegal and the Sudan and 30,000 from the French Caribbean. France simultaneously imported a labor force of nearly 300,000, both from elsewhere in Europe and from the colonies. Although France repatriated the great majority of the "native" troops, in 1926 there were still at least 10,000 Caribbean students and workers and 1,500 black African workers in Paris alone, along with hundreds of African American visitors and expatriates.[8] After the war, tales of encounter and connection, forged in the trenches and on the docks, traveled back to the United States with the American fighting forces. Some US blacks stayed in France to study or to perform, most gravitating to Paris – for Paris had simultaneously come to appreciate jazz and *l'art nègre*, partly through the performances of military music

units like James Reese Europe's 369th Infantry Regiment "Hellfighters" Band and postwar musicians including Palmer Jones's International Five, Louis Mitchell, Arthur Briggs, Cricket Smith, Eugene Bullard, Ada Smith, and Florence Embry Jones.[9] Looking just at the culture makers usually identified with the "Harlem Renaissance," it is striking that the exceptions are those who remained in the United States. Not even to mention visual artists, almost all of the major literary figures of the period, including Anna Julia Cooper, Claude McKay, Walter White, Gwendolyn Bennett, Countee Cullen, Langston Hughes, Alain Locke, James Weldon Johnson, Jessie Fauset, J. A. Rogers, Jean Toomer, Eric Walrond, and Nella Larsen, spent time abroad and especially in Paris in the 1920s. It is often overlooked that many early Francophone Antillean and African intellectuals (such as René Maran, Kojo Tovalou Houénou, Louis Achille, Léo Sajous, and Léon-Gontran Damas) were equally mobile in the period, in Europe, Africa, and in some cases the United States as well.

Still, these numbers are nowhere near the concentration of peoples of African descent in Harlem. It is important to recognize that the significance of Paris in this period is not a question of sheer population size. Instead, as Raymond Williams has argued, the European metropole after the war provided a special sort of vibrant, cosmopolitan space for interaction that was available neither in the United States nor in the colonies. It allowed "a complexity and a sophistication of social relations, supplemented in the most important cases – Paris, above all – by exceptional liberties of expression. . . . [W]ithin the new kind of open, complex and mobile society, small groups in any form of divergence or dissent could find some kind of foothold."[10] Paris is crucial because it allowed boundary crossing, conversations, and collaborations that were available nowhere else to the same degree.

At the same time the city resonates in the cultures of black internationalism because it came to *represent* certain kinds of crossings, certain extensions of the horizon, even for populations that did not travel. [. . .] To sketch its implications quickly, one might note – just in terms of interwar black US novelistic production alone – that to ask about the function of Paris is to ask a broader set of interrelated questions about the role of outernational sites even in texts that are putatively the canonical literature of "Harlem." It is as though certain moves, certain arguments and epiphanies, can only be staged beyond the confines of the United States, and even sometimes in languages other than English. In other words, why does James Weldon Johnson's *The*

Autobiography of an Ex-Colored Man (which predates the war, but only becomes a key text after its reprinting in the 1920s) place in Berlin the narrator's realization about using folk materials in classical composition? Why does Jessie Fauset's *Plum Bun* need that Paris ending; why is the last third of her *Comedy: American Style* set in the South of France? One thinks equally of Nella Larsen's *Quicksand*, with its crucial scenes in Copenhagen, Claude McKay's *Banjo* set in Marseilles, Du Bois's *Dark Princess*, so fascinated with the corridors of international power and intrigue, or Eric Walrond's *Tropic Death*, unraveling the intricacies of imperialism and labor migration in the Caribbean basin.

Many of the black literati invested in one way or another in the notion of Harlem as a worldwide black culture capital, and yet many of them came to view Paris as a special space for black transnational interaction, exchange, and dialogue. For African American intellectuals in particular, as Tyler Stovall phrases it, the role of Paris

> was both fascinating and deeply ironic. After all, the city was the seat of one of the world's great colonial empires, a place where anonymous French officials supervised the subjugation of millions of black Africans.... Outside of Marseilles, London, and some other British cities, one could not find a more diverse black population anywhere in Europe. More so than in the United States, even New York, African Americans found that in Paris the abstract ideal of worldwide black unity and culture became a tangible reality.... French colonialism and primitivism thus paradoxically combined to foster a vision of pan-African unity.[11]

A vision of internationalism, perhaps, though not exactly "worldwide black unity": in these transnational circuits, black modern expression takes form not as a single thread, but through the often uneasy encounters of peoples of African descent with each other. The cultures of black internationalism are formed only within the "paradoxes" Stovall mentions, with the result that — as much as they allow new and unforeseen alliances and interventions on a global stage — they also are characterized by unavoidable misapprehensions and misreadings, persistent blindnesses and solipsisms, self-defeating and abortive collaborations, a failure to translate even a basic grammar of blackness.

In part, as Stovall points out, black and brown encounters on the Seine were uneasy due to the African American habit of thinking about Paris as liberatory and "free of racism" precisely at the height of French colonial exploitation. Claude McKay took the "Renaissance" literati to task on this issue:

> The good treatment of individuals by those whom they meet in France is valued so highly by Negroes that they are beginning to forget about the exploitation of Africans by the French.... Thus the sympathy of the Negro intelligentsia is completely on the side of France. It is well-informed about the barbarous acts of the Belgians in the Congo but it knows nothing at all about the barbarous acts of the French in Senegal, about the organized robbery of native workers, about the forced enlistment of recruits, about the fact that the population is reduced to extreme poverty and hunger, or about the total annihilation of tribes. It is possible that the Negro intelligentsia does not want to know about all this, inasmuch as it can loosely generalize about the differences in the treatment of Negroes in bourgeois France and in plutocratic America.[12]

This blindness allowed the "Harlem Renaissance" intelligentsia to bask in its own vanguardist myths, as it employed the putative universality of the French "Rights of Man" to decry US racism. In effect, transnational black solidarity is traded in for a certain kind of national currency, an anti-racism in one country. In this configuration, the very notion of "*Paris noir*" is paradoxical because it represents the elision of black French culture in all its forms, whether that of the Francophone African and Antillian workers, performers, and students in the metropole, or that of the expressive traditions and struggles of the populations in the French colonies themselves.

What is seldom recognized in the many condemnations of the New Negro movement as a "failure" – as myopic, elitist, or insufficiently radical – is the degree to which the paradoxes of black Paris are in fact constitutive of black modern expression in general, which is shaped to a significant degree by what Kenneth Warren has termed the "necessary misrecognitions" of diasporic discourse.[13] Attempts to articulate the "race problem as a world problem," in Locke's phrase – to foster links among populations of African descent in order to organize the "darker peoples of the world" across the boundaries of nation-states and languages – are necessarily skewed by those same boundaries.[14] That is, the level of the international is accessed unevenly by subjects with different historical relations to the nation (for instance, in a collaboration between a US citizen marked by a context of violent racist exclusion, disenfranchisement, and segregation of a minority population, and a French West African citizen marked by a context of colonialism, invasive subjugation of a majority population, and Eurocentric structures of privilege and mobility). Thus, if the cultures of black internationalism are shaped by the imperatives of what Edward Said has called "adversarial internationalization" (attempts at organizing alliances to challenge the prevailing discourses of Western universalism), those cultures are equally "adversarial" to themselves, highlighting differences and disagreements among black populations on a number of registers.[15]

Another way to put this point is to note that the cultures of black internationalism can be seen only *in translation*. It is not possible to take up the question of "diaspora" without taking account of the fact that the great majority of peoples of African descent do not speak or write in English. I have outlined some of the reasons that it makes sense to situate this question in particular through the dialogues and encounters facilitated in the French metropole between the world wars; if, as I argue, that space is privileged and richly varied, it is by no means the exclusive prism of linguistic exchange. The larger point is that one can approach such a project only by attending to the ways that discourses of internationalism *travel*, the ways they are translated, disseminated, reformulated, and debated in transnational contexts marked by difference.

It should be evident that undertaking such a project necessitates unearthing and articulating an *archive*, in the sense not so much of a site or mode of preservation of a national, institutional, or individual past, but instead of a "generative system": in other words, a discursive system that governs the possibilities, forms, appearance, and regularity of particular statements, objects, and practices – or, on the simplest level, that determines "what can and cannot be said."[16] In terms of the cultures of black internationalism between the world wars, one must consider a great variety of texts: fiction, poetry, journalism, criticism, position papers, circulars, manifestoes, anthologies, correspondence, surveillance reports. One can come to terms with what archivist Robert Hill calls the "*stratification* of the deposits" in such a discursive field only by taking stock of not just the most durable and widely circulated, but also the most fleeting – the most time-bound – modes of expressive production.[17]

This particular archive turns especially on the multi-layered, high-stakes efforts between the wars to document the "fact" of blackness itself – to frame race as an object of knowledge production in the service of a range of

adversarial internationalizations. Writing in the mid-1920s, Walter Benjamin comments in one of the orchestrated fragments of *Einbahnstrasse* that

> [t]he construction of life is at present in the power far more of facts than of convictions, and of such facts as have scarcely ever become the basis of convictions. Under these circumstances, true literary activity cannot aspire to take place within a literary framework; that is, rather, the habitual expression of its sterility. Significant literary effectiveness can come into being only in a strict alternation between doing and writing; it must nurture the inconspicuous forms that fit its influence in active communities better than does the pretentious, universal gesture of the book – in leaflets, brochures, articles, and placards. Only this prompt language shows itself actively equal to the moment. Opinions are to the vast apparatus of social existence what oil is to machines: one does not go up to a turbine and pour machine oil over it; one applies a little to hidden spindles and joints [*Nieten und Fugen*] that one has to know.[18]

The "spindles and joints" of a print culture that aims to construct the "fact" of blackness, that attempts to intervene in conditions of great suffering and social upheaval, that strains to be "actively equal" to the exigencies of crisis and advocacy, are located above all at the stratum of periodical culture. Not surprisingly, the periodical print cultures of black internationalism were robust and extremely diverse on all sides of the Atlantic. If the list of journals and newspapers in the United States during the 1920s and 1930s was better known (including the *Negro World*, the *Messenger*, the *Crisis*, the *Crusader*, *Opportunity*, the *Emancipator*, the *Voice of the Negro*, *Fire!!*, the *Chicago Defender*, and the *Amsterdam News*), their counterparts in France and Africa (one might begin with *Le Paria*, *L'Action coloniale*, *Les Continents*, *La Voix des Nègres*, *La Race nègre*, *Le Courrier des Noirs*, *La Dépêche africaine*, *Légitime Défense*, *La Revue du monde noir*, *Le Cri des Nègres*, *L'Etudiant martiniquais*, *L'Etudiant noir*, and *Africa*) were quite keen to "link up" with English-language sources and just as energetic, albeit more ephemeral.

Taking up questions of the travels of discourses of black internationalism requires investigating in particular the multiplicity of translation practices – and transnational coverage more generally – that are so crucial to the fabric of this transatlantic print culture. A significant subset of these practices is the bilingualism espoused so frequently by black periodicals in this period. In Europe, the *Negro Worker* circulated a mimeographed French edition; in New

York, the *Negro World* published a French page edited by Theodore Stephens and a Spanish page edited by M. A. Figueroa; in Paris, a number of venues (*La Revue du monde noir*, *Les Continents*, *La Dépêche africaine*) tried to publish an English-language section. If translations are in the most basic sense the practice of linguistic connection – if, in other words, translation is one of the ways the "turbine" of the cultures of black internationalism is lubricated – then it is no coincidence that this situation caused such disproportionate consternation among French and British colonial authorities. In June 1928, to take one example, an internal correspondence from the political affairs branch of the French West African colonies to the Ministère des Colonies in Paris reported that *La Dépêche africaine*, published out of the French capital, had been reaching Senegal, Guinea, and the Ivory Coast. The administrator counseled that the relatively moderate periodical should continue on the list of "suspect publications" and added that *La Dépêche africaine*, "containing a page of articles in English, could be treated a priori much more rigorously than publications only in the French language."[19] In other words, black periodicals were a threat above all because of the transnational and anti-imperialist linkages and alliances they practiced: carrying "facts" from one colony to another, from the French colonial system to the British, from Africa to the United States.

[. . .]

Elsewhere I have noted the paradox that the term *diaspora* is not taken up in the cultures of black internationalism until the mid-1950s. I have attempted to sketch a genealogy of the term, an intellectual history of the reasons it is adopted at a particular moment in the African historiography of scholars such as George Shepperson and Joseph Harris.[20] That genealogy is not my task here. I do however take up the term *diaspora* in what follows as a term of analysis in the spirit of what I consider to be its particular intervention: it makes possible an analysis of the institutional formations of black internationalism that attends to their constitutive differences. Diaspora is a term that marks the ways that internationalism is pursued by translation. This is not to say that internationalism is doomed to failure, but instead to note that it necessarily involves a process of linking or connecting across gaps – a practice we might term *articulation*.

Stuart Hall's work offers the most suggestive theoretical elaboration of articulation in relation to the particular

archive at stake here. His well-known 1980 essay "Race, Articulation, and Societies Structured in Dominance" attempts to theorize the function of difference in a global capitalist mode of production. To understand capitalist production on a "global scale," Hall writes (drawing on the work of Louis Althusser and Ernesto Laclau), that Marx began to theorize

> an articulation [*Gliederung*] between two modes of production, the one "capitalist" in the true sense, the other only "formally" so: the two combined through an articulating principle, mechanism, or set of relations, because, as Marx observed, "its beneficiaries participate in a world market in which the dominant productive sectors are already capitalist." That is, the object of inquiry must be treated as a complex articulated structure which is, itself, "structured in dominance."[21]

Articulation here functions as a concept-metaphor that allows us to consider relations of "difference within unity," non-naturalizable patterns of linkage between disparate societal elements. The functional "unity" of specific and strategically conjoined structures, then, is emphatically

> not that of an identity, where one structure perfectly recapitulates or reproduces or even "expresses" another; or where each is reducible to the other. . . .
>
> The unity formed by this combination or articulation is always, necessarily, a "complex structure," a structure in which things are related, as much through their differences as through their similarities. This requires that the mechanisms which connect dissimilar features must be shown – since no "necessary correspondence" or expressive homology can be assumed as given. It also means – since the combination is a structure (an articulated combination) and not a random association – that there will be structured relations between its parts, i.e., relations of dominance and subordination.[22]

The notion of articulation is crucial not just because it combines the structural and the discursive but also because it has a flip side: such "societies structured in dominance" are also the ground of cultural resistance. Hall, following Antonio Gramsci, contends that ideology must be considered the key site of *struggle* over competing articulations.[23] In a transnational circuit, then, articulation offers the means to account for the diversity of black takes on *diaspora*, which Hall himself explicitly begins to theorize in the late 1980s as a frame of cultural identity determined not through "return" but through difference: "not by essence or purity, but by the recognition of a necessary heterogeneity and diversity; by a conception of 'identity' which lives with and through, not despite, difference."[24]

Another way to make this point is to note that a discourse of diaspora functions simultaneously as abstraction and as anti-abstraction. We have generally come to make recourse unquestioningly to its level of abstraction, grounding identity claims and transnational initiatives in a history of "scattering of Africans" that supposedly offers a principle of unity – as Paul Gilroy phrases it, "Purity and invariant sameness" – to those dispersed populations.[25] I am arguing here neither to disclaim this history of dispersal nor to substitute another abstraction (an alternative principle of continuity, such as the oceanic frame offered by Gilroy's *Atlantic*). Instead, I am emphasizing the anti-abstractionist uses of *diaspora*. This is an ideological task that cannot be simply "won" – it is continually necessary to attend to the ways the term always can be re-articulated and abstracted into evocations of untroubled essentialism or inviolate roots. Read as an anti-abstractionist term, *diaspora* points to difference not only internally (the ways transnational black groupings are fractured by nation, class, gender, sexuality, and language) but also externally: in appropriating a term so closely associated with Jewish thought, we are forced to think not in terms of some closed or autonomous system of African dispersal but explicitly in terms of a complex past of forced migrations and racialization – what Earl Lewis has called a history of "overlapping diasporas."[26] The use of the term *diaspora*, I am suggesting, implies neither that it offers the comfort of abstraction, an easy recourse to origins, nor that it provides a foolproof anti-essentialism: instead, it forces us to articulate discourses of cultural and political linkage only through and across difference in full view of the risks of that endeavor.

If a discourse of diaspora articulates difference, then one must consider the status of that difference – not just linguistic difference but, more broadly, the trace or the residue, perhaps, of what resists or escapes translation. Whenever the African diaspora is articulated (just as when black transnational projects are deferred, aborted, or declined), these social forces leave subtle but indelible effects. Such an unevenness or differentiation marks a constitutive *décalage* in the very weave of the culture, one that cannot be either dismissed or pulled out. Léopold Senghor has written suggestively about the differences and influences between US blacks and African blacks as spun out across such a gap:

Le différend entre Négro-Américains et Négro-Africains est plus léger malgré apparences. Il s'agit, en réalité, d'un simple décalage – dans le temps et dans l'espace.[27]

Despite appearances, the difference between Negro-Americans and Negro-Africans is more slight. In reality it involves a simple *décalage* – in time and in space.

Décalage is one of the many French words that resists translation into English; to signal that resistance and, moreover, to endorse the way that this term marks a resistance to crossing over, I will keep the term in French here.[28] It can be translated as "gap," "discrepancy," "time-lag," or "interval"; it is also the term that French speakers sometimes use to translate "jet lag." In other words, a *décalage* is either a difference or gap in time (advancing or delaying a schedule) *or* in space (shifting or displacing an object). I would suggest, reading somewhat against the grain of Senghor's text, that there is a possibility here in the phrase "in time *and* in space [italics added]" of a "light" (*léger*) and subtly innovative model to read the structure of such unevenness in the African diaspora.

The verb *caler* means "to prop up or wedge" something (as when one leg on a table is uneven). So *décalage* in its etymological sense refers to the removal of such an added prop or wedge. *Décalage* indicates the reestablishment of a prior unevenness or diversity; it alludes to the taking away of something that was added in the first place, something artificial, a stone or piece of wood that served to fill some gap or to rectify some imbalance. This black diasporic *décalage* among African Americans and Africans, then, is not simply geographical distance, nor is it simply difference in evolution or consciousness; instead it is a different kind of interface that might not be susceptible to expression in the oppositional terminology of the "vanguard" and the "backward." In other words, *décalage* is the kernel of precisely that which cannot be transferred or exchanged, the received biases that refuse to pass over when one crosses the water. It is a changing core of difference; it is the work of "differences within unity,"[29] an unidentifiable point that is incessantly touched and fingered and pressed.

Is it possible to rethink the workings of "race" in the cultures of black internationalism through a model of *décalage*? Any articulation of diaspora in such a model would be inherently *décalé*, or disjointed, by a host of factors. Like a table with legs of different lengths, or a tilted bookcase, diaspora can be discursively propped up (*calé*) into an artificially "even" or "balanced" state of "racial" belonging. But such props, of rhetoric, strategy, or organization, are always articulations of unity or globalism, ones that can be "mobilized" for a variety of purposes but can never be definitive: they are always prosthetic. In this sense, *décalage* is proper to the structure of a diasporic "racial" formation, and its return in the form of *disarticulation* – the points of misunderstanding, bad faith, unhappy translation – must be considered a necessary haunting. This reads against the grain of Senghor, if one can consider his Négritude one influential variety of this diasporic propping up. Instead of reading for the *efficacy* of the prosthesis, this orientation would look for the *effects* of such an operation, for the traces of such haunting, reading them as constitutive to the structure of any articulation of diaspora.

Recall that Hall points out the word *articulation* has two meanings: "both 'joining up' (as in the limbs of the body, or an anatomical structure) and 'giving expression to.'"[30] He suggests that the term is most useful in the study of the workings of race in social formations when it is pushed away from the latter implication, of an "expressive link" (which would imply a predetermined hierarchy, a situation where one factor makes another "speak"), and toward its etymology as a metaphor of the body. Then the relationship between factors is not predetermined; it offers a more ambivalent, more elusive model. What does it mean to say, for example, that one *articulates a joint*? The connection speaks. Such "speaking" is functional, of course: the arm bends at the elbow to reach down to the table, the leg swivels at the hip to take the next step. But the joint is a curious place, as it is both the point of separation (the forearm from the upper arm, for example) and the point of linkage. Rather than a model of ultimate debilitation or of predetermined retardation, then, *décalage*, in providing a model for what resists or escapes translation through the African diaspora, alludes to this strange ("two-ness" of the joint. It directs our attention to the "antithetical structure" of the term *diaspora*, its risky intervention. My contention, finally, is that articulations of diaspora demand to be approached this way, through their *décalage*. For paradoxically, it is exactly such a haunting gap or discrepancy that allows the African diaspora to "step" and "move" in various articulations. Articulation is always a strange and ambivalent gesture, because finally, in the body it is *only* difference – the separation between bones or members – that allows movement.

Notes

1 W. E. B. Du Bois, "To the Nations of the World," in *W. E. B. Du Bois: A Reader*, ed. David Levering Lewis (New York: Henry Holt, 1995), 639. See also Lewis, *W. E. B. Du Bois: Biography of a Race, 1868–1919* (New York: Henry Holt, 1993), 246–51.

2 Du Bois, "The Forethought," *The Souls of Black Folk* (1903), in *Writings* (New York: Library of America, 1986), 359.

3 Du Bois, "The Color Line Belts the World," *Collier's Weekly* (October 20, 1906): 30, collected in *W. E. B. Du Bois: A Reader*, 42.

4 Du Bois, "The Negro Mind Reaches Out," *Foreign Affairs* 3, no. 3 (1924), collected in *The New Negro* (1925; reprint, New York: Atheneum, 1989), 385.

5 Nathan Huggins, *Harlem Renaissance* (New York: Oxford University Press, 1971), 41.

6 Alain Locke, "The New Negro," in *The New Negro*, 13, 14.

7 Hubert Harrison, "Our International Consciousness," *When Africa Awakes* (1920; reprint, Baltimore: Black Classic Press, 1997), 100–1, 103.

8 Tyler Stovall, "Colour-Blind France? Colonial Workers during the First World War," *Race and Class* 35 (1993): 35–55; *The Marcus Garvey and Universal Negro Improvement Association Papers, vol. 1: 1826–August 1919*, ed. Robert A. Hill (Berkeley: University of California Press, 1986), 292n1; Philippe de Witte, "Le Paris noir de l'entre-deux-guerres, in *Le Paris des étrangers: depuis un siècle*, ed. A. Kaspi and A. Marès (Paris: Imprimérie Nationale, 1989), 157–69.

9 Reid Badger, *A Life in Ragtime: A Biography of James Reese Europe* (New York: Oxford University Press, 1919); Chris Goddard, *Jazz Away from Home* (New York: Paddington Press, 1979); Michael Haggerty, "Transes Atlantiques," *Jazz Magazine* 325 (January 1984): 30–1.

10 Raymond Williams, *The Politics of Modernism: Against the New Conformists* (London: Verso, 1989), 45.

11 Tyler Stovall, *Paris Noir: African Americans in the City of Light* (Boston: Houghton Mifflin, 1996), 90.

12 Claude McKay, *The Negro in America*, translated from the Russian by Robert Winter, ed. Alan McLeod (Port Washington, NY: Kennikat Press, 1979), 49.

13 Kenneth W. Warren, "Appeals for (Mis)recognition: Theorizing the Diaspora," in *Cultures of United States Imperialism*, ed. Amy Kaplan and Donald E. Pease (Durham, NC: Duke University Press, 1993), 404–5.

14 Locke, "The New Negro," 14.

15 Edward Said, "Third World Intellectuals and Metropolitan Culture," *Raritan* 9 (Winter 1990): 31.

16 David Scort, "Preface," in "The Archeology of Black Memory: An Interview with Robert A. Hill," *Small Axe* 5 (March 1999): 82. See also Michel Foucault, *The Archeology of Knowledge*, trans. A. M. Sheridan Smith (New York: Pantheon, 1972), 129.

17 Hill, "The Archeology of Black Memory," 120.

18 Walter Benjamin, "One-Way Street" (1928), in *Selected Writings, vol. 1: 1913–1926*, trans. Edmund Jephcott, ed. Marcus Bullock and Michael W. Jennings (Cambridge:

Harvard University Press, 1996), 444 (modified). The original is Benjamin, *Einbahnstrasse* (1928; reprint, Frankfurt am Main: Suhrkamp Verlag, 1955), 8.

19 Jules Carde, Direction des Affaires Politiques, letter to the Ministère des Colonies, June 26, 1928, *La Dépêche africaine* folder, Archives Nationales, Section d'Outre-Mer, Service de Liaison avec les Originaires des Territoires de la France d'Outre-Mer (abbreviated henceforth as SLOTFOM), series V, box 2 (abbreviated henceforth as "V, 2").

20 Brent Hayes Edwards, "The Uses of *Diaspora*," *Social Text* 66 (spring 2001): 45–73.

21 Stuart Hall, "Race, Articulation, and Societies Structured in Dominance" (1980), reprinted in *Black British Cultural Studies: A Reader*, ed. Houston A. Baker, Manthia Diawara, and Ruth H. Lindeborg (Chicago: University of Chicago Press, 1996), 33.

22 Ibid., 38.

23 Other work touching on the importance of the term in Birmingham cultural studies includes Jennifer Daryl Stack, "The Theory and Method of Articulation in Cultural Studies," in *Stuart Hall: Critical Dialogues in Cultural Studies*, ed. David Morley and Kuan-Hsing Chen (New York: Routledge, 1996), 112–30; and the interview with Hall, "On Postmodernism, and Articulation,"

131–50, in the same volume. Fredric Jameson offers a more idiosyncratic genealogy of the term (in his review essay "On 'Cultural Studies,'" *Social Text* 34 [1993]: 30–3), but elegantly notes the ways the term implies a "poetic" between the structural and the discursive (32).

24 Stuart Hall, "Cultural Identity and Diaspora," in *Identity, Community, Culture, Difference*, ed. Jonathan Rutherford (London: Lawrence and Wishart, 1990), 235.

25 Tommy Lott, "Black Cultural Politics: An Interview with Paul Gilroy," *Found Object* 4 (fall 1994): 56–7.

26 Earl Lewis, "To Turn as on a Pivot: Writing African Americans into a History of Overlapping Diasporas," *American Historical Review* 100 (June 1995): 765–87.

27 Senghor, "Problématique de la Négritude" (1971), in *Liberté III: Négritude et civilisation de l'universel* (Paris: Seuil, 1977), 274. The translation is my own.

28 Ranajit Guha, *Dominance without Hegemony: History and Power in Colonial India* (Cambridge: Harvard University Press, 1997) 13, 157. See also Guha, *Elementary Aspects of Peasant Insurgency in Colonial India* (Durham, NC: Duke University Press, 1999), 173, 330.

29 Senghor, "Problématique de la Négritude," 278.

30 Hall, "Race, Articulation, and Societies Structured in Dominance," 41.

5

Removal

Tiya Miles

Elizabeth Shoeboots was the head of her household, the mother of small children, and a survivor of enslavement. She was also among the thousands of Cherokees who faced the rude awakening of Indian Removal. Twice she was forced out of her home, made to recover and rebuild, first at the hands of slavecatchers and then at the hands of American soldiers. The expulsion of the Cherokees from the Southeast had its foundation in an illegal compact. In 1802 the US government entered into an agreement with the state of Georgia, promising to expel the Indians in the state's territory in exchange for Georgia's relinquishment of particular lands in the West. Over the ensuing twenty-five years, Georgia argued that the federal government was failing to fulfill this compact. Though the Cherokees did cede thousands of acres during these years, they still occupied lands that Georgia claimed. The ratification of the Cherokee Constitution in 1827 further incensed Georgia officials, who insisted that the notion of a sovereign Cherokee republic violated the state's rights to certain lands. Georgia then extended its jurisdiction into Cherokee territory, annulled Cherokee laws, and insisted that any white people in the Cherokee counties of the state of Georgia must seek the state's permission to remain there. The US Supreme Court cases *Cherokee Nation v. Georgia* (1831) and *Worcester v. Georgia* (1832) developed in response to Georgia's action of incorporating the Cherokee Nation. The Supreme Court decided in favor of Cherokee semisovereignty, defined as "domestic dependent nation[hood]" and deemed Georgia's action illegal. However, the outcome of the 1828 presidential election, won by celebrated Indian fighter Andrew Jackson, would render the Supreme Court decisions ineffectual.

A longtime and vehement proponent of Indian relocation, Jackson refused to enforce the Supreme Court's rulings and instead defended the state of Georgia. Jackson's first State of the Union address in December 1829 outlined a plan for Indian "removal" and urged Congress to enact it through legislation. This would be a national policy, affecting not only the Cherokees and other southeastern nations but also nations in the Midwest. Jackson argued in his address that the fact of American progress was to be commended, not regretted: "Philanthropy could not wish to see this continent restored to the condition in which it was found by our forefathers. What good man would prefer a country covered with forests and ranged by a few thousand savages to our extensive Republic, studded with cities, towns, and prosperous farms, embellished with all the improvements which art can devise or industry execute, occupied by more than 12,000,000 happy people, and filled with all the blessings of liberty, civilization, and religion?"[1] In Jackson's view, the removal of eastern Indians to a region west of the Mississippi was "not only liberal, but generous." They would be isolated and protected from the white man's influence, and their cultures would be better preserved. In the end, Jackson argued, this move West would be beneficial to the Indians, the impetus and opportunity for positive development:

Doubtless it will be painful to leave the graves of their fathers; but what do they [do] more than our ancestors did or than our children are now doing? To better their condition in an unknown land our forefathers left all that was dear in earthly objects. Our children by thousands yearly leave the land of their birth to seek new homes in distant regions, Does humanity weep at these painful separations from everything, animate and inanimate, with which the young heart has become entwined? Far from it. It is rather a source of joy that our country affords the scope where our young population may range unconstrained in body or in mind, developing the power and faculties of man in their highest perfection. . . . Can it be cruel that this Government when, by events which it can not control, the Indian is made discontented in his ancient home to purchase his lands, to give him a new and extensive territory, to pay the expense of his removal, and support him a year in his new abode? How many thousands of our own people would gladly embrace the opportunity of removing West on such conditions![2]

Jackson's address launched heated debates in the House and Senate. Supporters of the Cherokees and Indian tribes, such as missionary Jeremiah Evarts (whose pen name was William Penn) and journalist John Howard Payne, vehemently protested removal. In one of his famous William Penn essays, Evarts argued: "The American Indians, now living upon lands derived from their ancestors, and never alienated nor surrendered, have a perfect right to the continued and undisturbed possession of these lands. . . . These rights of soil and sovereignty are inherent in the Indians, till voluntarily surrendered by them; and cannot be taken away by compacts between communities of whites, to which compacts the Indians were not a party."[3] Nevertheless, the final votes in Congress favored the Indian Removal Act, with numbers as close as 28 to 19 in the Senate and 102 to 97 in the House. On May 28, 1830, Jackson signed the act into law.

Cherokee political leaders followed these developments closely, reprinting the congressional debates in the *Cherokee Phoenix* and writing articles in defense of Cherokee sovereignty. Cherokee people without official positions of leadership also protested and debated the issue. In October 1831 a delegation of Cherokee women appeared before the National Council to urge resistance to the new law. They asserted in their petition: "We believe that the present plan of the General Government to effect our removal West of the Mississippi, and thus obtain our lands for the use of the State of Georgia, to be highly oppressive, cruel and unjust. And we sincerely hope there is no consideration which can induce our citizens to forsake the land of our fathers of which they have been in possession from time immemorial, and thus compel us, against

our will, to undergo the toils and difficulties of removing with our helpless families hundreds of miles to unhealthy and unproductive country."[4] John Ross, principal chief of the Cherokee Nation, agreed with the women, as did the majority of Cherokees. By 1833, however, a minority faction of Cherokee leaders began to advocate removal. They argued that it could not be prevented, and thus it was in the best interest of the Cherokee people to accept the inevitable and negotiate a favorable treaty with the United States.

The leaders of this proremoval group were Major Ridge, his son John Ridge, and his nephews, Elias Boudinot and Stand Watie, friends and business partners of Shoe Boots. As internal dissension grew among Cherokees, the United States and the state of Georgia increased their pressure. In 1834 the federal government ceased payment of monies to the Cherokees that were their right by treaty, and in 1835 the state of Georgia enlisted the Georgia Guard to seize the Cherokee printing press and thus disable the publication of the *Cherokee Phoenix*. In the autumn of 1835, US officials took advantage of the opportunity that Cherokee discord presented. They met with members of the minority faction and their supporters, numbering almost two hundred in all, in the capital town of New Echota. There the members of this faction, that came to be known as the Treaty Party, signed the Treaty of New Echota, a document that sanctioned Cherokee removal in accordance with the Indian Removal Act and established that removal must occur within two years of the treaty's ratification. The Treaty of New Echota was blatantly fraudulent, since it bypassed the recognized channels of Cherokee government and lacked the support of the majority of the Cherokee population, numbering almost sixteen thousand. However, despite vehement Cherokee protests that included a petition of fifteen thousand signatures, the treaty was ratified by the US Congress in 1836.[5] Most Cherokees refused to believe that this was their fate: to be moved West, the direction that signified darkness and death in Cherokee culture, and to be forced into an unknown land against their will. For the next two years the majority of Cherokees continued to fight removal through political protest and the defiant act of living in their homeland. In 1838, when the designated two-year period had ended, they were pressed to abandon that land by force of arms.

If slavery is the monumental tragedy of African American experience and the trauma of continual return in the memory of black people, then removal plays the same role in American Indian experience. The theft and destruction of lives, lands, and cultures link these events as holocausts, and in the specific context of Cherokee history, slavery and removal are intimately connected. The expulsion of Cherokee people cleared the way for the expansion of American slavery into those abandoned lands; the expansion of slavery then contributed to the rapid growth of cotton production that would dramatically boost the US economy. At the same time, the presence of black slaves during removal made it possible for their Cherokee masters to survive the ordeal and to rebuild efficiently in the West. The institution of American slavery depended on Cherokee removal, even as the "success" of removal depended on slavery. The experience of Elizabeth Shoeboots and her family members, then, for whom slavery and removal were conjoined forces, in fact reflects a broader phenomenon. Ironically, or perhaps not, this historical moment, which so clearly revealed the interdependence of white supremacist systems, marked a negative turning point in relations between blacks and Cherokees. Removal would open a seemingly unbridgeable gulf between Cherokees and blacks because it exacerbated preexisting tensions and prejudices even while eliminating the historical bases of communication and negotiation.

Forced removal was carried out summarily by the US military and the local Georgia militia, with little regard for Cherokee dignity or life. On May 10, 1838, General Winfield Scott, the executor of removal, issued a warning to the Cherokee people: "My troops already occupy many positions . . . and thousands and thousands are approaching from every quarter to render assistance and escape alike hopeless. . . . Will you, then by resistance compel us to resort to arms . . . or will you by flight seek to hide yourself in the mountains and forests and thus oblige us to hunt you down?"[6] Women, children, and the elderly were rousted out of their cabins and directed at gunpoint by soldiers. Men were yanked from the fields, with many unable to locate and join their disheveled families. Forced to leave most of their possessions behind, the Cherokees were sometimes present as white Georgians immediately took ownership of their cabins, looting and burning cherished objects. Daniel Butrick, a missionary of the American Board, summarized the scene in his journal: "Women absent from their families on visits, or for other purposes, were seized, and men far from their wives and children were not allowed to return, and also children being forced from home, were dragged off among strangers. Cattle, horses, hogs, household furniture, clothing and money not with them

were taken and left."[7] One Georgia militiaman who was present reported: "I fought through the civil war and have seen men shot to pieces and slaughtered by thousands, but the Cherokee removal was the cruelest work I ever knew."[8]

According to a high-ranking officer, by June 1838 the fields and hills, valleys and riverbanks that Georgia claimed were now free of Cherokees. General Charles Floyd, a Georgia militia member in command of Cherokee expulsion from the state, reported to the governor on a job well done: "Sir: I have the pleasure to inform your excellency that I am now fully convinced there is not an Indian within the limits of my command, except a few in my possession, who will be sent to Ross' Landing tomorrow. My scouting parties have scoured the whole country without seeing an Indian, or late Indian signs. If there are any stragglers in Georgia, they must be in Union and Gilmer counties, and near the Tennessee and North Carolina line; but none can escape the vigilance of our troops. Georgia is ultimately in possession of her rights in the Cherokee country."[9] Being captured and commanded against their will were only the first traumas of the Cherokees' removal experience. Like captive Africans awaiting the slave ships or Japanese Americans during World War II, Cherokee people, numbering almost fifteen thousand, were loaded into "stockades," or concentration camps, until the appointed time of their departure.[10] There, crowded together in makeshift shelters in the moist summer heat, many fell ill. Though General Scott had planned for the expulsion of the Cherokees by steamboat in the summer, the heat was intolerable, and Chief John Ross requested permission for the remaining Cherokees to organize their own removal in the cooler autumn weather.

That next fall, the Cherokees divided into thirteen groups of nearly one thousand people, each with two appointed leaders.[11] They set out on multiple routes to cross Tennessee, Kentucky, Illinois, Missouri, and Arkansas at ten miles a day with meager supplies. Among these groups were black people and black-Cherokees, slave and free, who traveled with the Cherokees to remain near relatives, to escape enslavement in the white South, and to serve their masters. Whites who had married Cherokees as well as white missionaries like Butrick also made the journey. At certain points along the way, the straggling bands of travelers were charged fees by white farmers before they could cross privately owned land. The few wagons available to them were used to carry the sick, infants, and the elderly. Most walked. They walked through the fall and into the harsh winter months, suffering the continual deaths of loved ones to cold, disease, and accident. White Path, leader of the Cherokee rebellion against the new constitution back in 1827, became deathly ill during the march. According to an article in the *Kentucky Gazette*, dated November 1838, "White Path ha[d] been in the last stages of sickness for many days and ha[d] to be hauled and [was] helpless." He died on the Trail at the age of seventy-five.[12] Quatie Ross, wife of Principal Chief John Ross, also lost her life en route to Indian Territory. Rebecca Neugin, a small child at the time of removal, recounted her family's experience to historian Grant Foreman in 1932:

> When the soldiers came to our house my father wanted to fight, but my mother told him that the soldiers would kill him if he did and we surrendered without a fight. They drove us out of our house to join other prisoners in a stockade. . . . My father had a wagon pulled by two spans of oxen to haul us in. Eight of my brothers and sisters and two or three widow women and children rode with us. My brother Dick who was a good deal older than I was walked along with a long cow whip. . . . My father and mother walked all the way also. . . . There was much sickness among the emigrants and a great many little children died of whooping cough.[13]

Butrick, who continued to keep a journal during the march, also recorded in entry after entry the increasing rates of illness and death.

For those Cherokees who owned or had access to black women and men, the harsh impact of removal was blunted. In addition to bearing the hardships of the journey, slaves were enlisted to do the additional work of hunting for their masters, nursing the sick, preparing meals, guarding the camps at night, and hiking ahead of the group to ensure passable roads.[14] Butrick recorded in his journal the labors and deaths of a handful of blacks in his detachment. One elderly black woman, whose children had recently purchased her freedom, "died in the camps." Her son, Peter, and his wife were then sold to slave speculators. Along the Trail, one black man "cut some wood for the night," and a black woman, "our kind Nancy," was "employed . . . to wash and [dry] our clothes in the evening by the fire." An unnamed black man died on a February day that also took four Cherokee lives: "During this time five individuals have died, viz. one old Cherokee woman, one black man, and three Cherokee children, making in all since we crossed the Tennessee River 26 deaths."[15] Many people lost their lives during the Cherokee removal, and scholars attempting to count

those deaths have estimated four thousand. Historian and demographer Russell Thornton has argued that this figure is much too low. He in turn has offered his own estimate, which takes into account not only actual deaths but also the loss in population that resulted from a decline in the birthrate. Thornton estimates that the total Cherokee population loss due to forced removal was more than ten thousand people.[16]

Describing Cherokee removal by way of miles and deaths captures the quantitative hardship of the incident but misses its psychological and spiritual reverberations. In her novel *Pushing the Bear*, Cherokee poet Diane Glancy has reframed this event by imagining the inner journeys of those who walked. Glancy constructs a multivoiced history by weaving together the threads of diverse experiences. She balances the voices of Maritole, a young Cherokee woman and the main character of the novel, with Maritole's family members, Cherokee Christians, traders, elders, and spirits. Excerpts from historical documents such as property claims and government reports are also woven into the text, creating a narrative that is layered and expansive. Unlike Andrew Jackson's representation of removal as an improving exercise, Glancy depicts the affair as a nightmare. In Glancy's portrayal the walk West is a life-stealing march, which Maritole describes in the bleakest of terms: "We were marching west toward darkness, toward death. . . . The cold sat upon my bones. It was as though I had no clothing. It was as though I had no skin. I was nothing but a bare skeleton walking the path." Maritole's brother, Tanner, renames the Trail of Tears to express the reality of spiritual and physical death, saying, "Behind us for a hundred miles stretched the trail of ghosts of our dead ones."[17]

Glancy articulates the injustice of removal by underscoring the significance of place for the Cherokees, the relationship between land and identity. For at the center of the removal tragedy is the deep and life-sustaining relationship between Cherokee people and their land. So central is the land to this story that it becomes a character in Glancy's rendering, materialized by the maps that begin each chapter and by the words of the Cherokee characters. The use of maps in the book that trace the route of departure allows for the visual reenactment of displacement, even as it unmasks the force behind removal, since early maps were both expressions and tools of European colonialism. The conceptualization of the natural world as voiced by the characters emphasizes the importance of the land base depicted in the early maps, the homeland that is being left behind. In one instance while the people are walking the Trail, a holy man tries to comfort them by reciting the cure for lost voice: "These (five barks) cure them with: Cherry, a small acorn oak, flowering dogwood, bitter apple, big (white) willow." The other characters respond anxiously: "'What if those trees don't grow outside Cherokee land?'" and "'What if the words only work on land where we were born?'"[18] The intimate relationship, even union, of land and people is reiterated in a recurring and mutating phrase spoken by various characters in the novel: "we were the land."

As the families, friends, and neighbors of Glancy's imagination drag themselves across an unforgiving country, they consistently invoke their homeland, its places and stories. While Maritole tries to soothe an ailing friend, she whispers, "The old land won't leave us, Luthy. We carry it within us wherever we're going."[19] But even as the characters invoke their old home, they are desperately aware of their loss. One woman thinks to herself, "I felt a grief so deep it was nearly silent. We were the land. The red clay people with mouths that would talk. Sometimes I even thought I could hear the hens cackle on my farm. I looked over my shoulder. If only I could listen hard enough." The alienation the characters feel as they travel further from their homeland is exemplified in Maritole's dream of an empty landscape. "In the nights my spirit walked a slick road. I dreamed all the land was white as the inside of an apple. It would never be anything but white."[20]

As the characters in *Pushing the Bear* march from their home place to an unknown place, they wonder how a people can survive apart from their land when the people *are* the land. The conceptual framework introduced in Glancy's novel allows us to understand that Indian Removal was more than the relocation of bodies and possessions. It was the tearing of the flesh of the people from the same flesh of the land, a rupture of soul and spirit. This rupture contributed to the deterioration of tribal well-being, as factionalism and civil war fractured the Cherokees in the West. Concurrently, removal created a legacy of detachment between Cherokees and blacks that would lessen potential for cross-racial alliances and narrow the possibility of subverting racial hierarchies. In the Cherokee Nation West, the treatment of slaves became harsher and more rigid, since much of the flexibility that had endured in the East was extinguished by law.

Key to making sense of the decline in relations between Cherokees and blacks in the West is Glancy's paradigm of place. For Cherokees and other Native peoples, place was paramount in maintaining cultural values and moral relationships. Displacement, therefore, was likely to weaken those values and relationships. Removal separated Cherokees and blacks from the ground where they first encountered one another and developed bonds, and thus it damaged ties of connection that were inscribed and reinforced in the landscape. In their studies of place and its meanings for human societies, geographers David Lowenthal and Kenneth Foote have addressed the meaning and resonance of homeland. Lowenthal notes, in exploring the phenomenon of homesickness, that the intensity of a people's relationship to their homeland is due in part to the fact that the history of the people is tangible in the terrain.[21] Similarly, Foote explains that "the physical durability of landscape permits it to carry meaning into the future so as to help sustain memory and cultural traditions."[22]

Deriving meaning and tradition from the land is especially important to American Indian people, the only population indigenous to the United States. Land, specifically homeland, sustains Native identities and values, not just because it is the place where the people eat and sleep, but because it is a repository of the people's cultural ways, beliefs, and histories. Laguna Pueblo writer Leslie Marmon Silko explains in an essay titled "Interior and Exterior Landscapes: The Pueblo Migration Stories" that tribal stories hold the people's communal identity and are themselves held in place by the land. Each story is connected to a specific location in the Pueblo homelands, and a story is recalled when a person comes across a geographical marker that corresponds with that tale. In this intimate relationship between story, identity, and place, the earth itself sustains and reinforces who the people are.[23] N. Scott Momaday intimates a similar relationship in his personal, family, and tribal memoir, *The Way to Rainy Mountain*. Here he journeys through Kiowa history and culture in fragmentary episodes that intertwine landmarks, stories, and personal revelations. In his introduction to the book Momaday captures the ability of a geographical feature, in this case Rainy Mountain, to mark and contain the history of a people and thereby to restore personal and community life. Toward the conclusion of the book Momaday dwells on the indescribable and boundless power of place and the necessity for people to be in close relationship with the land: "Once in his life a man ought to concentrate his mind upon the remembered earth, I believe. He ought to give himself up to a particular landscape in his experience, to look at it from as many angles as he can, to wonder about it, to dwell upon it.

He ought to imagine that he touches it with his hands at every season and listens to the sounds that are made upon it. He ought to imagine the creatures there and all the faintest motions of the wind. He ought to recollect the glare of noon and all the colors of the dawn and dusk."[24]

Anthropologist Keith Basso also explores this relationship to homeland illustrated by Silko and Momaday. In his work with the Western Apache, Basso has found that landscape plays a profound role in reinforcing their identity and regulating group morality. Basso explains that one category of Western Apache stories, which he terms "historical narratives," are told to discourage unacceptable behavior and to set the listener on a path of self-correction and self-renewal.[25] These stories, cautionary tales that depict a person doing something wrong and that warn of the negative consequences of his action, are always tied to a location where the original event is said to have taken place and always include the name of that place within the narrative structure. The listener, the target of such a story, is moved to change through the sting and shame of rebuke. When a person who has been the target of an historical narrative passes by the location where that story took place, she is reminded of her mistake and encouraged again to live right. Often historical narratives are imparted to a younger person by an older relative, so that the stories are imbued not only with the lesson and location of the original event but also with the spirit and memory of the teller: "Apaches view the landscape as a repository of distilled wisdom, a stern but benevolent keeper of tradition, an ever-vigilant ally in the efforts of individuals and whole communities to put into practice a set of standards for social living that are uniquely and distinctively their own."[26]

In a sense these stories live in the land, since the landscape holds them steady and brings them to mind in the service of the people. It follows, then, that Western Apaches view the land as an enduring protector of community values. As Basso puts it, "grandmothers and uncles must perish but the landscape endures, and for this the Apache people are deeply grateful." One Western Apache man, Nick Thompson, made a blunt and evocative statement: "The land looks after us . . . the land keeps badness away." For Western Apaches, memories of community values are embedded in the land, and separation from that land leads to forgetfulness, transgression, and trouble. As Basso explains, "losing the land is something the Western Apache can ill afford to do, for geographical features have served the people for centuries as mnemonic pegs on which to hang the moral teachings of their history." The power of homeland and consequences of separation from it are not unique to Western Apaches. For Native people across a range of tribes, epistemologies and moral codes are tied to landscapes and places.[27]

Indian Removal disrupted the relationship between Cherokees, their homeland, and the stories that lived there. As a result, the cultural values embedded in those stories could no longer be reinforced through the visible markers of place. The two hundred years of history that Cherokees had shared with Africans in the Southeast would also have been inscribed in the landscape. Family and community memories involving black friends and relatives would have been marked and recalled by the locations where significant events happened; a Cherokee story about the effects of displacement serves as a metaphor for this connection between human relations and terrain. In "The Removed Townhouses," Cherokee people are separated from their relatives, first by the spirit world and then by federal removal policy. This story was recorded by ethnologist James Mooney between 1887 and 1890 in his meetings with Cherokee oral traditionalists in North Carolina:

> Long ago, long before the Cherokees were driven from their homes in 1838, the people on Valley river and Hiwassee heard voices of invisible spirits in the air calling and warning them of wars and misfortunes which the future held in store, and inviting them to come and live with the Nunnehi, the Immortals, in their homes under the mountains and under the waters. . . . The people were afraid of the evils that were to come, and they knew that the Immortals of the mountains and the waters were happy forever, so they counciled in their townhouses and decided to go with them. . . . They are there now, and on a warm summer day, when the wind ripples the surface, those who listen well can hear them talking below. When the Cherokees drag the river for fish the fish-drag always stops and catches there, although the water is deep, and the people know it is being held by their lost kinsmen, who do not want to be forgotten.

> When the Cherokees were forcibly removed to the West one of the greatest regrets of those along the Hiwassee and Valley rivers was that they were compelled to leave behind forever their relatives who had gone to Nunnehi.[28]

"The Removed Townhouses" tells of the sad end to a relationship that was already compromised by difference – the difference between the human world and the spirit world. The people on the Hiwassee and Valley Rivers were separated from their relatives because those relatives had joined the immortals. Still, the two groups were able to communicate through the river that linked them across that difference. Leaving the Cherokee homeland during removal meant severing that connection. In the new place, there would be no Hiwassee River, no historical landmark to serve as a repository of memory and a medium of communication.

The deterioration of relations between Cherokees and blacks postremoval can be understood in similar terms. Cherokees and blacks were already separated in the Southeast by the breach of race, as Cherokees began to own slaves and to codify racial definitions and hierarchies. At the same time though, individuals belonging to these groups were connected through the places where they lived together. Like the river in the story, those places could serve as channels for connection and negotiation. Removal meant tearing the people – Cherokee, black, and Afro-Cherokee – away from those places, thus cementing the distance between them. History has not recorded the many events, weighty and whimsical, that took place between Doll, her children, and other Cherokees who lived on the Etowah River. We do know, however, that the river would have served as a marker of those events, a reminder of the relationships that were born and nourished there. Relationships, like stories, belonged to places and were held fast by them. With the loss of those places, fragile relationships were left vulnerable to deterioration.

The despair that characterized the new western communities in 1840, along with an emerging culture of disconnection from the past, made it easier for some Cherokees to adopt Euro-American values to the detriment of the black people living among them. The ties of kinship, respect, and affection between Cherokees and individual blacks who had survived the early stages of slavery were weakened by the division of Cherokees from their homeland. The places where blacks and Cherokees had raised families together were now behind the state lines of Georgia and Tennessee. In a new landscape devoid of embedded mutual memories, the people were separated by a cavernous divide of race and caste.

The beleaguered Shoeboots family, along with many others, made this journey of no return. Doll went West before her daughters, transported by flatboat and steamship, with Major and Susannah Ridge and their slaves. In 1838 Elizabeth and her sister, Polly, walked the Trail of Tears with their young children and relatives. All crossed into another world. The Drennen Roll of 1851, which catalogs the Cherokees who emigrated during forced removal, lists Elizabeth and Polly side by side, each followed by the names of their dependents:

Lizzy Boot, All-se, Sally, Lotty, Morrison, Dahsegahyahge

Polly Boot, Mireah, Eliza Hammer, Louisa, Lizzy, Mary, Chahwahyoocah[29]

Uprooted from the Etowah River in the Cherokee Nation East, what would become of their family in the Cherokee Nation West?

Notes

1   Andrew Jackson, State of the Union Address, December 6, 1830, in *The Cherokee Removal: A Brief History with Documents*, ed. Theda Perdue and Michael Green (Boston: Bedford Books, 1995), 119–20.
2   Jackson, State of the Union Address, 120.
3   William Penn, "A Brief View of the Present Relations between the Government and People of the United States and the Indians within our National Limits," November 1829, in *Cherokee Removal* (see note 1), 97.
4   Cherokee Women, Petition, October 17, 1831, in *Cherokee Removal* (see note 1), 126.
5   Members of the Treaty Party refused to accept the legitimacy of the petition, arguing that a number of the signatures were falsified. Thurman Wilkins asserts that some names appeared more than once on the petition, while others belonged to babies; Thurman Wilkins, *Cherokee Tragedy: The Ridge Family and the Decimation of a People* 2nd ed. (Norman: University of Oklahoma Press, 1986), 292.
6   Quoted in Grant Foreman, *Indian Removal* (1932; reprint, Norman: University of Oklahoma Press, 1972), 286.
7   Daniel Butrick, *The Journal of Rev. Daniel S. Butrick, May 19, 1838-April 1, 1839, Monograph One* (1839; reprint, Park Hill, Okla.: Trail of Tears Association Oklahoma Chapter, 1998), 2.
8   James Mooney, *Historical Sketch of the Cherokee* (1897; reprint, Washington, D.C.: Smithsonian Institution, 1975), 124.
9   Foreman, *Indian Removal* 296.
10 Russell Thornton, "The Demography of the Trail of Tears Period: A New Estimate of Cherokee Population Losses," in *Cherokee Removal*, ed. William Anderson (Athens: University of Georgia Press, 1991), 80.
11 Mooney, *Historical Sketch of the Cherokee*, 126.
12 Quoted in Foreman, *Indian Removal*, 303.
13 Foreman, *Indian Removal*, 302–3.
14 Theda Perdue, *Slavery and the Evolution of Cherokee Society*, 1540–1866 (Knoxville: University of Tennessee Press, 1979), 71.
15 Butrick, *Journal*, 32–3, 54, 61, 58.
16 Thornton, "Trail of Tears," 91. The number of blacks who died along the Trail of Tears has not been estimated.

17   Diane Glancy, *Pushing the Bear: A Novel of the Trail of Tears* (New York: Harcourt Brace, 1996), 58, 86.

18   Glancy, *Pushing the Bear*, 128.

19   Glancy, *Pushing the Bear*, 179, 87.

20   Glancy, *Pushing the Bear*, 179, 191.

21   David Lowenthal, "Past Time, Present Place: Landscape and Memory," *Geographical Review 65* (January 1975): 1–36.

22   Kenneth Foote, *Shadowed Ground: America's Landscapes of Violence and Tragedy* (Austin: University of Texas Press, 1997), 33.

23   Leslie Marmon Silko, *Yellow Woman and a Beauty of the Spirit: Essays on Native American Life Today* (New York: Simon and Schuster, 1996), 25–47. For an in-depth exploration of place and its relationship to Native women's experiences and historical identities as well as black women's lives, see Catherine Griffin, " 'Joined Together in History': Politics and Place in African American and American Indian Women's Writing" (PhD diss., University of Minnesota, 2000).

24   N. Scott Momaday, *The Way to Rainy Mountain* (Albuquerque: University of New Mexico Press, 1969), 83.

25   Keith Basso, *Wisdom Sits in Places* (Albuquerque: University of New Mexico Press, 1996); Basso, "Stalking with Stories," in *Western Apache Language and Culture* (Tucson: University of Arizona Press, 1990), 99–137.

26   Basso, "Stalking," 129.

27   Basso, "Stalking," 127, 128, 130.

28   "The Removed Townhouses," in James Mooney, *Myths of the Cherokee* (1900; reprint, New York: Dover, 1995), 335–6. This story might be attributed to one or more of Mooney's major sources, the Cherokee storytellers named Swimmer and John Ax.

29   *Drennen Roll of the Cherokee Indians*, 1851 (Tulsa, Okla.: Indian Nations Press, 1851), Delaware District, nos. 1041, 1042.

6

Redefining Security: Okinawa Women's Resistance to US Militarism

Yoko Fukumura and Martha Matsuoka

On the eve of the gathering of the heads of state from the United States, France, Italy, Canada, the United Kingdom, Japan, Germany, and Russia (the "G8") in Okinawa in July 2000, a group of Okinawan women hosted an international meeting of women to strategize about women's responses to globalization and militarization. The International Women's Summit to Redefine Security was held in Naha and drew women from Okinawa, Japan, South Korea, the Philippines, the United States, and Puerto Rico. Following their summit, the women issued a statement:

> The purpose of this meeting was to challenge the principle of "national security" on which the economic policies of the G8 are based. These economic policies can never achieve genuine security. Rather, they generate gross insecurity for most peoples of the world and devastate the natural environment. These economic policies are inextricably linked to increasing militarization throughout the world. Militaries reap enormous profits for multinational corporations and stockholders through the development, production and sale of weapons of destruction. Moreover, militaries maintain control of local populations and repress those who oppose the fundamental principles on which the world economic system is based. (East Asia – US Women's Network Against Militarism 2000)

The statement sent two messages. First, national security interests do little for women in East Asia and the United States. Instead, principles of "national security" provide the rationale for an increased global militarization that privileges profit over people. In doing so, the global militarized economy breeds deep insecurity by increasing the economic and environmental vulnerability of local communities, particularly that of women and children. Second, women resisting the presence of US militarism in their respective communities were organizing across national borders to put forth alternative frameworks for global security and sustainability. Challenging the traditional paradigms of "security," the women instead assert a framework of security based on the following four key tenets (Reardon 1998):

- The environment in which we live must be able to sustain human and natural life;
- People's basic survival needs for food, clothing, shelter, health care, and education must be met;
- People's fundamental human dignity and respect for cultural identities must be honored; and
- People and the natural environment must be protected from avoidable harm.

With these principles in mind, women from Asia and the US gathered in Okinawa to raise awareness and visibility of the local Okinawan women's resistance to the US military and the negative impacts of globalization and militarization. Not only is the framework relevant to the struggle of East Asian women against the US military, it also illuminates examples of women struggling worldwide to survive increasing economic and environmental insecurity in a global context in which neoliberal economic policies push for the privatization of state assets, lower barriers to trade, and elimination of restrictions of transnational movement of capital. [. . .]

In Okinawa, this framework of alternative security emerges from a dynamic of material conditions facing women across East Asia who live with the ongoing presence of the US military. The emergence of women's resistance to militarism must be seen in context of the relationship between the US military presence and globalization in East Asia. In a revealing speech delivered at University of California, Los Angeles, in October 1998, then Secretary of Defense William Cohen remarked, "U.S. troops would be the most professional and most ready military in the world in order to protect the emerging and stabilizing capital markets around the globe." His remarks, in the wake of the Asian financial crisis, explicitly tie the presence of the US military to the future of globalizing economies and to the support and protection of national governments in the struggle to develop markets. Though his rhetoric made direct the link between the US military and globalizing economies, John Feffer (2000) argues that the relationship between the military and globalization in East Asia is much more complex than Cohen implies and that policies of globalization and US militarism "do not always mix well in East Asia." Feffer notes:

> Certain military imperatives, such as a regional missile defense system, have driven wedges between countries that neoliberals want to unite through free trade. Moreover, certain economic trends, such as the deregulation of financial markets, have weakened some of the very countries that U.S. troops and battleships are pledged to protect. Herein lies the central problem for U.S. policy toward East Asia: the tension between core military and economic objectives. U.S. military strategy in the region depends on the maintenance of the Cold War, with North Korea, China, or a set of new "threats" substituting for the Soviet Union. U.S. economic strategy, although initially forged in the crucible of the Cold War, is increasingly dependent on breaking down ideological divisions in the region. (22)

The combination of neoliberal economic policy and Cold War military strategies, or "gunboat globalization," Feffer argues, must be replaced by a multilateral policy framework that assumes the cooperation between and within countries in East Asia. Certainly, governmental actors are key in this transformation of policy, but Feffer also acknowledges the role of civic actors and activism that challenge military budgets, labor conditions, and employment security:

> A true multilaterialism – independent of the United States, economically equitable, and accountable to the citizens of the region – cannot be solely created by government officials. As transnational movements in East Asia are discovering, true multilaterialism must be built from the ground up. (22)

An examination of Okinawan women and their resistance to US militarism suggests that such a strategy to address globalization and militarization may be possible in Asia. Using the case study of Okinawa Women Act against Military Violence (OWAAMV), a nongovernmental, grassroots organization, this chapter examines the cultural, historical, political and economic context of antimilitarism in Okinawa. Drawing on the ideology and strategies used by OWAAMV women, we argue that their activism suggests alternative paths of security and development in the face of globalization and militarization.

[. . .]

Women's Resistance to the Military

When the world's media flocked to Okinawa in the summer of 2000 to cover the G8 Summit, Okinawans staged a prefecture-wide protest to raise awareness of the negative effects of the US military in Okinawa. Nearly 30,000 Okinawan people linked arms in protest to form a human peace chain around Kadena Air Base, the largest US Air Force base in the Pacific, timed for the arrival of President Clinton. Just days before, a young schoolgirl had been assaulted by a drunken US Marine while she slept in her home; the same week, another US serviceman committed a hit-and-run in which an Okinawan man was struck while crossing a street.

These Okinawan acts of resistance against the US military were not new, however. [. . .]

In 1995, about 85,000 people came together in Naha, the capital of Okinawa, in the largest public demonstration and rally in postwar Okinawa, to protest the brutal rape of a 12-year-old schoolgirl by three US servicemen. The rape, and specifically the girl's decision to report the rape to local authorities and make public the crime committed against her, catalyzed a resurgence of antimilitary activism in Okinawa. Carolyn Bowen Francis (1999) writes,

> Parents, teachers, and students, many of whom up until now remained silent on the troubling issue of the mammoth U.S. military presence, rose up as one, raising their

voices to declare, "No More!" in the largest, most broad based and longest lasting citizen protest in postwar Okinawan history. Their response sent unexpected tremors reverberating not only throughout Japan, but also throughout the U.S., ultimately shaking the very foundations of the U.S.-Japanese defense relationship spelled out in the U.S.-Japan Security Treaty and the more detailed U.S.-Japan Status of Forces Agreement. (189)

That nearly 1 in 10 people within the entire prefecture turned out for the demonstration signified a clear revival of the antimilitarism movement, which focused for the first time on the US military presence as an act of violence against women and children. Fueling the movement were protests of the legal procedures that privilege the US military. Following the rape, the accused were not turned over to the Japanese authorities for 25 days. The men eventually stood trial in Okinawa, were found guilty, and are now serving sentences of between six and one-half and seven years in Japan. Over the course of the trial and sentencing, the protests continued. Finally, on September 8, 1996, a year after the rape, the people of Okinawa went to the polls to vote on the first prefecture-wide citizen referendum in Japan's history. The nonbinding but highly symbolic referendum, asked, "Do you support the continued presence of US military in Okinawa?" Sixty percent of voters cast ballots; 90 percent voted "no," raising a loud voice against the presence of the US military in Okinawa (Johnson 1999, 12).

The visibility of the issues of women and children in the reemergence of antimilitarism was due to the active leadership role of Okinawan women, and in particular Okinawa Women Act Against Militarism (OWAAMV). Since its formation, campaigns and activities have reflected a perspective on militarism that recognizes women's rights as human rights and the military as an affront to human security. Keiko Itokazu, co-chair of OWAAMV and an elected member to the Okinawa Prefectural Assembly, says:

Our campaigning is not anti-U.S., but against military forces. The Japanese forcibly involved women in Okinawa in that wheel of destruction. During the war, not just women from Okinawa and the mainland but all over the region, Taiwan and Korea, were all called in to serve the requirements of the military. The military always forces women into this unproductive process of destruction; that is what their existence and logic is all about. Only with that sort of logic, war logic, could the destruction of our natural environment and the denial of women's human rights be possible. (Itokazu 1996, 11)

In a report to the International Conference on Violence against Women in War and Armed Conflict Situations OWAAMV argued that (1) even in times of "peace," the long-term military presence results in violence against women, (2) military facilities represent sites of violence, illustrated by deployment of US military forces from Okinawa to engage in conflict in Korea, Vietnam, and the Persian Gulf; (3) training facilities used by military personnel expose residents and civilians to physical and psychological domination and risk to safety; (4) the extent of violence against women is related to the attitudes of the host government, reflecting the status of women, human rights, and the legal system that is in place to protect the status of women in society; (5) violence against women and the violation of their human rights is related to the economic relationships between the country deploying the military presence and the country receiving the military presence; and (6) the military is a male-dominated structure that maintains constant war-making readiness, domination, and violence (Takazato 1997a).

Japanese feminist scholar Yayori Matsui (1998) further notes that OWAAMV's activism is drawn from a framework of alternative security.

Okinawan women challenge the very concept of security by asking whose security it is if women and children are raped and harassed by military men and put under fear and threat. They forcefully call for people's and women's security, not security of the state. They claim that violence against women cannot be prevented without confronting and doing away with U.S. military dominance and without achieving demilitarization in the Asia-Pacific region. They emphasize that the army itself is a mechanism of violence. They also broadened the concept of violence against women from war and armed conflict situations to cover the situations of long-term military presence, because women near military bases are constantly victimized by sexual violence, even if there is no war or armed conflict. (61)

Ueunten (1997) suggests that OWAAMV has been able to frame antimilitarism in a way that goes beyond nationalism, one which moves toward a broader sense of community reflecting the historical evolution of the Okinawan diaspora. The political and economic history of Okinawa, the international relationships between the United States and Japan, and the colonial legacy of both nations in Okinawa serve as a complex backdrop for any local antibase struggle. Traditional explanations using colonial theory to describe Okinawa's history and future have limited the historical and potential agency of Okinawans to define their own history and future. Ueunten argues, however, that the activism of OWAAMV challenges these explanations by putting forward a type of activism which recognizes and emerges from the implications of Okinawan history, culture, and political and economic conditions under Japanese and US rule.

[...]

Strategies for Action

OWAAMV has grown to approximately 200 members. Co-chairs are elected annually, and a 10-woman steering committee leads the group. The steering committee meets once a month and on an as-needed basis; the general membership meets every six months. OWAAMV supports itself through donations, honoraria, and membership dues of 2,000 yen per year (approximately $20). All decisions are made through consensus of the members. Co-chair Suzuyo Takazato (1999) notes that "in Okinawan culture, consensus is the only way. Though we as women quarrel and disagree on certain issues, we come together and move onward together."

Activities of OWAAMV reflect five key strategies: direct action and protest, education and awareness, building networks and alliances, electing women to public office, and youth development and leadership.

Direct action and protest

The emergence of OWAAMV and its continuing activities illustrate the central role of direct action and protest in women's organizing throughout Okinawa and the world. The experiences of direct action and protest provided the base for the formation of OWAAMV following the 1995 rape. Since then, the organization has undertaken other forms of direct action such as a 12-day women's sit-in protest and signature campaign in November 1998 to raise Okinawan awareness of military violence against women. On the fifth day of the sit-in, a 25-member delegation traveled to Tokyo to deliver an appeal with 55,000 signatures to the Japanese prime minister, the Foreign Ministry, and the US Embassy to protest the rape and the US military presence in Okinawa (Bowen Francis 1999, 192). Additional examples of direct action include organizing demonstrations such as the human chain formed around Kadena Air Base in 1999 and during the G8 Summit in July 2000.

Education and awareness

A core area of OWAAMV work focuses on raising awareness of the effects of the US military in Okinawa. Members have compiled a detailed chronology of acts of violence committed by US military members against Okinawans and documented the presence and impact of military toxics. With this research, they make presentations to women's organizations, peace and environmental groups, labor unions, churches, and student organizations within Okinawa and in mainland Japan in order to expand their membership and build their campaigns.

In mid-1998 OWAAMV began a campaign along with US-based environmental organizations to protect the endangered *dugong*, a species of manatee found off the western coast of Okinawa. The Okinawan women see the survival and preservation of the *dugong* as necessarily tied to the prevention of the construction of a proposed military heliport that would destroy the habitat of the *dugong* and as a way to preserve the delicate marine ecosystem of the coral reef. In addition, OWAAMV is involved in campaigns focused on the cleanup of toxic contamination at military installations. These campaigns include demands for access to information, adequate funding to conduct public health and toxics assessments, and the staff and money to clean up military sites when they close and to get pollution-prevention measures started at operating sites.

OWAAMV leaders recognize the necessity of building international pressure to push the Japanese government to take action on environmental cleanup of the military bases in Okinawa. In collaboration with another NGO, the Okinawa Environmental Network, a representative from OWAAMV attended the International Grassroots Summit on Military Base Cleanup held in Washington, DC, in October 1999. Together with activists from 10 countries in which the United States has military bases, a Host Country Bill of Rights was created to demand a set of guidelines to address the harm of toxics created by US military activities in host countries (Matsuoka 1999). These organized trips to participate in and speak at international events have been a large part of OWAAMV's work. Visits to and from international conferences are widely covered in the local Okinawan media, reflecting OWAAMV's commitment to building a cadre of media reporters, many of whom are women, to report on their struggles. In their visits to the United States in 1996 and 1998, delegates included columnists from the Okinawan press who provided daily reports from the delegation.

Following the 1995 rape, OWAAMV organized a four-city (San Francisco Bay Area, Boston, Honolulu, and Washington, DC) women's peace caravan through the United States and met with elected officials and community organizations to raise awareness of the effects of the US military on women and the environment in Okinawa. A similar peace caravan was organized in 1998, stopping in Los Angeles, San Diego, and Washington, DC. Both caravans included teachers, local government representatives, youths and community organizers.[13][. . .]

Issues of concern during the caravans and the congressional hearings were articulated in four key areas: (1) US military violence against women, including domestic abuse, rape, and prostitution; (2) environmental damage, including the need for cleanup of US bases in Okinawa and the public health effects of toxics; (3) Amerasian children; and (4) Status of Forces Agreements and Treaties that determine the scope and scale of US military presence in Okinawa. During its 1998 trip, the group presented the following specific demands at the Congressional briefing (Okinawa Women Act against Military Violence 1998):

- We call for a full investigation of all past US military crimes against women in Okinawa
- We call for the reduction and realignment, not the mere moving around of US military bases within Okinawa; moreover, we call for the removal of US military forces, especially the Marine force, from Okinawa
- We call for a halt of the plan to build a new offshore heliport base in Okinawa that will cause environmental destruction
- We call for full disclosure of all past military base toxic contamination in Okinawa, for the establishment of a toxic cleanup plan and for the clarification of responsibility for cleanup; to achieve these goals we call for the revision of the Status of Forces Agreement
- We call for the guarantee of the human rights of women and children and the necessary passage and enactment by each of the countries involved to realize that guarantee.

Other international educational strategies include organizing a delegation of women and youths to participate in the Hague Appeal for Peace talks in May 1999. A key objective was to demand action by the international courts to address issues of military violence against women in the Pacific. With the announcement that the G8 Summit would be held in Okinawa in July 2000, the group developed a set of activities and actions designed to develop alternative analyses and critiques of the global economic and military system. Recognizing the media opportunities provided by the G8 Summit, the group also agreed to organize an International Women's Summit as a way to focus media attention on militarization and its negative effects on women, children, and the environment in Okinawa. OWAAMV developed a series of local educational workshops to raise issues such as globalization and alternative security paradigms. At the invitation of the group, feminist scholar Betty Reardon led a workshop to discuss women's rights as human rights and to outline her framework of security, which is based on elements of human needs rather than national needs.

[. . .]

Paths to genuine security

Through its activism, OWAAMV continues to point to the US military's role in creating conditions of insecurity for women, children, and the environment. At the same time, the group recognizes that the military base lands held by the United States must be returned to local government control if alternative paths of development are to be achieved. The broad membership and support base of OWAAMV reflects its ability to organize across lines of class, nation, and the division between urban and rural. It also illustrates the resonance of militarism as a critical issue for women, and it positions antimilitary activism in a broader context of redefining national security. These themes of antimilitarism and security resonate with the ecological feminist framework developed by Seager (1993) and Kirk (1997). The framework identifies economic and political institutions as "perpetrators of ecologically unsound investment." Both argue that within this framework, it is possible to make global connections across lines of difference – race, class, and nation – to build alliances. Specifically, Kirk argues that an ecological feminism

> must oppose the structural/social economic adjustment policies of northern governments, as well as militarism and the culture of violence it generates and requires. This means opening up a public debate that challenges and opposes the values and practices of this economic system – its hazardous production processes as well as its consumerist ideology – rather, framing progress in terms of sustainability, connectiveness and true security. (361)

For Okinawan women, the opportunity to demonstrate these forms of alternative security is fast approaching. In late 1998, the Special Action Committee on Okinawa (SACO) report outlined a Base Return Action Program announcing the return of nine US military posts in Okinawa to the Japanese government by the year 2001; 14 by 2010; and 17 by 2015. On an island with little developable land, the closure of these military sites, including the immediate return of Futenma Air Station (1,200 acres), presents an opportunity to develop Okinawa's local economy. Plans emerging from the prefectural government have included such concepts as the "Multimedia Island," a plan to develop a multimedia industry in Okinawa. The concept argues that such a plan will "create jobs for 24,500 people or one percent of the entire labor population in the nation, which is expected to reach 2.45 million by 2010, in the area of information and communications." Other highlights of the reuse concept include the development of a resort in the northern part of the island, the establishment of a new urban development at Futenma Air Station, and the expansion of the Naha military port (Okinawa Prefectural Government 1998).

The alternative security framework put in practice by OWAAMV triggers a critique of such development approaches. It is unclear, for example, whether a "Multimedia Island" concept will address the key issues of meeting people's basic needs, ensuring that the environment will sustain human and natural life, honoring people's human dignity and respect of cultural identities, and ensuring that people and the environment be protected from avoidable harm. Beyond a critique of existing development proposals, OWAAMV must now face the challenges of how to create everyday examples and models of this alternative security framework. Based on the experiences of military base closure, conversion, and reuse in the United States and the Philippines, the challenge of creating development that will serve the local community is a daunting one. Three key considerations are (1) the cleanup of military toxics; (2) the need for a overall reuse plan that addresses the needs of local people, particularly women and children; and (3) a well-organized and powerful political force to ensure that cleanup and reuse processes are fully funded and implemented.

In the eight years between 1988 and 1995, the US Department of Defense closed 12 domestic military sites in the San Francisco Bay Area and transferred the land and facilities to local and other nonmilitary governmental bodies. The process of converting former military lands into civilian uses requires the cleanup of environmental toxics, the development of a reuse and redevelopment plan, and implementation of the plan. To date,

at least $1.6 billion have been spent on environmental cleanup alone at the sites (*Los Angeles Times* 2000). Hunters Point Naval Shipyard, in San Francisco, has been closed for more than 25 years and not fully reused because of the presence of military toxics. The problem of cleanup is partially technological as scientists and engineers work to find ways in which to clean up the toxics. But the problem is also highly political. In 2000, the United States plans to spend $1.72 billion on the cleanup of its domestic bases; all overseas bases will share $165 million (Matsuoka 1999). Okinawans have little access to the decision makers in Washington who allocate military base cleanup funding. While OWAAMV has documented the impact of military toxics and begun to develop relationships with US-based activists on issues of military toxics and cleanup, it is clear that more capacity must be developed in Okinawa to engage in activism specifically focused on issues of military toxics and cleanup.

Second, as former military land becomes available for local reuse, OWAAMV is poised to play a powerful leadership role in determining the scope and framework of local development plans. Toward this end, it is able to draw on earlier successful experiences. OWAAMV have helped develop community-serving projects including a Prefectural Women's Building that provides programs, services, and resources to and about women in Okinawa. Other efforts include a domestic violence and rape hotline and counseling center. Plans are under way to develop a women's shelter modeled after such successful shelters as the Asian Women's Shelter in San Francisco and My Sisters Place in South Korea. While not to the scale necessary to generate economic activity equal to an operating military base, the models established by the women represent possible approaches to develop other community-based projects and the locally controlled institutions that will further these projects. They are tangible, physical and relevant examples of development that reflect principles of alternative security and provide real critiques of development processes that have little to do with local resources.

Using these examples as prototypes, OWAAMV may be able to promote its agenda for alternative security and development. The task itself is daunting especially in the face of powerful political and economic interests that privilege US and Japanese corporate and government interests over the interests of the people. Yet as McCormack (1998) argues, the current development road consisting of military bases, public works, and tourism is unsustainable in the long term.

Okinawa now faces a choice between being incorporated in the nationstate-centered regional and global order as a hyper-peripheral hyperdependent backwater to be despoiled by the "slash-and-burn" of rampant development (*ran-kaihatsu*) or, alternatively, becoming a base for the creation of a 21st century's new, decentralized, sustainable and naturally balanced order. The latter could only be accomplished by a prodigious concerted effort, almost certainly of an international character. (7)

Third, the struggle of military base cleanup and reuse requires broad political support that spans Okinawa, Japan, and the United States. There are important lessons to be learned from earlier base conversion efforts. In the Philippines, women organized to develop a reuse plan for Subic that recognized the need for reuse activities that addressed the needs of women and children. Government officials, however, opted for a plan that emphasized the need to attract foreign investment, promoting development such as free trade zones, hotels, casinos, and large-scale resorts. Similar lessons from base reuse at the Alameda Naval Shipyard in California suggests that community-based plans require a strong organized constituency to build the political power necessary to get community plans adopted in formal reuse processes (Matsuoka 1999). Having reviewed the citizen-initiated reuse plan developed for the Subic base in the Philippines and met with activists involved in the Alameda base closure, OWAAMV is aware of what it will take to organize and develop the political will to support a citizen-based plan. Currently the organization's organizing strategies focus on mobilizing women around issues of women's rights as human rights, not of base conversion and reuse issues. Shifting focus to a base conversion agenda even with women's issues as a central focus will require a revisiting of organizing strategies. How OWAAMV chooses to develop its future organizing strategies remains an important question.

Conclusion

This chapter has attempted to outline the dimensions of Okinawan women's activism against militarization. It illustrates how women in Okinawa have built an organization as well as the leadership, networks, and power to influence the debates on military presence in Okinawa. Through this resistance and political activism, Okinawan women have developed a proactive stance toward political self-determination, democracy, and overall security for women and children. Their struggle is not only an act of resistance against the US military and the complicit government of Japan, but also a struggle to build a community-based vision of security in the face of increasing globalization. The movement has helped frame proactive development alternatives to the military industrial complex that exists in Okinawa and the Pacific region. Moreover, their resistance exemplifies what Feffer (2000) suggests may be a strategy of bottom-up multilateralism. Thus, some of the seeds of an alternative development path have been planted. But much remains to be done.

The possibility of reusing closed military sites presents an immediate opportunity and daunting test of OWAAMV's intention and ability to shape future local development in Okinawa. While women have put in place a framework and examples of community-based projects to meet the needs of women, children, and the environment, the scope and scale of these projects remains relatively small in relation to the ongoing presence and dominance of the US military. Yet these examples embody and emerge from a women's activism that has laid a path of resistance that has at its core an alternative vision of peace and security.

References

Bowen Francis, Carolyn. 1999. "Women and Military Violence." Pp. 189–203 in *Okinawa: Cold War Island*, ed. Chalmers Johnson. Cardiff, CA: Japan Pacific Resource Institute.

East Asia–US Women's Network against US Militarism. 1999. "Project Summary."

Feffer, John. 2000. "Gunboat Globalization: The Intersection of Economics and Security in East Asia." Special issue on Globalization, Militarism, and Armed Conflict. Okazawa-Rey and Kirk, co-editors. *Social Justice* 27(4): 45–62.

Itokazu, Keiko. 1996. "The World Can Learn from Our History." Pp. 10–17 in *Okinawa Dreams O.K.*, ed. Tony Barell and Rick Tanaka. Berlin: Zehdenicker Strase.

Johnson, Chalmers. 1999. "The 1995 Rape Incident and the Rekindling of Okinawan Protest against the American Bases." In *Okinawa: Cold War Island*, ed. Chalmers Johnson. Cardiff, CA: Japan Pacific Resource Institute.

Kirk, Gwyn. 1997. "Standing on Solid Ground: A Materialist Ecological Feminism." Pp. 345–63 in *Materialist Feminism: A Reader in Class, Difference and Women's Lives*, ed. Rosemary Hennessy and Chrys Ingraham. New York: Routledge.

Matsui, Yayori. 1998. "History Cannot Be Erased, Women Can No Longer be Silenced." *Women's Asia 21: Voices from Japan* no. 4. 26–32. Tokyo, Japan: Asia-Japan Women's Resource Center.

Matsuoka, Martha. 1999. "An Environmental Justice Framework for Base Conversion." Panel presentation to the International Grassroots Summit on Military Base Cleanup.
Washington, DC: October 25–29.

McCormack, Gavan. 1998. "Okinawan Dilemmas: Coral
Islands or Concrete Islands." Working Paper No. 45. The Japan
Policy Research Institute, San Diego, California.

Okinawa Prefectural Government, Military Base Affairs Office.
1998. "A Message from Okinawa: U.S. Military Bases in
Okinawa." Retrieved March 1999, http://www.pref.okinawa.jp.

Okinawa Women Act against Military Violence. 1998.
"Okinawa Women's American Peace Caravan." Pamphlet.

Reardon, Betty A. 1998. "Gender and Global Security: A
Feminist Challenge to the United Nations and Peace
Research." *Journal of International Cooperation Studies.* 6(1):
1–28.

Seager, Joni. 1993. *Earth Follies: Coming to Feminist Terms with
the Global Environmental Crisis.* New York: Routledge.

Takazato, Suzuyo. 1977. "The Military Mechanism: Systemic
Violence and Women." Okinawa Country Report to the
International Conference on Violence against Women in
War and Armed Conflict Situations, October 30–November
3, Tokyo.

——. 1999. Personal interview. July 24.

Ueunten, Wesley. 1997. "In the Shadow of Domination: The
Asian American and Okinawan Movements." Unpublished
manuscript, Department of Ethnic Studies, University of
California-Berkeley.

Part II

States, Citizenship, Rights

This analytic represents the emergence of research questions that force a rethinking of the state form, the citizens with which it engages and the rights it claims to guarantee, through an emphasis on the performative nature of subjectivity that focuses on the construction of new subjects in the contested interstices between law and society. It also marks the emergence of debates and conversations distinct from those informed by concerns with conceptions of the state's obligations to its citizens, the growth of bureaucracy and prescriptive regulation, and critiques of the shift from citizen to client in the clientelist state. While earlier work often implicitly conceived a maternal state as it examined contradictions, ambiguities, and contests over providing education, welfare, and services, more recent work has emphasized technologies of discipline in a carceral and punitive state. The articles in this analytic might usefully be viewed, in effect, as emphatic additions to the critique of an abstract, disembodied notion of citizenship and a state that responds dispassionately to each abstract citizen. From Peggy Pascoe's account of US states' control during the nineteenth century over the inheritance of property through statutes forbidding not just intermarriage, but unions between white women and men of color, to the articles by Leti Volpp and Moustafa Bayoumi on the racial profiling and denial of citizenship rights to groups held suspect by US officials after the 9/11 terror attacks, these articles attest to the importance of the role of the state in determining who possesses the right to have rights.

These articles critique the assumption of a free, rational subject/citizen participating in the public sphere, and remind us forcefully that, to paraphrase Volpp, not all citizens are equal. Citizenship, as the outcome of state processes of inclusion and exclusion, is highly contingent. In the United States, citizenship, in terms of life chances and the ability to exercise political and social rights of equal protection and opportunity, while substantially revised from the original republic of white male property owners, has always been limited by race and gender, notwithstanding occasional claims of a color-blind constitution. If the state is the mechanism of enforcement, marking the boundaries between citizens and noncitizens, and enacting sovereignty, the American nation – and nationalism – derives from the affective ideological union of those who, by virtue of the inherently racial understanding of citizenship rooted in our origins as a slave society, often cannot imagine themselves as citizens without denying others that status.

Laura Doyle's article locates the origins of the modern West's exclusionary, racialized notion of liberty and freedom in the seventeenth-century Atlantic world. Without discounting the slave trade and establishment of New World slavery as crucibles of modern racism, Doyle argues that Anglo-Atlantic literature and the work of such philosophers as Rousseau and Hegel identified freedom and liberty as the racial characteristic of Saxon peoples. The characterization of the internecine strife leading to the formation of the English nation as racial conflict provided a crucial blueprint for the racialized practices of citizenship taken up by the other articles in this analytic.

These articles suggest that the distinction between the state (as enforcer of laws of inclusion and exclusion) and the nation (as civic belief system), though analytically necessary, goes only so far. Racist constructions of the nation are enacted by state policy. Mae Ngai argues that immigration restrictions have been essential to twentieth-century ideas about and practices of citizenship, race, and the nation-state. Examining the construction of new subjects in the constitution of both the illegal alien and the white US citizen, Ngai demonstrates that the consensus for state policies of immigration restriction legislation during the 1920s rested on eugenics theories, and policy-makers' desire to maintain the integrity of a "white American race." Leti Volpp examines racial profiling and the wave of hate violence that developed in the wake of the attacks of September 11, 2001, and argues that the tragedy facilitated the consolidation of a new identity category that groups those who appear "Middle-Eastern, Arab, or Muslim." Suggesting that "citizenship is made of four distinct discourses – citizenship as former legal status, as rights, as political activity, and as identity/solidarity, she analyzes the shifting and multiple definitions and dimensions of citizenship within the power triangle of sovereignty, discipline, and government. Asking who is the disappeared and who is the "us" in US, Volpp argues that we need to start from the perspective that power both subordinates and constitutes one as a subject, and think of citizenship as a process of interpellation. Peggy Pascoe's analysis of state statutes criminalizing racial intermarriage suggests the state's role in consolidating property and providing for its orderly transmission from whites to whites. Through the mechanism of anti-intermarriage laws, as well as federal fugitive slave acts, which affirmed the property rights of slaveowning and nonslaveholding whites at the expense of the citizenship rights of free and enslaved blacks, the US State was a powerful exponent of racial capitalism. In a property owner's republic founded on chattel slavery, the state was merely reflecting and affirming the importance of being white for the possession of personal freedom.

Moustafa Bayoumi examines the legal history of the combination of Islam and immigration in the United States between 1909 and 1944 to cast a critical historical eye on the racing of religion in the post 9/11 era, and the special registration laws directed at people from disparate countries, united by little but that they were all Muslim majority nations. In a series of immigration cases in the first half of the twentieth century, while many relied on ocular proof alone to determine race, others were decided by claims of innate and immutable differences between the "Mohammedan world" and "the predominately Christian peoples of Europe." In "racing" religion through the legal mechanism of the state, special registration laws of 2002 reinscribed the cultural assumption that the terrorist is Muslim, foreign born, an alien in the United States, and that all Muslim men fitting this profile are potential terrorists.

Lauren Berlant examines the development of "infantile citizenship," characterized by a relationship of degraded dependency of the citizen on the state. Emphasizing the transnational conditions under which the nation becomes a more intense object of concern and struggle, Berlant examines the heteronormative public culture – elaborated across juridical, economic, and aesthetic projects – promoted by exponents of Reagan-era conservatism. Articulating a false narrative of ex-privileged heterosexuality, and obsessed with the private realm of family, intimate relationships, and religious and moral values, conservatives coupled citizenship and suffering by defining a citizen as a person traumatized by some aspect of sexual unease, racial discord, and economic insecurity in the United States. Countering the narrow and distorted version of citizenship analyzed by Berlant, Christopher Newfield's article seeks to empower critics of the dominant ideology of neoliberalism to reclaim the idea of freedom from conservative, market-based definitions. Seeking to understand the widespread demoralization and feelings of powerlessness in people who are formally and technically empowered, Newfield argues that markets unmodified by society undermine the personal agency that is critical for liberty and democracy. Challenging neoliberals' equation of unregulated commercial markets and political democracy and the claim that markets promote individual freedom, Newfield outlines a project of recouping citizenship as participation and agency.

Liberty's Empire

Laura Doyle

Liberty's Empire

In *The Social Contract* (1762), Jean-Jacques Rousseau likens revolution in the state to the rupture of a person's memory – and so gives a hint of the novel's work in Atlantic modernity:

> just as certain afflictions unhinge men's minds and banish their memory of the past, so there are certain violent epochs and revolutions in states which have the same effects on peoples . . . ; only instead of forgetting the past, they look back on it in horror, and then the state after being consumed by civil war, is born again, so to speak, from its own ashes, and leaps from the arms of death to regain the vigour of youth. (89)

Among his contemporaries, Rousseau's reflections would have recalled the English Revolution and its aftermath. For in the preceding century all of Europe had stood witness as the English fought a bloody civil war, beheaded their king, swerved from republic to Protectorate to Restoration to "bloodless" revolution, and finally fashioned themselves as a youthful "people" of vigorous free spirit, destined to win colonies from their European rivals and build the next western empire. The immensely popular eighteenth-century histories of England written by the Frenchman Paul de Rapin-Thoyras, the Scot David Hume and, most polemically, the Englishwoman Catharine Macaulay had both intensified and reflected the eighteenth-century Anglo-European preoccupation with English revolutionary history.

It is this revolutionary history, I argue, that the English-language novel most deeply encodes and that, in turn, racializes its plots. The kind of radical unhinging that, in Rousseau's account, follows both violent revolution and personal trauma creates the turning point in many English-language novels. Overwhelmed by force or betrayal, protagonists momentarily swoon into dissociation or seeming death, fall under threat of utter forgetting, yet rise (sometimes) into their full (e)state. This story tells not only a person's but also a people's history – and not just a people's but, more specifically, a race's. It makes race history out of violent deracination. For in what later became known as the Whig narrative of English history, the nation's ruptures and revolutions were explained as the effects of a uniquely Saxonist legacy of freedom; and in complex, implicit ways, the English-language novel from *Oroonoko* to *Quicksand* has taken up this racial legacy. Rousseau may in fact have borrowed his trope of the reborn state from a literary text that helped to define this Saxonist narrative: the enormously popular eighteenth-century, narrative poem, *Liberty* (1736), penned by that poet of the British nation, James Thompson, and read on both sides of the Channel as well as the Atlantic. Telling the story of Britain's revolutionary turn toward freedom, Thomson's poem contributed both to the racializing of this revolutionary "people" and to the novel's emergent "phoenix" plot of ruin and rebirth which would inscribe that racialization. He gives an epic account of liberty's migration from Greece to Rome and then, triumphantly, to the northern climes, where the "yellow-haired, the blue-eyed Saxon" (IV.670) of "the Gothic nations" (IV.742) carried liberty to England and the world. And he conjures the same phoenix image of rebirth, using it to mark the turning-point crisis in the progress-story of a free, Gothic-descended (if Briton-blended) people.[1] The narrator, Liberty herself, explains that in the English Revolution of the early seventeenth century "There was a flame / Broke out that clear'd, consum'd, renew'd the Land," a "Con-flagration" in which "KINGS, LORDS, COMMONS, thundering to the Ground, / Successive, rush'd – Lo! From their Ashes rose, / Gay-beaming radiant Youth, the *Phoenix-State*" (IV.1020–1, 1041–5).

Thompson's narration of freedom as a racial inheritance and of revolution as racial renewal later finds its most influential elaboration in the work of G. W. F. Hegel. Hegel likewise invokes the phoenix in his vision of a racialized, dialectical "spirit" that realizes the state's freedom telos. In Hegel's account, "the German Spirit is the Spirit of the new World" whose "absolute Truth" is the "self-determination of Freedom" (*History* 341). And it is by way of the Germanic Spirit of Freedom that the State "arises rejuvenated from the ashes of its embodiment, . . . exalted."[2] Here, too, the phoenix image representing the cataclysmic origins of the free state emblematizes the modern racial refashioning of identity, a refashioning in which novels have played a part.[3] Together, race and liberty fire both the revolutions and the fictions that remake citizens from the inside out, as Rousseau suggests in his analogy between the person's psyche and the nation's history. Herein lie the deepest roots of what we now call whiteness, whose purported superiority rests on its racially inherited, mastering capacity for freedom. To be white is to be fit for freedom, and the white man's burden is to lead others by forging the institutions and modeling the subjectivities required to practice proper freedom, even if along the way this requires enslaving, invading, or exterminating those others who may not (yet) be fit for freedom.

That is to say, in Atlantic modernity, race is a freedom myth. The project of this [study] is to understand how, why, and to what effect. In a way, novels tell the whole story, but to give us the light we need to read them, we must begin by uncovering the ways race first takes shape as a *revolutionary* formation in seventeenth-century England. In other words, the task entails a fundamental revision of our histories of race in the West. In the different history of race that I propose here, the Atlantic economy plays a crucial part, but not strictly along the lines that historians of race have drawn.[4] For, although the racial-ization of freedom was fed by the Atlantic slave trade and exploitive encounters with American Indians, this racialization and these contact-zone conditions are only part of the picture – and, initially, not the most import-ant *racial* part.

The original fashioning of race in English-language culture, at least, develops in an emergently transatlantic England in the 1620s through 1640s as what can rightly be called a postcolonial discourse – whether it was pure ideology or not – of Anglo-Saxon rights. It was an insur-gent discourse, and, as long as the Stuart kings were in power, to speak it was to be stripped of privileges, put in the Tower, or have one's ears cut off. In this ideology as it eventually was embellished, "outlandish" Norman conquerors had invaded England in 1066 and trampled, without utterly destroying, her Anglo-Saxon traditions. These traditions, brought to England by the fierce Gothic Saxons who had displaced the Rome-weakened Britons, included participatory government through the *witenagemot*, zealous protection of land and rights, and a populace of "freeborn" men. These were the pur-portedly native traditions and common laws that in the first decades of the 1600s the Society of Antiquaries worked to translate, print, and reassert – until this Society was banned by Stuart King James I in 1614.

The Society's work of unearthing of pre-Conquest or Anglo-Saxon legal and parliamentary traditions first found subscribers among members of the English Parliament claiming the "ancient" right to participate in state decision-making against the divine-right claims of James I; its discourse of native rights then got taken up in the later 1620s by a transatlantic coalition of merchants and Puritans who used it to challenge Royal monopoly rules and justify religious and colonial dissent – and who by the 1640s, with their new, unregulated wealth, helped to fund civil war and behead the King; and finally, espe-cially with the civil-war lapse of censorship controls, this Saxonist discourse found vociferous and widespread expression among a war-weary populace who went so far as to assert – in print – an inherent God-given freedom for every English soul, including those of women, Quakers, and the landless. Among such groups as the Diggers, this claim to freedom even threatened to turn universalist and leave race behind. But exactly because freedom's far-reaching implications were unthinkable and, furthermore, threatened both landed and mercan-tile wealth, the idea of freedom was ultimately re-contained, I argue, within an exclusionary Saxonist narrative. Revolu-tion in England was, as all kinds of agitators put it, decreed from within, in conformity to an Anglo-Saxon, Protestant conscience and habit of independence, now laudably "manifested" in print and bravely being recovered, in phoenix fashion, after generations of a Norman–Catholic oppression, lately renewed by Stuart tyranny (and, soon after, the Puritan Protectorate). The Protestant and Saxonist vocabularies of tender conscience and native birthright worked in this way to position liberty as an interior, racial inheritance, planted in the individual and constituting an irrevocable principle for the government of the state.

Thompson, Rousseau, and Hegel thus express what I propose is an Atlantic imaginary structured by this narrative in which the state, phoenix-like, falls into revolution, dissolves, reclaims its racial birthright to liberty, and is reborn into the freedom of a modern nation. What makes this narrative "Atlantic" is that the Anglo-Saxon race's entry into a "state" of liberty is from the beginning associated with an Atlantic crossing and trauma of exile that, moreover, resonates richly with Old Testament narratives of sea-crossing by another, affiliated, freedom-seeking race. The phoenix fall and rise entails, that is, a deracinating but ultimately racialized and triumphant Atlantic crossing. In *this* early Atlantic modernity, there is something that we can call racialism or nativism that is not yet ra*cist*, even though it soon provides the infrastructure for a racist and imperial "white" subjectivity in transatlantic culture. This revolutionary racialism enfolds race utterly into the notion of liberty. And ultimately it provides the "ancient" ballad structure, so to speak, for the full orchestral and eugenic racist symphonies of the nineteenth and twentieth centuries.

Only by recognizing this revolutionary understory of race can we fully appreciate its later force in transatlantic modernity and in the English-language novel. Attending to it, we can more cogently answer Paul Gilroy's call in *Black Atlantic* to "take the Atlantic as one single, complex unit of analysis" and "use it to produce an explicitly transnational and intercultural perspective" (15). We can also more fully interpret the racialized Atlantic performances catalogued by Joseph Roach in *Cities of the Dead*. Most broadly, we can see how English-language structures of narratives participate in the emergent differentiation between modernity and subalternity; we see how these texts articulate what Walter Mignolo calls the modernity/coloniality border, a border that is not so much geographical as onto-political, inflecting language, sorting persons, and creating divergent bodily and social experiences through a racialized liberty discourse [. . .]

Anglo-Atlantic and African-Atlantic narratives in English diverge radically, of course – as determined exactly by the racialization of liberty that deems one group free and the other not yet capable of freedom – even while the narrative trope of a sea-crossing and an experience of exilic self-loss underlies both sets of stories. Indeed, by the end of the eighteenth century Anglo-Atlantic and African-Atlantic authors were writing back and forth to each other in a vexed dialectic centering on this trope. Anglo-Atlantic authors do so less consciously. Their narratives frequently register the presence and sometimes the "freeing" work of African-Atlantic persons in the service of whites, yet then, in habitual gestures, subordinate and elide this presence. Think, for example, of the labors of Xury and Friday in Robinson Crusoe's two escapes from captivity, reframed by Crusoe as his liberation of them. That is, Anglo-Atlantic novels from the beginning practice what Toni Morrison calls Africanism, unwittingly manifesting how the production of white identity, articulated as free and modern, depends on an African-Atlantic presence and labor.[5] Meanwhile, however, the narratives' logic of liberty and their muffled acknowledgment of an African presence together create an opening for the articulation of the Black experience in English-language texts. Although, not surprisingly, given language differences and racist literacy laws, the trope of an Atlantic trauma first found *printed*, English-language expression in Anglo-Atlantic texts, African-Atlantic authors such as Olaudah Equiano, Harriet Jacobs, Pauline Hopkins, and others directly rewrite these Atlantic stories so as to make prior the African-Atlantic subjects' experience and highlight their enabling role – all in the name of the righteous principle of liberty.

And yet, in another twist, since the founding logic of freedom decrees that it can be claimed only under the sign of race, African-American writers must adopt the *race* plot of freedom, extending its genealogical idea to African peoples. Thus do African-Atlantic counter-narratives at once resist and embrace the racial order of Atlantic modernity. In this vexed dialectical way, a diverse range of Atlantic narratives develop an allegorical structure for the advent of an unanchored modern self who finds a steadying current, however, in the idea of race. They record the (re)patriation of the liberated individual within a racialized national community.

Within all of these narratives, the trope of an Atlantic crossing correlates with what I call a swoon moment – the phoenix fall – involving a bodily "undoing" or "ruin" that is often sexual or coded as feminine. The swoon appears as a tableau-moment in narrative after narrative, from Behn's *Oroonoko* to Richardson's *Clarissa* to Pauline

Hopkins's *Of One Blood*. Within the liberty plot, it is the moment when a character faints or momentarily collapses, overcome with an experience of violation by a terrorizing or tyrannizing, and certainly bodily-violating force. For African-Atlantic writers, the origin of the association between an Atlantic crossing and this scene of bodily ruin is literal and obvious. The middle-passage experience of violation is heralded not only when Equiano faints as he arrives on the Guinea slave ship but also in his apostrophe to his sister, when he anticipates that she will face the lust of the overseer; and it finds repeated enactment in Pauline Hopkins's liberty-plot novels, in swoons that unveil the history of rape as the most brutal racial event of the Atlantic and yet expose how that history ultimately undercuts racial distinctions. By the time that Nella Larsen writes *Quicksand*, in which Helga Crane's final swoon into the arms of Reverend Pleasant Green has already been prepared by her Scandinavian mother's sexual fall into the US racial economy, she is one of several African-Atlantic authors crafting a palimpsest of the ruinous, racialized liberty story of the Atlantic. Indeed in her final short story "Sanctuary," Larsen reframes the whole long Atlantic history that found expression in this ruinous scene in both traditions.

For Anglo-Atlantic writers, although the swoon in the wake of ruin often operates more sentimentally or metaphorically, it also nonetheless arises from the seventeenth-century English experience of migration, civil war, and radical public challenges to class and gender assumptions which forged an association between an Atlantic crossing and the sense of a psychological and corporeal "unhinging," to borrow Rousseau's word. The growth of American colonies had furthermore threatened to create the experience of freedom as *aporia*, for economically, geographically, and viscerally the colonies put new stress on the contours of Englishness. What Gordon Wood observes about "the precariousness of society" in the new nation of the United States was already beginning to be felt in the transatlantic seventeenth century – that is, "the loosening and severing of the hierarchical ties of kinship and patronage that were carrying them into modernity only increased their suspicions and apprehensions" since "they could not know then what direction the future was taking."[6] Writers such as Pauline Hopkins, Virginia Woolf, and Larsen offer meta-fictions of this vexed, violent legacy of African-Atlantic and Anglo-Atlantic history.

Thus in texts as different as Defoe's *Robinson Crusoe*, Susanna Rowson's *Charlotte Temple*, Equiano's *Interesting Narrative*, Hawthorne's *The Scarlet Letter*, Melville's *Billy Budd*, Pauline Hopkins's *Contending Forces*, and Virginia Woolf's *The Voyage Out*, the swoon marks the person's entry into the supposedly free republics of Atlantic modernity that also entails the assuming of a race identity. For all of these writers, African- and Anglo-Atlantic, the self in an Atlantic swoon moment faces an abyss, losing its old social identity as it faints – only to reawaken deracinated and yet newly racialized, "born again" from its own ashes, as Rousseau and Hegel say of the state. Because this bodily rupture of the self occurs within a colonial horizon of captivity or opportunity, the narratives merge the notion of "entry" as transatlantic arrival in a new society with "entry" as coercive physical or sexual violence. Perhaps most fundamentally, as suggested in Rousseau's references to the person's and nation's fall into the "arms of death" where each is nearly "consumed" before it "leaps" forward, this often-reiterated swoon moment in literary texts registers the violence of the Atlantic economy. In a sense it should be read against the event of the *Zong*: in 1783, the Captain of the *Zong* ordered 132 purchased Africans thrown overboard, apparently in his attempt to win the insurance money for their value. As Ian Baucom points out in *Specters of the Atlantic*, his book-length meditation on this event, the economy that calculated these enslaved persons' value at 40 pounds each also encompassed the lives of all of those traveling in this Atlantic circuit, for instance weighing the value of a limb of Lieutenant John Willis "who had the misfortune to lose his right thigh in actions against the French and Spanish Fleets," as the Lords Commissioners' report in their budget calculations, and so they relegate him to 5 shillings a day and half pay (Baucom 6–8). These calculations are *not* comparable – the Lieutenant gains some of the profit, so to speak, of his wounds, while the slave's loss of life profits someone else. Not comparable yet working in combination: the violent "afflictions" of the Lieutenant unfold together with the forced leap into the arms of death of the African; and African-Atlantic authors, in particular, undertake the work of wresting back into view this mass-murderous frame for the trope of the swoon.

At the same time, in the hands of all kinds of Atlantic authors, the placing of the swoon at the origin of a new political order comes implicitly to reference an older history and discourse: a classical set of associations between rape and the founding of republics. To recall this point is to recover yet another layer of the faded yet felt palimpsest that makes up the Atlantic imaginary. For the link between rape and republics reaches back, of course, to the story of Tarquin's rape of Lucretia as catalyst for the founding of Rome's republic.[7] In Livy's account, the final threat that Tarquin makes to Lucretia before he rapes her involves a slave, and all elitist assumptions about the slave are kept in place throughout the story. As Livy tells it, in order to persuade Lucretia to submit to his rape, Tarquin threatens to kill her and lay the body of a slave next to hers so that it appears she was killed after committing "foul adultery" (73, *History of Rome*). This is the threat that finally convinces her to submit – she would rather befoul her body than her family's name. Lucretia's submission to rape, followed by her spectacular suicide before Brutus, which fires him to fight the tyranny of the ruling Tarquins and leads to the famous founding of the Roman republic, thus takes shape as much against the threat of mingling with slaves from "below" as it does against the coercions of brute power from "above."

Modern Atlantic narratives tap all of these elements – including the logic of a submission that frees, or a death that, phoenix-like, gives birth to a republic – but they also encounter certain un-classical stumbling blocks. In modernity, slaves and women appear on the scene not only as catalysts but also as *potential* republican subjects. Because the ideology of the English Revolution has made the principle of liberty interior, and also because of the dissent enabled by print literacy, both the woman and the slave potentially have the means for claiming rights in a free society. Anglo-Atlantic women can draw on their claim to race membership to authorize their freedom to write – so that female historians such as Catharine Macaulay and Mercy Otis Warren argue precisely that, as women of a free race, they *must* speak and write freely. "Fortunate" men like Olaudah Equiano (as he deems himself) can find a way to write and therefore to send a written account of the crimes committed on the *Zong*, for example, as Equiano does to Granville Sharp. Yet, again, to do so, Equiano and other African-Atlantic writers must find ways to re-narrate the story of "their race" so as to establish a naturally free interiority for the Black subject. Thus in Hopkins's fiction, the violations that make her women collapse give rise, equivocally, to a world of African-American noble domesticity or the recovery of an ancient racial genealogy – to a plot of racial "uplift" within the order of the free republic.

Finally, the swoon symbolically marks the entry not only into a raced republic but also into what Juliet Flower McCannell calls its republican "regime of the brother." As many scholars have explored, the early modern shift from strict monarchy to "republics" founded on participatory government in many ways challenged the paternal order of patriarchy.[8] And yet somehow this shift did not wholly undo the subordination of women. Following the clues of political and literary texts (including those of Rousseau, Stendhal, Freud, Lacan, Duras, Rhys, and Jhabvala), McCannell suggests that, under republican rule, the order of the father is replaced by the order of the brother. Here, competition among brothers drives the narrative and demands either exclusion or proper marriage of sisters. In opening her analysis, McCannell mentions Samuel Richardson's story of Clarissa and her jealous brother James as a paradigmatic example.

I agree and will later elaborate on the ways that Richardson's novel offers a cautionary tale of the birth of a republic that, in effect, botches the task of emplacing yet still subordinating the sister within it. Yet I place additional emphasis on the way the fused discourses of race and freedom provide the terms of this sibling competition, and shape the pattern of "ruin" that emerges as a necessary pivot or condition within republican modernity. In this new order, men and women both vie for power by way of race. When we note that Clarissa challenges the violations of James and Lovelace precisely by way of a nativist claim to a "birthright" of freedom, we see how race enters the republican regime of the brother at its inception and, by giving the woman as well as the man a point of entry, trips up the brother's aim to rule in place of the father. Indeed, the incest plot that circulates in many novels expresses the trouble in this new "sibling" political relation, announcing the dangers to normative heterosexuality lurking within women's new claim to freedom under the sign of race "birthrights." As I read it, the repeatedly fictionalized scandal of brother-sister incest is the scandal of a claim to overly "intimate" sibling relations within this free, racial order – that is, an uncomfortably side-by-side position within the sphere of power. In texts as different as *Moll Flanders, Charlotte Temple, Wieland, Our Nig, Daniel Deronda, Of One Blood*, and *The Waves*, brothers and sisters symbolically or literally endure ocean crossings only to find themselves "too close" or somehow at odds on the competitive and racially-staked ground of freedom.

Ultimately, however, these English-language liberty narratives that pivot on ruin offer an object lesson for all subjects and all readers, even those who are apparently most secure – readers who identify with Arthur Dimmesdale or Daniel Deronda as well as those who are most like Clarissa Harlowe, Olaudah Equiano, Hester Prynne, or Helga Crane.[9] Narratives on both sides of the Atlantic, both sides of the color line, and both sides of the gender divide grapple with the revolutionary dispersal of community into an aggregate of independent individuals. In turn they reconstruct community as an interior, racial, bodily sensibility, which offers a stay against the centrifugal force of individualist freedom. At the same time these narratives strenuously negotiate, each one differently, with both the race-authorized liberation of women and the entrenched unfreedom of non-Anglo-Saxon persons in the lands of freedom.

It is not so much that these stories express "anxiety about consent as an adequate expression of the individual," as Gillian Brown puts it (Consent 133), as that they express a social and bodily destabilization experienced in the very making of this racialized, contractual, and possessive individuality.[10] For if, in a laissez-faire, individualist, contract-based, and geographically dispersed social order, freedom – theoretically – is the right of the racial "everyman," by the same token failure is also a possibility for everyone. Everyone is a *contingent* member of this race-empire of freedom. Everyone is free to rise, and free to fall, to rule or be ruined, financially and bodily. Even as the reach of this modern Atlantic society expands powerfully through colonies and commerce, the potential for falling symbolically and materially outside of it also oddly increases, for all it takes is a failure to be responsible for oneself as a wage-earning or property-owning, autonomous, "free" individual (or failure to be a woman married to such a one). Failure to be autonomous can mark one as a member of an inferior race, or it can authorize expulsion from the dominant race, or at least threaten loss of race protection and privilege. Conversely, the enactment of self-supporting, individual *autonomy* ratifies one's membership in the race community, as Theo Goldberg has also argued.[11] Strangely, individual freedom can only be had by way of a race group. Desiring freedom, and fearing a ruinous fall, modern selves bind themselves to race as a source of security, history, and identity.

In *The Social Contract*, Rousseau offers a reading, in effect, of this social logic when he lays out the necessary "alienation entailed by the social contract" (67). He labors earnestly to make sense of the apparently freely chosen self-deracination entailed in this making of oddly group-dependent individuals. To do so, he reverses the "before" and "after" of the historical process, positioning individuality as the "natural" and earliest human condition, before sociality, which a *certain* freedom then binds to the state. Overlooking the fact of infant dependency on adults (despite his aggrandizement of motherhood), he theorizes that the social contract "replace[s] the

physical and independent existence we have all received from nature with a moral and communal existence" (84). In this community "each man must be stripped of his powers, and given powers which are external to him, and which he cannot use without the help of others" (84). That is, this society that exposes and maximizes the vulnerability of each person in this way encourages their allegiance to the (racial) nation. Despite this allegiance's effect of dependency, Rousseau argues that participation in such a state still expresses freedom, for "obedience to a law one prescribes to oneself is freedom" (65). Thus, although the contract with a society based on freedom entails "the total alienation by each associate of himself and all his rights to the whole community" (60), those rights are understood to be held in trust. They are the citizen's, only *via* the laws of the community.

In thinking through the paradoxical relation between freedom and law within the republican state, Rousseau wrestles with the same questions that troubled the English Revolution and that came to propel the plots of novels: how can freedom be the founding principle of community? How can liberation from social bonds – from "subjecthood" under a king – create a bonded community of citizens? How can "a people" be "a people" by virtue of their individual autonomy? Like the English revolutionaries, and in tandem with novels, Rousseau, too, taps race as the notion that will cohere and naturalize this volatile, dispersed, and apparently voluntary socius. When he tells his readers, echoing Montesquieu, that "Freedom is not the fruit of every climate, and it is not therefore within the capacity of every people" (*SC* 124), he enacts modernity's contradictory harnessing of freedom to race, re-establishing the very organic community that his notion of contractual community has undone, or made anonymous and abstract. He dramatizes the impulse by which the threat of alienation calls forth a compensatory racialization. And he then articulates the turn by which this racialization becomes racist and colonialist when he excludes Africans and Native Americans from consideration – the latter of whom, he says, never developed farming or technology and "therefore always remained savages" – apparently outside the purview of the contract (quoted in Goldberg 46). The "capacity" for freedom distinguishes *a* people and concentrates, it seems, in certain peoples of the North.

Rousseau's turns of thought parallel those of Atlantic memoirs and novels, which likewise ameliorate and naturalize, by way of the racialization of freedom, the alienations entailed in the contractual republic. They reveal, without fully intending to, how a contractual society positions everyone as a lone outsider who *must join a race* if he or she wants security. The undoing quest for freedom is the necessary ritual for racial membership. In tracking this ideology as it unfolds in novels, we begin to see how race, that backward myth, came to drive modern revolutions and bind modern communities.

Of course the racialization of power and community is nothing new. Myths of noble races or ancient lineages are as old as the hills. What is new, and what comes to dominate after the seventeenth century, is a myth in which the capacity for *liberty* places the ruling "races" above others. *Liberty's Empire* recovers this racialization of liberty in English-language modernity, a racialization that has at once fostered revolutionary claims and justified violent slavery and colonization, even as it has buffered the existential aporia of an individualist notion of freedom. It is this racialization of liberty that has, I propose, helped to constitute subaltern coloniality as the alter-ego of the first-world nation-state. Thus I offer an account not of racism per se but of liberty's powerful intertwining of racialism and racism within the English-language transatlantic novel and, in turn, the English-language discourses of modernity.

In doing so, I bring together a set of English-language conversations about Atlantic modernity, race history, and the nation, including both Britain and the US, that have for too long proceeded in parallel lines. Historians of Britain have long considered the pamphlets and debates of the English Civil War the first articulation of democratic ideas of liberty, and, more recently, scholars of the seventeenth century have clarified the role, of a new transatlantic, mercantile network in the eruption of that Civil War. At the same time, scholars of race have traced the rise of Saxonism in England in this period. But no scholar that I am aware of has considered the tight bonding of these elements. And yet it is their profound co-formation that has intensified their powerful effects in Atlantic history – and created English-language stories of racial destiny.

Likewise, in recent studies of republicanism on both sides of the Atlantic, scholars have considered many of the elements of the emerging, English-language nation-state: ancient constitutionalism, the turn to documentary history, the pitting of commoner against aristocrat, the religious rhetoric of dissent, and, within both family and state, the redefinition of authority, contract, virtue, and independence.[12] Yet with the exception of Reginald Horsman, recent historians have overlooked or mis-understood the racial strain within these debates. American

scholars in particular have set aside the abundant evidence of American Saxonism gathered by earlier historians.[13] Because this scholarship often overlooks the earliest transatlantic genealogies of the rhetoric of liberty, which manifest its embeddedness in notions of birthright and race, it often casts the modern republic, and especially the American republic, as one of "political membership based on consent" by contrast to the Anglo-European ones "based on birthright."[14] This account reduces race in the US to an interloping ideology that illogically skews the formation of the liberal, contract state. But transatlantic seventeenth-century history reveals that race is of a piece with the discourses of consent and freedom. From their first articulation, the vocabularies of liberty, consent, birthright, and Saxonism were tightly intertwined – by way of the idea that liberty itself was a birthright – and they continued to be so throughout the founding of the United States.

The story I tell about the ways that modern nations implicitly racialize their individualist political identities is thus informed by and yet also diverges – in its emphasis on seventeenth-century, revolutionary racialism – from the accounts of political theorists who have addressed questions of race and citizenship, from C. L. R. James and Hannah Arendt to Etienne Balibar, Ann Laura Stoler, David Theo Goldberg, Theodore Allen, and Homi Bhabha. Likewise with my understanding of ideologies of race and whiteness as they emerge in the Atlantic Triangle: I am indebted to the work of W. E. B. DuBois, Ralph Ellison, David Brion Davis, Winthrop Jordan, Paula Giddings, Nancy Stepan, Toni Morrison, Robert Young, and David Roediger as well as many others, but ultimately I offer a different framework for understanding race on the Atlantic.[15] For, instead of treating Anglo-Saxonism only in terms of what it became – a form of racism – I study how it began – as a form of racialism. Here I build on the work of scholars of Anglo-Saxonism, such as Leon Poliakov, Samuel Kliger, Eleanor Adams, Roberta Brinkley, and Trevor Colbourn who document – without foregrounding – the link between Saxonism and freedom.[16] Although my account of the transatlantic co-formation of Saxonism and liberty certainly corroborates Etienne Balibar's and Theo Goldberg's arguments that the modern liberal nation-state has from the start been a racial state, it also rewrites the story of how this came to be by showing that, at least on the Atlantic, the state's earliest and most long-lived "racial contract" began as an equivocally revolutionary one, written under a broad range of pressures in which Africans and Native

Americans initially had an important economic but incipient racial part.

It needs saying that the history of religious, political, and scientific race thinking since the medieval period defeats any attempt to codify the meanings of race, especially in relation to the overlapping notions of nation, ethnicity, and class. The historian and theorist both trip over race's status as a cultural fiction and its susceptibility to the manipulations of the moment. From medieval notions of German-Catholic superiority over the Romans, to Victorian and contemporary Anglo-Saxon presumptions of superiority over Africans, that is, race distinctions have taken the shape required by the political surround. Moreover, in the eighteenth and nineteenth centuries in Europe, the word "nation" served sometimes as a synonym for, and sometimes as a subcategory of, race, even while it also named the official, political entity ruled by a single government within guarded borders. Eighteenth-century English writers, for instance, spoke of the "nations" of the Gothic "race," and they entered into heated debate about the best way to distinguish European "races," not strictly aligned with nations, from one another. They, too, found themselves negotiating with the migrations and histories of conquering that so muddle distinctions not only between races but also amongst the categories of race, nation, and class. Later, in the Victorian period, social commentators conveniently began to think of Britain's lower classes as distinct races, while Americans and Britons both assumed (and often still do) that their "original" citizens share an Anglo-Saxon "stock" bridging the two nations and the Atlantic – and creating their alliance as world leaders. These more recent conflations of race and nation indicate their co-development in Atlantic modernity within an imperial world-system. Race has sustained the imperial reach of the nation, providing both temporal continuity and socio-spatial integrity – in the face of rupture in both dimensions. That is, race articulated a genealogy for the nation (including as expressed in discursive skirmishes over which lineage was the true one), which in turn authorized its imperial projects, profits, invasions, and enslavements as part of a world-historical freedom struggle. At the same time, exactly against the distensions and dissensions – the loosening of the center – created by this imperial reach, race provided a principle of cohesion among "the English" or "Anglo-Saxons," even as it justified the exclusion or forced labor of all "Others" and generated oppositions between primitive and modern.

[. . .]

Notes

1 Although Thomson also narrates the mingling of Saxons with Britons on English soil, he clearly points to the Germanic Saxons as the catalyzing force in Britain's recovery of freedom.

2 *The Philosophy of History in the Philosophy of Hegel*, ed. Carl F. Friedrich, 59.

3 In this light, it would be interesting to consider Franco Moretti's argument, in *Way of the World*, about the focus on youth and the structure of *Bildungsroman* in the novel.

4 Beginning with Winthrop Jordan, most scholars have considered new encounters between Europeans and Africans, and especially within slavery and the slave trade, the source of racist and racial thinking in western modernity. See Jordan, *White over Black*.

5 See Morrison, *Playing in the Dark*.

6 Gordon Wood, *The Radicalism of the American Revolution*, 173.

7 For a full study of this connection, see Melissa Matthes, *The Rape of Lucretia and the Founding of Republics*. Also see Margaret Doody's discussion of rape as a part of a freedom plot embedded in classical Greek novels, although she does not then read English novels as freedom stories or interpret their seduction plots in these terms (*The True Story of the Novel*, esp. 73–81).

8 In historical studies, see especially the work of J. G. A. Pocock and Gordon Wood; for application of this analysis to the British novel, see James Thompson, *Models of Value*, Elizabeth Heckendorn Cook, *Epistolary Bodies*, Christopher Flint, *Family Fictions*, John P. Zomchick, *Family and Law*; and for the American novel, see Jay Fliegelman, *Prodigals and Pilgrims*, Cathy Davidson, *Revolution and the Word*, Julia Stern, *The Plight of Sympathy*, Philip Gould, *Covenant and Republic*, and Elizabeth Barnes, *States of Sympathy*.

9 Myra Jehlen long ago sketched the possibility that the plight of novels' heroines stands in for that of the modern citizen. Nina Auerbach specifically considered the ruined woman as a figuration of the ruined state in Victorian culture. More recently Ros Ballaster (*Seductive Forms*), Amanda Anderson (*Painted Faces*), Catherine Gallagher (*Nobody's Story*), and Gillian Brown (*Consent of the Governed*) have all considered the ways that the heroine's struggle or "fall" is emblematic, as an increasing number of studies on the novel do, but usually without developing this insight at length. Anderson's *Painted Faces* does so most completely.

10 See *The Political Theory of Possessive Individualism*, in which C. B. Macpherson traces this social formation to the seventeenth century in a way that prepares and supports my thesis here. Also see Melvin Yazawa, *Colonies to Commonwealth*, for full discussion of the new ideal of "independence" in the American republic which, as Yazawa points out, ultimately implied that "the citizen

was on his own" (144). He concludes that, accordingly, "the commitment to republicanism entailed nothing less than the forming of a new identity," disentangled from kinship community, a point that accords with my interpretation of the "swoon" experience in Atlantic narratives. I would add that a parallel discourse of independence circulated in England in the eighteenth century.

11 My suggestions here are in accord with Theo Goldberg's way of understanding how race defines citizenship to the core, with only a slight difference in emphasis. He argues that racialized exclusion from the state is predicated on the presumed "incapacity to fulfill rational and civilized needs and drives, a failure to deliver the goods" (*The Racial State*, 47). But I would add that, underlying this incapacity, according to the liberty plot, is the perceived absence of a drive toward liberty – including the active will to "free" commerce. I also offer a different history for how this logic came into being.

12 See, for instance, Pocock (*The Ancient Constitution and the Feudal Law*; *Virtue, Commerce, and History*), Caroline Robbins (*The Eighteenth-Century Commonwealthman*), Gordon Wood (*The Creation of the American Republic*; *The Radicalism of the American Revolution*), J. C. D. Clark (*The Language of Liberty*; *Revolution and Rebellion*), Melvin Yazawa (*From Colonies to Commonwealth*), and Michael Warner (*Letters of the Republic*). Although the title of Clark's book, *The Language of Liberty*, might suggest a close affinity between our projects, Clark wishes to highlight the ways that this language was driven largely by religious concerns, and he wishes to disconnect the liberty discourse from cultural revolutions related to race, class, and gender. I would point out, however, that the freedom language of religion was itself implicitly cultural and racial by way of its links to Saxonism.

13 See Horsman, *Race and Manifest Destiny*. For earlier scholarship see Trevor Colbourn and Bernard Bailyn. For insistent de-emphasis on race in "the language of liberty" see Clark's book by that title. See previous note.

14 This is the formulation of Deborah Gussman (Hawthorne binder #2, pp.58–9). Also see Peter H. Schuck and Rogers M. Smith, *Citizenship without Consent: Illegal Aliens in the American Polity*. By contrast, in *Empire for Liberty*, Wai-Chee Dimock names the ways in which liberty as an ideology served imperial ambition, although her focus is not on race as a vehicle in this ideology.

15 Although Robert Young briefly notes the association between Anglo-Saxon character and "qualities of Protestantism, freedom and liberty," he too quickly reduces this cluster of elements to what he calls "the Saxon supremacist view" and therefore misses the full import of its contradictory racial formation (129–30) in "Hybridism and the Ethnicity of the English" in *Cultural Readings of Imperialism*.

16 Poliakov most comprehensively tracks the medieval to modern sources of the notion of superior "Aryan" races, while Kliger, Smith, Adams, Brinkley, and (in the US

context) Colbourn focus more narrowly on Anglo-Saxonism. Poliakov's work, together with V. G. Kiernan's, draws attention to the medieval and early modern conflations of race, class, and nation, where all three categories overlapped and shifted depending on who had most recently conquered whom.

References

Anderson, Amanda, *Tainted Souls and Painted Faces: The Rhetoric of Fallenness in Victorian Culture* (Ithaca, NY: Cornell University Press, 1993).

Auerbach, Nina, *Communities of Women: An Idea in Fiction* (Cambridge, MA: Harvard University Press, 1978).

Ballaster, Ros, *Seductive Forms: Women's Amatory Fiction from 1684 to 1740* (Oxford: Clarendon Press, 1998).

Barnes, Elizabeth, *States of Sympathy: Seduction and Democracy in the American Novel* (New York: Columbia University Press, 1997).

Brown, Gillian, *The Consent of the Governed: The Lockean Legacy in Early American Culture* (Cambridge, MA: Harvard University Press, 2001).

Clark, J. C. D., *Revolution and Rebellion: State and Society in England in the Seventeenth and Eighteenth Centuries* (Cambridge: Cambridge University Press, 1985).

Clark, J. C. D., *The Language of Liberty 1660–1832: Political Discourse and Social Dynamics in the Anglo-American World, 1660–1832* (Cambridge: Cambridge University Press, 1993).

Cook, Elizabeth Heckendorn, *Epistolary Bodies: Gender and Genre in the Eighteenth-Century Republic of Letters* (Stanford, CA: Stanford University Press, 1996).

Davidson, Cathy, *Revolution and the Word: The Rise of the Novel in America* (Oxford: Oxford University Press, 2004).

Dimock, Wai-Chee, *Empire for Liberty: Melville and the Poetics of Individualism* (Princeton, NJ: Princeton University Press, 1991).

Doody, Margaret, *The True Story of the Novel* (New Brunswick, NJ: Rutgers University Press, 1997).

Fliegelman, Jay, *Prodigals and Pilgrims: The American Revolution against Patriarchal Authority 1750–1800* (Cambridge: Cambridge University Press, 1985).

Flint, Christopher, *Family Fictions: Narrative and Domestic Relations in Britain, 1688–1798* (Stanford, CA: Stanford University Press, 1998).

Friedrich, Carl F. (ed.), *The Philosophy of History in the Philosophy of Hegel* (New York: Random House, 1953).

Gallagher, Catherine, *Nobody's Story: The Vanishing Acts of Women Writers in the Marketplace, 1670–1920* (Berkeley: University of California Press, 1995).

Goldberg, Theo, *The Racial State* (Oxford: Wiley-Blackwell, 2001).

Gould, Philip, *Covenant and Republic: Historical Romance and the Politics of Puritanism* (Cambridge: Cambridge University Press, 1996).

Horsman, Reginald, *Race and Manifest Destiny: The Origins of American Racial Anglo-Saxonism* (Cambridge, MA: Harvard University Press, 2006).

Jehlen, Myra, *American Incarnation: The Individual, the Nation, and the Continent* (Cambridge, MA: Harvard University Press, 2002).

Jordan, Winthrop, *White over Black: American Attitudes toward the Negro, 1550–1812* (Chapel Hill: University of North Carolina Press, 1968).

Macpherson, C. B., *The Political Theory of Possessive Individualism* (New York: Oxford University Press, 1962).

Matthes, Melissa, *The Rape of Lucretia and the Founding of Republics: Readings in Livy, Machiavelli, and Rousseau* (University Park: Pennsylvania University Press, 2001).

Moretti, Franco, *Way of the World*, trans. A. Sbragia (London: Verso, 2000).

Morrison, Toni, *Playing in the Dark: Whiteness and the Literary Imagination* (New York: Vintage, 1993).

Pocock, J. G. A., *Virtue, Commerce, and History: Essays on Political Thought and History, Chiefly in the Eighteenth Century* (Cambridge: Cambridge University Press, 1985).

Pocock, J. G. A., *The Ancient Constitution and the Feudal Law: A Study of English Historical Thought in the Seventeenth Century* (Cambridge: Cambridge University Press, 1987).

Robbins, Caroline, *The Eighteenth-century Commonwealthman: Studies in the Transmission, Development, and Circumstance of English Liberal Thought from the Restoration of Charles II until the War with the Thirteen Colonies* (Indianapolis, IN: Liberty Fund, 2004).

Schuck, Peter H., and Rogers M. Smith, *Citizenship without Consent: Illegal Aliens in the American Polity* (New Haven, CT: Yale University Press, 1985).

Stern, Julia, *The Plight of Feeling: Sympathy and Dissent in the Early American Novel* (Chicago: University of Chicago Press, 1997).

Thompson, James, *Models of Value* (Durham, NC: Duke University Press, 1996).

Warner, Michael, *The Letters of the Republic: Publication and the Public Sphere in Eighteenth-Century America* (Cambridge, MA: Harvard University Press, 2006).

Wood, Gordon, *The Radicalism of the American Revolution* (New York: Knopf, 1992).

Wood, Gordon, *Creation of the American Republic, 1776–1787* (Chapel Hill: University of North Carolina Press, 1998).

Yazawa, Melvin, *From Colonies to Commonwealth: Ideology & the Beginnings of the American Republic* (Baltimore, MD: Johns Hopkins University Press, 1985).

Young, Robert, "Hybridism and the Ethnicity of the English," in K. A. Pearson, B. Parry, and J. Squires (eds), *Cultural Readings of Imperialism: Edward Said and the Gravity of History* (Basingstoke: Palgrave, 1998), 127–50.

Zomchick, John P., *Family and the Law in Eighteenth-Century Fiction: The Public Conscience in the Private Sphere* (Cambridge: Cambridge University Press, 2007).

The Johnson-Reed Act of 1924 and the Reconstruction of Race in Immigration Law

Mae M. Ngai

Although Congress legislated the first numerical restrictions in 1921, it would be nearly a decade before permanent immigration quotas were implemented. The intervening years were filled with contention and difficulty as Congress debated the design of a new system. All were keenly aware of the stakes: the new order would codify certain values and judgments about the sources of immigration, the desired makeup of the nation, and the requirements of citizenship.

The nativists who had led the drive for restriction believed there were serious flaws in the 3-percent quotas that were established in 1921. The law set the quotas according to the 1910 census because data from the 1920 census was not fully compiled at the time. Using 1910 as the base, the southern and eastern European countries received 45 percent of the quotas and the northern and western European countries received 55 percent. Although the quotas reduced southern and eastern European immigration by 20 percent from prewar levels, nativists believed it was still unacceptably high. They argued for a 2-percent quota based on the 1890 census. That was when, they argued, the sources of European immigration shifted, altering the racial homogeneity of the nation. The 1890 formula reduced the level of immigration to 155,000 per year and reduced the proportion of southern and eastern European immigration to a mere 15 percent of the total.[1]

But, the 1890 formula was crudely discriminatory and therefore vulnerable to criticism. Opponents of the bill pointed out that using the 1920 census figures, the most up-to-date, was conceptually more sound, but since that gave even greater weight to the newer immigrants, it

defeated the whole purpose of the quotas as far as the nativists were concerned. Proponents of restriction thus labored to devise a plan that would discriminate without appearing to do so. W. W. Husband, the commissioner general of immigration, advocated a plan to set quotas according to the rate at which each immigrant group became citizens. Naturalization was an indication of assimilation, Husband contended. Moreover, he believed that some nationalities "naturally" sought American citizenship, while others did not. Husband argued for disfavoring the immigration of those groups that resisted assimilation, rather than "advertising and going out into the highways and byways and dragging people into Americanization.... [W]hen you try to change [a man] by a hothouse process it does not work," he said. Not surprisingly, Husband found that the rate of naturalization was 67 percent among northern and western Europeans and 32 percent among southern and eastern Europeans.[2]

Another proposal was introduced by David Reed, the Republican from Pennsylvania and chair of the Senate immigration committee, and John Trevor, a leading restrictionist and head of an immigration-restriction coalition of patriotic orders and societies. Trevor, a New York lawyer, sat on the board of the American Museum of Natural History and was an associate of Madison Grant, author of the best-selling tract *The Passing of the Great Race*. In March 1924 Trevor submitted a proposal for quotas based on "national origin" to the Senate immigration committee. Like other restrictionists, Trevor warned that the new immigration threatened to lower the standard of living and dilute the "basic strain" of the American population. But Trevor turned the debate on its head by arguing that the quotas enacted in 1921 discriminated against native-born Americans and northwestern Europeans. Those quotas were based on the number of foreign-born in the population, leaving "native stock" Americans out of the equation. As a result, the 1921 act admitted immigrants from southern and eastern Europe on a "basis of substantial equality with that admitted from the older sources of supply," discriminating against "those who have arrived at an earlier date and thereby contributed more to the advancement of the Nation." To be truly fair, Trevor argued, the national origins of the *entire* population should be used as the basis for calculating the quotas. He calculated an apportionment of national origins quotas based on the nation's population in 1920, which gave 16 percent of the total to southern and eastern Europe and 84 percent to northern and western Europe. The quotas were nearly identical to those calculated at 2 percent of the foreign-born population in 1890, yet could be declared nondiscriminatory because they gave fair representation to each of the nation's "racial strains."[3]

In May, Congress passed an immigration act based on Trevor's concept of national origins quotas.[4] It restricted immigration to 155,000 a year, established temporary quotas based on 2 percent of the foreign-born population in 1890, and mandated the secretaries of labor, state, and commerce to determine quotas on the basis of national origins by 1927. The law also excluded from immigration all persons ineligible to citizenship, a euphemism for Japanese exclusion. Finally, Congress placed no numerical restrictions on immigration from countries of the Western Hemisphere, in deference to the need for labor in southwestern agriculture and American diplomatic and trade interests with Canada and Mexico.

Taken together, these three components of the Immigration Act of 1924 constructed a vision of the American nation that embodied certain hierarchies of race and nationality. At its core, the law served contemporary prejudices among white Protestant Americans from northern European backgrounds and their desire to maintain social and political dominance. Those prejudices had informed the restrictionist movement since the late nineteenth century. But the nativism that impelled the passage of the act of 1924 articulated a new kind of thinking, in which the cultural nationalism of the late nineteenth century had transformed into a nationalism based on race.

In the eighteenth and early nineteenth century, "race" and "nation" were loosely conflated in intellectual discourse

and in the public imagination. Race indicated physical markers of difference (especially color) but also often simultaneously referred to culture – commonalties of language, customs, and experience. *Race, people,* and *nation* often referred to the same idea. In the mid- and late nineteenth century, physical anthropology gave rise to "scientific" classifications that treated race as a distinctly biological concept. Social Darwinists believed civilization evolved to higher levels as a result of race competition and the survival of the fittest. Many, including Herbert Spencer and John Fiske, also held neo-Lamarckian views that cultural characteristics and behaviors acquired from the environment were inheritable. Of course, neo-Lamarckianism was two-faced, as it could both claim the inheritability of socially degenerate behavior and provide opportunity for race improvement. Thus, some social evolutionists believed that immigrants from the "backward" peoples or races of Europe might eventually become Americanized.[5]

The nativism of the late nineteenth and early twentieth century comprised a cultural nationalism in which cultural homogeneity more than race superiority was the principal concern. Restrictionists did not entirely discount the possibility of assimilation but complained that the high volume of immigration congested the melting pot, creating "alien indigestion." But by World War I, restrictionists spoke increasingly of "racial indigestion" and rejected the idea of the melting pot altogether. The shift in thinking evidenced the influence of eugenics, which had grown after the rediscovery of Mendelian genetics in the early twentieth century disproved Lamarckianism and severed environment from biology.[6]

The eugenicists were strict biological determinists who believed that intelligence, morality, and other social characteristics were permanently fixed in race. They believed racial boundaries were impermeable and that assimilation was impossible. In its most radical articulation, eugenics espoused social policy that advocated race breeding and opposed social reform because, as Charles Davenport, the founder of the Galton Society, said, the latter "tends to ultimately degrade the race by causing an increased survival of the unfit."[7] Witnesses who testified at congressional hearings frequently invoked race theories alleging the superiority of "Nordics" over the "Alpine" and "Mediterranean" races of southern and eastern Europe and warned that race-mixing created unstable "mongrel" races. During the 1920s the House committee retained a scientific expert, Harry H. Laughlin, the director of the Eugenics Institute at Cold Spring Harbor, New York, the research arm of the Galton

Society. Laughlin supplied Albert Johnson with copious amounts of data on "degeneracy" and "social inadequacy" (crime, insanity, feeblemindedness) showing the alleged racial inferiority and unassimilability of southern and eastern Europeans. Laughlin also cited the psychologist Robert Yerkes's intelligence tests conducted among soldiers during World War I as evidence of racial hierarchy. The army tests shocked contemporaries because they purported to show that the average white American male had the mental age of 13 (a score of 12 ranked as "moron"). Eugenicists seized upon Yerkes's study because it appeared to vindicate their innatist theory of intelligence: the tests indicated low intelligence among African Americans (10.4), and ranked Poles, Italians, and Russians barely higher (10.7 to 11.3).[8]

To the extent that historians have focused their attention on the legislative process leading to the 1924 act, the race-nativism of men like Madison Grant, Harry Laughlin, and John Trevor has dominated the story of the law. No doubt, scientific racism clarified and justified fears about immigration that were broadly based, and also enabled the descendants of the old immigration to redeem themselves while attacking the new immigrants.[9] But if the language of eugenics dominated the political discourse on immigration, it alone did not define the national origins quota system. Placing the eugenics movement in the foreground of the story of the Johnson-Reed Act has obscured from view other racial constructions that took place in the formulation of immigration restriction, some of which have turned out to be more enduring in twentieth-century racial ideology.

In fact, the national origins quota system involved a complex and subtle process in which race and nationality disaggregated and realigned in new and uneven ways. At one level, the new immigration law differentiated Europeans according to nationality and ranked them in a hierarchy of desirability. At another level, the law constructed a white American race, in which persons of European descent shared a common whiteness distinct from those deemed to be not white. In the construction of that whiteness, the legal boundaries of both white and nonwhite acquired sharper definition, Thus, paradoxically, as scientific racism weakened as an explanation for Euro-American social development, hereditarianism hardened as a rationale for the backwardness and unassimilability of the nonwhite races. Moreover, the idea of racial "difference" began to supplant that of racial superiority as the basis for exclusionary policies. Lothrop Stoddard, a leading race-nativist who explicitly advocated for white supremacy in *The Rising Tide of Color* in 1920, argued in 1927, "When we discuss immigration we had better stop theorizing about superiors and inferiors and get down to the bedrock of *difference*."[10]

The Invention of National Origins

It was one thing for David Reed and John Trevor to convince Congress that a system of quotas based on "national origins" was a conceptually sound and non-discriminatory way to align immigration with the composition of the American people. But it was quite another matter to actually design that system – to define the "national origins" of the American people and to calculate the proportion of each group to the total population.

The Johnson-Reed Act mandated the formation of a committee under the Departments of Commerce, Labor, and State to allocate quotas by 1927. Dr. Joseph A. Hill, an eminent statistician with a thirty-year tenure at the Bureau of Census, chaired the Quota Board, as the committee was known. Computing the national origins quotas was arguably the most difficult challenge of Hill's career: Congress would reject reports submitted by the Quota Board and postpone implementation of the quotas twice before finally approving a third report in 1929.

Indeed, the project was marked by doubt from the beginning. The law required quotas to be allocated to countries – sovereign nation-states recognized by the United States – in the same proportion that the American people traced their origins to those geographical areas, through immigration or the immigration of their forebears. Census and immigration records, upon which the Quota Board relied, however, were woefully incomplete. The census of 1790, the nation's first, did not include information about national origin or ancestry. The census did not differentiate the foreign-born until 1850 and did not differentiate the parental nativity of the native-born until 1890. Immigration was unrecorded before 1820, and not classified according to national origin until 1899, when the Immigration Service began designating immigrants by "race or people." Emigration was not recorded at all until 1907 and not recorded according to nationality until 1909. To complicate things further, many boundaries in Europe changed after World War I, requiring a translation of political geography to reattribute origins and allocate quotas according to the world in 1920.[11]

Before the Quota Board could address the data (or lack of it), it had to conceptualize the categories that comprised the national origins quota system. "National origin," "native stock," "nationality," and other categories were not natural units of classification; they were constructed according to certain social values and political judgments. For example, "native stock" did not refer to persons born in the United States but to persons who descended from the white population of the United States at the time of the nation's founding. The board defined the "immigrant stock" population as all persons who entered the United States after 1790 and their progeny.[12]

The law defined "nationality," the central concept of the quota system, according to country of birth.[13] Although the statute made no explicit reference to race, race entered the calculus and subverted the concept of nationality in myriad ways. Ironically, nationality did not mean "country of birth" as far as defining the American nationality was concerned. The law excluded nonwhite people residing in the United States in 1920 from the population universe governing the quotas. The law stipulated that "'inhabitants in continental United States in 1920' does not include (1) immigrants from the [Western Hemisphere] or their descendants, (2) aliens ineligible for citizenship or their descendants, (3) the descendants of slave immigrants, or (4) the descendants of the American aborigines."[14]

The Quota Board applied that provision according to race categories in the 1920 census: "white," "black," "mulatto," "Indian," "Chinese," "Japanese," and "Hindu."[15] It discounted from the population all blacks and mulattos, eliding the difference between the "descendants of slave immigrants" and the descendants of free Negroes and voluntary immigrants from Africa.[16] It discounted all Chinese, Japanese, and South Asians as persons "ineligible to citizenship," including those with American citizenship by native-birth. The provision also excluded the Territories of Hawai'i, Puerto Rico, and Alaska, which American immigration law governed and whose natives were United States citizens.[17] In other words, to the extent that the "inhabitants of the continental United States in 1920" constituted a legal representation of the American nation, the law excised all nonwhite, non-European peoples from that vision, erasing them from the American nationality.

On a practical level, eliminating nonwhite peoples from the formula resulted in larger quotas for European countries and smaller ones for other countries. For example, African Americans comprised 9 percent of the United States population in 1920; if they had been counted, and their "national origins" in Africa considered, 9 percent of the quota would have been allocated to west

African nations, resulting in 13,500 fewer slots for Europe.

Race altered the meaning of nationality in other ways as well. Formally the quota system encompassed all countries in the world, except for those of the Western Hemisphere. China, Japan, India, and Siam each received the minimum quota of one hundred; but the law excluded the native citizens of those countries from immigration because they were deemed to be racially ineligible to citizenship. Congress thus created the oddity of immigration quotas for non-Chinese persons of China, non-Japanese persons of Japan, non-Indian persons of India, and so on. With regard to the independent African nations, Ethiopia, Liberia, and South Africa received quotas of one hundred each, amounting to a concession of two hundred immigration slots for black Africans. European mandates and protectorates in Africa, the Near East and Far East – for example, Tanganyika, Cameroon, Palestine, New Guinea – each had their own quotas, which in practice served to increase the quotas of Great Britain, France, and Belgium, the nations with the largest colonial empires.

Thus, while the national origins quota system intended principally to restrict immigration from southern and eastern Europe and used the notion of national origins to justify discrimination against immigrations from those nations, it did more than divide Europe. It also divided Europe from the non-European world. It defined the world formally in terms of country and nationality but also in terms of race. The quota system distinguished persons of the "colored races" from "white" persons from "white" countries. The new taxonomy was starkly represented in a table of the population of the United States published in 1924, in which the column "country of birth" listed fifty-three countries (Australia to Yugoslavia) and five "colored races" (black, mulatto, Chinese, Japanese, Indians).[18] In this presentation, white Americans and immigrants from Europe have "national origins," that is, they may be identified by the country of their birth or their ancestors' birth. But, the "colored races" were imagined as having *no country of origin*. They lay outside the concept of nationality and, therefore, citizenship. They were not even bona fide immigrants.

Thus the national origins quota system proceeded from the conviction that the American nation was, and should remain, a white nation descended from Europe. If Congress did not go so far as to sponsor race breeding, it did seek to transform immigration law into an instrument of mass racial engineering. "The stream that feeds the reservoir should have the same composition as the contents of the reservoir itself," Hill said. "Acceptance of that idea doesn't necessarily imply a belief that the composition of the American people can not be improved, but it does probably imply a conviction . . . that it is not likely to be improved by unregulated immigration but rather the contrary."[19]

Like most of their contemporaries, members of Congress and the Quota Board treated race as self-evident of differences that were presumed to be natural. Few, if any, doubted the Census Bureau's categories of race as anything other than objective divisions of an objective reality, even though the census's racial categories were far from static. Such confidence evinced the strength of race-thinking generally as well as the Progressive faith in science, in this case, the sciences of demography and statistics. Indeed, few people doubted the census at all. Census data carried the weight of official statistics; its power lay in its formalization of racial categories. The census gave the quotas an imprimatur that was nearly unimpeachable and was invoked with remarkable authority, as when, during the floor debate in the House in 1924, Congressman William Vaile retorted to an opponent of the national origins principle, "Then the gentleman does not agree with the Census!"[20]

Demography, and the census itself, far from being the simple quantification of a material reality, grew in the late nineteenth and early twentieth century as a language of interpreting the social world. Census officials like Francis Amasa Walker and Richmond Mayo Smith took the census beyond its Constitutional function as an instrument of apportionment. As historian Margo Anderson observed, the classifications created for defining urban and rural populations, social and economic classes, and racial groups created a vocabulary for public discourse on the great social changes taking place in America at the time – industrialization, urban growth, and, of course, immigration.[21] In fact, the census was the favored form of scientific evidence cited by restrictionists and nativists during this period.

[. . .]

In a sense, demographic data was to twentieth-century racists what craniometric data had been to race scientists during the nineteenth. Like the phrenologists who preceded them, the eugenicists worked backward from classifications they defined a priori and declared a causal relationship between the data and race. Instead of measuring skulls, they counted inmates in state institutions. If statistics showed that immigrants were less healthy, less educated, and poorer than native-born Americans, the data were deemed to be evidence of the immigrants' inferior physical constitution, intelligence, and ambition.

Unlike Francis Walker, Joseph Hill did not aggressively campaign for restriction. He endorsed the national origins principle in a restrained way and otherwise scrupulously avoided taking political positions. Yet, like all scientists, he brought his own political views and values to his work – to the questions he asked, to the ways in which he classified data, and to the interpretations he drew from the data. In Hill's case, those politics had guided a proliferation of census data on the foreign-born that served the nativist movement.[22]

That is not to say that Hill's work was unscientific or unprofessional. To the contrary, he was a serious professional, who worked according to the established methods and disciplinary requirements of his field. As Nancy Stepan has pointed out, scientific racism's power lay, in large part, in its adherence to scientific methodology and disciplinary standards. If race science were merely "pseudo-science" it would have had far less currency.[23]

In fact, Hill agonized over the methodological problems in determining national origins. One of the most serious problems he confronted was the lack of reliable information about the national origins of the white, nativestock population. Hill deduced that roughly half of the white population in 1920 comprised descendants from the original colonial population, but the census of 1790 did not record data on place of birth. A study conducted by the Census Bureau in 1909, "A Century of Population Growth," classified the population of 1790 according to country of origin by analyzing the surnames of the heads of households recorded in the census. The study found 87 percent of the population to be English. Independent scholars believed the report was inaccurate, however, because it failed to take into account that some names were common to more than one country and that many Irish and German names had been Anglicized. It omitted Scandinavians from the national composition altogether. Hill also believed the report was "of questionable value."[24]

Nevertheless, Hill decided to use "A Century of Population Growth" because no other data existed. But Irish, German, and Scandinavian American groups criticized the report and lobbied Congress that the calculations in the Quota Board's first report slighted their populations.[25] Hill realized that the flawed report endangered the credibility of the entire exercise. With the help of a $10,000 grant from the American Council of Learned Societies, Hill enlisted Howard Barker, a genealogist, and Marcus Hansen, an immigration historian, to determine the national origins of the white population in 1790. Their conclusions, based on a more sophisticated method of analyzing surnames and reported to the Quota Board in 1928, adjusted the allocations of origins of the colonial stock considerably. Great Britain and Northern Ireland's share fell from 82 percent to 67 percent of the total, reducing its quota by ten thousand.[26]

Assuming for the moment that Barker and Hansen discerned the national origins of the population at 1790 with a fair degree of accuracy, determining the national origins of the American population from that base by following their descendants forward in time from 1790 to 1920 was an entirely different matter. The basic methodology employed by the Quota Board assumed an analysis of the population in terms of numerical equivalents, not actual persons. Hill explained that the Quota Board could not "classify people into so many distinct groups of individual persons, each group representing the number of individual persons descending from a particular country." He continued,

> Even if we had complete genealogical records that would not be possible because there has been a great mixture of nationalities through inter-marriage since this country was first settled. So when the law speaks of the number of inhabitants having a particular national origin, the inhabitant must be looked upon as a unit of measure rather than a distinct person. That is to say, if we have, for example, four people each of whom had three English grandparents and one German grandparent, we have the equivalent of three English inhabitants and one German inhabitant.[27]

Herein lay the fundamental problem of the whole project: its methodology assumed that national identities were immutable and transhistorical, passed down through generations without change. The Quota Board assumed that even if nationalities combined through intermarriage, they did not mix but remained discrete, unalloyed parts in descendants that could be tallied as fractional equivalents. The board's view of national origin drew from the concept of race defined by bloodline and blood quantum, which was available in the established definition of Negro. Rather than apply the "one-drop of blood" rule, however, the board conceived

of intermarriage between European nationalities in Mendelian terms. But is a person with three English grandparents and one German grandparent really the numerical equivalent of her ancestors? Or does that person perhaps develop a different identity that is neither English nor German but one that is syncretic, produced from cultural interchanges among families and communities and by the contingencies of her own time and place? By reifying national origin, Congress and the Quota Board anticipated the term "ethnicity," inventing it, so to speak, as Werner Sollors said, with the pretense of being "eternal and essential," when in fact it is "pliable and unstable." Sollors's view of ethnicity as a "pseudo-historical explanation" triggered by "the specificity of power relations at a given historical moment" fits well the notion of immigration quotas based on national origin.[28]

At the same time, the Quota Board ignored intermarriage between Euro-Americans and African Americans and Native American Indians, never problematizing the effect of miscegenation on the "origins" of the white population. Thus, even as the board proceeded from an assumption that all bloodlines were inviolate, it conceptualized national origin and race in fundamentally different ways.[29]

Even when considered on its own terms, the task of calculating national origins was beset by methodological problems. The Quota Board had to make a number of assumptions in order to fill the gaps in the data. Hill acknowledged that his computations involved "rather arbitrary assumptions," some of which did "violence to the facts." Most serious – and surprising, in light of Hill's longstanding interest in immigrant fecundity – of these was his decision to apply the same rate of natural increase to all national groups. Hill also weighted the population figures for each decade, giving each earlier decade greater numerical importance than the succeeding one, to allow for a larger proportion of descendants from earlier immigrants. The net result of these assumptions tilted the numbers towards the northern European nationalities.[30]

[...]

Lawmakers had invoked anthropology and scientific racism to create an immigration system based on national origins, but that had only gone as far as establishing a general ideological framework. It fell to civil servants in the executive branch to translate that ideology into actual categories of identity for purposes of regulating immigration and immigrants. Indeed, the enumeration and classification of the population *enabled* such regulation. As historian Vicente Rafael has pointed out, the value of such population schedules to the modern state lay in their "render[ing] visible the entire field of [state] intervention." Thus the invention of national origins was not only an ideological project; it was also one of state building.[31]

Sociologist John Torpey points out that nationality is a legal fact that, to be implemented in practice, must be codified and not merely imagined. While "citizen" is defined as an abstract, universal subject, the citizenry is not an abstraction but, in fact, a collection of identifiable corporeal bodies. As Partha Chatterjee has written, the modern nation-state is a "single, determinate, demographically enumerable form." This is part of the "logic of the modern regime of power," which pushes "the processes of government in the direction of administration and the normalization of its objects of rule."[32]

The national origins quota system created categories of difference that turned on both national origins and race, reclassifying Americans as racialized subjects simultaneously along both axes. That racial representation of the American nation, formalized in immigration quotas, reproduced itself through the further deployment of official data. The process of legitimation was evident in Joseph Hill's last monograph, "Composition of the American Population by Race and Country of Origin," written in 1936. Hill's analysis derived from the racial constructions embedded in immigration policy as it had evolved during the 1920s. It also reflected the distance Hill had traveled in his own thinking. After noting that "the population of the United States . . . is almost 90 percent white and almost 10 percent Negro," and that 68.9 percent of the "total white stock" in the United States derived from Great Britain and Northern Ireland, the Irish Free Republic, and Germany, Hill mused about the future of the "composite American." He speculated that if immigration were to be completely cut off, the foreign-born element of the population would disappear within seventy-five to one hundred years. Perhaps after another seventy-five years, the native population of foreign parentage would disappear. "[T]he white population would then be 100 percent native white of native parentage," he said. "Its composition by country of origin would not differ greatly from that of the present white population, but with the intermingling of national or racial stocks in the melting pot it would be a more homogeneous population. Few persons could then boast of unmixed descent from any single country or people."[33]

Joseph Hill readily assumed that the "composite American" would be white. The colored races had no place in his vision of the American nation, whether through intermarriage or by inclusion in a pluralist society. But if the elision of "American" and "white" was a predictable articulation of contemporary race thinking, Hill's assertion of a white American race represented an evolution in race ideology. Hill had rehabilitated the old trope of the melting pot, but with a new twist. Traditionally, the idea of the melting pot was based on cultural assimilation, the Americanization of immigrants from diverse European backgrounds through education, work, and social advancement. Nativists rejected that idea in the 1910s and the years immediately after World War I in favor of theories that emphasized race purity. Congress and the Quota Board invented national origins that paradoxically upheld both the inviolate nature of racial bloodlines and the amalgamation of the descendants of European nationalities into a single white American race. Hill presciently imagined that one consequence of restricting European immigration would be the evolution of white Americans.

[. . .]

Notes

1   Robert Divine, *American Immigration Policy, 1924–1952* (New Haven: Yale University Press, 1957), 5–6, 17.

2   "Restriction of Immigration," Hearings before the House Committee on Immigration and Naturalization (hereafter "House immigration committee"), 68th Congress, 1st Session (Washington, DC: GPO, 1924), 42–6, 293, 302, 1041–5.

3   John Trevor, "Immigration Problem," March 5, 1924, file 16, box 2, Reports, correspondence, and other records relating to immigration quota laws and national origins statistics, ca. 1920–1936, NN-374-63, Population Division, Records of the Census Bureau, RG 29, National Archives, Washington, DC (hereafter "Quota Board Papers"); idem, "Preliminary Study of Population," House Report 350, 68th Congress, 1st Session (Washington, DC: GPO, 1924), 26–9. See also "Europe as an Emigrant Exporting Continent," Hearings, House immigration committee, Mar. 8, 1924, 68th Congress, 1st Session, Appendix, tables 2 and 3.

4   Act of May 26, 1924 (43 Stat. 153).

5   Carl Degler, *In Search of Human Nature: The Decline and Revival of Darwinism in American Social Thought* (New York: Oxford University Press, 1991), 20–2; George Stocking, Jr., *Race, Culture, and Evolution: Essays in the History of*

Anthropology (Chicago: University of Chicago Press, 1982 [1968]), 234–69.

6   Divine, *American Immigration Policy*, 14; Degler, *In Search of Human Nature*, 41–4.

7   Degler, *In Search of Human Nature*, 43.

8   For example, see Harry H. Laughlin, "Analysis of the Metal and Dross in America's Melting Pot," Hearings, House immigration committee, Nov. 21, 1922, 67th Congress, 3d Session (Washington, DC: GPO, 1923), and "American History in Terms of Human Migration," Hearings, House immigration committee, Mar. 7, 1928, 70th Congress 1st Session (Washington, DC: GPO, 1928). On army tests, see Degler, *In Search of Human Nature*, 51; John Higham, *Strangers in the Land: Patterns of American Nativism, 1860–1925* (New Brunswick, NJ: Rutgers Univ. Press, 1988 [1955]), 275; *Stephen Jay Gould, The Mismeasure of Man*, rev. ed. (New York: Norton, 1996 [1981]), 227. The tests were highly flawed in the cultural assumptions of the questions and in the way they were administered. See Gould, 229–64.

9   Higham, *Strangers in the Land*, 270–7, 303, 313–15; John Higham, *Send These to Me, Immigrants in Urban America*, rev. ed. (Baltimore: Johns Hopkins University Press, 1984 [1975]), 44–7; Divine, *American Immigration Policy*, 45–9; Desmond King, *Making Americans: Immigration, Race, and the Origins of Diverse Democracy* (Cambridge, MA: Harvard University Press, 2000).

10 John S. Haller, *Outcasts from Evolution: Scientific Attitudes of Racial Inferiority, 1859–1900* (Urbana: University of Illinois Press, 1971), 124–8, 148–51. Stoddard quoted in Walter Benn Michaels, *Our America: Nativism, Modernism, and Pluralism* (Durham: Duke University Press, 1995), 65; see also Elazar Barkan, *The Retreat of Scientific Racism: Changing Concepts of Race in Britain and the United States between the World Wars* (New York: Cambridge University Press, 1992), 104.

11 LaVerne Beales, "Distribution of White Population as Enumerated in 1920 according to Country of Origin," Oct. 16, 1924, file 16, box 2, Quota Board Papers; Minutes of Quota Board meeting, May 25, 1926, file 19, ibid. The taxonomy of "races and peoples" used by the Immigration Bureau was not consistent with the modern understanding of nation-states. For example, the schedule differentiated "Polish" from "Polish (Hebrew)," distinguished "Italy (north)" from "Italy (south)," and listed Indians as "Hindu" or "Hindoo."

12 Joseph A. Hill, "The Problem of Determining the National Origin of the American People," address at the Social Science Conference, Hanover, NH (August 25, 1926), 7, file 17, box 2, Quota Board Papers.

13 Sec. 12(a).

14 Sec. 11(d).

15 The Census Bureau was well aware that contemporary anthropological and race theories classified "Hindu" as a "Caucasian" race. The 1910 census population schedule included a note with the table on race explaining that, anthropology notwithstanding, the Census Bureau considered Hindus to be a colored race. Joan Jensen, *Passage From India* (New Haven: Yale University Press, 1988), 252.

16 The discrepancy was noted by Boggs but not corrected. Memorandum, S. W. Boggs to W. W. Husband, Nov. 11, 1926, 3, file 30, box 3, Quota Board Papers.

17 Congress granted a limited form of citizenship to Puerto Ricans in 1917. Jones Act, ch. 190 (39 Stat. 951 [1917]); *Balzac v. Porto Rico*, 258 U.S. 298 (1922).

18 John Trevor, "An Analysis of the American Immigration Act of 1924," *International Conciliation* 202 (September 1924): 428–9.

19 Hill, "The Problem of Determining the National Origin of the American People," 3.

20 Melissa Nobles, *Shades of Citizenship: Race and the Census in Modern Politics* (Stanford: Stanford University Press, 2000); David Theo Goldberg, *Racial Subjects: Writing on Race in America* (New York: Routledge, 1997), 34; Vaile quoted by Margo Anderson, *The American Census: A Social History* (New Haven: Yale University Press, 1988), 147.

21 Anderson, *American Census*, 133–4.

22 Hill, "The Problem of Determining the National Origin of the American People," 2–3.

23 Nancy Stepan, *The Idea of Race in Science: Great Britain, 1800–1960* (Hamden, CT: Arcon Books, 1992) xvi.

24 Minutes, Quota Board meeting of June 23, 1926, file 19, box 1, Quota Board Papers; Joseph Hill, Memorandum for the Secretary, June 21, 1926, 3, file 15, box 1, Memoranda and Notes, 1906–40, Joseph Hill Papers; Joseph Hill, "Notes on Prof. Jameson's Paper on 'American Blood in 1775,'" typescript [1924–25], file 20, box 2, Quota Board Papers.

25 "National Origin Provision of the Immigration Act of 1924," Dec. 16, 1926, Senate Document no. 192, 69th Congress, 2d Session; "Immigration Quotas on the Basis of National Origins," Feb. 25, 1928, Senate Document no. 65, 70th Congress, 1st Session.

26 Hill, Memorandum for the Secretary, June 21, 1926, 3; American Council of Learned Societies, "Report of Committee on Linguistic and National Stocks in the Population of the United States," *Annual Report of the American Historical Association* (Washington, DC, 1931), 1:124. See also Anderson, *American Census*, 148–9.

27 Hill, "The Problem of Determining the National Origin of the American People," 5–6.

28 Werner Sollors, ed., *The Invention of Ethnicity* (New York: Oxford University Press, 1989), xiv–xvi.

29 On the persistent denial of the existence and scale of interracial marriage in the United States, see Gary Nash, "The Hidden History of Mestizo America," *Journal of American History* 82 (Dec. 1995): 941–64; see also Joel Williamson, *New People, Miscegenation and Mulattos in the U.S.* (New York: New York University Press, 1984); Peggy Pascoe,

"Miscegenation Law, Court Cases, and the Ideology Race in Twentieth Century America," *Journal of American History* 83 (June 1996): 44–69.

30 Hill, Memorandum for the Secretary, June 21, 1926, 2; Minutes, meeting of the Quota Board, May 25, 1926, 3, file 19, box 2, Quota Board Papers: Joseph Hill to Secretary of State, Secretary of Commerce, Secretary of Labor, Feb. 15, 1928, in "Immigration Quotas on the Basis of National Origins," Feb. 28, 1929, Senate Document no. 65, 70 Congress, 1st session, 9; LaVerne Beales, "Committee on Distribution of Population by National Origin," typescript, Dec. 1, 1924, file 16, box 2, Quota Board Papers.

31 Vicente Rafael, "White Love: Surveillance and Nationalist Resistance in the U.S. Colonization of the Philippines," in *Cultures of United States Imperialism*, ed. Amy Kaplan and Donald Pease (Durham: Duke University Press, 1993), 188.

32 John Torpey, *The Invention of the Passport: Surveillance, Citizenship and the State* (Cambridge: Cambridge University Press, 2000), 13; Partha Chatterjee, *The Nation and Its Fragments, Colonial and Postcolonial Histories* (Princeton: Princeton University Press, 1993), 19, 238.

33 Joseph Hill, "Composition of the American Population by Race and Country of Origin," *Annals of the American Academy of Political and Social Science* (Philadelphia, PA), November 1936: 1, 7–8.

9

The Citizen and the Terrorist

Leti Volpp

Introduction

In the wake of the terrorist attacks of September 11, 2001, there have been more than one thousand incidents of hate violence reported in the United States.[1] How do we understand this violence, and in particular, its emergence in a context of national tragedy? What are the seeds of this violence, and how has the political climate following September 11 allowed them to grow? Of course, there are no easy answers to these questions. I would suggest that September 11 facilitated the consolidation of a new identity category that groups together persons who appear "Middle Eastern, Arab, or Muslim."[2] This consolidation reflects a racialization wherein members of this group are identified as terrorists, and are disidentified as citizens.

The stereotype of the "Arab terrorist" is not an unfamiliar one. But the ferocity with which multiple communities have been interpellated as responsible for the events of September suggests there are particular dimensions that have converged in this racialization. I offer three: the fact and legitimacy of racial profiling; the redeployment of old Orientalist tropes; and the relationship between citizenship, nation, and identity.

I   On Racial Profiling

Before September 11, national polls showed such overwhelming public opposition to racial profiling that both US Attorney General John Ashcroft and President George W. Bush felt compelled to condemn the practice.[3]

There was a strong belief that racial profiling was inefficient, ineffective, and unfair.[4] This all seems a distant memory. There is now public consensus that racial profiling is a good thing, and in fact necessary for survival.[5] There are at least four ways in which this racial profiling has been practiced against persons who appear "Middle Eastern, Arab, or Muslim."

Subsequent to September 11, over twelve hundred noncitizens have been swept up into detention. The purported basis for this sweep is to investigate and prevent terrorist attacks, yet none of the persons arrested and detained have been identified as engaged in terrorist activity.[6] While the government has refused to release the most basic information about these individuals – their names, where they are held, and the immigration or criminal charges filed against them – we know that the vast majority of those detained appear to be Middle Eastern, Muslim, or South Asian.[7] We know, too, that the majority were identified to the government through suspicions and tips based solely upon perceptions of their racial, religious, or ethnic identity.[8]

The US Department of Justice has also engaged in racial profiling in what has been described as a dragnet – seeking to conduct more than five thousand investigatory interviews of male noncitizens between the ages of eighteen and thirty-three from "Middle Eastern" or "Islamic" countries or countries with some suspected tie to Al Qaeda, who sought entry into the country since January 1, 2000, on tourist, student, and business visas. These are called voluntary interviews, yet they are not free of coercion or consequences.[9] The Department of Justice has directed the US Attorneys to have investigators report all immigration status violations to the Immigration and Naturalization Service (INS), which includes minor visa violations. As a result, one student in Cleveland, Ohio has been criminally charged and indefinitely detained for telling the Federal Bureau of Investigation (FBI) that he worked twenty hours per week, when he actually worked twenty-seven.[10]

[. . .]

Airport officials, airlines, and passengers have also practiced racial profiling against those appearing "Middle Eastern, Arab, or Muslim."[11] Countless men have been kicked off airplanes, because airline staff and fellow passengers have refused to fly with them on board, despite US Department of Transportation directives to protect the civil rights of passengers.[12] And President Bush has said that he would be "madder than heck" if investigators find American Airlines racially profiled his Arab American Secret Service agent in removing him from a flight to the Crawford ranch.[13]

Lastly, since September 11, the general public has engaged in extralegal racial profiling in the form of over one thousand incidents of violence – homes, businesses, mosques, temples, and gurdwaras firebombed; individuals attacked with guns, knives, fists, and words; women with headscarves beaten, pushed off buses, spat upon; children in school harassed by parents of other children, by classmates, and by teachers.[14] We know of at least five people who have been killed since September 11 in incidents of hate violence: a Sikh Indian, killed in Mesa, Arizona; a Pakistani Muslim killed in Dallas, Texas; an Egyptian Coptic Christian, killed in Los Angeles, California; a Sikh Indian killed in Ceres, California; and an Indian Hindu killed near Dallas, Texas.[15]

These myriad attacks have occurred, despite Bush meeting with Muslim leaders, taking his shoes off before he visited the Islamic Center in Washington, DC, and stating that we must not target people because they belong to specific groups.[16] His statements have done little to disabuse people of their "common sense" understanding as to who is the terrorist and who is the citizen. This is connected to the fact that the government has explicitly engaged in racial profiling in terms of its targets of our "war on terrorism." Furthermore, President Bush and other top officials have characterized the war against terrorism as a battle for "civilization" – indeed, a "crusade."[17] While this characterization occasionally acknowledges the heterogeneity of Muslim practices, its ideological effect is the legitimation of the religious and

modern imperative to eradicate either from without or within the forces of despotism, terror, primitivism and fundamentalism, each of which are coded as Middle Eastern, Arab, and Muslim.[18] Through these actions and these statements, the American public is being instructed that looking "Middle Eastern, Arab, or Muslim" equals "potential terrorist."

[. . .]

While the Oklahoma City bombing certainly led to enormous concern about the militia movement in the United States, there was little consolidation of a national identity in opposition to Timothy McVeigh's terrorist attack. In contrast, post–September 11, a national identity has consolidated that is both strongly patriotic and multiracial. The multiracial consolidation of what it means to be American was represented in a cartoon, whereby various persons marked on their T-shirts as African American, Irish American, and Asian American dropped the hyphenated identities, so that all in the second frame had become "American."[19] This expansion of who is welcomed as American has occurred through its opposition to the new construction, the putative terrorist who "looks Middle Eastern." Other people of color have become "American" through the process of endorsing racial profiling. Whites, African Americans, East Asian Americans, and Latinas/os are now deemed safe and not required to prove their allegiance.[20] In contrast, those who inhabit the vulnerable category of appearing "Middle Eastern, Arab, or Muslim" and who are thus subject to potential profiling, have had to, as a matter of personal safety, drape their dwellings, workplaces, and bodies with flags in an often futile attempt at demonstrating their loyalty.

Racial profiling only occurs when we understand certain groups of people to have indistinguishable members who are fungible as potential terrorists. The Timothy McVeigh analogy helps clarify the strangeness of the present moment. Under the logic of profiling all people who look like terrorists under the "Middle Eastern" stereotype, all whites should have been subjected to stops, detentions, and searches after the Oklahoma City bombing and the identification of McVeigh as the prime suspect.[21] This did not happen because Timothy McVeigh did not produce a discourse about good whites and bad whites,[22] because we think of him as an individual deviant, a bad actor. We do not think of his actions as representative of an entire racial group. This is part and parcel of how racial subordination functions, to understand nonwhites as directed by group-based determinism but whites as individuals.[23] Racial profiling also did not happen because, as a white man, Timothy McVeigh was seen by many as one of "us" – as the *New York Times* editorialized at that time, there was "sickening evidence that the enemy was not some foreign power, but one within ourselves."[24]

[. . .]

[Racial profiling] cases belie what sadly does not also seem to be apparent: Very few persons who appear "Middle Eastern, Arab, or Muslim" are terrorists. Many men who fall into this category, including law professors, have been subjected to questioning. One friend of this author was profiled for reading too slowly. He was working his way through Heidegger while sitting in Newark Airport on his way to a legal history conference, and was questioned because someone had apparently reported a "Middle Eastern looking man" engaging in the suspicious activity of reading a book for an hour without turning the page. As Arundhati Roy has written, we are in a moment when "War is Peace, Pigs are Horses."[25] And reading Heidegger is a potential terrorist activity.

II   On Orientalist Tropes

We are witnessing the redeployment of old Orientalist tropes. Historically, Asia and the Middle East have functioned as phantasmic sites on which the US nation projects a series of anxieties regarding internal and external threats to the coherence of the national body.[26] The national identity of the United States has been constructed in opposition to those categorized as "foreigners," "aliens," and "others."

Edward Said describes Orientalism as a master discourse of European civilization that constructs and polarizes the East and the West. Western representations of the East serve not only to define those who are the objects of the Orientalizing gaze, but also the West, which is defined through its opposition to the East. Thus, for example, the West is defined as modern, democratic, and progressive, through the East being defined as primitive, barbaric, and despotic.[27] Similar discourses sustain American national identity. American Orientalism references North Africa, the Middle East, and Turkey, as well as East Asia. Collectively, and often indistinguishably, they function as the "East" to America's democratic and progressive "West." September 11 gave this discourse new currency

in relation to what are depicted as the barbaric regions of the world that spawn terror.[28]

Rather than understand Orientalism as solely a creature of purported racial difference, it is important to point out that American Orientalism, like European Orientalism, is gendered. Historically, the status of women in need of uplift was a source of justification for Western colonization of regions of the world[29] – "white men saving brown women from brown men."[30] The aftermath of September 11 witnessed the redeployment of this idea. One of the stated justifications for American intervention in Afghanistan – made by both President George Bush and First Lady Laura Bush – was that Afghan women needed to be saved from the Taliban and Islamic barbarism.[31] But long before the Feminist Majority Fund began campaigning on the issue of Afghan women, many women in Afghanistan had been starving and faced with violence not only because of the Taliban regime but also because of a long history of conflict in the region in which the United States has been deeply implicated.[32] We must remember where the Taliban came from, that US administrations thought that religious fundamentalists made better anti-Communist fighters, and so supported the mujahideen who became the Taliban.[33] Saving women from purdah has been propounded as a reason for bombardment, even while, ironically, the epidemic of hate violence in the United States has led to the seclusion of many women identified as "Middle Eastern, Arab, or Muslim" who otherwise face harassment and violence when they venture outside of their homes.[34] Furthermore, the long-term impact of the war on the "liberation" of the women of Afghanistan remains an open question.[35]

In part, the gendering of colonial and Orientalist discourses was achieved by collapsing non-Europeans and women into an undifferentiated field in which passion reigned, not reason.[36] The East was the site of passivity and irrationality, awaiting the conquest by the masculine and rational West.[37] This bifurcation continues to describe the way in which the United States genders the sites of its interventions, which in turn shapes the relationship of US national identity to race, gender, and sex.[38] We should understand nationalism to be constituted through the simultaneous interworkings of racism, sexism, and homophobia. Fliers have circulated in New York City depicting Osama Bin Laden being sodomized by the World Trade Center, with the caption, "You like skyscrapers, bitch?"[39] Post–September 11 nationalist discourses reinscribe both compulsory heterosexuality[40] and the dichotomized gender roles upon which it is based: the masculine citizen-soldier, the patriotic wife and mother, and the properly reproductive family.[41]

In 1997, Lauren Berlant presciently suggested that there was a coupling of the ideas of suffering and American citizenship.[42] National civic identity has been experienced as a trauma that conflates patriotism, suffering, and abhorrence for what is constructed as oppositional to "America." As Muneer Ahmad has recently written, cases of hate violence before September 11 – such as the murders of Matthew Shepard and James Byrd – were deemed incomprehensible.[43] In contrast, hate attacks after September 11 are understood as the result of displaced anger, the underlying sentiment with which most Americans agree. Thus, Ahmad argues, the former were understood as crimes of moral depravity, but the post–September 11 attacks are understood as crimes of passion, whereby the passion is love of nation. Perpetrators of post–September 11 hate violence, then, are guilty not of malicious intent but of only misdirecting their anger, so that there is something of an understanding of these acts.[44] This helps explain why many think it their patriotic duty to engage in racial profiling in the form of hate violence. The man arrested for the murder of Balbir Singh Sodhi, the Sikh Indian killed in Mesa, Arizona, reportedly shouted as he was arrested, "I stand for America all the way!"[45]

At the same time that the category of "loyal American" is, at this moment, a broad and encompassing one, there is also great heterogeneity in terms of who has been singled out as a potential terrorist.[46] In particular, Sikh men, who are religiously mandated to wear turbans, have been conflated with Osama Bin Laden and have suffered significant violence.[47] South Asian Americans have suddenly been subjected to racist attack and galvanized as a political community.[48] As a response to such a heterogeneous racial interpellation, the claim of racial or religious misrecognition ("I'm not Muslim")[49] rather than condemnation of violence regardless of its target, is both troubling and reminiscent of the actions of Chinese Americans who wore buttons during World War II that read "I'm Chinese, not Japanese," so they would not be targeted.[50] Others are importantly arguing that this is a moment for constructing coalitions.[51]

There are obviously enormous resonances in what has been happening to the treatment of Japanese Americans during World War II, whereby the fungibility of members of a racially defined community was considered to make it impossible to screen individually loyal citizens from enemy aliens.[52] Recently, the publisher of the Sacramento

Bee attempted to deliver a graduation speech at Cal State Sacramento. Booed and heckled, she was unable to finish her speech about the need for the protection of civil liberties; when she wondered what would happen if racial profiling became routine, the audience cheered. Witnesses described the event as terrifying; the president of the faculty senate was quoted in the New York Times as stating, " 'For the first time in my life, I can see how something like the Japanese internment camps could happen in our country.' "[53]

And, in fact, a Gallup poll found that one-third of the American public surveyed thought that we should intern Arab Americans.[54] Motivation for the internment of over 120,000 Japanese Americans was fear of what we today might call sleeper cells. The fact that the Japanese Americans did not attack after Pearl Harbor was understood to mean that they were patiently waiting to strike and therefore must be interned.[55] Japanese American internment constituted a pivotal moment in American Orientalism; the present moment is another.

III   On Citizenship and Identity

The shift in perceptions of racial profiling is clearly grounded in the fact that those individuals who are being profiled are not considered to be part of "us." Many of those racially profiled in the sense of being the targets of hate violence or being thrown off airplanes are formally citizens of the United States, through birth or naturalization. But they are not considered citizens as a matter of identity, in that they in no way represent the nation.

We can understand citizenship as made up of four distinct discourses: citizenship as formal legal status, citizenship as rights, citizenship as political activity, and citizenship as identity/solidarity. In focusing on the question of citizenship as identity, it is imperative to isolate two very different conceptualizations of this idea.

The prevalent idea of citizenship as identity focuses on the notion of what I consider *citizenship as a form of inclusion*.[56] Citizenship as a form of inclusion starts from the perspective of the citizen who proceeds to imagine fellow members who are to be included in a network of kinship or membership – those with whom the citizen feels affective ties of identification and solidarity. I want also to suggest that we must think about a very different idea of citizenship as identity, which we could call *citizenship as a process of interpellation*. Citizenship as a process of interpellation starts from the perspective that power both subordinates and constitutes one as a subject.[57] The focus, then, is not initially from the perspective of the citizen who includes, but foregrounds the role of ideology in either including one as a citizen or excluding one from membership, and then shifts to the standpoint of the subject.

For the idea of interpellation, I am relying on the work of Louis Althusser.[58] Depicting a scene in which the subject is hailed by an officer of the law, Althusser writes:

> Naturally for the convenience and clarity of my little theoretical theatre I have had to present things in the form of a sequence, with a before and an after, and thus in the form of a temporal succession. There are individuals walking along. Somewhere (usually behind them) the hail rings out: "Hey, you there!" One individual (nine times out of ten it is the right one) turns around, believing/suspecting/knowing that it is for him, i.e. recognizing that "it really is he" who is meant by the hailing. But in reality these things happen without any succession. The existence of ideology and the hailing or interpellation of individuals as subjects are one and the same thing.[59]

As Althusser writes, this is not a temporal process that takes place in sequence, but is rather how ideology functions: Individuals are "always-already subjects" of ideology.[60] Through positing an identity dimension of citizenship as a process of interpellation, I want to emphasize how certain individuals and communities are positioned as objects of exclusion ("Hey, you noncitizen!" (or foreigner, or enemy alien, or terrorist)). This process of interpellation of those who appear "Middle Eastern, Arab, or Muslim" is taking place through the racial profiling by both government officials and the US public.[61] As the individual is hailed in this manner and recognizes the hail, he or she is transformed into a subject of ideology – here, the subject of nationalist ideology that patrols borders through exclusions.

In the American imagination, those who appear "Middle Eastern, Arab, or Muslim" may be theoretically entitled to formal rights, but they do not stand in for or represent the nation. Instead, they are interpellated as antithetical to the citizen's sense of identity. Citizenship in the form of legal status does not guarantee that they will be constitutive of the American body politic. In fact, quite the opposite: The consolidation of American identity takes place *against* them.

While many scholars approach citizenship as identity as if it were derivative of citizenship's other dimensions, it seems as if the guarantees of citizenship as status,

rights, and politics are insufficient to produce citizenship as identity.[62] Thus, one may formally be a US citizen and formally entitled to various legal guarantees, but one will stand outside of the membership of kinship/solidarity that structures the US nation. And clearly, falling outside of the identity of the "citizen" can reduce the ability to exercise citizenship as a political or legal matter. Thus, the general failure to identify people who appear "Middle Eastern, Arab, or Muslim" as constituting American national identity reappears to haunt their ability to enjoy citizenship as a matter of rights, in the form of being free from violent attack.

Thus, the boundaries of the nation continue to be constructed through excluding certain groups. The "imagined community"[63] of the American nation, constituted by loyal citizens, is relying on difference from the "Middle Eastern terrorist" to fuse its identity at a moment of crisis. Discourses of democracy used to support the US war effort rest on an image of antidemocracy, in the form of those who seek to destroy the "American way of life."[64] The idea that there are norms that are antithetical to "Western values" of liberty and equality helps solidify this conclusion.

We can consider whether the way in which identity disrupts citizenship is inevitable. Race has fundamentally contradicted the promise of liberal democracy, including citizenship. While liberalism claimed to promise universal liberty and equality, these were in fact only guaranteed to propertied, European male subjects.[65] While some might believe in the promise of universality – that one can infinitely expand the ambit of who is entitled to rights and freedoms – race and other markers appear and reappear to patrol the borders of belonging to political communities. Despite the liberal universalizing discourse of citizenship, not all citizens are equal.[66] These events make apparent how identity in the form of foreignness, or perpetual extraterritorialization, means that the circling of wagons is an uneven process, that drawing tighter together takes place through the expulsion of some.

Recent theorizing about diasporic or transnational subjects, while productive in many regards, has on occasion minimized the continued salience of the nation, both in terms of shaping identity and in the form of governmental control. In particular, discussions charting the decline of the nation-state have led to unfortunate implications when two points are stretched to extremes: First, the idea that immigrant communities have complete agency in determining their location and their national identity; and second, the idea that the borders of the nation can be traversed with the greatest of ease and are so reduced as to become almost meaningless.[67]

Arjun Appadurai, in an essay titled *Patriotism and its Futures*, written at what was perhaps a more optimistic moment, suggests that we "need to think ourselves beyond the nation," for we now find ourselves in a post-national era.[68] America, he suggests, is "eminently suited to be a sort of cultural laboratory and a free trade zone" to test a "world organized around diasporic diversity."[69] Appadurai argues that the United States should be considered "yet another diasporic switching point, to which people come to seek their fortunes but are no longer content to leave their homelands behind."[70]

If only this were indeed a postnational era. In a response, titled *Transnationalism and its Pasts*, Kandice Chuh criticizes the evenness of power relations within and across national borders implied in Appadurai's post-nation.[71] Chuh emphasizes the link between transnationalism and state coercion, and reminds us of the forced removal and internment of Japanese Americans by the US government during World War II.[72] A transnational extension of Japan into the United States was relied upon to justify this dispossession. This memory is instructive to us now. We should remember that the idea of transnationality is not solely one where immigrants function as agents in maintaining diasporic ties, but can be one where a state or its people brands its citizens with foreign membership, extraterritorializing them into internment camps, or ejecting them from membership through violence against their bodies.[73]

We function not just as agents of our own imaginings, but as the objects of others' exclusions. Despite frequent rhetorical claims, this society is neither colorblind nor a happy "nation of immigrants." Certain racialized bodies are always marked and disrupt the idea of integration or assimilation.

Conclusion

Those who appear "Middle Eastern, Arab, or Muslim" and who are formally citizens of the United States are now being thrust outside of the protective ambit of citizenship as identity. But I want to shift focus here, to bodies that disappear: What of those members of this group who are not formally citizens? Those individuals who are noncitizens – currently being interviewed, deported, and detained – are made even more vulnerable by their noncitizen status and the power of immigration law to control their fate. They are even farther removed from the "us" of America because of the ways in which we understand citizenship to correlate with membership.[74]

The reaction to the American Civil Liberties Union (ACLU) offering to assist those going through interviews, as recorded on the ACLU hotline and reported in the *Detroit Free Press*, gives a sense of these sentiments:

FEMALE CALLER: How can you guys tell us that people who are not American citizens have rights? Bull crap!

MALE CALLER: What makes you think these people have rights? Those are Arabs; they have no rights. Deal with it![75]

Ariel Dorfman wrote, early after September 11, that the photographs of those missing in the World Trade Center reminded him of the photographs of the *desaparecidos* of Chile.[76] What might it mean to expand who occupies the category of our disappeared, from those killed in the World Trade Center, to consider also those noncitizens in detention? Our government has taken them, and we do not know where they are. Are those in detention our disappeared? If not, why not? I raise this to provoke a rethinking of what bodies are centered in our consideration and what bodies disappear.[77] Who is the "us" in the US?

Notes

1 As of February 8, 2002, 1717 cases of "Anti-Muslim incidents" had been reported to the Council on American-Islamic Relations (CAIR) since September 11, 2001, http://www.cair-net.org (last updated Feb. 8, 2001).

   My figure of one thousand incidents in all likelihood vastly underestimates the violence. Between September 11, 2001, and January 31, 2002, in six jurisdictions in the state of California alone, the state attorney general reported 294 incidents of anti-Arab hate crimes (defined as reported hate crimes against Arab Americans, Muslim Americans, Afghan Americans, Sikhs, South Asians, and others mistaken for Arabs or Muslims) under investigation. *See* Press Release, Office of the Atty. Gen., State of Cal, Dep't of Justice, Attorney General Releases Interim Report on Anti-Arab Hate Crimes, http://caag.state.ca.us/newsalerts/2002/02-014.htm (Feb. 28, 2002).

2 For a discussion of the equation of "Muslim" with "Middle Eastern" or "Arab," and the use of "Muslim" as if it were a racial category see Moustafa Bayoumi, *How Does It Feel to Be a Problem?*, AMERASIA J. 2001–2, at 69, 72–3.

3 *See Attorney General Seeks End to Racial Profiling*, N.Y. TIMES, Mar. 2, 2001, at A20; Steve Miller, *"Profile"*

Directive Rallies Two Sides: Bush Seeks Data on Police Stops, WASH. TIMES, Mar. 12, 2001, at A1.

4　*See, e.g.*, Reginald T. Shuford, *Civil Rights in the Next Millenium. Any Way You Slice It: Why Racial Profiling is Wrong*, 18 ST. LOUIS U. PUB. L. REV. 371 (1999).

5　*See* Sam Howe Verhovek, *Americans Give in to Race Profiling*, N.Y. TIMES, Sept. 23, 2001, at A1; *see also* Nicole Davis, *The Slippery Slope of Racial Profiling: From the War on Drugs to the War on Terrorism*, COLORLINES, Dec. 2001, at 2 (noting that 80 percent of Americans were opposed to racial profiling before September 11, but that polls now show that 70 percent believe some form of racial profiling is necessary to ensure public safety).

6　The Uniting and Strengthening America by Providing Appropriate Tools Required to Intercept and Obstruct Terrorism (USA Patriot Act) Act of 2001, Pub. L. No. 107–56, § 412, 115 Stat. 272, 274 (2001) grants the US Attorney General the power to take into custody any alien who is certified, on his reasonable belief, as a terrorist or person engaged in other activity that threatens the national security of the United States.

7　*See, e.g.*, Dan Eggen & Susan Schmidt, *Count of Released Detainees Is Hard to Pin Down*, WASH. POST, Nov. 6, 2001, at A10 ("Since Sept. 11, hundreds of people – many of them Middle Eastern men – have been detained in connection with the probe into the suicide hijackings...."); *see also* Susan Akram & Kevin Johnson, *The Civil Rights and Immigration Aftermath of September 11, 2001: The Targeting of Arab Americans*, ANN. SURV. AM. L. 9 (forthcoming 2002) (manuscript at 9, on file with author) (asserting the largest numbers of detainees are from Pakistan and Egypt, and pointing out that the detentions have apparently failed to produce any direct links to the terrorist acts).

8　MIGRATION POLICY INSTITUTE – NYU IMMIGRANT RIGHTS CLINIC, THE ROLE OF ETHNIC PROFILING IN LAW ENFORCEMENT AFTER SEPTEMBER 11TH 1, *at* http://www.nlg.org/post911/resources/NYU_project_descript.pdf (last visited Mar. 18, 2002) (stating that "media reports and anecdotal evidence strongly suggest that suspicions and anonymous tips – based purely on ethnic and/or racial stereotypes – have motivated the bulk of arrests made").

9　*See* Chisun Lee, *Why People of All Colors Should (Still) Resist Racial Profiling: "Let Us Not Be Suckers for Anybody,"* VILLAGE VOICE, Dec. 26, 2001 (describing the coercion involved in interviews); CNN, *INS Memo Cites Possible Detention for Those Questioned in Terror Probe* (Nov. 29, 2001), *available at* http://www.cnn.com/2001/US/11/29/inv.terrorism.interviews/ (describing an INS memo stating that interviewees could be held without bond if an immigration violation is suspected).

10　*See* e-mail from Reginald Shuford to Leti Volpp, Associate Professor, American University, Washington College of Law (Jan. 3, 2002 3:15 p.m. EST) (describing the case of the student) (on file with the author). Students here on non-immigrant F-1 visas may only work up to twenty hours per week or are considered to be in violation of the terms of their visa. *See* 8 CFR § 214.2 (f)(9).

11　US Congressman John Cooksey, in a radio interview about airline security, said that "any person who has 'a diaper on his head and a fan belt wrapper around the diaper' needs to be singled out for questioning." Dennis Camire, *Muslim Council Seeks Action Against Cooksey for Slur*, GANNETT NEWS SERVICE, Sept. 21, 2001, *available at* 2001 WL 5112923. Cooksey later said that he regretted his choice of words, but insisted on the use of racial profiling in airport security. *Id.*

12　Sasha Polakow-Suransky, *Flying While Brown*, AM. PROSPECT, Nov. 19, 2001, at 14 (describing the cases of passengers cleared for boarding by law enforcement officers, who were kicked off planes when pilots refused to fly with them, and subsequent U.S. Department of Transportation investigations); Niraj Warikoo, *Racial Profiling: Muslims and Arab Americans See Their Civil Rights Eroded*, DETROIT FREE PRESS, Oct. 24, 2001, http://www.freep.com/news/nw/terror2001/arab24_20011024.htm (describing flying while Arab). The anxiety airline passengers feel was documented in a CNN/USA Today/Gallup poll taken that showed that 58 percent of those surveyed backed more intensive security checks for Arabs, including those who are United States citizens, compared with other travelers, 49 percent favored special identification cards for such people, and 32 percent backed "special surveillance" for them. *See* Sam Howe Verhovek, *Once Appalled by Race Profiling, Many Find Themselves Doing It*, N.Y. TIMES, Sept. 24, 2001, *at* http://www.nytimes.com/learning/teachers/featured_articles/20010924Monday.html.

13　*See* Darryl Fears, *Turbulence on Flight 363: Prudence, or Profiling? Secret Service Agent Rebuts Airline Account of Boarding Clash*, WASH. POST, Jan. 13, 2002, at A3; Roland Watson, *Standoff on Flight Ban for U.S. Agent*, TIMES OF LONDON, Jan. 5, 2002, at 16.

14　*See* SOUTH ASIAN AMERICAN LEADERS OF TOMORROW, AMERICAN BACKLASH: TERRORISTS BRING WAR HOME IN MORE WAYS THAN ONE (2001), *available at* www.peopleforpeace.org/docs/BiasReport.pdf; *Hate Crime Reports Up in Wake of Terrorist Attacks*, CNN.com, Sept. 17, 2001, *at* http://www.cnn.com/2001/US/09/16/gen.hate.crimes/index.html (last visited May 15, 2002).

15　*See* Muneer Ahmad, *Homeland Insecurities: Racial Profiling the Day After 9/11*, 22 SOC. TEXT 72, 20:3 (Fall 2002); *Death for 11 Sept. Revenge Killer*, BBC News, Apr. 5, 2002, *at* http://news.bbc.co.uk/hi/english/world/americas/newsid_1912000/1912221.stm (last visited May 15, 2002).

16　*See* Dana Milbank & Emily Wax, *Bush Visits Mosque to Forestall Hate Crimes: President Condemns an Increase in Violence Aimed at Arab Americans*, WASH. POST, Sept. 18, 2001, at A1.

17　*See, e.g.*, Malcolm Beith, *Welcome to World War 1*, NEWSWEEK, Oct. 8, 2001, at 2 (describing George Bush's equation of the "war" on terrorism with a "crusade");

Michael Hirsh & Roy Gutman, *Powell's New War*, NEWSWEEK, Feb. 11, 2002, at 24. Katha Pollitt, *Egg on the Brain*, NATION, Mar. 4, 2002, at 10.

18 For a criticism of the persistence of the paradigm of the West's superiority over Islam in explaining the attacks of September 11, rather than understanding this "carefully planned and horrendous, pathologically motivated suicide attack and mass slaughter" as "the capture of big ideas" [using the word loosely] by "a tiny band of crazed fanatics for criminal purposes," see Edward W. Said, *The Clash of Ignorance*, ZNET, *at* http://www.zmag.org/terrorframe.htm (last visited May 15, 2002).

19 This cartoon was described in a lecture by Inderpal Grewal. Inderpal Grewal, Consumer Citizenship, Diasporic Communities & American Nationalism, Lecture at the University of California at San Diego Ethnic Studies Department Series on Transnational Feminism, Culture and Race (Nov. 14, 2001); *see also* Inderpal Grewal, *Transnational America: Feminisms, Diasporas, Neoliberalisms* (2005).

20 Grewal, *supra* note 20.

21 *See* Paola Bacchetta et al., *Transnational Feminist Practices Against War* (October 2001), http://home.earthlink.net/~jenniferterry/transnationalstatement.html (last visited Apr. 30, 2002). This statement [is] written collectively by feminist theorists Paola Bacchetta, Tina Campt, Inderpal Grewal, Caren Kaplan, Minoo Moallem, and Jennifer Terry.

22 *See* UCLA LAW SCHOOL STATEMENT OF CONCERNED FACULTY (making this point and opposing racial profiling) (on file with the author); *see also* Devon W. Carbado, (E)racing the Fourth Amendment, 100 MICHIGAN LAW REVIEW, 946–1004 (2002). (discussing the "good black"/bad black" dichotomy).

23 *See* Leti Volpp, *Blaming Culture for Bad Behavior*, 12 YALE J.L. & HUMAN., 89, 94–99 (2000).

24 Linda Greenhouse, *Exposed: Again, Bombs in the Land of the Free*, N.Y. TIMES, Apr. 23, 1995, § 4, at 1. For a critical analysis of how geopolitics of a "heartland" space operated to divide the "national" from the "international" in terms of "inside" and "outside" in discourses of the Oklahoma City bombing, see Matthew Sparke, *Outsides Inside Patriotism: The Oklahoma Bombing and the Displacement of Heartland Geopolitics, in Rethinking Geopolitics* 198, 199 (Gearóid Ó Tuathail & Simon Dalby eds., 1998).

25 *See* Arundhati Roy, *War is Peace*, OUTLOOK INDIA, Oct. 29, 2001, http://www.outlookindia.com/archivecontents.asp?fnt=20011029.

26 I borrow this metaphor from Lisa Lowe, who writes of the phantasmic role played by the figure of the Asian immigrant on which the US nation projects a series of complicated anxieties. *See* Lisa Lowe, *Immigrant Acts: On Asian American Cultural Politics* 18 (1996).

27 *See generally* Edward Said, *Orientalism* (1978); Edward Said, *Culture and Imperialism* (1993). In presenting this bifurcation, I do not intend to suggest that Orientalism was not a hybrid and contradictory process. For a discussion of the heterogeneity of Orientalism, see Lisa Lowe, *Critical Terrains: French and British Orientalisms* 1–29 (1991).

28 *See e.g.* Italian Prime Minister Silvio Berlusconi's comments about the superiority of Western civilization. Berlusconi boasted of the "supremacy" and "superiority" of Western civilization, called on Europe to recognize its "common Christian roots," and claimed links between Islamist terrorism and the antiglobalization movement as the enemies of Western civilization. John Hooper & Kate Connolly, *Berlusconi Breaks Ranks Over Islam*, GUARDIAN, Sept. 27, 2001, http://www.guardian.co.uk/waronterror/story/0,1361,558866,00.html (quoting Silvio Berlusconi).

29 Leti Volpp, *Feminism Versus Multiculturalism*, 101 COLUM. L. REV. 1181, 1196–7 (2001).

30 Gayatri Spivak, *Can the Subaltern Speak, in Marxism and the Interpretation of Culture* 271, 297 (Cary Nelson & Lawrence Grossberg eds., 1988).

31 Laura Bush, Radio Address to the Nation (Nov. 17, 2001), *at* http://www.whitehouse.gov/news/releases/2001/11/20011117.html; President George W. Bush Address to Joint Session of Congress and the American People (Sept. 20, 2001), *at* http://www.whitehouse.goy/news/releases/2001/09/20010920-8.html. *See, e.g.*, Judith Apter Klinghoffer, *Afghanistan: A Just War*, HIST. NEWS NETWORK, Jan. 21, 2002, http://historynewsnetwork.org/articles/article.html?id=518 (justifying the American war in Afghanistan "because it enabled Afghani women to claim their place in the sun").

32 *See* Bacchetta et al., *supra* note 22; Charles Hirschkind & Saba Mahmood, *Feminism, The Taliban, and the Politics of Counter-Insurgency*, 75 ANTHROPOLOGICAL Q. 75, 2 (2002), 339–54 (describing the United States' role in creating conditions in Afghanistan and the elision of this history in the linkage made between women's oppression, Taliban evil, and Islamic fundamentalism).

33 *See* Rasil Basu, *The Rape of Afghanistan*, ZNET, Dec. 30, 2001, http://www.zmag.org/terrorframe.htm (describing the role of the United States in supporting fundamentalist groups that destroyed women's rights that had been improved under Soviet occupation, and expressing skepticism as to the sudden concern of the American government with the plight of Afghan women). For more information on the history of US funding of the mujahideen in Afghanistan, see Eqbal Ahmad, *Terrorism: Theirs & Ours* 12, 22 (2001); Hirschkind & Mahmood, *supra* note 33; Amitava Kumar, *Nothing to Write Home About*, AMERASIA J., 2001–2 at 181, 187–8; Vijay Prashad, *War Against the Planet*, AMERASIA J., 2002, at 31, 31–9.

34 Ahmad, *supra* note 15, at 11.

35 I mean by "liberation" here both Feminist Majority Fund concerns as to women wearing the burqua, and concerns as to the impact of the war on consolidating fundamentalisms. On the former, see John Daniszewski, *Post-Taliban Kabul Marks International Women's Day Celebration*, L.A. TIMES, Mar. 9, 2002 at A3, describing the

observance of International Women's Day. *See also* Robert Fisk, *Brace Yourself for Part Two of the War for Civilisation*, ZNET, *at* http://www.zmag.org/terrorframe.htm (last visited March 5, 2002).

Fisk writes:

> With a headache as big as Afghanistan, reading through a thousand newspaper reports on the supposed "aftermath" of the Afghan war, I'd become drugged by the lies. Afghan women were free at last. . . . We could ignore the fact that, save for a few brave female souls, almost all Afghan women in Kabul continued to wear the burqua.

Id. On the latter, see Revolutionary Association of the Women of Afghanistan, Statement on the US Strikes on Afghanistan (2001), http://rawa.fancymarketing.net/usstrikes. htm. The statement from RAWA, which since 1977 has struggled for the rights of women in Afghanistan, provides:

> If until yesterday the US and its allies, without paying the least attention to the fate of democracy in Afghanistan, were supporting the policy of Jehadis-fostering, Osama-fostering and Taliban-fostering, today they are sharpening the dagger of the "Northern Alliance". . . . The continuation of US attacks and the increase in the number of innocent civilian victims not only gives an excuse to the Taliban, but also will cause the empowering of the fundamentalist forces in the region and even in the world.

36   *See* Ann Laura Stoler, *Race and the Education of Desire: Foucault's History of Sexuality and the Colonial Order of Things* 128–9 (1995); *see also* Jean L. Comaroff & John Comaroff, *Of Revelation and Revolution: Christianity, Colonialism, and Consciousness in South Africa*, 105–8 (1991).

37   *See* Meyda Yegenoglu, Colonial Fantasies: Towards a Feminist Reading of Orientalism, 11 (1998).

38   For an analogous argument in the context of European colonialism, see generally Ann McClintock, Imperial Leather: Race, Gender and Sexuality in the Colonial Contest (1995); Stoler, *supra* note 36.

39   Ahmad, *supra* note 15, at 10 (citing Elisa Byard, *Queerly Un-American*, NEWSLETTER OF THE INST. FOR RES. ON WOMEN & GENDER (Colum. U.), Jan. 2002, at 6).

40   On the relationship between nationalism and sexuality, see generally George L. Mosse, *Nationalism and Sexuality: Respectability and Abnormal Sexuality in Modern Europe* (1985).

41   Bacchetta et al., *supra* note 21.

42   *See* Lauren Berlant, *The Queen of America Goes to Washington City: Essays on Sex and Citizenship* 1 (1997).

43   *See* Ahmad, *supra* note 15, at 8. For a description of the murders of Matthew Shepard, a gay man tied to a wooden

fence, and James Byrd, a black man chained to and dragged by a pick-up truck, see Lu-in Wang, "Suitable Targets"? Parallels and Connections Between "Hate" Crimes and "Driving While Black," 6 MICH J. RACE & L. (2001), at 215 & nn. 21–2.

44   *See* Ahmad, *supra* note 15, at 8–9.

45   Joseph Trevino & Gendy Alimurung, *The Hate Files*, L.A. WEEKLY, Sept. 21, 2001, http://www.laweekly.com/ink/01/44/ cover-alimurung.shtml. The suspect, Frank Roque, was also reported as being suspected of shooting an Afghan family and a Lebanese gas station worker the same day. *See* Emil Guillermo, *The War Has Already Started in America*, ASIAN WK., Sept. 21, 2001, http://www.asianweek.com/ 2001_09_21/opinion_emil.html.

46   *See* Davis, *supra* note 5, at 2 (describing Latinos subjected to racial profiling post–September 11).

47   *See* website of the Sikh Coalition, *at* http://www.sikhcoalition. org/ListReports.asp (visited March 7, 2002) (listing 226 incidents and hate crimes).

48   Sarah Wildman, *All for One*, NEW REPUBLIC, Dec. 24, 2001, http://www.tnr.com/doc.mhtml?i=20011224&s=diarist 122401.

49   *See, e.g.*, Onkar Singh, *Attacks on Sikhs Worries Indians*, REDIFF, Sept. 17, 2001, http://www.rediff.com/us/2001/sep/ 17ny30.htm (describing rally where demonstrators carried placards that read "Sikhs are not Muslims" and "Bush, Educate the American people that Sikhs are not Muslims or Arabs").

50   *See, e.g.*, Sharon Boswell & Lorraine McConaghy, *Abundant Dreams Diverted*, SEATTLE TIMES, June 23, 1996, at B2.

51   For the argument that Arab and South Asian communities should use this moment as an opportunity to forge coalitions, see Ahmad, *supra* note 15, at 12–14. For a similar argument at an earlier moment, that of California post–Proposition 187 and Proposition 209, see Rosemary Marangoly George, *"From Expatriate Aristocrat to Immigrant Nobody": South Asian Racial Strategies in the Southern California Context*, 6 DIASPORA 30, 49–50 (1997).

52   *See generally* Eric K. Yamamoto et al., *Race, Rights and Reparation: Law and the Japanese American Internment* (2001); Natsu Taylor Saito, *Symbolism Under Siege: Japanese American Redress and the "Racing" of Arab Americans as "Terrorists,"* 8 ASIAN L.J. 1 (2001). On the relation of Japanese American internment and racial profiling post 9–11, see Jerry Kang, *Thinking Through Internment: 12/7 and 9/11*, AMERASIA J., 2001–2, at 43, 45–9 (arguing against racial profiling and for the recognition of how racism warps what we believe to be rational calculations).

53   Timothy Egan, *In Sacramento, a Publisher's Questions Draw the Wrath of the Crowd*, N.Y. TIMES, Dec. 21, 2001, at B1 (quoting Bob Buckley, computer science professor at California State University, Sacramento).

54   Gallup Poll Analysis: The Impact of the Attacks on America, http://www.gallup.com/poll/releases/pr010914c.asp

(showing that one in three Americans favors internment for people of Arab descent).

55 See Keith Aoki, *Civil Rights: Six Experts Weigh In*, TIME, http://www.time.com/time/nation/article/0,8599,186583,00. html (last visited Apr. 11, 2002).

56 See Linda Bosniak, *Citizenship Denationalized*, 7 IND. J. GLOBAL LEGAL STUD. 447, 456–88 (2000), at 479–88.

57 See Judith Butler, *The Psychic Life of Power: Theories in Subjection* 2 (1997).

58 See Louis Althusser, *Ideology and Ideological State Apparatuses, in Lenin and Philosophy and Other Essays*, 127, 170–177 (Ben Brewster trans., 1971). *See also* Frantz Fanon, *Black Skin White Masks*, 109 (Charles Lam Markmann trans., 1967).

59 Althusser, supra note 59, at 174–5.

60 *Id.* at 176.

61 Janet Halley understands interpellation to include not only a call from above, from a high center of power, for example, the police, but also "from below," for example, from within resistant social movements. *See* Janet Halley, *Gay Rights and Identity Imitation: Issues in the Ethics of Representation, in The Politics of Law* 115, 118 (David Kairys, ed., 3d ed. 1998). I would supplement this analysis with the claim that the "call from below" can include hate violence and hate speech.

62 See Bosniak, *supra* note 59, at 479 (asserting that the "feeling of citizenship" that we experience is "not merely a product of the ways in which citizenship is conceived and practiced in our legal and political worlds").

63 See Benedict Anderson, *Imagined Communities*, 7 (1991) (writing that the nation is "an imagined political community").

64 This is apparent in the name given by the administration to the bombardment of Afghanistan, and to the war on terrorism more generally: "Operation Enduring Freedom." For a discussion of how our ideas of freedom have come into existence and their relation to lines of power, truth, and ethics, see generally Nikolas Rose, *Powers of Freedom: Reframing Political Thought* (1999) (analyzing the relationship of freedom to contemporary governmentality).

65 See generally David Theo Goldberg, *Racist Culture* (1993); David Theo Goldberg, *The Racial State* (2002). *See also* Stuart Hall, *Conclusion: The Multi-cultural Question, in Un/settled Multiculturalisms: Diasporas, Entanglements, Transruptions* 209, 234 (Barnor Hesse ed., 2000) (observing that European imperialist expansion was presented in terms of a universalizing civilizing function, so that Western particularism was rewritten as a global universalism).

66 See Hope Lewis, *Lionheart Gals Facing the Dragon: The Human Rights of Inter/national Black Women in the United States*, 76 OR. L. REV. 567, 616–19 (1997) (discussing second-class citizenship of native-born and immigrant black women in the United States); Leti Volpp, *"Obnoxious to Their Very Nature": Asian Americans and Constitutional Citizenship*, 5 CITIZENSHIP STUD. 57, 62–67 (2001), *reprinted in* 8

ASIAN L.J. 71, 77–83 (2001) (describing how racialization of Asian Americans limits their enjoyment of citizenship as political activity and citizenship as identity).

67 Alex Aleinikoff similarly points out that while it has "become fashionable to predict the decline of the nation-state at the hands of sub-national and supra-national forces," the postnational perspective is not an accurate depiction of US models of rights and membership. T. Alexander Aleinikoff, *Between National and Post-National: Membership in the United States*, 4 MICH. J. RACE & L. 241, 243 (1999).

68 Arjun Appadurai, *Patriotism and Its Futures*, 5 PUB. CULTURE 411, 411 (1993) [hereinafter Appadurai, *Patriotism*]. A revised version also appears in Appadurai, *Modernity at Large: Cultural Dimensions of Globalization* (1996), at 158. Appadurai acknowledges that the nation-state, in its classical territorial form, is not yet "out of business." Appadurai, *Patriotism and Its Futures, supra*, at 421. Yet he also argues that today we are in a "postnational, diasporic world." *Id.* at 425.

69 *Id.* at 425.

70 *Id.* at 424.

71 Kandice Chuh, *Transnationalisms and its Posts*, 9 PUB. CULTURE 93, 95 (1996). I am indebted to Laura Kang for calling my attention to this juxtaposed reading of Appadurai and Chuh; see Laura H. Y. Kang, "Comfort Me": Mediated Affiliations and Disciplined Subjects in Korean/American Transnationality, Paper Presented at the American Studies Association Annual Meeting (Nov. 9, 2001) (on file with author). *See also* Partha Chatterjee, *Beyond the Nation? Or Within?*, 56 SOC. TEXT 57 (1998) (critically responding to Appadurai and suggesting that the postnational turn will in fact strengthen present inequalities, and arguing that strategies must first look within the nation-state to examine the relationship between civil society and modernity on the one hand and political society and democracy on the other).

72 Chuh, *supra* note 72, at 96–104.

73 Parenthetically, Mike Masaoka, Executive Director of the Japanese American Citizens League during World War II, suggested at that time that Japanese Americans brand themselves for easy identification and to prove their loyalty. He also suggested they create suicide battalions. *See* Chris K. Iijima, *Reparations and the "Model Minority" Ideology of Acquiescence: The Necessity to Refuse the Return to Original Humiliation*, 19 B.C. THIRD WORLD L.J. 385, 406 (1998).

74 On the correlation of citizenship with membership, see T. Alexander Aleinikoff, *The Tightening Circle of Membership*, 22 HASTINGS CON. L.Q. 915, 917–19 (1995) (suggesting a broader definition of membership); Hiroshi Motomura, *Whose Immigration Law? Citizens, Aliens and the Constitution*, 97 COLUM. L. REV. 1567, 1586 (1997) (reviewing Gerald L. Neuman, *Strangers to the Constitution: Immigrants, Borders, and Fundamental Law* (1996)). *See also*

T. Alexander Aleinikoff, *Citizenship Talk: A Revisionist Narrative*, 69 FORDHAM L. REV. 1689, 1692 (2001).

75   *See* Brian Dickerson, *ACLU Finds Intervention Not Welcome*, DETROIT FREE PRESS, Dec. 7, 2001, http://www.freep.com/news/metro/dicker7_20011207.htm (describing the response to an announcement by the Michigan chapter of the American Civil Liberties Union that it would provide free legal counsel to any of the 566 Middle Eastern men the FBI wanted to interview in the Detroit area). Of course, noncitizens do have rights under our Con-stitution, in its invocation of "persons" and not "citizens." *See* Susan Gzesh & Mae Ngai, Letter to the Editor, *In Crime, Immigrants, Citizens Have Same Rights*, CHIC. TRIB., Dec. 31, 2001, at 16.

76   *See* Ariel Dorfman, *America Looks at Itself Through Humanity's Mirror*, L.A. TIMES, Sept. 21, 2001, at B15.

77   For an example centering those currently detained, and, in fact, analogizing them to his parents, Russian immigrants jailed in the Palmer Raids, see Clancy Sigal, *John Ashcroft's Palmer Raids*, N.Y. TIMES, Mar. 13, 2002, at A25.

10

Race, Gender, and the Privileges of Property

Peggy Pascoe

Like a growing number of feminist scholars, I spend most of my time trying to understand the history of relationships between race and gender. These days, that is a pretty hot topic. For some time now, the best, and most sophisticated, work in this area has put race and gender relations in the context of what has come to be known as the "powers of desire"; in other words, it traces the connections between race, gender, and sexuality.[1] To mention only a few examples, I think of Hazel Carby's revealing study of the sexual politics of women's blues, of Antonia Castañeda's incisive critique of sexual violence in the Spanish Mexican conquest of California, or of Jacquelyn Dowd Hall's brilliant essay on rape and lynching.[2] When studies like these are combined with a remarkable constellation of recent disciplinary developments – the dynamic emergence of lesbian and gay studies, the coming of age of the history of sexuality, and the current poststructuralist preoccupation with the politics of "bodies" – the study of sex and sexuality suddenly seems to be everywhere.[3]

My own topic, the history of miscegenation law, would seem to be a prime candidate for interpretation along these lines.[4] Whenever and wherever I talk about my work, I encounter people who think that miscegenation laws were significant primarily because they reflected the ultimate American sexual taboo – that against sex between white women and black men.

There is, of course, no question that such a taboo has been pervasive in American society.[5] Certainly its power is threaded through the history of miscegenation laws. Although most experts agree that the overwhelming majority of interracial sexual relationships occurred

between white men and African American or American Indian women, miscegenation laws were clearly designed to control the behavior of white women.[6] One of the very first laws, passed in 1664 in Maryland, said so explicitly: it targeted relationships between two groups the lawmakers identified as "freeborn English women" and "Negro slaves."[7] Although most later miscegenation laws referred to "whites" in general rather than to white women in particular, they, too, were most likely to pass in the wake of scandals over the participation of white women in interracial relationships. Statistics on arrests and convictions are hard to come by, but, if the several dozen criminal cases which eventually reached appeals courts are any indication, the majority of couples dragged into criminal courts for violating miscegenation laws followed this same pattern: they were made up of white women and black men.[8]

And yet, the more I study the history of miscegenation law, the more intrigued I am with the parts of the story that have so far attracted much less attention than the American obsession with controlling the sexual behavior of white women.[9] The story I want to tell in this paper focuses more on marriage and property relations than on sex and sexuality, and more on white men and women of color than on white women and black men. And, perhaps just as important for the history of race and sex classification in American law, my story takes place not in the South, the region that has for so long stood as *the* paradigm for the study of race in America, but in the West, where the existence of a multicultural population provided both unprecedented opportunities for – and unprecedented challenges to – legal racial classifications. As historians Vicki

Ruiz and Ellen DuBois have pointed out in another context, paying more attention to the history of the US West is one way to move feminist scholarship beyond the limitation of its usual uniracial or bi-racial analyses.[10] In these few short pages, I'll need to be more suggestive than definitive: I'll briefly outline the structure of miscegenation laws, offer as a sample one case to consider, and merely mention some historical and contemporary variations on my theme.

Let me begin by outlining the laws. Although miscegenation laws are usually remembered (when they are remembered at all) as a southern regional development aimed at African Americans, they were actually a much broader phenomenon. Adopted in both the North and the South beginning in the colonial period, miscegenation laws grew up with slavery. They did not, however, reach maturity until after the Civil War, for it was only when slavery had been abandoned that miscegenation laws came to form the crucial "bottom line" of the system of white supremacy later embodied in segregation. Miscegenation laws gained this newfound importance just at the time that they were being extended to newly formed western states.

Although the laws were in many respects a national phenomenon, it was in the West, not the South, that they reached their most elaborate, even labyrinthine, development, covering the broadest list of racial categories. Thus, while the earliest miscegenation laws, passed in the South, forbade whites to marry African Americans, later laws, developed mostly in western states, expanded the list of groups prohibited from marrying whites by adding first American Indians, then Chinese and Japanese (both often referred to by the catchall term "Mongolians"), and then "Malays" (or Filipinos). And even this didn't exhaust the list. Oregon prohibited whites from marrying "Kanakas" (or native Hawaiians); South Dakota proscribed "Coreans"; Arizona singled out Hindus. The first western miscegenation law was passed by Texas in 1837, the last more than a century later, by Utah in 1939. By the 1920s, southern states like Virginia and Georgia were expanding their laws to include categories first listed by western states.[11]

To keep pace with this multiplication of racial categories, some states packed their laws with quasi-mathematical definitions of "race." Oregon, for example, declared that "it shall not be lawful within this state for any white person, male or female, to intermarry with any negro, Chinese, or any person, having one fourth or more negro, Chinese, or Kanaka blood, or any person having more than one half Indian blood."[12] Altogether,

miscegenation laws covered forty-one states and colonies. They spanned three centuries of American history: the first ones were enacted in the 1660s, and the last ones were not declared unconstitutional until 1967.[13]

Although it is their sexual taboos that attract attention today, the structure and function of miscegenation laws were, I think, more fundamentally related to the institution of marriage than to sexual behavior itself.[14] In sheer numbers, many more laws prohibited interracial marriage than interracial sex.[15] And in an even deeper sense, all miscegenation laws were designed to privilege marriage as a social and economic unit. Couples who challenged the laws knew that the right to marry translated into social respectability and economic benefits, including inheritance rights and legitimacy for children, that were denied to sexual liaisons outside marriage.

Miscegenation laws were designed to patrol this border by making so-called "miscegenous marriage" a legal impossibility. Thus criminal courts treated offenders as if they had never been married at all; that is, prosecutors charged interracial couples with the moral offense of fornication or some other illicit sex crime, then denied them the use of marriage as a defense. Civil courts guarded the junction between marriage and economic privilege. From Reconstruction to the 1930s, most miscegenation cases heard in civil courts were *ex post facto* attempts to invalidate relationships that had already lasted for a long time. They were brought by relatives or, sometimes, by the state, after the death of one partner, almost always a white man. Many of them were specifically designed to take property or inheritances away from the surviving partner, almost always an African American or American Indian woman.[16]

By looking at civil lawsuits like these (which were, at least in appeals court records, more common than criminal cases), we can begin to trace the links between white patriarchal privilege and property that sustained miscegenation laws. Let me illustrate the point by describing just one case, *In re Paquet's Estate*, decided by the Oregon Supreme Court in 1921.[17] The Paquet case, like most of the civil miscegenation cases of this period, was fought over the estate of a white man. The man in question, Fred Paquet, died in 1919, survived by his sixty-three-year-old Tillamook Indian wife, named Ophelia. The Paquet estate included twenty-two acres of land, some farm animals, tools, and a buggy, altogether worth perhaps $2,500.[18] Fred and Ophelia's relationship had a long history. In the 1880s, Fred had already begun to visit Ophelia frequently and openly enough that he had become one of many targets of a local grand jury that periodically threatened to indict white men who lived with Indian women.[19] Seeking to formalize the relationship – and, presumably, to end this harassment – Fred consulted a lawyer, who advised him to make sure to hold a ceremony that would meet the legal requirements for an "Indian custom" marriage. Accordingly, in 1889, Fred not only reached the customary agreement with Ophelia's Tillamook relatives, paying them fifty dollars in gifts, but also sought the formal sanction of Tillamook tribal chief Betsy Fuller (who was herself married to a white man); Fuller arranged for a tribal council to consider and confirm the marriage.[20] Fred and Ophelia lived together for more than thirty years, until his death. Fred clearly considered Ophelia his wife, and his neighbors, too, recognized their relationship, but because Fred died without leaving a formal will, administration of the estate was subject to state laws which provided for the distribution of property to surviving family members.

When Fred Paquet died, the county court recognized Ophelia as his widow and promptly appointed her administrator of the estate. Because the couple had no children, all the property, including the land, which Ophelia lived on and the Paquets had owned for more than two decades, would ordinarily have gone to her. Two days later, though, Fred's brother John came forward to contest Ophelia for control of the property.[21] John Paquet had little to recommend him to the court. Some of his neighbors accused him of raping native women, and he had such an unsavory reputation in the community that at one point the county judge declared him "a man of immoral habits . . . incompetent to transact ordinary business affairs and generally untrustworthy."[22] He was, however, a "white" man, and under Oregon's miscegenation law, that was enough to ensure that he won his case against Ophelia, an Indian woman.

The case eventually ended up in the Oregon Supreme Court. In making its decision, the key issue for the court was whether or not to recognize Fred and Ophelia's marriage, which violated Oregon's miscegenation law.[23] The court listened to – and then dismissed – Ophelia's argument that the marriage met the requirements for an Indian custom marriage and so should have been recognized as valid out of routine courtesy to the authority of another jurisdiction (that of the Tillamook tribe).[24] The court also heard and dismissed Ophelia's claim that Oregon's miscegenation law discriminated against Indians and was therefore an unconstitutional denial of the Fourteenth Amendment guarantee of equal protection. The court ingenuously explained its reasoning; it held that the Oregon miscegenation law did not discriminate because it "applied alike to all persons, either white, negroes, Chinese, Kanaka, or Indians."[25] Following this logic, the court declared Fred and Ophelia's marriage void because it violated Oregon's miscegenation law; it ordered that the estate and all its property be transferred to "the only relative in the state," John Paquet, to be distributed among him, his siblings and their heirs.[26]

As the Paquet case demonstrates, miscegenation law did not always prevent the formation of interracial relationships, sexual or otherwise. Fred and Ophelia had, after all, lived together for more than thirty years and had apparently won recognition as a couple from many of those around them; their perseverance had even allowed them to elude grand jury crackdowns. They did not, however, manage to escape the really crucial power of miscegenation law: the role it played in connecting white supremacy to the transmission of property. In American law, marriage provided the glue that set the transmission of property from husbands to wives and their children; miscegenation law kept property within racial boundaries by invalidating marriages between white men and women of color whenever ancillary white relatives like John Paquet contested them.[27]

The Paquet case, then, illustrates the significance of property in miscegenation cases. The next step is to understand that property, so often described in legal sources as simple economic assets (like land and capital) is actually a much more expansive phenomenon, one which took various forms and structured crucial relationships. Let me mention just three of the property relationships that appear and reappear in civil miscegenation cases. The first was suggested to me by the work of critical race theorists, who are nowadays arguing that race is in and of itself a kind of property.[28] As Derrick Bell, the scholar who has made this argument most explicitly, explains, most whites did – and still do – "expect the society to recognize an unspoken but no less vested property right in their 'whiteness.'" "This right," Bell maintains, "is recognized and upheld by courts and the society like all property rights under a government created and sustained primarily for that purpose."[29]

As applied to the Paquet case, this theme is easy to trace, for, in a sense, the victorious John Paquet had turned his "whiteness" (the best, and perhaps the only, asset he had) into property, and did so at Ophelia's expense. This transformation happened not once but repeatedly. One instance occurred shortly after the county judge had branded John Paquet immoral and unreliable. Dismissing these charges as the opinions of "a few scalawags and Garibaldi Indians," John Paquet's lawyers rallied enough white witnesses who would speak in his defense to mount an appeal which convinced a circuit court judge to declare Paquet competent to administer the estate.[30] Another example of the transformation of "whiteness" into property came when the Oregon Supreme Court ruled that Ophelia Paquet's "Indianness" disqualified her from legal marriage to a white man; with Ophelia thus out of the way, John and his siblings won the right to inherit the property.

The second property relationship I want to mention was illuminated for me by Nancy Cott, who was kind enough to share with me a work in progress in which she points out the etymological connection between the words "property" and "propriety."[31] Miscegenation law played on this connection by drawing a sharp line between "legitimate marriage" on the one hand and "illicit sex" on the other, then defining all interracial relationships as illicit sex. The distinction was a crucial one, for husbands were legally obligated to provide for legitimate wives and children, but men owed nothing to "mere" sexual partners: neither inheritance rights nor the legitimacy of children accompanied illicit relationships.

By defining all interracial relationships as illicit, miscegenation law did not so much prohibit or punish illicit sex as it did create and reproduce it. Conditioned by stereotypes which associated women of color with hypersexuality, judges routinely branded long-term settled relationships as "mere" sex rather than marriage. Lawyers played to these assumptions by reducing interracial relationships to interracial sex, then distinguishing interracial sex from marriage by associating it with prostitution. Describing the relationship between Fred and Ophelia Paquet, for example, John Paquet's lawyers claimed that "the alleged 'marriage' was a mere commercial affair" that did not deserve legal recognition because "the relations were entirely meretricious from their inception."[32]

It was all but impossible for women of color to escape the legacy of these associations. Ophelia Paquet's lawyers tried to find a way out by changing the subject. Rather than refuting the association between women of color and illicit sexuality, they highlighted its flip side, the supposed connection between white women and legitimate marriage. Ophelia Paquet, they told the judge, "had been to the man as good a wife as any white woman could have been."[33] In its final decision, the Oregon Supreme Court came as close as any court of that time did to accepting this line of argument. Taking the unusual step of admitting that "the record is conclusive that [Ophelia] lived with

[Fred] as a good and faithful wife for more than 30 years," the judges admitted that they felt some sympathy for Ophelia, enough to recommend – but not require – that John Paquet offer her what they called "a fair and reasonable settlement."[34] But in the Paquet case, as in other miscegenation cases, sexual morality, important as it was, was nonetheless still subordinate to channeling the transmission of property along racial dividing lines. Ophelia got a judicial pat on the head for good behavior, but John and his siblings got the property.

Which brings me to the third form of property relationship structured by miscegenation laws – and, for that matter, marriage laws in general – and that is women's economic dependence on men. Here the problems started long before the final decision gave John Paquet control of the Paquet estate. One of the most intriguing facts about the Paquet case is that everyone acted as if the estate in question belonged solely to Fred Paquet. In fact, however, throughout the Paquet marriage, Fred had whiled away most of his time; it was Ophelia's basket-making, fruit-picking, milk-selling, and wage work that had provided the income they needed to sustain themselves. And although the deed to their land was made out in Fred Paquet's name, the couple had used Ophelia's earnings, combined with her proceeds from government payments to Tillamook tribal members, to purchase the property and to pay the yearly taxes on it. It is significant, I think, that, although lawyers on both sides of the case knew this, neither they nor the Oregon Supreme Court judges considered it a key issue at the trial in which Ophelia lost all legal right to what the courts considered "Fred's" estate.

Indeed, Ophelia's economic contribution might never have been taken into account if it were not for the fact that in the wake of the Oregon Supreme Court decision, United States Indian officials found themselves responsible for the care of the now impoverished Ophelia. Apparently hoping both to defend Ophelia and to relieve themselves of the burden of her support, they sued John Paquet on Ophelia's behalf. Working through the federal courts that covered Indian relations and equity claims, rather than the state courts that enforced miscegenation laws, they eventually won a partial settlement. Yet their argument, too, reflected the assumption that men were better suited than women to the ownership of what the legal system referred to as "real" property. Although their brief claimed that "Fred Paquet had practically no income aside from the income he received through the labor and efforts of the said Ophelia Paquet," they asked the court to grant Ophelia the right to only half of the

Paquet land.[35] In the end, the court ordered that Ophelia should receive a cash settlement (the amount was figured at half the value of the land), but only if she agreed to make her award contingent on its sale.[36] To get any settlement at all, Ophelia Paquet had to relinquish all claims to actual ownership of the land, although such a claim might have given her legal grounds to prevent its sale and so allow her to spend her final years on the property. It is not even clear that she ever received payment on the settlement ordered by the court. As late as 1928, John Paquet's major creditor complained to a judge that Paquet had repeatedly turned down acceptable offers to sell the land; perhaps he had chosen to live on it himself.[37]

Like any single example, the Paquet case captures miscegenation law as it stood at one moment, and a very particular moment at that, one that might be considered the high-water mark of American courts' determination to structure both family formation and property transmission along racial dividing lines.[38] There is, of course, more to the story than that, so with the Paquet case now firmly in mind, let me range rather widely across time and space to mention a few historical and contemporary variations on its themes of race, gender, patriarchal privilege, and property.[39]

Consider, for example, that if the Paquet case had been argued fifty years earlier, in the early 1870s, its outcome might well have been different, for during Reconstruction, several state legislatures repealed their miscegenation laws, and, in a remarkable handful of cases heard in Alabama, Louisiana, and Texas, judges declared others inoperative.[40] The reasoning behind these decisions shows both the potential Reconstruction held for challenging white supremacy and the continuing influence of the gendered powers of traditional patriarchs. Having just lost the traditional system of social control embodied in slavery law (in which courts guarded the rights of white patriarchs as slaveowners), a few judges tried, I think, to fill the gap by reinforcing the system of social control embodied in marriage law (in which courts guarded the rights of white patriarchs as husbands); the result was that a few courts extended formal legal recognition to marriages between white men and newly freed black women.

Revealing as these decisions of the early 1870s were, however, they were also quite exceptional. Between 1875 and the 1920s, miscegenation laws found such firm footing in the courts that even the patriarchal powers of husbands were overwhelmed by the rise of the newly definitive racial classifications of the segregation era. Outside miscegenation courts, too, traditional white patriarchy was in the process of being replaced by a new form of male dominance.[41] The extent of the erosion of traditional white patriarchy can be seen in the fact that by the 1930s, the most significant civil challenges to miscegenation law came from an unprecedented source in a new type of case: lawsuits in which couples made up of white women and men of color went to court to win the formal right to marry.[42] These couples were, in effect, relying on a new – and less racially exclusive – definition of the role of husband to help them challenge the racial classifications at the core of miscegenation law.

It may well be significant (and, given the sheer range of miscegenation laws in the US West, it is certainly ironic) that these challenges to miscegenation laws found their firmest footholds in western state courts. The cases that would eventually set precedents for invalidating miscegenation laws first reached courts in the 1930s, and began to carry real force in 1948, when California declared its state miscegenation law unconstitutional.[43] After 1967, when the US Supreme Court held that miscegenation laws violated the Fourteenth Amendment, racial categories were erased from marriage law, and miscegenation laws became a thing of the past.[44] By the 1970s, then, fifty years after Ophelia Paquet ended up in court, the decision rendered in the Paquet case no longer made legal sense.

Today, most Americans have trouble remembering that miscegenation laws ever existed. The audiences I speak to are incredulous at the injustice and the arbitrariness of the racial classifications that stand out in the cases I tell them about; they express considerable relief that those "bad old days" are now over. I share their outrage, but I also find it intriguing that so few modern listeners notice that one of the themes raised in the Paquet case – the significance of marriage in channeling property transmission – not only remains alive and well, but has, in fact, outlived both the erosion of traditional patriarchy and the rise and fall of racial classifications in marriage law.

More than a generation after the demise of miscegenation laws (and despite repeated feminist reforms of marriage laws), the drawing of exclusionary lines around marriage is still going strong. Today the most prominent – though hardly the only – victims are lesbian and gay couples, who point out that the sexual classifications currently embedded in marriage law operate in much the same way that the racial classifications embedded in miscegenation laws once did: that is, they allow courts to categorize same-sex relationships as illicit sex rather than legitimate marriage and they allow courts to exclude same-sex couples from the property benefits of marriage, which now include everything from tax advantages to medical insurance coverage.[45]

These modern legal battles and the earlier ones fought by couples like Fred and Ophelia Paquet both suggest, I think, that focusing on the historical connections between property and the political economy of marriage in the US West offers a revealing window on the form and power of race and sex classifications in American law and race and gender hierarchies in American history.

Notes

1   The phrase comes from Ann Snitow, Christine Stansell, and Sharon Thompson, eds., *Powers of Desire: The Politics of Sexuality* (New York: Monthly Review Press, 1983).

2   Hazel V. Carby, "'It Jus Be's Dat Way Sometime': The Sexual Politics of Women's Blues," in Ellen Carol DuBois and Vicki L. Ruiz, eds., *Unequal Sisters: A Multicultural Reader in U.S. Women's History* (New York: Routledge, 1990), 238–49; Antonia I. Castañeda, "Sexual Violence in the Politics and Policies of Conquest: Amerindian Women and the Spanish Conquest of Alta California," in Adela de la Torre and Beatríz Pesquera, eds., *Building with Our Own Hands: New Directions in Chicana Scholarship* (Berkeley: University of California Press, 1993), 15–33; Jacquelyn Dowd Hall, "'The Mind That Burns in Each Body': Women, Rape, and Racial Violence," in *Powers of Desire*, 328–49. For additional collections including work of this kind, see John C. Fout and Maura Shaw Tantillo, eds., *American Sexual Politics: Sex, Gender, and Race since the Civil War* (Chicago: University of Chicago Press, 1993); and Carol S. Vance, ed., *Pleasure and Danger: Exploring Female Sexuality* (Boston: Routledge & Kegan Paul, 1984).

3   There is now an enormous literature in these areas. Among the best starting points are the following surveys and collections: Henry Abelove, Michele Aina Barale, and David M. Halperin, eds., *The Lesbian and Gay Studies Reader* (New York: Routledge, 1993); Martin Bauml Duberman, Martha Vicinus, and George Chauncey, Jr., eds., *Hidden from History: Reclaiming the Gay and Lesbian Past* (New York: Meridian, 1989); John D'Emilio and Estelle B. Freedman, *Intimate Matters: A History of Sexuality in America* (New York: Harper and Row, 1988); and Thomas Laqueur, *Making Sex: Body and Gender from the Greeks to Freud* (Cambridge: Harvard University Press 1990).

4   A word is in order about my use of the term "miscegenation." It is, I know, now customary for scholars to try to avoid the embarrassingly biological connotations of this term, which dates to the 1860s and means "race mixing," by referring to "cross-cultural" or "interracial" marriages. Those

terms, which work just fine for describing actual marriages, are inaccurate as characterizations of miscegenation laws, for the laws did not prohibit marriages between, say, Chinese immigrants and African Americans, but only marriages between groups designated as "white" and groups designated, in effect, as not "white." In this sense, the laws served as deliberate hand-maidens of a particular form of American white supremacy. In order to remind us that the laws were intended to reflect these notions, I will retain the term "miscegenation" when referring to the laws, using it in favor of the other major alternative, "anti-miscegenation," which seems to me to grant a certain legitimacy to the concept, as if the laws were aimed at a real biological phenomenon.

5   The most interesting recent work on this taboo explores shifts in its power and structure in different time periods. See especially Martha Hodes, *White Women, Black Men: Illicit Sex in the Nineteenth-Century South* (New Haven: Yale University Press, 1997); Hodes, "The Sexualization of Reconstruction Politics: White Women and Black Men in the South after the Civil War," in *American Sexual Politics*, 59–74; Robyn Weigman, "The Anatomy of Lynching," in *American Sexual Politics*, 223–45; and Hall, "Women, Rape, and Racial Violence."

6   On relationships between white men and women of color, see D'Emilio and Freedman, *Intimate Matters*, 85–108; Deborah Gray White, *Arn't I A Woman: Female Slaves in the Plantation South* (New York: Norton, 1985); Thelma Jennings, "'Us Colored Women Had to Go Through a Plenty': Sexual Exploitation of African-American Slave Women," *Journal of Women's History* 1 (Winter 1990), 45–74; Sylvia Van Kirk, *"Many Tender Ties": Women in Fur Trade Society, 1670–1870* (Norman: University of Oklahoma Press, 1980); and the essays by Johnny Faragher, Deena González, and Sylvia Van Kirk in Lillian Schlissel, Vicki L. Ruiz, and Janice Monk, eds., *Western Women: Their Land, Their Lives* (Albuquerque: University of New Mexico Press, 1988), 197–226. On white women as the special objects of miscegenation laws, see Karen Getman, "Sexual Control in the Slaveholding South: The Implementation and Maintenance of a Racial Caste System," *Harvard Women's Law Journal* 7 (Spring 1984), 114–52; A. Leon Higginbotham, Jr., and Barbara K. Kopytoff, "Racial Purity and Interracial Sex in the Law of Colonial and Antebellum Virginia," *Georgetown Law Journal* 77 (August 1989), 1994–2000; George M. Fredrickson, *White Supremacy: A Comparative Study in American and South African History* (New York: Oxford University Press, 1981), 103–5; Peter W. Bardaglio, *Reconstructing the Household: Families, Sex, and the Law in the Nineteenth-Century South* (Chapel Hill: University of North Carolina Press, 1995), 52–5; David H. Fowler, *Northern Attitudes towards Interracial Marriage: Legislation and Public Opinion in the Middle Atlantic and the States of the Old Northwest, 1780–1930* (1963; New York: Garland,

1987), 150–3, 166; and Peggy Pascoe, "Race, Gender, and Intercultural Relations: The Case of Interracial Marriage," *Frontiers* 12, no. 1 (1991), 6–7.

7 William H. Browne, ed., *Archives of Maryland*, vol. 1 (Baltimore: Maryland Historical Society, 1883), 533–4, cited in Fowler, *Northern Attitudes*, appendix, 381. As Barbara J. Fields points out, the fact that the law refers to freeborn English women rather than "white" women suggests that the law did not so much reflect racial categories already in place as show "society in the act of inventing race." Barbara J. Fields, "Slavery, Race, and Ideology in the United States of America," *New Left Review*, no. 181 (May–June 1990), 107.

8 My search of US appeals court cases involving miscegenation law between 1867 and 1947 shows that 61 percent of the seventy-seven criminal cases for which racial designations were listed involved pairings between white women and non-white men. Appeals cases are, of course, a very special – and in some respects, very limited – kind of source; for a longer discussion of their advantages and disadvantages, see note 17 below.

9 This article is part of a larger project, my book on the history of miscegenation law, *What Comes Naturally: Miscegenation Law and the Making of Race in America* (New York: Oxford University Press, 2008). In addition to the studies listed above, the following works are essential reading for those interested in the history of theoretical relationships between race and gender: Evelyn Brooks Higginbotham, "African-American Women's History and the Metalanguage of Race," *Signs* 17 (Winter 1992), 251–74; Tessie Liu, "Teaching the Differences among Women from a Historical Perspective: Rethinking Race and Gender as Social Categories," *Women's Studies International Forum* 14, no. 4 (1991), 265–76; and Ann Stoler, "Making Empire Respectable: The Politics of Race and Sexual Morality in Twentieth-Century Colonial Cultures," *American Ethnologist* 16 (November 1989), 634–60.

10 "Introduction" to *Unequal Sisters*, xii.

11 The most complete list of state miscegenation laws can be found in Fowler, *Northern Attitudes*, appendix, 336–439. To those familiar with late twentieth-century US "racial" groupings (or, for that matter, the structure of racial oppression in the nineteenth-century American West), there is a notable omission from the list of those prohibited from marrying whites, and that is Spanish/Mexicans. The fact that Spanish/Mexicans were not listed in the laws, however, did not always mean that they fell on the "white" side of the racial divide. In terms of legal theory, individual Spanish/Mexicans were categorized as racially "Caucasian" unless it could be proven that they had "native" or "African" "blood," in which case they came under the jurisdiction of miscegenation laws targeting American Indians and African Americans. In terms of actual practice, it appears that many couples made up of whites and Spanish/Mexicans believed that their marriages would be

prohibited by miscegenation law and, in fact, officials often refused to issue them licenses.

12 *Oregon Codes and Stats.*, 1901, Chap. 8, Sec. 1999 (1866).

13 The overall development of the laws can be followed in Robert J. Sickels, *Race, Marriage, and the Law* (Albuquerque: University of New Mexico Press, 1972); Byron Curti Martyn, "Racism in the United States: A History of the Anti-Miscegenation Legislation and Litigation" (PhD diss., University of Southern California, 1979); and Fowler, *Northern Attitudes*. The US Supreme Court decision which declared miscegenation laws unconstitutional is *Loving v. Virginia*, 388 US 1 (1967).

14 One of the first scholars to recognize this was Mary Frances Berry; see her fine discussion of the structure of miscegenation laws in "Judging Morality: Sexual Behavior and Legal Consequences in the Late Nineteenth-Century South," *Journal of American History* 78 (December 1991), 838–9. For this reason, I find the work of scholars who have explored the outlines of marriage as a social structure especially helpful in thinking through my topic. See especially Berry, "Judging Morality"; Nancy F. Cott, "Giving Character to Our Whole Civil Polity: Marriage and the Public Order in the Late Nineteenth Century," in Linda K. Kerber, Alice Kessler-Harris, and Kathryn Kish Sklar, eds., *U.S. History as Women's History: New Feminist Essays* (Chapel Hill: University of North Carolina Press, 1995), 107–21; Ramón Gutiérrez, *When Jesus Came, the Corn Mothers Went Away: Marriage, Sexuality, and Power in New Mexico, 1500–1846* (Stanford: Stanford University Press, 1991); and Verena Martinez-Alier, *Marriage, Class, and Colour in Nineteenth-Century Cuba: A Study of Racial Attitudes and Sexual Values in a Slave Society* (Cambridge: Cambridge University Press, 1974).

15 According to the list in Fowler, *Northern Attitudes*, appendix, forty-one states and colonies prohibited interracial marriage, twenty-two of which also prohibited one form or another of interracial sex, variously described as "adultery," "bastardy," "concubinage," "cohabitation," "illicit cohabitation," "fornication," "cohabiting in fornication," "illicit carnal intercourse," "sexual intercourse," or "sexual relations." Only one colony (New York) prohibited interracial sex ("adulterous intercourse") without also prohibiting interracial marriage, bringing the total number of jurisdictions which prohibited interracial sex to twenty-three.

16 My count of US appeals court cases involving miscegenation law between 1867 and 1947 shows that 81.8 percent of the eighty-eight civil cases for which racial designations are listed involved pairings between white men and non-white women. Although I have offered totals like these here and in note 8 above, readers should keep in mind that appeals court cases are not representative in any simple numerical sense; indeed, the reason cases end up in appeals courts in the first place is that they are in some respect unusual. There remains a pressing need for research into

the numbers of lower-court cases, especially the statistics on criminal arrests and convictions and the frequency with which miscegenation law was invoked in civil cases involving property relations.

17   I have selected the Paquet case from my working database of appeals court decisions, which includes every decision involving the interpretation of a miscegenation law issued by an appeals court and recorded in state, regional, or federal court reporters from 1860 through 1967. Appeals court decisions are both enticing and extremely tricky historical sources. Although cases that reach appeals courts are by definition somewhat atypical, they hold considerable significance for historians because the decisions reached in them set general policies later followed in more routine cases and because the texts of the decisions provide important clues to the ways judges thought through particular legal problems. I have relied on them here not only because of these interpretive advantages, but also for two more directly practical reasons. First, because appeals court decisions are published and indexed, it is possible to compile a list of them comprehensive enough to ensure maximum coverage. In the case of miscegenation law, ensuring coverage can be a considerable challenge. Because marriage was generally considered a matter of state rather than federal jurisdiction, the vast majority of cases came up in state courts, and finding them requires painstaking state-by-state or regional research. I was considerably aided in this process by Byron Curti Martyn's encyclopedic dissertation, "Racism in the United States: A History of the Anti-Miscegenation Legislation and Litigation," the bibliography of which includes references to many cases that did not appear in the usual legal reference sources. Second, the process of making an appeal often requires that documents that might otherwise be routinely discarded after a set period of time (such as legal briefs and court reporters' trial notes) are transcribed, typed or printed, and saved, allowing historians additional clues to the relationship between the specific local context and the larger legal issues. The Paquet case, for example, can be followed not only by reading the text of the appeals court decision, *In re Paquet's Estate*, 200 P. 911 (Oregon 1921); but also in the following archival case files: *Paquet v. Paquet*, file No. 4268, Oregon Supreme Court, 1920; *Paquet v. Henkle*, file No. 4267, Oregon Supreme Court, 1920; and Tillamook County Probate file No. 605, all in the Oregon State Archives; and in *US v. John B. Paquet*, Judgment Roll 11409, Register No. 8–8665, March 1925, National Archives and Records Administration, Pacific Northwest Branch.

18   Initial estimates of the value of the estate were much higher, ranging from $4,500 to $12,500. I have relied on the figure of $2,528.50 provided by court-appointed assessors. See Tillamook County Probate file No. 605, Inventory and Appraisement, June 15, 1920.

19   *Paquet v. Paquet*, Respondent's Brief, November 1, 1920, pp. 2–5.

20   Tillamook County Probate file No. 605, Judge A. M. Hare, Findings of Facts and Conclusions of Law, February 3, 1920; *Paquet v. Paquet*, Appellants Abstract of Record, September 3, 1920, pp. 10–16.

21   *Paquet v. Paquet*, Appellants Abstract of Record, September 3, 1920, p. 3.

22   Tillamook County Probate file No. 605, Judge A. M. Hare, Findings of Fact and Conclusions of Law, February 3, 1920.

23   Court records identify Fred Paquet as being of French Canadian origin. Both sides agreed that Fred was a "pure" or "full-blooded" "white" man and Ophelia was a "pure" or "full-blooded" "Indian" woman. *Paquet v. Paquet*, Appellant's First Brief, October 8, 1920, p. 1; *Paquet v. Paquet*, Respondent's Brief, November 1, 1920, p. 2.

24   The question of legal jurisdiction over Indian tribes was – and is – a very thorny issue. Relations with Indians were generally a responsibility of the US federal government, which, although it advocated shaping Indian families to fit white middle-class molds, had little practical choice but to grant general recognition to tribal marriages performed according to Indian custom. In the US legal system, however, jurisdiction over marriage rested with the states rather than the federal government. States could, therefore, use their control over marriage as a wedge to exert some power over Indians by claiming that Indian-white marriages, especially those performed outside recognized reservations, were subject to state rather than federal jurisdiction. In the Paquet case, for example, the court insisted that, because the Tillamook had never been assigned to a reservation and because Fred and Ophelia lived in a mixed settlement, Ophelia could not be considered part of a recognized tribe nor a "ward" of the federal government. As events would later show, both contentions were inaccurate: Ophelia was an enrolled member of the Tillamook tribe, which was under the supervision of the Siletz Indian Agency; the federal government claimed her as "a ward of the United States." See *US v. John B. Paquet*, Bill of Complaint in Equity, September 21, 1923, p. 3.

25   *In re Paquet's Estate*, 200 P. 911 at 913 (Oregon 1921).

26   *In re Paquet's Estate*, 200 P. 911 at 914 (Oregon 1921).

27   Although the issue did not come up in *Paquet*, children, in addition to the wife, could lose their legal standing in miscegenation cases, for one effect of invalidating an interracial marriage was to make the children technically illegitimate. According to the law of most states, illegitimate children automatically inherited from their mothers; but they could inherit from their fathers only if their father had taken legal steps to formally recognize or adopt them. Since plaintiffs could rarely convince judges that fathers had done so, the children of interracial marriages were often disinherited along with their mothers. A classic example is

the case of Juana Walker, decided in Arizona in 1896, in which Walker was declared illegitimate and thereby disinherited after the court decided that no legal marriage could have existed between her father John Walker, a "white" man, and his Pima Indian wife Churga. The chief beneficiaries of this decision were John Walker's brother William and his siblings. See *In re Walker's Estate*, 46 P. 67 (Arizona 1896). For a discussion of the Walker case, see Roger D. Hardaway, "Unlawful Love: A History of Miscegenation Law," *Journal of Arizona History* 27, no. 4 (1986), 378–9.

28 For introductions to critical race theory, see Kimberlé Crenshaw et al., eds., *Critical Race Theory: The Key Writings that Formed the Movement* (New York: New Press, 1995) and Richard Delgado and Jean Stefancic, "Critical Race Theory: An Annotated Bibliography," *Virginia Law Review* 79 (March 1993), 461–516. For particularly suggestive accounts of the relationships between "race" and property, see Derrick Bell, "Remembrances of Racism Past," in Herbert Hill and James E. Jones, eds., *Race in America: The Struggle for Equality* (Madison: University of Wisconsin Press, 1992), 73–82; Cheryl I. Harris, "Whiteness as Property," *Harvard Law Review* 106 (June 1993), 1707–1791; George Lipsitz, "The Possessive Investment in Whiteness: Racialized Social Democracy and the 'White Problem' in American Studies," *American Quarterly* 47 (September 1995), 369–87; Eva Saks, "Representing Miscegenation Law," *Raritan* 8 (Fall 1988), 39–69; and Patricia J. Williams, "Fetal Fictions: An Exploration of Property Archetypes in Racial and Gendered Contexts," in Hill and Jones, *Race in America*, 73–82.

29 Bell, "Remembrances of Racism Past," 78. See also Bell, "White Superiority in America: Its Legal Legacy, Its Economic Costs," *Villanova Law Review* 33 (1988), 767–79.

30 *Paquet v. Henkle*, Respondent's Brief, March 14, 1920, p. 6, Index to Transcript, August 25, 1920, p. 3. As is often the case in legal matters, the process itself was a convoluted one. The county court initially – and apparently automatically – granted Ophelia Paquet the right to administer the estate. After John Paquet objected to her appointment and challenged the validity of her marriage, the county judge removed Ophelia in favor of John Paquet. At that point R. N. Henkle, a creditor of the estate and a man said by John Paquet's lawyers to be acting for Ophelia, persuaded the county judge that John Paquet was unfit to carry out his duties; Henkle won appointment in his stead. John Paquet then appealed to the circuit court, which removed Henkle and reappointed John Paquet, who remained administrator of the estate while the marriage issue was being settled in the Oregon Supreme Court and thereafter.

31 Nancy F. Cott, "A Map of Marriage in the Public Order in the Late Nineteenth-Century United States" (unpublished paper, August 1993), p. 5. See also Cott, "Giving Character to Our Whole Civil Polity."

32 *Paquet v. Paquet*, Respondent's Brief, November 1, 1920, p. 7. Using typical imagery, they added that the Paquet relationship was "a case where a white man and a full blooded Indian woman have chosen to cohabit together illictly [sic], to agree to a relation of concubinage, which is not only a violation of the law of Oregon, but a transgression against the law of morality and the law of nature" (16).

33 *Paquet v. Paquet*, Appellant's First Brief, October 8, 1920, p. 2.

34 *In re Paquet's Estate*, 200 P. 911 at 914 (Oregon 1921).

35 *US v. John B. Paquet*, Bill of Complaint in Equity, September 21, 1923, pp. 4, 6–7.

36 *US v. John B. Paquet*, Stipulation, Decree, June 2, 1924.

37 Tillamook County Probate file No. 605, J. S. Cole, Petition, June 7, 1928. Cole was president of the Tillamook-Lincoln County Credit Association.

38 For a particularly insightful analysis of the historical connections between concepts of "race" and "family," see Liu, "Teaching the Differences among Women."

39 For a more extended discussion of twentieth-century developments, see Peggy Pascoe, "Miscegenation Law, Court Cases, and Ideologies of 'Race' in Twentieth-Century America," *Journal of American History* 83 (June 1996), 44–69.

40 Between 1866 and 1877, Arkansas, Florida, Illinois, Louisiana, Mississippi, New Mexico, South Carolina, and Washington state either repealed their laws or omitted them from state code compilations, though several would reenact them only a few years later. See Fowler, *Northern Attitudes*, appendix. Courts in Alabama, Louisiana, and Texas upheld particular marriages in *Burns v. State*, 17 Am. Rep. 34 (Alabama 1872); *Honey v. Clark*, 37 Tex. 686 (Texas 1873); *Hart v. Hoss*, 26 La. Ann. 90 (Louisiana 1874); *State v. Webb*, 4 Cent. L. J. 588 (Texas 1877); *Ex parte Brown*, 5 Cent. L. J. 149 (Texas 1877).

41 The most suggestive account I know of this redefinition of male dominance is Linda Gordon, *Heroes of Their Own Lives: The Politics and History of Family Violence* (New York: Viking, 1988), 56–7. On related topics, see Gail Bederman, *Manliness and Civilization: A Cultural History of Gender and Race in the United States, 1880–1917* (Chicago: University of Chicago Press, 1995); Michael Grossberg, *Governing the Hearth: Law and the Family in Nineteenth-Century America* (Chapel Hill: University of North Carolina Press, 1985); Elaine Tyler May, *Great Expectations: Marriage and Divorce in Post-Victorian America* (Chicago: University of Chicago Press, 1980); and Margaret Marsh, "Suburban Men and Masculine Domesticity, 1870–1915," *American Quarterly* 40 (June 1988), 165–86.

42 *Roldan v. Los Angeles County*, 129 Ca. App. 267 (California 1933); *Perez v. Lippold*, 198 P. 2d 17 (California 1948); *Oyama v. O'Neill*, 5 Race Relations Law Reporter 136 (Arizona 1959); *Davis v. Gately*, 269 F. Supp. 996 (1967).

43 *Perez v. Lippold*, 198 P. 2d 17 (California 1948).

44 *Loving v. Virginia*, 388 US 1 (1967). Given that so many twentieth-century challenges to miscegenation law had been taken to court by couples made up of white women and men of color, it is striking that the Loving case involved the criminal conviction of a white man and a black woman.

45 Court cases on the issue of same-sex marriage include *Anonymous v. Anonymous*, 325 NYS 2d 499 (New York 1971); *Baker v. Nelson*, 191 NW 2d 185 (Minnesota 1971); *Jones v. Hallahan*, 501 S.W. 2d (Kentucky 1973); *Singer v. Hara*, 522 P. 2d 1187 (Washington 1974); *De Santo v. Barnsley*, 476 A. 2d 952 (Pennsylvania 1984); *Dean v. District of Columbia*, 18 FLR 1141 and 1387 (1991–92); *Baehr v. Lewin*, 852 P. 2d 44 (Hawaii 1993). For legal commentary on the analogy between sex and race classification in marriage laws, see Mark Strasser, "Family, Definitions, and the Constitution: On the Antimiscegenation Analogy," *Suffolk University Law Review* 25 (Winter 1991), 981–1034; James Trosino, "American Wedding: Same-Sex Marriage and the Miscegenation Analogy," *Boston University Law Review* 73 (January 1993), 93–120; Andrew Koppelman, "The Miscegenation Analogy: Sodomy Law as Sex Discrimination," *Yale Law Journal* 98 (November 1988), 145–64; and Koppelman, "Why Discrimination against Lesbians and Gays is Sex Discrimination," *NYU Law Review* 69 (May 1994), 197–287. For a particularly fine analysis of the significance of sex classifications in contemporary, marriage law, see Nan D. Hunter, "Marriage, Law, and Gender: A Feminist Inquiry," *Law and Equality* 1 (Summer 1991), 9–30.

11

Racing Religion

Moustafa Bayoumi

The Jew is one whom other men consider a Jew: that is the simple truth from which we must start.

Jean-Paul Sartre

But what exactly is a black? First of all, what's his color?

Jean Genet

Late in 1942, as the Second World War raged overseas, a Yemeni Muslim immigrant named Ahmed Hassan quietly appeared one day in front of a United States District Court judge. The Michigan resident had come to court for a hearing regarding his petition for naturalization, and while we don't know what he wore that day, it was probably something carefully chosen to downplay his "extremely dark complexion," as described in the judge's decision (In re *Hassan* 1942, 844). Hassan, after all, was making his official appearance in front of the Court to prove that he was a white person and, therefore, eligible for citizenship.

Although Hassan was one of the first Arab Muslims to petition for American naturalization, his case was far from unique. Beginning in 1790 and until 1952, the Naturalization Act had limited citizenship to "free white persons" but without exactly defining what makes a person white. Thus, many people, primarily of Asian descent, had appeared in front of the courts before Hassan to argue that they were "white by law," to borrow a phrase from Ian Haney Lopez's book (1996) of the same name. The immigration laws had changed over the years. In 1870, for example, the Naturalization Act was amended to include "aliens of African nativity and to persons of African descent" (Act 1870), and in 1940, language was added to include "races indigenous to the Western Hemisphere." Nonetheless, certain Asians, beginning

with the Chinese, had been excluded from American citizenship since 1878 (Haney Lopez 1996, 42–5). In 1882, Congress passed the first Chinese Exclusion Act, and in 1917, most immigration from Asia was further curtailed with the establishment of what Congress called the "Asiatic Barred Zone" (Chin 1998, 15). The reasoning here was that the country should not admit people who had no chance of naturalization. Despite all these changes, it was still far from clear just what race Hassan was, especially with Yemen sitting squarely on the Arabian Peninsula in Asia.

Hassan certainly knew he had a fight ahead of him and was aware that the battle would be about his group membership and not his individual qualifications. He understood that the Court would want to know if Arabs were white or yellow, European or Asian, Western or Eastern. He probably knew that the Court would wonder if Arabs, as a people, could assimilate into the white Christian culture of the United States or if they were, by nature, unsuited to adapt to the republic where they now lived. After all, in previous "racial-prerequisite cases," as they are called, such political and cultural questions were commonly asked, although they traditionally narrowed in simply on the color of one's skin. Even then, as Haney Lopez tells us, the courts adopted shifting standards of whiteness, first using scientific knowledge (now largely discredited) or congressional intent and then adopting the test of "common understanding" (1996, 67–77).

We know that Hassan was aware of the impending questions and the legal history of immigration by the fact that he came to Court that day armed with affidavits stating that his coloring "is typical of the majority of the Arabians from the region from which he comes, which [in] fact is attributed to the intense heat and the blazing sun of that area" (In re *Hassan* 1942, 844). Under his arm were other affidavits, claims by unnamed ethnologists declaring that "the Arabs are remote descendants of and therefore members of the Caucasian or white race, and that [Hassan] is therefore eligible for citizenship" (846). He had done his homework. He had hope.

Whatever optimism he may have had, however, was soon dashed. Hassan's petition was denied. In his three-page decision dated December 14, 1942, Judge Tuttle straightforwardly stated that "Arabs are not white persons within the meaning of the [Nationality] Act" (In re *Hassan* 1942, 847). Interestingly, Tuttle based his determination of Hassan's whiteness not principally on the color of his skin but primarily on the fact that he was an Arab and Islam is the dominant religion among the Arabs. "Apart from the dark skin of the Arabs," explained the judge, "it is well known that they are a part of the Mohammedan world and that a wide gulf separates their culture from that of the predominately Christian peoples of Europe. It cannot be expected that as a class they would readily intermarry with our population and be assimilated into our civilization" (845).

Religion determines race. At least in 1942 it did, and so Arabs were not considered white people by statute because they were (unassimilable) Muslims. But by 1944, a mere seventeen months later, things changed radically. At that time, another Arab Muslim would petition the government for citizenship. His name was Mohamed Mohriez, and he was "an Arab born in Sanhy, Badan, Arabia," who came to the United States on January 15, 1921. Unlike Hassan, however, Mohriez would succeed in his petition. District Judge Wyzanski, who ruled in Mohriez's favor, made a point of explaining in his brief decision (delivered on April 13, 1944) that the global political leadership of the United States requires its adherence to the principles of equality that it espouses. After citing *Hassan* and stating his position ("the Arab passes muster as a white person"), the judge ended his decision by admitting that the "vital interest [of the United States] as a world power" required granting Mohriez's petition (Ex parte *Mohriez* 1944, 942, 943). Why? Wyzanski explained that his decision was necessary "to promote friendlier relations between the United States and other nations and so as to fulfill the promise that we shall treat all men as created equal" (943). If in *Hassan* religion produces race, then in *Mohriez*, politics directly sways legal racial determination.

The last of the Asian exclusion laws was repealed in 1952 in favor of a restricting quota system of immigration. In 1965, the law changed again, abandoning the quota system entirely and making the racial prerequisite cases, with their now antiquated racial language, look like history. But half a century after the *Hassan* decision, and following the terrorist attacks of September 11th, Arabs and Muslims have again been repeatedly forced to undergo state scrutiny and official state definition simply because of their group membership and not due to their individual qualifications. Reminiscent of the earlier racial prerequisite cases, today's post-September 11th state policies also teeter uncomfortably on race, religion, and contemporary politics, and the result has been mass exclusions and deportations of Arab and Muslim men from the United States in a strategy that, I argue, can properly be described as deliberate and racist.

Specifically, I am talking about the policy known as "special registration," a program of the Bush Administration's war on terror that draws on the history of the racial prerequisite cases for its authority and its practice. When it was first announced, special registration drew some critical commentary from journalists and legal scholars, but it has not been investigated in depth. It bears looking into, however, for an inquiry into its mechanism should reveal at least two things: the insufficiency of past critiques of legal racial formation (like Haney Lopez's) to address how political expediency affects state definitions of race and the fact that through special registration the government has, in effect, turned a religion, namely Islam, into a race. The rest of the essay will elaborate these points, but since the details of special registration are not well known, it is worth reviewing the program in detail before continuing.

What's So Special about Special Registration?

On September 11, 2002, the one-year anniversary of the terrorist attacks on the United States, the Bush administration established the National Security Entry-Exit Registration System (NSEERS) as part of its strategy in the war on terror. Since then, NSEERS, commonly known as "special registration," has been a controversial and poorly executed program, and it is particularly reviled in the American Muslim community, where the brunt of its enforcement is felt. Because parts of NSEERS were later suspended and augmented by another program, US-VISIT, special registration has largely disappeared from discussions on the war on terror. However, contrary to what many believe, special registration has not been completely eliminated by US-VISIT. Instead, it has only been subsumed under US-VISIT. However, the bulk of special registration's enforcement, which resulted in the mass expulsion of thousands of Muslims from the United States, occurred prior to the implementation of US-VISIT. For that reason, I will refer to special registration as a program in the past.

What exactly was special registration? It was a government-mandated system of recording and surveillance that required all nonimmigrant males in the United States over the age of sixteen who are citizens and nationals from select countries to be interviewed under oath, fingerprinted, and photographed by a Department of Justice official. These procedures applied to nonimmigrant visitors as they crossed the border and entered the United States. Until December 2, 2003, this also applied to those already in the country (what the Department of Justice termed "call-in" registration). All those who were required to register had to provide proof of their legal status to remain in the United States, proof of study or employment (in the form of school enrollment forms or employment pay stubs), and proof of residential address (such as a lease or utility bill). Some also had to supply any and all of their credit card numbers, the names and addresses of two US citizens who can authenticate their identity, and to answer questions regarding their political and religious beliefs. Before the program was modified, registrants also had to reregister within 40 days with a Department of Justice official if they remained in the country for more than 30 days, and then again annually. Additionally, special registrants could enter and exit from the United States only from specific ports of entry. Each and every time he entered and left the country, the nonimmigrant male had to go through the Byzantine and arduous registration process again.

It goes almost without saying that special registration was heavily burdensome on the registrant, and those who underwent it complained that they were treated as if they were guilty of a crime and had to prove their innocence, thus flipping an avowed tradition of American jurisprudence (innocent until proven guilty) on its head. The execution of the program also came under fire. When the deadline for the first call-in registration passed in December 2002, mayhem ensued, particularly in

southern California, where, according to the *Washington Post*, hundreds of men (almost 1,200 nationwide) were incarcerated in mass arrests on alleged immigration violations (US Detains 2003). Ramona Ripston, executive director of the American Civil Liberties Union (ACLU), compared special registration to World War II measures against Japanese Americans. "I think it is shocking what is happening. It is reminiscent of what happened in the past with the internment of Japanese Americans," she told *Reuters* (Hundreds 2002). Many of the men arrested had been in the country for over a decade and had families in the United States (with US citizen children), and many more complained that their status was, in fact, legal but that their paper work was incomplete due to Immigration and Naturalization Service (INS) backlogs (Lee 2002). Tens of thousands of lives have been disrupted by the special registration program, many more if we consider the collateral effect on families. Since its implementation in October of 2002, NSEERS has registered at least 83,519 men and boys domestically (and over 93,740 at points of entry) (DHS Factsheet 2003). Out of this number, 13,799 have been served with "Notices to Appear" subpoenas, meaning that deportation proceedings have begun in their cases. Not a single charge of terrorism has been levied as a result of special registration (Simpson et al. 2003; Charles 2004).

Just what is going on here? If special registration was meant to be a program to net terrorists, as the government claims, then it was clearly a colossal and expensive failure. The Department of Justice stated that "In light of the attacks against the United States on September 11, 2001, and subsequent events, and based on information available to the Attorney General, the Attorney General has determined that certain nonimmigrant aliens require closer monitoring when national security or law enforcement interests are raised" (Special Call-In 2002, 1). But the criterion for "closer monitoring" of certain people was based almost exclusively on a single fact: national origin. Kris Kobach, an architect of the program, is unapologetic about such broad-based selection. "We had to just use the very blunt instrument of nationality [for special registration]," he explains (quoted in Simpson et al. 2003). But the dull thud of this blunt program was its own stupidity since it was unlikely to result in the capture of a terrorist, who, if he or she were in the country already, would logically not bother to register before carrying out any nefarious activity. Since the mechanism (i.e., the profile) of the program was known, it was also highly unlikely to catch an incoming terrorist, who would again logically search for ways to circumvent special registration's categories.

Initially focused on citizens and nationals from five states (Iran, Iraq, Libya, Sudan, and Syria), the list of targeted nations requiring registration ballooned to 25 countries, some in North and East Africa (Egypt, Tunisia, Algeria, Morocco, Somalia, Eritrea), others in West Asia (Yemen, Kuwait, Saudi Arabia, United Arab Emirates, Qatar, Oman, Bahrain, Lebanon, Jordan), South Asia (Pakistan, Bangladesh, Afghanistan), Southeast Asia (Indonesia), and East Asia (North Korea). Six of these countries are listed by the State Department among the seven state-sponsors of terrorism (the initial five, plus North Korea. Cuba is the seventh, and its absence is telling). Two of these countries (Iraq and Afghanistan) have recently been invaded by the United States, and the vast majority of the rest are allies of the United States. This fact alone – that the overwhelming number of men who were subject to special registration were from friendly countries – is significant, for it proves that something else other than enemy nationality was operative here.

That special registration was a discriminatory program is incontrovertible. Ostensibly, it discriminated by gender, age, national origin, and citizenship status. The discrimination was, in all likelihood, entirely legal under the plenary power doctrine, a century-old Supreme Court decision that holds that Congress and the executive branch have sovereign authority to regulate immigration without judicial review (Chin 1998, 1–74; Olafson 1999, 433–53). That decision dates from 1898, upheld Chinese exclusion from the United States, and is still considered good law. Furthermore, according to legal scholar Gabriel Chin, the plenary power doctrine approves discrimination based not only on national origin but also on race:

> In immigration law alone, racial classifications are still routinely permitted. In recent decades, courts in the District of Columbia and the First, Second, Fifth, Seventh, Eighth, Ninth, Tenth, and Eleventh Circuits have said not only that aliens may be excluded or deported on the basis of race without strict scrutiny, but also that such racial classifications are lawful per se. Apparently no court has even hinted to the contrary. These circuits merely honor an unbroken line of Supreme Court decisions holding that "Congress may exclude aliens of a particular race from the United States" and, more broadly, that an alien seeking admission "has no constitutional rights regarding his application." (Chin 1998, 3–4)

It ought to be noted that in the publication of its rule in the *Federal Register* (2002b), the Department of

Justice cited key plenary power decisions to give special registration its legal legs on which to stand (52585). Since the Chinese exclusion cases provided the foundation for the plenary power doctrine, special registration thus has its own direct connection to Chinese exclusion.

One should also note that little unites the disparate group of special registration countries but that they are all Muslim majority nations. To argue, as the Department of Justice did, that what unifies the list is not Islam but the "heightened risk of involvement in terrorist" activity (presumably al-Qaeda membership) (*Federal Register* 2002a, 40582) just does not hold. By the government's own admission, al-Qaeda activity had already been discovered in France, the Philippines, Spain, Germany, and Britain, but no visitors from these countries were required to undergo special registration. Indeed, the case of Richard Reid, the so-called shoe bomber, who converted to Islam (and thus is not a "citizen or national" of a Muslim country), underscores the limitations – or falsity – of such an argument.

Special registration accomplished several things, nonetheless. It reinscribed, through a legal mechanism, the cultural assumption that a terrorist is foreign-born, an alien in the United States, and a Muslim, and that all Muslim men who fit this profile are potential terrorists. But special registration also did more than this. Special registration made legal and executive sense to the government because it participated in a long bureaucratic tradition found in American law of racial formation. Through its legal procedures, special registration was a political and bureaucratic policy that created a race out of a religion.

Racing Religion

How does special registration "race" Islam? To begin answering this question, we need to investigate the relationship between religious and racial difference in American politics and to understand how both racial and religious difference can be exploited in ways that are racist by definition. Racism is, of course, a complex social phenomenon that is difficult to sum up in just a few words. George Fredrickson, however, offers a useful definition in his book-length essay on the topic. According to Fredrickson, racism "exists when one ethnic group or historical collectivity dominates, excludes, or seeks to eliminate another on the basis of differences that it believes to be hereditary and unalterable" (Fredrickson 2002, 170). While racism may at times appear similar to religious clashes, Fredrickson sees them as, in fact, quite distinct for the important reason that in religiously based systems or conflicts, the opportunities for conversion have always been present as a way to defeat one's own marginal status. In a religious conflict, it is not who you are but what you believe that is important. Under a racist regime, there is no escape from who you are (or are perceived to be by the power elite). Thus, Fredrickson correctly finds racial and not religious division as driving the Spanish Inquisition's purity of blood laws. "Anti-Judaism became anti-Semitism," he explains, "whenever it turned into a consuming hatred that made getting rid of Jews seem preferable to trying to convert them, and anti-Semitism became racism when the belief took hold that Jews were intrinsically and organically evil rather than merely having false beliefs and wrong dispositions" (19). Jews and Muslims in medieval Spain were both collectively marked as dangerous and excludable because of a belief in their innate and hereditary natures. Exclusion was preferable to conversion.

How one's religion or culture is apprehended, for example, can also assume a racist character. During the Spanish Inquisition, certain cultural (not necessarily religious) practices labeled one as a Jew or a Muslim. Changing one's sheets on Friday could make one Jewish in the eyes of the Christian community (Kamen 1998, 62), just as sitting on the ground (as opposed to in a chair) proved one was Muslim (223). As the explanatory power of scientific theories of race has declined in our contemporary world, culture has again assumed a prominent role in determining and describing racial difference. As Etienne Balibar (1991) puts it, "[C]ulture can also function like nature, and it can in particular function as a way of locking individuals and groups a priori into a genealogy, into a determination that is immutable and intangible in origin" (22).

Racism, however, should not be seen as something that is necessarily irrational or is a "consuming hatred," as Fredrickson describes it. While these certainly are historic realities, racism must also be understood as a careful ideology that is, unfortunately, politically useful, particularly in circumstances where one is called upon to define oneself against another. It determines the other, and it does so through various institutions, the law being a primary one among them. It also has historically led to three different categories of material consequences: exploitation, extermination, or exclusion (Fredrickson 2002, 9). All three, unfortunately, have their precedents in American history, as Michael Omi and Howard Winant point out in *Racial Formation in the United States*:

From the very inception of the Republic to the present moment, race has been a profound determinant of one's political rights, one's location in the labor market, and indeed one's sense of "identity." The hallmark of this history has been racism, not the abstract ethos of equality, and while racial minority groups have been treated differently, all can bear witness to the tragic consequences of racial oppression. The examples are familiar: Native Americans faced genocide, blacks were subjected to racial slavery, Mexicans were invaded and colonized, and Asians faced exclusion. (Omi and Winant 1986, 1)

Here is a short history of racism in the United States, from extermination (of Native Americans) to exploitation (slavery and colonization) to exclusion (of Asians). It is in the last of these, exclusion, where special registration operates.

With its broad-brush focus on national origin, special registration juridically excludes thousands of Muslims by category and creates a barrier that repels even more. Special registration creates a vast, new legal geography of suspicion for the United States government, a geography that in some way mirrors the "Asiatic barred zone" of the 1917 Immigration Act. It may not prevent visitors from entering, but it makes it onerous to penetrate the border. Perhaps it would be more correct to say that special registration, rather than barring entry, draws a burdensome zone around Muslim-majority countries.

But special registration again does more. In requiring that citizens and nationals of those countries suffer through its burdens, special registration collapses citizenship, ethnicity, and religion into race. Under the special registration guidelines, immigration officers are charged with the authority to register whoever they have reason to believe should be specially registered. This procedure extends to nonimmigrant aliens who the inspecting officer has "reason to believe are nationals or citizens of a country designation by the Attorney General" (*Federal Register* 2002b, 52592). In a memo to regional directors and patrol agents, the INS clarified that this included cases such as "a nonimmigrant alien who is a dual national and is applying for admission as a national of a country that is not subject to special registration, but the alien's other nationality *would* subject him or her [sic] to special registration" (Memorandum 2002). Numerous reports since special registration began have indicated that birthplace is used as the trigger to determine the "reason to believe" one should be registered.

The implications of every national being required to register means that if you happen to hold dual citizenship with, say, Sweden and Morocco, or if you were born in Morocco but are not its citizen, or if you were born out of Morocco but to parents who are Moroccan, then you qualify. Swedish citizenship, even if it is your only citizenship, is no protection from special registration if you were born or your parents were born in one of the listed countries. The reason why this in particular is troubling is that, considering the broad geography of special registration, it makes descent or inheritability of Islam (and gender) the defining criterion. And that inheritability has nothing to do with enemy nationality since most of the listed nations are considered allies of the United States. Nor has it anything to do with belief or political affiliation since it says nothing about each individual's worldview. Rather, it is only about one's blood relationship to Islam. Through that blood relationship, legal barriers have been established to exclude as many Muslims as possible, and that fact consequently turns Islam into a racial category.

The Arabian Gulf of Racial Difference

Troubling as all this is, the relationship of Islam to racial definition in the United States is not new with special registration, and it is important to review this past to understand the history that special registration has to the political and racial logic of the United States. In fact, the combination of Islam and immigration has its own legal history in the United States, and we can discover that by surveying some of the key racial prerequisite cases from 1909 to 1944, particularly cases like *Hassan* and *Mohriez* in which the petitioners are Muslim or come from countries with Muslim majorities. While we may be accustomed to thinking of racial definition as being determined by the color of one's skin, what we observe here is that religion in general, and Islam in particular, plays a role in adjudicating the race of immigrants seeking naturalization in the United States. The various immigration acts that constitute the body of racial exclusion laws did not explicitly place religion inside a logic of race, but the courts did repeatedly note the religion of an applicant, and that in itself was often a deciding (if not the deciding) factor in determining the race of the petitioner. Although the physical attributes of the applicants were often discussed, the main question surrounding many of these cases, as in the *Hassan* decision cited earlier, was actually about the ability to assimilate to the dominant, Christian culture.

The cases are worth a look. An initial review reveals, as one might expect, that many of the cases did rely

simply on ocular proof to determine race. Race, it would appear, was the color of one's skin, no more and no less. This seems to be the case with the Syrian Costa George Najour, who in 1909 went before the district judge to petition for citizenship. The judge was impressed that Najour "is not particularly dark, and has none of the characteristics or appearances of the Mongolian race, but, so far as I can see and judge, has the appearance and characteristics of the Caucasian race" (In re *Najour* 1909, 735). Najour's petition was granted.

Similarly, skin tone is called into question when, in 1909, four Armenians petitioned for naturalization. "I find that all were white persons in appearance, not darker in complexion than some persons of north European descent traceable for generations," writes the district judge in that case (In re *Halladjian* 1909, 835). Likewise, in *US v. Dolla* (1910), the Circuit Court of Appeals makes the determination that in this case it lacks jurisdiction, but not without first noting the facts of the case, with a novelist's detail. The Court states that Dolla, an Afghan who lived in Calcutta before coming to the United States, has a "complexion that is dark, eyes dark, features regular and rather delicate, hair very black, wavy and very fine and soft." It continues:

> On being called on to pull up the sleeves of his coat and shirt, the skin of his arm where it had been protected from the sun and weather by his clothing was found to be several shades lighter than that of his face and hands, and was sufficiently transparent for the blue color of the veins to show very clearly. He was about medium or a little below medium in physical size, and his bones and limbs appeared to be rather small and delicate. Before determining that the applicant was entitled to naturalization the presiding judge closely scrutinized his appearance. (*US v. Dolla* 1910, 102)

His race was written on his body, just above his tan line.

In the case of the Syrian Tom Ellis (1910), the judge notes that "ethnologically, [Ellis] is of Semitic stock, a markedly white type of race," although the judge does concede that "the words 'white person' . . . taken in a strictly literal sense, constitute a very indefinite description of a class of persons, where none can be said to be literally white, and those called white may be found of every shade from the lightest blonde to the most swarthy brunette" (1003). Ellis, too, was admitted.

In Ex parte *Shahid* (1913), the petitioner was, once again, a Syrian, yet this time "in color, he is about that of walnut, or somewhat darker than is the usual mulatto or one-half mixed blood between the white and the Negro races" (813). *Shahid* is most interesting because the judge acknowledges the limitations of phenotypical race. "One Syrian may be of pure or almost pure Jewish, Turkish, or Greek blood, and another the pure-blooded descendant of an Egyptian, an Abyssinian, or a Sudanese. How is the court to decide? It would be most unfortunate if the matter were to be left to the conclusions of a judge based on ocular inspection" (814). Taking up the argument that "free white persons" meant "Europeans," the judge goes on to acknowledge that that definition, too, is problematic since that "would exclude persons coming from the very cradle of the Jewish and Christian religions" (816) Although he seems bothered by such a line of thought ("such arguments are of the emotional ad captandum order that have no place in the judicial interpretation of a statute"), the judge relies on the strict application of the separation of powers to devolve himself of any greater comment on the matter. *Shahid* will be excluded, he explains, not because of his race but simply on his "own personal disqualifications" (817).

The first time a Syrian is denied naturalization because of his race occurs with Ex parte *Dow*, in 1914. Again, the Court finds it necessary to write the skin of the applicant. "In color he is darker than the usual person of white European descent, and of that tinged or sallow appearance which usually accompanies persons of descent other than purely European" (Ex parte *Dow* 1914, 487). Dow is first denied naturalization because, "following the reasoning set out in Ex parte *Shahid*," the Court here construed "free white person" to mean "inhabitants of Europe and their descendants" (489). The district judge laments this, for Dow, he argues, is a capable man, but making law is beyond the power of the Court. To prove his point, the judge mixes nation, religion, and race in an exasperated (and racist) appeal. "No race in modern times has shown a higher mentality than the Japanese. To refuse naturalization to an educated Japanese Christian clergyman and accord it to a veneered savage of African descent from the banks of the Congo would appear as illogical as possible, yet the courts of United States have held the former inadmissible and the statute accords admission to the latter" (489).

Dow is appealed, and at first affirmed, as geography takes precedence over skin color. ("There is no known ocular, microscopic, philological, ethnological, physiological, or historical test that can settle the question of the race of the modern Syrian; but the applicant and his associates are certainly Asiatics in the sense that they are of Asian nativity and descent and are not Europeans" [In re *Dow* 1914, 362].) On further appeal to the Fourth Circuit Court of Appeals (*Dow v. United States* 1915), the decision is reversed, and Dow is finally admitted citizenship. In fact, the Syrian community mobilized every resource it had for the Dow case, as described by Alixa Naff (1985, 256).

All these cases take place before *US v. Thind* (1923), the Supreme Court case that Haney Lopez cites as shifting the reasoning of the courts. Prior to *Thind*, the courts depended largely on so-called scientific knowledge to determine whiteness. After *Thind*, the notion of common understanding of what whiteness is held sway. It would seem, then, that in the bulk of the cases I have thus far discussed, race is understood primarily as the color of one's skin and secondarily as geographically determined. Skin color influences the decisions in *Najour, Halladjian, Dolla, Ellis, Shahid, Dow*, and others. In discussions of race, this is to be expected. Geography, too, plays a role in these cases, but what about religion?

All of the Syrians to come before the Court during the racial exclusion era were Christian, and the Court often found it important to underline this fact in every instance it could. In *Ellis*, the court reiterated the fact twice in the first paragraph of its decision. "The applicant is a Syrian, a native of the province of Palestine, and a Maronite. . . . It may be said, further, that he was reared a Catholic, and is still of that faith" (In re *Ellis* 1910, 1002). In *Halladjian*, the court not only draws attention to the confessional traditions of the Armenians but uses their Christianity as proof of their eligibility for naturalization. "Race . . . is not an easy working test of 'white' color," averred the court (In re *Halladjian* 1909, 840), which then moved to discuss eligibility in terms of "ideals, standards, and aspirations." "In the warfare which has raged since the beginning of history [sic] about the eastern Mediterranean between Europeans and Asiatics, the Armenians have generally, though not always, been found on the European side. They resisted both Persians and Romans, the latter somewhat less strenuously. By reason of their Christianity, they generally ranged themselves against the Persian fire-worshippers, and against the Mohammedans, both Saracens and Turks" (In re *Halladjian* 1909, 841). The decision goes so far as to explain why Armenians are part of the Eastern Church and to excuse them for it. "Present war and their remoteness are said to have prevented the Armenian bishops from attending the Council of Chalcedon in the fifth century. Thus, they say that they were misled as to the pronouncement of that Council, and so a schism arose without heresy on their part" (841). Whereas Catholicism was a liability for a long time for Italians and Irish in the United States, it was considered favorably with regard to the Armenians, illustrating the shifting boundary of acceptability. "During the Crusades and afterwards many Armenians came into the obedience of the Roman Catholic Church, while retaining distinctive rites and customs" (841). Religion becomes the ultimate arbiter of admissibility, though, the court argues, without prejudice. "These facts are stated, without reproach to the followers of Mohammed or Zoroaster, because history has shown Christianity in the near East has generally manifested a sympathy with Europe rather than with Asia as a whole" (841). Christianity turns Armenians white.

[. . .]

After *Thind*, who is referred to not as an Indian but as a "high caste Hindu," the decisions adopt more explicit language regarding religion (as science is discarded and replaced with culture). Another case involving the right of Armenians to naturalize comes before the Court in 1925. The case of *US v. Cartozian* (1925) references both *Ozawa v. United States* (another Supreme Court decision from 1922 disallowing Japanese to naturalize) and *Thind* in its decision. It argues that "it is now judicially determined that mere color of the skin of the applicant does not afford a practical test as to whether he [the petitioner] is eligible to American citizenship" (*US v. Cartozian* 1925, 919). Thus, the court feels emancipated from judging hue and tone and relies largely on religion (and assimilation) in its determination. "Although the Armenian province is within the confines of the Turkish empire, being in Asia Minor, the people thereof have always held themselves aloof from the Turks, the Kurds, and allied peoples, principally, it might be said, on account of their religion, though color may have had something to do with it" (921). In *Wadia v. US* (1939), the Court substitutes "ethnicity" for "race," calling Wadia "of the Parsee race," and feels compelled to disclose facts that must be important to its deliberations, including that "he was a follower of Zoroaster" (7).

By the 1940s, we have the two notable petitions of *Hassan* and *Mohriez*. Unlike the petitioners mentioned directly above, Hassan and Mohriez are both Muslim (at least by name). What makes their cases noteworthy is not just their faith community but the short span of time between when an Arab Muslim is considered nonwhite (Hassan) and when an Arab Muslim is officially considered white (Mohriez). It is this abrupt shift, mirrored in

the sudden creation of a Muslim race by special registration, that should concern us, for it illustrates not just the capricious nature of racial formation but also the depth to which contemporary American politics creates race, rather than race always creating politics.

[. . .]

[P]olitics matters a great deal, and it always has, as Yale historian Rogers Smith understands. Smith has exhaustively examined thousands of citizenship cases in the United States and has come to the conclusion that inclusion in the United States has not been determined by an overarching theory of liberalism or by republican notions of citizenship. Rather, "American citizenship laws have always emerged as none too coherent compromises among the distinct mixes of civic conceptions advanced by the more powerful actors in different eras" (Smith 1997, 6). The point is to recognize how labor or civil unrest or, especially for our purposes, war aids in producing citizenship and inclusion, which in the history of the United States, functions through political power and along the definitional axis of race.

One of the most painful examples of race-in-flux during American history must be Japanese internment during World War II. The signing of Executive Order 9066 resulted not only in the internment of over 110,000 people of Japanese ancestry, but also in the removal of the protections of citizenship, at the stroke of a pen, for over 70,000 of them. Race trumped nationality. If you were born in the United States to Japanese parents prior to February 18, 1942, for example, you were an American citizen. But on February 19, you had become an enemy alien.

There are other cases as well, situations which resolved into inclusion rather than exclusion. In 1943, for example, following the US's entry into the war, Congress repealed the Chinese Exclusion Acts (but set a paltry quota of 100 Chinese immigrants a year). President Roosevelt described the measure "as important in the cause of winning the war and of establishing a secure peace," (*INS Monthly Review* 1943, 16) and told Congress that Chinese exclusion had been an "historic mistake" (*INS Monthly Review* 1943, 17). Whereas Asians had been since 1917 an undifferentiated mass of people living in a barred zone of immigration, Chinese were now politically and ontologically distinct (especially from Japanese) and had achieved a type of honorary white status as evidenced by their (limited) ability to immigrate and naturalize. In his decision on Mohriez's petition, Judge

Wyzanski shows he is aware of this fact. The end of the Mohriez decision reads:

> And finally it may not be out of place to say that, as is shown by our recent changes in the laws respecting persons of Chinese nationality and of the yellow race, we as a country have learned that policies of rigid exclusion are not only false to our professions of democratic liberalism *but repugnant to our vital interests as a world power.* (Ex Parte *Mohriez* 1944, 942)

Sometimes politics, and not just personal or cultural prejudice, produces race.

The Armenian State of Exception

The point that I have been making in this article is not only . . . that the law produces race, but also that we need to examine racial formation through law and policy as a rational system of administration and domination rather than as an example of individual prejudice or capriciousness to understand its full impact. Only then can we possibly imagine new political formations that will not be dependent on race as a principle of political domination. Moreover, what special registration proves is that any group can be racialized through America's traditions and then be sent into administrative hell through the bureaucracy of the state (what Hannah Arendt calls "rule by Nobody" [Arendt 1969, 81]). Racialization operates through a legal past and enables a legal machinery to provide differential rights, particularly to immigrants, who are the most vulnerable owing, in part, to the plenary power doctrine.

In the case of special registration, we can also witness the bizarre memory of a bureaucracy. American history has long operated through a kind of racial logic that has its own inertia (call it tradition) as well as its own morphability (call it political expediency), and at times both sides of American race policy will career right into each other. Under special registration, this is precisely what happened. As the cases of *Halladjian* and *Cartozian* illustrated, Armenians – as a Christian people who live in the Middle East – were a particular conundrum for the courts. In fact, in *Hassan*, the judge cites the case of Cartozian in his decision. Judge Tuttle writes:

> The court there [in *Cartozian*] found, however, that the Armenians are a Christian people living in an area close to the European border, who have intermingled and intermarried with Europeans over a period of centuries. Evidence was also presented in that case of a considerable amount of intermarriage of Armenian immigrants to the United States with other racial strains in our population. These facts serve to distinguish the case of the Armenians from that of the Arabians. (In re *Hassan* 1942, 846)

And yet, in a twist that can only reveal the strange pull of history on a bureaucracy, the Justice Department published the list of the third "call-in" group for registration on December 16, 2002. Designating Pakistan and Saudi Arabia as countries whose male citizens would be subject to special registration, the Department also included Armenia on its list. Without comment, Armenia was dropped the next day (Cooperman 2002).

Race, Terror, and Bureaucracy

Special registration is not necessarily a nefarious plot to racialize Islam, but it is a bureaucratic and cultural response to political turmoil. This is not to say that religious bigotry no longer exists. If we consider the words of deputy undersecretary for defense, Lieutenant General William Boykin, who claims that "my God [is] a real God," and a Muslim's God is "an idol," and that the United States must attack radical Islamists "in the name of Jesus" (Three Star Bigotry 2004; Holding the Pentagon 2004), we find that his statements participate not in racializing Islam but in older traditions of religious prejudice that, sadly, are still with us. Moreover, we should not exonerate special registration from the charge of being a legal method of racial formation, even if it does not subject all Muslims to its procedures and despite the fact that not every Muslim majority country is included on its list. In fact, what special registration accomplishes is the production of a typology of Muslims for the war on terror, and by defining one type, it colors the whole population. What it produces is a kind of racial anxiety among Muslims, non-Muslims from Muslim countries, and those who are perceived to be Muslim. Every immigrant male in these groups must dis-identify from the Muslim-as-terrorist figure, sometimes officially (as with special registration) or unofficially, as political policy and cultural attitudes bleed into each other. Suspicion is coded into law through race.

In fact, like Operation TIPS (which asked us to spy on our neighbors), special registration is best understood as a form of political theater. It allows a new bureaucracy (homeland security) to parade itself as being hard at work. The public is both the cast and the audience in this play. While it is acted out, we are propelled into living in an increasingly militarized and surveyed society. And when government actions impact Muslim populations so visibly, the public understands what is politically acceptable (even if criminally prosecutable) behavior. Meanwhile, the government bureaucracy can mobilize statistics and bodies to prove that it is cleansing the country of a terrorist threat, all at the expense of Muslims in the United States.

What has been particularly disheartening, however, is the academic silence around special registration while it proceeds apace. Without outspoken critique, special registration will continue to race Muslims and to bind whiteness in the United States with political exigency and with notions of culture and Christianity. However, as Arendt (1969) says, "[N]either violence nor power is a natural phenomenon . . . they belong to the political realm of human affairs whose essentially human quality is guaranteed by man's faculty of action, the ability to begin something new" (82). Now is the time to begin something new.

References

Act of July 14, 1870., Sec. 7, 16 Stat. 254, 256.

Arendt, Hannah. 1969. *On Violence*. New York: Harcourt.

Balibar, Etienne. 1991. Is There a Neo-Racism? In *Race, Nation, Class*, edited by E. Balibar and E. Wallerstein, 17–28. New York: Verso.

Charles, Deborah. 2004. U.S. Changes Post–9/11 Foreign Registration Rule. *Reuters*, December 1.

Chin, Gabriel. 1998. Segregation's Last Stronghold: Race Discrimination and the Constitutional Law of Immigration. *UCLA Law Review* 46, no. 1: 1–74.

Cooperman, Alan. 2002. Armenians in U.S. Not on INS List. *Washington Post*, December 18.

Department of Justice. December 1. *http://www.dhs.gov/dhspublic/display?content=3020* (last visited April 17, 2006).

DHS Factsheet. 2003. Changes to National Security Entry-Exit Registration System (NSEERS).

Dow v. United States 226 F. 145 (4th Cir. 1915).

Ex parte *Dow* 211 F. 486 (E.D.S.C. 1914).

Ex parte *Mohriez* 54. F. Supp. 941 (D.Mass. 1944).

Ex parte *Shahid* 205 F. 812 (E.D.S.C. 1913).

Federal Register. 2002a. 67 no. 114: 40581–6.

——. 2002b. 67 no. 155: 52584–93.

Fredrickson, George. 2002. *Racism: A Short History*. Princeton: Princeton University Press. *Law* 12, no. 1: 27–55.

Genet, Jean. 1960. *The Blacks: A Clown Show*. Translated by Bernard Frechtman. New York: Grove Press.

Haney Lopez, Ian. 1996. *White by Law*. New York: New York University Press.

Holding the Pentagon Accountable for Religious Bigotry. 2004. *New York Times*, August 26, editorial.

Hundreds of Muslim Immigrants Rounded up in Southern California. 2002. *Reuters*, December 19.

In re *Dow* 213 F. 355 (E.D.S.C. 1914).

In re *Ellis* 179 F. 1002 (D. Or. 1910).

In re *Halladjian* 174 F. 834 (C.C.D. Mass. 1909).

In re *Hassan* 48 F. Supp. 843 (E.D. Mich. 1942).

In re *Najour* 174 F. 735 (N.D. Ga 1909).

INS Monthly Review. 1943 1 no. 1: 12–16.

Kamen, Henry. 1998. *The Spanish Inquisition: A Historical Revision*. New Haven: Yale University Press.

Lee, Chisun. 2002. Detainees Protest Mass Arrests. *Village Voice*, December 25–31.

Memorandum for Regional Directors. 2002. September 30 (on file with the author).

Naff, Alixa. 1985. *Becoming American: The Early Arab Immigrant Experience*. Carbondale: Southern Illinois Univ. Press.

Olafson, Meredith K. 1999. The Concept of Limited Sovereignty and the Immigration Law Plenary Power Doctrine. *Georgetown Immigration Law Review* 13, no. 2: 433–53.

Omi, Michael, and Howard Winant. 1986. *Racial Formation in the United States*. New York: Routledge.

Ozawa v. United States 260 U.S. 178 (1922).

Sartre, Jean-Paul. 1948. *Anti-Semite and Jew*. Translated by George Becker. New York: Schocken.

Simpson, Cam, et al. 2003. Immigration Crackdown Shatters Lives. *Chicago Tribune*, November 16.

Smith, Rogers. 1997. *Civic Ideals*. New Haven: Yale University Press.

Special Call-In Registration Procedures for Certain Non-Immigrants. 2002. Department of Justice. November 26. *http://www.ice.gov/doclib/pi/specialregistration/CALL_IN_ALL.pdf*. (last visited April 17, 2006).

Three Star Bigotry. 2004. *Los Angeles Times*, August 25, editorial.

US v. Cartozian 6 F. 2d 919 (D.Or 1925).

US v. Dolla 177 F. 101. (5th Cir. 1910).

US v. Thind 261 U.S. 204 (1923).

US Detains Nearly 1,200 during Registry. 2003. *Washington Post*, January 16.

Wadia v. US 101 F. 2d 7 (2nd Cir. 1939).

12

The Intimate Public Sphere

Lauren Berlant

Something strange has happened to citizenship. During the rise of the Reaganite right, a familial politics of the national future came to define the urgencies of the present. Now everywhere in the United States intimate things flash in people's faces: pornography, abortion, sexuality, and reproduction; marriage, personal morality, and family values. These issues do not arise as private concerns: they are key to debates about what "America" stands for, and are deemed vital to defining how citizens should act. In the process of collapsing the political and the personal into a world of public intimacy, a nation made for adult citizens has been replaced by one imagined for fetuses and children. How did these changes come to be, and why?

The story can be told many ways. During this period, a cartoon version of a crisis in US citizenship has become established as a standard truth. In the cartoon version of the shaken nation, a citizen is defined as a person traumatized by some aspect of life in the United States. Portraits and stories of citizen-victims – pathological, poignant, heroic, and grotesque – now permeate the political public sphere, putting on display a mass experience of economic insecurity, racial discord, class conflict, and sexual unease.

This coupling of suffering and citizenship is so startling and so moving because it reveals about national power both its impersonality and its intimacy. The experience of social hierarchy is intensely individuating, yet it also makes people public and generic: it turns them into *kinds* of people who are both attached to and under-described by the identities that organize them. This paradox of partial legibility is behind much of the political and personal anger that arises in scenes of misrecognition in everyday life – at work, on the street, at home, under the law, and even in aesthetic experience. Yet the public rhetoric of citizen trauma has become so pervasive and competitive in the United States that it obscures basic differences among modes of identity, hierarchy, and violence. Mass national pain threatens to turn into banality, a crumbling archive of dead signs and tired plots.

This exhaustion of cultural struggle over the material and symbolic conditions of US citizenship is a desired effect of conservative cultural politics, whose aim is to dilute the oppositional discourses of the historically stereotyped citizens – people of color, women, gays, and lesbians. Against these groups are pitted the complaints not of stereotyped peoples burdened by a national history but icons who have only recently lost the protections of their national iconicity – politicians who are said to have lost their "zone of privacy"; ordinary citizens who are said to feel that they have lost access to the American Dream; white and male and heterosexual people of all classes who are said to sense that they have lost the respect of their culture, and with it the freedom to feel unmarked.

Indeed, today many formerly iconic citizens who used to feel undefensive and unfettered feel truly exposed and vulnerable. They feel anxious about their value to themselves, their families, their publics, and their nation. They sense that they now have *identities*, when it used to be just other people who had them.[1] These new feelings provoke many reactions. One response is to desire that the nation recommit itself to the liberal promise of a conflict-free and integrated world. Another is to forge a scandal, a scandal of ex-privilege: this can include rage at the stereotyped peoples who have appeared to change the political rules of social membership, and, with it, a desperate desire to return to an order of things deemed normal, an order of what was felt to be a general everyday intimacy that was sometimes called "the American way of life." To effect either restoration of the imagined nation, the American ex-icon denigrates the political present tense and incites nostalgia for the national world of its iconicity, setting up that lost world as a utopian horizon of political aspiration.

These narratives of traumatized identity have dramatically reshaped the dominant account of US citizenship. They also show that politics by caricature can have profound effects: on the ways people perceive their own social value and the social value of "Others"; on the ways they live daily life and see their futures; and on mainstream political discourse, which exploits the national identity crises it foments to claim a popular mandate for radical shifts in norms of ideology and political practice.[2]

The Queen of America Goes to Washington City attends to the ways in which these rhetorics of a traumatized core national identity have come to describe, and thereby to make, something real. It tracks the triumph of the Reaganite view that the intimacy of citizenship is something scarce and sacred, private and proper, and only for members of families. It focuses on the ways conservative ideology has convinced a citizenry that the core context of politics should be the sphere of private life. In so doing, it develops a different story about what has happened to citizenship in both the law and daily life during the last few decades. The privatization of citizenship has involved manipulating an intricate set of relations between economic, racial, and sexual processes. This chapter begins to lay out some aspects of their relation.

Here is another way of telling the story. My first axiom is that there is no public sphere in the contemporary United States, no context of communication and debate that makes ordinary citizens feel that they have a common public culture, or influence on a state that holds itself accountable to their opinions, critical or otherwise. By "ordinary citizens" I mean ones without wealth and structural access to brokers of power. The antiwar, antiracist, and feminist agitations of the sixties denounced the hollow promises of the political pseudo-public sphere; then, a reactionary response grew dominant, which claimed that, in valuing national criticism over patriotic identification, and difference over assimilation, sixties radicals had damaged and abandoned the core of US society.

A conservative coalition formed whose aim was the privatization of US citizenship. One part of its project involved rerouting the critical energies of the emerging political sphere into the sentimental spaces of an amorphous opinion culture, characterized by strong patriotic identification mixed with feelings of practical political powerlessness. A number of different forces and themes converged to bring about this end: the antifederal but patriotic nationalism of Reagan Republicanism, which sought to shrink the state while intensifying identification with the utopian symbolic "nation"; a rhetorical shift from a state-based and thus political identification with nationality to a culture-based concept of the nation as a site of integrated social membership; the expansion of a mass-mediated space of opinion formation that positions citizens as isolated spectators to the publicity that claims to represent them; the marketing of nostalgic images of a normal, familial America that would define the utopian context for citizen aspiration. Much of this agenda continues beyond the Reagan years, as Clintonite liberalism strives to find a middle ground on the right.

This set of successful transformations has reinvigorated the idea of the American Dream. It would be all too easy to ridicule the Dream, and to dismiss it as the motivating false consciousness of national/capitalist culture. But the fantasy of the American Dream is an important one to learn from. A popular form of political optimism, it fuses private fortune with that of the nation: it promises that if you invest your energies in work and family-making, the nation will secure the broader social and economic conditions in which your labor can gain value and your life can be lived with dignity. It is a story that addresses the fear of being stuck or reduced to a type, a redemptive story pinning its hope on class mobility. Yet this promise is voiced in the language of unconflicted personhood: to be American, in this view, would be to inhabit a secure space liberated from identities and structures that seem to constrain what a person can do in history. For this paradoxical feeling to persist, such that a citizen of the Dream can feel firmly placed in a zone of protected value while on the move in an arc of social mobility, the vulnerability of personal existence to the instability of capitalism and the concretely unequal forms and norms of national life must be suppressed, minimized, or made to seem exceptional, not general to the population. This sets the stage for a national people imagining itself national only insofar as it feels unmarked by the effects of these national contradictions.

The fear of being saturated and scarred by the complexities of the present and thereby barred from living the

"Dream" has recently produced a kind of vicious yet sentimental cultural politics, a politics brimming over with images and faces of normal and abnormal America. In the patriotically-permeated pseudopublic sphere of the present tense, national politics does not involve starting with a view of the nation as a space of struggle violently separated by racial, sexual, and economic inequalities that cut across every imaginable kind of social location. Instead, the dominant idea marketed by patriotic traditionalists is of a core nation whose survival depends on personal acts and identities performed in the intimate domains of the quotidian.

It is in this sense that the political public sphere has become an intimate public sphere. The intimate public of the US present tense is radically different from the "intimate sphere" of modernity described by Jürgen Habermas. Habermas portrays the intimate sphere of the European eighteenth century as a domestic space where persons produced the sense of their own private uniqueness, a sense of self which became a sense of citizenship only when it was abstracted and alienated in the nondomestic public sphere of liberal capitalist culture. In contrast, the intimate public sphere of the US present tense tenders citizenship as a condition of social membership produced by personal acts and values, especially acts originating in or directed toward the family sphere. No longer valuing personhood as something directed toward public life, contemporary nationalist ideology recognizes a public good only in a particularly constricted nation of simultaneously lived private worlds.[3]

This vision of a privatized, intimate core of national culture rings dramatic changes on the concept of the body politic, which is rarely valued as a *public*.[4] In the new nostalgia-based fantasy nation of the "American way of life," the residential enclave where "the family" lives usurps the modernist promise of the culturally vital, multiethnic city; in the new, utopian America, mass-mediated political identifications can only be rooted in traditional notions of home, family, and community. Meanwhile, the notion of a public life, from the profession of politician to non-family-based forms of political activism, has been made to seem ridiculous and even dangerous to the nation. Downsizing citizenship to a mode of voluntarism and privacy has radically changed the ways national identity is imagined, experienced, and governed in political and mass-media public spheres and in everyday life.

The Queen of America asks why it is, and how it has come to be, that a certain cluster of demonic and idealized images and narratives about sex and citizenship has come to obsess the official national public sphere. It asks why the most hopeful national pictures of "life" circulating in the public sphere are not of adults in everyday life, in public, or in politics, but rather of the most vulnerable minor or virtual citizens – fetuses, children, real and imaginary immigrants – persons that, paradoxically, cannot yet act as citizens. It asks why acts that are not civic acts, like sex, are having to bear the burden of defining proper citizenship. It asks why a conservative politics that maintains the sacredness of privacy, the virtue of the free market, and the immorality of state overregulation contradicts everything it believes when it comes to issues of intimacy. It asks why the pursuit of some less abstracted and more corporeal forms of "happiness" – through sex and through multicultural and sexual identity politics – has come to exemplify dangerous and irresponsible citizenship for some and utopian practice for others.[5] Meanwhile, it also asks to what degree liberals and the left have absorbed the conservative world view, relinquishing the fight against structural inequality for a more labile and optimistic culturalist perspective.

Each chapter to follow tracks a controversial guiding image of US citizenship through the process of its privatization; and each highlights some pilgrimages to Washington, the capital space which stands in for the nation, acting as its local form. These secular pilgrimages measure the intimate distances between the nation and some of the people who seek to be miraculated by its promise. We will see that in the reactionary culture of imperiled privilege, the nation's value is figured not on behalf of an actually existing and laboring adult, but of a future American, both incipient and pre-historical: especially invested with this hope are the American fetus and the American child. What constitutes their national supericonicity is an image of an American, perhaps the last living American, not yet bruised by history: not yet caught up in the processes of secularization and sexualization; not yet caught in the confusing and exciting identity exchanges made possible by mass consumption and ethnic, racial, and sexual mixing; not yet tainted by money or war. This national icon is still tacitly white, and it still contains the blueprint for the reproductive form that assures the family and the nation its future history. This national icon is still innocent of knowledge, agency, and accountability and thus has ethical claims on the adult political agents who write laws, make culture, administer resources, control things.

But most important, the fetal/infantile person is a *stand-in* for a complicated and contradictory set of anxieties and desires about national identity. Condensed into the image/hieroglyph of the innocent or incipient American, these anxieties and desires are about whose citizenship – whose subjectivity, whose forms of intimacy and interest, whose bodies and identifications, whose heroic narratives – will direct America's future. But the abstract image of the future generated by the national culture machine also stands for a crisis in the present: what gets consolidated now as the future modal citizen provides an alibi or an inspiration for the moralized political rhetorics of the present and for reactionary legislative and juridical practice.

These questions – of sex and citizenship, of minor and full citizens, and of mass national culture – have long been concerns regarding the United States (from Tocqueville's suspicion of democracy's infantilizing effects to the infantilized masculinity of the cold war).[6] But the national nervous system has become especially animated by the right-wing cultural agenda of the Reagan revolution.[7] One effect of this revolution has been to stigmatize these long-standing anxieties as "victim politics," a phrase that deliberately suppresses the complexity, ambivalence, and incoherence of social antagonism in the everyday life of contemporary citizenship.

The right-wing cultural agenda of the Reagan revolution – a phrase that resonates throughout this book – is my name for the public discourse around citizenship and morality that a complex bloc of activists has engendered during roughly the last two decades.[8] I have suggested that it bases its affirmative rhetoric on a nationalist politics of intimacy, which it contrasts to threatening practices of nonfamilial sexuality and, by implication, other forms of racial and economic alterity. The Reagan revolution not only has suffused "the personal" with political meanings well beyond those imagined in the "sexual revolution" of the 1960s, but it has had three other important consequences. First, it has helped to create some extremely limiting frames for thinking about what properly constitutes the practice of US citizenship. One famous example of this process is Peggy Noonan and George Bush's image of the American people as "a thousand points of light."[9] This brightly lit portrait of a civic army of sanctified philanthropists was meant to replace an image of the United States as a Great Society with a state-funded social safety net. It sought to substitute intentional individual goodwill for the nationstate's commitment to fostering democracy within capitalism. Practical citizenship is here figured as something available to good people with good money. Now

the Christian Coalition and the Republican Party are promoting legislation to put this fantasy into institutional practice by, among other things, advocating the transfer of federal entitlement programs for the "deserving poor" to private, voluntary, "faithbased" organizations.[10]

In addition, following the Reaganite tendency to fetishize both the offensive example and the patriotic norm, the increasingly monopolistic mass media act as a national culture industry whose mission is to micromanage how any controversial event or person changes the meaning of being "American." The constant polling used by this media apparatus, which includes the solicitation of testimony on talk radio and television, along with telephone interviews, has paradoxically enabled the standards and rhetorics of citizenship to become so privatized and subjective that even privileged people can seem legitimately to claim "outsider," if not "minority," status.[11] With political ideas about the nation sacrificed to the development of feelings about it, nationality has become a zone of trauma that demands political therapy.

The third consequence of the Reaganite cultural revolution involves the way intimacy rhetoric has been employed to manage the economic crisis that separates the wealthy few from everyone else in the contemporary United States. By defining the United States as a place where normal intimacy is considered the foundation of the citizen's happiness, the right has attempted to control the ways questions of economic survival are seen as matters of citizenship. This use of intimacy is extremely complicated. First, it helps displace from sustained public scrutiny the relation between congealed corporate wealth and the shifting conditions of labor; second, it becomes a rhetorical means by which the causes of US income inequality and job instability in all sectors of the economy can be personalized, rephrased in terms of individuals' capacity to respond flexibly to the new "opportunities" presented to them within an increasingly volatile global economy; third, it enables the hegemonic state-business class to promote a virulent competition between the native-born and immigrant poor. Even when economic issues are explicitly joined to institutions of intimacy – as in the current emphasis on family-oriented state entitlements for the middle classes – the "economic" foregrounds personal acts of saving and consumption over what happens in the workplace and the boardroom.

As discussions of the politics of sex and bodily identity in the United States have become so fascinating and politically absorbing, a concern with the outrages of American class relations has been made to seem trite and unsexy. It is my view that a critical engagement with what ought to constitute the social privileges and obligations of citizenship must be reorganized around these questions – of national capitalism, metropolitan and rural poverty, environmental disintegration, racist thinking and ordinary concrete practice, and other banalities of national evil. Questions of intimacy, sexuality, reproduction, and the family – the concerns of this book – are properly inter-related with these questions of identity, inequality, and national existence. No doubt these issues and institutions of intimacy will continue to be central to the disposition of national life, but as separate entities they should no longer overorganize the terms of public discussion about power, ethics, and the nation.

The materialist litany that the previous paragraph just begins to recite has been made to seem orthodox, boring, facile, or an occasion for paralyzed mourning.[12] Numerous efforts have been devoted to neutralizing these issues, all of which aim to separate out considera-tion of the economic conditions of citizenship from questions of culture and subjectivity. It almost goes without saying that the wealth of the wealthy classes in the United States is protected by this divisive rhetoric. The suggestion that capitalism is always on the brink of failing – as the current rhetoric of downsizing and scarcity would claim – terrorizes many workers into feeling competitive with each other and into overvalorizing individual will, as though personal willpower alone would be enough to make "market democracy" deliver on its "promise." Likewise, the utopia of a color-blind and gender-consensual society has been used as an alibi to make cases of egregious inequality seem like exceptions to a national standard, rather than a structural condition. In addition, the political alliance between business culture and the Christian right enables legitimate polit-ical dissent and outrage to be recast as immorality and even blasphemy.[13] Finally, the use of intimacy as a distraction from critical engagement with a general matrix of ordinary hard hierarchy actually impairs discussions of intimacy itself, in its broader social contexts.

The hegemonic achievement of Reaganite conservatism is also evident in its effects on its adversaries on the left. For example, a growing number of scholars and activists who speak from identity movements celebrate the ways US subalterns develop tactics for survival from within capitalist culture: forms of activity like gay marriage, critically-motivated acts of commodity consumption, and identity-based economic investment zones are said to make marginalized social groups more central, more legitimate and powerful in capitalist society. Yet for all the importance of survival tactics, a politics that advo-cates the subaltern appropriation of normative forms of the good life makes a kind of (often tacit) peace with exploitation and normativity, as well as with the other less happy and frequently less visible aspects of capitalist culture outlined above.[14]

In addition, many radical social theorists see the polit-ical deployment of intimacy crises as merely ornamental or a distraction from "real" politics. They have become alienated by the intensities of the sex and identity wars, which seem to be disconnected from more important and public questions of equity, justice, and violence in political life in general.[15] But they have been misdirected by a false distinction between the merely personal and the profoundly structural.[16] These forms of sociality too often appear to be in separate worlds of analysis and commitment, with catastrophic political consequences for critical engagement with the material conditions of citizenship.[17] It is the purpose of *The Queen of America* to challenge both the terms of the Reaganite revolution and the ways it has been opposed. Above all, it is to interfere with the intimate image of the national body that has, like a sunspot, both illuminated and blinded the world of mass politics and national fantasy in the contempor-ary United States.

[. . .]

On the Heterosexuality of the Queen

In the quasi-queer film *Boys on the Side* (dir. Herbert Ross, 1995), a heterosexual man who is speaking to a lesbian about his longing for a woman they both desire says, "I think heterosexuality's going to make a comeback." His joke would be an ironic throwaway line were it not for the film's commitment to associating heterosexuality with "life" and lesbian desire with the virtue of abstinence and the tragedy of death by AIDS. (This takes some doing, since the AIDS transmitted in the film originates in a heterosexual one-night stand, but no matter.) The defining sexual event of the generation currently coming to national power in the United States was the sexual revolution, with its accompanying shift in the availabil-ity of birth control/abortion: this was a revolution, largely, in heterosexuality. While gay- and lesbian-rights movements were contemporary with the sexual revolu-tion, the revolution that dominated the public-sphere dis-cussion of sex and feminism was not mainly concerned with nonheterosexual forms of identity or behavior. In contrast, for the current generations entering into sexuality, the defining issue is AIDS and other forms of disease and death. The transformation in national sexual culture from thinking about sexuality in terms of lives already in progress to imagining sexuality in the shadow of deaths to be avoided registers a shift in the contours of national personhood that is widely experienced, but little narrated. This is a revolution that has forced a generation of sexual subjects to become conscious of a much larger variety of life practices, and to see that these constitute a field of choices and identifications ordinary people make.

No one coming into sexuality in contemporary America can avoid thinking about gay, lesbian, bisexual, transsexual, transgendered, or other categories of sexuality. Some might share with their parents a nostalgia for a time when sex practice seemed to flow naturally from the life-building hopes children are taught to have for the stable reproductive family and for wedding presents. These are the people for whom the desire for heterosexuality to make a "comeback" actually makes some sense. To them, a "comeback" would mean that you would not have to think about sexual preference; it would mean that only the rare and unfortunate people who have the non-dominant sexuality would have to imagine it, and then keep it to themselves.

Many of us, however, experience the world as permeated by the practices and narratives of what Michael Warner has called heteronormative culture – a public culture, juridical, economic, and aesthetic, organized for the promotion of a world-saturating heterosexuality.[18] The phenomenal forms of heteronormative culture will vary as people locate themselves differently in racial, class, gender, regional, or religious contexts, contexts which mark the experience of sexualization with specific traumatic/liberatory intensity. But nowhere in the United States has heterosexuality gone into a decline or "left" in a way that makes the idea of a comeback even remotely plausible. It has been and remains culturally dominant. There is a vast culture industry constantly generating text and law on behalf of heterosexuality's preservation and extension into resistant or unincorporated domains of identification and fantasy. Take, for example, *The Crying Game* (dir. Neil Jordan, 1992), with its offer of a celibate same-sex couple in heterosexual drag as the fantasy solution to the problem of sexual and postcolonial violence. Or take sex education, which has again become controversial now that its tendency is to speak of things not conjugally heterosexual, like different sexual preferences and nonreproductive sexual practices. According to the cultural agenda of the radical

right, sex education, when it happens at all, should be a great terrorist device for breaking in straight sexual subjects who fancy each other but don't have sex, as in *The Crying Game*: if not, it will be seen simply as an immoral mechanism for promoting sex.

Yet it is a sexual and political fact that heterosexual life no longer seems the only mentionable one in the United States. This is what continues to fuel a state of sexual emergency, through homophobic and racist policies in the state and federal system, along with various forms of defensiveness, rage, and nostalgia among ordinary citizens who liked it better when their sexuality could be assumed to be general for the population as a whole. Heterosexuality has never "left": it has had to become newly explicit, and people have had to become aware of the institutions, narratives, pedagogies, and social practices that support it.

The false history of ex-privileged heterosexuality – the story that it went out of fashion – tells us something important about how nationality and sexuality meet up in the official public sphere. Identity is marketed in national capitalism as a property. It is something you can purchase, or purchase a relation to. Or it is something you already own that you can express: *my* masculinity, *my* queerness, for example (this is why bisexuality has not made it fully into the sexual star system: it is hard to *express* bisexuality). Michel Foucault and scholars like Judith Butler and Jonathan Ned Katz have shown how sexuality is the modern form of self-intelligibility: I am my identity; my identity is fundamentally sexual; and my practices reflect that (and if they don't, they require submission to sexual science, self-help, or other kinds of law).[19] The account of the total correspondence between acts and identities that marked the controversy over gays in the military manifested the juridical understanding of sexuality: my perverse act expresses my perverse identity; the state has a compelling interest in protecting the family by repressing my perversion; hence, no gays in the military; and hence, no privacy protection for any non-reproductive sexual practice or identity. Insofar as the politics and the medical crisis brought into collective awareness by AIDS has made it impossible to draw an absolute public boundary between US citizens and gay people, and as that increasing consciousness makes people aware of and more interested in gay, lesbian, and queer culture, it has also helped broaden the conservative rage against non-heteronormative forms of sexual activity and identity, which include all kinds of nonreproductive heterosexual activity, and sex and childbirth outside marriage.

But identity need not be simply a caption for an image of an unchanging concrete self. It is also a theory of the future, of history. This leads to the second way sexuality has met up with national fantasy. I have described the first way in the regulation of "perversion" on behalf of a heterofamilial citizenship norm. The second is in the way the generational form of the family has provided a logic of the national future. When the modal form of the citizen is called into question, when it is no longer a straight, white, reproductively inclined heterosexual but rather might be anything, any jumble of things, the logic of the national future comes into crisis.

This crisis of the national future, stimulated by sexual politics, comes at a time when America feels unsure about its value in a number of domains: in world military politics, in global economics, in ecological practice, and in the claim that the nation has a commitment to sustaining justice, democracy, and the American Dream when there seems to be less money and reliable work to go around. Along with sex-radical politics and feminism, multiculturalism and transnational capitalism and the widening social inequities that have accompanied it have called the national narrative into question. *What will the American future look like?* Suddenly no narrative seems to flow naturally from the identity people thought was their national birthright: of course, that birthright was partly protected because it was tacit. But let us think for a minute about this birthright, its corporeal norms, and the future it purported to produce.

Here is a brief story about the history of birthright citizenship in the United States, beginning with a familiar kind of long view. In the eighteenth century, the United States came into being via a democratic revolution against a geographically distant monarchial authority and an economically aggressive colonial marginality. The fantasy of a national democracy was based on principles of abstract personhood (all persons shall be formally equivalent) and its rational representation in a centralized state and federal system. The constitutional American "person" was a white male property owner: more than that, though, was unenumerated in the law.

These abstract principles of democratic nationality have always been hypocritical.[20] From the beginning, entire populations of persons were excluded from the national promise which, because it was a promise, was held out paradoxically: falsely, as a democratic reality, and legitimately, as a promise, the promise that the democratic citizenship form makes to people caught in history. The populations who were and are managed by the discipline of the promise – women, African Americans, Native Americans, immigrants, homosexuals – have long experienced simultaneously the wish to be full citizens and the violence of their partial citizenship. Of course, the rules of citizenship constantly change, both in the law and in the public sense of how persons ought to be treated, protected, and encouraged to act. But it is not false to say that over the long term some of us have been American enough to provide labor but not American enough to be sustained by the fullest resources of democratic national privilege.

During the twentieth century, however, changes in the economy and in the juridical and everyday life politics of identity have forced the birthright assumptions of US nationality into a vulnerable explicitness, and this very explicitness is making the patriots of the ex-tacit nation very unhappy. In response, a virulent form of revitalized national heterosexuality has been invented, a form that is complexly white and middle class, for reasons I address throughout. I found, when circulating chapters from this book, that some readers feel I am too hard on heterosexuality. I do not mean to be coming out against it. I simply do not see why the nation has to have an official sexuality, especially one that authorizes the norm of a violent gentility; that narrows the field of legitimate political action; that supports the amputation of personal complexity into categories of simple identity; that uses cruel and mundane strategies both to promote shame for non-normative populations and to deny them state, federal, and juridical supports because they are deemed morally incompetent to their own citizenship. This is the heterosexuality I repudiate.[21]

Feminist politics has long authorized my dedication to producing new contexts for understanding the politics, economics, and everyday practices of intimacy; its conjuncture with queer and materialist theory and activism is the context for this book's project. Queer/feminist activity in and outside the academy has enticed its participants to develop new names, analytics, contexts, and institutions for politics, practices, and subjectivities. It has broadened the notion of what sexuality is beyond the public/private divide, and has challenged a notion of gender that can overorganize how to understand machineries of domination, a notion that has tended to push questions of sexuality, race, class, and ethnicity to an ever-receding horizon of what "we" feminists promise to understand "later." This kind of commitment to conjunctural practice has also challenged the forms and styles of writing, research, and representation that typically buttress professional credentials, pushing me to work rigorously beyond my expertise in ways that feel at once risky and absolutely necessary.

[. . .]

Notes

1 On this point, see Cindy Patton's brilliant analysis, "Refiguring Social Space."

2 [C]artoons have a long and hallowed place in the production of critical discourse in the US public sphere. But political cartoons have used the body to represent, *in extremis*, the distorting tendencies of power and identity that political culture engenders. . . .

3 Habermas, *The Structural Transformation of the Public Sphere*, 27–37, 43–51, 151–75, 231–50.

4 My argument that the Reaganite right has attempted to privatize citizenship by reframing it as an intimate form of social membership might seem to suggest that the dominant nation now uncannily repeats the conservative politico-familial mood of the US postwar period. . . . See Corber, *In the Name of National Security*; Rogin, *Ronald Reagan, the Movie*; Dolan, *Allegories of America: Narratives, Metaphysics, Politics*; Meyerowitz, *Not June Cleaver*; May, *Homeward Bound*; Omi and Winant, *Racial Formation in the United States*. For a prophetically longer view of the emergence of intimacy as the index of normativity in the United States, see Sennett, *The Fall of Public Man*.

5 For an aligned project of understanding the ambiguous impulses at play in the contemporary United States, involving identity, nationality, commodity identification, and public-sphere intimacy forms, see Gilroy, "'After the Love Has Gone.'"

6 Tocqueville, *Democracy in America*; see also Rogin, *Ronald Reagan, the Movie*.

7 I take the logic of the nervous system as an image of the social machinery of politics and subjectivity from Taussig, *The Nervous System*.

8 On the popular contexts of right-wing culture in the everyday of the nation see Diamond, *Roads to Dominion*; and Grossberg, *We Gotta Get Out of This Place*.

9 President Bush used the phrase (penned by speechwriter Peggy Noonan) "a thousand points of light" to describe the new, defederalized, post-welfare-state nation both in his speech accepting the presidential nomination and in his inaugural speech five months later. See the *New York Times* 19 August 1998: A14, and 21 January 1989: A10.

10 See Gillespie and Schellhass, *Contract with America*; Moore, *Restoring the Dream*; Christian Coalition, *Contract with the American Family*.

11 Much has been written about the ways media conglomerates are advancing the US public sphere's atrophy. See especially the special issue of *The Nation* titled "The National Entertainment State," vol. 262, no. 22: 3 June 1996. For earlier and fuller analyses of the material, as opposed to psychic, subordination of the citizen to private "public" media interests in a complicated collusion with the security sector of the federal government, see Schiller, *Information and the Crisis Economy* and *Culture, Inc*; and Mowlana, Gerbner, and Schiller, *Triumph of the Image: The Media's War in the Persian Gulf – A Global Perspective*.

12 In particular the influential work of Chantal Mouffe, from which I have learned much, presumes the inefficacy of class rhetorics for the progressive revitalization of citizenship discourse. Mouffe chooses an antiessentialist form of identity politics, which focuses on the contingencies of identity, and its potential for alliance building, in her reconstruction of citizenship. However, the unassimilability of class discourse to identity politics could just as easily be the *model* for what a conjunctural alliance politics might look like: Mouffe's exclusion of the economic (and class experience) from the realm of cultural politics seems a critical flaw in her imagination of new social movements. See Mouffe, "Preface, Democratic Politics Today" and "Democratic Citizenship and the Political Community," in *Dimensions of Radical Democracy*, 1–14, 225–39.

13 For example, the nonprofit organization Focus on the Family, headed by the radio and print journalist and minister, Dr. James C. Dobson, lobbies for family values in everyday life and the national public sphere with sacred verve and rational clarity. See his magazines *Focus on the Family* and *Citizen*, the latter of which gives encouragement, explanation, argument, and tactical maps for being effective in the political public sphere. See also note 10.

14 For texts that imagine a mutual transformation of subaltern and capitalist culture see, for example, *The Black Public Sphere*, ed. The Black Public Sphere Collective (Chicago: University of Chicago Press, 1995), especially Austin, "'A Nation of Thieves': Consumption, Commerce, and the Black Public Sphere," 229–52; D'Emilio, "Capitalism and Gay Identity"; Griggers, "Lesbian Bodies in the Age of (Post) mechanical Reproduction"; Sedgwick, *Epistemology of the Closet*. Queer theory in particular has generally occupied the scene of tactical subversion rather than anticapitalist radicalism: for critical analyses of this tendency, see Hennessey, "Queer Visibility in Commodity Culture"; Lauren Berlant and Michael Warner, "Sex in Public." For a critique of the capitalist optimism of cultural studies in general, see Berland, "Angels Dancing."

15 This includes most liberal and materialist social theory, and would require an interminable note.

16 To break down analytic distinctions between political, economic, and cultural domains of experience and analysis has long been a project of a certain strain of Marxist cultural theory. In my own development, the promise and challenge of *Social Text* 1 (winter 1979) remains vital. See especially Jameson, "Reification and Utopia in Mass Culture"; and John Brenkman, "Mass Media: From Collective Experience to the Culture of Privatization." See also Jameson, "Five Theses on Actually Existing Marxism."

17 For an analytic that engages the ways the dominant media of the contemporary US public sphere produce national

knowledge via a series of discrete, unrelated events (thus frustrating the formation of a critical culture) see Hansen, foreword, in *Public Sphere and Experience*. Taken as a whole, Negt and Kluge's work on fantasy, experience, and political life is central to the thinking in this book. See especially chapter 1, "The Public Sphere as the Organization of Collective Experience," 1–53.

18 Warner, introduction, *Fear of a Queer Planet*.

19 The literature of "identity" is, again, very large: some examples from it include Foucault, *The History of Sexuality*, v. 1–3; Butler, *Gender Trouble*; Katz, *The Invention of Heterosexuality*; Danielsen and Engle, *After Identity*, especially essays by Halley ("The Politics of the Closet") and Coombe ("The Properties of Culture and the Politics of Possessing Identity"); Rouse, "Questions of Identity"; and Spivak, *Outside in the Teaching Machine*. For an essay that opens new comparative ways of thinking about identity as property in the self, see Petchesky, "The Body as Property."

20 The bibliography on the historical relation between US citizenship and corporealized quasi nationality or subnationality is substantial. I summarize it in *The Anatomy of National Fantasy*, 11–17, 222–3. For an important politico-philosophical engagement with the means by which a culture of democratic rights hypocritically produces a turbulent politics of race, gender, and ethnicity, see Balibar, *Masses, Classes, Ideas*.

21 Elshtain argues strenuously against the current US drive to consign "shameful" identities to the private or to use shame to draw the boundary between full and incompetent citizenship, a desire she sees as making democracy impossible. See *Democracy on Trial*, especially chapter 2, "The Politics of Displacement," 37–63.

References

Balibar, Etienne. *Masses, Classes, Ideas: Studies on Politics and Philosophy after Marx*. New York: Routledge, 1994.

Berland, Jody. "Angels Dancing: Cultural Technologies and the Production of Space." *Cultural Studies*. Ed. Lawrence Grossberg, Cary Nelson, and Paula Treichler. New York: Routledge, 1992. 39–55.

Berlant, Lauren. *The Anatomy of National Fantasy: Hawthorne, Utopia, and Everyday Life*. Chicago: U of Chicago P, 1991.

Berlant, Lauren, and Michael Warner, "Sex in Public." *GLQ* 3 (1996): 159–252.

Brenkman, John. "Mass Media: From Collective Experience to the Culture of Privatization." *Social Text* 1 (Winter 1979): 94–109.

Butler, Judith. *Gender Trouble: Feminism and the Subversion of Identity*. New York: Routledge, 1990.

Christian Coalition. *Contract with the American Family: A Bold Plan by the Christian Coalition to Strengthen the Family and Restore Common-Sense Values*. Nashville: Moorings, 1995.

Coombe, Rosemary J. "The Properties of Culture and the Politics of Possessing Identity: Native Claims in the Cultural Appropriation Controversy." *After Identity*. Ed. Dan Danielsen and Karen Engle. New York: Routledge, 1995. 251–70.

Corber, Robert J. *In the Name of National Security: Hitchcock, Homophobia, and the Political Construction of Gender in Postwar America*. Durham: Duke UP, 1993.

Danielsen, Dan, and Karen Engle. *After Identity: A Reader in Law and Culture*. New York: Routledge, 1995.

D'Emilio, John. "Capitalism and Gay Identity." *Powers of Desire: The Politics of Sexuality*. Ed. Ann Snitow, Christine Stansell, and Sharon Thompson. New York: Monthly Review, 1983. 100–13.

Diamond, Sara. *Roads to Dominion: Right-Wing Movements and Political Power in the United States*. New York: Guilford, 1995.

Dolan, Frederick M. *Allegories of America: Narratives, Metaphysics, Politics*. Ithaca: Cornell UP, 1994.

Elshtain, Jean Bethke. *Democracy on Trial*. New York: Basic, 1995.

Foucault, Michel. *The History of Sexuality*. Vols, 1–3. Trans. Robert Hurley. New York: Pantheon, 1978, 1985, 1986.

Gillespie, Ed, and Bob Schellhass, eds. *Contract with America: The Bold Plan by Rep. Newt Gingrich, Rep. Dick Armey, and the House Republicans to Change the Nation*. New York: Times, 1994.

Gilroy, Paul. "'After the Love Has Gone': Bio-Politics and Etho-Poetics in the Black Public Sphere." *The Black Public Sphere*. Ed. the Black Public Sphere Collective. Chicago: U of Chicago P, 1995. 53–80.

Griggers, Cathy. "Lesbian Bodies in the Age of (Post) mechanical Reproduction." *Fear of a Queer Planet: Queer Politics and Social Theory*. Ed Michael Warner. Minnesota: U of Minnesota P, 1993. 78–192.

Grossberg, Lawrence. *We Gotta Get Out of This Place: Popular Conservatism and Postmodern Culture*. New York: Routledge, 1992.

Habermas, Jürgen. *The New Conservatism: Cultural Criticism and the Historians' Debate*. Trans. Shierry Weber Nicholsen. Cambridge: MIT P, 1989.

——. *The Structural Transformation of the Public Sphere: An Inquiry into a Category of Bourgeois Society*. Trans. Thomas Burger. Cambridge: MIT P, 1989.

Halley, Janet E. "The Politics of the Closet: Legal Articulation of Sexual Orientation Identity." *After Identity: A Reader in Law and Culture*. Ed. Dan Danielsen and Karen Engle. New York: Routledge, 1995. 24–38.

Hansen, Miriam. Foreword. *The Public Sphere and Experience: Toward an Analysis of the Bourgeois and Proletarian Public Sphere*. Ed. Oskar Negt and Alexander Kluge. Trans. Peter Labanyi.

Hennessy, Rosemary. "Queer Visibility in Commodity Culture." *Social Postmodernism*. Ed. Linda Nicholson and Steven Seidman. Cambridge: Cambridge UP, 1995. 142–83.

Jameson, Fredric. "Five Theses on Actually Existing Marxism." *Monthly Review* 47, no. 11 (April 1996): 1–10.

——. "Reification and Utopia in Mass Culture." *Social Text* 1 (winter 1979): 130–48.

Katz, Jonathan Ned. *The Invention of Heterosexuality*. New York: Dutton, 1995.

May, Elaine Tyler. *Homeward Bound: American Families in the Cold War Era*. New York: Basic, 1988.

Meyerowitz, Joanne, ed. *Not June Cleaver: Women and Gender in Postwar America, 1945–1960*. Philadelphia: Temple UP, 1994.

Moore, Stephen, ed. *Restoring the Dream: The Bold New Plan by House Republicans*. New York: Times, 1995.

Mouffe, Chantal. Preface, "Democratic Politics Today"; and "Democratic Citizenship and the Political Community." *Dimensions of Radical Democracy: Pluralism, Citizenship, Community*. New York: Verso, 1992. 1–14, 225–39.

Mowlana, Hamid, George Gerbner, and Herbert I. Schiller. *Triumph of the Image: The Media's War in the Persian Gulf – A Global Perspective*. Boulder: Westview, 1992.

Negt, Oskar, and Alexander Kluge. *Public Sphere and Experience: Toward an Analysis of the Bourgeois and Proletarian Public Sphere*. Foreword by Miriam Hansen. Trans. Peter Labanyi, Jamie Owen Daniel, and Assenka Oksiloff. Minneapolis: U of Minnesota P, 1993.

Omi, Michael, and Howard Winant. *Racial Formation in the United States: From the 1960s to the 1990s*. 2nd ed. New York: Routledge, 1994.

Patton, Cindy. "Refiguring Social Space." *Social Postmodernism: Beyond Identity Politics*. Ed. Linda Nicholson and Steven Seidman. New York: Cambridge UP, 1995. 216–49.

Petchesky, Rosalind P. "The Body as Property: A Feminist Revision." *Conceiving the New World Order: The Global Politics of Reproduction*. Ed. Faye D. Ginsburg and Rayna Rapp. Berkeley: U of California P, 1995. 387–406.

Rogin, Michael Paul. *Ronald Reagan, the Movie: And Other Episodes in Political Demonology*. Berkeley: U of California P, 1987.

Rouse, Roger. "Questions of Identity: Personhood and Collectivity in Transnational Migration to the United States." *Critique of Anthropology* 15, no. 4 (1955): 353–80.

Schiller, Herbert I. *Culture, Inc: The Corporate Takeover of Public Expression*. New York: Oxford UP, 1989.

——. *Information and the Crisis Economy*. Norwood, NJ: Ablex, 1984.

Sedgwick, Eve Kosofsky. *Epistemology of the Closet*. Berkeley: U of California P, 1990.

Sennett, Richard. *The Fall of Public Man*. New York: Norton, 1976.

Spivak, Gayatri Chakravorty. *Outside in the Teaching Machine*. New York: Routledge, 1993.

Taussig, Michael. *The Nervous System*. New York: Routledge, 1992.

Tocqueville, Alexis de. *Democracy in America*. Vol. 1. Trans. Henry Reeve. Ed. Philips Bradley. New York: Vintage, 1945.

Warner, Michael. Introduction. *Fear of a Queer Planet*. Minneapolis: U of Minnesota P, 1993. vii–xxxi.

Democratic Passions: Reconstructing Individual Agency

Christopher Newfield

US democracy has been driven by neoliberal economics for the past thirty years, and any discussion of democratic possibilities must begin there. Neoliberalism was spearheaded by American conservatives, but it is also the basic philosophy of the New Democrats who continue to control the Democratic party. The term "neoliberalism" crosses the wandering US boundary between liberal and conservative and illuminates an underlying consensus on political economy that has dominated electoral politics under both major parties. This consensus has persuaded many people that market-based economic transactions can subordinate and in many cases replace political democracy. This is because they allegedly offer the freest forms of choice in their everyday activity, where choice is defined as essentially economic.

The Market Ideal

There is almost nothing new about neoliberalism. It carries on a classical liberalism whose core features have remained stable for about two centuries. One of these core features is the ideal of the "self-regulating market." This term has been fully analyzed by economic historian Karl Polanyi. "A market economy," he wrote, "is an economic system controlled, regulated, and directed by market prices; order in the production and distribution of goods is entrusted to this self-regulating mechanism." Economic liberalism's second core feature follows directly from this, and that is that the market must remain autonomous from society and its politics: "Nothing must be allowed to inhibit the formation of markets, nor

must incomes be permitted to be formed otherwise than through sales. Neither must there be any interference with the adjustment of prices to changed market conditions. ... Neither price, nor supply, nor demand must be fixed or regulated" by government action. Polanyi noted that, for economic liberals, the state could intervene in markets only to help markets supersede the state: "Only such policies and measures are in order which help to ensure the self-regulation of the market by creating conditions which make the market the only organizing power in the economic sphere."[1]

Polanyi was describing the ideology that supported nineteenth-century industrialization in England, but it should sound familiar to anyone who has been following US economic policy discussions or the globalization debates. Globalization is regularly used as a euphemism for emancipating economic activity from the societies and populations that conduct it. Again, there is nothing new about this. Polanyi claimed that the fundamental economic revolution was not an industrial but a market revolution. The market revolution meant that markets, which had been "embedded" in society for all of prior human history, had revolted against society and declared their independence. Polanyi called this a utopian project, and it is a third feature of market economies: they cannot *in fact* transcend their embeddedness in society, but instead continually aspire to this transcendence. They tirelessly arouse the population against any infringement on market self-regulation. Polanyi also elaborated a fourth core feature of market economies: they cause levels of suffering, injustice, and inequality that produce a popular backlash, whose major form in Polanyi's time was fascism.

With this background in mind, we can understand why American neoliberals have worked so hard for so long to construct their enormous and expensive apparatus for installing the market ideal in society.[2] The work is simply never done, and it is always on the verge of coming undone.[3] Self-regulating markets do not exist, cannot exist, have not existed, and will not exist. Self-regulating markets are more openly managed by concentrated corporate power than ever before. And yet the effort to get entire societies to aspire to "free markets" has dramatically shifted power from governments to markets, most triumphantly in the United States.

I agree with Polanyi and many others that the ideal of self-regulating markets is impossible, undesirable, and socially destructive. But if we are right, why is the market ideal, though slain any number of times, so undead? Why is the self-regulating market so powerful while the Left's ideal – markets embedded in democratic social relations – seems so weak?

Part of the answer is that the popularity of the market ideal is an illusion created by promarket spin control: polling data actually suggests weak public support when the "market" is described as "business" or "big companies" or "corporate money" and the like.[4] A further explanation of the power of market ideals would have many other dimensions, including the obvious wealth and related political power of the business institutions that benefit from it.

I'm going to devote this essay to looking at still another, central part of the explanation. The past and present of market ideology suggests that its popularity hinges on its ability to represent freedom. Demonstrations that markets damage social justice unless society's interests are protected through democratic intervention, although true in my view, simply fail to address the market appeal to freedom. The Left has generally (though with important exceptions) neglected to construct nonmarket models of *individual* freedom, models that work with the systems of democracy and social justice that the Left rightly cares about.[5]

I am motivated by my concern that the glaring absence of equality in US life, coupled with the widespread claim that the market has delivered freedom, has muted demands for expanded forms of *social* freedom. I am interested in the widespread demoralization that accompanies procedural democracy in the United States. I am interested in the everyday feeling of powerlessness in people who are formally and technically empowered. I am interested in this experience of weak or pointless personal agency both because it feels bad, thereby

limiting individual capacity, and because it prevents full "participation," thereby gutting democracy and leaving its forms. I am alarmed that democracy continues to feel and act like a burden on individuality. Most political theory accepts this as inevitable. But this means accepting the continuing decline of democracy.

In response, I am going to make two arguments. First, I will suggest how self-regulating markets damage the individual autonomy and agency they claim to protect. Second, I'll describe forms of *social* autonomy that are both the prerequisite to a fully democratic society and suppressed by self-regulating markets.

The Market Claim to Freedom

Liberal theorists have never sought democracy through the political system alone. They have regarded even the US Constitution as by itself unequal to the task of sustaining a social order. Liberalism has not settled for the "constituted" power of the state, or for the "constituent" strength of the democratic masses, or for some combination of the two.[6] It has also invoked the market as a necessary arena of democratic self-regulation and of freedom. The success of liberal thought in Western societies can be measured by the currency of the belief that political activity sustains social order through its interaction with market activity.

In keeping with the tradition of economic liberalism, neoliberalism formulates the centrality of markets through a pair of equations. The first equates deregulated commercial markets with political democracy. For example, Francis Fukuyama's emblematic essay, "The End of History and the Last Man," attributed the end of the cold war to the spreading belief that "free markets" were the same as "representative democracy."[7] Fukuyama was consolidating an already common view of market deregulation as enhancing the economic power of ordinary people. For example, airline deregulation has long been credited with lowering prices and increasing the access of ordinary Americans to air travel; its main architect, Cornell economist Alfred Kahn, has been described as a latter-day Jefferson – "the father of cheap airfares."[8] Such views build on at least a century of developments in marketing, advertizing, and kindred fields that have defined the United States as the world's most advanced "consumer society." Consumption is widely regarded as something like democratic choice. Business's devotion to sales is seen as devotion to popular demand. Economic policy is one long "kitchen debate" that defines development much like Richard Nixon's praise of American capitalism to Nikita Khrushchev on the grounds of its labor-saving household appliances. The United States is not a social democracy but rather a market democracy and a consumer democracy. As a result, most US political leaders now assume that markets are better than government at perceiving demand, better at designing the service, better at building the product, better at customer delivery, and better at responding to feedback.[9] Under neoliberalism, markets have successfully put this question to governments: What aspect of democracy – meaning responding to the everyday needs of ordinary citizens – can *you* do better than *we* do?

Neoliberalism's second equation claims that markets promote individual freedom. It defines the "freedom to choose" as market choice – the choice of goods to consume, the choice of means of production. Individual agency may be small in market practice, but it is a giant in market theory. Thirty years of conservative calls to "get the government off our backs" have forged powerful associations between the ideal of self-regulating markets and the always popular vision of individual liberty. Neoliberalism borrows a language of popular economic revolt against political tyranny, a language that in the United States harkens back at least to the Boston Tea Party, in which ordinary, enterprising citizens fight the economic coercion of a regulative government. In the 1990s, conservatives were joined by market liberals like Bill Clinton, Tom Peters, and most of the mainstream media in accepting the view that markets were both the most efficient medium of transmitting economic information *and* the natural ally of human creativity.[10]

Although its causes are complex, the outcome is clear: by the early 1990s the market had become the friend not of the plutocrat and monopolist but of the citizen and employee. Peters confessed, "I love markets. I admit it. I love radical decentralization. I am an enemy of elaborate plans. An ally of hasty action. An enemy of excessive order. A friend of disorderly trial and error – especially error."[11] What kind of an economy encourages professional consultants to confess *love* for markets? One that has managed to equate markets with freedom, with the feeling of one's own unlimited possibilities, with a belief in action without government's fixed determinations. This market liberates individuals from capitalist discipline, the better to liberate capitalism itself. Mediterranean societies, Peters continued, "were the first, according to Hayek, to accept 'a person's rights to dispose [of property], thus allowing individuals to develop a dense network of commercial relations.' . . . The right to dispose of one's assets

provides the basis for dealing with – or not dealing with – others of one's choosing."[12] For neoliberalism, markets transform the raw material of private property into the material and spiritual reality of personal freedom. Hayek's history rests on the same idealization that produces Peters's love, but that only enhances its psychological appeal.

Liberty has always been liberalism's ace in the hole, and neoliberal arguments have carried on the tradition. Ideological success always depends on laying out a positive ideal effect that will draw people in spite of their misgivings about your program. People are more likely to accept your cuts in Medicare payments, for example, if you tie them to expanding the freedom to choose physicians. Another ingredient of ideological success is removing your ideal from the zone of debate. You will have trouble if your enemy attacks your ideal in the name of their better version of it. It is better for you if you can get your enemy to ignore your ideal and fail to claim it for themselves.

Neoliberalism owes some of its success to the Left's tendency to make this tactical mistake. Market critics have tended to target neoliberalism's first equation and have found that markets are often undemocratic and damage basic equity and equality. These arguments are extremely important, but they are simply beside the point of the second equation of markets with freedom. Showing that markets damage equality and direct political participation, the classical components of democratic states, does not amount to showing that markets damage liberty. To make matters worse, market critics actually *reinforce* the massively popular neoliberal equation of markets and liberty when they criticize individualism as a market ideal or equate individual rights with neoliberalism.[13]

An example of how the Left tacitly enforces the link between personal freedom and markets is its polarization of the positions of sociologists Anthony Giddens and Pierre Bourdieu. At one time they adhered to similar versions of democratic socialism. Giddens now celebrates "the new individualism," the stress on "self-fulfillment, the fulfillment of potential," as part of his "Third Way" acceptance of market mechanisms. Bourdieu, by contrast, rejects market-based governance. He calls instead for "a social order which would not have as its sole law the pursuit of egoistical interests and the individual lust for profit, and which will find a place for collectives oriented towards the *rational pursuit of collectively elaborated and approved goals*."[14] Bourdieu's rejection of market governance involves the rejection of individualism as irrational selfishness that destroys social justice.

But must Bourdieu yoke the term "individual" to the term "lust for profit"? Is self-fulfillment really dependent on egoistical interests and exploitation? Aren't there ways of fulfilling individual potential that are democratic rather than market-based, that in fact make democracy possible and meaningful? Don't we in fact need self-fulfilled citizens to do valid collective planning, and valid collective planning to support self-fulfillment? Perhaps Bourdieu would say yes to these, but I can't find any evidence in his attacks on neoliberalism. I find myself in the apparently awkward position of agreeing with Bourdieu on the value of social planning and with Giddens on the value of self-fulfillment.

Neoliberal theory has worked hard to produce this polarity, which is enormously convenient for the ideal of the self-regulating market. The polarity says that liberty and democracy are fundamentally at odds. States that incline toward democracy incline toward restricting liberty, for liberty inherently leads toward antisocial egoism. That means, in a common American theme, that the defense of liberty requires the suppression of states. The most desirable default becomes the marketplace, which is said to deliver both democracy and liberty through a mechanism inherently superior to state and anarchy. If you seek Bourdieu-like control of bad market outcomes, then you must side with the state against liberty; if you seek liberty with Giddens, then you must oppose the justice-seeking state. The only winner in this argument is the ideal of the self-regulating market.

Neoliberalism has used this theme to move far down the road to political ascendancy. But it has also achieved something more. By inducing the liberal tension between liberty and equality in the heart of left-wing antimarket argumentation, it has pulled the Left off of its highest ground. The crux of leftist political insight during these recent liberal centuries has been that liberty and equality and democracy go hand in hand. You cannot have genuine liberty without equality, or equality without liberty.[15] This conceptual truth appears clearly in moments of revolution in which the masses demand democracy in the name of their own liberation. Democracy, and the equality that enables it, is sought for the sake of freedom and not order. It is only later, as Antonio Negri points out, that the masses' "constituent power," having formed a state, finds itself reduced to the form of a law.[16] In its own proper form and desire it seeks its own freedom, including the freedom to make and remake its own law. The task of a fully democratic society is to preserve the "constituent power" that seeks its own freedom. There is no genuine democracy, in other words, that does not express this collective freedom.

The market ideal succeeds for at least two reasons of strategy: it claims to represent individual liberty, and it induces its left-wing opponents to encourage this view. By installing the conflict between liberty and equality as national common sense, neoliberalism immeasurably strengthens the market ideal while discrediting the Left's vision of democracy as in conflict with freedom. Radical democrats lose political power and, all too often, commit the huge intellectual error of repressing their defining attachment to individual liberty.

Market Determinism

It would be easier to see the connection between democracy and individual liberty if we could specify the limits of market liberty. As part of the process of forging the link between markets and freedom, neoliberalism has had to ignore or discredit the possibility that a common feature of markets is coercion or determinism. Market determinism is a version of what Raymond Williams once called "abstract determinism." By this Williams meant the experience that the economy is run by forces outside of anyone's and everyone's control.[17] "The strongest single reason for the development of abstract determinism," he wrote, "is the historical experience of large-scale capitalist economy, in which many more people than marxists concluded that control of the process was beyond them, that it was at least in practice external to their wills and desires, and that it had therefore to be seen as governed by its own 'laws.' "[18] Free choice was not, for Williams, the general experience of people in markets.

In the wake of market triumph, how do we now talk about the way markets produce this loss of control? Categorical rejection of markets as such is ineffective and wrong. "Markets," as exchanges among people, are inevitable and valuable. On the level of everyday exchange, markets provide freedom largely in the form of consumer choice. Markets make goods available by linking producers and consumers through price signals and other forms of information that keep the entire economic system in motion. Market critics can accept such propositions without feeling that they weaken our case. But choice and information are only two features of markets; they are also hierarchical and regulated structures. The freedom of the isolated purchase is a popular icon of market behavior but it does not accurately represent the overall operation of a market system.

[...]

As for consumer choice, it is the most expensively choreographed social act in the United States. Any firm in any industry spends as much of its cash flow as it can afford to narrowing the consumer's conscious range of possibility to its own product. Recent advances in niche marketing have focused the address of particular campaigns on demographic groups as small as one person. The flashing ad in the margin of your Web browser may be seen only by you, having been generated by the cookie-trail of your previous computer purchases. The obvious goal is to hook you and not to free you up. Marketing never succeeds at eliminating independent choice, but dependence on one firm is its Platonic ideal. Market competition requires that firms seek the reduction of consumer independence. Markets cannot not present themselves as independence's special patron.

The same goes for virtually every other aspect of business life, where success requires maximum control of your environment's independent variables. The uncertain, the unknown, the uncontrolled, the truly independent are your enemies. They will steal your employees, your customers, your suppliers, your regular revenues, your profits, everything you care about. Your job is to reduce everyone's power except your own. Reduce labor's bargaining power so you can keep wages down. Increase your supplier's dependence on your business so you can control their pricing. Damage your competitor's leverage with a new product by flooding the market with your imitation. Reduce the visibility of their brand by saturating the airwaves with yours. Increase the price of electricity by artificially reducing its supply; time your reductions for maximum effect by, for example, taking a plant offline in the middle of a heat wave.[19] Such lists could go on for hundreds of pages. They illustrate ordinary, everyday market calculation. The general goal of this calculation is to protect your position by minimizing the independence of everyone and everything else.

[...]

An identical pattern marks globalization, in which "free trade" produces increasing levels of dependence on foreign capital in "developing nations." Wealthy nations make market rules from their position of superior market power, and these relations often amount to a neocolonial authority over the poorer region or country. Again, this restriction on the poorer country's options is not an accident but is the deliberate aim of neoliberal policy. When the policy is thwarted, Western wrath is instantaneous. In 1998, Malaysian Prime Minister Mahathir Mohamad responded to capital flight by instituting, among other things, a tax on investment returns that favored investors who left their money in place for at least one year. "Essentially, you've got a Government that makes its own rules," one fund manager exclaimed indignantly.[20] Investors earn far more money by making rules for others, rules that may be procedurally fair but clearly favor one party or position. Market success routinely involves reducing the independence of variables, which means relentless and effective attacks on others' independence.

Markets, of course, do not *intrinsically* require dependence any more than they guarantee freedom: like any system, they offer a mixture of both. The mixture is what the strong defense of markets denies.[21] It is certainly true that markets offer freedom to people in the right market position. The right position is usually a compound of access to capital, brand visibility, social status, product advantage, good timing, and other network effects of competitive advantage. Freedom follows from a superior position. It is not a *general* ability of people in markets but is contingent on unusual wealth or institutional power – on executive status in a large corporation, on distinctive professional status, on banking connections from a previous job, on unique product design, and so on. Markets offer certain individuals *contingent* freedom: the individual's effective freedom is contingent on her advantageous position in the market.[22]

[...]

Although market deregulation proceeds in the name of more individual opportunity, it in fact turns previously guaranteed choices into contingent ones. For example, many firms have replaced "defined benefit" pensions, which pay out according to a set formula, with "defined contribution" pensions, in which individuals pay into a fund whose outputs depend on its fortunes in the market. This increases the freedom of movement of one's pension's market value but it decreases one's own autonomy from market movements. Deregulation increases the market's deterministic power over individuals, whether or not the individual benefits financially. Fixed, formulaic pensions sheltered the individual from the market, which meant shelter from the wills of vastly more powerful market actors like corporate boards and pension fund managers. Fixed pensions offered an increasingly rare freedom of choice within the pension's limits. Deregulation has meant that many benefits of citizenship, assured in the political sphere, have been redefined as returns on competitive investment, won in the economic sphere. An "entitlement," after all, offered an individual right, and that right defined a scope of free operation. Markets eliminate these rights and their contractual freedoms.

Market freedom is contingent on market position; different positions offer their inhabitants very different possibilities for controlling markets. The *majority* experiences their contingent freedom as insufficient power to control markets, as weak and fitful freedom, as market determinism. Although market movements are shaped by elaborate webs of law and policy, and although these laws can be changed, market theory withholds the power of change from ordinary actors. The minority possibility of changing markets by pulling strings in remote, invisible, and superior locations does not ease the majority experience of determinism on the ground. Once again, this is not an unfortunate by-product of self-regulating markets, but rather is their stated goal: market ideals reject mass control of economies, which must take place in the political realm, and revere minority control of economies by those who, having passed "market tests," have acquired concentrated power.

Neoliberal market theory is hostile to economic democracy, so much so that it overrides a central liberal political value. Liberalism has always opposed contingent freedom in the political sphere on the grounds that freedom is an individual right held by the individual regardless of her particular social situation (wealth, race, creed, color, sexual orientation, national origin). Such guarantees actually increase the complexity of the political system by increasing independence and potential variability. Yet liberals routinely defend contingent freedom in markets, where one's capacity is directly dependent on one's market situation. Although countless stories and studies show that people with different economic resources have very different life chances, neoliberals still claim that individual freedom is either unaffected by one's market position or is affected only in justifiable ways. Neoliberals, in short, are in the conflicted position of advocating uniform freedom in law and politics while defending contingent freedom in the economy.

Given these features of markets, there's no reason why the Left should concede any part of the neoliberal claim

that markets generally sponsor a freedom that states and publics do not. To the contrary, the market, unmodified by society, reduces the systemic complexity and suppresses the personal agency that underlines liberty and democracy alike.

Unburdened Agency

Nonmarket democracy is democracy that operates independently of self-regulated (stratified, heavily managed) markets. This democracy has at least two major elements. The first is procedural equality across the whole mix of social terrains. I plan to talk about a psychological measure of nonmarket democracy that I believe is more basic, but procedural equality is important. Great benefits follow from the real implementation of the liberal ideals of due process and equality under the law. The ideal of procedural equality appears under a variety of names: in addition to due process in the law, market actors seek "transparency" of information when they make investments; markets rest their claims for efficiency on the basis of every actor making his or her decisions on the basis of identical knowledge. Allegedly efficient markets are themselves dependent on state-sponsored forms of procedural equality, and so is virtually every form of justice. It should also be noted that procedural equality depends on good bureaucratic administration.[23] The subjective elements I am more interested in cannot "scale up" to a municipal or national level without the dense networks of regulations that often affront individuality while being crucial to any kind of equal treatment.

One of liberalism's historical weaknesses is its tendency to describe certain inconsistencies in its ideal of due process as tolerable and necessary. Walzer follows in these footsteps by asking us to accept many undemocratic steps in complex governance. An even more serious liberal flaw is its elevation of equal treatment over equal outcomes. When the two are in conflict liberals generally side with regularized process rather than equitable impact. For example, liberals have generally been unwilling to defend affirmative action as a "quota system" that produces racial proportions settled by democratic deliberation. They speak instead of outreach programs, admission by class percentile, and so on as removing barriers to equal opportunity. In contrast, I understand Left democratic traditions as seeking equality of outcome in any arena that affects life chances. I favor differentiated equality of outcome, but the questions that always arise are what do we mean by equal outcomes and how are we going to measure it?

In my view, the most profound measure of equal outcomes is subjective. Do the affected individuals feel outcomes are equal enough to allow their own freedom? In other words, are outcomes equal enough to allow them to feel their *unburdened agency*?

I am interpreting democratic theory as requiring three things. Individuals must (1) control the whole, (2) in collaboration with the whole society, and (3) without the impairment or burdening of their individual powers. The first two phrases reiterate Walzer's and nearly every other definition of mass democracy. The third phrase is the crucial one. It must be noted that I do not mean that an individual has direct control over all outcomes. One *cannot* say one's powers are impaired because one's unilateral goal is blocked. The term "unburdened agency" means that the individual's wish or position is present in and is transmitted through the entire decision chain without rejection or repudiation.[24]

Traditional notions of democratic citizenship have always involved some version of unburdened powers. They tend to measure these in the quasi-quantitative terms of equivalence. The concept of equal protection, for example, means that no one's treatment – and no one's agency – will be the same across social positions. This tradition of citizenship insists that one's placement, specialization, connections, access, or *office* in society will not affect one's substantive powers. The system can be highly differentiated without becoming *inequitably* differential. I agree that equity and equality must be evaluated in terms of due process, as traditional notions insist, *and* also in terms of the individual experience of agency. This means, to satisfy due process, that one's agency is unburdened if one's experience of it is not diminished by *any special fact of one's position*. Democracy depends on this experience of unburdened agency in the sense of an experience of having one's identity, passions, and interests recognized and then passed on into a larger collaborative system. Complex systems, in order to be democratic, cannot simply point out the burden of complexity. They must find ways of preserving the agency of each member in the course of complex contact.

In defining equal outcomes through unburdened agency, I am not dismissing the more objective and quantifiable measures of interpersonal equality that include analysis of personal income, access to health care and education, and equal numbers of minutes waiting for women's and men's restrooms. Those measures are important, but they have unfortunately eclipsed the deeper level of equality's impact on subjective experience, in particular the experience of freedom. Burdened agency is agency that has little or no effect on the outcome of processes that it addresses. Only part of this burden can be measured quantitatively. It is intensely subjective and interpretive. It consists of the *feeling* of blockage, of futility, of helplessness, of lacking power, of not being recognized, of not being respected, of not being properly counted. We are used to demanding objective measures of burdens and sufferings, and while those forms of accounting must continue and must improve, they encourage us to ignore or downplay personal testimonials to agency's condition. Individuals routinely provide their own data on the extent of their burdens, and some of the process of democratization consists of learning to take this personal data seriously. In spite of our enormous cynicism about people's self-descriptions, self-descriptions of one's burdens (and other conditions) are simply irreplaceable – they are not reducible to accounts provided by others, be they sociologists, policy analysts, police, social workers, family members, lovers, or friends.[25] Descriptions of the burden on agency must come finally from the agent him or herself. It is in fact one of the greatest burdens on agency that we have become so unable to trust the accounts of it coming from the agents themselves.

These reflections lead to some straightforward additional principles, following on the numbering of the series above. Democracy means (4) the coordination of differentiated and even conflicting subsystems across boundaries such as class and race. This coordination is democratic to the extent that its various subsystems or local cultures are (5) permeable and (6) of *equal* status such that (7) individual agency from any domain can be equitably transmitted through to any other, thus (8) offering individual members the experience of an agency unburdened by the collective process.

Complications are of course unavoidable.[26] But for too long the Left has let its brilliant grasp of the complications deter it from developing models for unburdening individual agency within complex democracies.

The Practice of Contact

A superb portrait of freedom in groups appears in *Times Square Red, Times Square Blue*, a book about contemporary New York City by novelist Samuel R. Delany.[27] Delany's topic is the Guiliani administration's "redevelopment" of Times Square, and he cuts between the larger social forces at work and his personal experience of the changes they have wrought. Redevelopment destroyed a range of low-cost venues for public interaction, many of them illegal and most regarded as antisocial by the powers that be. Delany describes the codified and yet spontaneous, pleasure-based social lives that passed in the bars, clubs, and porn theaters of the old Times Square area, where he conducted an important part of his own sexual and social life over several decades. He contrasts this with the large-scale redevelopment, which rests on a much more restrictive idea of desirable public conduct. To show that redevelopment was unnecessary and repressive, Delany describes how the former citizens of Times Square had found ways to combine personal and public life that made external controls invasive and unnecessary.

How can Delany make this case, especially given his candor about the local scourges of addiction, illness, and crime? First, Times Square society is *not* a self-regulating market, for it is regulated by the directed activity of its members. Transactions are face-to-face and resemble precapitalist market exchanges of goods and services that avoid commodification and higher management. Some participants pay for sex but most do not, giving and receiving according to mutual arrangements. Although there is nothing anarchistic about public sex, which Delany describes as highly choreographed, its practitioners make and change most of their own rules.[28]

The sign of this power of rule making is what the more regulated market terms sexual perversity. Perversity designates the unmanaged range of practices that includes oral sex, mutual masturbation, and open voyeurism; in short, sex across every imaginable body type, functionality, and above all social class. Perversity is a name for this very unusual range of choices, an epithet commonly applied to self-authorized personal decisions. In the market ideal, markets operate according to impersonal laws. Delany shows that everyday users operate on principles so different from those that have redeveloped Times Square that they comprise an alternative kind of market behavior. No cash is exchanged, no accumulation takes place, no class inequalities occur: in the *capitalist* sense, it is not market behavior at all.

Sexual exchange generally expresses some kind of interest and some anticipated benefit. Delany's own interests are remarkably nonphobic and varied, and include interest in normally "undesirable" people – the mentally and physically disabled, malformed, or ill. Delany specifies the core of sexual interest in terms that are especially relevant to our discussion:

There are as many different styles, intensities, and timbres to sex as there are people. The variety of nuance and attitude blends into the variety of techniques and actions employed, which finally segues, as seamlessly, into the variety of sexual objects the range of humankind desires. . . . We do a little better when we sexualize our own manner of having sex – learn to find our own way of having sex sexy. Call it a healthy narcissism, if you like. This alone allows us to relax with our own sexuality. Paradoxically, this also allows us to vary it and accommodate it, as far as we wish, to other people. I don't see how this can be accomplished without a statistically significant variety of partners and a fair amount of communication with them, at that, about what their sexual reactions to us are. . . . When Lacan says, "One desires the desire of the other," self-confidence is, generally speaking, the aspect of it desired.[29]

Unlike a self-regulating market, sexual exchange works through ranges restricted only by the practitioners. Desire is variable within one person, is changeable, is nonlinear, is not exactly predictable. Delany insists on the nonmonogamous and polymorphous nature of interest; interest is fundamentally polymorphous wherever it is not controlled, as it usually is, by the great intrapsychic manager, shame.[30] The still more basic point is that the most satisfying form of exchange depends on what I've been calling unburdened agency. "Healthy narcissism" is the state of feeling no limit on one's basic capacity. It is also the thing we desire in others and that triggers our desire – their self-confidence, their own refusal to experience social life as a burden. Sex is the meeting of two temporarily and partially unburdened agents, whose social ties support the unburdening. This condition of strong agency, so often derided as wishful and naive by professionals and theorists, lies at the core of human pleasure. This is also the extraordinary, the charmed core of a just society, where relationships express the freedom and agency of their members.

The crucial question is how to find the kind of social system that supports healthy narcissism, pleasure, and self-confidence. Delany takes for granted that it will involve addressing unequal power relations within the complex systems that support such phenomena as Times Square redevelopment. Society is always a net situation, and "in a net situation," Delany writes, "information comes from several directions and crosses various power boundaries, so that various processes – modulating, revisionary, additive, recursive, and corrective (all of them critical, each of them highlighting different aspects) can compensate for the inevitable reductions that occur along the constitutive [linear] chains."[31] But Delany also thinks that "networking" is only one of the ways to exist in social nets. People in net situations might be networking, or, on the other hand they might be engaging in "contact."[32]

Some oversimplified contrasts will help here. Networking is formally structured. Contact is not. "Contact is the conversation that starts in the line at the grocery counter with the person behind you while the clerk is changing the paper roll in the cash register. It is the pleasantries exchanged with a neighbor who has brought her chair out to take some air on the stoop. It is the discussion that begins with the person next to you at the bar. . . . It can be two men watching each other masturbating together in adjacent urinals of a public john – an encounter that, later, may or may not become a conversation."[33] Networking occurs in professional societies where, for example, a senior member of your field likes a paper she hears you present and helps you get it published. Contact occurs when you, a struggling writer, start a conversation with the man standing next to you at the remainder table in your local bookstore, continue by complaining about the treatment your genre receives from reviewers, and end by discovering your new acquaintance is one of those reviewers who winds up praising your book in his next column.[34] "Networking tends to be professional and motive-driven. Contact tends to be more broadly social and appears random. . . . Networking is heavily dependent on institutions to promote the necessary propinquity. . . . Contact is associated with public space and the architecture and commerce that depend on and promote it."[35]

[. . .]

Although networking and contact interact and overlap, they part company on the issues of scarcity, loss, and agency. Networks are devices for managing scarcity. Networks are similar to self-regulating markets in which everyone competes for goods distributed according to general laws. . . . Networks offer opportunity along with the spectacle of continuous and massive failure.

Individuals manage network scarcity in familiar ways. Most blame themselves and see their failure as outside their control. They come to experience themselves as in need of defense against further loss, which encourages, and yet they feel dependent on the same network against which they defend themselves. Individuals look to superiors rather than to peers for meaningful help. They largely cede to superiors their power to make general rules for

the disposition of people and things. They become small branch offices of self-policing. The network in this way shapes and reduces individual autonomy without overt coercion. The resulting states of reduced capacity are so common we rarely notice them, and yet we cope by abandoning whatever agency doesn't fit. As small-scale markets, networks manage scarcity in a way that generates the routine experience of absent control. The member's habituation to noncontrol is a primary burden on their agency.

[. . .]

Contact's contingency, indeterminacy, intimacy, and open interest allow each person to face the other as an approximate and provisional peer. The parties may come from quite various social positions – one guy in the bookstore reviews for national newspapers and the other is a twenty-year-old nobody – but they are peers for the duration of the contact. They are two people looking for dollar books, and they are as close or remote, equal or unequal, as their conversation. The twenty-year-old may get something he wants from the contact because of the other's network, but he does not approach him as he would in a network, where he would be a junior person approaching a senior, the one who lacks approaching the one who has. The relationship is not controlled by the dominant party, and it doesn't require general management to regulate the effects of inequality. The partial relief from domination allows a partial lowering of defenses. While individuals never fully escape negative affects like fear and shame that inhibit interest, contact is a situation in which the individual feels a reduced need to defend herself against her own interest. Contact allows the individual to experience herself as one who creates the interaction through her own agency. Contact offers unburdened agency; and offers it not simply to the winners in marketlike competition but to everybody.

The freedom experienced in contact is social. Contact offers individuals the experience of public relations in which their autonomy is not sacrificed. It is any ordinary experience of small-scale linkages to others that we can make and unmake as we go through the day. Contact is generally local because it involves someone on the same bus bench or gym pool, but it contains the experience of unrepressed interaction that serves as the positive benchmark for social experience. Having experienced freedom in public, most of us are reluctant to sacrifice it for better regulation or even equity. Apparently democratic procedures that block the circulation of our interest no longer feel democratic. Delany is particularly emphatic that contact must and does take place across social barriers, class barriers above all.[36] Ordinary contact offers the experience not only of unburdened agency but of agency unburdened by barriers of unequal power and conflicting interests.

Contact encourages the individual to measure her agency by its capacity to transmit itself through social spaces normally charged by polarity and stratification. With the temporary, provisional, and partial lifting of immediate barriers, her baseline standard for wider society is that it furnish unburdened interest. This experience goes by many names, and one is Delany's idea of "pleasantness." The individual moves from one interest to the next without barriers signaled by blockage and deprivation. Contact focuses the self on the enjoyment it takes from the continuous coexistence of irreducible differences in a democratic mass. Contact offers an experience in which the liberal opposition between liberty and equality does not exist. Contact is the repeated revelation that, contrary to much current democratic theory, strong agency can thrive on complexity.

The Agency Project

I started by suggesting that market critics have erred when they have assumed that individual agency is alive and well and/or an effect of the market ideal. Neoliberalism has done so well in large part by championing liberty while quietly tailoring it to a highly managed corporate economy. In the current contest, I've said, the Left must insist on personal, individual agency; one as radical as we can imagine. I have in mind an agency that, without naively seeking atomistic escapes from discourse and organizations, and while seeking better collective action, can first imagine itself acting without these. It would be an agency that is not shame based, that is not only in the service of a defensive ego, that can act in collectives with a sense of its own freedom, that does not seek mastery at the expense of relations, that will not restrict these collectives because of the freedom it has not received.

[...]

I will end with a few pushy imperatives. I'd like to see a democratic agency project, one that builds on identity politics and our current ambivalent pursuit of philosophically adequate political agency. This will mean

attracting others with our openly delighted embrace of the material practices of "self-composition." This will need to be a theme for which we never apologize – it means self-creation as something like a UN-sanctioned human right, hardly mentioned in the current process of globalization. We will need to endorse what allows this unshamed self-creation: the centrality of identity and identity politics in individual life. We will need to explain why Toni Cade Bambara was right to say "Revolution begins with the self, in the self."[37] We will need to rearticulate important moments of radical humanism, as when Jean-Paul Sartre wrote "we must militate in our writings in favor of the freedom of the person *and* the socialist revolution. It is our job to show tirelessly that they imply each other."[38] We will of course need to maintain our grasp of systemic forces, coercion, contradiction, and negative affect while nonetheless stressing what Alaine Touraine has called "offensive identity" – not "an appeal to a mode of being but the claim to a capacity for action and for change."[39] We will need to rework some New Left / social movement themes to counter an age of corporate liberation – themes like alienation as a major problem, identity-based subordination as a destructive injustice, difference as basic and wonderful, self-management as a key to happiness. The result will be, once again, to show how market freedom – individual agency always mediated by corporations – is not as good as democratic freedom; that without the latter justice and life are lost. The democratic version of freedom means individual agency for all. Elaborating this is a crucial part of moving toward the postcorporate world for which artists and writers and cultural academics have so often stood.

Notes

1 Karl Polanyi, *The Great Transformation: The Political and Economic Origins of Our Time*, 2nd ed. (1944; Boston: Beacon Press, 2001), 71–2.

2 I am using the term "market ideal" as shorthand for the "ideal of the self-regulating market."

3 One example is the Indonesian riots following the Asian financial crisis of 1997, when the International Monetary Fund forced the population to cut further into basic necessities like food and shelter to pay foreign creditors for loans that they would have lost in what was looking like a large number of ordinary bankruptcies.

4 A *Business Week*/Harris poll conducted in August 2000 found that 73 percent think executives are paid too much, 74 percent think big companies have too much political influence, 87 percent think "entertainment and popular

culture are dominated by corporate money which seeks mass appeal over quality," and 95 percent think companies "owe something to their workers" and communities and not just to shareholders (Aaron Bernstein, "Too Much Corporate Power?" *Business Week* 11 [September 2000]: 144–58). Sometimes the mass media takes note of this widely held economic populism. In September 2000, Paul Krugman observed that "ordinary people, when push comes to shove, feel that sometimes the market just isn't fair – and have sympathy for those who protest that unfairness" (Paul Krugman, "Britain's Stormy Petrol," *New York Times*, September 17, 2000, sec. 4, p. 19). Local resistance to corporate behavior is fairly common, and includes fighting new Wal-Mart stores, forcing Starbucks to increase the price at which it buys its coffee, antisweat-shop protests against Nike and other clothing manufacturers, anti-WTO protests in various cities – the list continues to grow. This is more evidence for the view that neoliberal-ism must maintain itself through constant intervention in public discourse.

5   I use the term "nonmarket" to refer to exchanges that are not exclusively subject to the principles and management of capitalist economic institutions. Nonmarket exchanges interact with market forces but are not determined by them. They may work on a smaller scale and involve "face-to-face" relationships among individuals, but the crucial feature is that they are not primarily controlled by financial criteria.

6   For definitions of constituted and constituent power, a dis-cussion of the many theories of their interrelation, and a passionate, comprehensive defense of constituent strength as authentic democracy, see Antonio Negri, *Insurgencies: Constituent Power and the Modern State*, trans. Maurizia Boscagli (1992; Minneapolis: University of Minnesota Press, 1999).

7   Francis Fukuyama, "The End of History and the Last Man," *The National Interest* (summer, 1989): 3–18.

8   Jon E. Hilsenrath: "The Outlook: The Pros and Cons of Power Price Caps," *Wall Street Journal*, June 4, 2001, A1.

9   As I write, outright market failure has not dented market dogma. Commenting on California state government's efforts to intervene in the "deregulated" electricity markets that produced exponential wholesale price increases and rolling blackouts, businessman and former Democratic gubernatorial candidate Al Checchi asserted that "California politicians and bureaucrats cannot reasonably expect to purchase, finance, transmit, or generate electricity more efficiently than their private-sector counterparts" ("Deeper and Deeper We Get in Risky World of Power," *Los Angeles Times*, February 16, 2000, B9).

10   Here one usually sees a citation to master guru F. A. Hayek, from his mid-century arguments against Soviet state planning such as *The Road to Serfdom* (Chicago: University of Chicago Press, 1956), to his exploration of the market as a discovery process in *The Fatal Conceit: The Errors of Socialism*, ed. W. W. Bartley (Chicago: University of Chicago Press, 1989).

11   Tom Peters, *Liberation Management: Necessary Disorganiza-tion for the Nanosecond Nineties* (New York: Knopf, 1992), 484.

12   Ibid., 499. Markets and personal choice meet around "decentralization," which Peters associates with a good kind of chaos and unknowability, because these force experimentalism and thwart the tyranny of planning.

13   This trend is certainly not universal: liberals and radicals have sometimes objected to the claim that individual free-dom interferes with democracy and justice. For example, Will Kymlicka writes, "Various critics of liberalism – including some Marxists, communitarians, and feminists – have argued that the liberal focus on individual rights reflects an atomistic, materialistic, instrumental, or conflictual view of human relationships. I believe that this criticism is profoundly mistaken, and that individual rights can be and typically are used to sustain a wide range of social relationships. Indeed, the most basic liberal right – freedom of conscience – is primarily valuable for the protection it gives to intrinsically social (and noninstru-mental) activities" (Kymlicka, *Multicultural Citizenship* [Oxford: Oxford University Press, 1995], 26). The radical feminist Ellen Willis makes a similar point: "In a way it's true that feminism is bourgeois. Women's demand for self-determination is rooted in the idea of the autonomous individual, and it is the institution of wage labor that made it possible for women to conceive of independence from men. . . . There is a common theme in leftists' reduc-tive view of bourgeois liberties, their contempt for mass culture, and their dismissal of sexual politics. I think all these antipathies reflect a puritanical discomfort with the urge – whatever form it takes – to gratification now, an assumption that social concern is synonymous with altruism and self-sacrifice" (Willis, *Beginning to See the Light: Sex, Hope, and Rock-and-Roll*, 2nd ed. [Hanover, NH: Wesleyan University Press, 1992], xix, xx). But the Left can dismiss thinkers like Kymlicka as liberals and Willis as a second-wave feminist, thus failing to engage with their important claims for the individual.

14   Anthony Giddens, *The Third Way: The Renewal of Social Democracy* (Cambridge: Polity Press, 1998), 37; Pierre Bourdieu, *Contre-feux: Propos pour servir à la résistance contre l'invasion néo-liberale* (Paris: Editions Raisons d'Agir, 1998), 117–18. Both texts are cited in Alex Callinicos, "Social Theory Put to the Test of Politics: Pierre Bourdieu and Anthony Giddens, *New Left Review* 236 (July/August 1999): 82, 91.

15   This is the point of what Etienne Balibar called "egalliberty," an "impossible" but necessary term. "If it is absolutely true that equality is *practically* identical with freedom, this means that it is materially impossible for it to be otherwise, in other words, it means that they are necessarily always *contradicted together*. . . . There is no example of conditions

that suppress or repress freedom that do not suppress or limit – that is, do not abolish – equality, and vice versa" (Balibar, "'Rights of Man' and 'Rights of the Citizen': The Modern Dialectic of Equality and Freedom," in *Masses, Classes, Ideas: Studies on Politics and Philosophy Before and After Marx*, trans. James Swenson [New York: Routledge, 1994], 48).

16 Antonio Negri, *Insurgencies*, 3.

17 The abstract determinist holds that "some power (God or Nature or History [or markets]) controls or decides the outcome of an action or process, beyond or irrespective of the wills or desires of its agents" (Raymond Williams, *Marxism and Literature* [Oxford: Oxford University Press, 1977], 84).

18 Ibid., 86.

19 For example, see Doug Smith, Carl Ingram, Rich Connell, "Duke Shaped Power Market, Three Tell Panel, *Los Angeles Times*, June 23, 2001, A1.

20 Mark Landler, "The Ostrich that Roared," *New York Times*, September 4, 1999, B2, quoting Henry Lee, the managing director of Hendale Asia, based in Hong Kong.

21 The weaker claim, that deregulated markets are better than socialism, blocks discussion of mixed economies only when it imports the strong, untenable version.

22 For example, people are free to go to college in the United States, but their actual access to a particular college is contingent not simply on their own efforts (measured imperfectly by such measures as their grades in high school) but on where they live, parental income, racial and other identity factors, and so on. The problem is not that people lack *identical* opportunities: it is impossible to put everyone in a differentiated system in the equivalent position. Rather, the problem is that most people lack agency that is on par with that of the market – an equivalent *agency* that would allow them to control their position.

23 All complex systems require some version of bureaucratic administration. For a strong defense of its democratic value, see Paul du Gay, *In Praise of Bureaucracy: Weber, Organization, Ethics* (London: Sage, 2000). Du Gay is particularly eloquent on Weber's insistence that bureaucracy be separated from politics.

24 I use the term "unburdened agency" because I don't think individual agency has a positive content that can be applied in a general way. I do not use the term "free agency," for example, because I don't think individual agency can be unrestricted, open, unconditioned, or undetermined within the systems in which it inevitably operates.

25 Policy makers, professionals, pundits, and sometimes the general population have an extremely hard time taking individual self-descriptions at face value. One of the major jobs of expert knowledge is to distrust personal statements and provide allegedly more public and objective languages to describe it. Expert knowledge systematically burdens individuality as it enters public systems, forcing this

individuality to express itself in reductive languages. We support this process by assuming that people are so biased in favor of themselves that we can trust little that they say about themselves. Workplace performance reviews generally come from supervisors and not candidates, because the supervisor is thought to be more objective about the candidate's performance than the candidate. Psychotherapy has a hard time taking the client's self-descriptions at face value, or deepening their insight without showing they mean something like the opposite of what their user thought. The "client-centered" therapy of Carl Rogers and others has little credence among theorists. In the academic humanities, critical theory is equally cynical about individual self-description, given its legitimate and illuminating concerns with the subject's entrenched narcissism, the workings of the unconscious, the operations of aggression and power, and the treachery of language, among many others.

26 All persons have an unconscious. Their motives and desires will be opaque and confusing even to them. All signals have noise. Interpretation will always be necessary, and interpretation will not be "rational" or generalizable. Transparency and linear control will *never* take place. The unburdened agent will never have the feeling of unconditioned sovereignty. But these are the inevitable features of complexity and translation; they are already the conditions of all transmitted agency.

27 Samuel R. Delany, *Times Square Red, Times Square Blue* (New York: New York University Press, 1999). For a parallel treatment of redevelopment and sexual repression, see Michael Warner, *The Trouble with Normal: Sex, Politics, and the Ethics of Queer Life* (New York: The Free Press, 1999), especially chapter 4. Warner's advocacy of "sexual autonomy," his calls for sex's public elaboration, his sense of the value of variation, and his analysis of shame as a repressive force overlap with Delany's perspective.

28 "Another point that people lose track of: Public sex situations are not Dionysian and uncontrolled but are rather some of the most highly socialized and conventionalized behavior human beings can take part in" (Delany, *Times Square Red*, 158).

29 Delany, *Times Square Red*, 45–6.

30 Here I am following psychologist Silvan Tomkins, who defines interest as a positive affect whose orientation is "track, look, listen." Interest is a fundamental reflex – prior, for Tomkins, to drives – that opens the self to the world and enables all intellectual and perceptual development. "The function of this very general positive affect," he writes, "is to 'interest' the human being in what *is necessary* and in what it is *possible* for him to be interested in" (*Affect, Imagery, Consciousness*, 1:337, 342). Tomkins continues: "For some time now, both Psychoanalysis and Behaviorism have regarded interest as a secondary phenomenon, a derivative of the drives, as though one could be interested

only in what gave or promised drive satisfaction. We have turned this argument upside down. It is interest or excitement . . . which is primary, and the drives are secondary. . . . Excitement, rather than being a derivative of drives, is the major source of drive amplification" (1:342). (See also *Shame and Its Sisters: A Silvan Tomkins Reader*, ed. Eve Kosofsky Sedgwick and Adam Frank (Durham: Duke University Press, 1995), 75–6.

31 Delany, *Times Square Red*, 122.

32 As I discuss these terms, I'm going to contrast them in a way that Delany explicitly warns against. I heed his warning that "we must not let [their] opposition sediment onto some absolute, transcendent, or ontological level that it cannot command" (*Times Square Red*, 129). Contact and networking coexist, overlap, and regularly work together, and there are times when they cannot be told apart. My goal is not to replace networking with contact, but to help make visible the features of contact in a society in which it tends to be absorbed or trivialized by networking.

33 Delany, *Times Square Red*, 123.

34 Delany is recounting a bit of "SF folklore" about Ray Bradbury's random encounter with Christopher Isherwood in a bookstore, who then helped launch Bradbury's career (*Times Square Red* 134–5).

35 Delany, *Times Square Red*, 129.

36 Delany begins the book's second essay, ". . . Three, Two, One, Contact: Times Square Red," in this way: "The primary thesis underlying my several arguments here is that, given the mode of capitalism under which we live, life is at its most rewarding, productive, and pleasant when large numbers of people understand, appreciate, and seek out interclass contact and communication conducted in a mode of general good will" (*Times Square Red*, 111).

37 Toni Cade Bambara, "On the Issue of Roles," *The Black Woman: An Anthology*, ed. Toni Cade Bambara (New York: New American Library, 1970), 109.

38 Jean-Paul Sartre, "Introduction," *Les Temps Modernes* 1 (October 1945); cited in Arthur Hirsh, *The French New Left: A History and Overview* (Montréal: Black Rose Books, 1982), 42.

39 Alaine Touraine, *Return of the Actor: Social Theory in Postindustrial Society*, trans. Myrna Godzich (Minneapolis: University of Minnesota Press, 1988), 81.

Part II

States, Citizenship, Rights

This analytic represents the emergence of research questions that force a rethinking of the state form, the citizens with which it engages and the rights it claims to guarantee, through an emphasis on the performative nature of subjectivity that focuses on the construction of new subjects in the contested interstices between law and society. It also marks the emergence of debates and conversations distinct from those informed by concerns with conceptions of the state's obligations to its citizens, the growth of bureaucracy and prescriptive regulation, and critiques of the shift from citizen to client in the clientelist state. While earlier work often implicitly conceived a maternal state as it examined contradictions, ambiguities, and contests over providing education, welfare, and services, more recent work has emphasized technologies of discipline in a carceral and punitive state. The articles in this analytic might usefully be viewed, in effect, as emphatic additions to the critique of an abstract, disembodied notion of citizenship and a state that responds dispassionately to each abstract citizen. From Peggy Pascoe's account of US states' control during the nineteenth century over the inheritance of property through statutes forbidding not just intermarriage, but unions between white women and men of color, to the articles by Leti Volpp and Moustafa Bayoumi on the racial profiling and denial of citizenship rights to groups held suspect by US officials after the 9/11 terror attacks, these articles attest to the importance of the role of the state in determining who possesses the right to have rights.

These articles critique the assumption of a free, rational subject/citizen participating in the public sphere, and remind us forcefully that, to paraphrase Volpp, not all citizens are equal. Citizenship, as the outcome of state processes of inclusion and exclusion, is highly contingent. In the United States, citizenship, in terms of life chances and the ability to exercise political and social rights of equal protection and opportunity, while substantially revised from the original republic of white male property owners, has always been limited by race and gender, notwithstanding occasional claims of a color-blind constitution. If the state is the mechanism of enforcement, marking the boundaries between citizens and noncitizens, and enacting sovereignty, the American nation – and nationalism – derives from the affective ideological union of those who, by virtue of the inherently racial understanding of citizenship rooted in our origins as a slave society, often cannot imagine themselves as citizens without denying others that status.

Laura Doyle's article locates the origins of the modern West's exclusionary, racialized notion of liberty and freedom in the seventeenth-century Atlantic world. Without discounting the slave trade and establishment of New World slavery as crucibles of modern racism, Doyle argues that Anglo-Atlantic literature and the work of such philosophers as Rousseau and Hegel identified freedom and liberty as the racial characteristic of Saxon peoples. The characterization of the internecine strife leading to the formation of the English nation as racial conflict provided a crucial blueprint for the racialized practices of citizenship taken up by the other articles in this analytic.

These articles suggest that the distinction between the state (as enforcer of laws of inclusion and exclusion) and the nation (as civic belief system), though analytically necessary, goes only so far. Racist constructions of the nation are enacted by state policy. Mae Ngai argues that immigration restrictions have been essential to twentieth-century ideas about and practices of citizenship, race, and the nation-state. Examining the construction of new subjects in the constitution of both the illegal alien and the white US citizen, Ngai demonstrates that the consensus for state policies of immigration restriction legislation during the 1920s rested on eugenics theories, and policy-makers' desire to maintain the integrity of a "white American race." Leti Volpp examines racial profiling and the wave of hate violence that developed in the wake of the attacks of September 11, 2001, and argues that the tragedy facilitated the consolidation of a new identity category that groups those who appear "Middle-Eastern, Arab, or Muslim." Suggesting that "citizenship is made of four distinct discourses – citizenship as former legal status, as rights, as political activity, and as identity/solidarity, she analyzes the shifting and multiple definitions and dimensions of citizenship within the power triangle of sovereignty, discipline, and government. Asking who is the disappeared and who is the "us" in US, Volpp argues that we need to start from the perspective that power both subordinates and constitutes one as a subject, and think of citizenship as a process of interpellation. Peggy Pascoe's analysis of state statutes criminalizing racial intermarriage suggests the state's role in consolidating property and providing for its orderly transmission from whites to whites. Through the mechanism of anti-intermarriage laws, as well as federal fugitive slave acts, which affirmed the property rights of slaveowning and nonslaveholding whites at the expense of the citizenship rights of free and enslaved blacks, the US State was a powerful exponent of racial capitalism. In a property owner's republic founded on chattel slavery, the state was merely reflecting and affirming the importance of being white for the possession of personal freedom.

Moustafa Bayoumi examines the legal history of the combination of Islam and immigration in the United States between 1909 and 1944 to cast a critical historical eye on the racing of religion in the post 9/11 era, and the special registration laws directed at people from disparate countries, united by little but that they were all Muslim majority nations. In a series of immigration cases in the first half of the twentieth century, while many relied on ocular proof alone to determine race, others were decided by claims of innate and immutable differences between the "Mohammedan world" and "the predominately Christian peoples of Europe." In "racing" religion through the legal mechanism of the state, special registration laws of 2002 reinscribed the cultural assumption that the terrorist is Muslim, foreign born, an alien in the United States, and that all Muslim men fitting this profile are potential terrorists.

Lauren Berlant examines the development of "infantile citizenship," characterized by a relationship of degraded dependency of the citizen on the state. Emphasizing the transnational conditions under which the nation becomes a more intense object of concern and struggle, Berlant examines the heteronormative public culture – elaborated across juridical, economic, and aesthetic projects – promoted by exponents of Reagan-era conservatism. Articulating a false narrative of ex-privileged heterosexuality, and obsessed with the private realm of family, intimate relationships, and religious and moral values, conservatives coupled citizenship and suffering by defining a citizen as a person traumatized by some aspect of sexual unease, racial discord, and economic insecurity in the United States. Countering the narrow and distorted version of citizenship analyzed by Berlant, Christopher Newfield's article seeks to empower critics of the dominant ideology of neoliberalism to reclaim the idea of freedom from conservative, market-based definitions. Seeking to understand the widespread demoralization and feelings of powerlessness in people who are formally and technically empowered, Newfield argues that markets unmodified by society undermine the personal agency that is critical for liberty and democracy. Challenging neoliberals' equation of unregulated commercial markets and political democracy and the claim that markets promote individual freedom, Newfield outlines a project of recouping citizenship as participation and agency.

14

Domestic Life in the Diggings

Susan Lee Johnson

"I have heard of Miners at some diggins subsisting for days on Acorns of which we have a very fine kind in this Country," Helen Nye wrote to her mother in 1853. Nye, a Massachusetts-born white woman whose husband was a merchant at Don Pedro's Bar in Tuolumne County, went on to explain how immigrant men learned to make use of the oak tree's bounty: "The Indians make great account of gathering [acorns] for their winter store." Newcomers to the Sierra Nevada foothills watched the autumn harvest with interest. And though they preferred to purchase rather than hunt for or gather their own provisions, in hard times, and especially on prospecting tours, they might follow Miwok practices. While looking for new diggings in Tuolumne County during November of 1849, for example, William Miller and his Anglo companions baked acorns for supper, and a few days later, farther south in Mariposa County, the clergyman Daniel Woods and his prospecting party boiled a kettle of acorns with a bit of venison for their evening meal. In general, though, Gold Rush immigrants saw the food that Miwoks most valued as something to be eaten only in dire circumstances. As Charles Davis explained to his daughter in 1852, while acorns, grass, and wild oats abounded in the Sierra foothills, "these serve for Wild Indians and Wild Animals."[1]

As Davis's disdain for Miwok sustenance suggests, cooking and eating could be sites of contestation, as well as of communion, in the Southern Mines. That was because culinary practices fit into a larger constellation of activities in the diggings that signaled for many a world of confusion – men mending trousers and caring for the sick, Anglos dining on acorns and frijoles.

Edmund Booth captured one aspect of that confusion when he complained to his wife in 1850, "Cal. is a world upside down – nothing like home comforts and home joys." Booth was a New Englander by birth and an Iowan by migration, and he wrote to his wife, Mary Ann, from the Tuolumne County town of Sonora. He lived at a boardinghouse there kept by a young Mexican man and two African American men from Florida. Edmund told Mary Ann that his daily routine began when he awoke from a night's sleep on the bare ground, rolled up his blankets, and sat down to a breakfast of coffee, meat, butter cakes, and applesauce. Then he walked half a mile below the town to the diggings. "The evening passes," he wrote, "in reading, talking, thinking of home, or as I am now – writing." Booth stayed in towns and at boarding-houses more frequently than did many placer miners, perhaps in part because he was deaf and thus lived most safely in densely populated communities of hearing people.[2] But if Booth's privations were less severe than those of most gold seekers, what did he mean when he complained to his wife about the absence of "home comforts and home joys"? Why did California in the 1850s seem like a world standing on its head?

To answer these questions, one must ponder the multiple meanings of such common activities as eating acorns, digging gold, thinking of home, and inhabiting a race or a gender.[3] Even in so short a time as the Gold Rush years and even in so small a place as the Southern Mines, meanings proliferated, evolved, collided. By attending to daily life in the diggings – to the work people did to maintain and enrich themselves and to the ways they filled the rest of their Gold Rush hours – one can begin to comprehend why so short a time was so transformative and why so small a place was so volatile. While native people in the Southern Mines lived in communities with roughly equal numbers of women and men, among immigrant peoples, skewed sex ratios meant drastically altered divisions of labor in which men took on tasks that their womenfolk would have performed back home. Analyzing how immigrant men parceled out such work and how they thought about what they were doing shows us much about the content of gender in the Gold Rush.[4] [. . .]

Skewed sex ratios in the diggings were accompanied by an extraordinary demographic diversity: people came to California from many parts of the world, producing and reproducing ideas about color, culture, and nation that, on US soil, often coalesced into conversations about race.[5] Race, like gender, is a changing set of ideas about human difference and hierarchy, and a relation in which those ideas are put into practice. In Gold Rush California, its meanings pulsed through everyday life like an erratic heartbeat. For instance, the way that certain tasks, such as cooking or laundry, came to be associated with particular groups of non-Anglo American men demonstrates how constructions of race could be mapped onto constructions of gender in the diggings.[6]

Not everyone in the Southern Mines dug gold, but everyone did perform, or relied on others who performed, life-sustaining and life-enhancing tasks such as procuring provisions, preparing meals, and providing companionship. Since few could reproduce in California the divisions of labor that made the performance of these tasks seem more or less predictable and culturally coherent back home, Gold Rush participants devised new ways to provide for their needs and wants. But all the while they wondered and worried about what it meant, for example, that Anglo men were down on their knees scrubbing their shirts in a stream, that Mexican women were making money hand over fist selling tortillas on the streets of Sonora, or that French men seemed so good at creating homey cabins in the diggings.

Distinguishing between two kinds of work – domestic and personal service work, on the one hand, and work in the mines, on the other – may seem to reify categories of labor. Surely placer mining sustained and enhanced human life as much as baking bread or caring for the sick did. In making such distinctions, one invokes the discursive division between home and the workplace that accompanied the growth of industrial capitalism in the nineteenth century, especially in the northeastern and urban United States. One also echoes more recent Marxist-feminist delineations of productive and reproductive labor, which have placed "reproductive" chores (often women's work) on a par with those "productive" chores (often men's work) assumed to constitute true economic activity. But impulses similar to those that split home life off from labor in the nineteenth century – impulses scrutinized by twentieth-century feminists – also led most Gold Rush participants to view mining as qualitatively different from and more important than their other daily tasks. This makes intuitive sense, especially since immigrants traveled hundreds or thousands of miles to dig gold or to profit from those who did. Yet performing this privileged activity required that miners pay attention to the exigencies of everyday life. And, in fact, evidence shows that gold seekers paid great heed to their more immediate desires – for shelter, for food, for company, for pleasure, for some way to make sense of what was for most a novel situation. [. . .] So the distinction, drawn here between mining labor and domestic and personal service work is at once heuristic *and* grounded in some, but not all, relevant historical circumstances.[7]

In the end, though, the distinction serves yet another purpose. During the 1980s, historians learned to use poststructuralist analyses of language that show how binary oppositions work – oppositions such as the one between productive and reproductive labor. In the productive/reproductive labor distinction, for example, the leading term (productive or "breadwinning" work) takes primacy, while its partner (reproductive or "domestic" work) is weaker or derivative. This hierarchical relation mirrors some social relations of dominance and subordination based on gender and race. So foregrounding reproductive or domestic labor in a history of a mining area, where mining labor might be assumed to take precedence, is itself a gesture toward unsettling that hierarchical relation.[8]

[. . .]

One of the first needs immigrants had to meet was that for shelter.

By far the most common material Gold Rush immigrants used for shelter was canvas, and this may have been even more true in the Southern Mines than in the Northern Mines. When J. D. Borthwick, a Scottish artist and writer, toured the diggings in 1852 and 1853, he noted that in the north, "log cabins and frame houses were the rule, and canvas the exception; while in the southern mines the reverse was the case."[9] Winters farther south were milder, which accounts for some of the difference, and the persistence of placer mining – which characterized the southern region throughout the 1850s and which necessarily encouraged transience – may explain it as well. Placer miners were always on the move, taking up new claims when old ones gave out or situating themselves near riverbeds during the dry months and on smaller creeks in the rainy season; they relocated so often that "vamos the ranch" was often the first "Spanish" English-speaking miners learned.[10]

Though most did live in canvas homes, the word "tent" actually described a wide variety of structures. Some people lived in cramped quarters, such as the Chinese men Borthwick saw in 1852, the first year of mass Chinese immigration to California, and who were organized "in a perfect village of small tents." Likewise, the Pennsylvanian Enos Christman shared with two others a nine-foot-square dwelling that ran up to a ridge pole in the center. [. . .][11] Tents like these were not only small; they also offered little protection. John Doble's canvas home in Calaveras County got damp with every rainfall, and, since it had no fastenings, camp dogs ran in and out with impunity, sometimes carrying off mouthfuls of provisions.[12]

So when miners stayed still for any length of time, they built more elaborate shelters. For instance, although the Belgian Jean-Nicolas Perlot and his five French companions lived at first in a small tent and a brush hut, within a year the four men who remained in partnership built a typical structure, "a sort of cabin of tree trunks, topped with canvas to form [a roof] composed of two tightly stretched pieces of canvas, one six inches above the other."[13] Such canvas-topped cabins were ubiquitous in the Southern Mines. In them, immigrants could set up rough bedsteads and construct fireplaces, though at least two Anglo men remembered how improvised chimneys forced smoke into their living quarters instead of drawing it out.[14] Heavy rain could impair the draft of even a well-built fireplace, and Welsh-born Angus McIsaac, situated near Mariposa, noted in his diary that men living with such irritants often compared their smoky cabins to scolding wives or leaky ships.

[. . .]

For the most part miners fended for themselves. Once they constructed cabins or pitched tents, inhabitants had to organize domestic labor such that all stayed reasonably well fed and healthy. By far the preponderance of evidence about camp life describes the subsistence strategies of Anglo

American men – particularly diary-writing northerners. Still, a handful of sources generated by French- and Spanish-speaking immigrants, as well as descriptions of non-Anglo camps by Anglo writers, help round out the picture of daily sustenance in the diggings. Then too, multiethnic, multiracial tents and cabins were by no means rare in the Southern Mines, and white men who worked in partnership with men of color, for example, sometimes left a record of shared domestic duties.

Probably the most common type of household in the Southern Mines during the boom years of the Gold Rush was that of two to five men who constituted an economic unit: they worked together in placer claims held by household members, alternating tasks and placing the gold in a common fund from which they purchased food and other necessities. Profits, when there were any, were divided among the partners.[15] But such households were not universal. Often the men of several cabins would band together, for example, to dam a river and work its bed. In this case, domestic concerns were the province of the cabinmates, while the larger group distributed the proceeds of labor in the diggings. Likewise, a household might include members who worked separately and did not pool resources, but did share household tasks and provisions. The variations on these themes were endless, and the unpredictability of placer claims meant that a miner might find himself in a variety of domestic situations over the course of a year or two in California. At times he might even end up, as Anglos put it, "on his own hook," mining and tenting alone. But most men spent a good deal of time living and working in cooperation with other gold seekers.[16]

These generalizations probably hold for most white men, both North American and European, and most free African Americans during the Gold Rush. It is likely that they hold for a large number of Mexican and Chilean and perhaps some Chinese men as well. But for those North Americans, Latin Americans, and early-arriving Chinese who went to California under conditions of slavery, debt peonage, or contract labor, other domestic arrangements may have obtained. And whenever women of any background were present in the camps or whenever men lived in or near towns with boardinghouses and restaurants, daily subsistence was a different matter.

All types of households in the Southern Mines, save those of Miwoks, relied on tenuous market relations to supply most of their basic needs. (In time, even Miwoks would turn to the market for many provisions.) Out in the camps, men traded in gold dust for provisions at the nearest store, generally a tent or cabin located a fair hike

from home and stocked with freight hauled overland to
the mines from Stockton.[17] In the first year of the Gold
Rush, some goods came straight from Mexico, as
merchants in northern Sonora emptied their shelves
and hurried their wares on pack animals to the mines.
Rancheros from southern California also bypassed the new
trade routes, driving their cattle directly to the diggings
and reaping healthy profits.[18] But Stockton was a conduit
for most trade goods. Beef, pork, beans, flour, potatoes,
and coffee ranked high on miners' lists of provisions
purchased. In flush times, they might also be able to buy
onions, dried apples, or a head of cabbage, though fresh
fruits and vegetables were the hardest items to find.[19]

Limited foodstuffs spelled monotonous meals for
most, but also encouraged people to exchange cooking
techniques. Men from Europe and the United States, for
example, sometimes adopted Mexican practices. Perlot and
his French companions, en route to the mines in 1851
and low on provisions, met a party of Mexicans who were
eating what looked to Perlot like turnips dipped in salt
and pepper, fresh tortillas, and hearty beefsteaks cooked
on sticks over an open flame. The Mexican men gave Perlot
some raw meat, and he returned with it to his own
party's fire, proclaiming, "Messieurs . . . in this country,
this is how beefsteak is cooked."[20] Howard Gardiner,
a Long Islander, was less enthusiastic about the
Mexican-style foods he learned to prepare during lean
times, recalling that he and his partners lived "more like
pigs than human beings." But those meals based around
pinole, a fine flour of parched corn that had been
pounded in a mortar, sustained him until he was able to
buy what seemed to him more appropriate Anglo fare.[21]
While not all English-speaking miners were as disdain-
ful as Gardiner was, the contrast between Perlot's and
Gardiner's responses to Mexican dishes would be echoed
in later conflicts between Anglo Americans, on the one
hand, and Spanish- and French-speaking immigrants,
on the other. Just as Gold Rush shelters took on gendered
meanings, so too could Gold Rush food become racialized in its procurement, preparation, or consumption –
recall Charles Davis's comment about fare that was fit only
for "Wild Indians and Wild Animals."

[. . .]

[Many] miners tried to supplement store-bought provisions by hunting and fishing, and a few gathered greens
in the hills or planted small gardens. Not all who hunted
met with success. Moses Little managed to bring down
some quail just in time for Christmas dinner during

the lean winter of 1852, but he spent most of his shot at
target practice. Timothy Osborn, another white New
Englander, and his cabinmates were similarly ineffective
in late 1851 despite the abundance of deer, antelope, and
bear near their Tuolumne County camp. They depended
instead on neighboring Texans, "genuine backwoods-men,"
to supply them with venison.[22] William Miller had better
luck. He and his fellow white partners were camped
near a group of free black men in the fall of 1849, and in
addition to coming together to dam the river and work
its bed, the two parties went out deer hunting with one
another and otherwise shared provisions. Heavy rains foiled
the plans of the damming company, but the African and
Anglo American residents of the camp continued to
exchange gifts of fresh venison. By Christmas, one of the
black men, Henry Garrison, had moved into Miller's
tent, and all parties spent the holiday together indulging
in a "Splendid Dinner" and dancing to the music of
Garrison's fine fiddle playing.[23]

Fewer men planted gardens or gathered greens. So
visitors were astonished by Perlot's singular store of
herbs and vegetables. After serving salad to an incredulous miner in the mid-1850s, Perlot took him on a
stroll: "I led him a hundred paces from the house . . . where
I gathered chervil; a few steps farther to a place where cress
was growing well . . . ; a little farther, I found lamb's
lettuce," and so on. One of Perlot's partners, the French
Louvel, had planted the garden the year before. On
seeing it, the newcomer exclaimed, "My God, . . . how
stupid can you be! to suffer four years as I have, without
having had an idea as simple as that."[24] A few others had
that same idea. William Miller planted cabbage and
onions in 1849; the preacher Woods put in potatoes,
turnips, and cabbage the next spring; and the following
year A. W. Genung cultivated two acres from which he
boasted he could raise a thousand dollars worth of
vegetables – a claim that had as much to do with their
scarcity and high price in the diggings as with his
confidence as a gardener.[25]

Still, most immigrant men suffered from the dietary
deficiencies created by their ignorance of the wild plants
that Miwok women gathered and by their unwillingness
to grow more familiar crops. Perhaps they hesitated to
plant vegetables because their campsites were temporary
or because kitchen gardens were generally women's
responsibility back home. Whatever the reason, their
reluctance made them sick. George Evans, for example,
could not fathom why he was too ill to work in the mines
during the winter of 1850, until doctors told him he had
scurvy: "They advised me to get all the vegetables

afforded by these hills." So he had friends gather what looked to him like wild cabbage and onions, and he bought some Irish potatoes and a bottle of lime juice. Within two days, his health took a clear turn for the better.[26]

Evans, given his condition, was wise to eat his vegetables raw, but miners cooked most of their food and had to determine among themselves how to share culinary duties. What evidence exists about such divisions of labor reveals more about Anglo American men than other Gold Rush participants, but Europeans and free African Americans, at least, seem to have followed similar practices. The Belgian Perlot claimed, in fact, that most men in the diggings organized cooking in like fashion: "The rule generally observed between miners in partnership . . . was to do the cooking by turns of a week." Similarly, John Doble explained to a correspondent, "sometimes one does the cooking and sometimes another and one only cooks at a time and cooks for all who are in the Cabin." Moses Little approved of this common arrangement: "As we take turns to do the cooking we shall know how things are done."[27]

Indeed, there were many things to do. A man's "cook week" began on Sunday, when he prepared for the days ahead, as Little recorded: "It being my week to cook I have been somewhat busy – more so than on other Sabbath – Coffee to burn A box full of nuts to fry Bread to bake & Beef to cut up & take care of." George Allen's Sunday journal entries note a similar round of tasks – boiling meat, making bread, stewing grapes, cooking rice and beans, frying doughnuts, baking apple pie and bread pudding. During the week, the cook continued to make large quantities of staple foods like bread and beans, in addition to getting up three meals a day. Little, for example, described his evenings as punctuated by the rhythm of domestic duties: "I sit & mended a shirt while my bread is baking & my Beef boiling"; and two nights later, "I am writing My Beans are stewing & Bread baking."[28] The days around New Year's 1850 must have been the cook week of Henry Garrison, the African American fiddle player who lived with William Miller and his dancing partners, because Miller's journal for that period is filled with references to Garrison cooking breakfast, making apple pudding ("the Best Pudding I had Eaten Since Leaving home," Miller wrote), and stirring up a "Beautiful Stew" of squirrel meat. Miller must have looked forward to Garrison's cook weeks, because at least one of his other partners had trouble even lighting a fire, to say nothing of preparing meals for the men.[29] Domestic competence was hardly universal in the diggings, but men valued it when they found it among their comrades.

[. . .]

Anglos did occasionally write about Chinese men, who arrived in the Southern Mines in large numbers toward the end of the boom years of the Gold Rush. But white observers were more apt to note how odd they found Chinese foods, cookware, and eating implements than to describe how Chinese men divided up domestic work. Borthwick, the Scottish traveler, visited Chinese camps in both the Northern and the Southern mines, and claimed that Chinese men "treated in the same hospitable manner" all those who approached them. On each visit, Chinese miners invited Borthwick to eat with them, but the traveler declined, finding their dishes "clean" but "dubious" in appearance. He added that he much preferred "to be a spectator," a role chosen by many a white man in his dealings with Chinese miners. The spectacle Borthwick described was that of a Chinese camp at dinnertime, with men "squatted on the rocks in groups of eight or ten round a number of curious little black pots and dishes, from which they helped themselves with their chopsticks."[30] Borthwick's word picture evoked white men's visions of the Chinese; there was something both delicate and animal-like in the circle of squatting Chinese and their curious cookware. While his words said as much about white visions as about Chinese practices, they did suggest that Chinese miners working in large parties broke into smaller groups of men who shared meals and that they used cooking and eating utensils from their homeland.

Some white men were more gracious than Borthwick when invited to join Chinese circles. John Marshall Newton was camped with a partner near five hundred Chinese miners in Tuolumne County in 1852. After helping the Chinese secure their title to a claim that had been challenged by English miners, Newton fancied himself a "hero" in his neighbors' eyes. The Chinese men did bring him plates of "rice flavored with sweetmeats" and other small gifts. They also invited him for meals, a practice Newton described with nostalgic flavor and a dash of exoticism: "many a pleasant dinner have I had eating their outlandish dishes." No doubt the Chinese miners appreciated Newton's assistance in what often proved for them an inhospitable local world. But however much they credited his actions, they also relished making him the butt of dinnertime jokes. Invariably when Newton sat down to eat, someone would hand him chopsticks. "Of course I could do nothing with them," Newton remembered, and so "the whole 500 seeing my awkwardness would burst out into loud laughter."[31]

To the Chinese miners, their neighbor must have looked a bit like an overgrown child fumbling with his food. Still, despite this momentary, ritual reversal of a dynamic in which Anglo American men disproportionately held the power and resources necessary to ensure survival in the diggings, more often Chinese men found it expedient to curry favor with whites. In a situation where white men missed more than anything "home comforts and home joys," Chinese men could turn Anglo American longings to their advantage. Indeed, although Newton sometimes offered his Chinese neighbors cups of coffee, neither he nor other white men whose personal accounts are readily accessible left behind evidence of having shared their own meals with Chinese miners; the dinner invitations flew in one direction, from the Chinese to their Anglo neighbors. Howard Gardiner, for example, the one who loathed Mexican foods, lived for a time by himself near the tent of a Chinese man. Sometimes Gardiner would stay late working on his claim, and when he went home, he recalled, "I found that the Celestial had preceded me and prepared supper."[32] Gardiner's neighbor must have found some benefit in looking after the white man. Meanwhile, for Gardiner the arrangement seemed so unremarkable – so familiar, perhaps – that he granted it only passing mention. In everyday events like these, where men of color performed tasks white men associated with white women, Gold Rush race relations became gender relations as well.

[. . .]

California *was*, for many, a "world upside down." Even in hotels and restaurants, all the help might be male. When Hinton Rowan Helper – who would soon be known as a southern critic of slavery but who first took aim at California – passed through Sonora and breakfasted there, he noted that the male proprietor and two male workers cleared the table. "Women have no hand in these domestic affairs," he exclaimed. "There is not a female about the establishment." In case the reader missed the point, he added, "All the guests, owners and employees are men." (The breakfast was dull, too – pork, beans, and flapjacks.)[33] The future governor Lucius Fairchild himself became such an employee for a time and felt compelled to explain the situation to his family: "Now in the states you would think that a person . . . was broke if you saw him acting the part of *hired Girl*. . . . but here it is nothing, for all kinds of men do all kinds of work." Besides, he went on, "I call *bob around the table*, saying 'tea or Coffee Sir.' about as fast as most *hombres*."

Although Fairchild insisted it all meant nothing in California, his explanation suggested that it meant a great deal – white men bobbing around tables waiting on other white men. If he could act the part with such enthusiasm, did gender and race have less to do with bodies and essences than with performing tasks and gestures? No doubt Fairchild thought he could tell a "natural" hired girl from one just "acting the part." But the anxiety such situations produced could be striking. Fairchild, for example, compared his own performance not to that of "real" women but to that of other *hombres* – as if the English word might not adequately insist upon his own essential manhood.[34]

[. . .]

In the diggings, too, non-Anglo men provided many of the services the largely male population wanted. Helen Nye, the white woman whose husband was a merchant at Don Pedro's Bar, was in a good position to keep track of the demand, in particular, for non-Anglo cooks. Her home on the Tuolumne River was also a boardinghouse, but she did not prepare the meals. In letters to her mother and sisters, Nye explained her absence from the kitchen in a variety of ways. Once she intimated that her husband and a boarder had decided to hire a French cook, seemingly over her objections. On another occasion, she wrote that although she wanted to help out, "about all who hire as Cooks prefer to do the whole and have the regular price." In yet another letter, she complained that the cook Florentino had "left in a kind of sulky fit" and that his job landed in her hands: "I found it was too much as it kept me on my feet all the day." "If we were a private family I should prefer to do it," she reasoned, but keeping a boardinghouse was a different matter. The shifting ground of Nye's explanation suggests that she worried about what her female relatives might think of her circumstances. Whether or not Nye herself wanted to stay out of the kitchen, the male cooks kept on coming. Florentino got over his fit and returned to Don Pedro's Bar, and he was preceded and followed by others – a fellow named Scippio, for example, and an African American man whom Nye, in spite of her stated wish to help with the cooking, disliked because he worked slowly, forcing her to assist. And although she implied that her husband made hiring decisions, she once revealed her own hand in the process by writing to her sister, "I think I shall try a Chinese cook next they are generally liked."[35] Nye's compulsion to explain her relationship to domestic duties – like Fairchild's to explain his – and her inconsistent descriptions indicate that novel divisions of labor could unsettle notions of womanliness as well as manliness. What *did* it mean for a white woman to turn over cooking to a black man, a French man, a Chinese man? For a Chilean *patrón* to wait tables alongside his *peónes*?

It was confusing – the way that gender relations, race relations, and labor relations coursed into and out of customary channels in California, here carving gullies out of hard ground, there flowing in familiar waterways, whereby women waited on men, darker-skinned people served lighter-skinned people, and a few held control over the labor of many. Beyond food preparation, other kinds of domestic and personal service work became sites of such confusion. This was especially true of laundry and sewing as well as the care of convalescing men, activities that were often gendered female in immigrants' homelands.

Washing and mending clothes was an endless preoccupation for miners, who spent much of their time shoveling dirt, sand, and gravel. Out in remote camps, men did their own laundry in rivers and streams. Although most left no record of using anything but water to clean their clothes, some used a plant of the lily family, the bulb of which has the properties of soap. John Doble may have learned this trick from a native man who stopped to wash his pants, shirt, and vest at the river where Doble was working. Likewise, Mrs. Lee Whipple-Haslam recalled that Indians taught her mother to use the soap plant, while the French journalist Derbec claimed that Mexican men often made use of such bulbs.[36] Like ways of cooking, washing techniques could be shared across the various populations in the diggings. In this, native peoples and those from nearby held a premium on knowledge of how best to use the local environment.

Miners, particularly Anglos, did their laundry on Saturday afternoon, after half a day of work in the mines, or else on Sunday. Some found that digging gold was such dirty work that they had to wash themselves and their clothes more often, as Leonard Noyes recalled: "every morning we would take a swim, put on our blue drilling pants and shirt work all day in the mud go home at noon. Jump into the water wash mud off, put on our flannels and let our cloathes dry while we got dinner – at night go through the same motions." It must have been a common scene in the diggings – men bathing naked together in the river and walking about camp in flannel drawers, trousers draped over bushes and drying in the sun. Some men hated the work – both Enos Christman

and Howard Gardiner called laundry "detestable" – but others seemed to revel in the washing-and-bathing ritual. Timothy Osborn, in particular, looked forward to his Saturday afternoon plunge into the slow, deep waters of the Merced River, allowing himself to be drawn out into a swift current that whirled him downstream until rapids forced him to scamper up the bank and return to his friends.[37]

If washing and bathing proved a site of homosocial bonds among some Anglo American men, so too did sewing. Although John Doble moaned to a female correspondent about the task – "One thing troubles us old Bachelors sorely and that is mending our clothes" – others recorded the repair of shirts, pants, and socks without complaint. Most knew that sewing was work that could be done while beans were boiling or friends were "spinning long yarns," and it also passed the time when sickness or bad weather confined miners to their tents.[38] Some even elevated the care of clothing to a moral imperative, as did William Miller when he wrote in his diary, "I am sorry to say there is one in my Camp who... chooses to Lay Down and Sleep rather then mend his Cloths, or eaven wash them... he does not Improve his time as he Should." But it was the Reverend Woods who articulated the gendered meanings that some men could not help attaching to their rainy-day sewing circles. In January of 1850 Woods wrote, "In our visits to each other these days, like the ladies at home, we often take our sewing with us. Today I took a pair of stockings to darn, one of my shoes to mend, and the 'Democratic Review' to read. While we plied our needles, our tongues were equally busy speaking of mutual friends and hopes."[39] Busy tongues and needles, mutual friends and hopes – these were intimate terms for an everyday task shared among miners.

Still, while some seemed to enjoy such scenes, many jumped at the chance to turn over the care of personal belongings to someone else.

[. . .]

Usually, laundry establishments were sites of benign interactions, but ones nonetheless that bespoke some of the social hierarchies of the Gold Rush. Non-Anglo men joined Mexican women in the laundry business. In particular, those men who were subject to systematic harassment as miners, such as the Chinese, worked in washhouses, but so did other men of color. An older African American in Calaveras County, for example, ran a laundry as early as 1850. Although free blacks in the diggings did not face the strictures of the foreign miners' tax, they did face countless daily insults and informal prohibitions, which might have encouraged entry into the commercial domestic sphere.[40] Friedrich Gerstäcker recalled that the Calaveras County man charged half the going rate for shirts – twenty-five cents each rather than half a dollar each – and yet "lived exceedingly well by it." The demand for laundry services must have been great, because when Gerstäcker went to pick up his wash at this man's establishment, he found a huge pile of clean but unironed and unmarked shirts, which the proprietor told him to sort through on his own. In frustration, Gerstäcker randomly picked out six wrinkled shirts that he liked. The laundryman, not one to coddle his white customers, just shrugged, "Ebery gen'leman did the same."[41]

As the number of Chinese immigrants to California increased after 1852, and as the state government reinstated a foreign miners' tax (the first tax, imposed in 1850 and directed primarily at Spanish- and French-speaking miners, had been repealed), Chinese men moved into the laundry business.[42] Documentation for how and why Chinese started opening washhouses is frustratingly slim. Most scholars acknowledge that the process began during the Gold Rush and assume that it is explained by the absence of women in California and the harassment that encouraged some Chinese to provide goods and services to miners rather than engaging in mining themselves. Historians argue that both ethnic antagonism and the low capital and equipment requirements of washing accounts for the prevalence of Chinese laundries in California. And they remind readers that washing was women's, not men's, work in South China – that the "'Chinese laundryman' was an American phenomenon."[43]

[...]

Care of the sick proved another kind of work that encouraged men to stretch, twist, invert, or even temporarily abandon customary ideas and practices. If one ignored the near absence of all women save Miwoks in the diggings, one could see much that was familiar. Timothy Osborn thought so: "A mining camp very closely resembles a country village, in its domestic concerns ... sickness ... excites the enquiry of neighbors, and the little exchanges by way of mutual relief is one of the beauties of camp life." William McCollum, a doctor from western New York State, went even further, claiming that the sick and destitute got along better in California than anywhere else in the world: "There is fellow-feeling there, a spirit of active, practical

benevolence." According to McCollum, men made charity offerings for the ill on a scale that matched the extravagance of the Gold Rush itself: "$1000 could be raised easier there ... than $5 in any of our large villages."[44]

Enthusiastic as some men could be about such "fellow-feeling" in 1849 or 1850, those who wrote reminiscences decades later could be positively enraptured. Benjamin Butler Harris, recalling the manly democracy of the diggings (and misquoting Shakespeare) was breathless: "Was this Utopia? Was it the Isle of the Blest? What largeheartedness, what floods, what gushes, what warm glows of friendship and kindness one for the other. One touch of their grand natures made them all akin." In Harris's memory, such male homosocial desire could transcend even racial and ethnic hatred. During the winter of 1849, scurvy was common in the mines. Harris thought the disease was particularly widespread among Mexicans, and he remembered that at one point seven hundred in his camp were "sheltered, doctored, nursed, and maintained by miners' subscriptions alone." Recalling this scene prompted Harris to condemn the "bigot," the "loud-mouthed Pharisee" of the "civilized" world in favor of those "whole-souled pioneers" who constituted "a superior society." Elsewhere Harris's reminiscences are filled with accounts of Mexican and French resistance to the foreign miners' tax, of Indian-immigrant conflicts, of the Australian "flood of scoundrels" that "polluted the mines" (floods could bring danger as well as pleasure), belying his romantic constructions of ubiquitous male harmony in the diggings.[45] But something about the way men cared for one another prompted Osborn and McCollum and then Harris after them to celebrate the manly benevolence they saw manifest in the mines.

[...]

Notes

1 Helen Nye to Mother, Jan. 6, 1853, Helen Nye Letters, Beinecke Library, Yale Univ., New Haven (hereafter cited as Beinecke Library); Journal entry, Nov. 12, 1849, William W. Miller Journal, Beinecke Library; Daniel B. Woods, *Sixteen Months at the Gold Diggings* (London: Sampson Low; New York: Harper and Brothers, [1851]), 86; Charles Davis to Daughter, Jan. 1, 1852, Charles Davis Letters, Beinecke Library.

2 Edmund Booth, *Edmund Booth, Forty-Niner: The Life Story of a Deaf Pioneer* (Stockton, Calif.: San Joaquin Pioneer and Historical Society, 1953), 22, 31, 33.

3 See Denise Riley, "*Am I That Name?*": Feminism and the Category of "Women" in History (Minneapolis: Univ. of

Minnesota Press, 1988), esp. 6; and Evelyn Brooks Higginbotham, "African-American Women's History and the Metalanguage of Race," *Signs* 17, no. 2 (Winter 1992): 251–74, esp. 253–6.

4   See Mary P. Ryan, *Cradle of the Middle Class: The Family in Oneida County, New York, 1790–1865* (Cambridge: Cambridge Univ. Press, 1981); essays collected in J. A. Mangan and James Walvin, eds., *Manliness and Morality: Middle-Class Masculinity in Britain and America, 1800–1940* (Manchester: Manchester Univ. Press, 1987), and Mark C. Carnes and Clyde Griffen, eds., *Meanings for Manhood: Constructions of Masculinity in Victorian America* (Chicago: Univ. of Chicago Press, 1990); E. Anthony Rotundo, *American Manhood: Transformations in Masculinity from the Revolution to the Modern Era* (New York: Basic Books, 1993); George Chauncey, *Gay New York: Gender, Urban Culture, and the Making of the Gay Male World, 1890–1940* (New York: Basic Books, 1994); and Gail Bederman, *Manliness and Civilization: A Cultural History of Gender and Race in the United States, 1880–1917* (Chicago: Univ. of Chicago Press, 1995).

5   See Thomas C. Holt, "Marking: Race, Race-Making, and the Writing of History," *American Historical Review* 100, no. 1 (Feb. 1995): 1–20. See esp. Barbara Jeanne Fields, "Ideology and Race in American History," in *Region, Race, and Reconstruction: Essays in Honor of C. Vann Woodward*, ed. J. Morgan Kousser and James M. McPherson (New York: Oxford Univ. Press, 1982).

6   See Mrinalini Sinha, "Gender and Imperialism: Colonial Policy and the Ideology of Moral Imperialism in Late Nineteenth-Century Bengal," in *Changing Men: New Directions in Research on Men and Masculinity*, ed. Michael Kimmel (Newbury Park, Calif.: Sage Publications, 1987), 217–31.

7   See Joan Kelly, "The Doubled Vision of Feminist Theory," in *Women, History, and Theory* (Chicago: Univ. of Chicago Press, 1984), 51–64. See also the essays collected in Zillah Eisenstein, ed., *Capitalist Patriarchy and the Case for Socialist Feminism* (New York: Monthly Review Press, 1979); and Heidi Hartmann, "The Family as the Locus of Gender, Class, and Political Struggle: The Example of Housework," *Signs* 6 (Spring 1981): 366–94. For a trenchant analysis of the gendering of work in a different historical context, see Dana Frank, *Purchasing Power: Consumer Organizing, Gender, and the Seattle Labor Movement, 1919–1929* (New York: Cambridge Univ. Press, 1994). Also Evelyn Nakano Glenn, "From Servitude to Service Work: Historical Continuities in the Racial Division of Paid Reproductive Labor," *Signs* 18, no. 1 (Autumn 1992): 1–43.

8   See Glenn; and Joan Scott, "Deconstructing Equality-versus-Difference: Or, the Uses of Poststructuralist Theory for Feminism," *Feminist Studies* 14, no. 1 (Spring 1988), 33–50. For other discussions of domestic themes in the Gold Rush, see David Goodman, *Gold Seeking: Victoria and*

California in the 1850s (Stanford: Stanford Univ. Press, 1994), 149–87; Laurie F. Maffly-Kipp, *Religion and Society in Frontier California* (New Haven: Yale Univ. Press, 1994), esp. 148–80; Malcolm J. Rohrbough, *Days of Gold: The California Gold Rush and the American Nation* (Berkeley: Univ. of California Press, 1997), esp. 91–105.

9   J. D. Borthwick, *The Gold Hunters* (1857; Oyster Bay, NY: Nelson Doubleday, 1917), 291. Cf. George W. B. Evans, *Mexican Gold Rush Trail: The Journal of a Forty-Niner*, ed. Glenn S. Dumke (San Marino, Calif.: Huntington Library, 1945), 244.

10   See, e.g., Journal entry, Jan. 10, 1851, George W. Allen Journals, Beinecke Library; Journal entry, March 28, 1853, Angus McIsaac Journal, Beinecke Library; Doten, 1:76–7 (Doten writes, "we vamosed aqui for the rich gulsh").

11   Borthwick, 252, and see 143, 302; Enos Christman, *One Man's Gold: The Letters and Journal of a Forty-Niner*, ed. Florence Morrow Christman (New York: Whittlesey House, McGraw-Hill, 1930), 132.

12   John Doble, *John Doble's Journal and Letters from the Mines: Mokelumne Hill, Jackson, Volcano and San Francisco, 1851–1865*, ed. Charles L. Camp (Denver: Old West Publishing, 1962), 40, 54.

13   Jean-Nicolas Perlot, *Gold Seeker: Adventures of a Belgian Argonaut during the Gold Rush Years*, trans. Helen Harding Bretnor and ed. Howard R. Lamar (New Haven: Yale Univ. Press, 1985), 100–1, 153.

14   Harvey Wood, *Personal Recollections of Harvey Wood* (Angels Camp, Calif.: Mountain Echo Job Printing Office, [c. 1878]), 16.

15   See e.g., Moses F. Little Journals, Beinecke Library, items 12 and 14, passim; John Amos Chaffee and Jason Palmer Chamberlain Papers, Bancroft Library, Univ. of California, Berkeley (hereafter cited as Bancroft Library), Chamberlain Journals 1 and 2, passim; *The Journals of Alfred Doten, 1849–1903*, 3 vols., ed. Walter Van Tilburg Clark (Reno: Univ. of Nevada Press, 1973), 1:91–250 passim; Perlot, 89–292 passim. Secondary accounts that address such issues include Rodman W. Paul, *California Gold: The Beginning of Mining in the Far West* (1947; reprint, Lincoln: Univ. of Nebraska Press, 1965), 72–3; John Walton Caughey, *The California Gold Rush* (1948; reprint, Berkeley: Univ. of California Press, 1975), 177–201; Ralph Mann, *After the Gold Rush: Society in Grass Valley and Nevada City, California, 1849–1870* (Stanford: Stanford Univ. Press, 1982), 17. US Bureau of the Census, Seventh Federal Population Census, 1850, National Archives and Records Service, RG-29, M-432, reels 33, 35, 36.

16   See, e.g., Journal entries, Oct. 20–Nov. 3, 1849, Miller Journal; Journal entry, Jan. 16, 1853, McIsaac Journal; Journal entries, June 11–29, 1850, Allen Journals; Perlot, 215, 259–61; Doten, 1:76, 81; Doble, 94.

17   See, e.g., Doble, 38–9; Doten, 1: 115–27; Helen Nye to Mother, Jan. 6, 1853, Nye Letters Account book entries, 1852–3, Little Journals, item 13.

18 Leonard Pitt, *The Decline of the Californios: A Social History of the Spanish-Speaking Californians, 1846–1890* (Berkeley: Univ. of California Press, 1966), 54, 104–5; Albert Camarillo, *Chicanos in a Changing Society: From Mexican Pueblos to American Barrios in Santa Barbara and Southern California, 1848–1930* (Cambridge: Harvard Univ. Press, 1979), see, e.g., Journal entries, July 3 and Sept. 10, 1850, Timothy C. Osborn Journal, Bancroft Library.

19 See sources cited n. 17 above, and Charles Davis to Daughter, Jan. 5, [1852], Davis Letters; Perlot, 153, 154, 159–60; Howard C. Gardiner, *In Pursuit of the Golden Dream: Reminiscences of San Francisco and the Northern and Southern Mines, 1849–1857*, ed. Dale L. Morgan (Stoughton, Mass.: Western Hemisphere, 1970), 95, 107, 164–5; Doble, 58.

20 Perlot, 56–7; cf. Evans, 200.

21 Gardiner, 95; cf. William Perkins, *Three Years in California: William Perkins' Journal of Life at Sonora, 1849–1852*, ed. Dale L. Morgan and James R. Scobie (Berkeley: Univ. of California Press, 1964), 106.

22 Journal entries, Dec. 21, 24, 25, 1852, Little Journals, item 12; Journal entries, Nov. 25, 27, 1851, Osborn Journal.

23 Journal entries, Oct. 13–Dec. 25, 1849, passim, Miller Journal. On the decline of game animals near Sonora over the early years of the Gold Rush, see Perkins, 261–2. For examples of men fishing, particularly during the fall salmon run, see Journal entries, Oct. 16–19, 1850, Allen Journals; Journal entry, Oct. 18, 1850, Osborn Journal; Journal entry, Oct. 19, 1852, P. V. Fox Journals, Beinecke Library.

24 Perlot, 272.

25 Journal entry, Nov. 26, 1849, Miller Journal; Woods, 123; A. W. Genung to Thomas, April 22, 1851, A. W. Genung Letters, Beinecke Library. On other gardens, see Doten, 1:85, 147–8. 151; Doble, 94.

26 Evans, 260–1. See Perkins, 262; Borthwick, 57; Doble, 58; Journal entries, Aug. 12–24, 1851, Chamberlain Journal no. 1; Benjamin Butler Harris, *The Gila Trail: The Texas Argonauts and the California Gold Rush*, ed. Richard H. Dillon (Norman: Univ. of Oklahoma Press, 1960), 123 (on scurvy among Mexican miners); Lucius Fairchild, *California Letters of Lucius Fairchild*, ed. Joseph Schafer (Madison: State Historical Society of Wisconsin, 1931), 48, 63; Étienne Derbec, *A French Journalist in the California Gold Rush: The Letters of Étienne Derbec*, ed. Abraham P. Nasatir (Georgetown, Calif.: Talisman Press, 1964), 121–2, 140–1.

27 Perlot, 260; Doble, 245; Journal entries, Aug. 24, Sept. 6, 1852, Little Journals, item 12.

28 Journal entries, Oct. 24, Nov. 22, 24, 1825, ibid.; Journal entries, July 14, 1850, Jan. 12, Feb. 9, 1851, Allen Journals. And see Journal entry. Aug.

29 Journal entries, Dec. 22, 30, 1849, Jan. 1, 4, 5, 1850, Miller Journal.

30 Borthwick, 255–6, 302–3.

31 John Marshall Newton, *Memoirs of John Marshall Newton* (n.p.: John M. Stevenson, 1913), 48–50.

32 Gardiner, 166. Although Gardiner spent most of his time in the Southern Mines, this actually took place in the Northern Mines.

33 Hinton Rowan Helper, *The Land of Gold. Reality Versus Fiction* (Baltimore: Henry Taylor, 1855), vi, 169.

34 Fairchild, 139. On gender as performative, see Judith Butler, *Gender Trouble: Feminism and the Subversion of Identity* (New York: Routledge, 1990), esp. 24–5, 33, 134–41.

35 Helen Nye to Sister Mary, Dec. 26, 1852, Feb. 8, March 14, 1853, May 20, 1855, Nye Letters. On Chinese cooks, see also Evans, 274.

36 Doble, 58; Derbec, 142; Lee Whipple-Haslam, *Early Days in California: Scenes and Events of the '50s as I Remember Them* (Jamestown, Calif.: Mother Lode Magnet, [1925]), 3–4.

37 Leonard Withington Noyes Reminiscences, Essex Institute, Salem, Mass., transcription at Calaveras County Museum and Archives, San Andreas, Calif., 37, 35; Christman, 132; Gardiner, 69; Journal entries, Aug. 10, 17, 31, 1849, Osborn Journal.

38 Doble, 245; Journal entries, Sept. 9, Nov. 22, 1852, Little Journals, item 12; Journal entries, Feb. 1, 8, 1851, Allen Journals; Journal entries, March 2–3, 1850, Miller Journal.

39 Journal entry, Jan. 1, 1850, Miller Journal; Woods, 98.

40 Lapp, 49–93.

41 Friedrich W. C. Gerstäcker, *Narrative of a Journey round the World* (New York: Harper and Brothers, 1853), 225.

42 On the arrival of large numbers of Chinese starting in 1852, and on the reimposition of the foreign miners' tax, see chap. 5, "Dreams That Died."

43 See Ronald Takaki, *Strangers from a Different Shore: A History of Asian Americans* (Boston: Little, Brown, 1989), 92–4; and also Paul Ong, "An Ethnic Trade: The Chinese Laundries in Early California," *Journal of Ethnic Studies* 8, no. 4 (Winter 1981): 95–113.

44 Journal entry, Sept. 6, 1849, Osborn Journal; William McCollum, *California as I Saw It. Pencillings by the Way of Its Gold and Gold Diggers. And Incidents of Travel by Land and Water*, ed. Dale L. Morgan (1850; reprint, Los Gatos, Calif.: Talisman Press, 1960), 160–1.

45 Harris, 113, 123, 132–4, 136. The term "male homosocial desire," of course, is Eve Kosofsky Sedgwick's: *Between Men: English Literature and Male Homosocial Desire* (New York: Columbia Univ. Press, 1985).

"Women's Sweat": Gender and Agricultural Labor in the Atlantic World

Jennifer L. Morgan

[...]

Hard labor, daily and relentless, underlaid all ideologies of race and reproduction and all experiences of birth, parenting, and loss under slavery. The obscene logic of racial slavery defined reproduction as work, and the work of the colonies – creating wealth out of the wilderness – relied on the appropriation of enslaved women's children by colonial slaveowners. But, at the risk of stating the obvious, reproductive work did not alone define daily life. The effort of reproducing the labor force occurred alongside that of cultivating crops. And even as enslaved women engaged in a process of community formation that was simultaneously resistant and acquiescent and ultimately the inevitable byproduct of their dispossession and oppression, they struggled to protect their bodies and their spirits from the ravages of unrelenting hard labor.

An overdetermined connection between women and the domestic has dominated the ways we think about women's work. The very phrase conjures the domestic – cleaning, childcare, food preparation – and inevitably leans in the direction of the family. Images of enslaved female house servants tend to populate the collective imaginary with as much tenacity as do gentle-hearted mammies. But as slaveowners perused the bodies of their newly purchased human property, they quickly made decisions about the kind of work each was capable of performing and in almost all cases put women to work cultivating land. To be exempted from the field in favor of the house was a fate open to very few enslaved women, particularly in the colonial period, when the

luxury of large houses and the niceties of china, silver, and fine furniture were still part of the slaveowners' imaginary future rather than their tangible present. It was far more likely that women would end up in the fields. Indeed, the entire system of hereditary racial slavery depended on slaveowners' willingness to ignore cultural meanings of work that had been established in England and to make Africans work in ways the English could not conceive of working themselves.[1] Once slaveowners received almost equal numbers of African men and women from slave traders, they inverted the gender ideology that they applied to white women and work.[2] As more and more enslaved persons were brought to the Americas, African women and girls found themselves in the fields. Early American slaveowners felt no compunction about using women for this kind of hard labor. As Thomas Nairne calculated the cost to the crown of sponsoring settlers to Carolina in the first decade of the eighteenth century, he speculated on the wealth that would be produced by transported settlers. "I will suppose for the present, that white Women and Children are of no Advantage (tho' 'tis not altogether so) and only reckon Men fit to Labour, and the Slaves of both Sexes."[3] During the crucial frontier period of slavery in the mid-eighteenth-century Georgia lowcountry, for example, a contemporary stated that "in the planting and cultivation of fields the daily tasks of a good Negro Woman" was exactly the same as that of a man.[4] Another planter, outfitting a Florida plantation in 1769 wrote, "very strong and able wenches will do as much work as any man."[5] And on the island of Barbados, eighteenth-century Codrington Plantation owners calculated the monetary value of enslaved male and female field hands equally at £56.[6] As the role of African women in all manner of cultivation, production, and marketing in African societies was reduced to a singular drudgery on a white man's lands, the narrowing of their lives and skills would compound the violation of this new manner of work. It is ironic that the reliance of slaveowners on African women as fieldworkers made their economic role as significant to the American economy as it had been in Africa; African women on both continents produced the agricultural goods that were the base of the respective economies.[7] As they cleared fields and cultivated and harvested crops, enslaved West African women found themselves performing familiar tasks whose cultural meaning had radically changed.

The invisibility of enslaved women in the iconography of early American slave labor is a modern omission. For the men who put black women to work in the fields and for the women who worked there, women's capacity for backbreaking labor was hardly incidental. Indeed, it was central to developing racialist ideology; the "natural" difference between "Negroes" and Englishmen often was evidenced by black women's supposed ability to labor ceaselessly. As Europeans registered their "wonder" at African difference, the image of the black woman who "slaved" for lazy African men was both recurrent and necessary. The intellectual and social milieu from which English slaveowners emerged supported an approach to the organization of labor that fully exploited enslaved women's real and imaginary capacity for grueling agricultural toil.

The diverse labor needs of the early American settlement have been well documented. While often rhetorically reduced to their most important export, "sugar islands" and other staple crop-producing colonies were actually sites of a wide array of work – ranging from road building to navigating small craft to blacksmithing and tailoring to carpentry and butchering. While clearly it would be wrong to present the sole undertaking of the early American slave society as producing monoculture crops, it would not be far from the truth to suggest that enslaved women found themselves confined to the monotony and drudgery of the field more regularly than their male counterparts.

As [. . .] planters moved from tobacco culture toward sugar, for example, almost all planters enslaved nearly equal numbers of men and women, and it was not uncommon for slaveowners to own more women than men. [. . .] English incorporation of colonial settlements and racial

slavery into the parameters of acceptable labor management required some dramatic ideological maneuverings and a fundamental restructuring of the notion of women's work; a similar transformation of thinking about men's labor did not occur. Outnumbered by women two to one, the men on John Waterland's plantation would have been diverted to craft and stock work because the four women would amply cover his twenty acres of land. But once Waterland faced his mortality, Jude, Maria, Mall and Hagar became more than simply workers; they were workers with riches embedded in their intimate behaviors. Calculating their contribution to his wealth, along with their enduring value, Waterland attached Mingo and Hagar to the land in his bequest to his eldest son. The others would ultimately be dispersed between his wife and children, but together Hagar, Mingo, and their progeny would, with luck, carry young Nicholas Waterland far into the future.[8]

[. . .]

Forced to accommodate a demography that was determined on the African coast, slaveowners throughout the colonies struggled to bring their assumptions about gender and labor into line with this new labor force. The work of constructing colonial settlements, of manufacturing the goods and products ancillary to staple crops for export, further complicated the relationship between labor and gender. [. . .]

By the mid-eighteenth century, these practices were solidified on plantations like the Roaring River plantation in Jamaica, where, for example, 76 percent (seventy of ninety-two) of enslaved women were field workers compared with only 33 percent (twenty-eight of eighty-four) of enslaved men. These women, it should be noted, were also the parents of forty-three boys and thirty-six girls, most of whom were too young to work at the time of the plantation's inventory in 1756.[9]

Because of what we know about depressed fertility and increased infant mortality, we can safely say that most enslaved women found fieldwork, rather than childbirth or parenting, to be that which they experienced in common. Cutting eighty acres of cane was not the same as cultivating subsistence crops, but important connections existed between the rhythm of working plantations both large and small on the sugar islands and the mainland colonies. On small estates, both women and men worked the land. On larger plantations, however, enslaved men worked in the boiling house, tended cattle, or made barrels and worked with wood, leaving fieldwork to women. The refusal to allow enslaved women to occupy skilled or artisanal positions meant that the mobility that accompanied such work was also denied them.

The work of the field was, in part, responsible for the low fertility of enslaved women. However, many women still shouldered the burden of fieldwork alongside the difficulties of parenting under slavery. Robert Rumball enslaved twelve children, eleven women, and only five men on his 89-acre plantation in Barbados. The women Rumball owned lived on the small sugar plantation that had a sugar works. Two white female indentured servants did the domestic work. The work of sugar processing and animal husbandry (the plantation also contained a curing house and forty-two assorted livestock) fell to the five male indentured servants and most of the five enslaved men. This left the backbreaking work of the field to the eleven enslaved women – Grete Jugg, Wasshaw, Backoe, Great Marrea, Dido, Violettoe, Lille, Hagar, Affee, Frowna, and Little Marea – many of whom were also mothers to the twelve children who appear in Rumball's inventory under the heading "Negroe Children." Childbirth simply meant that the demands of the field had to coexist with the emotional and physical pull of parenthood.[10]

In the late seventeenth and early eighteenth centuries, then, cane fields were places in which women constituted a high proportion of the total work force. Indeed, in some places, the field became a female space as balanced sex ratios across the English sugar islands led to female majorities in the fields. Even when women's proportional representation in the slave trade declined, in many places – notably Jamaica – sex ratios on the plantations remained quite balanced. Thus, even though they were outnumbered in the population as a whole, women constituted more than half the work force – half the visible source of sugar's cultivation. On the Mesopotamia plantation in Jamaica, which enslaved 322 men and 216 women, the majority of fieldworkers were women (182 of 359); close to half the enslaved men worked as drivers, craft and stock workers, stock keepers, or marginal workers.[11] Similarly, on the eighteenth-century Beaulieu plantation in Saint-Domingue, there were eighty-seven men and fifty-four women, but women outnumbered men on the field more than two to one.[12] Despite the fact that men were imported at a ratio of 163 to 100 women over the course of the slave trade to Jamaica (1655–1807), on the estates, work gangs were close to even with ratios of approximately 105 men to 100 women.[13] Even where the larger population was still demographically weighted toward men, slaveowners'

understanding of gender and work among the enslaved explained the preponderance of women seen in work gangs. On both small and large plantations, women spent their working lives in the field. On the sugar islands as well as in Carolina's rice swamps and Virginia's tobacco fields, occupational diversity existed almost solely for enslaved men.[14]

In the colonial period, slaveowners throughout the Americas became quite willing to put African women permanently to work in the fields, but they balked at allowing them access to any skilled tasks. Skilled work that supported domestic economies such as dairy work or weaving primarily remained the purview of white women – planters' wives who oversaw the work of overseers' wives or female servants.[15] Black women found themselves on the bottom of the work pyramid on the sugar plantations, exposed to hard labor and drudgery with little chance of escape to more skilled or protected positions. Women of African descent were presumed to be fully capable of the heavy lifting and wielding of rudimentary tools that fieldwork required and were found throughout the French Caribbean cutting cane. On the sugar islands of the French Caribbean, women were regularly assigned the fieldwork dismissed by one ecclesiastic observer as "the easiest of all labor."[16] They prepared the fields for planting, cut cane and did the often dangerous work of feeding sugar cane into the mills, a job that could maim or kill if it was not done with perfect timing and that, despite the need for precision, was often relegated to the evening, after enslaved women had worked a full day on the fields. It is not surprising that accidents were "certainly frequent among female slaves . . . particularly at night, when, exhausted by hard labor during the daytime, they fall asleep while passing the cane."[17]

Slave labor was not, of course, limited to sugar cultivation. Women worked on coffee plantations and cultivated indigo as well. An early eighteenth-century observer in Saint-Domingue for example, wrote of a sexual division of labor on the island's indigo fields; men hoed while women stooped to plant seeds and cover them with earth.[18] In seventeenth-century French Guiana, slaveowners sent enslaved women – even in advanced states of pregnancy – to do the public works projects such as road and fortress construction known as corvée labor. Returning from her corvée labor early after becoming ill, an enslaved woman named Doué gave birth to a stillborn son in April 1690; his death marked the limited expectations that shaped a life controlled by the demands of work.[19]

The connection between femininity and domesticity elicits images of cooks and child minders, but the reality was that few women of African descent escaped the field. During a 1706 raid on the island of St. Christopher, French forces absconded with a large number of enslaved persons. When they enumerated those they had lost, the English provided the occupational category each laborer filled and thus left an occupational breakdown for the island's forced laborers at a juncture when St. Christopher had already been settled for more than seventy years and four decades had passed since the turn to sugar cultivation. Of the captives, 64 percent had been field hands, 10 percent had worked in sugar factories, 14 percent had been domestics, and 12 percent had been artisans, overseers, or other "skilled" laborers.[20] Forty years earlier, planters would have been even less willing to divert ablebodied workers from fieldwork to the care and production of domestic luxuries.

Periods of gender parity would wax and wane according to the internal logic of the slave trade, leaving those West African women who survived the Middle Passage in a gender minority.[21] While Barbados was distinct in maintaining female majorities/gender parity during the entire slavery period, women enslaved on the other English sugar islands would continue to find themselves outnumbered in the quarters even as they labored in the fields alongside mostly other women. They were vulnerable to both white and black men, and their time spent in the fields would have been the only time in which they might achieve anything even approximating the female space that defined daily life in most West African cultures. In the context of closely supervised gang labor, the connection between their centrality to agricultural production in West Africa and to fieldwork in the Americas would be at best a numbing reminder of the violent contraction of their unfolding futures. Moreover, women's connections with each other and their sense of collective identity must have grown as a result of the sex ratios of the cane fields. In this regard, a world only nominally defined by their identity as parents presaged the community of mutual support, healing, and resistance evidenced among enslaved women in the antebellum American south.[22] Still, it is difficult to fully imagine the ways in which shifting meanings of gender and backbreaking agonies of hard labor came together to assign meaning to women's work in the colonial cane fields.

The slaveowners who made their way from Barbados and elsewhere in the West Indies to the mainland colony of Carolina in the 1670s constructed a labor system that mirrored the sugar fields in many ways. The Barbadian planters who introduced slavery to South Carolina

caused the mainland colony to become a slave society from the very moment of its settlement.[23] Although indentured servants accompanied the initial white settlers and landowners, there was never any question that Africans and their descendents would perform the bulk of the colony's hard labor. Englishmen and women in Carolina cemented the connection between hard labor and black bodies even before their arrival. When South Carolina was chartered, land grants were awarded on the basis of the numbers of servants and slaves that settlers brought with them to the colony. Those with the means transported large numbers of laborers to increase the size of their land grants without fear that in the new colony their status as slaveowners would be undermined. In correspondence concerning the particulars of the settlement plan, the lords proprietors had been quick to clarify that land would be allocated equally for "Negroes as well as Christians"; in other words, those who brought slaves would be rewarded uniformly, in terms of land, with those who brought servants.[24] White settlers coming from the West Indies, where black labor had long since displaced white servitude, were obvious beneficiaries of this landgrant system. The future of Carolina was inextricably linked to enslavement, assuring settlers that land entitlements would be based on generous headrights. The care taken to ensure privilege for slaveowners who settled in the new colony illustrates two implicit assumptions on the part of the new settlers: black laborers would constitute wealth and black laborers would produce wealth on the mainland.

While landgrants were distributed equally regardless of the race of a white servant or a Negro slave, the lords proprietors did distinguish between male and female laborers. First settlers would be granted 100 acres for the importation of white or black women, and 150 acres for white or black men. Rewarded proportionately more for the import of men than women, newly arrived slaveowning settlers were not blind to the gender conventions that prevailed around them regarding notions of hard labor. During the first twenty-five years of settlement, enslaved men outnumbered enslaved women by two to one.[25] Most of the early settlers to the colony who received warrants for land between 1672 and 1695 for transporting slaves, or servants and slaves, brought only men or male majorities. (35 percent and 25 percent respectively.) However, more than 20 percent brought pairs of men and women, and others brought only women or a majority of women. (9 and 5 percent respectively.) Put another way, enslaved women were considered an investment valuable enough to offset disparities in land acquisition by 65 percent of all the first settlers who went to the expense of transporting laborers to the new settlement alongside themselves and their families.[26] In this moment at which slaveowners themselves momentarily controlled the ratios of men and women imported into a colony, it is particularly telling that women were a logical and consistent choice for transport to the new colony. The proof that women would work in Carolina's fields would be confirmed, and not only by looking backward to Barbados's sugar plantations. In the early years of the colony a brisk trade in Native American slaves also confirmed women's place in the mainland colony. Enslaved Indian women outnumbered men by close to five to one in the first decades of the colony's history, mostly because slaves obtained as a result of intertribal wars were more likely to be women and children – men were killed rather than taken as prisoners. John Wright enslaved fifteen black men and seventeen women, only four of whom were of African descent. Perhaps wishing to offset the black majorities that defined the English island colonies, some looked to a different kind of female labor. When writing a promotional pamphlet for the colony, John Norris wrote that a small-scale settler should bring money to purchase "Two Slaves; a good *Negro* man and a good *Indian* woman," while a wealthier settler should plan to purchase

> Fifteen good *Negro* Men. . . . Fifteen *Indian* Women to work in the Field. . . . Three *Indian* Women as Cooks for the Slaves and other Household-Business and Three *Negro* Women to be employ'd either for the Dairy, to attend the Hogs, Washing, or any other employment they may be set about in the family.[27]

The correlation between sex and race was rarely this extreme, nor would the intended designation of black women as domestics become a reality for more than a fraction of enslaved African women in the colony, but of the 4,300 enslaved persons in the colony in 1708, 1,400 were Native American. The vast majority of those 1,400 were women who worked alongside African and Afro-Caribbean women in the new colony.[28]

As the seventeenth century ended, the headright was reduced to 50 acres per laborer, male or female. The desire to reward the first generation of settlers – those willing to risk an uncertain future in the colony – had led to the generous landgrants in the 1670s and 1680s; but the removal of gendered distinctions of labor by 1685 reflected the shifting understanding of gender, race, and labor on the part of the colonial settlers. It was perhaps

in deference to that shift that Peter Hearne Sr., imported a "negro woman" only three months after he brought a single "negro man" to the colony in 1683. Hearne's choice of a woman would necessarily have been conditioned by the transparent relationship between race and reproduction for seventeenth-century slaveowners. For those women and men transported to the new colony, the confusion of the frontier was possibly abated by clarity about the role they would be performing. The assumption that their working bodies promised more than just their labor on the land must have been as clear to Jone and Andrew, transported together in April of 1673, as it was more than twenty years later to Sam, Tony, Bess, and Jany, who arrived in the colony with their owner and his wife in 1695.[29]

[. . .]

During the first twenty-five years of the eighteenth century, deerskin trading, cattle raising, and the production of naval stores gradually gave way to methods of acquiring wealth that were far more ecologically invasive and, for enslaved women and men, cost much more in human terms. By 1708, the Carolina colony had become the only mainland colony with a black majority as the settlers turned their resources and attention to rice cultivation and transported rapidly expanding numbers of enslaved persons from the West African coast. In 1700 half of the enslaved persons in Carolina were African born; by 1710 that proportion had grown to two thirds.[30] The colony's transition to rice production brought with it a complicated change in women's work; both to the rhythms and rigors of their labors and to the cultural milieu in which they performed them. African laborers cleared the forested lands that soon gave way to rice plantations. Women and children worked alongside men. Enslaved Africans brought more than simple hard labor to the process of transforming the land; in both large and small ways they brought expertise that was recognized and exploited by white settlers albeit in ways that would ultimately destroy them. An observer described black male workers laboring after dark (when the winds had died down) "lopping and fireing," while women and children cut down shrubs and bushes. In 1679, Jean Barbot observed cultivation techniques among the Wolofs on the Senegal Coast. "They set fire to what is found on the land left fallow in previous years, then afterwards. . . . they turn it over and mix up the earth and the burnt material."[31] In 1707, John Archdale remarked that "little Negro Children" performed valuable complementary labor on plantations; their work, essential but light, freed adults for larger, more physically strenuous, jobs.[32]

The colony was beginning its unstoppable journey toward rice culture; it is a great irony that that journey both depended upon African expertise and was devastating to black bodies. In the small cattle-raising outposts of the backcountry, black women had used large mortar and pestles to process the rain-fed rice they grew on dry land. Free-ranging cattle, tended by men, cleared the fields after harvesting in an indigenous complementarity learned on the West African coast. When slaveowners took note of the crop, the move from garden to plantation happened with alarming speed and devastating results. As rice culture developed and the colony expanded in the early eighteenth century, the numbers of enslaved persons brought to Carolina directly from the West African coast rose rapidly.[33] In 1706, only 24 Africans entered the colony by ship. Four years later, 107 persons were forcibly transported from West Africa. By 1725, that number approached 2000 per annum.[34] [. . .]

Slave import levels fluctuated greatly over these years (from 25 to 600 per annum between 1706 and 1723) and women whose pasts likely included labor in Barbados or elsewhere in the Americas were joined in small numbers by those coming from the West African coast. Childbirth and parenting must have occasionally provided a bridge that connected women and men whose pasts were so divergent and whose futures were now necessarily conjoined. As they parented, or mourned the conditions that made parenting impossible, they would also be caught up in the overwhelming demands for their labor in the forests or on the fields. Faced with cargoes they could not control, slaveowners' connection to a Barbadian tradition of slave-holding helped to create the ideological room for women in the fields. The fact that women provided valuable labor, and more valuable children, meant that as the colonial economy developed, slaveowners in Carolina followed the example set by decades of slaveownership in the English Caribbean and did not shirk from using women as laborers on Carolina plantations. Through their presence, their work, and their children, enslaved African women unwillingly contributed to the developing definitions of slavery and control in colonial South Carolina.

[. . .]

Throughout the slaveowning south and Caribbean, one of the consequences of white commitment to slave labor was an unwillingness to invest heavily in more efficient but delicate equipment that would make the agricultural work done by the enslaved less labor intensive. The significant differences in the lives of enslaved people that accrued from the staple crops they cultivated were mediated, especially for the women who found themselves in fields of tobacco, rice, sugar, and coffee, by the work of the hoe. In the antebellum period, Frances Kemble described enslaved women as "hoeing machines," and recently, historian Leslie Schwalm has suggested that the hoe itself might be considered the "universal implement of slavery," one with particular significance for women across the Americas.[35] With the advent of rice culture in South Carolina, another implement served to reinscribe the difference and particularities of cultivation and culture in the lives of African and African American women – the mortar and pestle.[36]

The particular role of African women in the harvesting and processing of rice cannot be underestimated. In order to make rice edible, the indigestible outer husk must be removed while keeping the inner kernel whole. This involves a delicate balance of strength and finesse that was undertaken completely by hand until the advent of mechanized threshing in the 1760s and 1770s. Until that time, the only way to mill rice was with the mortar and pestle that was used by African women in Senegambia and Sierra Leone, and in South Carolina. Many questions have been raised about how rice culture was brought to South Carolina. Rice was a crop with which Englishmen were unfamiliar, and for some time the introduction of the crop with its complex system of water management – the use of dikes and dams to periodically flood and drain the fields – was attributed to some combination of planter ingenuity and grain brought by the captain of a slave ship from Madagascar. But the connection between West African slaves (particularly those from the Senegambia region, who came with a long tradition of both dry and tidal rice-cultivation skills) and the introduction of rice to the colony is compelling. Recent scholarship has cemented the link between the knowledge Africans from the Senegambia region brought, however involuntarily, to South Carolina and the development of the wet growing techniques that transformed the physical and economic landscape of the lower South.[37]

The turn to rice culture in the colony had devastating effects on enslaved women and men. Rice is among the most onerous and labor intensive food crops, and the duration of the growing season and the dangerous and repellent nature of the work placed it at the extreme end of any continuum of forced agricultural labor in the early Atlantic world. Cultivating the crop over the duration of its 14-month growing season involved clearing the land of trees, bushes, and shrubs in January and February; planting acres of seeds by hand and foot; weeding constantly with hoe and hand: spending weeks in knee- and waist-deep water scaring birds away from the ripening crop; harvesting and stacking the rice over the course of three to four weeks; and finally threshing, winnowing, and pounding the rice to remove the kernel from the husk. Runaway numbers peaked during the hoeing and weeding seasons of June through early August as enslaved men and women stole away in search of respite from the "laborious and tedious" task of hand-picking grass from around the rice shoots that had taken root.[38] But the pounding of the harvested rice had to be the most arduous and dangerous work over the course of the season of rice. Not until the 1770s would technology begin to replace the exhausting work of pounding rice by hand.[39] Slaveowners were mindful of the toll that this work took on the health and lives of those they enslaved:

> The worst comes last for after the Rice is threshed, they beat it all in the hand in large wooden Mortars . . . which is a very hard and severe operation as each Slave is tasked at Seven Mortars for One Day, and each Mortar contains three pecks of Rice. Some task their Slaves at more, but often pay dear for their Barbarity, by the loss of many . . . valuable Negroes.[40]

The constant work of lifting a ten-pound pestle, arms over one's head, for hours a day was exhausting, so much so that the task was often divided into two separate sessions in the mornings and evenings. The act of pounding the rice required not only physical strength but acumen as well. Pounding too strenuously would leave one with less-valuable broken rice and bring castigation on the worker whose exhaustion level was costing the plantation owner his profits. The information necessary to cultivate and harvest rice drew heavily on female West African expertise, as women who had for generations begun their day with the pounding of a small amount of rice for daily use found their relationship with the crop utterly transformed – beginning with the need to teach men how to efficiently and carefully perform this task.

The skills needed to cultivate rice successfully were transferred from African to Englishman and from women to men to women again. Women, whose knowledge of rice cultivation in Senegambia had been passed from mother to daughter for generations, found themselves in the difficult position of transferring their knowledge to men,

whose enslavement would now be exacerbated by the indignity of performing women's work and the penalty for not performing it well. As Pearson has written, in the process of meeting the demands of the crop, slaveowners "dissolved the gender division of labor" that had characterized the early years of the colony as well as the West African past.[41] The introduction and construction of the tidewater cultivation levees, sluices, and dikes that transformed swamps into rice fields demanded an astounding amount of labor from enslaved women and men. Over the course of fifty years, the enslaved workers on a single seventeenth century Carolina plantation moved over 6 million cubic feet of earth in the construction of the rice fields, creating "an earthwork approximately one-half the size of Monks Mound, the largest prehistoric Indian mound in North America."[42] In the aftermath of the War of Independence, white observers noted the connection between the design of rice irrigation systems and military engineers' fortifications, a link that was often materialized as enslaved men worked alongside military engineers in the construction of canals, thus cementing the connection between constructing irrigation systems and male knowledge.[43] While men had historically performed much of this work in Western Africa, the conviction held by South Carolina slaveowners that men and women would have "the same day's work in the planting and cultivating of the fields" suggests that slaveowners did not exempt women from the heavy work of moving earth to create the rice fields.[44] In this, enslaved women would follow the lead of the men, whose familiarity with hydraulic design was so essential to South Carolinian planters.

Rice culture in South Carolina differs from staple crop cultivation elsewhere in the New World not only because of the grueling demands of the crop but because of the relationship between indigenous African female knowledge and rice cultivation. As Judith Carney has so eloquently illustrated, the aural rhythm of a woman at her mortar and pestle pounding rice for the day's consumption announced the new day all over the West African coast. Women's expertise was of paramount importance at every stage of the crop's cultivation in the West African rice region – from seed selection to the use of the long- and short-handled hoe to the use of the mortar and pestle to the construction and design of the fanner baskets for winnowing and, finally, to cooking. For the first generations of enslaved persons in the colony, that sound would continue to punctuate the day. As relatively isolated laborers on the colonial frontier, enslaved women and their families might even have relished the familiarity wrought by the steady rhythmic cadences of the mortar and pestle at the start of the day. But as South Carolina slaveowners wrested the crop from household use and applied it to plantation agriculture, the cadence of the mortar and pestle would resonate in entirely different ways. As Carney writes:

> A task performed daily by African women in less than an hour became transformed with commodity production into extended hours of daily toil by male and female slaves over an abbreviated period of the year. The pounding of rice, the preparation of a food that signals daybreak and the re-creation of community life in West Africa, underwent a radical transformation on eighteenth-century rice plantations. As workers arose to the first of two pounding periods, the striking of the pestle represented a new conception of time and labor, calibrated by the dictates of planter and market.[45]

The continuity between rice culture in the lowcountry and on the West African coast and the essential role of women's knowledge in that transmission should not suggest that women had less difficult work in the rice fields. Among the enslaved in North America, those who toiled in the South Carolina rice fields suffered the highest mortality. The work was grueling, the tasks stretched the workday out until well into the night, and the toll that the pounding of rice took on the bodies of the enslaved was so extensive that slaveowners took careful notice of the destruction of their human property. One late-eighteenth-century planter reasoned that the value of the hulled rice did not outweigh that of his laborers and wrote to his overseer that "if the Rice made at Goose-Creek is not yet beat out, I wd. Wish to have it sold in the rough, to save Labour of the Negroes."[46] Nonetheless, the unique connection between the African past and the Carolinian present must be accounted for in the lives of enslaved women in Carolina. The connection between women's knowledge and the life of Carolina planters raises intriguing questions about the ability of these women to negotiate spaces of autonomy. The task system of labor conceded to the enslaved by South Carolina slaveowners allowed for the development of slave economies and created a clear distinction between time in the service of the slaveowner and time in the service of oneself. The task system itself had African antecedents and may have developed from the transfer of knowledge and skills between the enslaved and the slaveowner.[47] Indeed, the parameters of the task system, which was in place as early as 1712, may have given rise to the natural increase among the enslaved that was evident in the

early years of Carolina's settlement. We know that the space that resulted from task labor generated gardens and markets: perhaps it generated a different relationship to the future that children embodied as well.

On the other hand, in the accounting of rice and women's lives, the balance should tip toward misery. Women in the Carolina lowcountry watched as one of the most essential cadences of their former lives was utterly transformed. The quotidian task that had given shape to their morning would in its transformation become a reminder of all that no longer existed. Not just the mortar and pestle but also the weaving and basketry that once served the household and the life of the community would be transfigured by the rapacious demands of the slaveholder.[48] Not unlike the birth of a child, the agricultural work that gave meaning to one's life now gave meaning to someone else's life. But opportunities to reconfigure the balance of power in slave societies were everywhere and constituted an ongoing narrative thread in the history of racial slavery. Childbirth and the identifiable skills brought to cultivation and processing crops were themselves possible spaces in which to maneuver, even as they simultaneously concentrated the misery and violation enslaved women and men endured.

Notes

1 David Eltis, *The Rise of African Slavery in the Americas* (Cambridge: Cambridge University Press, 2000), 220.

2 Eltis, *Rise of African Slavery*, 85–113; and Hilary McD. Beckles, *Natural Rebels: A Social History of Enslaved Black Women in Barbados* (New Brunswick, NJ: Rutgers University Press, 1989), 29.

3 Thomas Nairne, *A Letter from South Carolina* (London, 1710), in Jack P. Greene, ed., *Selling a New World: Two Colonial South Carolina Promotional Pamphlets* (Columbia: University of South Carolina Press, 1989), 68.

4 Johann Martin Bolzius, "Reliable Answers to Some Submitted Questions Concerning the Land Carolina," *William and Mary Quarterly* 3rd ser. 14 (April 1957): 223–61, 257. This source was first published in 1751.

5 Ira Berlin, *Many Thousands Gone: The First Two Centuries of Slavery in North America* (Cambridge, Mass.: Harvard University Press, 1998), 168.

6 Harry J. Bennett, *Bondsmen & Bishops: Slavery and Apprenticeship on the Codrington Plantations of Barbados, 1710–1838* (Berkeley: University of California Press, 1958), 16.

7 Eltis, *Rise of African Slavery*, 92.

8 Will of John Waterland, February 3, 1660, RB6/14: 532, BA.

9   Richard Sheridan, *Sugar and Slavery: An Economic History of the British West Indies* (Baltimore: Johns Hopkins University Press, 1973), 257.

10 Will of Robert Rumball, September 14, 1660, RB6/14: 493, BA.

11 Richard S. Dunn, "Sugar Production and Slave Women in Jamaica," in *Cultivation and Culture: Labor and the Shaping of Slave Life in the Americas*, ed. Ira Berlin and Philip D. Morgan (Charlottesville: University Press of Virginia, 1993), 62.

12 Bernard Moitt, "Women, Work, and Resistance in the French Caribbean During Slavery, 1700–1848," in *Engendering History: Caribbean Women in Historical Perspective*, ed. Verene Shepard, Bridget Brereton, and Barbara Baily (New York: St. Martin's Press, 1995), 159. Moitt goes on to argue that by the nineteenth century, female-majority field gangs were ubiquitous throughout the French Caribbean, a demographic situation acknowledged by historians but still under-theorized (162).

13 Dunn, "Sugar Production and Slave Women," 50–1.

14 For women's participation in work gangs in eighteenth-century Barbados, see Barbara Bush, *Slave Women in Caribbean Society, 1650–1838* (Bloomington: Indiana University Press, 1990), 121–4. For a discussion of labor and culture, see Ira Berlin and Philip Morgan, "Labor and the Shaping of Slave Life in the Americas," in *Cultivation and Culture; Labor and the Shaping of Slave Life in the Americas*, ed. Ira Berlin and Philip Morgan (Charlottesville: University Press of Virginia, 1993), 1–48; and David Barry Gaspar, *Bondmen & Rebels: A Study of Master-Slave Relations in Antigua with Implications for Colonial British America* (Baltimore: Johns Hopkins University Press, 1985), 93–128.

15 Eltis, *Rise of African Slavery*, 102.

16 Jean Pierre Labat, *Nouveau voyage aux isles de l'Amérique* (Paris: Guillaume, 1722), 3: 432; cited in Bernard Moitt, "Slave Women and Resistance in the French Caribbean," in *More Than Chattel: Black Women and Slavery in the Americas*, ed. David Barry Gaspar and Darlene Clark Hine (Bloomington: Indiana University Press, 1996), 239.

17 Labat, *Nouveau voyage*, 4: 206; cited in Moitt, "Women, Work, and Resistance," 165.

18 Elie Monnereau, *Le Parfait indigotier ou description de l'indigo* (Marseilles, 1765), cited in David Geggus, "Indigo and Slavery in Saint-Domingue," *Plantation Society in the Americas* 5 (1998): 191–2.

19 Moitt, "Women, Work, and Resistance," 162.

20 Richard S. Dunn, *Sugar and Slaves: The Rise of the Planter Class in the English West Indies, 1624–1713* (Chapel Hill: University of North Carolina Press, 1972), 198.

21 For balanced sex ratios in late seventeenth- and early eighteenth-century English sugar islands, see Dunn, *Sugar and Slaves*, 315–17. It is interesting that at the beginning of the nineteenth century, men outnumbered women in only six of sixteen British Caribbean slave societies. In Demerara-Essequibo (where the ratio was 130:100), in Berbice (128:100) and in Trinidad (123:100), the demographics were particularly skewed. In the Bahamas (104:100), St. Vincent (102:100), and Jamaica (100.3:100), they were closer to "normal." See Barry Higman, *Slave Populations of the British Caribbean, 1807–1834* (Baltimore: Johns Hopkins University Press, 1984), 117.

22 See Deborah Gray White, *Ar'n't I a Woman? Female Slaves in the Plantation South* (New York: W.W. Norton, 1985), 119–41.

23 Richard S. Dunn, "The English Sugar Islands and the Founding of South Carolina," *South Carolina Historical Magazine* 72 (April 1971): 81–93.

24 Lord Ashley to Sir John Yeamans, May 1670, in Langdon Cheves, ed., *The Shaftesbury Papers and Other Records relating to Carolina* (Charleston: South Carolina Historical Society, 1897), 164.

25 Peter H. Wood, *Black Majority: Negroes in Colonial South Carolina from 1670 Through the Stono Rebellion* (New York: W.W. Norton, 1974), 25.

26 Alexander S. Salley, *Warrants for Land in South Carolina, 1672–1711* (Columbia: University of South Carolina Press, 1973).

27 John Norris, *Profitable Advice for Rich and Poor* (London, 1712), in Jack P. Greene, *Selling a New World: The Colonial South Carolina Promotional Pamphlets* (Columbia: University of South Carolina Press, 1989), 128, 132, emphasis in original.

28 Mortgage of John Wright to Samuel Wragg, 15 June 1714, Charleston County Wills, #45, SCDAH; cited in Philip D. Morgan, *Slave Counterpoint: Black Culture in the Eighteenth-Century Chesapeake and Lowcountry* (Chapel Hill: University of North Carolina Press, 1998), 482. On Indian slavery, see Wood, *Black Majority*, 38–43; and Theda Perdue, *Slavery and the Evolution of Cherokee Society, 1540–1866* (Knoxville: University of Tennessee Press, 1979), 28.

29 Warrant for land for Peter Hearne, Sr., April 1683; Warrant for land for Mrs. Dorcas Smith, April 1673; Warrant for land for Francis Blanchart, July 1695; all in Salley, *Warrants for Land*.

30 Morgan, *Slave Counterpoint*, 61. Russell Menard has asserted that equating rice with the rise in the importation of enslaved Africans is an oversimplification. Rather, using the work of Clarence Ver Steeg, he argues that the combination of naval stores and rice production, or "the general expansion of Lowcountry exports," together created the demand and economic means for the growth in slave imports. Russell R. Menard, "The Africanization of the Lowcountry Labor Force," in *Race and Family in the Colonial South*, ed. Winthrop Jordan and Shelia Skemp (Jackson: University Press of Mississippi, 1987), 94.

31 John Gerar William de Brahms, *Report of the General Survey in the Southern District of North America*, ed. Louis de Vorsey, Jr. (Columbia: University of South Carolina Press,

1971), 93–94, quoted in Timothy Silver, *A New Face on the Countryside: Indians, Colonists, and Slaves in South Atlantic Forests, 1500–1800* (Cambridge: Cambridge University Press, 1990), 106–7. *Barbot on Guinea: The Writings of Jean Barbot on West Africa, 1678–1712*, ed. P. E. H. Hair, Adam Jones, and Robin Law, 2 vols. (London: Hakluyt Society, 1992), 1: 91; and Daniel C. Littlefield, *Rice and Slaves: Ethnicity and the Slave Trade in Colonial South Carolina* (Urbana: University of Illinois Press, 1991), 103–4.

32 John Archdale, "A New Description of that Fertile and Pleasant Province of Carolina, by John Archdale, 1707," in Alexander-Salley, ed., *Narratives of Early Carolina, 1650–1708* (New York: Charles Scribner's Sons, 1911), 310. He particularly discussed enslaved children's suitability for feeding silkworms. Planters' experiments in silk production were abandoned in the face of the successful introduction of rice to the colony. Silver, *New Face*, 147.

33 On the stages of Carolina's socioeconomic development, see Peter Coclanis, *The Shadows of a Dream: Economic Life and Death in the South Carolina Lowcountry, 1670–1920* (New York: Oxford University Press, 1989), 48–110, especially 61–3; Wood, *Black Majority*; and Clarence Ver Steeg, *Origins of a Southern Mosaic: Studies of Early Carolina and Georgia* (Athens: University of Georgia Press, 1975), 114–30.

34 Peter H. Wood, "'More like a Negro Country': Demographic Patterns in Colonial South Carolina, 1700–40," in *Race and Slavery in the Western Hemisphere: Quantitative Studies*, ed. Stanley Engerman and Eugene Genovese (Princeton, NJ.: Princeton University Press, 1975), 144.

35 Leslie Schwalm, *"A Hard Fight for We": Women's Transition from Slavery to Freedom in South Carolina* (Urbana: University of Illinois Press, 1997), 21.

36 I borrow the phrase "cultivation and culture" from the volume of the same name: *Cultivation and Culture: Labor and the Shaping of Slave Life in the Americas*, ed. Ira Berlin and Philip Morgan (Charlottesville: University Press of Virginia, 1993).

37 Judith Carney's examination of the transmission of rice culture from Africa to America provides the most complete and compelling argument. Carney, *Black Rice*, 78–98. In addition, see Wood, *Black Majority*, 35–62; Littlefield, *Rice and Slaves*, 74–114; Joyce Chaplin, *An Anxious*

Pursuit: Agricultural Innovation and Modernity in the Lower South, 1730–1815 (Chapel Hill: University of North Carolina Press, 1993), 266; Edward A. Pearson, "'A Countryside Full of Flames': A Reconsideration of the Stono Rebellion and Slave Rebelliousness in the Early Eighteenth-Century South Carolina Lowcountry," *Slavery and Abolition* (August 1996), 22–50, esp. 33–4; and Michael A. Gomez, *Exchanging Our Country Marks: The Transformation of African Identities in the Colonial and Antebellum South* (Chapel Hill: University of North Carolina Press, 1998), 93.

38 Mark Catesby, *Natural History* (London, 1731, 1747), in *The Colonial South Carolina Scene: Contemporary Views, 1697–1774*, ed. H. Roy Merrens (Columbia: University of South Carolina Press, 1977) 100.

39 In 1787 Jonathan Lucas patented a water-driven mill for removing the husk from rice kernels. Judith Carney, *Black Rice: The African Origins of Rice Cultivation in the Americas* (Cambridge, Mass.: Harvard University Press, 2001), 132. For a discussion of the impulse on the part of slaveowners to develop mechanized milling of rice, see Chaplin, *All Anxious Pursuit*, 251–62.

40 Alexander Garden to Royal Society, April 20, 1755, Guard Book I, Royal Society of Arts, London; cited in Philip Morgan, *Slave Counterpoint*, 153. See also 151.

41 Pearson, "'A Countryside in Flames,'" 34. The skill of the processor resulted in more or less broken rice in the final product. Carney, *Black Rice*, 127.

42 Leland Ferguson, *Uncommon Ground: Archaeology and Early African America, 1650–1800* (Washington: Smithsonian Institute Press, 1992), xxiv. See also Carney, *Black Rice*, 91–7.

43 Chaplin, *Anxious Pursuit*, 267.

44 Bolzius, "Reliable Answers," 257.

45 Carney, *Black Rice*, 135.

46 Peter Manigault to John Owen, February 20, 1794, Peter Manigault Letter-book, South Caroliniana Library, University of South Carolina; cited in Chaplin, *Anxious Pursuits*, 252.

47 Carney, *Black Rice*, 99–101.

48 Dale Rosengarten, *Row upon Row: Sea Grass Baskets of the South Carolina Lowcountry* (Columbia: University of South Carolina and McKissick Museum, 1986); and Gomez, *Exchanging Country Marks*, 93.

Fashioning Political Subjectivities: The 1909 Shirtwaist Strike and the "Rational Girl Striker"

Nan Enstad

On November 23, 1909, 20,000 shirtwaist makers, 85–90 percent of them women, walked off their jobs in hundreds of factories across New York City. The dramatic strike captured the public eye as popular magazines and the city's many newspapers scrambled to cover the most salient events of this female-dominated conflict. The popular press focused on the elaborate fashions and festivity of many of the strikers, bearing witness to the visible participation of working "ladies" in the strike. They printed police reports about strikers' violence on the picket lines and represented the strikers as fashionably dressed hell-raisers. This coverage served in part to undermine working women's claims as political actors, because such ladies did not meet middle-class expectations for the proper demeanor of public participants. To Sarah Comstock, reporter for *Collier's* magazine, well-dressed and smiling strikers did not seem to have the seriousness of rational, political actors, nor the visible poverty that would legitimate their claims of low wages. Thus, they did not "look as if they had any grievance." Comstock could not see women with identities based in working ladyhood as political subjects, even when they enacted the recognized political script of a strike.

It should not be surprising that public discussion of the mass strike recurrently focused on women's styles. Fashion already carried a diverse range of cultural meanings that would have political valences in the context of a strike. For Enlightenment thinkers, democratic political exchange depended on the capacity of participants to act *rationally*. The nineteenth-century middle class built upon these ideas and created the notion of a "public sphere" in which rational white men could

engage in such exchange. They defined the public in opposition to the concept of a "private," feminine, and irrational realm. These concepts did not describe the reality of nineteenth-century politics, which consistently defied such boundaries, but they did shape normative expectations about the nature of political subjectivity as well as legal barriers to political participation.[1] [...] To many, the elaborate dress of shirtwaist strikers signaled femininity and irrationality: two qualities that disqualified a person from being a political subject. In addition, many saw elaborate fashion on working-class women as evidence of wealth and desires "beyond their station," invalidating their claims that wages were too low. Women's flamboyant fashion thus would become a lightning rod for political debate about the central contests of the strike: women's right to act politically and the legitimacy of their claims about workplace conditions.

Labor leaders responded to this publicity and tried to make the mass strike of young, working women intelligible and favorable to a largely middle-class public. They portrayed the strikers as serious, "thinly clad," non-violent victims of police abuse, constructing an ideal political subjectivity that countered the damaging publicity. The leaders represented women as political subjects despite their gender, class, and ethnicity by declaring that the strikers *acted* like political participants recognized by the wider culture. Specifically, labor leaders combined Enlightenment ideals about rational political participation with quite different, charity-based notions of "needs." They depicted striking women as bringing rational claims to unionization, but bolstered their worthiness by emphasizing their abject poverty and exceptional physical need. In so doing leaders erased the participation of working ladies in the strike, and promoted strikers in ways that ran counter to many working-class women's proud identities rooted in consumer culture. Working ladyhood, as we have seen, expressly rejected the condescension and the stigma of impoverishment so often associated with the "poor working girl." Leaders' representations were calculated to counter damaging portrayals of women as irrational or greedy, but also tried to reform working women's appearance and cultural practices to more closely resemble this ideal image.

This chapter argues that the public debate about the strike, including labor leaders' contributions, constricted the intelligibility of working ladies' own attempts to claim formal political subjectivities. That is, existing ideals of what a political subject looked like obscured working ladies' identities. While labor leaders rendered crucial assistance and legitimation to the strikers and their cause, their efforts to cast the women in the most "positive" light contributed to a widespread failure to recognize the diversity of political subjectivities. Historians, drawing principally on labor union records, have replicated this failure. As strikers thronged the public streets of New York City, demonstrated in parades and mass meetings, and picketed in front of factories, they challenged established assumptions about the identity and appearance of political actors and access to public space. These working-class, largely immigrant women comprised a subordinated group long denied an active voice in recognized political forums. By occupying the arena of labor politics through a mass strike, they demanded a voice. But the strike was not an arena of free will or total agency. Women did not magically transcend the structures that had limited their political participation in the past and enter a space of free expression when they walked off their jobs.[2] Rather, they worked within and against oppressive structures even as they struck. Indeed, even as the strike challenged certain hierarchies in US society, the public debate and striking women's limited ability to influence print media replicated existing inequalities, and curtailed the degree to which these women achieved a recognized public voice in the union and in the society at large.

[. . .]

Historians of this strike have taken leaders' strategic representations of striking women to be factual descriptions. The strikers appear in historical accounts much as they did in labor leaders' strategic but partial representations: serious, thinly clad, nonviolent. This is partly because none of the existing histories closely examined the public debate about the strike, the context in which leaders formed their representations. Indeed, no historical account makes systematic use of the newspapers in which this debate was largely waged. As a result, fashion does not figure in any of the strike histories, despite its centrality to the public debate and the visible participation of working ladies in the strike. Historians have based their accounts primarily or exclusively on labor leaders' records and dismissed the popular press coverage as "biased."

[. . .]

When newspaper records and leaders' accounts are viewed together, they provide considerably more evidence about the strike debate than when seen in isolation. This chapter examines available sources to reveal a dramatic public debate over whether the striking women were legitimate political actors with sound grievances, and the ways the strike itself was a terrain of limited agency for the women. [. . .]

The broad contours of the strike were as follows: conflicts began several months before the 1909 general strike in the Triangle and Leiserson factories. Employers claimed a slack season and laid off women workers who had been organizing with local 25 of the ILGWU, but then advertised for new workers, effectively locking out the pro-union women. The workers began picketing to persuade others not to take their places. The picketers met great resistance from police and thugs hired by the employers; many were arrested, and the WTUL began to assist them. The conflict hit the popular press on November 5, after the police arrested a wealthy WTUL member, Mary Dreier, while she walked the picket line. On November 22, the ILGWU held a mass meeting to discuss a general strike. Clara Lemlich, a striking worker from the Triangle factory, interrupted to make a speech that would become famous in labor history, moving that the shirtwaist workers go out on general strike. The motion passed unanimously, and the next day thousands of workers walked off their jobs. The numbers overwhelmed even the most optimistic of the ILGWU and WTUL leaders: the union was unprepared to handle workers from so many shops. Each shop had to organize picketing, decide on specific grievances and demands, and settle individually through discussions with employers. SP members and suffragists stepped in to help the ILGWU and WTUL manage the thousands of workers needing to join the union, form picketing brigades, decide upon grievances, and petition for strike benefits, The AFL sent a representative to assist them. Because police and thugs severely challenged women's picketing, many leaders also supervised picket lines and attended night court, where magistrates tried arrested picketers. Leaders produced a great deal of publicity about the strike by writing articles and creating promotional events calculated to capture the attention of the press. Meanwhile, manufacturers formed their own association to fight the strike collectively.

In mid-January, the strike committee and manufacturers' association agreed to a compromise to end the strike; it granted workers better wages and working conditions, but did not include union recognition. The striking workers overwhelmingly rejected this compromise. Their insistence on union representation, rather than simply improvements in workplace conditions, fractured the uneasy alliance of leaders. The AFL representative and many prominent suffragists broke ranks with the strikers and claimed that the workers were swayed by the Socialists. By mid-February, ILGWU leaders officially declared the strike over, and strikers from 150 shops went back without agreements. Because the improvements experienced by many did not include a change in the structure of power or decision-making, conditions soon deteriorated. Despite the strike's mixed results for the shirtwaist workers, it inaugurated a chain of large strikes in garment industries that established women as important members in the ILGWU.[3]

The strike debate soon focused on the dramatic, gendered conflicts over public space on the picket lines. Striking women experienced daily challenges to their right to act politically as picketers. Employers hired thugs to harass and attack picketing workers, police readily arrested them, and city magistrates imposed harsh fines and jail sentences on those arrested. Leaders reported that thugs initiated physical confrontations with picketers, and police would then arrest women strikers for disorderly conduct. Police also arrested strikers for using the word "scab" and for congregating in groups rather than maintaining lines. Police even arrested one group of strikers on the request of an employer because "they were standing in front of my factory."[4] The terms and tactics used by employers, police, and court magistrates to oppose picketing merged typical and time-honored strike-breaking techniques with particularly gendered attacks designed to undermine women's basic claim to political subjectivity. Police violence, mass arrests, and harsh sentences were

standard fare for workers who sought a political voice through strikes. Because the striking women were working class and mostly immigrants, police and thugs did not feel compelled to treat them with the deference due to white, middle-class women. The women also faced tactics that capitalized on the historic association of unescorted women in public space with disorder, including sexual disorder.

Shirtwaist picketers regularly encountered accusations or insinuations that they were prostitutes; their public activity called into question their sexual respectability. This began during the conflict at the Triangle and Leiserson shops that preceded the general strike, when manufacturers hired female prostitutes as well as male thugs to harass the picketers. Employers knew that women who occupied public space without male escorts already jeopardized their sexual reputations. Regulatory norms originating in bourgeois conceptions of public and private deemed women sexually virtuous only when they were contained in the private realm. Indeed, in the nineteenth century, prostitutes were commonly referred to as "public women." For this reason, some middle-class people believed that working women were, or soon would be, compromised in virtue.[5] When these women picketed, their overtly political action challenged the normative definition of public space even more intensely. Manufacturers knew that hiring prostitutes to stand on the same corners as the pickets would intensify the association between female picketing and disreputable behavior. This tactic apparently drew too much protest from observers and neighborhood businesses and did not persist into the general strike. However, Mary Brown Sumner, in an article for The Survey, noted that in the general strike, " 'Streetwalker' is one of the terms that the police and the thugs apply daily to the strikers, in fact it has become in their vocabulary almost synonymous with striker."[6] By calling picketing women "streetwalkers," police and thugs repeated the discourse that had historically served to keep women from public life,[7] not only insulting picketers by associating them with a stigmatized group, but also resolutely denying them a political subjectivity. To the police, women in public were not political actors, but "public women."

Successful picketing was crucial to the strike effort, and it was on the picket lines that striking women most visibly enacted political subjectivities. The first function of picketing was to bring work in shops to a halt by preventing scabs from taking strikers' places. This alone would pressure owners to deal with them through union agreements. Picketing also effectively brought shop floor struggles out from behind the closed doors of the factory and into the public space of the street. The second function of picketing, then, was to demand public recognition of workplace struggles and insist that control of labor conditions was not the private prerogative of owners but a political matter in which the larger community had an interest. Thus, the opposition from thugs and the police had potentially grave consequences. Striking women had to picket, because it was imperative that they stop production and make the strike a public issue.

Ironically, the extreme repression that striking women encountered on the picket lines functioned to increase debate about women's political subjectivities. The cumulative effect of the violence and arrests by thugs and police was to recognize that striking women did indeed act politically. In addition, a direct outcome of the pitched battle over the picket lines was increased public attention to, and press coverage of, the strike. As police arrested hundreds of young women, the newspapers scrambled for stories of recent skirmishes. Their representations of these events became central to the public debate about women's right to be political actors and the legitimacy of their grievances. Newspapers sensationalized the conflict and selectively reported daily arrests and magistrates' decisions, making some courtroom proceedings part of public knowledge about the strike. Leaders responded to both the repression and the newspaper coverage by launching a concerted public relations campaign to promote their view of the strikers.

Identifying a singular meaning or effect of newspaper coverage on the strike is impossible. First, the papers were not all alike. Some, like the *New York Times* and the *New York Tribune*, targeted a more middle-class audience and tended to foreground business interests. Others, such as the *New York Evening Journal* and the *New York World*, catered to a wide audience that included many working-class people and had reputations as "sensational rags." The various papers covered the strike somewhat differently. Editorials and letters to the editor introduced multiple perspectives and gave certain papers "pro-union" tones, while others clearly espoused "anti-union" positions.[8] Second, we cannot determine a single effect of newspaper coverage because the same stories often portrayed the striking women in multiple or even contradictory terms. In addition, the same stories could be read in different ways, depending on the social positions and cultural competencies of readers. While some coverage was definitely negative, the papers did include some prostrike letters and editorials, report divergent court decisions on the legalities of picketing, and regularly quote strike leaders at length.

Nevertheless, leaders' objections to newspaper coverage of strike events were justified. Because newspapers were market-driven, news reports hinged on the novelty of the events. Intense competition for readers prompted all of the papers to foreground those aspects of the strike that were most surprising, dramatic or titillating. As they did so, despite their diversity and differences, *all* of the papers utilized tropes emerging from dominant middle-class views on gender, class, and order which precluded taking striking women seriously as political actors. Specifically, the city newspapers represented striking women as constituting a feminine, irrational disorder: fashion-oriented, interested only in fun, and violent on the picket lines.

Much of the popular press's emphasis on dress and demeanor may not have sprung from a conscious anti-union sentiment, but simply from a desire to write "good copy." Among the novel elements of the strike the papers emphasized, the most fundamental was that the strikers were predominantly female. Newspapers rarely mentioned male strikers or leaders, despite the fact that men comprised up to 15 percent of the striking workers, and nearly all of the ILGWU leadership. Rather, they focused on the transgressive element of working-class women acting politically in the public sphere. The battle as represented in the press was primarily between young, female strikers and the combined forces of young, female scabs and male authorities: police, magistrates, and employers. The focus on the female-dominated nature of the strike did not in itself damage the cause. However, the ways newspapers emphasized this fact directed readers' interests to the alleged disorderly conduct of women on the lines, rather than to a consideration of their claims.

For example, newspapers disproportionally listed names and addresses of arrested female strikers at the ends of articles. Comparison with similar reporting in the *New York Call*, the Socialist daily paper, suggests that the popular press omitted the names of many of the male strikers and almost all of the scabs or thugs arrested. This could give an impression that striking women were the only ones arrested. [. . .]

Some articles mentioned clothing in seemingly neutral descriptions that had a similar effect. For example, a *New York Sun* reporter described the fashions of women in public space: "In the streets outside [strike] headquarters young women in furs and feathered hats gathered in groups."[9] While refraining from negative comment, this article nevertheless suggested that women's appearance was somehow significant to their political claims, inviting readers to evaluate striking women's actions in different terms than they did men's in similar situations.

Newspapers regularly reported on the proceedings in night court, where magistrates heard the cases of arrested women. Those reports both prompted public discussion of women's right to picket, and promoted a view of women as violent on the picket lines. Papers particularly printed widely variant decisions that revealed disagreements among magistrates on the definition of peaceful picketing. Magistrate Krotel upheld women's right to picket early in the strike when he dismissed women arrested for standing in front of a factory. However, the very same night Magistrate Corrigan sentenced a striker to five days in the workhouse for a similar offense and publicly declared that he would "deal severely with any strikers brought before him." Most of the strikers were charged with "disorderly conduct," a sufficiently loose charge that could bend to fit the occasion. Magistrate Butts dismissed a case in which the striker was charged with disorderly conduct for "shouting and causing a crowd to collect." His comments criticized the police and other magistrates for their ready use of the charge: "These strikers have the right by fair and peaceable means, by reason of argument to win over to their cause those who are working, in order to obtain better conditions in their manner of livelihood. I hold that in order to constitute disorderly conduct it must be shown that the defendant was liable to provoke a breach of the peace under the existing conditions." In contrast, Magistrate Barlow reportedly said, "If these girls continue to rush around and cry 'scab' I shall convict them of disorderly conduct. There is no word in the English language so irritating as the word scab."[10] The papers thus made courtroom battles a matter of public concern, and raised the question of what constituted acceptable behavior on the lines.

At the same time, however, papers printed magistrates' most dramatic or extreme statements, most of which chastised the strikers for (alleged) unlawful or immoral behavior. Collectively, these comments represented young striking women as "girls" who were out of control. Magistrate Cornell revealed his association between the strike and female, even sexual, disorder when he verbally harangued a picketer, saying, "Why do you paint your face?" The newspapers all picked up this story and reported somewhat different versions of it. In some, the magistrate sent an officer to rub his finger on the young woman's face to see if she wore makeup; in others, the

young woman herself wiped her finger on her face to prove that she did not.[11] Certainly, whether the striker wore makeup or not should not have been an issue in deciding her innocence or guilt. But the fact that Magistrate Cornell seized upon this is revealing. Many people in 1909 associated makeup with prostitution or the theater, both of which offered women less than virtuous means to make money. (Both also featured women in public.) Among many working-class women, however, the practice of wearing makeup was acceptable and widespread, and did not carry such overtones. The magistrate's question insinuated that the picketer lacked sexual respectability. The incident occurred in night court, and Magistrate Cornell knew that most of the women present who were not connected to the strike were arrested prostitutes, or as one strike commentator put it, "the painted street girl."[12] Like the employer who hired prostitutes to harass the pickets, Cornell disparaged the picketers' public actions by associating them with "public women," calling into question the legitimacy of their political subjectivity.

Some newspaper articles abandoned the tone of neutrality, and explicitly focused on the dress and demeanor of striking women in ways likely to delegitimate working women's claims to political subjectivity, particularly for a middle-class readership schooled in Enlightenment ideals of rational political participation. Articles characterized striking women not as producers making political claims, but as consumers having fun. Under the headline 40,000 WORK GIRLS AT EASE, one *New York Sun* article described the strikers as an "unwonted leisure class of 40,000, all in holiday attire, all excitedly gossiping, visiting, shopping."[13] Striking workers undoubtedly did feel an exhilaration from successfully walking off their jobs, being momentarily released from the drudgery of monotonous toil, and joining with other workers at strike headquarters. Labor history is replete with examples of workers creating a holiday atmosphere in a strike, complete with wearing their very best clothes.[14] However, this article obscured women's identities as workers when it called them a "leisure class" and emphasized socializing and shopping, rather than their workplace grievances. Some accounts represented the walkout itself as a frolic: "The girls went out with a whoop.... Laughing and shouting, the girls dropped their work and ran for their hats and coats." One announced a mass meeting to be held two weeks into the strike as a "party," noting that it "was going to be a whopper." Another article claimed that at strike headquarters, "All were in the highest of spirits, though many of them admitted that they had no grievances, but said they did not want to remain at work when the others struck."[15]

Reporters described employers, in contrast, as rational men attending to the crisis in meetings. A particularly damaging *New York Times* headline at the beginning of the strike read GIRL STRIKERS DANCE AS EMPLOYERS MEET: THE WAISTMAKERS ARE HOLDING IMPROMPTU PARTIES IN THEIR HEADQUARTERS. The article reported the creation of the Association of Waist and Dress Manufacturers, an organization formed to oppose the strike, as well as the many resolutions passed at the first meeting, including a resolution against the closed shop. In contrast, the *Times* stated that strikers "seemed to be in good spirits yesterday and held impromptu dances in several of the halls where they met."[16] Clearly, in this story manufacturers, not strikers, hold "somber meetings" and pass "somber resolutions" in order to rationally promote their interests. Indeed, one reporter noted that a middle-class WTUL leader "seems to take the matter much more seriously than the many thousands of women who look to her for direction and information." This coverage provided support for some manufacturers' strategic interpretation of the strike, represented well in one owner's statement: "The strike is altogether silly."[17]

The popular press also undermined women's legitimacy as political actors by representing them as an irrational mob, emotionally under the sway of union leaders. One reporter claimed that on the first day of the strike, "the excited girls created the din of a howling mob, setting the entire neighborhood in an uproar." Strikers formed "stampede[s]" and "hysterical swarms," and went "wild with excitement" whenever addressed by leaders. Yet another claimed the strikers acted with "hysterical optimism," and that strike headquarters were a "clamorous jam." Newspapers also regularly reported that women attacked police in direct inversions of public order. In the most dramatic article, the *New York World* reported that one hundred "petticoated antagonists" mobbed two policemen, ripping and ruining their uniforms.[18] Of course, we must maintain skepticism about the accuracy of such stories. But the overall picture painted by this coverage was of young women irrationally out of control in public, rather than of citizens making political claims.

Popular descriptions of picketing particularly associated fashion with a distinctively feminine irrational disorder. Comstock, the *Collier's* reporter, provided an image of ruined clothing to sensationalize her description of picketing:

Picketing and its results have furnished more excitement than any other phase of this spectacular strike.... But although the instructions run "moral suasion," somehow other elements have crept in: witness the hurling of pie and the kicking of shins as example. Just where the trouble begins it is hard for an outsider to say; but girl has met girl, and presently there have been a torn plume, a bedraggled bow, a detached cluster of puffs, and an officer on the spot, then a patrol wagon and a group of strikers whirled off to the station, thence to Jefferson Market Court.[19]

On November 26, only three days into the strike, the *New York World* reported a "riot" between strikers and strike breakers in front of a large shop on Greene Street on the Lower East Side. The paper described the picketing women as an "army of Amazons" who fought the equally aggressive scabs in an "Amazonian melee," throughout which witnesses could reportedly hear "steady grinding and ripping sounds produced by tearing clothing and scratching faces." The next day, similar stories of the event appeared in the other papers. A *New York Tribune* article claimed that picketers and scabs used "the most approved feminine tactics" in their fight: "Hair was pulled out of heads by the handful, hats and coiffures were torn, tresses were disarranged, and many received marks of the fight from the nails of their antagonists." The *New York Times* claimed that the "riot" continued for two hours "while dresses were torn, faces scratched and the headgear of many girls on both sides were wrecked." Newspaper articles reported later altercations in similar terms. One described a "riot" in which "the girls kicked, scratched and pummelled each other until the street was littered with torn and tattered millinery. Bleeding faces and blackened eyes were the general rule."[20]

Torn and disheveled clothing in these descriptions probably signified irrationality and disorder, as well as gender deviance, to middle-class readers. Certainly, women were expected to keep their clothing intact. In addition, such details could be titillating for an audience that was primed to see working women in public – that is, "streetwalkers" – in sexual terms. Finally, such coverage served to erase strikers' individuality and cast them as a mob of virtually indistinguishable puffs, furs, and feathers, or as one article said, "shirtwaist whirlpools."[21] The press's coverage of the picket line battles then, whatever its intentions, undermined women as political subjects: it implied that women were not really producers but consumers; they were not rational; indeed, they were hardly individuals.

[. . .]

Newspaper coverage of women's fashion also tapped middle-class fears of disorder. For the white middle class, striking women's consumption of fashion, unbridled by middle-class values, held decisively sexual overtones. Middle-class contemporaries worried that desires for higher wages and clothing would escalate uncontrollably, until they could only be satisfied by a prostitute's income. The deserving poor, in middle-class eyes, should not dress "above their station." Newspaper articles focused on whether women had too much or not enough, rather than on their participation, as political actors, in decision-making processes. The articles in general did not treat striking women as political actors making claims but rather invoked the limits of their citizenship by focusing attention on their consumption as women.

These news articles were not the newspapers' only contribution to the public debate. Several female columnists countered the representation of striking women's fashion in newspaper reports with their own, prostrike editorials. This provided readers with a diversity of representations that could indicate that the meaning of the fashionable, striking women was more a matter of debate than a matter of fact. The columnists were middle-class suffragists, and they understood how damaging portrayals of striking women as fashionable and frivolous would be to middle-class readers' opinions. They provided a counterpoint to the predominant image of the strikers, but their defense did not represent them as political actors but as impoverished women in need of uplift.

Female columnists accepted the idea that fashionable dress signaled frivolousness and lack of need; they therefore categorically denied charges that working women dressed fashionably. Beatrice Fairfax, reporting on one parade, insisted that the strikers "were all quietly and suitably dressed, there was no attempt at finery. Some of them were hatless."[22] Dorothy Dix went further and reported that the strikers were

> young girls who had no pleasure, no amusements, who never had a full meal, or a pretty dress – girls to whom the buying of a new pair of cheap shoes is a matter of saving and scraping, and self-denial and economy, and the acquiring of one of the hundreds of dainty shirtwaists, that passes through their hands, an utter impossibility.[23]

Many shirtwaist workers certainly were impoverished, but their meager incomes did not prevent them from experiencing pleasure or obtaining pretty dresses. However, an image of young women who had "no pleasure" and

who made "no attempt at finery" fit nicely the preconception of the "deserving poor," consistent with an image of the strike in which, in the *Collier's* reporter's words, "mothers [wiped] their eyes with their aprons . . . [and] babes . . . wept bitterly for a soup bone to suck." Such representations assured middle-class readers that striking women challenged poor working conditions but not the class structure itself. Middle-class journalists who supported the strikers thus represented them less as political actors than as the needy poor, and they ignored the participation of working ladies in the strike.

[. . .]

Strike leaders had little choice but to deal with the issue of clothing: the extensive press coverage of striking women's fashion carried powerful and potentially damaging associations. Like the middle- and upper-class suffragists, strike leaders understood this, but their claims differed significantly from the suffragists as well. No leader in the SP, WTUL, or ILGWU claimed that the strikers had never had any pleasure or a "pretty dress." Perhaps they feared such a statement would ring false for anyone who had seen the strikers and would undermine leaders' credibility. Instead, they emphasized the poor *quality* of the clothing and avoided the issue of fashionable or "pretty" styles. This emphasis contained an important element of truth. [I]nexpensive, mass-produced clothing that working women could purchase was decidedly substandard in quality: while the *styles* were similar to those available for middle- and even upper-class women, the garments were cheaply made. Additionally, working women often spent the whole of their available income for a suit (skirt and jacket), shirtwaist, petticoats, shoes, and hat, and did not have the considerable sum of money necessary for a functional winter overcoat. Picketing in December and January was indeed a hardship for such inadequately dressed women. Typical articles by strike leaders ignored the style of clothing and portrayed the strikers as "thin, pale-faced, ill-clad" or as "insufficiently clad and fed." Others described their "scanty clothes" and their "thin and poorly nourished bodies and insufficient clothing," helping create an overall picture of women as impoverished and on the "verge of starvation."[24]

[. . .]

Labor leaders catered to the middle class when they obscured strikers' elaborate fashions and emphasized impoverishment, but they also represented women as serious political participants. To do so, they promoted an image of the strikers as rational subjects in keeping with Enlightenment ideals and excluded aspects of working women's culture that did not fit such an image. Theresa Malkiel reflected this concern when writing for the *New York Call*'s special strike issue:

> An uprising of women, a girls' strike! The average reader smiled as he read the first news of it. The average reader still thought that girls are flippy, flighty little things, working for pin money and more interested in the style of hairdressing for the coming season than they would be in any organization, let alone a trade union.

Malkiel reassured readers that "It is not for riches or luxuries" that women struck, but simply for "a living wage, a little more freedom, the right to co-operate with each other for their common defense." Unlike Dix, who wrote for the popular press, Malkiel included political participation in the list of women's demands. The popular press tended to represent the strikers as having feminine fun on strike; in direct contrast, Malkiel showed the strikers rationally taking personal risks, not partying or "whooping" when they walked off their jobs: "Of the 47,000 workers employed in the industry 35,000 laid down their scissors, shook the threads off their clothes and calmly left the place that stood between them and starvation."[25]

Leaders countered popular press representations of women's violence on the picket lines by representing them as peaceful and powerless victims of thugs, police, and magistrates. They described the striking women as "frail" or "tiny" strikers falling victim to "great big scabs," a "huge henchman," or a "burly" and "six footed [sic] policeman."[26]

[...]

Such "feminine" traits historically functioned as signs of women's "dependence" and were integral to women's consignment to the "private" sphere. Leaders thus created a contradictory representation of striking women as rational and thinly clad, yet frail and powerless victims. As they challenged women's historic exclusion from public life, they also replicated notions rooted in class and gender hierarchies. They depicted striking women in terms consistent with the historical political subject, yet they also incorporated gendered images of powerlessness that mollified the middle class and built upon a history of working women as charity subjects. Thus, they represented striking women *both* as citizens and as clients. In

each aspect of this representation, however, they found it necessary to obscure women's fashionable dress.

Strike leaders' strategic representations of working women as powerless *were* effective in garnering a positive response from some white middle-class people. Working women who claimed political subjectivities profoundly challenged class, gender and race hierarchies; but *as clients* striking women's political claims directly threatened shop owners' interests without appearing to threaten the class position of those who pitied them or took up their cause. Casting striking women as supplicants, leaders tacitly placed middle-class observers in the powerful position of judge and, potentially, benefactor. Indeed, the strategic representation of striking women as helpless not only garnered support for the shirtwaist strike, it culminated in a wave of protective legislation in the 1910s that limited women's work hours but not men's. The coalition of reformers and unions argued that women workers were frail "future mothers," powerless and oppressed and therefore in need of state protection. In this way, working women gained "a voice," that is, a recognized identity in relation to public and state power, partly via claims of utter defenselessness. Leaders' strategies thus inflected the development of a welfare system as well as union ideologies.[27]

There were two main problems with the labor leaders' strategy. First, it stood in uneasy relationship to the structure of unions, which ideally demanded for workers an ongoing voice in the decision-making process. Some supporters did not pay much attention to this and believed the strikers would be satisfied if their demands for higher wages and improved conditions were met. This limitation in the strategy was revealed when the workers turned down the January compromise agreed to by the strike committee and manufacturers. The compromise would meet the strikers' demands concerning wages, hours, and conditions – in Dix's terms, the "little [they asked] of their employers." However, it would not recognize the union, and thus would not grant women a voice in grievance procedures or in future contracts. The strikers rejected it unanimously, revealing an insistence on democratic participation that exceeded that of their leaders and prompting a split in the fragile alliance of strike supporters. Many of the middle- and upper-class suffragists, along with Eva McDonald Valesh, the AFL representative, withdrew their support and charged that the strike was controlled by Socialists. For them, strikers were now stepping beyond their place.[28] For the suffragists, striking women now challenged the class system; for the AFL representative, they challenged the skilled craft union basis of the AFL, which reserved full union membership and the living wage for men.

The second problem with the leaders' strategic representation of the strikers as thinly clad, rational, and powerless was that it did not match the way many working women saw themselves. The intervention of leaders in the popular debate about the strike is understandable. The visible culture of working ladies could undermine women's already shaky claims to a political voice in the eyes of many working- and middle-class people. Middle-class columnists' defense served to position strikers as charity cases who needed *only* philanthropy and pity rather than as political actors who deserved to participate in workplace decisions. Labor leaders thus faced entrenched assumptions and formidable foes. However, by erasing women's subcultural practices rather than building upon their meanings, they represented women in terms that striking ladies might find conflicted at best, insulting at worst. This would prove to have an ongoing impact on the ways labor leaders addressed working women.

[...]

When labor leaders obscured working ladyhood, then, they implicitly (and sometimes explicitly) asked working women to change fundamentally in order to take part in the labor union. While they represented strikers strategically to win public favor, many leaders believed that the ideal of a serious and rational subjectivity was indeed necessary for sustained political participation. In fact, some sought to reform working women's cultural practices of ladyhood – fashion and dime novel reading – because they believed such practices prevented the women both from being accepted as political actors and from attaining the requisite ability for rational thinking. Leaders did not simply describe actual women strikers, rather they called the "rational girl striker" into being. [...] Of course, working women did not necessarily recognize the leaders' address as fitting them, even if they were union members. Nevertheless, they certainly recognized that the address was meant for them; for those who participated in ladyhood it could make union discourse contradictory rather than simply emancipatory.

[...]

Labor publications aimed at working women actively promoted the ideal of the rational girl striker and not only erased but attacked women's popular culture activities,

particularly the primary components of ladyhood: fashion and dime novels. Such articles and stories appeared in the WTUL journal *Life and Labor* and the ILGWU journal *Ladies Garment Worker*.[29] Both of these publications originated within a year of the shirtwaist strike, and most of the articles and stories attempted to foster attitudes and identities that leaders believed were conducive to long-term union participation. Some working women did read these publications, especially those quite active in union activities, such as shop chairladies.

[...]

Leaders' representations of the rational girl striker were both strategic efforts to shape public perceptions, and evidence of a larger campaign to hail working women as political subjects. Labor leaders understood the threat of women's fashion to the public image of the strikers. They combined elements of the Enlightenment subject with charity-based ideals to paint strikers as poor and needy, wearing thin and tattered clothing, and bringing rational grievances to public attention in a serious and calm way. They then worked to get striking women to resemble this image.

[...]

The more than 20,000 striking women thus faced a number of limitations and constraints as they walked off their jobs and claimed political voices. Their historic exclusion from public life meant that many working-class and middle-class observers did not see them as legitimate political actors. They faced gendered efforts by police and courts to obstruct picketing that built upon their questioned status as political actors. Additionally, they did not have access to the popular press in which the debate about them raged, nor did they have any direct influence over the Socialist *New York Call*. While the ILGWU, the WTUL and the SP joined forces to provide critical support for women in their political efforts, they also stepped forward to represent and advocate *for* them. These representations conflicted with the ways that the many working ladies in the strike presented themselves to the public.

Thus, the 1909 shirtwaist strike was not a moment of transcendent freedom in which strikers threw off their chains and acted out of free will. Rather, women workers found the strike itself to be a limited cultural terrain, much like other social arenas they occupied. Their agency came not from autonomy, but from their creative use of limited resources. They used these resources, including the cultural contradictions in the various ways they were addressed, to claim formal political identities as strikers. Indeed, the fact that the role of working ladies was *obscured* by strike leaders does not mean that they had *no* role. Leaders' attempts to control the workers or even to influence them were themselves greatly limited in the strike. The large number of strikers – tens of thousands – and the relatively unplanned nature of the strike meant that the alliance of leaders was often overwhelmed in its many duties. Women had considerable latitude to construct subjectivities as strikers from the available cultural resources, particularly leaders' interpellations and the established practices of ladyhood. Their very different story of the strike is buried in the historical record under the official version promoted strategically by leaders. Released from seeing the official record as equivalent to the strikers' stories, it is possible for us to unearth women's formal political subjectivities.

Notes

1 See Steven Seidman, ed., *Jürgen Habermas on Society and Politics: A Reader* (Boston: Beacon Press, 1989); Nancy Fraser, "What's Critical About Critical Theory? The Case of Habermas and Gender" and Iris Marion Young, "Impartiality and the Civic Public: Some Implications of Feminist Critiques of Moral and Political Theory," both in Seyla Benhabib and Drucilla Cornell, *Feminism as Critique: On the Politics of Gender* (Minneapolis: University of Minnesota Press, 1987), 31–55, 56–76; Mary Ryan, *Civic Wars: Democracy and Public Life in the American City during the Nineteenth Century* (Berkeley: University of California Press, 1997); Miriam Hansen, *Babel and Babylon: Spectatorship in American Silent Film* (Cambridge: Harvard University Press, 1991), 9.

2 See especially Ava Baron, ed., *Work Engendered: Toward a New History of American Labor* (Ithaca: Cornell University Press, 1991); David R. Roediger, *The Wages of Whiteness: Race and the Making of the American Working Class* (London: Verso, 1999).

3 My understanding of strike chronology is drawn primarily from Louis Levine, *The Women's Garment Workers: A History of the International Ladies Garment Workers' Union* (New York: B. W. Huebsch, 1924); Helen Marot, "A Woman's Strike – An Appreciation of the Shirtwaist Makers of New York," *Proceedings of the Academy of Political Science* (Oct. 1910): 199–28.

4 *New York Evening Journal*, November 26, 1909, 1.

5 "The Girl Who Comes to the City," *Harper's Magazine* (July 1908): 693. See Laura Hapke, *Tales of the Working Girl: Wage-Earning Women in American Literature, 1890–1925*

(New York: Twayne Publishers, 1992); Hazel Carby, "Policing the Black Woman's Body in an Urban Context," *Critical Inquiry* 18 (Summer 1992), 738–55.

6 Sumner, "The Spirit of the Strikers," *The Survey* 13: 553, 551.

7 See Judith Butler, "Implicit Censorship and Discursive Agency" in *Excitable Speech: A Politics of the Performative* (New York: Routledge, 1997), 127–63.

8 See Michael Emery and Edwin Emery, *The Press and America: An Interpretive History of the Mass Media*, 6th ed. (New York: Prentice Hall, 1988), 253–4.

9 *New York Sun*, November 30, 1909, 5.

10 *New York Evening Journal*, November 26, 1909, 1; *New York World*, December 21, 1909, 3; *New York Times*, December 24, 1909, 3. Magistrate Breen, in contrast, dismissed a striker arrested for calling a strike breaker a "scab," and declared it legal to use the word. See *New York World*, December 25, 1909, 9.

11 *New York World*, December 24, 1909, 4; *NewYork Tribune*, December 25, 1909, 2; *New York Sun*, December 25, 1909, 10.

12 *New York Evening Journal*, December 31, 1909, 9. See also Kathy Peiss's discussion of the phrase "painted woman" in *Hope in a Jar: The Making of America's Beauty Culture* (New York: Henry Holt, 1999), 30–1.

13 *New York Sun*, November 30, 1909, 5.

14 See for example Norwood, *Labor's Flaming Youth*; Hall, "Disorderly Women"; Michelle Perrot, *Workers on Strike: France 1871–1890* (New Haven: Yale University Press, 1987).

15 *New York Evening Journal*, November 24, 1909, 1; *New York Sun*, December 6, 1909, 1; *New York Tribune*, November 25, 1909, 4. See also *New York Tribune*, November 28, 1909, 5.

16 *New York Evening Journal*, December 6, 1909, 5; *New York Times*, November 28, 1909, 3.

17 *New York Sun*, November 30, 1909, 5; *New York Tribune*, November 26, 1909, 10.

18 *New York World*, November 23, 1909, 2; *New York World*, November 24, 1909, 1; *New York World*, January 13, 1910, 3.

19 Sarah Comstock, "The Uprising of the Girls," *Collier's* (December 25, 1909): 15–16.

20 *New York World*, November 26, 1909, 1; *New York Tribune*, November 27, 1909, 4; *New York Times*, November 27, 1909, 3; *New York World*, January 19, 1910, 2.

21 *New York Sun*, December 6, 1909, 1.

22 Beatrice Fairfax, "Bravo, Little Sisters, Keep to the Fight," *New York Evening Journal*, December 19, 1909, 18.

23 Dorothy Dix, "Shirtwaist Strike Shows Woman's Need of the Ballot," *New York Evening Journal*, January 6, 1910, 17.

24 Miriam F. Scott, "What the Women Strikers Won," *Outlook*, July 2, 1910, 480; Marot, "A Woman's Strike," 126; "When You Go Out Shopping Remember the Shirt-Waist Girl," *Ladies' Garment Worker* 1 (1) (Apr. 1910): 1; William Mailly, "How Girls Can Strike," *Progressive*

Woman 3 (33) (Feb. 1910); Teresa Malkiel, "The Jobless Girls," *New York Call*, December 29, 1909 (special issue): 2; see also Sue A. Clark and Edith Wyatt, *Making Both Ends Meet* (New York: Macmillan, 2007), 85.

25 Malkiel, "The Jobless Girls," 2.

26 Ibid.; Tom Price, "Fighting to Live," *International Socialist Review* 10 (8) (Feb. 1910): 679.

27 Linda Gordon and Nancy Fraser, "A Genealogy of *Dependency*: Tracing a Keyword of the U.S. Welfare State," *Signs* 19 (2) (Winter 1994): 309–36. See Linda Gordon, *Pitied But Not Entitled: Single Mothers and the History of Welfare,* *1890–1935* (New York: Free Press, 1994); Barbara Nelson, "The Origins of the Two-Channel Welfare State: Workmen's Compensation and Mother's Aid," in Linda Gordon, ed., *Women, the State, and Welfare* (Madison: University of Wisconsin Press, 1990), 123–51.

28 *New York Times*, January 4, 1910, 20.

29 See Theresa S. Malkiel, *The Diary of a Shirtwaist Striker* (Ithaca, NY: ILR Press, 1990); a sampling of Barnum's columns, "Talks With the Girl Who Works," are *New York Call*, March 6, 1909, 8; March 13, 1909, 8; March 20, 1909, 8; April 17, 1909, 8; May 1, 1909, 8.

17

The Age of the CIO

Michael Denning

To name a period – the "depression," the "thirties," the "New Deal," the "age of Roosevelt," "modernism," the "streamlined years," the "age of the CIO" – is already to argue about it. Much of the argument about this period has revolved around the issue of periodization itself. If the crash of 1929 is widely accepted as the beginning of the crisis, the "end" of the "thirties" is hotly disputed. W. H. Auden dated the end of the "low dishonest decade" in his famous poem "September 1, 1939," and many literary and cultural historians critical of the Popular Front have followed suit. Within five short years, they argue, the left cultural renaissance was over, lost in the betrayals of the Moscow Trials, the Nazi-Soviet Pact, and the onset of global war. For these memoirists and historians, the thirties tell a cautionary tale: a story of impetuous youthful radicalism, of seduction and betrayal, of a "god that failed."

For others, more sympathetic to thirties radicalism, the glory days were already over by the time *Waiting for Lefty* hit Broadway in the spring of 1935. For these critics, the 1935 American Writers' Congress betrayed the young writers of the John Reed Clubs; the documentaries of Frontier Films failed to carry out the radical promise of the Workers Film and Photo League; and the Popular Front was a liberal sentimental façade replacing the radical vigor of the early 1930s. Malcolm Cowley's memoir of the 1930s ends in the summer of 1935, summarizing the last half of the decade in twenty pages; similarly, Daniel Aaron's durable history abandons its narrative in 1935 and concludes by looking at the disenchantment of half a dozen figures.[1]

For a third group, closer to the perspectives of the Popular Front itself, the thirties ended with the Henry Wallace campaign of 1948 and the onset of the Cold War. For them, the rise of McCarthy, the Hollywood blacklist, and the execution of the Rosenbergs mark the end of the period as clearly as the Moscow Trials, the Spanish Civil War, and the Nazi-Soviet Pact did for the various anti-Communists.[2]

All of these attempts to date the end, to mark the betrayal of the hopes born out of the depression, remain tied to the time of biography, the scarring of private lives by public events. However, to begin to capture the complexities of this period, we need several time frames: the conjunctural, the generational, and the epochal. A "conjuncture" was Gramsci's useful term for the immediate terrain of struggle: "[W]hen an historical period comes to be studied," Gramsci notes, "the great importance of this distinction becomes clear. A crisis occurs, sometimes lasting for decades. This exceptional duration means that incurable structural contradictions have revealed themselves . . . and that, despite this, the political forces which are struggling to conserve and defend the existing structure itself are making every effort to cure them, within certain limits, and to overcome them. These incessant and persistent efforts . . . form the terrain of the 'conjunctural,' and it is upon this terrain that the forces of opposition organise."[3]

The decades following 1929 – the age of the CIO – are just such a crisis. The crash of 1929 triggered what Gramsci called a "crisis of hegemony" in the United States, a moment when social classes became detached from their traditional parties, a "situation of conflict between 'represented and representatives'." The years of depression and war saw a prolonged "war of position" between political forces trying to conserve the existing structures of society and the forces of opposition, including the Popular Front social movement, who were trying to create a new historical bloc, a new balance of forces. The eventual post-war "settlement," marked by the famous 1950 General Motors-UAW contract, which *Fortune* called the "Treaty of Detroit," depended on the defeat of the Popular Front and the post-war purge of the left from the CIO and the cultural apparatus. If the metaphor of the front suggests a place where contending forces meet, the complementary metaphor of the conjuncture suggests the time of the battle.[4]

From this point of view, the history of the Popular Front might be seen as a series of offensives and retreats on the "terrain of the conjunctural." The first great surge was the revolutionary season from the summer of 1933 through 1934, with remarkable unrest among the unemployed, veterans (the Bonus Army march), and farmers (the Farmer's Holiday movement), culminating in a wave of strikes following the National Industrial Recovery Act, including the left-led general strikes of 1934 in Toledo, Minneapolis, and San Francisco. [. . .] This was the moment of the "proletarian avant-garde" as young communist writers and artists produced a wave of little magazines and exhibitions.

The second great surge began in the fall of 1936 and continued through the spring and summer of 1937: kicked off by the CIO victories in Akron and Flint, it was the year of "sit-down fever." The elections of Popular Front governments in Spain (February 1936) and France (May 1936) raised the hopes of socialists around the world; Franco's revolt against the Spanish Republic in July 1936 led to two years of US organizing in solidarity with the Spanish Loyalist government. These were the years when the term "Popular Front" emerged as the characteristic name of the movement. [. . .]

The defeat of the Spanish Republic in early 1939, the Nazi-Soviet Pact of August 1939, and the onset of war in Europe were deeply discouraging, and marked a crisis for the Popular Front. Nevertheless, during the fall of 1940 and the spring and summer of 1941, there was an often-overlooked resurgence. Although it had made little headway since 1937, the CIO led one of the largest strike waves in US history in 1941, winning both at Ford's River Rouge plant and against the firms that made up Little Steel. [. . .] Nineteen forty-one also marked the beginning of the modern civil rights movement: the March on Washington Movement, led by A. Philip Randolph, won black workers jobs in the defense industries and led to the creation of the FEPC (Fair Employment Practices Commission). In 1941, the New York Popular Front elected the first black city council member, Adam Clayton Powell, and the first Communist city council member, Pete Cacchione. The spring of 1941 saw the opening of the Mercury Theatre's production of Richard Wright's *Native Son*, as well as the release of *Citizen Kane*. Duke Ellington's "socially conscious" revue, *Jump for Joy*, played in Los Angeles through the summer of 1941. In June 1941, the Nazis invaded the Soviet Union, and in December the Japanese bombed Pearl Harbor, bringing the US into the war; very quickly, the social struggle was subordinated to war mobilization.[5]

The fourth surge was from the summer of 1943 through the election of 1944: the wartime Popular Front. In the face of a summer of hate strikes and race riots in 1943, the "labor victory front" linked the call for a second front in the anti-fascist war to a vision of post-war decolonization and a social democratic "century of the common man." The formation of CIO-PAC to support Roosevelt marked the labor movement's most ambitious electoral campaign, outlining a "people's platform" for the post-war world. In New York, Powell was elected to Congress, and Benjamin Davis was elected to the city council in his place. An important defeat at this stage was Roosevelt's choice of Truman over Henry Wallace for vice president.

The Popular Front's final offensive was from V-J Day in August 1945 through 1946, when the CIO launched a massive strike wave: by 1 February, 1946 over a quarter of the CIO's membership was on strike in what was the "most massive strike episode in American history." There were general strikes in a half-dozen US cities, including Houston, Pittsburgh, and Oakland, and a series of bitter strikes in the Hollywood studios. The CIO launched Operation Dixie, an attempt to organize the South, and the Popular Front social movement seemed to be moving again. But the fall of 1946 saw the beginning of the end: the first Republican Congress since 1932 was elected, and Truman dismissed Henry Wallace as secretary of commerce. With the announcement of the Truman Doctrine and the Marshall Plan in the spring of 1947, the Cold War had begun in earnest. Within a year, the anti-labor Taft-Hartley Act was passed (June 1947), repealing the rights labor had won during the New Deal and requiring a non-Communist affidavit from union officers; and a revived House Committee on Un-American Activities called the Hollywood Ten to testify (fall 1947). [. . .] By 1949, a Gallup Poll found that support for socialism had dropped to 15 percent. Though a Popular Front subculture persisted through the

1950s, blacklisted and in internal disarray, the backbone of the Popular Front social movement was broken.[6]

In another sense, however, the culture of the Popular Front, the culture of the "thirties," lasted well into the post-war era.

[...]

The Popular Front might in this way be seen as a structure of feeling, to use Raymond Williams's phrase. This concept reminds us that decades are by no means the most adequate way of periodizing cultural history; between the punctual events of a decade and the wider horizon of an epoch (modernism or Fordism) lies the generation. Williams himself suggested the affinity between a structure of feeling and a generation when he argued that "one generation may train its successor, with reasonable success, in the social character or the general cultural pattern, but the new generation will have its own structure of feeling. . . . [T]he new generation responds in its own ways to the unique world it is inheriting." To see the Popular Front as a structure of feeling is thus to see it as a political and cultural charter for a generation. This is why many figures who broke decisively with the Communist Party, like Richard Wright or Elia Kazan, did not really break with the Popular Front, and continued to produce works within a Popular Front structure of feeling: there is a clear continuity between Kazan's minor acting role in *Waiting for Lefty* and his direction of the 1954 film *On the Waterfront*, one of the greatest "proletarian" dramas.[7]

[...]

However, if the notion of a structure of feeling is to be more than a way of characterizing the mood of a generation, the fundamental task remains, as Fredric Jameson has noted, "that of coordinating new forms of practice and social and mental habits (this is . . . what . . . Williams . . . had in mind by the notion of a 'structure of feeling') with the new forms of economic production and organization thrown up by the modification of capitalism." Thus, in order to understand the rise and fall of the Popular Front social movement, the conjunctural and generational frames must be accompanied by an epochal one: one must triangulate the conjuncture and the generation with those larger narratives that make up our sense of cultural history, in this case the narratives of modernism and postmodernism, Fordism and post-Fordism. That the moment of the Popular Front – the age of the CIO – is

usually visible only as an interregnum, a dead end, the "thirties," is a result, I suggest, of its seeming to fall outside those larger stories of modernism and post-modernism, Fordism and post-Fordism. However, the Popular Front, the age of the CIO, stands, not as another epoch, but as the promise of a different road beyond modernism, a road not taken, a vanishing mediator. It was a moment of transition between the Fordist modernism that reigned before the crash, and the postmodernism of the American Century that emerged from the ruins of Hiroshima.[8]

"Modern times," the half-century between the 1890s and the 1940s, were what economic historians have called a "long wave" in capitalist development, comprising a period of growth and expansion from the late 1890s to World War I and a period of stagnation and contraction from World War I to World War II. "In a purely economic sense, capitalism seemed set for a long and untroubled future around 1900," Eric Hobsbawm writes. "The international capitalist economy . . . had, by and large, . . . an astonishing run for its money . . . until 1914." These "modern times" that emerged from the deep depression of the 1890s had been built on the defeat of the Populists and Knights of Labor; on a racial regime of segregation and sharecropping based on black disenfranchisement, Jim Crow legislation, and lynching; on the massive importation of migrant laborers from Southern and Eastern Europe; and on the exercise of imperial muscle in the Caribbean and the Pacific. Politically, the Republican Party dominated the nation, holding the White House from the McKinley election of 1896 until 1932, with the brief interlude of Woodrow Wilson, who came to power only when Taft and Theodore Roosevelt split the Republican Party.[9]

This economy was built on the technologies of oil, rubber, and steel fabricated into the automobile, and on the patterns of work and leisure to which Ford gave his name: the reorganization of work by the assembly line and the remaking of leisure by the family car and the five-dollar day. The opening of the Highland Park assembly line in 1915 stands as the symbolic inauguration of the Fordist labor process, combining the production of standardized parts using standardized machine tools, a continuous assembly line which brought the work to the worker in massive plants, and a workforce of semiskilled machine operators controlled by engineers and designers, embodying the Taylorist dream of separating conception from execution. The announcement of the five-dollar, eight-hour day for all workers who could pass Ford's Sociological Department's examination of "the clean and wholesome life" on 1 January 1914 marked the symbolic initiation of Fordist mass consumption, the sense that mass production requires a working-class consumer.

Thus, modernism itself might be understood as the culture of Fordism, schizophrenically divided between the functionalist machine aesthetic of Ford himself, who wished to produce one generic car, reduced to essentials, without frills or useless parts, in any color the customer wanted "as long as it is black," and the aesthetic of packaging pioneered by Alfred Sloan of General Motors, who captured Ford's market by offering new styles, new models, new colors. But modernism also became the name of the cultural ferment of the early decades of the century. The experimental avant-gardes mixed sexual and artistic radicalism with sympathies for the revolutions in Mexico and Czarist Russia, and had a lasting impact on the more widespread youth countercultures of the 1910s and 1920s, what Malcolm Cowley later called a "revolution in morals which began as a middle class children's revolt." For modernism marked a transformation of gender relations: part of the generational revolt against the "Victorian" was a refusal of the patriarch. The first two decades of the century were a high point of the woman's movement: these years were dominated by the struggle for women's suffrage, by the emergence of a "new woman," and by the invention of a new term – "feminism." There were close connections between women's rights, sexual radicalism, and the artistic renaissance: indeed, in 1917, the New York *Evening Sun* was noting that "some people think women are the cause of modernism, whatever that is."[10]

Thus, modernism came to be the expression of the dreams, discontents, and cultural contradictions of the disaffected young people of the predominantly Anglo bourgeoisie as they came to grips with the changes in the corporate economy and the changes in proper sexuality and gender roles, with the new imperialism, with the "foreign hordes" of immigrant workers. They had broken from the genteel tradition because they were caught directly between capital and labor: they were the settlement house activists, the social scientists like Walter Wykcoff who disguised themselves to see how the other half lives, the journalists like John Reed and Mary Heaton Vorse who went from Harvard and Provincetown to witness revolutionary struggles in Paterson, New Jersey, Lawrence, Massachusetts, Mexico, and Russia, and the experimental, expatriate writers and artists like Ernest Hemingway, Gertrude Stein and T. S. Eliot. They dominated the renaissance in American culture because they

attempted to represent the world of Fordism, to capture the new.

The age of the CIO grew out of the crisis of this modernism, a crisis figured by the crash of 1929. The CIO had itself emerged in the heartland of the Fordist economy and culture, in the industries that mass-produced automobiles and radios. Its unions were built by the children of the modernist migration, challenging the strikebreakers and private police of Ford, General Motors, US Steel, General Electric, and Westinghouse. The Liberty League, the now largely forgotten alliance of capitalists led by the Du Ponts, dominated the Popular Front imagination, as did the giant fortunes of J. P. Morgan, Henry Ford, William Randolph Hearst, and the Mellons. The culture of the age of the CIO was built by the children of the modernist arts, struggling to assimilate and transcend its legacy of formalist experiment. The opening shots of the cultural front were the narratives of modernist disenchantment, like Malcolm Cowley's *Exile's Return* and Caroline Ware's *Greenwich Village*. The young artists and intellectuals of the age of the CIO inherited the mantle of modernism, naming their clubs for the legendary John Reed, but, as I will argue later, they sought to create a new social modernism, a "revolutionary symbolism."

Nevertheless, the success of the CIO and the Popular Front social movement depended on the world of Fordism and modernism; and as the continental shelf of Fordism and modernism began to slip in the midst of the Second World War, revealing the first glimpses of the world we now call post-Fordism or postmodernism, the fault lines in the Popular Front social movement began to appear, cracks first evident in the 1943 riots in the war-boom cities across the continent. By the time these fault lines had entirely reshaped US society, the Popular Front social movement had vanished, together with its vision of a social democracy.

There were four aspects of this midcentury earthquake: the shift from modern to postmodern gender relations and household formations; a racial revolution that inaugurated a postmodern racial regime; the largest internal migration in US history, a migration of black and white southerners to the North, remaking the industrial working class; and the "third technological revolution" and the emergence of a post-Fordist economy. Despite the attempts by Popular Front activists to respond to these changes, each dis-organized the Popular Front social movement.

The question of whether the Second World War was a watershed in the history of US gender relations and household formations remains a contentious point among historians of women: the very visibility of the recruitment of women workers into the war industries, and the popular iconography of Rosie the Riveter that accompanied that recruitment, has made it difficult to assess whether the changes that took place were superficial or lasting.[11] Moreover, changes in the social organization of sex and gender are hard to register by decades or even by generations; conceptions of manhood and womanhood, of parenting and growing up, change slowly, even glacially. So it is difficult to correlate these changes with changes in culture and the arts, let alone with changes in political regimes.

Nevertheless, there are periods of intensified conflict between men and women, children and parents, periods of gender strife – which the early part of the century called "sex antagonism," the middle part of the century, the "battle of the sexes," and the end of the century, "sexual politics" – rooted in changes in the sexual division of labor. As the literary historians Sandra Gilbert and Susan Gubar put it: "the sexes battle because sex roles change, but, when the sexes battle, sex itself (that is, eroticism) changes." Transformations in the way work is done and divided, whether wage work, childrearing work, the work of consumption, or the unwaged work of maintaining a household, lead to an unsettling of customary stories of manhood and womanhood, in forms and ideologies of sexuality.[12]

Thus, whether or not the changes wrought by Rosie the Riveter have been overemphasized, it seems clear that the period between 1929 and 1948 marked a moment of crisis and transformation in the sexual organization of work, in gender relations, and in household formations. The modernist gender system, forged from the revolt of young women and young men against Victorian patriarchy and manifest in the emergence of what Lois Banner has called "fashion culture," was rocked by the crash of 1929. If the depression years were not a moment of feminist militancy, they were surely a time of gender strife and change: many commentators at the time noted the crisis in masculinity that accompanied the massive unemployment of the depression; the birthrate "dropped precipitously" by 1933; there was a renewed ideological attack on married women workers, who became a scapegoat for the depression; and there was a national outcry about the state of mothering and the evils of "momism" during the war years. These two decades saw the beginnings of what might be seen as the shift from a modern to a postmodern gender formation.[13]

First, there was a remarkable increase in the proportion of *married* women working for wages. Despite the

depression campaign to eliminate married women from the labor force and to strengthen the "marriage bar," the percentage of married women in the wage-labor force increased between 1930 and 1940; and by 1950, the rate was twice what it had been in 1930. As one historian has noted, "it is no wonder that even as early as the 1920s, social commentators shifted their attention from the plight of the single working woman to that of the married woman." In large part, this increase in married women workers was a consequence of the shifts in the overall occupational structure; it was not that women joined men in occupations, but that sectors of the economy employing women grew in the midcentury decades. As several studies have shown, even in the wartime mass-production industries, job segregation by sex continued, as women worked in women's departments and in jobs newly defined as "women's jobs," and those gains did not, for the most part, survive the war. Thus, the lifting of the marriage bar in teaching and clerical work by about 1950 was responsible for much of the increase in married women workers.[14]

Second, there was a marked decrease in domestic service. In the early part of the century, more women worked in domestic service than in any other occupation, and domestic service was racially and ethnically structured: in the Northeast, most domestic workers were European immigrant women; in the South, most were African Americans; in the Southwest, most were Chicanas; and in the West, most were Asian. The Second World War marked a dramatic decline in domestic service, particularly among white women. The major growth in women's employment came in clerical work and in commercial services. By 1930, clerical work was already the single most important occupational group for white women, despite the fact that married women were largely excluded from it. With the disappearance of the marriage bar by 1950, women of the depression cohort who had had greater high-school education swelled the ranks of clerical workers (women of color remained excluded from clerical work until the 1960s).[15]

These changes in women's employment were part of far-reaching shifts in household structure. If the household is the basic unit of social reproduction, the transformation from Fordism to post-Fordism has seen the growing commercialization of the household's reproductive functions; as a result, there have been remarkable shifts in the kinds of households and in the relations within households. With the decline in child labor and the rise in schooling in the first half of the century, relations between parents and children altered, as children were less a resource, contributing to the household budget, than an investment requiring resources: this paralleled a long-term decline in the birth rate. The decline in domestic service was matched by a rise in commercial services, particularly food service: the 1930s mark both the growth and feminization of commercial food service.[16]

Moreover, the expansion of the state apparatuses in this period is in large part due to the increasing involvement of the state in the household: the early welfare state was in part devised by "progressive maternalists," and the conflict between mothers and social workers runs throughout the working-class fiction of the period. The WPA day nurseries, established to provide relief work for teachers, nurses, and nutritionists, marked the first federal support of child care, and the 1941 Lanham Act funded the construction of child-care centers for war workers.[17]

These commercial and state interventions in the household accompanied the rise of a new sexual economy. The "companionate marriage," a phrase that dates from the mid 1920s, was built around birth control and the right of divorce, and placed an "unprecedented emphasis on the importance of sexual gratification in marriage." In turn, new households based on gay and lesbian sexual ties emerged, and the Second World War saw the development of an urban gay and lesbian subculture which would become a fundamental part of the postmodern household formation.[18]

These changes in work patterns and household structures had profound consequences for the Popular Front social movement, which remained closely linked to the characteristic household form of the mass-production industries, with its emphasis on the "family wage" of the male worker. This is not to say that women were not central to the Popular Front: in New York, the women workers of the garment trades were at the heart of the Popular Front, and this was, as we shall see, why *Pins and Needles* became a key cultural icon of the moment. Moreover, since the Popular Front was in many ways a community-based social movement – epitomized perhaps in the citywide general strikes of 1934 and 1946 – the key community organizers were often women. Finally, though the entry of women into the wartime mass-production industries was often tense and difficult, it rarely manifested itself in anti-women hate strikes. For the most part, the CIO unions actively recruited and supported women workers.[19]

Nevertheless, the forms of organizing that would come to dominate post-Fordism – the organization of clerical and service workers, and the sexual politics of the women's movement and the gay and lesbian movements

– did not emerge in the Popular Front. Women were usually imagined as "auxiliaries" in the struggle, and only rarely did a Popular Front feminism develop. Perhaps the first explicit Popular Front feminism appeared in the work of Mary Inman and Elizabeth Hawes. Inman's controversial study of women's oppression, *In Woman's Defense*, was serialized in the *People's World*, the voice of the California Popular Front in 1939 and 1940; and Elizabeth Hawes's labor feminism took shape in her "News for Living" columns in *PM*, the New York Popular Front tabloid. The first organizational forms of Popular Front feminism came after the Second World War: the Congress of American Women was formed in November 1945 and the 1945 equal pay bill became a key focus for both the CIO and women's groups. But these initiatives fell victim to the Cold War. Similarly, the Popular Front social movement never developed a self-conscious political struggle for gay or lesbian rights; however, when the first gay political organization, the Mattachine Society, was formed in 1950, all its founders, most notably its early leader Harry Hay, were Popular Front activists who had met through the left-wing labor school, the People's Educational Center, where Hay taught courses in music.[20]

The second aspect of the midcentury earthquake that shook the Popular Front was the racial revolution of the 1940s, the transition from a modern racial regime to a postmodern one. The racialization of peoples had long been a fundamental aspect of settler colonial societies like the United States. Since land was cheap and labor expensive, various forms of forced and imported labor reigned, class structures were racialized, and the white settlers developed racial ideologies of creole exceptionalism. Nevertheless, as Stuart Hall reminds us, this history is not a single, uninterrupted story: there is no racism, only *racisms*. In the United States, the modern racial formation emerged in the years after the Civil War. The end of the systems of forced labor in the 1860s – US slavery, Russian serfdom, and Australian transportation – marked not only a remarkable expansion of global labor migration and the rise of the "new imperialism" in the late nineteenth century, but also the birth of the modern racial systems with their legal codes of segregation, exclusion, reservations, and anti-miscegenation. In the United States, the end of Reconstruction and the restoratian of white supremacy in the South were accompanied by the Chinese Exclusion Act of 1882, the Dawes Act of 1887, which undermined the tribal land ownership of Americans Indians, and the colonial conquests of Hawaii, Puerto Rico, and the Philippines.[21]

This racial regime of modernism began to unravel in the midst of World War II. Nineteen forty-two and 1943 were years of exceptional racial conflict. In early 1942, 110,000 Japanese Americans were evacuated to assembly centers at racetracks and fairgrounds and were then interned in camps in remote desert areas of the West. In the spring and summer of 1942, race riots over public housing and "hate strikes" – white workers refusing to work with black workers – broke out throughout Detroit. Similar hate strikes occurred in Mobile, Baltimore, and Gary in 1943, culminating in the long transitworkers strike in Philadelphia in the summer of 1944, in which white streetcar employees walked out to protest the upgrading of black workers: 5,000 federal troops were called in to restore order. In June 1943, young Chicanos, Filipinos, and African Americans wearing zoot suits were stopped, stripped, and beaten by white servicemen in Los Angeles. These "zoot-suit riots" went on for a week and spread across the country in cities where servicemen were stationed: in Philadelphia, twenty-five whites attacked four blacks wearing zoot suits on 12 June. The zoot-suit riots triggered a wave of race riots throughout the summer of 1943: in San Diego, Philadelphia, Chicago, Evansville, Beaumont, Detroit, and Harlem.[22]

The internment camps, hate strikes, and race riots were symptoms of a dramatic reshaping of the American racial regime, a postmodern rewriting of the color line that derived from new relations to Asia and Latin America and the emergence of a powerful civil rights movement. The war with Japan marked the beginning of thirty-five years of war in Asia, as the United States was covertly or overtly involved in wars and insurrections in the Philippines, Korea, Indonesia, Vietnam, Cambodia, and Laos. The Asian American communities were deeply affected by the mobilizations and migrations that accompanied these wars. During the Second World War, while Japanese and Korean Americans were regarded as enemy aliens, Filipinos were allowed to become citizens for the first time, and the Chinese Exclusion Acts were repealed.[23]

The war was also a watershed in hemispheric relations. The 1942 Bracero Program recruited thousands of Mexican agricultural workers to release US farmworkers for the war plants and military; and by 1956 Mexican Americans made up a quarter of all US farmworkers. Puerto Rico's "Operation Bootstrap" of 1945 marked the beginning of the major migration of Puerto Ricans to the mainland.

Meanwhile, the national March on Washington Movement to protest the racist hiring practices of the new defense industries marked the beginning of a powerful new African American civil rights movement. Organized by the foremost black labor leader, A. Philip Randolph, the March on Washington Movement held demonstrations across the country to prepare for the 1 July 1941 march. Though the march was called off when Roosevelt met with Randolph and agreed to outlaw discrimination in the defense industries, the organization and militancy of African Americans continued to grow: the NAACP's membership multiplied ninefold during the war and the Congress on Racial Equality (CORE) was founded in 1943.[24]

In many ways, the Popular Front was more prepared for the racial realignments of the war years than for the gender realignments. The Popular Front social movement had been built around a politics of anti-racism and anti-imperialism and had struggled for an interracial movement. Moreover, the infrastructure of the Popular Front was made up of an intricate network of ethnic fraternal associations, foreign-language newspapers, and arts clubs that supported a kind of "cultural nationalism," emphasizing the distinctive histories of the peoples of the United States. The CIO unions, particularly the left-led unions, had actively worked to organize African American, Asian American, and Latino workers, and fought against the hate strikes and zoot-suit riots. One of the major successes of the wartime CIO was the ILWU's organization of Filipino and Japanese American plantation workers in Hawaii. The campaign to strengthen and enforce the Fair Employment Practices Commission (FEPC) continued throughout the war years. Though the Communist Party did not protest the internment of Japanese Americans and even suspended their Japanese American members, the West Coast Popular Front spoke out against the camps: Louis Goldblatt, the secretary-treasurer of the California CIO and Harry Bridges's right-hand man, was one of the few who testified against the internment order at the start, and Carey McWilliams, perhaps the leading intellectual of the California Popular Front, became one of the few white critics of the camps, spending three years visiting them, writing about them, and speaking against them on the radio. From Paul Robeson's 1939 version of Earl Robinson's "Ballad for Americans" to Frank Sinatra's 1945 version of Earl Robinson's "The House I Live In," the anthems of the Popular Front were pleas for racial and ethnic tolerance.[25]

Nevertheless, the Popular Front was dramatically dis-organized by the central cause of the racial realignment of the 1940s: the massive migration of white and black southerners to the war-industry cities of the North and West, a migration that remade the working classes. It was the largest internal migration in US history: not only did southwesterners – "Okies" and "Arkies" – continue to pour into California, but a million people left the southern Appalachians in each of the two decades of the 1940s and 1950s. One historian has estimated that between 8 and 12 million white southerners left the South in the quarter century after 1945. In addition, 4.5 million black southerners left the South's Black Belt between 1940 and 1970, between 12 and 15 percent of the South's black population; 90 percent of black southerners moved to six states: California, Illinois, Michigan, Pennsylvania, Ohio, and New York. In some ways, the full extent of the black migration is disguised by the additional migration to cities within the South. At the peak of southern sharecropping in 1920, half of all black Americans lived on farms; by 1984, that had dropped to 1 percent.[26]

The effect of the migration on US national culture was tremendous; the years after midcentury saw a "southernization" of American culture. Before 1954, the South was another country, another people, the land of the defeated Confederacy, ruled by large landowners and home to a system of sharecropping and segregation. One of the characteristic forms of pre-World War II national culture was the "southern", as much a genre as the western, including mythical tales of the Civil War like *Gone with the Wind* and sensational fictions of sharecropper life like Erskine Caldwell's salacious bestsellers. The migration of millions of southerners transformed the national culture. The most successful popular musics in the post-war years were those that had been called "race" and "hillbilly" and were now renamed "rhythm and blues" and "country." Similarly, a southern "regional" writer whose works were largely out of print at the end of the war, William Faulkner, became recognized as the leading "national" novelist, winning a Nobel Prize. In part, this was because Faulkner was one of the few white writers who dealt with the legacy of slavery and the racial divide. [. . .]

The relations between black and white Americans took on a dramatic new centrality in the culture as a whole; what had earlier often seemed to be a problem of the Jim Crow South was now a national divide. The cities that emerged from the migration were extremely segregated: sociologists who study residential segregation by statistical measures of "relative isolation" have found that the highest rate of isolation ever recorded for an ethnic group – Milwaukee's Italians in 1910 – was the same as the lowest rate for black Americans in 1970 (in San Francisco). A history of urban disinvestment, slum clearance in neighborhoods adjoining white neighborhoods, and the construction of high-density public housing to contain the black population, combined with the government subsidy of mortgages and highways to build white suburbs, created a new Black Belt Nation, not the Black Belt of the cotton South, but an archipelago of cities across the continent: this *de facto* apartheid became the dominant social fact of American social life in the second half of the twentieth century.[27]

The South-to-North migration and the world it created dis-organized the Popular Front social movement. The race riots and the hate strikes of the war years were emblems of these tensions, as the CIO unions, which had signed a no-strike pledge for the duration of the war, were experienced by the new workers as an alien power: not their representatives, but part of the discipline of the workplace. Just at the moment when the CIO working class, those Italian, Polish, Slavic, and Jewish ethnics of whom Robeson and Sinatra sang, gained a measure of cultural, political, and economic power, they were faced with a new working class. Whereas the CIO working class had deep roots in European radicalisms – Jewish socialism and communism, Italian anarchism, and Finnish communism, among others – the southern migrants came with little history of left-wing radicalism. The white populism of the South and Southwest was in some cases inflected by the residual socialism of the Debsian party – Woody Guthrie is an emblem of that tradition – but more often tinged with the Klan. There were exceptions, but even the militant unionism and underground Communism of rural sharecroppers, miners, and textileworkers was based in a cultural world foreign to the urban Popular Fronts of the North. If the ethnic fraternal lodges of the IWO served as a seed bed for the CIO and the Popular Front, the black and white holiness and Pentecostal churches of the southern and southwestern migrants rarely became part of the Popular Front social movement.[28]

Moreover, the cultural divide between the predominantly Catholic and Jewish workers of the CIO generation and the new southerners, black and white, was tremendous; this conflict stood at the center of the great proletarian novel of midcentury, Harriette Arnow's epic narrative of the migration of the Nevels family from Kentucky to Detroit, *The Dollmaker*. It could also be seen in the divide between the swing of Frank Sinatra, Benny Goodman, and Count Basie, and the rhythm and blues of Hank Williams, Muddy Waters, and Elvis Presley. By the 1960s, an anthem written by the Oklahoma migrant Woody Guthrie, "This Land Is Your

Land," had not only displaced the Earl Robinson anthems sung by Paul Robeson and Frank Sinatra, but Irving Berlin's "God Bless America" as well. The failure of the CIO's southern initiatives – both the pre-war Textile Workers Organizing Committee aimed at the largest group of southern industrial workers, and the post-war Operation Dixie – loomed larger and larger as Dixie became America.[29]

If this religious, ethnic, and cultural divide within the working classes broke up the fragile alliances built by the Popular Front, the emerging labor processes of post-Fordism weakened the industrial home of the CIO unions. As Robert Hill has noted, "the word 'automation' was coined around 1946 by the automobile industry to describe the introduction of automatic devices and controls to mechanize production." The development of these computer-controlled machine tools transformed the labor process of the semiskilled machine operatives, who were the heart of the CIO mass-production unions, weakening the shop-floor systems of power that industrial unionism had won and reducing the size of the labor force. As industrial production shifted from economies of scale to economies of scope, avoiding the rigidities of large-scale production by subcontracting and small-batch production, employment shifted away from goods production: in 1947, there was an even balance between employment in goods and services; by 1981, two-thirds of all workers were in services. Nineteen fifty-six was the first year when white-collar workers outnumbered blue-collar workers. The CIO's inability to organize clerical and service workers, and to invent a labor feminism that spoke to the women working in the new offices, the "factories" of post-Fordism's information industries, was to weaken the Popular Front social movement.[30]

The Popular Front social movement grew out of the crisis of Fordist modernism, and it built a remarkable coalition for economic justice and civil rights and liberties. Its political defeat in the post-war settlement was due both to the dis-organizing social transformations of midcentury and the strength of its adversaries. The capitalist revival in the years after the war sustained the anti-Communist crusade at home and abroad, and clinched the victory of Henry Luce's vision of an American Century over Henry Wallace's social democratic vision of a People's Century. Nevertheless, as Stuart Hall reminds us, "social forces which lose out in any particular historical period do not thereby disappear from the terrain of struggle; nor is struggle in such circumstances suspended." If the Popular Front was defeated on the political terrain, and the age of the CIO gave way to the American Century, it nevertheless continued to have a deep influence on US culture.[31]

Notes

1 Ira Levine, *Left-Wing Dramatic Theory in the American Theatre* (Ann Arbor: UMI Research Press, 1985), pp. 131, 177; Barbara Foley, *Radical Representations: Politics and Form in U.S. Proletarian Fiction, 1929–1941* (Durham NC: Duke University Press, 1993), p. 127. Malcolm Cowley, *The Dream of the Golden Mountains: Remembering the 1930s* (New York: Viking, 1980); Daniel Aaron, *Writers on the Left: Episodes in American Literary Communism* (New York: Harcourt, Brace & World, 1961); Paula Rabinowitz, *Labor and Desire: Women's Revolutionary Fiction in Depression America* (Chapel Hill: University of North Carolina Press, 1991); William Alexander, *Film on the Left: American Documentary Film from 1931 to 1942* (Princeton, NJ: Princeton University Press: 1981); Russell Campbell, *Cinema Strikes Back: Radical Filmmaking in the United States, 1930–1942* (Ann Arbor: UMI Research Press, 1982).

2 Larry Ceplair and Stephen Englund, *The Inquisition in Hollywood: Politics in the Film Community, 1930–1960* (Berkeley: University of California Press, 1983), and Nancy Lynn Schwartz, *The Hollywood Writers' Wars* (New York: Alfred Knopf, 1982). See also Robbie Lieberman, *"My Song Is My Weapon": People's Songs, American Communism, and the Politics of Culture 1930–1950* (Urbana: University of Illinois Press, 1989); and Frances K. Pohl, *Ben Shahn: New Deal Artist in a Cold War Climate, 1947–1954* (Austin: University of Texas Press, 1989).

3 Antonio Gramsci, *Selections from the Prison Notebooks* (London: Lawrence and Wishart, 1971), p. 178.

4 Gramsci, *Prison Notebooks*, p. 210. For a rich elaboration of Gramsci's notions of conjuncture and crisis, see Stuart Hall, *The Hard Road to Renewal* (London: Verso, 1988).

5 James J. Matles and James Higgins, *Them and Us: Struggles of a Rank-and-File Union* (Boston: Beacon Press, 1974), pp. 128, 130. Godfrey Hodgson, *America in Our Time* (New York: Vintage, 1978), p. 77. Judy Kutulas, *The Long War: The Intellectual People's Front and Anti-Stalinism, 1930–1940* (Durham, NC: Duke University Press, 1995), p. 184.

6 Robert H. Zieger, *The CIO 1935–55* (Chapel Hill: University of North Carolina Press, 1995), p. 223. See George Lipsitz, *Rainbow at Midnight: Labor and Culture in the 1940s* (Urbana: University of Illinois Press, 1994), pp. 99–154; Nelson Lichtenstein, "From Corporatism to Collective Bargaining: Organized Labor and the Eclipse of Social Democracy in the Postwar Era," in Steve Fraser and Gary Gerstle, *The Rise and Fall of the New Deal Order,*

1930–1980 (Princeton, NJ: Princeton University), p. 122. Gallup Poll quoted in Godfrey Hodgson, *America in Our Time* (New York: Vintage, 1978), p. 77.

7 Raymond Williams, *The Long Revolution* (New York: Harper and Row, 1966), pp. 48–9.

8 Fredric Jameson, *Postmodernism, or, The Cultural Logic of Late Capitalism* (Durham, NC: Duke University Press, 1991), p. xiv.

9 Hobsbawm quoted in David Gordon, Richard Edwards, and Michael Reich, *Segmented Work, Divided Workers: The Historical Transformation of Labor in the United States* (Cambridge: Cambridge University Press, 1982), p. 103.

10 Malcolm Cowley, *Exile's Return: A Literary Odyssey of the 1920s* (1934, rpt. New York: Penguin, 1976), p. 64; Peter Wollen, *Raiding the Icebox: Reflections on Twentieth-Century Culture* (Bloomington: Indiana University Press, 1993), pp. 1–71; Nancy Cott, *The Grounding of Modern Feminism* (New Haven: Yale University Press, 1987), pp. 13–16. Sandra M. Gilbert and Susan Gubar, *No Man's Land: The Place of the Woman Writer in the Twentieth Century. Volume 1: The War of the Words* (New Haven, Conn.: Yale University Press, 1988), p. vii.

11 Susan Hartmann, *The Home Front and Beyond: American Women in the 1940s* (Boston: Twayne, 1982), pp. 21, 86. Maureen Honey, *Creating Rosie the Riveter: Class, Gender and Propaganda during World War II* (Amherst: University of Massachusetts Press, 1984), p. 2.

12 Sandra M. Gilbert and Susan Gubar, *No Man's Land: The Place of the Woman Writer in the Twentieth Century. Volume 2: Sexchanges* (New Haven, Conn.: Yale University Press, 1989), p. xi.

13 Lois W. Banner, *American Beauty* (New York: Alfred Knopf, 1983).

14 Alice Kessler-Harris, *Out to Work: A History of Wage-Earning Women in the United States* (New York: Oxford University Press, 1982), pp. 258–9. Claudia Goldin, *Understanding the Gender Gap: An Economic History of American Women* (New York: Oxford University Press, 1990), p. 26.

15 Kessler-Harris, *Out to Work*, p. 270. Hartmann, *The Home Front and Beyond*, p. 94.

16 Dorothy Cobble, *Dishing It Out: Waitresses and their Unions in the Twentieth Century* (Urbana: University of Illinois Press, 1991).

17 See Molly Ladd-Taylor, *Mother-Work: Women, Child Welfare, and the State, 1890–1930* (Urbana: University of Illinois Press, 1994); Paula Rabinowitz, *Labour and Desire: Women's Revolutionary Fiction in Depression America* (Chapel Hill: University of North Carolina Press, 1991), p. 35. Geraldine Youcha, *Minding the Children: Child Care in America from Colonial Times to the Present* (New York: Scribner, 1995), p. 309.

18 Steven Mintz and Susan Kellogg, *Domestic Revolutions: A Social History of American Family Life* (New York: Free Press, 1988), p. 115. John D'Emilio, *Sexual Politics, Sexual Communities: The Making of a Homosexual Minority in the United States, 1940–1970* (Chicago: University of Chicago Press, 1983).

19 Elizabeth Faue, *Community of Suffering & Struggle: Women, Men, and the Labor Movement in Minneapolis, 1915–1945* (Chapel Hill: University of North Carolina Press, 1991), p. 12. Annelise Orleck, *Common Sense and a Little Fire: Women and Working-Class Politics in the United States, 1900–1965* (Chapel Hill: University of North Carolina Press, 1995). See Ruth Milkman, *Gender at Work: The Dynamics of Job Segregation by Sex during World War II* (Urbana: University of Illinois, 1987); Amy Kesselman, *Fleeting Opportunities: Women Shipyard Workers in Portland and Vancouver during World War II and Reconversion* (Albany: State University of New York Press, 1990); Nancy Gabin, *Feminism in the Labor Movement: Women and the United Auto Workers, 1935–1975* (Ithaca, NY: Cornell University Press, 1990); and Dorothy Sue Cobble, "Recapturing Working-Class Feminism: Union Women in the Postwar Era," in Joanne Meyerowitz, ed., *Not June Cleaver: Women and Gender in Postwar America, 1945–1960* (Philadelphia: Temple University Press, 1994).

20 See Sharon Hartman Strom, " 'We're No Kitty Foyles'," and "Challenging 'Woman's Place': Feminism, the Left, and Industrial Unionism in the 1930s," *Feminist Studies* 9.2, Summer 1983, pp. 359–86. Cobble, "Recapturing Working-Class Feminism"; Harriet Hyman Alonso, "Mayhem and Moderation: Women Peace Activists during the McCarthy Era," in Joanne Meyerowitz, ed., *Not June Cleaver: Women and Gender in Postwar America*; Amy Swerdlow, "The Congress of American Women: Left-Feminist Peace Politics in the Cold War," in Linda K. Kerber, Alice Kessler-Harris, and Kathryn Kish Sklar, eds., *U.S. History as Women's History* (Chapel Hill: University of North Carolina Press, 1995); D'Emilio, *Sexual Politics, Sexual Communities*, pp. 57–74; Stuart Timmons, *The Trouble with Harry Hay: Founder of the Modern Gay Movement* (Boston: Alyson Publications, 1990).

21 Carey McWilliams, *Brothers under the Skin* (Boston: Little Brown, 1945), p. 317.

22 See Margaret Crawford, "Daily Life on the Home Front: Women, Blacks and the Struggle for Public Housing," in Donald Albrecht, ed., *World War II and the American Dream* (Cambridge, Mass.: MIT Press, 1995); Zieger, *The CIO*, pp. 154–5; *In Transit*, pp. 252–9. See Mauricio Mazón, *The Zoot-Suit Riots: The Psychology of Symbolic Annihilation* (Austin: University of Texas Press, 1984).

23 Ronald Takaki, *Strangers from a Different Shore: A History of Asian Americans* (Boston: Little, Brown, 1989), pp. 357–405.

24 Herbert Garfinkel, *When Negroes March: The March on Washington Movement in the Organizational Politics for FEPC* (New York: Free Press, 1959). Manning Marable, *Black American Politics: From the Washington Marches to Jesse Jackson* (London: Verso, 1985), pp. 79–87; James Farmer,

Lay Bare the Heart: An Autobiography of the Civil Rights Movement (New York: Arbor House, 1985), pp. 67–168.

25   Sanford Zalburg, *A Spark is Struck! Jack Hall and the ILWU in Hawaii* (Honolulu: University of Hawaii Press, 1979).

26   Hodgson, *America in Our Time*, p. 62. Reynolds Farley and Walter R. Allen, *The Color Line and the Quality of Life in America* (New York: Oxford University Press, 1989), pp. 113–14.

27   Douglas S. Massey and Nancy A. Denton, *American Apartheid: Segregation and the Making of the Underclass* (Cambridge, Mass.: Harvard University Press, 1993), pp. 33, 57.

28   See Mark Naison, "Claude Williams," in Buhle, Buhle, and Georgakas, *Encyclopedia*; Robin D. G. Kelley, *Hammer and Hoe: Alabama Communists during the Great Depression* (Chapel Hill: University of North Carolina Press, 1990), pp. 107–8, 114–15, 196; James N. Gregory, *American Exodus: The Dust Bowl Migration and Okie Culture in California* (New York: Oxford University Press, 1989), pp. 158–62, 191–221.

29   See Michael Goldfield, "The Failure of Operation Dixie: A Critical Turning Point in American Political Development?" in Gary M. Fink and Merl E. Reed, *Race, Class, and Community in Southern Labor History* (Tuscaloosa: University of Alabama Press, 1994); Ira Katznelson, Kim Geiger, and Daniel Kryder, "Limiting Liberalism: The Southern Veto in Congress, 1933–1950," *Political Science Quarterly* 108.2, 1993, pp. 283–306.

30   Robert Hill, "Afterword" to C. L. R. James, *American Civilization* (Cambridge: Blackwell, 1993), p. 337; David Noble, *Forces of Production: A Social History of Industrial Automation* (New York: Alfred Knopf, 1984); Daniel Bell, *The Coming of Post-Industrial Society* (1973, rpt. New York: Penguin, 1976), pp. 130, 134; David Harvey, *The Condition of Post-Modernity* (Oxford: Basil Blackwell, 1989), p. 157.

31   Stuart Hall, "Gramsci's Relevance for the Study of Race and Ethnicity," in David Morley and Kuan-Hsing Chen, eds, *Stuart Hall: Critical Dialogues in Cultural Studies* (London: Routledge, 1996), p. 423.

Work, Immigration, Gender:
New Subjects of Cultural Politics

Lisa Lowe

Hello, my name is Fu Lee. I am 41 years old, married, and I have a 9-year-old daughter. I have been living in Oakland Chinatown since I left Hong Kong 12 years ago. . . .

My eyes hurt from straining under poor lighting; my throat hurt because of the chemical fumes from the fabric dye. Sometimes, I would wear surgical masks so I don't have to breathe in all the dust from the fabric. My back never stopped hurting from bending over the sewing machine all day. Our boss was like a dictator. He was always pushing us to work faster. There was a sign in the shop that said, "No loud talking. You cannot go to the bathroom." When we did talk loudly or laugh during work, he would throw empty boxes at us and tell us to go back to work. When there was a rush order, we had to eat lunch at our work station.

Last year, my employer closed his shop and left us holding bad paychecks. We found out that he had filed for bankruptcy and had no intentions of paying us our meager wages. The twelve Chinese seamstresses including myself were so mad. After working so hard under such horrendous working conditions, we should at least get our pay.

With the help of Asian Immigrant Women Advocates, we began searching for ways to get our pay. . . .[1]

Mrs. Fu Lee's testimony at a community hearing initiated by Asian Immigrant Women Advocates (AIWA) in Oakland, California, describes the conditions of many Asian immigrant women working in the San Francisco Bay Area garment industry: low-waged or unpaid labor, forced increases in productivity through long workdays or speedups, repetitive manual labor, occupational hazards and environmental toxins, and no union or collective bargaining protections. Before the Lucky Sewing Co. closed shop and left the sewing women with bad paychecks, Mrs. Lee and the other seamstresses were to have been paid $5 a dress; the subcontractor was paid $10 a dress, yet each dress was sold by Jessica McClintock, Inc. for $175. In the San Francisco Bay Area garment industry, women sew clothing that their meager wages, when they receive them, will not permit them to buy as commodities. The women work under physical conditions that are unsafe, unhealthy, and fatiguing. Furthermore, the policy of paying the worker by piece exploits the immigrant women in ways that extend beyond the extraction of surplus value from hourly low-waged factory labor. The incentive to complete as many pieces as possible makes certain that the sewing woman will work overtime without compensation and will intensify her productivity even if it results in exhaustion or personal injury. Because many are non-English- or little-English-speaking women and consider their employment options limited, because eight out of ten Chinatown immigrant families with multiple wage earners say they would "barely get by" if there were but one breadwinner in the family, these women are forced to accept the payment conditions dictated by the employer.[2]

Mrs. Lee, in collaboration with AIWA and the other women workers, has produced an important testimony that at once connects her life as a Chinese immigrant woman with her struggle as a worker who desires economic justice. Struggles for empowerment are often exclusively understood within the frameworks of legal, political, and economic institutions; the subjectivity of

Mrs. Lee can be comprehended in relation to systemic oppression and systemic change. Yet an important link in this relation is the production of individual and collective subjectivities through cultural forms and practices. In this sense, Mrs. Lee's testimony is compelling not only for the facts it relates, but also for the way it poses relations between those facts. The narrative progression charts a movement from being an aggrieved seamstress to forging a collective campaign for back pay; it inspires identification that has helped to build community solidarity around the immigrant garment workers. In addition, Mrs. Lee's testimony conveys the manner in which the factory extracted surplus value not only through her "labor" as an abstract form, but from using and manipulating her body itself: from her eyes that strained under poor lighting, her throat that hurt because of the chemical fumes from the fabric dye, and her back that ached from being bent over the sewing machine all day. Where Mrs. Lee's narrative evokes her conscious, embodied relation to work, it also refuses the isolation of each part as separate sites to be instrumentally exploited; her narrative integrates the sites of bodily exploitation as constitutive parts of the value of her labor, as well as of the process in which she becomes a "political" subject. Furthermore, as the narrative moves from her description of embodied exploitation to the decision to take collective political action, it alludes to her experiences as a woman, as a mother, as a Chinese immigrant, and as a worker, also refusing the atomization of the conditions that issue from patriarchal subordination, racialized immigration, segregation, and labor exploitation, Mrs. Lee's narrative does not reduce her political identity or actions to one cause or origin; instead it brings together the dimensions of her material and political subjectivity and, in that process, illuminates the intersecting axes of exploitation she inhabits and the differentiating operations of contemporary capital that exploit precisely through the selection and reproduction of racially, culturally, gendered-specific labor power.

Forms of individual and collective narrative are not merely representations disconnected from "real" political life; neither are these expressions "transparent" records of histories of struggle. Rather, these forms – life stories, oral histories, histories of community, literature – are crucial media that connect subjects to social relations. To consider testimony and testimonial as constituting a "genre" of cultural production is significant for Asian immigrant women, for it extends the scope of what constitutes legitimate knowledges to include other forms and practices that traditionally have been excluded from

both empirical and aesthetic modes of evaluation. Yet as Chandra Talpade Mohanty has observed of third world women's narratives, they are in themselves "not evidence of decentering hegemonic histories and subjectivities. It is the way in which they are read, understood, and located institutionally which is of paramount importance. After all, the point is not just 'to record' one's history of struggle, or consciousness, but how they are recorded; the way we read, receive, and disseminate such imaginative records is immensely significant."[3] "The way we read, receive, and disseminate" Mrs. Lee's testimony may be, in one context, to cite it as evidence in a hearing to protest the abuse of Asian immigrant garment industry workers; in this context, Mrs. Lee's testimony contributed to AIWA's campaign that succeeded in establishing Jessica McClintock's responsibility for the subcontractor. In another, and not mutually exclusive, context, the way we read Mrs. Lee's testimony may be to place it in relation to other cultural forms that make use of different techniques of narration. Such a reading need not level the differences between evidential forms that gain meaning on the horizon of the "empirical" and literary or art forms that are more commonly interpreted on the horizon of the "aesthetic." The aim is not to "aestheticize" the testimonial text, but rather to displace the categorizing drive of disciplinary formations that would delimit the transgressive force of articulations within regulative epistemological or evaluative boundaries. This mode of reading and reception seeks to situate different cultural forms in relation to shared social and historical processes, and to make active the dialectic that necessarily exists between those forms because of their common imbrication in those processes. It is to understand Asian American cultural production critically and broadly, and to interpret the interconnections between testimony, personal narrative, oral history, literature, film, visual arts, and other cultural forms, as sites through which subject, community, and struggle are signified and mediated. While specifying the differences between forms, this understanding of cultural production troubles both the strictly empirical foundations of social science and the universalizing tendencies of aesthetic discourse. In this mode, we can read testimony as more than a neopositivist "truth," as a complex mediating genre that selects, conveys, and connects "facts" in particular ways, without reducing social contradiction or compartmentalizing the individual as a site of resolution. Likewise, we can read literary texts like the novel not merely as the aesthetic framing of a "private" transcendence, but as a form that may narrate the dissolution or impossibility of the "private" domain in the context of the material conditions of work, geography, gender, and race. In this sense, cultural forms of many kinds are important media in the formation of oppositional narratives and crucial to the imagination and rearticulation of new forms of political subjectivity, collectivity, and practice.

This notion of cultural production as a site for the formation of new political subjects serves to focus the next section, in which I discuss the current construction of Asian immigrant women's work within the context of what we might term the "racialized feminization of labor" in the global restructuring of capitalism. The location of Asian immigrant women's work – at the intersection of processes of immigration, racialization, labor exploitation, and patriarchal gender relations – marks that work as irreducible to the concept of "abstract labor" and distinguishes the subjectivity it constitutes as unassimilable to an abstract political identity or to a singular narrative of emancipation implied by that identity. Hence, it is often in cultural forms and practices, broadly defined, that we find the most powerful articulation of this complex subjectivity, and through those forms and practices that an alternative "politicization" of that subject is mediated. Furthermore, the focus on women's work within the global economy as a material site in which several axes of domination intersect provides the means for linking Asian immigrant and Asian American women with other immigrant and racialized women. Asian immigrant and Asian American women are not simply the most recent formation within the genealogy of Asian American racialization; they, along with women working in the "third world," are the "new" workforce within the global reorganization of capitalism. In this sense, the active affiliations of Asian immigrant and Asian American women are informed by, yet go beyond, Asian American cultural identity as it has emerged within the confines of the US nation. They are linked to an emergent political formation, organizing across race, class, and national boundaries, that includes other racialized and immigrant groups, as well as women working in, and immigrating from, the neocolonized world.

[. . .]

Since the 1980s, the globalization of capitalism has shifted many manufacturing operations to Asia and Latin America and has reorganized a mode of production that at one time employed a US male labor force, white and black, in industrial manufacturing, and formerly employed white working-class and racialized women in assembly, blue- and pink-collar, and service work. In the search for ever cheaper, more "flexible," labor pools, this reorganization also produces a greater "pull" for new Asian and Latino immigrants, especially for Asian and Latina women, to fill the insecure assembly and service sector jobs in the United States that have emerged largely as a result of restructuring and "reengineering." Just as the displacement of US workers as well as increased immigration to the United States are an index of global capitalist restructuring, so, too, has restructuring exacerbated both anti-immigrant nativism and the state's "need" to legislate "undocumented aliens" and "permanent resident aliens" who have entered since 1965. Thus, the proletarianization of Asian and Latina immigrant women is a current instance of the contradiction between the globalization of the economy and the political needs of the nation-state; it takes place in conjunction with a gendered international division of labor that makes use of third world and racialized immigrant women as a more "flexible," "casual," "docile" workforce. Transnational industry's use of Asian and Latina women's labor – in Asia, Latin America, and the United States – is the contemporary site where the contradictions of the national and the international converge in an overdetermination of neocolonial capitalism, anti-immigrant racism, and patriarchal gender stratification.

In this sense, the global restructuring of the capitalist mode of production can be understood to constitute a new social formation, one whose domain has extended beyond the nation-state to global markets and international circuits of exchange. In *Reading Capital*, Louis Althusser and Etienne Balibar extend Marx's original formulation of the relationship between the "mode of production" and the "social formation," by defining a social formation as the complex structure in which more than one mode of production, or set of economic relations, may be combined.[4] Their elaboration suggests not only that the situations of uneven development, colonialist incorporation, and global restructuring and immigration are each characterized by the combination of several simultaneous modes of production, but that each constitutes a specific, historically distinct social formation, which includes economic, political, and ideological levels of articulation. The need to understand the differentiated forms through which capital profits through mixing and combining different modes of production suggests, too, that the complex structures of a new social formation may indeed require interventions and modes of opposition specific to those structures. One of the distinct features of the global restructuring of capital is its ability to profit not through homogenization, but through the differentiation of specific resources and markets that permits the exploitation of gendered and racialized labor within regional and national sites. Part of this differentiation involves transactions between national and international sites that formalize new capital accumulation and production techniques specifically targeting female labor markets. This occurs where women are disciplined by state-instituted traditional patriarchy, whether in Malaysia or Guatemala, or by racialized immigration laws that target female immigrants in particular, such as in California. The global racialized feminization of women's labor is a new social formation characterized by the exploitation of women both in export-oriented production zones in Asia and Latin America, *and* near the center of the market in the Silicon Valley electronics industry, in the Los Angeles manufacturing district, and in the San Francisco Bay Area garment industry.

While some analysts of transnationalism argue that global capitalism has reached a near-universal extension and has incorporated all sectors into its logic of commodification, the situations of Asian and Latina women workers suggest that transnational capitalism, like nation-state capitalism and colonial capitalism before it, continues to produce sites of contradiction and the dynamics of its own negation and critique.[5] For in the complex encounters between transnational capital and women within patriarchal gender structures, the very processes that produce a racialized feminized proletariat both displace traditional and national patriarchies and their defining regulations of gender, space, and work, and racialize the women in relation to other racialized groups. These displacements produce new possibilities precisely because they have led to a breakdown and a reformulation of the categories of nation, race, class, and gender, and in doing so have prompted a reconceptualization of the oppositional narratives of nationalism, Marxism, and feminism. The shift toward the transnationalization of capital is not exclusively manifested in the "denationalization" of corporate power or the nation-state, but, perhaps more importantly, it is expressed in the reorganization of oppositional interventions against capital that articulate themselves in terms and relations other than the singular "national," "class," or "female" subject. Asian, Asian immigrant, and Asian American women occupy some of the sites of contradiction in the current international division of labor, and their agencies are critical to US women of color activism, cross-border labor organizing, and third world and immigrant women's struggles.

Although Asian immigrant women have been in the United States since the nineteenth century, the greater numbers of Asian women immigrated after the mid-twentieth century, and the specific recruitment of women as a labor force has intensified since the Immigration and Nationality Act of 1965.[6] Since that time, along with African American and Mexican American women, Asian immigrant women have constituted an important low-paid workforce within the United States, "occupationally ghettoized" in menial, domestic, and reproductive labor, textile and garment industries, hotel and restaurant work, and a current mix of mass production, subcontracting, and family-type firms. Because of their material, gender, and racial differentiation from the abstract citizen proposed by the US political sphere, they remain at a distance from its nationalist narratives. Immigration laws help to produce a racially segmented and gender-stratified labor force for capital's needs, inasmuch as such laws seek to resolve these inequalities by deferring them in the promise of equality on the political terrain of representation. While the official narratives of immigrant inclusion propose to assimilate immigrants as citizens, the conditions of Asian immigrant women in the United States directly contradict these promises of incorporation, equal opportunity, and equal representation. Asian "American" women, even as citizens, continue to be located at the cultural, racial, and political boundaries of the nation. Indeed, I use quotation marks here to signal the ambivalent identification that both US-born Asian and Asian immigrant women have to the nationalist construction "American." For Asian immigrant women, the American contract of citizenship is quite evidently contradictory; if it proposes the state as the unified body in which all subjects are granted equal membership, it simultaneously asks that differences – of race, class, gender, and locality – be subordinated in order to qualify for membership in that democratic body.

At the same time, as a group formed through the intersecting processes of racialization, class exploitation, and gender subordination, Asian immigrant women are also differentially situated in relation to the political narratives of social movements organized around single forms of domination: for example, the liberal feminist critique of patriarchy, the trade union analysis of capitalism from the standpoint of class exploitation, and the critique of racism and internal colonialism from the standpoint of racialized minority subjects. From the early post-World War II years through the 1960s, political economy in the United States was dominated by the notion of development, and in that period, opposition to exploitation was often articulated in terms of class issues.[7] The late 1960s marked, however, the beginning of a period in which the articulation of opposition became increasingly mediated by analyses of other forms of domination, not only capitalism and imperialism, but also patriarchy and racism.[8] Emerging out of this earlier moment in the capitalist mode of production, US oppositional social movements of the 1970s – feminist, labor, civil rights, and ethnonationalist – produced narratives of political development for the subjects resisting domination within this earlier mode. According to these narratives, the "woman," "worker," and "racial or ethnic minority" subjects were said to develop from a prehegemonic pre-classidentified position to that of politicized participants who could "grasp" their exploitation in relation to their function within patriarchy, capitalism, and racism. Asian immigrant and Asian "American" women, like other racialized women, have a different political formation than that prescribed by *either* narratives of liberal capitalist development and citizenship or the narratives proposed by these oppositional movements of the 1970s. The isolation of one axis of power, such as the exploitation of labor under capitalism, masks the historical processes through which capitalism has emerged in conjunction with, and is made more efficient by, other systems of discrimination and subordination: patriarchy, racism, and colonialism.[9] The Asian "American" woman and the racialized woman are materially in excess of the subject "woman" posited by feminist discourse, or the "proletariat" described by Marxism, or the "racial or ethnic" subject projected by civil rights and ethnonationalist movements. This excess and differential places Asian American and other racialized women in critical, and dialectical, relationships to the subjects of feminism, Marxism, and ethnic nationalisms. In this sense, Asian immigrant and Asian American women may be said to constitute the dialectical sublation of these earlier models of political subjectivity.

[...]

US women of color have located themselves in relationship to intersecting dominations, and these locations have been powerfully translated into critical practices. From the 1980s, work by Audre Lorde, Cherríe Moraga, and the collective Asian Women United of California, for example, exemplify "situated" non-totalizing perspectives on conjoined dominations, as well as the emergence of politicized critiques of those conjunctions.[10]

The necessary alliances between racialized and third world women within, outside, and across the borders of the United States grow out of the contemporary conditions of global capitalism under which immigrant women working in the garment industries of Los Angeles are virtually part of the same labor force as those employed in Asia or Latin America. The sweatshops of the garment industry located in San Francisco and Los Angeles, for example, employ immigrant women from Mexico, El Salvador, Guatemala, Hong Kong, South Korea, Thailand, and the Philippines, while in these countries of origin, US transnational corporations are also conducting garment assembly work.[11] Women migrate from countries of origin formerly colonized by the United States, or currently neocolonized by US corporate capital, and come to labor here as racialized women of color. In this sense, despite the obstacles of national, cultural, and linguistic differences, there are material continuities between the conditions of Chicanas and Latinas working in the United States and the women working in *maquiladoras* and low-cost manufacturing zones in Latin America, and Asian women working both within the United States and in Asian zones of assembly and manufacturing.

Thus, recent immigrant communities constitute the most evident sites for racialized women in the United States to intersect with women in the neocolonized world whose experiences are doubly determined by exploitation that traverses national boundaries. The important ongoing work of organizations like AIWA in the San Francisco Bay Area, in which second- and third-generation Asian American women work for the empowerment of immigrant Asian women workers in the garment, hotel, and electronics industries, and the Garment Workers' Justice Center in Los Angeles and La Mujer Obrera in El Paso, suggests some ways of thinking about the mutual processes of politicization that occur between racialized immigrant women in the United States and women in the third world. [...] AIWA is an innovative example of cross-generational women of different national origins, classes, and language backgrounds organizing in ways that address the particular conditions of Asian immigrant women workers.[12] While AIWA organizes Asian immigrant women around the more traditional labor issue of workers' rights – as in the successful campaign to pressure garment manufacturer Jessica McClintock, Inc. – AIWA also focuses on bringing Asian American and Asian immigrant women together as members of Asian communities, and addresses issues that are of concern "outside" of the workplace, such as child care, health care, language, and literacy. [...]

Whereas AIWA works with Asian immigrant and Asian American women, other projects create and maintain solidarity across racial and ethnic groups and across national boundaries: groups like the Border Workers Regional Support Committee (CAFOR) and the Coalition for

Justice in the Maquiladoras (CJM) have helped Mexican *maquiladora* workers organize against US – and Japanese-owned parent companies. The Support Committee for the Maquiladora Workers in San Diego organizes activists, a number of whom are Asian immigrant women, to assist in documenting the exploitative, unsafe working conditions of the *maquiladoras* and to provide various support services for the mostly female Mexican workers.[13] Recently, the Support Committee assisted in retrieving the back wages for workers formerly employed at Exportadora de Mano de Obra in Tijuana, Mexico, through building pressures at a variety of sites, including bringing a suit in US courts against the parent company, National O-Ring, a division of American United Global Corporation. One hundred and eighty workers had lost their wages when National O-Ring suddenly closed the Exportadora plant in Tijuana, an act precipitated by the women workers having brought charges of sexual harassment against the company president. "Solidarity among workers should cross the border as easily as companies move production," says Mary Tong, director of the Support Committee for Maquiladora Workers. Labor organizing projects are changing both in response to the modes of global restructuring and to the changes in immigration and immigrant communities over the past two decades; new strategies aim to take on the difficult work of forging understanding and political solidarity between women and men across racial and national boundaries.

[...]

Mah was too busy even to look up when I offered her lunch. She said she didn't have an appetite, so I put the aluminum packet of food on the water pipe, where it'd stay warm, and her thermos on the already-filled communal eating table.

She wanted to teach me to do zippers so I could sew another dozen for her at home. . . .

Back home, I started with the darts. I sewed the facing to the interfacing, the front to the back; then I had trouble with the zipper. I wasn't used to the slick gabardine fabric; my seams didn't match up, and the needle kept sliding over to the metal teeth. I undid the seam and tried again. This time the needle hit the metal zipper tab and jammed. I gave up afraid I might break the needle. Mah broke a needle once and its tip flew up and lodged so close to her eye that Luday and Soon-ping had to walk her over to Chinese hospital.[14]

Fae Myenne Ng's novel *Bone* (1993), like Mrs. Lee's testimony with which we began, portrays Chinatown sewing women who provide labor for a transnational

consumer market in which they do not participate, and who bring home work and solicit the help of children and relatives, making the "private" domestic space of the immigrant home an additional site of labor. The lives of the Leong family in Ng's novel are legibly imprinted by conditions of Mah's work as a sewing woman: from the central motif of the sewing machine in all their lives, to the vulnerability of the immigrant home to capitalist penetration, to the tense contrast between the father Leon's difficulty staying steadily employed and Mah's "overemployment." The marriage of Leon and Mah mediates the changes in Chinatown's immigrant community, gender, and work, as sweatshops first made use of Chinese male labor during the garment industry's growth in the 1920s to 1940s, then turned increasingly to female labor after the 1946 modification of the Magnuson Act permitted Chinese wives and children to enter as nonquota immigrants and the Immigration Act of 1965 abolished Asian national origin quotas.[15] Finally, the family relations in *Bone* allegorize the conditions of immigrant life within the contradictions of the liberal nation-state as capitalism extends globally: the immigrant's lack of the civil rights promised to citizens of the nation permits the "private" space of the immigrant home to become a workplace that prioritizes the relations of production over Chinese family relations. In contradistinction to the traditional novel whose progressive narrative reconciliation of the individual to the social order symbolically figures the "private" domain as the resolution of struggles and conflicts in the nation, *Bone* "digresses" backward in time, narrating instead the erosion of the "private" sphere under the material pressures of racialized and gendered relations of production in a transnationally divided social space. From the breakdowns in communication between the parents to the various "flights" of the three daughters (emotional, mortal, and physical), the novel allegorizes how the affective, cultural ties in the Leong family bear the weight of immigration laws, geographical segregation, and global flows of exchange.

In associating a literary text like *Bone* with Mrs. Lee's testimony, I emphasize that a relation exists between these literary and evidential forms of narrative owing to their dialectical relationship to common historical and social processes. Both forms emerge in relation to a shift in the mode of production that expands by means of a deepened racialization, gendering, and fracturing of the labor force. Both elaborate the contradictions of this shift – in which the global "pulls" that bring immigrant women to work near the market's center also increase the regulation and segregation of those women by national laws and capital – but neither form seeks to resolve those contradictions in the development of a singular identity. Indeed, both Lee's testimony and Ng's novel suggest that the exploitation of immigrant seamstresses depends exactly on the cultural, racial, and gendered qualities of the workforce, rather than on the reduction of their work as interchangeable "abstract labor" without characteristics; furthermore, as immigrant women, it is precisely those characteristics that are the material trace of their historical disenfranchisement from the political realm and that differentiate the seamstresses from the concept of the "abstract citizen."[16] Therefore, in both immigrant narratives, opposition to garment industry exploitation is redressed neither through notions of the national citizen nor through strict identification with the proletarian-class subject of traditional trade unions. In other words, both Lee's testimony and Ng's novel refuse the separation of the economic, the political, and the cultural spheres dictated by the modern state, and neither narrative resolves in the formations of abstract subjects predicated on the modern separation of spheres. Rather, immigrant opposition articulates itself in forms and practices that integrate yet move beyond the political formations dictated by the modern institutions separating the political and economic spheres; the immigrant testimony and novel are cultural forms through which new "political" subjects and practices are narrated, and through which new "political" actions are mediated. In their common interruption of the modern separation of spheres and the political formations dictated by that separation, these cultural forms produce conceptions of collectivity that do not depend on privileging a singular subject as the representative of the group, conceptions of collectivity that do not prescribe a singular narrative of emancipation. Engagement with these cultural forms is not regulated by notions of identity or by modes of identification; a dialectic that presupposes differentiation and that crosses differences is always present as part of the process of engagement.

This dialectic of difference marks these texts as belonging to a new mode of cultural practice that corresponds to the new social formation of globalized capitalism. The contradictions of Asian American formation emerged in relation to the modern nation-state's attempt to resolve the contradictions between its economic and political imperatives through laws that excluded Asian immigrant laborers as "non-white aliens ineligible to citizenship" from the nineteenth to the mid-twentieth century. In that period, Asians entered along the economic axis, while the state simultaneously excluded Asians along racial and citizenship lines, and thus distanced Asian Americans, even as citizens, from membership in the national culture. While

official US cultural narratives aimed at reconciling the citizen to the modern nation-state, the material differentiation of Asian immigrants through racialization provided the conditions for Asian American cultural nationalism to emerge in the 1970s in contradiction to that official culture; Asian American cultural nationalism is contestatory in the field of culture to the degree that culture operates in and for the modern state. Insofar as this notion of culture as an institution of the modern state remains in force, even today in its complex imbrication with "postmodern" global extensions and distortions, Asian American cultural nationalism as an oppositional mode continues to have significance in relation to both residual and recast modes of the "modern." For transnational capital is "parasitic" on institutions and social relations of the modern nation-state, deploying its repressive and ideological apparatuses, manipulating the narratives of the liberal citizen-subject, as well as rearticulating modern forms of gender, temporality, and spatialization. This is nowhere clearer than in the contradiction within which global expansion precipitates the proliferation of anti-immigrant legislation, combining refortified policing of borders with ideological appeals to the racial basis of citizenship. Hence, Asian American cultural nationalism that emerged in opposition to racial exclusion continues to address these modern institutions within transnational capitalism. Yet at the same time, the current global restructuring – that moves well beyond the nation-state and entails the differentiation of labor forces internationally – constitutes a shift in the mode of production that now necessitates alternative forms of cultural practice that integrate yet move beyond those of cultural nationalism.

[...]

Notes

1 From Asian Immigrant Women's Advocates, *Immigrant Women Speak Out on Garment Industry Abuse: A Community Hearing Initiated by Asian Immigrant Women Advocates* (Oakland, CA: AIWA, 1 May 1993), 5. Mrs. Fu Lee is one of twelve women who were not paid by a sweatshop contracted by manufacturer Jessica McClintock, Inc. AIWA organized a long-term campaign that secured pay for these women and revealed garment industry abuse of immigrant women workers.

2 See Chalsa Loo, *Chinatown: Most Time, Hard Time* (New York: Praeger, 1991).

3 Chandra Talpade Mohanty, "Cartographies of Struggle: Third World Women and the Politics of Feminism," in *Third*

World Women and the Politics of Feminism, ed. Chandra Talpade Mohanty, Ann Russo, and Lourdes Torres (Bloomington: Indiana University Press), 34.

4 Louis Althusser and Etienne Balibar, "On the Basic Concepts of Historical Materialism," in *Reading Capital* (London: Verso, 1979).

5 On transnationalism and the capitalist mode of production, see, for example, David Harvey, *The Condition of Postmodernity* (Oxford: Basil Blackwell, 1990); Fredric Jameson, *The Geopolitical Aesthetic: Cinema and Space in the World System* (Bloomington: Indiana University Press, 1992). For analyses of third world and racialized women's work in the global economy, see Aihwa Ong, *Spirits of Resistance and Capitalist Discipline: Factory Women in Malaysia* (Albany: State University of New York Press, 1987); Swasti Mitter, *Common Fate, Common Bond: Women in the Global Economy* (London: Pluto, 1986); Maria Mies, *Patriarchy and Accumulation on a World Scale: Women in the International Division of Labor* (London: Zed Press, 1986).

6 Sucheta Mazumdar, "General Introduction: A Woman-Centered Perspective on Asian American History," in *Making Waves*, ed. Asian Women United of California (Boston: Beacon Press, 1989).

7 See Arturo Escobar, "Imagining a Post-Development Era? Critical Thought, Development and Social Movements," *Social Text* 31–2 (1992): 20–56.

8 See Nancy Hartsock, "The Feminist Standpoint: Toward a Specifically Feminist Historical Materialism," in *Money, Sex, and Power* (Boston: Northeastern University Press, 1985); Catherine Mackinnon, "Feminism, Marxism, Method, and the State: An Agenda for Theory," *Signs* 7 (1982): 515–44; Robert Blauner, *Racial Oppression in America* (New York: Harper, 1972); Mario Barrera, *Race and Class in the Southwest* (Notre Dame: University of Notre Dame Press, 1979); Rodolfo Acuna, *Occupied America: A History of Chicanos* (New York: Harper, 1981).

9 Chela Sandoval, "U.S. Third World Feminism: The Theory and Method of Oppositional Consciousness in the Postmodern World," *Genders* 10 (spring 1991): 1–24; Angela Davis, *Women, Race, and Class* (New York: Random House, 1981); Evelyn Nakano Glenn, "Racial Ethnic Women's Labor: The Intersection of Race, Gender, and Class Oppression," *Review of Radical Political Economics* 17, no. 3 (1983): 86–109. Moreover, the critique established by many women of color has consistently argued against both the hierarchization of oppressions as well as the false unification of women of color as impediments to theorizing and organizing movements for social change.

10 See Audre Lorde, "The Master's Tools Will Never Dismantle the Master's House," in *This Bridge Called My Back: Writings by Radical Women of Color*, ed. Cherríe Moraga and Gloria Anzaldúa (Watertown: Persephone Press, 1981); Asian Women United of California, *Making Waves: An Anthology of Writings by and about Asian American Women* (New York: Beacon, 1989). On the subject "women of color," see Norma Alarcón, "The Theoretical Subject(s) of 'This Bridge Called My Back' and Anglo-American Feminism", in *Making Face, Making Soul/Haciendo Caras: Creative and Critical Perspectives by Women of Color*, ed. Gloria Anzaldúa (San Francisco: Aunt Lute, 1990). See also Donna Haraway, "Situated Knowledges," *Feminist Studies* 14, no. 3 (fall 1988): 575–99.

11 See Committee for Asian Women, *Many Paths, One Goal: Organizing Women Workers in Asia* (Hong Kong: CAW, 1991); June Nash and Maria Patricia Fernandez-Kelly, eds., *Women in the International Division of Labor* (Albany: State University of New York Press, 1983); Maria Patricia Fernandez-Kelly, *"For We Are Sold, I and My People": Women and Industry on Mexico's Frontier* (Albany: State University of New York Press, 1983); Edna Bonacich, "Asians in the Los Angeles Garment Industry," in *New Asian Immigration in Los Angeles and Global Restructuring* (Philadelphia: Temple University Press, 1994); Richard P. Appelbaum, "Multiculturalism and Flexibility: Some New Directions in Global Capitalism," in *Mapping Multiculturalism*, ed. Avery Gordon and Christopher Newfield (Minneapolis: University of Minnesota, 1996); and Laura Ho, Catherine Powell, and Leti Volpp, "(Dis)Assembling Workers' Rights along the Global Assembly-line: Human Rights and the Garment Industry," *Harvard Civil Rights–Civil Liberties Law Review* 31, no. 2 (summer 1996): 383–414.

12 Asian Immigrant Women's Advocates (AIWA), 310 8th Street, Suite 301 Oakland, CA 94607.

13 Support Committee for Maquiladora Workers, 3909 Center Street, Suite 210, San Diego, CA 92103; see Kyungwon Hong and Mary Tong, "Aguirre v. AUG: A Case Study," in *Multinational Human Resource Management: Cases and Exercises*, ed. P. C. Smith (Tulsa, OK: Dame Publishing, forthcoming).

14 Fae Myenne Ng, *Bone* (New York: Hyperion, 1993), 178–9.

15 For a study of San Francisco Chinatown, see Victor G. Nee and Brett de Bary Nee, *Longtime Califoran': A Documentary Study of an American Chinatown* (New York: Pantheon, 1972).

16 Lowe, *Immigrant Acts*, 24–8.

Global Cities and Survival Circuits

Saskia Sassen

Global Cities and Survival Circuits

When today's women migrate from south to north for work as nannies, domestics, or sex workers, they participate in two sets of dynamic configurations. One of these is the global city. The other consists of survival circuits that have emerged in response to the deepening misery of the global south.[1]

Global cities concentrate some of the global economy's key functions and resources. There, activities implicated in the management and coordination of the global economy have expanded, producing a sharp growth in the demand for highly paid professionals. Both this sector's firms and the lifestyles of its professional workers in turn generate a demand for low-paid service workers. In this way, global cities have become places where large numbers of low-paid women and immigrants get incorporated into strategic economic sectors. Some are incorporated directly as low-wage clerical and service workers, such as janitors and repairmen. For others, the process is less direct, operating instead through the consumption practices of high-income professionals, who employ maids and nannies and who patronize expensive restaurants and shops staffed by low-wage workers. Traditionally, employment in growth sectors has been a source of workers' empowerment; this new pattern undermines that linkage, producing a class of workers who are isolated, dispersed, and effectively invisible.

Meanwhile, as Third World economies on the periphery of the global system struggle against debt and poverty, they increasingly build survival circuits on the backs of women – whether these be trafficked low-wage workers and prostitutes or migrant workers sending remittances back home. Through their work and remittances, these women contribute to the revenue of deeply indebted countries. "Entrepreneurs" who have seen other opportunities vanish as global firms entered their countries see profit-making potential in the trafficking of women; so, too, do longtime criminals who have seized the opportunity to operate their illegal trade globally. These survival circuits are often complex; multiple locations and sets of actors constitute increasingly far-reaching chains of traders and "workers."

Through their work in both global cities and survival circuits, women, so often discounted as valueless economic actors, are crucial to building new economies and expanding existing ones. Globalization serves a double purpose here, helping to forge links between sending and receiving countries, and enabling local and regional practices to assume a global scale. On the one hand, the dynamics that converge in the global city produce a strong demand for low-wage workers, while the dynamics that mobilize women into survival circuits produce an expanding supply of migrants who can be pushed – or sold – into such jobs. On the other hand, the very technological infrastructure and transnationalism that characterize global industries also enable other types of actors to expand onto the global stage, whether these be money launderers or people traffickers.

[…]

New Employment Regimes in Cities

Most analysts of postindustrial society and advanced economies report a massive growth in the need for highly educated workers but little demand for the type of labor that a majority of immigrants, perhaps especially immigrant women, have tended to supply over the last two or three decades. But detailed empirical studies of major cities in highly developed countries contradict this conventional view of the postindustrial economy. Instead, they show an ongoing demand for immigrant workers and a significant supply of old and new low-wage jobs that require little education.[2]

Three processes of change in economic and spatial organization help explain the ongoing, indeed growing, demand for immigrant workers, especially immigrant women. One is the consolidation of advanced services and corporate headquarters in the urban economic core, especially in global cities. While the corporate headquarters-and-services complex may not account for the majority of jobs in these cities, it establishes a new regime of economic activity, which in turn produces the spatial and social transformations evident in major cities. Another relevant process is the downgrading of the manufacturing sector, as some manufacturing industries become incorporated into the postindustrial economy. Downgrading is a response to competition from cheap imports, and to the modest profit potential of manufacturing compared to telecommunications, finance, and other corporate services. The third process is informalization, a notable example of which is the rise of the sweatshop. Firms often take recourse to informalized arrangements when they have an effective local demand for their goods and services but they cannot compete with cheap imports, or cannot compete for space and other business needs with the new high-profit firms of the advanced corporate service economy.

In brief, that major cities have seen changes in their job supplies can be chalked up both to the emergence of new sectors and to the reorganization of work in sectors new and old. The shift from a manufacturing to a service-dominated economy, particularly evident in cities, destabilizes older relationships between jobs and economic sectors. Today, much more than twenty years ago, we see an expansion of low-wage jobs associated with growing sectors rather than with declining ones. At the same time, a vast array of activities that once took place under standardized work arrangements have become increasingly informalized, as some manufacturing relocates from unionized factories to sweatshops and private homes. If we distinguish the characteristics of jobs from those of the sectors in which they are located, we can see that highly dynamic, technologically advanced growth sectors may well contain low-wage, dead-end jobs. Similarly, backward sectors like downgraded manufacturing can reflect the major growth trends in a highly developed economy.

It seems, then, that we need to rethink two assumptions: that the post-industrial economy primarily requires highly educated workers, and that informalization and downgrading are just Third World imports or anachronistic holdovers. Service-dominated urban economies do indeed create low-wage jobs with minimal education requirements, few advancement opportunities, and low pay for demanding work. For workers raised in an ideological context that emphasizes success, wealth, and career, these are not attractive positions; hence the growing demand for immigrant workers. But given the provenance of the jobs these immigrant workers take, we must resist assuming that they are located in the backward sectors of the economy.

The Other Workers in the Advanced Corporate Economy

Low-wage workers accomplish a sizable portion of the day-to-day work in global cities' leading sectors. After all, advanced professionals require clerical, cleaning, and repair workers for their state-of-the-art offices, and they require truckers to bring them their software and their toilet paper. In my research on New York and other cities, I have found that between 30 and 50 percent of workers in the leading sectors are actually low-wage workers.[3]

The similarly state-of-the-art lifestyles of professionals in these sectors have created a whole new demand for household workers, particularly maids and nannies, as well as for service workers to cater to those professionals' high-income consumption habits. Expensive restaurants, luxury housing, luxury hotels, gourmet shops, boutiques, French hand laundries, and special cleaning services, for example, are more labor-intensive than their lower-priced equivalents. To an extent not seen in a very long time, we are witnessing the reemergence of a "serving class" in contemporary high-income households and neighborhoods. The image of the immigrant woman serving the white middle-class professional woman has replaced that of the black female servant working for the white master in centuries past. The result is a sharp tendency toward social polarization in today's global cities.

We are beginning to see how the global labor markets at the top and at the bottom of the economic system are formed. The bottom is mostly staffed through the efforts of individual workers, though an expanding network of organizations has begun to get involved. Kelly Services, a Fortune 500 global staffing company that operates in twenty-five countries, recently added a home-care division that is geared toward people who need assistance with daily living but that also offers services that in the past would have been taken care of by the mother or wife figure in a household. A growing range of smaller global staffing organizations offer day care, including dropping off and picking up schoolchildren, as well as completion of in-house tasks from child care to cleaning and cooking. One international agency for nannies and au pairs (EF Au Pair Corporate Program) advertises directly to corporations, urging them to include the service in their offers to potential hires.

Meanwhile, at the top of the system, several global Fortune 500 staffing companies help firms fill high-level professional and technical jobs. In 2001, the largest of these was the Swiss multinational Adecco, with offices in fifty-eight countries; in 2000 it provided firms worldwide with 3 million workers. Manpower, with offices in fifty-nine different countries, provided 2 million workers. Kelly Services provided 750,000 employees in 2000.

The top and the bottom of the occupational distribution are becoming internationalized and so are their labor suppliers. Although midlevel occupations are increasingly staffed through temporary employment agencies, these companies have not internationalized their efforts. Occupations at the top and at the bottom are, in very different but parallel ways, sensitive. Firms need reliable and hopefully talented professionals, and they need them specialized but standardized so that they can use them globally. Professionals seek the same qualities in the workers they employ in their homes. The fact that staffing organizations have moved into providing domestic services signals both that a global labor market has emerged in this area and that there is an effort afoot to standardize the services maids, nannies, and home-care nurses deliver.

Producing a Global Supply of the New Caretakers: The Feminization of Survival

Immigrant women enter the migration process in many different ways. Some migrate in order to reunite their families; others migrate alone. Many of their initial movements have little to do with globalization. Here I am concerned with a different kind of migration experience, and it is one that is deeply linked to economic globalization: migrations organized by third parties, typically

governments or illegal traffickers. Women who enter the migration stream this way often [. . .] take over tasks previously associated with housewives.

The last decade has seen a growing presence of women in a variety of cross-border circuits. These circuits are enormously diverse, but they share one feature: they produce revenue on the backs of the truly disadvantaged. One such circuit consists in the illegal trafficking in people for the sex industry and for various types of labor. Another circuit has developed around cross-border migrations, both documented and not, which have become an important source of hard currency for the migrants' home governments. Broader structural conditions are largely responsible for forming and strengthening circuits like these. Three major actors emerge from those conditions, however: women in search of work, illegal traffickers, and the governments of the home countries.

These circuits make up, as it were, countergeographies of globalization. They are deeply imbricated with some of globalization's major constitutive dynamics: the formation of global markets, the intensifying of transnational and translocal networks, and the development of communication technologies that easily escape conventional surveillance. The global economic system's institutional support for cross-border markets and money flows has contributed greatly to the formation and strengthening of these circuits.[4] The countergeographies are dynamic and mobile; to some extent, they belong to the shadow economy, but they also make use of the regular economy's institutional infrastructure.

Such alternative circuits for survival, profit, and hard currency have grown at least partly in response to the effects of economic globalization on developing countries. Unemployment is on the rise in much of the developing world; small and medium-sized enterprises oriented to the national, rather than the export, market have closed; and government debt, already large, is in many cases rising. The economies frequently grouped under the label "developing" are often struggling, stagnant, or even shrinking. These conditions have pressed additional responsibilities onto women, as men have lost job opportunities and governments have cut back on social services. In other words, it has become increasingly important to find alternative ways of making a living, producing profits, and generating government revenues, as developing countries have faced the following concurrent trends: diminishing job prospects for men, a falloff in traditional business opportunities as foreign firms and export industries displace previous economic mainstays, and a concomitant decrease in government revenues, due both to the new conditions of globalization and to the burden of servicing debts.[5]

The major dynamics linked to economic globalization have significantly affected developing economics, including the so-called middle-income countries of the global south. These countries have had not only to accommodate new conditions but to implement a bundle of new policies, including structural adjustment programs, which require that countries open up to foreign firms and eliminate state subsidies. Almost inevitably, these economies fall into crisis; they then implement the International Monetary Fund's programmatic solutions. It is now clear that in most of the countries involved, including Mexico, South Korea, Ghana, and Thailand, these solutions have cost certain sectors of the economy and population enormously, and they have not fundamentally reduced government debt.

Certainly, these economic problems have affected the lives of women from developing countries. Prostitution and migrant labor are increasingly popular ways to make a living; illegal trafficking in women and children for the sex industry, and in all kinds of people as laborers, is an increasingly popular way to make a profit; and remittances, as well as the organized export of workers, have become increasingly popular ways for governments to bring in revenue. Women are by far the majority group in prostitution and in trafficking for the sex industry, and they are becoming a majority group in migration for labor.

Such circuits, realized more and more frequently on the backs of women, can be considered a (partial) feminization of survival. Not only are households, indeed whole communities, increasingly dependent on women for their survival, but so too are governments, along with enterprises that function on the margins of the legal economy. As the term *circuits* indicates, there is a degree of institutionalization in these dynamics; that is to say, they are not simply aggregates of individual actions.

Government Debt: Shifting Resources from Women to Foreign Banks

Debt and debt-servicing problems have been endemic in the developing world since the 1980s. They are also, I believe, crucial to producing the new countergeographies of globalization. But debt's impact on women, and on the feminization of survival, has more to do with particular features of debt than with debt *tout court*.

A considerable amount of research indicates that debt has a detrimental effect on government programs for women and children, notably education and health care. Further, austerity and adjustment programs, which are usually implemented in order to redress government debt, produce unemployment, which also adversely affects women[6] by adding to the pressure on them to ensure household survival. In order to do so, many women have turned to subsistence food production, informal work, emigration, and prostitution.[7]

[...]

The ratios of debt to GNP in many of the highly indebted poor countries exceed sustainable limits; many are far more extreme than the levels considered unmanageable during the Latin American debt crisis of the 1980s. Such ratios are especially high in Africa, where they stand at 123 percent, compared with 42 percent in Latin America and 28 percent in Asia.[8] Such figures suggest that most of these countries will not get out of their indebtedness through structural adjustment programs. Indeed, it would seem that in many cases the latter have had the effect of intensifying debt dependence. Furthermore, together with various other factors, structural adjustment programs have contributed to an increase in unemployment and in poverty.

Alternative Survival Circuits

It is in this context – marked by unemployment, poverty, bankruptcies of large numbers of firms, and shrinking state resources to meet social need – that alternative circuits of survival emerge, and it is to these conditions that such circuits are articulated. Here I want to focus on the growing salience of the trafficking of women as a profit-making option and on the growing importance of the emigrants' remittances to the bottom lines of the sending states.

Trafficking, or the forced recruitment and transportation of people for work, is a violation of human, civil, and political rights. Much legislative effort has gone into addressing trafficking: international treaties and charters, UN resolutions, and various bodies and commissions have all attempted to put a stop to this practice.[9] Nongovernmental organizations have also formed around this issue.

Trafficking in women for the sex industry is highly profitable for those running the trade. The United Nations estimates that 4 million people were trafficked in 1998, producing a profit of $7 billion for criminal groups.[10] These funds include remittances from prostitutes' earnings as well as payments to organizers and facilitators. In Poland, police estimate that for each woman delivered, the trafficker receives about $700. Ukrainian and Russian women, highly prized in the sex market, earn traffickers $500 to $1,000 per woman delivered. These women can be expected to service fifteen clients a day on average, and each can be expected to make about $215,000 per month for the criminal gang that trafficked her.[11]

It is estimated that in recent years, several million women and girls have been trafficked from and within Asia and the former Soviet Union, both of which are major trafficking areas. The growing frequency of trafficking in these two regions can be linked to increases in poverty, which may lead some parents to sell their daughters to brokers. In the former Soviet republics and Eastern Europe, unemployment has helped promote the growth of criminal gangs, some of which traffic women. Unemployment rates hit 70 percent among women in Armenia, Russia, Bulgaria, and Croatia after the implementation of market policies; in Ukraine, the rate was 80 percent. Some research indicates that need is the major motivation for entry into prostitution.

The sex industry is not the only trafficking circuit: migrant workers of both sexes can also be profitably trafficked across borders. According to a UN report, criminal organizations in the 1990s generated an estimated $3.5 billion per year in profits from trafficking migrants. Organized crime has only recently entered this business; in the past, trafficking was mostly the province of petty criminals. Some recent reports indicate that organized-crime groups are creating strategic intercontinental alliances through networks of coethnics in various countries; this facilitates transport, local distribution, provision of false documents, and the like. These international networks also allow traffickers to circulate women and other migrants among third countries; they may move women from Burma, Laos, Vietnam, and China to Thailand, while moving Thai women to Japan and the United States. The Global Survival Network reported on these practices after it conducted a two-year investigation, establishing a dummy company itself in order to enter the illegal trade.[12]

Once trafficked women reach their destination countries, some features of immigration policy and its enforcement may well make them even more vulnerable. Such women usually have little recourse to the law. If they are undocumented, which they are likely to be, they will not be treated as victims of abuse but as violators of entry, residence, and work laws. As countries of the global north attempt to address undocumented immigration and trafficking by clamping down on entry at their borders, more women are likely to turn to traffickers to help them get across. These traffickers may turn out to belong to criminal organizations linked to the sex industry.

Moreover, many countries forbid foreign women to work as prostitutes, and this provides criminal gangs with even more power over the women they traffic. It also eliminates one survival option for foreign women who may have limited access to jobs. Some countries, notably the Netherlands and Switzerland, are far more tolerant of foreign women working as prostitutes than as regular laborers. According to International Organization for Migration data, in the European Union, a majority of prostitutes are migrant women: 75 percent in Germany and 80 percent in the Italian city of Milan.

Some women know that they are being trafficked for prostitution, but for many the conditions of their recruitment and the extent of the abuse and bondage they will suffer only become evident after they arrive in the receiving country. Their confinement is often extreme – akin to slavery – and so is their abuse, including rape, other forms of sexual violence, and physical punishment. Their meager wages are often withheld. They are frequently forbidden to protect themselves against AIDS, and they are routinely denied medical care. If they seek help from the police, they may be taken into detention for violating immigration laws; if they have been provided with false documents, there will be criminal charges.

With the sharp growth of tourism over the last decade, the entertainment sector has also grown, becoming increasingly important in countries that have adopted tourism as a strategy for development.[13] In many places, the sex trade is part of the entertainment industry, and the two have grown in tandem. Indeed, the sex trade itself has become a development strategy in some areas where unemployment and poverty are widespread, and where governments are desperate for revenue and hard currency. When local manufacturing and agriculture no longer provide jobs, profits, or government revenue, a once marginal economic wellspring becomes a far more important one. The IMF and the World Bank sometimes recommend tourism as a solution to the troubles of poor countries, but when they provide loans for its development or expansion, they may well inadvertently contribute to the expansion of the entertainment industry and, indirectly, of the sex trade. Because it is linked to development strategies in this way, the trafficking of women may continue to expand in these countries.

Indeed, the global sex industry is likely to expand in any case, given the involvement of organized crime in the sex trade, the formation of cross-border ethnic networks, and the growing transnationalization of tourism. These factors may well lead to a sex trade that reaches out to more and more "markets." It's a worrisome possibility, especially as growing numbers of women face few if any employment options. Prostitution becomes – in certain kinds of economies – crucial to expanding the entertainment industry, and thereby to tourism as a development strategy that will in turn lead to increased government revenue. These links are structural; the significance of the sex industry to any given economy rises in the absence of other sources of jobs, profits, and revenues.

Women, and migrants generally, are crucial to another development strategy as well: the remittances migrant workers send home are a major source of hard-currency reserves for the migrant's home country. While remittances may seem minor compared to the financial markets' massive daily flow of capital, they are often very significant for struggling economies. In 1998, the latest year for which we have data, the remittances migrants sent home topped $70 billion globally. To understand the significance of this figure, compare it to the GDP and foreign currency reserves in the affected countries, rather than to the global flow of capital. For instance, in the Philippines, a major sender of migrants generally and of women for the entertainment industry in particular, remittances were the third largest source of foreign currency over the last several years. In Bangladesh, which sends significant numbers of workers to the Middle East, Japan, and several European countries, remittances totaled about a third of foreign-currency transactions.

Exporting workers is one means by which governments cope with unemployment and foreign debt. The benefits of this strategy come through two channels, one of which is highly formalized and the other a simple by-product of the migration process. South Korea and the Philippines both furnish good examples of formal labor-export programs. In the 1970s, South Korea developed extensive programs to promote the export of workers, initially to the Middle Eastern OPEC countries and then worldwide, as an integral part of its growing overseas construction industry. When South Korea's economy boomed, exporting workers became a less necessary and less attractive strategy. The Philippine government, by contrast, expanded and diversified its labor exports in order to deal with unemployment and to secure needed foreign-currency reserves through remittances.

The Philippines Overseas Employment Administration (POEA) has played an important role in the emigration of Filipina women to the United States, the Middle East, and Japan. Established by the Filipino government in 1982, POEA organized and supervised the export of nurses and maids to high-demand areas. Foreign debt and unemployment combined to make the export of labor an attractive option. Filipino workers overseas send home an average of almost $1 billion a year. For their parts, labor-importing countries had their own reasons to welcome the Filipino government's policy. The OPEC countries of the Middle East saw in the Filipina migrants an answer to their growing demand for domestic workers following the 1973 oil boom. Confronted with an acute shortage of nurses, a profession that demanded years of training yet garnered low wages and little prestige, the United States passed the Immigration Nursing Relief Act of 1989, which allowed for the importation of nurses.[14] And in booming 1980s Japan, which witnessed rising expendable incomes but marked labor shortages, the government passed legislation permitting the entry of "entertainment workers."

The largest number of migrant Filipinas work overseas as maids, particularly in other Asian countries.[15] The second largest group, and the fastest growing, consists of entertainers, who migrate mostly to Japan. The rapid increase in the number of women migrating as entertainers can be traced to the more than five hundred "entertainment brokers" that now operate in the Philippines outside the state umbrella. These brokers provide women for the Japanese sex industry; which is basically controlled by organized gangs rather than through the government-sponsored program for the entry of entertainers. Recruited for singing and entertaining, these women are frequently forced into prostitution as well.

The Filipino government, meanwhile, has also passed regulations that permit mail-order-bride agencies to recruit young Filipinas to marry foreign men. This trade rapidly picked up pace thanks to the government's organized support. The United States and Japan are two of the most common destinations for mail-order brides. Demand was especially high in Japan's agricultural communities in the 1980s, given that country's severe shortage of people in general and of young women in particular, as the demand for labor boomed in the large metropolitan areas. Municipal governments in Japanese towns made it a policy to accept Filipina brides.

A growing body of evidence indicates that mail-order brides frequently suffer physical abuse. In the United States, the Immigration and Naturalization Service has recently reported acute domestic violence against mail-order wives. Again, the law discourages these women from seeking recourse, as they are liable to be detained if they do so before they have been married for two years. In Japan, foreign mail-order wives are not granted full legal status, and considerable evidence indicates that many are subject to abuse not only by their husbands but by their husbands' extended families as well. The Philippine government approved most mail-order-bride brokers before 1989, but during Corazon Aquino's presidency, the stories of abuse by foreign husbands led the Philippine government to ban the mail-order-bride business. Nonetheless, such organizations are almost impossible to eliminate, and they continue to operate in violation of the law.

The Philippines may have the most developed programs for the export of its women, but it is not the only country to have explored similar strategies. After its 1997–1998 financial crisis, Thailand started a campaign to promote migration for work and to encourage overseas firms to recruit Thai workers. Sri Lanka's government has tried to export another 200,000 workers in addition to the 1 million it already has overseas; Sri Lankan women remitted $880 million in 1998, mostly from their earnings as maids in the Middle East and Far East. Bangladesh organized extensive labor-export programs to the OPEC countries of the Middle East in the 1970s. These programs have continued, becoming a significant source of foreign currency along with individual migrations to these and other countries, notably the United States and Great Britain. Bangladesh's workers remitted $1.4 billion in each of the last few years.[16]

Conclusion

Globalization is not only about the hypermobility of capital and the ascendance of information economies. It is also about specific types of places and work processes. In order to understand how economic globalization relates to the extraction of services from the Third World to fulfill what was once the First World woman's domestic role, we must look at globalization in a way that emphasizes some of these concrete conditions.

The growing immiserization of governments and economies in the global south is one such condition, insofar as it enables and even promotes the migration and trafficking of women as a strategy for survival. The same infrastructure designed to facilitate cross-border flows of capital, information, and trade also makes possible a range of unintended cross-border flows, as growing numbers of traffickers, smugglers, and even governments now make money off the backs of women. Through their work and remittances, women infuse cash into the economies of deeply indebted countries, and into the pockets of "entrepreneurs" who have seen other opportunities vanish. These survival circuits are often complex, involving multiple locations and sets of actors, which altogether constitute increasingly global chains of traders and "workers."

But globalization has also produced new labor demand dynamics that center on the global cities of the north. From these places, global economic processes are managed and coordinated by increasing numbers of highly paid professionals. Both the firms and the lifestyles of these professionals are maintained by low-paid service workers, who are in growing demand. Large numbers of low-wage women and immigrants thus find themselves incorporated into strategic economic sectors in global cities. This incorporation happens directly, as in the case of low-wage clerical and blue collar workers, such as janitors and repair workers. And it happens indirectly, through the consumption practices of high-income professionals, which generate a demand for maids and nannies as well as low-wage workers in expensive restaurants and shops. Low-wage workers are then incorporated into the leading sectors, but under conditions that render them invisible.

Both in global cities and in survival circuits, women emerge as crucial economic actors. It is partly through them that key components of new economies have been built. Globalization allows links to be forged between countries that send migrants and countries that receive them; it also enables local and regional practices to go global. The dynamics that come together in the global city produce a strong demand for migrant workers, while the dynamics that mobilize women into survival circuits produce an expanding supply of workers who can be pushed or sold into those types of jobs. The technical infrastructure and transnationalism that underlie the key globalized industries also allow other types of activities, including money-laundering and trafficking, to assume a global scale.

Notes

1 For more detailed accounts of each of these configurations please see my "Towards a Feminist Analytics of Globalization," in Saskia Sassen, *Globalization and Its*

Discontents: Essays on the Mobility of People and Money (New York: The New Press, 1998); and my article, "Women's Burden: Countergeographies of Globalization and the Feminization of Survival," *Journal of International Affairs*, vol. 53, no. 2 (spring 2000) pp. 503–24.

2   Frank Munger, ed., *Laboring Under the Line* (New York: Russell Sage Foundation, 2002); Laurance Roulleau-Berger, ed., *Youth and Work in the Postindustrial City of North America and Europe* (Leiden and New York: Brill, 2002); Hector R. Cordero-Guzman, Robert C. Smith, and Ramon Grosfoguel, eds., *Migration, Transnationalization, and Race in a Changing New York* (Philadelphia: Temple University Press, 2001); see generally for data and sources, Saskia Sassen, *The Global City* (Princeton, NJ: Princeton University Press, 2001), chapters 8 and 9.

3   See Sassen, 2001, chapters 8 and 9.

4   (E.g., Saskia Sassen, *Guests and Aliens* [New York: The New Press, 1999]). See also Max Castro, ed., *Free Markets, Open Societies, Closed Borders?* (Berkeley: University of California Press, 2000); and Frank Bonilla, Edwin Melendez, Rebecca Morales, and Maria de los Angeles Torres, eds., *Borderless Borders* (Philadelphia: Temple University Press, 1998).

5   See Kathryn Ward, *Women Workers and Global Restructuring* (Ithaca, NY: School of Industrial and Labor Relations Press, 1990); Kathryn Ward and Jean Pyle, "Gender, Industrialization and Development," in *Women in the Latin American Development Process: From Structural Subordination to Empowerment*, ed. Christine E. Bose and Edna Acosta-Belen (Philadelphia: Temple University Press, 1995), pp. 37–64; Christine E. Bose and Edna Acosta-Belen, eds., *Women in the Latin American Development Process* (Philadelphia: Temple University Press, 1995); Lourdes Beneria and Shelley Feldman, eds., *Unequal Burden: Economic Crises, Persistent Poverty, and Women's Work* (Boulder, Colo.: Westview Press, 1992); York Bradshaw, Rita Noonan, Laura Gash, and Claudia Buchmann, "Borrowing Against the Future: Children and Third World Indebtness." *Social Forces*, vol. 71, no. 3 (1993), pp. 629–56; Irene Tinker, ed., *Persistent Inequalities: Women and World Development* (New York: Oxford University Press, 1990); and Carolyn Moser, "The Impact of Recession and Structural Adjustment Policies at the Micro-Level: Low-Income Women and Their Households in Guayaquil, Ecuador," *Invisible Adjustment*, UNICEF, vol. 2 (1989).

6   See Michel Chossudovsky, *The Globalisation of Poverty* (London: Zed/TWN, 1997); Guy Standing, "Global Feminization Through Flexible Labor: A Theme Revisited," *World Development*, vol. 27, no. 3 (1999), pp. 583–602; Aminur Rahman, "Micro-credit Initiatives for Equitable and Sustainable Development: Who Pays?" *World Development*, vol. 27, no. 1 (1999), pp. 67–82; Diane Elson, *Male Bias in Development*, 2nd ed. (Manchester, 1995). For an excellent overview of the literature on the impact of the debt on women, see Kathryn Ward, "Women and the Debt," paper presented at the Colloquium on Globalization and the Debt, Emory University, Atlanta (1999). On file with author at kbward@siu.edu.

7   See Diana Alarcon-Gonzalez and Terry McKinley, "The Adverse Effects of Structural Adjustment on Working Women in Mexico," *Latin American Perspectives*, vol. 26, no. 3 (1999), 103–17; Claudia Buchmann, "The Debt Crisis, Structural Adjustment and Women's Education," *International Journal of Comparative Studies*, vol. 37, nos. 1–2 (1996), pp. 5–30; Helen I. Safa, *The Myth of the Male Breadwinner: Women and Industrialization in the Caribbean* (Boulder, Colo.: Westview Press, 1995); Nilufer Cagatay and Sule Ozler, "Feminization of the Labor Force: The Effects of Long-term Development and Structural Adjustment," *World Development*, vol. 23, no. 11 (1995), pp. 1883–94; Erika Jones, "The Gendered Toll of Global Debt Crisis," *Sojourner*, vol. 25, no. 3, pp. 20–38.

8   See Richard C. Longworth, *Global Squeeze: The Coming Crisis for First World Nations* (Chicago: Contemporary Books, 1998).

9   See Janie Chuang, "Redirecting the Debate over Trafficking in Women: Definitions, Paradigms, and Contexts," *Harvard Human Rights Journal*, vol. 10 (winter 1998); *Trafficking in Migrants*, International Office of Migration quarterly bulletin, Geneva: IOM, 1998.

10   See, generally, the Foundation Against Trafficking in Women (STV) and the Global Alliance Against Traffic in Women (GAATW). For regularly updated sources of information on trafficking, see http://www.hrlawgroup.org/site/programs/traffic.html. See also Sietske Altink, *Stolen Lives: Trading Women into Sex and Slavery* (New York: Harrington Park Press, 1995); Kamala Kempadoo and Jo Doezema, *Global Sex Workers: Rights, Resistance, and Redefinition* (London: Routledge, 1998); Susan Shannon, "The Global Sex Trade: Humans as the Ultimate Commodity," *Crime and Justice International* (May 1999), pp. 5–25; Lap-Chew Lin and Wijers Marjan, *Trafficking in Women, Forced Labour and Slavery-like Practices in Marriage, Domestic Labour and Prostitution* (Utrecht: Foundation Against Trafficking in Women [STV], and Bangkok: Global Alliance Against Traffic in Women [GAATW], 1997); Lin Lim, *The Sex Sector: The Economic and Social Bases of Prostitution in Southeast Asia* (Geneva: International Labor Office, 1998).

11   For more detailed information, see the STV-GAATW reports; IOM 1996; CIA, "International Trafficking in Women to the United States: A Contemporary Manifestation of Slavery and Organized Crime," prepared by Amy O'Neill Richard (Washington, DC: Center for the Study of Intelligence, 2000). www.cia.gov/csi/monograph/women/trafficking.pdf

12   See Global Survival Network, "Crime and Servitude: An Expose of the Traffic in Women for Prostitution from the Newly Independent States," at www.globalsurvival.net/femaletrade.html, November 1997.

13 Nancy A. Wonders and Raymond Michalowski, "Bodies, Borders, and Sex Tourism in a Globalized World: A Tale of Two Cities – Amsterdam and Havana," *Social Problems*, vol. 48, no. 4 (2001), pp. 545–71. See also Dennis Judd and Susan Fainstein, *The Tourist City* (New Haven: Yale University Press, 1999).

14 See generally, Satomi Yamamoto, "The Incorporation of Women Workers into a Global City: A Case Study of Filipina Nurses in the Metropolitan New York Area," (2000). On file with the author at syamamot@uiuc.edu.

15 Brenda Yeoh, Shirlena Huang, and Joaquin Gonzalez III, "Migrant Female Domestic Workers: Debating the Economic, Social and Political Impacts in Singapore," *International Migration Review*, vol. 33, no. 1 (1999), pp. 114–36; Christine Chin, "Walls of Silence and Late 20th-Century Representations of Foreign Female Domestic Workers: The Case of Filipina and Indonesian Houseservants in Malaysia," *International Migration Review*, vol. 31, no. 1 (1997), pp. 353–85; Noeleen Heyzer, *The Trade in Domestic Workers* (London: Zed Books, 1994).

16 Natacha David, "Migrants Made the Scapegoats of the Crisis," *ICFTU Online* (International Confederation of Free Trade Unions, 1999). www.hartford-hwp.com/archives/50/012.html

Part IV

Religion, Spirituality, and Alternate Ways of Being in the United States

Within hours of the destruction of New York's World Trade Center towers by two hijacked passenger planes, and the subsequent crash of two additional airliners into the Pentagon and a remote field in southwestern Pennsylvania, anguished commentary raced around the globe centering on the question of who had carried out such a spectacularly violent attack. Commentators also wondered why. When it quickly became known that the attack had been implemented by 19 young men who considered themselves agents of Al-Qaeda, a militant Islamicist organization countering alleged US interference in the Muslim world, reporters, writers, artists, politicians, and ordinary citizens joined in a world-wide discussion about the apparent global increase in religious fundamentalisms of all kinds. That discussion also posed questions about the nature of the relationship between fundamentalism and contemporary political events in a world increasingly affected by the secular forces of a rampant, transnational capitalism. This discussion was only rendered more urgent when the US government declared war on terrorism, linked Al-Qaeda to Iraq, which it branded part of an "axis of evil," and thereby cloaked its subsequent military actions in the language of righteous religious crusade.

Journalists and commentators turned often to the world's scholars of religion who had been working for some time already on how best to understand the full range of practices, beliefs, and organizations that claim, and have claimed, the categorical status of "religion" throughout the course of world history. Critical scholarship on religion has been animated by efforts to rethink the field's object of study in the wake of the same intellectual and

political trends that have transformed American Studies, including poststructuralist literary theory, postmodern critiques of Enlightenment liberalism and rationality, and race-based and gender analysis, as well as postcolonial critique. At stake in this discussion has been the larger theoretical question of how to understand the specificity of "religion" as a category of human behavior as well as how to trace the nature of the relationship between religions and everyday social, political, and economic acts.

Scholars of religion associated with American Studies have actively participated in these trends and, as a consequence, have begun to generate a body of work that is revivifying and transforming a path of inquiry that was once central to an American Studies preoccupied with the extended consequences of the Puritan errand in the wilderness. A new analytic is thus emerging within American Studies that is characterized by the same fundamental tension that has informed the critical study of religion more generally. On the one hand, we see a desire to take religion seriously as a force with a specificity all its own – one that needs to be understood from within. At the same time, this analytic is informed by an equally powerful impulse to investigate how religious life has developed within, intersected with, and altered the non-religious social and material conditions of everyday life. The few articles we have been able to collect here cannot fully represent the richness of these approaches. Still, they are intended to show how an attention to religion as such causes the familiar objects and concerns of American Studies to wheel into view in altered form – when engaged from a perspective willing to attend to the particular alterities of religious ways of knowing, and the different ways they have migrated globally as the world's people have been increasingly set in motion.

In the article, "Snakes Alive: Religious Studies between Heaven and Earth," Robert Orsi focuses meta-critically on the consequences of the fact that the specific moral frameworks of Western Christianity have characterized modern intellectual approaches to the study of religion and thereby limited how religions have been identified, construed and explained. Pointing to the origins of these frameworks in the colonial politics of the West and an accompanying fear of racial and ethnic otherness, Orsi asks what true respect for radical religious otherness and the diversity of forms in which it appears would look like and what it might mean for inquiries into the history and cultures of the United States.

In arguing for the importance of "getting religion" in their article of the same name, Janet Jakobsen and Ann Pellegrini critique the emerging tendency within American cultural studies of the 1990s to attend to the rise of fundamentalism alone. Suggesting in opposition to this trend that scholars of religion need to look more broadly at the relations between the "religious" and the "secular" because they are always mutually constituting, they then move to examine how, in the American context, the distinction "religious/secular" covers over another distinction, that between the Christian and non-Christian. This means that in the United States, not only do the religious and the Christian substitute for each other, but also the secular is "always already modeled in the particular image of the Christian, or at least a particular strain of the Christian, reformed post-Enlightenment Protestantism." This move, Jakobsen and Pelligrini argue, both enables and justifies the market vision of freedom as freedom precisely *from* religion and renders those who are non-Christian or Christian in another way merely "minorities."

Just as Orsi and Jakobsen and Pellegrini attend to the ways in which religious life confounds familiar categorical oppositions including that between the sacred and the secular so, too, does Leigh Schmidt in his article, "From Demon Possession to Magic Show," where he traces aspects of the encounter between religion and the Enlightenment as that conflict migrated across the Atlantic. Combining a history of philosophy and religious thought with a more performative theoretical framework that attends to the actual practices of religious life, Schmidt treats the supposed deanimation of the religious world in the United States not simply as a national matter of changing ideology or belief but rather as a gradual, uneven, and conflicted process effected by myriad

practices that produced quite different bodies with different ways of "living between heaven and earth."

Evelyn Higginbotham shows us that taking religion seriously forces us to reconceptualize the intertwined history of race, class, and mass culture more carefully. Through an analysis of highly popular religious race records of the 1920s and 1930s, Higginbotham calls for a rethinking of black vernacular culture that would challenge the assumption that black working-class culture is to be found most authentically in urban blues culture. Rather, she argues, the emotional folk orality of black working-class culture, which was embedded in both the evangelical churches of the black South and in the sermon and gospel records issued to urban audiences by Okeh, Victor, Vocalion, and Paramount, challenged the ethics and aesthetics of the black middle class and forged an enduring connection between race consciousness, creative expression, the black church, and American consumer capitalism. Equally significantly, Higginbotham shows that black working-class culture cannot be conceptualized monolithically but must be understood as itself riven by a "contestation of cultures" and conflicting value systems.

Elizabeth McAlister's treatment of Haitian Catholicism in New York similarly complicates familiar historical narratives and categorical oppositions. Indeed her account of the complex relations among Italian and Haitian Catholics around the feast of Our Lady at the Church of Our Lady of Mount Carmel in East Harlem contests older histories of immigration, assimilation, citizenship, and national belonging. Tracing the complex nature of Haitian participation in a religious festival originated and still controlled by the families of an older wave of Italian immigrants, McAlister demonstrates how the Haitians continue the practice of Catholicism at the church but always in active, diasporic relationship to Haiti itself and to its older Voudou religious traditions. In effect, their translocative religious practice is also ironically a strategy to create a new black ethnicity and alternative American identity in contra-distinction to that of *African*-Americans. Here, we see clearly the constitutive tension of this new analytic, that is, the importance of attending to religion qua religion as well as the need to understand how religion is both transformed by and transforms the social and political situation within which it emerges.

Melani McAlister is similarly interested in the space where religion and politics meet. Tracing what she calls the "the post-Vietnam figuration of Israel" through several discursive locations in American cultural production, she demonstrates how a complex image of Israel, constructed gradually over the course of the 1970s, 1980s, and 1990s, functioned as a stage upon which the war in Vietnam could be refought and potentially won. This image was produced at least initially by conservative white Christian fundamentalists like Hal Lindsey in his 1970 best-selling novel, *The Late Great Planet Earth*. Indeed Israel became an object of obsessive fascination among evangelicals as the prophesied home of the immanent Second Coming of Christ. Called as a result to an investment in the politics of Zionism, Christian fundamentalists were asked by churches and preachers to involve themselves as well in the American political sphere more generally.

This they did with a vengeance, developing a particular interest in military and foreign affairs that was then sutured to a muscular, masculinist politics modeled on the aggressive Israeli response to the murder of Israeli Olympic athletes at Munich and the generalization of that approach in Israel's relations with the Palestinians. The resultant wedding of moral discourse to military power, McAlister argues, ensured that after Munich, Entebbe, and the fall of Saigon, Israel "became a prosthetic for Americans" as the "long arm of Israeli vengeance extended the body of an American nation no longer sure of its own reach."

Snakes Alive: Religious Studies between Heaven and Earth

Robert A. Orsi

At the end of an account of his two-year sojourn among snake-handling Christians in southern Appalachia, Dennis Covington, who at the time was a Georgia-based reporter for the *New York Times*, describes the night he realized that he could not join the snake handlers whom he had come to love and respect in their faith. I want to borrow this instance of one man's discovery of radical religious otherness – a discovery that led him to turn away in sorrow and disappointment from his friends – as an opening onto the question of how critical scholarship in religion is not only possible but compelling, exciting, and revealing, especially given the challenges – moral, political, and epistemological – that have so profoundly shaken scholarship in the humanities in the last quarter century.

We scholars of religion go among people in other times or in other places who are working on their worlds with (among other things) religious tools they have found, made, or inherited, in relationships with each other and with gods, spirits, ancestors, and other significant beings. Mostly we do not share these ways of living and imagining, or do not quite share them, or even if we do share them or once did, we train ourselves to approach them now in another spirit and with different questions. Yet we want to understand these persons in their worlds in order to discover something about human life and culture, about religion and about ourselves; we would not be doing this work unless we believed that we would learn something essential about questions and problems that press themselves upon us with great urgency. How is any of this possible? How is it possible given legitimate concerns about the political implications of studying other cultures, our disturbing awareness

of the limits of Western rationalities for understanding (let alone assessing) other ways of construing the world, or simply given the formidable linguistic, historical, and existential difficulties of making one's way into a religious world that one does not share?

Critical scholarship on something called "religion" (as opposed either to theological reflection within a religious tradition or polemical commentary on religions, one's own or someone else's) first appeared in the early modern era in the West amid the ruins of the religious wars between Protestants and Catholics and just when Europeans were encountering the ancient religious cultures of Asia, Africa, and the Americas. The study of religion then developed through the ages of European colonialism and industrialism. Discourse about "religion" and "religions," in which the dilemmas, judgments, hatreds, and longings of modern Christian history were inevitably if unconsciously embedded – nineteenth- and early-twentieth-century scholarship on "Hindu" ritual, for instance, echoed with anti-Catholic contempt for corporal religious idioms and revealed less about religious practices in south Asia than about internecine European hatreds – became one medium for construing the peoples dominated by European nations, at home (in factories, on slave plantations, in urban working-class enclaves) and abroad. Discourse about "religions" and "religion" was key to controlling and dominating these populations, just as religious practice and imagination were central to the way that the dominated themselves submitted to, contested, resisted, and reimagined their circumstances. So the history of the study of religion is also always a political history, just as the political and intellectual history, of

modernity is also always a religious history. The epistemologies, methods, and nomenclature of scholarship in
religion are all implicated in this history.[1]

Within this political and historical frame, the academic study of religion has been organized around a distinct and identifiable set of moral judgments and values
that are most often implicit and commonly evident
more in convention and scholarly ethos than in precept.
Theorizing about "religion" has proceeded in accordance with these embedded moral assumptions even as
religious studies has increasingly claimed and vehemently insisted on its "scientific" status in the secular university. The usually unacknowledged imperative of these
values in the working life of the discipline has limited the
range of human practices, needs, and responses that count
as "religion." It is true that over the past twenty years
in response to criticism from various quarters the discipline has intermittently made room for less socially
tolerable forms of religious behavior within the scope
of its inquiries. But the social and intellectual pressures against this are great and the odd inclusion of an
anxiety-provoking ritual or vision has not fundamentally
changed the meaning of "religion" in "religious studies."
It is understandably preferable to write and think about
people and movements that inspire us rather than those
that repel us, that make us anxious, that violate cherished
social mores, and that we want to see disappear.
However understandable this may be, though, the question is how this hidden moral structure limits the study
of religion.

Scholars of religion, moreover, are often requested by
journalists, law-makers, and fellow citizens to map the
complex and frequently troubling landscape of contemporary religious practice and imagination in a way that
makes normative distinctions among religious behaviors
and that reassures people that despite the wildly pro-
fligate and varied nature of religions on the world stage
today, only some are really religions, while other apparently religious expressions – such as the fury unleashed
against the World Trade Center in 2001 in the name of
Islam – represent perversions or distortions of "true" religion. A lot of public talk about "religion" in the media
works to stir up terrible but also thrilling anxiety, which
is not surprising in a country enthralled and titillated by
movies and stories of gothic horrors, imaginative creations
that rose up from the bloody soil of the violence between
Protestants and Catholics in the founding age of
American culture. These frissons of titillating anxiety in
the media call forth the need – and create the occasion
– for expressions of reassurance and authority.[2]

People want to be reassured that the men who flew their
planes into the World Trade Center on September 11, 2001,
were not representatives of "real" or "good" Islam, or that
the Christians gunning down abortion doctors do not
reveal anything about contemporary American Christianity, or that priests abusing the children in their care cannot have anything to do with Catholicism. Such concerns
are understandable, and there are important distinctions
to be made in all these cases. Islam is a rich and complicated religious culture now and in the past; in the fall of
2001 and since, many Americans were appropriately
concerned that Muslim fellow citizens and visitors not be
persecuted by baseless identification with the acts of
terrorists. Evangelical Christians span the political spectrum and most of them abhor the vigilantism of the very
radical religious Right. Some of the commentary on the
clerical abuse scandal in the media and in the courts
does draw on deep anti-Catholic roots to malign a faith
because of the actions of a few. How can we scholars of
religion face the world today or our students, who are
so troubled by that world, and not make such moral
distinctions?

I am not here to argue for relativism, for scholarship
that ignores or denies its perspectives or politics, or least
of all for learning that does not address the haunting and
urgent questions of our times, nor am I suggesting that
"Islam," "evangelical Christianity," or "Catholicism" are
each respectively one unified coherent entity. But the tools
that scholars of religion use to make moral distinctions
among different religious expressions were crafted over
time in the charged political and intellectual circumstances within which the modern study of religion
came to be, and before introducing or reintroducing
moral questions into our approach to other people's
religious worlds, before we draw the lines between the
pathological and the healthy, the bad and the good, we
need to excavate our hidden moral and political history.
Otherwise, the distinctions that we make will merely be
the reiteration of unacknowledged assumptions, prejudices,
and implications in power.

Dennis Covington first entered the culture of snake
handlers on assignment from the *Times* to cover the trial
of a minister accused of attempting to kill his wife by
forcing her hand into a box of poisonous snakes.[3] Drawn
by a religious idiom that fused domains that others considered irreconcilable – heaven and earth, spirit and snake,
above and below, vulnerability and control – and that
generated experiences of tremendous visceral power,
Covington stayed on. He came to see snake handling as

a way for poor, displaced people in a ravaged land to contend with and to surmount, at least once and a while, with the snakes in their hands, the violence and danger that bore down on them in their everyday lives. Covington vividly describes local life and religious practice, and he does not stay aloof from the people he writes about (although some scholars working in the same area and many of the people with whom Covington spoke about their practices later challenged his descriptions and interpretations). He smells the "sweet savor" of the Holy Spirit moving in the room when the snakes are taken out of their boxes – a smell like "warm bread and apples" discernible just beneath the reptile fug – and finally he takes up serpents too. Until the last night of the time he spent with the snake handlers, Covington offers a worthy model for an engaged, interpersonal, participatory religious study.

But on this last evening, at the Church of the Lord Jesus Christ in Kingston, Georgia, Covington is appalled when his photographer, a young woman well known by then to the handlers, is verbally assaulted – by a minister Covington had considered his spiritual father – for what this minister and others in the congregation saw as her usurpation of the place assigned to men in church by Holy Scripture. Covington rises to witness against this denial of spiritual equality to women, but his mentor silences him. Then another preacher, the legendary figure Punkin' Brown, who was known among other things for wiping his sweat away with rattlesnakes bunched in his hand like a handkerchief, reached into the serpent box, pulled out a "big yellow-phase timber rattler, which he slung across his shoulders like a rope." As he does so, Punkin' Brown makes a sound that Covington records as "haaagh," an explosive, angry grunt, and as he bears down into his nasty, woman-hating sermon, the preacher uses this sound to set the cadence of his attack and to underscore his rage. Covington makes sure we hear this. "Haaagh" appears ten times on a single page – and it is thus – "haaagh!" – that he reestablishes the border between himself and the handlers that he had up until then so courageously been tearing down.

Covington signals and solidifies his new position vis-à-vis the handlers with a change in rhetoric. Before this evening in Kingston he had seen an eerie, otherworldly beauty in the moans and movements of the handlers. His descriptions of women taking up serpents, sobbing and trembling as they drew bundles of snakes close to themselves in religious "ecstasy," in particular are charged with a fierce (and unacknowledged) erotic intensity. But now he gives us Punkin' Brown, a vile, primitive force,

"strutting" about the sanctuary with the big snake across his shoulders, his body contorted, his face flushed with blood and hate. The evangelist brushes his lips with the serpent and wipes his face with it and always there is the brutal "haaagh!" like "steam escaping from an *underground vent*" (I have added this emphasis). Punkin' Brown has become a nightmare figure, a subterranean creature, a snake himself.[4]

Covington believes that he was saved at the last minute from descending into such strangeness himself. He tells us he was all set to give up his work at the newspaper, stock his car trunk with snakes, and head out across the land as an itinerant, snake-handling evangelist. But the "haaagh!" brought him to his senses and restored his world to him. This appears to be the existential impulse behind the abrupt change in voice – to shield himself from otherness and to impose closure on a two-year experience that threatened in the end to penetrate the boundaries of his own subjectivity. The description of Punkin' Brown – or rather, the construction of "Punkin' Brown", not the man but the character in this drama of Covington's imagination – is a barrier enacted in the language of the text against the compulsive attraction of otherness. "Punkin' Brown" makes the world safe again for Covington and his readers. Protected now against this alien – who would ever confuse the author or oneself with this wild creature, one's own fantasies, needs, and hopes with his? – Covington can find Punkin' Brown ridiculous, "grotesque and funny looking, with his shirttail out and a big rattlesnake draped over his shoulder." His description of "Punkin' Brown" is humiliating. The work of rendering Punkin' Brown into "Punkin' Brown" first secures the identity of the observer as safely separate from the other and then establishes the observer's superiority.[5]

Before moving on I want to say something about what I just called the compulsive attraction of otherness – not of difference that can be bridged but otherness that cannot and that offers only the alternatives of surrender or repulsion. Punkin' Brown died some years ago in church with a snake in his hands (his friends maintain it was not the bite that killed him but a heart weakened by the venom of many prior snakebites). Brown appears to have been a compelling man. But the wider reality here is that Americans have long been deeply fascinated by such powerfully complex religious figures, who blur gender or racial categories, for example, or do forbidden and dangerous things with their bodies or with others' bodies. Brown and his fellow snake-handling Christians were the subject of several television shows and documentaries, of many research projects, and tourists came from around the county to watch them in action. Brown believed that it was God present before him that caused him to pick up snakes at meetings; he embodied, in other words, the enduring power of sacred presence in the modern world and in modern persons' imaginations and memories, from which presence is disallowed. Americans want to be protected from these religious actors, but at the same time they want access to some of their power, an unstable mix of desire and prohibition.

Having turned Punkin' Brown into a snake, Covington makes another move. At stake that night in Georgia, he maintains on the closing page of the book (so that the handlers will not have the opportunity to say anything further for themselves), was not simply the role of women in the church. Nor was it the rightness of taking up serpents, even though this is how Punkin' Brown understood the conflict. If the Bible is wrong about women, the preacher believed, then it is wrong about the Christians' invulnerability from poisonous snakes too, so that we who take up such serpents will die, and so will our beloved family members. ("This wasn't a *test* of faith," a Tennessee minister commented on Punkin' Brown's death, "this *is* our faith.") Rather, according to Covington, at issue that night in Georgia was "the nature of God." Punkin' Brown's God, Covington reassures himself and his readers, is not, cannot be, my, our God. This is the final, and most damning, step in the rendering of Punkin' Brown as radical other: he has been cast out of the shared domain of the sacred.[6]

What has happened here? How could a writer who managed to bring the alien world of snake handlers so close end by repositioning them at the margins of culture? Covington has inscribed an existential circle, taking a long detour to reestablish the prejudices against snake handlers many readers started out with, alongside whatever fascination drew them to the work as well. I want to explore how this happens, how the religious figure that confounds and challenges us with his or her difference is silenced and securely relegated to otherness, and then I want to propose another way of approaching religions.

It seems to be virtually impossible to study religion without attempting to distinguish between its good and bad expressions, without working to establish both a normative hierarchy of religious idioms (ascending from negative to positive, "primitive" to high, local to universal, infantile to mature, among other value-laden dichotomies familiar to the field) and a methodological

justification for it. These resilient impulses take on special significance in light of the well-known inability of the field to agree on what religion is: we may not know what religion is but at least we can say with certainty what bad religion is or what religion surely is not. The mother of all religious dichotomies – us/them – has regularly been constituted as a moral distinction – good/bad religion.[7]

One of the main sources or contexts for the development of this moralizing imperative in the study of religion had to do with the way that the nascent discipline of religious studies was situated in American higher education as this was taking modern shape in the late nineteenth and twentieth centuries. The academic study of religion in the United States developed within a university culture struggling with the conflicting claims of Christian authority (widely accepted in the culture) and secular learning. Christians did not speak with a single voice in the United States and so whatever compromises were sought in response to this intellectual and cultural tension had to be acceptable within the broader social context of American denominational and theological diversity, to Calvinists, Arminianists, Quakers, Spiritualists, Christian Scientists, and so on. The solution to the dilemma from the early Republic until the years after the Second World War, according to a distinguished historian of religion in American higher education, was "morally uplifting undergraduate teaching," on the one hand, and voluntary, extracurricular religious activities on the margins of academic life, on the other, in order to satisfy the concerns of Christians inside and outside the academy. Morally uplifting undergraduate teaching: *ethics* came to stand for Christianity in American university culture but ethics defined in a broad, universal, nondogmatic, nonsectarian, and nondenominational way designed to appeal to a broad clientele. A modern and liberal creed, what the historian just cited acidly but justly calls "pious nonsectarianism," became the official religious culture of the American academy.[8]

[. . .]

The true religion long established within American academic culture – what another historian calls a domesticated Christianity tailored "for use in public life" – now became the "religion" studied in the academy.[9]

It was inconceivable that "religion" would be anything but good religion in this social and intellectual setting, "good" meaning acceptable in belief and practice to this domesticated modern civic Protestantism. Proponents of the academic study of religion claimed a place in university culture by asserting that the study of "religion" – meaning the denominationally neutral version of Christianity recast as an ethical system – was good and even necessary for American democracy. Outside the walls of the academy, the winds of religious "madness" howled (in the view of those inside) – fire-baptized people, ghost dancers, frenzied preachers and gullible masses, Mormons and Roman Catholics. "Religion" as it took shape in the academy was explicitly imagined in relation to these others and as a prophylactic against them.

Fear was central to the academic installation of religious studies. Religious difference overlapped with ethnic and racial otherness, and this combination produced and fed upon the pervasive and characteristically American idea that dangers to the Republic were germinating in the religious practices of dark-skinned or alien peoples congregated in areas beyond the oversight of the Christian middle class. Religious paranoia has been as deep in the American grain as political paranoia, deeper even because it came first; religious paranoia always shadows times of political fear. Early American scholars of religion, searching diligently for scientific laws of religious behavior, explicitly committed themselves to the project of social order. [...]

"Primitive" is an important word here. One way that [...] scholars of religion contributed to social order was by constructing and authorizing scales of religious practice and imagination that went from "primitive" to modern – where modern or mature meant the domesticated Protestantism tolerable within the academy – and mandating movement up the developmental ladder as prerequisite for modern life. (Such culturally obtuse schemas attained substantial psychological authority later in the century in models of religious "faith development.") American psychologists of religion created categories and terms to pathologize unacceptable forms of religious behavior and emotion – a scientific nomenclature of containment – and countered bad religious expressions with a normative account that designated as "religion" that component of human personality that moved it toward emotional, spiritual, and existential maturity, unity, success, and happiness. Sociologists of religion correlated unacceptable religious behaviors with certain environments and "types" of people – immigrants, migrants, African Americans, women, children, poor rural folk. "Religion," on the other hand, was socially integrative. These sociologists emphasized "religion's" role as the pivot of social stability and solidarity and relegated to categories other than "religion" any phenomenon that did not serve this consensual function.

Normative terms were presented as analytical categories, and their implicit moral and cultural assumptions went unchallenged. Such was the authority of "real" or "good" or "true" religion in the academy.

All this had dreadful social consequences when it converged with broader racist discourse in the world outside the academy. It contributed to destructive federal policies toward Native Americans. Northerners who wanted to temporize about (or even to justify) the grim realities of lynching used sociological accounts of African American popular religious culture, defined in racist terms, as mitigating explanation. Teaching domesticated Protestantism as "religion" would protect American democracy and inoculate the young against the contagion of American religious imaginings, which scholarship would contain and enclose by nomenclature and analysis. No wonder religious practitioners often do not recognize what passes for "religion" in religious studies.

The point here is not simply that the normative account of real religion that took shape within the academy or at the anxious intersection of the academy with the extravagance of American religious life excluded from the study of religion ugly, violent, or troublesome matters (although it certainly does this). Rather the entire notion of "religion" had been carefully demarcated to preserve it from ambivalence and ambiguity, from anything not in accordance with certain sanctioned notions of self and society. Religion came to be gridded along a graph of diametric opposites, and the possibility that religion can transgress these various dualities, that it does its cultural, psychological, and political work precisely by disregarding boundaries between one self and another, or between past, present, and future, or between the natural and the supernatural, is disallowed.

So what is real religion?

[...]

True religion [...] is epistemologically and ethically singular. It is rational, respectful of persons, noncoercive, mature, nonanthropomorphic in its higher forms, mystical (as opposed to ritualistic), unmediated and agreeable to democracy (no hierarchy in gilded robes and fancy hats), monotheistic (no angels, saints, demons, ancestors), emotionally controlled, a reality of mind and spirit not body and matter. It is concerned with ideal essences not actual things, and especially not about presences in things. [...] Whatever this is, it is not "good religion." All the complex dynamism of religion is thus stripped away, its boundary-blurring and border-crossing propensities

eliminated. Not surprisingly, there is only one methodology and one epistemology for studying this 'religion,'
critical, analytical, and "objective" (as opposed to "subjective," existentially engaged, or participatory).

In this way the discipline reflects the religious politics
of the United States as well as the particular history of
American higher education. The embedded, hidden
others against whom the "religion" in religious studies as
constituted are the religions on the American landscape
that appeared so terrifying and un-American to the
guardians of the culture – Mormonism, Catholicism,
certain forms of radical Christian evangelicalism, Pentecostalism, among others. The discipline was literally
constructed by means of the exclusion – in fact and in
theory – of these other ways of living between heaven and
earth, which were relegated to the world of sects, cults,
fundamentalisms, popular piety, ritualism, magic, primitive religion, millennialism, anything but "religion."

The academic study of religion is not an American
phenomenon, of course. American academics who study
religion participate in an international network of scholars institutionalized in various sorts of academic arrangements, scholarly exchanges, and symposia. But in this
broader context, too, liberal notions of religion allied to
particular political agendas came to be authoritative.
Scholars shaped in liberal Christian traditions played
important roles in the formative period of the modern
development of the discipline in Europe and in Asia; a
vision of "religion" that developed out of liberal and
modernist Christianity acquired a normative status in the
work of nineteenth- and twentieth-century scholars of
comparative religion. Nineteenth-century scholars of
south Asian religions, for example, "invented what might
be called a Euro-Buddhist canon," according to anthropologist H. L. Seneviratne, "by portraying a rationalized
and sanitized Buddhism in keeping with the imperatives
of the sociology of their own intellectual life."[10]

Indeed, this Christianity was seen as the telos of the
evolution of world religions. At the World Parliament of
Religions in Chicago in 1893 an authoritative and
hypostasized "Christianity" – identified by its superior
moral teachings – was compared with other essentialized
religious entities – ("Islam," "Buddhism," and so on) –
to create a class of "world religions" identified by
enlightened liberal and rational characteristics and to
set Christianity up as the highest realization of global
religious culture. The Columbian exposition performed
this distinction spatially, by putting the world religions
into massive buildings and everyone else on the Midway.
While representatives of the former traded pieties, a
carnival atmosphere took hold of the latter space,
where religions marked as other were depicted in mock
demonstrations of cannibalism and human sacrifice. As
the colonial period came to a close, scholars proposed a
broadly inclusive, universal religion of man as the goal
of both the study and the practice of religions, aspiring
to gather the world's many different traditions into a
single, global narrative of the progressive revelation of the
Christian God.[11]

Given the commitment within modern scholarship on
religion to the evolutionary model – from primitive to
modern, infantile to mature, religions – many practitioners
insisted that the academic study of religion itself make
a positive contribution to human culture and to the
betterment of life on earth, to facilitate relations across
cultures and to deepen human tolerance. This seemed
particularly imperative after the Second World War,
when many figures in the discipline held that academic
study of religions had a role to play in the reconstruction
of Western culture devastated by war and totalitarianism.
A hard-core group, comprised mainly of European
scholars, held to an "empiricist" vision of the field and
insisted that the renewed emphasis on the moral responsibility of professors of religious studies represented
the intrusion of theology and normative ethics into the
discipline, but their voices were overwhelmed by the
ameliorative imperative. Both in content and method
the academic study of religion has been preoccupied
with the study and defense of "good" religion for a long
time.[12]

[...]

Any approach to religion that foregrounds ethical
issues as these are now embedded in the discipline
obstructs our understanding of religious idioms because
religion at its root has nothing to do with morality.
Religion does not make the world better to live in
(although some forms of religious practice might); religion does not necessarily conform to the creedal formulations and doctrinal limits developed by cultured and
circumspect theologians, church leaders, or ethicists;
religion does not unambiguously orient people toward
social justice. Particular religious idioms can do all of
these things. The religiously motivated civil rights movement is a good example of a social impulse rooted in an
evangelical faith and dedicated to a more decent life for
men and women. But however much we may love this
movement and however much we may prefer to teach it
[...] this is not the paradigm for religion, nor is it the

expression of religion at some idealized best. There is a quality to the religious imagination that blurs distinctions, obliterates boundaries – especially the boundaries we have so long and so carefully erected within the discipline – and this can, and often does, contribute to social and domestic violence, not peace. Religion is often enough cruel and dangerous, and the same impulses that result in a special kind of compassion also lead to destruction, often among the same people at the same time. Theories of religion have largely served as a protection against such truths about religion.

It is the challenge of the discipline of religious studies not to stop at the border of human practices done in the name of the gods that we scholars find disturbing, dangerous, or even morally repugnant, but rather to enter into the otherness of religious practices in search of an understanding of their human ground. Practitioners must find a way of honoring their own moral and political values while not masking the common humanity that both researcher and religious adept share – share with a man Punkin' Brown, for instance, who was, after all, as his friend pointed out, "just a man." The point of engaging other religious worlds should not be to reassure ourselves and our readers that we are not them, that Punkin' Brown and I belong to different species.

But in attempting such a morally and existentially demanding engagement with the men and women they study, practitioners of religious studies will run into a problem. Although the discipline authorizes an implicit account, freighted with moral value, of what religion is, religious studies in its quest for academic legitimacy has also explicitly insisted that scholars adhere to canons of critical and analytical scholarship as defined by the secular academy. Scholars of religion must maintain a remove that is understood to be the necessary precondition for analysis and interpretation. (This is why there is such trepidation in the discipline about studying one's own tradition.) Scholars of religion are trained to keep their lives out of their research; not to do so exposes them to charges of subjectivism, of writing autobiographically (which is a critical comment!), journalistically, or theologically.

Religious studies acquired its contemporary shape in the American academy after the Second World War in explicit distinction from – and rejection of – seminaries and schools of theology. The severity of the injunction against theology, and more broadly against the moral and religious presence of the scholar in the conduct or presentation of his or her research (other than to articulate the discipline's domesticated Protestant moral assumptions), reflects this origin. Theology is the reflection upon the thought and practice of a religious tradition by its adherents; religious studies is an outsider's discipline by definition, aspiring to critical knowledge through strategy of distance. But of course this paradigm is under attack now, from several different quarters.

Among the most severe contemporary critics of religious studies are evangelical Christian academics of various denominational affiliations who have felt that the hegemony of the liberal definition of religion and the dominance of liberal approaches to research have precluded their own full participation in the discipline or in the wider university culture. Evangelical perspectives have survived in the liberal university, according to these critics, only to the extent that evangelicalism denies its own distinctiveness, severs its connections to the believing community, and becomes a branch of cultural studies. Could a Christian biologist, grounded in a particular faith community and certain of the truth of Scripture, conduct her research according to her faith? Would such an alternative be allowed in the academy, which is otherwise so open by its own account of itself to the perspectives of the marginalized, oppressed, and voiceless? The liberal secular university, in the view of these evangelical critics, is the site of manifold prohibitions masquerading as permissions. Liberal piety opens the space for anything to be studied critically as long as the critical perspective brought into play is not religiously particular, and thus theology, which is always particularist, has been exiled by academic liberalism.

Religious studies is an egregious expression of this prohibitive environment since it sets out to study matters of greatest concern to others from a nonconfessional point of view – ostensibly demanding, indeed, the suppression of the researcher's own values in the process. Could a Christian scholar of religion frame her classes by what she understood to be the authoritative witness of her church? But how does one assess one's understandings of Christian history or doctrine apart from the guidance of tradition as articulated in a believing community? Some have even seen religious studies as corrosive of religious practice generally on college campuses: writing as an evangelical and neoconservative critic of the discipline, D. G. Hart notes that "religious studies reflects the very same intolerance of religious points of view or normative religious judgments that characterizes the university's culture of disbelief," with the result that "the academic study of religion is a failure when it comes to making the university a more hospitable place for religion."[13]

[. . .]

Christian critics [like Hart] now sense that the moment is right for a challenge: insurgent groups of younger conservative Christian scholars, many of them trained and credentialed in departments of religious studies at secular universities, have set out to undermine the authority of older, modernist, liberal scholars and perspectives in biblical studies, philosophy of religion, theology, and even religious history. The notion of a critical and unaffiliated study of religion has come to seem almost fusty to some, a vestige of modernist confidence long ago chastened by postmodernism, and indeed, ironically, or perversely (depending on one's politics), the Christian critique of the liberal, secular university echoes themes of radical critics of modernity. Scholar of education Warren A. Nord, for instance, has suggested that what multiculturalism means is that education "should give voice to various subcultures – religious subcultures included – which currently have little say in the world of intellectual and educational elites." George Marsden argues in a polemical "Concluding Unscientific Postscript" to his history of the secularization of learning in American higher education that "the widespread current critiques of scientific objectivity provide a context for reconsidering the near exclusion of religious perspectives from the academic life of American universities of Protestant heritage." Once one admits that "everyone's intellectual inquiry takes place in a framework of communities that shape prior commitments," there is little reason for excluding explicitly religious claims from the teaching and research that take place in the academy. Confessional pedagogy slips its nose into the academic tent through the opening created by postmodernism.[14]

An alternative account of contemporary university culture maintains that it is Christianity in any form, modern or postmodern, that stands as an obstacle for intellectual work, generally and particularly in the study of religion. Marsden claims that contemporary university culture is anti-Christian, and surely anyone who has spent any time in this world must agree that there is a measure of truth in this charge. Some of this is simply prejudice; some of it is a reaction against the long Christian domination of thinking about other religions in the world; some of it is a way for university intellectuals to draw an unmistakable boundary for themselves – and for their students – between the culture of learning they value and a surrounding society that can be anti-intellectual on explicitly Christian grounds. [. . .]

But for some the critique of Christianity is linked with a broader political and epistemological agenda and is meant to challenge the hegemony of Western ways of knowing and living. Articulated by scholars who have worked in cultures that endured the burden of Christian authority under colonial regimes, this perspective on Christianity is politically charged. Christianity is understood to have been indispensable to Western imperialism, providing its cultural legitimacy, moral confidence, and epistemological grounding while spiritually underwriting the military and economic campaigns of the Western powers. Intellectuals, including scholars of religion, crafted the philosophical framework that constituted native populations as empty of culture and therefore not only open to but actually requiring Western conquest and domination for their own good. Representations of native cultures as either primitive, proto-Christian, or crypto-Christian were the intellectuals' contribution to imperialism.

The postcolonial world since the 1950s has exposed the cruelty of Western intellectual authority, unmasking practices of domination and exploitation enclosed within the culture of enlightened reason and liberal tolerance. Intellectuals in Asia, Africa, and South America have challenged the canons of Western culture. The task for American university intellectuals now, some say, is to rethink American culture from the perspective of the once-dominated other and from alternative and once-oppressed vantage points, a process of defamiliarizing and decentering as the first step to reinterpretation. Globalism as an economic, demographic, and political reality demands an intellectual reorientation, a reimagining of the place of the United States in world culture. Western styles of knowledge, which typically give priority to detachment over engagement, textuality over vocality, mind over body, are to be exposed to radically different ways of understanding and inhabiting reality.

In the context of this broader criticism of Western knowing and given the history of religious studies' implication in Western power at home and abroad, the challenge now, say scholars of religion working from this political vantage point, is to become radically aware of the discipline's implicit Western and Christian biases, of the hidden, normative Christianity within the basic methodologies and philosophical orientations of religious studies, and to expunge them. Just as postcolonial intellectual culture calls into question central tenets of Western thought, so a new kind of moral inquiry must be open to construals of the "ethical" that are profoundly at variance with Christian ideals and formulations.

One example of what this sort of ethical inquiry would look like is Karen McCarthy Brown's now-classic discussion of Haitian vodou morality in *Mama Lola: A Vodou Priestess in Brooklyn*. Unlike the radical distinction made within Christianity between absolute good and absolute evil, a boundary authorized and presided over by a singular deity and an authoritative clergy equipped with the varied tools of moral discipline, Brown maintains that vodou asserts multiplicity, diversity, and contradiction. Vodou notions of subjectivity understand the self to be multifarious, the site of conflicting energies, capacities, and possibilities without the Christian insistence on consistency in self-presentation. "A moral person, in Vodou," writes Brown, is one who lives "in tune with his or her character, a character defined by the spirits said to love that person." Such moral "flexibility," she adds, "is provided in the midst of moral dilemmas by the support these favorite spirits offer to different and sometimes contradictory values.[15]

[...]

Brown and other scholars who have spent personally and intellectually formative years in other cultures call us to juxtapose the language of American reality with the reality of those other worlds. They propose to bring the religious, and moral vision of the colonized into creative tension with the moral sensibility and religious idioms of the colonizer. The goal is a creole scholarship that draws from the epistemological, aesthetic, religious and moral idioms of different cultures to decenter and rethink the idioms of the West. Christianity itself – as well as the normative, dualistic crypto-Christian categories of religious studies – looks very different when viewed from Mama Lola's living room in Brooklyn or her ancestral home in Haiti.

It may appear that there is little common ground between the evangelical and the postcolonial critiques of the liberal paradigm for studying religion, but surprisingly and perhaps ironically there are significant convergences. Proponents of both perspectives propose that the universalistic ambitions of Western enlightened rationality give way to local orientations: there is no essential, singular truth, only situated truths. Both understand the scholar herself to be situated at a particular cultural location that fundamentally shapes her vision, and both place passion and commitment at the center of research methodology and pedagogy. Stanley Hanerwas has said that the confessional teacher "witnesses"

in the classroom, makes his or her faith present and invites students into a dialogue about it, holds it up as a lens for examining and challenging the dominant arrangements of culture. Critical anthropologists also propose a radical critique of Western culture as an appropriate classroom stance. They draw on the experiences of people in distant places, and especially their often-disastrous encounters with Christianity, to frame students' examinations of Western religions and their assessments of the claims of Western reason. Conversion – to Christianity or to other religions – is not necessarily the explicit goal of either evangelical or postcolonial pedagogies, but there is a heightened existential edge to this kind of teaching as compared with the older critical liberal model, so that students may find themselves attracted to the religious worlds represented in both of these classrooms. The evangelical and the political critiques challenge the authority of liberal Protestantism in the discipline of religious studies and demand that scholars in the field transgress, in method and in the subjects they choose, the authoritative boundaries of religious studies.

I find both critiques compelling and welcome the challenge each represents to the way we have gone about the study of religion in the United States. But I am not sure that either one ultimately avoids the pitfall to which Covington succumbed in reestablishing his barrier against Punkin' Brown. Evangelical and postcolonial scholars themselves rely on the constitution of others in doing their work – the Christian other, in the case of postcolonial critics (for whom non-Western religions are valued in part as expressions of not-Christianity, a perspective that often informs how these religions are described and interpreted), and for evangelicals, either the liberal, secular other or, just as likely, ways of being Christian other than those espoused by evangelicals. The postmodern Christian scholar in the postliberal university would presumably assess Punkin' Brown's Christianity from the perspective of a distinct set of Christian beliefs and perspectives, much as Covington himself did in his own criticism of the snake handler. (Covington's argument at the end is a liberal Christian theological one about God and human equality.) Encountering such a figure would be a ripe moment for normative theological engagement and criticism, the explication of the scholar's own faith through a dialectical interplay between his or her religious world and the religious world of the other. Covington secured the boundary between himself and Punkin' Brown by evoking God as his witness, explicitly placing himself in a debate within the Christian community over the "nature of God," in his words, and the role of women in the church and society. The confessional professor too might witness to her own faith by affirming that in her reading of Scripture, God sanctions the participation of women in religious life. She might say that the God of the handlers is not the God of the New Testament, as indeed Covington did say. How much closer does this get us to understanding the world of the snake handlers, which is the goal of scholarship in religion?

I find it even harder to imagine what postcolonial professors might make of Punkin' Brown given the resolutely anti-Christian animus of so many of them. His rage against women and his apparent determination to dominate them (religiously and probably otherwise too – although this is not the picture that emerges in other studies of the man) disclose what many consider to be the inherent social aggressiveness of Christianity. A cultural critic might help us understand Punkin' Brown's impulse to dominate in global and domestic perspectives. He or she might shift the focus of analysis away from the nature of God to the sorts of social conditions that shaped Punkin' Brown. But the internal power of the man's religious imagination, his relationship with Jesus crucified, and his deep desire to experience the real power and presence of the Spirit with the re-threatening snake in his hands – Brown's passionate love of God in the snakes – might be missed by observers tone-deaf to matters of faith and religious practice, especially to Christian faith and practice.

Punkin' Brown and others like him are just too valuable precisely *as others*, as the unassimilable and intolerable, to be easily surrendered. So long as the point of religious scholarship, even implicitly or unconsciously, is to seal the borders of our own worlds of meaning and morals, whatever these might be – liberal or conservative, Christian or not – against such others, it will be impossible to relinquish the "Punkin' Browns" constituted in the field or in the archives. The challenge facing the discipline today, however, is not to find new others, as both the evangelical and postcolonial approaches do, but to get beyond "otherizing" as its basic move.

There is another alternative to the liberal paradigm that guards more assiduously against the moralistic impulse to construct figures of otherness. This alternative – which I think of as a third way, between confessional and theological scholarship, on the one hand, and radically secular scholarship on the other – is characterized by a disciplined suspension of the impulse to locate the other (with all her or his discrepant moralities, ways of knowing, and

religious impulses) securely in relation to one's own cosmos. It has no need to fortify the self in relation to the other; indeed, it is willing to make one's own self-conceptions vulnerable to the radically destabilizing possibilities of a genuine encounter with an unfamiliar way of life. This is an in-between orientation, located at the intersection of self and other, at the boundary between one's own moral universe and the moral world of the other. And it entails disciplining one's mind and heart to stay in this in-between place, in a posture of disciplined attentiveness, especially to difference.

This in-between ground upon which a researcher in this third way stands belongs neither to herself nor to the other but has come into being between them, precisely because of the meeting of the two. This is ground that would not have existed apart from the relationship between researcher and her subject. (Covington forgets that Punkin' Brown was responding to *him* that night; the preacher would not have given that sermon had Covington and his friends not entered his world in the way they did. Covington represents his own presence as a provocation that revealed the real nature of the snake handlers, the depths of their faith, but what it revealed was the snake handlers in relation to Covington.) On this ground, not owned by either party, each person experiences the taken-for-granted world as vulnerable, decontextualized, realigned. Ideally, after such an exchange, neither party is the same as when the exchange opened (which is exactly the problem with the evangelical and postcolonial approaches and with Covington: they wind up just where they started). Scholarship in the third way is transformative. Such a movement onto the ground in-between universes of meaning would not permit the kind of closure Covington imposes on Punkin' Brown and his world. It requires that the scholar of religion abandon the security offered by the discipline, by its implicit and explicit moral certainty as this is embedded in its theoretical apparatuses, and to proceed instead by risk, suspension, and engagement.

To illustrate what I have in mind here, I want to take an example, David Haberman's study of the Ban-Yatra pilgrimage in ancient and contemporary northern India, *Journey through the Twelve Forests: An Encounter with Krishna*.[16] Like Covington's, this is an intensely personal narrative. It recounts Haberman's deep existential involvement with the Hindu pilgrims he journeys with through Braj, as the pilgrimage area is called. Haberman never forgets who he is, and he is always mindful of the history of Western relations with India and of the implications of Western religious and philosophical pre-occupations in mapping the landscape of "Hinduism." A sophisticated theorist of postcolonial culture, he is aware that as a contemporary student of Hinduism he steps into and attempts to challenge a tradition of interpretation with its roots in the period of empire. A scholar of the third way remains resolutely aware of the history of religious scholarship in his or her area, conscious that the analytical terminology he or she works with (whatever it is) is formed and marked by this history.

Braj is dotted with sites central to narratives about Krishna – the grove he frolicked in with his consort, Radha, for example, and the prison cell where he was born. Believers claim that Braj *is* in some sense the body of the god: the landscape is so intimately connected to Krishna that it is he. The god's body is thus uniquely present to the pilgrims during their arduous journey through Braj. This trope of physical presence becomes a central device of Haberman's work. Early in the journey Haberman begins to develop awful blisters on his tender feet, and for the rest of the pilgrimage he must contend with terrible pain and rely on the assistance of fellow pilgrims. Just as the god's body is everpresent in Braj, so is the ethnographer's in his experience and account of the pilgrimage, which as a result becomes a journey through the possibilities and limitations of temporality. On the levels of religious understanding and existential experience, pain is the pathway for Haberman into the intersection between worlds, the suspensive space where a new kind of understanding of other religions is possible.

Haberman could see that many of his fellow pilgrims were also in pain. But this did not prevent them from taking a deep sensual pleasure at sites commemorating Krishna's own pleasures, an incongruity that Haberman found confusing at first. How could these weary bodies stumbling into the groves of Krishna's delight experience joy and pleasure, and how could the anthropologist with his inflamed foot? But as he enters into this apparent disjuncture of pain and pleasure, deprivation and sensuality, stress and celebration, Haberman comes to see it as the dynamic of the pilgrimage. His confusion, disorientation, and pain become means of comprehension (as Clara could have told him). Haberman shows us what Covington might have done differently, at greater personal risk to himself and cultural disorientation to his readers, that night in Georgia. Covington might have used the distress and even revulsion occasioned in him by Punkin' Brown's performance as such a pivot of reflection. By suspending the need to guard himself against whatever fears and revelations Brown's performance

evoked, Covington could have been led to discover the common source of both the violence and the beauty of this startling religious idiom. He might have reflected on the roots of Brown's anger; he might have explored the intersection between desire and rage as these swirled around each other in the snake handlers' world, or looked at the convergence of love and pain in the handlers' experience or on the intersection of the sacred and the obscene, and come to grips with his own attraction to snake handling. Instead, he turns away, and asserts a principled commitment to the spiritual equality of women. This commitment may be readable in itself, but Covington does not see how invoking it where and when he does amounts to a refusal to engage his subject.

The key moment in Haberman's account for my purposes – his version of the Punkin' Brown encounter – comes when he finds himself standing on bleeding feet in a place called Charan Pahari, the "Mountain of the Foot," where Krishna is said to have left a footprint in a white stone that had been softened by his music. The stone is lovingly, regularly bathed by the god's devout with water and smeared with red powder. Haberman's account of his visit to this spot begins with an acknowledgment of otherness. There is a quality to the site that causes him to step out of his role as pilgrim and to admit his place – and confusion – as observer: "Such claims [as that Krishna had stepped on this stone] are naturally met with some doubt on the part of the outsider." He moves still further out in the second half of this sentence: "especially considering the economic benefits gained by the attendants busily collecting money from the pilgrims." A moral distance has opened between him and the caretakers of the shrine. This is the "haaagh" experience: suspicion, detachment, and doubt overwhelm compassion, attention, and understanding.[17]

Haberman might have turned away at this moment in disgust at the venality of the shrine keepers and the gullibility of the devout, as other visitors to India have done. There are indeed good reasons to be suspicious of what goes on at a shrine, in India and elsewhere. Shrine priests do not scruple to take advantage of people in considerable emotional need and religious excitement. Moreover, as countless Western critics have pointed out whenever they have encountered such human practices, the money spent on feeding, dressing, and adoring the gods in this way might better be spent on people's health, clothing, or education. Religious discomfort in this way is transmuted into moral criticism through a posture of pragmatic superiority. Liberal scholars of religion have been as bemused by immigrant Catholics' devotion to the saints as by Hindus in this regard. So this could have been the boundary of Haberman's journey, the point at which he stopped at otherness and confirmed it, and many readers would have understood and even shared his moral concerns.

But he turns back to the experience of the people he is observing and forces himself – and his readers – to recognize that there are many worlds, many different ways of making and inhabiting reality. He writes, "upon observing several women bow down and touch their heads to this stone, come up with tears streaming down their faces, and hug each other crying, 'O Sister, O, Sister!' I began to think that questions [about the venality of the shrine keepers or the ontological reality of the stone's imprint] . . . were inappropriate." Since "reality is not set for human beings [and] multiple realities or worlds of meaning are available to us," moral judgment is rendered problematic. "Judgments of realities are difficult," Haberman continues, although not impossible or unnecessary, "because there is no-where to stand that is not situated in a particular reality, which by its very nature regards other realities with suspicion."[18] The challenge then becomes to set one's own world, one's own particular reality, now understood as one world among many possible other worlds, in relation to this other reality and to learn how to view the two in relation to each other, moving back and forth between two alternative ways of organizing and experiencing reality. The point is not to make the other world radically and irrevocably other, but to render one's own world other to oneself as prelude to a new understanding of the two worlds in relationship to one another.

Ironically, it is Haberman's constant awareness of his difference that permits him to enter so deeply into the intersection of the two worlds; indeed, there would be no intersection without awareness of difference, no in-betweenness. Covington portrayed himself initially as having passed over entirely to the culture of snake handling, but that apparent immersion ends up telling us less about either his own or Punkin' Brown's world than Haberman's intersectional strategy tells us about Braj. This is where the pleasure, excitement, and risk of religious studies are, its delights as well as its dangers. The space is dangerous because one cannot, after all, simply abandon one's deepest values or tolerate the intolerable, even though something awful and intolerable might make sense in someone else's world. It is delightful because, by staying in the place in between – indeed, prolonging one's stay there by refusing initial opportunities for closure – one comes to know something about the other

and about oneself through relationship with the other. Haberman identifies this as an erotic methodology, borrowing from French psychoanalytic theorist Jacques Lacan an understanding of desire as that which arises from lack and rejects closure. The erotic orientation to another's religion resists ending the tension provoked by the unexpected proximity of two diverse worlds. It is this delight in difference that sets religious studies apart from the more conventional orientations of liberal academics, evangelical theologians, and postcolonial critics alike.

[. . .]

The classroom is where many of us perform a significant portion of our daily intellectual work; it is where we invite others to join us in our questions. Our students come to us from many different worlds, bearing many different histories. This was true even in the Bible Belt, where I taught for more than a decade: the world's cultures are well represented in midwestern classrooms. Furthermore, "Christian" students bring complex Christianities into the classroom. Many of them – and here I can say *especially* in the Bible Belt – have had truly ruinous experiences in their churches and Christian homes. They are already quite familiar with the power of Christian faith to scar them and, if they have been fortunate, with its powers of liberation and salvation. These students from Bible-reading homes are often sick of witnesses and revivals, of experiencing the "truth" as a prescription about the doable, thinkable, or possible. In response, some have put together intricate Christian understandings that draw on neo-paganism, snippets of Asian religions, popular psychology, and contemporary science fiction. Others simply will have nothing more to do with religion, finding their way instead to religious studies classrooms in hopes of securing the tools to help them reflect critically on their experiences. "Christianity," when it is used in the authoritative singular, as if it had secure, discernible boundaries, makes sense only as a symbol for political or cultural mobilization and the domination of others. The social reality of our classrooms, as of American culture, is that there are many, many Christianities.

Students in this polytheistic world are not well served by a professor's witnessing to a singular truth, nor will they be inevitably awakened by denunciations of their Christianities by postcolonial critics. Nor will students be helped by normative accounts of religion that neglect or exclude all the humiliating, destructive, beautiful, mysterious, and terrifying dimensions of it that they know from their own experience. It is difficult to see these

"Christian" students as agents of Western hegemony, since like Punkin' Brown their families have so often been on the receiving end of cultural domination; postcolonial cultural criticism becomes another form of imperial witnessing when it is conducted without a vivid sense of the worlds Americans come from and the varieties of Christianity they have known. Religious witnessing in any case will always fail in the university, where the expectation is appropriately for discussion, critical analysis, and open exchanges (an ideal often enough abandoned but no less desirable or admirable for that). Moral inquiry without communication and conversation is nothing but a covert compulsion.

[. . .]

Since moral reflection is in fact the conversations that constitute it, then the presence of many different histories, memories, and experiences converging in our classrooms is a unique opportunity for religious studies. Moral inquiry and religious study proceed in this context not by constituting the other – "Punkin' Brown," "Hinduism," "cult members," "popular" religion, and so on; rather, they work through the recognition of difference and a revisioning of one's own story through the lens of the other openly engaged. [. . .] Like the discipline itself, the religious studies classroom exists in suspension too. The understanding of other religious worlds and of the moral impulses of these worlds comes only through the multiplicity of stories told and stories attended to and to the new possibilities that emerge in the places between heaven and earth, between lives and stories, and between people and their gods.

Notes

1   My discussion of the history of the modern Western study of religion is based on a rich literature on the subject that has begun to emerge in the past decade (with some distinguished predecessors). Among the works that have most shaped my understanding are Talal Asad, *Genealogies of Religion: Disciplines and Reasons of Power in Christianity and Islam* (Baltimore: Johns Hopkins University Press, 1993); David Chidester, *Savage Systems: Colonialism and Comparative Religion in Southern Africa* (Charlottesville: University Press of Virginia, 1996); Richard King, *Orientalism and Religion: Post-colonial Theory, India, and "the Mystic East"* (New York: Routledge, 1999); Hans G. Kippenberg, *Discovering Religious History in the Modern Age*, trans. Barbara Harshay (Princeton: Princeton University Press,

2002); Bruce Lincoln, *Theorizing Myth: Narrative, Ideology, and Scholarship* (Chicago: University of Chicago Press, 1999); Donald S. Lopez Jr., *Prisoners of Shangri-La: Tibetan Buddhism and the West* (Chicago: University of Chicago Press, 1998); Lopez, *Curators of the Buddha: The Study of Buddhism under Colonialism* (Chicago: University of Chicago Press, 1995); Russell T. McCutcheon, *Manufacturing Religion: The Discourse on Sui Generis Religion and the Politics of Nostalgia* (New York: Oxford University Press, 1997); Tomoko Masuzawa, *In Search of Dreamtime: The Quest for the Origin of Religion* (Chicago: University of Chicago Press, 1993); Ashis Nandy, *Intimate Enemy: Loss and Recovery of Self Under Colonialism* (Oxford: Oxford University Press, 1989); Nandy, *Time Warps: Silent and Evasive Pasts in Indian Politics and Religion* (New Brunswick, N.J.: Rutgers University Press, 2002); Mary Louise Pratt, *Imperial Eyes: Travel Writing and Transculturation* (New York: Routledge, 1992); J. Samuel Preus, *Explaining Religion: Criticism and Theory from Bodin to Freud* (New Haven: Yale University Press, 1987); Leigh Eric Schmidt, *Hearing Things: Religion, Illusion, and the American Enlightenment* (Cambridge, Mass.: Harvard University Press, 2001); Jonathan Z. Smith, *Imagining Religion: From Babylon to Jonestown* (Chicago: University of Chicago Press, 1982); Smith, *Drudgery Divine: On the Comparison of Early Christianity and the Religions of Late Antiquity* (Chicago: University of Chicago Press, 1990); Michael Taussig, *Shamanism, Colonialism, and the Wild Man: A Study in Terror and Healing* (Chicago: University of Chicago Press, 1987); Ann Taves, *Fits, Trances, and Visions: Experiencing Religion and Explaining Experience from Wesley to James* (Princeton: Princeton University Press, 1999); Mark C. Taylor (ed.), *Critical Terms for Religious Studies* (Chicago: University of Chicago Press, 1998); Peter van der Veer, *Imperial Encounters: Religion and Modernity in India and Britain* (Princeton: Princeton University Press, 2001); Steven M. Wasserstrom, *Religion after Religion: Gershom Scholem, Mircea Eliade, and Henry Corbin at Eranos* (Princeton: Princeton University Press, 1999).

2   On the history of the gothic in American culture see Mark Edmundson, *Nightmare on Main Street: Angels, Sadomasochism, and the Culture of Gothic* (Cambridge: Harvard University Press, 1997) and Edward J. Ingebretsen, *Maps of Heaven, Maps of Hell: Religious Terror as Memory from the Puritans to Stephen King* (Armonk, NY: M.E. Sharpe, 1996). For a powerful study of the eruption of this ancient memory of religious horror in the present see Lawrence Wright, *Remembering Satan* (New York: Knopf, 1994).

3   Dennis Covington, *Salvation on Sand Mountain: Snake Handling and Redemption in Southern Appalachia* (Reading, Mass.: Addison-Wesley, 1995). For other accounts of this culture that include some trenchant criticism of

Covington's work see David L. Kimbrough, *Taking Up Serpents: Snake Handlers of Eastern Kentucky* (Chapel Hill: University of North Carolina Press, 1995) and Fred Brown and Jeanne McDonald, *The Serpent Handlers: Three Families and Their Faith* (Winston Salem: John F. Blair, Publisher, 2000).

4   Covington, *Salvation on Sand Mountain*, describes the "sweet savor" of the snakes, a phrase used by the handlers themselves, on p. 162; the description of Punkin' Brown at the service is on p. 234, as is the comparison of Brown's "haaagh" with the underground vent. When he first introduces Brown, Covington tells readers that the preacher is "mired in the Old Testament, in the enumerated laws and the blood lust of the patriarchs" (209).

5   Covington, *Salvation on Sand Mountain*, 235.

6   Covington, *Salvation on Sand Mountain*, 239. The Tennessee minister is quoted by Brown and McDonald, *The Serpent Handlers*, 20.

7   On this point see also Smith, *Imagining Religion*, 6.

8   George M. Marsden, *The Soul of the American University: From Protestant Establishment to Established Nonbelief* (New York: Oxford University Press, 1994), 34, 85, and 89.

9   Marsden, *The Soul of the American University*, 243; D. G. Hart, *The University Gets Religion: Religious Studies in American Higher Education* (Baltimore: Johns Hopkins University Press, 1999), 29.

10   H. L. Seneviratne, *The Work of Kings: The New Buddhism in Sri Lanka* (Chicago: University of Chicago Press, 1999), 2 and passim; on this subject see also Stephen R. Prothero, *The White Buddhist: The Asian Odyssey of Henry Steel Olcott* (Bloomington: Indiana University Press, 1996).

11   See John P. Burris, *Exhibiting Religion: Colonialism and Spectacle at International Expositions, 1851–1893* (Charlottesville: University Press of Virginia, 2001) and Richard Hughes Seager, *The World's Parliament of Religions: The East/West Encounter, Chicago, 1893* (Bloomington: Indiana University Press, 1995).

12   See Eric J. Sharpe, *Comparative Religion: A History*, 2d ed. (LaSalle, Ill.: Open Court, 1986), 266–93.

13   Hart, *The University Gets Religion*, 241.

14   Warren A. Nord, *Religion and American Education: Rethinking a National Dilemma* (Chapel Hill: University of North Carolina Press, 1995), 8. Marsden, *The Soul of the American University*, 429–30.

15   Karen McCarthy Brown (ed.), *Mama Lola: A Vodou Priestess in Brooklyn* (Berkeley: University of California Press, 2001), 241.

16   David L. Haberman, *Journey through the Twelve Forests: An Encounter with Krishna* (New York: Oxford University Press, 1994).

17   Haberman, *Journey*, 168–9.

18   Haberman, *Journey*, 169.

From Demon Possession to Magic Show: Ventriloquism, Religion, and the Enlightenment

Leigh Eric Schmidt

In *Saducismus Triumphatus: Or, Full and Plain Evidence Concerning Witches and Apparitions* (1681), Joseph Glanvill marveled at those so possessed by the devil that they became his mouthpiece: "For *Ventriloquy*, or speaking from the bottom of the Belly, 'tis a thing I think as strange and difficult to be conceived as any thing in Witchcraft, nor can it, I believe, be performed in any distinctness of articulate sounds, without such assistance of the Spirits, that spoke out of the *Dæmoniacks.*" By the late eighteenth and early nineteenth centuries, ventriloquism, loosened from the confines of theological debates over demonology, had become a salient category in rationalistic discussions of religion and had taken center stage as a form of enlightened entertainment. This expanded construction of ventriloquy provided a tangible way of thinking about revealed religion as rooted in illusion – that, indeed, various wonders of the devout ear such as divine calls, the voices of demonic possession, prophecy, mystical locutions, oracles, and even the sounds of shamanic spirits had their origins in vocal deceptions that empiricists could pinpoint and magicians could demonstrate. The new ventriloquism, in its sober appraisal of all sectarian enthusiasm and religious credulity, made suspect the very claim that God could speak to or through the human. In performative practice, the ventriloquist's art shifted the focus of learned attention from the divine struggle over the soul to the protean malleability of personal identity, the fears and attractions of imposture, and the sheer pleasures of amusement.[1]

Despite varied pressures of reform in the early modern world, magical practices proved highly resilient, particularly in their old dance with natural philosophy. The Enlightenment did not so much assault magic as absorb and secularize it; with the help of the market, legerdemain was transformed into a widely distributed commodity of edifying amusement. The enlightened magician cultivated such newly codified arts as ventriloquism and the display of phantasmagoria, turning the old juggler's repertory into an object lesson on religious illusion and epistemological trickery (with the consequent need to hone technical knowledge and skeptical rationality). In the expanding marketplace of late-eighteenth- and early-nineteenth-century entertainment – in theaters, museums, inns, coffeehouses, and concert halls – magic was given renewed prominence as a stage art explicitly allied with philosophical experiment rather than supernatural power. The old forms of magic – alchemy, astrology, palmistry, healing, and treasure-seeking – persisted and often enough even flourished, but, from the late eighteenth century on, the magician increasingly appeared as one of the alluring celebrities of the Enlightenment, a wizard arrayed against wizardry, an exposer of "supernatural humbugs." This skeptical pose became characteristic of leading American illusionists from P. T. Barnum to Houdini to the Amazing Randi.

Through closely examining the reformulation of ventriloquism from a demonological category to a technique of enlightened magic, this essay circles around two larger points. First, it looks at how rationalists went about creating a universal, naturalistic category for explaining (away) religious phenomena, especially the "irrational" voices of popular Christian experience. It locates the formation and diffusion of such knowledge in the intersections of philosophy and entertainment, scientific experiment and magical display, print and performance. For the learned, ventriloquism provided a grounds for suspicion and contest; knowledge of the art came to supply a ready-at-hand script for the performative exposure of the "superstitious" beliefs of others. Second, whereas most scholars, in keeping with the wider emphasis on the "ocularcentrism" of modernity, have drawn attention to the optics of modern science, technology, consumption, and surveillance, this essay foregrounds the "aural culture" of the Enlightenment. To the visual moorings of modernity need to be added the complementary concerns with the disciplining of the ear, the science of acoustics, the voices of revelation and madness, the perceptual "illusions" of hearing, the technologies of the auditory, and the aesthetics of sound. Amid the putative visual dominance of the modern sensorium, the sudden popularity of ventriloquism as both philosophy and entertainment at the end of the eighteenth century gave expression to the continuing strength of these aural fascinations among the learned. The assumed eclipse of orality by the visuality of print has left hearing's complex history far more muffled than hearkened to, submerged under the reigning narrative of the eye's modern hegemony.[2]

What the enlightened strove, in particular, to contain was the explosive aurality of popular Christianity – all the internal and external voices that beckoned the faithful from George Fox and John Bunyan to John Woolman, Lorenzo Dow, and Jarena Lee, all the "hearsay" of the demonic and the miraculous. As Tom Paine concluded with characteristic bluntness, "I totally disbelieve that the Almighty ever did communicate anything to man, by any mode of speech, in any language, or by any kind of vision." To destroy the anathema of immediate revelation – what Ethan Allen mocked as a "heavenly dictating voice" – the enlightened resorted to various devices: some textual and historical (such as the attack on the biblical record or on the Sibylline prophecies), some medical (such as the detailed pathologizing of enthusiasm or the delineation of the illusions of the diseased ear), some acoustical (such as the wide-ranging pursuit of the mechanics and technologies of sound), some political (such as the unmasking of the oracular impostures of tyrannical priests), and some playful (such as the use of rational amusements like ventriloquism and the phantasmagoria). As part of this multilayered critique, the sportive magic of the Enlightenment was serious business, offering up the skeptical professions of the *philosophes* in a performative and entertaining mode.[3]

An Enlightenment Theory of the Origins of Religion: or, How to Turn Supernatural Voices into Aural Illusions

From late antiquity into the eighteenth century, ventriloquism was deeply embedded in Christian discourses about demon possession, necromancy, and pagan idolatry. The term itself, in its Greek and Latin derivations, meant literally one who speaks from the belly, and it long held a place among many other specialized markers for different types of divination, prophecy, and conjuring. As Reginald Scot explained in *The Discoverie of Witchcraft* (1584), "*Pythonists*" or "*Ventriloqui*" speak in a "hollowe" voice, much different from their usual one, and are "such as take upon them to give oracles" or "to tell where things lost are become." In demonological discussions, such nomenclature referred to one who had "a familiar spirit," who spoke during trances or fits in an apparently diabolical voice, or who claimed soothsaying powers.[4]

Much of the formative discussion of ventriloquy in the Christian tradition focused on the story of the Witch of Endor recounted in 1 Samuel 28 in which King Saul, who formerly had sought to suppress all magical diviners, disguises himself and visits a sorceress in hopes of summoning up the ghost of Samuel and discerning the future of his battle against the Philistines. With the help of the necromancer, Saul hears the prophet Samuel speak from beyond the grave – an apparent success for the soothsayer that made for considerable anxious commentary in the patristic literature and long afterward.[5] Why would God allow necromancy, a practice repeatedly abominated, to be used for divine purposes? Was this whole scene not accomplished through the power of the devil? Was this apparitional voice of Samuel real and prophetic or only a diabolical illusion created by the enchantress to trick a weakened Saul? The story bundled many compelling theological issues together, but one of the most intriguing to centuries of interpreters was the question of the ventriloquized voice, who was speaking and by what means or powers.

In the early modern versions of this debate about Samuel's ghost, interlocutors swung, as in the larger controversies over witchcraft, between those who saw the power of the demonic and the supernatural on display and those who supported increasingly skeptical explanations. Reginald Scot's work, a leading harbinger of dissent from long-standing demonic readings, shifted the blame, comparing the woman's powers to that constant Protestant bugbear of Catholic "magic." [. . .]

Among Scot's lengthy explanations for the whole affair, he offered this image of magical illusion: "This *Pythonist* being *Ventriloqua*; that is, Speaking as it were from the bottome of hir bellie, did cast hir selfe into a transe, and so abused *Saule*, answering to Saule in Samuels name, in hir counterfeit hollow voice." In direct opposition, Joseph Glanvill, who, as a member of the Royal Society, was committed to establishing an empirical base for the defense of Christian supernaturalism against emergent mechanists and materialists, argued that it was "a *real Apparition*" and thought that the ventriloquial explanation was nonsense: "It cannot certainly in any reason be thought, that the Woman could by a natural knack, speak such a Discourse as is related from *Samuel*, much less that she could from her Belly imitate his Voice, so as to deceive one that knew him as *Saul* did." For Glanvill – as with the Mathers, Henry More, and George Sinclair – the contention that necromancers, witches, and demoniacs were mostly frauds was "threadbare Sophistry." Diabolical as well as prophetic utterances were part of a biblical world of spirits, apparitions, and wonders that Glanvill and his various allies stood ready to defend against the incipient challenges of medical materialists and other skeptical debunkers of witchcraft.[6]

The scriptural debate over the Witch of Endor and the sources of Samuel's voice had its lived counterpart in the "sacred theater" of possession that haunted seventeenth-century Protestants and Catholics alike.[7] In the context of such dramatic religious phenomena, *ventriloquy* was one of the terms used to debate whether or not Satan was speaking through the possessed: was it a "familiar spirit" who was making people roar out in low and unnatural voices, taunt ministers and godly neighbors, or mimic the cries of animals in what amounted to an infernal menagerie (dogs, cats, horses, or roosters)? Or, were those afflicted with such trances, voices, and bellowings fraudulent or diseased? [...]

Skeptics from Reginald Scot on were inevitably contemptuous of all such trickeries of the voice. In *Leviathan* (1651), Thomas Hobbes, arguing for a naturalistic view of wonders and for the prevalence of religious imposture, was predictably biting about ventriloquy, seeing such vocal forms as part of the "false miracles" of enchanters by which they were "able to make very many men believe" that their own voice "is a voice from Heaven." In the hands of philosophical rationalists, ventriloquism was being fashioned into an anti-enthusiast weapon, another way of exposing Christian wonders and delimiting superstition. "Some Counterfeits can speak out

of their Bellies with a little or no Motion of their Lips," the Anglican Francis Hutchinson explained in 1718 in an essay attacking the reality of witches, apparitions, and possessions. "They can change their Voices, that they shall not be like their own. They can make, that what they shall say be heard, as if it was from a different Part of the Room, or as if it came from their own Fundament." "Such persons are call'd," he said, "*Engastriloques*, or *Ventriloquists*."[8]

[...]

The decisive turn toward the Enlightenment construction of ventriloquism was made in 1772 by Joannes Baptista de La Chapelle. That year La Chapelle – mathematician, encyclopedist, inventor, and another member of the Royal Society – published his 572-page opus, *Le Ventriloque, ou l'engastrimythe*. Part of much wider currents within the Enlightenment to establish a natural history of superstitions, oracles, miracles, fetishes, priestly cheats, and pious frauds, La Chapelle's treatise took its place in a stream of works by such writers as Bernard le Bovier de Fontenelle, Antonius van Dale, John Trenchard, and Charles de Brosses and emerged as especially influential in the interpretation of vocal deceptions, revelatory voices, and mediumistic phenomena. Translated into Dutch (1774), Italian (1786), and Russian (1787) and widely abstracted in the new encyclopedias, La Chapelle's tome provided much of the basic analysis of ventriloquism across Europe and North America for the next century. It was the main source for the 1797 entry on the subject in the *Encyclopedia Britannica* (and its ensuing American incarnation); it was used by Charles Brockden Brown as the background on the topic for his major fictional creation of Carwin, the rogue ventriloquist, in *Wieland* (1798) and in the serialized, fragmentary sequel *Memoirs of Carwin the Biloquist* (1803–1805); it provided all of the material for one of the first American expositions of the art, a small pamphlet published in Morristown, New Jersey, in 1799; it influenced a mix of philosophic interpreters from Dugald Stewart to David Brewster to Eusebe Salverte; and its stories even became staples of popular how-to guides by the mid-nineteenth century. La Chapelle, more than anyone else, reinvented ventriloquism as a general category for the rationalistic explanation of supernatural voices. He gave it renewed currency as an idea; others would then turn his philosophic observations into a system of rational recreation, a widely recognized form of stage entertainment.[9]

La Chapelle began in the thicket of the age-old Christian debate about the Witch of Endor and the apparitional voice of Samuel, and then he cut through the whole tangle. Taking up the side that the soothsayer was a studied impostor, who, through the art of ventriloquy, had the ability to feign voices and to create the aural illusion of the supernatural, La Chapelle expanded this into a blanket explanation for superstition that moved from the artifice of the ancient oracles to credulity and fanaticism among his contemporaries. He moved the debate out of the biblical narratives, the scriptural commentaries, and the theological territory of demonology into the domain of experimentation, acoustics, and anatomy (it was the physiology of the mouth and throat, not the belly, argued La Chapelle, that deserved attention for finding the "causes" of this vocal phenomenon). Ventriloquism, he concluded, was an art, a practiced technique of modulation, misdirection, and muscular control, which required neither supernatural assistance nor any special endowments of nature. Locating two contemporaries who had developed ventriloquial skills for their own amusement – one a Viennese baron who dabbled in puppetry and mimicry and another a nearby grocer named Saint-Gille who always enjoyed a good practical joke – La Chapelle built his explanatory framework on scientific report and empirical observation, particularly of the grocer. Unlike previous writers, he anchored his attack on religious imposture in experimental exhibitions; instead of going to view the possessed, he closely observed a magical performer. That was a fateful shift of perspective.

La Chapelle insisted that Saint-Gille was an honest man and hence a reliable source, but the grocer certainly had a roguish streak, confounding people with his amateur illusions time and again. One story, aptly titled "Les Religieux dupés," was particularly important for La Chapelle's purpose of establishing his point that ventriloquism was a generative force of religious delusion, that it was an important technique for creating "an appearance of revelation." Taking refuge in a monastery during a storm, Saint-Gille learns that the brothers are in mourning over the recent death of one of their members; visiting the tomb in the church, he projects a ghostly voice of the dead friar – one that laments the indifferent prayers of his fellows for his suffering soul in Purgatory. Soon the ventriloquist has the whole community praying for forgiveness, falling on the floor in fear and astonishment, and trying desperately to make amends to their lost brother. Overawed by the divine evidences he finds in the ghostly voice, the prior even tells Saint-Gille that such apparitions effectively put to flight all the skeptical reasonings of the philosophers. But then Saint-Gille, La Chapelle reports in all seriousness, lets the duped in on the trickery – telling them that it had all been done by the art of ventriloquy, that he himself is the all-too-human source of this oracle. In the consummate act of the enlightened magician, Saint-Gille takes the devout back to the church and turns it into the scene of their awakening from illusion, showing them his techniques of mystification. La Chapelle, thus reaffirming the ease with which the senses are deceived and the need for critical reason, drew out the doubled moral of the story, "The art of the ventriloquists is then admirable for establishing and destroying superstition."[10]

[...] The point to La Chapelle was that he had found one of the originating causes of religious phantasms and that now, so identified, ventriloquism could be turned with delicious irony from being a buttress of superstition to a tool of the Enlightenment. The study of nature had yielded up the secrets of the sorcerer's power as well as the ancient springs of political and religious despotism, and now those demystified illusions could be turned into a Baconian exercise of enlightened entertainment, a didactic amusement that would enact rationality's triumph over superstition and truth's routing of fraud. [...]

With La Chapelle's expansive reformulation of ventriloquism, the art now illumined many of the issues that were the lifeblood of eighteenth-century intellectual life. One was epistemology. Predictably the Scottish Common-Sense thinkers, whose arguments for the reliability of human perception were so prized for American Protestant didacticism, became especially concerned about the art's apparent challenge to empiricism. Both Thomas Reid and Dugald Stewart addressed the issue in their massive philosophies of the mind, Reid briefly, Stewart at some length, and both saw these vocal deceptions in the context of their larger efforts to discipline the senses. The impressions that the mind received through the senses, Reid acknowledged, were "limited and imperfect," but they were not inherently "fallacious," so empirical knowledge was both widely reliable and also capable of ongoing refinement. Ever the enemy of skeptics, Reid affirmed that the senses were not "given to us by some malignant demon on purpose to delude us" but rather "by the wise and beneficent Author of nature, to give us true information of things necessary to our preservation and happiness." Reid's confident pledge was that the drag of credulity and the power of deception weakened as experience deepened and learning grew. Improving, training, and augmenting the senses were crucial parts of this Baconian enterprise.[11]

The acoustic deceptions of ventriloquists (or gastrilo-quists, as Reid called them) were thought to be contain-able within this framework. Writing in 1785, before ventriloquism had been formalized as a stage perform-ance or as "an engine for drawing money," Reid admitted that he (unlike La Chapelle) had not had "the fortune to be acquainted with any of these artists," but hazarded that the vocal illusions possible were "only such an imperfect imitation as may deceive those who are inattentive, or under a panic." The powers of imperson-ation paled before the minute discriminations of "an attentive ear," always "able to distinguish the copy from the original"; human senses, if imperfect, emerged from these vocal tricks unscathed, perhaps even sharpened in their discernment. [. . .] Likewise, Dugald Stewart, who was able to frequent ventriloquists' exhibitions and pined to see more (especially the celebrated Alexandre Vattemare), thought deceptions of this variety finally had "but narrow limits," at least for the philosophically disciplined viewer: "In the progress of entertainment, I have, in general, become distinctly sensible of the impo-sition; and have sometimes wondered that it should have misled me for a moment." What Reid, Stewart, and their varied allies imagined was a fine-tuned discipline of hearing, a carefully trained ear that would minimize the power of both "acoustic illusions" and "wonderful rela-tions," that would, in effect, keep people from hearing things in credulous ways. The perceptual disciplines that the ventriloquists demanded would help further the aural culture of a highly reasonable Christianity.[12]

The immediate religious struggles on which such experimental observations fed were the battles over what the enlightened like to call popular enthusiasm and credulity. Dugald Stewart, for example, placed his consideration of ventriloquism in his *Elements of the Philosophy of the Human Mind* (3 vols., 1792–1827) at the end of a long section on "sympathetic imitation" in which he considered the human propensity for copying others and the weighty influence that the imagination has on the body. Here he took up "the contagious nature of convulsions, of hysteric disorders, of panics, and of all different kinds of enthusiasm" and the joined importance of imitation and imagination in explaining "these various phenomena." Animal magnetism was his leading example of the power of the imagination in rendering people sus-ceptible to "theatrical representations," but that was part of a longer train of popular enthusiasms and religious frenzies (such as the Quakers, the Camisards, and the Cambuslang revival) for which sympathy, imitation, and imagination provided guiding categories of explanation.

The Scottish Enlightenment was hardly any more moderate than the French when it came to retuning the resonances of popular Christian piety.[13]

Ventriloquism was relevant to this discussion for Stewart because of the crucial role that "the imagi-nation of the spectator or of the hearer" played in the human susceptibility to both deception and enthusiasm. Whereas some wanted to emphasize the formal acoustic dimensions of vocal illusions, for Stewart the point was the way in which the ventriloquist "manages the imaginations of his audience" through misdirection, counterfeiting, and theater. Stewart accented the complicity of the deceived, the ways in which their own imaginations were excited, making up for any gaps in the artifice, finally yielding "without resistance, to the agreeable delusions practised on [them] by the artist." The ven-triloquist was thus like the mesmerist or the revivalist in bringing the imaginations of his spectators under his own skillful management. [. . .] In between such images of the ventriloquist's enormous power to manipulate people's enthusiastic imaginations and the confident assertions that ventriloquism finally only advanced the rationalistic disciplines of modernity existed a core Enlightenment concern: the triumphant progress of the new learning faced the obduracy of popular religion.[14]

No one explored such tensile propositions about rea-son and religious voices with greater depth than Charles Brockden Brown in *Wieland; or, The Transformation* and in *Memoirs of Carwin, the Biloquist*. Brown, like Tom Paine, had journeyed from a Quaker upbringing into deistic skepticism, and Carwin's ventriloquist act is one emblem of Brown's religious disavowals. The representation of Carwin partakes of La Chapelle's doubled perspective: this knowledge abetted the Enlightenment's ambition for a new mode of hearing deaf to the sounds of supernatural promptings and at the same time underscored the dis-heartening power of enthusiasm and the ease of impos-ture. The Wieland family, steeped via their father in a long history of radical Protestant sectarianism, proves an easy target for Carwin's deceptions after his arrival at their tranquil home. Clara and her brother Theodore, for all their cultivation of republican virtue and education, retain active religious imaginations and are all too ready to attribute supernatural agency to Carwin's mysterious voices. The pious Theodore, after all, had long sought "the blissful privilege of direct communication" with God, "of listening to the audible enunciation" of the divine will. Clara, somewhat more cautious, is torn by the appear-ance of the marvelous: "My opinions were the sport of eternal change. Sometimes I conceived the apparition to be more than human. I had no grounds upon which to build a disbelief." Carwin, too late, will provide the naturalistic grounds for presuming "auricular deception" through his learned exposition of ventriloquy or, what Brown calls interchangeably, *biloquism* (aptly capturing the divided, "double-tongued" quality of this vocal trickery). Earlier Carwin, tipping his hand, had tried to make the Wielands aware of "the power of mimicry," but they had remained impervious to his "mode of explaining these appearances," incapable of absorbing such knowledge.[15]

Similar credulity within Carwin's own family started him in the cultivation of this art. "A thousand superstitious tales were current in the family," Carwin avers. "Apparitions had been seen, and voices had been heard on a multitude of occasions. My father was a confident believer in supernatural tokens. The voice of his wife, who had been many years dead, had been twice heard at midnight whispering at his pillow." Seeing in such popular religious beliefs an opening to manipulate his father, Carwin feels emboldened to move from simple mimicry and the ventriloquizing of distant voices to feigning utterances of the dead and even God. Put to the test, both his own family and the Wielands fail badly at suspicion; Carwin's studied art dupes them all (with murderous consequences for the Wielands as Theodore is eventually thrown into such madness by these "divine" voices that he murders his wife and children). The whole episode, the apparently repentant Carwin tells Clara as he reveals the technical knowledge of his enlightened magic, provides a potent "lesson to mankind on the evils of credulity," on the fatality of religious illusions.[16]

Ventriloquism offered a playful way for rationalists and deists to scorn the continuing ferment of enthusiasm and prophecy – all the innovative voices of evangelical awakening, all the personal discoveries of divine "calling" amid these outpourings of the Spirit. "No other instrument" but deft ventriloquy was necessary to "institute a new sect," Carwin learns from a European mentor. "Can you doubt these were illusions?" Clara's uncle asks her with appropriate skepticism after hearing about the voices. "Neither angel nor devil had any part in this affair." The philosophic knowledge of ventriloquism provided an assumption of suspicion, a strategy of disenchantment, a sardonic hedge against prophecy and demonism; it tendered a naturalistic vocabulary to sustain such incredulity in the face of the clamoring voices of religious inspiration and the sweeping rise of revivalistic fervor. Yet, Brown always had it both ways: Enlightenment dreams that philosophical experiments

with ventriloquism would unmask popular "superstitions" blended into the new masquerades made possible with such "rational" forms of recreation. The mesmerizing impostor Carwin was less interested finally in taming the enthusiastic imagination than manipulating "the ignorant and credulous" for his own ends of wealth, power, and pleasure. In Carwin, Brown created the sort of charlatan who bared the "irrationality" hidden in La Chapelle's embrace of the illusionist Saint-Gille as a philosophical ally. In this juggling of the Enlightenment and magic, reason easily slipped into humbug, and such subversions from within made the natural philosopher's hope of containing the eruptive voices of democratized Christianity all the more a pipe dream.[17]

The uses to which ventriloquial theory could be put ultimately extended far beyond such "local" applications within European and North American Christianity. It provided a naturalistic lens on religions across the board and came specifically to provide a way of making sense of indigenous shamans encountered through colonial contact. La Chapelle and his varied heirs had all seen ventriloquism as an ancient conspiracy of priests, as one of the chief means employed among Egyptians, Greeks, and other pagans "to effect the apparition of their gods," but Dugald Stewart made a significant extension of the construct by concluding his remarks on the subject in *Elements of the Philosophy of the Human Mind* with an account of Captain George Lyon's travels among the Eskimos. Lyon's story was then picked up by David Brewster in his *Letters on Natural Magic*, quickly becoming part of the ventriloquist's echo chamber.[18]

Stewart and Brewster read Lyon's "curious" narrative of exploration with their new explanatory tools, ready to incorporate these "savages" and their "male wizards" into their peculiar account of superstition's natural history. Lyon himself had licensed this reading, finding "all the effect of ventriloquism" in the varied imitations that he saw enacted among the Eskimos by "an ugly and stupid-looking young glutton." Speaking wryly of a diviner's possession by a spirit named Tornga and the "hollow" voice that replaced the shaman's own, Lyon reported what he heard in diction shaped by ventriloquial categories: "Suddenly the voice seemed smothered, and was so managed as to sound as if retreating beneath the deck, each moment becoming more distant, and ultimately giving the idea of being many feet below the cabin, when it ceased entirely." Brewster, Stewart, and Lyon saw no mystery in this, no threat of difference, no hint of the ecstatic or the demonic, only the natural curiosity of the ventriloquist's illusion, only what Euro-American stage magicians had by now rendered a harmless and humorous simulation. "The Eskimaux of Igloolik," it turned out, were simply, as Brewster said, "ventriloquists of no mean skill." Philosopher and explorer thus joined together to make ventriloquism a vagrant hypothesis ready to explain Eskimo "wizards" as readily as Delphic oracles or sectarian enthusiasts. Decades later one of the major ethnographers among the Chukchees and Eskimos still included in his massive field report a section on "ventriloquism and other tricks" in his discussion of religious practices. [. . .] Through the category of ventriloquy, the learned were able to take "possession" of shamanism itself, to perform their own interpretive sleight of hand of transforming the strange into the familiar, ritual into art(ifice).

"Every Man . . . His Own Magician": Performances of Suspicion

In his vision of the model college for increasing "the knowledge of Causes, and secret motions of things" in the *New Atlantis*, Francis Bacon dreamed of magical performance becoming an instrument of science. Not the gnostic occultist, but the common juggler would become part of the advancement of empiricism.[19]

[. . .]

Bacon's utopian dreams found partial fulfillment in the new celebrity magicians of the late eighteenth and early nineteenth centuries. Many of these illusionists expressly presented their dexterous tricks as philosophical recreations and mechanical experiments, illustrative of natural principles, not of occult powers or diabolic alliances. Their explanations of their own deceptions were designed to destroy any lingering beliefs about magicians holding "intelligence with supernatural beings"; as conjurers of the Enlightenment, they would help keep people from being "imposed on" by both charlatans and priests. The arts of the juggler were thus widely refashioned into "a most agreeable antidote to superstition, and to that popular belief in miracles, exorcism, conjuration, sorcery, and witchcraft."[20]

Among the most renowned of these enlightened magicians were the operators of the phantasmagoria or magic lantern ghost shows, such as the French magus Étienne Gaspard Robertson who took a well-known technology and widely popularized it in the late 1790s. Made a spectacle across Europe, the phantasmagoria

were quickly exported by various performers to North America, flourishing in the United States in the first quarter of the nineteenth century (and well beyond that through ongoing reinvention and improvement). Like Saint-Gille, Robertson chose a cloistered chapel surrounded by the tombs of monks for one of his grandest displays of simulated apparitions, creating a sublime spectacle of both Gothic horror and demystifying reason. As an 1802 playbill of one of Robertson's imitators proclaimed, "This SPECTROLOGY, which professes to expose the Practices of artful Impostors and pretended Exorcists, and to open the Eyes of those who still foster an absurd Belief in GHOSTS OR DISEMBODIED SPIRITS, will, it is presumed, afford also to the Spectator an interesting and pleasing Entertainment." The naturalistic implications of such displays were not lost on deistic debunkers of revealed religion. In *The Age of Reason*, Paine latched onto such shows to illustrate his larger attack on prophecy and miracle: "There are performances by sleight-of-hand, and by persons acting in concert that have a miraculous appearance, which when known are thought nothing of. And besides these, there are mechanical and optical deceptions. There is now an exhibition in Paris of ghosts or spectres, which, though it is not imposed upon the spectators as a fact, has an astonishing appearance." Deistic skepticism about the divine showmanship of miracles found performative corroboration in the entrepreneurial showmanship of enlightened magicians like Robertson.[21]

Ventriloquism was the close ally of the phantasmagoria. Its rise as a stage art was coeval with the ghost shows, coming into its own between 1795 and 1825. Before that, such vocal talents did not constitute a distinct performative genre, but mingled with the assorted entertainments at fairs and markets, the shows of acrobats, jugglers, mimics, freaks, musicians, mountebanks, and puppeteers.[22] The new performers of ventriloquism were adepts of mimicry, mastering impressions of multiple voices, natural sounds, and animal cries (in effect, recreating the devil's menagerie of familiars in secular form); they were also experts at "throwing" the voice, making it seem to come from various distances and places (under the floor, from the ceiling, up a chimney, out of a pocket or hat); they achieved such illusions through clever misdirection, precise modulation, and well-nigh motionless lips or "speaking without appearing to speak"; they cleverly played off these other voices and invisible beings, badgering, flirting, capering; and they were also puppeteers, sometimes using wooden dolls and automata to create stage doubles (such magical figures echoed the "puppets" used in witchcraft and foreshadowed the "dummies" that eventually became the *sine qua non* of vaudeville acts of the late nineteenth century). In all, ventriloquists were masters at animating the inanimate; they were bearers of aural astonishment – of sounds uncertain, confounding, low, tremulous, intermittent, and bestial. [. . .]

In the United States, ventriloquism became an established stage art in the first decade of the nineteenth century and remained a popular staple of antebellum theater and entertainment thereafter. One Boston physician, in bragging of his assiduous dedication to science in 1823, suggested the scope of this rational amusement in the early republic: "Our constant devotion to anatomical pursuits has prompted us to improve every opportunity of witnessing these exhibitions, with the sole object of understanding the rationale." In his rounds he estimated that he had gone to observe close to thirty different ventriloquists! Leading the way in this new host of performers was John Rannie, a Scottish actor and magician, who, as the first ventriloquist to tour the United States, put on innumerable American shows between 1801 and 1811. Like the many ventriloquists after him, he crisscrossed the republic, making appearances from New York to New Orleans, from Newburyport, Massachusetts, to Natchez, Mississippi.[23]

Much of Rannie's variegated act was the usual juggler's show of card tricks, knife swallowing, and slack-wire walking, but he also stood out as an exemplar of stage magic's entanglement with rational religion. He commonly presented himself as a magician of the Enlightenment cultivating philosophical experiments, with ventriloquism as his most prodigious talent in that line. Ventriloquism, Rannie explained in a Boston advertisement in 1804, "is one of the most singular phenomena that has been contemplated by the most enlightened sages." He described the scriptural notion of familiar spirits and then informed his potential viewers that "when the witch at *Endor* raised the apparition of Samuel," it was "by the power of Ventriloquism" that the "artful woman" occasioned "a voice to come from the Ghost, which Saul took to be the voice of the prophet himself." How the woman "managed" this voice "as she pleased," Rannie promised, would be "clearly demonstrated in the course of this evening's exhibition."[24]

Such propositions evidently did not sit well with some of Boston's Protestant faithful, long accustomed as they were to opposing both players and jugglers as dissolute influences. By early August, Rannie was lamenting in his advertising how hard it was "to remove the cobwebs of imposition from the eyes of ALL mankind" and how his shows were being scorned by certain "disciples of

illiberality." Comparing himself melodramatically to Copernicus in his confrontation with reigning orthodoxies, Rannie insisted that he had come "before the public, with both the ability and intention of exposing, and, if possible, exterminating the very dregs of fanaticism," only to find that many in Boston had "the self-sufficience of an Ostrich" with their unseeing heads stuck in a bush. [. . .]

One of the first American expositors of ventriloquism, having heard of Rannie's feats in and around Boston, wanted to make sure that the right point was sinking in with the credulous: "The intention of this work was not only to amuse and instruct," William Pinchbeck explained in one of his two manuals on enlightened magic in 1805, "but also to convince superstition of her many ridiculous errors, – to shew the disadvantages arising to society from a vague as well as irrational belief of man's intimacy with familiar spirits, – to oppose the idea of supernatural agency in any production of man." [. . .] Surveying the widening array of enlightened magic on display in the early republic – phantasmagoria, ventriloquism, automata, and even an "Acoustic Temple" that revealed "how the Pagan priests by making use of tubes deceived the people" with oracles – Pinchbeck rejoiced in the progress of scientific ingenuity, "the parent of manufactories." His own mission, he related after debunking the story of a churchyard apparition as just one more chimera, was to "convince the world that in order to support wisdom, and banish folly, whenever any uncommon sounds are heard, or any unnatural visions seen, it is indispensably necessary to search into the secret causes of such sounds and visions." Along with book peddlers and publishers, such entrepreneurial magicians and their expositors became agents of the "Village Enlightenment," blending illusionist performance with the business of print in the wider democratization of experimental knowledge and critical reason.[25]

The lingering influence of enlightened magicians like Rannie and Pinchbeck was significant. That Yankee trickster and anti-Calvinist Universalist P. T. Barnum was only the most visible heir in an extensive company. Barnum built his empire around one of the grand institutions of democratized Enlightenment and entertainment, the American Museum, in which a major part of the spectacle was – as Neil Harris has shown – the question of how things worked, the hidden operations of his attractions. [. . .] Barnum's selling of hoax and illusion, including ventriloquism, was intimately connected to his inculcation of a healthy skepticism, his desire to goad inquiry and expose credulity through respectable entertainment. Indeed, Barnum opened his monumental chronicle of *The Humbugs of the World* (1866) with praise for an illusionist who first "astonished his auditors with his deceptions" and then later showed "how each trick was performed, and how every man might thus become his own magician." For Barnum, as with Rannie before him, the performative exposure of "supernatural humbugs" – whether mediums, ghosts, prophets, or oracles – helped put people on their guard, made them ever ready to detect imposture, religious and otherwise. From Robertson and Philipstal, to Rannie and Pinchbeck, to Barnum and Houdini, to Mulholland and Randi, magic was not a form of hermetic knowledge, not a spiritual quest for harmonial powers, but a playground of skeptical rationality and bold enterprise.[26]

As with Captain Lyon's encounters with the Eskimos, such enlightened forms of magic often ended up having a shaping influence on popular Christian exchanges. The new ventriloquy and its allied knowledges supported habits of suspicion and provided performative techniques for "exposing" the religious claims of others.

[...]

Exposing the "imposture" and "priestcraft" of *other* faiths became something of a sport in antebellum America, and the natural magic of the Enlightenment provided a common script for these encounters, whether with Mormons, Catholics, or Spiritualists. In his travels in the 1830s, Tocqueville was intrigued not only by the strength of Christianity in the United States, its capacity to sustain the associational bonds that made democracy work, but also by the frailties of that faith. Antebellum Americans were prone, Tocqueville noted, to an "almost wild spiritualism," but they were also ever eager to "laugh at modern prophets," to arraign supernatural claims at the bar of their own critical reason and individual judgment. The extension of rationalistic suspicion threatened to taint the country with "an almost insurmountable distaste for whatever is supernatural." Tocqueville feared, as Melville did later, that Americans were given to "a sort of instinctive incredulity." Though these reservations in Tocqueville's account would be easy to discount, it is important to recognize how widely Enlightenment forms of knowledge and suspicion were diffused, how popular they could be. As the sphere of Christianity widened, so too did the magic circle of the Enlightenment. In a Barnumesque culture in which "every man might...become his own magician," in which the widening knowledge of illusion often fueled a harsh game of disenchantment, any new faith was hard won, built on a series of incredulous disavowals, sustained amid a welter of exposures and counterexposures – a small raft in a sea of suspicion.[27]

Ventriloquism's modern transformation points us to some other ways of thinking about the American Enlightenment and its fate. The Enlightenment was an encyclopedia, a web, the reach of which is hardly measured by the failure of organized deism, the success of evangelicalism, or the Protestant absorption of Scottish moral philosophy. The lingering force of that vast network of learning can be gauged in any number of cultural realms in the nineteenth-century United States. Two quick sketches – one of medical psychology, the other of commercial entertainment – will have to suffice here to illustrate the rippling effects of the enlightened way of reimagining the voices of popular Christian piety.

The fate of these altered voices echoed the larger process by which the travails of the soul became matters of the self – one in which the divine struggle of demonic possession passed into a bleak diagnosis of the divisibility of personal identity. As much as epistemological uncertainty, this had been Thomas Reid's underlying dread, that the unity of the self was being fractured by Humean skepticism. What Reid saw as the potentially "dangerous" abilities of the ventriloquist – the powers of impersonation and doubling – were a cultural emblem of those splittings, that someone might be "two or twenty different persons," that personal identity could be "shivered into pieces" and hence the integrity of individual moral responsibility lost. The new ventriloquism of the late eighteenth century imagined the final erasure of demons and spirits and their replacement by a profusion of naturalized voices, stark images of divided, multiple, or counterfeited selves. The Enlightenment construction of ventriloquism helped broker the much larger transition to hearing the voices of religious experience as psychological illusions or symptoms of inner fragmentation. This interpretive construct was one small token of the growing power of naturalism to translate the Christian drama of possession and vocal presences into the delusions of double consciousness and the proliferating diagnoses of dementia – monomania, hallucination, erotomania, and dissociation. As much as their British and French counterparts, antebellum American theorists like Amariah Brigham contributed to the pathologizing of religious excitements and various forms of devotional intensity.[28]

The second trajectory is that the new ventriloquism managed to submerge its oracular, demonic, and Christian precursor within the expanding culture of commodified leisure. The illusionist technologies of the Enlightenment, like the phantasmagoria, helped lay the groundwork for a whole complex of modern entertainments. Ventriloquism shared in this luxuriant growth; as a commercial amusement, it passed into vaudeville, cinema, radio (incongruously enough), and television; it even became a pop culture icon with Edgar Bergen and Charlie McCarthy. Within this vast culture of showmanship, it takes something of an excavation even to discern the old meanings of ventriloquism. As E. B. Tylor remarked of the naturalistic abandonment of an animistic universe in his monumental study of *Primitive Culture* (1871), in "old times" the ventriloquist "was really held to have a spirit rumbling or talking from inside his body"; now he was a stage entertainer; no longer a shaman, he was a showman. "How changed a philosophy it marks," concluded Tylor, "that among ourselves the word 'ventriloquist' should have sunk to its present meaning."[29] The enlightened magician and his philosophical expositors made ventriloquism an easy and entertaining trick, a show of mastered simulation, available for the price of admission. In that, ventriloquism was indicative of the larger absorption of the sacred into the mediated, spectacular, and domesticated forms of modern consumption.

Notes

1 Joseph Glanvill, *Saducismus Triumphatus: Or, Full and Plain Evidence Concerning Witches and Apparitions* (London: J. Collins, 1681), 2: 64. Ventriloquism's history has been told primarily by practitioners. By far the best example of that genre is Valentine Vox, *I Can See Your Lips Moving: The History and Art of Ventriloquism* (North Hollywood: Plato Publishing, 1993). Otherwise the scholarship is dominated by critical theorists, who, interested in the polyphony of discrepant "voices" within texts and in the problem of authorial voice, have taken up ventriloquism as a trope. See, for example, Annabel Patterson, " 'They Say' or We Say: Protest and Ventriloquism in Early Modern England," in *Historical Criticism and the Challenge of Theory*, ed. Janet Levarie Smarr (Urbana: University of Illinois Press, 1993), 145–66; David Goldblatt, "Ventriloquism: Ecstatic Exchange and the History of Artwork," *Journal of Aesthetics and Art Criticism* 51 (1993): 389–98; and Christopher Looby, *Voicing America: Language, Literary Form, and the Origins of the United States* (Chicago: University of Chicago Press, 1996), 165–74.

2 On modern ocularcentrism, see especially Martin Jay, *Downcast Eyes: The Denigration of Vision in Twentieth-Century French Thought* (Berkeley: University of California Press, 1993); David Michael Levin, ed., *Modernity and the Hegemony of Vision* (Berkeley: University of California Press, 1993). For the most sustained theorizing of the sensorium and sound, though presented within the near universal framework of the triumph of visuality, see Walter J. Ong, *The Presence of the Word: Some Prolegomena for Cultural and Religious History* (New Haven: Yale University Press, 1967). On religious orality, especially preaching, see the work of Harry S. Stout, particularly, "Religion, Communications, and the Ideological Origins of the American Revolution," *William and Mary Quarterly* 34 (1977): 519–41.

3 Thomas Paine, "The Age of Reason," in *The Complete Writings of Thomas Paine*, ed. Philip S. Foner (New York: Citadel, 1945), 1: 596; Ethan Allen, *Reason the Only Oracle of Man*, ed. John Pell (New York: Scholars' Facsimiles and Reprints, 1940), 231.

4 Reginald Scot, *The Discoverie of Witchcraft* (1584; reprint, London: Rowan and Littlefield, 1973), 101.

5 For background on the problems the Witch of Endor created for Christian commentaries, see Valerie I. J. Flint, *The Rise of Magic in Early Medieval Europe* (Princeton: Princeton University Press, 1991), esp. 18–21, 54–6; Lynn Thorndike, *A History of Magic and Experimental Science* (New York: Columbia University Press, 1923), 1: 352, 448, 470–1.

6 Scot, *Discoverie*, 114, 121; Glanvill, *Saducismus*, 2: 64.

7 On possession as "sacred theater," see Clarke Garrett, *Spirit Possession and Popular Religion: From the Camisards to the Shakers* (Baltimore: Johns Hopkins University Press, 1987), esp. 4–6, 86–7.

8 Thomas Hobbes, "Leviathan, or the Matter, Form, and Power of a Commonwealth Ecclesiastical and Civil," in *The English Works of Thomas Hobbes of Malmesbury* (London: Bohn, 1839–1845), 3: 434; Francis Hutchinson, *An Historical Essay Concerning Witchcraft* (London: Knaplock, 1718), 8–9. See also Hobbes, "Elements of Philosophy," in *Works*, 1: 498; John Webster, *The Displaying of Supposed Witchcraft* (London: J.M., 1677), 165–6.

9 For the author's notation on La Chapelle in *Wieland*, see Charles Brockden Brown, *Wieland; or, The Transformation and Memoirs of Carwin, the Biloquist*, ed. Emory Elliot (Oxford: Oxford University Press, 1994), 181n–182n. For the 1799 pamphlet (not available through the Charles Evans imprints, but preserved at the New Jersey Historical Society), see *Amusement-Hall: Or, A Collection of Diverting Stories and Extraordinary Facts, with an Account of the Art of Ventriloquism; and Other Entertaining Matter* (Morristown, N.J.: n.p., 1799), 10–19. For the influence on Salverte, see Eusebe Salverte, *The Occult Sciences: The Philosophy of Magic, Prodigies and Apparent Miracles*, trans. Anthony Todd Thomson (London: Bentley, 1846), 1: 157–62, 283–4. La Chapelle hitherto has not been written into the history of the naturalistic study of religion

alongside other Enlightenment speculators such as Trenchard, Hume, and Fontenelle.

10 Joannes Baptista de la Chapelle, *Le Ventriloque, ou l'engastrimythe* (Paris: Duchesne, 1772), 341, 471–8.

11 Thomas Reid, "Essays on the Intellectual Powers of Man," in *The Works of Thomas Reid* (Charlestown, Mass.: Etheridge, 1813), 2: 83, 309, 322.

12 Reid, *Works*, 2: 319–20; Dugald Stewart, "Philosophy of the Human Mind," in *The Works of Dugald Stewart* (Cambridge: Hilliard and Brown, 1829), 3: 168–9.

13 Stewart, *Works*, 1: 108, 137–51.

14 Stewart, *Works*, 3: 166–71; David Brewster, *Letters on Natural Magic* (London: John Murray, 1842), 171–2. There were at least seven American editions of Brewster's *Letters* between 1832 and 1845. For the point that the illusion was less about acoustics than the misdirection of the imagination Stewart was drawing especially on an anonymous review of John Gough's research in *Edinburgh Review* 2 (April 1803): 192–6. See also John Gough, "Facts and Observations to Explain the Curious Phenomenon of Ventriloquism," *Journal of Natural Philosophy, Chemistry, and the Arts* 2 (June 1802): 122–9.

15 Brown, *Wieland*, 32, 69–70, 152, 165. *Wieland* is among the most widely commented upon novels of the early national era, but scholars have been imprecise in contextualizing the book's central illusionist practice of ventriloquism and the religious meanings that flow from it. For a basic contextualization of this dimension of the novel, see "Historical Essay," in Charles Brockden Brown, *The Novels and Related Works of Charles Brockden Brown*, ed. Sydney J. Krause, S. W. Reid, and Alexander Cowie (Kent State: Kent State University Press, 1977), 1: 325–6. Readings that I have found especially insightful for my purposes include: Jay Fliegelman, *Prodigals and Pilgrims: The American Revolution against Patriarchal Authority, 1750–1800* (Cambridge: Cambridge University Press, 1982), 235–48; Jon Butler, *Awash in a Sea of Faith: Christianizing the American People* (Cambridge, Mass.: Harvard University Press, 1990), 225–8; Steven Watts, *The Romance of Real Life: Charles Brockden Brown and the Origins of American Culture* (Baltimore: Johns Hopkins University Press, 1994), esp. 54–8, 82–9, 184–5; Bernard Rosenthal, "The Voices of *Wieland*," in *Critical Essays on Charles Brockden Brown*, ed. Bernard Rosenthal (Boston: G. K. Hall, 1981), 104–25. Rosenthal and Watts both do an especially fine job of locating the novel within Brown's wider deistic suspicions about revealed religion.

16 Brown, *Wieland*, 194, 234.

17 Brown, *Wieland*, 163, 243. On the religious hothouse, see especially Nathan O. Hatch, *The Democratization of American Christianity* (New Haven: Yale University Press, 1989); Butler, *Awash*; Gordon S. Wood, "Evangelical America and Early Mormonism," *New York History* 61 (1980): 359–86.

18 Brewster, *Letters*, 5, 176–8; Stewart, *Works*, 3: 171–3; Dugald Stewart, "Observations on Ventriloquism," *Edinburgh Journal of Science* 9 (1828): 250–2. For the original account, see George Francis Lyon, *The Private Journal of Captain G. F. Lyon of H.M.S. Hecla, during the Recent Voyage of Discovery under Captain Parry* (London: Murray, 1825), 149–50, 359–74.

19 Francis Bacon, *The Works of Francis Bacon*, ed. James Spedding, Robert Ellis, and Douglas Heath (London: Longman, 1859), 3: 156, 162, 164.

20 *Breslaw's Last Legacy; Or, the Magical Companion*, 5th ed. (London: Lane, 1791), viii–ix; John Beckmann, *A History of Inventions and Discoveries*, trans. William Johnston (London: Longman, 1817), 3: 269–70. See also William Hooper, *Rational Recreations in which the Principles of Numbers and Natural Philosophy Are Clearly and Copiously Elucidated*, 4 vols. (London: Davis, 1784); Philip Astley, *Natural Magic: Or, Physical Amusements Revealed* (London: n.p., 1785); Guiseppe Pinetti, *Physical Amusements and Diverting Experiments* (London: n.p., 1784); [Henri Decremps], *The Conjurer Unmasked; Being a Clear and Full Explanation of all the Surprizing Performances Exhibited as well in this Kingdom as on the Continent*, trans. Thomas Denton (London: Stalker, 1788).

21 Paine, *Complete Writings*, 1: 508. For the ghost shows, see X. Theodore Barber, "Phantasmagorical Wonders: The Magic Lantern Ghost Show in Nineteenth-Century America," *Film History* 3 (1989): 73–86 (playbill on p. 79); Xenophon Theodore Barber, "Evenings of Wonders: A History of the Magic Lantern in America," 2 vols. (Ph.D. diss., New York University, 1993); Pecor, *Magician*, 85–6, 104–12; Erik Barnouw, *The Magician and the Cinema* (New York: Oxford University Press, 1981), 19–34; Terry Castle, "Phantasmagoria: Spectral Technology and the Metaphorics of Modern Reverie," *Critical Inquiry* 15 (autumn 1988): 26–61; Richard D. Altick, *The Shows of London* (Cambridge, Mass.: Belknap Press of Harvard University Press, 1978), 117, 217–20; Robert M. Isherwood, *Farce and Fantasy: Popular Entertainment in Eighteenth-Century Paris* (New York: Oxford University Press, 1986), 50–2, 199–201. For Robertson's own account, see Étienne Gaspard Robertson, *Mémoires recreatifs scientifiques et anecdotiques* (Paris: n.p., 1831), 1: 272–310. Like ventriloquism, the phantasmagoria were also incorporated into the natural history of superstition. See Salverte, *Occult Sciences*, 1: 265–92; Brewster, *Letters*, 5–6, 57–85.

22 Vox, *History and Art*, 41–8; Isherwood, *Farce*, 197–8; Altick, *Shows*, 36.

23 "Ventriloquism," *Boston Medical Intelligencer*, 67. The best study of stage magic in North America for this period is Pecor's *Magician on the American Stage*. Pecor tracks the travels, shows, and venues of various magicians, including several of the early ventriloquists (such as Rannie and Potter) and documents the development of magic as professional theater. I am indebted to his work for substantiating the geographic range of these itinerant performers.

See also H. J. Moulton, *Houdini's History of Magic in Boston, 1792–1915* (Glenwood, Ill.: Meyerbooks, 1983), 1–44.

24 *Columbian Centinel*, 14 July 1804, 3. See also [John Rannie], *The European Ventriloquist's Exhibition* (Portsmouth: S. Whidden, [1808]). For Rannie's shows within the wider theatrical history of the period, see David Grimsted, *Melodrama Unveiled: American Theater and Culture, 1800–1850* (Chicago: University of Chicago Press, 1968), 100–1; George C. D. Odell, *Annals of the New York Stage* (New York: Columbia University Press, 1927), 2: 143–44, 209–10, 344.

25 William Frederick Pinchbeck, *The Expositor; Or Many Mysteries Unravelled* (Boston: n.p., 1805), A2, 31–4, 38–40, 53–60, 81–2, 90–1; William Frederick Pinchbeck, *Witchcraft, Or the Art of Fortune-Telling Unveiled* (Boston: n.p., 1805), 10, 13–15, 47–9, 70. On the democratization of the Enlightenment through print, see David Jaffee, "The Village Enlightenment in New England, 1760–1820," *William and Mary Quarterly* 47 (July 1990): 327–46.

26 Barnum, *Humbugs*, v, 294. On Barnum's "operational aesthetic" and uses of deception, see Neil Harris, *Humbug: The Art of P. T. Barnum* (Chicago: University of Chicago Press, 1973), 33–89, 211–23. For Heth and ventriloquism, see Philip B. Kunhardt Jr., Philip B. Kunhardt III, and Peter W. Kunhardt, *P. T. Barnum: America's Greatest Showman* (New York: Knopf, 1995), 20–2.

27 Alexis de Tocqueville, *Democracy in America* (New York: Vintage Books, 1945), 2: 4, 10, 142.

28 Reid, *Works*, 2: 114, 320, 338–44, 357, 360; Amariah Brigham, *Observations on the Influence of Religion upon the Health and Physical Welfare of Mankind* (Boston: Marsh, Capen, and Lyon, 1835). On earlier efforts to medicalize enthusiasm, see especially Michael Heyd, *"Be Sober and Reasonable": The Critique of Enthusiasm in the Seventeenth and Early Eighteenth Centuries* (Leiden: Brill, 1995). On the larger translation of religious idioms into psychological ones, see, for example, Ian Hacking, *Rewriting the Soul: Multiple Personality and the Sciences of Memory* (Princeton: Princeton University Press, 1995), esp. 142–58.

29 Edward B. Tylor, *Primitive Culture: Researches into the Development of Mythology, Philosophy, Religion, Language, Art and Custom* (New York: Holt, 1889), 2: 132–4, 182. On ventriloquism's thriving as a commercial entertainment, see Vox, *History and Art*, esp. 90–133.

Rethinking Vernacular Culture:
Black Religion and Race Records
in the 1920s and 1930s

Evelyn Brooks Higginbotham

If black religious culture in its varied beliefs and practices has fostered bright and shining stars such as Martin Luther King, Jr., Malcolm X, Marian Anderson, Aretha Franklin, Jesse Jackson, and Cornel West, then as this list of names suggests, black religious culture has played a significant role in the contestation of ideologies in African-American communities. This contestation occurs between the middle class and working class, and it also occurs within the working class itself. Unfortunately, the trend in recent scholarship has not given the religious culture of the working class the attention it deserves. Some of the most imaginative and analytically sophisticated studies tend to privilege the secular life of black working-class communities. Such studies often draw upon the "race records" of the 1920s and 1930s, linking blues records with socioeconomic processes of migration and urbanization. They focus on the lyrics of the blues and the lives of blues singers as emblematic of sexual freedom, iconoclastic values, and an overall culture of resistance to the hegemony of middle-class ideology.[1] Implicitly, if not explicitly, the blues is deemed the "authentic" signifier of African-American culture.[2] Blues culture, working-class culture, and "blackness" become virtually synonymous. The religious culture of the working poor, when visible at all, appears as an anomaly or false consciousness. The blues and church are thus counterposed as cultural icons of class division. Perhaps this representation of working-class religion stems from the belief that African-American Christianity is white-derived, middle-class in orientation, and thus less authentically black. Or conversely, perhaps religion among the poor is not taken seriously because it is perceived as otherworldly,

lower-class escapism, having no ideological implications and playing no strategic role in struggles over moral and cultural authority.

The race records of the 1920s and 1930s are useful for analysis, since they included not only the blues but also the explicitly religious articulations of the black working class.[3] Companies such as Okeh, Victor, Vocalion, and Paramount recorded vernacular discourses of religion in the form of sermons and gospel music, called gospel blues, as eagerly as they recorded the raunchiest blues lyrics.[4] The religious records tapped into the cultural repertoire of storefront Baptist churches and the rising numbers of Holiness and Pentecostal churches in urban ghettos. Langston Hughes recalled his impressions of the Holiness churches in Chicago around the time of World War I: "I was entranced by their stepped-up rhythms, tambourines, hand clapping, and uninhibited dynamics, rivaled only by Ma Rainey singing the blues at the old Monogram Theater."[5] Just as Hughes had juxtaposed the songs of the church with the blues, this odd coupling of the sacred and profane appeared regularly in newspaper advertisements for race records. Paramount Records informed the readers of the *Chicago Defender* that they could "get these Red-Hot Blues and Inspiring Spirituals" through mail order. Okeh included in a single advertisement blues singer Lonnie Johnson and gospel singer Jessie May Hill. Featuring Johnson's "Mean Old Bed Bug Blues," the advertisement read: "Bedbugs big as a jackass bite you and stand and grin. Then drink a bottle of bed bug poison and come and bite you again. The Hottest Blues You Ever Heard." Yet the same advertisement listed "Sister Jessie May Hill and Sisters of the Congregation singing 'Earth Is No Resting Place.' "[6]

If, as some scholars suggest, advertising's juxtaposition of religious and blues records served as an affront to the pious, the coupling nonetheless offers an analytical rubric for disentangling the working class from its exclusive identification with blues culture. Clearly, the church was just as indigenous to the working poor as was the blues. On one level the popularity of the sermons and gospel songs speaks to an emotional folk orality that contested the ethics and aesthetics of the black middle class. Not through the counterculture of the blues, but rather through vernacular discourses of religion, the black poor waged a struggle over cultural authority that ultimately subverted the hegemonic values and aesthetic standards of the traditional Protestantism of the black middle class. On another level the religious race records speak to the existence of multiple and conflicting subcultures within the black working class, indicating differences of consciousness, values, and lifestyle even among the most poor. The religious culture of the poor, as evidenced in the Pentecostal and Holiness churches, for example, embraced a strict moral code that denounced the fast and free lifestyle of blues culture.[7] In the dialect, imagery, and rhythms of the black poor, the religious race records repudiate sexual freedom, gambling, drinking, womanizing, and general defiance of the law. Nina Simone reminisced about her working-class family: "Mama and them were so religious that they wouldn't allow you to play boogie-woogie in the house, but would allow you to use the same boogie-woogie *beat* to play a gospel tune."[8]

The religious race records of the 1920s gave a new public dimension to black religion and especially to the working-class churches. The records validated the creative energies of the rural folk, turned urban proletariat, as an alternate, competing voice within African-American communities. At the most prosaic levels, the ascendant voice of southern folk culture challenged the middle-class ideology of racial uplift as pronounced by educated religious leaders of the late nineteenth century. The latter group had defined racial progress not merely in the context of black–white relations but also in the context of a class-based contestation over group beliefs and practices. Educated religious leaders emphasized written texts and rational discourses in the struggle for the advancement of their people.[9] These religious leaders articulated sentiments similar to W. E. B. Du Bois's viewpoint that the black colleagues brought African Americans "in contact with modern civilization."[10] Commitment to collegiate education figured prominently in

their belief in an intellectual and professional vanguard – the Talented Tenth as Du Bois characterized the black elite at the turn of the century.

As time and schooling distanced African Americans further and further from their slave past, many became self-conscious, conflicted, even critical of the culture of their forebears. From gentle persuasion to ridicule and punishment, white and black missionary teachers sought the demise of the older forms of singing and worship. In 1870, Elizabeth Kilham, a white northern teacher among the freedman, acknowledged the impact of education on the younger generation:

> The distinctive features of negro hymnology, are gradually disappearing, and with another generation will probably be obliterated entirely. The cause for, this, lies in the education of the younger people. . . . Already they have learned to ridicule the extravagant preaching, the meaningless hymns, and the noisy singing of their elders. Not perhaps as yet, to any great extent in the country; changes come always more slowly there, but in the cities, the young people have, in many cases, taken the matter into their own hands, formed choirs, adopted the hymns and tunes in use in the white churches. . . .[11]

It is interesting that Kilham, while praising the shift to white hymns, conceded the slowness with which blacks in the countryside assimilated. Bishop Daniel Alexander Payne of the African Methodist Episcopal Church recalled his frustrating experience in a rural church in South Carolina.

> After the sermon they formed a ring, and with coats off sung, clapped their hands and stamped their feet in a most ridiculous and heathenish way. I requested the pastor to go and stop their dancing. At his request they stopped their dancing and clapping of hands, but remained singing and rocking their bodies to and fro. This they did for about fifteen minutes. I then went, and taking their leader by the arm requested him to desist and to sit down and sing in a *rational* manner. I told him also that it was a heathenish way to worship and disgraceful to themselves, the race, and the Christian name.[12] (my emphasis)

Payne's plea for a "rational manner" of singing formed part of the larger assimilationist project of ridding the black community of sensuality, intemperance, "superstition," and the emotional style of worship practiced in the hush harbors of the slave era. His emphasis on a calm, intellectually oriented religious expression signaled the growing class and cultural differences that would surface prominently as rural southern migrants poured into the northern cities. For Bishop Payne, loud and emotive behavior constituted more than an individual's impropriety or doctrinal error. It marked the retrogression of the entire racial group. In the midst of heightened racial discrimination and social Darwinist thought, educated leaders decried the moaning and bodily movements of black worship.[13] Educated African Americans such as James Trotter posited that vocal and instrumental music in the form of the "noble organ . . . sacred chant, the prayer or thanksgiving, uttered in melodious song by the choir or by all the congregation" served as an antidote to "the cares and wild passions" of the world. For Trotter music functioned as a civilizing force, a "source of refinement and pleasure . . . to the possessor himself, and by which he may add to the tranquillity, the joys, of his own and the home life of his neighbors and friends."[14]

Literacy and published texts came to be linked increasingly to the expression of religious culture. The Reverend Sutton Griggs, a college-educated Baptist minister and novelist, typified the black middle class in its preference for print discourse, thus implicitly devaluing the interpretative authority of illiterate leaders. He proclaimed, "To succeed as a race, we must move up out of the age of the voice. . . ."[15] Educated leaders perceived the medium of print as a source of communication and power. They made continual appeals for the publication of texts that would present the African-American side of history and instill pride in their people. They commonly used the term "distinctive literature," referring to any text that was written and/or published by African Americans.[16] Yet the phenomenal rise in literacy among African Americans in the decades after the Civil War occurred with unsettling consequences for traditions of black worship. Calling attention to the clash between literate and oral traditions in the postbellum South, Elsa Barkley Brown describes the conflict surrounding the introduction of printed songbooks in the First African Baptist Church in Richmond. The adoption of hymnals superseded the older practice of "lining out hymns," a practice increasingly labeled "unrefined" and a vestige of slave culture by educated blacks and whites. Lining out had not required literacy, but only an able song leader to introduce each verse of song, which in turn was followed by the congregation's repetition of the verse. The introduction of hymnals, however, disadvantaged the illiterate, since it reconfigured the collective voice to include the literate only. For the illiterate, asserts Elsa Barkley Brown, "it was the equivalent of being deprived of a voice, all the more significant in an oral culture."[17] [. . .]

An entire genre of race literature arose in the late nineteenth century for the purpose of "uplifting" the black masses culturally, politically, and economically. The rise of literacy had been foundational to the evolution of a black reading public, and it was this very readership that constituted the race market so crucial to the success of church-based entrepreneurship. Many local religious presses as well as the large denominational ones (the AME Book Concern, the AME Sunday School Union Press, the AME Zion Book Concern, the AME Zion Publication House, the National Baptist Publishing Board, and the Sunday School Publishing Board of the National Baptist Convention, USA, Inc.) figured significantly in the production of hymnals, church literature, newspapers, and to a lesser extent works of fiction. For example, the earliest novels of Frances Ellen Watkins Harper appeared in syndicated form in the *Christian Recorder* of the AME Church.[18] Literature produced by African Americans strove to negate the pejorative racial images prevalent in film, media, art and scholarly and popular books. Photographs in black-owned periodicals often depicted middle-class men and women in the act of reading. Captions to such photographs made reference to the cultivation of the "higher arts" and sought to convey images of refinement and civility, material comfort and respectability. The conflation of musical taste and literature culture is apparent in the 1904 issue of the *Voice of the Negro*, which featured a photographic series of "representative" black men and women. A caption to a photograph of a young black woman read: "An admirer of Fine Art, a performer on the violin and the piano, a sweet singer, a writer – mostly given to essays, a lover of good books, and a home making girl."[19]

It is no small irony, then, that the newly urbanized southern folk ushered in the "age of the voice" at the height of the renaissance of the black literati.[20] During the 1920s and 1930s the black working class effected the shift to an emotional folk orality that challenged the cultural authority of the black middle class. The migrants built storefront churches, established sects and cults, and "infiltrated" and transformed many of the "old-line" Baptist and Methodist churches with the gospel blues, a twentieth-century musical innovation with roots in the slave past.

[. . .]

The public emergence of a folk orality can be attributed to both the massive migration of southern blacks to northern cities and to a triumphant American commercialism, which during the 1920s turned its gaze upon black consumers. Through advertising, department stores, catalog shopping, and installment buying, the new commercial culture made its impact on the Great Migration. The recently arrived migrants soon became a consuming public, hungry for their own musical styles and for an array of products with a racial appeal.[21] They swelled the ranks of the race market and reconfigured black supply and demand well beyond the small entrepreneur and communities of readership at the turn of the century. [. . .]

Race-consciousness, creative expression, and the black church itself became implicated in America's growing corporate capitalism. Nowhere is this more evident than in the nexus between working-class religion and the record industry. The record industry tapped into the cultural repertoire of the black working-class churches, drawing upon and promoting the very folk traditions that the middle class had sought to eradicate. While the commodification of black religious culture and the attendant reality of white-controlled profits speak to the problematic aspects of the race records industry,[22] it cannot be denied that this commodification was made possible by the matrix of exchange inherent in the black working-class church. The church was and is at once the producer of musicians and music forms as well as a consumer market with changing tastes. Technological advancement and the consequent rise of the record and broadcast industries, along with mass advertising in the national black press, e.g., the *Chicago Defender*, all worked together to effect the commodification of the religious experience.

[. . .]

If African-American religion succumbed to the commercialism and consumerism of the 1920s, it did so while harnessing new venues for working-class cultural production. A new public voice, indeed a charismatic authority, rivaled the authority of the educated black leadership. The nineteenth century had witnessed the ascendancy of the middle class as the literate public voice of the race. The twentieth century witnessed the ascendancy of the black working class as the oral narrator of modernity.[23] Growing working-class consumerism, coupled with black middle-class disdain for the cultural styles of the poor, had initiated this important shift to working-class orality within the black public sphere. Even the Reverend Sutton Griggs, who had earlier admonished his people to "move up out of the age

of the voice," recorded sermons on the Victor label during the 1920s.[24] However, the rise of race records should not imply a false dichotomy between reading and oral/aural constituencies. More often than not, the two constituencies were one and the same, since record consumers looked primarily to black newspapers for the advertisement of new record releases and for coverage on the personal lives and public appearances of recording stars.

Blues scholar Paul Oliver notes that religious records enjoyed a popularity equal to that of the blues, and possibly greater.[25] Produced in three-minute and six-minute sound bites, these records attempt to re-create the black worship experience, presenting highly emotional preaching, moaning, ecstatic audience response, vocal and instrumental accompaniment. Oliver recounts their unrestrained quality: "The preacher develops his subject, often speaking in a direct address at first and moving to a singing tone as he warms to his theme. . . . Urged on by the murmurs, cries, shouts of approval and encouragement from the congregation, he might struggle for the right words, 'straining' with constricted throat . . . 'moaning,' 'mourning,' 'whooping.' "[26]

Building on patterns from the folk tradition and thus rejecting a rational, dispassionate style, the recorded sermons and religious songs were especially appealing to the waves of rural migrants who poured into northern cities, uprooted and in search of cultural continuity.[27] Record companies catered to the migrants' preference for a "down-home," i.e., more rural, southern style by adopting such phrases as "old-fashioned," "real Southern style" and "old-time" in their record titles and advertisements. Paramount proudly announced its "latest new electric method" of record production in its advertisement for *Old Time Baptism* by the Reverend R. M. Massey. [. . .] The Reverend J. C. Burnett's sermon, the *Downfall of Nebuchadnezzar*, sold eighty thousand records within months of its release in November 1926. Interestingly, the sermon begins in the tradition of the slaves with the lining out of the hymn *I Heard the Voice of Jesus Say*.[28] The sale of Burnett's record quadrupled the normal sale of a Bessie Smith record. By the end of the 1930s, the number of black preachers, male and female, on record had soared from six to seventy, while more than 750 sermons had been recorded.[29]

Also popular during the 1920s and early 1930s were the religious records of male and female singers, especially those identified with the storefront Baptist, Holiness, and Pentecostal churches. The strictly musical records outlived the sermons in their appeal to consumers.[30] Arizona Dranes, the blind vocalist, who sang for Okeh

Records, played in a piano style reminiscent of ragtime and boogie-woogie as she rendered the songs of black Pentecostalism to record consumers across the nation. The records of Sanctified singers (Paul Oliver's term for female singers in the Pentecostal and Holiness churches) such as Jessie May Hill, Leora Ross, Bessie Johnson, Melinda Taylor, and Rosetta Tharpe with her gospel hybridization of jazz and swing, were widely distributed in black communities.[31] Sanctified singers did not limit themselves to the piano, but employed secular accompaniment – guitars, jug bands, and tambourines. Oliver notes that blues singers even cut religious records, after record promoters convinced them of the lucrative nature of the religious market. Classic blues queens, such as Bessie Smith, Sara Martin, Clara Smith, and Leola Manning claimed at least one sacred song in their repertoire of otherwise secular recordings.[32]

The standard hymn, with its implicit connotations of order and respectability, yielded ineluctably to improvisation and earthy rhythms. The capitulation of middle-class notions of assimilation and respectability to the new "gospel blues" occurred most glaringly in the black Baptist church.[33] This shifting emphasis is epitomized by the musical styles of Marian Anderson and Mahalia Jackson, both of whose musical talents were discovered and nurtured in the church. During the first two decades of the twentieth century, the talents of the future opera star Marian Anderson grew to maturity under the influence of the musical traditions of Philadelphia's Union Baptist Church. By age thirteen she was promoted to the adult choir, having sung in the junior choir since she was six. Her sense of music and its cultural meaning was informed by traditional hymnody and orchestral performances. Black hymnody in this setting is reminiscent of Houston Baker's discussion of the "mastery of form." Baker identifies such mastery as a strategy efficaciously adopted in the name of group advancement, but clearly based upon the acknowledgment of an appeal to white America's hegemonic cultural styles and values, i.e., the nation's *standards*.[34] The church's annual concerts frequently engaged tenor Roland Hayes who "sang old Italian airs, German Lieder, and French songs exquisitely." Anderson recalls in her autobiography that "even people with little understanding of music knew it was beautiful singing, and they were proud Mr. Hayes was one of their own and world famous."[35]

Mahalia Jackson's talents were cultivated in the musical traditions of the southern black church. She began her singing career in New Orleans, the birthplace of jazz. She performed in an up-tempo rhythm expressive of what

Michael W. Harris terms "indigenous black religious song in a down-home manner."[36] Her singing group, while popular in the South, met with initial disfavor after she migrated to Chicago in 1927 at the age of sixteen. In his study of the rise of gospel blues, Harris notes that Jackson was once thrown out of a church – the minister shouting, "Get that twisting and jazz out of the church."[37] [...]

Mahalia Jackson's gospel blues appealed greatly to the swelling numbers of poor, Deep South migrants to Chicago. Jackson gave new voice to an old spirituality as she regularly performed at storefront churches. By 1932 she was receiving invitations from the established, old-line churches and would soon sing at the annual meetings of the National Baptist Convention.[38] The gospel blues had subverted the central, if not hegemonic position of standard hymnody even in these churches. Far less concerned about the gaze of white America in the projection of an African-American image, the gospel blues evoked the call and response of blacks themselves.

Nor did church leaders continue to link inextricably racial progress with their congregants' mastery of Western expressivity and styles of decorum. At issue here is more than the contestation between middle-class and working-class cultures; it is rather the interpenetration of the two. While both Marian Anderson and Mahalia Jackson enjoyed enormous fame throughout their lives, the musical repertoire of urban black Baptist churches came increasingly to identify (although not without contestation) the old-line voice with European hymns, while associating the modern with the more spontaneous, emotive style of downhome religious culture.[39] The transition of black church discourses symbolized the responsive soundings of a people in transition from an old to a new order. The commodification of black religious culture roared along with the 1920s as a marker of the decade's preoccupation with the black vernacular.[40]

Yet the contestation of cultures occurred not merely between the working class and the middle class. Division and dispute occurred within the working class itself. While the musical form of gospel blues incorporated the rhythmic patterns and sounds of secular blues, ragtime, and jazz, the lyrical content of gospel blues were embedded in institutions and belief structures that repudiated secular blues themes. Enjoying a prominence that was not confined to a particular congregation or region, men such as the Reverends E. D. Campbell, A. W. Nix, J. M. Gates and women such as the Reverends Leora Ross and Mary Nelson brought messages of doom and salvation to African Americans throughout the nation. Through recorded sermons and songs they drew upon biblical passages in their denunciation of crime, liquor, dancing, women's fashions, gambling, and fast living in general.[41] In *Better Get Ready for Judgement* the Reverend Mary Nelson sings in a strong a capella voice, condemning the hypocrites, drunkards, liars, and adulterers.[42] The recordings constituted vernacular discourses of religion, calling attention to the conditions of ghetto life in the everyday language of the poor and uneducated.

[. . .]

Themes of justice to the wicked and proud abound in the recorded sermons. Against the background of moaning voices and cries of amen, Reverend Burnett began his blockbuster hit, the *Downfall of Nebuchadnezzar*, by prophesying the inevitable ruin of people who hold themselves in high estimation and manipulate the weak. Burnett's message serves as a promise to the oppressed: God will bring down the liars, backsliders, and rich men.[43] A similar theme can be found in Reverend J. M. Gates's record, *Samson and the Woman*. Despite the title, the sermon focuses not on gender but on class and race relations. Gates, like Burnett, targets those people who think that their positions of strength, privilege, and power over others will last forever. Those on top will be leveled in time, he proclaims repeatedly in the sermon.[44] Gates was one of the most popular of the recorded preachers, holding contracts with five different record companies during the 1920s. Titles of his recorded sermons reveal concern about rising crime, e.g., *The First Born Was a Murderer, Did You Spend Christmas in Jail?, Death Might Be Your Santa Claus, No Room in the Jail-house*, and *Dying Gambler*. Whether sung or preached, the religious race records condemned the growing disorder, alienation, and criminal elements in the urban setting, but they did so in the common, everyday language of the black working class.[45] The vernacular discourses of religion constituted a moral idiom for distinguishing the personal and collective identity of the "righteous" from other working-class identities (e.g., blues people). The messages in the recorded sermons and songs articulated shared meanings and constraints for evaluating and interpreting social reality. They sought to establish boundaries around the lives of the black poor in the effort to shield them from dangers that were perceived as emanating from both outside and inside their own communities.

At issue here are not only conflicting value systems but internally generated norms. This latter point is often overlooked by scholars who too readily attribute efforts

to restore "moral order" to the intentionality, ideology, and disciplinary mechanisms of the middle class. The middle class certainly played a role in disciplining the poor and in policing black women's bodies, as Hazel Carby perceptively discusses, but so, too, did Pentecostal churches.[46] Nor were notions of "moral panic" situated solely within a 1920s bourgeois ideology. The quest for moral order is replete in the sermons, gospel songs, and religious institutions of the working class. The storefront Baptist, Pentecostal, and Holiness churches along with a variety of urban sects and cults, e.g., Father Divine's Peace Mission movement and Daddy Grace's United House of Prayer, were doubtless more effective than middle-class reformers in policing the black woman's body and demanding conformity to strict guidelines of gender roles and sexual conduct.[47] Within these religious traditions, an impassioned embrace of outward emotion and bodily movement went hand-in-hand with the rejection of sexual contact outside of marriage, secular dancing, and worldly indulgence.

In conclusion, I offer these comments on religion and race records in order to ponder competing values and moral discourses within the black working class. Juxtaposing the sacred and profane forces a rethinking of the oft-rendered image of a working class that is the monolithic and coherent bearer of an "authentic" black consciousness. Black working-class culture, as the generative site of the blues and the zoot suit, produced as well Pentecostalism and the Nation of Islam.[48] Religious culture, like the blues, found expression in the black vernacular.

Notes

1   See, for example, Houston A. Baker Jr., *Blues, Ideology, and Afro-American Literature: A Vernacular Theory* (Chicago: University of Chicago Press, 1984); Hazel V. Carby, "Policing the Black Woman's Body in an Urban Context," *Critical Inquiry* 18 (Summer 1992): 738–55; Carby, "'It Jus Be's Dat Way Sometime': The Sexual Politics of Women's Blues," in *Unequal Sisters: A Multicultural Reader in U.S. Women's History*, ed. Vicki L. Ruiz and Ellen Carol DuBois, 2nd ed. (New York: Routledge, 1994), 330–41.

2   See Ann duCille's important critique that this emphasis has caused the blues to be thought of as a "metonym for authentic blackness." Ann duCille, "Blues Notes on Black Sexuality: Sex and the Texts of Jessie Fauset and Nella Larsen," *Journal of the History of Sexuality* 3 (January 1993): 418–44, esp. 419–20. Published since the presentation of this paper at the Race Matters Conference in April 1994 is Farah Griffin's rich interdisciplinary study of the

migration narrative. See Farah Jasmine Griffin, *"Who Set You Flowin'?": The African-American Migration Narrative* (New York: Oxford University Press, 1995), 61–3. Griffin draws some of her analysis of working-class religion from an earlier version of this paper, in particular Evelyn Brooks Higginbotham, "'Out of the Age of the Voice': The Black Church and Discourses of Modernity" (paper delivered at the Conference on the Black Public Sphere in the Era of Reagan and Bush, University of Chicago, October 14, 1993.

3   I am focusing on religious records in contradistinction to the interesting work of scholars of religion who locate religious inflections (theology and theodicy) in blues and rap. For example, Jon Michael Spencer finds in the blues and Michael Dyson finds in rap and in the songs of Michael Jackson moral reflections on evil, hypocrisy, suffering, justice, and biblical lore. See Jon Michael Spencer, *Blues and Evil* (Knoxville: University of Tennessee Press, 1993), xxviii, 35, 43–53. Michael Eric Dyson, *Reflecting Black: African-American Cultural Criticism* (Minneapolis: University of Minnesota Press, 1993), 35–60.

4   I am indebted to the following scholars for their pioneering work on race records in both the blues and religious traditions: Paul Oliver, *Songsters and Saints: Vocal Traditions on Race Records* (Cambridge: Cambridge University Press, 1984); Robert M. W. Dixon and John Godrich, *Recording the Blues* (New York: Stein & Day, 1970); Jeff Todd Titon, *Early Downhome Blues: A Musical and Cultural Analysis* (Urbana: University of Illinois Press, 1977); Tony Heilbut, *The Gospel Sound: Good News and Bad Times* (New York: Simon & Schuster, 1971).

5   Hughes is quoted in Lawrence Levine, *Black Culture and Black Consciousness: Afro-American Folk Thought from Slavery to Freedom* (New York: Oxford University Press, 1978), 180.

6   The advertisement appeared in the *Chicago Defender*, October 8, 1927, 8.

7   See the following: Cheryl Townsend Gilkes, "'Together and in Harness': Women's Traditions in the Sanctified Church," *Signs: Journal of Women in Culture and Society* 10 (Summer 1985): 679; Arthur Huff Fauset, *Black Gods of the Metropolis: Negro Religious Cults of the Urban North* (Philadelphia: University of Pennsylvania Press, 1944); Melvin D. Williams, *Community in a Black Pentecostal Church: An Anthropological Study* (University of Pittsburgh Press, 1974); Arthur E. Paris, *Black Pentecostalism: Southern Religion in an Urban World* (Amherst: University of Massachusetts Press, 1982).

8   Levine, *Black Culture*, 200.

9   Evelyn Brooks Higginbotham, *Righteous Discontent: The Women's Movement in the Black Baptist Church, 1880–1920* (Cambridge, Mass.: Harvard University Press, 1993), 42–6.

10 W. E. Burghardt Du Bois, "The Talented Tenth," in Booker T. Washington et al., *The Negro Problem: A Series of Articles by Representative Negroes of Today* (New York: James Pott, 1903), 54–5.

11 Elizabeth Kilham, "Sketches in Color," is quoted in Dena J. Epstein, *Sinful Times and Spirituals: Black Folk Music to the Civil War* (Urbana: University of Illinois Press, 1977), 277.

12 Daniel Alexander Payne, *Recollections of Seventy Years* (New York: Arno Press and the *New York Times*, 1969), 253–4.

13 Levine, *Black Culture*, 162–6; also see analysis of the "politics of respectability" in Higginbotham, *Righteous Discontent*, 187–99.

14 James M. Trotter, *Music and Some Highly Musical People* (Chicago: Afro-American Press, 1969; reprint of 1880 ed.), 58–9, 285.

15 Sutton Griggs is quoted and discussed in Wilson Jeremiah Moses, *The Golden Age of Black Nationalism, 1850–1925* (New York: Oxford University Press, 1978), 170–93.

16 Virginia W. Broughton, "Need of Distinctive Literature," *National Baptist Union* 13 (December 1902).

17 Elsa Barkley Brown, "Negotiating and Transforming the Public Sphere: African American Political Life in the Transition from Slavery to Freedom," *Public Culture* 7 (November 1994): 135–6; Levine, *Black Culture*, 24.

18 Frances Smith Foster, ed., *Minnie's Sacrifice; Sowing and Reaping; Trial and Triumph: Three Rediscovered Novels by Frances E. W. Harper* (Boston: Beacon Press, 1994), xxiv–xxvi.

19 For a discussion of the role of photographic imagery in racial reconstruction, see Henry Louis Gates, Jr., "The Trope of a New Negro and the Reconstruction of the Image of the Black," *Representations* 24 (Fall 1988): 141.

20 For discussion of the literati during the Harlem Renaissance, see David Levering Lewis, *When Harlem Was in Vogue* (New York: Oxford University Press, 1989; originally published by Knopf, 1981), 119–55.

21 For a discussion of black consumerism during the 1920s and 1930s, see Liz Cohen, *Making a New Deal: Industrial Workers in Chicago, 1919–1939* (New York: Cambridge University Press, 1990), 147–58.

22 For a discussion of the inability of a black-owned record company, the Black Swan Company, to compete successfully against the large white corporations, such as Victor and Paramount, see Dixon and Godrich, *Recording the Blues*, 13, 21–32, 44.

23 Here I am reminded of Houston Baker's brilliant discussion of the "blending . . . of class and mass – *poetic mastery discovered as a function of deformative [subversive] folk* sound – constitutes the essence of black discursive modernism." Houston A. Baker, Jr., *Modernism and the Harlem Renaissance* (Chicago: University of Chicago Press, 1987), 93; the oral narrative in literature is described by Henry Louis Gates, Jr., as the "speakerly text." See Gates, *The Signifying Monkey: A Theory of African-American Literary Criticism* (New York: Oxford University Press, 1988), xxv–xxvi, 181.

24 Sutton Griggs, *A Hero Closes a War*, Victor 21706-B (1928), and *A Surprise Answer to Prayer*, Victor 21706-A (1928); Oliver, *Songsters and Saints*, 146–7.

25 Paul Oliver discusses the popular appeal of the recorded sermons of black Baptist, Holiness, and Pentecostal preachers in Oliver, *Songsters and Saints*, 140–228; Dixon and Godrich, *Recording the Blues*, 38, 56–7.

26 Oliver, *Songsters and Saints*, 155.

27 Record companies began to scour southern cities and hamlets in the mid-1920s in search of down-home religious and secular talent. Jeff Titon argues, however, that part of the return to the old-time was part of a "folk" vogue that swept American culture in the post–World War I period as a counter-voice to the increasing sophistication and slickness of urbanity and the Jazz Age of the 1920s. Titon argues that race records must be seen as a part of this larger vogue, which also included "hillbilly" music, Broadway plays about mountain life in North Carolina and Kentucky during the 1923–4 season, and a general romanticization of a simpler, agrarian society. Titon, *Early Downhome Blues*, 215–16, 243–5.

28 See the analysis of recorded sermons in Michael Harris's biography of Thomas A. Dorsey: Michael W. Harris, *Rise of Gospel Blues: The Music of Thomas Andrew Dorsey in the Urban Church* (New York: Oxford University Press, 1992), 156–63.

29 Oliver, *Songsters and Saints*, 140–5, 155, 159.

30 Recorded sermons seem to have enjoyed the greatest popularity between 1926 and 1931. The onset of the Great Depression caused a precipitous decline in the release of sermonic records. Gospel music records continue to be popular to this day. Moreover, gospel queens outlasted the classic blues singers of the 1920s in popularity. Dixon and Godrich, *Recording the Blues*, 85; Oliver, *Songsters and Saints*, 188–98, 203–5; Heilbut, *The Gospel Sound*, 9–35.

31 Oliver, *Songsters and Saints*, 183–7. See advertisements for Rev. Leora Ross's *Dry Bones in the Valley* and *A Gambler Broke in a Strange Land*, Okeh 8486, and Jessie May Hill's *The Crucifixion of Christ* and *God Rode in the Windstorm*, Okeh 8490, in the *Chicago Defender*, August 27, 1927, and September 24, 1927; also Jerma Jackson, "Testifying at the Cross: Thomas Andrew Dorsey, Sister Rosetta Tharpe, and the Politics of African-American Sacred and Secular Music" (Ph.D. diss., Rutgers University, 1995), 157–80, 263–71.

32 Oliver, *Songsters and Saints*, 203–5.

33 Harris, *Rise of Gospel Blues*, 182–208.

34 Baker, *Modernism and the Harlem Renaissance*, 93.

35 Anderson notes that her church made possible her initial training at the studio of Giuseppe Boghetti by helping to pay the costs for instruction. Marian Anderson, *My Lord, What a Morning* (New York: Viking Press, 1956), 7, 23–38, 49.

36 Michael Harris notes that Mahalia Jackson received voice training from gospel-blues songwriter Thomas Dorsey, then music director at Pilgrim Baptist Church in Chicago but formerly a blues lyricist and piano accompanist to Ma Rainey, Bessie Smith, and other blues queens. Harris, *Rise of Gospel Blues*, 259–60.

37 Quoted in ibid., 258; Mahalia Jackson noted in her autobiography: "In those days the big colored churches didn't want me and they didn't let me in. I had to make it my business to pack the little basement-hall congregations and store-front churches and get their respect that way. When they began to see the crowds I drew, the big churches began to sit up and take notice." Mahalia Jackson, *Moving' On Up* (New York: Hawthorn Books, 1966).

38 Harris, *Rise of Gospel Blues*, 258–71.

39 Ibid., 269–70.

40 The new urban context of the 1920s unleashed strivings for "authentic" racial expression in music (blues and jazz), in literature (Harlem Renaissance writers such as Zora Neale Hurston and Langston Hughes), and in political movements such as Marcus Garvey's Universal Negro Improvement Association. Black church culture must be situated in this historical context.

41 Oliver, *Songsters and Saints*, 145, 155, 159.

42 Ibid., 146; Rev. Mary Nelson, *Better Get Ready for Judgement*, Vocalion 1109-B.

43 Rev. J. C. Burnett, *The Downfall of Nebuchadnezzar*, Columbia 14166 (1926).

44 Gates, *Samson and the Woman*, Victor 21125 (1927).

45 Gates, *The First Born Was a Murderer*, Victor 21125 (1927); *Death Might Be Your Santa Claus*, Okeh 8413 (1926); *Did You Spend Christmas in Jail?*, Okeh 8753-A; *No Room in the Jailhouse*, Okeh 8753-B (1929); and *Dying Gambler*, Okeh 8387 (1926); Oliver, Harrison, and Bolcom, *The New Grove Gospel*, 194–95.

46 Carby, "Policing the Black Woman's Body," 739–55.

47 Hans A. Baer and Merrill Singer, *African-American Religion in the Twentieth Century: Varieties of Protest and Accommodation* (Knoxville: University of Tennessee Press, 1992), 147–78, 215–21; Jill Watts, *God, Harlem U.S.A.: The Father Divine Story* (Berkeley: University of California Press, 1992), 161–2.

48 "I knew that our strict moral code and discipline was what repelled them most," stated Malcolm X in reference to the fact that many blacks came to hear him but far fewer joined the Muslims. He continued: "No Muslim who followed Elijah Muhammad could dance, gamble, date, attend movies, or sports, or take long vacations from work." Malcolm X with the assistance of Alex Haley, *The Autobiography of Malcolm X* (New York: Ballantine, 1973), 221; for a brilliant analysis of the zoot suit culture that attracted the young Malcolm, see Robin D. G. Kelley, "The Riddle of the Zoot: Malcolm Little and Black Cultural Politics During World War II," in *Malcolm X: In Our Own Image*, ed. Joe Wood (New York: St. Martin's Press, 1992), 155–82.

23

The Madonna of 115th Street Revisited: Vodou and Haitian Catholicism in the Age of Transnationalism

Elizabeth McAlister

Reclaimed by the Virgin

Every year on the fifteenth of July, the tall, wrought-iron gates of the big, brick Church of Our Lady of Mount Carmel in East Harlem swing open to welcome thousands of religious pilgrims. Women and men, children and the elderly, throng to the church for evening Mass, after which they follow a larger-than-life statue of the Virgin Mary through the New York City streets in a long, night-time procession. After a midnight Mass they spend the night in the church, or go home and come back early the next day, dressed in the Madonna's colors of blue and white and carrying flowers, letters, rosaries, and money. In this way, the faithful celebrate the feast day of Our Lady and perform devotions for one of the many appellations of the Blessed Mother.

In 1995, ten-year-old Marie-Carmel wore a puffy, sky-blue satin dress whose many layers and petticoats made her look as though she were the topmost decoration on a multitiered cake. She sat patiently through the Mass, listening to the priest while she wrestled with her squirming baby brother on her lap. Her long, dark hair was carefully oiled and braided, each braid ending in a shiny blue and gold ribbon tied in a bow. As she rose with her family to join the line to receive Holy Communion, she faltered and tripped, and her mother had to catch her by the arm and help her up. Marie-Carmel looked down in embarrassment and studied her patent-leather Mary Janes as she approached the priest.

When Marie-Carmel lifted her head to receive the Host, her knees buckled and she staggered backward, wheeling into an aunt standing behind her. After she took communion, the family helped Marie-Carmel out of the church for some fresh air in the courtyard. They smiled and waved away the concern of the deacon who approached them about the little girl. "She'll be fine, thank you," said her mother, "it's just that she hasn't eaten today."

She turned to her sister and to me, as I was a friend of the family and had come to join them. Beginning in French, she finished in her mother tongue, Haitian Creole: "*C'est la Vierge. Li vin manifeste nan tét ti-moun nan*" (It's the Virgin. She manifested herself in the child's head.)" To indicate her continuing protection over the little girl, Notre Dame du Mont Carmel (Our Lady of Mount Carmel) had, briefly, possessed her namesake, Marie-Carmel.

The little girl's fall inside the church yielded two different interpretations, delivered in three languages. The family explained to the deacon, in English, that the girl was simply hungry.[1] But the deeper reality for the family had to do with their long relationship with the Virgin. That meaning was expressed in Haitian Creole, with, as a nod to me, a *blan* (foreigner), a translation in French.[2] This ten-minute drama at the church in East Harlem was only a small part of a much larger story about the involvement of Notre Dame du Mont Carmel in the life of a new immigrant family from the island nation of Haiti. It is a story about migration and religious expression, production, and performance, and like language itself, it contains multiple levels of meaning for various audiences.

Thousands of Haitian people have been making the yearly pilgrimage to the Church of Our Lady of Mount Carmel in East Harlem for the last two decades. It is surely the largest annual religious gathering of Haitians in North America. It takes place at the same moment when thousands in Haiti flock to a mountainside waterfall at a village called Sodo (pronounced "So-DOE"), for the Fèt Vièj Mirak (Feast of the Miracle Virgin). Temporarily relaxing class, color, and political boundaries during the pilgrimage, the feast day of the "Miracle Virgin" also brings Haitian people in New York together for two days to pray, sing, and socialize in a particularly Haitian style. In this sense, Marie-Carmel's small drama in church was also part of an even wider story about Haitian religiosity in the United States.

For several years I have been following that story through the words and actions of the Haitian people who come to visit Our Lady of Mount Carmel. The stories here will not only feature individual women and men expressing their devotion, but will also consider the role of social forces in their religious lives. These social forces extend back to the legacies of French colonization and the lasting effects of slavery and the ways that Afro-Haitian religion appropriated Roman Catholicism to form what Haitians call "le mélange" (the mixing) and what anthropologists call "religious syncretism." Another shaping factor is the postcolonial or, more properly put, the neocolonial relationship between Haiti and the United States. This relationship has contributed to the creation of the Haitian *djaspora*, or "diaspora," which, since the fall of Jean-Claude Duvalier in 1986, has been increasingly shaped by the phenomenon of transnational migration – the frequent movement back and forth of migrants from home countries to host countries.

What, then, can this pilgrimage tell us about immigrant religiosity? What do Roman Catholic devotions mean in the ritual vocabulary of Afro-Haitian religious culture? What meanings do these same devotions acquire in the United States? This chapter tries to answer these questions by focusing on the Haitian experience of the feast.

[...]

Revisiting 115th Street: Religious Borderlands

The story of the Haitian devotion at the Church of Our Lady Mount Carmel in East Harlem is only the latest chapter in the ongoing history of that feast. Although the annual July feast at 115th Street now attracts thousands of Haitians, the church was built in 1884 by the Roman Catholic Pallottine order as a mission church to minister to the Italian immigrant population of that era. Italian

Harlem nourished itself with the love and protection of La Madonna del Carmine, continuing a tradition they had known back in Italy. Robert Anthony Orsi's book *The Madonna of 115th Street: Faith and Community in Italian Harlem, 1880–1950*, paints a lyrical and sensitive portrait of the ways the *festa* for the Madonna shaped people's lives – especially the mothers, wives, daughters, and sisters in the community for whom the Blessed Virgin was mother, goddess, protector, and role model. Her feast day, July 16, grew to be a major ritual marker in Italian New York, helping Italians forge an American identity based largely on their Catholicism (Orsi 1985). Although the mission of the church officially remains the same – to minister to Italian immigrants – now only 750 Italian Americans are left in its neighborhood (Laurino 1995).[3]

The ethnic flavor of the area began to change when Puerto Ricans started migrating into East Harlem just before World War II. By 1963, eleven public housing projects were built in the vicinity of the Church of Our Lady of Mount Carmel for twelve thousand low-income black and Latino families (Orsi 1992, 326; Bourgois 1995, 51). The neighborhood transformed into Spanish Harlem, the strong "Nuyorican" community affectionately known as "El Barrio" that now shares its territory with Mexicans, Dominicans, and West Africans.

The Italian immigrant families that moved to East Harlem between the 1880s and the 1920s had prospered by the 1950s, and as the Puerto Rican families moved in, the Italians emigrated to middle-class suburban communities with lawns and fences. Many of them still come back to the church to organize the feast, to attend the novena still prayed in Italian beforehand, to celebrate a special Mass for the dead, or to bless a bride or groom the day before their wedding. But these days, the majority of the pilgrims form a sea of coffee-, mahogany-, and cinnamon-colored bodies, clad in sky blue and white, praying and singing in French and Haitian Creole. The Haitians' presence at the feast is actually part of a larger social drama that is playing itself out among the Virgin, the Pallottine order, the Italian Americans who organize the event, their Puerto Rican (and other Latino) neighbors, and the Haitian pilgrims. Haitians have become actors on a multiethnic social stage that is vastly more diverse than their relatively homogeneous home ground.[4]

This Catholic church and its surrounding neighborhood have become a religious borderland of sorts. During the feast for Our Lady, Masses are said every hour in Latin, Italian, Spanish, English, French, or Haitian Creole. There are a very few Latino pilgrims in attendance, and only a handful of Irish Americans who search out the

Tridentine Mass still said there. But this feast, which is sponsored and produced by Italian Americans, has come to be peopled by new immigrants, who turn the space of the large church into a site of Haitian religious activity.

Haitians at East 115th Street

[...]

The Haitian community, as did (and do) the Italians, begins to celebrate the feast nine days before July 16 with a novena – a series of daily prayers to the Virgin at the 115th Street church. Their numbers increase until the two days before the feast is celebrated, the fifteenth and sixteenth of July. The activity at the church begins to build throughout the day of the fifteenth. The Italian American ladies who form the religious articles committee unpack the goods they sell on behalf of the church: statues, medallions, scapulars, prayer cards, crosses, and crucifixes. Soon pilgrims pull up in cars, step down from buses, and climb the stairs leading from the subway. For the two days of the feast the sidewalks leading from the Lexington Avenue IRT trains become rivers of people wearing "Sunday best" outfits of the light blue associated with the Blessed Mother (and with ritual begging in Vodou), or white, a color of ritual purity for Catholic and Vodouist alike. They stroll on the arms of husbands, children, old people, and friends. Boys dressed in little suits and ties gallop ahead, racing little girls wearing dresses of satin tiers of sugary-looking cloth.

[...]

Pilgrims arrive throughout the day, and by nine o'clock that evening the huge church is filled to capacity for the Latin Mass; more than two thousand are in attendance. Hundreds more gather together in the courtyard and spill out into the sidewalk for the candlelight procession behind the larger-than-life statue of Our Lady of Mount Carmel.

Soon a great popping can be heard; this is the fireworks that announce and salute the Virgin at various places on the procession route. The smell of gunpowder fills the air, and the Haitian ladies, candles in their hands, lift their hands upward in a posture learned from Charismatic Catholicism.[5] The noise and smell of the firecrackers "heat up" the prayers, as each pilgrim hopes that the fireworks will carry his or her message to the Virgin. But the sound of bursting gunpowder is also an aural semiotic sign for Ezili Dantò, the goddess who "walks behind" the Vièj Mirak. In Vodou services for Dantò and the rest of the spirits in the Petwo rite to which she belongs, whips are cracked and gunpowder is lit to create the slaps and pops that Petwo spirits like. When the fireworks go off in front of the Madonna on 115th Street, not a few women falter and clutch at those around them, fighting off spirit possession.

Each July fifteenth, the statue of Our Lady is brought out of the church and she is paraded along a route designated by the church priests. Past Second Avenue after a left to Saint Ann's Church on 110th Street, more fireworks are lit, and more prayers launched heavenward. Some pilgrims take the opportunity to go inside and visit Saint Ann. Just as she is the mother of Mary in Roman Catholicism, in Vodou cosmology she is Grann Ezili, an older form of Ezili. A few Haitian pilgrims have come to East Harlem specifically to see her. "The power starts with the mother," confided one woman. "Me, I come to the fèt to pran woulib [take a ride] on the procession." She uses the mystical power of the feast day to strengthen her request to the older feminine power, Grann Ezili/ Saint Ann.

The procession winds down Second Avenue from Saint Ann's back up First Avenue, past 116th to 118th Street, pausing at various points along the way to light firecrackers. Many of these stopping places are homes of the Italian American families still in the neighborhood, who contribute time and money to the feast. They have decorated the brownstones, some in the old style of hanging linens from the windows, others by placing blue candles and statues along their steps. The fireworks are a sort of salute to patronage that the Haitian community understands from their own Carnival and Rara celebrations, where music is played for the contributions of local gwo nèg, or "big men" (McAlister 1995).

During the procession some families walk together and sing hymns like "Ave Maria," "Louange a Toi," and "Chez Nous Soyez Reine," or the Lord's Prayer in French. Others crowd toward the float bearing the Madonna, touching the blue and white plastic fringe as they walk. Candles in hand, the pilgrims wear the brown scapulars of Our Lady of Mount Carmel. Bearing a brown scapular when she originally appeared, the Blessed Virgin promised that whosoever wore her scapular at the moment of death would escape the fires of eternal damnation.

When the procession reaches the church, every seat is filled for the midnight Mass. The courtyard is a scene of another sort, one close in mood to the mountain celebrations at Sodo. Each year several women bring food, which they ritually distribute among the pilgrims. Standing in the vicinity you may be handed delicious *soup joumou* (pumpkin soup), rice and beans, *griyo* (fried pork, the ritual food of Ezili Dantò), soda, and black, sugary Haitian coffee. The women who bring the food explain that they are continuing a tradition they keep at Sodo, inherited from their mothers, a form of ritual feeding of the poor. In late-night New York there are no homeless or needy people around this church, so other Haitian pilgrims stand in for the poor and consume the food with gusto. The menfolk stand around drinking rum or whiskey, talking politics among themselves. [...]

On the day of the sixteenth, the feast day proper, a 9:00 A.M. Mass is followed by another procession. Throughout the day, a quick Mass is said every half-hour in a different language, as hundreds of people arrive at the church, hand flowers to the workers in the sacristy, light candles, pray to the saints, attend Mass, and receive communion. Pilgrims pass in front of the various statues, praying out loud in the Haitian style, asking for the intercession of the Blessed Mother.

Some pilgrims bring a practical orientation born out of their Afro-Creole religious culture. "Never come into the church through the back door from the courtyard," one woman instructs me. "You should not approach the saint from her back – she has to see you walking in." Other pilgrims come to perform spiritual work that is meaningful in the ritual logic of Vodou. They leave money near the statues, either dollar bills or ritual amounts of coins. A few leave candles or sprinkle Florida Water, the cologne commonly used in Vodou for its sweet, spiced scent. Occasionally the priests have found plates of food as offerings to the *lwa*, the spirits of Vodou. Many leave notes and letters stuffed in Jesus' hands, on Saint Lucy's plate of eyes, and in the folds of the gowns of Saint Damien and Cosmos. The priests walk the length of the church from time to time, collecting the money and sweeping up the letters into piles (which they later throw away). Some of the letters are written to the Virgin for help in a specific problem, related to good health, jobs, or love. Other letters are formulas for spiritual work with *lwa*. One, with a name written seven times with three *X*s and the word *Jistis*, is asking Ezili Dantò for justice. Another name, written repeatedly on one side of a scrap of paper, is echoed by a name listed on its reverse. Here Ezili is asked to reconcile two enemies, or two lovers.

[...]

Religious Culture, Diaspora, and Transnational Migration

In many ways, Haitians' experience of the Mount Carmel feast is similar to that of their Italian predecessors at the church. In fact, their general positions as immigrant populations run parallel. Like Italians fleeing from *la miseria* (poverty) at the end of the last century, Haitians have come to the United States to escape the structural violence of *la mizè*, the poverty of the poorest country in the Western Hemisphere. Both agricultural peoples, arriving Italians and Haitians were (and are) similarly independent, family-centered, and devoted to local religious forms. The Italian emphasis on *rispetto* (respect) and dependence on *padroni* (patrons) (Orsi 1985) is similar to the Haitians' social hierarchies, articulated through patronage and loyalty to a *patron*, or *gwo nèg*.

There are, however, major differences between the experiences of these two communities that visit this shrine for the Madonna. For example, compared to the Haitians, Italian immigrants fit better the classic pattern of nineteenth-century migration. "Uprooting" themselves from the home country, they were "transplanted" to the United States and gradually created a new, Italian American national identity (Handlin 1951, Orsi 1992, 316). In contrast, many Haitians in the contemporary United States perceive themselves to be living *nan djaspora*, "in the diaspora," defined against Haiti as an essential location of its own, regardless of whether they live in Miami, Montreal, Paris, or Senegal. Haiti itself is real, tangible, and, in fact, often a place of partial residence. From local points "in the diaspora," Haitians live transnational lives. That is, they live embedded in international networks, sustaining social relations that link their societies of origin with their new settlement (Basch et al. 1994). Haitian transmigrants typically work jobs in New York to support homes in Haiti, keeping their children in Haitian schools until they are young teens. They return to Haiti during periods of illness or unemployment; for vacations; for important family events like baptisms, marriages, or funerals; and sometimes for national celebrations like the inauguration of a president, the yearly Carnival or Rara, or the pilgrimage to Sodo for Fèt Vièj Mirak. After decades in the United States, the elderly may return to spend their last years at home. Family roles shift between the two countries, so that children come of age and migrate north, and old folks retire and return southward to home. Both opportunity and tragedy can be the occasion to *janbe dlo*, or "cross over the water."[6]

It is the US Immigration Act of 1965 and its liberalizing entrance policies that allowed for the legal immigration of large numbers of non-European peoples. We can look to this moment as a pivotal occasion that heralds the vast increase in migrants from developing countries, many of whom have brought new religious traditions – Hinduism, Buddhism, Islam, and numerous local, "traditional" spiritualities – to the United States. But this legislation cannot be the sole explanation for the increase of Caribbean (and other) immigrants. It does not explain, for one thing, why so many thousands of people would want to leave their homelands and cultures and come live in the *djaspora* in cold and hostile environments.

Such drastic movement of people is linked to economic conditions. The past several decades can be characterized in terms of new levels of capital penetrations into "Third World" economies, the development of export processing, and the increased migration of people from the peripheries to the centers (Wallerstein 1974, 229–31; Nash 1983, 3–69; Sassen-Koob 1982). Individual actors who maintain lives in two nation-states at once are engaging in a creative strategy that maximizes their position in the present configuration of global capital. It is more practical, for example, for many women to work as nurses in New York and send remittances back to Haiti to raise small children so that they will become *kretyen vivan* (good people, or literally "living Christian") and not *gate* (ruined) by the harshness of New York life. In this way we can see that economic conditions are affecting both the flow of transmigrant activities and "the manner in which they come to understand who they are and what they are doing" (Basch et al. 1994,)

It is increasingly true that in order to understand religious life for some new immigrants, we must also understand their continued relationship with the religious world of their home countries (Levitt 1998). Unlike the earlier Italian immigrants of East Harlem, who shifted their religious focus from the churches of the old country to East 115th Street, Haitians join congregations and undertake pilgrimages *nan djaspora*, and also continue religious activities when they move to Haiti. They often plan business or vacation trips to coincide with opportunities to perform religious work at one of the many important spiritual sites at home. When they arrive, they are labeled *djaspora* by the townspeople who could not afford to leave.

As spaces where other Haitians congregate, religious sites in diasporic locations become inflected with meanings that span both home and host nations. Working with Cubans at a shrine church in Miami, Thomas Tweed (1997) suggests that we can usefully understand diasporic religious communities as translocative (moving symbolically between the homeland and the new land) and transtemporal (relating to a constructed past and an imagined future). [. . .]

The pilgrimage to Our Lady of Mount Carmel in East Harlem expands the saint's influence in the Haitian world. Rather than substituting the New York feast for the ones they left behind in Haiti, they add the Harlem location as another site of spiritual work. In this way East Harlem is opened up as one more place in the expansive "religioscape" of transnational Haitian religious culture.[7] During the pilgrimage to the Vièj Mirak in New York, the Haitian population reterritorializes spiritual practice, reinscribing sacred, translated space onto their new landscape of settlement.[8] Haitians in diaspora reach out to Our Lady of Mount Carmel and Ezili Dantò, powerful nationalist symbols, extending prayers for family and friends throughout the *djaspora* and in Haiti. Temporally they include concern for the dead and departed in Haiti as well as the hoped-for children of the future. Insofar as the Haitian population is able to return to Haiti [. . .] the activities at the shrine are those of an actively transnational religious culture.

[. . .]

Vièj Mirak: Mont Carmel in Haiti

Many of the pilgrims at the New York Church of Our Lady of Mount Carmel, if they are in Haiti in July, would go to one of the pilgrimage sites for the Vièj Mirak back home. The biggest one, at Sodo in Ville Bonheur, attracts thousands of pilgrims who come for summer vacation and stay for weeks around the time of the July sixteenth feast. This small village is located high in the mountain range between Mirebalais and Saint Marc, with a population that is probably under three thousand (Laguerre 1989, 84). During the month of the feast, the town swells with pilgrims and vacationers, who rent rooms and houses from the villagers.

It is for the Fèt Vièj Mirak that many *djaspora* are willing to plan their international travel, don the light blue clothing of the ritual beggar pilgrim or the burlap sacks of penitence, and ride for seven hours on a *bourik* (donkey) into the mountainous Haitian countryside. Although Notre Dame du Perpetuel Secours (Our Lady of Perpetual Help) is the official patron saint of Haiti, the chapel for Notre Dame du Mont Carmel at Sodo is the most popular pilgrimage of the country.

"Sodo" is the Creole spelling of "Saut d'Eau," which in French means "waterfall." The great waterfall of Sodo was created during an earthquake on May 7, 1842 (Rouzier 1891, 262; cited in Laguerre 1989, 86). Farmers in the region understood "sodo" to be a natural dwelling place of various water spirits in Afro-Haitian cosmology: the serpent Danbala Wèdo and his rainbow wife Ayida Wèdo, Simbi Dlo (Simba of the water), and others. It is indeed a beautiful place. White, frothy mineral water falls hundreds of feet, bounces off boulders, and runs through twisting tree roots into pools below. As the cool spray splashes off the rocks, tiny rainbows glisten in the air. Pilgrims, hot from the seven-hour ride through the mountains, step under the falls and are sometimes possessed by the spirits. Their faltering steps and wide-eyed expressions become the visual currency of the ubiquitous foreign photographers who ring the falls, fighting for the best spots for their tripods in the undergrowth.[9]

In July 1849, some time after the creation of the waterfall, rumors began to circulate that a peasant farmer had sighted the Virgin Mary in a nearby palm tree. President Faustin Soulouque, Haiti's ruler from 1847 to 1859, appointed members of his legislative cabinet to study the apparition. After satisfying himself with their report, he ordered the (now) lemon-yellow chapel built in honor of Notre Dame du Mont Carmel (Laguerre 1989, 87).[10]

Since the apparition, the pilgrimage at Sodo has been not only a center of spiritual power but also a place of celebration. Haitians of all classes travel to Sodo in July with their families. Struggling entrepreneurs arrive early to set up food stalls, market stands, and gambling houses. Rich vacationers build or rent houses and arrive in private cars with the family to spend a few weeks enjoying the festivities. Among these, the *djaspora* from the United States are easily recognizable. They arrive wearing the latest fashions from Brooklyn or Miami, the women in shorts and halter tops with blonde streaks in their permed hair and long acrylic nails painted with designs. Young men likewise adopt the styles of Black American popular culture, often crossed with a Jamaican sensibility they learn through their contact with the Jamaican youth in their own West Indian neighborhoods. They wear athletic shoes, baseball hats, and the red, green, and gold belts of the Rastafari looped through their baggy jeans.[11] This small mountain village turns into a crossroads of the global Haitian diaspora each July, as returning pilgrims also come from Zaire, Martinique, Guadeloupe, the Bahamas, Boston, and Montreal.

[...]

The Haitian Religious Continuum

The chapel and the waterfall at Sodo are both important and impressive. However, *manbo* and *oungan* who serve the spirits of Vodou insist that the most powerful spot is the actual place where the Madonna appeared. Called Nan Palm (In the Palm Grove), this site stands near the entrance to the village. It is here that the Virgin dwells with her counterpart Ezili Dantò, the powerful Afro-Haitian goddess. Dantò's co-existence with the Vièj Mirak is an example of the great mystery of le mélange, or the syncretism of African and Catholic symbolisms. Like Mexico's Virgin of Guadalupe, who appeared to an Indian man at the shrine of an Aztec goddess, Notre Dame du Mont Carmel at Sodo is a powerful national figure resonant with multiple layers of meaning. When pilgrims make the trip through the mountains to Sodo, they visit the church, the waterfall, and the palm grove – a threefold spiritual site.[12]

The *manbo* I have worked with tell me that Notre Dame du Mont Carmel "walks a path" with Ezili Dantò, a *lwa* or *mistè* "mystery" who has become one of the most important divinities in the culture.[13] While she can be represented by Mont Carmel, Ezili Dantò is most often represented in popular Haitian iconography as Notre Dame du Czestochowa, the Black Virgin of Poland, whose face bears two scars running down her cheek. Like both Czestochowa and Mont Carmel, Ezili Dantò carries a baby in her arms. Dantò's baby is not the infant Jesus but, interestingly, a daughter. Some call her "Anayiz," others "Ti-Gungun." Dantò is known as a single mother, a hard-working black woman, and a powerful warrior and fighter. A symbol of nationalist pride, she is said to have been a leader in the slaves' victorious war of independence against Napoleon's army, when she earned the scars she carries (Brown 1991, 229).

Sometimes Dantò is described as a lesbian, and she is thought to choose which men will live as effeminate homosexuals. When she possesses people (for she can "ride" both women and men), she drinks *kleren* cane liquor and demands to eat pork, often the ears and feet of the roasted pig. In her incarnation as Ezili Ge Wouj (Red Eyed Ezili), she speaks without the use of the front of her tongue, saying only "ke ke ke ke," and pantomiming her meanings. Some say her tongue was cut out during the Haitian revolution so she would not betray her side's secrets (Brown 1991, 229).

When pilgrims go to the East Harlem shrine or to Nan Palm at Sodo and light a candle, sing to the Virgin, and *fè demann* (make requests), they are addressing

Notre Dame du Mont Carmel and Ezili Dantò *at the same time*. This overlapping, simultaneous practice of Catholicism and Vodou has puzzled outsiders – both Haitian intellectuals and foreigners – for generations. Within anthropology, "syncretism" was the theoretical concept developed by Melville Herskovits (1941) and then Roger Bastide (1960) to understand the processes of change that arose with culture contact. Syncretism came to describe an "impure" religious tradition, saturated with local, unorthodox strains. Recent terms used to describe cultural mixings have included "creolization," "symbiosis," and "inter-culture" (Stewart and Shaw 1994, Desmangles 1992).

The received way of thinking about Vodou and Catholicism is to imagine them as a pair of binary opposites. It is true that Haitian Catholics have affirmed their own status by stressing their apartness from Vodou. A Catholic who is not at all involved in serving the *lwa* identifies as a *fran katolik* (straight Catholic), and there are some in the Haitian upper classes who know nothing of Afro-Haitian religion. The upper classes were (and are) generally literate, French-speaking, politically enfranchised, light-skinned, and emphatically Catholic. On the stage of cultural politics, Vodou was (and is) held up as the pagan, Satanic superstition of the poor, dark, non-literate, and disenfranchised majority. Politically, then, Catholicism has always positioned itself in opposition to Vodou.[14]

In practice, it may be more helpful to imagine these two traditions occupying either end of a continuum, with Roman Catholicism on one end and Vodou on the other.[15] Any given actor in Haiti falls somewhere along the continuum, some as Catholics, some as Vodouists, and the vast majority living their lives in the middle, going through the rites of passage of the Catholic church while simultaneously maintaining contact with Vodou healers and the *lwa*, especially in times of crisis.

Even this continuum model must be complicated with further qualifications. Elsewhere, I have written that both the Afro-Haitian religion and the Catholicism that evolved in Haiti were constructed in dialectical relation to the other in a process of creolization. In this sense there is simply no "pure Catholicism" or "pure Vodou" in Haiti. To a degree that some advocates in each tradition might not like to admit, each has incorporated the other into its philosophies and practices. Each tradition is therefore constitutive and revealing of the other (McAlister 1995, 179).[16]

While one tradition may be bound up in the other, the Haitian cultural politics that divides the enfranchised from the disenfranchised insists on seeing each as a separate religion. This same politics governs the behavior of actors in public space. It can be useful to understand the Haitian majority as being "bicultural" or "bireligious," a population able to speak both of the religious languages operating within the culture (Murphy 1988, 124). People strategically employ "religious code-switching" to translate the logics of Catholicism and Vodou back and forth to suit the social situation at hand. For this reason it may make sense to view the religious worldview of the vast majority as "Haitian religious culture," a term that "reflects a religion in two-way communication with the structures of authority around it" (Davis 1982). It is a religious culture that contains within it shifting sets of possible elements, complicated yet bounded by the theologies and practices of both Roman Catholicism and Vodou.

[...]

The fact that people do the spiritual work of Afro-Haitian religion in church settings does not mean that they are not also fully participating Catholics. For the Haitians, the pilgrimage at 115th Street is very much respected as a Catholic event, and any spiritual work that is done explicitly for the *lwa* is done discreetly. Vodou remains an unspoken presence at the feast in New York, and each sign that carries meaning within Vodou can also be read as a form of Catholic devotion. Wearing light blue clothing, saying prayers during fireworks, distributing pork in the churchyard, writing letters to the Virgin – all these things have a place in the ritual vocabulary of Catholicism, even if they are seen by the priests at the church as the quaint expressions of the "folk."

The spiritual works of Vodouist Catholics are achieved in a process of religious code-switching through the subtle use of language, the nuanced use of color, and discreet offerings of spiritual significance. It is possible, then, to communicate with Ezili Dantò through Mont Carmel on the public stage without detection, even by fellow community-members standing at one's side. Devotions to Our Lady that are also spiritual work for Ezili Dantò are masked with a discretion that has come from generations of experience with colonial and postcolonial repression from France and Rome. Because of the historical circumstances involving the church's repression of Vodou, then, it is quite possible to serve Ezili Dantò through the coded performance of Catholicism.

[...]

The Haitian presence at the shrine for Our Lady of Mount Carmel began as a spontaneous devotion; no church institution initiated or invited the Haitian participation. Not even the sponsoring Pallottine order ministers to the Haitians as a group, except for holding a monthly Mass in French. Part of this has to do with diocesan politics and the territorial jurisdictions of the church. The Haitian leadership is located in Brooklyn and Queens, in the Brooklyn diocese. The feast in East Harlem falls into the New York archdiocese, covering Manhattan, Rockland, and Westchester. With only thirty-five priests of Haitian descent living and serving in the United States, there is a shortage of priests with Haitian cultural fluency. Yet the pilgrims at Mount Carmel do not seem to be concerned.

A small, informal group of committed Haitians prints the text of the Mass in French and distributes it during the feast. The priests at Mount Carmel explain that they offer two Masses in French out of the eight that are said that day "as a courtesy." They have also appointed a Haitian man quasideacon, endowing him with some, but not all, of the responsibilities of that position. Yet the pilgrims who come to the feast have not played a great role in organizing it. The pilgrimage is, for the Haitians, a matter apart from their regular church activities. It is an affair between themselves and the Virgin.

The community of Haitians at the Church for Our Lady of Mount Carmel is what makes this site a translocative one – symbolically engaged with both home and host countries. The image of the festivities back in Haiti at Sodo is a quietly spoken reference. Ezili Dantò, the powerful feminine divinity who fought for Haitian independence, forms the backdrop for prayers and conversation about the various transmutations of Haitian national politics – the fall of Duvalier, the election of Aristide, the coup d'ètat, and the US military "intervasion" – as well as US elections and immigration legislation. People can see old friends, be seen by new friends, and ritually distribute their Haitian foods to enthusiastic recipients. By sharing this important date with one another, actors build a religious community of sorts, maintaining the nostalgia for Haiti and reaffirming the dream of eventual return. As they would at Sodo, they can stay up late to *bay blag* (tell jokes) and sleep in groups in the church on the night before the feast. They can pray the rosary together in French and relax into the common codes of their culture. In one of the few times of liminal community solidarity, they can enjoy the deeply satisfying company of their sisters and brothers from Haiti around them as they pray, sing, and speak to their common mother, the Vièj Mirak.

Catholicism and the Haitian Strategy of Alterity

bell hooks (1989) has noted that scholars may be more comfortable focusing on international or postcolonial issues than addressing race and class differences at home. She points out that language that diasporizes and internationalizes US minorities can obscure understandings of structured inequalities of class and race in the national arena. While they are dubbed "*djaspora*" when they return to Haiti, in the United States the Haitian population is engaged in a struggle over questions of identity and definition that are inseparable from American processes of racialization.

Immigrants who establish themselves in the United States enter an increasingly plural society, where ethnic identity is structured through various processes that include race, class, religion, language, and gender as well as the politics of nationalism. Recent scholarship by David Mittelberg and Mary C. Waters (1992) suggests that immigrants' identities in the United States will be formed out of a dialectic of sorts. Identity will be made up of the category into which the receiving society assign them on one hand and the "cognitive map" of the immigrants themselves on the other. Mittelberg and Waters offer the hypothetical case of a Polish immigrant. Americans, familiar with other Polish Americans, assign him or her to the category "Polish." The Polish American population becomes what is referred to as the "proximal host," the group to which the receiving society would assign the immigrant. The newly arrived Pole is different, of course from Polish Americans, but most likely perceives a series of historical similarities and begins to develop a Polish American self-understanding and identity (ibid., 416).

But what if the receiving society assigns the new immigrant to a proximal host that the immigrant does not recognize? Afro-Caribbean immigrants are caught in this problematic position. As black immigrants they are offered the label "African American." But here the proximal host to which the dominant society assigns them is not the identity that they understand themselves to have. They understand themselves to be historically and culturally distinct from Black Americans. Yet social scientists have shown that groups defined through race will have the least amount of choice in self-identification. Groups of black African descent will inevitably be labeled "black." In contrast, "white ethnics" like Irish Americans or Italian Americans have a considerable amount of choice in the ways they may cast their identity (ibid.).

Scholars of race have demonstrated that there is no such thing really, as "race," but rather that racializations and racisms are processed in historical evolution, changing through time and across space (Hall 1978). We can see the ways in which the former slaveholding societies of Latin America, the West Indies, and the United States have all developed differently racialized configurations. When Haitians arrive in the United States, they carry cognitive maps charting a complete sense of Caribbean racialization in which people are located along a color continuum, mitigated by class and family lineage. Race in the United States has been constructed along a color line, making people either black or white. Haitian Americans' identity and subjective positions of racialization must be seen as being superimposed onto their new experience of United States constructions of race. Part of the challenge people of color face when they emigrate is in assessing and renegotiating a newly found racial status in North America.

Unpacking the complexities of Haitian American identity, Caroll Charles (1990) argues that the categories of race, class, and ethnicity by which Haitians identify themselves are expressions of their social consciousness, and are part of a process of rejection and redefinition of categories of race and ethnicity ascribed in the United States. Charles's work reveals Haitians' tendency to disaffiliate with African Americans. Haitians are acutely aware that Black Americans have been assigned again and again to the lowest status position in the United States. Haitian immigrants see that meanings of blackness in the United States are subordinated, that blacks represent the bottom of United States society. Haitians reject this placement and tend to dismiss US meanings of blackness, while affirming their own race and culture.

Although Haitians self-identify as black, they link their blackness through Haitian history to Africa and not via the United States. Haitian racial identity is closely connected to pride in the Haitian revolution of 1791–1804, which created the first black-ruled nation in the Americas. The revolution was fought by slaves said to be inspired by Vodou and fortified by magical weapons. Blackness and militarism became key tropes of Haitian nationalism, along with allusions to Afro-Creole spiritual power. Citizens of the black nation that defeated Napoleon's army, Haitians carry a deep sense of national pride that is linked to blackness and independence (Charles 1990; see also McAlister 1995).

The paths that they chart reveal Haitians in the United States to be actors constructing their own identity as a population. Two important performative elements

they have available to use in carving out their own identities are language and religion. A common Haitian American tactic is to display, use, and value their Francophone (and Creolophone) abilities. By referring to themselves as "Frenchies" and speaking French in public, Haitians display a foreign-born status that is at once an upper-class marker in Haitian society (Charles 1990, Mittelberg and Waters 1992). By continuing to participate in Catholic congregations and public feasts, Haitian Americans distinguish themselves further from African Americans, whom they generally view as members of the black Protestant church establishment.[17]

It is thus possible to view the Haitian devotion at the Church of Our Lady of Mount Carmel and at other pilgrimages to the Blessed Mother in the United States as a partial strategy in the Haitian American struggle to create an American identity, "a self-constitution through the strategy of alterity within the broader context of American racial semiotics" (Orsi 1992, 321). By maintaining Frenchness, Creoleness, and Catholicism, and by dressing in conservative, French-influenced fashions and hair styles, Haitians broadcast their difference from African Americans. By displaying and practicing their Catholic culture with its Latin and French linguistic attributes, Haitians can underscore to themselves, their children, and the larger society that they are fully Haitian, Afro-Caribbean, Catholic, immigrant – and not African American. In a sense, Haitian Americans can be said to be struggling to create a new black ethnicity in the United States.

While this conservative Francophile strategy is a long-standing one for Haitians throughout the diaspora, it is worth noting that this is not the only stance possible for Haitian American identity. Since the fall of Duvalier in 1986, the *racine* (roots) movement has created an alternative Haitianized identity. This politically progressive movement cultivates a peasant, "folksy" style and an explicitly pro-Vodou ethos. There are also many important political and social alliances between African American and Haitian American groups, each working out of a pro-black consciousness (McAlister 1995a).

Nevertheless, while the pilgrimage is a place to perform spiritual work, it is also an occasion to perform Catholicism on the public stage, regardless of where each person stands on the Catholic-Vodou continuum in Haitian religious culture. Catholicism becomes one ritual performance among others in the larger cultural repertoire. This performance is a continuation of a stance developed in slavery and throughout the postcolonial history of Haiti in the face of church repression of

African-based spirituality. In the US context, the perform-ance becomes one element in the Haitian strategy to redefine American categories of race and ethnicity.

Italians and Haitians: Race and Religious Symbiosis

The arrival of both Italians and Puerto Ricans into the United States has been racially charged, each in a specific way. Robert Orsi (1985, 160) writes of the "racial inbetweenness" of late-nineteenth-century Italian immi-grants, arguing that Italians were initially viewed as unassimilable "African racial stock." Tallulah, Louisiana, became the bloody scene of race hatred when five Sicilian men (targets of a terrorism historically reserved for African Americans) were lynched "because they had violated the protocols of racial interaction." Italian Americans created an identity in reaction to early racism against them and, in turn, larger issues about their position with respect to other dark-skinned peoples. Immigrants from Italy learned that "achievement in their new environment meant successfully differentiating themselves from the dark-skinned other" (Orsi 1992, 314–17).

In New York Puerto Rican people have also been met with a racialized hatred (Orsi 1992, Díaz-Stevens 1993, Bourgois 1995). When Puerto Rican migrants moved into Italian Harlem in the pre-World War II period, the Italians reacted with hostility to this "other dark-skinned other," and three-way violence broke out between African Americans, Italian Americans, and Puerto Ricans. Insofar as organized crime syndicates held sway in the Italian community, they forced local landlords to main-tain white-only segregated buildings (Bourgois 1995, 60).[18] They could not, however, stop the public housing projects being built in the neighborhood, which were replacing Italian families with black and Latino ones. "We had to leave when the 'goombas' moved in," an Italian American pilgrim returning to Our Lady of Mount Carmel told me. Italians spoke with disdain of the "so-called Puerto Ricans" who as Latins were culturally and linguistically similar, yet whose arrival threatened Italian control of East Harlem and soon turned *cara Harlem* into *el barrio* (Orsi 1992, 326).

Despite the important place reserved for Our Lady of Mount Carmel in their devotions, Puerto Ricans quickly sensed that they would find no welcome at the feast on 115th Street. "Puerto Ricans knew to stay away, because on these days and nights Italian Americans were in the

grip of a profound experience of their own power and identity (conflicted and polysemous as this was) and would not tolerate the appearance of 'outsiders' among them, especially those 'outsiders' who lived in the neigh-borhood" (ibid., 330). The Italians were determined to maintain the Italian ethnic flavor of the feast, ensuring that the *festa* not become a *fiesta*. Even at the present writing, few Puerto Rican pilgrims attend the July sixteenth festivities.

By the time Haitian immigrants began to attend the feast in large numbers in the 1970s, the Italian battle for territory was over. Most Italian American families had moved out of East Harlem, and for them the July feast had become another sort of pilgrimage – a nostalgic visit to the old neighborhood where their parents' American journey began (ibid.). Today Italian American families return to the feast with video cameras; after Mass they line the sidewalks to film the old neighborhood for posterity. The feast is still produced and controlled by the Pallottine order, and the Italian American old guard organizes the feast committees. But the fact is that without hundreds of Haitian bodies at the processions and thousands of Haitians who come to Mass, the feast of Our Lady would not be possible.

The Italians producing the feast receive the Haitians very differently from the way they did the Puerto Ricans a generation ago. The Haitians' arrival from outside the neighborhood and their departure afterward makes their yearly "invasion" less threatening than that of the Puerto Ricans who overtook East Harlem as residents (see also McGreevy 1996). The Italians make gestures welcoming the Haitians, adding a French Mass "as a courtesy," and flying the Haitian flag next to the Italian one in the parade. They comment on how prayerful and devoted the Haitians are. "Look how they pray, the beautiful way they dress, they come from all over, they are so devoted to the Blessed Mother," said one lay worker approvingly. They sense *rispetto* (respect) for the Blessed Mother in the little suits and "Wedding-cake" dresses that make up the Haitian "Sunday best."

The Italians express hostility toward Puerto Rican *santeros* (priest in the Yoruba-based religion called *La Regla de Ocha*) when they come to do spiritual work at the church. They describe *Ocha* as "satanism" while at the same time denying that the Haitians are involved in Vodou.[19] Florida Water, candles, and fried pork set near the altars are left only by "a few crazy ones" (Orsi 1992, 334). The elderly Italian American women are nevertheless anxious about the new influx and express fear to one another about the statue's safety in the midst of the newest pilgrims. Some advocate restricting Haitian access to the nave of the church (Bourgois 1995, 347).

Despite Italian anxieties, the Haitians are accommodated and even respected at the church. Language has been an important marker shaping the respect the Italians have for the Haitians. Well versed in the Tridentine Mass, the Haitians chant the prayers in Latin along with the priests, which impresses the Italians. In the respect and prayerfulness of the Haitians, the Italian Americans recognize a conservative, pre-Vatican II religiosity, and identify them as "traditional Catholics" (Orsi 1992, 333). The Haitians' Creole impresses the Italians, on whom the difference between French and Creole is lost. The Italian Americans recognize the Haitian strategies of racial alterity and emphatically assert that "Haitians are not considered as black people" (Orsi 1992, 334). In a sense, the two communities find sympathetic reflection in one another.

For the days of the feast, Haitians and Italians form a sort of symbiosis, each allowing the other to extend once again a cherished event from their past into the future. Italians and Haitians engage in a kind of pact, and each community fills the needs of the other. While the Italian Americans produce the feast, they maintain control over their old neighborhood and the shrine church, one of the three most important Marian sites in all the Americas. Meanwhile, the Haitians are consumers at the shrine. They arrive with flowers, make donations, and buy religious articles – scapulars, statues, and prayer cards. They sing the Mass in Latin and French, and their presence fills the streets in the procession. Without having to organize and produce it, they use the feast as a public stage upon which to serve the Virgin and perform their ethnicity. When it is all over the Haitians retreat, leaving the Italian community to itself. In the often racially tense landscape of New York, this week represents a smooth collaboration that suits everybody involved. For one week each year, the Italian American community of East Harlem becomes a sort of "religious host," welcoming Haitians from near and far. Each community allows the other to preserve their myths, their hopes, and their own deep sense of identity.

[. . .]

Conclusions

In this chapter I set out to illustrate that in order to understand religious life for some new immigrants, we must understand their continuing relationships with the religious cultures of their home countries. The Haitian diaspora represents an actively transnational population, embedded in social, political, and financial networks that span home and host countries. The Fèt Vièj Mirak on East 115th Street is a religious event whose meaning also spans New York and Haiti. But rather than substituting the New York feast for the one they left behind at Sodo, Haitians add the Harlem location as another possible site of spiritual work. In this way East 115th Street is opened up as one more site in the expanding "religioscape" of transnational Haitian religious culture. During the pilgrimage for Notre Dame du Mont Carmel in New York, the Haitian population reterritorializes spiritual practice, reinscribing sacred space onto their new landscape of settlement.

The pilgrimage to Mont Carmel in East Harlem expands the saint's influence in the Haitian world. Haitians in diaspora reach out to Our Lady of Mount Carmel and Ezili Dantò, both nationalist divinities, extending prayers for family and friends throughout the *djaspora* and in Haiti. By attending the feast by the thousands, the New York Haitian population has collectively placed the Church of Our Lady of Mount Carmel on an invisible community map. In stepping onto the public stage of the Catholic feast, they orient themselves within the shifting "ethnoscape" of New York City. They make sense of the confusing complexity of this ethnic landscape by locating the church as a center of spiritual power where they will be welcome. [. . .] When national populations spread through migration to new localities, they bring their divinities with them, re-territorializing their religious practices. The supernatural world assents, and comes to bear up communities in transition.

Notes

In this article, I capitalize the term Black American to refer to the specific national group that is regularly designated as a category separate from other Americans.

1 Before the Second Vatican Council of the 1960s, it was customary to fast until taking communion. While this particular family no longer observed that tradition, it did serve as an implicit, legitimating explanation for Marie-Carmel's fainting.

2 Although I speak Creole fluently, older Haitians often address me in French, as they might any non-Haitian, for French is more widely spoken worldwide and is also a marker of prestige. In Haitian Creole, foreigners are always called *blan,* implying "whiteness." An Anglo-American woman like

me is a *fanm blan,* while an African American woman would be a *nègès blan,* a "black white/foreigner." In Creole, blackness is normative, hence the word for "man" is *nèg,* connoting "black man." A Haitian man is always a *nèg,* even if he is of European descent, in which case he is a *nèg blan,* a "white black man," or a *nèg milat,* a "mulatto black man." Much has been written on Haitian codes of racialization, which are different from those in both the United States and other parts of Latin America and the Caribbean (see Nicholls 1979, Dupuy 1989).

3 Robert Orsi (personal communication, New York, July 1992) notes that the last Italian religious supply shop closed in 1990.

4 The vast majority of Haitians are black people of African descent. There is also a small minority of *Ayisyen blanc,* or "European Haitians," *milat,* or "mulatto Haitians," and a tiny but economically significant sector of *Siryen,* a gloss for the Lebanese, Palestinian, Syrian, and Israeli diaspora merchant community in Port-au-Prince.

5 Interview, Father Guy Sansariqc, head of the Haitian Apostolate, Brooklyn, June 1996.

6 Tragedy can include forced deportation, for example. Increasingly the United States and weaker nations are collaborating in an institutionalized transnational policy whereby persons convicted of crimes are deported to their home country after serving their sentences in US jails. This policy was made possible by Title 3 of the Illegal Immigration Reform and Immigrant Responsibility Act of 1996, and represents a new era in international relations.

7 Arjun Appadurai (1990, 6) writes of the disjoined flows that are set in motion with increased globalization: "ethnoscapes, mediascapes, technoscapes, financescapes and ideoscapes." It is possible here to think of "religioscapes" as the subjective religious maps (and attendant theologies) of diasporic communities who are also in global flow and flux.

8 Important religious sites dot the New York landscape, and include intersections where offerings can be made to Papa Legba, *lwa* of the crossroads; public parks where trees and rocks are used for their spiritual power; cemeteries where the recently dead can be honored; and churches housing the saints, where Creole Mass is spoken. Other pilgrimages are also mapped onto the metropolitan area as well: for example, thousands of Haitians take chartered buses to the Church of Czestochowa in Pennsylvania for the Feast of the Assumption. For a treatment of sacred urban lanscape in Afro-Cuban tradition, see David Hilary Brown (1989, 353–57).

9 See, for example, Carole Devillers (1985) and the Winter 1992 issue of *Aperture* (vol. 126) that focused on Haiti.

10 He was subsequently crowned emperor of the Haitian Republic and the de facto head of its Roman Catholic church (see n. 16 below). Sodo is still a site of political manipulations. During the period after the fall of Jean-Claude Duvalier, the ruling junta members built cinder-block

vacation houses among the wooden and straw houses right next to the falls in order to maintain a visible public presence at the site.

11 For the only ethnographic work to date on Rastafari in New York City, see Hepner (1998).

12 Another spot, called Fey Sen Jan, was the site of a ritual the night before the Mont Carmel feast in Ville Bonheur, but it has virtually disappeared (Laguerre 1989, 84; interview with Manbo Gislene, New York City, July 1994).

13 In French her name was written "Erzulie Dantor," and it appears that way often in Vodou flags, songs, and other works of art, as well as in priests' notebooks and other sacred writings. The etymological history of her name merits future research.

14 Throughout Haitian history, the Catholic church has launched waves of repression against Vodou practitioners in "anti-superstition campaigns" (see Desmangles 1992).

15 This understanding applies to religion the theories on Creole linguistics worked out by Lee Drummond (1980).

16 Although the history is too lengthy to elaborate here, it is important to note that with Haitian Independence in 1804, ties were officially cut to the Vatican, and a Catholicism in Haiti evolved with its own national flavor. In 1860 a concordat was signed reopening the relationship with Rome. By that time, Afro-Haitian spirituality had established itself as the worldview of the vast majority of Haitians.

17 Haitians also tend to send their children to Catholic schools in relatively high numbers (see Lawrence 1997).

18 In his ethnography *In Search of Respect: Selling Crack in El Barrio,* Philippe Bourgois (1995, 48–76) chronicles the largely Puerto Rican-controlled drug trade that ravaged the neighborhood around the Church of Our Lady in the 1980s. He argues that this area of Manhattan has long been a site of "crime, violence and substance abuse," from the early Dutch tobacco farms to the heroin and cocaine trades of Italian crime families to the Latin crack dealers. While it is dangerous to attempt to describe drug-dealing networks because of the potential for stereotyping, it is important to be conscious of the realities of both legal and extralegal economic spheres and subcultures and their influence on wider communities.

19 See Andrew Parker et al. (1992).

References

Aperture. 1992. 126 (Winter): 40–7.

Appadurai, Arjun. 1990. "Disjuncture and Difference in the Global Cultural Economy." *Public Culture* 2 (2): 1–24.

Basch, Linda, Nina Glick-Schiller, and Cristina Szanton Blanc. 1994. *Nations Unbound: Transnational Projects, Postcolonial Predicaments, and Deterritorialized Nation-States.* Langhorne, Pa.: Gordon and Breach.

Bastide, Roger. 1960. *The African Religions of Brazil: Towards a Sociology of the Interpenetration of Civilizations*. Baltimore: Johns Hopkins University Press.

Bourgois, Philippe. 1995. *In Search of Respect: Selling Crack in El Barrio*. New York and Cambridge: Cambridge University Press.

Brown, David Hilary. 1989. "Garden in the Machine: Afro-Cuban Sacred Art and Performance in New Jersey and New York." Ph.D. dissertation, Yale University.

Brown, Karen McCarthy. 1991. *Mama Lola: A Vodou Priestess in Brooklyn*. Berkeley: University of California Press.

Charles, Carolle. 1990. "Distinct Meanings of Blackness: Haitian Migrants in New York City." *Cimarron* 2 (3): 129–38.

Davis, Nathalie Z. 1982. "From 'Popular Religion' to Religious Cultures." Pp. 312–343 in *Reformation Europe: A Guide to Research*, edited by Steven Oziment. St. Louis: Center for Reformation Research.

Desmangles, Leslie G. 1992. *The Faces of the Gods: Vodou and Roman Catholicism in Haiti*. Chapel Hill: University of North Carolina Press.

Devillers, Carole. 1985. "Haiti's Voodoo Pilgrimages of Spirits and Saints." *National Geographic* 167 (March): 394–408.

Díaz-Stevens, Ana-María. 1993. *Oxcart Catholicism on Fifth Avenue: The Impact of the Puerto Rican Migration upon the Archdiocese of New York*. Notre Dame, Ind.: University of Notre Dame Press.

Drummond, Lee. 1980. "The Cultural Continuum: A Theory of Intersystems." *Man* 15: 352–74.

Dupuy, Alex. 1989. *Haiti in the World Economy: Class, Race, and Underdevelopment Since 1700*. Boulder, Colo.: Westview Press.

Hall, Stuart, ed. 1978. *Policing the Crisis: Mugging, the State, and Law and Order*. New York: Holmes and Meier.

Handlin, Oscar. 1951. *The Uprooted*. New York: Grosset and Dunlap.

Hepner, Randal L. (1998) "The House That Rasta Built: Church-Building and Fundamentalism Among New York Rastafarians." Pp. 197–234. In *Greetings in Diaspora: Religious Communities and the New Immigration*, edited by R. Stephen Warner and Judith G. Wittner. Philadelphia: Temple University Press.

Herskovits, Melville. 1941. *The Myth of the Negro Past*. Boston: Beacon, 1958.

hooks, bell. 1989. "Critical Interrogation: Talking Race, Resisting Racism." *Inscriptions* 5: 159–64.

Laguerre, Michel. 1989. *Voodoo and Politics in Haiti*. New York: St. Martin's Press.

Laurino, Maria. 1995. "Sharing a Saint: The Two Worlds of Our Lady of Mount Carmel." *New York Times*, July 23, sect. 13, p. 5, col. 3.

Lawrence, Stewart. 1997. "U.S. Immigrants in the Catholic Schools: A Preliminary Assessment." Unpublished paper, Catholic University of America, Washington, DC.

Levitt, Peggy. 1998. "Local-Level Global Religion: The Case of U.S.-Dominican Migration." *Journal for the Scientific Study of Religion*, 3: 74–89.

McAlister, Elizabeth. 1995. "Men Moun Yo; Here Are the People: Rara Festivals and Transnational Popular Culture in New York City." Ph.D. dissertation, Yale University.

McGreevy, John. 1996. *Parish Boundaries: The Catholic Encounter with Race in the Twentieth-Century Urban North*. Chicago: University of Chicago Press.

Mittelberg, David and Mary C. Waters. 1992. "The Process of Ethnogenesis Among Haitian and Israeli Immigrants in the United States." *Ethnic and Racial Studies* 15 (3): 412–35.

Murphy, Joseph. 1988. *Santeria: An African Religion in America*. Boston: Beacon Press.

Nash, June. 1983. "The Impact of the Changing International Division of Labor on Different Sectors of the Labor Force." Pp. 3–69. In *Women, Men, and the International Division of Labor*, edited by June Nash and Patricia Fernandez-Kelly. Albany: SUNY Press.

Nicholls, David. 1979. *From Dessalines to Duvalier: Race, Color and National Independence in Haiti*. New York: Cambridge University Press.

Orsi, Robert Anthony. 1985. *The Madonna of 115th Street: Faith and Community in Italian Harlem, 1880–1950*. New Haven: Yale University Press.

——. 1992. "The Religious Boundaries of an Inbetween People: Street Feste and the Problem of the Dark-Skinned Other in Italian Harlem, 1920–1990." *American Quarterly* 44 (3): 313–41.

Parker, Andrew, Mary Russo, Doris Sommer, and Patricia Yaeger, eds. 1992. *Nationalisms and Sexualities*. New York: Routledge.

Rouzier, Sèmexan. 1891. *Dictionnaire Géographique d'Haiti*. Paris: Charles Blot.

Sassen-Koob, Saskia. 1982. "Recomposition and Peripherialization at the Core." *Contemporary Marxism* 5: 88–100.

Stewart, Charles, and Rosalind Shaw. 1994. *Syncretism/Anti-Syncretism: The Politics of Religious Synthesis*. New York: Routledge.

Tweed, Thomas A. 1997. *Our Lady of the Exile: Diasporic Religion at a Cuban Catholic Shrine in Miami*. New York and Oxford: Oxford University Press.

Wallerstein, Emmanuel. 1974. *The Modern World System*. New York: Academic Press.

24

The Good Fight: Israel after Vietnam, 1972–80

Melani McAlister

In the spring of 1967, as the war between Israel and the neighboring Arab states was brewing, newspapers and television in the United States reported on the progress of a very different conflict. In Vietnam, the US military was enmeshed in the second year of Operation Rolling Thunder, the bombing campaign that dropped eight hundred tons of bombs a day on North Vietnam. Troop call-ups had increased, and the antiwar movement was conducting a ceaseless round of protest and confrontation with authorities. As the war escalated, television news in particular brought it home, making Vietnam "the living room war." A new generation of young reporters – David Halberstam, Seymour Hersh, Peter Arnett, Morley Safer – were accompanying US troops nearly everywhere in the field. They filled the expanded evening newscasts (which had been lengthened from fifteen to thirty minutes beginning in 1963) with dramatic, highly visual, and controversial reporting that was virtually uncensored by US military authorities. While most Americans still described themselves as firmly in support of the war, doubts were spreading. That May, General Westmoreland, the commander of US troops in Vietnam, was called home to appear before Congress, in a move that commentators assumed was intended to shore up political support for the war. Although the general was received warmly by Congress, he did little to quell the public's doubts. *Newsweek* pointed out that, while Westmoreland had claimed to be explaining the situation in Vietnam, he had "never touched the fundamental questions causing all the concern in the first place. . . . Was the U.S. really prepared to fight a long war of attrition in Asia?"[1]

These questions echoed more general concerns, just beginning to emerge in mainstream debates, about the nature of US power. As the Vietnam War dragged on, even some members of the foreign policy establishment began to wonder whether the United States was beginning to look more like an imperial power that an anticolonial one. Shortly after Westmoreland's appearance, no less an official than Secretary of Defense Robert McNamara made this rather remarkable observation: "The picture of the world's greatest superpower killing or seriously injuring a thousand noncombatants a week, while trying to pound a tiny backward country into submission on an issue whose merits are hotly debated is not a pretty one."[2] On the other hand, General Westmoreland and other military officials argued that the war could and would be won, even against an "unconventional" enemy, if only the United States followed a purposeful and sustained application of military force, backed by a willingness to sustain losses.[3] This debate over Vietnam policy would soon become a debate over Middle East policy as well, as US officials and the American public faced the oil crises of the 1970s.

In May 1967, the escalating tensions between Egypt and Israel eclipsed public concern about Vietnam, at least for a while. In the Situation Room in the White House, the map of Vietnam was replaced with a map of the Middle East.[4] Then, in June, the Israelis surprised the world with their extraordinarily rapid victory over the forces of Egypt, Syria, and Jordan. Before war broke out, experts had suggested that the Arab forces were distinctly stronger and more battle-ready than they had been in either 1948 or 1956.[5] But doubts about the outcome were quickly put to rest; six days after the war began, Arab nationalists were humiliated, and Israel emerged as the preeminent military power in a region where the political and territorial map had been suddenly redrawn.

Whatever complicated feelings the 1967 war engendered among African Americans and American Jews, most news accounts focused simply on the drama of Israel's victory. Newspapers and TV news told of the rapid successes of the Israeli army, detailing the "stunning pre-dawn air-strikes, the "remarkable military triumph," and the "brilliant planning and execution of the Israeli attack."[6] Headlines such as "How Israel Won the War" highlighted the media's focus on the pragmatic details of the battle. Politically, Israel clearly had the vast majority of public support: in Washington, two hundred pro-Arab demonstrators (including some Black Muslims and members of the Student Nonviolent Coordinating Committee) faced more than twenty thousand pro-Israeli demonstrators.[7] Comparisons with US actions in Vietnam were not lost upon observers. One columnist sarcastically proposed that the world should establish an agency to allocate wars so that they would not exhaust public attention by running simultaneously. A television comedian joked that the Israeli general Moshe Dayan should be hired to put a quick end to the fighting in Vietnam.[8] The conservative news magazine *U.S. News & World Report* made much the same point, quoting the observations of an unnamed US military official: "The Israeli performance was proof of the only sound military strategy: When a country decides to go into a war, it goes in 'wham' – to win."[9]

Just over six months later, the illusion of any such rapid victory in Vietnam was shattered when North Vietnam and its allies launched the Tet Offensive. Eventually, US and South Vietnamese troops repelled the attack decisively, but only after having fought Vietnamese communist forces in the courtyard of the American embassy in Saigon, with television cameras there to record every moment of the battle. For the American public, which had been told for years that the United States was winning – had almost won – the war, the fact that the communists had enough strength to launch such a daring campaign was in itself a shock. Thus at virtually the same moment that officials like Robert McNamara were bringing the antiwar movement's critique of the morality of US power into the mainstream debate, serious questions emerged about the efficacy of that power. In other words, just as the United States began to look like an imperial power in the eyes of some of its citizens, it began to look like an imperial power in decline, unable or unwilling to shore up its own ambitions.

In the following decade, Israel came to be constituted as an icon in the post-Vietnam debate about the nature of US world power. Just as the Arab oil embargo had figured prominently in arguments for a global managerialist model, Israel and its military played a key symbolic role for those who advocated the remilitarization of US policy. As questions raged both about the morality of the US war in Vietnam and about the role of the US military more generally, Israel came to provide a political model for thinking about military power and a practical example of effectiveness in the use of that power.

For many American Jews and others, Israel had long stood as a very different kind of symbol: a reconstructed community built out of the ashes of the Holocaust. While not all Jews shared this sense of solidarity, most people who felt strong ties to Israel before 1967 did so because of their conviction that a precious haven was being created. In the 1970s, however, some Americans came to invest emotionally and politically in Israel for very different reasons, and precisely through the more militarized image that emerged in the wake of Vietnam. This investment, which solidified the political ties between the United States and Israel, had a profound effect on foreign policy. Over the course of the decade, a dominant view emerged that it was at once morally just and in US national interests to act not only *with* Israel but also *like* Israel on key international issues.

This new image of Israel was interconnected with domestic politics, but not in the way that many commentators have imagined. Both the Israeli lobby and American Jews have of course played an important role in framing US Israeli relations, but they did not – could not – construct US cultural or political interests out of whole cloth. Israel played a rhetorical role in an argument about US foreign policy and American identity. That argument itself was also connected to problems of gender: as feminism and women's political activism shook American culture to its core in the 1970s, the fascination with military power served to reassert a certain kind of masculinity. In the 1960s, black radicals had used Islam and Arab culture to assert their own masculinity against a civil rights movement perceived as too accommodating and overly feminized; in the 1970s, white evangelicals and political conservatives mobilized Israel as part of a challenge to the liberal and left-wing advances of feminism and the antiwar movement of the 1960s and early 1970s.

I trace here the significance of the post-Vietnam figure of Israel through several locations. [. . .] and detail the rising fascination with modern-day Israel in the subculture of conservative Christian fundamentalism. As the New Christian Right emerged and gained cultural recognition and political power over the course of the 1970s, its writers and preachers began to talk more and more about the role of the Middle East in the great end-time battles predicted in biblical prophecy. Israel was central to their scenario, and the fundamentalists' deep interest in the details of the contemporary Arab-Israeli conflict arose from an increased sense that the end times would be heralded by events in the Middle East. These religious concerns connected to a broader interest in Israel that developed as the battle against terrorism came to dominate US headlines in the 1970s. I argue that Israel's response to terrorism was the source of a nearly endless public fascination, in large part because of how Israel figured into questions about declining US military power. The meanings of Israel developed in conjunction with the concept of the "Vietnam Syndrome," the conservative reinterpretation that viewed the American defeat in Vietnam as a failure of political will.

Overall, I suggest that each of these dynamics, diverse as they were, included a dual focus on the importance of Israel as a moral exemplar and Israel as an admired military power. The chapter concludes by suggesting that this militarized image of Israel has not been sufficiently acknowledged as a factor in the New Right coalition that came together in the 1980 elections. As New Right revisionism came to dominate public understanding of what had happened in Vietnam, it had a new understanding of Israel as its subtext. Thus, several *different* discursive sites, each with its own institutional history and modes of representation, worked together in the 1970s to remake the dominant meanings of Israel in the United States. Over the course of the 1970s, Israel, or a certain image of Israel, came to function as a stage upon which the war in Vietnam was refought – and this time, won.

[. . .]

Prophecy and Israel

Three years after the Six-Day War, in 1970, a small religious publishing house released a thin book about biblical prophecy that would soon transform the cultural and religious landscape of the decade. The author, a relative unknown who had graduated from Dallas Theological Seminary and then toured the country as a lecturer for Campus Crusade for Christ, was Hal Lindsey. His exegesis of the relationship between the biblical

prophecies of Armageddon and contemporary political events was titled *The Late Great Planet Earth (LGPE)*; by the end of the decade, it had sold more than ten million copies, making it the best-selling book of the 1970s. (By 1998, estimates for total sales ranged between eighteen and twenty-eight million copies.)[10]

LGPE was an unusual book in a long tradition of Christian publishing. For decades, evangelical authors had analyzed the prophetic and apocalyptic books of the Hebrew Scriptures, particularly Daniel and Ezekiel, and of the Christian New Testament, particularly Revelation. An interest in prophecy was especially common among fundamentalists, who identified themselves as literal interpreters of the Bible. Like earlier authors, Lindsey viewed the biblical prophecies of the "last days" and the war of Armageddon in light of contemporary politics, focusing on the Middle East. *LGPE*'s fundamental argument was that certain key world events, which would signal the battle of Armageddon and the Second Coming of Christ, were beginning to happen in the 1970s, and that the nation of Israel (and its allies and enemies) would be central to those developments. As Bible analysis, Lindsey's book added little to the established framework of evangelical prophecy interpretation as outlined in scholarly texts and as taught in the nation's Bible college and seminaries. Indeed, some of his fellow students at Dallas Theological Seminary complained that Lindsey had simply repackaged his lecture notes.[11]

But if Lindsey's theories were derivative, his "repackaging" made impressive innovations at the level of style. *LGPE* was a very different sort of narrative than its predecessors, which were often academic, inbred books aimed at audiences of the already-converted. [. . .] Lindsey's breezy, upbeat style attempted to make the exegesis of complex biblical passges – and the accompanying discussion of contemporary politics – accessible and nonintimidating. Mobilizing the language of the sixties counterculture (or at least those popularized versions of the counterculture that had migrated into the mainstream), Lindsey tried to structure his discussion like an imagined rap session, sprinkling his prose with headlines like "Tell It Like It Will Be" (7), "Dead Men Do Tell Tales" (52), and "What Else Is New?" (86).

[. . .]

Although it aimed at a mass market of the young and the worried, *LGPE* initially made its reputation by selling to committed evangelicals. Released by a small Midwestern publishing house, Zondervan, it rode a rising tide of interest in religious and inspirational writings. These writings included a proliferation of books directed specifically at evangelicals, who by 1976 numbered almost eight million in the United States.[12] In the early 1970s, religious publishing had become the fastest-growing segment of the American publishing industry, even though books with religious themes rarely showed up on bestseller lists. Before the advent of universal product codes, the major lists (such as in the *New York Times*) were compiled by polling general-interest bookstore managers; since religious books were sold primarily through church conferences and small religious bookstores, they usually did not show up in the sampling polls. It was in this subcultural market that *LGPE* was first distributed; only later, after it had already sold half a million copies, did Bantam pick it up for release in a mass-market edition.[13] From then on, Lindsey's book was distributed at convenience and grocery stores, as well as in major bookstores, where it was often shelved alongside the "occult" and "New Age" paperbacks that were also selling at a brisk pace.[14]

Marketed to a mainstream audience as doomsday exotica, *LGPE* brought evangelical prophecy interpretation to bear on a detailed discussion of contemporary international politics. Unlike some analyses, which assumed that signs of the end times could be read primarily through the supposed moral degeneration of the United States, *LGPE* focused on events in the Middle East, Russia, and, to a lesser degree, Europe and China. Lindsey assumed that, however much his readers knew of scriptural texts, they were far less familiar with the outlines of Middle East politics; his response was to freely mix Scripture, historical background, and political advice. The "prophetic calendar" was moving forward, Lindsey insisted; the Second Coming of Christ was imminent and would take place in modern-day Israel. According to the Bible, three things had to happen before Christ would return: "First, the Jewish nation would be reborn in the land of Palestine. Secondly, the Jews would repossess Old Jerusalem and the sacred sites. Thirdly, they would rebuild their ancient temple of worship upon its historic site" (40). By 1970, two of those events had occurred, and both had involved a major Middle Eastern war. Arguing that the Bible predicted yet another conflict, *LGPE* included a map of the Middle East, marked with arrows indicating the expected invasion routes into Israel by the "Russian confederacy" from the north and the "Pan Arabic assault" from the south (144, 148).

Lindsey's detailed analysis of the world situation implied that white evangelicals needed to pay careful attention to politics – an unusual position in 1970. For the most part, white evangelical and fundamentalist churches had remained aloof from political life since the 1920s, when the Scopes Monkey Trial had subjected fundamentalist beliefs about evolution to public ridicule. Focusing on personal sin and inner salvation, fundamentalist doctrine had discouraged too much focus on "this world," as opposed to God's kingdom.[15] Black churches, on the other hand, which might well be called evangelical in doctrine, had been swept into political life during the civil rights movement, but had organized themselves more as big-tent Christians than specifically as evangelicals. The segregation of church life and the fact that both black and white evangelicals were concentrated in the South made race a particularly charged issue, since black Christians often squared off against evangelical whites over civil rights.

Most scholars have traced the increasing politicization of white evangelicals in the 1970s to their opposition to civil rights combined with concerns over a few other key domestic issues, particularly the changing educational environment (the Supreme Court ban on school prayer, new tax codes for religious schools, and curricular issues in the public schools) and the extensions of the liberal state. Many white fundamentalists and evangelicals also perceived a threat to their values in the antiwar and student movements. And they were profoundly affected by the public visibility of feminist movements – from the famous Miss America pageant demonstration in 1968 to Congress's approval of the Equal Rights Amendment (ERA) in 1972 to the *Roe v. Wade* abortion rights decision in 1973. In their eyes, "women's lib" had become perhaps the most influential, and threatening, social movement to emerge out of the 1960s.[16]

These issues were undeniably important to fundamentalists, but the US position in the world mattered to them as well. One tangible connection arose from the fact that evangelicals were disproportionately represented in the US military. Southerners had for many years played a key role in the military leadership and were more likely to be among the midlevel officers in Vietnam. This southern overrepresentation in the military did not mean, of course, that any particular southern soldier was a fundamentalist. But by the early 1970s, both rank-and-file soldiers and military officers were declaring their religious convictions, countering the traditional marginalization of religion in military culture. Bible studies, prayer groups, and Christian breakfast meetings soon became routine at the Pentagon, as evangelical officers consciously increased their public visibility. At the same time, from the late 1960s on, fundamentalist preachers consistently and vocally supported US involvement in Vietnam.[17]

In 1970, however, the opening up of white evangelicals to politics was still in its infancy, and Lindsey's enthusiasm about the links between Bible prophecy and the details of the Arab-Israeli conflict was remarkable precisely for its worldliness. The brew of political analysis and apocalyptic urgency proved potent, and after *LGPE*, evangelical intellectual life would never be the same. The book's unexpected popularity was at once a foreshadowing and an exemplar of the emerging white evangelical politicization – a development that would consistently include a strong investment in modern Israel's military battles.

Lindsey's focus on Israel was not an innovation; it drew on a long history of passionate evangelical interest in the politics of Zionism. Certain basic doctrines had changed little since the late nineteenth century, including the commitment to biblical inerrancy and the premillennialist view that Christ must return before the thousand-year reign of peace predicted in the Bible could begin. Still drawing on the interpretations popularized in the 1909 Scofield Reference Bible, evangelicals held that the Bible's accuracy could be tested and confirmed by political developments, especially those concerning Israel.

[. . .]

This focus on Israel as an instrument in God's plan for human history had bolstered evangelicals' consistent support for Zionism in the early part of the century. An even greater enthusiasm was generated with the founding of Israel in 1948. While mainline Protestants had been divided on the issue of Israel (in the years just before and after the creation of the state, they debated the partition plan, the conduct of the 1948 war, the status of Jerusalem, and the situation of the Palestinian refugees), evangelicals and fundamentalists saw the establishment of a Jewish state in Palestine as a clear validation of prophecy and of God's action in history.[18] As William Culberson of the Moody Bible Institute wrote in 1960, Israel's rebirth was "the most striking of all the signs" of an imminent Rapture.[19]

If the founding of Israel was one sign, it was not the only one, and in the years after the initial excitement over the creation of Israel had worn off, the contemporary Middle East had appeared to be something of a backwater, even to evangelicals who had an interest in prophecy. Then, in 1967, the Israeli army's taking of

Jerusalem galvanized evangelical observers. The war, the seemingly miraculous Israeli victory, and the transformation in the status of Jerusalem (a formerly divided city now entirely controlled by Israel) made contemporary Israeli-Arab politics look imminently and urgently relevant to evangelicals. [. . .]

Thus while the mainstream media had focused on the logistics of Israeli victory in the 1967 war, and while Jews wrote of its effect on their emotional relation to Israel, Christian evangelicals interpreted the event as evidence of the quickening pace of God's action in human history. Lindsey argued that the 1967 war proved the final war of Armageddon would likely be triggered by the Arab-Israeli conflict. "It is [the Arabs'] . . . fierce pride and smoldering hatred against Israel that will keep the Middle East a dangerous trouble spot" (76). For Jerry Falwell, then a young minister in Lynchburg, Virginia, the war also inspired the beginning of what would become a long standing interest in Israel; he took his first of many trips to the Holy Land shortly thereafter.[20] And in 1970, Billy Graham, the nation's most well-known and most influential evangelist, released the feature-length film *His Land*. Featuring upbeat tunes by the young Christian singer Cliff Barrows, and criticized, even at the time, for its simplistic support of current Israeli policies, the film was the beginning of the multimedia presentation of evangelical interest in Israel.[21]

[. . .]

The strong connection between Israel and evangelicals left many American Jews increasingly worried about what they saw as the anti-Semitism of evangelical teachings. The status of Jews within evangelical theology was, at the very least, ambiguous. In the prophecy literature, Jews held a multifaceted and complex position: on the one hand, most evangelicals were quick to point out that Jews had failed to recognize Christ, and that the collective failure of the chosen people to do so was a cause of particular displeasure to God. On the other hand, dispensationalists believed that at the end times, God would once again be dealing directly with his "earthly people," the Jews, as opposed to his "spiritual people," the Church.[22] Thus the destiny of the Jews as God's chosen people and their central role in God's plan for humanity was a matter of doctrine. (For this reason, perhaps, converted Jews – Derek Price, Charles Lee Feinberg – played a particularly visible role in the prophecy-interpretation genre.) But in a religious tradition in which "earthliness" or "worldliness" was often despised, the positioning of Jews as merely God's people on earth, as opposed to in heaven, certainly seemed like a demotion of Jewish "chosenness." Evangelicals also generally presumed the mass conversion of large numbers of Jews during the tribulation, and the terrible deaths of many others. As one sociologist has pointed out, whatever else these prophecy interpretations suggest, at the very least they indicate the "instrumentality" of Jews for premillennialists.[23] But beyond this particular theological interest in Jewish conversion at the end times – and here one must note that evangelicals viewed all those who had not been converted to Christianity as both recalcitrant and doomed – there was little direct anti-Semitism in the prophecy literature and a good many statements of God's love for the Jewish people.

Anti-Semitism was present in fundamentalist thinking, however, as became clear in a now infamous comment made in 1980 by Bailey Smith, then president of the Southern Baptist Convention. Speaking before a gathering of ministers in Dallas, Smith remarked disparagingly on the ecumenical trends of the major political parties: "It is interesting at great political rallies how you have a Protestant to pray, a Catholic to pray, and then you have a Jew to pray. With all due respect to those dear people, my friends, God Almighty does not hear the prayer of a Jew." The comment reached the national media and set off a storm of criticism. Although Smith's comment sounded like profound anti-Semitism, it might also be interpreted as simple fundamentalist exclusiveness. As William Martin has pointed out, had Smith been asked, he likely would have also argued that God was equally deaf to Hindus, Muslims, and Buddhists.[24] At the very least, however, Smith's statement indicated a stunning insensitivity to Jewish concerns and a more general lack of appreciation for pluralism in American life.

As Smith was being criticized roundly in the US media, Israeli officials and American Jews worked together to craft a response. Smith was immediately invited to come to Israel as a guest of the Israeli government. After his trip, Smith announced, "The bottom line is that you're going to read my name many times in the future in activities supporting the Jewish people and Israel."[25] Of course, there was conflation of Jewishness with Israel here, one aided by the apparently savvy decision to sponsor Smith's Holy Land trip. In order to deal with Jews and Jewishness, Smith had to go first through Jerusalem. American Jews, and their varied concerns about church and state, civil liberties, domestic policy issues, and so on, were marginalized in this equation. Sidestepping the theological issue of conversion an the political issue of

pluralism, evangelical Christian relations with Jewishness were forged through, and exemplified by, their relations to the Israeli state.

Modern Israel's attention to American evangelicals, and evangelicals' attention to Israel, proved useful for both sides. Still, the primary reason for evangelical interest remained biblical. All agreed, drawing on Genesis 12:1–3, that God would bless those who blessed Israel and curse those who cursed it. In their enthusiastic study of Israeli military capacity and their detailed examination of maps, invasion routes, and attack strategies, evangelicals were first and foremost searching for clues to the end times.

[. . .]

After 1967, evangelicals looked around and saw a world spinning out of control; immersed in the post-Vietnam discourse of failure, they harbored doubts not only about the social fabric of American society but also about the nature of US power in the world. In that moment, white evangelicals entered the world of politics for the first time in decades. And they developed a specific (and perhaps otherwise unexpected) interest in military and foreign policy issues, related to their almost obsessive fascination with the question of how and when the last great war – the war to end all wars – would come about. The Apocalypse at Armageddon would be horrific and frightening, but it would also be the one truly just war, with Jesus himself fighting on the side of righteousness.

Terrorism in the News

The evangelical interest in Israel as the site of earth's final battle did not occur in a vacuum. It paralleled, and intersected, a more secular focus on Israel's visible contemporary battles in what soon came to be known as the "war against terrorism." That conflict began in earnest after the 1967 war; as a result of Israel's occupation of Arab territories, Palestinians began to take a more militant stance in the struggle over land. It was during the Olympic Games in Munich, West Germany, however, that the Palestinian-Israeli conflict was brought home to the world. There, on the morning of September 5, 1972, eight Palestinian guerrillas sneaked into the Olympic compound, broke into the rooms of the Israeli team, and took nine Israeli team members and their coaches hostage. In the process, they killed one athlete and one coach; about eighteen others had escaped through a back window. The guerrillas were members of Black September, a strike force for the Palestine Liberation Organization (PLO), though officially disavowed. In return for releasing their hostages, they demanded the release of two hundred Palestinians held in Israeli jails.[26]

Once the attack began, sports reporters from all over the world suddenly became political correspondents. As tense negotiations between the Palestinians and West German authorities continued throughout the day, ABC, the US network covering the games, began continuous live coverage. Sportscaster Jim McKay anchored the broadcast for sixteen straight hours, with the assistance of announcer Howard Cosell. Peter Jennings, a young Middle East correspondent for ABC who was in Munich to do feature stories, managed to sneak into the Italian athletes' quarters and report by phone.[27] Officially, the compound was sealed off, but the high-mounted television cameras captured extraordinary footage: one gunman, his head covered by a dark hood, as he came out to the balcony of the dormitory to examine the situation outside; then German sharpshooters dressed in athletic gear, positioning themselves around the building.

Away from the cameras, the situation grew more and more desperate. From the first, the Israeli government had refused to release any prisoners or to negotiate with Black September. German officials took a gamble: they promised the Palestinians safe passage out of the country, then looked for an opportunity for sharpshooters to pick off the guerrillas. The plan went wrong, and at the airport a gun battle broke out between the Palestinians and German police. Several of the Palestinians were killed, and three surrendered. Before the battle was over, the Palestinians killed all of their hostages, who were tied up and blindfolded in waiting helicopters. One group died when a guerrilla shot into a helicopter and then tossed in a grenade; the second group was machine-gunned down. At first, the information from the airport was confusing. One German official told reporters that all the Israelis had been freed alive; that news was greeted with joy in both the United States and Israel. When the truth came out a few hours later, the response was shock and anger.[28]

The massacre at Munich had an extraordinary impact in the United States. Accounts of the attack and the Israeli deaths dominated US news for more than a week. Reports dissected the Israeli refusal to negotiate, why and how the West Germans had bungled their attack, as well as the controversial decision to continue the

Olympic Games in the wake of the murders. American media also detailed the heroism of some of the Israelis during the initial moments of the attack (the two men killed in the dormitory had both died trying to protect their teammates), as well as the names and life stories of the dead.[29] Many accounts pointed out the terrible irony that these deaths had happened at Munich, where the West Germans had been self-consciously trying to counter the memories of the Nazi games of 1936.[30]

Earlier in the spring, Palestinians and their allies had killed dozens of people in terrorist attacks, including both Israelis and international travelers, but none of those events carried the emotional force that Munich had for Americans.[31] Perhaps, as some commentators suggested, it was because the spirit of the Olympics had been destroyed. Or perhaps it was the fact that, this time, US television was on the scene, reporting events as they happened. ABC won twenty-nine Emmys for its work in news and sports at Munich, as well as accolades from the Senate floor to the *New York Times*.[32] Live terrorist TV was born at the Munich Olympics.

Observers in the United States once again made comparisons to Vietnam. By this time, however, the hope of a military victory in Vietnam had all but disappeared. Despite President Nixon's promise of "peace with honor," the war already had spread into Cambodia and Laos, and increasingly people talked about the impossibility of winning against an "unconventional" enemy, one that they believed broke the rules of war by bringing women and children into the battle. For liberals, Vietnam was often mentioned as an example of the limits of military power for solving conflict.

The day after the Olympic massacre, ABC news anchor Howard K. Smith made just such a link, suggesting that the lessons of Vietnam could be used in the Middle East. Despite the Olympic killings, he said, both Israel and the Arab states still had an interest in negotiating a settlement rather than continuing their conflict. Peace was inevitable, Smith said. "The retreat from violence may be slow, but in the end, sheer weariness with a crisis that has long outlasted any national interest is going to prevail in the Middle East – as it will in Vietnam."[33] Senator George McGovern, the Democratic nominee for president, also drew the comparison, speaking at a campaign rally in Los Angeles. His message was apparently simple: "Stop the killing!" he said. "Stop the killing everywhere around the world!" But in fact, the politics of the Vietnam connection were quite politically charged. Some people remained skeptical of the implicit moral equivalence suggested in that formulation, and the next day, at another meeting with a group of rabbis, one rabbi asked McGovern if he really meant to imply that US pilots in Vietnam could be compared to Arab terrorists. No, McGovern replied, they were on different moral levels. Still, he insisted, killing was killing, and he expressed his "own horror and indignation at the killing that is taking place . . . in Vietnam."[34]

These comments built upon an interpretation of the lessons of the war that had, by the early 1970s, become the dominant one among liberals and some moderates. The quagmire in Vietnam, they argued, was an indication of the changing nature of world power. The United States still relied too heavily on force in situations where political, economic, or diplomatic solutions were more likely to be effective.[35] This "global managerialist" model was certainly committed to maintaining the power and influence of the United States, and to pursuing what its adherents considered to be US economic and political interests. Its proponents insisted, however, that the United States must come to terms with the political realities of a multipolar world, one in which diplomacy and negotiation, rather than military power, should be the key to maintaining US interests.

But just as the debate over Vietnam was far from settled, the response to Munich was also quite divided. Conservatives had a different take than liberals, and mainstream reactions were ambivalent and inconsistent. Even as some observers suggested that the solution to excessive violence was negotiation, others anticipated and supported an Israeli counterattack. When, in response to the Olympic killings, Israeli war planes bombed ten villages in Lebanon and Syria that Israel claimed were guerrilla strongholds, leaving scores of people dead, *CBS Evening News* rather smugly reported the words of one senior Israeli official: "I hope they got the message." Editorialists generally announced themselves able to "understand" and "sympathize" with the Israeli actions, even as they worried that instability and violence in the Middle East would increase.[36]

The instability and violence that did in fact follow were widely reported: the 1973 Arab-Israeli war; the outbreak of civil war in Lebanon; and several major terrorist attacks, in Israel and elsewhere, in 1974 and 1975, including an attack on Israeli schoolchildren at Maalot and the taking hostage of several OPEC oil ministers in Vienna.

Then in June 1976, four hijackers claiming to be affiliated with the Popular Front for the Liberation of Palestine (PFLP) began what would arguably become the most famous incident of terrorism in a decade obsessed

with terrorism. The hijackers, who included two West German radicals and at least one South American, plus several Palestinians, took over an Air France flight from Tel Aviv and forced it to fly to Entebbe, Uganda. There, with the apparent collusion of Ugandan president Idi Amin, the hijackers moved 259 hostages (including the crew) to an old unused terminal at the Entebbe airport, from where they began negotiations, demanding that Israel and several other states release Palestinian or pro-Palestinian prisoners held in their jails.

By 1976, hijacking had already become a dominant international concern. Since 1968, a total of twenty-nine hijackings had been staged by Palestinian or pro-Palestinian groups, while other groups, including several in Latin America as well as the Symbionese Liberation Army (SLA) and the Weathermen in the United States, had carried out kidnappings or assassinations. For many observers, however, there was a particularly close association between Palestinians and terrorism not only because of Munich but also as a result of a widely reported series of hijackings and airport killings in the early 1970s. Perhaps the most infamous of these was Skyjack Sunday in 1970. In one day, the PFLP commandeered three different international flights and forced them to land in Jordan (a fourth attempt failed). Three days later, yet another flight was hijacked. Nearly 450 passengers were held hostage for six days; eventually, all were released.[37]

Realizing that the Palestinian case was damaged by the furious public response to these events, the main faction of the PLO, Arafat's Al Fatah, had pledged after Munich to end all guerrilla or terrorist activity outside of Israel and the occupied territories. The initial goal of the violence had been to bring attention to the Palestinian cause as an independent issue in the Arab-Israeli conflict. After the defeat of the Arab armies in 1967, Palestinians had begun to take leadership in their own movement, and the PLO developed from a front organization controlled by Arab states into a genuinely autonomous Palestinian umbrella. In the wake of the 1967 war and the Israeli occupation of the West Bank and Gaza, and in the context of the appropriation of their land and the ongoing military and political oppression in the occupied territories, many Palestinians believed that violence against Israeli and other civilians was justified. However, the goal of gaining world attention had also included the hope of gaining world sympathy; that hope had been severely undermined by the strong moral condemnation of terrorism in the United States and Europe. Still, the disavowal of international terrorism by major Palestinian organizations did not protect them from blame when smaller factions, such as the PFLP, took matters into their own hands; for those who paid little attention to the political differences among Palestinians (and this included almost everyone in the United States), the distinctions were unintelligible.[38]

Shortly after the PFLP-allied hijackers brought their hostages to Entebbe in late June 1976, the Israelis began planning a secret rescue operation. They were faced with a delicate diplomatic situation, however, since in any such rescue attempt, French or American citizens could possibly be killed. Then, over the course of the week in Uganda, the hijackers inadvertently opened the way for unilateral Israeli action by releasing all the hostages except for the 104 Israeli citizens. Just after midnight on July 4, 1976, Israeli commandos flew the long flight to Uganda and surprised the guerrillas and the Ugandan military. They attacked, killing all the hijackers and loading the hostages into planes bound for Israel. During the raid, which lasted about ninety minutes, three hostages and one Israeli soldier were killed. The Israeli soldier who died, the ground commander of the strike forces, was a young lieutenant colonel named Jonathan Netanyahu. He immediately became a national hero. His brother, then living in the United States with his parents, moved back to Israel shortly thereafter. There, the future prime minister Benjamin Netanyahu's first major public role in Israeli life was that of brother to a national martyr.[39]

Immediately, Israelis poured nearly $3 million in unsolicited contributions into a voluntary fund for the Ministry of Defense, which had recently faced budget cuts. The US news media reported with a sense of awe the unrestrained enthusiasm of Israelis for their military. "Aircraft flew over Jerusalem," *Newsweek* enthused, "skywriting, 'All our respect to Zahal' – the Hebrew acronym for Israeli Defense Forces."[40]

The significance of this support could not have failed to register in a nation that had just watched the disastrous final pullout of American troops in Vietnam the year before. As the North Vietnamese had marched into Saigon, US officials fled, while desperate Vietnamese allies tried to fight their way onto the helicopters. By 1976, the public image of the US military was quite low, and the assessment of Vietnam as a misguided intervention and an unwinnable war was commonplace. In contrast, American observers were riveted by the Israeli raid, and almost as enthusiastic as the Israelis themselves. Newspapers and journalists from across the political spectrum – from the *Nation* to the *National Review* – expressed their support.[41] The US ambassador to the United Nation, William Scranton, defended Israel's

action against criticisms that Israel had violated Uganda's territorial integrity: "Under such circumstances," he said, "the government of Israel invoked [*sic*] one of the most remarkable rescue missions in history, a combination of guts and brains that has seldom if ever been surpassed. It electrified millions everywhere and I confess I was one of them."[42] Secretary of State Kissinger was, simply, "immensely pleased."[43]

In fact, given the coincidence of the date (the Fourth of July, on the American Bicentennial), neither public officials nor journalists were above making grandiose statements implying that the Israelis and the hijackers had orchestrated their crisis with the United States in mind. As one State Department official effused, "The Israelis gave us a very special birthday present this July 4th."[44] Another observer, flush with a vicarious victory, indulged in biblical rhetoric, saying that the Israelis had given a gift to all the world for the US Bicentennial. That gift, he said, was "the Eleventh Commandment. thou shalt not bow down to terrorism."[45]

[. . .]

In the United States, as in Israel, the Entebbe hijacking was understood as a criminal action inflicted on the innocent. The Palestinian hijackers and their allies likely had a different view, seeing themselves as guerrilla warriors fighting a war on international territory, with civilians less as targets than as weapons. But American responses to Palestinian actions had hardened considerably since Munich. When the eleven athletes were murdered at the Olympics, it led to a surprising number of calls for Israel and the Palestinians to negotiate an end to their ongoing conflict. Four years later, when scores of people were taken hostage, but no one killed (until the rescue raid), links to the larger political conflict were all but invisible.

American interest in the rescue was framed partly as human drama, but also as a discussion of the issue of will. "Once again, and most strikingly," editorialized the *National Review*," the Entebbe operation showed that in political and military matters, *will* is the decisive factor."[46] As with the framers of National Security Council document 68 in 1950, who had insisted that the cultivation of will was necessary if the United States was going to challenge the "perversions" of the Soviet Union and establish postwar American hegemony, the question of American will was once again paramount. Israel's relative strength of will was taken as the point of contrast, as American observers quickly constructed the lessons of

Entebbe for the United States, with US failures in Vietnam as the implicit backdrop. Right after the raid, the military-oriented *Aviation Week and Space Technology* suggested that, while it would not always be possible to duplicate the circumstances of Entebbe, the basic formula – "an uncompromising attack on the international outlaws, wherever they find sanctuary, delivered with the best technical means available" – should become policy.[47] And not only conservatives made the point. Walter Mondale, accepting his nomination for vice president at the Democratic National Convention in August, got one of "the biggest roars of applause" of the five-day event when he said, defiantly, "We reject . . . the idea that this nation must sit by passively while terrorists maim and murder innocent men, women, and children."[48]

Despite all the talk about will, however, Entebbe was important to Americans less because the Israelis had exhibited will than because they had won. At Maalot in 1974, the Israelis had shown great force of will by sending in commandos to rescue a group of schoolchildren held hostage, but most of the children were killed in the rescue attempt, and Maalot, despite its iconographic status in Israeli national mythology, was not widely discussed in the United States.[49] Similarly, the US rescue of hostages on the *Mayaguez* in 1975 (in which forty-one Marines died trying to rescue thirty-nine crewmen of a ship seized by the Cambodians) did not evoke nearly as much enthusiasm, precisely because, despite an extraordinary display of the will to fight, the Marines had not managed a clear-cut victory.[50] *U.S. News & World Report* made this clear when it enriched its coverage of Entebbe with a sidebar on the failed US rescue mission into a North Vietnam prison camp in 1970.[51]

In fact, the implicit and explicit comparisons of Entebbe with Vietnam enabled the reinterpretation of the Vietnam War being mounted by conservative intellectuals, who in the mid-1970s had begun to promote the idea of a "Vietnam Syndrome." The concept reiterated an older interpretation of the war, which insisted that the United States could have won in Vietnam with sufficient application of military power. But it was also a claim about the war's legacy: in the wake of its failure to use force properly, the nation was afflicted with a profound failure of nerve. Against those who argued that realism required the United States to recognize a multipolar world, conservatives insisted that realism required a different calculation. The conservative academic theorist Jeane Kirkpatrick (who would go on to become the US ambassador to the United Nations in the first Reagan administration) summarized this view in a 1977 interview:

"We are daily surrounded by assertions that force plays no role in the world. Unfortunately it does, in most aspects of society, especially in international relations. Therefore a culture of appeasement which finds reason not only against the use of force but denies its place in the world is a profoundly mistaken culture – mistaken in the nature of reality."[52] In the later 1970s, this interpretation of reality increasingly began to take on the mantle of "common sense." After Entebbe, it did not have to build an argument from scratch; conservatives could – and often did – simply gesture toward the example of Israel. For those who diagnosed the Vietnam Syndrome, Entebbe was a clear example of the positive and successful use of force. Enthusiasts took Israel as a model for American action; they focused on the importance of Israel as both a moral exemplar and an admired military power. Indeed, it was the harnessing of moral discourse *to* military power – in a period in which both were undergoing radical critiques – that made the combination so potent. After Entebbe, and after Saigon, Israel became a prosthetic for Americans; the "long arm" of Israeli vengeance extended the body of an American nation no longer sure of its own reach.

America's Israel

In May 1979, Kevin Phillips, a leading conservative intellectual who had worked for Richard Nixon, published a widely cited article on the emerging phenomenon of neoconservatism. In his assessment of the state of conservative politics in the late 1970s, Phillips argued that, despite the media attention they had received, neoconservatives would never manage to achieve real political power. The neoconservative movement, as he defined it, was made up of well-known intellectuals and activists, including Irving Kristol, Daniel Patrick Moynihan, and Norman Podhoretz. He described this group as "distressed ex-liberal Democrats" who had been disenchanted with McGovern in 1972 and who needed a banner to rally around. Several elements, Phillips said, made this specific strain of conservatism "a nonstarter in North Carolina or South Boston," including the "New York city parochialism" and the "intellectualism" of its leaders. In addition, Phillips argued – with more than a suggestion of anti-Semitism – that necoconservatism had "disproportionately Jewish antecedents" and thus focused too strongly on Israel. While he disagreed with those who had suggested that neoconservatism's origins were *primarily* with Jews who had become hawks on issues of Israeli security, Phillips argued that "necoconservatism's strong preoccupation with Israel does suggest a genesis and a partial *raison d'être* not deeply shared by the country as a whole."[53]

This provocative and impressively misguided assessment appeared about eighteen months before the 1980 elections that swept Ronald Reagan to power on a landslide, ushering in a conservative resurgence that fundamentally reshaped the American political landscape. After 1980, neoconservatives *were* influential – active in the Reagan administration, cited in the press, interviewed on television, and consulted for their policy views. Despite what Phillips had said, "real political power" was theirs indeed. Phillips had believed that a concern with Israel was "not deeply shared," outside neoconservative circles, and thus would marginalize the conservative movement. He imagined a focus on Israel as a rather esoteric foreign policy investment, derived from special interest group politics and based on ties essentially ethnic or religious – something akin, perhaps, to Irish American support for the Irish Republican Army. Ten or twelve years earlier, he might have been right, but by 1979, something fundamental had changed in non-Jewish Americans' perceptions of Israel.

The same month that Phillips published his article, Jerry Falwell, working with several other activists of the New Right (including Paul Weyrich, who had founded the Heritage Foundation), announced that he and his colleagues had begun a new organization, the Moral Majority. They were not simply a religious (Christian) organization, Falwell said, but instead were willing to work with anyone "who shared our views on the family and abortion, strong national defense, and Israel." Shortly thereafter, Falwell issued the Moral Majority's platform statement, which listed ten tenets of the new organization. Number 6 read: "We support the state of Israel and the Jewish people everywhere. . . ."[54] As evangelicals and fundamentalists organized themselves, they surprised a great many people in the conservative camp who, like Phillips, had paid little attention to evangelical theology and thus never would have believed that Israel would have mattered in "North Carolina" or in Falwell's Virginia. Like so many others, Phillips did not see how the issue of US support for Israel, far from being an obstacle, helped to secure the conservative coalition that came together to elect Reagan in 1980.

[. . .]

While the question of whether it was the evangelical vote that won the election for Reagan has been hotly debated by scholars and political activists alike, there is little question that Israel was a key issue for the conservative Christians who were involved in the organizing. Thus it was perhaps a case of preaching to the choir when, in early 1981, some prominent leaders of the Christian Right sent a telegram to President Reagan after he took office: "We are concerned about morality and reaffirmation of principles of faith," they wrote, "not only on the domestic American scene but also in terms of our international affairs. From our religious, moral, and strategic perspective, Israel supremely represents our values and hopes for security and peace in the Middle East."[55]

The importance of Israel as an issue in the 1980 elections has often been overlooked. Many evangelical Christians had been educated in detail about the Middle East over the previous decade, and by the year of Reagan's election they shared with many American Jews, and not just conservative Jews, a commitment to supporting Israel both politically and militarily. Of course Israel was not by far the only issue tying conservative factions together; among other things, they also shared a dislike of Carter and of communism. But Israel certainly was one issue, and one that far too often has been ignored or dismissed.

Israel also played another role in the rise of a widespread conservative political culture in the late 1970s. For many people, Israel was less the recipient of profound personal allegiance than it was an icon of positive militarism. For the conservative intellectuals who diagnosed the Vietnam Syndrome, Israel was one example of the positive use of force. In addition, Israel emerged as a strategic asset for the United States, especially after its victory in the 1973 war. A new generation of defense planners in the Pentagon argued that Israel could serve American interests in the Middle East precisely because it had the strongest military in the region and could serve effectively to back US political and military goals. After 1973, every branch of the military was involved in strengthening strategic ties, by exchanging military and intelligence information. Journalist Wolf Blitzer has argued that these strategic ties also played a role in the dramatic rise of US military and economic aid to Israel in this period: "If Israel were to be demonstrated to provide a useful military and strategic service to the United States, . . . the aid becomes justified on the basis of self-interest as well as national morality."[56] As a strategic asset, Israel could support an active, even aggressive, US posture in the Middle East.

Beyond (and connecting to) these developing policy interests, there lay the more general public enthusiasm for Israel that crystallized after Entebbe. This enthusiasm involved a kind of appropriation: Israel was a model of tough, effective military power used in a just war against terrorism. (Christian evangelicals told the story of Israel as the protagonist in another just war, that of Armageddon.) The fact that Israel was seen as fighting the good fight and doing it well – made it an icon of all that the Vietnam War was not for Americans. As media and popular culture in the United States focused more on Israel in the 1970s, the image that emerged became implicated in the rethinking of Vietnam that was also a significant component of the conservative resurgence.

[. . .]

This transformation was the result of an unplanned, uncoordinated, yet quite powerful conjuncture of diverse interests and images. What is perhaps most striking about this history is the remarkable differences in the institutions and practices that constituted it. American Jews, evangelical Christians, military policymakers, and traditional conservative intellectuals all developed their interests in Israel and its military for different reasons, and they did so from diverse sociopolitical locations, with different access to cultural capital, and with varying levels of self-consciousness. The increased identification with Israel that many American Jews felt after 1967 did not immediately seem to map with the evangelical belief that Israel was at the heart of Armageddon prophecy. And prophecy interest overlapped with – but was far from identical to – the mainstream media investments in Israel as the answer to Vietnam. What emerged at these intersections was an increased US investment in an image of a militarized Israel, one that represented revitalized masculinity and restored national pride. In the context of the decade's debate about global managerialist versus conservative militarist models of US world "leadership," Israel's image served to strengthen right-wing views, though the conservative argument would not achieve full hegemony until after the Iran hostage crisis in 1979–80. To tell the history of this transformation, then, is to find the unexpected points of convergence – the overlap and reinforcement that transformed ideologically charged narratives into the "common sense" of an era.

Notes

1 "The Home-Front War," *Newsweek*, May 8, 1967, 31–6, quote on 36.

2 Paul Boyer et al., *Enduring Vision*, 987. See also Ronald Spector; *After Tet*.

3 Hendrik Hertzberg, "Why the War Was Immoral."

4 "Foreign Relations," *Time*, June 16, 1967, 15.

5 "Middle East: The Scent of War," *Newsweek*, June 5, 1967, 47; "Intermission: 'Too Late and Too Early,'" *Newsweek*, June 12, 1967, 39.

6 "The Quickest War," *Time*, June 16, 1967, 22; "The Three-Day Blitz from Gaza to Suez," *U.S. News and World Report*, June 19, 1967, 33; "Terrible Swift Sword," *Newsweek*, June 19, 1967, 24. See also "U.S. Believes Israel Can Hold Its Own," *Chicago Tribune*, June 6, 1967, sec. 1:8.

7 "The People," *Time*, June 16, 1967, 18; Joseph Zullo, "Call March Urging U.S. to Back Israel," *Chicago Tribune*, June 6, 1967, sec. 1:7.

8 Russell Baker, "Needed: Agency to Allocate Wars," *Chicago Tribune*, June, 1, 1967, sec. 1:10; Edward Tivnan, *The Lobby*, 69.

9 "The Three-Day Blitz from Gaza to Suez," *U.S. News and World Report*, June 19, 1967, 33.

10 Hal Lindsey, *Late Great Planet Earth*. All subsequent page references are in parenthesises in the text. Ten million copies reported sold: Edwin Mc-Dowell. "Publishers: A matter of Faith," *New York Times Book Review*, April 6, 1980, 18. Best-seller of the decade: Mark Silk, "Religious Books: Seven That Made a Difference," *New York Times Book Review*, March 30, 1976, 21. William Martin also repeats this claim, without attribution, in *With God on Our Side*. Later sales: Leo Ribuffo. "God and Contemporary Politics"; Paul Boyer, *When Time Shall Be No More*, 6.

11 Paul Boyer, *When Time Shall Be No More*, 126–7.

12 Dwight Wilson, "Armageddon Now!" quoted in Paul Boyer, *When Time Shall Be No More*, 2.

13 Ray Walters, "Paperback Talk," *New York Times Book Review*, April 6, 1980. Some of the publishing history from jacket and inside cover of Zondervan edition thirteenth printing, August 1971. (In 1988, Zondervan was acquired by Harper and Row, later to become HarperCollins, and *LGPE* was reissued in 1990 once again under the Zondervan imprint.)

14 McDowell, "Publishers: A Matter of Faith," Walters, "Paperback Talk." 45–6.

15 Most histories of the fundamentalist and evangelical movements address this long retreat from politics. See, for example, James Reichley, "The Evangelical and Fundamentalist Revolt."

16 Nancy Ammerman, "North American Protestant Fundamentalism," 95–7; Robert Liebman, "Making of the New Christian Right," 230; Martin, *With God on Our Side*, 100–43.

17 Anne Loveland, *American Evangelicals and the U.S. Military*, 122–66.

18 Hertzel Fishman, *American Protestantism and a Jewish State*, 83–122. 140–50.

19 "Could the Rapture Be Today?" *Moody Monthly*, May 1960, quoted in Paul Boyer, *When Time Shall Be No More*, 187.

20 Grace Halsell, *Prophecy and Politics*, 72–3; Merrill Simon, *Jerry Falwell and the Jews*, 57–100, esp. 61–5.

21 *His Land*, videocassette; Paul Boyer, *When Time Shall Be No More*, 206.

22 See also John F. Walvoord, "Future of Israel," 332; and Lindsey, *Late Great Planet Earth*, 131.

23 Charles Strozier, *Apocalypse*, 204.

24 Martin, *With God on Our Side* 215.

25 Halsell, *Prophecy and Politics*, 122, Wolf Blitzer, *From Washington to Jerusalem*, 198.

26 The description of these events is drawn from several sources: from contemporary newspaper and television accounts, particularly ABC and CBS evening coverage September 6–9, 1972, as well as Serge Groussard, *Blood of Israel*.

27 Marc Gunther, *House that Roone Built*, 19.

28 "Honor and Death at the Olympics," *Time*, September 18, 1972, 28.

29 For example, "A Father Three Weeks, He's Slain," *Atlanta Constitution*, September 6, 1972, A1; "Israel's Dead Were the Country's Hope," *Time*, September 18, 1972, 26, "Israeli Team Had Eighteen Athletes and Coaches," *New York Times*, September 6, 192, A19.

30 Shana Alexander, "Blood on the Playground," *Newsweek*, September 18, 1972, 35.

31 On May 8, Palestinian hijackers had commandeered a plane to Israel's Lod airport in Tel Aviv. They were eventually overtaken by Israeli soldiers disguised as mechanics; two were killed and two were captured. On May 30, three members of the Japanese guerilla organization, the Red Army, armed with machine guns and grenades, had massacred twenty-eight and injured seventy-two when they opened fire at the Tel Aviv airport.

32 Marc Gunther, *House That Roone Built*, 8–11.

33 Howard K. Smith commentary, *ABC News*, September 6, 1972.

34 *ABC News*, September 6, 1972; "McGovern Blames Egypt, Lebanon," *Atlanta Constitution*, September 7, 1972, Azo. Others who drew the connection between Munich and Vietnam included Stephen Rosenfeld. "Terror as a Tactic of Many Aspects," *New York Times*, September 8, 1972, Azz; Nicholas von Hoffman, "Munich: A History of Terror Written in Blood," *Washington Post*, September 8, 1972, B1; David Broder, "Munich and Vietnam," *Washington Post*, September 10, 1972–276.

35 Jerry Sanders makes this argument in *Peddlers of Crisis*, 191–276.

36 *CBS Evening News*, September 8, 1972; "Israeli Retaliation," *Washington Post*, September 12, 1972, A20; "Retribution and Justice," *New York Times*, September 11, 1972, 30; "'Eliminate This Scourge': Israel Begins Drive against Terrorism," *Atlanta Constitution*, September 11, 1972, B5. William Raspberry criticized the Israeli raid from a liberal perspective, "Arab-Israel Grievance," *Washington Post*, September 13, 1972, A15. The editors of the *National Review* criticized it from the Right, "Political Olympics," September 29, 1972, 1047–8.

37 For summaries of these events, see Steve Posner, *Israel Undercover*; Edgar O'Ballance, *Language of Violence*; and Michael Bar-zohar and Eitan Haber, *Quest for the Red Prince*. Some numbers also from Terrance Smith, "With Life at Stake, How Can Terrorists Be Dealt With?" *New York Times*, July 11, 1976, Week in Review, 1.

38 On the PLO in this period, see Manuel Hassassian, "Policy and Attitude Changes in the PLO"; Shaul Mishal, *PLO under Arafat*, 15–23, 36–48; and Baruch Kimmerling and Joel S. Migdal, *Palestinians*, 220–5. Claire Sterling's right-wing popular book *The Terror Network* includes a summary of Palestinian actions in Europe in the early 1970s (113–30).

39 O'Ballance, *Language of Violence*, 239–58. See also "Raiders Free 106 Hostages," *Atlanta Journal-Constitution*, July 4, 1976, A1; Drama in Hijacking of Jet to Uganda," *New York Times*, July 1, 1976, 1.

40 "Hijacking Rescue Lifts Israeli Spirit," *New York Times*, July 7, 1976, 1; The Fallout from Entebbe," *Newsweek*, July 19, 1976, 41; quote from "How the Israelis Pulled It Off," *Newsweek*, July 19, 1976, 46.

41 "Israel's Skill and Daring," *Nation*, July 17, 1976, 37; James Burnham, "Reflection on Entebbe," *National Review*, August 6, 1976, 834. Similarly, support was expressed by the African American paper the *New York Amsterdam News* ("A Right to Be Wrong," July 10, 1976, A–4); and by the conservative *U.S. News and World Report* ("'Israeli Raid in Uganda Was Justified'; Interview with Adrian Fisher," July 9, 1976, 30).

42 "Rescue by Israel Acclaimed by US at Debate in UN," *New York Times*, July 13, 1976; also "Vindication for the Israelis," *Time*, July 26, 1976, 39.

43 *CBS Evening News*, July 7, 1976, Marvin Kalb reporting.

44 *CBS Evening News*, July 5, 1976, Marvin Kalb reporting.

45 "Israel Rescue Brings Tributes Tears of Joy," *New York Times*, July 5, 1976, 2.

46 Burnham, "Reflections on Entebbe," 834.

47 "Israel Points the Way," *Aviation Week and Space Technology*, July 12, 1976, 7. And the *Atlanta Journal-Constitution* editorialized: "Israel's flagrant violation of Uganda's sovereignty was a deeply satisfying performance for all of us who still hope that the nice guys of this world do not necessarily always finish last." July, 7, 1976, A4.

48 Tom Wicket, "Talking Tough on Terrorism," *New York Times*, July 20, 1976, editorial page, 31.

49 The guerrillas captured eighty-five students; in the rescue attempt, twenty-six students were killed, and more than sixty wounded, *New York Times*, May 15, 1974, May 16, 1974.

50 The Mayaguez incident is discussed briefly by David C. Martin and John Wolcott, *Best Laid Plans*, 36.

51 "When U.S. Rescue Mission Fizzled," *U.S. News and World Report*, July 19, 1976, 32.

52 Noted in Sanders, *Peddlers of Crisis*, 162.

53 Kevin Phillips, "The Hype That Roared," 55. On the rise of the New Right, see Michael Kazin, *The Populist Persuasion*, 221–60.

54 David Snowball, *Rhetoric of the Moral Majority*, 16; on the multiple origin stories of the organization, see 50–3. See also Reichley, "Evangelical and Fundamentalist Revolt."

55 Blitzer, *Between Washington and Jerusalem*, 193. On Reagan, see Paul Boyer, ed., *Reagan as President*, and Robert Dallek, *Ronald Reagan*.

56 Ibid., 73. Blitzer was the Washington correspondent for the *Jerusalem Post* for fifteen years starting in the mid–1970s. He joined CNN in 1990.

References

Ammerman, Nancy. "North American Protestant Fundamentalism." In *Media, Culture, and the Religious Right*, edited by Linda Kintz and Julia Lesage, 55–114.

Bar-Zohar, Michael, and Eitan Haber. *The Quest for the Red Prince*. New York: William Morrow, 1983.

Blitzer, Wolf. *Between Washington and Jerusalem: A Reporter's Notebook*. New York: Oxford University Press, 1985.

Boyer, Paul. *When Time Shall Be No More: Prophecy Belief in Modern American Culture*. Cambridge, Mass.: Harvard University Press, 1992.

———, ed. *Reagan as President: Contemporary Views of the Man, His Politics, and His Policies*. New York: Ivan R. Dee, 1992.

Boyer, Paul, et al. *The Enduring Vision: A History of the American People*. Vol. 2. New York: Heath, 1996.

Dallek, Robert. *Ronald Reagan: The Politics of Symbolism*. Cambridge, Mass.: Harvard University Press, 1999.

Fishman, Hertzel. *American Protestantism and a Jewish State*. Detroit: Wayne State University Press, 1973.

Groussard, Serge. *The Blood of Israel: The Massacre of the Israeli Athletes, the Olympics, 1972*. New York: William Morrow, 1975.

Gunther, Marc. *The House That Roone Built: The Inside Story of ABC News*. Boston: Little, Brown, 1994.

Halsell, Grace. *Prophecy and Politics: Militant Evangelists on the Road to Nuclear War*. Westport, Conn.: Lawrence Hill, 1986.

Hassassian, Manuel S. "Policy and Attitude Changes in the Palestine Liberation Organization, 1965–1994: A Democracy in the Making." In *The PLO and Israel: From Armed Conflict to Political Solution, 1964–1994*, edited by Avraham Sela and Moshe Ma'oz, 73–96. New York: St. Martin's Press, 1997.

Henry, Carl F., ed. *Prophecy in the Making*. Carol Stream, Ill.: Creation House, 1971.

Herzberg, Hendrik. "Why the War Was Immoral." In *Vietnam: Ten Years After*, edited by Robert E. Long, 113–19. New York: H. W. Wilson, 1986.

Kazin, Michael. *The Populist Persuasion: An American History*. Ithaca: Cornell University Press, 1995.

Kimmerling, Baruch, and Joel S. Migdal. *Palestinians: The Making of a People*. New York: Free Press, 1993.

Liebman, Robert. "Making of the New Christian Right." In *The New Christian Right: Mobilization and Legitimization*, edited by Robert Liebman and Robert Wuthnow.

Lindsey, Hal, with C. C. Carlson. *The Late Great Planet Earth*. Grand Rapids, Mich.: Zondervan, 1970.

Loveland, Anne. *American Evangelicals and the U.S. Military, 1942–1993*. Baton Rouge: Louisiana State University Press, 1996.

Martin, David C., and John Walcott. *Best Laid Plans: The Inside Story of America's War against Terrorism*. New York: Harper and Row, 1988.

Martin, William. "Waiting for the End." *Atlantic Monthly*, June 1982, 31–37.

———. *With God on Our Side: The Rise of the Religious Right in America*. New York: Broadway Books, 1996.

Mishal, Shaul. *The PLO under Arafat: Between Gun and Olive Branch*. New Haven, Conn.: Yale University Press, 1986.

Neuhaus, Richard, and Michael Cromartie, eds. *Piety and Politics: Evangelicals and Fundamentalists Confront the World*. Washington, DC: Ethics and Public Policy Center, 1987.

O'Ballance, Edgar. *Language of Violence: The Blood Politics of Terrorism*. Novato, Calif.: Presidio, 1979.

Phillips, Kevin. "The Hype That Roared." *Politics Today*, May/June 1979, 54–58.

Posner, Steve. *Israel Undercover: Secret Warfare and Hidden Diplomacy in the Middle East*. Syracuse, NY: Syracuse University Press, 1987.

Reichley, James. "The Evangelical and Fundamentalist Revolt." In *Piety and Politics: Evangelicals and Fundamentalists Confront the World*, edited by Richard Neuhaus and Michael Cromartie, 69–97.

Ribuffo, Leo P. "God and Contemporary Politics." *Journal of American History 79* (March 1993): 1515ff.

Sanders, Jerry. *Peddlers of Crisis: The Committee on the Present Danger and the Politics of Containment*. Boston: South End Press, 1983.

Simon, Merrill. *Jerry Falwell and the Jews*. Middle Village, NY: Jonathan David, 1984.

Snowball, David. *Continuity and Change in the Rhetoric of the Moral Majority*. New York: Praeger, 1991.

Spector, Ronald. *After Tet: The Bloodiest Year in Vietnam*. New York: Free Press, 1993.

Strozier, Charles. *Apocalypse: On the Psychology of Fundamentalism in America*. Boston: Beacon Press, 1994.

Tivan, Edward. *The Lobby: Jewish Political Power and American Foreign Policy*. New York: Simon and Schuster, 1987.

Walvoord, John F. "The Future of Israel." In *Prophecy in the Making*, edited by Carl Henry, 327–43.

Getting Religion

Janet R. Jakobsen and Ann Pellegrini

We wonder about "religion" and what it might mean to "get religion" in any number of ways. We certainly (at one time in our lives, at least) got religion, and we sometimes wonder if the resistance on the part of some left intellectuals to getting religion isn't based on a desire to distance oneself from those early experiences of "getting it." We also wonder about religion in the ever popular "public sphere." Why, for example, do homosexuals "get it" so often – from religion, that is — but also the topic of this essay is to ask why do homosexuals "get it" – religion, that is – from that most secular of institutions, the Supreme Court? Why are the terms in which the Court establishes the regulation of sexuality so often religious, so that when it comes to homosexuals, at least, what the court seems to be handing out is not justice but religion? Finally, we also wonder about the implications of "getting it" for scholars of cultural studies or the intellectual left (a group within which we would include ourselves).[1] What would it mean if they/we did "get it"? This question is a complicated one (rather than simply referring to a lacuna in the scholarship that can be easily filled in). What the attempt to simply take up the study of religion fails to ask is, what does it mean to take on religion as an "object" of cultural study? This is not the same question as, "What is religion?"

In a footnote to the article in which Fredric Jameson refers to cultural studies as a "desire," he expresses a desire of his own, a desire for religion, for its analysis and apparently for its representation. He does so through the invocation of none other than Cornel West. Jameson writes, "But it is important to stress, as Cornel West does, that religion (and in particular fundamentalism) is a very large and basic component of American mass culture and in addition that

it is here decidedly underanalyzed and underrepresented" (1995, 295, n. 12). Fundamentalism here appears as the exemplary instance of American religion and in its parenthetical reference as that which is set off from the American public (and hence most in need of explanation by the scholar).[2] Because we're concerned that the contemporary focus on something called the "religious right" is not politically sufficient, we've wanted to question both the wish and the containment captured by the parenthetical bracketing of "fundamentalism": What does it leave in place? Unexamined? Unmarked? Thus, we turned not to religion per se and especially not to fundamentalism so-called, but rather to the secular (and in particular the liberal middle), and we "got religion."

We are arguing for the diacritical relation between the "religious" and the "secular." This suggestion – that the religious and the secular are mutually constituting, acquiring their definition and meaning in relation to each other – will not be very controversial.[3] However, we also contend that "religious/secular" is a distinction without a difference, or, to put it another way, a distinction that covers over the difference "Christian/non-Christian." But not because, or not simply because, in the American context (official claims to religious pluralism or Judaeo-Christian values notwithstanding) the religious and the Christian may be flashed as signs of one another.[4] But also because the secular as such is always already modeled in the particular image of the Christian, or at least of a particular strain of the Christian, reformed post-Enlightenment Protestantism. The difference "religious/secular" cannot simply be mapped onto the difference "Christian/non-Christian." As we will see, the secular sometimes changes places with reformed Protestantism.

Intervention 1

The reason the secularization story is crucial for our concerns here is that it is often told specifically in terms of "freedom," freedom from the church and freedom also in relation to the market, where, for example, John Guillory (1993) argues (and he's careful in his choice of language here) the market provided a site of interaction between producers and consumers that "felt like" freedom from ecclesiastical authority. The invention of the secular in relation to the religious is specifically about instituting the market (as freedom). Weber, however, in The Protestant Ethic and the Spirit of Capitalism, *tells a story that could line up with Guillory's, but that is different from the common progressive secularization story, by reminding us that Reformation preceded Enlightenment, instituting a form of rationalization that was to Weber decidedly irrational and yet extremely effective as a means of disciplining the body to work with and in the particular (ir)rationality of the market. This form of regulation, "this-worldly asceticism," takes place in order to demonstrate freedom in the other world of salvation, and it takes place as a discourse of "freedom" from the church. Thus, Weber is concerned that we recognize the specific and extensive disciplines that were instituted under the name of "freedom" from the church.*

> [I]t is necessary to note, what has often been forgotten, that the Reformation meant not the elimination of the Church's control over everyday life, but rather the substitution of a new form of control for the previous one. It meant the repudiation of a control which was very lax, at that time scarcely perceptible in practice and hardly more than formal, in favour of a regulation of the whole conduct which, penetrating to all departments of private and public life, was infinitely burdensome and earnestly enforced. (1930, 36)

These disciplines are those that Foucault has identified as peculiar to modernity and, thus, in these post-Foucauldian times we might call market freedom a technology of body regulation. It may "feel" like freedom, and it becomes so naturalized as part of the market that it becomes unnoticed, both as restraint and as specifically "reformed" Protestant.

Out of this "irrational" rationalization comes the rationality of the Enlightenment as secular, and the intertwining of the

secular and the religious is forgotten, but not lost, meaning that it can still be operative. The secular is even at its moment of institution not necessarily "free" from the religious. If the modern disciplines, or in Weber's terms, "regulations," of the body are the site of religious authority, or even more strongly in Weber's terms, of "church control," then the new(ly secular) state in enforcing body regulation is also maintaining religious authority. Body regulation is, thus, the site of connection between reformation in religion and the formation of the secular state. It is not a coincidence, then, that Chief Justice Warren Burger makes the following connections, "During the English Reformation when powers of the ecclesiastical courts were transferred to the King's Courts, the first English statute criminalizing sodomy was passed" (Hardwick 196–7). We'll come back to Burger's snapshot of the history of sodomy later.

As a way to expose how particular Christian claims undergird applications of the secular, we want to turn to two Supreme Court cases that involve the regulation of the body, *Bowers v. Hardwick* (1986) and *Romer v. Evans* (1996). It is important to recognize the Supreme Court as the idealized representation of secularism, the site of the separation of church and state, the site, indeed, whereby that separation is performatively produced.

Both *Hardwick* and *Romer* bear on the subject of homosexuality and, to the extent that heterosexuality is constituted in relation to homosexuality, bear also on the subject of heterosexuality. Of course, one important difference is that the privileged term, "heterosexuality," not unlike this other privileged term, "Christianity," works best when it does not proclaim itself too openly.[5]

Intervention 2

Thus, we hope to investigate two important points in looking at the Supreme Court as the site of secularism – 1) the moments at which religion makes an appearance at this most secular of sites; and 2) the ways in which even where it doesn't explicitly appear, but takes the form of (reformed) Protestant body regulation, it remains (shall we say) active.

Issued ten years apart, the dispensations in *Hardwick* and *Romer* could not be more different – or so it seems. *Hardwick* upheld the constitutionality of Georgia's sodomy statute as applied to "consensual homosexual sodomy" only, remanding the matter of heterosexual sodomy to a footnote. Writing for the majority, Justice

White pronounced the disavowal: "We express no opinion on the constitutionality of the Georgia statutes as applied to other acts of sodomy" (*Hardwick* 188n2). Coming immediately after he has just written, still in the same footnote, the words "consensual homosexual sodomy," we are left to fill in the blank for those other acts of sodomy Justice White will not or cannot utter in the open: heterosexual.

This silence was not an innocent one. A 1968 amendment to Georgia's sodomy statute made the prohibition on sodomy facially neutral for the first time: "A person commits the offense of sodomy when he performs or submits to any act involving the sex organs of one person and the mouth or anus of the other. . . ." (qtd. 188n1 [a]). The statute is an equal opportunity prohibition.

By contrast, *Romer* struck down Colorado's Amendment 2, deeming that law, which was passed by Colorado voters in 1992, an unconstitutional abridgment of equal protection. Though never enforced, Amendment 2 would have repealed local and statewide ordinances that prohibited discrimination on the basis of – and here we quote the all-bases-covered terms of Amendment 2 — "homosexual, lesbian or bisexual orientation, conduct, practices or relationships." Further, it would have prohibited the passage of any future such ordinances. Writing for the majority, and joined by Justices Ginsburg, Souter, O'Connor, Stevens, and Breyer, Justice Kennedy deftly rejected the ruse by which antidiscrimination ordinances and equal rights protections were recast as "special rights":

> We cannot accept the view that Amendment 2's prohibition on specific legal protections does no more than deprive homosexuals of special rights. To the contrary, the amendment imposes a special disability upon those persons alone. Homosexuals are forbidden the safeguards that others enjoy or may seek without constraint. . . . We find nothing special in the protections Amendment 2 withholds. These are protections taken for granted by most people either because they already have them or do not need them. (*Romer*, 1626–7)

Kennedy concluded his opinion by holding that "Amendment 2 classifies homosexuals not to further a proper legislative end but to make them unequal to *everyone else*" (emphasis added; 1629) – and everyone else he does not name, but we can infer, again, as heterosexual.

The majority opinion is thunderously silent on the case of *Hardwick*, which is nowhere mentioned in the ruling,

thus sustaining the state's ability to regulate bodies in their sexual acts.[6] This is a silence Scalia will exploit in his scathing dissent, to which Chief Justice Rehnquist and Justice Thomas signed their names. In that dissent, he points out the striking nonappearance of *Hardwick* and implicitly reconfirms the constitutionality of proscribing homosexual sodomy. He imputes homosexuality as a matter of conduct, and so reduces bodies to their sexual acts and discriminates which citizen bodies constitute the "public at large" (as he writes) and which do not.

Intervention 3

We want to look at the work that the "public at large" does for Scalia here, because it is precisely the construction of a supposedly secular and middle (not right-wing), in fact, "tolerant" place. To quote Scalia, the problem with homosexuals is that "quite understandably, they devote [their disproportionate] political power to achieving not merely a grudging social toleration, but full social acceptance, of homosexuality." Importantly, Scalia establishes the disproportionate nature of this power through a series of antisemitic images right out of the "Protocols of the Elders of Zion," effecting a substitution (in no way an innocent one and not a recent twinning) of homosexual for Jew. He writes, "Because those who engage in homosexual conduct tend to reside in disproportionate numbers in certain communities [spatial concentration], have high disposable income [concentration and accumulation of capital] and of course care about homosexual rights issues more than the public at large [exclusive or self-interested], they possess political power greater than their numbers [political will out of majority control]" (1634). Most obviously, this "public at large" is built through the assumption, or perhaps we should say supersession, of a Christianity both invoked and unnamed in Scalia's images. Just as importantly, what homosexuals should be allowed is the "toleration" so frequently offered by the liberal middle. This is not a right-wing point.

In fact, Scalia is concerned only for this middle and their "sexual mores," calling Amendment 2 "a modest attempt by seemingly tolerant Coloradans to preserve traditional sexual mores against the efforts of a politically powerful minority to revise those mores through law." This concern for "values" is part of the process of the invention of religion in relation to the secular at the turn to modernity.[7] Over the course of the development of modernity, reason is (re)invented in relation to religion to replace the God-term, and religion now operates within the "limits of reason alone." This ordering of the terms is not merely a reversal but a (re)invention of each term in relation to the other, a relation that is both oppositional and homologous. Even as reason is defined in contradistinction to religion, religion establishes the parameters to which reason must aspire. Reason was, and had to be, universal, in both its opposition and its homology with religion, while religion in its homology with reason was invented as the universal category underlying Christianity and itself based on an assent to a set of reasonable principles. Morality thus becomes the primary articulation of the religious in modernity, of religion as reason.

It is hard to resist the notion that the anti-Semitic recoding of homosexuality is where Scalia was heading all along. He asserts in the first line of his dissent: "The Court has mistaken a Kulturkampf for a fit of spite" (1629). Among other things, this suggests that the twinning of "the Jew" and "the homosexual" in Scalia's dissent is not an incidental feature of his logic, but one of its structuring conditions.

Scalia makes a case for the eminent reasonableness of anti-gay discrimination.[8] Against the majority's implicit appeals to an American tradition of tolerance, Scalia conserves the Americanness of opposition to homosexuality: "The Court's opinion contains grim, disapproving hints that Coloradans have been guilty of 'animus' or 'animosity' toward homosexuality, as though that has been established as Unamerican" (1633). Unlike the majority opinion, which skirts the sodomitical territory of *Bowers v. Hardwick*, Scalia draws on *Hardwick* to reassert while overriding a status/conduct distinction. He takes for granted "our moral heritage that one should not hate any human being or class of human beings" (1633).

Intervention 4

Thus, it is important to note that this entire discourse takes place under the terms of tolerance, not hate. The claiming of tolerances contributes to the construction of a "center" where people can experience themselves as "not hating anyone" and still vote for legislation that belies the proclamation.

"Our moral heritage" notwithstanding, Scalia goes on to list "certain conduct" one can reasonably consider "reprehensible": "murder, for example, or polygamy, or cruelty to animals," concluding that "one [that impersonal

disembodied one] could exhibit even 'animus' toward such conduct" (1633). And it is this and only this – "animus" – that he claims Amendment 2 does.[9]

This is a familiar story: Love the sinner but hate the sin.[10] If "love the sinner, hate the sin" smacks of Catholic theological dispositions, better to say it is catholic with a lowercase "c," in that it admits the universalizing move by which non-Christians might be invited to leave minority status behind and disappear into the majority's ranks. The bribe is that they acquiesce to the only barely suppressed Christian assumptions and norms that sustain by constituting the distinction (that isn't one) religious/secular.

Although *Romer* is certainly a victory for gay rights, it is a limited one. The majority's silence on the matter of *Hardwick* leaves the status/conduct distinction operational. Thus, the specific mode of the assertion of values through body regulation stands in that heavy silence.

Let's turn back to the moral arguments supplied by Justices White and Burger in *Hardwick* against any constitutional protection for consensual homosexual sodomy. We are interested in tracing their appeal to the "obviousness" of tradition, which, for White and Burger at least, requires no further argument. This is what Althusser might call the "obviousnesses [of] the obvious" ("Ideology," 171–2). In their race through Western history, both justices draw on the "ancient roots" (White's term) of proscriptions against homosexual sodomy, arguing on that basis for the continuing moral claims against such conduct. Thus, White moves from "ancient roots" to laws of the original thirteen states to there being "no cognizable roots in the language or design of the Constitution for homosexual sodomy as a fundamental liberty" (194). Against the backdrop of White's continuous history, to assert that "a right to engage in such conduct is deeply rooted in this Nation's history and tradition is, at best, facetious" (194).

Though White never names the particular moral values assumed by his interpretation of this "Nation's history and tradition," the continuous record he poses is one shaped by and through Christian theological responses to sodomy (though, unlike White, Christian theological treatments of sodomy are not unfazed by the spectre of heterosexual sodomy). However, if White will not fully name or cite the "notions of morality" that inform and shape the law (and that the dissenting justices actually call him to do), he yet thinks the moral claims of law a reason sufficient unto itself: "The law, however, is constantly based on notions of morality [*Read: religion*], and if all laws representing essentially moral choices are to be invalidated under the Due Process Clause, the courts will be very busy indeed" (196).

If Justice White is so fully under the thrall of the obvious that he does not stop to mention by name just whose "moral notions" and whose "essentially moral" choices the law represents and that he, in the name of the law, sustains, Justice Burger, in a concurring opinion, cuts to the chase. In his thumbnail sketch of sodomy and Western civilization, he writes:

> As the Court notes . . . the proscriptions against sodomy have very "ancient roots." Decisions of individuals relating to homosexual conduct have been subject to state intervention throughout the history of Western Civilization. Condemnation of those practices is firmly rooted in Judaeo-Christian moral and ethical standards. Homosexual sodomy was a capital crime under Roman law. (196–7)

Was it for this that ancient Greek and Latin texts have been canonized, have been deemed classics, so that we moderns may all the more thoroughly forget their very different moral compass and misrecognize the ancients for ourselves?

And on and on through the English Reformation and the first "secular" statute condemning sodomy until he approaches the Georgia Legislature's first enactment of a law against sodomy in 1816, a statute which, he writes, "has been continuously in force in one form or another since that time" (197). From here, for Burger, it is but a day to 1986 and the upholding of that statute. However, Burger's condensed history – "in one form or another" – writes over Georgia's 1968 revision of the sodomy law, which made the prohibition facially neutral and applied it equally to homosexual and heterosexual sodomy. This is a facial neutrality against which the majority turns the other cheek.

Despite Burger's invocation of "Judaeo-Christian moral and ethical standards," we should not mistake the hyphen for inclusion or some sign of religious pluralism. Rather, the hyphen condenses the story of Judaism's supersession by Christianity and passes off a wished-for assimilation of difference into the one as an instance of religious pluralism.

Intervention 5

Of course, Judaism is not silent on this question, and complex relations are invoked in the term "Judaeo-Christian," *but Burger is in fact stunningly silent on the issue of Jewish Law, citing a book entitled* Homosexuality and the Western Christian Tradition *as the source of the "ancient roots" of this "tradition." Thus, he implies (all too familiarly) that Judaism is simply the "ancient roots" of a dominant Christian "tradition."*

If to be "traditionally" American is to be Christian in a certain way, then non-Christians, or even those who are Christian in another way, will always be "minorities" that can only be "tolerated" within the "larger" American public. Moreover, members of "religious minorities" are American only insofar as they agree with dominant American, i.e., Christian, "values." So the points of similarity or overlap in values, not the differences, among traditions become the publicly acceptable articulation of all "religions." These claims also pose the secular as the site of the intersection between "religion" and "values" such that any alternative configurations of these relationships – values, for example, that are not necessarily "Christian" – are erased, thus allowing references to values that are effectively marked as religious and Christian without the need to name them directly as such. This move is at once universalizing and specifying, or more accurately it enacts the universalization of a specific set of values, such that all values that travel under other names can be conflated with Christian values or those that cannot be so condensed are simply placed outside the realm of recognizable values. They simply are not values. So, for example, Katie Cannon (1988) argues that Black womanist ethics, despite being in Cannon's case expressly theological, are often not recognized as moral, are labeled immoral or amoral, precisely because they are in resistance to capitalism, rather than enacting the dominant US Protestant ethic that supports capitalist endeavor. In other words, even Protestant Christian values, if not in line with the secular-market version of Christianity, are unrecognizable as values.

To be sure, the dissenting justices in *Hardwick* – Blackmun, Brennan, Marshall, and Stevens – explicitly criticize the sectarian claims of Burger. Offering a spirited defense of secular values, the values of the secular, Blackmun argues: "The legitimacy of secular legislation depends instead on whether the State can advance some justification for its law beyond its conformity to religious doctrine" (211). Along the way, however, Blackmun seems to draw the secular in religion's image and to redraw, this time with positive feeling, sexual values into religious values by imputing sexuality as one site for the expression of "man's spiritual nature, of his feelings and of his intellect." (207).

Intervention 6

Even as the religious once again reappears in the assertion of the secular, the particular means by which Blackmun makes this assertion, declaring the need of "secular law" for "some justification beyond its conformity to religious doctrine" (note: the conformity remains) is precisely the progress narrative of the Enlightenment in which reason both depends upon and supposedly moves beyond religion. This site of the true beyond, we have argued, is the site of the market-reformed-Protestantism. Secularization configured in this way is "progress" – the more secular, the more rational, the more enlightened/emancipatory/progressive.[11] We (left, progressive, cultural studies scholars) have all, over the last few decades, been well schooled in questions about the progress narrative of the Enlightenment, and yet it has also been extremely difficult to give up, particularly given that both the contemporary university and left (progressive?) social movements are in some sense products of this narrative. Moreover, there has been, at least from left/progressive sites, much less questioning of the secularization narrative, in part, because the secular is seen as a bulwark against the irrational regressive aspects of religion. When you're facing something depicted as "the Christian right" as the primary danger, secularism can look pretty good. So, part of our concern here is to question whether this depiction of the contemporary situation, a depiction that focuses on the right rather than, say, the middle, is the most politically useful. When "we" place ourselves on the side of reason, we must remember that so does the middle, Scalia's "public at large," which has at best "grudging social toleration" to offer, a toleration that is all the more insidious because it claims not to be the "hate" of the right wing. But in fact "tolerance" more effectively undergirds body regulation than does "hate."

"The Court has mistaken a Kulturkampf for a fit of spite."

Intervention 7

So, if the secular is not a safe space, free from religion, free from "getting it," what are, as a friend of ours once said, "nice post-Christian homosexual girls" like us supposed to do? To answer this question we must also ask: Why would cultural studies both desire a theory of religion and yet have trouble getting it? We read this refusal as not simply a knee-jerk reaction, but instead as something better termed symptomatic (and what else could desires relegated to footnotes be?). The persistence of this refusal despite admonitions like Jameson's indicates that there is something

more going on, that the refusal is somehow motivated, not just by prejudice (prejudging, knowing always already what one is going to find when one "studies" religion) but by something deeper. We would suggest that this something deeper is about the status of knowledge and "study," including cultural study, itself. The only means of getting a more complicated picture of what is happening in the contemporary practice and invocation of religion is to challenge the interwoven terms of the modernization and secularization story, but to do so is to challenge the very basis of knowledge production. Thus, the study of "religion," if undertaken in this complex manner, can tell us something about the current political situation and the role of body regulation, as we have suggested through our readings of the Supreme Court. But it also has broader implications that point toward the possibility of refiguring the relations of knowledge production, refiguring them not because religion is somehow different from reason, but because religion and reason participate in the same regime of knowledge and power. Thus, "getting religion" opens up a set of problems, not easily solved but important to name because of their wide-ranging implications for study, for the possibility of articulating values that are not (always already) circumscribed by the market, and for progressive social movement. Getting (or giving) the more complex story of "religion" offers an opening through the impasse sensed in a number of disciplines that without Enlightenment narratives values are simply unavailable, and the choices are to (re)turn to modern values out of necessity, turn to a politics of realism or ressentiment, or turn to a religion that supposedly counters modernity. Getting religion creates an opening not because somehow turning from reason to religion solves the problem, but because religion is the unnamed part of the story that sets up the impasse.

Our admonition that cultural studies scholars need to stop refusing to get religion (and note, we can only recommend this as a double negation: stop refusing) goes hand in hand with this other wish: That, where cultural studies and its practitioners are concerned, getting religion might itself take the form of a refusal, a refusal of the ways in which knowledge continues to be conducted and the ways in which particular constellations of knowledge/power continue to conduct us.

Notes

1 By "left intellectuals" we mean that loose concatenation of those who might identify their scholarship with Marxian

analysis and social movement, but also with those so-called "new" social movements – feminist, antiracist, queer, etc. – that have played a large role in post-war politics. These sites are also sometimes gathered under the rubric of "progressive" social movements, a name that we sometimes invoke because it can connect Marxist and new social movements more accurately than does the term "left"; and yet just what it might mean to name something "progressive" – given the tie between the progress and secularization narratives of the Enlightenment – is one of our central questions. Insofar as cultural studies can be said to have a politics and given its genealogy when traced to the Birmingham school, it can be seen as tied to this same loose concatenation. While our own political and intellectual commitments may be overlapping here and while "cultural studies" as a field may have emerged from the "culture and society" moment in which post-war Marxists tried to recognize the import of working-class cultural activity as well as social structure, we also recognize that not all those who currently take up studies of the cultural have such political ends in mind.

2   In one sense "fundamentalism" is a perfect container for this ambivalent desire because it allows for a focus on religion, but a religion that remains "other" to the scholar. We're concerned that invoking this container for the ambivalence feeds a focus on the "right" that is not politically effective.

3   This is an argument Janet E. Halley makes for the classifications "homosexual" and "heterosexual" ("Construction," 83). Her analysis of the classificatory scheme at work in *Hardwick* has been influential for the argument we are unfolding here.

4   Halley has suggested that the "homosexuality is like race" arguments made by some gay rights advocates have enabled, as if on the other side, the opponents of affirmative action to "flash homosexual and black as signs of one another," and so discredit both equal rights for homosexuals and civil rights for blacks and other racial minorities as "special rights" (English Institute Talk).

5   See Halley, "Construction"; Sedgwick, *Epistemology*; Halperin, *Saint Foucault*.

6   Halley suggests that the majority in *Romer* "could not have uttered this silence [around *Hardwick*] if they thought that the constitutionality of criminal statutes proscribing homosexual sodomy *a fortiori* produces the constitutionality of every species of anti-gay discrimination" ("Status/Conduct Distinction," 221).

7   For more on the "invention of religion" see Baird (forthcoming).

8   He then uses this distinction to differentiate between giving favored status to people who are homosexual (which he says Amendment 2 would still permit) and giving them this favored status because of homosexual "conduct." The people who are homosexual might be favored insofar as they also happen to be people who are "senior citizens or members of racial minorities" (1633).

Out of the list of attributes Amendment 2 named – "orientation, conduct, practices, and relationship" – Scalia has singled out conduct. He even seems to construe the political activity of "those who engage in homosexual conduct" as itself a form of "homosexual, lesbian [and] bisexual . . . conduct."

9   Is "animus" the "fit of spite" he says the majority has mistaken for a Kulturkampf? Consider the odd inversion and, then, substitutions of Scalia's rhetoric. We might have expected him to write that the Court has mistaken a fit of spite for a Kulturkampf, not the other way around. But not only does he deny that Amendment 2 represents "animus," but he also wants to shift the agents of Kulturkampf from the presumptively heterosexual electoral majority who approved Amendment 2 to homosexuals – and their allies on the Court. By Scalia's own reasoning, the Kulturkampf is one performed by homosexuals whose single-minded pursuit of homosexual rights does not stop at achieving "grudging social toleration," but aims at nothing short of "full social acceptance" (1634). The majority writing in *Romer* gets aligned with this homosexual "minority," which seeks to impose its will on the "public at large." Thus Scalia: "This court has no business imposing upon all Americans the resolution favored by the elite class from which the members of this institution are selected" (1634).

10   However, given all the work categorizing conduct can do to distinguish non-homosexuals from homosexuals, is homosexual conduct ever only a matter of acts? Isn't it also a way to constitute through silent exclusion a class of non-homosexuals, aka "heterosexuals"?

11   Religion here becomes configured as both irrational and regressive; thus, if religion "reappears," as theories of the contemporary "resurgence of religion" claim it has over the past few decades, this is a sign of regression.

References

Althusser, Louis. "Ideology and Ideological State Apparatuses." *Lenin and Philosophy and Other Essays by Louis Althusser.* Trans. Ben Brewster, 127–86. New York: Monthly Review Press, 1971.

Baird, Robert J. *Inventing Religion in the Western Imaginary* Princeton: Princeton University Press, forthcoming.

Cannon, Katie Geneva. *Black Womanist Ethics*. Atlanta: Scholars Press, 1988.

Guillory, John. *Cultural Capital: The Problem of Literary Canon Formation*. Chicago: University of Chicago Press, 1993.

Halley, Janet E. Paper presented at the English Institute, Harvard University, Cambridge, MA. September 27, 1997.

——. "The Construction of Heterosexuality." *Fear of a Queer Planet: Queer Politics and Social Theory*, ed. Michael Warner, 82–102. Minneapolis: University of Minnesota Press, 1993.

———. "The Status/Conduct Distinction in the 1993 Revisions to Military Anti-Gay Policy." *GLQ* 3:2–3: 159–252.

Halperin, David M. *Saint Foucault: Towards a Gay Hagiography*. Oxford: Oxford University Press, 1995.

Hardwick, Bowers v. 478 U.S. 186 (1986).

Jameson, Fredric. "On Cultural Studies." *The Identity in Question*, ed. John Rajchman, 251–95. New York: Routledge, 1995.

Romer, Evans v. 116 S. Ct. 1620 (1996).

Sedgwick, Eve Kosofsky. *Epistemology of the Closet*. Berkeley: University of California Press, 1990.

Weber, Max. *The Protestant Ethic and the Spirit of Capitalism*, trans. Talcott Parsons. New York: Scribners, 1930.

Part V

Performances and Practices

The reconfiguration of American Studies includes a de-ontologizing of the objects of cultural analysis. Rather than assuming that culture always exists as a set of *things*, it now appears as an interweaving flow of shifting practices and relations. Cultural production has been shown to be not only an intertextual but a fundamentally collective practice. Where traditionally much attention has been focused on artists, texts, and objects (e.g., Romare Bearden, *Beloved*, the Brooklyn Bridge), recent work attends to the collective practices that produce these objects, to performances that resist the reduction to definitive texts, and to the performative effects of the practices of everyday life. The insinuation of commodity desire in mass culture, the subversive gesture of the ducktail tipping off the neckline of a conk, the persistence of political histories that animate a popular song, the flickering simultaneity of presence and absence that characterizes the cinematic image – all these effects are revealed through an analytic attention to performances and practices in the cultures of the United States.

Richard Ohmann carefully details the intertwining of hegemonic practices and mass culture as advertising comes to provide the economic basis for newspapers and magazines between 1880 and 1900. While the "age of Barnum" clearly prepared audiences for professionally produced entertainment spectacles, it was not until magazines such as *McClure's* and *Munsey's* identified a large national readership that had cultural aspirations but was not hereditarily affluent, delivered a mix of domestic advice and uplifting stories (fiction and nonfiction), built large subscription lists through low cover prices, and paid for the whole package through an increasingly visual approach to large-scale advertising. Advertising was the economic practice that underlay the entire industry and the cultural practice that hegemonically linked cultural advancement to commodity desire.

Style – the commonality among the flowing lines of the zoot suit and the emphatic details of the conk, the blisteringly fast runs of bebop soloists and the twirls and leaps of the lindy hop – links together the performance of a specific black hipster identity with a resistance to the political structures that had shaped the mainstream options of assimilation and the black bourgeoisie. Returned to its historical context, hipster style underlay "a subversive refusal to be subservient." Even the broad grins and snapping towels of a shoeshining Tom can be understood as a particular performance that extracted nickels and dimes from whites longing for submissive service. Robin Kelley's analysis of Malcolm X's memoir reveals the roots of mature political activism in the youthful insistence on stylish presentation.

As George Lipsitz shows us, performance can also maintain and renew counter-memories of historical conflict, even when using the forms and objects of commercial culture. When working-class blacks in New Orleans sew feathers and beads on costumes and call their parade groups tribes, they are borrowing a commercialized vision of Native American culture – drawn not from Indian sources but from Buffalo Bill – to produce a resistant practice. Aesthetic forms – songs, costumes, dance steps – carry history with them, even when borrowed from distorted sources. But the forms themselves come alive in performance. The Mardi Gras Indians use commercial culture for unconventional purposes and give coded expression to the values that shape their everyday lives. In so doing, they perform an imagined commonality of resistance to white imposed practices of for-profit production.

Conversely, second-generation South Asian youth in New York borrow from black culture to negotiate their own contradictory placement in the racialized class hierarchy of the United States. Sunaina Maira demonstrates how young Indian Americans blend bhangra remix music with hip-hop stylings to map out a tenuous yet relatively autonomous space between the cultural nostalgia of their parent's generation and commercialized urban culture. In so doing, they defer the question of their specific place in the black/white racialized binary of American culture. In Los Angeles, queer Latino performance artists display the conjunctural complexity of their identities in multilayered dramatic scenarios that confront authority in both its familiar patriarchical form and its state police form. David Román's insistence on the simultaneous analysis of gendered, sexualized, and racialized structures mirrors the intersectional approach to characterization employed by these performers. Román finds that a differential oppositional consciousness develops in these practices that echoes a Brechtian concept of engaged performance. The oppositional consciousness produced in and through these performances challenges the audience to recognize differences rather than collapsing them into Manichaean oppositions.

The ghost of literature and literary forms of analysis continue to haunt the de-ontologized approach to performances and practices. The analytical framework of authors with works and words in books still shapes much of our approach to not only literature but also film. The production and circulation of language remains the model for most of our concepts of cultural production. We close our section on performances and practices, therefore, with Takayuki Tatsumi's forced encounter between Disney (*Peter Pan*) and Oshima (*In the Realm of the Senses*) in Japanese avant-pop literature and Eva Cherniavsky's insistence on the materialist (and indeed economic) production of white female stardom in 1930s Hollywood. Both of these studies insist that our attention be focused on the mutually subverting determinants of racialized otherness, sexual desire, technological capabilities, and economic demands in the production of narratives and images. Both of these articles situate their objects of analysis in the context of cultural and economic empire. Tatsumi describes a continual, almost unending process of trans-Pacific rewriting, where US popular culture meets Japanese art porn and produces an ironic reflection on power and longing. Cherniavsky reveals the filmic techniques that allowed white female stars to become almost dematerialized while functioning ever more powerfully as desirable commodities, signifying the spreading power of the US economy across Europe.

26

The Origins of Mass Culture

Richard M. Ohmann

[...]

Like mind and body, mass culture and our form of society are inseparable; it is impossible to imagine one without the other. To ask what the effects of mass culture are and whether it is good or bad for us is to freeze events and stand outside them with a slide rule and a list of (someone's) do's and don't's, turning away from the complex social process in which individuals and groups try, over time, to make the best of the circumstances in which they find themselves. Asking whether we want the kind of mass culture we have is almost the same as asking whether we like the social relations of advanced capitalist society.

The expenditure of $40 billion a year on advertising is both a cause and an effect – really, many causes and effects. It represents the achievement of many aims by many people, along with the defeat or frustration of aims that others have pursued. More complicated still: Jane Jones may genuinely *want* the promises about a new sleeping pill that a TV commercial brings her. Her aims may harmonize with those of the pharmaceutical company and the ad agency; but only because the kind of life she leads, which is integrally bound up with TV advertising and the circulation of commodities, has given her money problems, anxiety at work, rebellious kids, and other experiences she doesn't want, all of which add up to insomnia. In a world made up of such situations it seems almost pointless to ask in a broad way what the function of advertising is.

In this situation it helps to look back. Like mind and body, mass culture and advanced capitalism evolved together. By going back, we can consider what needs led some to produce and others to consume mass culture in the first place, and how that culture in turn opened up some avenues for social and personal development while closing off others. In this way it is possible to pry apart the fusion of cause and effect that we see whenever we look about us: the advertiser can sell Bill Black an image of himself as a carefree male (lost with his buddies in West Virginia, but here's a place we can get steaks and Löwenbrau), because he has already learned from a million other commercials to fill vacancies in his life through commodities, because advertisers have long since inscribed that nexus on his mind, because *they* have to expand sales to cope with the productive capacity that manufacturers have achieved partly by making Bill's job mechanical, which in turn makes him long for autonomy and market-free social relations, which desire has over decades been fixed to an image of the home as a place of care and refuge, which image in turn drew him into marriage with impossible hopes, and the burden of these hopes on his wife, along with her own ad-inflated aspiration to be superwoman, has made her resentful and no fun to be with. . . . And so on and on.

Of course there was never a bright day in September when some Edison of the marketplace invented all these connections and changed our society from traditional to modern. And there is no moment in the past to which we can look for an uncontaminated cause and a newborn effect. But it's my contention that causes, effects, needs, and strategies show themselves more plainly in times of rapid emergence than in times of elaboration and refinement. Broadcasting is a routine fact of our lives now, and alternatives to the technology and the social relations embedded in it are unimaginable, even though we see their pliability as television supplements radio, as cable companies challenge networks, as interactive TV emerges over the horizon. But in the early 1920s, nothing about the forms, technologies, uses, and power relations of broadcasting was settled, and everyone could see that a new shuffling of the social deck was in progress, with battles to be won and lost. I hope to find such clarity about mass culture, more broadly, by looking at an earlier time when some of its main structures and processes were initiated through a ten- or fifteen-year period of intense change.

[. . .]

Now, a definition: mass culture in societies like this one includes voluntary experiences, produced by a relatively small number of specialists, for millions across the nation to share, in similar or identical form, either simultaneously or nearly so, with dependable frequency; mass culture shapes habitual audiences, around common needs or interests, and it is made for profit.

[. . .]

[T]he point of a definition like this one is not to dispute other people's categories or labels, nor to settle substantive questions by fiat. I wish only to be as clear as I can about my subject, in an area filled with terminological variety and conceptual overlap. Of course I do also hope to have marked off an area of human activity that readers will recognize as a unified field, not the result of intellectual gerrymandering. I hope I have succeeded in specifying, through the definition, features of mass culture that are truly distinctive rather than incidental. [. . .] And I mean it to indicate an area of experience that is recognizably contemporary, so that one may also find a time in the past when it did not exist, and a time when it came into being.

A time when it did not exist: I have encountered no claim that mass culture arose in the US before the end of the eighteenth century. To be sure, historians of particular cultural forms are fond of pushing back to firsts. James Playsted Wood traces advertising to street cries of the Greeks, "thousands of years ago."[1] Frank Presbrey says that Babylonian merchants used these techniques, and even entertains the possibility that they inscribed ads in stone. And he identifies as the first printed advertisement in English a poster by Caxton, offering for sale a set of rules for the conduct of the clergy at Easter.[2] Less ambiguously,

the first book to be printed in the American colonies appeared in 1640, the first newspaper in 1690, the first magazine in 1741. But for many decades after even the last of these dates, there was nothing in the colonies or the new Republic that distantly resembled a modern mass culture.

[. . .]

Newspapers and magazines were a negligible part of this culture. There were but ninety-two of the former in 1790,[3] and no more than seven of the latter.[4] Their circulations were small, and they tended to be unstable enterprises, especially magazines. Books were another matter: by the end of the eighteenth century, well over a thousand new titles (books and pamphlets) appeared each year, and even by mid century some came out in printings of several thousand. Until about the time of the Revolution, however, most belonged to the earnest discourses of religion and politics; they were not meant to be entertaining. And ordinary people read few of them: reading was for the Bible, *The Pilgrim's Progress*, and a few other texts that one might live by. Culture was immediate, oral, participatory.

That began to change fairly early in the nineteenth century; people entered into experiences that had some of the characteristics of mass culture. For the first time, thousands of people who did not know each other came together as audiences. In sport, for example, a crowd estimated at more than 50,000 watched the famous race between Eclipse and Sir Henry, in 1823. The next year, a similar crowd lined New York harbor to watch a boat race for a $1000 prize. Foot racing became a professional sport, with paid admission, and in 1835 a much publicized contest to see if any runner could run ten miles in less than an hour drew twenty or thirty thousand people.[5] But sporting events were not formally organized and regulated, repeated daily or weekly for large paying audiences, and surrounded with an aura of printed publicity and statistics until at least a decade after 1876, when the National Baseball League was founded. These early spectacles were just that: more comparable to the public feats of an Evel Knievel than to the continuous marketing of events to fans that marks our century.

In fact, one might characterize most large public entertainments around mid century as spectacles, thus emphasizing the way they stood out front the fabric of daily life rather than merging into its pattern. Many were irregular experiences billed as the greatest ever, within some category, and the appeal was to people's sense of the extraordinary or unique. Barnum's American Museum (opened in New York in 1842) epitomized this kind of attraction, bringing under one roof 600,000 exhibits and acts whose only uniting theme was their oddity: famous paintings, giants and midgets, serpents, George Washington's nurse, white elephants. Every visitor to New York had to take in this wonder; everyone in the country knew about it.

The American Museum was there every day; many events happened only once, or just once in a given place, or once a year. Thousands came together to watch balloon ascensions, Fourth of July displays, circuses. There was little distinction between art and entertainment. (This line would later be drawn with care, effort, and money by the patrons of art museums and symphonies, the studied culture of class.) Jenny Lind's mid-century tour drew multitudes who would never have heard of her had it not been for Barnum's hype. (Her ninety-five concerts grossed a total of $712,161.)[6] Tens of thousands met her boat at the wharf and milled around her hotel. There was a brisk market in souvenirs and commodities named after or associated with her. Her visit was the prototype of the sensational, never-to-be-matched event.

Scheduled entertainments, like theater, also ran to the spectacular. Shakespeare, farces, and melodramas mixed with acrobatic performances, feats of strength, and equestrian dramas. And the regular repertoire itself was sold to audiences increasingly through the celebrity of famous actors and actresses: Kean, the Kembles, the Booths. Even highly stereotyped performances such as melodramas and minstrel shows offered themselves as novel, bizarre, sensational.[7]

There is no question that Americans began to learn the role of a mass audience through what might be called the Age of Barnum. They learned to pay for amusement, learned to expect that it would be provided by professionals (and strangers), learned to accept publicity as the forerunner and framer of a major event, learned that they *must* have certain experiences – or at least know about them – to feel adroit in the medium of the social. They developed a vocabulary of the new and the celebrated. But this was not yet a national culture, and, more importantly, it came in staccato bursts of the extraordinary, rather than in measured, formulaic portions delivered to the neighborhood theater, the sports park, or the home itself. Also, these were face-to-face experiences, the audience all in one place, rather than dispersed and forming a crowd only through the mediation of the printing press or an electronic impulse.

What, then, of the print media? Without doubt, a transformation of newspapers and their place in the life of the nation occurred in the 1830s. Even before that, the small-town weekly had integrated itself into the lives of most Americans; Robert Gross notes that in 1827 the *Yeoman's Gazette* of Concord, Massachusetts had a circulation of 1100 in and around a town whose population was only about 1500. By 1840 there were 1400 of these papers around the country.[8] But a production resembling the modern daily emerged only after 1830, and did so in a dramatic way, much as happened later with the magazine.

Most urban dailies sold for six cents, up to that time, and sold a few hundred copies, chiefly to merchants and other affluent people, whose political views they represented. In 1833, a compositor named Benjamin Day hit upon the idea of bringing out his *New York Sun* at a penny; it was soon followed by the *Transcript* and by James Gorden Bennett's *New York Herald*. These papers revolutionized the business and brought together a new readership, as one can tell from the numbers: in 1830 the circulation of all eleven New York dailies amounted to about 25,000; by 1835 the three leading penny papers alone sold 44,000 copies a day. As penny papers sprang up around the country, the national circulation of all dailies went from 78,000 in 1830 to 300,000 in 1840.[9]

This boom derived from more than simply the drop in price. Day, Bennett, and the rest of the new editors sharply altered the nature of the product and its place in readers' lives. For one thing, they were the first to collect and convey news itself, in the modern sense – the first to send reporters out on beats, to keep track of crime and high society, to acknowledge the daily life of the city. Moreover, they largely divorced themselves from the political factions whose mouthpieces newspapers had been, proclaiming their independence and groping toward what would eventually become the practices of objectivity. Most readers ceased to consult newspapers primarily for business and editorial opinion, and went there instead for a conspectus on themselves and their immediate world. The ads, too, had a different appeal, speaking to readers as consumers of clothing, patent medicines, and the like, rather than as businessmen who needed to know about the arrivals of ships. Naturally, with the lower selling price of the papers, ads also paid a much greater share of costs. And, since the new editors had hit on the idea of selling readers to advertisers, they also aggressively pursued new readers: most strikingly, they sent newsboys to hawk papers in the streets, whereas earlier editors had depended on subscriptions. The newspaper itself became part of the spectacle of city life.

In all these ways it drew closer to a form we would recognize. Yet it still belonged to a different epoch. A total circulation of 300,000 in 1840 represented a quantum leap, but that still amounted to just one daily for every 57 people in the country. Most never saw or had a chance to buy one; this was a phenomenon of the city. And it was local in another sense, too: Though by the 1850s a few papers (Greeley's *Tribune*; the *Springfield Republican*) had readers scattered around the nation, most did not circulate far from home. And their content was different from place to place, aside from some of the political news. A reader in Baltimore saw none of the same text as a reader in Boston, and very likely none of the same ads. Physically, these papers were drab: four pages of unbroken columns, with no large headlines and no graphics except for tiny, stylized logos in the ads. They made no appeal to the eye.

The developments that formed the modern newspaper and made it a national medium took place gradually over the next five decades. By 1860, some stories from papers like the *Herald* and the *Tribune* were reprinted around the country, as were dispatches from Civil War battlegrounds. The development of the telegraph after 1840 and the formation of the Associated Press in 1848 prepared the way for this spread of identical news. Journalism began to emerge as a profession, with its own practices and organizations, and its ethic of empiricism. Syndication of features became common in the 1880s; comics arrived in the 1890s. That was the first time Americans had available in the format of the newspaper a homogeneous national experience of *the* news, of opinion, of household advice, and of entertainment.

Gradually, through this period, the paper became modern in other ways too. Ad agencies began selling space to clients in "lists" of dailies from all over, so that national advertising became feasible. Advertisers were also responsible for constant pressure on the "column rule" and for ingenious schemes to draw the eye of the reader. Publishers finally realized that their product, too, could sell itself visually, and by the 1890s halftone reproductions of photographs had supplanted engravings in this effort. Hearst and Pulitzer capitalized on and extended these practices, along with the "yellow" journalism that made the newspaper unequivocally a form of entertainment, whatever else it was. Finally, it was only in the 1890s that advertising began to provide more than half the revenue for newspapers, and that ads for national brands took a prominent place alongside classifieds and ads for local merchants and department stores. In short, the newspaper became a channel of national mass culture about the same time as did the magazine, in spite of a longer and richer evolution.

Anyone wishing to identify a form of national mass culture well before this time could make the strongest case for books (though it is a bit anomalous to imagine mass culture existing in just one medium). Such a case would not have to depend upon the presence and regular use of a Bible in most households, supplemented by a few other texts central to the old, theocentric culture. Nor would it have to rest on the almost universal use of a household standby such as Webster's *Speller*, which had sold 30 million copies by 1860, nor even on the phenomenon of *Uncle Tom's Cabin*, which sold 300,000 within a year of its 1852 publication, 3 million before the Civil War, and perhaps more hardbound copies than any new book before or since. Rather, one could note that there was a surge of cheap, paperback publishing after 1841, when the weekly paper, *New World*, brought out a supplement that included the entire first volume of a Charles Lever novel, for 50 cents. A rival paper, *Brother Jonathan*, quickly published the same novel at 25 cents, and a race was on that led to sales of many novels in newspaper format at 12½ cents, and some for as little as 6 cents. Major book publishers like Harper's met the competition with paperbacks sold almost as cheaply, and for a while dozens of pirated novels by Scott, Bulwer, Balzac, Hugo, Sue, Dickens, and the like, as well as some by American writers, were available at prices anyone could afford. Few sold as many as 30,000 copies, and the original paperback entrepreneurs went out of business within a few years. But the cheap book was now established, and a new readership for books created, so that publishing exploded as an industry through the rest of the 1840s and the 1850s:[10] the value of books made and sold in the United States tripled from 1840 to 1856, and, given the drop in price, the number of copies sold must have increased far more than that.[11] Over succeeding decades, a number of entrepreneurs exploited the techniques of inexpensive production and the presence of a large audience habituated to reading. The famous dime novels began appearing in the 1860s, and the following two decades brought a flood of cheap "libraries" – that is, series of reprints – selling for anything from 10 to 50 cents a volume. In 1877 there were fourteen libraries, and the most frenetic publisher in this format, George Munro, was bringing out a novel a day.[12]

Nineteenth-century book publishing resembled modern mass culture in other ways than sheer volume of production and low cost. People who liked a particular kind of experience could repeat it regularly and indefinitely. Individual authors kept their fans satisfied with repeat performances, across the cultural spectrum: Cooper's novels were selling 40,000 copies a year by 1860, and Mrs E.D.E.N. Southworth, the most popular novelist of the century, turned out fifty or so romances beginning in 1854, almost all of which sold over 100,000 copies. The other "scribbling women" were not far behind, and writers like Longfellow and Irving, remembered more generously today, appeared in innumerable editions that sold well. Books were everywhere available: before the Civil War there were 3000 booksellers, and after it, books began to make their way into department stores and other outlets (often at discount).[13] Subscription sales developed into an almost equally large system of distribution, reminding one of book clubs and of series like Hawthorn Romances today. Some novels were expensively advertised, creating a modern sort of cultural imperative. And most books with large sales were novels (in many years, more than 1000 new and old novels were published): this was unequivocally a form of entertainment. Finally, books had almost the same material appearance in the mid nineteenth century as they do today.

For all that, one might almost as convincingly hold that book publishing was the last culture industry to attain modernity. Not until after World War II did it become part of the large corporate sector, and adopt the practices of publicity and marketing characteristic of monopoly capital. Throughout the nineteenth century and well into the twentieth, publishing houses were either family businesses operating (at least, to hear them tell it) more for the love of books than for profit, or fly-by-night opportunists, or a mixture of both. Most ran their enterprises in a haphazard and highly individualistic fashion, and the history of cheap publishing can be viewed as little more than a series of coups and bankruptcies. Price wars periodically racked the industry, along with intense and ingenious races to be first on the streets with a new book. Distribution was chaotic, with leadership sometimes assumed by the publishers themselves, but often by wholesalers, jobbers, printers, local or regional correspondents, bookstores, even department stores buying out random lots of surplus books and selling them at a few cents apiece. Equally chaotic relations between publishers and authors marked the period, running from virtual slave labor to the payment of huge advances and royalties of over 20 percent. It was not uncommon for less well known authors to have to pay for or subsidize the costs of production; on the other hand, some famous authors like Longfellow *chose* to buy and keep the plates of their books, thus maintaining full control. Finally, nineteenth-century publishing was one of the few capitalist industries grounded in piracy.

I think it fairest to adopt neither of the two positions, but recognize that book publishing went through extremely uneven development for over a century. It achieved some of the methods of mass culture early, but failed to consolidate them into a stable and controlled enterprise with enduring relations to a mass public. The practice which, more than any other, made books a mass medium was the large-scale production of cheap paperbacks, and that came to an abrupt *end* in the 1890s, just as an integrated mass culture emerged. Books were out of step with the rest of the culture industry: a telling statistic is that, across the entire period from 1850 to 1914, which surely embraces the rise of mass culture, book publishing's share of all manufacturing value declined from 1 percent to one-fourth of 1 percent, even as it was quadrupling in absolute value.[14] This makes sense: books came first, and for many decades they held the largest share of the cultural market; but when other forms of cultural production (newspapers, magazines, spectator sports) transformed themselves, and new ones (movies, records) appeared, books were crowded into a smaller corner of leisure time and of the market.

But I do want to claim that in the final fifteen years of the nineteenth century – the inaugural moment, I argue, of our national mass culture – book publishing, too, underwent some changes that brought it into greater conformity with the other modern culture industries. It undertook practices of rationalization and control, efforts to rein in the anarchic competition of earlier decades. Publishers gradually learned how to stabilize the sales effort. They acquired their own staffs of traveling salesmen, and greatly increased both the amount and the flamboyance of their advertising. They began to shape their product and create its market, rather than just publishing what appealed to them and hoping for the best. As a result, hardback sales of 100,000 and more became common in the 1890s. Given the economics of publishing, successes like these were necessary to cover the inevitable failures and to make substantial profits. Publishers concentrated their efforts more on achieving the big hit, and less on grinding out series of cheap books. These efforts were rewarded with marketing sensations like *Trilby*, *Ben Hur*, *Black Beauty*, *Freckles*, *Quo Vadis*, *David Harum*, and *The Red Badge of Courage*. This new emphasis in the industry was punctuated by the first regular publication of regional best seller lists in the *Bookman* in 1895, and national best seller lists in 1897.

At the same time, publishers were accepting, and even creating, checks on the cutthroat competition that had long characterized their business. Many of them supported a stronger copyright law, one that gave protection to foreign books for the first time, and thus eliminated the main source of free raw material for paperback publishers. It passed in 1891, finally ending piracy, and making for more durable arid amiable relations with authors. They also reluctantly began dealing with literary agents, who first appeared at this time and whose intervention helped regularize relations with authors. It was in the 1890s, too, that publishers increasingly generated ideas for books themselves and pressed writers to execute their plans, rather than just competing for finished manuscripts. Most significantly, perhaps, publishers recognized the need to cooperate; by 1900 the leaders of the industry had formed the American Publishers' Association, and were encouraging retailers to form the American Booksellers' Association, which organized in 1901. The two groups immediately agreed on a system of retail pricing, of discounting to the trade, and of what we now know as remaindering, designed to end the fratricidal price competition that had long made the business so risky. This agreement failed, mainly because it did not include department stores, but a key principle of advanced capitalism had been established, and would eventually take hold.[15] In this context, the decline of paperback publishing in the 1890s can be seen as part of a successful attempt by major houses to get rid of ill-mannered entrepreneurial competitors. Book publishing was now a smaller part of the cultural environment, but it had acquired many of the characteristic forms and practices of a twentieth-century culture industry.

Few of the ambiguities and reversals that mark the development of book publishing obscure the birth of modern magazines. Their transformation was dramatic, and obvious to all; that is one reason for taking them as paradigmatic in this study. A typical magazine of the 1830s, to pick a starting point, claimed a circulation measured in hundreds, for a few pages of solid columns of print, with few or no ads. These magazines reached audiences that were at most regional; they rarely made a profit, and they usually died young. There were no national magazines at all before 1850. Even after the railroad linked the two coasts in 1869, and after the Postal Act of 1879 made cheap distribution possible, magazines were not a main feature of American culture, and they barely resembled their counterparts of the late twentieth century.

Yet by 1900 they very much did. And "everyone" was reading them. Any aficionado of historical discontinuities could delight in the events of 1893; even the sober historians of American magazines feel compelled to call it a "revolution."[16]

And although I think it bears a different kind of scrutiny than they have given it, 1893 was indeed a year when something happened. At that time the leading respectable monthlies – *Harper's*, *Century*, *Atlantic*, and a few others – sold for a quarter or 35 cents, and had circulations of no more than 200,000. In the middle of the panic of 1893, S. S. McClure brought out his new monthly at an unprecedented 15 cents. John Brisben Walker, editor of the old *Cosmopolitan*, quickly dropped his price to $12\frac{1}{2}$ cents. And in October, with much hoopla, Frank Munsey cut the price of his faltering monthly from a quarter to a dime. Its circulation went from 40,000 that month to 200,000 the following February to 500,000 in April, and to a circulation that Munsey called the largest in the world by 1898. These entrepreneurs – Munsey most consciously – had hit upon a formula of elegant simplicity: identify a large audience that is not hereditarily affluent or elite, but that is getting on well enough, and that has cultural aspirations; give it what it wants; build a huge circulation; sell lots of advertising space at rates based on that circulation; sell the magazine at a price *below* the cost of production, and make your profit on ads. An unnamed publisher is reported as saying, with only slight exaggeration, "If I can get a circulation of 400,000 I can afford to give my magazine away to anyone who will pay the postage."[17]

But if this is the economic principle behind the mass magazine of our century (and up until recently, it has been), the decision to fix 1893 as the critical moment is only a narrative convenience. It credits McClure and Munsey with too much, and makes a development that could only have occurred over time seem instantaneous and magical. I would venture to say that no major form of cultural production ever springs at once from the brain of a single person: television plagiarized from radio and the movies; radio took its content from newspapers, vaudeville, and the concert hall; moviemakers drew upon a variety of entertainments like the photograph, stereopticon, and magic lantern, which appealed through their re-presentation of real life. Munsey and McClure also fused and elaborated practices that were well established before 1893.

For instance, the elite monthlies had earlier concocted the blend of genres that editors of the 1890s adapted for a wider audience: fiction, articles about the famous, historical pieces, cultural articles and reviews, and so on. Furthermore, some of them had long since abandoned their aristocratic scruples about advertising. The *Atlantic* began to take a few ads as early as 1860. Soon after *Scribner's Monthly* was founded, in 1870, its business manager, Roswell Smith, actively sought ads.

[...]

Scribner's did not in fact attract a lot of advertising for a while; this was an idea whose time had not yet come. But after the magazine changed its name to the *Century* in 1881, its ad pages multiplied. This example shattered the reserve of some other class monthlies, *Harper's* in particular, which averaged about ten pages of ads in 1885, but about seventy-five pages in 1890, in which year it passed the *Century*.[18] Munsey could not have missed the point.

A second forerunner was the popular weekly. Usually spoken of as a "paper" rather than a magazine (and printed in newspaper format, though on better paper), it too found advertising quite acceptable. Advertising in *Harper's Weekly*, for instance, went from about half a quarto page per issue in its first year (1857), to a page in 1862, to two pages in 1867, and three pages in 1872. The weeklies also pioneered display ads: the 1 June 1872 issue of *Harper's Weekly* (circulation about 150,000) included pictorial ads for lawn mowers, corsets, furniture, jewelry, a toy engine, statuary, a freezer, a carriage, roofing, shotguns, engines, and sewing machines.

By the end of the 1880s, *Youth's Companion* (circulation about 400,000) had in effect an advertising department, which got up full-page pictorial ads for presentation to manufacturers, many of whom went along with the new idea. Most famously, it sold to Mellin's baby food the plan for a full-page and full-color ad, a lithograph of Perrault's "The Awakening of Cupid": both the color and the price ($14,000) were firsts.[19] This movement toward the visual characterized the whole content of the magazine, as well as that of other major weeklies like *Frank Leslie's Illustrated Newspaper*. There was apparently an insatiable appetite among subscribers for engravings of Civil War scenes; Leslie maintained the visual emphasis after the war, with many full-page engravings per issue. The balance began to shift in some of these periodicals, from pictures as secondary to the text (illustrations) to pictures as the heart of a feature, with the text as a gloss. Walker's *Cosmopolitan* was a leader in adding photo-engravings to the visual display; Munsey developed this innovation into virtually the equivalent of the modern photo-essay.

The "mail-order journals" also anticipated Munsey's idea, and probably influenced it. So ephemeral were they that few libraries in the country have preserved any of them, and my supplier of old magazines, who had three warehouses full, had not heard of even the major titles. Thus I rely on Mott's definition of this genre: "a yearly subscription rate of twenty-five to fifty cents, poor printing (usually in the folio size), cheap serial fiction, and varied but undistinguished household departments."[20] The first of these was the *People's Literary Companion*, started in 1869 by E. C. Allen, who made Augusta, Maine a center for such publications. By the 1890s there were apparently hundreds of them; Allen himself put out twelve. They contributed two ideas to the composite of the modern magazine. First, not only were they cheap, but the publishers spent little effort soliciting renewals, preferring to continue sending the magazines free to one-time subscribers, and in effect selling this list to the advertisers who paid the freight. Hence editorial content was completely subordinate to the advertising relationship. Second, these magazines apparently went to millions of people who could not have afforded and would not have liked the class monthlies. Allen and his competitors discovered that there was truly a mass audience for magazines: *Comfort*, the leader among them, carried perhaps a million "subscribers" through the 1890s and into this century. [...]

If the credit given to Walker, McClure, and Munsey ignores periodicals directed at a working class audience, it also ignores those produced for women. Not only had *Godey's Lady's Book* been the circulation leader at mid century (followed closely by *Peterson's*, another women's magazine); it had latched onto a central ideology of that time – progress – in a version tailored to the advancement of women. It took up the cause of labor-saving devices like the sewing machine, anesthesia, women doctors, exercise and education for women. It was prettily illustrated, with engravings hand-colored by an army of 150 employees. Still, it was a crude production by later standards, and hampered by the primitive infrastructure of the society; its publication tended to be irregular, and its arrival even more so as it was shipped by boat and stage and vulnerable to bad weather as well as bad roads.[21]

These difficulties had long been surmounted in 1883, when Cyrus H. Curtis decided to transform the women's pages of his *Tribune and Farmer* into a separate magazine called the *Ladies' Home Journal*. A combination of brilliant editorial conception (executed for a while by Mrs Curtis, then, after 1889, by Edward Bok) and vigorous advertising pushed the circulation of the *Journal* to

200,000 in 1885, 400,000 in 1888, and 600,000 in 1891. It sold for a nickel until 1889, then for the same ten cents, or a dollar a year, that Munsey "hit on" in 1893. It welcomed advertising, and displayed it handsomely, not all on separate pages at beginning and end, but set in amongst the editorial contents. It may have been the first magazine to change its cover design with each issue (in the early 1890s), thus signalling the contradictory fusion of novelty and sameness which has since been crucial to the ideological subtext of magazines, and of mass culture in general.

The *Journal* not only took the lead in perfecting the format and economic formula of the modern magazine, but also approximated it in editorial content by 1893. Munsey and the others did not regard the *Journal* as a magazine; it and its editor were the butt of many jokes and lampoons during this period. This ridicule had a basis in both gender and class. Through its early years, the *Journal* gave its audience practical household advice, moral counsel of the Dear Abby sort, and instruction in how to be respectable. Readers and editors of the cultural monthlies found this blend embarrassingly intimate, lowbrow, and feminine. And indeed, the *Journal* did frankly address its audience as one that needed counsel in matters taken for granted at homes where the affinity was for *Harper's* or the *Atlantic*. It penetrated into areas of personal and social concern previously kept apart from culture in the medium of magazines, if not in other sectors of American society. But Curtis, and especially Bok, understood that the kind of propriety (read, class standing) they nourished through instruction in fashion, home design, and entertaining, as well as through departments like "Side Talks with Girls," needed the counterpoint of literary culture. At first, the latter was difficult to bring into the magazine, since recognized writers did not want to be associated with the former. But Curtis inveigled writers like Louisa May Alcott, Elizabeth Stuart Phelps, Mrs A. D. T. Whitney, and Will Carleton into Contributing, and advertised their names widely on his "List of Famous Contributors." Bok further extended the list to include Howells, Stockton, Addams, Kipling, Twain, Harte, Jewett, and more than one president of the United States, as well as many artists of note. By the mid nineties, the *Journal* was a previously unimaginable blend of intimate domestic chatter (though it dropped the subtitle, "And Practical Housekeeper" in 1889) and upper middle class literary culture. If one magazine should get more credit than another for discovering the twentieth century, it is the *Ladies' Home Journal*.[22]

What actually happened in 1893, then, was the broadening of a "revolution" already underway. Munsey, McClure, and Walker fused a number of business and editorial practices that were working well enough, but separately. They took from the weeklies the idea of a lively pictorial appearance, from these and a few of the monthlies a willingness to hustle ads and let them be splashy, from the women's magazines and the mail order journals the idea of a very low price that would attract a large audience of people with only a little extra money to spend. Some publishers of magazines from each of these genres had already discovered that such an audience could be delivered to advertisers at prices that would pay a major share of costs. And from the literary monthlies, the entrepreneurs of 1893 took the idea of offering this audience participation in a mainstream of national culture, though they rechanneled that stream in such a way that it no longer implied life membership in an elite club; it was no longer a culture rooted in family, old money, the past.

So there was no spontaneous generation of this mass cultural form, one day in 1893. But, having restored the change to the category of process, rather than invention, I must reemphasize the fact that this process ran its course very quickly, as historical changes go. I would say that there were no modern, mass circulation magazines in 1885, and that by 1900 there were in the neighborhood of twenty – enough to make them a highly visible and much noted cultural phenomenon. The numbers bear out the claim: at the end of the Civil War the total circulation of monthlies seems to have been at most 4 million. It was about 18 million in 1890, and 64 million in 1905. To bring these figures down to scale, in 1865 there may have been one copy of a magazine each month to every ten people in the country. By 1905 there were three copies for every four people, or about four to every household. And for a contrast, while monthly magazine circulation more than tripled between 1890 and 1905, the total circulation of newspapers and weekly periodicals rose only from 36 million to 57 million – the two forms together having less circulation than the monthlies.[23] By this measure, monthly magazines had become the major form of repeated cultural experience for the people of the United States.

Because of that, and because this culture industry took shape so rapidly, the history of monthly magazines can stand as a paradigm case. Such a concentrated development gives focus to the questions with which I began this chapter: Where did mass culture come from? What does it do in and to societies like ours? But I hope I have also made the point that magazines are not otherwise a special case – that the same processes of commercializing the "product," regularizing its availability, and attracting large audiences to it took place also in public entertainments such as sport, newspaper publishing, and book publishing; and that they culminated in modern forms of cultural production at roughly the same time.

[...]

Notes

1   James Playsted Wood, *The Story of Advertising* (New York: Ronald Press, 1958), p. 18.

2   Frank Presbrey, *The History and Development of Advertising* (Garden City, NY: Doubleday, Doran & Company, 1929), pp. 3, 16.

3   Robert A. Gross, "Comments on Ohmann," *Berkshire Review*, vol. 16, no. 106, 1981.

4   Frank Luther Mott, *A History of American Magazines, 1741–1850* (New York: Appleton, 1930), p. 29.

5   Foster Rhea Dulles, *America Learns to Play; A History of Popular Recreation, 1607–1940* (New York: Peter Smith, 1952), pp. 140, 142–3.

6   Ibid., p. 127.

7   For the best account see "William Shakespeare in America," in Lawrence W. Levine, *Highbrow/Lowbrow; The Emergence of Cultural Hierarchy in America* (Cambridge, Mass.: Harvard University Press, 1988).

8   Robert A. Gross, "Comments on Ohmann," p. 106.

9   Michael Schudson, *Discovering the News; A Social History of American Newspapers* (New York: Basic Books, 1978), p. 18.

10 I take this account from John Tebbel, *A History of Book Publishing in the United States*, vol. 1 (New York: R. R.

Bowker, 1972), pp. 243–5, and from C. Hugh Holman, "'Cheap Books' and the Public Interest," in Ray B. Browne, Richard H. Crowder, Virgil L. Lokke, and William T. Stafford, eds, *Frontiers of American Culture* (Lafayette, Ind.: Purdue University Studies, 1968), pp. 26–30.

11 Tebbel, *History of Book Publishing*, vol. 1, p. 221.

12 John Tebbel, *The Media in America* (New York: Thomas Y. Crowell, 1974), p. 250.

13 Tebbel, *History of Book Publishing*, vol. 1, p. 206, 222, 247.

14 John Tebbel, *A History of Book Publishing in the United States*, vol. 2 (New York: R. R. Bowker, 1975), p. 12.

15 Ibid., pp. 123–6,

16 Frank Luther Mott, *A History of American Magazines, 1885–1905*, vol. IV (Cambridge, Mass.: Harvard University Press, 1957), p. 6; Theodore Peterson, *Magazines in the Twentieth Century* (Urbana, Ill.: University of Illinois Press, 1956), p. 7.

17 Presbrey, *The History and Development of Advertising*, p. 471. Jackson Lears, *Fables of Abundance; A Cultural History of Advertising in America* (New York: Basic Books, 1994), p. 201.

18 Ibid., pp. 469–70; Wood, *The Story of Advertising*, p. 198.

19 Presbrey, *The History and Development of Advertising*, p. 471.

20 Mott. *History of American Magazines*, vol. IV, pp. 364–5.

21 See Ruth E. Finley, *The Lady of Godey's* (Philadelphia: J. B. Lippincott, 1931).

22 Mott, *History of American Magazines*, vol. IV, gives a good sketch of the *Journal's* early years, pp. 536–45. See also Edward Bok, *The Americanization of Edward Bok; The Autobiography of a Dutch Boy Fifty Years After* (New York: Charles Scribner's Sons, 1921); Edward Bok, *A Man From Maine* (New York: Charles Scribner's Sons, 1923); and Salme Harju Steinberg, *Reformer in the Marketplace; Edward W. Bok and The Ladies' Home Journal* (Baton Rouge, La.: Louisiana State University Press, 1979).

23 Presbrey, *The History and Development of Advertising*, p. 488.

27

The Riddle of the Zoot: Malcolm Little and Black Cultural Politics during World War II

Robin D. G. Kelley

[. . .]

"I Am at the Center of a Swirl of Events"

The gangly, red-haired young man from Lansing looked a lot older than fifteen when Malcolm Little moved in with his half-sister Ella, who owned a modest home in the Roxbury section of Boston. Little did he know how much the world around him was about to change. The bombing of Pearl Harbor was still several months away, but the country's economy was already geared up for war. By the time US troops were finally dispatched to Europe, Asia, and North Africa, many in the black community restrained their enthusiasm, for they shared a collective memory of the unfulfilled promises of democracy generated by the First World War. Hence, the Double V campaign, embodied in A. Philip Randolph's threatened march on Washington to protest racial discrimination in employment and the military, partly articulated the sense of hope and pessimism, support and detachment, that dominated a good deal of daily conversation. This time around, a victory abroad without annihilating racism at home was unacceptable. As journalist Roi Ottley observed during the early years of the war, one could not walk the streets of Harlem and not notice a profound change. "Listen to the way Negroes are talking these days! . . . [B]lack men have become noisy, aggressive, and sometimes defiant."[1]

The defiant ones included newly arrived migrants from the South who had flooded America's Northeastern and Midwestern metropolises. Hoping to take advantage of opportunities created by the nascent wartime economy, most found only frustration and disappointment because a comparatively small proportion of African Americans gained access to industrial jobs and training programs. By March of 1942, black workers constituted only 2.5 to 3 percent of all war production workers, most of whom were relegated to low-skill, low-wage positions. The employment situation improved more rapidly after 1942: by April of 1944, blacks made up 8 percent of the nation's war production workers. But everyone in the African American community did not benefit equally. For example, the United Negro College Fund was established in 1943 to assist African Americans attending historically black colleges, but during the school year of 1945–6, undergraduate enrollment in those institutions amounted to less than 44,000. On the other hand, the number of black workers in trade unions increased from 150,000 in 1935 to 1.25 million by the war's end. The Congress of Industrial Organizations' (CIO) organizing drives ultimately had the effect of raising wages and improving working conditions for these black workers, though nonunion workers, who made up roughly 80 percent of the black working class, could not take advantage of the gains. The upgrading of unionized black workers did not take place without a struggle; throughout the war white workers waged "hate strikes" to protest the promotion of blacks, and black workers frequently retaliated with their own wildcat strikes to resist racism.[2]

In short, wartime integration of black workers into the industrial economy proceeded unevenly; by the war's end most African Americans still held unskilled, menial jobs. As cities burgeoned with working people, often living in close quarters or doubling up as a result of housing shortages, the chasm between middle-class and skilled working-class blacks, on the one hand, and the unemployed and working poor, on the other, began to widen. Intraracial class divisions were exacerbated by cultural conflicts between established urban residents and the newly arrived rural folk. In other words, demographic and economic transformations caused by the war not only intensified racial conflict but led to heightened class tensions within urban black communities.[3] For Malcolm, the zoot suit, the lindy hop, and the distinctive lingo of the hep cat simultaneously embodied these class, racial, and cultural tensions. This unique subculture enabled him to negotiate an identity that resisted the hegemonic culture and its attendant racism and patriotism, the rural folkways (for many, the "parent culture") which still survived in most black urban households, and the class-conscious, integrationist attitudes of middle-class blacks.

"The Zoot Suit of Life"

Almost as soon as Malcolm settled into Boston, he found he had little tolerance for the class pretensions of his neighbors, particularly his peers. Besides, his own limited wardrobe and visible "country" background rendered him an outsider. He began hanging out at a local pool hall in the poorer section of Roxbury. Here, in this dank, smoky room, surrounded by the cracking sounds of cue balls and the stench of alcohol, Malcolm discovered the black subculture which would ultimately form a crucial component of his identity. An employee of the poolroom, whom Malcolm called "Shorty" (most likely a composite figure based on several acquaintances, including his close friend Malcolm Jarvis), became his running partner and initiated him into the cool world of the hep cat.[4]

In addition to teaching young Malcolm the pleasures, practices, and possibilities of hipster culture, Shorty had to make sure his homeboy wore the right uniform in this emerging bebop army. When Malcolm put on his very first zoot suit, he realized immediately that the wild sky-blue outfit, the baggy punjab pants tapered to the ankles, the matching hat, gold watch chain, and monogrammed belt were more than a suit of clothes. As he left the department store he could not contain his enthusiasm for his new identity. "I took three of those twenty-five-cent sepia-toned, while-you-wait pictures of myself, posed the way 'hipsters' wearing their zoots

would 'cool it' – hat dangled, knees drawn close together, feet wide apart, both index fingers jabbed toward the floor." The combination of his suit and body language encoded a culture that celebrated a specific racial, class, spatial, gender, and generational identity. East Coast zoot suiters during the war were primarily young black (and Latino) working-class males whose living spaces and social world were confined to Northeastern ghettos, and the suit reflected a struggle to negotiate these multiple identities in opposition to the dominant culture. Of course, the style itself did not represent a complete break with the dominant fashion trends; zoot suiters appropriated, even mocked, existing styles and reinscribed them with new meanings drawn from shared memory and experiences.

While the suit itself was not meant as a direct political statement, the social context in which it was created and worn rendered it so. The language and culture of zoot suiters represented a subversive refusal to be subservient. Young black males created a fast-paced, improvisational language which sharply contrasted with the passive stereotype of the stuttering, tongue-tied Sambo; in a world where whites commonly addressed them as "boy," zoot suiters made a fetish of calling each other "man." Moreover, within months of Malcolm's first zoot, the political and social context of war had added an explicit dimension to the implicit oppositional meaning of the suit; it had become an explicitly un-American style. By March 1942, because fabric rationing regulations instituted by the War Productions Board forbade the sale and manufacturing of zoot suits, wearing the suit (which had to be purchased through informal networks) was seen by white servicemen as a pernicious act of anti-Americanism – a view compounded by the fact that most zoot suiters were able-bodied men who refused to enlist or found ways to dodge the draft. Thus when Malcolm donned his "killer-diller coat with a drape-shape, reat-pleats and shoulders padded like a lunatic's cell," his lean body became a dual signifier of opposition – a rejection of both black petit bourgeois respectability and American patriotism.[5]

The urban youth culture was also born of heightened interracial violence and everyday acts of police brutality. Both Detroit and Harlem, two cities in which Malcolm spent considerable time, erupted in massive violence during the summer of 1943. And in both cases riots were sparked by incidents of racial injustice.[6] The zoot suiters, many of whom participated in the looting and acts of random violence, were also victims of, or witnesses to, acts of outright police brutality. [. . .]

The hipster subculture permeated far more than just sartorial style. Getting one's hair straightened (the "conk" hairdo) was also required. For Malcolm, reflecting backward through the prism of the Nation of Islam and Pan-Africanism, the conk was the most degrading aspect of the hipster subculture. In his words, it was little more than an effort to make his hair "as straight as any white man's."

> This was my first really big step toward self-degradation: when I endured all of that pain, literally burning my flesh to have it look like a white man's hair. I had joined that multitude of Negro men and women in America who are brainwashed into believing that the black people are "inferior" – and white people "superior" – that they will even violate and mutilate their God-created bodies to try to look "pretty" by white standards.[7]

Malcolm's interpretation of the conk, however, conveniently separates the hairstyle from the subculture of which it was a part, and the social context in which such cultural forms were created. The conk was a "refusal" to look like either the dominant, stereotyped image of the Southern migrant or the black bourgeoisie, whose "conks" were closer to mimicking white styles than those of the zoot suiters. Besides, to claim that black working-class males who conked their hair were merely parroting whites ignores the fact that specific stylizations created by black youth emphasized difference – the ducktail down the back of the neck, the smooth, even stiff look created by Murray's Pomade (a very thick hair grease marketed specifically to African Americans), the neat side parts angling toward the center of the back of the head.

More importantly, once we contextualize the conk, considering the social practices of young hep cats, the totality of ethnic signifiers from the baggy pants to the coded language, their opposition to war, and emphasis on pleasure over waged labor, we cannot help but view the conk as part of a larger process by which black youth appropriated, transformed, and reinscribed coded oppositional meanings onto styles derived from the dominant culture. For

> the conk was conceived in a subaltern culture, dominated and hedged in by a capitalist master culture, yet operating in an "underground" manner to subvert given elements by creolizing stylization. Style encoded political "messages" to those in the know which were otherwise unintelligible to white society by virtue of their ambiguous accentuation and intonation.[8]

"But There Is Rhythm Here"

Once properly attired ("togged to the bricks," as his contemporaries would have said), sixteen-year-old Malcolm discovered the lindy hop, and in the process expanded both his social circle and his politics. The Roseland Ballroom in Boston, and in some respects the Savoy in Harlem, constituted social spaces of pleasure free of the bourgeois pretensions of "better-class Negroes." His day job as a soda fountain clerk in the elite section of black Roxbury became increasingly annoying to him as he endured listening to the sons and daughters of the "Hill Negroes," "penny-ante squares who came in there putting on their millionaires' airs." Home (his sister Ella's household) and spaces of leisure (the Roseland Ballroom) suddenly took on new significance, for they represented the negation of black bourgeois culture and a reaffirmation of a subaltern culture that emphasized pleasure, rejected work, and celebrated a working-class racial identity. "I couldn't wait for eight o'clock to get home to eat out of those soul-food pots of Ella's, then get dressed in my zoot and head for some of my friends' places in town, to lindy-hop and get high, or something, for relief from those Hill clowns."[9]

For Malcolm and his peers, Boston's Roseland Ballroom and, later, Harlem's Savoy, afforded the opportunity to become something other than workers. In a world where clothes constituted signifiers of identity and status, "dressing up" was a way of escaping the degradation of work and collapsing status distinctions between themselves and their oppressors. In Malcolm's narrative, he always seemed to be shedding his work clothes, whether it was the apron of a soda jerk or the uniform of a railroad sandwich peddler, in favor of his zoot suit. At the end of his first run to New York on the Yankee Clipper rail line, he admitted to having donned his "zoot suit before the first passenger got off." Seeing oneself and others "dressed up" was enormously important in terms of constructing a collective identity based on something other than wage work, presenting a public challenge to the dominant stereotypes of the black body, and reinforcing a sense of dignity that was perpetually being assaulted. Malcolm's images of the Roseland were quite vivid in this respect: "They'd jampack that ballroom, the black girls in wayout silk and satin dresses and shoes, their hair done in all kinds of styles the men sharp, in their zoot suits and crazy conks, and everybody grinning and greased and gassed."[10]

For many working-class men and women who daily endured backbreaking wage work, low income, long hours, and pervasive racism, these urban dance halls were places to recuperate, to take back their bodies. Despite opposition from black religious leaders and segments of the petite bourgeoisie, black working people took the opportunity to do what they wished with their own bodies. The sight of hundreds moving in unison on a hardwood dance floor unmistakably reinforced a sense of collectivity as well as individuality, as dancers improvised on the standard lindy hop moves in friendly competition, like the "cutting sessions" of jazz musicians or the verbal duels known as "the dozens." Practically every Friday and Saturday night, young Malcolm experienced the dual sense of community and individuality, improvisation and collective call and response:

The band, the spectators and the dancers, would be making the Roseland Ballroom feel like a big rocking ship. The spotlight would be turning, pink, yellow, green, and blue, picking up the couples lindy-hopping as if they had gone mad. "*Wail, man, wail!*" people would be shouting at the band; and it *would* be wailing, until first one and then another couple just ran out of strength and stumbled off toward the crowd, exhausted and soaked with sweat.[11]

It should be noted that the music itself was undergoing a revolution during the war. Growing partly out of black musicians' rebellion against white-dominated swing bands, and partly out of the heightened militancy of black urban youth – expressed by their improvisational language and dress styles, as well as by the violence and looting we now call the Harlem Riot of 1943 – the music that came to be known as "bebop" was born amid dramatic political and social transformations. At Minton's Playhouse and Monroe's Uptown a number of styles converged; the most discerning recognized the wonderful collision and reconstitution of Kansas City big band blues, East Coast swing music, and the secular as well as religious sounds of the black South. The horns, fingers, ideas, and memories of *young* black folk (most, keep in mind, were only in their early twenties) like Charlie Parker, Thelonius Monk, Dizzy Gillespie, Mary Lou Williams, Kenny Clarke, Oscar Pettiford, Tadd Dameron, Bud Powell, and a baby-faced Miles Davis, to name only a few, gave birth to what would soon be called "bebop."

Bebop was characterized by complex and implied rhythms frequently played at blinding tempos, dissonant chord structures, and a pre-electronic form of musical "sampling" in which the chord changes for popular Tin Pan Alley songs were appropriated, altered, and used in conjunction with new melodies. While the music was not intended to be dance music, some African American youth found a way to lindy hop to some remarkably fast tempos, and in the process invented new dances such as the "apple jack."

Although the real explosion in bebop occurred after Malcolm began his stay at Charleston State Penitentiary, no hip Harlemite during the war could have ignored the dramatic changes in the music or the musicians. Even the fairly conservative band leader Lionel Hampton, a close friend of Malcolm's during this period, linked bebop with oppositional black politics. Speaking of his own music in 1946, he told an interviewer, "Whenever I see any injustice or any unfair action against my own race or any other minority groups 'Hey Pa Pa Rebop' stimulates the desire to destroy such prejudice and discrimination."[12] Moreover, while neither the lindy hop nor the apple jack carried intrinsic political meanings, the social act of dancing was nonetheless resistive – at least with respect to the work ethic.[13]

"War and Death"

From the standpoint of most hep cats, the Selective Service was an ever-present obstacle to "the pursuit of leisure and pleasure." As soon as war broke out, Malcolm's homeboys did everything possible to evade the draft.

[. . .]

We can never know how many black men used subterfuge to obtain a 4F status, or how many [. . .] complied with draft orders but did so reluctantly. Nevertheless, what evidence we do possess suggests that black resistance to the draft was more pervasive than we might have imagined. By late 1943, African Americans comprised 35 percent of the nation's delinquent registrants, and between 1941 and 1946, over 2,000 black men were imprisoned for not complying with the provisions of the Selective Service Act.[14]

While some might argue that draft dodging by black hipsters hardly qualifies as protest politics, the press, police, and white servicemen thought otherwise. The white press, and to a lesser degree the black press, cast practically all young men sporting the "drape shape" (zoot suit) as unpatriotic "dandies."[15] And the hep cats who could not escape the draft and refused to either submerge their distaste for the war or discard their slang faced a living nightmare in the armed forces. Zoot suiters and jazz musicians, in particular, were the subject of ridicule, severe punishment, and even beatings. Civilian hipsters fared no better. That black and Latino youth exhibited a cool, measured indifference to the war, as well as an increasingly defiant posture toward whites in general, annoyed white servicemen to no end.

[...]

"I Think Life a Commodity Bargained For"

Part of what annoyed white servicemen was the hipsters' laissez-faire attitude toward work and their privileging of the "pursuit of leisure and pleasure." Holding to the view that one should work to live rather than live to work, Malcolm decided to turn the pursuit of leisure and pleasure into a career. Thus after "studying" under the tutelage of some of Harlem's better-known pimps, gangsters, and crooks who patronized the popular local bar Small's Paradise, Malcolm eventually graduated to full-fledged "hustler."

Bruce Perry and other biographers who assert that, because Malcolm engaged in the illicit economy while good jobs were allegedly "a dime a dozen," we should therefore look to psychological explanations for his criminality, betray a profound ignorance of the wartime political economy and black working-class consciousness. First, in most Northeastern cities during the war, African Americans were still faced with job discrimination, and employment opportunities for blacks tended to be low-wage, menial positions. In New York, for example, the proportion of blacks receiving home relief *increased* from 22 percent in 1936 to 26 percent in 1942, and when the Works Progress Administration shut down in 1943, the percentage of African Americans employed by the New York WPA was higher than it had been during the entire depression.[16] Second, it was hard for black working people not to juxtapose the wartime rhetoric of equal opportunity and the apparent availability of well-paying jobs for whites with the reality of racist discrimination in the labor market. Of the many jobs Malcolm held during the war, none can be said to have been well-paying and/or fulfilling. Third, any attempt to understand the relationship between certain forms of crime and resistance must begin by questioning the dominant view of criminal behavior as social deviance. As a number of criminologists and urban anthropologists have suggested, "hustling" or similar kinds of informal/illicit economic strategies should be regarded as efforts to escape dependency on low-wage, alienating labor.[17]

The zoot suiters' collective hostility to wage labor became evident to young Malcolm during his first conversation with Shorty, who promptly introduced the word "slave" into his nascent hipster vocabulary. A popular slang expression for a job, "slave" not only encapsulated their understanding of wage work as exploitative, alienating, and unfulfilling, but it implies a refusal to allow *work* to become the primary signifier of identity. [...] Implied, too, is a rejection of a work ethic, a privileging of leisure, and an emphasis on "fast money" with little or no physical labor. Even Shorty chastised Malcolm for saving money to purchase his first zoot suit rather than taking advantage of credit.[18]

Malcolm's apprenticeship in Boston's shoeshine trade introduced him to the illicit economy, the margins of capitalism where commodity relations tended to be raw, demystified, and sometimes quite brutal. Success here required that one adopt the sorts of monopolist strategies usually associated with America's most celebrated entrepreneuers. Yet, unlike mainstream entrepreneurs, most of the hustlers with whom Malcolm was associated believed in an antiwork, anti-accumulation ethic. Possessing "capital" was not the ultimate goal; rather, money was primarily a means by which hustlers could avoid wage work and negotiate status through the purchase of prestigious commodities. Moreover, it seems that many hustlers of the 1940s shared a very limited culture of mutuality that militated against accumulation. On more than one occasion, Malcolm gave away or loaned money to friends when he himself was short of cash, and in at least one case "he pawned his suit for a friend who had pawned a watch for him when he had needed a loan."[19]

Nevertheless, acts of mutuality hardly translated into a radical collective identity; hustling by nature was a predatory act which did not discriminate by color. Moreover, their culture of mutuality was a male-identified culture limited to the men of their inner circle, for, as Malcolm put it, the hustler cannot afford to "trust anybody." Women were merely objects through which hustling men sought leisure and pleasure; prey for financial and sexual exploitation. "I believed that a man should do anything that he was slick enough, or bad and bold enough, to do and that a woman was nothing but another commodity." Even women's sexuality was a commodity to be bought and sold, though for Malcolm and his homeboys selling made more sense than buying. (In fact, Bruce Perry suggests that Malcolm pimped gay men and occasionally sold his own body to homosexuals.)[20]

At least two recent biographies suggest that the detached, sometimes brutal manner with which Malcolm treated women during his hipster days can be traced to his relationship with his mother.[21] While such an argument might carry some validity, it essentially ignores the gendered ideologies, power relationships, and popular culture which bound black hipsters together into a distinct, identifiable community. Resistance to wage labor for the hep cat frequently meant increased oppression and exploitation of women, particularly black women. The hipsters of Malcolm's generation and after took pride in their ability to establish parasitical relationships with women wage earners or sex workers. And jazz musicians of the 1940s spoke quite often of living off women, which in many cases translated into outright pimping.[22]

[. . .]

Hustling not only permitted Malcolm to resist wage labor, pursue leisure, and demystify the work ethic myth, but in a strange way the kinds of games he pulled compelled him to "study" the psychology of white racism. Despite the fact that members of this subaltern culture constructed a collective identity in defiance of dominant racist images of African Americans, the work of hustling "white folks" often required that those same dominant images be resurrected and employed as discursive strategies. As a shoeshine boy, for example, Malcolm learned that extra money could be made if one chose to "Uncle Tom a little," smiling, grinning, and making snapping gestures with a polishing rag to give the impression of hard work. Although it was nothing more than a "jive noise," he quickly learned that "cats tip better, they figure you're knocking yourself out." The potential power blacks possessed to manipulate white racial ideologies for their own advantage was made even clearer during his brief stint as a sandwich salesman on the Yankee Clipper commuter train:

> It didn't take me a week to learn that all you had to do was give white people a show and they'd buy anything you offered them. . . . We were in that world of Negroes who are both servants and psychologists, aware that white people are so obsessed with their own importance that they will pay liberally, even dearly, for the impression of being catered to and entertained.

Nevertheless, while Malcolm's performance enabled him to squeeze nickels and dimes from white men who longed for a mythic plantation past where darkeys lived

to serve, he also played the part of the model Negro in the watchful eye of white authority, a law-abiding citizen satisfied with his "shoeshine boy" status. It was the perfect cover for selling illegal drugs, acting as a go-between for prostitutes and "Johns," and a variety of other petty crimes and misdemeanors.[23]

In some respects, his initial introduction to the hustling society illumined the power of the trickster figure or the signifying monkey, whose success depended not only on cunning and wiles, but on knowing what and how the powerful thought. Yet the very subculture which drew Malcolm to the hustling world in the first place created enormous tension, as he tried to navigate between Sambo and militant, image and reality. After all, one of the central attractions of the zoot suiters was their collective refusal to be subservient. As Malcolm grew increasingly wary of deferential, obsequious behavior as a hustling strategy, he became, in his words, an "uncouth, wild young Negro. Profanity had become my language." He cursed customers, took drugs with greater frequency, came to work high, and copped an attitude which even his co-workers found unbecoming. By the war's end, burglary became an avenue through which he could escape the mask of petty hustling, the grinning and Tomming so necessary to cover certain kinds of illicit activities. Although burglary was no less difficult and far more dangerous than pulling on-the-job hustles, he chose the time, place, and frequency of his capers, had no bosses or foremen to contend with, and did not have to submit to time clocks and industrial discipline. Furthermore, theft implied a refusal to recognize the sanctity of private property.

Malcolm's increasingly active opposition to wage labor and dependence upon the illicit economy "schooled" him to a degree in how capitalism worked. He knew the system well enough to find ways to carve out more leisure time and autonomy. But at the same time it led to a physically deleterious lifestyle, reinforced his brutal exploitation of women, and ensured his downward descent and subsequent prison sentence. Nevertheless, Malcolm's engagement with the illicit economy offered important lessons that ultimately shaped his later political perspectives. Unlike nearly all of his contemporaries during the 1960s, he was fond of comparing capitalism with organized crime and refused to characterize looting by black working people as criminal acts – lessons he clearly did not learn in the Nation of Islam. Just five days before his assassination, he railed against the mainstream press's coverage of the 1964 Harlem riot for depicting "the rioters as hoodlums, criminals, thieves, because they were abducting some property." Indeed, Malcolm insisted that dominant notions of criminality and private property only obscure the real nature of social relations: "Instead of the sociologists analyzing it as it actually is . . . again they cover up the real issue, and they use the press to make it appear that these people are thieves, hoodlums. No! They are the victims of organized thievery."[24]

"In a Blue Haze of Inspiration, I Reach the Totality of Being"

Recalling his appearance as a teenager in the 1940s, Malcolm dismissively observed, "I was really a clown, but my ignorance made me think I was 'sharp.'" Forgetting for the moment the integrationist dilemmas of the black bourgeoisie, Malcolm could reflect:

> I don't know which kind of self-defacing conk is the greater shame – the one you'll see on the heads of the black so-called "middle class" and "upper class," who ought to know better, or the one you'll see on the head of the poorest, most downtrodden, ignorant black men. I mean the legal minimum-wage ghetto-dwelling kind of Negro, as I was when I got my first one.[25]

Despite Malcolm's sincere efforts to grapple with the meaning(s) of "ghetto" subculture, to comprehend the logic behind the conk, the reat pleat, and the lindy hop, he ultimately failed to solve Ralph Ellison's riddle. In some ways this is surprising, for who is better suited to solve the riddle than a former zoot suiter who rose to become one of America's most insightful social critics of the century?

When it came to thinking about the significance of *his own* life, the astute critic tended to reduce a panoply of discursive practices and cultural forms to dichotomous categories – militancy versus self-degradation, consciousness versus unconsciousness. The sort of narrow, rigid criteria Malcolm used to judge the political meaning of his life left him ill-equipped to capture the significance of his youthful struggles to carve out more time for leisure and pleasure, free himself from alienating wage labor, survive and transcend the racial and economic boundaries he confronted in everyday life. Instead, "Detroit Red" in Malcolm's narrative is a lost soul devoid of an identity, numbed to the beauty and complexity of lived experience, unable to see beyond the dominant culture he mimics.

This is not at all to suggest that Malcolm's narrative is purposely misleading. On the contrary, precisely because his life as a pimp, prostitute, exploiter, addict, pusher, and all-purpose crook loomed so large in his memory of the 1940s, the thought of recuperating the oppositional meanings embedded in the expressive black youth cultures of his era probably never crossed his mind. Indeed, as a devout Muslim recalling an illicit, sinful past, he was probably more concerned with erasing his hustling years than reconstructing them. As bell hooks surmises, Malcolm's decision to remain celibate for twelve years probably stems from a desire to "suppress and deny those earlier years of hedonistic sexual practice, the memory of which clearly evoked shame and guilt. Celibacy alongside rigid standards for sexual behavior may have been Malcolm's way of erasing all trace of that sexual past."[26]

In the end, Malcolm did not need to understand what the zoot suit, bebop, lindy, or even hustling signified for black working-class politics during the war. Yet his hipster past continued to follow him, even as he ridiculed his knob-toed shoes and conked hair. His simple but colorful speaking style relied on an arsenal of words, gestures, and metaphors drawn in part from his street-corner days. And when he lampooned the black bourgeoisie before black working-class audiences, he might as well have donned an imaginary zoot suit, for his position had not changed dramatically since he first grew wary of the "Hill Negroes" and began hanging out in Roxbury's ghetto in search of "Negroes who were being their natural selves and not putting on airs."[27] There, among the folks today's child gangstas might have called "real niggaz," fifteen-year-old Malcolm Little found the uniform, the language, the culture which enabled him to express a specific constellation of class, racial, generational, and gendered identities.

What Malcolm's narrative shows us (unintentionally, at least) is the capacity of cultural politics, particularly for African American urban working-class youth, to both contest dominant meanings ascribed to their experiences and seize spaces for leisure, pleasure, and recuperation. Intellectuals and political leaders who continue to see empowerment solely in terms of "black" control over political and economic institutions, or who belittle or ignore class distinctions within black communities, or who insist on trying to find ways to quantify oppression, need to confront Ellison's riddle of the zoot suit. Once we situate Malcolm Little's teenage years squarely within the context of wartime cultural politics, it is hard to ignore the sense of empowerment and even freedom thousands of black youth discovered when they stepped onto the dance floor at the Savoy or Roseland ballrooms, or the pleasure young working-class black men experienced when they were "togged to the bricks" in their wild zoot suits, strolling down the avenue "doin the streets up brown."

Whatever academicians and self-styled nationalist intellectuals might think about Malcolm Little's teenage years, the youth today, particularly the hip hop community, are reluctant to separate the hipster from the minister. Consider, for example, W.C. and the MAAD Circle's sampling of Malcolm's voice to open their lyrical recasting of the political economy of crime, "If You Don't Work, U Don't Eat," in which Los Angeles rapper Coolio asserts, "A hustle is a hustle, and a meal is a meal/that's why I'm real, and I ain't afraid to steal." Or consider Gangstarr's video, "Manifest," in which the lead rapper, "Guru," shifts easily between playing Malcolm – suit, rimmed glasses, and all – rapping behind a podium before a mosque full of followers, to rollin' with his homeboys, physically occupying an abandoned, deteriorating building which could have easily been a decaying Roseland Ballroom. Not coincidentally, beneath his understated tenor voice switching back and forth between sexual boasting and racial politics, one hears the bass line from Dizzy Gillespie's bebop classic, "A Night in Tunisia." Through an uncanny selection of music, an eclectic mix of lyrics, and a visual juxtaposing of young black men "hanging out" against Malcolm the minister, Guru and D. J. Premier are able to invoke two Malcolms, both operating in different social spaces but sharing the same time – or, rather, timelessness. While some might find this collapsing of Malcolm's life politically and intellectually disinguous, it does offer a vehicle for black (male) youth to further negotiate between culture as politics and culture as pleasure.

But "collapsing" the divisions Malcolm erected to separate his enlightened years from his preprison "ignorance" also compels us to see him as the product of a *totality of lived experiences*. As I have tried to suggest, aspects of Malcolm's politics must be sought in the riddle of the zoot suit, in the style politics of the 1940s which he himself later dismissed as stupidity and self-degradation. This realization is crucial for our own understanding of the current crisis of black working-class youth in urban America. For if we look deep into the interstices of the postindustrial city, we are bound to find millions of Malcolm Littles, male and female, whose social locations have allowed them to demystify aspects of the hegemonic ideology while reinforcing their ties to it. But to understand the elusive cultural politics of contemporary black urban America requires that we return to Ellison's riddle posed a half century ago and search for meaning in the language, dress, music, and dance styles rising out of today's ghettos, as well as the social and economic context in which styles are created, contested, and reaccented. Once we abandon decontextualized labels like "nihilism" or "outlaw culture" we might discover a lot more Malcolm X's – indeed, more El Hajj Malik El Shabazz's – hiding beneath hoods and baggy pants, Dolphin earrings and heavy lipstick, Raiders' caps and biker shorts, than we might have ever imagined.

Notes

1 Roi Ottley, *"New World A-Coming": Inside Black America* (Boston: Houghton, Mifflin, 1943), 306. On black politics during the war, see Richard Dalfiume, *Fighting on Two Fronts: Desegregation of the Armed Forces, 1939–1953* (Columbia, Mo.: University of Missouri Press, 1969) and "The 'Forgotten Years' of the Negro Revolution," *Journal of American History* 55 (June 1968), 90–106; Herbert Garfinkel, *When Negroes March: The March on Washington Movement in the Organizational Policies for FEPC* (Glencoe, Ill.: Free Press, 1959); Lee Finkle, "The Conservative Aims of Militant Rhetoric: Black Protest during World War II," *Journal of American History* 60 (December 1973), 692–713; Peter J. Kellogg, "Civil Rights Consciousness in the 1940's," *The Historian* 42 (November 1979), 18–41; Neil A. Wynn, *The Afro-American and the Second World War* (New York: Holmes and Meier Publishers, 1975); John Modell, Marc Goulden, and Magnusson Sigurdur, "World War II in the Lives of Black Americans: Some Findings and an Interpretation," *Journal of American History* 76 (December 1989), 838–48; Harvard Sitkoff, *A New Deal for Blacks: The Emergence of Civil Rights as a National Issue* (New York: Oxford University Press, 1978), 298–325, and Sitkoff, "Racial Militancy and Interracial Violence in the Second World War," *Journal of American History* 58 (December 1971), 661–81; Robert Korstad and Nelson Lichtenstein, "Opportunities Found and Lost: Labor, Radicals, and the Early Civil Rights Movement," *Journal of American History* 75 (December 1988), 786–811; Herbert Shapiro, *White Violence and Black Response: From Reconstruction to Montgomery* (Amherst, Mass.: University of Massachusetts Press, 1988), 301–48.

2 Manning Marable, *Race, Reform, and Rebellion: The Second Reconstruction in Black America, 1945–1990*, 2nd ed. (Jackson, Miss.: University Press of Mississippi 1991), 14–17; Philip S. Foner, *Organized Labor and the Black Worker, 1619–1981* (New York: International Publishers, 1981), 239, 243; Daniel R. Fusfeld and Timothy Bates, *The Political Economy of the Urban Ghetto* (Carbondale, Ill.: Southern Illinois University Press, 1984), 48; William H. Harris, *The Harder We Run: Black Workers since the Civil War* (New York: Oxford University Press, 1982), 113–22;

George Lipsitz, *"A Rainbow at Midnight": Labor and Culture in the 1940s* (Urbana: University of Illinois Press, 1994), 14–28; Nelson Lichtenstein, *Labor's War at Home: The CIO in World War II* (New York: Cambridge University Press, 1982), 124–6.

3 Eugene Victor Wolfenstein, *The Victims of Democracy: Malcolm X and the Black Revolution* (Berkeley and Los Angeles: University of California Press, 1981), 175–6.

4 Bruce Perry, *Malcolm: The Life of a Man Who Changed Black America* (Barrytown, N.Y.: Station Hill Press, 1991), 48–9; Malcolm X, with Alex Haley, *The Autobiography of Malcolm X* (New York: Grove Press, 1964), 56, 38–41; Wolfenstein, *Victims of Democracy, 154–7.*

5 Cosgrove, "The Zoot-Suit," 78, 80; LeRoi Jones, *Blues People: Negro Music in White America* (New York: William Morrow, 1963), 202; Eric Lott, "Double V, Double-Time: Bebop's Politics of Style," *Callalloo* 11, no. 3 (1988), 598, 600; Ben Sidran, *Black Talk* (New York: Holt, Rinehart and Winston, 1971), 110–11; Tyler, "Black Jive and White Repression," 31–66.

6 Dominic J. Capeci, Jr., *Race Relations in Wartime Detroit* (Philadelphia: Temple University Press, 1984), and *The Harlem Riot of 1943* (Philadelphia: Temple University Press, 1977); Harvard Sitkoff, "The Detroit Race Riot of 1943," *Michigan History* 53 (Fall 1969), 183–206; Shapiro, *White Violence,* 310–37.

7 Malcolm X, *Autobiography,* 54.

8 Kobena Mercer, "Black Hair/Style Politics," *New Formations* 3 (Winter 1987), 49; also see Lawrence Levine, *Black Culture and Black Consciousness: Afro-American Folk Thought from Slavery to Freedom* (New York: Oxford University Press, 1977), 291–2.

9 Malcolm X, *Autobiography,* 59–60.

10 Ibid., 72 (first quote), 49.

11 Ibid., 51; see Jervis Anderson, *This Was Harlem: A Cultural Portrait, 1900–1950* (New York: Farrar, Straus & Giroux, 1981), 307–14.

12 Quoted in Lott, "Double V, Double-Time," 603. See also Ira Gitler, *Swing to Bop: An Oral History of the Transition in Jazz in the 1940's* (New York: Oxford University Press, 1985); Jack Chambers, *Milestones 1: The Music and Times of Miles Davis to 1960* (Toronto: University of Toronto Press, 1983); Ira Gitler, *Jazz Masters of the 1940's* (New York: Collier Books, 1966); Jones, *Blues People,* 175–207; Frank Kofsky, *Black Nationalism and the Revolution in Music* (New York: Pathfinder Press, 1970), chapter 1; Robert Reisner, *Bird: The Legend of Charlie Parker* (New York: Citadel Press, 1962); Sidran, *Black Talk,* 78–115; John Wilson, *Jazz: The Transition Years, 1940–1960* (New York: Appleton-Century-Crofts, 1966).

13 See Paul Gilroy, "One Nation under a Groove: The Cultural Politics of 'Race' and Racism in Britain," in David Theo Goldberg, ed., *Anatomy of Racism* (Minneapolis: University of Minnesota Press, 1990), 274;

Tera Hunter, "Household Workers in the Making: Afro-American Women in Atlanta and the New South, 1861–1920" (Ph.D. diss., Yale University, 1990), 92–3; and Katrina Hazzard-Gordon, *Jookin': The Rise of Social Dance Formations in African-American Culture* (Philadelphia: Temple University Press, 1990).

14 Cheryl Greenberg, *Or Does it Explode? Black Harlem in the Great Depression* (New York: Oxford University Press, 1991), 164–8; George Q. Flynn, "Selective Service and American Blacks during World War II," *Journal of Negro History* 69 (Winter 1984), 14–25. Gill, "Dissent, Discontent, and Disinterest," 156–7; E. U. Essien-Udom, *Black Nationalism: A Search for Identity* (Chicago: University of Chicago Press, 1962), 80–1; Sidran, *Black Talk,* 82.

15 See especially, Tyler, "Black Jive and White Repression," 34–9 passim.

16 Gerald R. Gill "Dissent, Discontent and Disinterest: Afro-American Opposition to the United States Wars of the Twentieth Century" (unpublished book manuscript, 1988), 166–7, 198–202; Fusfeld and Bates, *Political Economy,* 45–6.

17 Carol B. Stack, *All Our Kin: Strategies for Survival in a Black Community* (New York: Harper and Row, 1974); Betty Lou Valentine, *Hustling and Other Hard Work: Life Styles in the Ghetto* (New York: The Free Press, 1978); Peter Linebaugh, *The London Hanged: Crime and Civil Society in the Eighteenth Century* (London: Allen Lane, The Penguin Press, 1991); Steven Box, *Recession, Crime, and Punishment* (Totowa, N.J.: Barnes and Noble Books, 1987); Jason Ditton, *Part-Time Crime: An Ethnography of Fiddling and Pilferage* (London: Macmillan 1977); Richard C. Hollinger and J. P. Clark, *Theft by Employees* (Lexington, Mass.: Lexington Books, 1983); Cyril Robinson, "Exploring the Informal Economy," *Crime and Social Justice* 15, nos. 3 and 4 (1988), 3–16.

18 Malcolm X, *Autobiography,* 44, 51; Wolfenstein, *Victims of Democracy,* 157. Julius Hudson, "The Hustling Ethic," in Thomas Kochman, ed., *Rappin' and Stylin' Out: Communication in Urban Black America* (Urbana, Ill.: University of Illinois Press, 1972), 414–16.

19 Wolfenstein, *Victims of Democracy,* 155; Perry, *Malcolm,* 72. Horace Cayton and St. Clair Drake, *Black Metropolis: A Study of Negro Life in a Northern City,* 2nd ed. (New York: Harper and Row, 1962), II, 570–611 passim.

20 Malcolm X, *Autobiography,* 134; Perry, *Malcolm,* 77–8, 82–3.

21 Perry; *Malcolm,* 51–2; Wolfenstein, *Victims of Democracy,* 162–3.

22 See, for example, Miles Davis with Quincy Troupe, *Miles: The Autobiography* (New York: Simon and Schuster, 1989), 87–189 passim; Charles Mingus, *Beneath the Underdog* (Harmondsworth, England: Penguin, 1969); and for some postwar examples beyond the jazz world, see Elliot Liebow, *Tally's Corner: A Study of Negro Streetcorner*

Men (Boston: Little, Brown and Co., 1967), 137–44; Christina Milner and Richard Milner, *Black Players: The Secret World of Black Pimps* (New York: Little, Brown, 1972).

23 Malcolm X, *Autobiography*, 47–8, 75.

24 "Not Just an American Problem, but a World Problem," in Perry, ed., *Malcolm X: The Last Speeches*, 161.

25 Malcolm X, *Autobiography*, first quote, 78, second quote, 55.

26 bell hooks, "Sitting at the Feet of the Messenger: Remembering Malcolm X," in *Yearning: Race, Gender and Cultural Politics* (Boston: South End Press, 1990), 84.

27 Malcolm X, *Autobiography*, 43.

28

Mardi Gras Indians: Carnival and Counter-Narrative in Black New Orleans

George Lipsitz

More than fifty years ago, alarmed by the rise of commercial culture and the attendant eclipse of literature and folklore, the great cultural critic Walter Benjamin envisioned a world without stories. Benjamin complained that in such a world, "It is as if something that seemed inalienable to us, the securest of our possessions, were taken from us; the ability to exchange experiences." Certainly, subsequent events have more than justified Benjamin's pessimism.[1] Social and economic changes have undermined the ascribed roles and inherited customs historically responsible for most story-telling traditions. A commodified mass-culture industry covers the globe, replacing traditional narratives with mass-produced spectacles, while the "ability to exchange experiences" often degenerates into the necessity to consume the same cultural commodities.

Yet story-telling persists, even inside the apparatuses of commercial mass culture. Indeed, commerical culture expressly depends upon the residues of local popular narratives for its determinate forms and themes. Blues and reggae music form the unacknowledged subtext of most contemporary popular music. Suppressed ethnic, class, and gender rage undergirds much of the comedy displayed on motion-picture screens around the world, while vernacular art and popular oral traditions provide the raw materials for much of mass culture's visual and aural stimuli. Outside of popular culture, personal and collective memories of region, race, class, gender, and ethnicity continue to provide the raw materials for shared stories. But the pervasiveness of popular narrative forms and themes is not just a matter of the sedimented residue of historical communities and cultures. Mass society and commercial culture provoke a new popular narrative response, one that draws upon both old and new forms of cultural creation. By circulating the stories of particular communities and cultures to a mass audience, the culture industry invites comparison, interpretation, and elaboration. Culture consumers find profound meaning in stories fashioned outside their own communities, and they inevitably re-examine their own traditions in light of what they discover about other cultures.

[. . .]

The Mardi Gras Indians of New Orleans offer an important illustration of the persistence of popular narratives in the modern world, providing a useful case study about the emancipatory potential of grass-roots cultural creation. Every Mardi Gras day, "tribes" of anywhere from fifteen to thirty working-class, black males dress as Plains Indians and take to the streets of New Orleans. They parade through black neighborhoods, displaying their costumes and flags, singing and chanting in a specialized argot, while treating themselves to the hospitality offered in neighborhood bars and private homes. The Indians work all year designing and sewing their costumes, but generally they show them in public only on Mardi Gras Day and St. Joseph's Day. Organized into a rigid status hierarchy of official positions (spy boy, flag boy, wild man, third chief, second chief, big chief, and council chief), the tribes celebrate their own worthiness in chants and songs, while remaining vigilant for competing tribes who might challenge them with aggressive word play to compare costumes, dances, or singing and rhyming ability.[2] Although tribe members must be chosen directly by the group leader, the organizations represent entire neighborhoods. They practice all year in neighborhood bars, and they draw a group of neighborhood residents into the streets behind them as a "second line" of supportive singers and dancers.[3]

On the surface, the core practices of the Mardi Gras Indians resemble quite conventional behaviors by other groups. Under the aegis of carnival, they form secret societies, wear flamboyant costumes, speak a specialized language, and celebrate a fictive past. Carnival revelers all around the world engage in the same practices to release tension from the repressions and frustrations of everyday life. But what distinguishes the Mardi Gras Indians is their use of conventional forms for unconventional purposes. Drawing upon dominant icons and images, they invert them and subvert them. What for other groups might be a symbolic and temporary release from deep-seated repressions functions very differently for the Indian tribes. *Rather than merely expressing utopian desires, the Indian spectacle gives coded expression to values and beliefs that operate every day in the lives of black workers in New Orleans.* Although it takes place in response to the rituals and timetables of European carnival traditions, the Indian spectacle is not primarily European. It presents visual and narrative references to Native American Indians, but it bears little resemblance to genuine Indian celebrations and ceremonies. It draws its determinate modes of expression from African culture and philosophy, but it is not a purely African ritual. Instead, *it projects a cultural indeterminacy*, picking and choosing from many traditions to fashion performances and narratives suitable for arbitrating an extraordinarily complex identity.

The working-class blacks who create the Mardi Gras Indian tribes collectively author an important narrative about their own past, present, and future. Drawing upon the tools available to them – music, costumes, speech, and dance – they fashion a fictive identity that gives voice to their deepest values and beliefs. They replicate many traditional folk practices such as the aggressive festivity of carnival, the ritualistic observance of holidays, and the celebration of a heroic lineage. They tap literary and oral traditions of story-telling through song lyrics, chants, word games, and names. But their collective narrative goes beyond literature and folklore. It draws upon a myriad of contradictory images and icons to fashion a syncretic unity. In the aesthetics of their performance, the Mardi Gras Indians balance the competing claims of commercial culture and folk culture, of America and Africa, of resistance and accommodation, and of spontaneity and calculation. Their art stems less from ancient story-telling traditions or aesthetic intentions than from the necessity imposed upon them by oppressive social conditions. Their utopian projections originate less from abstract images of an ideal future than from a determination to read the lessons of solidarity and struggle from the past and present into the future. If the practices of story-telling, and the qualities of criticism and creativity embedded with them, are to survive in the modern world, it will likely be through the multidimensional practices of artists and individuals like the Mardi Gras Indians.

The Mardi Gras Indian narrative does not always take the form of pure narrative – of a sequence of events taking place over time in a cause-and-effect relationship – but its central recurring theme is a story of heroic warriors resisting domination. The Indians tell about past Mardi Gras days when challenges from other groups forced them to bring to the surface the bravery and solidarity they must repress in everyday life. Song lyrics, chants, and costumes celebrate brave tribes who "won't kneel, won't bow, and don't know how."[4] This Indian imagery draws upon many sources. In slavery times, Indian communities offered blacks a potential alternative to a society in which to be black was to be a slave and to be white was to be free. In New Orleans, black slaves mingled with Indians in local markets, and interactions between Native American Indians and blacks gave many Louisiana blacks a historical claim to a joint Indian and Afro-American heritage. In addition, more than twenty black spiritualist churches in New Orleans venerate the Native American Indian Chief Black Hawk as a martyr, in keeping with the teachings of Leith Anderson, a half Mohawk woman who preached the doctrine of "spirit returning." But the evidence tying the Mardi Gras Indians to direct Indian ancestry is slight.[5] New Orleans "tribes" wear the headresses and costumes of Plains Indians, not of Southeastern Indians, and with the exception of some styles of bead work, few of their practices replicate the crafts of local Native American Indian tribes. South American and Caribbean carnival traditions feature Indians prominently, and some of the New Orleans chants more closely resemble French and Spanish carnival phrases than they do any known Native American Indian tongue.[6] As one Mardi Gras Indian told a researcher

We're not real Indians, we just masquerade as Indians really, and we just give our tribe a name, and different positions and things like that. But as for real Indians, like you'd have to go to Arizona or Texas or something like that to talk to a real Indian, and on a reservation or something like that, but he wouldn't tell you the things I'm telling you because what we're doing is just something that we copies behind the Indians really.[7]

In fact, the touring "Wild West" shows of Buffalo Bill Cody and other late nineteenth-century popular culture entrepreneurs were probably the real impetus for the creation of these mock Indian tribes. Carnival parades in New Orleans began in 1827, but blacks did not generally dress up as Indians until Becate Batiste formed the Creole Wild West tribe in the early 1880s.[8] Donning headdresses and face paint enabled Afro-Americans to circumvent the local laws that made it illegal for blacks to wear masks, but the Indian imagery held important symbolic meaning for them as well. One former Chief of the Golden Blades tribe suggests that *both* blood ties and consumer tastes played a role in the formation of an early Indian tribe, telling a reporter, "In 1895, Robert Sam Tillman got the idea to mask Injun by seeing a Wild West show that came through N'Awlins. Brother Tillman came from Indians himself, and in 1897 he started the [Yellow] Pocahontas tribe."[9] But to see the identification with Indian culture as more a matter of choice than a matter of blood lines hardly lessens its significance. While carnival masking for all groups proclaims a generalized "right to be other" (as Bakhtin asserts), the Mardi Gras Indians adopt a very specific sense of otherness. Most other carnival celebrants might dress as pirates or crows or cowboys in any given year to escape from their everyday identities, but the Indians are always Indians. Furthermore, the Indian image calls attention to the initial genocide upon which American "civilization" rests. It challenges the core dualism of American racism that defines people as either white or black. To perpetuate collective consciousness about Indians in this context is to perpetuate memories about runaway slaves seeking shelter. Other revelers may use carnival masking to escape the repressions of their everyday existence, but the Indian tribes' disguise brings out into the open dimensions of repression that the dominant culture generally tries to render invisible. Of course, this kind of inversion runs the risk of being captured by the very forms it seeks to satirize. Native American viewers might not appreciate the Mardi Gras Indian appropriation of demeaning stereotypes; too many groups in American history have used the image of the Indian for their own purposes, and what comprises symbolic emancipation for one group

might consequently oppress another. But images in negotiation with power are often ambiguous, complicated, and implicated in the crimes they seek to address.

In both content and form of presentation, the Mardi Gras Indian narratives and imagery revolve around self-affirmation and solidarity. Members of Indian tribes might be construction workers, dock hands, bakers, or porters oppressed by both their race and their class in everyday life, but in their rehearsals and performances as Indians they become part of a community of resistance and self-affirmation. They treat life as precious, celebrating its joys and pleasures, even while mourning the dead. Their song lyrics, costumes, speech, and dances all reinforce the same values – grace, strength, elegance, precision, happiness, composure, and dignity.[10] But the key to their collective story rests in more than specific words and images; it comes from the aesthetics of their performance. The Mardi Gras Indian narrative is eloquent and compelling because the forms used to convey it correspond to its basic message, and because the daily lived experience of its adherents reinforces its core values.

In its aesthetics, the Mardi Gras Indian narrative resonates with the culture and philosophy of African music. Of course, they are Afro-Americans and make distinctly Afro-American music, but the Africanisms within Mardi Gras Indian music raise important ideological and artistic issues. Ethnomusicologist John Miller Chernoff identifies the definitive feature of the African musical sensibility as a "functional integration" of music and culture. In African communities, audience handclapping is seen as a vital part of a musical performance, not merely a response by the spectators. Similarly, during African rituals, music is joined with dance, drama, and visual representation to form a fused art made up of interdependent elements. These musical performances blend with lived experiences, accompanying day-to-day events rather than providing a break from them as a self-conscious form of leisure or enlightenment. Finally, music-making in Africa is a functional group activity – a means for organizing and communicating tradition by giving different social groups rights and privileges connected to specific songs.[11]

The Mardi Gras Indian ritual draws upon these African sensibilities in significant ways. The neighborhood residents who attend weekly practice sessions and who follow the tribes into the streets as their "second line" function as active participants in the performance, not just as passive spectators. Second liners beat on bottles with sticks, shake tambourines attached to long poles, and dance to rhythmic chants in an interactive call and response with the singers and dancers in the tribe. Years ago, the second line had an additional function – to protect the costumes and persons of the Indians when the parade entered hostile neighborhoods.[12] In addition, the tribes function as more than musical aggregations. While they do offer opportunities for leisure, recreation, and creative expression, they also serve as mutual-aid societies providing burial insurance, bail money, or other forms of assistance.[13] Most important, the Indians use artistic expression as a means of reinforcing desired behaviors within their community. As Chernoff says about African music,

> the practice of art is an explicitly moral activity because African art functions dynamically to create a context of values where criticism is translated into social action. The meaning of the music is externalized through an event in which participation parallels the musician's artistic purpose: an artist's coolness lends security to intimacy, and the rhythms of an ensemble become the movement of an event when people dance.[14]

In New Orleans, as in Africa, this translation of criticism to action takes place through a fusion of music, dress, speech, and dance.

Fewer than twenty songs make up the basic corpus of Mardi Gras Indian music, although each song has many variants. New songs have become popular and old songs have disappeared, but year in and year out, on Mardi Gras Day and in rehearsals throughout the year, the Indians rework familiar words and melodies.[15] All the tribes sing all of the songs, changing the words to insert the distinctive histories and features of their own group. Musical traditions from around the globe appear in Mardi Gras Indian music. Songs like "Handa Wanda" and "Get Out the Way" involve an interaction between leader and chorus by means of antiphony, or "call and response," a form which originated in West Africa, but which has become a basic feature of Afro-American and Euro-American popular music. In "Don't Like That Song," the leader and chorus exchange groups of phrases in the performance style of Anglo-American Protestant hymn singing. "Indian Red," the song used to end all rehearsals and to begin the Mardi Gras Day procession, contains Caribbean phrases and styles.[16]

The structural forms of Mardi Gras Indian songs relate directly to their functions. The limited corpus of songs ensures a great deal of repetition, but it also places a premium on subtlety and improvisation. As Chernoff points out about African music

People can hear the music for years and always find it fresh and lively because of the extent to which an African musical performance is integrated into its specific social situation. In traditional African music-making situations, the music is basically familiar, and people can follow with informed interest the efforts of the musicians to add an additional dimension of excitement or depth to a performance. Relatively minor variations stand out clearly and assume increased importance in making the occasion successful.[17]

These musical principles reflect philosophical and moral stances. Unlike the Euro-American musical tradition which places a premium on individual authorship of finite texts, the African tradition manifest in Mardi Gras Indian music values dialogue and conversation between artists and audiences to adapt old texts to new situations. The "audience" participates in the creation of this music by singing responses to the leader, by handclapping, and by dancing or chanting in a way that acknowledges the creativity of the musicians. As Chernoff explains, "The music works more by encouraging social interaction and participation at each performance than by affirming a fixed set of sanctioned concepts or beliefs."[18]

But it is not merely an abstract philosophy that emerges from the Indian music; the musical forms employed by the tribes reflect concrete social relations. Thus the "call and response" between the leader and the tribe in "Handa Wanda" represents the symbiotic relationship between the individual and the group. The chiefs have certain concrete responsibilities – in life and in songs – and when appropriate they take the lead both musically and socially. But each individual plays an important role in the tribe, replete with occasions to show off individual skills and attributes for the benefit of the entire group. Similarly, the form of "Indian Red" mirrors the social organization of Indian tribes. Only the chief can sing lead on this song, but his responsibility is to call forth the other members of the tribe by naming their roles – spy boy, flag boy, trail chief, etc. In most tribes, each "rank" has three people in it, and coincidentally "Indian Red" employs a triple meter.[19] The song "Big Chief Wants Plenty of Fire Water" tells a story about a chief who likes to drink, but the Indian tribes and the audiences know that it is used to take up a collection to buy wine for the Indians.[20] Obviously reflective of Anglo and mass-media stereotypes about Indians and alcohol, this song is one of the places where the metaphor employed undermines the culture of anti-racism intended by the Mardi Gras Indian ritual. Yet the act that accompanies it

– hospitality and treating within the community – affirms self-worth and solidarity at the same time.

Like their music, the Mardi Gras Indians' costumes and insignia serve both expressive and functional purposes. Most generally, their beads, feathers, designs, and colors celebrate the bounty of life. Plumes and feathers extend outward magnificently, laying claim to dominion over all the space around them, just as bright colors and rhinestones command spectators' fields of vision. This sartorial display draws upon both the Euro-American sensibility of carnival as a time of pleasure before the deprivations of Lent, as well as on the celebration of life's pleasures ritualized in Afro-American funerals in New Orleans. But it is impossible to understand the full meaning of the Indian suits from their appearances alone. To the Indians, these costumes have meaning only as coded reflections of a complex social process.

Designing and sewing Indian suits is a year-round endeavor; as soon as one carnival ends, the Indians begin to prepare for the next. No one wears the same suit two years in a row; indeed no one wears the same *color* suit two years in a row. Each member of the tribe selects his own colors and designs his own suit, although tribes generally adopt at least one theme color that appears in all of the costumes.[21] Although specialized craftspersons may be asked to assist others with drawing or other particular tasks, Indians are responsible for all their own beading and sewing. The sense of craft is so strong among them that using sewing machines risks unqualified disapproval. Individual expression is encouraged and prized, but most of the sewing takes place in collective work sessions involving the sharing of skills, advice, and opinions.[22] Like music rehearsals, these sewing sessions bring the group closer together and provide an opportunity for passing along skills, attitudes, and traditions.

The costumes and insignia also serve as part of the tribe's communications system. Flags display the names of treasured symbols of each group, but they are also used by the flag boys to signal directions along the line of march, to warn of the approach of other tribes, and even to encourage changes in rhythms for the chants, songs, and dances.[23] The Indians also send a message to the community via the costume of their chief, whose prestige rests largely on the beauty of his suit. One of the stock songs of the Indians boasts "My big chief got a golden crown." The entire tribe takes pride in the chief's appearance as well as responsibility for his protection. Many tribes have body guards in plain clothes accompanying the line of march, and most have a "wild man" whose sole job is to clear the path for the chief and to make sure that no one attacks his costume.[24]

The same calculated playfulness that informs Mardi Gras Indian music and dress makes itself felt in its language as well. Les Blank captures the logic of this speech beautifully in his 1978 documentary film *Always for Pleasure*, in which he has an informant reel off a dazzling set of rhymes in "Indian talk." When asked how he knows what to say, the man replies, "It's no script, no set language; you say what you feel."[25] Of course, most viewers of Blank's film (like most readers of this book) could say what they feel all day and never come up with "Wild Tchoupitoula, uptown ruler, blood shiff ahoona, won't kneel, won't bow, don't know how." Such words come "spontaneously" only to those whose preparation is so thorough that the language has become completely internalized. But the seeming inaccessibility of "Indian talk" plays an important role within the subculture, drawing lines between insiders and outsiders, and cultivating an active sense of ambiguity capable of serving many purposes.

[...]

Song lyrics also connect contemporary heroism to traditional figures. Thus the Wild Tchoupitoulas' "Brother John," pays tribute to John "Scarface" Williams (a rhythm-and-blues singer and Mardi Gras Indian who died from a knifing shortly after carnival in 1972) by comparing him to "Cora" who "died on the battlefield." An earlier song by Willie Turbinton of the Wild Magnolias (based on a chant by the Magnolias' chief Bo Dollis), told the story of a rebellious slave named Corey. In the 1920s jazz musician Danny Barker recorded a song "Corrine Died on the Battlefield," a song which Paul Longpre of the Golden Blades claims told the story of a woman named Cora Anne who masked as queen of the Battlefield Hunters, but who died of gunshot wounds incurred when she got caught in a crossfire between the Hunters and the Wild Squatoolas.[26] Cora thus refers to at least four people living more than a hundred years apart, three of them male and one female. The story touches on the histories of at least five tribes and appeared in four separate songs. There is no one authentic Corey; the purpose of all this borrowing is precisely to fashion a collective narrative embracing a wide range of actual events and individuals. No one lyricist or story-teller can control the narrative about Corey; it filters through the community, undergoing significant changes, yet retaining important continuities.

Language, costumes, and music combine to shape the fused art of Mardi Gras Indian pageantry, but it is largely through dancing that each of these separate forms becomes part of a larger totality. Indians who chant "two way pockaway" ("get out of the way") will dance differently from those chanting "handa wanda" ("we're not looking for trouble"). Dancing offers an opportunity to display the beauty of one's costume; conversely, costume design anticipates the movements of street dancing. Musical selections not only have their own lyrics, melodies, and rhythms, but they also have specific dance steps that accentuate their other meanings.

In recent years, dancing has taken on even greater importance among the Mardi Gras Indian tribes as a symbolic form of combat. At one time the tribes carried real hatchets and spears and used the aggressive festivity of carnival as a cover for gang warfare. After a day of drinking and marching they would meet to settle grudges and rivalries on the "battlefield" – an empty lot at the intersection of Claiborne and Poydras streets. But when urban renewal destroyed the basis for neighborhood competitions, and when police vigilance made violent acts on carnival day more difficult, a new spirit began to emerge. Aesthetic rivalries took the place of street fighting, and dancing became a key way of demonstrating one's superiority over others. When Indians challenge each other in the streets, they draw an imaginary line between them and compete by dancing as close as possible to it without crossing. Their dance enacts a mock fight replete with attacks on territory and each other's bodies. The dancers capable of giving the appearance of fighting without resorting to actual combat win the highest esteem from their tribe and from other spectators.[27]

The transformation of actual violence into symbolic aesthetic competition has many precedents and parallels in Afro-American communities all across the nation, but it has a special history in New Orleans. Art Neville, a rhythm-and-blues musician who has played with the Hawketts, the Meters, and the Neville Brothers (and whose "Uncle Jolly" formed the Wild Tchoupitoulas tribe in 1972), remembers music as a viable alternative to gang fighting in the public housing project where he grew up in the 1940s and 1950s. "We used to do the doo-wop thing," Neville recalls, referring to the close harmonies and scat singing favored by his friends and relatives at that time. "There were gangs from different neighborhoods and some would fight. I was with a gang that did the singing, so I didn't have nothing to worry about."[28]

Yet dancing means much more to the Indian tribes than the mere displacement of aggressive tendencies. Dancing is a communications system in its own right. In parade situations, certain steps by the spy boys and flag boys alert the rest of the tribe to the presence of hostility ahead.[29] Second liners and tribe members create the rhythms for chants and songs with their dancing, every bit as much as the beating of tambourines and sticks conveys a beat for the dancers. Willie Turbinton of the Wild Magnolias remembers that it was the dancing of the Indians that attracted him to them in the first place. When he was eleven years old Turbinton saw his first Indian tribe and remembers, "It just always intrigued me. There were certain steps and certain moves they'd make that were synonymous with the kind of rhythm they played."[30] Turbinton liked the Indian costumes and language, and he was fascinated by the rituals that gave each member of the tribe a particular significance. But he felt drawn into the spectacle most strongly by the ways that the rhythms made him want to dance. "It was the kind of groove that you couldn't resist," he recalls. "The pulse affected you. You find yourself patting your foot, and if you're shy, you just feel it inside yourself."[31]

[...]

Much of the power of the Mardi Gras Indian ritual stems from its force as a counter-narrative challenging the hegemony of New Orleans' social elite. During Mardi Gras, New Orleans "high society" celebrates its blood lines and mythologizes itself as the heir to a powerful tradition of mysticism and magic. The elite mask themselves in expensive costumes and ride motorized floats along the city's main thoroughfares, throwing beaded necklaces and souvenir doubloons to crowds of spectators. The Indians subvert this spectacle by declaring a powerful lineage of their own, one which challenges the legitimacy of Anglo-European domination. Their costumes are made, not bought. They avoid the main thoroughfares and walk through black neighborhoods. They define the crowds along their route as participants, not just as spectators. Their fusion of music, costumes, speech, and dance undermines the atomized European view of each of those activities as distinct and autonomous endeavors, while it foregrounds an African sensibility about the interconnectedness of art and the interconnectedness of human beings.

Yet the degree to which this counter-narrative actually threatens the hegemony of the dominant culture is open to dispute. One can well imagine how easily those in power might dismiss black workers in outlandish costumes drinking and dancing in the streets on Mardi Gras Day.

Certainly within the black community, the ambiguities and multi-layered symbolism of the Indian ritual might well obscure the historical and social power realities behind its genesis, as the traditional internal rivalries it has provoked have demonstrated. The dominance of males and the peripheral role allotted to females within the Indian ritual reinforces traditional gender roles. [...] Furthermore, even if one were to claim that the Indian ritual served an oppositional purpose within black New Orleans, there would be no guarantee that this particular counter-narrative could transcend specific experiences of race, region, and class to speak to people with different values and histories. The forms and styles fashioned by the Indians seem so rooted in the specific history and culture of New Orleans that it is difficult to imagine how their practice could be representative of counter-narratives generated under different conditions.

[...]

Like all subordinated groups, the Indians lack access to significant power and resources, and their organizations do serve purposes of mutual aid and self-affirmation denied them in other spheres. Their ritual may have started in relative isolation from the "largely imposed character of mass media culture," but their present-day and future audiences have been saturated with competing images and sounds from other cultures through the mass media. They seem to exemplify Jameson's contention that truly "popular" art exists only in specialized and marginalized circumstances, far removed from the centers of mainstream commerce and culture.

Yet the same forms of commercial culture that destroy the organic basis for traditional folklore enable people to escape the prejudices and parochialisms of their own communities. The same forces that relegate ethnic, linguistic, and subcultural minorities to the margins of contemporary culture, also transmit the oppositional sensibilities of marginal groups to a mass audience. The same feelings that motivate people to fashion autonomous signs and symbols within folkloric traditions impel them to put the stamp of their own experience on the ideas and images circulated within commercial culture. Most important, the internal properties of the electronic mass media favor precisely the kinds of dynamic cultural creation basic to the entire Mardi Gras Indian activity. Commercial culture destroys the sense of "origins" and "authenticity" prized by Euro-American music and folklore, but its biases toward repetition, non-linear reasoning, and immediacy make it a viable conduit

for oppositional narratives like those created by the Mardi Gras Indians. Nothing illustrates this tendency more convincingly than the way in which New Orleans musicians have inserted Mardi Gras Indian music into American and international popular music.

As early as the 1920s, jazz musicians from New Orleans recorded Mardi Gras Indian songs. Danny Barker and his Creole Cats did "My Indian Red" and "Chocko Mo Fendo Hando" on the King Zulu label, while Louis Dumaine and his Jazzola Eight performed "To Wa Bac a Wa" for Vic Records.[32] In 1954, Sugar Boy Crawford inserted Indian music into mainstream popular culture when his song "Jock-A-Mo" became a big regional hit. Although not an Indian himself, Crawford created "Jock-A-Mo" by combining two songs he remembered hearing them sing when he was growing up near the "battlefield" on Claiborne and Poydras streets.[33] Dave Bartholomew's 1957 "Can't Take It No More" begins with chanting evocative of Indian call and response.[34] In 1965, the Dixie Cups, a female trio from New Orleans, reached the national top-twenty list with "Iko Iko" – which like "Jock-A-Mo" originated with the Mardi Gras Indians. In a story that illustrates how commercial and folk cultures can intersect, Barbara Hawkins of the Dixie Cups relates how "Iko Iko" became a record:

> We were clowning around the studio while the musicians were on break, it was just the three of us using drumsticks on ashtrays and glasses singing "Iko Iko." We didn't realize that [producers] Jerry and Mike (Leiber and Stoller) were in the control room with the tape rolling. They came out and said that's great, they had never heard it before, all they added was a calypso box. We had never planned on recording it.[35]

Hawkins described the song as "the type of thing the Indians have always used, inventing new words as they march along."[36] In the late 1970s, Hawkins herself came full circle with the Indians, marching as Queen of the Wild Magnolias on Mardi Gras Day.

[...]

In 1986, rock singer Cyndi Lauper delayed the release of her "True Colors" album in order to include "Iko Iko" on it. Lauper had been listening to playbacks of her rendition of Marvin Gaye's 1960s antiwar, anti-racist "What's Going On," and she began to be reminded of another song. Eventually, she realized that the rhythms she had been using in "What's Going On" fit perfectly into "Iko Iko," which came to Lauper through listening to the Neville Brothers, Doctor John, and the Dixie Cups.[37] On the surface, her connection might seem absurd. The profound political lyrics of "What's Going On" bear little resemblance to the nonsense rhymes of "Iko Iko." The life experience of a white woman rock star from New York seems to have little in common with the historical struggle against racial and class domination waged by the Mardi Gras Indians. Yet Lauper's intuition led her to the right place. "What's Going On" and "Iko Iko" *are* both about fighting racism and exploitation. The magnificent plumes and bright colors of the Mardi Gras Indians express in their way what the multicolored hair and self-parodying costumes of Cyndi Lauper represent in another way. The proto-feminist blend of adolescent female voices and adult sexual desires in the Dixie Cups' "Iko Iko" serves as a legitimate progenitor to Lauper's own breakthrough hit in 1985, "Girls Just Want to Have Fun."

That Lauper came to "Iko Iko" through the apparatuses of commercial culture raises intriguing questions about the supposedly diminishing power of popular narratives. It illustrates how marginalized cultures can insinuate their oppositional values into the texts of popular culture and create allies among people with similar though not identical experiences. It is no more ridiculous for Cyndi Lauper to appropriate "Iko Iko," than it was for nineteenth-century, working-class blacks to use the Wild West Show, Mardi Gras, and gang-fighting as a basis for an oppositional subculture. As part of the history of rock and roll, as part of the historic opposition to hierarchy and exploitation in America, "Iko Iko" offered a logical source of inspiration and celebration for Lauper. The critics may be right when they talk about the decline of traditional narratives, the marginalization of "popular" art, and the "largely imposed character of mass media culture." But people fight with the resources at their disposal, and frequently their pain leads them to quite innovative means of struggle. They do not all have the same story, and they often fail to understand the stories of others. They often suffer terrible oppression and anguish as they search for a narrative capable of making sense out of their existence. But story-telling survives, even when the story-tellers develop coded and secret ways of communicating with one another, inside and outside of commercial culture. For all of his pessimism, even Walter Benjamin understood this. In the same essay in which he fretted about the demise of story-telling, Benjamin offered a phrase which he meant figuratively, but which has a literal meaning as well. "Indeed," Benjamin observed, "each

sphere of life has, as it were, produced its own tribe of storytellers."[38]

Notes

1   Walter Benjamin, *Illuminations* (New York: Schocken Books, 1969), 83.
2   David Elliott Draper, "The Mardi Gras Indians: The Ethnomusicology of Black Associations in New Orleans," (Ph.D. dissertation, Tulane University, 1973), 7, 27, 38, 40.
3   Draper, "The Mardi Gras Indians," 35, 54.
4   Les Blank, *Always for Pleasure*, Flower Films, 1978.
5   See Jason Berry, "Controversy Swirls Around Mardi Gras Indian Origins," *New Orleans Times-Picayune*, February 17, 1984. sec. 1, 6.
6   Jason Berry, Jonathan Foose, and Tad Jones, *Up from the Cradle of Jazz* (Athens and London: University of Georgia Press, 1986), 210, 218.
7   Helen Joy Mayhew, "New Orleans Black Musical Culture: Tradition and the Individual Talent" (MA Thesis, University of Exeter, 1986), 187–88.
8   Berry, Foose, and Jones, *Up from the Cradle of Jazz*, 210.
9   Jason Berry, "Pomp and Circumstance of the Mardi Gras Indians," *Dynamic Years*. n. 16. March 1981.
10 Draper, "The Mardi Gras Indians," 42. John Miller Chernoff identifies grace, strength, elegance, precision, happiness, composure, and dignity as key elements in performances by African chiefs on p. 150 of his wonderful book *African Rhythms and African Sensibility* (Chicago and London: University of Chicago Press, 1979).
11 Chernoff, *African Rhythm and African Sensibility*, 33–4.
12 Draper, "The Mardi Gras Indians," 54. See also Alan Lomax, *Mr. Jelly Roll* (Berkeley: University of California Press, 1950, 1973), 12.
13 Draper, "The Mardi Gras Indians," 23. See also John Blassingame, *Black New Orleans, 1860–1880* (Chicago and London: University of Chicago Press, 1973).
14 Chernoff, *African Rhythm and African Sensibility*, 143.
15 Draper, "The Mardi Gras Indians," 218, 360.
16 Draper, "The Mardi Gras Indians," 227, 276, 286. Berry, Foose, and Jones, *Up from the Cradle of Jazz*, 213.
17 Chernoff, *African Rhythm and African Sensibility*, 61.
18 Chernoff, *African Rhythm and African Sensibility*, 125.
19 Draper, "The Mardi Gras Indians," 362, 363.
20 Finn Wilhelmsen, "Creativity in the Songs of the Mardi Gras Indians of New Orleans, Louisiana," *Louisiana Folklore Miscellany*, v. 3, 1973, 58.
21 Draper, "The Mardi Gras Indians," 130, 166, 167.
22 Draper, "The Mardi Gras Indians," 122, 166, 167.
23 Draper, "The Mardi Gras Indians," 103.
24 Draper, "The Mardi Gras Indians," 51, 53, 54.
25 Blank, *Always for Pleasure*.
26 Berry, Foose, and Jones, *Up from the Cradle of Jazz*, 224, 235.

27   Ibid. 216. Draper, "The Mardi Gras Indians," 36, 38.

28   Don Palmer, "Gumbo Variations," *The Sobo News*, August 11, 1981, 23.

29   Draper, "The Mardi Gras Indians," 103.

30   Berry, Foose, and Jones, *Up from the Cradle of Jazz*, 220.

31   Ibid.

32   Draper, "The Mardi Gras Indians," 389.

33   Jeff Hannusch, *I Hear You Knockin'* (Ville Platte: Swallow Publications, 1985), 262.

34   Helen Joy Mayhew, "New Orleans Black Musical Culture: Tradition and the Individual Talent" (MA thesis, University of Exeter, 1986), 215.

35   Shepard Samuels, "The Dixie Cups," *Wavelength*, May 1982, 18.

36   Ibid.

37   Jon Bream, "Cyndi Lauper," *Minneapolis Star and Tribune*, December 7, 1986.

38   Benjamin, *Illuminations*, 85.

29

To Be Young, Brown, and Hip: Race, Gender, and Sexuality in Indian American Youth Culture

Sunaina Marr Maira

The massive beats of a new sound reverberated in New York City nightlife in the mid-1990s, a mix of Hindi film music and bhangra, a North Indian and Pakistani dance and music, with American rap, techno, jungle, and reggae. The second-generation Indian American youth subculture that introduced this "remix music" has become a recognized part of the city's broader popular culture, heralded to the mainstream by concerts at the Summerstage series in Central Park, articles in the local news media, and documentaries by local independent filmmakers. This chapter explores the tension between the production of cultural nostalgia and the performance of "cool" in this subculture, showing how the dialectic between these structures of feeling reveals the contradictory cultural politics of authenticity for Indian American youth (Williams 1977).

Bhangra remix music constitutes a transnational popular culture in the Indian/South Asian diaspora; it emerged among British-born South Asian youth in the mid-1980s and has since flowed between New York, Delhi, Bombay, Toronto, Port-of-Spain, and other nodes of the South Asian diaspora (Gopinath 1995). While this "remix youth culture" has emerged in other urban areas in the United States that have large Indian American populations, such as Chicago and the Bay Area, its expressions are shaped by local contexts. There has not as yet been much comparative work on this topic, but it is clear that Manhattan lends this youth culture distinctive features, including particular sonic elements: DJ Tony of TS Soundz in Chicago pointed out to me that while Chicago remixes tend to use house and techno music, New York deejays favor remixes with rap music, and participants in this local subculture tend to adopt a more overtly "hoody," hip-hop-inspired style (see Sengupta 1996).

The New York subculture based on Indian music remixes includes participants whose families originated in other countries of the subcontinent, such as Bangladesh and Pakistan, yet insiders often code events that feature this music as the "Indian party scene" or "desi scene." While participants in the desi scene share certain South Asian cultural codes and common experiences in the United States, aspects of ethnic and national identity play out in particular ways for different national and religious, not to mention regional, groups. The "scene" is a differentiated one: Indian American youth who are not in college also attend these parties, and there are "Indian parties" held outside Manhattan, for instance, on campuses in New Jersey and Long Island that have large South Asian student populations. Manhattan, however, provides a particular context for desi parties because of the presence of city clubs, such as the Madison, the China Club, or SOB.'s (Sounds of Brazil), that draw large droves of South Asian American youth who get down to the beats of bhangra. SOB.'s, a world music club in downtown Manhattan, has been home to one of the most well known regular "bhangra parties" since March 1997, when DJ Rekha launched "Basement Bhangra," the first Indian remix music night to be featured monthly on the calendar of a Manhattan club – and the first to be hosted by a woman deejay.

[. . .]

Indian Remix Music and the Manhattan "Desi Scene"

The emergence of this vibrant Indian American (and South Asian American) youth culture in Manhattan in the mid-1990s was partly due to the presence of the large local Indian immigrant community in the area. New York City is one of the primary receiving areas for Indian immigrants to the United States because of two major factors. First, the local labor market offers a range of employment opportunities, from engineering jobs in industries in nearby New Jersey and Connecticut to employment in hotels, motels, banking, insurance, public health, and garment and jewelry businesses, as well as the import/export trade (Lessinger 1995). New York City also has traditionally favored small, family-owned retail businesses over national chain stores, which accounts for the increasing number of Indian entrepreneurs, some of whom run the newsstands that dot the city and others of whom own small businesses that serve the growing South Asian American market – for example, travel agencies and law firms that are advertised in Indian community newspapers and the restaurants and grocery stores in midtown Manhattan and in Jackson Heights, Queens. Working-class Indian immigrants or middle-class Indians who could not find the jobs they had hoped for sometimes find employment in the service sector or unskilled labor market (Lessinger 1995). The taxi industry has absorbed many South Asian immigrant men, particularly from agricultural regions in the Punjab; in 1992, the Taxi and Limousine Commission of New York City reported that 43 percent of Manhattan-based yellow cabs were driven by South Asians, equally represented by Indians, Pakistanis, and Bangladeshis (Advani 1997), and in 1999–2000, that figure was close to 60 percent (Esser et al. 1999–2000). The second factor that has motivated many Indian immigrants to settle in New York City, at least initially, is that many have immigrated through family reunification categories, especially during the 1980s and 1990s. These are immigrants who have chosen to live close to relatives already settled in the area or in localities with a large number of other Indian families, such as Jackson Heights in Queens or Edison in New Jersey.

[. . .]

Understanding a subculture and its rituals, such as those of the desi party scene in New York, helps explain why a popular culture based on music in particular has such strong appeal for youth. Simon Frith (1992, p. 177) has written that "for young people . . . music probably has the most important role in the mapping of social networks, determining how and where they meet and court and party." In other words, in societies with commercialized popular cultures, music has become a ritual that is important in the socialization of youth. Frith argues that by providing a subtle and complex means of individual and collective expression, "[music] is in many respects the model for their involvement in culture, for their ability to see beyond the immediate requirements of work and family and dole" (1992, p. 177). His insight also suggests that subcultures – expressions of distinctive identities organized around particular rituals or commodities – exist in relationship to the broader context of "culture," against which the web of social meanings, relationships, and material experiences of particular subcultures are defined. Popular culture is saturated with ideologies about youth that are racialized, gendered, and classed, but it also offers an arena in which youth may reappropriate or symbolically transgress existing racial, gendered, and class boundaries.

[. . .]

By sampling Indian music, second-generation youth draw on sounds from Hindi movies and Indian music that their parents introduced them to when they were children in order to inculcate an "Indian" identity. By remixing these with rap and reggae and by donning hip-hop gear or brand-name clothes, Indian Americans display the markers of ethnicity and material status used in a multiethnic, capitalist society. To understand the collision of racialized, gendered, and ethnicized imaginings with material aspirations in this remix popular culture, I first outline the cultural contradictions facing second-generation youth that are enacted at "desi parties" in Manhattan and that are part of the popular discourse used to explain these events, and then suggest more layered interpretations that reveal gendered tensions and underlying racial and material processes.

The performances that remix youth culture in New York makes possible, while not enabling wider systemic change, fulfill an immediate social and affective need for desi youth and have a pragmatic and not just expressive dimension. Les Back (1994), analyzing the "intermezzo culture produced in the fusion of bhangra and reggae in Britain," argues that in the alternative public sphere of the dance, "liminal ethnicities are produced that link together different social collectivities" (cited in Sharma 1996, p. 36). Since this popular culture involves events that are almost exclusively attended by South Asian youth, it is often condoned by parents who would be more hesitant to allow their children to go to regular clubs or parties with non–South Asian friends, especially while youth are still in high school or living at home. [. . .]

Parental approval, at least during the initial years of this desi party scene, seems a largely unintentional benefit for youth seeking to participate in the rituals of American youth popular culture, such as clubbing, dating, and performances of subcultural style. [. . .]

After the party is over, youth must return to the constraints of interacting with their parents, peers, and communities (Cohen 1997; Gelder 1997). Sanjay Sharma points out that the "liminal ethnicities" represented by British Asian dance culture, if created at all, may be limited to the "transitory and contingent spaces of the dance floor" (Sharma 1996, p. 36). Hybridity, though fashionable in cultural theory and also, literally, in "ethnic chic," is not always easy to live, for social institutions and networks continue to demand loyalty to sometimes competing cultural ideals that second-generation youth may find difficult to manage. For many, liminality is an ongoing, daily condition of being betwixt and between cultural categories (Turner 1967; 1987, pp. 101, 107) that is symbolically expressed in remix culture. This is, however, only one of several spaces that Indian American youth negotiate, and other contexts elicit a more bounded, fixed notion of Indianness.

The performance of a visibly hybrid ethnicity occurs in specific contexts and is not always optional; it belongs to a range of performances of cultural scripts in every-day life. Indian American youth still switch among multiple identities, as they did when moving between high school and family, only now perhaps they change from the baggy pants and earrings that they wear among peers to conservative attire on the job, or from being in secret relationships at college to acting as dutiful daughters on visits home. These transitions clearly have a gendered dimension, and the negotiation of ethnic identity and national culture is embodied differently by women and men, as is visibly enacted in the remix music subculture.

A revealing source of tension within this Indian American world of dance parties and social gatherings is the contestation of sexual and gender roles and of racialized images of desire. Many of the young people I interviewed noted that a "hoody" or streetwise hip-hop image was not considered as appealing for women in this subculture as it was for men, and that the predominant style associated with desirable femininity was designer-inspired urban fashion. Slinky club wear that allows a flash or more of leg or midriff is the style popular among many young women at desi parties; at the time of my study, this meant hip-hugger pants, halter tops, and miniskirts. Some women sport a diamond nose stud or nose ring in a nod to ethnic style. A glamorous femininity is pervasive – kohl-lined eyes, dark lipstick, and arched eyebrows – and an emphasis on slimness, if not sheer thinness. This feminized image had become the look for many hip-hop women artists in the 1990s, some of whom moved away from androgynous rapper style to the "ghetto fabulous" look (George 1998, p. 119), The Indian American remix subculture, however, showed little variation in the cod-ing of female style and, more important, an underlying preoccupation with the stylistic coding and regulation of Indianness, and implicitly of Blackness, especially for women.

[. . .]

Notions of style and body image are embedded in deeper contradictions in the gender constructions and heterosexual roles that are played out in remix youth culture and that are contested by some who find this constricting. Often this contestation is enacted not only in gendered but also in racialized terms, with an under-lying concern about appropriate femininity and the perils of racial border crossing. Manisha, whose friends were mainly African American and Latino and who often dressed in hip-hop gear – with a gold "Om" pen-dant dangling around her neck – reflected, "Guys can get away with [the 'hoody' look] but girls who are consid-ered 'cool' dress prettier. I think the guys are intimidated by that [girls with a hip-hop look], it's taken as a sign of being closer to Latinos or Blacks, of being outside of the Indian circle, as I am . . . the guys may think we're rougher, or not as sweet." This "sweet," more conven-tionally feminine look, often associated with the ethni-cally and racially coded marker of long, straight hair, is also rife with contradictions; an ambivalence about the appeal of "innocent" femininity creates yet another doubling in these enactments of desire. While most men favor for Indian American women the demure, feminized image over the androgynous hip-hop look, the former presentation is in turn passed over on the dance floor for women who perform a more sexualized style – the "hoochy mamas." Yet these women are considered "loose," that is, not the type of woman an Indian

American man would like to marry. Among men, however, a somewhat wider range of images of male desirability seems to apply, although these are no less racialized than for women.

For some women who go to these "Indian parties," what is most frustrating is the discomfort they feel being subjected to aggressive male advances and female heterosexual competitiveness. Reena, for example, said she enjoys the music and socializing, "but it's also a lot of competition, in the sense that you have all these hoochy mamas in there with their tight-fitting dresses and stuff like that and trying to be all up on everyone. I just remember getting into my brother's car and being like, I'm just way too mature for this, because like guys [are] coming up to me, 'Hey, baby, what's your number?'" Reena's comment highlights the problems of heterosexual objectification in club culture, even while young women may take pleasure in vamping it up in their "tight-fitting dresses." Her observations of sexual play in this remix youth culture have to be situated in relation to the contradictory expectations of immigrant families that daughters successfully negotiate mainstream society while simultaneously performing the role of primary bearers of culture (Agarwal 1991). The chastity of daughters becomes emblematic not just of the family's reputation but also, in the context of the diaspora, of the purity of tradition and ethnic identity, a defense against the promiscuity of "American influences" (Bhattarcharjee 1992; Das Dasgupta and Dasgupta 1996; Gibson 1988; Mani 1993).

[...]

In the desi party subculture, a different set of norms for heterosexual appeal operate for young men than for young women, for "doing gender" is more explicitly tied to negotiations of material status for desi males (Leblanc 1999, p. 141). Several youth pointed explicitly to the need for men who belong to this subculture to flaunt brand-name "gear" to signal their buying power and thus their appeal in the heterosexual dating market. The *behavior* of Indian American men, however, is not read as a marker of ethnic authenticity. While the women I spoke to often criticized men who projected a sexualized or promiscuous image in the party scene as unreliable and unappealing for long-term relationships, they did not consider these men "less Indian" for their hypersexuality. Machismo becomes linked to nationalism, however, and in some cases even to specific regional identifications, through practices that are common in club culture generally but are framed within the desi party scene

by a discourse of ethnic marginalization and internal differentiation.

[...]

Dharmesh, a young man whose family lives in New Jersey, remarked that Indian American youth who grew up with Blacks and Latinos, and even some who did not, on coming to college often acquire "the style, and the attitude, and the walk" associated with urban Black and Latino youth culture. Hip-hop is not just "the Black CNN" but has become the channel for youth culture information in general, as Peter Christenson and Donald Roberts point out: "Of all the current popular music styles, the rap/hip hop culture most defines the pop cultural cutting edge, thus providing adolescents concerned with 'coolness' and peer status much crucial information on subjects such as the latest slang and the most recent trends in dance and fashion" (1998, p. 111; see also Perkins 1996, p. 13). The music and media industries have helped make hip-hop a language increasingly adopted by middle-class and suburban youth (Giroux 1996; Kleinfeld 2000; Roediger 1998), with White consumers accounting for about 75 percent of rap album sales (Christenson and Roberts 1998, p. 111). Hip-hop culture is resignified by Indian American "homeboys" when it crosses class boundaries, as Sujata, a woman who grew up in suburban Connecticut, pointed out: "A lot of them are like total prep school, but they put on a, like, it's this preppie boy–urban look, you know, it's like Upper East Side homeboy, you know. Huge pants, and then, like, a nice button-down shirt, you know."

[...]

The question of hybridity is doubly complicated for desi youth in New York, for they are reworking hip-hop not only into their own youth culture but into a *remix* youth culture, one that expresses the cultural imaginaries of second-generation youth from an immigrant community of color. Fundamentally, desi youth turn to hip-hop because it is key to marking their belonging in the multiethnic urban landscape of New York City. Sharmila noted that for many second-generation men, hip-hop style connotes a certain image of racialized hypermasculinity that is the ultimate definition of cool. "South Asian guys give more respect to African Americans than to Whites because they think the style is cool. The guys look up to them because it's down [fashionable]. They think, 'I'm kinda scared of them but I want to look like them because they're cool.'" Ravi, who began going to Indian parties while in high school in California and who has continued to do so in New York, reflected, "The hip-hop culture has just really taken off. It's really appealed to the Indians, maybe just listening pleasure, the way it sounds, I guess. Maybe the toughness it exudes." Roediger points out that "in a society in which the imagination of Blackness so thoroughly frames what both attracts and repulses whites," American male youth often "identify with violence, scatology, and sexism in rap rather than with Black music and culture more broadly" (1998, pp. 359, 361). Black style is viewed as the embodiment of a particular machismo, the object of racialized desire and, simultaneously, of racialized fear. The desi youth subculture not only is engaged with essentialized definitions of what it means to be truly Indian but also invests this ideal with essentialized definitions of what it means to be cool and to be "young, urban, and black" (Banerjea and Banerjea 1996).

[. . .]

The Racial Politics of "Cool"

The appropriation of Black style obviously has different meanings for youth depending on the particular racial and class locations they occupy; an understanding of the politics of cool is necessarily conjunctural. Codes of hip(-hop)ness at work in Asian American youth subcultures are always in relationship to the racialization of Asians and the Black/White racial paradigm of the United States. Dorinne Kondo (1995, p. 53), commenting on urban Asian Americans who identify with African Americans and borrow their dialect, observes, "If you are Asian American or Latino, especially on the East Coast, white and black are the poles, and if you don't identify with one, you identify with the other." Gary Okihiro (1994) probes more deeply into the positioning of Asian Americans within this racial binary by addressing the political implications of the question "Is yellow Black or White?" – or, if you will, is brown Black or White? Okihiro (1994, p. 34) notes that Asian Americans, Native Americans, and Latinos are classified as either "near-whites" or "just like blacks," depending on the operation of model minority myths or their subordination as minorities: "Asian Americans have served the master class, whether as 'near-blacks' in the past or as 'near-whites' in the present or as 'marginal men' in both the past and the present. Yellow [or brown] is emphatically neither white nor black; but insofar as Asians and

Africans share a subordinate position to the master class, yellow is a shade of black, and black, a shade of yellow." [. . .] The turn to hip-hop by desi youth in New York could be considered a "racial project" in Michael Omi and Howard Winant's sense of the term – an ideological link between structures and representations of race, connecting "what race means in a particular discursive practice and the ways in which both social structures and everyday experiences are racially organized, based upon that meaning" (1994, p. 56).

This racial project can be seen as a response to the Black/White racial binary and the attempts of second-generation Indian Americans to position themselves in relation to the monochromatic racial boundaries of the United States.

[. . .]

Remix youth culture's sampling of hip-hop allows desi youth to hold the two impulses of ethnicization and participation in the U.S. racial formation in a delicate balance. As a racial project, it defers the question of "Black or White" through the ambiguity of adopting Black style in an ethnically exclusive space. If the production of cool symbolically crosses racial boundaries, it is still, for some youth, only a transitional flirtation with Black popular culture, and one that has been, for many, almost an American rite of passage in adolescence (Roediger 1998). Jeffrey Melnick observes that the crossing of racial boundaries through music tends to wane as adolescents move into adulthood and is "temporally bounded by the fact that . . . teenagers have to grow up into a labor economy deeply invested in racial division" (1996, p. 227). Sunita, who grew up in Queens and in Stamford, Connecticut, believed many desi youth immersed in hip-hop culture "at the back of their minds are thinking, this is not long-term." She commented that the appropriation of what is perceived by the mainstream to be an oppositional style is mediated by the often unstated but always present location of class status, and she remarked, "I know for me there's this cushion, my parents are supporting me, they're paying for my college . . . you know [the identification] is only up to a certain point, there are big, distinct differences." This was exemplified by a conversation I had with an Indian American man in his mid-twenties at a conference organized by the New York chapter of the Network of Indian Professionals (NETIP). He had been immersed in the desi party scene, but as an adult in the workforce, he felt unmoored. What would replace the desi subculture that he had identified with when he was younger? Clearly, his question was partly answered by the conference itself, sponsored by an organization formed largely to support networking and heterosexual liaisons among young, upwardly mobile Indian Americans.

In New York, many college students I spoke to seemed to envision a future in which they would move into the professional, college-educated class, in order to realize their immigrant parents' aspirations for upward mobility. Unlike the creators of hip-hop, the youth who participate in the Indian remix subculture are not necessarily using it to recognize limited options for economic mobility. Most Indian American youth I spoke to did not view this remix popular culture as resistance to a system of economic and racial stratification; in fact, several seemed bent on succeeding within that system. Although as youth of color they are often targets of racial discrimination, many did not believe that would translate into economic discrimination in their own lives. Second-generation youth who grew up in less affluent, racially diverse neighborhoods, however, often know what it is like to live in communities struggling for city and state resources, and regardless of class location, many of these youth have experienced racial harassment, sometimes because they are mistakenly identified as Black or Latino.

[. . .]

Second-generation youth who participate in the desi youth culture are not unaware of the contradictions of consuming Black style and are often uneasy about the politics of this "cultural appropriation" in light of anti-Black racism. DJ Baby Face articulated this paradox clearly at an Indian party held in the cavernous tunnels of a Manhattan club, with the beat of Indian remix pounding against the walls: "Blacks are the scapegoat for Indians, but when it comes to fashion and style, we hold them high, they have power." His succinct observation reveals the underlying politics of being cool – the group emulated in style is also the one on whose back immigrants tread to preserve their sense of superior status.

[. . .]

Some theorists argue that the turn to hip-hop among desi youth is explained in part by the alienation of second-generation youth from the model minority leanings of their parents, including the stereotype's manifestation as anti-Black racism. Singh is hopeful that second-generation youth have been socialized into a different kind of race politics, mediated through Black popular music: "Unlike their parents, they have African American friends and have developed a better understanding of how racism and poverty operate in American society. . . . [M]aybe the deep sense of 'alienation' expressed in contemporary black music resonates with their own sense of rebellion against their parents' double standards: an insistence on seeing African Americans harshly through the prism of caste even as they cloak themselves in the highest ideals of fairness and equal opportunity" (1996, p. 98). Some of the youth I spoke to expressed an awareness of race politics that had grown out of friendships and everyday social interactions with other youth of color, and had developed into a critique of institutional and community racism. Yet I distinguish between an "alienation" felt by youth who are politically or economically disenfranchised or critical of the status quo – a "structural alienation" – and a resistance arising out of a generational difference – a "social-psychological alienation" (Epstein 1998, pp. 5–6). Adolescent rebellion against parents and the generational ideologies they represent is a trope that has long been embedded in theories of adolescence and coming-of-age narratives in the United States, even while these have varied by gender, ethnic, and class location (Erikson 1968; Mead 1961). Rebellion through popular music, moreover, is a familiar rite of youth culture – often a particularly masculinized one (Whitely 1997) – that may offer Indian American youth a cultural form to express their distancing from parents. For some Indian American youth, however, a style that subverts their parents' expectations and racial prejudices may simultaneously be an expression of their own critique of the racialized caste stratification of US society.

Desi youth's turn to hip-hop in the 1990s is rooted in a larger history of appropriation of Black music by non-African Americans as part of the reinvention of ethnic identity by various groups. The resonant connections between the work of cultural studies theorist George Lipsitz (1994) and anthropologist Michael Fischer (1986) on this issue provide interesting insights into the implications of Indian American hip-hop. Lipsitz, commenting on White American artists who were drawn to African American and Latino musical traditions, writes, "Black music provided them with a powerful critique of mainstream middle-class Anglo-Saxon America as well as with an elaborate vocabulary for airing feelings of marginality and contestation. For Indian American youth, this alienation may be partly a result of what Fischer calls "ethnic anxiety," a deep desire to maintain a sense of difference in the face of homogenization and to redefine the relationship between self and community (1986, p. 197). The ethnic anxiety of second-generation youth may be a response to ethnic identity politics in the United States, assimilationist pressures, and their own experiences as objects of racism. Lipsitz argues that for certain American musicians of Greek, German, or Jewish descent, this anxiety sometimes arises from a political understanding of relationships of racial dominance and subordination; engagement with Black music may signal the re-creation of a "moral vision" of the meanings of community and tradition (Fischer 1986, p. 197). For Indian American youth, the turn to hip-hop is not always based on clearly articulated political dissent or moral outrage, but it may at least provide a discourse for coding an alienation from parents that is bound up with struggles over what it means to be Indian in the United States. This alienation may not simply be a rejection of parents' racial ideologies but may also express an ambivalence toward the upwardly mobile path their parents have attempted to carve out for them, with its burden of suitable educational fields and careers.

[...]

References

Advani, A. G. 1997. Against the tide: Reflections on organizing New York City's South Asian taxicab drivers. Pp. 215–22 in *Making more waves: New writing by Asian American women*, edited by E. H. Kim, L. V. Villanueva, and Asian Women United of California. Boston: Beacon Press.

Agarwal, P. 1991. *Passage from India: Post-1965 Indian immigrants and their children: Conflicts, concerns, and solutions*. Palos Verdes: Yuvati.

Back, L. 1994. *X amount of sat sri akal: Apache Indian, reggae music and intermezzo culture*. South Asia Seminar Series, ICCCR, Universities of Manchester and Keele, United Kingdom.

Banerjea, K., and P. Banerjea. 1996. Psyche and soul: A view from the "South." Pp. 105–24 in *Dis-Orienting rhythms: The politics of the new Asian dance music*, edited by S. Sharma, J. Hutnyk, and A. Sharma. London: Zed Press.

Bhattacharjee, A. 1992. The habit of ex-nomination: Nation, woman, and the Indian immigrant bourgeoisie. *Public Culture* 5(1): 19–44.

Christenson, P. G., and D. F. Roberts. 1998. *It's not only rock & roll: Popular music in the lives of adolescents*. Cresskill, NJ: Hampton Press.

Cohen, S. 1997. Symbols of trouble. Pp. 149–62 in *The subcultures reader*, edited by K. Gelder and S. Thornton. London: Routledge.

Das Dasgupta, S., and S. Dasgupta. 1996. Women in exile: Gender relations in the Asian Indian community. Pp. 381–400 in *Contours of the heart: South Asians map North America*, edited by S. Maira and R. Srikanth. New York: Asian American Writers' Workshop.

Epstein, J. S. 1998. Introduction: Generation X, youth culture, and identity. Pp. 1–23 in *Youth culture: Identity in a postmodern world*, edited by J. Epstein. Malden, MA: Blackwell.

Erikson, E. H. 1968. *Identity: Youth and crisis*. New York and London: W. W. Norton and Company (1994 edition).

Esser, D. et al. 1999. Reorganizing organizing: Immigrant labor in North America – Interview with New York Taxi Workers' Alliance. *Amerasia* (Special Issue – Satyagraha in America: The political culture of South Asians in the U.S. Eds. Biju Mathew and Vijay Prashad) 25(3): 171–181.

Fischer, M. 1986. Ethnicity and the post-modern arts of memory. Pp. 194–233 in *Writing culture: The poetics and politics of ethnography*, edited by J. Clifford and G. Marcus. Berkeley: University of California Press.

Frith, S. 1992. The cultural study of popular music. Pp. 174–86 in *Cultural studies*, edited by L. Grossberg, C. Nelson, and P. A. Treichler. New York: Routledge.

Gelder, K. 1997. Introduction to part three. Pp. 145–48 in *The subcultures reader*, edited by K. Gelder and S. Thornton. New York: Routledge.

George, N. 1998. *Hip hop America*. New York: Penguin.

Gibson, M. A. 1988. *Accommodation without assimilation: Sikh immigrants in an American high school*. Ithaca: Cornell University Press.

Giroux, H. A. 1996. White panic and the racial coding of violence, and Racism and the aesthetic of hyper-real violence: Pulp Fiction and other visual Tragedies. Pp. 27–54 and 55–88 in *Fugitive cultures: Race, violence, and youth*. New York: Routledge.

Gopinath, G. 1995. "Bombay, U.K., Yuba City": Bhangra music and the engendering of diaspora. *Diaspora* 4(3): 303–21.

Kleinfeld, N. R. 2000. Guarding the borders of the hip-hop nation: In the 'hood and in the burbz, white money feeds rap. True believers fear selling out. *New York Times*, July 6, A1, A18–A19.

Kondo, D. 1995. Bad girls: Theater, women of color, and the politics of representation. Pp. 49–64 in *Women writing culture*, edited by R. Behar and D. A. Gordon. Berkeley: University of California Press.

Leblanc, L. 1999. *Pretty in punk: Girls' gender resistance in a boys' subculture*. New Brunswick: Rutgers University Press.

Lessinger, J. 1995. *From the Ganges to the Hudson: Indian immigrants in New York City*. Boston: Allyn and Bacon.

Lipsitz, G. 1994. *Dangerous crossroads: Popular music, postmodernism, and the poetics of place*. London: Verso.

Mani, L. 1993. Gender, class, and cultural conflict: Indu Krishnan's *Knowing her place*. Pp. 32–36 in *Our feet walk the sky: Women of the South Asian diaspora*, edited by the

Women of South Asia Descent Collective. San Francisco: Aunt Lute Books.

Mead, M. 1961. *Coming of age in Samoa*. 3d ed. New York: William Morrow.

Melnick, J. 1996. R 'n' B skeletons in the closet: The men of doo wop. *Minnesota Review* 47: 217–29.

Okihiro, G. 1994. Is yellow black or white? Pp. 31–63 in *Margins and mainstreams: Asians in American history and culture*. Seattle: University of Washington Press.

Omi, M., and H. Winant. 1994. *Racial formation in the United States: From the 1960s to the 1990s*. 2d ed. New York: Routledge.

Perkins, W. E. 1996. The rap attack: An introduction. Pp. 1–45 in *Droppin' science: Critical essays on rap music and hip hop culture*, edited by W. E. Perkins. Philadelphia: Temple University Press.

Roediger, D. 1998. What to make of Wiggers: A work in progress. Pp. 358–366 in *Generations of Youth: Youth cultures and history in twentieth-century America*, edited by J. Austin and M. N. Willard. New York: New York University Press.

Sengupta, S. 1996. To be young, Indian and hip: Hip-hop meets Hindi pop as a new generation of South Asians finds its own groove. *New York Times*, June 30, section 13: "The City," p. 1.

Sharma, S. 1996. Noisy Asians or "Asian noise"? Pp. 32–55 in *Dis-Orienting rhythms: The politics of the new Asian dance music*, edited by S. Sharma, J. Hutnyk, and A. Sharma. London: Zed Press.

Singh, A. 1996. African Americans and the new immigrants. Pp. 93–110 in *Between the lines: South Asians and post-coloniality*, edited by D. Bahri and M. Vasudeva. Philadelphia: Temple University Press.

Turner, V. 1967. *The forest of symbols: Aspects of Ndembu ritual*. Ithaca: Cornell University Press.

——. 1987. *The anthropology of performance*. New York: Performing Arts Journal Publications, 1987.

Whitely, S. 1997. Introduction. Pp. xiii–xxxvi in *Sexing the groove: Popular music and gender*, edited by S. Whitely. London: Routledge.

Williams, R. 1977. *Marxism and literature*. Oxford: Oxford University Press.

Teatro Viva! Latino Performance and the Politics of AIDS in Los Angeles

David Román

[. . .]

Latino gays and lesbians in theatre perform their art and activism from the multiple positions that inform their Latino gay/lesbian identities. Their performances enact the "oppositional consciousness" that Chicana lesbian Chela Sandoval has theorized as a tactic utilized by marginalized people to resist hegemonic inscription:

> The differential mode of oppositional consciousness depends upon the ability to read the current situation of power and of self-consciously choosing and adopting the ideological form best suited to push against its configurations, a survival skill well known to oppressed peoples.[1]

Sandoval argues against a political identity reduced to a single or fixed perception by dominant culture and the identity politics engendered by such configurations. Rather, oppositional consciousness accommodates a tactical privileging of one component of identity without disturbing the notion of identity as a dynamic process. While Sandoval writes specifically within the context of US Third World feminism, oppositional consciousness, as she explains, "is also a form of consciousness in resistance well utilized among subordinated subjects under various conditions of domination and subordination."[2] As I hope to make clear, Latino gay performers can be best understood in light of Sandoval's theory. Moreover, as Sandoval's theory begins to suggest, one of the benefits of the differential mode of oppositional consciousness is the possibility of forging links with others experiencing social marginality. With Sandoval's theory in mind, I will argue how in one localized (albeit enormous) social space – Los Angeles – counter-hegemonic coalitions based on a model of affinity politics are materializing through performance. I draw my examples from the performances of Latino gay and lesbian artists working in Los Angeles, in particular, Luis Alfaro's solo and collaborative works. These Latino performers offer a much needed voice in the work of what Antonio Gramsci has called the "historical bloc of organic intellectuals," the counter-hegemonic practices of subordinate groups working as a coalition or "bloc" against existing power relations. In this sense, these performers participate in a cultural and artistic process that George Lipsitz has outlined in his insightful reading of popular music in East Los Angeles. Lipsitz is interested in tracing the ways that Chicano artists produce music that is "accessible from both inside and outside the community" and in placing this work within its sociopolitical context. If, as Lipsitz argues, the music of Chicanos "reflects a quite conscious cultural politics that seeks inclusion in the American mainstream by transforming it," Latino gay performers must also work against the grain of the Latino heterosexist mainstream in order to dismantle it as well.[3] Latino gay performers often must maneuver between Latino conventions on the one hand, and dominant white gay traditions on the other. In terms of the theatre, their work may involve an interreferential allusion to the already parodic and satirical models of Culture Clash, thus furthering and enhancing the intertextual dialogues within Latino theatre, or may suggest an affinity with politicized white gay male performers in Southern California, such as Tim Miller or Michael Kearns, all the while expressing the oppositional consciousness first articulated by US Third World feminists.

Such a varied and deliberate tactic goes one step further than the bifocality that Lipsitz argues for popular music in East Los Angeles. Lipsitz reads the cultural performances of Chicano musicians through anthropologist Michael M. J. Fischer's concept of bifocality or reciprocity of perspectives. Bifocality, Lipsitz writes, is a process of self-respect: "prevented from defining themselves because of pervasive discrimination and prejudice, but unwilling to leave the work of definition to others, [Chicano musicians] adopted a bifocal perspective that acknowledged but did not accept the majority culture's image of Chicanos."[4] Sandoval's theory of oppositional consciousness provides the basis for the explication of how Latino gay performers must adjust through a *multifocality* in order to resist the stereotypes imposed by dominant heterosexist ideologies. This multifocal perspective is keenly attuned to the multiple sites of their discrimination stemming from their ethnicity, sexuality, class background, HIV status, or gender.

Luis Alfaro's performance work is a case in point. In his solo piece, *Downtown*, Alfaro – a Chicano playwright, performer, and community activist – performs various characters who live in the Pico-Union district, the heavily populated and impoverished Latino neighborhood in downtown Los Angeles, where he grew up.[5] *Downtown* is a nonlinear montage of multicharacter monologue, movement, autobiography, and sound. In *Downtown*, Alfaro investigates the rhythms of his neighborhood reconfiguring Los Angeles from his working-class Latino background and his gay identity. Alfaro scrutinizes Los Angeles by laying bare the glorification of the city and the glamorization of its people fabricated by Hollywood and offered for mass consumption by the entertainment industry. He provides snapshots of his neighborhood and family – from skyscrapers and alleys, undocumented workers and the 18th Street Gang, to local junkies and his tias Ofelia, Tita, and Romie – that suggest the formation of his politicized identity. But rather than offering a historical chronicle of his own political trajectory, Alfaro stages these stories as unrelated vignettes linked only as indelible memories of a vast urban and psychic landscape.

No comfortable claims are made for and about a Latino gay male identity in *Downtown*; instead Alfaro stages the multiple and often contradictory configurations that construct the possibility for the oppositional consciousness that emerges from a self-conscious and self-articulated Latino gay male perspective. Like Culture Clash, Alfaro draws from Latino culture, but he diffuses the centrality of his ethnicity by cultivating a deliberately gay perspective. From his marginality he offers a cultural politics that foregrounds ethnicity or sexuality depending on his point of emphasis at any given moment in time. As a result of this oppositional consciousness, Alfaro destabilizes the privileged status that his ethnicity or sexuality may hold as the constitutive force of his identity.

Downtown begins with Alfaro situated against a scrim onto which drive-by film shots of downtown Los Angeles street corners are projected; Petula Clark's classic pop hymn "Downtown" provides the soundtrack. The interplay between Petula Clark's escapist view of urban life and the harsh black and white images of downtown LA sets the tone for Alfaro's bittersweet relationship to the city. Alfaro first positions himself as part of this landscape by joining the nameless pedestrians projected upon the scrim. He then breaks the illusion by stepping out of the image to speak of the experience. Alfaro at once invokes the crisis of modernity – Walter Benjamin's reading of Baudelaire being "jostled by the crowd" – and the oral tradition of the epic poet composing and reciting the myths of an era. Such lofty posturing – flaneur and bard – is given a camp poignancy and a postmodern twist with Petula Clark's resounding "you can forget all your troubles, forget all your cares, so go downtown" refrain. Alfaro's man about town – Latino, gay, and poor – can't escape the omnipresence of the pop culture that infuses the neighborhood. In his performance, Alfaro will manipulate such realities by appropriation, commenting all the while on both the process of creating art and on the equally trying challenge of fashioning an identity.

With the ominous and always scrutinizing sounds and lights of a police helicopter hovering over the neighborhood in the background, Alfaro begins his first monologue, "On a Street Corner," with reminiscences of formative occasions from his childhood. He offers headlines:

> A woman got slugged.
> A man got slapped.
> A clown threw toys.
> A drunk staggered.
> An earthquake shook.[6]

which are then further abbreviated to simple gestures first spoken and then performed on his own body: "A Slap. A Slug. A Shove. A Kick. A Kiss." Initially sounding like non sequiturs, these gestures will be recontextualized throughout the performance and serve as the leitmotifs of the piece, physical reminders of the battles Latinos face daily. While the LAPD surveillance helicopters patrol the neighborhood, a plastic rotating Virgin Mary doll from Tijuana surveys the Alfaro household – "she would turn and bless all sides of the room." The Virgin Mary doll becomes a symbol of kinship, a token from the homeland that comforts and distracts from the urban hardships of downtown LA, the reminder of the family mantra ingrained in the young boy's consciousness: "You see, blood is thicker than water, family is greater than friends, and the Virgin Mary watches over all of us." At one point, ten-year-old Luis offers the doll to his ailing Tia Ofelia, who has breast cancer, in order to drive away *La Bruja Maldita*, who was "slowly eating at her insides." When the boy innocently asks to see her chest, Tia Ofelia slaps him so hard on the face that even he could feel *La Bruja Maldita* eating away at his heart. Soon after his tia dies and is buried, the Crips firebomb the 18th Street Gang, living underneath her old apartment. Rummaging through the charred remains of the apartment building, he finds what's left of the rotating Virgin Mary, now useless and empty of its meaning.

Alfaro tells the story of the Virgin Mary in order to call into question the cultural belief systems of his Latino and Catholic family. This scene offers a poignant and deeply affectionate send-up of the assumptions impoverished Latinos maintain in order to endure the hardships of everyday life – inadequate health care, gang warfare, and an LAPD that essentially quarantines their neighborhoods through its aggressive surveillance. Alfaro, while critical of this system of exploitation vis-à-vis the church and the state, cannot deny the power of its influence. He ends this section with the familiar iconography of the neighborhood, expanding the connotations of his background to accommodate his emerging sexual identification:

When I was eighteen, I met this guy with a rotating Virgin Mary. He bought it in Mexico, so, of course, I fell in love. His skin was white. He ate broccoli and spoke like actors on a TV series. It was my first love and like the *Bruja Maldita*, he pounded on my heart. He taught me many things; how to kiss like the French, lick an earlobe and dance in the dark. He was every "Brady Bunch"/ "Partridge Family" episode rolled into one. He gave me his shirt and I told him about the fields in Delano, picking cherries one summer and my summer in Mexico. Once my grandmother sent me a crate of grapes. We took off our clothes, smashed them all over our bodies and ate them off each other. When he left, the *Bruja Maldita's* hand replaced his in my heart and she pounded on me.

And she laughed like Mexican mothers at a clothes line. And I covered my tears with a smile that was like the veils at Immaculate Conception. But my sorrow was so strong that relatives nearby would say, "*Ay Mijo*, don't you see? Blood is thicker than water, family is greater than friends, and the Virgin Mary watches over all of us." (*Blackout*).

The conflicting interpretations of the signification of the iconography – for the Latino the Virgin Mary as a sign of kinship, for the white gay man a sign of kitsch; for the Latino the "Brady Bunch" as a sign of normalized family structures, for the white gay man a popular entertainment – set off the imbalance that will eventually bring back the pounding of the *Bruja Maldita* against the young man's heart. In "Virgin Mary" Alfaro demonstrates the forces that shape the construction of his Latino gay male identity. The performer, over a decade later, offers this construction to his audience in order to demonstrate the tensions that give shape to his desire – "A Slap. A Shrug. A Kiss." The scene ends without resolution, only with the melancholy recognition of his desire and its problematic reception in two conflicting social fields of power: the kinship systems of his Latino family and of an imagined gay community.[7]

In subsequent scenes, Alfaro includes fictionalized portraits of various characters from the neighborhood that extend beyond his immediate family. He inhabits the voices and movements of Latinos in the barrio, people he encounters on the street who give him a sense of himself and who inform the performance of the desperate economic conditions of the neighborhood. In these scenes, he foregrounds different aspects of the urban Latino experience and gives voice to the underrepresented thousands who populate LA's downtown. While these portraits contribute to the overall social milieu of *Downtown*, their main purpose is to convey to his audience his political consciousness. Alfaro imagines the emotional psyches of his characters and offers these poetic constructions to the audience as his points of connection with the people in his neighborhood; these are moments of both epiphany and affinity. In these moments, *Downtown* can be understood in light of Ramon Saldívar's theory of how Chicano narrative functions as an "aesthetically and ideologically memorial to and partial reconstitution of the forgotten history of a people's oppression and struggles."[8] In the section titled "Lupe," for example, Alfaro opens by describing his venture through the sweatshops where undocumented Latina women labor for less than minimum wage, working twelve-hour shifts on a six-day week. He spots Lupe, who has a face "brown like my father's" and who "paid a *coyote* $150 to smuggle her across the border." He shifts from his performance persona to the voice of Lupe. To mark the transition he puts on a dress. We meet Lupe as she's about to go out on the town on a Saturday night. Lupe's downtown – full of cumbias, *Bohemias*, and street corner lunatics – begins as a temporary refuge from the buzz of the sewing machines of the sweatshops. With her boyfriend she finds romance, but the promise of downtown – "you can forget all your troubles, forget all your cares, so go downtown" – is haunted by the distant sound of the machines "singing to me to come down to the other side of downtown and punch in, punch in, punch in." With fingers bleeding, sirens sounding, and the helicopter always overhead, Lupe fights to hang on to the romance of the city and the bargain of the border. Alfaro ends this portrait with her resounding, albeit temporary, triumph: "Tonight they can all be on fire. Because tonight there is no job. Tonight there is no stitch. No needle, no fabric, no pattern, no nothing. Because tonight is Saturday night and my dress is too tight and my name is Lupe (*blackout*)."

The "Lupe" section concludes with Alfaro still in character. The identification process of the Latino gay man with the young undocumented worker suggests an intracultural affinity that recognizes both class oppression and gender specificity. Alfaro's performance of Lupe is staged neither as the omniscient privilege of the creative agent's insight which escapes the character, nor as "classic" drag, where the male temporarily puts on a dress in an imagined transgression which by the end only reinforces gender binarism.[9] Instead, Alfaro's performance of Lupe seems to reveal more about his own persona and his choices of affinity. Lupe is neither mocked nor parodied. Lupe's oppression and her defiance are presented as interrelated to his own. Such is the tactic of performative oppositional consciousness. In "Lupe" Alfaro plays against preconceived notions of drag as gay performance in order to highlight the experiences shared by Latinos in the barrio. His performance can be interpreted as a political tactic which challenges the alienation of the oppressed by demonstrating the affinities between and among people living in the barrio. The performance moves beyond the autobiographical performance of an individual subject and enacts instead a collective cultural unity based on the recognition of a shared but distinct oppression. The multifocalities of the performer and the character – the specificity of class, gender, sexuality, and ethnicity – join in performance to build the coalition

necessary to counter hegemonic configurations of oppression that insist on the conflation of differences.

In "Federal Building," Alfaro describes his involvement in the March 1, 1990, artist chain-gang protest regarding censorship and the crisis at the National Endowment for the Arts. Over seventy artists and their supporters marched from the County Museum of Art to the downtown Federal Building, where civil disobedience turned into performance pieces staged en route. Artists dressed as criminals carried huge images of banned artists and engaged spectators to read quotations about freedom of speech. Guerrilla theatre vignettes, bilingual performances, and press conferences contributed to the militant defense of artistic freedom that resulted in twenty-seven arrests.

For Alfaro the Federal Building – "the big beautiful marble structure on Los Angeles Street" – is an emblem of his relationship with the city that dates back to his early years when his father would drive the family by the halls of justice "looking for distant Mexican relatives with phony passports ready for a life in Our Lady Queen of the Angels." Like the helicopter that opens and closes *Downtown*, the Federal Building is omnipresent: always visible and always threatening to reveal its power. Like the rotating Virgin Mary doll, the building is a symbol of surveillance:

> We have a long history together, this *ruca* and I. She has watched me grow up and play on her steps. Watched me low ride in front of her. Watched me spit at her face at an immigration demonstration that I don't understand but comprehend enough to know that my dad can go back any time, just never when he wants to.

The personal context of the building resurfaces for Alfaro when he returns to protest with artists and members of ACT UP/LA, shouting in both English and Spanish such chants as "Art is not a crime," "Alto a la censura," and "AIDS funding now." Unlike some of the other protesters, Alfaro has been here before. The downtown Federal building has always been for him a microcosmic icon of his relationship with the city; a place where the notion of home shifts to and from a sense of belonging or displacement. The specific circumstances articulated in the first half of the "Federal Building," where long-standing Latino issues such as immigration and deportation were introduced as evidence of nationalist muscle, now resurface as HIV issues with the discriminatory policies and procedures of the INS. And while the performer's ethnicity was the initial political identity foregrounded, by this point in "Federal Building" Alfaro's political tactic is to foreground his sexuality. By the end of this section, however, Alfaro demonstrates how both facets of his identity – sexuality and ethnicity – are enmeshed in his desire for, and denial by, the downtown Federal Building and the home that it has symbolically represented:

> I didn't get arrested because my government wants to control the content of art, or because a Republican congressman from Orange County thinks AIDS activists are a "dying breed." I got arrested because [former] Mayor Sam Yorty told me we were all the mayor. Because a black and white can stop you anywhere, any time, for whatever reason. Because big marble buildings stare down with a *chale* stare. Because I've never owned anything in my life – much less a city. (*blackout*)

In "Federal Building" Alfaro demonstrates how AIDS issues for people of color cannot be understood without an analysis of race and class. Although he joins the others in the spirit and mission of the protest, his personal investment in the Federal Building extends beyond the specifics of the moment and involves the complex contextual history of his relation to Los Angeles as a Latino gay man. And yet, Alfaro's arrest *does* result from his protest against censorship and AIDS bigotry and not this personal backdrop. The arresting officer who "puts handcuffs on me while hundreds of people blow whistles and yell 'shame, shame, shame'" has no idea why Alfaro is there, only that he is "trespassing on government property." The personal agenda articulated in performance is unavailable to "the man in the helmet and plastic gloves." For the arresting officer Alfaro is only one more protester. But for the spectator, manipulated by the performative tactics of oppositional consciousness, Alfaro's political identity is more complex. The oppositional consciousness model that forms the basis of this performance – the continual dynamic shift in focus from Latino to gay, for example – at its most successful, challenges the spectator to recognize differences rather than collapsing them. The operative dynamic of oppositional consciousness in Alfaro's performance suggests the possible affinities between performer and audience while simultaneously forcing the spectator to consider the specificity of their own subject positions.

In "Federal Building" Alfaro demonstrates how his multifocal identity and politics of oppositional consciousness work in the best interests of coalition movements. The demonstrators all chant various causes and concerns – anticensorship, AIDS, queer visibility and rights – in both English and Spanish. That Alfaro's performance in "Federal Building" is then about a performance, or more specifically an activist performance, suggests the deeply interdependent nature of his politics and his art. In reclaiming and recontextualizing downtown Los Angeles, Alfaro participates in the counter-hegemonic practice of both self-individualization and community formation. *Downtown* ends with Alfaro reciting (and enacting through gesture) a litany of epiphanic moments that encapsulate the characters introduced throughout the performance; each moment is prefaced by "one strong shove":

> One strong shove and the LAPD lets me know who is in charge . . .
> One strong shove and my fingers are bleeding . . .
> One strong shove and the sound of a helicopter or ambulance in the middle of the night lets me know I'm alive.
> One strong shove and a helicopter light has found me in downtown. (*Alfaro gestures shoves in silence. Blackout.*)

Caught once again in the glare of surveillance, Alfaro disappears into the darkness of the stage. The theatre then becomes the site of refuge, a place where identity can be explored or contested, created and shared. The theatre remains, however, a site of contestation, a place where queer Latinos, who have historically been marginalized, can intervene in the ideological systems which render them invisible or disposable. His work is, as Jan Breslauer explains in describing Los Angeles performance art, "a theatre of liberation."[10]

As with many other plays and performances by gay men of color, AIDS issues in *Downtown* are thoroughly connected with the prevailing issues of class and race bias. AIDS is experienced as one component in a complex system of exploitation and oppression. Through performance Alfaro stages affinities across boundaries of racial and gender difference in order to foreground the "historical bloc" necessary to intervene in the hegemonic scripts of dominant culture. While the material within Alfaro's performances displays many of Chela Sandoval's ideas, the productions of his performance begin to materialize Sandoval's theory toward a cogent model for political praxis. Although *Downtown* is usually produced as a solo artist evening, Alfaro has performed the piece in various group shows, ranging from *True Lies*,[11] director David Schweizer's full-scale production of three separate solo performance pieces at the Los Angeles Theatre Center, to stripped-down versions at Chicano or gay and lesbian art festivals in the Los Angeles area. In these settings, Alfaro's work as often received as either the gay piece or the Latino piece, or in the case of the LATC production, the gay and Latino piece. From this perspective, Alfaro's performance risks the appropriation of mainstream production, where either the work may be interpreted as an exercise in multiculturalism and therefore carries the burden of representation, or where his presence may be singled out as the performance of difference and therefore normalizes the assumptions inherent in the other performances staged. While such risks are real and have their own specific ramifications depending upon the production and the audience, the design of *Downtown* nonetheless allows Alfaro to contextualize difference *and* point toward a politics of affinity even in these settings.

The same weekend that Culture Clash premiered *S.O.S.* in downtown Los Angeles, Alfaro joined two other Los Angeles-based Latino performers, Monica Palacios and Alberto "Beto" Araiza, to premiere their collaboration *Deep in the Crotch of My Latino Psyche* at the Fourth Annual Gay and Lesbian Performance Festival at Highways. Palacios, a self-described "Latin Lezbo Comic" with a solo show of the same name, is a veteran of both comedy clubs and alternative performance venues. Her work is specific to her experience as a Chicana lesbian, but she sets out to refute the rigid sexual scripts expected of all women in Latino culture.[12] Araiza – an actor, playwright, and director – has poured his solo show *Meat My Beat* throughout North America and Europe. *Meat My Beat* chronicles Araiza's travels through urban gay male culture and addresses his experiences of living with HIV. Together in *Deep in the Crotch of My Latino Psyche*, they begin to negotiate through performance a Latino gay and lesbian politics.

In scenarios that vary from stand-up, melodrama, satire, and personal testimony, the three performers critique the institutions of both Latino culture and mainstream gay communities. As "Latino homos without a home" in either world, they take to the stage to carve out a niche and claim their rights. They contest the idea of a monolithic Latino gay experience by underlining the vast differences among them, from their own performance styles to their HIV status. *Deep in the Crotch of My Latino Psyche* closely resembles *S.O.S.* in style; short skits that may involve all three performers, solos, or combinations of two. But unlike Culture Clash, these performers insist on rupturing the gender binarism of the *chingón/chingada* polarity and critiquing Latino homophobia and the silence around AIDS.

Deep in the Crotch of My Latino Psyche, as its title indicates, is a humorous and provocative exploration of Latino lesbian and gay sexuality. Their promotional slogan "Comedy, Drama, Pathos, and Piñatas!" further accentuates the humor. The performance, however, also seriously engages a number of political issues. Palacios, for example, contributes a solo, "Tom Boy Piece," which addresses her coming-out process. Araiza includes two sections on AIDS and HIV in the Latino community, "HIVato" and "Safos." Araiza's solo sections participate in the larger cultural project expanding the theatrical representations of people with HIV and AIDS to include Chicanos. Cultural critic Alberto Sandoval's concern with the paucity of staged AIDS work by Latinos resonates for Araiza, who explicitly positions himself as HIV-positive in performance. Araiza's two solo sections are quasi-autobiographical monologues about living with HIV in the barrio. Alfaro also focuses his monologues on the experience of survival; however, he addresses it from a different angle. He offers a number of solos, including a lyrical AIDS memorial, "Where Are My Heroes? Where Are My Saints?" which, in its meditation on his experience of being gay and Latino in the public sphere, references the loss of a community besieged by AIDS. This dialectic between loss and survival now informs what it means for him to be Latino, gay, and presumably uninfected. In "Isolation" – the most effective piece of the performance – the three actors, with only their upper torsos lit, sit on stools and face the audience as an ominous voice-over interrogates them at length about their personal lives. The performers must raise their hands in silence to answer the interviewer's questions, which range in tone and intensity from "Have you ever lied about your nationality?" and "Have you lost a lover to AIDS?" to "Do you prefer flour to corn tortillas?" and "Have you ever put on make-up while driving your car?"[13] By the end of this scene, composed of nearly fifty questions, spectators – whether Latino or non-Latino, gay or non-gay – cannot possibly consider Latino gay and lesbian sexuality within a comfortable categorization. Latino gay identities are presented as dynamic and contradictory. The material production of performance, stripped down here to its most basic, demystifies the performance process and facilitates the effective representation of both the silence around homosexuality in Latino culture and the real and living bodies of Latino queers. The interactions among these very different Latino performers in *Deep in the Crotch of My Latino Psyche* demonstrate Chela

Sandoval's claim that "self-conscious agents of differential consciousness recognize one another as allies, country women and men of the same psychic terrain."[14]

Alfaro, Araiza, and Palacios, three of the driving forces behind VIVA!, have collaborated on various "behind the scenes" efforts to gain visibility for Latino gays and lesbians. *Deep in the Crotch of My Latino Psyche* is but one of the many tactics that demonstrate the inseparable nature of their art and activism. Perhaps their most impressive collaboration so far has been the AIDS Intervention Theatre project Teatro VIVA!, an AIDS outreach program that provided bilingual prevention information in both traditional (community centers and theatres) and nontraditional sites (parks, bars, community fairs and bazaars, art galleries, and private homes). Funded in the early 1990s with a $50,000 grant from the United States Conference of Mayors, Teatro VIVA! presented short skits on such HIV/AIDS issues as transmission, prevention, safer sex negotiation skills, popular misconceptions about AIDS, daily considerations of people with HIV and AIDS, and local community resources. The main component of the program was its bilingual mobile teatro presentations, performed in agitprop minimalist style, allowing for flexibility in response to the varying aspects of each venue. These teatros, presented by three performers, Refugio Guevera, Ron Sandoval, and Frank Castorena (also known to some as the Divas from VIVA), were then followed by a question-and-answer period which allowed for more detailed discussions about AIDS. Araiza, the project director for the first grant, reported that over 5,000 individuals – including nearly 2,000 self-identified gay and bisexual Latinos – viewed the Teatro VIVA! AIDS Outreach Project. Forty presentations were given within Los Angeles County between July 1991 and April 1992.

[. . .]

The proven success of Teatro VIVA!, while localized in Los Angeles to help combat AIDS among Latino gay and bisexual men, hints that the political landscape is changing. Consider that Teatro VIVA! was refunded in 1993 by the County of Los Angeles AIDS Program Office through the gay men of color consortium, with Palacios and Alfaro serving as codirectors. Consider as well that at the time of this grant, 6,510 people were confirmed with AIDS in Los Angeles County. Nationally, by 1993, Latinos accounted for 29 percent, nearly one-third, of all cases reported to the Centers for Disease Control.[15]

Beginning in 1991, Teatro VIVA! set out to provide Los Angeles Latinos life-saving HIV-prevention information through the combined methods of AIDS educational performance and Chicano agitprop theatre, two historically distinct traditions. The theatre, of course, is only one of the many sites of contestation in the fight against AIDS and performance, only one of the many means possible to counter AIDS and its mystifications in dominant culture. But performance holds the capacity to articulate resistance and generate social change. The work of Alfaro, Palacios, and Araiza – individually and in collaboration, in the theatre and on the streets – provides one model for Latinos and our supporters to engage at once in the tactics of oppositional consciousness and in the coalition building available through an affinity politics. The name Teatro VIVA! translates in the most pragmatic and descriptive sense as "VIVA's theatre," the theatre component of the Latino gay and lesbian arts organization VIVA! However, I employ "teatro viva" here in the literal sense of "theatre" and the imperative modality of the present subjunctive of the verb "to live" to convey, quite simply, an acclamation for theatre and life.

[. . .]

Notes

1 Chela Sandoval, "U.S. Third World Feminism: The Theory and Method of Oppositional Consciousness in the Postmodern World," *Genders* 10 (1991): 1–24.

2 Sandoval, 16. Yvonne Yarbro-Bejarano, "Expanding the Categories of Race in Lesbian and Gay Studies," in *Professions of Desire: Lesbian and Gay Studies in Literature*, ed. George E. Haggerty and Bonnie Zimmerman (New York: MLA Publications, 1994).

3 George Lipsitz, *Time Passages: Collective Memory and American Popular Culture* (Minneapolis: U of Minnesota P, 1990), 159.

4 Ibid., 154.

5 See Mike Davis, *City of Quartz: Excavating the Future in Los Angeles* (London: Verso, 1990).

6 All quotes are from the author's unpublished performance text. *Downtown* premiered at Highways Performance Space in Santa Monica, California, November 30 and December 1–2, 7–9, 1990.

7 Kath Weston, *Families We Choose: Lesbians, Gays, Kinship* (New York: Columbia University Press, 1991).

8 Saldívar is describing specifically Tomas Rivera's foundational Chicano novel, *Y no se lo tragó la tierra/And the Earth Shall Not Devour Him*. See his *Chicano Narrative: The Dialectics of Difference* (Madison: University of Wisconsin Press, 1990), 77.

9   See chapter 1 of Sue-Ellen Case, *Feminism and Theatre* (New York: Routledge, 1988). But see also Marjorie Garber, *Vested Interests: Cross-dressing and Cultural Anxiety* (New York: Routledge, 1991).

10   Jan Breslauer, "California Performance," *Performing Arts Journal* 41 (1992): 87–96.

11   Alfaro's *Downtown* was performed as *Pico-Union* on a bill with Chloe Webb's *Walkin' the Walls* and Rocco Sisto's rendition of Dario Fo's *The Tale of the Tiger*. *True Lies* was performed at the Los Angeles Theatre Center from July 25–September 8, 1991.

12   See Yvonne Yarbro-Bejarano's contribution to *Entiendes? Queer Readings/Hispanic Writings*, ed. Emilie Bergmann and Paul Julian Smith (Durham: Duke University Press, 1995).

13   All quotes are from the authors' unpublished performance script. *Deep in the Crotch of My Latino Psyche* premiered at Highways Performance Space, July 9–11 and 14–16, 1992.

14   Chela Sandoval, 15.

15   AIDS statistics were provided by the staff at the AIDS Information Library in Philadelphia.

Waiting for Godzilla: Toward a Globalist Theme Park

Takayuki Tatsumi

The Multicultural and Transgeneric Poetics of Chaotic Negotiation

In the late 1990s, American and Japanese cultures entered a new phase of interaction: from then onward, essentially chaotic and transculturally infectious negotiations occur between orientalism and occidentalism; between the western belief in eternity and the Japanese aesthetics of the moment; between a western productionist and idealist sensibility and a Japanese high-tech-consumerist and posthistorical mentality; or even between the science-fictional Japan of the American imagination and Japanese science fiction itself. The creative clash between cultures has made it easier for us to envision a new kind of theme park beautifully constructed within global space. Its features can be found in Philip K. Dick's alternate postwar America, controlled through yin-yang in *The Man in the High Castle* (1962); Sakyo Komatsu's postwar junkyard in *The Japanese Apache* (1964); William Gibson's "Walled City," simulated in cyberspace in his fifth novel. *Idoru* (1996); Toshihiko Yahagi's "Mount Fuji," reconstructed by nuclear acupuncture in *A-Japan!* (1997); Kyoji Kobayashi's phantasmagoric kabuki production, *Sekai-za* (The World Theater), featured in *The Day of Kabuki* (1998), which won a Yukio Mishima Award; Neal Stephenson's post-Tolkienian and postorientalist version of Manila in *Cryptonomicon* (1999); and Mark Danielewski's globally labyrinthine haunted house, constructed in his first meganovel, *House of Leaves* (2000).

In order to detail what I would like to call a globalist theme park built by the nuclear imagination, it will be useful here to talk about some narratives by Erika Kobayashi, the self-proclaimed avant-pop girl, born in 1978 in Tokyo, whose post-Pynchonesque comic strip video narrative *Bakudan-Musume no Yuutsu* (Bombastic Melancholy: A Story of Ms. Downer, the Human Bomb) (1999) has received numerous national and international awards and is highly admired in the United States and Russia. I have called it post-Pynchonesque, simply because her characterization has much in common with the rocket man Tyron Slothrop, one of the central figures in Pynchon's *Gravity's Rainbow*, who serves as a human radar, hypersensitive to and hypersexually connected with the destination of v2 rockets. What is more, Kobayashi confesses to have been directly influenced by David Blair's nonlinear video narrative *WAX, or The Discovery of Television among the Bees*, which we can interpret as a post-cyberpunkish take on *Gravity's Rainbow*. Theoretically speaking, while the nuclear imagination that expanded through the Godzilla series could well have inspired Komatsu and Pynchon to write their major novels, it is the post-Pynchonesque narratology made possible through Gibson and Blair that very naturally led Kobayashi to create her own avant-pop work, which deals with the impossible romantic love affair between Ms. Downer, a humanoid atomic bomb, and her boyfriend. Note that the rise of the Godzilla series, which featured a mutant dinosaur revived by a nuclear explosion, took place in the mid-1950s; around the turn of the millennium Kobayashi's "Bombastic Melancholy" is foregrounding Ms. Downer as a nuclear weapon herself. While nuclear disaster began as an essential tragedy in the mid-twentieth century, it has gradually transformed itself into a kind of literary motivation for black comedy. In this respect, I cannot help but appreciate Erika Kobayashi as an avant-pop black humorist endowed with a postnuclear imagination, capable of blurring the cultural distinctions between the All-American Disneyland and the All-Japanese Godzillaland.

Thus I cannot resist the temptation to discuss her first novella "Neversoapland," printed in the autumn 2000 issue of Kawade Publishers' quarterly *Bungei* and published in book form by the same publisher in March 2001. Take a look first at the strange title, and you will be disturbed by its extraordinary combination of concepts, for the title consists of our familiar term "Neverland" in the sense of J. M. Barrie and the Japanese-English coinage "Soapland," signifying a contemporary brothel – what used to be called a Turkish bath in Japan until the mid-1980s. Thus you are also invited to interpret "Neversoapland" primarily as a pornographic version of *Peter Pan*.

The story opens quite shockingly: "I have played the role of Wendy for fifteen years" (3). Sounding like an orthodox fairy tale, the story then abruptly introduces an extremely bizarre murder, shamelessly copying the scenario of *Ai so Koriida* (In the Realm of the Senses) directed by Nagisa Oshima. You may understand the extent of its impact simply by looking at Kathy Acker's homage to the film, *The Empire of the Senseless*, which inspired her young followers, like Eurudice, to weave new avant-porn texts. Oshima's film itself is an adaptation of the famous true story of Ms. Abe Sada, the maid who in 1936 killed and castrated her lover, Kichizo, as an act of love; the two had shut themselves in for what turned out to be six nights of sexual indulgence culminating in Kichizo's death and mutilation. A similar scandal occurs in Kobayashi's "Neversoapland" with Wendy's neighbors, a notoriously lustful couple, when the wife, Haruneko, suddenly bites off her husband's genitals. Journalists, all curious to know what in fact happened, storm the narrator Wendy, "How do you think of the accident, old woman?" (12).

Yes, this novella starts with a tremendously blasphemous mélange of the canonical fairytale *Peter Pan* and the hardcore pornography of *In the Realm of the Senses*. The narrator, Wendy, however, is not an adolescent girl, as in the original J. M. Barrie tale, but an old woman imitating the life style of Samantha, the beautiful young witch in the famous TV soap opera *Bewitched* (ABC, 1964–72) – an old woman, that is, who decides not to become mature. Thus, "Neversoapland" centers on an old-fashioned romantic love affair between Wendy and her husband Peter, an old man affected with Alzheimer's disease who is always wetting his pants. On one hand, Peter

murmurs: "Wendy, I find it more and more difficult to remember things. . . . But Wendy, probably it means that I'm now approaching childhood. Recently I have felt strongly that I'll end up by becoming the real Peter Pan" (25). On the other hand, Wendy is so anxious to visit a "Neverland" designed for children that her fear of sexuality increases day by day, and she becomes more and more particular about cleanliness. Then, whenever she is having a bath together with him, Wendy becomes afraid of Peter's erection. "Anyhow," she says, "I've never had sexual intercourse with anyone. This means I can't be mature forever. I will definitely become a child sooner or later" (33).

Despite this asceticist and puritanist way of life, however, the narrator and her spouse get involved in an extremely pornographic narrative. Wendy's elder brother meditates so deeply upon the relationship between the quantity of sperm he has produced and his longevity that he becomes a woman. Wendy herself is afflicted with the horrific fantasy of being raped by a swan. She sees a number of penises start jumping in the air just like a school of flying fish. In her fantasy, Wendy's beloved "Asian" husband transfigures himself into Peter Pan.

Through her postmodern and postcolonialist logic of mimicry, Erika Kobayashi's concept could well enrage Oshima fans as well as Disney freaks. For her mostly avant-porn imagination is as subversive as the atomic bomb and Godzilla. Nevertheless, think twice, and you will undoubtedly remember J. M. Barrie's original characterization of Peter Pan as an amnesiac, just like a person with Alzheimer's: "Every child is affected thus the first time he is treated unfairly. All he thinks he has a right to when he comes to you to be yours is fairness. After you have been unfair to him he will love you again, but he will never afterwards be quite the same boy. No one ever gets over the first unfairness; no one except Peter. He often met it, but he always forgot it" (128). Indeed, whenever Peter Pan gets fascinated with a new adventure, he is most likely to forget his most important friends and enemies. "Who is Captain Hook? . . . Who is Tinker Bell?" (232).

Peter Pan is permitted to remain in Neverland, precisely because he is amnesic, exempted from any kind of trauma, without which you cannot become mature. Accordingly, the All-American Disneyland, in which Neverland plays the central role, gives people the best chance to forget traumas and recuperate innocence. Without such a hyperreal theme park the American people could not have recovered from the trauma of the Vietnam War. Thus the multiplication of Disneylands all over the world will implant within all of us the seed of amnesia. Disneyland's amnesia is nonetheless complicated: the prototype Disneyland in Anaheim – built in 1955, one year after the debut of Godzilla in 1954 – embraced in its center, especially with its attraction the "Swiss Family Treehouse" in Adventureland, the apparently racist discourse of hardcore orientalism, through which the visitors are trained to see "Japan" as an exotic Far Eastern country providing them with a number of marvelous adventures. Yes, Disneyland, from the beginning, has been not only All-American but also radically orientalist.

As if faithfully repeating this exoticist scenario of Disneyland, William Gibson once suggested to me in 1988 that the Japanese are all living in the future, and Larry McCaffery, in his 1994 essay, affirms the essential similarity between Disneyland's postwar hyperreality and Japan's traditional "floating world." If you take into account these neo-Japonistic statements, made at the peak of Japan bashing, it becomes easier to assume that what we call the age of Pax Japonica in the 1980s must have given the United States the worst trauma since the Vietnam War, and that North American writers and intellectuals have attempted to invent the best discursive strategy for resolving and neutralizing this nightmare. Thus the ideology of the best theme park in the world strongly requires us to always "exoticize," so you will enjoy the highest stage of amnesia, which will erase every trace of national trauma. The multiplication of Disneylands since the 1980s promotes not only globalization as a form of Americanization, but also exoticization as a prescription for conquering national trauma and enjoying global amnesia. But, as Hubert Selby Jr. and Darren Aronofsky beautifully depict in their film *Requiem for a Dream* (written by Selby in 1978 and filmed by Aronofsky in 2000), in which the classic theme park Coney Island is transformed from utopia to dystopia, the American Dream could well become not simply a globalist dream but also a globalist nightmare.

From this perspective, Kobayashi's avant-pornographic ambition gives us an opportunity to criticize, deconstruct, and reexoticize the American standard represented by Disneyland, which has globally naturalized the avant-pop reality studio, spectacle-centered society. Her heroine Wendy makes up her mind to retain her innocence until her death, dreaming of living life in peace in Neverland together with the amnesic Peter. Now we have to read carefully Wendy's response to the Haruneko couple's erotic scandal simulating *In the Realm of the Senses*. Wendy declares that if Peter has an erection, she will respond by "cutting off [his] penis with a kitchen knife." She continues: "Then, I will be taken to

court, surrounded by TV cameras. . . . Next, I will definitely be raped . . . not only by swan but also by the whole TV crew" (29). And, ironically, Peter has a "silent erection" in the final sequence of the novella.

We are therefore automatically invited to the unwritten climax in which Wendy, acting the role of Abe Sada, castrates Peter, transforming the pornographic version of *Peter Pan* into the fairy tale version of *In the Realm of the Senses*. Thus Kobayashi's "Neversoapland" convinces us that the most amnesic theme park may contain within itself the most traumatic labyrinth. However hyperreal it seems on the surface, Disneyland has ironically kept growing into both the most innocent playground and the most bureaucratic panopticon. Is this novella a blasphemous appropriation of Disneyland by an ignorant Japanese writer? No, I do not think so. For it was Walt Disney who both entertained American children and committed himself so deeply into the FBI's investigation of suspected communists that he betrayed his left-wing colleagues in Hollywood. Despite its ironic commentary upon the American Dream, Neversoapland turns out to have been so faithful to the contradictory spirit of Walt Disney that it succeeds in disclosing the power of blackness hidden within the political unconscious of Disneyland, that is, of the United States itself. This is why I argue that Kobayashi is one of the contemporary artists whose postnuclear imagination in the wake of Godzilla brilliantly reveals an aspect of the chaotic negotiation between the discourse of Japan's hyper-occidentalism and that of North America's postorientalism.

Always Exoticize!

While ultraconservative western essentialists might dismiss these kinds of chaotic and transcultural negotiations as being nothing but "trash," this "trash" in fact has complex meanings. As Donald Kuspit points out, "Capitalism joins forces with trash culture to destroy human dignity, indeed, to eliminate the very idea and possibility of it."[1] From the perspective of conservatives, Kuspit's "human dignity" seems to mean western white phallocentric dignity. An Australian journalist praised the prophetic nature of Sakyo Komatsu's *Nippon Chinbotsu* (Japan Sinks) after the Osaka-Kobe Earthquake, saying: "At a time when government white papers are laughable, perhaps it should not be surprising that trash can make sense."[2] If one redefines the term "trash" to apply to invisible culture and paraliterature, it becomes applicable not only to popular fiction in the United States but also to all nonwestern literary discourses, including Japanese literature. While nonwestern artists have started their careers by imitating western works of art, their art of "mimicry" has domesticated and even outgrown the other. They paved the way not only for the late capitalist synchronicity between different cultures but also for the highly chaotic and splendidly creative negotiations between western and nonwestern cultures that have recently occurred.

We can reconfirm this creative potential of "mimicry" by tasting the multicultural artistic fruit of miscegenation and metamorphic cross-fertilization between western and nonwestern cultures. Examples include Kiju Yoshida's reorientalization (1988) of Emily Brontë's novel *Wuthering Heights*; David Henry Hwang and Philip Glass's collaborative opera *The Voyage* (1992), on the life of Christopher Columbus; Wayne Wang's film *Smoke* (1995), a visual adaptation of Paul Auster's tale; Roland Emerich's remake of *Godzilla* (1998), and the Japanese unit t.o.L's post-cyberpunkish post-anime *Tamala 2010* (2002). These contemporary films and performances reveal the ways Asian and/or Asian-American directors adopt and adapt Euro-American texts but also the ways Euro-American directors reappropriate Asian narratives.

This trend leads me to reconsider the history of Godzilla as emblematic of the history of these unpredictable and mostly chaotic interchanges. In the 1950s the film *Godzilla* started its career as a typically occidentalist adaptation of Hollywood's dinosaur-like creature movies. In the late 1990s, after a multimillion-dollar deal between Toho Studios and America's Tri-Star Films, the monster Godzilla achieved its present status of the international superhero. I believe this superhero will keep entertaining us, around the new turn of the century, as a multicultural, transgeneric, and postorientalist monster of postmodern representation.

One could therefore agree with Mark Jacobson that "the green of Gojiro (Godzilla)" is not the color that God splashed upon the spectrum, but that of men, "the green we have created" (110) in the globalist age. This vision beautifully coincides with the superb metaphor that Don DeLillo, in *Underworld* (1997), uses for one of the New York skyscrapers (perhaps the World Trade Center): "They were on the roof of a new building, forty stories, it loomed over the reservoir in the park and they stood a while watching runners in the night. . . . Miles thought they resembled fleeing crowds in a Japanese horror film . . . and he came up with a name for the forty-story building . . . Godzilla Towers, he thought they ought to call it" (388, emphasis mine). It is noteworthy that DeLillo's character skillfully avoids an orthodox nickname such as

"The Tower of Babel." On reading this passage, I felt the imperialistic godhead peculiar to Japan had been dramatically displaced by the global Godzilla, who was now reordering the whole earth.

Of course, if we compare skyscrapers to this famous Japanese monster, you may automatically feel like relating this metaphor to the awful terrorist attack on September 11, 2001. Nevertheless, what I would like to emphasize here is that, as Mark Jacobson suggested, Godzilla's color is exactly the greenness of the whole earth radically refigured as a global theme park, and that the "Godzilla Towers," as Don DeLillo named them, perfectly symbolize the nodal point of the chaotic negotiations between postorientalism and hyperoccidentalism, which undoubtedly point toward the narratives to come.

Notes

1   Kuspit, "Art and Capital," 478.
2   Hartcher, "Trashy Novel Was a Sign," 11.

References

Acker, Kathy, *Empire of the Senseless*. New York: Grove Press, 1988.
Barrie, J. M. *Peter Pan*. 1911. New York: Penguin/Puffin Classics, 1994.
Blair, David, dir. WAX, *or The Discovery of Television among the Bees*, 1991. Videocassette. Tokyo: Uplink, 1993.
Danielewski, Mark Z. *House of Leaves*. New York: Pantheon, 2000.
DeLillo, Don. *Libra*. New York: Penguin, 1998.
——. *Underworld*. New York: Scribner, 1997.
Dick, Philip K. *The Man in the High Castle*. New York: Putnam, 1962.
Gibson, William. *Idoru*. New York: Penguin, 1996.
Hartcher, Peter. "Trashy Novel Was a Sign of Things to Come." *Financial Review* (Australia), August 28, 1995, 11.
Jacobson, Mark. *Gojiro*. 1991. New York: Penguin, 1992.
Kobayashi, Erika. *Bakudan-Musume no Yuutsu* (Bombastic Melancholy). Tokyo: Tokyo Analog Project, 1999.
——. *Neversoapland*. 2000. Tokyo: Kawade Publishers, 2001.
Komatsu, Sakyo. *Nippon Apacchi-Zoku*. 1964. Introduction by Takashi Ishikawa. Tokyo: Kadokawa Shoten Publishers, 1971.
——. *Nippon Chinbotsu* (Japan Sinks). Tokyo: Kobunsha Publishers, 1973.
Kuspit, Donald. "Art and Capital: An Ironic Dialectic." *Critical Review* 9.4 (fall 1995): 469–82.
McCaffery, Larry, ed. *Avant-Pop: Fiction of a Daydream Nation*. Boulder: Black Ice, 1994.
Pynchon, Thomas. *Gravity's Rainbow*. New York: Viking, 1973.
Stephenson, Neol. *Cryptonomicon*, New York: Avon Press, 1999.
t.o.L (tree of Life), dir. *TAMALA 2010*. Tokyo: Kinetique, 2002.

Hollywood's Hot Voodoo

Eva Cherniavsky

In one of the cabaret performances folded (however loosely) into the narrative of *Blonde Venus* (1934), Helen Faraday (Marlene Dietrich) arrives on stage disguised in a full-body gorilla costume. Seemingly stalking the chorus line of nubile women in blackface, who nevertheless lead it forward in chains, the gorilla then appears to escape its bonds and make its way to stage center, where the feral body is stripped away and Dietrich rises up and out of the cast-off form. Dressed in a lavishly sequined bodice trimmed with ostrich feathers that outline and amplify her buttocks (in back) and cascade between her legs (in front), Dietrich dons a platinum blonde Afro wig (adorned with sequined arrows) and proceeds to "put over" the lyrics of "Hot Voodoo": "Did you ever happen to hear of Voodoo? / Hear it and you won't give a darn what you do. / Tomtoms put me under a cult of voodoo, / and the whole night long / I don't know the right from wrong." Certainly, this scene has not suffered from critical inattention, generating, as it has, a wide range of commentaries focused alternately or conjointly on the politics of artifice and the articulation of female sexuality with race.

[. . .]

While the conversation on *Blonde Venus* is certainly more complex and nuanced than this, one advantage of sketching the critical terrain in such broad strokes is to make more palpable the limits of the exchange: the ways, for instance, that performance becomes synonymous with "illusion," that critique means disclosure, that race remains an exclusively thematic concern for cinema. As always, the areas of the most banal consensus register the most profound impasses – and my interest in this chapter lies with a critical conversation on race and classic Hollywood cinema that has tended to engage with race as a narrative trope that carries over to cinema from other areas of cultural representation (e.g., the visual arts, elite and popular literatures, state/administrative discourses). [. . .] We can talk about race in cinema (as a question of representation), but there would seem to be nothing specific to the way that cinema mediates race: nothing that cinema can tell us about the (re)production and effects of racial embodiment that close study of another medium would not also reveal; nothing that cinema's mediation of race can tell us about the (re)production and effects of embodiment in film. Moving with and against the insights of feminist film scholarship, this chapter strives to rethink this curiously inert relation between cinema and race, in which each term appears historically and theoretically constituted, prior to their encounter. I argue that the blackness at once hyperbolically attributed to Dietrich in "Hot Voodoo" and emphatically (if still incompletely) purged from her shimmering white form is not simply an index to the racialization of promiscuous femininity in the cultural imaginary but the refraction of the white female body's insertion as commodity-image within the first mass medium and, more particularly, within the international circuits of distribution and consumption forged by US film producers.

Images

Critical to any revisionist discussion of race and cinema is a theory of the filmic image – if only because the Metzian understanding of the image as lack has been largely hegemonic for a psychoanalytic feminist film criticism that stresses, in turn, the figuration of the female star as the embodiment of that lack. In this analytic frame, so decisively posed in Laura Mulvey's influential writing, the consideration of the white female body is oriented to investigating fetishism (the visual and narrative management of women's lack) and, by extension, to cultivating critical distance (unveiling the operations of fetishism, as the only alternative to one's conscription by the fetishizing gaze). [...]

As Steven Shaviro observes, the insistence on the image as lack rejoins the modernist conviction in the critical force of distance, in a phobic ordering of film study that both evacuates the image and enjoins us to back away from the peculiar excess of appearance that this fundamental emptiness makes possible.

> But is it really *lack* that makes images so dangerous and disturbing? What these theorists fear is not the emptiness of the image, but its weird fullness, not its impotence so much as its power.... Much has been written about the "lost object" as a mainstay of cinematic desire. To the contrary: the problem for the cinema spectator is not that the object is lost or missing, but that it is never distant or absent enough. Maurice Blanchot suggests that the image is not a representational substitute for the object so much as it is – like a cadaver – the material trace or residue of the object's failure to vanish completely. (17)

Drawing substantially on Walter Benjamin as well as on Blanchot, Shaviro goes on to elaborate the significance of the camera's break with systems of perception that place the human subject at their center. For Shaviro, the key point is that the camera sees blindly – sees everything. Thus "the camera does not invent, and does not even represent; it only passively records. But this passivity allows it to penetrate, or to be enveloped by, the flux of the material world. The *automatism and non-selectivity* of mechanical reproduction make it possible for cinema to break with traditional hierarchies of representation and enter directly into a realm of matter, life, and movement" (32, my emphasis). Shaviro's point, of course, is not that the image makes its object fully/newly present but quite the contrary: that it confounds the very distinction between absence and presence, Symbolic and Real. In Shaviro's account, the image is not only non-referential but also, crucially, "nonsignifying," in the sense that the real-time cinematic images, their sensational immediacy for the spectator, and the involuntary bodily responses they provoke, remain necessarily in

excess of the signifying systems to which the spectator refers her visual input in the production of meaning.

So it is that Shaviro as spectator is "confronted and assaulted by a flux of sensations that I can neither attach to physical presences nor translate into systematized abstractions. I am violently, viscerally affected by *this* image and *this* sound, without being able to have recourse to any frame of reference, any form of transcendental reflection, or any Symbolic order" (32). In this model of spectatorship, cinema suspends our constitution of the world as object, as objects dissolve into images that we can no longer hold at the proper distance, images that are at once overproximate and incalculably remote. "On the one hand," he notes, "I am no longer able to evade the touch or contact of what I see, but on the other, the image is impalpable, I cannot take hold of it in return, but *always find it shimmering just beyond my grasp*" (46, my emphasis). It follows from this displacement of objects that cinema in Shaviro's reading is precisely *not* reducible to ideology – to a subject-making apparatus. Scopophilia is the inverse of "mastery," the event of the spectator's "forced, ecstatic abjection before the image," enabled by a gaze that is "passive and not possessive" (Shaviro 49, 54).

[...]

In a passage central to Shaviro's exposition, Walter Benjamin reflects:

> Every day, the urge grows stronger to get hold of an object at very close range by way of its likeness, its reproduction. Unmistakably, reproduction as offered by picture magazines and newsreels differs from the image seen by the unarmed eye. Uniqueness and permanence are as closely linked in the latter as are transitoriness and reproducibility in the former. *To pry an object from its shell, to destroy its aura, is the mark of a perception whose "sense of the universal equality of things" has increased to such a degree that it extracts them even from a unique object by means of reproduction.* (223, my emphasis)

Shaviro writes as though his terms were perfectly consonant with Benjamin's, and certainly, both are preoccupied with how cinema deranges the distance between viewing subject and aesthetic object, sacrificing the "total," humanist "picture" in the process; both are concerned with the material, tactile qualities of cinema and with how the medium overtakes the spectator, whose "thoughts ... [are] replaced by moving images."

However, Benjamin stresses that the breakdown of the auratic object, its dis- and reassembly elsewhere/anywhere, occurs as ever-larger segments of the object world submit to capitalist abstraction. [...] In other words, for Benjamin it matters that the reproductive operations of the camera are continuous with the logic of commodity production in ways that it does not seem to matter for Shaviro. [...]

From this perspective, however, Mitsuhiro Yoshimoto offers an equally important updating of Benjamin, when he argues for the special properties of the "commodity-image." In an analysis of a "global image culture" that resonates complexly with Shaviro's discussion of the cinematic image, Yoshimoto notes how the advent of the digital image unmoors images from objects by unsettling distance through speed:

> The synthetic image of the computer does not represent the object's real-time presence in the past [as in the photographic image] but presents the object which does not exist anywhere except as an effect of its own image. As digitally processed images are instantaneously transmitted without a loss of fidelity, a spatial distance is replaced by speed of circulation. . . . The collapse of a hierarchical relation of the object and the image dissolves the past as a temporal category while the future is transformed into the possible present. (111)

Significantly, for Yoshimoto, the loss of distance in the production and circulation of the image is keyed to a later historical moment, inaugurated not with the advent of cinema but with the shift from analog to digital technology. Nevertheless, it is quite possible to argue that the increasing salience of "commodity-images" Yoshimoto associates both with digital processing and with flexible accumulation represents less a reordering of commodity culture than an intensification of processes endemic to capitalism itself. [...]

Elaborating on the effects of information-based capitalism on film, Yoshimoto contends that images are not simply convertible into capital but that, like capital, they reproduce themselves through circulation:

> The image is the basic commodity in the global economy. . . . as commodities become commodity-images, new cycles of consumption and capital accumulation emerge: I-M-I (circulation of commodity-images) and M-I-M (circulation of money) [alongside and (or) in place of what Marx identifies as C-M-C (circulation of commodities) and M-C-M (circulation of money)]. One of the implications of these new formulas is the following: in the age

of global image culture, *it is not only money but also image that circulates without being consumed.* While in C-M-C, the starting and end points of the cycle are qualitatively different [the process is finite, insofar as the commodity is consumed], in I-M-I as in M-C-M, that difference becomes merely quantitative. Capital now accumulates not only through the circulation of money but also through the circulation of images without end. As money begets more money, images also bring forth more images. (115–16, my emphasis)

Plainly enough, the global circulation of cinematic images in the earlier decades of the twentieth century functioned in relation to industrial commodity production and consumption more as a supplement than as an alternative: commodity-images were hardly supplanting commodities (or conversely, we might say, the commodity was not yet becoming "commodity-image"), although certainly the dissemination of commodity-images helped forge the circuits through which industrial commodities would move. [...]

In Yoshimoto's analysis, the global dissemination of the image is an index to the virtual temporality of "instantaneous transmission," which represents, in turn, the condition of possibility for globalization itself. Thus, as he notes, "to some extent, 'globalization of image culture' or 'global image culture' is a misleading phrase or oxymoron since on a fundamental level globalization and image are inseparable each from the other" (109).

[...]

As Hollywood cinema gained a controlling share of the market in Australia, South America, and certain regions of Asia through reconstituting the channels of imperial commerce, it also anticipated a broader shift from political domination to cultivating economic dependencies (from colonialism to neocolonialism) that ensued during the twentieth century with the European powers' divestment of their colonial possessions.

[...]

[C]olonialism and its legacies are not only a theme for cinema but decisive for the medium's organization and its transglobal circulation. [...] Hollywood both participates from an early moment in the highly uneven integration we call globalization (it is suggestive, if not perhaps strictly accurate, that the post-World War I American film corporations have been described as "multinationals") and should also remind us of the extent to which globalization is imperialism by another name (Thompson, *Exporting Entertainment* 149).

Both mainstream journalism and industry publications in the post-1916 period overtly, indeed, on occasion, hyperbolically, acknowledged the relation of Hollywood cinema to the development of markets for other US commodities. Observing that the United States would need significantly to develop its overseas trade once World War I was ended, an article in *Colliers* goes on to reflect: "Well, consider what the American moving picture is doing in other countries. It is familiarizing South America and Africa, Asia and Europe with American habits and customs. It is educating them up to the American standard of living. It is showing them American clothes and furniture, automobiles and homes. And it is subtly but surely creating a desire for these American-made articles" (cited in Thompson, *Exporting Entertainment* 121–2). This upward education is almost certainly part of what a 1915 trade publication article meant to invoke in its celebratory prediction of the postwar film industry: established in South America and in a Europe grown dependent on its products, with a "bigger than ever" domestic market, "American-made films will not only lead the world – *they will constitute it*" (cited in Thompson, *Exporting Entertainment* 54, my emphasis). [. . .]

Bodies

The body and affect of the star have been central to mediating "a certain universality," as well as to determining a film's market value. As Tino Balio points out, while B movies were rented to exhibitors for a flat fee, the superior A product was made available for a percentage of the gross, and it was the cachet of its star(s) that largely established what the rental rate would be (144–5). Thus constituted as commodity-image – that is, as the avatar of a person "pr[ied] from [her] shell" and reckoned on a scale of abstract equivalence – the movie star was arguably the linchpin creation of the Hollywood film industry. [I]n the context of modernity, "race" (in the sense of nonuniversal, nonwhiteness) signifies the body's improper relation to capital: where the European colonizer claims an inalienable property in the body (one may commodify one's bodily or intellectual labor, but not one's flesh), the bodies of the colonized are made in varying degrees susceptible to abstraction and exchange. More particularly, plantation slavery is a limit case, where the "raced" body, made legally alienable, turns inside

out – because fully opened to and penetrated by the abstracting force of capital. Here my interest lies with the implications of slavery (in particular) and colonialism (more generally) for an understanding of embodiment and "image culture" – or, in other words, for an understanding of bodies as "commodity-images." What effects are engendered when the mechanically reproduced white body loses its legal and historical protections from exchange? In what sense can the mechanically reproduced body remain "white"?

[. . .]

If cinema marks the inaugural appearance of the white body in the inorganic, depthless form of the commodity-image, as I am proposing, then one might well anticipate how this body yields a set of contradictions that cannot be addressed, much less resolved, on purely narrative terms. Richard Dyer's discussion of white racial embodiment and the techniques of light takes an important step in considering how white corporeality is managed at the level of the cinematic medium. In his detailed account of the emergence and standardization of lighting patterns for white actors, Dyer demonstrates how white skin, in general, and white women, more particularly and conspicuously, are lit so as to diffuse rather than absorb the light: the white (female) star is always, to a greater or lesser degree (but it is usually greater) a radiant presence on the screen. Now for Dyer the white woman's "glow" is significant for the way it idealizes the white female subject in a gesture traceable across media, from religious iconography to Hollywood film. In a surprising turn, Dyer undercuts his welcome focus on race and the cinematic medium by claiming all the same that there is nothing specific to how cinema mediates race – that cinema simply extends the conventions developed in other representational media. But if it is true that cinema adapts its aesthetics from a wider cultural tradition, there is nothing given or self-evident in its selection of the particular codes and practices it continues (as the next section details), nor does the simple fact of continuity imply the identity of effects across media. So I draw on Dyer's account of the syntax of white embodiment in film to argue the reverse: cinema's mediation of whiteness, rather than the participation in an overarching "idealization" of whiteness that finds its genesis in something equally sprawling and transhistorical (in Eurocentrism, say), has everything to do with the organization of the cinematic medium. Primed by Dyer to remark the white body's glow (as opposed to what he describes as the black and brown body's "shine," its absorption of light), I find equally remarkable the extent to which this glowing skin remediates the white body's depthless condition as commodity-image and restores at least partially the protections of white embodiment at the very point of their erosion: visually, the radiant white body has been pried from its shell in the most literal sense (the edges of the body soften or dissolve), yet in this diffuse, unsettled, unquantifiable state it also refuses its measure on a scale of "the universal equality of things." In this way, the cinematically (re)mediated white body is overtaken by "systematized abstraction" and (seemingly) released from its condition of possibility as abstracted commodity-image. Moreover, as it suffuses and eclipses the objects that surround it, the dissipated body of the glowing star exists in a relation of spatial unrest to her mise-en-scène – an unrest that reproduces within the frame of the image the loss of proper distance that characterizes, for Shaviro, the spectator's relation *to* this image.

The Soft Style

In Hollywood trade publications of the 1920s and 1930s, as well as in the standard film histories of the period, the racial syntax that preoccupies Dyer – the lighting of white skin for glow – is addressed in specifically non-racial terms, as a preference for the "soft style" of cinematography. In their independent and collaborative writing, David Bordwell and Kristin Thompson offer an invaluable account of the changing technological environment in and sometimes against which the soft style emerged as normative for Hollywood productions. Certainly a number of factors favored the development of the soft style in its most conspicuous form during the silent era, among them the use of incandescent lighting and low-contrast developing solutions (Bordwell 342), but it is also evident that a soft, slightly (or significantly) diffused quality to the cinematic image was, more than a simple consequence of the state of the technology, a very deliberately, sometimes obsessively cultivated effect that entailed gauze filters, mesh screens, and special lenses (Thompson, "Major Technological Changes" 288). Contemporary "sources do not discuss the reasons for this usage, aside from the idea of beauty," Thompson notes. "But one purpose was probably to isolate the figures from the background, concentrating the spectator's attention on the face" (288). While "women usually got heavier gauzing" than men, "certain men were associated with glamor as well" (291). Citing an "idea of beauty" as

the impetus to the soft style, these sources would seem to affirm Dyer's association of glow with idealization (less so Thompson's reference to "glamor," which carries sharper commercial overtones). Yet even the dominance of such an apparently transcendent aesthetic is more surprising, when one weighs the extent to which it slowed production, raised costs, and conflicted expressly with other emergent production norms. "Clearly, soft-style cinematography did not promote efficiency. When workers are hanging giant gauzes, calculating special exposure and developing methods, or buying extra lenses, shooting time and expenses go up" (291). Equally telling, "the soft style . . . presented particular problems for the continuity system. Frequent changes in degree of contrast or fuzziness from shot to shot would call attention to editing and other stylistic devices" (292).

[...]

To understand the choice of this particular aesthetic (rather than simply to enumerate the aesthetic advantages of the choice), I argue that we should situate the enthusiasm for softness in the context of the deep and abiding contradiction of a medium that commodifies white bodies and in so doing threatens precisely to eradicate what constitutes the prestige and attraction of white embodiment. Whatever else its merits (its obvious signing of "artfulness," for example), the choice of a soft style allows cinema simultaneously to revoke and to extend the protections of white personhood, by opening whiteness to exchange but not to (re)appropriation. Glowing skin signals the softening of bodily limits that enables the "extraction" (through mechanical reproduction) of abstract value from the white body, even as it refuses the reduction of that body to an object among others – to a consumable artifact on the order of the cars and clothes and interior decor that surround this body on the screen. Inasmuch as the mechanically reproduced object is defined by its new and unprecedented mobility, so that, in Benjamin's phrase, it comes to "meet the beholder . . . in his own particular situation," we could say that cinema traffics in this encounter with (various forms of) eroticized white embodiment while also subtracting the white body from the prospect of end use, or consumption. At the same time, however, and quite apart from the workings of plot or narrative, this shimmering body visually immerses itself into the world of commodities and the (implied) pleasures of consumption. In my variation on Marx's dancing tables, the glowing white body of the star steps forth and speaks its visual hail: "You can meet me here, in this intimate darkness, but you cannot possess me (take me out of circulation and use me up). What can be yours is my ecstasy – my abandoned relation to the world of commodities." My argument is that whiteness manifests in Hollywood cinema as the impossible lure of protection from the invasive forces of capital (the prying open of human shells) through ecstatic consumption.

[...]

In the context of these meditations on images, markets, bodies, and the soft style that normalizes the conversion of white bodies into commodity-images for a global market, I want to return to the signal moment of Dietrich's transmutation from ape to Venus. For nearly all the film's critics, this performance animates contradictions that are pivotal for *Blonde Venus* and for the broader consideration of (white) women's position within a patriarchal imaginary. [...]

The film's overt preoccupation with domesticity and publicity, marriage and prostitution, makes it possible to read the narrative, strictly on its own terms, as concerned with an errant female protagonist, who seeks to constitute and dispose of her own value in a public, performative domain, only to be brutally, if implausibly, reprivatized in the end. To do so is to miss how the narrative attends to the circulation of the white female body as mechanically reproduced image and thus addresses the medium through which it circulates (cinema) at least as much as the arena of live performance it represents (the stage). We learn that (at the very least) two images of Helen are circulating in the press: the first, taken from the wanted poster, improbably features her in full Blonde Venus regalia; the second, which accompanies the engagement notice, is a publicity shot of the performer in a black top hat. Twice we see Johnny inspect these images of his mother, and we witness, as well, two detectives debate whether the image on the wanted poster resembles the woman they pursue. In all three instances, the focus of the commentary concerns the relation of the image to the embodied woman and the range of the responses – in contrast to the detectives, Johnny declares the image from the wanted poster "pretty good," but initially fails to recognize the top-hatted woman as his mother – suggests that the images "extracted" from the female body cannot be stabilized by reference to that body and in fact, quite the contrary, seem to render the "original" body elusive, harder rather than easier to locate in real time and space.

This attention to images as mechanical reproductions of the female body that proliferate according to their own, autonomous logic (I-M-I) obtains at the visual as well as the narrative level: *Blonde Venus* is replete with images of Dietrich that cite Venus with a difference. At the moment where Helen, only just become aware of Ned's early return from Europe, is startled by his footsteps, we see her luminous face, half obscured by the outsized fur collar of her jacket; like her own skin, the irregular borders of the pelt reflect the light, so that she appears to us, once again, as bound in furs (or feathers) and yet too soft, too fluid to bind. One eye is covered, while the other again declines to meet our look and searches a distant periphery. In another, equally salient instance, where the image of Venus reproduces itself for no other reason, one can surmise, except the inevitability of its reproduction, Helen's scarves catch the breeze and we see the ostrich feathers again, at once amplifying her buttocks and raised in a phallic salute.

Venus repeats again, dimly, in Helen's Paris performance, which stands in many respects as an apparent inversion of the motifs of "Hot Voodoo": Dietrich now appears in a rhinestone-studded white tuxedo, complete with white-silk top hat. The look is cool and cosmopolitan, instead of hot and feral; the decor spare, instead of tropical, and with the exception of the tails on the long white jacket of her suit, which again invoke, however timidly, the ostrich trim, Dietrich seems to have attained to the condition of "disengaged" whiteness that has elsewhere in the film eluded her. The glow that in "Hot Voodoo" suffused primarily her face and head here engulfs and softens her entire body; her face, in particular, manifests the softness-with-definition of a more standardized aesthetic, so that we can also read in the transit from "Voodoo" to Paris a reflection on the normalization of "glow" become possible and prevalent at the moment of the film's production.

With only a few, brief exceptions (in particular, a short sequence where it tracks her, from below, as she moves, backward, up a flight of stairs), the camera sits level with Dietrich or above her, thus returning her body to human proportions. If it is possible to read Paris as achieving the whitening of Dietrich's commodity-image, its release from abstraction through (henceforth) standardized practices of softening and diffusion, still this sequence dwells obsessively – and with only marginally less anxiety than "Hot Voodoo" – on the implications of the female body's mechanical reproduction. Critics have noted Dietrich's fashioning as "mannish" woman, or lesbian, as well as the film's self-awareness on this point.

Yet to note that the hot femininity of "Voodoo" here gives way to the cold, lesbian styling of the Paris performance is to beg the question of how lesbianism itself codes in *Blonde Venus*. Reading the mannish attire in the context established by the lyrics, I suggest that the primary association of lesbianism is with nonreproductivity but also, by extension, with lawless reproduction. "If the hens refused to lay / Or if bulls gave milk someday / Do you think I'd care? / That's their affair, / I couldn't be annoyed" – and the lyrics proceed, in this fashion, to enumerate comic scenarios, not simply of gender inversion but of reproductive inversions, in which the copy precedes the original (in another of the verses, it is children who bring forth their parents) and bodies produce without regard for their "natural" limit(ation)s (e.g., bulls give milk). Dietrich's much-referenced "coldness" in this scene may have less to do with her apparent renunciation of affective ties and (or) with the urbane detachment of the woman who desires "like a man" than with her studied indifference to the terms of (her) mechanical reproduction: caught up in a process of abstraction that derives from her body what was never proper to it, nevertheless, she assures us, she "couldn't be annoyed." The irony is that this cultivated distance from the image collapses the very distinction it sets out to protect; the wholly indifferent subject is finally eclipsed by the image she disowns, as subjectivity would seem minimally to require the very thing she abdicates – an investment in her being-in-the-world.

I have been arguing that the body of the star is hyperbolically white because never sufficiently white – and that Hollywood's Hot Voodoo consists in resignifying the body's invasion by capital as the condition of its emancipation. The interest of *Blonde Venus* lies in its preference for performing the ritual rather than simply effecting the voodoo – for rehearsing the production of the white female body (rather than simply producing it) and so, perversely, unlearning Hollywood cinema's grammar of white embodiment at the very moment of its most thoroughgoing institutionalization.

References

Balio, Tino. "Selling Stars." In *Grand Design: Hollywood as a Modern Business Enterprise, 1930–1939*, ed. Tino Balio. Berkeley and Los Angeles: University of California Press, 1993: 143–78.

Benjamin, Walter. *Illuminations: Essays and Reflections*. Ed. Hannah Arendt. Trans. Harry Zohn. New York: Schocken Books, 1969.

Bordwell, David, "Deep-Focus Cinematography." In *The Classical Hollywood Cinema: Film Style and Mode of Production to 1960*, ed. David Bordwell, Janet Staiger, and Kristin Thompson, New York: Columbia University Press, 1985: 341–52.

Dyer, Richard. *Heavenly Bodies: Film Stars and Society*. London: Macmillan, 1986.

——. *White*. New York: Routledge, 1997.

Mulvey, Laura. *Visual and Other Pleasures*. Bloomington: Indiana University Press, 1989.

Shaviro, Steven. *The Cinematic Body*. Minneapolis: University of Minnesota Press, 1993.

Thompson, Kristin. *Exporting Entertainment: America in the World Film Market, 1907–1934*. London: British Film Institute Publishing, 1985.

——. "Major Technological Changes of the 1920s." In *The Classical Hollywood Cinema: Film Style and Mode of Production to 1960*, ed. David Bordwell, Janet Staiger, and Kristin Thompson. New York: Columbia University Press, 1985: 281–93.

Yoshimoto, Mitsuhiro. "Real Virtuality." In *Global/Local: Cultural Production and the Transnational Imaginary*, ed. Rob Wilson and Wimal Dissanayake. Durham, NC: Duke University Press, 1996: 107–18.

Films

Blonde Venus. Dir. Josef von Sternberg. Paramount, 1932.

Part VI

Body-Talk

In this analytic we note the emergence of multiple conservations in American Studies that focus on the body as a site for commodification and discipline as well as a marker for definitions of normalcy. In a protracted crisis over identity and subjectivity, body-talk has loudly joined the conversation over the contested intersectionalities of the thing formerly known as the self. Body-talk has come to mediate multi-modal conversations on identity, subjectivity, and lived-experience. Each of these articles mediates a historicity – offering a clearer sense of a historical period through an emphasis on the body as a contested site of power and meaning-making. For these writers, the body is a barometer of how power and meaning are made.

In contemporary popular discourse, the power of the lingua franca of the body stems from its multiple references – harking back to things that are much older as well as providing a way to talk about the human self that is not seemingly about the subject or identity. Scholarship on the body has critiqued enlightenment common sense about the self and the body, challenging assumptions of reason/rationality and the primacy of the self. Hence, this scholarship relates to modernist thinking and the moves of the last century around the decentering and fragmentation of that Cartesian subject.

This analytic has emerged particularly from the transformation of an older set of analytics in scholarship on race, gender, and sexuality. Newer scholarship, deeply influenced by Foucaultian turns in African Americanist, feminist, and queer theory, has pursued questions about the relationship between materiality and bodies, asking how the body is constructed through contested social and cultural practices, and how such practices inform lived and bodily experience. In a field long concerned with definitions of sexuality, able-bodiedness, and beauty, where bodies appear as normative images and the body becomes a site for determining normalcy and its antithesis, newer work extends these interests through a focus on technologies of self-fashioning, along with those of discipline and control.

The commodification of human bodies as chattel lay at the very heart of the emergence of a modern market economy. Walter Johnson examines the process of commodification as slaves are prepared for sale in the New Orleans market, and what happens when bodies move through the slave pen; whether slaves, or the traders or buyers who participated in a shared fantasy of gentility and status through their positions as slaveholders. As bodies were prepared, polished, fattened, and dressed, and families were dismantled and repackaged with fabricated histories, slaves were stripped of their history. Their identities were evacuated to fit individuals into the categories of the market. Saidiya Hartman brings a telescopic focus to an examination of the processes of serpentine modes of power as it moves and twists in the nineteenth-century US South. For Hartman, dominant notions of political agency cannot comprehend the positionality, limitations, or possibilities for those subjected to the terror and social death of slavery. Only by suspending enlightenment notions of agency can one begin to imagine the slave experience of the body and performance as sites of pleasure and resistance in such practices as stealing away.

Nyan Shah brings a queer and critical perspective to the state's record of normative policing as he focuses on sodomy charges and the policing of sexuality among internal and external nomadic subjects – seasonal workers, including foreign immigrants, tramps, and local casual laborers – engaged in agricultural work on the Pacific Coast in the early twentieth century. Arguing that the correlation of national identity and sexual normalcy was a new development in the early twentieth century, he explores the development of categories of deviance and normality in police and prosecutors' readings of criminality in social interactions between white adolescent males and Asian migrants. The surveillance of borderlands created racialized and sexualized typologies of masculinities. For Shah, the state constructed a formidable defense of American normality and masculinity, along with "an immense legal archive that records its success" in defining and maintaining security. Yet, Shah suggests, this same archive that has been harnessed to create normalized legal subjects can be reinterpreted to expose rifts and crevices where competing narratives have left residual traces.

Lennard Davis argues that while disability studies has generally confined discussions exclusively to impairment and disease, scholars need to engage a larger picture of the development of notions of normalcy that include disability along with any nonstandard behaviors. He examines the emergence of the concept of "normal" in Western society between 150 and 200 years ago, and the ways in which it was bound up with the emergence of statistics, linguistic standardization, and the rubric of nationalism. Challenging distinctions between the world of the body and that of the body politic, Lennard argues that with the concept of a norm, representation is possible and notions of the equality of citizens is founded not on ethics but the quasi-science of norms. As major changes in medical science between 1750 and 1850 dovetailed with political ferment, disease was defined as excess and lack. Attributing political meaning to physical conditions, the body became tied to national identity and allegiance, as in discussions of eugenics. For Davis, the disability movement needs to examine the ways in which bourgeois definitions of rights create disabilities and seek to solve problems created by such definitions.

Virginia Blum explores constructions of beauty and desirability in the complex cultural phenomenon of plastic surgery, through tracing her own experience of becoming a patient, defined by a "deformity," in a surgery instigated by her mother when she was an adolescent. Arguing that the aesthetic gaze is additionally a transformative gaze, Blum analyzes the male construction of the female subject in the relationship between the male surgeon and the female patient. Emphasizing the vulnerability of the body and psyche to the positional and institutional power that plastic surgeons and the industry hold over women's bodies, Blum asks where this cultural power is located.

Mimi Nguyen explores the ways in which cyborgs and mutants in digital space enable acts of imagining strategies and tactics to escape the disciplined body. She further explores the dangers of inhabiting other bodies and ways in which race is reified in comics that otherwise celebrate the denaturalization of norms. Digital space represents a situation that potentially disrupts the presumption of an expressive relationship between embodiment and social identity. By releasing the body from social powers and offering users the ability to wear a body that doesn't refer to the physical appearance of the user/performer, Nguyen argues that the cybernetic interface poses significant challenges to some essentialisms as cyborg subjects generate new bodies and design new selves. The prosthesis of digital space enables a mobility that promises autonomy and inclusivity that allows the user to choose and fuse new parts in a potentially endless process of consumption and self-invention. Yet for Nguyen, the fantasy of redemptive identification risks appropriating the imagined experience of racial or national otherness and depoliticizes the social powers that produce difference. Asking whether the queer subject can conceptualize an avatar that isn't an escape, Nguyen examines the possibilities in comics that imagine disruption rather than escape.

Turning People into Products

Walter Johnson

Slave traders were sometimes accused of selling people who were dead. J. B. Alexander, for instance, did not have time to get very far from the slave market with the slave he had just bought before a man whom he did not know walked up to him and "remarked to him that he had bought a dead Negro." Alexander asked the man what he meant. The man replied that he could see that "the boy was sick," too sick to be cured – already dead. The man, it turned out, was in a position to know dead slaves when he saw them. He had been a slave trader for almost thirty years.[1] The lawyers for the hapless Dixons invoked a similar set of images in the suit brought by the couple against the slave dealer who had sold them Critty and Creasy. As the Dixons' lawyers saw it, the trader was "an experienced jockey" who had resorted "to all of the nostrums and arts of his profession, such as cod liver oil, stimulants, etc. to fatten and keep up these dying consumptives until he could get them off his hands."[2] Essentially, they charged the dealer with sending the dead to market.

The imagery used by the lawyers – the imagery of forbidden nostrums and secret arts – had much more to do with the world of the occult than with the supposedly rational workings of the slave trade. But what served the lawyers for the Dixons as an accusation of improper conduct might have summoned up a vision of the perfect sale for a slave trader: an otherwise lifeless body quickened into motion by the magic of the market. By this dark magic, this necromancy, new people could be made out of the parts of old ones: slaves could be detached from their pasts and stripped of their identities, their bodies could be disciplined into order and decorated

for market, their skills could be assigned, their qualities designated, their stories retold. Slaves could be remade in the image of the irresistible power of their salability – fed, medicated, beaten, dressed, hectored, and arrayed until they outwardly appeared to be no more than advertisements for themselves. The dead, their bodies disjointed from the past and their identities evacuated, would walk to sale.[3]

Slave Making

In the daily practice of the slave pens, slaves were treated as physical manifestations of the categories the traders used to select their slaves – No. 1, Second Rate, and so on. After gathering individuals into categories and attributing to those categories an independent existence in "the slave market" by which they could be compared to all other categories (and all other goods), the traders turned those categories around and used them to evaluate the individuals of whom they were supposedly composed.[4] Thus could slave trader J. M. Wilson walk into a Louisiana courtroom, declare himself "familiar with the prices of slaves in this market" (that is, with the price categories that traders used to do their business), and testify to the value of Clarissa and her family without ever having seen them. Similarly, slave trader J. W. Boazman could testify to the value of "Negroes bought about September 1851" in supporting a slaveholder's claim that the death of a woman he owned at the hands of a careless contractor had cost him a thousand dollars. Thus could slave trader David Wise testify to the value of a human eye: "Being asked if the girl had a filter on her eye if it would impair her value, he says it would impair its value from $25 to $40."[5] In switching the pronoun from "her" to "it," Wise revealed in a word what his business was about: turning people into prices. He used the tables of aggregates which *reflected* the market valuation of people to *project* that valuation.

The price tables made traders like Boazman and Wise capable of extraordinary feats of comparison, but it was their daily business to guide the buyers beyond comparison to selection: to get them to single out the one slave especially suited to their purposes from the many nominally similar slaves available in the market. In the daily practice of the slave pens, then, real slaves had a double relation to the abstract market in the traders' imaginations. On the one hand, they were to be transformed into exemplars of the category to which they had been assigned; but once the categories of comparison had been established and embodied, the slaves were supposed to become once again visible as individuals – comparable to all of those who inhabited the same category, yet different enough to attract a buyer's eye and seal the sale. This daily dialectic of categorization and differentiation was the magic by which the traders turned people into things and then into money.

Traders began to package their slaves for market before they ever reached the slave pens. As they neared their destination, the traders removed the heavy chains and galling cuffs from their slaves' arms and legs and allowed the slaves to wash and rest and heal. The traders shaved men's beards and combed their hair, they plucked gray hairs or blackened them with dye – the "blacking" that appears in their account books was perhaps intended for this purpose. Slave trader John White was clearer about what he did with the tallow he bought: it was "for the girls' hair."[6] The rituals of preparation continued once slaves had reached the market. In the slave pens the traders increased rations of bacon, milk, and butter, a fattening diet one trader referred to as "feeding up."[7] To keep the slaves' muscles toned, the traders set them to dancing and exercising, and to make their skin shine with the appearance of health, the traders greased the slaves' faces with "sweet oil" or washed them in "greasy water."[8]

The traders also hired doctors to visit their pens regularly. "Scarcely a day passes . . . but what I go to his establishment, it being on the road to my office," testified Dr. J. H. Lewis of J. M. Wilson's slave pen. Dr. John Carr spoke similarly of the slave yard owned by Hope H. Slatter in the 1840s: "is generally in the habit of calling there and sitting for an hour in the afternoon . . . he usually visited all the slaves." When Slatter's yard passed into the possession of Bernard and Walter Campbell, Carr continued as the yard's doctor: "was the attending physician at Campbell's establishment . . . is in the habit of visiting Campbell's establishment two or three times a day."[9] These accounts may be exaggerated, for these doctors had as much experience in the courts as they did in the slave market, and it was part of their ongoing business relation with the traders to emphasize the good care received by slaves in the pens. But even if they overstated the frequency and quality of their slave-market ministrations, it is clear that sick slaves in the pens often received professional treatment. At the time of his death and estate settlement, slave dealer Elihu Cresswell was carrying debts for having slaves' teeth pulled and providing them with medicine. In his account book John White recorded the twenty-five dollars he paid a physician to look after his slaves in 1845, and regularly noted prescriptions and treatment for slaves in the pens – chloride of lime, capsules, cupping, medicine. The New Orleans slave yards kept by Cresswell and Benjamin Screws both had separate rooms set aside for the sick. Fear of contagion more than charity might have motivated the traders' concern, but the separation of the sick was often accompanied by medical care. Frank, for example, was "nursed" back to health from yellow fever in slave dealer Calvin Rutherford's "private house," and Solomon Northup was treated for smallpox in the hospital, as, according to an 1841 city law, all slaves suffering from infectious disease were to be.[10]

In the slave pens, however, medical treatment was a trick of the trade, nothing more. These expenditures were speculations like any others the traders made, tactical commitments to slaves' bodies that were underwritten by the hope of their sale. When that hope ran out, so seemingly did the traders' concern. John White's reckoning of his chances of curing and selling Harriet, for instance, can be tracked through the pages of his account book – capsules for Harriet on February third, cupping Harriet on the fifth, burial of her child on the fourteenth, brandy for Harriet on the sixteenth, burial for Harriet on the nineteenth, the sale of Harriet's surviving children on the twenty-first. Harriet was treated when it seemed possible to save her, comforted (or quieted) with alcohol when it did not, and buried when she died. Her children, less valuable than she had been, were not treated at all and were quickly sold when their care became the trader's responsibility and their presence in the yard a threat to his other property.[11] There was always an alternative to caring for sick slaves: selling them quickly.

Their bodies prepared, the slaves in the pens were packaged for sale. The traders' account books document their extensive daily attention to presentation: entries for dresses, shoes, stockings, and head coverings for the women; suits with undershirts, drawers, socks, boots, and sometimes a hat for the men. In October of 1857 John White bought forty identical blue suits for the men in his yard.[12] The clothes masked differences among the slaves; individual pasts and potential problems were covered over in uniform cloth. The sick and the well, those from far away and those from nearby, the eager, the unattached, and the angry – all looked alike in the trader's window-dressed version of slavery.

The clothes suggested not only comparability but also cleanliness and chastity. Eyre Crowe's famous drawing of slaves lined out for sale in New Orleans shows women with long-sleeved blouses and covered heads, men in black suits with top hats. Noting the kerchiefs tied around their heads "in a mode peculiar to the Negress," northern writer Joseph Ingraham pronounced the women he saw in the market "extremely neat and 'tidy.'" "Their appearance had little of the repulsiveness we are apt to associate with the slaves," wrote Robert Chambers, another northern visitor to the slave pens.[13] None of the poverty and toil that characterized the daily life of American slaves, none of the bareness that contributed so powerfully to the historical sexualization of black bodies, was immediately apparent in the slave market. These people were dressed as ideal slaves, exaggerated in the typicality of their appearance, too uniform, too healthy, too clean. Through the daily practice of the pens, individual slaves were turned into physical symbols of their own salability – nothing else about them was immediately apparent.

[...]

Their bodies treated and dressed, the slaves were turned out for sale divided by sex. "Men on one side, women on the other": the phrase runs through descriptions of the slave market like a leitmotif. "Here may be seen husbands separated from wives by only the width of the room, and children from parents, one or both," wrote John Brown, reenvisioning the family ties that were erased by the traders' practice.[14] Even when the traders kept track of family ties, they often severed them in the slave market. Of the seven slaves bracketed with the label "Overton purchase" in John White's "slave record" for 1846, two were sold together, one sent home as unsalable, and the rest sold individually in Louisiana,

Tennessee, and Alabama. Families were likewise carefully bracketed on the bill of lading for a shipment of slaves received by Seraphim Cucullu in the winter of 1836. But they were indiscriminately separated as Cucullu sold them over the course of the spring. Cucullu's account-book record of the buyers of his divided slaves is a testament to the commitment of his employees to his instructions "that price might be the guide and to sell for the best of his interests."[15] That meant selling slaves the way the buyers wanted them, according to sex-specific demand rather than according to family ties.

The lengths to which slave traders could go in dismantling and repackaging slave families in the image of the market were limited by Louisiana law. The original *Code Noire* forbade the separation by sale of children under the age of ten from their mothers, and in 1829 the law was explicitly extended to outlaw the importation of thusly separated slaves.[16] While the 1829 law should not be ignored (it is a good example of slaveholders negotiating a hard bargain with their own consciences and of the tendency of paternalism to limit its already meager promises to protection of the very young), its effect should not be overemphasized. What the law did was to give legal credence to the categories according to which slave traders did their business. Who, after all, would favor a trade in motherless children? Not the slave traders. The vast majority of family-separating sales occurred in the upper South, out of the effective reach of the law. And the vast majority of these involved the removal of the parent; slave traders, especially those who traveled long distances, had little use for small children.[17] By the 1850s, as single women became a featured category of trade, orphaned children became a recognizable portion of the population in upper South slave communities.[18] Trader John White left four of Mary Cole's children (aged two to ten) behind when he took Cole and her three older children to New Orleans in 1846. Trader J. W. Boazman explained a similar choice this way: "servants are less valuable with children than without." But if the traders wanted to trade in children who had been separated from their mothers, there was little to keep them from adhering to the letter of the law by making orphans rather than finding them. It is hard to read slave trader David Wise's statement that "witness has often sold little children..." without wondering about his own role in the qualification he quickly added "... who had lost their mother."[19] The 1829 law, then, provided the maximal rhetorical effect with the minimal practical disruption of the slave trade. It stripped "the slave family" of its existing members, their history, their ties and affinities and substituted a more salable definition – a mother and a young child.

As well as packaging the slaves into salable lots, the traders packed them into racial categories. By the time they turned their slaves out for sale, the traders had transformed the market categories they used to talk to one another into the racial categories they used to talk to the buyers. In their back-and-forth market reports the traders described slaves as Prime, No. 1, No. 2, and so on, but on ninety percent of the Acts of Sale recorded by New Orleans notaries they used words like Negro, Griffe, Mulatto, or Quadroon.[20] These words were explicitly biological: they bespoke pasts that were not visible in the slave market by referring to parents and grandparents who had been left behind with old owners. But they did so by referring to something that the buyers would be able to see: skin color.

Brushed, dressed, and polished, divided by sex (or lamely protected by law), assigned a new history and a racial category, the people in the pens were lined out for sale by height: "The men were arranged on one side of the room, the women on the other, the tallest were placed at the head of the row, then the next tallest, and so on in order of their respective heights," remembered Solomon Northup.[21] Around the walls of the slave pens, the slaves were arranged to reflect the traders' buyer-tracking tables. As the slaves were hectored into line at the beginning of every day, there were no husbands or wives apparent among them, no old lovers or new friends; there were only men and women, field hands and house servants, Negro, Griffe, and Mulatto, tall, medium, and short.

Having done all they could to make real people represent the constructed categories of the marketplace, the traders began to try to turn them into money. Value in the slave market emerged out of the play of similarity with difference, the choice of one slave from among many similar slaves made a sale. To sell a slave, the traders had to peel back their own representations of com-modified similarity and slip beneath them a suggestion of personal distinction that would make one slave stand out to a buyer who was trying to distinguish himself from all of the other buyers in the market. The traders had to make a pitch. In the slave pens, the traders pitched their slaves by telling stories that seemed to individualize and even humanize the depersonalized slaves. They breathed the life of the market into the bodies, histories, and identities of the people they were trying to sell, by using a simulacrum of human singularity to do the work of product differentiation.

[. . .]

Some of the stories the traders told were quite simple, advertisements that were put forward as qualifications, accounts of past work through which buyers could view a certain future: first-rate cotton picker, experienced drayman, cooper, carpenter, cook, nurse, and so on. And some were more detailed: in the words of a slave trader's handbill, "Bill, Negro man, aged about 28 years, excellent servant and good pastry cook"; or, in the words of a witness to a trader's pitch, "[He] said that said slave was a first rate cook, a very good washer and could plait plain shirts very well & that Mr. Hewes would be satisfied in every respect with having purchased said Negress."[22] However brief, these lists of skills referred to the experience and judgment of former owners, to a past distant from the slave pens. But they insinuated them-selves into the present as trustworthy representations of past experience, drawing whatever authenticity they had (enough to convince Mr. Hewes) from the constant bab-ble of talk about slaves that characterized the social life of southern slaveholders. The traders were taking hold of slaveholders' fantasies about the slave market, wrapping them around the slaves they had for sale, and selling them back to the buyers as indications of those buyers' own good fortune and discernment.

And the traders' pitches went well beyond work. They could spin a detailed fantasy out of a list of supposed skills: "Sarah, a mulatress, aged 45 years, a good cook and accustomed to housework in general, is an excellent and faithful nurse for sick persons, and in every respect a first rate character." Sarah, as sold, was gentility and paternalism embodied – good meals, a clean house, a companion who would wait faithfully by the bed of an ailing (vulnerable) owner. "Dennis, her son, a mulatto, aged 24 years, a first rate cook and steward for a vessel, having been in that capacity for many years on board one of the Mobile packets; is strictly honest, temperate, and is a first rate subject."[23] Dennis would bring with him a hint of river-boat grandeur: the plush seats and ornate surroundings; the graceful service and extensive menu; the pleasure of traveling first class.[24] And Dennis was trustworthy: he had worked on a boat but not run away; he might be hired out or given the run of the house. His purchase would make good sense; his service would be in good taste. And, though Dennis and his mother were put up for sale separately, they could be bought together by someone who cared enough to do so.

The slave traders could line their families out separately and then knit them together again in the sales pitch. They could package and sell the negation of their own way of doing business by offering the buyers a chance to rejoin families that had been sundered in the market. Slave-market paternalism thus replayed the plots of proslavery propaganda and fiction: the good-hearted slave at the side of the dying master; the slave who could be trusted to master himself; the slaveholder's saving interventions in the life of the unfortunate slave. As representations of individual slaves, the traders' pitches drew their authenticity from slaveholders' shared fantasies of gentility, reciprocity, and salvation. The traders' stories helped the buyers to mirror their shared fantasies in the individual slaves who stood before them, to imagine that they were distinguishing themselves through the purchase of the slave they chose.

[...]

The traders had to be equally ready to spin unruly evidence of slaves' inward feelings back into the comforting conventions of proslavery rhetoric. When a woman who was missing two fingers mounted the stand in Richmond, the auctioneer quickly explained that the doctor had removed the first finger for a medical reason and she had herself cut off the second because it pained her. The disquieting specter of a woman who would choose to mutilate her hand rather than be sold was brushed over with the reassuring image of a slave so stupid and imitative that she would cut off one finger because the doctor had cut off another.[25] Anton Reiff, a visitor to New Orleans, remembered seeing a woman crying on the auction stand and recorded what he was able to learn about her in his diary: "Her master was in debt and was obliged to sell her to pay some mortgage. She had always lived with the family. She was about 35 years old. Her grief (to me) was heartrending. She wept most bitterly."[26] The loyal slave sold for her owner's debts: whether or not the story Reiff recorded was true, it was effective. The woman's tears became part of the auctioneer's pitch, and Anton Reiff, standing in the slave market, felt his heart rent by a convention of proslavery paternalism.

All of these stories may have been believed by the traders who told them; most of them may have been true, but their veracity is less important than their form. The traders' stories, redolent with the comforting commonplaces of slaveholding culture, guided the buyers' eyes to what they were supposed to see. The slave traders' stories suggested that the buyer of a particular slave would be a man with a sharp eye for the main chance, or a taste for the exceptional, or a singular capacity to do

right. As they packaged their slaves in stories about the distant past, the traders were telegraphing suggestive accounts of the slaveholding futures that were for sale in the pens. Along with the virtues of their slaves, the traders were scripting those of their buyers.

Some of the people the traders sold were not slaves at all. Eulalie had been living as free for decades when she, her six children, and ten grandchildren were taken by force from their home in Pointe Coupeé, Louisiana, sold at auction in New Orleans, and then placed in a slave pen for "safe keeping." Euphémie and her seven children were held in a New Orleans slave pen, advertised for sale in the New Orleans *Bee*, and sold at public auction. She had been living as a free person for over twenty years. Though they lost years of their life to the slave traders, these women and their families had nearby friends and relatives who could help them reconstruct their histories and successfully sue to have their freedom restored on the grounds that whatever claim there was to their ownership had long since lapsed through disuse.[27] The hopes of other free people sold as slaves, however, were even more attenuated.

The shades of legality in which the traders dealt sometimes crossed into outright kidnapping. The list of those who managed to send word out of slavery must stand as a partial list of the kidnapped: John Merry, a free man from Illinois, was arrested as a slave in St. Louis and shipped to New Orleans to be sold; Solomon Northup, a free man from New York, was lured with lies to Washington, drugged, threatened with death, and put on a boat for New Orleans, where he was sold in the yard of slave dealer Theophilus Freeman; Albert Young was freed by his Alabama owner's will but nevertheless carried to New Orleans by the will's executor and sold to the New Orleans dealers McRae, Coffman & Co.; John Wesley Dunn, another free man, was charged with stealing an "old coat" in Baltimore, jailed, sold to slave dealer Hope H. Slatter, and carried to New Orleans, where he was sold again. Messages sent by Merry and Northup reached their friends, and they were freed from slavery through the intervention of the courts. Young's suit also reached the courts, but his freedom was voided on the grounds that his emancipation was not legal under Alabama law. The letter Dunn sent for help may never have reached his father, to whom it was addressed.[28]

None of these stolen people could have been sold if their histories were known, so they were sold with new ones. These were only the most extreme cases of the creative power of the traders' market practice. Or, at least, they seem the most extreme, because lying about a slave's origins seems more abject than ignoring them, selling a person under an uncertain title seems more mendacious than selling with a clear title, and kidnapping a free person seems more shocking than selling a slave. But the extremity of these stories represents the regularity of what slave traders did every day for four hundred years, what they did hundreds of thousands of times during the antebellum period. Just as kidnapping made slaves of free people, the traders' packaging created slaves who did not previously exist out of the pieces of people who formerly did. By detaching slaves from their history and replacing human singularity with fashioned salability, the traders were doing more than selling slaves: they were making them.

Ultimately, however, the rites of the market had to be enacted by the slaves. From the time the buyers entered the yard in the morning to the time they left at night, the slaves were expected to enact carefully scripted roles. Solomon Northup remembered Theophilus Freeman hectoring his slaves to perform and "threatening" them with beatings if they stepped out of their assigned roles. In the slave pens, wooden boards with holes drilled through them or wide leather straps attached to a handle, were substituted for the mortifying lash, because paddles raised blisters but left no permanent scars. The traders' instruments of torture enforced the story they were trying to tell without leaving a trace of its source.[29] Northup also remembered Freeman "holding out various inducements," which left even fewer traces than beatings. The historian Michael Tadman has discovered that slaves were sometimes promised small cash rewards "if they would try to get homes and not do anything against the interest of their sales." As well as the entries for calico dresses and pantaloons, slave trader John White recorded regular cash outlays to slaves to make sure that the costumes he had bought were inhabited with the right spirit. Northup remembered that Freeman used his slaves' own hopes to fund his inducements. Instructing Northup to hold up his head and look "smart," Freeman told Northup that he "might, perhaps, get a good master" if he "behaved."[30]

[...]

The traders instructed slaves to give ages that accorded with their polished bodies and to hide pasts that might make buyers wary. Slaves who had run away or been ill were told to hide their histories. Those who were being sold for their skills were told to "exaggerate their accomplishments." Slaves in the pens were instructed to appear happy and active, William Wells Brown remembered, "some were set to dancing, some to jumping,

some to singing, and some to playing cards. This was done to make them seem cheerful as possible." Solomon Northup remembered that Theophilus Freeman "exhorted us to appear smart and lively" and provided Northup with a violin that he might give the others music to dance by. Following the conventions of antebellum racism, slaves were made to demonstrate their salability by outwardly performing their supposed emotional insensibility and physical vitality.[31]

These carefully prepared performances made it difficult for the buyers to sort representation from reality, and like other slave-importing states, Louisiana had strong warranty laws designed to rebalance the relationship between seller and buyer.[32] The asymmetry of information in the slave market had been addressed in the Louisiana *Civil Code* by the law of redhibition, or "the avoidance of sale on account of some vice or defect in the thing sold." As a justice of the Louisiana Supreme Court put it in 1859, these laws were "evidently created as a matter of policy and . . . founded upon the difficulty which purchasers of slaves recently brought from another state experience in procuring proof of their bodily condition and the comparative ease with which the proof of that fact could be made by the vendors."[33] Specific provisions of the *Civil Code* limited actions for redhibition to those cases in which the problem was not apparent upon "simple inspection" and not explicitly exempted from the general warranty. The sales of slaves (and animals) could be voided for "vices" of either body or character. Leprosy, madness, and epilepsy were considered absolute vices of body, their bare existence sufficient cause to void a sale. Other diseases were considered in proportion to the disability they caused. Vices of character, as defined by Louisiana law, were limited to cases in which it could be proven that a slave had committed a capital crime, was "addicted to theft," or "in the habit of running away." A habit of running away was established by proving that a slave had run away "twice for several days, or once for more than a month." Warranty suits had to be preceded by an attempt at "amicable return" of the unwanted slave(s) and filed within one year of the date of purchase. Under an 1834 addition to the law, buyers of recently imported slaves did not have to prove that the "vice" was existent at the time of the sale if it became evident within two months (for questions of character) or two weeks (for illness or infirmity).[34]

[...] Most slave traders appear to have played the odds, preferring to sell risky slaves as sound ones and counting on the buyers' difficulties in returning a slave and filing a suit to make good their risk.

Returning slaves, after all, cost dissatisfied buyers even more money than they had already spent in the market: the cost of transportation for the slave, the buyer, and usually a sympathetic witness; the cost of having depositions taken or of getting people to court, including exceptional charges for expert witnesses like physicians; court costs and lawyers' fees; the possibility of losing. Indeed, the relative frequency with which buyers who lived at some distance from New Orleans appeared in court to sue slave traders suggests that the traders may have been choosing their targets carefully, identifying the out-of-town buyers for whom returning an unwanted slave would be the most difficult and steering them toward slaves about whom the traders themselves had suspicions.[35]

[. . .]

[T]hose who returned slaves to the pens usually had the law on their side, and many traders accepted returns rather than risking suits. One slave salesman stated that such a practice was a matter of course in the pen where he worked: "Mr. Slatter's instructions were never to misrepresent Negroes and to exchange them at any time rather than go to a lawsuit."[36] It is hard to imagine the man saying anything else – that Slatter told him to lie to customers, sell them sick slaves, and refuse to take them back, for example – with a thousand dollar suit hanging in the balance. But even if accepting returned slaves was not a hard-and-fast rule, it was a practice common enough to have generated a common resolution: slaves who had been returned to the traders were often resold to other buyers, sometimes for prices higher than the traders had received the first time around.[37]

No matter what they eventually did when faced with a returned slave, traders did the daily work of preparing and selling their slaves in the shadow of the law. The representations traders made in the marketplace could be subject to subsequent legal action; vices they managed to conceal at the time of sale could later emerge as the grounds for a suit; credulous buyer could turn sedulous litigant. The traders had to consider the law when they decided who to sell to whom. John White's slave record book listed a number of slaves as "in my hands unsold" at the end of every season. Some people the slave traders just could not sell.[38] Every year White's firm sent a few slaves back to central Missouri after unsuccessfully offering them for sale in New Orleans: five sent in 1846; six in 1851; five more in 1852.[39] No doubt those were small numbers to John White, who sold a hundred or more slaves in a season. But they were momentous decisions to the small number they affected. Slaves who could not be sold sometimes ended up in the places from which they had been taken in the first, place, restored to their families and communities. "Sent home," one of White's entries reads.

The daily practice of the pens lay at the juncture of an unknown past and a promised future. As a justice of the Louisiana Supreme Court put it when considering the necessity of the enforcement of redhibition law: "The condition of a Negro at a trader's quarters, well dressed, well fed, unworked – in a word well cared for in every material respect for the express purpose of making a favorable impression on purchasers – is not necessarily a conclusive criterion of the future or the past condition and capability of that same Negro when undergoing the necessary hardships of ordinary slave service." The traders' daily business was to shape the real people they had in their hands to reflect the abstract market they had in their heads, and then to punctuate their categories of comparison with the value-producing practice of differentiation: the special clothes and spatial arrangement, the articulated human connections, the singular story. In the pens the traders medicated and fed and shined and shaved and plucked and smoothed and dressed and sexualized and racialized and narrated people until even the appearance of human singularity had been saturated with the representations of salability. This was the traders' version of necromancy – the magic that could steal a person and inhabit their body with the soul of another – the forcible incorporation of a slave with the spirit of a slaveholder's fantasy.

But though they went to great lengths to replace people with packaging, the traders did not have to fool anyone. Indeed, the traders could no more force their self-revealing representations upon a skeptical buyer than they could do their deadly business without the resistant bodies of living slaves. By replacing biography with salability, the traders did not have to do anything more than shape the discussion. Under the traders' watchful eyes, visible physical coordinates replaced invisible historical identities as the most accessible means for buyers to make their comparisons. Faced with the uncertainties of the slave pens, slave buyers turned to race as the best way to do the business of slavery.

Notes

1 *Alexander v. Hundley*, #5276, 13 La. Ann. 327 (1858), testimony of T. R. Davis, UNO.

2   *Dixon v. Chadwick*, #4388, 11 La. Ann. 215 (1856), plaintiff's brief, UNO.

3   On slavery, sale, life, and death see Orlando Patterson, *Slavery and Social Death: A Comparative Study* (Cambridge: Harvard University Press, 1982); Igor Kopytoff, "The Cultural Biography of Things: Commoditization as Process," in Arjun Appadurai, ed., *The Social Life of Things: Commodities in Cultural Perspective* (Cambridge: Cambridge University Press, 1986), 64–91; and Akhil Gupta, "The Reincarnation of Souls and the Rebirth of Commodities: Representations of Time in 'East' and 'West,'" *Cultural Critique* (Fall, 1992), 187–211.

4   For the evolution of the market from a place to a power see Jean-Christophe Agnew, *Worlds Apart: The Market and the Theater in Anglo-American Thought, 1550–1750* (Cambridge: Cambridge University Press, 1986).

5   *Coulter v. Cresswell*, #2734, 7 La. Ann. 367 (1852), testimony of J. M. Wilson and David Wise, UNO; *Peyton v. Richards*, #3523, 11 La. Ann. 63 (1856), testimony of J. W. Boazman, UNO.

6   John Brown, *Slave Life in Georgia: A Narrative of the Life, Sufferings, and Escapes of John Brown, a Fugitive Slave Now in England*, L. A. Chamerovzow, ed. (London, 1855; Savannah, GA: The Beehive Press, 1991), 112; William Wells Brown, *Narrative of William Wells Brown, A Fugitive Slave, Written by Himself* (1847), in Gilbert Osofsky, ed., *Puttin' on Ole Massa* (New York, 1969), 193. For "blacking" see *Ledger of Accounts*, Tyre Glen Papers, RASP, and John White, *Day Book*, April 19, 1845, UMC; for tallow see White, *Day Book*, January 4, 1845, UMC.

7   For fattening diet see White, *Day Book*, January 5, 29, April 12, 13, May 2, 1845, June 12, 1846, *passim*, UMC; for the quotation see A. J. McElveen to Ziba Oakes, September 8, 1856, reproduced in Edmund Drago, ed., *Broke by the War: Letters of a Slave Trader* (Columbia, SC, 1991).

8   John Brown, *Slave Life in Georgia*, 95–96; William Wells Brown, *Narrative*, in Osofsky, ed., *Puttin' on Ole Massa*, 194; Moses Roper, *A Narrative of the Escape and Adventure of Moses Roper* (London, 1838), 62; Henry Bibb, *Narrative of the Life and Adventures of Henry Bibb, An American Slave, Written by Himself* (New York, 1845), in Osofsky, ed., *Puttin' on Ole Massa*, 115.

9   *Dohan v. Wilson*, #5368, 14 La. Ann. 353 (1859), testimony of Dr. J. H. Lewis, UNO; *Stillwell v. Slatter*, unreported Louisiana Supreme Court case #4845 (1843), testimony of Dr. John J. Carr, UNO; *Murphy v. Mutual Benefit & Fire Insurance Company of Louisiana* #2244, 6 La. Ann. 518 (1851), testimony of Dr. John J. Carr, UNO. See also *Mulhollan v. Huie*, #3200, 12 La. 241 (1838), testimony of Abraham R. Jones, UNO; *Peterson v. Burn*, #912, 3 La. Ann. 655 (1848), testimony of William B. Williams, UNO; *Kock v. Slatter*, #1748, 5 La. Ann. 734 (1850), testimony of Dr. M. Mackie, UNO.

10 *Succession of Cresswell*, #2423, 8 La. Ann. 122 (1853), UNO; John White, *Day Book*, 1846, *passim*, UMC; *Perkins v. Shelton*, unreported Louisiana Supreme Court case #5654 (1859), testimony of E. F. Harrot, UNO; *Lynch and Wiesman v. McRae*, unreported Louisiana Supreme Court case #270 (1859), UNO; Solomon Northup, *Twelve Years a Slave*, Joseph Logsdon and Sue Eakin, eds. (Baton Rouge: Louisiana State University Press, 1968), 55; ordinance XLVII, articles 2 and 3 (passed June 8, 1841), in *Digest of the Ordinances and Resolutions of the General Council of the City of New Orleans* (New Orleans, 1845), 28.

11 White, *Day Book*, February 3, 5, 14, 16, 19, 21, 1846, UMC.

12 N. C. Folger to John White, bill for clothing purchased in New Orleans, dated October 1, 1857 (and totaling $585.25), Chinn Collection, MHS; John White, *Day Book*, *passim*, UMC; Tyre Glen account with Bragg and Stewart, 1833, Tyre Glen Papers, RASP; Whitehead and Loftus Account Book, 1835–1837, Floyd Whitehead Papers, DU; *Succession of Cresswell*, unreported Louisiana Supreme Court case #3521 (1954), UNO. See also Charles Ball, *Fifty Years in Chains: Or the Life of an American Slave* (New York, 1859), 70–81; Roper, *Narrative*, 63; Bibb, *Narrative*, in Osofsky, ed., *Puttin' on Ole Massa*, 116, 136.

13 Eyre Crowe, "The Slave Market in New Orleans," *Harper's Weekly Magazine*, January 24, 1863, 197; Joseph Holt Ingraham, *The Southwest by a Yankee* (New York: Harper & Brothers, 1835), II, 193, 197; Robert Chambers "Journal," October 1853, in Frederick Law Olmsted, *The Cotton Kingdom: A Traveler's Observations on Cotton and Slavery in the American Slave States* (New York, 1862), II, 597.

14 Brown, *Slave Life in Georgia*, 100; see also Northup, *Twelve Years a Slave*, 51.

15 White, *Slave Record*, 1846, UMC; *Gourjon v. Cucullu*, #2324, 4 La. 115 (1852), list of Negroes on board brig *Seraphim*, Compte de Vente du 94 esclaves reçu par le brick *Seraphim*, and testimony of Charles Tremot, UNO.

16 *Code Noire*, sections 8 and 9, quoted in Judith Kelleher Schafer, *Slavery, the Civil Law, and the Supreme Court of Louisiana* (Baton Rouge: Louisiana State University Press, 1994), 165; *Laws of Louisiana, 1829, 1st Session, 9th Legislature* reproduced in Henry J. Levoy, ed., *The Laws and General Ordinances of New Orleans* (New Orleans, 1857), 269.

17 Michael Tadman, *Speculators and Slaves: Masters, Traders, and Slaves in the Old South* (Madison: University of Wisconsin Press, 1989), 153–4.

18 Brenda Stevenson, *Life in Black and White: Family and Community in the Slave South* (New York: Oxford University Press, 1996), 182–3, 224.

19 White, *Slave Record*, 1846, UMC; *Coulter v. Cresswell*, #2734, 7 La. Ann. 367 (1852), testimony of J. W. Boazman and David Wise, UNO.

20 Robert Fogel and Stanley Engerman, eds., *The New Orleans Slave Sample, 1804–1862*, database available from the Inter-University Consortium for Political and Social Research.

21 Northup, *Twelve Years a Slave*, 51. See also John Brown, *Slave Life in Georgia*, 96–100.

22 "Sale of valuable Servants," 1838, mss 44 f. 86. HNO; *Hewes v. Baron*, #1641, 7 Mart. (N.S.) 134 (1828), testimony of Edward Durin, UNO.

23 Slave Sale Broadside, May 13, 1835, Lower Mississippi Valley Collection, Hill Memorial Library, LSU.

24 For the role of steamboats in shaping notions of "the good life" see Louis C. Hunter, *Steamboats on the Western Rivers: An Economic and Technical History* (Cambridge: Harvard University Press, 1949), 390–418.

25 James Redpath, *The Roving Editor, or Talks with Slaves in the Southern States* (New York, 1859), 252. On race and slavishness as imitation see Ariela Gross, "Pandora's Box: Slave Character on Trial in the Antebellum Deep South," *Yale Journal of Law and the Humanities*, 7 (1995), 283–8.

26 Anton Reiff, *Journal*, 42 (February 18, 1856), LSU.

27 *Eulalie, f.w.c. and her Children v. Long and Mabry*, #3237, 9 La. Ann. 9 (1854), testimony of Pierre Pouche, L. M. Foster, and the decision of the Supreme Court, UNO; *Euphemié, f.w.c. v. Juliet and Jourdan*, unreported Louisiana Supreme Court case #6740 (1865), plaintiff's petition, testimony of Juliette Maran, decision of the Supreme Court, UNO; see also *Eulalie, f.w.c. v. Long and Mabry* #3979, 11 La. Ann. 463 (1856), and *Andrinette, f.w.c. and her Children v. Maran*, f.w.c., unreported Louisiana Supreme Court case #6741 (1865), UNO. The acronym "f.w.c." stands for "free woman of color" and indicates the presumption of freedom which was granted under Louisiana law to anyone who appeared to be "mulatto" and sued for their freedom. For "f.w.c." (and "f.m.c"), these cases, and those of others whose suits for freedom were heard by the Louisiana Supreme Court see Schafer, *Slavery, the Civil Law, and the Supreme Court of Louisiana*, 220–249.

28 *Merry, f.m.c. v. Chexnaider*, #1877, 8 Mart. (N.S.) 699 (1830), plaintiff's petition and decision of the Supreme Court, UNO; Northup, *Twelve Years a Slave*, 12–20; *Young, f.m.c. v. Egan*, #4075, 10 La. Ann. 415 (1855); John Wesley Dunn to Charles Dunn, January 3, 1845, John Wesley Dunn Letter, 81–73-L, HNO. See also Schafer, *Slavery, the Civil Law, and the Supreme Court of Louisiana*, 250–288.

29 Northup, *Twelve Years a Slave*, 25. See also John Brown, *Slave Life in Georgia*, 97–98; Bibb, *Narrative*, in Osofsky, ed., *Puttin' on Ole Massa*, 115; Frederika Bremer, *Homes of the New World: Impressions of America*, trans. Mary Howlitt (New York, 1853), II, 535.

30 Obediah Fields, memorandum, February 11, 1828, quoted in Tadman, *Speculators and Slaves*, 101; White, *Day Book*, December 30, 31, 1844, January 8, 1845, *passim*, UMC;

Northup, *Twelve Years a Slave*, 36; see also Bibb, *Narrative*, in Osofsky, ed., *Puttin' on Ole Massa*, 101.

31 L. M. Mills interview in John Blassingame, ed., *Slave Testimony: Two Centuries of Letters, Speeches, Interviews, and Autobiographies* (Baton Rouge: Louisiana State University Press, 1977), 503; Brown, *Narrative*, in Osofsky, ed., *Puttin' on Ole Massa*, 196; Bibb, *Narrative*, in Osofsky, ed., *Puttin' on Ole Massa*, 95, 139; Brown, *Slave Life in Georgia*, 99–100; Northup, *Twelve Years a Slave*, 36.

32 For the general point about slave-importing states see Andrew Fede, "Legal Protection for Slave Buyers in the U.S. South: A Caveat Concerning *Caveat Emptor*," *American Journal of Legal History*, 31 (1987), 322–58. For the specifics of Louisiana law see Judith Kelleher Schafer, "'Guaranteed against the Vices and Maladies Prescribed by Law': Consumer Protection, the Law of Slave Sales, and the Supreme Court in Antebellum Louisiana," *American Journal of Legal History*, 31 (1987), 306–21, and Schafer, *Slavery, the Civil Law, and the Supreme Court of Louisiana*, 127–79.

33 *Dohan v. Wilson*, #5368, 14 La. Ann. 353 (1859), decision of the Supreme Court, UNO.

34 Thomas Gibbes Morgan, ed., *Civil Code of the State of Louisiana* (New Orleans, 1853), articles, 2496–508, 2512.

35 See, for example, *Rist v. Hagan*, #4503, 8 Rob. 106 (La. 1844); *Peterson v. Burn*, #912, 3 La. Ann. 655 (1848); *Slater v. Rutherford*, #1021, 4 La. Ann. 382 (1849); *Executors of Haggerty v. Powell*, #2215, 6 La. Ann. 533 (1851); *Coulter v. Cresswell*, #2734, 7 La. Ann. 367 (1852); *Person v. Rutherford*, #3585, 11 La. Ann. 527 (1856), UNO.

36 *Kock v. Slatter*, #1748, 5 La. Ann. 734 (1850), testimony of James Blakeny, UNO.

37 For returned slaves resold see *Stewart v. Sowles*, #725, 3 La. Ann. 464 (1848); *Peterson v. Burn*, #912, 3 La. Ann. 655 (1848); *Kock v. Slatter*, #1748, 5 La. Ann. 734 (1850); *Romer v. Woods*, #1846, 6 La. Ann. 29 (1851); *Person v. Rutherford*, #3585, 11 La. Ann. 527 (1856); *Gatlin v. Kendig*, #6894, 18 La. Ann. 118 (1866). For higher prices and sale in different states see White, *Slave Record*, 1851, *passim*, UMC. The other thing the traders did was return slaves themselves. Their legal rights were the same as any other slaveholders, and they could sue when they were dissatisfied or call previous owners "in warranty" when they were sued.

38 White, Slave Record, *passim*.

39 White, *Slave Record*, 1846 (David Overton, Megan Wells, Esther Taylor, Runel Causey, Berry), 1851 (Mary Ellette and her five children), 1852 (Abram Godwin, Kate King, and her three children), UMC.

Redressing the Pained Body: Toward a Theory of Practice

Saidiya V. Hartman

Lu Lee's owner encouraged the enslaved to have Saturday night dances even though he was a religious man and thought it wrong to dance. Lee remembered him saying, "Seek your enjoyment, niggers got to pleasure themselves someway." As argued earlier, the promotion of innocent amusements and harmless pleasures was a central strategy in the slave owner's effort to cultivate contented subjection. However, the complicity of pleasure with the instrumental ends of slaveholder domination led those like Mary Glover to declare emphatically, "I don't want [that] kind of pleasure." Generally, the response of the enslaved to the management and orchestration of "Negro enjoyment" was more complex than a simple rejection of "innocent amusements." Rather, the sense of operating within and against these closures made the experience of pleasure decidedly ambivalent. If "good times" were an index of the owner's profit and dominion, what possibilities could pleasure yield? For those like John McAdams, pleasure was less a general form of dominance than a way of naming, by contradistinction, the consumption and possession of the body and black needs and possibilities. It was more than a tendency for understatement that led McAdams to characterize his experience and that of other slaves as "no pleasure, as we had to work just as soon as [we] got large enough to work."[1]

Not only was pleasure posed in contrast to labor, but the negation or ambivalence of pleasure was to be explained by the yoking of the captive body to the will, whims, and exploits of the owner and by the constancy of the slave's unmet yearnings, whether for food or for freedom. Yet McAdams's remarks also suggest that "lack" insufficiently describes the vexed state of pleasure, since slaves also lived for Saturday night dances. The value attached to having a good time was its facilitation of collective identification: "We made good use of these nights as that was all the time the slaves had together to dance, talk, and have a good time among their own color."[2] And yet pleasure was ensnared in a web of domination, accumulation, abjection, resignation, and possibility. It was nothing if not cunning, mercurial, treacherous, and indifferently complicit with quite divergent desires and aspirations, ranging from the instrumental aims of slave-owner designs for mastery to the promise and possibility of releasing or redressing the pained constraints of the captive body. It is the ambivalence of pleasure and its complicity with dominative strategies of subjection that is the theme of this chapter.

The struggles waged against domination and enslavement in everyday life took a variety of forms, including opportunities seized in the domain of permissible and regulated amusements. If these occasions were designed, as Frederick Douglass argued, to "better secure the ends of injustice and oppression," they also provided a context in which power was challenged and claims made in the name of pleasure, need, and desire.[3] Pleasure was fraught with these contending investments in the body. As Toby Jones noted, the Saturday night dances permitted by the master were refashioned and used for their own ends by the enslaved: "The fun was on Saturday night when massa 'lowed us to dance. There was a lot of banjo pickin' and tin pan beatin' and dancin' and everybody talk bout when they lived in Africa and done what they wanted."[4]

Within the confines of surveillance and nonautonomy, the resistance to subjugation proceeded by stealth: one acted furtively, secretly, and imperceptibly, and the enslaved seized any and every opportunity to slip off the yoke.

In these pages, I outline the clandestine forms of resistance, popular illegalities, and "war of position" conducted under the cover of fun and frolic. Here I do not mean to suggest that everyday practices were strategies of passive revolution but merely to emphasize that peregrinations, surreptitious appropriation, and moving about were central features of resistance or what could be described as the subterranean "politics" of the enslaved. With this in mind, I endeavor in this chapter to illuminate the social struggle waged in "the Negro's enjoyment" and the challenges to domination launched under the rubric of pleasure. Yet, in order to do this, we must, first, situate performance within the context of everyday practices and consider the possibilities of practice in regard to specific forms of domination; second, defamiliarize fun and frolic or the performance of blackness in order to make visible the challenges that emerge in this arena; and, third, liberate the performative from the closures of sentiment and contented subjection in order to engage the critical labor of redress.[5]

The Centrality of Practice

Exploiting the limits of the permissible, creating transient zones of freedom, and reelaborating innocent amusements were central features of everyday practice. Practice is, to use Michel de Certeau's phrase, "a way of operating" defined by "the non-autonomy of its field of action," internal manipulations of the established order, and ephemeral victories. The tactics that comprise the everyday practices of the dominated have neither the means to secure a territory outside the space of domination nor the power to keep or maintain what is won in fleeting, surreptitious, and necessarily incomplete victories.[6] The refashioning of permitted pleasures in the effort to undermine, transform, and redress the condition of enslavement was consonant with other forms of everyday practice. These efforts generally focused on the object status and castigated personhood of the slave, the pained and ravished body, severed affiliations and natal alienation, and the assertion of denied needs. Practice is not simply a way of naming these efforts but rather a way of thinking about the character of resistance, the precariousness of the assaults waged against domination, the fragmentary character of these efforts and the

transient battles won, and the characteristics of a politics without a proper locus.

The everyday practices of the enslaved encompassed an array of tactics such as work slowdowns, feigned illness, unlicensed travel, the destruction of property, theft, self-mutilation, dissimulation, physical confrontation with owners and overseers that document the resistance to slavery.[7] These small-scale and everyday forms of resistance interrupted, reelaborated, and defied the constraints of everyday life under slavery and exploited openings in the system for the use of the enslaved. What unites these varied tactics is the effort to redress the condition of the enslaved, restore the disrupted affiliations of the socially dead, challenge the authority and dominion of the slaveholder, and alleviate the pained state of the captive body. However, these acts of redress are undertaken with the acknowledgment that conditions will most likely remain the same. This acknowledgment implies neither resignation nor fatalism but a recognition of the enormity of the breach instituted by slavery and the magnitude of domination.

Redressing the pained body encompasses operating in and against the demands of the system, negotiating the disciplinary harnessing of the body, and counterinvesting in the body as a site of possibility. In this instance, pain must be recognized in its historicity and as the articulation of a social condition of brutal constraint, extreme need, and constant violence; in other words, it is the perpetual condition of ravishment. Pain is a normative condition that encompasses the legal subjectivity of the enslaved that is constructed along the lines of injury and punishment, the violation and suffering inextricably enmeshed with the pleasures of minstrelsy and melodrama, the operation of power on black bodies, and the life of property in which the full enjoyment of the slave as thing supersedes the admittedly tentative recognition of slave humanity and permits the intemperate uses of chattel. This pain might best be described as the history that hurts – the still-unfolding narrative of captivity, dispossession, and domination that engenders the black subject in the Americas.

If this pain has been largely unspoken and unrecognized, it is due to the sheer denial of black sentience rather than the inexpressibility of pain. The purported immunity of blacks to pain is absolutely essential to the spectacle of contented subjection or, at the very least, to discrediting the claims of pain.[8] The black is both insensate and content, indifferent to pain and induced to work by threats of corporal punishment. These contradictions are partly explained by the ambiguous and precarious status of the black in the "great chain of being" – in short, by the pathologizing of the black body – this abhorrence then serves to justify acts of violence that exceed normative standards of the humanely tolerable, though within the limits of the socially tolerable as concerned the black slave. In this regard, pain is essential to the making of productive slave laborers. The sheer enormity of this pain overwhelms or exceeds the limited forms of redress available to the enslaved. Thus the significance of the performative lies not in the ability to overcome this condition or provide remedy but in creating a context for the collective enunciation of this pain, transforming need into politics and cultivating pleasure as a limited response to need and a desperately insufficient form of redress.

The Closures of Sentiment

[…]

Generally, the representation of the performative has been inscribed in a repressive problematic of consensual and voluntarist agency that reinforces and romanticizes social hierarchy. The pastoral has been the dominant mode of this problematic of repression. In the social landscape of the pastoral, slavery is depicted as an "organic relationship" so totalizing that neither master nor slave could express "the simplest human feelings without reference to the other." Thus the master and the slave are seen as, if not peacefully coexisting, at the very least enjoying a relationship of paternalistic dependency and reciprocity. In this instance, paternalism minimizes the extremity of domination with assertions about the mutually recognized humanity of master and slave. Even the regime of production becomes naturalized as "the rhythms of work," as if slave labor were merely another extension of blacks' capacity for song and dance. The lure of the pastoral is in reconciling sentiment with the brute force of the racial-economic order. Thus, the brutality and antagonisms of slavery are obscured in favor of an enchanting reciprocity. The pastoral renders the state of domination as an ideal of care, duty, familial obligation, gratitude, and humanity. The ruthless use of labor power and the extraction of profit are imagined as the consensual and rational exchange between owner and slave. This is accomplished by representing direct and primary forms of domination as coercive and consensual – in short, by representing slavery as a hegemonic social relation.

[…]

Within the enclosures of the avowedly total and reciprocal relations of master and slave in which the simplest expression of human feelings is impossible without reference to the other, the fetish or artifice of the slave's consent and agency effectively links the exercise of will and contented subjection.[9] Not surprisingly, song and dance and a range of everyday acts, seemingly self-directed but actually induced by the owner, are the privileged expressions of this consenting agency. The paternal endowments of will, voice, and humanity deny the pained and punitive constitution of the slave as person and the necessary violence of racial slavery. Thus the performative is rendered as little more than scenes of revelry and good times that lighten the burden of slavery and bonded labor represented as an extension of leisure; thereby emphasizing the festive and celebratory character of servitude.[10] Most often these practices, when not envisioned as concessions of slaveholders designed to "win over" or to debase the enslaved, have been rendered through the idyllic lens of the pastoral, in which the "off times," not bondage and coerced labor, define slave life.[11] Certainly Douglass was aware of this double bind; it was responsible for the anxiety that accompanied his discussion of slave recreations. He negotiated it by identifying recreation with abasement and stressing the importance of interpretation and contextual analysis in uncovering the critical elements or "implicit social consciousness" of slave culture.

The Character of Practice

In light of this, how might we reconsider the performative in order to illuminate the social relations of slavery and the daily practices of resistance that traverse these relations or represent the critical labor of these practices without reproducing the contented subject of the pastoral or the heroic actor of the romance of resistance? To render everyday practices with any complexity requires a disfigurement and denaturalization of this history of the subject as romance, even if a romance of resistance. This requires that we forgo simply celebrating slave agency and instead endeavor to scrutinize and investigate the forms, dispositions, and constraints of action and the disfigured and liminal status of the agents of such acts. In contrast to approaches that foreclose performance in the troubled frame of autonomy, arrogating to the enslaved the illusory privileges of the bourgeois subject or self-possessed individual, or performance as evidence of the harmonious order of slaveholder hegemony and the slave's consent to that order, or performance as a reprieve from the horrors of the system, what is considered here are precisely the ways in which performance and other modes of practice are determined by, exploit, and exceed the constraints of domination.

[. . .]

If the forms of power determine what kinds of practice are possible within a given field, what are the prospects for calculated action given that the very meaning of slave property is "being subject to the master's will in all things" and that issues of consent, will, intentionality, and action are utterly meaningless, except in the instance of "criminal" acts. Bearing this in mind, what possibilities for agency exist that don't put the enslaved at risk of a greater order of pain and punishment since the slave is a legal person only insofar as he is criminal and a violated body in need of limited forms of protection? In this case, the assignation of subject status and the recognition of humanity expose the enslaved to further violence in the case of criminal agency or require the event of excessive violence, cruelty beyond the limits of the socially tolerable, in order to acknowledge and protect the slave's person. Is it possible that such recognition effectively forecloses agency and that as subject the enslaved is still rendered without will or reinscribed as the object of punishment? Or is this limited conferral of humanity merely a reinscription of subjugation and pained existence? Does the designation of "criminal" or "damaged property" intensify or alleviate the onus of anguished and liable person?

In short, what I am trying to hint at here is the relation of agent and act – in particular, the anomalous status of the slave as subject and the circumscribed action characteristic of this condition. The cleavage or sundering of the slave as object of property, pained flesh, and unlawful agent situates the enslaved in an indefinite and paradoxical relation to the normative category "person." One must attend to this paradox in order to discern and evaluate the agency of the enslaved because the forms of action taken do not transcend this condition but rather are an index of the particular figurations of power and modes of subjection.

Yet it is also important to remember that strategies of domination don't exhaust all possibilities of intervention, resistance, or transformation. Therefore, it is necessary to investigate what possibilities exist given these determinants, the myriad and infinitesimal ways in which agency is exercised, the disposition or probability of certain acts, and the mechanisms through which these "ways of operating"

challenge and undermine the conditions of enslavement. Is the agency of the enslaved to be located in reiterative acts that undermine and discursively reelaborate the conditions of subjection and repression?[12] Is it founded upon the desire to negate constraint, to restage and remember the rupture that produced this state of social death, to exceed this determinate negation through acts of recollection, or to attend to the needs and desires of the pained body?

Performing Blackness

[. . .]

The import of the performative [. . .] is in the articulation of needs and desires that radically call into question the order of power and its production of "cultural intelligibility" or "legible bodies."[13] Thus issues of redemption and redress are central to these practices, and the intended or anticipated effect of the performative is not only the reelaboration of blackness but also its affirmative negation. It is important to remember that blackness is defined here in terms of social relationality rather than identity; thus blackness incorporates subjects normatively defined as black, the relations among blacks, whites, and others, and the practices that produce racial difference. Blackness marks a social relationship of dominance and abjection and potentially one of redress and emancipation; it is a contested figure at the very center of social struggle.[14]

Therefore, "performing blackness" conveys both the cross-purposes and the circulation of various modes of performance and performativity that concern the production of racial meaning and subjectivity, the nexus of race, subjection, and spectacle, the forms of racial and race(d) pleasure, enactments of white dominance and power, and the reiteration and/or rearticulation of the conditions of enslavement. It is hoped that "performing blackness" is not too unwieldy and, at the same time, that this unruliness captures the scope and magnitude of the performative as a strategy of power and tactic of resistance. The interchangeable use of performance and performativity is intended to be inclusive of displays of power, the punitive and theatrical embodiment of racial norms, the discursive reelaboration of blackness, and the affirmative deployment and negation of blackness in the focus on redress. I have opted to use the term "performing blackness" as a way of illuminating the entanglements of dominant and subordinate enunciations of blackness and the difficulty of distinguishing between contending enactments of blackness based on form, authenticity, or even intention.

These performances of blackness are in no way the "possession" of the enslaved; they are enactments of social struggle and contending articulations of racial meaning. The unremitting and interminable process of revision, reelaboration, mimicry, and repetition prevents efforts to locate an originary or definitive point on the chain of associations that would fix the identity of a particular act or enable us to sift through authentic and derivative performances, as if the meaning of these acts could be separated from the effects they yield, the contexts in which they occur, or the desires that they catalyze, or as if instrumental amusements could be severed from the prospects of pleasure or the performative from scenes of torture. Moreover, these performances implicitly raise questions about the status of what is being performed – the power of whiteness or the black's good time, a nonsensical slave song, or recollections of dislocation.

The emphasis on the joining of race, subjection, and spectacle is intended to denaturalize race and underline its givenness – that is, the strategies through which it is made to appear as if it has always existed, thereby denying the coerced and cultivated production of race. (This was particularly the case in the antebellum period, in which race was made an absolute marker of status or condition and being black came to be identified with, if not identical to, the condition of enslavement.) The "naturalization" of blackness as a particular enactment of pained contentment requires an extremity of force and violence to maintain this seeming "givenness." The "givenness" of blackness results from the brutal corporealization of the body and the fixation of its constituent parts as indexes of truth and racial meaning. The construction of black bodies as phobogenic objects[15] estranged in a corporeal malediction and the apparent biological certainty of this malediction attest to the power of the performative to produce the very subject which it appears to express.[16] What I am trying to argue here is not that the black body exists prior to the discourses and practices that produce it as such but that what is particular to the discursive constitution of blackness is the inescapable prison house of the flesh or the indelible drop of blood – that is, the purportedly intractable and obdurate materiality of physiological difference.

Thus despite the effort to contextualize and engage blackness as a production and performance, the sheer force of the utterance "black" seems to assert a primacy, quiddity, or materiality that exceeds the frame of this approach. The mention of this "force" is not an initial step in the construction of a metaphysics of blackness or an effort to locate an "essence" within these performances but merely an acknowledgment of the sheer weight of a history of terror that is palpable in the very utterance "black" and inseparable from the tortured body of the enslaved. It acts as a reminder of the material effects of power on bodies and as an injunction to remember that the performance of blackness is inseparable from the brute force that brands, rapes, and tears open the flesh in the racial inscription of the body. In other words, the seeming obstinacy or the "givenness" of "blackness" registers the "fixing" of the body by terror and dominance and the way in which that fixing has been constitutive.

[...]

If blackness is produced through specific means of making use of the body, it is important to consider this "acting on the body" not only in terms of the ways in which power makes use of the body but also in terms of pleasure. Pleasure is central to the mechanisms of identification and recognition that discredit the claims of pain but also to those that produce a sense of possibility – redress, emancipation, transformation, and networks of affiliation under the pressures of domination and the utter lack of autonomy. Much attention has been given to the dominative mode of white enjoyment, but what about forms of pleasure that stand as figures of transformation or, at the very least, refigure blackness in terms other than abjection? Certain ways of making use of the body are diacritically marked in practice as "black" or as self-conscious forms of racial pleasure: "having a good time among our own color," to quote McAdams. These acts become productions of race focused on particular patterns of movements, zones of erotic investment, forms of expression, and notions of pleasure. Race is produced as an "imaginary effect" by a counterinvestment in the body and the identification of a particular locus of pleasure, as in dances like the snake hips, the buzzard lope, and the funky butt. This counterinvestment in all likelihood entails a protest or rejection of the anatomo-politics that produces the black body as aberrant. More important, it is a way of redressing the pained constitution and corporeal malediction that is blackness.

Defamiliarizing the "Negro's Enjoyment"

The sense of black community expressed by "having a good time among our own color" depends upon acts of identification, restitution, and remembrance. Yet the networks of affiliation enacted in performance, sometimes referred to as the "community among ourselves," are defined not by the centrality of racial identity or the self-sameness or transparency of blackness nor merely by the condition of enslavement but by the connections forged in the context of disrupted affiliations, sociality amid the constant threat of separation, and shifting sets of identification particular to site, location, and action. In other words, the "community" or the networks of affiliation constructed in practice are not reducible to race – as if race a priori gave meaning to community or as if community was the expression of race – but are to be understood in terms of the possibilities of resistance conditioned by relations of power and the very purposeful and self-conscious effort to build community.

Despite the "warmly persuasive" and utopian quality that the word "community" possesses, with its suggestion of a locality defined by common concern, reciprocity, unity, shared beliefs and values, and so on, it cannot be assumed that the conditions of domination alone were sufficient to create a sense of common values, trust, or collective identification.[17] The commonality constituted in practice depends less on presence or sameness than upon desired change – the abolition of bondage. Thus, contrary to identity providing the ground of community, identity is figured as the desired negation of the very set of constraints that create commonality – that is, the yearning to be liberated from the condition of enslavement facilitates the networks of affiliation and identification.

[. . .]

"Community among ourselves" is an articulation of an ideal and a way of naming the networks of affiliation that exist in the context of difference, disruption, and death.[18] The significance of becoming or belonging together in terms other than those defined by one's status as property, will-less object, and the not-quite-human should not be underestimated. This belonging together endeavors to redress and nurture the broken body; it is a becoming together dedicated to establishing other terms of sociality, however transient, that offer a small measure of relief from the debasements constitutive of one's condition.[19] Here it is useful to think about the production of these shared identifications and interests as being constantly refigured and negotiated and as fractured by differences and antagonisms rather than defined by stasis and continuity. Rather than invoking community as an ideal of homogeneity or selfsameness or as arena of idealized values in opposition to the conflicts and violence of the social order, we must grapple with the differences that constitute community and the particular terms of community's enactment in their specificity in order to fully understand the value of "having a good time among their own color." In other words, the networks of affiliation or "politics of identification" enacted in practice traverse a range of differences and create fleeting and transient lines of connection across those differences.

The common set of identifications experienced in "having a good time among their own color" or "talking about when we were free in Africa" is not fixed but a fleeting, intermittent, and dispersed network of relations. These relations can neither be reduced to domination nor explained outside it. They exceed the parameters of resistance in creating alternative visions and experiences of subjectivity, though they do indeed challenge the dominant construction of blackness. This shared set of identifications and affiliations is enacted in instances of struggle, shared pleasures, transient forms of solidarity, and nomadic, oftentimes illegal, forms of association.

Politics without a Proper Locus

[. . .]

In order to illuminate the significance of performance and the articulation of social struggle in seemingly innocuous events, everyday forms of practice must be contextualized within the virtually unbounded powers of the slave-owning class, and whites in general, to use all means necessary to ensure submission. Thus it is no surprise that these everyday forms of practice are usually subterranean. I am reluctant to simply describe these practices as a "kind of politics," not because I question whether the practices considered here are small-scale forms of struggle or dismiss them as cathartic and contained.[20] Rather, it is the concern about the possibilities of practice as they are related to the particular object constitution and subject formation of the enslaved outside the "political proper" that leads me both to question the appropriateness of the political to this realm of practice and to reimagine the political in this context. (As well, I take seriously Jean Comaroff's observations that "the real politick of oppression dictates that resistance be expressed in domains seemingly apolitical.")[21]

[. . .]

The historical and social limits of the political must be recognized in order to evaluate the articulation of needs and the forwarding of claims in domains relegated to the privatized or nonpolitical. If the public sphere is reserved for the white bourgeois subject and the public/private divide replicates that between the political and the nonpolitical, then the agency of the enslaved, whose relation to the state is mediated by way of another's rights, is invariably relegated to the nonpolitical side of this divide. This gives us some sense of the full weight and meaning of the slaveholder's dominion. In effect, those subjects removed from the public sphere are formally outside the space of politics.

The everyday practices of the enslaved generally fall outside direct forms of confrontation; they are not systemic in their ideology, analysis, or intent, and, most important, the slave is neither civic man nor free worker but excluded from the narrative of "we the people" that effects the linkage of the modern individual and the state. The enslaved were neither envisioned nor afforded the privilege of envisioning themselves as part of the "imaginary sovereignty of the state" or as "infused with unreal universality."[22] Even the Gramscian model, with its reformulation of the relation of state and civil society in the concept of the historical bloc and its expanded definition of the political, maintains a notion of the political inseparable from the effort and the ability of a class to effect hegemony.[23] By questioning the use of the term "political," I hope to illuminate the possibilities of practice and the stakes of these dispersed resistances. All of this is not a preamble to an argument about the "prepolitical" consciousness of the enslaved but an attempt to point to the limits of the political and the difficulty of translating or interpreting the practices of the enslaved within that framework. The everyday practices of the enslaved occur in the default of the political, in the absence of the rights of man or the assurances of the self-possessed individual, and perhaps even without a "person," in the usual meaning of the term.

[...]

Notes

1   John McAdams, in George P. Rawick, ed., *The American Slave: a Composite Autobiography* (Westport, Conn.: Greenwood, 1973), 41 vols., Texas Narratives, suppl. 2, vol. 7, pt. 6, p. 2461; Lu Lee, in ibid., suppl. 2, vol. 6, pt. 5, p. 2297; Mary Glover, in ibid., suppl. 2, p. 1518.

2   McAdams, in ibid., suppl. 2, vol. 7, pt. 6, p. 2467.

3   Frederick Douglass, *Life and Times of Frederick Douglass* (New York: Collier, 1962), 147.

4   Toby Jones, in Rawick, *The American Slave*, Texas Narratives, vol. 4, pt. 2, p. 249.

5   The hyperbolic enactment of power central to domination links performance and everyday practice.

6   Michel de Certeau, *The Practice of Everyday Life* (Berkeley: University of California Press, 1984), 21.

7   Raymond A. Bauer and Alice H. Bauer, "Day to Day Resistance to Slavery," in *American Slavery: The Question of Resistance*, ed. John H. Bracey, August Meier, and Elliot Rudwick (Belmont, Calif.: Wadsworth, 1971), 37–60.

8   Elaine Scarry, *The Body in Pain* (New York: Oxford University Press, 1985), 33.

9   See Raymond Williams, *The Country and the City* (New York: Oxford University Press, 1973), 36–8; and Eugene Genovese, *Roll, Jordan Roll: The World the Slaves Made* (New York: Vintage, 1972), 3.

10 The pastoral is a comic romance generically about the reconciliation of opposing forces. Hayden White has argued that the mode in which a story is told reveals it to be a story of a particular kind. In White's schema of historical styles, when history is emplotted in the comic mode, its mode of explanation tends to be organicist and its ideological implications conservative. The focus on reconciliation, integrative and synthetic processes, and a conservative vision of good society, in this case the humanity of slavery, is certainly appropriate to our understanding of the pastoral. The features of the pastoral are replicated in the very terms of the historical imagination. So what is explained comes to mirror the very terms of explication. See Hayden White, *Metahistory: The Historical Imagination in Nineteenth Century Europe* (Baltimore: Johns Hopkins University Press, 1973), and *Tropics of Discourse: Essays in Cultural Criticism* (Baltimore: Johns Hopkins University Press, 1978). Roger D. Abrahams's work on the corn shucking as slave performance describes slavery as an "American pastoral" and the members of the plantation as "engaged in a vigorous common enterprise in which nature was placed at the service of the owners and tillers of the land. . . . Hands and masters played a role in a set piece which turned the system of power relationships of the plantation into a comedy and pastoral romance." *Singing the Master: The Emergence of African American Culture in the Plantation South* (New York: Pantheon, 1992), 24.

11 For representations of slave culture in this mode, see Abrahams, *Singing the Master*, and Charles Joyner, *Down by the Riverside: A South Carolina Slave Community* (Urbana: University of Illinois Press, 1984), 127.

12 See Judith Butler, *Bodies That Matter* (New York: Routledge, 1993), 223–42.

13 Ibid., 14. See also Judith Butler, *Gender Trouble: Feminism and the Subversion of Identity* (London: Routledge, 1990), 128–31.

14 Michael Omi and Howard Winant, in accordance with their definition of race as an "unstable and 'decentered' complex of social meanings constantly being transformed by political struggle," argue that "the meaning of race is defined and contested throughout society, in both collective action and personal practice. In the process, racial categories themselves are formed, transformed, destroyed and reformed." *Racial Formation in the United States* (New York: Routledge and Kegan Paul, 1986), 61–73.

15 Frantz Fanon, *Black Skin, White Masks*, trans. Charles Lam Markham (New York: Grove, 1967), 109–40; Butler, *Gender Trouble*, 24.

16 Paul Gilroy, "Sounds Authentic: Black Music, Ethnicity, and the Challenge of a Changing Same," *Black Music Research Journal* 11 (1991): 17. Performance "produces the imaginary effect of an internal racial core or essence by acting on the body through specific mechanisms of identification and recognition." Gilroy's definition of performance is very similar to Judith Butler's: "Acts, gestures and desire produce the effect of an internal core or substance, but produce this on the surface of the body, through the play of signifying absences that suggest, but never reveal, the organizing principle of identity as a cause. Such acts, gestures, enactments, generally construed, are performative in the sense that the essence or identity that they otherwise purport to express are [*sic*] fabrications manufactured and sustained through corporeal signs and other discursive means." *Gender Trouble*, 136.

17 Raymond Williams defines community as follows: "Community can be the warmly persuasive word to describe an existing set of relationships, or the warmly persuasive word to describe an alternative set of relationships. What is most important, perhaps, is that unlike all other terms of social organization (state, nation, society, etc.) it seems never to be used unfavourably, and never to be given any positive opposing or distinguishing term." *Keywords: A Vocabulary of Culture and Society* (New York: Oxford University Press, 1976), 76.

18 John W. Blassingame, *The Slave Community: Plantation Life in the Antebellum South* (Oxford: Oxford University Press, 1979), 315–17. Blassingame notes that "masters frequently noticed the sense of community in the quarters; they reported that slaves usually shared their few goods, rarely stole from each other, and the strong helped the weak.
Group solidarity in the quarters enabled the slaves to unite in the struggle against the master." Ibid., 315–17.

19 Drucilla Cornell, "The Postmodern Critique of Community," in *The Philosophy of the Limit* (New York: Routledge, 1992); Iris Marion Young, *Justice and the Politics of Difference* (Princeton: Princeton University Press, 1990), 226–56.

20 Neither liberal nor Marxist notions of the political subject are suited to the particular situation of the enslaved. The Marxist model is concerned with a different model of oppression-exploitation and the free worker and does not offer an analysis of racial oppression. Ironically, "Marxist" interpretations of slavery have been quite conservative in their analysis of slavery and have focused on paternalism rather than domination, total relations rather than racial subordination, and paternalism rather than terror.

21 Jean Comaroff, *Body of Power, Spirit of Resistance: The Culture and History of a South African People* (Chicago: University of Chicago Press, 1985), 261.

22 Karl Marx, "On the Jewish Question," in *The Marx-Engels Reader*, ed. Robert C. Tucker (New York: W. W. Norton, 1978), 34.

23 Anne Showstack Sasson writes that the word "political" only acquires its full sense in relation to the potential of a class to found a new integral state. Even when considering the possibilities of other political entities not defined by class, what is key is a notion of strategic action and systemic analysis. *Gramsci's Politics* (Minneapolis: University of Minnesota Press, 1987), 185.

Between "Oriental Depravity" and "Natural Degenerates": Spatial Borderlands and the Making of Ordinary Americans

Nayan Shah

In October 1926, Police Chief A. W. Reynolds raided a ranch four miles northeast of Porterville, California, in the foothills of the Sierra Mountains, and arrested forty-eight-year-old ranch hand Arjan Singh for attempting the "crime against nature" on a seventeen-year-old white "local boy," Alexander Quinn. The local newspaper reported Singh's arrest as a "statutory crime," but Alexander Quinn was hardly shielded from police suspicions. The Porterville police arrested Quinn and held him in jail on the charge of vagrancy pending a hearing in juvenile court. Although Singh declared that he would fight the sodomy charge, at the trial he pled guilty and was sentenced to five years in prison.[1]

Arjan Singh and Alexander Quinn were among thousands of seasonal field workers – foreign migrants, tramps, and casual local laborers – engaged in the year-long cycle of planting, pruning, and harvesting up and down the Pacific Coast in the early twentieth century.[2] This narrative culled from Tulare County Superior Court records could be considered predictable. Arjan Singh's arrest for sodomy fit a pattern of intergenerational, working-class, same-sex relations that early-twentieth-century sociologists, sexologists, and labor economists have conventionally described as situational "homosexuality" common in "mining districts, lumber camps, wheat fields, and fruit ranches." Sodomy was considered a prevailing immoral practice "wherever a large number of men [were] grouped together apart from women."[3] The prosecutor, Assistant District Attorney W. C. Haight, blamed the crimes on socializing between "low down whites and Hindus of the same type." Haight's ability to explain the crimes did not diminish his outrage at Singh's "disgusting Oriental depravity" or temper his ambivalence toward Quinn's behavior. Despite the newspaper's invocation of statutory crime, the prosecutor appeared reluctant to treat Quinn as an innocent victim.[4] What made the Porterville case simultaneously predictable and outrageous?

Like many other prosecutors and police, Haight anticipated immorality and criminality in the social interactions between white adolescent males and Asian migrants. Suspicions had turned the spatial locations of contact – the streets, alleys, boardinghouses, labor camps, and ranches where migrant workers congregated – into borderland spaces characterized by disorder, conflict, and murky social and sexual ties between males. In these borderland spaces of migrant life, the police suspicion of illicit and immoral activity remade transient domestic and leisure spaces into sites of public scrutiny. Two years prior to the sodomy arrest, Singh had been convicted of liquor possession and at the time was reputed for "making his house attractive to depraved boys by having liquor on hand."[5] At the trial, Haight pointedly established the illicit reputation of Singh's house and demonstrated the legal ramifications of de-privatizing a residence. Charging Quinn with vagrancy was a means to punish his association with an allegedly immoral foreign man and his presence in a transient's house that was defined as a disreputable and illicit resort. Policing by the liberal state strictly defined the boundaries of public and private in society. However, in borderland migrant spaces the feverish redefining of the borders of the public, the semipublic, and the private kept the boundaries unclear and unsettled.

The surveillance of spatial borderlands brought another set of ambiguous identities into play: the containment of normative American masculinity from the threats of other interloper masculinities, cast as foreign and degenerate. To this end, prosecutors and judges in the early twentieth century created racialized and sexualized typologies of masculinity to police the relationships of roaming male youth and foreign migrants. Their immediate purpose was to identify the dangers posed to male youth, but the effect was to ensure a future for American normative masculinity.[6] Yet the sexual ambiguity of male youth confounded the jurists, forcing them to consider whether sodomy was an act of violation or invitation, to judge whether a youth was innocent, criminal, or delinquent. The protection of a specific male victim, however, was secondary to the protection of society and civilization and the affirmation of American normative masculinity. As David Bell has argued, the emphasis on public victimization "often deployed in state and legal discourses" on sodomy normalizes the common good and recodes all suspect intimacies as spectacles of public discipline.[7] In the Porterville case, Haight hailed Singh's imprisonment as the removal of a "menace to society" and a "blessing to the community."[8] In political and cultural discourse, Asian men were generally perceived as the importers of "unnatural" sexual practices and pernicious morality.[9] The putative threat posed by the social practices of "amoral" alien migrants, domestic transients, and male adolescents thus simultaneously unsettled and shored up the constitution of normal American masculinity.

Very little of the texture of these tensions bubbles to the surface in the discreet and pithy newspaper accounts of the Porterville case and similar California cases. The court records, however, pulsate with the interests, suspicions, and imperatives of policing, and the corresponding production and regulation of borderland spaces and identities and the threats to normative American masculinity. This article examines how a series of California court cases in the 1910s and 1920s recast the boundaries of American masculinity through tackling the ambiguities of adolescent delinquency and deploying the categories of normality, degeneracy, and natural sex. Understanding how those spaces and identities were constituted and policed necessitates an exploration of how and why the legal statutes – sodomy, statutory rape, and

vagrancy laws – were reinterpreted and combined in this era to both explain and punish the dangers of male migrant social and sexual relations. The combination of sodomy, statutory rape, and vagrancy in these cases has particular analytical significance since most historical studies of law and society in the late-nineteenth- and early-twentieth-century United States often isolate the legal prosecution of vagrancy, sodomy, and statutory rape protections as separate problems and as the regulation of distinctive social bodies.[10]

Correlating American national identity with sexual normalcy was a new development of the twentieth century. The categories of deviance and normality and the new definitions of sexual identity shaped the policing of male adolescents' relationships with both external and internal nomadic subjects – the foreigners and transients who were the subject of vagrancy and sodomy prosecution. Policing and judicial reasoning converted these social dangers into the categories of delinquents, vagrants, and degenerates and developed heightened surveillance of the spatial borderlands of interaction. The judicial process revealed how unsettled the ideas of masculinity, adolescence, and normative sexual behavior were. Case by case, the legal archive underlined racialized sexualities that endangered the state as well as national masculinity. Even as the prosecutors, judges, and legal commentators strove in each individual case to put borders around normal masculinity, the process and dilemmas of adjudicating the cases repeatedly subverted any hope of fixed borders.

Sodomy, Statutory Protections, and the Problem of Consent

Until 1976, California law defined the felony charge of sodomy as a "crime against nature" and explicitly prohibited all genital-anal penetration. In sodomy prosecutions in California the penetrator was charged with the "crime against nature" but the status of the "penetrated" was ambiguous. Sex acts between females and males were occasionally punished under sodomy statutes, but historians have noted that since the 1880s in the United States, the prosecution of sodomy mostly involved two males, usually an adult male and a male youth or child.[11] At the turn of the nineteenth century, the greater police and prosecutorial interest in punishing adult male sexual conduct that involved youth paralleled the rise of legislation that created statutory protections for females with regard to rape.

In the last decades of the nineteenth century and the first decades of the twentieth century, US society was undergoing a cataclysmic shift in social consciousness and legal protections for girls and their sexual relations with adult men. Against the backdrop of prolific popular cultural and political representations of child prostitution, female abduction, child marriage, and white slavery, Progressive-era voluntary organizations and municipal government developed a web of social regulatory programs from juvenile courts to homes for unwed mothers to protect and discipline female youth.[12] Jurisdictions in California were at the vanguard of policing and protecting adolescents, and the courts became a key arena for disciplining and rehabilitating youth.[13] State legislatures created statutory rape protections for girls and rapidly revised age-of-consent standards. In the late nineteenth century, in tandem with trends nationwide, the California legislature had increased the age of consent for sexual intercourse for females from the age of ten in 1872 to fourteen in 1883 and sixteen in 1897. The legislature was deadlocked in lifting the age to eighteen until 1913, the year after women exercised suffrage in the state.[14] Despite this highly publicized movement to regulate the sexual activity of young females and their male partners, the California legislators were remarkably silent on similar age standards in sodomy cases. Judges and district attorneys stepped into the breach and formulated legal rules about how to try charges of, and who to protect in cases of, the "crime against nature," often borrowing from more-developed case law on female rape.[15]

Statutory rape protections were supposed to shield girls from interrogation about sexual history, conduct, and comportment. These protections were unevenly enforced, often resulting in greater scrutiny and interrogation of girls and young women. In practice, underage girls were often expected to explain their conduct, behavior, dress, and social history in order to prove their innocence. Defense attorneys, social workers, and even judges often pressed underage females to explain whether the particular sex act and sexual partner was invited, consensual, or forced. Yet raising the age of consent thresholds and creating statutory rape protections for girls carried an implicit understanding that both female and male adolescents possessed sexual maturity and the physical capacity for sexual activity that outstripped their social maturity and moral capacity to make decisions about sexual partners and sexual acts. Underwriting the new protections that defined the age boundary for consensual sex between males and females was a conventional understanding of male aggression and female vulnerability.

It was understood that female youth could be forced, persuaded, or duped into sexual relations with male adults and believed that the law must intervene to protect the girl before she would be capable of consent.[16]

In an era when cultural and legal borders of age and legitimate sexual participation for females were being fixed in statute, however, there existed striking ambiguity and uncertainty about how to judge the vulnerability of male youth. In the early-twentieth-century California state courts, the issue of how to adjudicate the innocence or culpability of male adolescents in sodomy cases emerged repeatedly. A 1912 California State Supreme Court decision in the appeal of *People v. Dong Pok Yip* became the ruling precedent for applying statutory protections for male youth and was frequently and authoritatively cited in subsequent sodomy cases.[17] The case involved a Chinese man, Dong Pok Yip, who befriended nine-year-old Albert Hondeville at the Antioch wharf and taught him to fish. Later in the afternoon, Rodrigues, a Portuguese American bookkeeper with offices overlooking the wharf, observed the two "walking hand-in-hand." Suspicious, Rodrigues followed them behind the oil tanks to a brush of willows, where he described them as "stooping . . . with the boy in front and the Chinaman" behind him with his "hands on the sides of the boy's waist." Although he could not testify to penetration of Albert, Rodrigues claimed to see the back of the boy's overalls hung down and that the "Chinaman's" trousers were unbuttoned in front.[18]

At the trial, the eyewitness Rodrigues explained that Dong Pok Yip was "trying to use the boy as a female."[19] This claim gendered the incident into a "crime against nature" by transforming the boy into a passive object that could be sexually acted upon and penetrated. By rendering the boy as a feminized victim, attorneys and judges could analogize the sexual victim status of underage females to the legal experience of male youth. In the appeal to the California State Supreme Court, State Attorney General US Webb elaborated on the analogy of statutory assault. Webb argued that the boy was "overpowered," and that the circumstances were similar to those where a "Schoolteacher takes indecent liberties with a female pupil" or a man lays "hold of" a woman and kisses "her against her will."[20] The supreme court agreed and ruled that "consent" must be distinguished from "submission," despite the perception that the "boy was ignorantly indifferent and passive in the hands of the defendant." They argued that a "child of tender years or retarded mental development . . . in the hands of a strong man might be easily overawed into submitting without actually consenting."[21]

The statutory age standards applied from the law on female rape, however, had to contend with the legal category of a criminal accomplice. California statute in 1911 specified that in order to be charged as a criminal accomplice one must be fourteen or above. Female age of consent at the time was sixteen and was raised two years later to eighteen. In sodomy prosecutions, the criminal accomplice became the category for the males who engaged in consensual sex. In 1923, the California Supreme Court affirmed in *People v. Carter Singh* that the age standard of an accomplice created a different baseline of statutory protections for male youth – "a child under the age of fourteen years is presumed incapable of committing a crime and cannot therefore be deemed an accomplice."[22]

[...]

Above this age threshold of fourteen, defense and prosecution attorneys struggled over how an individual could be designated an accomplice. The exchange of money or gifts for a sexual act constituted the most decisive material evidence of consent. The problem of consensual sodomy emerged in cases of male youth between the ages of fourteen and twenty-one implicated in activities that raised concerns of prostitution and hustling. In the early twentieth century, male street hustling was identified as a social problem for urban adolescent delinquents. Physicians, psychologists, sociologists, social workers, and sexologists studied the nature of individual pathology and social deviance that led male youth to prostitute their bodies to men. Encounters and transactions between men and male youth were thus seen as part of an ensemble of criminal and sexual activity, on a sliding scale from petty theft, truancy, loitering, intoxication, drug addiction, and socializing with female prostitutes.[23]

The street-level transactions of migrant males allowed the law to define adolescent males as criminal accomplices to adult men. In one incident, on Friday night, February 10, 1918, two police officers were patrolling downtown Sacramento. The officers observed Stanley Kurnick, a "nineteen year old boy of Austrian descent," in the company of a forty-year-old "Hindu," Jamil Singh; both were ranch hands who found temporary work in the surrounding Sacramento and San Joaquin valleys. Their conversation on a street corner led Jamil to offer Stanley seventy-five cents for a meal and to share his room at the Colusa Rooming House. Later that night the police followed a lead from a street informer to their room.

Officer Parker "looked through the keyhole and saw a boy lying face downward on the bed with his clothes partly off" and the "Hindu," also with his clothes partly off, lying on top of the boy, "going through the motions" of a man "having sexual intercourse." The officers broke open the door and arrested both men.[24]

Officer Parker's improbable strategy of looking through the "keyhole" was emblematic of sodomy arrests in which the police officer's account produced the third-party corroboration of the accomplice's testimony that was critical to conviction. This characteristic voyeurism, with its framing of anal intercourse, made sodomy a staged, witnessed, and profoundly public act. Sodomy was of such implicit public interest that at the trial neither the prosecution nor the defense attorneys compelled the police officers to explain their interest, justify their search without a warrant, or disclose their source of information. The protection of public morality justified police intervention into the "private" rooms of boardinghouses. In 1918 Sacramento, police surveillance of boardinghouses, brothels, pubs, and gambling houses had increased sharply under federal and public pressure to "clean up" the town in preparation for the construction of a military base. The ostensible concerns about the impact of female prostitution, venereal disease infection, and immoral gambling on male servicemen also drew more police officers into the downtown district and intensified their scrutiny of the interaction of foreign migrants and male youth. In such an atmosphere of intensified moral policing, boardinghouses became recalibrated as "semipublic" spaces along with an array of public leisure sites.

This scrutiny, however, produced different public exposure and punishment for the males involved. When Judge Glenn sentenced Jamil Singh to seven years in San Quentin, he wrestled with how to interpret Stanley Kurnick's behavior and his legal culpability. Glenn offered his opinion that Singh was "probably not any worse than the young man," and pronounced both "equally guilty." Yet he offered defenses for Kurnick's conduct – "he is a young man" and "probably of low mentality."[25] The prosecutors had charged Kurnick as "an accessory to the carnal act of the Hindu" and sent his case to juvenile court. From the prosecution's perspective, the accomplice charge signaled a perception of the delinquent youth as having unformed ethics, yet also the potential for reform that would be enhanced by the confidentiality of juvenile legal proceedings. Judge Glenn's assessment of Kurnick's culpability had much to do with his very suspect association with a foreign man and the heightened suspicion of illicit activity.

The credibility of the "accomplice" hinged on the circumstances and the social status of the adult defendant of the alleged crime. In September 1913, a San Francisco case involving circumstances that transpired in a middle-class home had a very different result upon appeal. In the San Francisco Superior Court, Samuel Robbins, a fifty-six-year-old white bookkeeper, was convicted by the reluctant testimony of sixteen-year-old Sidney, who claimed that Robbins attempted to penetrate him while in a locked bathroom in his house but was interrupted by the housekeeper, Mrs. Nute, trying to open the door. In the appeal to the California Supreme Court, however, the majority of justices argued that Mrs. Nute's testimony, though casting suspicious light on the defendant, did not sufficiently corroborate Sidney's accusation.[26] In overturning Robbins's conviction, the judges gave no credence to Sidney's explanation of trauma and his narration of the assault. The decision implicitly characterized Sidney as an unreliable accomplice and the producer of a false accusation. The judges decided not to heed Mrs. Nute's testimony, because she was a "prying" servant woman who had not expressly witnessed the actual crime.

Instead, the supreme court justices worried about Samuel Robbins's reputation, fearing that "friendship of a middle aged man for the lad" could be misinterpreted as criminal intent or activity. They argued that "in these days of the 'big brother movement' thousands of men throughout the country are systematically cultivating the friendship of boys, to the end that the influence of mature thought and association with men may aid in the development of the best qualities of the children."[27] The judicial intervention focused upon a key middle-class reform strategy for taming delinquent youth. Middle-class reformers advocated the sublimation of sexual energies into physical fitness, organized sports, and scouting, which were expected to impart proper socialization through adult mentorship and gender training into responsible and healthy adults.[28] Ironically, the same activities produced a homosocial environment and possibilities for intimate relations between males. The judges' decision, however, revealed the anxiety that men of middle-class privilege would be considered suspect in their association with boys and young men. The judges maintained that middle-class white men could impart moral development and should, therefore, not "be convicted of degrading crimes upon mere suspicion plus the story of an accomplice."[29] The judges accepted the defense's interpretation that it was "natural" that after a game of tennis the man and boy washed hands together in the bathroom and locked the door after themselves as

a "simple precaution . . . to prevent" any interruption from cleansing their bodies.[30] Such homosocial activities between white men and white boys could be perceived as natural, moral, and pedagogically appropriate.

The difference between "natural" intergenerational male friendship and "unnatural" sexual predation thus depended upon the reputation of the adult. The defense attorneys use of "natural" homosociality and modesty from female view reinforced Robbins's credibility. The judges refused the inference that Robbins may have taken advantage of that familiarity and instead let Sidney bear the trauma of sexual predation bereft of state protection. Branding Sidney an unreliable accomplice was all the more startling because Sidney had no history of juvenile delinquency or deceit. Robbins's defense succeeded because his white racial identity and respectable middle-class status overrode suspicions and accusation of sexual assault.

In contrast, the social associations of Asian migrant men with "American" or provisionally "American" youth were perceived as inherently dangerous and catalyzed suspicions of sexual immorality. The same week of Jamil Singh's arrest in downtown Sacramento, police surveillance led to the arrest of another South Asian man for sodomy. On February 13, 1918, eighteen-year-old Hector McInnes, a Native American who was originally from Truckee in the Sierra Mountains, befriended Tara Singh on the streets of downtown Sacramento. Tara gave Hector fifty cents for a meal and to rent a room at a lodging house on L Street run by a Japanese innkeeper, Koro Shigo. Tara followed Hector and was assigned to the adjoining room. In the early morning hours of Friday, February 15, police officers Malone and Weisler went to Shigo's boarding house pursuing anonymous leads "on the streets" that there "was a boy up there, with a Hindu." The officers found Hector naked in bed alone, and the doors between the adjoining rooms locked.[31] Under pressure from the police, Hector later testified in court that Tara came into his room at nine o'clock that night; Hector had taken off his pants, left his shirt on, and was ready to sleep. Hector claimed that Tara climbed into bed, began to "feel around" his body and then lay on top of Hector, attempting to penetrate him. Despite Tara Singh's denial that he had "never saw [Hector] that night" he was convicted of attempted sodomy.[32] In this case, the circumstantial evidence of the interracial association between an Asian migrant man and a male youth in public and their retreat to adjoining rented rooms overwhelmed any concerns that Hector McInnes's testimony was uncorroborated. In the arraignment hearing, Judge Henderson acknowledged that "the difficulty of these cases lies in the character of the boys who allow themselves to be used," making "their testimony not worthy of belief."[33] These doubts of credibility did little to dissuade the overwhelming suspicions of the dangers of migrant vagrancy that shaped police intervention and state prosecution.

Vagrancy, Nomadic Subjects, and Spatial Borderlands

In the late nineteenth and early twentieth centuries, vagrancy laws became a general umbrella under which migrants and delinquents could be policed, disciplined, and criminalized. The demands of capitalist development created mobile populations, but politicians and moral reformers condemned the social dynamics of unsteady work and temporary housing that were generated in the wake of human mobility. A vagrant was a transient, lacking reliable work, home, or family. Idleness was alone considered a badge of immorality, but vagrancy encompassed a range of disreputable behavior that could be criminalized. In nineteenth-century legal statutes, the crime of vagrancy explicitly identified the unproductive, disreputable, and sexualized character of its policing targets. In 1891 the California legislature amended the 1872 vagrancy statute that criminalized being an "idle or dissolute person, who wanders about the streets at late or unusual hours of the night," with characterization of a "lewd or dissolute person who lives about houses of ill-fame."[34] Vagrancy was thus not just temporary misfortune, unemployment, and poverty but was defined as an aversion to productiveness, an unwillingness to rehabilitate, and a failure of self-discipline. Vagrants were characterized as "lewd or dissolute persons" who were prone to habits of immorality – intoxication, prostitution, gambling, sodomy, or cross-dressing. In California, the shift from an explicit condemnation of prostitution to a broad policing of sex occurred when the vagrancy law was simplified in 1903 to criminalizing an "idle, lewd, or dissolute person."[35]

US legal and historical studies have analyzed the use of vagrancy laws in three ways. The first sees it as a device of labor regulation that has been used since English common law and revived in the nineteenth and early twentieth centuries to force black freed people in the South into wage work and to stifle European, Asian, and Mexican immigrants as well as white native-born workers from labor organization, protest, and bargaining in the North, Midwest, and West.[36] The second arena of scholarly interest recognizes that vagrancy law criminalizes

"having a certain personal condition or being a person of specified character" rather than criminalizing a specific act. Police surveillance and arrests could be made on reputation and general suspicion of future criminal activity.[37] The third specifically ties "vagrancy" with sexual and moral charges. The vagrancy complaint could combine with or substitute for specific charges of pimping, sodomy, sex perversion, lewdness, intoxication, indecent assault, or solicitation. Nationwide in the twentieth century, police and justice courts combined these policing targets into a generalized "vag lewd" charge. It was a notoriously vague and broadly applied misdemeanor charge that police employed in sweeps of parks, bars, clubs, toilets, and streets and "became the most deployed criminal sanction against same-sex intimacy" according to legal scholar William Eskridge.[38]

The police surveillance for potential vagrancy also produced scrutiny about the activities and movements of migrants and created the atmosphere to pursue suspicions of interracial social contact and, potentially, the felony charge of sodomy. Male migrant sociability thrived in the nodal hubs of transportation and the urban spaces where transients congregated between jobs. Vagrancy policing spatially mapped spaces of presumed safety and danger and recast social contact in terms of morality and immorality. Encounters between males occurred in the border spaces of streets, alleys, parks, and squares. Police walked the streets on their neighborhood beats, observing public activity and the social relations of the street. The police regulation layered public social spaces of everyday social encounter with nefarious and illicit implications. It also remade the interior spaces of public accommodations – saloons, clubs, halls, hotels, and boardinghouses – into semipublic arenas in which police could intervene upon suspicion. The policing of potential criminal activity included the regulation of improper social and sexual activity, resulting in arrests for soliciting prostitution, public drunkenness, property crime, public disturbance, lewdness, and sodomy. The geography of the rapidly urbanizing town and city provided the setting and spaces for casual, fortuitous, and dangerous encounters between men and boys of different ethnicities, classes, and ages.

[. . .]

Normal Man and Natural Degenerate

Early-twentieth-century jurisprudence and legislative politics intensively criminalized a range of sexual acts, practices, and persons. By elaborating upon the illegitimacy of the "unnatural" practices of sodomy and the specific dangers of migrants and vagrants, the contours of "natural" and "normal" male sexuality were constructed. The defense of normal masculinity and sexuality emerged under the threat of alleged degeneracy. James Kerr, a prominent legal scholar who edited the compendium of the *Codes of California* in 1921, illustrated the intensity of the threat when he railed against contemporary judicial decisions that left open the possibility of consensual sodomy as a "travesty of justice." He feared that "a degenerate person or a person of depraved and low character and mind, by consent to the beastly act, could nullify the will of the legislature."[39] In Kerr's reasoning, society must be defended from the "degenerate" and perverse individual, whose consent to anal penetration not only inverted masculinity but also undermined the political and social order. The ferocity of Kerr's response indexed the severity of the perceived threat. Consensual sodomy produced an "alternative mode of being," and its very viability "denaturalized" heterosexuality as the only "true identity."[40] Kerr's demand for the blanket illegitimacy of all male-to-male sexual relations was imperative to fortify the vision of normal male sexuality. Statutory protections for male youth were not enough. Kerr argued for the criminality of all acts of sodomy and the necessity of statutory protections for female youth that buttressed an ideology of natural sex, guiding male sexual activity into regulated sex, marital union, and procreation with adult females.

Although Kerr may have denied and deferred the question of consensual sex between males by nullifying its legitimacy, judges and prosecutors could not ignore its widespread existence. Like sociologists, psychologists, and social workers of the era, they instead created social categories to identify normalcy, degeneracy, and delinquency.[41] A striking example of how these categories converged and were reassembled is the 1928 Stockton case of "sex perversion," a newly created felony category that the California legislature established in 1921 to criminalize oral sex. In the 1910s the legislature had repeatedly attempted to criminalize oral-genital contact in response to its frequent prosecution in county courts, the California State Supreme Court ruling that only anal penetration constituted the "crime against nature," and the dissatisfaction of the frequent police recourse to the misdemeanor "vagrancy" charge to punish it.[42] In 1928, Stockton police arrested thirty-one-year-old Jack Lynch and seventy-year-old Keshn Singh for engaging in "sex perversion," specifically for being caught with Singh's penis in Lynch's mouth. The prosecution designated Keshn Singh as the accomplice who had paid Lynch fifty cents and "upon whom Lynch practiced his vulgar employment."[43]

In the court record, Assistant District Attorney H. C. Stanley deployed the categories of degeneracy, normalcy, and amorality within the framework of the "ordinary American" in order to identify the internal and external threats to American identity. At the sentencing hearing, Stanley, doubting that intoxication impaired Singh's judgment, instead believed his actions evidenced intrinsic amorality that was incompatible with American ethical behavior, despite Singh's having lived in the United States for twenty-three years. Stanley argued that Singh showed no remorse about the "wrong" of his action and he "does not seem to be a person that regards such a practice as the ordinary American would." Stanley advocated Singh's incarceration as a preventive measure to stop him from "prostituting other men by furnishing himself as a subject to be acted upon, whether for or without compensation."[44] Judge George Buck agreed and sentenced Singh to four years at San Quentin. As an amoral foreigner, Singh was cast as incapable of ever becoming an "ordinary American."

On the other hand, Jack Lynch appeared to have the lineage of an "ordinary American," a white man who was born in Wisconsin. But he also possessed all the characteristics of a vagrant – he was unmarried at age thirty-one, migrated from the upper Midwest to California in 1924, had temporarily worked in lumber camps and restaurants throughout the state, and had a long criminal record in California, which included vagrancy arrests and petty theft conviction, as well as the admission to arresting officers that he had practiced oral sex on men in Modesto and Stockton previous to this arrest. Stanley concluded that Lynch was a "natural degenerate," and that his record of vagrancy and habitual sex perversion made him unlikely to "be cured" of his "vulgar" practices that was "the incidental characteristic of the vagrant, who can never be regarded as a fit subject for society."[45] The case, a rare prosecution of two adult males, paired the amoral alien man who incited practices of sexual perversion with the condensation of the vagrant, degenerate, and sex pervert in the body of the white, native-born man. Neither man was considered a victim of the crime; rather, the work of policing their behavior served to ultimately isolate degenerate and amoral subjects from American society and incarcerate unfit subjects of society.

Racial difference had incited police suspicion, but it was the new sexual identities that framed the legal prosecution.

The categories of degenerate and pervert fortified an understanding of the normal. While some white middle-class men such as Samuel Robbins could sidestep the indictment of sodomy through their ability to preserve their reputations as moral subjects and normal men, many more men were suspect because of how they were cast as either innately degenerate, through an enumerated criminal history, or amoral foreigners, by their "proven" reputation. In the Lynch and Singh oral sex perversion case, the policing of sex between white males and migrant/vagrant men, white identity was not as it may have first appeared – the sign of the always-innocent victim. Police and prosecutors thus deployed whiteness strategically in scrutinizing social contacts between so-called Americans and foreigner nomadic males, but the fundamental goal became to isolate "natural degeneracy" and amoral foreigners from contaminating American society.

The internal threat of the vagrant degenerate and the external threat of the amoral foreigner most perniciously converged in the potential corruption of male youth. During the 1910s and 1920s, California courts were interpreting the degree of male vulnerability and victimhood on perceptions of age, consciousness, and the ability to narrate sexual transgression. The characterization of the vulnerable and innocent male victim became that of someone who was acted upon without will or knowledge. A child under the age of fourteen occupied this category, as did an unconscious male of an indeterminate youthfulness. Harvey Carstenbrook's silence and protestations that he had no consciousness of sexual assault demonstrated how the age boundaries could be flexed to accommodate unconscious males. Above the age of an accomplice and below the age of legal adulthood, male youth were in a more precarious position in the courtroom. Sidney, Stanley, Alexander, and Hector, ironically because of their reluctant and coerced testimony of sexual assault by adult men, aroused suspicion of their potential consent and complicity. In practice in the lower courts, judges, attorneys, and juries interpreted the conscious choice of teenage males to socialize and participate with adult men on the double-edge of statutory protections. In fact, the parallel prosecution of some of these male youth for vagrancy and other misdemeanor charges in juvenile courts demonstrated how the legal proceedings served to rechannel the conduct of adolescent males and rehabilitate them into respectable sociality and sexuality.

In these early-twentieth-century California court cases, the variability of the ethnic and racial identity of the male youth (European immigrant youth, Native American, and native-born white youth) demonstrated the broadening of subjects for the project of social rehabilitation into moral and normal American men. While the racial boundaries for the social rehabilitation of male youth were malleable, the court cases underscored and justified the insurmountable racial boundary that perpetually defined Asian men as foreigners to the American nation. The amoral Asian could never be an "ordinary American" and was already defined as an unfit subject for American society and at the outer limits of the continuum between the "natural man" and the "natural degenerate." The "foreigner" and the "degenerate" were not legal categories, but were culturally and politically potent contextual categories that served both to identify and to explain moral peril. Racial ascription of external threats such as "Oriental depravity" and "Hindu sodomites" had the taxonomic function of harnessing suspicion and identifying and amplifying targets for both the official police and the informal policing of community residents. But it did not produce a categorical certainty. Not all foreigners were immoral and degenerate; however, an alleged tendency to immorality reinforced racialized suspicions. In sentencing hearings and judicial decisions, the interpretation of criminal behavior shifted focus from the criminal act to criminal identities. And the very process of fixing individual behavior into broad social categories was undergoing transformation. Categories of ethnicity and race had been employed descriptively and analytically, but they were being harnessed to new categories such as degeneracy and normality. These categories were accruing salience in court decisions and were enabling a reconsideration of new liberal life forms. By the mid-twentieth century the broad categories of "normal" and "degenerate" would become interchangeable with the binary opposition of heterosexual and homosexual."[46]

The policing of degeneracy and anxious fixing of categories of unnatural sex and social conduct in spatial borderlands, both urban and rural, illuminated how liberal governance produced authoritative rule and social subjects to regulate the reproduction of a society of normal and ordinary Americans. The conjunction of external danger (amoral foreign migrant), internal danger (degenerate vagrant), and the identification of subjects for flexible rehabilitation (delinquent youth) became the ensemble of social figures that required policing and prosecution. On these grounds, liberal legal adjudication of sodomy and vagrancy in the early twentieth century gave way to a greater coherence of social figures that could be governed. Legal scholar Judith Grbich has encouraged scholarly investigation into "the ways in which legal reasoning transforms the embodied imaginings" of particular lives into that "which passes for the 'normative.' "[47] The process of transforming "embodied imaginings" into normative subjects also produced a wide array of liberal life forms, both valorized and denigrated, that were shaped by legal, political, and cultural logics into a regulative field. In early-twentieth-century US political and legal liberalism, the most valued and valorized life forms were the normal man and ordinary woman, who were seen to constitute normal American sexuality and "fit subjects for society." The healthy, fit, reproductive capacities of normal men and women were affirmed as simultaneously "natural" and "civilized" by the legal regulations that both shaped consensual and contractual monogamous marriage and the curtailment of putatively unnatural habits and vice.

Liberal governance and the policing of liminal social spaces also produced life forms that defined the boundaries of, and threats to, American normalcy – the vagrant, the degenerate, and the delinquent – all of whom inhabited the expansive repertoire of the "abnormal" in law and social life. As Christopher Tomlinson has recognized, these new social subjects of liberal rule generate a paradoxical process of fortifying "the authority of normality and the deviancy of the abnormal."[48]

Theorizing from the geographical specificity of the Mexican American borderlands, Gloria Anzaldúa offered an analytical approach that incisively interprets the density of human associations that straddle spatial and social boundaries. Anzaldúa recognized the strategies of social survival in the borderlands by the "the squint-eyed, the perverse, the queer, the troublesome, the mongrel, the mulatto, the half breed, the half dead; in short those who cross over, pass over or go through the confines of the 'normal.' "[49] This process of traversing the boundaries and confines of the normal embraces the heterogeneity of borderland bodies and practices, which flourish upon and within national borders.

Borderlands historian Emma Perez encourages us to challenge the exclusions of racialized sexualities and the dominant historical narratives that have "chosen to ignore or negate the populations who are on the margins, outside of normative behavior."[50] Perez's self-conscious approach meshes queering with borderlands analysis by encouraging the mining and reinterpreting of the borderlands legal archive for lost and silenced heterogeneities. By casting a queer and critical borderlands perspective on the state's records, Perez advocates reassembling alternative histories embedded in the legal archive of normalization.

This essay critically examines how legal codes, court cases, and jurisprudence contributed to both the sociological and aesthetic knowledge for identifying and regulating aliens, vagrants, and degenerates in spatial borderlands.[51] The policing of internal and external nomadic subjects revealed the ambiguity and insecurity of cross-racial and cross-class intimacy and intensified the fixing of social boundaries and social status. The state's imperative forged a seemingly unassailable defense of American normality and masculinity and an immense legal archive that records its success at maintaining security. Through the process of abstracting legal subjects and rules of law, the legal archive can be harnessed to create authoritative and normalized legal subjects. But the very same repository can also be reinterpreted to expose rifts and crevices where competing narratives have slipped. These residual traces in the case records contradict and confound the normalizing of legal subjects. Just as the judges and prosecutors recognized that they could not guarantee that the borders of normative masculinity or American identity would hold no matter how vigilantly they attempted to curtail specific sexual acts, partners, or practices, so too our own examination should not mistake the indictment and incarceration of nomadic subjects as acquiescence to normativity. Instead, we can continue to reassess the moments throughout when the borders blur and nomadic subjects deflect the normalizing project of making ordinary Americans.

Notes

1   *People v. Arjan Singh*, Case No. 2464, 1926, Tulare County Superior Court; "Two Statutory Cases Are Up for Hearings; Probe of One Hindu's Case Results in Another Being Arrested," *Porterville Evening Recorder*, October 9, 1926.

2   Bruce La Brack, *Sikhs of Northern California, 1904–1975* (New York: AMS Press, 1988), 123–24; David Vaught, *Cultivating California: Growers, Specialty Crops, and Labor, 1875–1920* (Baltimore: Johns Hopkins University Press, 1999).

3   Ranjani Kanta Das, labor economist and special agent of the U.S. Department of Labor, charged to study South Asian migrants on the Pacific Coast. Rajani Kanta Das, *Hindustani Workers on the Pacific Coast* (Berlin: Walter De Gruyter and Co., 1923), 83. Other noteworthy scholarship included Carleton H. Parker, *The Casual Laborer and Other Essays* (New York: Harcourt, Brace, and Howe, 1920); Nels Anderson, "Juvenile and Tramp," *Journal of American Institute of Criminal Law and Criminology* 14 (August 1923): 30; Josiah Flynt, "Homosexuality among Tramps, Appendix A," in Havelock Ellis, *Studies of the*

Psychology of Sex, vol. 4, *Sex Inversion* (Philadelphia 1904). Recent historical scholarship that has situated this history of male homosociality and homosexuality includes Peter Boag, *Same Sex Affairs: Constructing and Controlling Homosexuality in the Pacific Northwest* (Berkeley: University of California Press, 2003); Dee Garceau, "Bunkies, Cross-Dressers, and Family Men: Cowboy Identity and the Gendering of Ranch Work," in *Across the Great Divide: Cultures of Manhood in the American West*, ed. Matthew Basso et al. (Minneapolis: University of Minnesota Press, 2000).

4   *People v. Arjan Singh*; "Two Statutory Cases Are Up for Hearings."

5   *People v. Arjan Singh*.

6   David Campbell, *Writing Security: United States Foreign Policy and the Politics of Identity*, rev. ed. (1992; Minneapolis: University of Minnesota Press, 1998), 1–13.

7   David Bell, "Sexual Citizenship," in *Mapping Desire: Geographies of Sexualities*, ed. David Bell and Gill Valentine (New York: Routledge, 1995), 311–13.

8   *People v. Arjan Singh*.

9   The interpretation of "foreign" incitement to vice was typical in all areas, from legislative hearings to published medical studies. For instance, see U.S. Congress, *Senate Reports of the Immigration Commission*, 61st Cong., 3rd sess., 1911, Doc 753, 86; Immigration Commission Reports, Importation and Harboring of Women for Immoral Purposes, S. Doc. No. 61–753, 86 (3rd sess., 1911); Alfred J. Zobel, "Primary Gonorrhea of the Rectum in the Male," *American Journal of Urology* 45.1 (November 1909). For the contextualization of these threats in immigration, labor, and urban vice literature, see Chris Friday, *Organizing Asian American Labor* (Philadelphia: Temple University Press, 1994); Boag, *Same-Sex Affairs*; Nayan Shah, *Contagious Divides: Epidemics and Race in San Francisco's Chinatown* (Berkeley: University of California Press, 2001).

10 The history of sodomy prosecutions has identified and regulated the male homosexual body and mapped the formation of urban sexual subcultures. Vagrancy law was frequently deployed to police transients, migrants, and vagabonds and to regulate public space in small towns and cities. Historically associated with the control of labor, vagrancy arrests policed the leisure activities and intervened in working-class and migrant social spaces under the pretext of preserving public order. The history of statutory age protections for sexual relations focused on protecting female youth from male adults. No statutory legislation at this time protected male youth the way that highly publicized legislative protections for female youth at the turn of the century did.

11 George Chauncey, *Gay New York: Gender, Urban Culture, and the Making of the Gay Male World, 1890–1940* (New York: Basic Books, 1994); and Nan Alamilla Boyd, *Wide Open Town: A History of Queer San Francisco to 1965* (Berkeley: University of California Press, 2003).

12 Kathy Peiss, *Cheap Amusements: Working Women and Leisure in Turn-of-the-Century New York* (Philadelphia: Temple University Press, 1986); David J. Langum, *Crossing Over the Line: Legislating Morality and the Mann Act* (Chicago: University of Chicago Press, 1994); Mara L. Keire, "The Vice Trust: A Reinterpretation of the White Slavery Scare in the United States, 1907–1917," *Journal of Social History* 35.1 (2001): 5–41; Ruth Rosen, *The Lost Sisterhood: Prostitution in America, 1900–1918* (Baltimore: Johns Hopkins University Press, 1982); Pamela Haag, *Consent: Sexual Rights and the Transformation of American Liberalism* (Ithaca: Cornell University Press, 1999).

13 Municipal and county jurisdictions across the United States, including those in California, Oregon, Illinois, New York, and Massachusetts, were at the vanguard of creating partnerships between public agencies and private voluntary associations that both policed juvenile delinquents and protected adolescents.

14 William M. McKinney, ed., "Rape," *California Jurisprudence: A Complete Statement of the Law and Practice of the State of California*, vol. 22 (San Francisco: Bancroft–Whitney Company, 1925), esp. 361–5.

15 Jane E. Larson, "'Even a Worm Will Turn at Last': Rape Reform in Late-Nineteenth-Century America," *Yale Journal of Law and the Humanities* 9.1 (1997); Mary E. Odem, *Delinquent Daughters: Protecting and Policing Adolescent Female Sexuality in the United States, 1885–1920* (Chapel Hill: University of North Carolina Press, 1996).

16 Larson, "Even a Worm," 19–20; Odem, *Delinquent Daughters*.

17 The case is cited in the following appellate cases: *People v. Samuel P. Robbins* 171 Cal., 466 (1915); *People v. Kangiesser* 186 P. 388 (Cal. Dist. Ct. App. 1919); *People v. Carter Singh* 62 Cal. App. 450 (Dist. Ct. App. 1923). For summaries of the case law, see Curtis Hillyer, *Consolidated Supplement to the Codes of the State of California, 1927–1931*, pt. 2 (San Francisco: Bender-Moss, 1932), 6922–23, 6929–30; James M. Kerr, *The Codes of California*, vol. 4, *Penal Code 1920* (San Francisco: Bender-Moss, 1921), 277–78, 384–85, 390.

18 Transcript at 1, 4–7, *People v. Dong Pok Yip*, 164 Cal. 143, 145–46, 1912, California State Archives.

19 *People v. Dong Pok Yip*, 22.

20 Ibid., 13, 14.

21 Ibid., 147.

22 *People v. Carter Singh*.

23 Lilburn Merrill, "A Summary of Findings in a Study of Sexualisms among a Group of One Hundred Delinquent Boys," *American Journal of Urology and Sexology* 15 (1919): 259–69; A. J. Jones and Lee Janis, "Primary Syphilis of the Rectum and the Gonorrhea of the Anus in a Male Homosexual Playing the Role of the Female Prostitute," *American Journal of Syphilis, Gonorrhea, and Venereal Disease* 28 (July 1944): 453–7; F. A. Freyhan, "Homosexual Prostitution: A Case Report," *Delaware State Medical Journal* (May 1947): 92–4.

24 *People v. Jamil Singh*, Case No. 6029, 2–3, 7–9 (1918); Records of the Superior Court, Criminal Division, County of Sacramento, Sacramento Archives and Museum Collection Center (hereinafter "SAMCC").

25 Ibid., 15.

26 *See People v. Kangiesser.*

27 *People v. Robbins*, 145–46.

28 Dominick Cavallo, *Muscles and Morals: Organized Playgrounds and Urban Reform, 1880–1920* (Philadelphia: University of Pennsylvania Press, 1981), 15–48; Martha H. Verbrugge, *Able-Bodied Womanhood: Personal Health and Social Change in Nineteenth-Century Boston* (New York: Oxford University Press, 1988).

29 *People v. Robbins*, 145–6.

30 Ibid., 145.

31 *People v. Tara Singh*, Case No. 6039, 7 (1918), Records of the Superior Court, Criminal Division, County of Sacramento, SAMCC.

32 *People v. Tara Singh*, 9–10.

33 Ibid., 3.

34 1891 Cal. Stat. 117 sec. 5, 7; William N. Eskridge Jr., *Gaylaw: Challenging the Apartheid of the Closet* (Cambridge, Mass.: Harvard University Press, 1999), 30.

35 See Arthur Sherry, "Vagrants, Rogues, and Vagabonds – Old Concepts in Need of Revision," *California Law Review* 48 (1960): 557–60; "Use of Vagrancy Type Laws for Arrest and Detention of Suspicious Persons," *Yale Law Journal* 59 (1950): 1351.

36 See Ahmed A. White, "A Different Kind of Labor Law: Vagrancy Law and the Regulation of Harvest Labor, 1913–1924," *University of Colorado Law Review* 75 (2004): 668–743; Amy Dru Stanley, *From Bondage to Contract: Wage Labor, Marriage, and the Market in the Age of Slave Emancipation* (New York: Cambridge University Press, 1998); Linda K. Kerber, *No Constitutional Right to Be Ladies: Women and the Obligations of Citizenship* (New York: Hill and Wang, 1998), 47–80.

37 Forrest W. Lacey, "Vagrancy and Other Crimes of Personal Condition," *Harvard Law Review* 66 (1953):

1203–26; William O. Douglas, "Vagrancy and Arrest on Suspicion," *Yale Law Journal* 70 (1960): 1–14.

38 Eskridge, *Gaylaw*, 31; Boyd, *Wide Open Town.*

39 Kerr, *Codes of California*, 277–8.

40 Campbell, *Writing Security*, 3.

41 Jennifer Terry, *An American Obsession: Science, Medicine, and Homosexuality in Modern Society* (Chicago: University of Chicago Press, 2000).

42 Concern for the absence of statutes for oral sex led the state legislature in 1915 to pass a statute criminalizing fellatio and cunnilingus specifically; the State Supreme Court overturned the statute because it violated an "anti-Spanish" state constitutional amendment that required laws to be written in English. See Sharon Ullman, *Sex Seen: The Emergence of Modern Sexuality in America* (Berkeley: University of California Press, 1997); Christopher Brunnette, BA thesis.

43 *People v. Jack Lynch and Keshn Singh*, Case No. 4680 (1928), San Joaquin County Superior Court.

44 Ibid.

45 Ibid.

46 Terry, *An American Obsession.*

47 Judith E. Grbich, "The Body in Legal Theory," *At the Boundaries of the Law: Feminism and Legal Theory*, ed. Martha A Fineman and Nancy Thomadsen (New York: Routledge, 1991), 69.

48 Christopher Tomlinson, "Subordination, Authority, and Law: Subjects in Labor History," *International Labor and Working Class History* 47 (spring 1995): 56–90.

49 Gloria E. Anzaldúa in *Borderlands/La Frontera: The New Mestiza* (San Francisco: Aunt Lute Press, 1987).

50 Roderick Ferguson, *Aberrations in Black: Toward a Queer of Color Critique* (Minneapolis: University of Minnesota Press, 2003).

51 For a parallel process of tracking sociological knowledge and the racialized sexualization of African Americans, see Roderick Ferguson, *Aberrations in Black* (University of Minnesota Press, 2003).

36

The Rule of Normalcy: Politics and Disability in the USA [United States of Ability]

Lennard J. Davis

When my book *Enforcing Normalcy* was published in 1996, it received a positive review in an English periodical, but the reviewer did raise an Anglo-eyebrow at my use of the word "normalcy," noting that the word "normality" was preferred in England. Indeed, of normalcy" *Fowler's* comments that it is "a word of the 'spurious hybrid' class. . . . and seems to have nothing to recommend it."[1] Blanching at this degree zero of recommendation, I consulted my American reference works and found to my relief that although in some dictionaries "normality" was the preferred usage, "normalcy" was acceptable, and in others there was no distinction made between the two words.[2] I found out that President Harding was rumored to have coined the word in a speech entitled "Return to Normalcy," for which neologism he was much ridiculed, although *Fowler's* notes "there is no ground for the charge made against President Harding of having coined it; others had used it long before he did."[3] And after he did, one might add.

While I was relieved not to have made such a noticeable, front-page lexical blunder, nevertheless, like any obsessive academic, I got to thinking. I realized that my horror of appearing in print with a grammatical "error" was accentuated by my awareness of my working-class origins, my low-budget Bronx public school education, and my fear of being "outed" as a nonstandard English speaker, branded with the dreaded "[*sic*]" trailing after my solecisms like a tin can maliciously tied to a dog's tail. Although I have generally "passed" in a world of largely middle- and upper-class academics, I still bear the hidden injuries of class. Then, of course, I had to factor in my parents' deafness, and my "passing" in a hearing world

which by and large, until I began to write about this part of my life, had no idea that I was in fact culturally deaf. Further, I had to acknowledge that I am, like my son, somewhat dyslexic, at least in the realm of spelling and mathematics.

In other words, this near-slip in usage made me realize that something as superficial as the choice of a word in a title had a whole legacy tied up with disability and normalcy. Thinking more on it, I began to realize that a notion of correct and incorrect language usage, the notion of a preferred word – "normality" over "normalcy" – was after all a linguistic aspect of the very normalizing process I had been exposing in *Enforcing Normalcy*, the same book that was now being accused of abnormal forms of the word "normal."

When we say that "normality" is preferred over "normalcy," what exactly do we mean? We mean that some or a preponderance of experts in the field have agreed that a certain word is more "normal" than another word. How is the norm determined? By usage, to an extent. By logic, to an extent. By reference to grammatical patterns worked out from other languages like Latin and Greek. In other words, by social convention. For example, since "normalcy" is credited by the *Oxford English Dictionary* as having an American origin, we can imagine that the neologism would be discounted by some British lexicographers as a colonial malapropism, only another example in the decline of the empire's standards.

If we think of the distinction between prescriptive grammar, the body of didactic rules that tells us how to write and speak, versus descriptive grammar, which aims to describe how language is used in a variety of settings, we can understand how truly socially constructed are grammatical "norms." Prescriptive grammar arose in the seventeenth and eighteenth centuries in an attempt to regularize the English language, which had no grammar, to the level of the revered Latin and Greek, which being dead languages had to have grammars and rules so that they could be taught in schools. Scholars at the time had fretted over the fact that English had no grammar, so the grammatical conventions of Latin were applied in a procrustean way to English, whether they fit or not.[4] During this time, the first English dictionaries were compiled, so that spelling and meaning could be normalised, and so that printers could standardise their productions. In other words, language was regularized, and the effort of speaking and writing came under the jurisdiction and control of a class of scholars, men and women of letters, and other professionals who tried to make spoken language, in its transformational complexity, fit into rather arbitrary, logical categories. As Georges Canguilhem wrote, when French grammarians of the Enlightenment "undertook to fix the usage of the French language, it was a question of norms, of determining the reference, and of defining mistakes in terms of divergence, difference."[5]

Why I am mentioning grammar and language usage in the context of a discussion of disabled or abnormal bodies is worth considering. When we think about normality, people in disability studies have generally made the error, I would say, of confining our discussions more or less exclusively to impairment and disease. But I think there is really a larger picture that includes disability along with any nonstandard behaviors. Language usage, which is as much a physical function as any other somatic activity, has become subject to an enforcement of normalcy, as have sexuality, gender, racial identity, national identity, and so on. As Canguilhem writes, "there is no difference between the birth of grammar . . . and the establishment of the metric system. . . . It began with grammatical norms and ended with morphological norms of men and horses for national defense, passing through industrial and sanitary norms."[6]

Let me backtrack here for a moment and rehearse the argument I made in *Enforcing Normalcy* so that I can make clear to readers of this essay the direction in which I am going. In that book, I claimed that before the early to mid-nineteenth century, Western society lacked a concept of normalcy. Indeed, the word "normal" only appeared in English about a hundred and fifty years ago, and in French fifty years earlier Before the rise of the concept of normalcy, I argued, there appears not to have been a concept of the normal, but instead the regnant paradigm

was one revolving around the word "ideal." If one has a concept of the "ideal" then all human beings fall below that standard and so exist in varying degrees of imperfection. The key point is that in a culture of the "ideal," physical imperfections are not seen as absolute but as part of a descending continuum from top to bottom. No one, for example, *can* have an ideal body, and therefore no one has to have an ideal body.

Around the beginning of the nineteenth century in Europe, we begin to see the development of statistics and of the concept of the bell curve, called early on the "normal" curve. With the development of statistics comes the idea of a norm. In this paradigm, most bodies fall under the main umbrella of the curve. And those that do not are at the extremes – and therefore are "abnormal." Thus, there is an imperative on people to conform, to fit in, under the rubric of normality. Rather than being resigned to a less-than-ideal body in the earlier paradigm, people in the past hundred and fifty years have been now encouraged to strive to be normal, to huddle under the main part of the curve.

Is it a coincidence, then, that normalcy and linguistic standardization begin at roughly the same time? If we look at that confluence in one area in particular, we see that language and normalcy come together under the rubric of nationalism. As Benedict Anderson has pointed out, the rise of the modern nation took place largely in the eighteenth and nineteenth centuries when the varieties of polyglotism that had made up a politically controlled area were standardized into a single "national" language. Without this linguistic homogeneity, a notion of the modern nation-state would have had great difficulty coming into being. In addition, national literatures, both in prose and poetry, were made possible through the standardization of languages, the prescriptive creation of "normal" language practices.[7]

While few now object to Anderson's thesis that language practices had to be standardized, homogenized, and normalized to allow for the creation of the modern nation-state, I think that the next step, which I want to propose in this essay, might be more objectionable. I would claim that for the formation of the modern nation-state not simply language but bodies and bodily practices also had to be standardized, homogenized, and normalized.[8] In this sense, a national physical type, a national ethical type, and an antinational physical type had to be constructed. Here we see much work done in the nineteenth century on racial studies, studies of pathology, deviance, and so on – all with the aim of creating the bourgeois subject in opposition to all these abnormal occurrences.

This is where I want to return to my putative linguistic solecism. In thinking about the difference, or lack of difference, between normalcy and normality, I began to think of the suffixes which make all the difference in those two words. "-cy" seems to indicate a state of being, as does "-ity," but there are resonating differences. Both "-ity" and "-cy" turn adjectives into nouns – as "sexuality," "ethnicity," "formality," as well as "malignancy," "pregnancy" "immediacy." However, I would suggest, without insisting absolutely, that the use of "-cy" seems more strongly to denote a permanent state, as it does in "idiocy," "complacency," "malignancy."[9] But interestingly enough, many words that describe not simply a corporeal state but a political state use the suffix – "democracy," "autocracy," "plutocracy," or "aristocracy."[10] My thought, then, was to salvage my own oversight by making a valid distinction, much in the way that Jacques Derrida talked about "difference" and "differance." I would call "normality" the alleged physical state of being normal, but "normalcy" the political-juridical-institutional state that relies on the control and normalization of bodies, or what Foucault calls "biopower." Thus, like democracy, normalcy is a descriptor of a certain form of governmental rule, the former by the people, the latter over bodies.

This distinction allows us to think through ableism in a somewhat different way than we have in the past. Rather than conceptualizing ableism as a trait or habit of thought on the part of certain somatically prejudiced people, we can consider ableism to be one aspect of a far-ranging change in European and perhaps global culture and ideology that is part of Enlightenment thought and part of modernization. Further, and I think this is important, we can begin to move away from the victim-victimizer scenario with which ableism, along with racism, sexism, and the other "isms" have been saddled and which leaves so little room for agency. Instead, one can see ableism as an aspect of modifications of political and social practice that have both positive and negative implications and that can be changed through a political process.

Let us look at the development of bourgeois representative democracy as an example of how ideological structures can shape notions of the body. The feudal model of society encouraged, for its own ends, the notion of inequality, a notion that the king or queen represented an ideal below which all subjects fell. The feudal system was based on a hierarchical notion of perfection, power, and wealth massed at the top of the social and political pyramid, less perfection, power, and wealth in the aristocracy, and even less in the peasantry. This model seeks to justify such inequality through the institutions of religion, of the patriarchal family, and of the violence inherent in the visible trappings of the state. Enlightenment writers like Jean-Jacques Rousseau, Voltaire, Adam Smith, and Thomas Jefferson rejected the concept of an idealized ruler holding all the power and wealth in favor of a representative government that postulates individuals who are equal to all other individuals. Thus the ruling entity, whose power derives from a social contract, is theoretically made up of individuals no different in kind from any other individual. Thus it can be, for example, that a well-known statue of George Washington can show a button missing on his coat without fear of diminishing his authority, which does not derive from his embodying an ideal but from the delegated power of a social contract.

Yet, such a notion of an individual equal to other individuals, as expressed in the phrase of the Declaration of Independence of the United States of America that "all men are created equal," has at base several contradictions. First, how is it possible that someone can be an individual and yet be the same as other individuals? This paradox is contained in the word "identity," which signifies both individual existence and similarity with others. In order to postulate a government, at least theoretically, in which citizens are individuals equal to other individuals, one needs a notion of the average citizen. This being is seen as representative of all citizens. Likewise, in a representative democracy, one has to postulate that the elected officials "represent" each of these equal individuals.

The word "represent" conveys a further paradox. If the elected representative is a stand-in for any citizen, then he or she must act to convey the opinion of that individual. So the representative must both convey and literally "be" or represent the existence of the citizen. But to be truly representative, a government would have to have one elected official for each citizen. The notion of an individual representative representing groups of citizens contains the fundamental paradox of representative democracy: how is it possible to represent an individual citizen when one is elected by a majority or plurality of a segment of voters?

None of these issues was a problem for feudal or monarchical governments, since no representation of citizens had to take place. One did not have to postulate individuals but rather groups, classes, realms of control. Yet in order to represent, as a painter would for example, one has to visualise, create, postulate a simulacrum of a citizen.

This is where we see the development of the average citizen, "*l'homme moyen*," by Adolphe Quetelet at the beginning of the nineteenth century. As noted in the previous chapter, Quetelet physically measured people's bodily dimensions in order to come up with the proportions of the average man. He wrote, "If one seeks to establish, in some way, the basis of a social physics, it is he whom one should consider."[11] Thus, the average citizen is constructed to dissolve difference and hierarchy, all of which is reconciled in this statistical figure of equality. But the average citizen, like the average family with 2.5 children, is a kind of fiction, a created character that fits the national mold.

During the same period, statisticians began to come up with the concept of the norm and the normal. We may say of the norm, as a concept, that it is the perfect ideological and technical solution to the paradox of the individual. The norm provides an efficient explanation that reconciles the contradiction required in representative democracy concerning the notion of the represented individual. The paradox of how it is possible to be an individual equal to other individuals, and the further paradox of how to represent such individuals, is taken care of through the concept of the norm and the bell curve. Individual instantiations become statistically possible. Each entry has an existence and integrity, each person is an individual with his or her place on the bell curve. Yet, at the same time, each person is part of a continuum and fits into the whole. In addition, there is an average, a normal citizen who can be described. These are the hypothetical people whose cumulative characteristics fall under the center of the curve. Thus, the concept of the norm permits the idea of individual variation while enforcing a homogeneous standard or average.

Further, with the concept of a norm, representation is made possible, since the average citizen can be seen, postulated, and consulted in this way. Individuals can be represented in government as a collective. Indeed, the very idea of voting in an election for a representative has much to do with the formulation of an ideology of the norm. A collective voting decision can be thought of as nothing more than the tabulation of individual variations, and the result is the election of a person who is supposed to represent a norm of opinion or sentiment. Especially in a parliamentary election with many parties contending, the results can describe a kind of bell curve of opinion. The House of Representatives in the United States was conceived as a kind of living embodiment of this sense of the norm. Thus, representative democracy is normalcy or, to try another neologism, normocracy.

The point I am trying to make is that bourgeois, representative democracy implies normalcy – that the two are really one form of government. As Canguilhem writes, "Between 1759, when the word 'normal' appeared [in French], and 1834 when the world 'normalized' appeared, a normative class had won the power to identify ... the function of social norms, whose content it determined, with the use that that class made of them."[12] Democracy needs the illusion of equality, and equality needs the fiction of the equal or average citizen. So with the creation of representative democracy comes the need for an ideology that will support and generate the aims of normalcy.

If democracy fosters notions of individualism, equality, and liberty, it also requires an ideology that reconciles those aims with the aims of capitalism, under whose watchful eye bourgeois democracy has been shaped. Capitalism conceptualizes equality as equality among workers rather than financial equality – since the latter would eliminate the differences in capital between ruling classes and workers and therefore eliminate capitalism. As philosophers like Jurgen Habermas have pointed out, there is a fundamental paradox in Enlightenment thinking. Enlightenment philosophers have argued for equality, freedom, and liberty in an ethical sense, hoping to have a society in which all people are theoretically free as regards rights. However, the unequal distribution of wealth required by capitalism seems a stark contradiction to these ethical goals.

So capitalism must explain logically or through ideology why it is just and fair that some people should have so much wealth and by virtue of that wealth, so much power to influence government. The concepts behind normalcy allow for such an explanation. If one takes the bell curve as a model, one notices that all variations fall into the unremitting logic of this distribution. Indeed, even random instantiations fall into a bell curve, as Francis Galton demonstrated through his construction of the *quincunx*, a device which allowed steel balls to fall randomly through a series of pegs and accumulate at the bottom of the device. Galton could demonstrate that, because the balls always accumulated in a bell curve pattern, the normal curve was in effect a law of nature. Therefore, it is logical to say that something like individual wealth will conform to the curve of normal distribution – on the one side will be the poor, in the middle people of means, and on the other extreme the very wealthy. So the very theory that allows the individual to be instantiated in the collective on an equal basis also allows for wealth to be unequally distributed. Equality and normalcy demand, by the unbending laws of mathematics, that there will always be inequality.

Equality among citizens is therefore not based on an ethical notion of equality but on a quasi-scientific one. Once the ethical notion is reconditioned by the statistical one, the notion of equality is transformed. Indeed, the operative notion of equality, especially as it applies to the working classes, is really one of interchangeability. As the average man can be constructed, so can the average worker. All working bodies are equal to all other working bodies because they are interchangeable. This interchangeability, particularly in nineteenth-century factories, means that workers' bodies are conceptualized as identical. So the term "able-bodied" workers came to be interchangeable with able-bodied citizens. This ideological module has obvious references to the issue of disability. If all workers are equal, and all workers are citizens, then all citizens must have standard bodies to be able to fit into the industrial-political notion of democracy, equality, and normality. Clearly, people with disabilities pose problems to work situations in which work is standardized and bodies are conceptualized as interchangeable.[13]

Up to this point, I have been discussing what might be regarded as political considerations with reference to their implications for disability issues. But I hope that this discussion makes clear that there is no neat division between the world of the body and the world of the body politic. Indeed, what I have been stressing is that the rather neat divisions made between the technologies of the body and the machinations of the political world are ones that serve the very interests and ideologies being critiqued. So it is possible to talk about the way that medical discussions of illness and disability can partake of political and ideological imperatives as well.[14] One of the striking issues that comes up in looking at early medical conversations around the concept of normality is the way these conceptualizations dovetail with the political issues already discussed.

A major change in medical discourse occurred between about 1750 and 1850 around the definition of the normal and the pathological, as Georges Canguilhem details in his book *On the Normal and the Pathological*. The change was essentially from one system in which health and illness fought in a Manichean way over a body to another system in which disease and health were not seen as opposed forces but were conceptualized as part of a continuum. In the former, health and disease were sharply demarcated. In the latter, disease or health was measured by a lack or an excess. As the French physician

Broussais writes, "the phenomena of disease coincided essentially with those of health from which they differed only in terms of intensity."[15] So disease becomes associated with prefixes like "hyper" or "hypo," becoming in essence an extreme of normal health. According to John Brown writing in the 1780s, "it has been proved that health and disease are the same state depending upon the same cause, that is excitement, varying only in degree."[16]

In other words, a theory of a norm extends to and develops within medicine. In this theory, disease is actually a significant deviation from a moderate norm. Words like "intensity" or "excitement" connote disease, whereas health has been described by René Leriche as "the silence of the organs."[17] That disease can be quantified is illustrated by Samuel Lynch, who created a "veritable thermometer of health" which rated excitability in terms of the numbers zero to eighty, with perfect health in the middle at forty.[18]

Since the norm implies a theory of moderation, and since, as we have seen, this theory arose during the ascendancy of the middle classes and the rise of bourgeois democracy in the Western world, it makes sense to look carefully at the rhetoric of medicine here. In that formulation, the normal tranquil body is silent, operating with its moderate methods. Disease involves excess, excitability, noise, attention, irritation, stimulation. One can see in this rhetoric, as Susan Sontag saw in the metaphors surrounding illness, that a parallel is being drawn between the human body and the body politic. Perhaps it is no coincidence that this theory underlying normalcy, the rule of the norm, occurred exactly when Europe was trying to assimilate the specter of violent revolutions and insurrections.

Indeed, Auguste Comte saw such a parallel and thought approvingly that Broussais's ideas concerning medicine could be extended to "moral and intellectual activities" and applied to "the collective organism," which can use it "to confirm or perfect sociological laws."[19] Comte, too, emphasized that "the analysis of revolutions could not illuminate the positive study of society without the logical initiation resulting, in this respect, from the simplest cases presented by biology."[20] As Canguilhem observes, "[by] stating in a general way that diseases do not change vital phenomena, Comte is justified in stating that the cure for political crises consists in bringing societies back to their essential and permanent structure, and tolerating progress only within limits of variation of the natural order defined by social status."[21]

The conclusion then becomes quite clear. If the norm regulates society by creating equal bodies, then medical theory, following suit, defines disease as a lack of regulation, an excess, that must be returned to a silent norm. The theory then can work back to politics, so that a revolution is an excess, an excitability, in society, causing disease, that must be returned to a state of health, which implies moderation, silence, and invisibility. Broussais's formulation that irritation is "normal excitation transformed by its excess,"[22] is a telling remark made in 1822, just after the excessive excitation of the revolutionary and republican period had ended in France and the stability of the monarchy had been restored.

It is important to see that ideological ways of thinking about social unrest and physical health have the power to shape the perception of each other. If we think of hysteria, mental illness, mental retardation, blindness, deafness, or physical deformity during this period, we can see that there are often political valences attributed to such conditions. Certainly, books like James Trent's *Inventing the Feeble Mind*, David Rothman's *The Discovery of the Asylum*, Douglas Baynton's *Forbidden Signs*, and Martin Pernick's *The Black Stork*, among many others, show us how physical conditions are attributed political significance. Further, issues of national identity and allegiance are tied to physical issues, as we see in many of the eugenic discussions concerning the poor, women, foreigners, people of color, Jews, the Irish, Italians, gypsies, and so on.

A related consequence of this model of health, in which disease is linked to excesses or lacks, is that the patient, the person with an illness, is no longer a valuable reporter of somatic information. Rather, an individual's disease is determined in the laboratory by the expert. Levels of chemicals in the blood, urine, or tissue tell the expert whether the patient is in good health or not. Likewise, it is the laboratory that determines the norms to which the individual patient's body chemistry should match. Since these quantitative measures are not available to the patient, the patient is in no position to evaluate himself or herself. Likewise, statistics measure the invisible numbers of the state and determine the health or illness of the economy, the national debt, employment, and so on. In the case of the state, a new generation of specialists can determine, better than can an individual, how the collectivity is performing. In the case of the patient, the doctor, with the help of the laboratory, takes on the function of informing the patient whether she or he is or is not healthy.

In either of these scenarios, the autonomy of the individual is weakened, as is any sense of agency. The results are by now familiar to most of us. In the case of the state, although we individually may be financially strapped, we are told that the economy is doing well. The average citizen is made to feel that statecraft is too specialized for ordinary people to do anything about, and complacency and resignation is the proper role of the citizen. In this sense the citizen becomes the citizen-patient who must silently submit to the role of the specialist – medical or bureaucratic. In medicine, the case is similar. Although an individual is feeling fine, a doctor can alert the patient to a dangerously high level of cholesterol or estrogen or a lack of thyroid hormone. These ideologies fit nicely together to make both medically and socially compliant bodies – both of which are necessary for a rule by normalcy whether in the physician's office, the workplace, or on the streets.[23]

It may not be so far-fetched to claim even further that representative bourgeois democracy requires a consistent and controlled level of institutionalization for bodies. Foucault's work has shown us the extent to which the medical, institutional, personal, and political realms are all blurred under forms of enforced compliance. One of the side effects of the creation of norms in medicine is the need for each person to be linked to a doctor. Under the rule of normalcy, each person must have a physician who can monitor the hidden levels of health or illness in his or her body. Thus the physician becomes instrumental in determining whether each citizen is "normal" or "abnormal."

Individuals cannot self-report on their participation in the bell curve, since much of the data and the analysis of the data will be unavailable to him or her. For example, how can you know if your height or weight are normal? You must first have experts determine the normal height or weight in your particular nation. If you are, as I am, a 5'7" male living in the United States, then you will discover you are below average in height. If you are the same height in Mexico, you will discover you are above average. But you cannot determine this yourself with any accuracy. Nor can you determine whether you have prostate cancer or high blood pressure by yourself. Diagnosis and care become part of one's individual social identity. Each citizen must be part of a cradle-to-grave health care system in order to participate in the collectivity.[24]

An interesting situation arises with the necessity of the one-doctor-per-person model. The problem of representation is inverted. While we saw that it was really not possible to have an elected official represent each person, it is however possible for each person to be administered by a single doctor. Here, representation is not adequate, since no collectivity can replace the individual's medical history or identity. While I can elect a representative to stand in for me, I cannot choose a medical representative to act in the place of my body. Yet when patients are treated, they are not treated as individuals but as instantiations of norms. If my blood sugar rises above a certain measurable level, I am a diabetic; if below a certain level, I am hypoglycaemic. If I don't experience symptoms, I still violate the norm. So while normalcy requires that I appear in person, as an individual, before my health-care giver, I am treated by reference to a laboratory and statistically determined medical norms. Thus the paradox of the normal curve – that it contains equal individuals, yet groups them into a collective based on statistically based similarities – continues in force.

Linked to this is the imperative to be normal in health matters. The major drugs and therapies today are aimed at bringing abnormal bodies, as defined by quantitative measures, into line with agreed upon norms. A good deal of the energy of being alive becomes devoted to this imperative to conform physically. Through exercise, dieting, corrective surgery, the use of prostheses, and so on, contemporary citizens use up the hours left over from work and leisure activities, which can be seen simply as a prolongation of the workday,[25] so that there is no time or energy to engage in activity or analysis. In other words, the hegemony of normalcy creates compliant and disciplined bodies, to use Foucault's terms, which meet the needs of a bureaucratic, corporate state.

The fact that medical costs now make up the largest area of entitlements in the United States indicates that the relation between the medical and the political is not simply academic. Healthcare, as Bill Clinton discovered, is about much more than health – it is about money, business, trade, and power. Indeed, the overlap between the institutions of government and the medical system becomes more profound each day. A new entity – the patient-citizen – is now a reality. The patient-citizen, governed by the norm of representation and by the hegemony of normalcy, passes in one lifetime through a series of institutions – day care, primary, secondary, and higher educational facilities, corporate employment, managed care, hospitals, marriage and family, and finally nursing homes – all of which are based around legal, juridical, medical, and cultural normalizing concepts. The interlocking demands of these normalizing institutions are overwhelming and even totalitarian. Has there ever been such a total control of people in history? Arguably even in the most unfair feudal rule by a single all-powerful despot the ability to control all aspects of the mind and

body seem trivial compared to the rule of normalcy as it has developed over the past two hundred years.

In the midst of this system, the person with disabilities is only one casualty among many. Under normalcy, the fact is that no one is or can be normal, as no one is or can be equal. Everyone has to work hard to make it seem that they conform, and so the person with disabilities is singled out as a dramatic case of not belonging. This identification makes it easier for the rest to think they fit the paradigm.

As the media unfolds endless tales of their version of people with disabilities – take the three Academy Award nominees for 1997 alone, *Shine, The English Patient,* and *Slingblade,* all disability films – for the examination and comfort of people who believe themselves to be able-bodied, society groans on in singling out disability as the Other by which it defines itself. Whether we are talking about AIDS, low birth weight babies, special education issues, euthanasia, and the thousand other topics listed in the newspapers every day, the examination, discussion, anatomizing of this form of "difference" is nothing less than a desperate attempt by people to consolidate their normality. As Leriche suggests, the sick person must be studied to "advance knowledge about the normal,"[26] or, one might add, to create the normal person. Indeed, Freud's fascination with psychopathology laid the foundation for a superstructure describing mental health. Freud's interest in deviant minds created the framework for his psychology of the normal mind.

At the same time, the move of people with disabilities to frame the struggle in terms of civil rights and equality is something one might want to question. Obviously, a civil rights paradigm is better than one that relies on pity, the reverse side of discrimination. However, if, as I have been arguing, normalcy and equality go together, then a critique of normalcy that does not critique ideological notions of equality will end up falling prey to the same problems experienced by all who are oppressed by the rule of normalcy. In other words, people with disability may get their equal rights in their respective United States of Ability and join the ranks of the "privileged" normals (or normates, to use Rosemarie Thomson's term), but with that will come the repercussions of that complex agenda. To become part of the solution, one may become part of the problem. Equal access and equal rights are certainly important, but equality is a two-edged sword that carves out ethical space but also cuts down bodies to convenient and usable size. It should be the goal of a liberating movement based on disability rights to know the way in which rights create disability and how disability can help find a way to solve the problem posed by bourgeois definitions of rights.

Notes

1 R. W. Burchfield, *Fowler's Modern English Usage* (Oxford: Oxford University Press, 1965), 395.

2 Ironically, the person who made the first dictionary in English, Samuel Johnson, was himself a very nonstandard human. He had many disabilities, including Tourette Syndrome, which may have accounted for his obsessive behavior in compiling words.

3 [???]

4 See also H. Aarslef, *The Study of Language in England, 1780–1860* (Princeton: Princeton University Press, 1967); and Murray Cohen, *Sensible Words: Linguistic Practice in England, 1640–1785* (Baltimore: Johns Hopkins Press, 1977).

5 Georges Canguilhem, *On the Normal and the Pathological*, trans. R. Fawcett (New York: Zone Books, 1991), 150.

6 Canguilhem, *On the Normal*, 150.

7 Benedict Anderson, *Imagined Communities: Reflections on the Origin and Spread of Nationalism* (London: Verso, 1983).

8 I am following Foucault's lead in this claim. Foucault talked about the control of deviant bodies – criminal, sexual, and medical. In some sense, Foucault never fully accounted for why these bodies were considered deviant. He never really explained the ontology of deviance. My emphasis here is on deviance as pressured by concepts of the norm. In other words, the creation of the modern sense of deviance for bodies is located in the work of statisticians, medical doctors, and eugenicists attempting to norm physical variation.

9 I am sure that one can find many examples in which "-cy" does not express a permanent state. One could argue that "immediacy" can hardly be permanent or that "pregnancy" is certainly a state that has an end. But one could counterargue that each of these is an absolute state. A malignancy generally does not become benign, and one cannot be a little pregnant. So that while time can end the "-cy" state, it does not diminish it. In any case, as will be seen, my definition here serves propaedeutic and hortatory purposes more than linguistic ones.

10 I would be the first to recognize that my philology is probably spurious. The "-cracy" in these terms derives from kratein, "to rule." But for my polemical purposes, I will equate the "-cy" in "democracy" with that in "normalcy."

11 Theodore M. Porter, *The Rise of Statistical Thinking, 1820–1900* (Princeton: Princeton University Press. 1986).

12 Canguilhem, *On the Normal*, 151.

13 It is interesting that this formulation of an average worker is not only a necessity for capitalism, but is so for socialism or communism as well. Marx, for example, used Quetelet's idea of the average man to come up with his formulations of labor value or average wages. For more on this, see my *Enforcing Normalcy*, 28–9.

14 What follows are largely some thoughts on and reactions to my reading of Georges Canguilhem's book *On the Normal and the Pathological*, which I had failed to read when I wrote *Enforcing Normalcy*. This book is central to any study of normality, and the fault is clearly mine for having omitted it in my study. However, I would add that no conclusion I reached would have been altered by reading Canguilhem's work. If anything, my book would have been strengthened by the observations of this writer.

15 Canguilhem, *On the Normal*, 18.

16 Canguilhem, *On the Normal*, 24.

17 Canguilhem, *On the Normal*, 46.

18 Canguilhem, *On the Normal*, 25.

19 Canguilhem, *On the Normal*, 18.

20 Canguilhem, *On the Normal*, 18.

21 Canguilhem, *On the Normal*, 28.

22 Canguilhem, *On the Normal*, 22.

23 A larger point to made, and one that is far beyond the scope of this essay, is that in effect holistic, traditional practices of medicine based on accumulated experience, such as the traditions of Native American, Chinese, or Maori medicine, has been eliminated by this new kind of practice in which treatment can only be accomplished after laboratory work which isolates specific locations of disease. The suppression of indigenous medical practice in favor of a rationalized medical discourse can certainly be analyzed as an aspect of the suppression of indigenous people, colonial subjects, and women.

24 One has only to look at the social pressures forcing one to "have" a doctor; to "have" regular checkups; to find the hidden diseases that may be incipiently growing without one's knowledge. The ideological impulse is to place the responsibility for one's health on the individual rather than the community. Diet rather than control of pesticides, regular checkups rather than reduction of pollution, sunscreen rather than ozone-saving measures, cochlear implants rather than the widespread use of sign language and interpreters – are examples all of which point to the way ideology functions on the patient-citizen.

25 Max Horkheimer and Theodor W. Adorno, trans. John Cumming, *Dialetic of Enlightenment* (New York: Herder and Herder, 1972), 137.

26 Canguilhem, *On the Normal*, 52.

37

The Patient's Body

Virginia L. Blum

Surgery

It wasn't until the morning of the surgery that the surgeon admitted he might have to break the bone after all. I hesitated. Then I murmured, "Only if you have to," as though I hadn't known from the moment he brought up the possibility that it was inevitable. The bridge would be broken. He'd known all along, and only now, as the pre-op sedatives were beginning to take effect at 6:30 in the morning – after waiting in anticipation for three months, fantasying the beautiful future of my face, after going to bed early and having no food or water in my stomach since the previous evening – only now did he divulge the whole truth about the surgery. They need to reel us in slowly.

I came in and out of consciousness during the surgery, which was performed under a local anesthetic. Not long after I awoke in my hospital bed, feeling a kind of weight and intensity in the middle of my face, I was handed a mirror. My nose was in a cast and heavily bandaged, but what struck me immediately was that the bottom of my nose was now flat where once it had been rounded. Even then, recognizing on some level that too much was missing, I was in that postsurgery haze of pure expectation – when the result could be anything. After surgery, you lie in bed waiting for your day. Instead of obscuring your face, the bandages seem more like a blank field of possibility – of the beauty promised, of the happy ending to the surgical story.

This relationship between the male surgeon and the female patient is so powerful that more than twenty years later, as an interviewer, I found that surgeons

continued to have the same effect on me. Regardless of the professional career, the expertise, the presumed "grown-up" resistance to their blandishments and insinuations, no matter how big the desk between us or how sophisticated my insights – no matter how enlightened I am as to the way they harness cultural power over women's bodies in the service of their practice – these surgeons continued to be able to tell me who I am, to construct an identity for me that emerges in relation to an aesthetic standard they come to represent as the ultimate body critics (and perfecters). In their hands lies the route to the promised world of tens. Many of us can say no to the surgeon (most people never consider surgery), but it's more difficult to rise entirely above a culture where ten is something worth being.

During my interviews with plastic surgeons I found that, despite my role as interviewer, at times they assessed me as potential surgical material. Having spent a great deal of time in their offices, I am now hyperconscious of a general institutionalized distribution of power that has very little to do with the aesthetic particulars of each woman's face and body. Unless they asked, I rarely informed the surgeons that I have had surgery. For one thing, I hardly wanted them to comment on the outcome or recommend further surgery. I wanted them to interact and respond outside a surgeon-patient dynamic, which would have been all too available for them once they could position me as "patient." For the most part, the surgeons did not talk to me as though I was a prospective patient. They respected the interviewing boundary; my body remained beyond the scope of the interview – at least as a subject of discussion. Nevertheless, there were those who could not help but overstep, who seemed compelled to see me as a patient despite the institutional imperatives against doing so (the original exchange of letters, the process of signing consent forms, turning on a tape recorder). It was at these moments that I gained (harrowingly) much deeper insight into how men's and women's bodies perform in relation to preassigned roles of those who get to look, operate, impress upon, and make versus those who are looked at, assessed, receptive, and changed. It was as though the still-powerful cultural, allegorical roles of masculinity and femininity were ever straining against the fragile boundaries of the professional situation. The remainder of this chapter will concentrate on just this tension between my positions as interviewer and patient and how the interview process itself made me realize how perilously close I always am to lapsing back into the patient position. The demands of my damaged and vulnerable body continue to defy the rigors of half a lifetime of cultural inquiry and feminist protest.

Damage

Viewing themselves as "healers" of cosmetic defects and emotional desperation, plastic surgeons need not interrogate their own psychological necessity for intervening in the appearance of healthy bodies. We could argue that cosmetic surgery is markedly different from the life-saving efforts of, say, the general surgeon, because in cosmetic surgery we find harm being done to a healthy body, cuts being made, blood flowing for no known medical reason. This is why plastic surgeons tend to justify their practice through the claim of psychological necessity. Psychological damage takes over for physical impairment. Healthy bodies begin to appear "diseased." In countries with national health programs, this argument is taken quite literally. In Great Britain, for example, a woman can still receive a state-funded breast augmentation if a qualified psychologist deems it necessary to her emotional well-being. The sociologist Kathy Davis documents at length the criteria established in the Netherlands (also under national health insurance) to evaluate the "necessity" for the cosmetic operation:

For example, a breast lift was indicated if the "nipples were level with the recipient's elbows." A "difference of four clothing sizes between top and bottom" was sufficient indication that a breast augmentation or liposuction was in order. A sagging abdomen which "made her look pregnant" was enough reason to perform a tummy tuck.

For a face lift, the patient had "to look ten years older than his or her chronological age." (35)

While this program of government-subsidized cosmetic surgeries impressively levels the playing field between those who can pay out of pocket and those who cannot, such an approach to determining a patently aesthetic "necessity" colludes with the idea that people might need to put themselves at surgical risk in order to heal their self-esteem. Plastic surgeons operate under the pretext that the damage has already been done in the form of the cosmetic defect, hence they are simply correcting a problem that originated elsewhere. They can overlook the damage inflicted by them under their supervision in their operating room. They can project onto the other, the patient, the psychological damage as well.

It is possible that plastic surgeons are acting out in a socially sanctioned way their aggression on bodies that have been shaped by forces other than their scalpel. Such "forces" are either natural (what the patients were born with) or surgical (the results of other surgeons' work) or traumatic (car accidents, etc.); whatever might be the cause of the body's appearance, it induces in the surgeon a form of rivalry. This would explain the extraordinary level of in-fighting and competition among the surgeons, which include their readiness to "correct" the mistakes of other surgeons. Indeed, open any plastic surgery journal or women's magazine and you will find plastic surgeons bemoaning the failures of other surgeons as they extol their own corrective techniques. While it is certainly admirable that medical professionals are as attentive to psychological forms of impairment and dysfunction as they are to physiological forms, I suggest that we also consider what kind of gratification might be in it for plastic surgeons. How might their sincere regard for patients join with and disguise this double action of damaging and repairing?

Moreover, whose aesthetic prevails? Whose body, ultimately, is it? When friends ask my advice, I tell them to go to the surgeon whose surgical results look like what you want on your own face or body. Many surgeons criticize their colleagues who reproduce a particular look on every face and body touched by their scalpel. They talk at length about tailoring the change to the individual. But then I look at their own work, and all their patients as well look like members of a not-so-extended family. There's a surgeon whose face-lifts I would recognize anywhere. His procedure is always the same: yank up that brow, stretch back those nasolabial folds, insert a silastic implant into the chin. His patients look uncannily alike in their "after" photographs, staring brightly into the camera, chins stiffly prominent, every element on their faces that could crease or fold now permanently affixed as though by a rubber band.

Pathological Concern

"Do you think you're attractive?" one surgeon asked me.

"I'm okay," I replied. Of course, this is the stock response – one always replies "okay" to such a question – or "reasonably" or something neutral. One must be prudently modest. Think of all those models and actresses who "confess" to their aching insecurities. "I've always hated my mouth," Michelle Pfeiffer admits. Are we supposed to accept at face value that she dislikes her most celebrated feature? That she really believes she looks like a duck?

At the same time one must not cross the line into flagrant self-doubt, because then you will be pathologized as "disordered" by those who specialize in body-image disturbance; you will be said to suffer from a psychological affliction, body dysmorphic disorder, an extreme dissatisfaction with one's appearance, that they will promptly and efficiently try to "cure." Surgeons are trained to be wary of such individuals. But throughout the literature on body dysmorphic disorder, one is aware of an extraordinary insensitivity to the fact that some people are considered more attractive than others and that some people are considered unattractive by a significant number of people with whom they interact. How do body-image theorists reconcile their pathologization of beauty-obsessed people with their own work suggesting that the good-looking profit in all respects.

The cognitive behaviorist Katherine Phillips claims to have proved that body dysmorphic disorder (BDD) is biological in origin. Not only does she advocate treating it with a combination of antidepressants; she is also optimistic that brain scans will eventually locate the very scene of pathology. She concedes that BDD can seem related to "normal appearance concerns." But, in order to qualify as having BDD, you need to spend more than an hour a day engaged in BDD-related behaviors. Phillips considers (briefly) the cultural origins of preoccupation with appearance. She argues that while body dysmorphia may be exacerbated by the excessiveness of beauty culture, it is by no means caused by it. Her proof is that if the appearance-centeredness of the culture were to blame, more women would suffer than men and, in fact, it's the reverse. Yet, we could speculate that since men are not supposed to care as much about their appearance, it would only stand to reason that more men than women would be diagnosed as disordered for caring so much. "Normal" for Phillips seems to mean those of us who respond to magazine articles on "perfect thighs in this lifetime" and the possibility of going ' "from so-so to supersexy' " (182). To respond to a cultural preoccupation with appearance is, of course, normal. But you can care too much. Then you have a disorder. Plastic surgeons follow a logic similar to that of Katherine Phillips. Normal, apparently, is to want your ethnic nose fixed.

I wound up with one of those noses surgeons display as the "before" picture for a botched surgery. My turned-up nose became Roman. It twisted to one side. It hooked. The tip was flattened out from the removal of too much cartilage. Allegra Kent describes her own disastrous result: "My new face was grotesque. It was shockingly distorted. It was not me. The doctor had done a bad job, and I recuperated slowly. My mother's obsession with externals and what could be done about them had been played out on me" (80). Both our mothers assumed that surgery was a kind of miracle, that there was no dreadful aesthetic risk involved, that these (urgent) beautification rituals inevitably made one more beautiful. Afterward, my mother and I complained, but the surgeon dismissed us as having absurd expectations. There was only so much he could do – "the bones have to go somewhere," as he put it to my mother in response to her wondering how my nose had gone from turned up to turned down. Many years later, as I was going under anesthesia for my second rhinoplastic surgery, I heard the operating surgeon say to his nurse: "Look what some joker did to this poor girl's nose." Nevertheless, the first surgeon considered his work successful – or at least he claimed as much in the face of our dissatisfaction. While I may have been condemned as a perfectionist by surgeon number one (expectations out of line with predictable outcome), surgeon number two identified me as a legitimate case for correction.

Role Reversals

"Do you think you're attractive?"

What does it mean for a plastic surgeon to turn to a woman he doesn't know (and who's not there for surgery!) and ask her if she thinks she's attractive? Does he imagine he has the right by virtue of what he does – territorial rights, to be exact, over all women's bodies? He also knows (who knows better?) that it is the essential question for women. To be attractive for women means they get what they want. But what is it that women truly want – beauty or its putative social rewards? After undergoing extensive plastic surgery to make her ugly body beautiful, Fay Weldon's protagonist Ruth in *The Life and Loves of a She-Devil* is still dissatisfied because she remains too tall. " 'You must be satisfied now,' Dr. Black [one of her surgeons] was saying to this blond, simpering doll on stilts, 'if grown men are fighting over you. . . . You are beautiful, you are popular, you can go to a party and cause infinite trouble: you are the showgirl type. The balding businessman's dream' " (261). Not quite perfect enough, Ruth demands further (life-threatening) surgery. Dr. Black doesn't understand, because Ruth already has everything he imagines women could want – mainly, to be desired by most men. This, he takes for granted, is why women want to be beautiful. Certainly, Ruth wants to appeal to men (particularly her philandering ex-husband), but it is ultimately her ideal image of her body that she pursues. In other words, what women may want in the end is just beauty itself. While the number of potential partners may increase, this is perhaps not the goal but rather the proof of beauty, the approving stares and the expensive gifts and the proposals simply registered on the checklist of beauty's accomplishments. Just as the measure of a religion's truth is often made according to the numbers of its adherents, a beautiful woman achieves value through discipleship.

This is what Freud has to say on the subject of what he calls the secondary narcissism of the beautiful woman: "Strictly speaking, it is only themselves that such women love with an intensity comparable to that of the man's love for them. Nor does their need lie in the direction of loving, but of being loved. . . . Such women have the greatest fascination for men, not only for aesthetic reasons, since as a rule they are the most beautiful, but also because of a combination of psychological factors" ("On Narcissism" 89). The love object, then, is neither the partner nor the self (in any permanent sense) but instead the body and only when it's beautiful. Freud seems to have captured a cultural turning point when just being beautiful took over as the object of desire. We generally assume that women want beauty as a means to certain ends, the various benefits that become more available to beautiful women: more financially successful partners and the material pleasures they bring. But it is possible that the accomplishment of the lifestyle serves merely as an index of her value on the open market of desirability. What appear to be the cultural rewards, in

other words, are just the evidence of – the thing she has, the only thing she wants – her beauty. It is not surprising that beauty has come to this pass.

In *Beauty Secrets*, Wendy Chapkis describes the received relationship between beauty and its benefits:

> Real life and real appearance are not enough when the goal is to live in a travel poster with a beautiful person at your side and in your flesh. If only we were more stylish, if only we had more money, if only we had accomplished something more remarkable, if only we were really beautiful, then life could begin.
>
> But as it is, we know we are too flawed to deserve it – yet. Meanwhile we wait, buying the props if we can afford them, trying to turn ourselves into closer approximations of the beautiful. We wait, aware that beautiful people are not old. (140)

What is most telling about Chapkis's wish-list is how the chain of "if onlys" culminates in beauty itself. The travel poster is the ubiquitous cultural metonymy for "the place" of success, which entails becoming beautiful in a beautiful place. When success looks like a place and place is just an appearance – the place where you are perfectly beautiful – then most of us can simply try to be "closer approximations of the beautiful," never truly "inside" the pictured paradise.

"One day," Fay Weldon writes, "we vaguely know, a knight in shining armor will gallop by, and see through to the beauty of the soul, and gather the damsel up and set a crown on her head, and she will be queen" (*She-Devil* 63). But in the end Weldon's *She-Devil* heroine, Ruth, doesn't even really want the knight – she just wants to be the queen of beauty; the knight, her ex-husband, in all his defeated confusion, merely guarantees her sovereignty. It's not that the man in the heterosexual woman's fantasy of beauty is incidental; no, he is central. He is part of the package.

What am I saying, exactly? That beauty is its own end? It seems almost too astonishing; at the same time it is such an obvious consequence of a culture that bombards women on all sides with beauty regimes, beauty solutions, beautiful images – the exigency, in other words, of beauty. It was inevitable that the thing women needed in order to be "successful" as women has ascended to the thing itself. If you tell us enough times and you show us enough appealing examples, then we will begin to believe utterly in beauty as its own reward.

As we are increasingly influenced by the ubiquity of beautiful female bodies on television, in movies, on the cover of virtually every magazine in the supermarket, it is no wonder that the identification with the image of beauty itself is so compelling. The art historian Francette Pacteau discusses the connection between men's near fetishistic representations of beautiful women and women's fascination with these images. She advances the perplexing possibility that "man-made images of female beauty are, at least in part, a product of the man's attempt to meet the desire of the woman – to accede to being *her* desire, by presenting her with an ideal image of herself" (190). Contrary to the commonly received notion that it is men who dictate the demand for and the terms of this female beauty, Pacteau intriguingly suggests that to some extent men are giving women what men think women want – representations of female beauty. These images serve women's demand for identification with beautiful images.

Art historian Lynda Nead emphasizes the emergence of the female nude as the favorite subject of nineteenth-century painting, which suggests not only the new centrality of the female body as the object of the gaze but also the circulation and availability of images of the female body. Thus, what I point to as the overinvestment in beauty as its own goal is the historically specific result of both identifying women with (beautiful) visual images and raising women to identify with the image of their own beauty.

"*Do you think you're attractive?*"

What am I supposed to do with the "think" in that sentence? What if he had asked me, "Are you attractive?" A yes or no question that people feel as though they can't answer about themselves. To ask us if we "think" we are attractive implies the power of the mind over the body. If you feel beautiful, then you are. But the plastic surgeon's very role in life is to overturn dramatically this already quite impoverished cultural fiction.

A beautiful woman in my family loves to assert that beauty doesn't make you happy – "Just look at Elizabeth Taylor," she will urge. As though Taylor's beauty interfered with her pursuit of happiness. So invested is my relative in this myth that she kept secret from me her own rhinoplastic surgery – even when I was about to have surgery myself (that first surgery). It was her cousin who accidentally spilled the beans, because he didn't know the degree to which women guard their beauty secrets. When I confronted her with her cousin's story, she conceded that, yes, she'd had a revision, but only a very little one, only a slight refinement of the tip.

It is impossible ever to tap into the whole truth of these family fictions, but what I learned from her was that narcissism is shameful, and what could be more narcissistic than having cosmetic surgery?

"*Do you think you're attractive?*"

To be asked by a plastic surgeon whether you think you are attractive is a reversal of the real question hanging between the surgeon and the patient – Does *he* think you're attractive? When he asked me, "Do you think you're attractive?" what naturally sprang to mind was his opinion, not mine. Whatever I thought, he was going to tell me the truth; moreover, his question brought to light what I work hard at forgetting when I am in the company of these surgeons – the degree to which they are immediately, reflexively almost, pronouncing aesthetic judgment on me as I walk through the door. When he asked me, "Do you think you're attractive?" I felt as though I were being quizzed by a teacher who knew in advance the correct answer.

"Have you had your nose done?" he pursued.

I think back to that first surgeon pinching the tip of my nose between his thumb and forefinger. "I was checking the cartilage, in case she was Hispanic," he explained to us. "Hispanic noses don't have the right consistency for reshaping." My mother was instantly impressed with his cross-cultural expertise in the distribution and pliability of nasal cartilage. Afterward she kept referring to that moment when she had witnessed his expertise in practice, when he had pinched my nose. These surgeons trade on the cultural conviction of their ability to analyze the body's surfaces like a form of corporeal exegesis. It takes so little. A soothsayer of the body, reading my parts, my ethnicity – as though it weren't obvious. My last name is Blum. Not exactly Hispanic-sounding.

"*Have you had your nose done?*" He smiled. It wasn't a casual question. He may as well have been pinching my nose between his thumb and forefinger.

"Yes," I told him. He wanted to know who had (re)operated on me.

"Um, yes, I know him," he commented. He asked me to turn off the tape recorder. It was my turn to be scrutinized – as though the lamp had suddenly swung across the desk from his face to mine. He chain-smoked in my face in his small office.

My anxiety – that any moment any one of them could turn on me, tumble me off my high horse and into the muck of defective female plastic flesh – was lived out with this particular surgeon. My reaction was an extreme version of the pervasive and understood relationship between heterosexual men and women in Western culture. We are always dependent on their restraint, their charity, their ability to refrain from taking advantage of the power reposed in them. This surgeon simply acted upon the power any one of them had.

Just the same, where this power is located is not altogether clear. The power he assumed in that massive reversal was a power I attributed to him as male, as plastic surgeon, to evaluate me aesthetically. He could not have the power unless I turned it over. But I was helpless to withhold it. In other words, while his power cannot happen without my complicity, my complicity is an inevitable corollary and consequence of his cultural power. There is no choice involved in this relationship. If his effect happens only through my response, I can at the same time argue that my response wells up uncontrollably to the positional power he commands over my body. Recall that I could have turned the tables once again. I could have made his face and body an object of my gaze – I could have asked him if he had had surgery. Why didn't I ask him about his eyes, for example, because certainly they appeared operated on? But I instinctively withdrew, and it is this "instinctive" withdrawal that is ultimately structural. This institutional power is inextricably tethered to the degree to which women are the perfect subjects of and for cosmetic surgery.

I will illustrate my point through my various encounters with plastic surgeons. Early on, I was alerted to my vulnerability when a Kentucky plastic surgeon, discussing the kinds of cosmetic procedures he would and would not perform, remarked that he would do only "really bad noses," for example, "real honkers," as he put it. Then, in an offhand manner, he added: "I wouldn't do your nose, for instance." Now, I didn't take this as a compliment; rather, he was using my nose as an example of features that weren't sufficiently displeasing for him to bother reshaping them. As he emphasized, in light of his practice, which was predominantly reconstructive rather than cosmetic, the cosmetic procedures had to be such that he "could make a significant difference." Whether his comment was indifferent or aesthetically evaluative was irrelevant to my stunned recognition that he was looking at me in that way – that he could not help but appraise me, moreover that anyone who walked into that office was subject to his professional look. This particular circumstance applies to men and women alike. Given the surgeon's customary experience of the doctor/patient relationship taking place within his office,

it was no wonder that he would see me in light of my context – that very office.

They see us all with an aesthetic gaze that is additionally a transformative gaze – what they can do for the defective face and body. Many surgeons acknowledged that often they found themselves looking at people with an eye to what aesthetic revisions they might want to make. "When I went to church more frequently," a surgeon said, "I used to while away the time looking at people and wondering what I would do if they consulted me. And that's a lot of fun." By way of showing me an example of too-heavy eyelids, one surgeon handed me a picture of his nineteen-year-old daughter. "She'll probably need something done in another ten years," he pointed out. What might this be like for the daughter of a plastic surgeon? I felt bad for her. I had noticed her photograph early on in the interview – it was a large photograph and prominently displayed. I had mistaken the gesture of the enormous photograph for a father's pride; rather, she was there as a strategy for personalizing defects. See (I could imagine him explaining genially to a patient), my own daughter suffers from this defect; in another few years, she will need the very surgery you require today. He allowed that I had eyelids. But later in the interview, as he commented on some pictures of face-lifts and noted how impossible it is to correct the nasolabial folds, he pleasantly added, "You have them already, and you're a young person."

Aesthetic Judgment

I was already wearing a mask when I entered the operating room. This was the first time I was meeting the surgeon in person, so he had no idea what I looked like. This mask covered my face from the top of my nose to my chin. Nevertheless, as he inserted a cadaver-harvested septum into the patient's nose, he asked me if I'd had my nose done – a nose he had not yet glimpsed. I was a Jewish woman raised in Southern California, writing a book on plastic surgery; I suppose it was a likely assumption. He, too, wanted to know the name of the surgeon. It was a casual question. Just as casually, after describing the transformations he was making in this woman's facial contours via the addition of a number of silastic implants, he asked me what my jawline was like, if I had a strong chin.

I was sent off to a private room to view a videotape of the surgeon describing his silastic implantation technique. He looked different to me in the tape – older, with a narrower face. Had something been done in between the filming and now? Was he surgically altered, or was I just projecting onto his face his own aesthetic fantasy? Was I seeing him as his own work-in-progress simply because I was caught inside his world at that moment – a world in which all faces are simply variations on a particular surgical theme? After surgery, he came into the room and showed me slides of his work – a series of implant miracles where flat, narrow, chinless faces suddenly bulged with the eminences of jawlines and cheekbones – tiny little features like rosebud mouths and narrow-set eyes now caught amid the mountainous terrain of their plastic bone structure. Out of the blue, he announced: "You have great eyes, full lips, good jawline and chin, a cute nose, but you need cheek implants to widen your face."

I laughed. I wasn't offended. I half expected him to say something of the kind. It was endearing in a way, thoroughly ingenuous. This is what he does – he adds bits to people's faces to make them more nearly match the current fashion in bone structure. My face is too narrow. I need cheek implants. In order to do what he does for a living, he cannot help but view the world around him as divided into those who do and don't need augmentation of their bone structure. It wasn't in the least aggressive. I had the feeling, in fact, that he would give me the surgery for a reduced rate, as a courtesy. He wants to make people happy.

I realized that I had to phrase my refusal cautiously – this is his life's work, after all. I told him I wasn't comfortable with the thought of foreign substances in my face. He looked bewildered, slightly wounded. "What do you mean?" "It's just me," I mumbled apologetically.

Most of his slides were impressive. I remarked on the extreme changes for the better in his patients' appearance. I hesitated, however, over one set of before and after shots. The young woman started out fine, but I didn't much care for her after photo. I was trying to figure out what had gone wrong. I wondered if perhaps she had gained weight, because her cheeks seemed too round. The surgeon interjected: "This woman has a facial shape just like yours. See the difference I made with the cheek implants." I stared. She had chipmunk cheeks. This is what he wanted for me. I explained to him that I didn't care for the changes. He was immediately uneasy. "Well, that's okay," he said. "You probably like it because it's like your own face and so that's what you're accustomed to looking at." It was unlikely, I observed, that I would use my own face as any kind of standard. "I'm confident about the work I did on her," he assured me. "It's all right

that you don't like it, because I don't have any doubts about it."

Suddenly, I understood that he was anything but confident – that the point of showing me all of these slides was to win my approval. I was his perfect audience, both because I know a great deal about surgery (enough, in other words, to validate my judgment) and because I am not a surgeon myself. There is a danger in revealing one's work to another surgeon because of the element of rivalry that inevitably surges through the relationship between two "master artists," especially, perhaps, two male artists. I am a woman, and I am not a surgeon. Yet, because I have interviewed other surgeons, reviewed a great deal of the literature, in other words, momentarily borrowed their prestige, my approval goes a long way toward shoring up the surgeon's self-esteem.

As Susan Bordo puts it in "Reading the Male Body," what feminists commonly dismiss as the male objectification of women (in pornography) may not be desubjectifying at all. Quite the contrary, for the fantasy to thrive, the woman *must* be a subject who accepts the male body and its performances on any terms:

> The attempt is to depict a circumscribed female *subjectivity* that will validate the male body and male desire in ways that "real" women do not. The category of "objectification" came naturally to feminism because of the continual cultural fetishization of women's bodies and body parts. But here it is perhaps the case that our analysis suffered from mind/body dualism. For the fact that women's bodies are fetishized does not entail that what is going on in their minds is therefore unimplicated or unimportant. Rather, an essential ingredient in porn . . . is the depiction of a subjectivity (or personality) that willingly contracts its possibilities and pleasures to one – the acceptance and gratification of the male. (276)

Bordo's analysis of a male construction of female subjectivity coincides with what I experienced at the hands of the surgeons. It is not that they are just objectifying my body (and those of their patients) as so much meat for their transformational miracles. There also needs to be an appreciative subject of the surgery who can afterward look in the mirror and recognize the surgeon's skill. While surgeons may be objectifying the body, they depend on the living subject who can evaluate outcome, insist upon a revision, go to another surgeon (where both patient and surgeon will pool their scorn for the "lesser" surgeon), then praise the "greater" surgeon to all her friends and family as a miracle worker.

38

Queer Cyborgs and New Mutants: Race, Sexuality, and Prosthetic Sociality in Digital Space

Mimi Nguyen

Long ago I learned my lessons from the comic books. I learned that mutant bodies were powerful but vulnerable bodies; vulnerable because such powers made one a target for social control, prejudice, enmity, and evil-doers seeking recruits, vulnerable because these energies threaten to overcome and eclipse the fragile vessel of the body. In 1980 the Marvel universe introduced the super-hero team called the New Mutants, a multicultural crew of misfit teens led by an ascetically thin Vietnamese refugee Xi'an Coy Manh, the daughter of a South Vietnamese colonel with an evil twin (and also mutant) brother and a criminal ganglord uncle. Recruited by Professor Xavier for his New England School for Gifted Youngsters and called Karma in her X incarnation, she was a grim and conscientious figure, able to seize control of other people's minds and bodies – a fortuitous alteration of her genetic code in the aftermath of her mother's exposure to mutagenic chemical defoliants used during the war. The luckless subjects of her power would become extensions of her will and her senses – prosthetic mannequins speaking in her voice, attacking their fellows with their physical strength or armor where she had little of both. Though she could possess several subjects simultaneously, her control would be fragmented and sometimes awkward, distributed among the hosts. In many ways, it was a curious power that left her vulnerable to physical threat and harm. Her own flesh was not protected by any aspect of her power, and she was forced to find some discrete corner or shield herself with the bodies of her more physically powerful team members. And the experience drained her; often she would eventually collapse from the exhaustion of controlling

another's mind and body. If she remained in possession of her subject for too long, she would begin to leak into the subject, or the subject into her – and her distinct personality and memories would be melded with those of the host. Nine issues into the series Karma had been captured by an enemy called the Shadow King and disappeared, only to reappear herself possessed by his disembodied spirit and of monstrously large proportions, having lost both her psychic strength and bodily control.

When I was young I sought to develop my own psionic strengths, hoping perhaps my mother, too, had been exposed to the same chemical substances. This did not seem wholly unreasonable; after all, like Coy Manh I had relatives in the former South Vietnamese army, a brother with definite potential for evildoing, and an enduring sense of being a categorical mistake. Like the mutant teenagers that populated the Marvel universe, I felt my birthright was to exist "outside" the normative social body of central Minnesota. I reasoned that this awkward, preadolescent exterior – garbed in mismatched, secondhand clothes and thick eyeglasses – would serve me well as a secret identity for the while; but my real self (which would arrive with puberty, as it did in the comic books) would be eruptive, powerful, and wield a mastery of my body and my surroundings that I didn't yet possess. No revelations were forthcoming, however, and after a while I consoled myself with the assurance that there were dangers I would never be then forced to face, so frighteningly realized by Karma's own possession and loss of self.

For years the appeal of comic-books faded away, and punk rock had come and gone as my chosen venue for social mutancy. But in a Boston comic-book shop, between sessions at an MIT conference on race and digital space, I discovered an old back issue of the New Mutants series, with a cover featuring a possessed Karma as an enormous puppetmaster, dangling and jerking her chosen avatars (her former New Mutants team members) at the ends of their strings. Because story arcs in comic books are ruled by fateful coincidence and constant resurrection, I recognized this encounter for what it was – a fortuitous link between the mutant in my imaginary and the cyborg in my work. It made sense: both Karma and the cyberspatial body represent popular cultural visions of the intersection between organic bodies and technologies, and the powers and dangers involved in the transgression. The mutant body and the cyborg body act as metaphors, representations of social structures and cultural systems in a seemingly new, complex, and contradictory configuration. She is an image of our notions about body and bodies in a moment of transformation, creating the imaginary spaces that the mutant/cyborg inhabits and posing new human possibilities and problematics.

In this essay I examine representations and images of the mutant/cyborg subject in feminist and queer science fictions; even progressive cyborgs need to be resituated within the material and ideological conditions of their origins to make sense of their political motives and possibilities. With comic book in hand, the following group of commentaries traces this intersection and transgression in science fiction and cyberspatial culture through two very queer concerns: our prostheses and our mobility. From the Greek, *prostithensis* means "to add" – *pros*, "in proximity," and *tithensis*, "to place" – a word, a part to something else. The prosthesis – a human-machine encounter enhancing movement, function, or activity – is often conceptualized as the interface allowing increasing freedom, mobility, and speed. As such, a prosthesis connotes several meanings: an artificial part replacing what has been irrevocably lost; an addition to the principal body enhancing movement, function, or activity; the intimate interpenetration of the biological with the mechanical. But the prosthetic subject describes both the incorporation of these meanings and a particular kind of doubling – the worker whose mechanized labor is assisted by robotic arms or machinery; the abstract citizen who, desiring the protection of the state, gives up the particularity of her body; the comic book avatar, a mutant who temporarily possesses the bodies and minds of others; the lesbian or transgendered subject, equipped with a harness and a dildo, resignifying the phallus and sexual meanings and practices; and the virtuality of a material body in digital

space, interpenetrated by informational patterns and protruding machinery (keyboard, mouse, monitor). As technologies of the self, prostheses are both literal and discursive in the digital imaginary. They are a means of habitation and transformation, a humanmachine mixture engaged as a site of contest over meanings – of the self and the nonself, of the strange and the familiar, of the parameters of mobility and its limits. At this interface the body is at stake – where it begins or ends, what it means, what is replaceable (and what is not), what its limits might be, what dangers may lurk in the encounter.

Locating my inquiry at the intersection of the imagination and material reality, I begin with the New Mutant Karma to interrogate the premises of what I call the "recombinant liberal subject" of cyberspatial fantasy – an abstract, sovereign subject released from social location. It is this capacity for inclusivity, attributed to the imagined neutrality of the cyborg in cyberspaces, that allows feminist and queer theorists to reimagine a radical subjectivity that celebrates fluidity and mobility. I then focus on feminist and queer interventions in science fictions and queer practices that seek to disrupt the "straight" taxonomy of sex/gender/desire, with profound consequences for representations of race and the cyborg subject. At this juncture I ask, What effects do our prostheses – whether figured as abstract personae in a global public or fantastical bodies of mixture and masquerade, as projective fantasies of control or sliding, shifting walls of invisibility – have upon subjectivity and social relations? What are the implications of feminist and queer conceptualizations of digital space and prosthetic sociality for the examination of race, not in isolation, but in critical, complex, and contradictory articulation with gender and sexuality? Is there a vanishing point at which, as Karma so powerfully worries with her fiction, the body ever really disappears?

"Your Mind – Your Body – Belong to Karma!"

While a minor character in the Marvel pantheon, Karma is massively traumatized: she grew up during the war in Vietnam as bombers and bullets flew overhead; her parents were imprisoned in a reeducation camp until she freed them with her powers; their escape on an overcrowded fishing boat was violently marked by the attack of Thai pirates; too weak from hunger to use her powers, she was forced to watch while the pirates murdered her father and raped the women, including her mother; her mother then died the day the survivors were rescued by the US

Navy; responsible for herself and her young siblings Leong and Nga, she moved to New York City where her ex-general, secret crimelord uncle kidnapped Leong and Nga in an effort to force her cooperation in his schemes. Originally gathered to fight "evil mutants" who (of course) sought to subjugate humanity, these teenage New Mutants are nonetheless viewed with fear and suspicion by the non-mutant population. Flanked by her teammates, Karma is an admittedly odd figure; often she holds her head in her hands, the only outward indication of the use of her powers. (The others erupt into black masses of solar energy, transform into animals, project spirit forms, or burst out at breakneck speed.) In the comics her powers are visually rendered as a kind of boundary-breaking psychic ray – it extends multihued (but usually in shades of fuchsia) from her furrowed brow to envelop her usually unwilling but violent opponents, traversing panels to intervene in other spaces. In the fashion of all comic-book characters, who are given both to lengthy exposition and statements of the obvious, she might declare, "Your day is done, villain! Your mind – your body – belong to *Karma!*"

Taken as a kind of evidence – and because comic books often wage battles across titles and temporalities – Karma can be read as a warning about the dangers of prostheses and possession, self-transformation and the boundaries of limitless mobility. For decades, both cyberpunk and corporate science fictions (and the intersection of both) predicted anarchic affairs between automaton and autonomy, negotiating the possible achievement of total liberty from the body (or derisively, the meat) or regulation. These fictions produced a cybernetic fantasy of the recombinant liberal subject – an abstract, sovereign subject reconstituted by the interpenetration of the virtual-systems interface with liberal humanist discourse, the transcendent figure of the technological sublime. That is, because both textual and graphical virtual interfaces make possible the decoupling of public persona from the materiality of the body, digital space can be made to sanction a body politic in which subject formation is understood as divorced from assigned or ascribed characteristics or social location. The appearance of the skin, the distribution and texture of hair, the bone structure of features, the contours of the body, the quality of grooming, the coterminous interplay of surfaces – the visual apprehension of race, gender, class, sexuality, and the like falls apart. To the extent that liberalism deems these to be constraints undermining autonomy and utopian subjectivity, digital space promises their removal through the absence or mitigation of presence.

But the figure of Karma substantiates the dangers of abstraction. Her powers might be said to mirror the powers of the recombinant liberal subject in digital space, enabling an escape from the flesh and the possession of other bodies, but the hope that this genetic cyborg can be read as an autonomous social agent is circumscribed.[1] The history of this cyborg is continuously apprehended in the present: the source of her powers, her ability to possess other bodies and minds, can be traced to a series of technological interventions in the war and to her DNA.[2] The history of Karma, but also of Xi'an Coy Manh (her "secret identity"), is thus embedded in the historical reality of the biochemical weaponry of the US military-industrial complex, and necessarily references a disturbing past of neocolonialism and medical experimentation. She is a cyborg whose creation could have easily resulted in physical deformity or damage – as it did for others whose exposure to the chemical defoliants did not end so fortuitously – and yet she is nonetheless a freak. She is a cyborg *because* she is Vietnamese. Her adventures are constant reminders of this past – she joins the New Mutants and acts as Professor Xavier's secretary so that she might continue to provide for her siblings, who somehow contrive to be kidnapped again and again by various villains, including their uncle. As a "new mutant," she displays the arrogance of the war's engineers not on the surfaces of her body but from *within*, projecting these properties of possession and control onto others. As a New Mutant, her powers mirror the conditions of her creation. Against the utopian technological discourse in which the body is rendered inconsequential and immaterial, her *particular* body in all its permutations is the instrument of (and not the impediment to) her powers.

And far from being an abstract subjection position ensuring autonomy and mobility, the "new mutant" reinscribes the difference and the social powers that the recombinant liberal subject disavows. Her genetic mutation does not allow Karma unusual access to freedoms. On the contrary, because of the dangers and risks that accompany her powers, she must demand discipline from her prosthesis. As a cyborg, Karma must pass for human or risk being the object of fear and hostility, but to do so she must deny the history of her genetic mutation in an attempt to approximate the ideal (nonmutant) or be marked (by the *X*) as an "illegitimate" human being. The trauma of passing is realized in the "secret identity," which is *not* the mutant superhero but *the persona of normalcy*. This secret identity – and its recombinant liberal counterpart in digital space – implicates the social powers that produce, situate, and constrain legitimate/

illegitimate subjects. This subject who suppresses is provided a kind of prophylaxis, to borrow from Lauren Berlant – a prosthetic status as abstract "person" that disguises her particularity.[3] But the impossibility of this disembodiment erupts repeatedly. While Karma may pass for human, she cannot otherwise pass as other than Asian; the consequences of the first kind of passing may bear upon the second, in which her body is already marked as "foreign" in the West, and vice versa. The objectification of the Vietnamese by the US military as "mere gooks" during the intervention – and thus justifying the usage of napalm and biochemical defoliants – suggests that the hope to pass for human is precarious and a historical contingency. For the body that is understood as too much body – too much sex, too much skin, too much history – the ideal of the unmarked liberal subject is violence.

But the mobility attributed to the recombinant liberal subject is not limited to abstraction; in the release of the body from social powers, the ability to wear a body that does not reflect or refer to the physical appearance of the user/performer is perhaps the most popular aspect of science fictions. And when superpowers fail to manifest, digital space provides. The emergence of the cybernetic interface has posed an incipient and significant challenge to some essentialisms as cyborg subjects generate new bodies and design new selves in the choosing and fusing of new parts in a potentially endless process of consumption and self-invention; the prosthesis of digital space enables a mobility that promises both autonomy and inclusivity. But however transgressive (and some avatars might be within certain parameters), these are choices that may simultaneously participate in the reconstruction of a recombinant liberal subject – continuously accumulating surplus (material and cultural) capital in late modernity. Such modes of cross-identification and cybernetic drag are coded as safe or entertaining, divorced from social consequence or political conditions. Even as "warranting" (the process of making the physical body legible) becomes problematic in digital space, the corporeal codes or tokens of "identity tourism" or cross-identification can still be fetishized, and the relations of power that produce and circulate such narratives about specific bodies are concealed, made invisible in electronic environments. These codes do not require the physical body that authorizes them into digital space to match, to be *warranted*, but they invoke bodies nonetheless, and in very specific ways.

This may easily become the occasion for (a desire for) escape, a wish for a post-body future in which one might enjoy the exoticism of otherness or dodge complicity by inhabiting that space of difference. Indeed, the fantasy of becoming "other" (or some approximation of her) is a feature of modern commodity culture and contributes to the apprehension of mobility for the liberal subject. The contemporary spectacle of multiculturalism appropriates racial and national otherness for use in a range of fantasies of identification. Lisa Nakamura describes this as "identity tourism"; writing of the Lambda MOO environment, she observes that "Asian-ness is co-opted as a 'passing' fancy, an identity-prosthesis that signifies sex, the exotic, passivity when female, and anachronistic dreams of combat in its male manifestation."[4] In these userbuilt environments, Nakamura suggests that the transgender and transracial "identity tourist" who occupies the space of the "other" is engaged in a fantasy of social control. The popular avatars that Nakamura discusses – the samurai, ninja, or mail-order bride – are deeply implicated as codes in contemporary anxieties about gendered labor and transnational capital. That many of the persons who adopt the identity of an "Asian Doll" in electronic environments are, as Nakamura surmises, white men, would then suggest that the performance of transracial and transgender performance does not necessarily disrupt social (or geopolitical) relations *between* specific bodies; digital space allows for the nonmimetic act to be ideologically contained by the abstraction of virtual reality. Released from an empirical referent, the digitized token is circulated as "play" and severed from the sociopolitical and ideological processes that produce it. Nonetheless, these codes reference a body politic and frameworks of cultural intelligibility that, in this case, spectacularize already hypervisible bodies.

To what degree, then, does the autonomy of the recombinant liberal subject depend upon the suppression of other subjects, throwaway cyborgs used as servants, laborers, or toys? Maintaining multiple subjectivities drains Karma, and she is always in fear of losing control of her prosthesis, or worse, abusing its capacity. Her twin brother Tran developed similar abilities, and enjoyed the power over others. Having both saved and spared his life on numerous occasions she was forced to absorb the essence of her evil twin (effectively killing him) when he threatened innocents (having possessed Spiderman) under the guiding criminal thumb of their ex-general uncle. And when possessed by a mind more powerful than her own after a raging battle of wills, Karma grows enormous, gorging to satisfy the appetites of the Shadow King, the disembodied mind of an Egyptian crimelord once trapped in the astral plane who inhabits her body for his own vicarious purposes, fulfilling fantasies of consumption, disguise, and desire. In the throes of this possession, she traps her former team members – who had thought her dead – and pits them against one another in a gladiatorstyle battle for an audience of the international elite. Always a risk when using other bodies as a personality, she is submerged in the appropriation of *her* physical form; the Shadow King even dresses her physical body like a geisha in an enormous kimono and top-knot. Possessed, she becomes her own enemy; could the dangers of inhabiting other bodies be more obvious?

The Queer Appeal of Cyborgs

Because of this fluidity, this mobility, feminist and queer appropriations of science fictions are rewriting gender and sexuality in cyberspaces, fashioning pervert avatars in drag and powerful cyborg selves in a space perceived as boundaryless. If digital space makes possible a Cartesian abstraction or the commoditization of the flesh, it also suggests that there is no necessary mimetic or expressive relation of psychical identifications to physical bodies. Digital space represents a situation in which the interiority of subjectivity is no longer easily located on the subject's flesh, potentially disrupting the (presumption of an) expressive relationship between embodiment and social identity. The image in digital space does not necessarily refer to an actually existing object/subject or body; the virtual medium is a medium for discontinuity. The detachment of public personae from the physical location/material of the body can have the effect often attributed to drag or transgender identifications, denaturalizing gender norms and making possible the articulation of a plurality of sexual subjectivities.

It is at this juncture of theory and technology that many feminist and queer scholars have engaged cybernetic politics as a space of identity play and gender reconstruction.[5] A *Wired* editorial extols the virtues of cyberfeminism "based on the idea that, in conjunction with technology, it's possible to construct your identity, your sexuality, even your gender, just as you please."[6] Others argue that "[a]ll the things that separate people, all the supposedly immutable facts of gender and geography, don't matter quite so much when we're all in the machine together."[7] Thus, digital space is hailed as a liberatory space, disrupting the social determinism of the body from the identifications of the self, allowing for sex play/gender fuck transcending the unidirectional implication of "sexual orientation" and gender norms. This radical potential is

often identified with the gender trouble instigated by Judith Butler – that is, that gender does not constitute a metaphysics of presence, that a particular gender is not inherent to a particular sexed body, and that sex and gender do not thus exist in a one-to-one expressive relation to each other, that sex itself is a gendered construct.[8] The appeal of drag as a metaphor for subversion in digital space is located in the act of cross-identification and *self-conscious* performance. Utilizing various modes of performance, drag is theorized as the revelation of the prosthetic nature of gender. Rather than a "bad copy," drag is the disclosure of *no* original, of the fabrication of gender as essence through the repetition of its expectations and signifying systems by the "wrong" sex.[9] Both drag and digital space make possible the nonmimetic mapping of bodies, dislocating embodiment from social identity or self. Both imagine new ways of making subjects – including cyborgs as drag queens or genderqueer rebels – seemingly free of social imperatives. Drawing upon Butler's arguments, feminist and queer scholars like Thomas Foster, Allucquere Roseanne (Sandy) Stone, Cynthia Fuchs and many others have argued that the cyborg offers an imaginative site for radical potential because "nothing in a cyborg body is essential."[10] This crucial recognition – that nothing in a body, cyborg or not, is essential – does not, however, null the body.

As such, feminist and queer science fictions do negotiate the body in digital space in complex ways. In Melissa Scott's novel *Trouble and Her Friends*, a group of gay and lesbian computer hackers have been implanted with "brainworms," neural-electrical connections that allow them to directly interface their nervous systems with cybernetic networks – the now-familiar prosthetic capacity for "jacking in" in cyberpunk science fiction.[11] Of them the main protagonist India Carless, a white lesbian hacker (with a suggestively "colorful" name), abandons the shadow world of brainworms, dollie slots, and hacking ICE (Intrusive Countermeasures Electronic) when an electronic surveillance act is passed by the US Congress (notably, against an international treaty). She is compelled to return to the networks when someone adopts her former code name – Trouble – to wreak havoc. The specter of government regulation inspires a crisis of identity for her circle of friends, who are also faced with the choice to "go straight, moving out of the shadows into the bright lights of the legal world, the legal nets."[12] The dangers of "going straight" are clear – whether assimilation into the mainstream of computer technicians and system operators, legally bound to follow a set of rules and conventions, or assimilation into the mainstream of heteronormativity and "wholesome" values. In contrast, digital space represents for the characters a space of liberation as queer individuals whose mobility is constrained and regulated in "real life" – it is a place where "a woman could easily be as hard and tough as any man,"[13] where their skills are the measure of their worth, not their sexualities. Nevertheless there is prejudice in the world of hackers too, including a kind of corporeal disgust for those hackers who've had the "brainworm" implanted. At one point Trouble speculates that "maybe that was why the serious netwalkers, the original inhabitants of the nets, hated the brainworm: not so much because it gave a different value, a new meaning, to the skills of the body, but because it meant taking that risk, over and above the risk of the worm itself. Maybe that was why it was almost always the underclasses, the women, the people of color, the gay people, the ones who were already stigmatized as being vulnerable, available, trapped by the body, who took the risk of the wire."[14] The novel groups women, queers, and people of color as a category of individuals willing to take more risks with the body because this "stigmatized" body has not been historically available as a vehicle for liberal subjectivity. The hope of "escaping" these social constraints (and acts of violence) is articulated in this novel as a possibility located in the antiessentialist ether of digital space; but this imagined capacity for radical inclusion, attributed to the prosthetic sociality afforded by cyberspace, treads dangerous ground. This is a queer cyborg subjectivity enabled by a purported universality in which digital space facilitates not only an escape from social location but also the reappropriation of the queer cyborg as a recombinant liberal subject. Whether in the replication of a universal antagonism (binary gender), in statements of solidarity or in the hope for gender and/or sexual insurrection, these accounts are often characterized by a critical lack of attention to examining the boundaries drawn around gender and/or sexuality as a social category to the exclusion of other vectors of analysis.

Nor is the transgender subject necessarily any more suited to resolving this dilemma. Sandy Stone suggests that in cyberspace, "the transgendered body is the natural body. The nets are spaces of transformation, identity factories in which bodies are meaning machines, and transgender – identity as performance, as play, as wrench in the smooth gears of the social apparatus of vision – is the ground state."[15] While aptly articulating the challenge to gender expressivity that digital space and virtuality may pose, the seeming elevation of a singular or "natural" subject/body should give us pause, as should the seeming

reduction of identity to performance and play. Having dismantled the mythology of a natural woman located in biological or psychic substance in both patriarchal and feminist discourse, or the universality of "queer" as a signifier for fluid and mobile sexual or intellectual practices, can the substitution of another body – however self-consciously constructed – as a universal subject provide a new paradigm for future identification? Where is the agency of this body located? Is it in the act of passing among other nonmimetic bodies? Is the transracial body *also* a natural body? And in considering this last question, to what extent can digital drag acts and the queer challenges these pose to traditional relations between sex and gender ideologically and politically occlude – if not contain – an emergent discourse (and conflict) with transracial performance?

In these science fictions mutant bodies and cyborg bodies are analogized as minoritarian bodies, subjected and subjugated, but the limits of this analogy are striking. Moreover, these "stigmatized" bodies are differently disciplined through sometimes conflicting and sometimes collaborating operations and structures; the work of intervening in these operations and structures must account for these different modalities of social subjection. In one problematic instance, the blurred boundaries of human-machine have inspired allusions to Gloria Anzaldúa's work to describe deracinated cyborg subjects with a gendered and racialized geopolitical vocabulary; for instance, the iconography of the borderland and mestiza in Sandy Stone's theoretical project is used to describe *all* agents participating in electronic virtual communities.[16] The representation of the mestiza as a privileged figure transcending racial and ethnic boundaries – or those boundaries between physical and virtual space – is also the problematic relocation of a specific configuration of history, gender, race, sexuality, and nation. What are the consequences of theorizing the cyborg as mestiza for the actually existing (racial) mestiza? For the mestiza who works in the *maquiladoras* (factories) of multinational electronics industries, the mestiza who is "in the machine," but in a radically different relation? What are the consequences of equalizing the imaginative gap between physical and virtual space with the juridical sociopolitical division of the US-Mexican border? To what extent does the particularity of race (or racialized gender) as a social or subjective force disappear in order to extend the metaphor of hybridity? Far from allowing a neutral or transgressive subject position of liberty or autonomy, this powerful fantasy of the hybrid cyborg subject can function as a technology for seeming to become "other" while allowing for the reassertion of the agency and fluidity of the liberal self. The argument that "bodies don't matter here" might be another kind of prosthesis in and of itself – the deliberate disdain of a tangled materiality for a uniformly prophylactic body, encased in hard plastic and disguised as a safe sociality because in digital space, *everybody has one*. It is a queer erasure indeed.

Overkill

Just where does the science fiction end and the cyborg possibilities begin? Feminist and queer fictions of digital space and technological transformations of the body blur the boundaries in the search for a utopian space, simultaneously producing and contesting the political terms of liberalism. In particular, the novel *Nearly Roadkill: An Infobahn Erotic Adventure* uses practices of gender play to conceptualize virtual reality and digital space in a curious blend of liberal humanism and postmodern queer theory.[17] Transgender theorist Kate Bornstein and Caitlin Sullivan's collaborative work explicitly probes the possibilities for transgendered performances in contemporary cybernetic technologies (which are also suggested by Bornstein in her nonfiction "guide" to sexual subversion, *The Gender Workbook*),[18] while demonstrating the limits of the drag/transgender metaphor for digital embodiment. Set in the near future, the central characters, Winc and Scratch, are ordinary users (i.e., not hackers) who enjoy the performance of a host of differently sexed and gendered identities in chat rooms, message boards, and instantaneous private exchanges. In the course of their online flirtations and flings in various textually rendered bodies, they examine the nonmimesis of gender, sex, and desire and fall in love. They do not reveal their physical bodies to either the readers or each other until halfway through the novel, at which point we learn that Winc is a male-to-female transsexual whose gender identity remains fluid and unfounded and Scratch is a butch lesbian. Notably their whiteness, unlike their complicated negotiations with gender and sexuality, is invisible and implied in the absence of explicit racial markers. During the course of the novel Winc and Scratch inadvertently become rebel icons for a larger community of users, having refused both to mimetically reproduce themselves in their online gender and sexual performances and to register their "real" identities with the US government. Corporations have pressured the government to pursue this program

of registration as a mutual venture of the public and private sectors, making it possible to gather demographic data and to tailor advertisements and strategies of surveillance for individual users based on the given information. Against the enthusiastic endorsement of actual cyberlibertarians like R. U. Sirius – for whom "commerce is the ocean that information swims in"[19] – these fictional queer agents are seeking an escape from the commoditization of being and compulsory consumption. Against the "natural" order of the corporation (made "natural" through sheer ubiquity) in digital spaces, Winc and Scratch seek to resist the field of invisibility cloaking the corporate logo and capital through which the contemporary social body travels.[20]

Winc and Scratch are postmodern queer hero(in)es, and their virtual and actual acts of performance and "becoming" are clearly meant to be read as modes of transgressive mobility and fluidity, colored with the liberation of desire. While the state and transnational capital are located as nodes of power creating and regulating gendered citizen consumers, digital space is envisioned as an untamed and radically decentered expanse in danger from commercial colonization. They are the ultimate, technologically enhanced drag performers, imaginatively speeding through digital guises and urban spaces eluding captures of all kinds. And while themes of anticorporate resistance are not new to science fiction, it is rare that such resistance is spearheaded by a queer couple who simply want to fuck however they choose. The valence of choice becomes the pivotal antagonism of the novel: between government/corporation and the individual, assigned gender and gender fluidity, regulation, and liberty.

Perhaps nowhere is the extent of virtual systems' premise of unfettered mobility more evident than in an appeal for democratic liberal pluralism, made later in the novel as the characters discuss the implications of their rebellion. Weighing their options, Winc and Scratch argue that digital space is where "anyone who can't speak up because they were always afraid of being put in their place" is granted the freedom to do so – to speak out, to act up.[21] But while Winc and Scratch imagine that anybody – female, black, Latino, "Asians getting off the boat in California," gay, lesbian – can live more freely in digital space, "there is almost no consideration of how this technology might be used by blacks, Latinos, or Asians, despite their inclusion in the list of social subjects who might share [their] attitude toward the Internet."[22] The implications of this conversation are otherwise ignored. How might these other subjects – who are hardly a homogeneous bunch – access, use, and interpret the mobility offered by digital space? And would this necessarily entail a *desire to escape location or engage in identity play,* and if so, could we be assured that the meanings attached to these acts would be the same, or familiar to Winc and Scratch?

What is also not acknowledged is that at least some of these "others" are subjects of an abject modernity, encompassing vulnerable (biological) bodies, militarized borders, and microchip assembly lines.[23] As such, the recombinant liberal subject can be read as an autonomous social agent *on the condition* of the making of other kinds of cyborgs, highly gendered and racialized workers mechanized and merged as interchangeable parts, widgets in a different order of machinic-organic assemblage. So while the question of race and transracial performance is always already implicated in the electronic environment – whether figured as invisible labor or identity play – it is overwhelmed by the spectacular and celebratory narrative of gender and sexual cross-identifications in the novel. When race *is* invoked it is always problematically aligned as a category either parallel to gender or altogether alien.

In the midst of an online dialogue about gender uncertainty and the context of ambiguity while occupying one of her online personae, Leila, Scratch muses, "There's this civil rights march in my neighborhood once a year. All of us, black and white, march in it. Suddenly people smile at me who wouldn't give me the time of day otherwise. The colors of our skin don't matter then, because it's *that* day, that march." Assuming "Leila" is black, and unaware that she is a persona animated by Scratch, Winc replies, "I hadn't even considered your race. Ouch." "Exactly. You probably assumed I was white, right?" Scratch then "wearily" replies, "It's OK, it happens all the time. One of the cool things for black folks online is they are assumed to be white, too. Not that they want to be white, but they're assumed to be 'in the club,' without having to prove credentials at the door."[24]

This brief passage juxtaposes a field of racial discourses in complicated and sometimes contradictory ways. In the first instance the force of racism is located in the alleged fixity of visual knowledge. Its apparent counterstrategy is situated in the technologically enhanced ability to pass, extended by digital space to all persons of color. Passing here is construed as transgressive because it traverses boundaries of social identity, and because it exposes the categories as arbitrary. Yet passing is not a secured set of political effects or meanings, but instead encompasses a range of exercises and radically different implications for different subjects seeking to pass through different and uneven relations of power. The ability to pass is interpreted here as a deliberate strategy to reap certain benefits and avoid harassment, though the privileged body (white, male, heterosexual) retains its social power as the neutral body. In appropriating the rhetoric of disembodied abstraction, the asymmetry of corporeality ascribing universalism to some bodies and particularism to others is problematically reproduced in digital space. As a counterstrategy, passing in this instance depends upon the silence and invisibility of the minoritarian subject even as "the humiliating positivity of the particular" is attached to her body. Because this prosthetic of abstraction – facilitating the claim to legitimacy and mobility – is a relative privilege, the reproduction of the "bodiless citizen" of liberal humanism as a transcendent cyborg position in virtual systems is a clear danger, permitting the black body only an incorporeal participation in the dominant cultural body. Even as liberty is imagined as effortless mobility, it sets the terms of prosthetic sociality and places limits upon marked subjects who have no previous claim to abstraction. The presence of race is a disruption in a space that claims an asymmetrical neutrality. Oddly enough, Scratch, whose transgendered performances deliberately inspire anxiety, does not ask the obvious question, Why not be disruptive?

The answer – or *her* answer – is contained within the same conversation. Raised in this passage is the assurance that racial difference is easily surmounted – that in the visual absence of epidermis or because of an assumed political solidarity, race as an organizing principle and/or disruption disappears and "the colors of our skin don't matter." Scratch, feigning fatigue and passing as black, reiterates the sovereignty of the recombinant liberal subject – the "cool thing" about online sociality is that it allows "black folks" to adopt the prosthetic of whiteness. Here again race is imagined as *only* a superficial visual regime, and racism is abstracted from its historicity in ideological apparatus and social relations. However, even as Scratch asserts that cyberspace allows black people to pass as white, she herself passes as black by signifying race at all. The social transgression of her genderfuck is aligned with her passing, functioning to position transgender drag on an expressive level approximating that of racial otherness. The theoretical celebration of blurred boundaries and pluralism masks the act of appropriation here, disguised as empathy or the denaturalization of racial categories. The passage thus performs the elision of whiteness as transparency – and not necessarily as an effect or privilege of power – even while positing gender as functionally and politically "the same" as race, *even while* reductively assigning race a merely visual affect/effect and the positivity of particularity. These moves position the two kinds of racial drag in lopsided and slippery opposition; for while the prosthesis of neutral whiteness allows black people to passively participate as abstract individuals, Scratch's own transracial performance functions, like her drag, as self-conscious transgression. Thus, the structural and discursive distinction between the black subject who passes as white and the white subject who passes as black is not disavowed but *reconstituted* in an unfolding power play, displaced, by the drag metaphor, in which the white subject reasserts her agency (and appropriation) as privilege and her "special" knowledge (about civil rights, the suffering of African Americans, etc.) as authority.

When Winc and Scratch do finally interact face to face, Scratch admits to a seemingly endless desire to occupy multiple personae, a desire that she is uniquely able to fulfill online, in which she juxtaposes racial identity with animal: "I wish I were black because I hate my skin and probably next week being a wolf would be even better."[25] For her, both blackness and animalness signify escape from the felt abjection of inhabiting her particular body – and their juxtaposition has an imperial archive that is obscured in the "play" of the virtual interface. Such fantasies of identifying with and knowing "others" through a proximity, or, in the case of digital space, *approximation* of the "other," reify a racial being while simultaneously establishing a normative (e.g., white) self against which racial otherness is performed as radical difference. For Scratch, that radical distance from her sense of self can best be articulated as blackness or animalness in a romantic appeal to a state of being prefigured as more real, more authentic, more primal, perhaps – an appeal that has a lengthy history in colonial and imperial relations. As a queer subject whose mobility is deemed her weapon, her willingness to occupy blackness is represented as an empathic, rather than preemptive, identification. This fantasy of redemptive identification appropriates/approximates the (imagined) experiences of racial or national otherness while depoliticizing the social powers that produce them. This racial difference is fixed in order for Scratch to imagine herself as a transgressive subject, redefined by her consumption of this otherness in which blackness becomes a fetish-object *through which she comes to know her self.*[26] The list of "Latinos, Asians, et cetera" cited elsewhere in the novel as a multicultural vision of digital potential is nominally fulfilled by Scratch's appropriation of *all* difference as her drag and/or her desire.

In a novel that otherwise celebrates digital space as the denaturalization of gendered and sexual norms and the proliferation of multiplicity, race is both mythologized as radical difference ("I want to be black because I don't want to be me") and radical similarity ("I can pass for black because color doesn't matter here"). Winc and Scratch are queer agents whose universality (as rebels, as countercultural heroes) reanimates the production of an abstract, sovereign subject that is instrumentalized in a liberal humanist discourse of digital space.[27] Their protests and play are limited to the language of individual rights and the promise of mobility, and freedom is defined as individual license and couched in the rhetoric of "choice." It is an emancipatory project that reproduces the liberal cyborg subject as the ideal condition of personhood, with a twist. If the transgender body is the *natural* body in the cybernetic interface because its nonmimetic logic is universalized, then transgender *in this instance* becomes the neutral subject position that secures liberty and autonomy, and digital space is the field of fantasy in which particularities are rendered equivalent, even while racial positivity (especially when articulated as nonwhiteness) continues to figure (if sometimes inadvertently) as surplus, difference, or disruption. Resting on the liberal premise of equality, the antiessentialism of cross- or transgender identification in digital space can thus subsume and mask the differential reception and meanings of racial or transracial identification. That race, gender, and sexuality are simultaneous modalities of social subjection does not mean that they operate analogously, or that the technologies of their regulation or the strategies for their transgression and destabilization will be commensurate. This queer practice cannot destabilize racial categories as a scientific concept, biological or metaphysical essence, or even as a system of classification simply by refusing to acknowledge its borders; and this queer cyborg subject may designate a flexible space that accommodates various and fluctuating positions, but its ambiguity also creates a space of ahistoricity, of social forces and cultural asymmetries once again rendered invisible.

Can this queer cyborg subject conceptualize an avatar that isn't an escape? After all, as a young girl I was inclined toward revenge – feelings of betrayal aside, this was not an identification with abstract bodilessness. There was no small part of me that sought to recuperate my body, this ill-fit, awkward thing, through the exercise of my hoped-for mutant powers. As such, Karma might provide an alternate route of the politicization of the queer cyborg subject. It is significant that as a New Mutant she wears a uniform, but not a mask; in refusing to do so, she deliberately forsakes her "secret identity," the abstract prosthesis of normalcy, passing, or identity play. So rather than imagine escape, we might imagine disruption, like Karma reading the histories of our mutant/cyborg/queer bodies into the matrix to indict the social powers and material conditions that produced the regulatory apparatus of deviance and normalcy.

[. . .]

The Future of Cyborgs and Mutants

What digital space could then mean for our politics is both problematic and profound. What had previously been established as separate domains (the virtual and the real) are mutually informed processes of signification; and our prostheses are not just symbolic but instead symptomatic of our contemporary contradictions. The fetish of digital space, of the body released from history or mimesis or materiality, manifests for progressive discourses both the hope for liberation from prior meaning and the desire to become the instrument of resolution. Digital space, as a redemptive technology of new life forms, may reproduce a modernizing or progressive idealism that reiterates the limits of transgression in the *political* coding of race (as difference) as disruptive. The cyborg may designate an elastic and progressive space that accommodates multiple and fluctuating positions, including social misfits, drag queens and kings, and transgendered rebels, but its ambiguity must not resubordinate the subjects (recalling Winc and Scratch's list of Latinos, Asians, etc.) for whom such claims are made by erasing the historicity of those social forces and relations of power that generated the desire to be "free" in the first place.

The progressive, feminist, and queer discourses of digital space examined here are limited in scope – in defining freedom as license, liberation as choice, and identity as self-fashioned. They adhere to liberal democratic models of subjectivity and publicity premised on the imagined absence of social forces and the micro- and macropolitics of power. The fact of incoherence – of signs and signifiers mismatched, of bodies disappeared or made anew (or seemingly so), of social identity detached from material flesh – does not necessarily signal the disruption of a more hegemonic reality, and such incoherence can be easily accommodated by equally fluid rearticulations of power.[28] A more useful approach

to digital space would necessarily find ways to discuss the production of signs and circuit boards simultaneously, study the material and ideological labor of the technological imaginary, and examine the differential ways in which the blurring of flesh machine manifests across free trade zones and troublesome histories of colonial fantasy.[29] To otherwise affirm an antiessentialist subject while asserting a unified subjectivity through the valence of the transcendent cyborg, endlessly shifting and ambiguous but somehow outside of social forces or relations of power and capital, is a posture of erasure and danger.

And because her name, after all, invokes return and reprisal, I want to look to Karma one last time for a guiding lesson about agency, control, and the ambivalent instrumentality of our prostheses. As a "new mutant" she is a marginal being whose existence poses a question and a threat to the normative social body and to the status quo of human relations, but not simply because of her powers – these cannot be isolated from the historical conditions of her creation as a Vietnamese mutant subject. While her psychic powers disallow a reductive conflation of body with subjectivity, or a necessary expressive relation between interiority and exteriority, she grounds the play of self and nonself in a nuanced contest of social forces and circuits of power. No matter how powerful her prosthesis, her marginalized body is vulnerable; rather than allow for total mobility, her mutant superpowers – literally and figuratively marked with an X for excess, for exclusion, for ex-human – illustrate the dangers of reproducing an abstract subject through the discourses of antiessentialism or liberal humanism. So while the celebration of porosity between mind and body in discourses of technological mobility would pose a subject who is able to transcend the flesh, Karma's creation as a mutant subject and its constitutive conditions must be *looked at* rather than *looked through*. Last spotted as a pinkhaired lesbian film student, she defected from superhero-dom because she could no longer abide by the comic book universe of binarisms, which allowed little room for contradiction or complexity. Mobility and fluidity are not the apex of freedoms, as Karma learns the hard way (the only way in the comic books), and there are consequences and dangers involved in the prosthesis. After all, the possibilities and limitations of her prosthetic abilities make Karma a more critical queer cyborg subject *in her Vietnameseness*, distinct not because of an essence but because of the epistemic and corporeal violence involved in the production of her existence, because of the contours of her historically specific biotechnological transformation from human girl to *something more*.

But even if no cyborg is ever born innocent – like Karma, born of a neocolonial encounter and possessed of a comparable power to occupy other bodies – this does not mean we may not simultaneously take *some* pleasure in our cyborgs and yet interrogate the conditions of their existence, as science or fiction. Against a nostalgic discourse of authentic selves or organic interaction, of natural bodies and traditional communities, what might instead be revealed in digital space is the constructedness of all selves, interaction, bodies, and communities; what must be attended to are the structures and relations that produce different kinds of subjects in position with different kinds of technologies.[30] While the cyborg bodies we create to navigate these new spaces will not resolve the material realities or social contradictions of their manufacture, they provide a rich assemblage of myths, legends, fears, fantasies, codes, and tools with which to interrogate which bodies matter and why. In doing so we might be better equipped to imagine or even achieve alliances among mutants and cyborgs alike.

Notes

1　The term *genetic cyborg* is also used by Mark Oehlert in his essay, "From Captain America to Wolverine: Cyborgs in Comic Books, Alternative Images of Cybernetic Heroes and Villains," in *The Cyborg Handbook*, ed. Chris Hables Gray (New York: Routledge, 1995), 219–32.

2　Among the original New Mutants, Xi'an Coy Manh is the only member who might be read as a symptom of modernity's violence. The others – a wary Cherokee woman able to manifest images from others' mind as spirit forms; a naive Appalachian boy who becomes a flying, invulnerable human cannonball; an insecure Scottish human-wolf shapeshifter; and a black Brazilian boy who inexplicably draws upon the sun to become a roiling energy mass – are simply mutants with no particular explanation for their abilities.

3　Lauren Berlant, "National Brands, National Body: Imitation of Life" in *The Phantom Public Sphere*, ed. Bruce Robbins (Minneapolis: University of Minnesota Press, 1993), 176.

4　Lisa Nakamura, "Race in/for Cyberspace: Identity Tourism and Racial Passing on the Internet," in *The Cybercultures Reader*, ed. David Bell and Barbara M. Kennedy (New York: Routledge, 2000), 718. Lauren Berlant identifies this code crossing as "borrowing the corporeal logic of an other, or a fantasy of that logic, and adopting it like a prosthesis"; see Berlant, "National Brands," 200.

5　Alternately, cyberfeminist theorist Sadie Plant has argued that the electronic environment provides a pre-oedipal

space that reflects a "feminine subjectivity" of weaving and webs, destroying patriarchal control: "[A]t the peak of his triumph, the culmination of his machinic erections, man confronts the system he built for his own protection and finds it is female and dangerous"; see Plant, "On the Matrix: Cyberfeminist Simulations," in Bell and Kennedy, eds., *The Cybercultures Reader*, 335.

6　Hari Kunzu, quoted in Jeff Ow, "The Revenge of the Yellowfaced Cyborg: The Rape of Digital Geishas and the Colonization of Cyber-Coolies in 3D Realms' *Shadow Warrior*," in *Race and Cyberspace*, ed. Beth E. Kolko, Lisa Nakamura, and Gilbert B. Rodman (New York: Routledge, 2000), 52.

7　Shannon McRae, "Coming Apart at the Seams: Sex, Text, and the Virtual Body," in *Wired Women: Gender and New Realities in Cyberspace*, ed. Lynn Cherny and Elizabeth Reba Weise (Seattle: Seal Press, 1996), 262.

8　See Judith Butler, *Bodies That Matter: On the Discursive Limits of "Sex"* (New York: Routledge, 1993), and Judith Butler, *Gender Trouble: Feminism and the Subversion of Identity* (New York: Routledge, 1990).

9　The fact that such gestures may be performed by the "wrong" sex suggests that there is no "right" or "wrong" body for any given gender identity; moreover, that the argument for "nature" is actually a political one, the normalization of social control and its violence. Against what Butler calls a "metaphysics of substance," or the articulation of gender as a coherent essence located within the sexed body, gender is instead revealed as a historical affect of a regulatory heterosexual matrix – or in effect, a technology of the self revealed as prosthetic. It would be a mistake to conflate performativity (as a modality of power as discourse or expressivity) with performance (as a deliberate display) in characterizing acts of cross-identification.

10　Cynthia Fuchs, " 'Death is Irrelevant': Cyborgs, Reproduction, and the Future of Male Hysteria," in Gray, ed., *The Cyborg Handbook*, 283.

11　Melissa Scott, *Trouble and Her Friends* (New York: Tor Books, 1994). Thomas Foster makes a similar argument in his essay " 'Trapped by the Body?' Telepresence Technologies and Transgendered Performance in Feminist and Lesbian Rewritings of Cyberpunk Fiction," in Bell and Kennedy, eds., *The Cybercultures Reader*, 439–59.

12　Scott, *Trouble*, 33–4.

13　Ibid., 210.

14　Ibid., 128–9.

15　Sandy Stone, *The War of Desire and Technology at the Close of the Mechanical Age* (Cambridge, MA: MIT Press, 1995), 180.

16　Sandy Stone, "Will the Real Body Please Stand Up? Boundary Stories about Virtual Cultures," in Bell and Kennedy, eds., *The Cybercultures Reader*, 524.

17　Kate Bornstein and Caitlin Sullivan, *Nearly Roadkill: An Infobahn Erotic Adventure* (New York: High Risk Books, 1996).

18 Kate Bornstein, *My Gender Workbook* (New York: Routledge, 1998).

19 R. U. Sirius, quoted in Vivian Sobchack, "New Age Mutant Ninja Hackers: Reading Mondo 2000" in *Flame Wars: The Discourse of Cyberculture*, ed. Mark Dery (Durham, NC: Duke University Press, 1994), 27.

20 Their cyberspatial maneuverings and their constant travel in the "real world" to escape detection and capture echo the blurred impermanence – and its anarchic, nomadic possibilities – suggested by Sandy Stone: "[S]ome people are getting harder to track. Not by getting physically shifty, but by dissolving, by fragmenting – by being many persons in many places simultaneously, . . . by refusing to be one thing, by *choosing* to be many things"; see Stone, "Split Subjects, Not Atoms, or, How I Fell In Love With My Prosthesis," in Bell and Kennedy, eds., *The Cybercultures Reader*, 400.

21 Bornstein and Sullivan, *Nearly Roadkill*, 135.

22 Foster, "Trapped?" 452.

23 As Coco Fusco notes, the so-called digital revolution has "reorganized what used to be known as the Third World, making those territories into low-end markets and low-wage labor pools for multinational corporations" (Coco Fusco, "At Your Service: Latinas in the Global Information Network" (1998) online at <http://www.hkw.de/forum/foruml/doc/text/fusco-isea98.html>.

24 Bornstein and Sullivan, *Nearly Roadkill*, 74.

25 Ibid., 195.

26 In an incisive interrogation of cross-racial empathy, Sara Ahmed notes that "[blackness] become[s] a means through which [a woman] can know herself (as black), by providing what is lacking in her self. Passing for black is a technique of knowledge insofar as it remains tied to the narrativization of the white female subject's knowledge of herself through her sympathetic incorporation of others (by assuming an image of blackness, it becomes known as that which is lacking in the white self)"; see Ahmed, *Strange Encounters: Embodied Others in Post-Coloniality* (New York: Routledge, 2000), 133.

27 In describing digital space as nomadic and themselves as guerillas, their "adherence to modernist myths of extreme dislocation and refusal of 'home' ground" can replicate the "appropriation of the margins by the center in the name of a supposedly radical theoretical practice." Caren Kaplan, "The Politics of Location as Transnational Feminist Practice," in *Scattered Hegemonies: Postmodernity and Transnational Feminist Practices*, ed. Caren Kaplan and Inderpal Grewal (Minneapolis: University of Minnesota Press, 1994), 146.

28 In an earlier essay, I noted that "virtual harassers" to my Asian American feminist resources website made a point not only of willing my prosthetic body into view, but also of identifying themselves as white straight men. Accordingly, I noted that privilege is not necessarily disrupted by attention drawn to its particularity. I further noted, "The violence of normalization depends upon making natural uneven relations of power and the bodies to which authority accrues; but because fluidity is also a crucial component of gendered and racial hegemony, denaturalizing the social character or the morphological particularity of masculinist hegemony and its attendant racial order by no means guarantees collapse." See Mimi Nguyen, "From Paper to Pixels: Tales of An Asiatic Geek Girl," in *Technicolor: Race and Technology in Everyday Life*, ed. Thuy Linh-Tu and Alondra Nelson with Alicia Headlam Hines (New York: New York University Press, 2001).

29 To quote Kaplan in "The Politics of Location," "In a transnational world where cultural asymmetries and linkages continue to be mystified by economic and political interests at multiple levels, feminists need detailed, historicized maps of the circuits of power" (148).

30 On a broader scale, what has been located as the source of identity – whether the imagined rational self or some substance of gender, sexuality, or race – can be shown to be (also) effects of institutions, practices, and discourses.

Part VII

Mediating Technologies

One of the traditionally strong areas of research in American studies centers on questions of technology in cultural context. Classics like Leo Marx's *The Machine in the Garden*, Anthony F. C. Wallace's *Rockdale*, and Jeffrey Meikle's *Twentieth Century Limited* each worked to situate technological development as a relatively independent factor within cultural history, revealing important ways in which culture is materialized. More recent work opens up questions of the agency of technology in culture to explore technologies as particular sites where power and knowledge can be seen in their interlocking complexity. In this new work the agency of technology is not necessarily an effect of its mechanical workings. The representational effects of the materialization of culture are emphasized as much as the cultural assumptions that shape its formation. We call this analytic *mediating* technologies, not because this scholarship focuses on the media per se, but because new work in this area emphasizes the active mediations, the agentive connections that technologies construct in flows of culture. This work recognizes that technologies always mediate flows of culture, even as particular ways of doing and making are the products of cultural expectations, beliefs, and needs. Once technologies are conceptualized as nodes in cultural networks, as mediating flows of power and knowledge rather than merely objects or even systems to be understood in themselves, it becomes possible to see connections between cloth production and war, the racialization of modern subjects and the automobile, the deconstruction of a singular national identity and the rise of the neo-network era in television, among other previously surprising linkages. In none of these cases

does technology function in a linear or monocausal fashion. Machines might exert agency, but American Studies has rarely made room for simplistic technological determinism. Technologies are always embedded in other practices, always mediating subjectivities, representations, knowledge, and economic production.

Two seventeenth-century spinning wheels sit in a museum made of an old fort garrison. Why? Is this just an accident of collecting? A sloppy attempt to create some sort of resonating past for historical tourists, perhaps? Laurel Thatcher Ulrich refutes those charges with a careful article that details the links between spinning, Irish immigration and Anglo-Indian war. As she makes clear, "The story of cloth-making in colonial New England is a story about empire as well as rural economy, about Atlantic trade as well as household production, and about Irish migration as well as English expansion." The technologies of cloth-making mediated among flows of labor, wealth, and violence.

The impact of print culture on the American revolution is well established. But does that fact suggest something immutable about the agency of print in politics? No. As Michael Warner shows us, Puritan literature focused on interpretations of scripture and learned sermons. In this context, print culture functioned as a mediating technology of the self, devoted to the examination of the soul. Beneath that official literature, however, spread a counter-print culture of news, gossip, and business information that eschewed the soul for more worldly concerns. When John Adams wrote of the significance of print for spreading ideas of democracy, he was making a claim about the agency of print technology. But the meaning and function of print had changed tremendously from the period before. Like all other technologies, print is contingent, not purely autonomous in its agency. In the revolutionary era, print technology mediated the connections among business, the interest in the self, and the growing insistence on self-government in the colonies.

If mediating technologies focus our attention on the materialization of culture, few examples resonate the effects of that concatenation more powerfully than does the daguerreotype. As Alan Trachtenberg points out, the original power of this imaging technology was built on its physicality. These physical qualities were not a barrier blocking the more perfect realization of an image of the self. Instead they contributed to the conundrum of portraiture. The daguerrean objectification of a person's likeness captured the ephemerality of the soul in the materialization of its visage. In the process, it functioned as an "engine . . . a self-contained mechanical entity requiring no external power." The daguerreotype powered profound questions about identity, meaning, and life. In the process, it helped to "destabilize the idea of self and character which underlay American liberal individualism in the nineteenth century."

A focus on technologies traditionally results in a narrative of progress or development. Philip Deloria's juxtaposition of Indians and automobiles shows the power of mediating technologies to disrupt the narrative arcs that assume a certain "naturalness" associated with Indians and an equally problematic "progress" connected to automobiles. In Deloria's words, "the pairing of Indians and automobiles has continued to tweak non-Native anxieties about progress and its costs." From Geronimo's Cadillac to the Jeep Cherokee, from Natives using cars to forge pan-tribal associations to whites splurging on gas-guzzling SUVs, automotive technologies mediate discourses of race, progress, and autonomy.

Biomedical technology might seem to participate more simply in narratives of progress. After all, the Human Genome Project claims to help us understand who we are ontologically as humans. But genes do not create meaning in isolation. As Sarah Chinn reminds us, "Without culturally defined judgments of normal or ab/subnormal outcomes, genes cannot be labeled as normal or abnormal in any way but the most trivial aspect." Not only does the growing sophistication of DNA research interrupt our understanding of disease, it mediates our understanding of racial identities as well. What kind of difference does DNA evidence make in our understanding of difference? What does it mean that a branch of the Jefferson-Hemings family now proudly proclaims its mixed heritage after decades of passing as white?

Perhaps the most powerful mediating technology of the past five decades has been television. One of TV's most important cultural functions over that period has been the forging of a coherent national identity. Herman Gray argues that by virtue of its economic structure, television has always mediated differences in the construction of its audience. In the network era, this mediation resulted in a cohesive white, middle-class, heterosexual, domestic national identity. Gray gracefully details the demand for race- and class-specific televisual narratives that increased over time and produced a market for multiple networks catering to racially demarcated audiences. The neo-network era of television demonstrates "the failure of a liberal pluralist vision of a national imaginary achieved through the management of cultural difference."

Two Spinning Wheels in an Old Log House

Laurel Thatcher Ulrich

The two spinning wheels that sit in the garret of the William Damm Garrison in Dover, New Hampshire, have lost their story. They could be exchanged for similar pairs in dozens of period houses in New England and no one would know. It is their setting that gives them resonance. The old garrison is one of the treasures of northern New England. Built sometime before 1695 on a narrow point of land thrusting into New Hampshire's Great Bay, it is a rare example of a form of log construction once common to the area. Unlike the chinked cabins of later frontiers, it was made of massive timbers squared in a waterpowered sawmill until they lay one atop the other like quarried stone. Their weight attests not only to the size of the trees that once covered coastal New England but to the violence that accompanied English attempts to turn those trees into lumber, ships, and fortunes.

When Ellen Rounds discovered the garrison in 1887, it was a derelict outbuilding open to wasps and weather. She repaired its roof and sashes, patched its plaster, and over the next thirty years filled its three rooms and garret with eight hundred "precious mementoes of ye olden time." In 1915, she donated the house and its contents to a new museum endowed by Annie Woodman "for the promotion of Education and Science and Art and the increase and dissemination of general and especially historical knowledge." The trustees put the house on rollers and pulled it three miles to the center of town, siting it on a broad back lawn between two brick mansions provided in Woodman's will. To shelter it from weather and protect visitors from the jarring sight of its rough, unpainted facade, they encased it in a trellised gazebo connected to the other houses by a columned walkway that reached across the grass in a graceful semicircle. The garrison became the connecting link between the natural history exhibits and Indian relics in the first of the museum's buildings and the decorative arts galleries in the second.[1]

The columned walkway is gone, but the gazebo, lined with wire mesh to protect it from nesting pigeons, is freshly painted and inviting. Entering its trellised shade, visitors confront the weathered timbers of the old house and the historical pieties of the nineteenth century. Guns protrude from portholes on either side of the battened door. Inside, a glass case displays a bit of charcoal, an iron key, the piece of a hoe, an ox shoe, and the bolt from a lintel excavated from a house burned in a French and Abenaki attack of 1689. Nearby are gentler mementos of colonial life, a wooden bowl on a rough pine table, a clutter of trivets and iron pots, and, in a little room beyond the parlor, spinning wheels and a cradle. There are more wheels in the garret.

Ascending on treads worn almost to rungs, visitors emerge into the speckled light of an imagined age of homespun. Under the eaves are the two spinning wheels, one for flax and one for wool. Beside them is an old loom, partly rigged. A pile of weaver's reeds, or slays, sits on the breast of the loom. Three niddy-noddies, strange-looking implements once used for winding yarn into skeins, hang behind it. A framing post displays four hetchels, fierce-looking combs used for processing flax. In the sloping space beside them, a mane of brittle straw spills from the arm of a flax brake. On the opposite side of the garret, crammed in among farm tools, barrels, and an ancient rope bed, is a more obscure set of tools – a broken quill winder, a homemade skein winder, and the inner workings of a click reel.

The clutter of tools in the old garrison brings together two stories that at first glance seem separate, one about cloth-making, the other about war. New Hampshire colonists coexisted peacefully with their Indian neighbors during the first fifty years. But population growth in the Puritan colonies to the south, a disastrous betrayal at the end of King Philip's War, and almost constant conflict between England and France on the northern frontier changed things. Between 1689 and 1725, the fragile English enclaves in northern New England were under almost constant threat. Some English families fled the region. More resolute men, like William Damm, persisted. To stay put, to raise flax, to pasture sheep, and to establish sons and daughters on nearby farms were as essential to English victory as sending troops up the Cocheco River to Winnepesauki or over the mountains to Norridgewock.

The Algonkians whose land became New England buried material objects with their dead. Layering graves with woven mats and bark, they folded their loved ones into fetal position, arranging wampum, hoes, thimbles, tobacco pipes, glass bottles, baskets, and iron kettles at their heads and feet.[2] The English insisted on the poverty of the grave ("dust thou art, and to dust shalt thou return") while obsessively counting every spoon, sow, and plowshare left to the living. When William Damm died in 1718, inventory-takers appointed by a probate court moved through his house, yard, and barn, meticulously accounting for every possession, even the bed he died in and the last tools he touched, in pounds, shillings, and pence. The record they created tells us that toward the end of his life – and probably much earlier – he owned two "spinning wheels," a "Lining wheel," wool cards, a hetchel, and two looms.

The tools now in the house probably looked different from those Damm owned, but he would have understood their use. Textile equipment changed little from the late Middle Ages to the early nineteenth century. But the same tool used in much the same way can have different meanings in different settings. That is why the display in the garrison is so compelling. Ellen Rounds inadvertently connected Horace Bushnell's idealized age of homespun with the brutality and violence of colonial war. Murals painted about the time of Damm's death in the stairway of a grand house in Portsmouth, New Hampshire, the provincial capital, enlarge the connection by juxtaposing images of an Irish spinner, two Indian "kings," and an English monarch. The story of

cloth-making in colonial New England is a story about empire as well as rural economy, about Atlantic trade as well as household production, and about Irish migration as well as English expansion.

[. . .]

When John Damm arrived in Massachusetts in 1633, spinning wheels and looms were rare. When trade with England was disrupted in the 1640s by the English civil war, the Massachusetts General Court passed legislation encouraging colonists to sow flax and enlarge their small flocks of sheep, but it was commerce, not agriculture, that rescued them. As one writer explained, "when one hand was shut by way of supply from England, another was opened by way of traffic . . . to the West Indies . . . whereby among other goods much cotton-wool was brought into the country . . . which the inhabitants learned to spin." West Indian cotton remained part of household production throughout the colonial period.[3] For some Englishmen, the prevalence of cotton accentuated the marginality of New World production. One official dismissed the coarse druggets and serges made in New England, arguing that "these, as well as their homespun linen, which is generally half cotton, serve only for the use of the meanest sort of people."[4]

Probate records from Plymouth Colony show the gradual development of household production in southern New England. Before 1649, only 15 percent of estates listed spinning wheels. By 1660 that had risen to 40 percent as entries like "two Blanketts being homemade" began to appear alongside English textiles, some inventions even finding it necessary to distinguish "Inglish ticken" (English ticking). The reference in one man's inventory to "homade Cloth which the family hath needed to have worne before now had it bine Got Reddy" shows the difficulties of cloth-making in a still undeveloped economy. Some families solved the problem by pooling resources. Josiah Winslow of Marshfield owned just "the half of 23 yards and an halfe of homespun cloth at the Fullers." This reference to homespun cloth at the fullers is intriguing, since in English usage homespun was usually defined as a coarsely woven, *unmilled* fabric. In America, the words *homespun* and *homemade* were used interchangeably.[5]

[. . .]

The colonial official who asserted that only the "meanest sort of people" *wore* homespun may have been correct, but well-to-do families were just as likely to produce it. John Reyner, pastor of the Congregational Church in Dover, New Hampshire, and a graduate of Magdalen College, Cambridge, owned six spinning wheels at his death in 1669. His estate also included, in addition to imported fabrics, twenty pounds of yarn and thirty-one yards of "homemade cloth." Dover's ruling elder, a man with the fearsome name of Hatevil Nutter, was also well equipped with wheels, wool, and cotton. Such families not only had the raw materials but the labor necessary for cloth-making. In 1694, Richard Martyn, a wealthy merchant and member of the New Hampshire Council, bequeathed his wife "that web of cloth which is now Spining in the house & Hannah Harriss her time till said web be Spun." The servant wasn't spinning the cloth, of course, but the yarn to make it. Once that was done, Martyn could take it to a local weaver, a man like John Fabes of Portsmouth, whose own estate contained forty yards of "homspun cloth," six yards of "very course Carsy," and five yards of serge.[6]

William Damm's inventory suggests that he, too, was a weaver. When the inventory was taken in 1718, the "backroom" of his garrison contained "2 pr looms." A pair of looms, like a pair of scissors or a pair of pants, was one object rather than two, but the presence of *two* pairs is quite unusual. There is further evidence of cloth-making in the inventories of Damm's relatives.[7] When Martha Damm's father, James Nute, died in 1691, his inventory contained wheels, cards, thirty pounds of cotton wool, ninety-five pounds of yarn, and forty-six yards of cloth. Ninety-five pounds of yarn could have produced as much as two hundred yards of cloth, not much by English standards but a hefty supply for this time and place. The 1700 inventory of Martha's brother-in-law also contained wheels, yarn, wool, and unspun cotton. One can imagine a small industry here with production extending from one household to another, Nute and his sons-in-law paying for West Indian cotton with lumber cut and sawed on their own land, the women cleaning, carding, and spinning it, and William Damm or an apprentice making it into fabric.[8]

The importance of cloth-making to Damm's household is confirmed in a complaint filed by the oldest son, Pomfret, claiming that before the inventory was taken his siblings had "taken away & concealed . . . a great weeb of wolling Cloath and a great deall of sheps woll & flacks [flax]."[9] But if Damm was a weaver, he was also a farmer, lumberman, and miller. His inventory lists "neat cattle," oxen, sheep, swine, and horses, a "breaking plough," a "horse plough," a dung fork, a harrow,

scythes, sickles, saws, axes, chisels, wedges, gouges, a draw knife, a grinding stone, a cooper's adze, a gun, a carbine, and part-interest in two sawmills. This combination of implements was not unusual. Even in Damm's native Cheshire, rough cloth was often made by farmer-weavers.[10]

[. . .]

Although most Americans can recognize a spinning wheel when they see one, few understand how it works. A spinning wheel doesn't operate the way a coffee mill or a meat grinder might. That is, one doesn't feed wool or flax into one end and take yarn out the other. The basic operation takes place outside the machine between the spinner's thumb and fingers.

To demystify the process it helps to experiment with a bit of fiber. The wad of cotton from the top of a medicine bottle will do. Flatten it out, then tear a strip about an eighth of an inch wide. Gently pull on one end so that it grows longer and thinner. This step is called "drawing." As you draw, twist the tip of the extended fiber until it forms the beginning of a tiny thread. Spinning is nothing more than a continuous process of drawing and twisting. Keeping both things going at once is the difficult part. As Elizabeth Barber has observed, a spinner needs four hands – one to hold the fiber, another to draw it out, a third to twist it, and a fourth to hold on to the new thread, since letting it go while spinning allows it to "ball up in a snarl like an angry rubber band and then start coming apart." Because humans weren't made with four hands, somebody invented the spindle. A spindle is a weighted stick that can be spun like a top. Attaching a leader of yarn to the shaft, a spinner gave the spindle a quick turn, then dropped it, letting it twist the yarn as it fell. When the spindle stopped, she wound the newly spun yarn onto the shaft and started the process over again.[11]

A spinning wheel is a mechanical device for keeping a spindle in motion. Spinning on a large wheel like the one in the garrison was much like spinning with a drop spindle. The spindle was attached horizontally to the post, then connected by a single cord to the drive wheel. Using one hand to give the wheel an occasional turn, the spinner drew out her fiber with the other. As the thread lengthened, she stepped backward inch by inch until she had gone as far as her arm could reach. Then she reversed the action of the wheel, winding the yarn onto the spindle as she moved toward it. This back-and-forth motion explains why some people called the spindle wheel a "walking wheel." Wheels like this developed from those used in cotton manufacturing in Italy in the late Middle Ages, though in northern Europe and the British Isles they were adapted for spinning wool. Some spinners used a wooden peg called a "wheel finger" to turn the wheel, as the owner of the wheel in the garret must have done. Still visible is a worn spot where she hit the same spoke over and over again.[12] The wool wheel displayed on the main floor of the garrison has been fitted with an "accelerating head," a device invented in the early nineteenth century, but it is otherwise identical to those made in Europe since the Middle Ages.

With a spindle wheel as with a drop spindle, a worker had to pause frequently to wind her yarn. Bobbin-flyer wheels solved that problem. First used in the Italian silk industry, they traveled in the late fifteenth century to southern Germany where they were used in flax production. A spinner using a flax wheel like those in the garrison threaded a leader of yarn through the tip of a hollow bobbin and out onto one or more of the metal hooks attached to a U-shaped device called a flyer. As the bobbin turned, it automatically wound the newly spun yarn onto the shaft. By the early seventeenth century many flyer wheels also had foot treadles that allowed a spinner to sit as she worked, using both hands to draw. Some writers call these "Saxony wheels." The name does not appear in New England inventories.

Treadle wheels were so convenient that one wonders why they didn't replace walking wheels. The reason is that different fibers required different handling. Although wool for home production was spun much finer than the bulky yarn used today in craft-weaving, it was generally spun thicker than flax. More important, the long drawing out that was characteristic of the walking wheel helped compensate for the short fibers and natural curliness of wool. Conversely, fuzzy wool might clog a bobbin. Combed flax, on the other hand, was straight and stiff, individual filaments sometimes measuring more than fifteen inches. The flax was usually combed into a cone-shaped bundle supported by a distaff. The distaff arm on the wheel in the garrison is broken, though someone has fitted it with a distaff made from the branch of a chokecherry bush. An intact wheel now at the American Museum of Textile History shows how it may once have looked.[13]

The drive wheel on the wool wheel has slender spokes set into a rim bent by steaming. In contrast, the rim of the flax wheel is composed of four short planks joined together and turned on a lathe. Weight rather than size

gives it momentum. Its legs, posts, and spokes are also more decorative than those on the wool wheel. In England and the Continent, the turnings on flax wheels became so elaborate that one English writer dubbed them "Gentle Woman's Wheels," arguing that their busy posts and spindles were better adapted to "shew the Art of the Turner, then to add any goodness to the working."[14] The most expressive feature was usually the U-shaped frame that held the flyer. The horizontal section, called the "mother of all," supported two upright posts called "maidens" that ended in elaborate finials. Our flax wheel stops short of gentility, but it is more decorative than the wool wheel.

[. . .]

Some writers refer to spinning as unskilled work. They have obviously never tried it. A good spinning wheel helped, but a spinner's ability to draw evenly, maintain the right tension on the yarn, and control the speed of twisting was what really determined the quality of the finished product. Flax, hemp, cotton, worsted, and wool demanded different techniques, as did yarns destined for warping, weaving, knitting, lace-making, shoe-binding, or embroidery. Some fabrics required loose, almost hollow spinning, others smooth, tightly twisted thread. A fleece that had been scoured to remove the natural lanolin handled differently than one spun "in the grease." English sources tell us that kerseys were spun "thick by great spinning," while wool destined for jersey was "wasshed out of his oile and spun cleane."[15] Even the weather added complications. Too much humidity caused wool to frizz and axles to stick; too little produced static in the fiber and a wobbling wheel. The spindle wheel in the attic of the garrison, made with a wooden, rather than an iron, axle and without any device for adjusting tension, was probably especially vulnerable to changes in the weather. The word *homespun* is itself evidence that spinning was an important determinant of the quality of a fabric.

The other tools in the garrison remind us that spinning was one operation among many. Spun yarn had to be wound and measured into skeins, using a hand-cranked reel or a simple niddy-noddy. After winding, skeins were washed or dyed, then placed on an adjustable yarn-winder or "swift" from which they could be wound into balls for knitting, onto spools for warping, or onto the tiny bobbins called "quills" that were fitted into the weaver's shuttle. Weaving was the final process. A children's puzzle published in England around 1800 illustrates these steps. In one scene a woman spins wool on a walk-ing wheel while another uses a "quill wheel" and "swift" much like those in the garrison.

Some New England looms were built like the one in the puzzle, with cantilevered beams extending from a single set of uprights. More commonly they were constructed with two identical frames (hence the phrase "pair of looms") joined at the ends with crossbars. Although the loom in the garrison was made in the early nineteenth century, its construction is little different from looms made in Europe in the late Middle Ages. Built like a house with its joints mortised and pegged, it was designed to withstand the constant motion of the swinging bar used to beat in the weft. It was used at least some of the time for weaving linen. One can still see tiny ridges on the beater bar where the taut threads rubbed against the wood. The weaver warped such a loom by threading hundreds of warp threads or "ends" through a slotted frame called a "sley," then through heddles, finally winding them around a warp beam at the far end of the loom. Near the weaver's feet a second beam took up the finished cloth as it was woven. The width of the loom was determined by the reach of the weaver's arms. Throwing the shuttle through the raised warp with one hand, he caught it with the other, then pressed down the treadles to reverse the position of the threads. English broadlooms were constructed in much the same way but because they were twice as wide, they required two weavers.[16]

As D. C. Coleman has explained, the English woolen industry did not succeed through technical innovation – it "was one of the more technologically stagnant and conservative industries in European economic history" – but through a capacity to organize household labor. Because cloth-making involved so many steps, the work could be subdivided again and again "yet remain, in respect of its central processes, capable of being carried on in the home," or, more accurately, in hundreds of homes linked by the entrepreneurial energies of clothiers.[17] As commercial production expanded, sorting, carding, spinning, dyeing, and weaving not only took place in different workshops but in different parts of the country. Spinning was the most time-consuming task. Since it typically took eight to ten spinners to keep one weaver supplied with thread, jobbers sought workers wherever they could find them, in depressed agricultural areas, in the more mountainous parts of Ireland, and even in poorhouses and orphanages.[18]

[. . .]

In 1713, Massachusetts and New Hampshire officials traveled to Casco Bay near present-day Portland, Maine, to ratify "Articles of Pacification" signed by representatives of several Abenaki groups. Offering lawful subjection to Queen Anne, the Abenaki ostensibly promised colonists free liberty of hunting, fishing, and development in the "Eastern parts." At a conference held at Portsmouth in July 1714, officials from both colonies ratified the articles of peace with gifts of blankets, "fine white shirts," gunpowder, lead, rum, tobacco, and biscuits. Land speculators rejoiced. These new lands were opening at the very time Protestants in northern Ireland were struggling under burdens of taxation, uncertain land tenure, and falling prices.[19]

In Portsmouth, Archibald Macpheadris, an ambitious young merchant newly arrived from Ireland, would soon take advantage of these opportunities. In 1716, he married Sarah Wentworth, the teenage daughter of one of the key participants in the treaty conferences, and began to erect an impressive new house on Portsmouth harbor that was a radical contrast to Damm's log fortress and unlike anything New Hampshire had seen before. Hiring a builder fresh from London, he built in brick in the latest Palladian style. In a 1717 letter to Irish associates, he outlined a plan to send vessels to Cork, Belfast, Dublin, and Waterford to bring over "Servants & Good farmers" for the new plantations. The rivers had "more Salmon & all manner of fish than in any place in the World," he wrote, "& plenty of Good Middow & timber of all Sorts." A man who knew the business might cure a thousand tons of salmon in season, creating a good estate for himself in two years' time. Such a scheme would not only benefit New England; it would provide new sales for Irish linen.[20]

[. . .]

Two hundred families from northern Ireland arrived in Boston in 1718 and 1719. One group spent a miserable winter on Casco Bay before seeking grants on the Merrimack River in New Hampshire. They named their new town Londonderry for the Irish city where thirty years before Protestants had held back Catholic troops supporting James II. They, like Macpheadris, believed that Protestant courage in northern Ireland had assured a victory for William of Orange. Now Irish men would help secure a Protestant victory in North America. In his inaugural sermon, their pastor borrowed the words of the Old Testament prophet Ezekiel: "Moreover, I will make a covenant of peace with them; it shall be an everlasting covenant with them; and I will place them, and multiply them, and will set my sanctuary in the midst of them for evermore."[21]

Because the Penacook had withdrawn into the lake country of northern New Hampshire, Irish settlers at Londonderry thrived. Those in Maine did not. Irish migration had hardly begun when Indians living on the upper Saco complained to Samuel Jordan, the proprietor of the Massachusetts truck house, that the new colonists were using hanging nets or seines to catch "all sorts of fish," destroying their own catch. Men from Ulster did indeed know how to catch and cure salmon, but they were unprepared for Abenaki resistance.[22]

A tense conference at Georgetown in 1720 turned into a festival of incomprehension. The Abenaki complained about the establishment of a settlement called Cork on the east of the Kennebec River. The commissioners were outraged about "insults" offered the new planters. When the English tried to talk about procedure, asking if the Indian leaders were actually authorized to speak for their people, the Abenaki spokesman deflected the question: "We desire that the people may be removed from Merry Meeting," the bay on the Kennebec where the Irish had settled. "That's no answer," the commissioners retorted. Mugg held up a string of wampum and asked again that the settlers be removed. The commissioners weren't interested in his complaint; they wanted reparations for dead cattle and for threats made to peaceful colonists. They told the Abenaki leaders that if they couldn't govern their young men, the settlers would be forced to take their own satisfaction. If the Abenaki wanted back the four men the English had already taken, they must bring in two hundred skins within twenty-five days. The English had good title to these lands going back seventy years.[23]

The colonial negotiators concluded the conference with a threat. "If you will constrain us, by your repeat'd Insults, to any Violent proceedings, we have force Enough; & wil pursue you to your Headquarters (which we are well acquainted with, & can Easily take Possession of) & will not leave you till we have cut you off Root and Branch from the Face of the Earth." The language was biblical, the speech itself a direct allusion to the last chapter of Malachi in the Old Testament: "For behold, the day cometh, that shall burn as an oven; and all the proud, yea, and all that do wickedly, shall be stubble: and the day that cometh shall burn them up, saith the Lord of hosts, that it shall leave them neither root nor branch."[24]

In 1722, Massachusetts once again declared war, calling the Abenaki "Robbers, Traitors and Enemies to his Majesty King George." Two years later provincial troops pushed to the presumed headquarters of the Kennebec Indians at Norridgewock, where they burned buildings, killed the French priest, and slaughtered more than eighty people, a third of the village. The remaining inhabitants fled, bleeding, to the French mission at St. Francis where they gathered strength for new attacks. A Massachusetts commander lamented that though his troops had accomplished "such a slaughter of them at Norridgewock as has not been known in any of the late wars," the depredations continued.[25] It took almost forty years for the English to subdue the Abenaki. Not until the final victory over French Canada would Maine's river valleys be safe for settlement.

Northern New Hampshire, too, remained Abenaki territory, but on the lower Merrimack, the Irish flourished. For a time, they even imagined establishing a linen industry. In 1728, Londonderry's town fathers appointed a sealer of "weights, measures, leather and all sorts of Good sufficient linen Cloth." A resolution in the New Hampshire legislature in 1731 confirmed the necessity for such an office when it deplored the "deceit practiced by persons travelling in this Province by selling of Foreign Linnens under pretence they were made at Londonderry." Although production was never very large, the reputation for quality persisted for several decades.[26]

[. . .]

There is [. . .] a curious shift in nomenclature in New England probate inventories beginning about 1730. Earlier inventories differentiated spinning wheels by size or intended use. There were "large" and "small" wheels, "great" and "little" wheels, "wool" and "linen" (or more commonly "wooling" and "lining") wheels. Although eighteenth-century inventory-takers continued to use these terms, "Dutch wheel" gradually edged out "linen wheel" in western Connecticut and some parts of Massachusetts. In central Connecticut, the new term was "foot wheel." Coastal Massachusetts and New Hampshire inventories showed an occasional "Irish wheel." While this is too broad a change to attribute to a small group of settlers in a corner of New Hampshire, it suggests that treadle wheels may have become more common in the eighteenth century and that in areas bordering New York, people attributed the new design to the Dutch rather than the Irish. The difference between a Dutch wheel and an Irish wheel was probably primarily aesthetic. An Irishman traveling in Holland in the 1720s said that the spinning wheels he found there were "much after the same form with ours in Ireland, called Dutch Wheels, only they are made firmer and the rims heavier."[27]

[...]

It was probably Hayes who sometime in the middle of the eighteenth century enlarged the narrow windows in the old garrison and gave them double-hung sashes like those that survive today. He may also have improved the interior woodwork, though he seems not to have changed the basic plan. There is surprisingly little difference between his inventory, taken in 1777, and that taken at Damm's death sixty years before. In 1718, Damm owned twenty-three ewes and seventeen lambs; sixty years later, Hayes had fifteen sheep and twelve lambs. Both men owned unspun sheep's wool, a comb or "hatchell" for processing flax, two kinds of spinning wheels, and unfinished "webs" of cloth.[28] Yet in the half century between the two inventories, the nature of New England cloth-making had changed.[29] This change cannot be discerned in the fabric of Damm's house or in the design of the spinning wheels now in it. It is a broad change, visible all over New England and in some other parts of North America as well, in the relationship between spinning wheels and looms in household inventories.

In Essex County, Massachusetts, almost half of households had spinning wheels by 1700, but only 6 percent had looms. That is exactly what one would expect to find in an artisan production system where families spun their own yarn and had it woven by a skilled neighbor. But between 1700 and 1730 loom ownership tripled while wheel ownership stayed about the same. The same thing occurred a bit earlier in western Massachusetts. When Edward Taylor arrived in Hampshire County in 1671, barely 35 percent of inventories listed spinning wheels, and looms were so rare as to be virtually invisible. By the time he died in 1729, two-thirds of households had wheels and an astonishing 20 percent had looms. Samples of other probate districts show even higher ratios of looms to wheels. In East Greenwich, Rhode Island, and Woodbury, Connecticut, in the 1730s there was one household with a loom for every two households with wheels. The same thing occurred in New Hampshire by 1750. If this were the West of England or the linen precincts of Ulster, one would suspect that yarn was being gathered from miles around by merchant clothiers. But New England in this period had no markets in yarn, and its very few clothiers were fullers and dressers of finished cloth. In New England, a high ratio of looms to

wheels meant dispersed household production. Women had begun to weave.[30]

The account book of John Gould of Topsfield, Massachusetts, shows how this happened. Gould was a master weaver, the descendant of English artisans who came to Ipswich in 1640, but in the early eighteenth century he was unable to pass the craft on to his sons. His account book notes the employment of only two journeymen or apprentices between 1697 and 1724. Neither stayed long. Random entries suggest that his steadiest helper was his daughter Mary, who at the age of twelve wove a coverlet that took "a fortnight" to make. Later entries mention a daughter Phebe and two nieces. The wives and daughters of weavers had probably always done some work at the loom, but that practice accelerated in the early eighteenth century and then spread beyond artisan families.[31]

Scattered evidence of female weavers appears even in Manasseh Minor's diary. On January 5, 1718, he reported dryly, "bety ford Cam to weav." Whether she was working for him or only using his loom, we do not know. Farmers' and weavers' account books from other parts of New England have similar entries. In Providence, Rhode Island, two unmarried sisters, Tabitha and Joanna Inman, appear to have had a cooperative enterprise. One sister owned a wool wheel, the other a flax wheel and a loom. There are even references to female weavers among Christian Indians. When Josiah Cotton traveled through southern New England in 1726, he stayed at the Bridgewater home of Hannah James, a woman who used to attend his Indian church at "Mattakees." In Cotton's view one mark of James's civility was that her children could read. Another was that she lived in "a high House of the English Fashion" with "2 Looms in it."[32]

Because William Damm died just on the cusp of this change, it is tempting to think that the second weaver in his household may have been his daughter Leah, the only child still unmarried at his death. Leah continued to live in the garrison after her marriage to Samuel Hayes, but she was dead by 1754 when Hayes, and his second wife, Joanna Critchet, signed a contract with a Dover man for the services of his daughter. The girl was to serve faithfully for seven years. In return Hayes and his wife promised to "learn her [to] read, & to knit, & to weave if Capable & also other household work." That weaving was listed alongside "other household work" tells the story.[33] Cloth-making lost its artisan identity as it became a female occupation.

In New Hampshire weaving passed into the female domain in exactly the same period that the colony's woodworking economy was maturing. Between 1715 and 1768, shipments of pine boards from the port of Portsmouth increased from one million to twelve million board feet. Men clearing land for new townships rafted timber down the tributaries of the Piscataqua, supplying raw materials for a shipbuilding industry that by 1740 was the second or third largest in New England. Specialized woodworking trades also expanded. Portsmouth merchants were exporting house frames to Lisbon as early as 1715. In the 1720s, they added chairs to the cargoes of foodstuffs and lumber they sent to the West Indies. In 1752, a Portsmouth ship bound for Newfoundland carried eight desks carefully packed in cases. By 1768, Portsmouth stood just behind Boston as an exporter of household furniture. As farmers brought more land under cultivation, opportunities for craft work expanded. Barrel makers supplied casks for salted meat, cordwainers turned the hides that were a byproduct of the meat trade into shoes sold at market. Although some men continued to weave, especially in the Scots-Irish towns, there too weaving gradually slipped into the female domain as wood crafts became dominant. In Bedford, John Dunlap, son of a Scots-Irish weaver, became a skilled furniture maker. In Londonderry, Samuel Gregg came home from fighting the French to "learn to make foot wheels." In Newington, a man named William Damm, nephew of the builder of the garrison, became a skilled turner and chair maker.[34]

New Hampshire's story fits well into new scholarship in economic history. Historians are less disposed than they once were to describe a linear transformation from subsistence agriculture to market production. As economic historian Jan de Vries has observed, the expanding commerce of the eighteenth century affected different regions in different ways. In some parts of Europe, putting-out industries captured child and female labor, simultaneously creating new goods and new markets for those goods. In other parts of the Atlantic world, farmers and their sons concentrated on market production, while children and women produced less saleable commodities for family use. The end result was an "industrious revolution" that transformed the Western world.[35] The New England story is intriguing because it contrasts so markedly with Pennsylvania, where continuing immigration of artisan weavers from the British Isles and continental Europe kept weaving in the male domain into the nineteenth century. In the Chesapeake, however, women began to weave almost as early as in New England and for much the same reason. Weaving had little commercial value and was designed to supplement rather than replace foreign imports. In later chapters, we

will see what women did with their seemingly marginal occupation. Here it is enough to note that they took up weaving in the second quarter of the eighteenth century as an extension of household work.[36]

Perhaps someday the scholars who have taught us so much about the development of furniture trades in colonial New Hampshire will turn their attention to anonymous wheels like those in the garrison. No one knows who made them, but they do have a story. It begins with the transfer of textile technology from the continent to the British Isles in the sixteenth and seventeenth centuries and from Britain to America in successive waves of immigration. It is a story about conquest as well as settlement, about imperial objectives and Protestant vision, and about the distribution of work in colonial households. These old spinning wheels not only symbolize women's household labor but the shaping of male identity in market production.

[. . .]

Notes

1 *Dedication Ceremonies on July 26, 1916, The Annie E. Woodman Institute at Dover, New Hampshire* (Concord, NH: Rumford, 1916), 3–7, 15–19, 31–2.

2 Susan Gibson, "Introduction," and Christina B. Johannsen, "European Trade Goods and Wampanoag Culture in the Seventeenth Century," in *Burr's Hill: A Seventeenth-Century Wampanoag Burial Ground in Warren, Rhode Island*, ed. Susan Gibson (Providence: Haffenreffer Museum of Anthropology, Brown University, 1980), 22, 23, 27.

3 Rolla Milton Tryon, *Household Manufactures in the United States, 1640–1860* (1917; repr., New York: Augustus M. Kelley, 1966), 28–33, 44–6, 61–4; Eric Kerridge, *Textile Manufactures in Early Modern England* (Manchester, UK: Manchester University Press, 1985), 24, 75, 124–5; Florence M. Montgomery, *Textiles in America 1650–1870*, New York: Norton, 1984), 206.

4 E. B. O'Callaghan and B. Fernow, eds., *Documents Relative to the Colonial History of New York*, vol. 5 (Albany, NY: Weed Parsons and Company, 1855), 598, quoted in Tryon, *Household Manufactures*, 78.

5 Tryon, *Household Manufactures*, 25; William Harris Papers, *Collections of the Rhode Island Historical Society* 10 (Providence, 1902): 147; *Calendar of State Papers, Colonial Papers*, vol. 13 (London: Kraus Reprints, 1964), 255; Harris, 147; Public Record Office, Great Britain; *Calendar of State Papers, Colonial Papers* 13:255.

6 *New Hampshire Provincial and State Papers*, vol. 31 (Concord, NH: n.p., 1911), 376; New Hampshire Probate

Records, New Hampshire State Archives, Concord, New Hampshire, nos. 43, 32, 198, and books 1:122, 10:32; John Scales, *Colonial Era History of Dover, New Hampshire* (Dover, 1923; repr., Heritage, 1989), 314; Noyes, Libby, and Davis, *A Genealogical Dictionary*, 516, 427; Collections of the Dover Historical Society, vol. 1 (1894), 53, 79, 152, 153, 156, 160.

7   Hampshire County Probate Records, 5:87–8, Hampshire County Courthouse, Northampton, Massachusetts.

8   New Hampshire Probate Records, nos. 212, 220; Sybil Noyes, Charles Thornton Libby, and Walter Goodwin Davis, *A Genealogical Dictionary of Maine and New Hampshire* (Portland, Maine: Southworth-Anthoensen Press, 1928), 181, 403, 515.

9   William Damm Estate, New Hampshire Probate Records, no. 437.

10 Kerridge, *Textile Manufactures*, 176–7.

11 Elizabeth Wayland Barber, *Women's Work: The First 20,000 Years* (New York and London: Norton, 1994), 36–9, 90; Rachel Brown, *The Weaving, Spinning, and Dyeing Book*, 2d ed. (New York: Knopf, 1997), 225–8.

12 Brown, *Weaving*, 230–1; Maureen Fennell Mazzaoui, *The Italian Cotton Industry in the Later Middle Ages 1100–1600* (Cambridge: Cambridge University Press, 1981), 78–9; Peter Kriedte, *Peasants, Landlords and Merchant Capitalists: Europe and the World Economy, 1500–1800* (Cambridge: Cambridge University Press, 1983), 32–6; Charles Singer et al., *A History of Technology* (Oxford: Clarendon, 1956), 2:202–3; Kerridge, *Textile Manufactures*, 5–10.

13 Brown, *Weaving*, 232–3; Patricia Baines, *Linen: Hand-spinning and Weaving* (London: Batsford Ltd., 1989), 28–30, 37–50; Museum of American Textile History, Lowell, Massachusetts, 1959.1.152.

14 Bud Kronenberg, *Spinning Wheel Building and Restoration* (New York: Van Nostrand Reinhold, 1981), 25–8; Randle Holme, *Academy of Armory, 1688* (Menston, England: Scholar, 1972), 3:286.

15 Kerridge, *Textile Manufactures*, 5, 14–24; Baines, *Linen*, 50–9, 109. For a typical reference to spinning as unskilled work, see Jan de Vries and Ad van der Woude, *The First Modern Economy* (Cambridge: Cambridge University Press, 1997), 597.

16 Kerridge, *Textile Manufactures*, 172.

17 D. C. Coleman, "Textile Growth," in N. B. Harte and K. G. Ponting, *Textile History and Economic History* (Manchester: Manchester University Press, 1973), 1–10. Also see Peter Kriedte, Hans Medick, Jurgen Schlumbohm, *Industrialization before Industrialization: Rural Industry in the Genesis of Capitalism*, trans. Beate Schempp (Cambridge and New York: Cambridge University Press, 1981), and Maxine Berg, *The Age of Manufactures: Industry, Innovation, and Work in Britain, 1700–1820* (Oxford, UK: Blackwell, 1985).

18 Kerridge, *Textile Manufactures*, 158–61, 194–6, 201–3; G. E. Fussell and K. R. Fussell, *The English Countrywoman:*

A Farmhouse Social History, A.D. 1500–1900 (New York: Blom, 1971), 45; Herbert Heaton, *The Yorkshire Woollen and Worsted Industries* (Oxford: Clarendon, 1965), 334–8, 345; G. D. Ramsay, *The Wiltshire Woollen Industry in the Sixteenth and Seventeenth Centuries* (New York: Kelley, 1943; repr., 1965), 12–15, 90–9; Jane Gray, "Gender and Uneven Working-Class Formation in the Irish Linen Industry," in *Gender and Class in Modern Europe*, ed. Laura L. Frader and Sonya O. Rose (Ithaca, NY, and London: Cornell University Press, 1996), 36–46.

19 New Hampshire Provincial Papers, vol. 3 (Manchester, 1869), 542–6; Nicholas Canny, *Kingdom and Colony: Ireland in the Atlantic World 1560–1800* (Baltimore and London: Johns Hopkins University Press, 1988), 129–30; Minutes of "A Meeting with the Delegates of the Eastern Indians," in Colonial Papers, Massachusetts State Archives, Boston, microfilm, roll 29:36–52.

20 Alexander Macpheadris Papers, Portsmouth Atheneum, Portsmouth, New Hampshire.

21 Canny, *Kingdom and Colony*, 105; Edward L. Parker, *The History of Londonderry* (1851; repr., Londonderry, NH: Town of Londonderry, 1974), 1–29.

22 Bunny McBride and Harald E. L. Prins, "Walking the Medicine Line: Molly Ockett, a Pigwacket Doctor," in *Northeastern Indian Lives 1632–1816*, ed. Robert S. Grumet (Amherst: University of Massachusetts Press, 1996), 321–6, 345 n. 8.

23 "Council of Kennebeck Indians," Georgetown, 25 Nov. 1720, microfilm, Massachusetts Archives 29:68–74.

24 Malachi 4:1.

25 Colin G. Calloway, *The Western Abenaki of Vermont, 1600–1800* (Norman and London: University of Oklahoma Press, 1990), 123.

26 Martha Coons and Katherine Koob, *All Sorts of Good Sufficient Cloth: Linen-Making in New England 1640–1860* (North Andover, Mass.: Merrimack Valley Textile Museum, 1980),12–18.

27 John Horner, *The Linen Trade of Europe during the Spinning-Wheel Period* (Belfast: M'Caw, Stevenson & Orr, 1920), 17–18; G. B. Thompson, *Spinning Wheels* (Belfast: Ulster Folk Museum, 1966), 19–20, 31.

28 Strafford County Probate Records, Strafford County Courthouse, Dover, New Hampshire, 1:249–53.

29 On Londonderry wheels, see Coons and Koob, *Good Sufficient Cloth*, 51; Caleb Stark, *The History of the Town of Dunbarton, Merrimack County, New Hampshire* (1860), 248; Samuel Gregg, *Autobiography of Major Samuel Gregg* (n.p. 1806), photocopy, Textile Department, Museum of American Textile History, Lowell, Massachusetts.

30 Laurel Thatcher Ulrich, "Wheels, Looms, and the Gender Division of Labor in Eighteenth-Century New England," *William & Mary Quarterly*, 3d ser. 55 (1998): 3–38.

31 Benno M. Forman, "The Account Book of John Gould, Weaver, of Topsfield, Massachusetts, 1697-1724," *Essex Institute Historical Collections* 105 (1969): 36, 39; John

Gould Account Books, 1697–1724, Essex Institute, Salem, Massachusetts, 91, 93.

32 *The Diary of Manasseh Minor*, ed. Frank Denison Miner (n.p., 1915), 144; *The Early Records of the Town of Providence* (Providence: 1894, 1901), 7:130–5, 16:236–42; Josiah Cotton, "Some Inquiries Made among ye. Indians in the General Visitation begun Septr. 4: 1726," Curwen Papers, American Antiquarian Society, Worcester, Massachusetts; Daniel R. Mandell, *Behind the Frontier: Indians in Eighteenth-Century Eastern Massachusetts* (Lincoln: University of Nebraska Press, 1996), 200.

33 Katharine F. Richmond, *John Hayes of Dover, New Hampshire* (Tyngsboro, Mass., 1936), 1:46; *Collections of the Dover, N.H., Historical Society* (Dover, NH: Scales and Quimby, 1894), 1:16, 39; New Hampshire Probate Records, 18:492–3.

34 Gloria L. Main, "Gender, Work, and Wages in Colonial New England," *William and Mary Quarterly*, 3d ser., 51 (1994): 62–3, 65; Daniel Vickers, *Farmers and Fishermen: Two Centuries of Work in Essex County, Massachusetts, 1630–1830* (Chapel Hill: University of North Carolina Press, 1994); James Garvin, "That Little World, Portsmouth," in *Portsmouth Furniture: Masterworks from the New Hampshire Seacoast*, ed. Brock Jobe (Boston: Society for the Preservation of New England Antiquities, 1993), 15–21; Brock Jobe, "Furniture Making in Eighteenth-Century

Portsmouth," in *Portsmouth Furniture*, ed. Jobe, 43, 46–9, 55, 285–91; Charles S. Parsons, *The Dunlaps and Their Furniture* (Manchester, NH: Currier Gallery of Art, 1970) 1–8; Gregg, *Autobiography*, 8.

35 Jan de Vries, "Between Purchasing Power and the World of Goods: Understanding the Household Economy in Early Modern Europe," in *Consumption and the World of Goods*, ed. John Brewer and Roy Porter (London and New York: Routledge, 1993), 107, 108; Main, "Gender, Work, and Wages," 62–5; Vickers, *Farmers and Fishermen*, 247–59. On the gender division of labor, see Merry Wiesner-Hanks, " 'A Learned Task and Given to Men Alone': The Gendering of Tasks in Early Modern German Cities," *Journal of Medieval and Renaissance Studies* 25 (1995): 89–106; and Judith M. Bennett, "Medieval Women, Modern Women: Across the Great Divide," in *Feminists Revision History*, ed. Ann-Louise Shapiro (New Brunswick, NJ: Rutgers Univ. Press, 1994), 58–9.

36 Adrienne D. Hood, "The Gender Division of Labor in the Production of Textiles in Eighteenth-Century Rural Pennsylvania (Rethinking the New England Model):" *Journal of Social History* 27 (1994): 537–60, and "The Material World of Cloth: Production and Use in Eighteenth-Century Rural Pennsylvania," *William & Mary Quarterly*, 53 (1996): 43–67; and personal communication from Jean Elliott Russo.

The Cultural Mediation of the Print Medium

Michael Warner

In 1765, in the early stages of an imperial crisis and of his career as a lawyer, John Adams wrote a brief retrospect of the political and legal history of the West. Appearing unsigned and untitled in four installments in the *Boston Gazette*, the essay depicts the history of power as a history of knowledge. It tells modern history as a story of human self-determination rising through reflection. Much of the power of such a narrative for Adams, as later for D'Alembert and other Enlightenment intellectuals, was that it offered him a political self-understanding. But Adams' history offers a more particular self-understanding in two main respects: its history of self-determination yields a protonationalist consciousness of America; its history of reflection takes the form of a history of letters. Writing at the very moment when America was emerging as a symbolic entity, Adams perfects a story of America's history. It is a history of literature, and its telos is emancipation.[1]

This is how it works. According to Adams, the papal and feudal political systems of Europe rested in the last analysis on what might be called a hegemony of letters: "All these opinions, they [the clergy and the feudal lords] were enabled to spread and rivet among the people, by reducing their minds to a state of sordid ignorance and staring timidity; and by infusing into them a *religious* horror of letters and knowledge" (1:112). Because the entire political system of feudal Europe depends on such a relation of populace and letters, a history of letters can be a history of emancipation. For the same reason, the emancipation for which the world has longed can be realized in America. "From the time of the reformation, to the first settlement of *America*," Adams writes,

"knowledge gradually spread in Europe, but especially in *England*; and in proportion as *that* increased and spread among the people, *ecclesiastical* and *civil* tyranny, which I use as synonimous expressions, for the *cannon* and *feudal* laws, seem to have lost their strength and weight. The people grew more and more sensible of the wrong that was done them, by these systems; more and more impatient under it; and determined at all hazards to rid themselves of it . . . IT was this great struggle, that peopled America" (1:113). The puritan colonists emerge as the heroes in a political history of enlightenment.

Adams is aware that the civic humanist terms of such a history conflict with the terms of American Protestantism's self-understanding. Yet he presses his point by arguing that the reason for the Puritans' emigration "was not religion *alone*, as is commonly supposed." Rather, he claims, it was that they "had become intelligent in general, and many of them learned"; "to many of them, the historians, orators, poets and philosophers of *Greece* and *Rome* were quite familiar: and some of them have left libraries that are still in being, consisting chiefly of volumes, in which the wisdom of the most enlightened ages and nations is deposited" (1:113–114). We are perhaps unaccustomed to seeing the Puritans described as republican classicists in this way. And the history of racial and sectarian conflict in New England has taught us to be skeptical of Adams' claim that they committed "no other crime than their knowledge, and their freedom of enquiry and examination" (1:114). But the story is a powerful one. Treating enlightenment republicanism as the latent meaning of Puritan history, and employing terms that are simultaneously world-historical and national,

Adams' revisionist history became a pillar of American nationalism, and has remained so to the present.

[...]

Between Puritanism and Adams' history of Puritanism, the cultural meaning of letters has begun to change, as has their relation to power. No longer a technology of privacy underwritten by divine authority, letters have become a technology of publicity whose meaning in the last analysis is civic and emancipatory. It will be recalled that the struggles leading to the colonial revolution were largely undertaken by writers. At the same time that colonists were engaging in violent crowd actions, organized law-breaking, and boycotts, they also engineered a newspaper and pamphlet war in a way that was arguably more integral to the American resistance than to any other revolution. Those who organized the revolutionary struggle and were placed in power by it were men of letters. Their paper war articulated and helped to mobilize an intercolonial and protonational public – a public that remained a public of readers. And it was through the texts of that paper war that the democratic revolution in the colonies had such far-reaching impact both on the continent and in the New World. The transformation of letters that lies behind Adams' history was no mean affair.[2]

For Adams too the republican destiny of letters takes on a national importance in the context of a global revolution. And indeed, the rising sense in the colonies of letters' importance had important transatlantic parallels. After 1695 printers had rapidly moved out into English towns such as Manchester, Birmingham, Liverpool, Bristol, and Canterbury. Just at the moment when colonists were setting up shop and establishing weekly newspapers, their counterparts in the English provinces were doing the same, and London printers were beginning to produce dailies. The appearance of the press in places like Annapolis, New York, and Charleston, therefore, figures in narratives that involve the British empire as well as Europe and its empires. The growth of the trade, for one thing, was clearly supported by the financial revolution of the 1690s, with its new methods of capitalization. And the new forms of print discourse sutured emergent forms of political and social organization. Printers were simultaneously products of the transformation of the West and agents in the creation of the West's self-identification, producing the universalizing discourses of the Enlightenment and of the democratic revolutions. American colonists such as Adams made major contributions to those discourses, so the historical horizon of modernity must be made visible in any account of the printing activities of the North American English creoles.[3]

What, then, was the relation between republican enlightenment and printing? Adams implicitly poses the question by arguing that they are identical. In this sense his history is also a theory of print: insofar as his narrative has a plot, the unity and progress of that plot stem from the nature of print. For while he argues that learning and the press bring about changes in the political world, Adams assumes that printing's purposes, uses, and meaning do not themselves undergo change. The press is a powerful instrument for enlightenment precisely because its nature is *not* contingent. If it were variable in its nature, it might in some circumstances support despotism rather than liberty, and the history of enlightenment would lack a propulsive logic. It would have been hard, for example, for Adams to argue for the democratically enlightening character of print and yet account for the ancient use of printing among the Chinese and the Uighur Turks – who represent, for eighteenth-century thinkers such as himself, the very types of Oriental despotism.

In order to pose our question with regard to Adams' rhetoric – to ask, in other words, what was the relation between printing and the Enlightenment, or between printing and republicanism – we have to assume that the purposes, uses, and meaning of print do change. The rhetoric of Adams' history would thus be seen as a part of a transformation in the character of print, though his history presupposes the contrary. The establishment of newspapers, the rise of empiricism, capitalism, the Enlightenment, the novel, the democratic revolutions, the rise of a bureaucratic state – all these bear important relations to print; but they might entail transformations *of* print, not just social changes affected by a medium with its own unchanging logic.

[...]

New England

Printers and readers were more numerous in New England than elsewhere. But, as Kenneth Lockridge has argued, high literacy in early New England did not result in the modernizing orientation toward letters. Printing seems to have been put to conservative uses.[4] Certainly the special tradition of Puritan culture conferred its own features on print and writing. Books that were read in the devotional tradition had a strong public value in the New England towns, where in fact it was not uncommon for committees to inspect each home to make sure that it had a Bible.[5]

The reading of these works was a technology of the self. Cotton Mather, for example, records in his diary the uses of the German pietists' writings: "I would endeavour as in Reading their Books, I find the Passages of a raised and noble Piety occurring, to pant and strive after a lively Impression thereof, on my own Mind. And in this Way I would seek a particular praeparation for Services which I may do, in the coming on of the Kingdom of God."[6] The ideal that Mather articulates here contains a norm for subjectivity: reading, ideally, is a way of internalizing that is simultaneously a feature of literacy and a feature of the sacred order. He takes it as a moral imperative for himself but also for the community: "In visits to credible Families, I will bespeak little Studies and Bookshelves for the little Sons that are capable of conversing with such things; and begin to furnish their Libraries and perswade them to the Religion of the Closet."[7]

The religion of the closet prescribes not only that books will be useful, but that their utility will lie in a practice of internalization. In the official text of the Massachusetts laws the colony's citizens were reminded, "When Laws may be read in men's lives, they appear more beautiful than in the fairest Print, and promise a longer duration, than engraven in Marble."[8] On the basis of the same perception, one minister could write, "The life of *Reading*, is in the *performance* of our duty in what we learn. *Words* are but *empty sounds*, except we draw them forth in our *lives*. *Printed Books* will do *little good*, except Gods Spirit print them in our hearts."[9] Implicit here are assumptions about printing technology that differ radically from those underlying John Adams' history of enlightenment. Sacred internalization renders the nature of print in such a way that the publication of broadsides or newspapers could only be seen as inferior uses accidental to the godly effort to "print" the divinely ordained laws "in our hearts." In this case we do not see individuals emancipated by print; instead, it is the individual who is printed from an authoritative stamp.

In the diary entry just quoted, Mather used the same figure to connect the nature of print with its normative effects: he speaks punningly of the "Impression" that reading should make on his mind. I want to make a strong claim about this metaphor as an indicator of the meaning of print in Puritan culture. At the very least, the idea of an authoritative stamp – as opposed to far-flung

distribution, let us say – is the standard metaphoric use that Puritan rhetoric makes of printing. Such metaphors cannot be sharply distinguished from the objective facts of printing, for there are any number of ways in which printing might be distinguished from other technologies, and to describe it as a definitive impression has as much validity as any. The rhetoric of impression names the literal and defining features of the print medium in a way that already defines the social value of print. Here the emphasis is on the perfect reception by the copy of a master original. Puritan typography and Puritan typology, in other words, could be mutually reinforcing. Insofar as print is construed, valued, and used according to the perception of a relation between type and antitype – a relation that obtains both between copy and original as well as between text and animated reading – it expresses the character of authority. Constituted in the context of this symbolic logic, print seems eminently suited to the devotional text. One would not construe the distinctive features of the medium in the same way if the object were a shipping report.

Perceiving a relation between private reading and the religion of the closet, Mather became a tireless promoter not only of his own innumerable screeds, but of devotional literature of all kinds. "There is an old *Hawker*," he once wrote in his diary, "who will fill this Countrey with devout and useful Books, if I will direct him; I will therefore direct Him, and assist him, as far as I can, in doing so."[10] With such help, the Boston and Cambridge presses produced a moderate but steady stream of cheap broadsides, devotional steady sellers, execution accounts, sensational reports, and almanacs – all of which combined in various degrees the rhetorical pleasures of leisure reading with the disciplinary discourse of sacred exegesis.

The Massachusetts presses also produced a different kind of trade, often in conjunction with the European Protestant market: learned theological works produced and mainly consumed by the ministerial class. Such works differ from the popular trade not only in their subject matter or in their typically higher price, but in their mode of consumption. These are the works that were accumulated to form the libraries essential to the status and collective identity of the clergy. Learned lawyers and other nonclerical men of letters were rare in New England until James Otis' generation, and the popular, cheap literature consisted almost entirely of ephemera or a relatively small number of steady sellers. The New England library as a substantial collection, therefore, was clerical, and ministers well understood the relation between bibliotechnical capital and professional authority. Mather, for one, was seldom so happy as when he was able to purchase the library of a deceased fellow minister. Edward Taylor, unable to buy many books because of their expense and his remote residence, laboriously copied a library of books which he carefully bound.[11] The discourse that comprises the theological works of the clerical library is highly self-referential, and the books appear to have been read in an intensive and cross-indexical manner – digested for sermons, cited for authority, attacked in polemic. The theological literature exhibits the discursive mode of the library, which can itself be understood as a metonym for the corporate clerisy.

It has often been claimed that New England was an oral society.[12] In an important sense this is true, though not in the way that is usually meant. The conventional distinction between oral and literate societies, in which oral means *preliterate* and innocent of the exploitation that comes through writing, I would reject as sentimental and ideological.[13] It conceals norms not only about language, but about personhood and social relations. New Englanders, far from being ignorant of letters, used them with an intensity equalled by very few other cultures in the world at the time. Yet in an important ideological way it was an oral society. New Englanders accorded a disciplinary privilege to speech and in most contexts insisted on seeing writing as a form of speaking. A case in point is the response of Obadiah Gill and his collaborators to Robert Calef's skeptical treatise on the witch trials:

Is there any among the Children of men, that have Sold themselves to serve the Interest of Satan to purpose? Let it be their Study by their *Slanders* to Blast the Reputation of those, in whom the Honour of God, and of His Religion, and the Salvation of Souls is much concerned. This we take to be the Grand Aim and End of all that Robert Calef can call his own, throughout his whole *Treatise*. And now, vent thy malice; speak what thou hast to Accuse them of; they shall come off with flying Colours.[14]

Gill here demonstrates a desire to consider his writing not only as speech, but as speech in a setting of exemplary and disciplinary personal presence. He wants to imagine the exchange of pamphlets as an unmediated relation between persons, in which the godliness invested in himself and the ministers will dictate the outcome. Hence the command to Calef – "speak what thou hast" – which creates a fictive scenario of speech in order rhetorically to cancel any sense of practical liberty that the print medium might occasion. The same vocative

scenario can be seen governing Cotton Mather's practice to the end of his career – notably in the smallpox inoculation controversy, where he emphatically represents his opponents as assaulting his person. He once remarked that his sermons would be more powerful if "Preached a Second Time in the way of the Press."[15] And although he tells us that he gave away his books by the score, he also notes that when giving a book away he liked to instruct the recipient: "Remember, that I am speaking to you, all the while you have this Book before you!"[16]

This disciplinary fiction was part of the trade politics of print. Calef, after all, had been forced to send to England to have his attack on Mather printed, and a similar piece by Thomas Brattle evidently circulated only in manuscript. A group of disgruntled ministers in Boston charged in 1700 that the printer Bartholomew Green was so "in aw of the Reverend Author" – Increase Mather, Cotton's father – as not to print anything hostile to him.[17] Whether the accusation is entirely true or not, such struggles over personality and access to print demonstrate that an ethic of personal presence serves as the ground of print. Mather's defenders say of the charge that "It was highly rejoycing to us, when we heard that our *Book-sellers* were so well acquainted with the Integrity of our Pastors, as not one of them would admit any of those *Libels* to be vended in their shops."[18] The critical ministers and the Mathers agree in seeing the printing of a work as an act in a relation between specific persons, and the possibility that print might function as a public mediation is not even entertained.

In 1722, as a new set of print practices was only just emerging, the Reverend Thomas Symmes published a sermon which included a preface that comments extensively on the scene of print in New England society. The chief advantage of the "Art of Printing," he explains, is that by its means, "as many of the eminent Servants of God *being dead, yet speak unto us*; so many other worthy Persons, and especially . . . the Ministers of the Gospel are still blest with Opportunities of rendring their Usefulness more *extensive* and *durable*."[19] The attributes of extension and durability are the classically distinctive features of writing, and print's superiority to script is seen as lying mainly in its greater extension. Extension and durability determine print as a derivative of speech that introduces to the immediacy of speech the dimensions of space and time. In other forms of print discourse, writing's dimensions of space and time appear as exoticism and antiquarianism; here Symmes's terms for those dimensions – extension and durability – bear connotations less of curiosity than of ministerial power.[20]

Symmes encourages his fellow clergy to make more use of print. In a revealing moment he explains that the reason they do not is that they hope to "escape the scourge of the tongue." If the scourge of the oral is the restraint on the press, it is also the validation of the press. Symmes argues that no one need fear superfluous or bad publications, for such works "we are under no obligation in the World to patronize, admit under our roof, or touch with one of our Fingers."[21] Space and time, in the Puritan ideology, do not sever print from the speaking body and its fingers – they bring it inexorably under a metonymic discipline. Because New England culture structured print in this way, print discourse had not become the basis for the community's self-representation – as it would be for John Adams and his contemporaries – except in its covert identification with the community of white males.

The typological and ministerial virtues of print were only one symbolic context for understanding print. I have already indicated that the world of seaport commerce gave printing a set of features that could hardly be incorporated with those picked out by Symmes, Mather, and their fellow clergy. And since the way print was construed always had consequences for imagining society and its norms, there were stakes of power in these symbolic differences. The New England printing trade and its cultural settings were anything but monolithic; the trade, for example, displayed a much greater specialization than in the Southern colonies. As early as 1700 a book-buyer in Boston would have had a choice among nineteen booksellers and seven printers. Unlike Virginia, where book owning remained a sign of wealth and distinction, New England had some kind of printed artifact for almost all white families. As David Hall points out, in the same period in which the *Virginia Almanac* was printed in press runs of 5,000 copies (and even this figure is much larger than that of the average press run), New Englanders were buying 60,000 copies of a single almanac and supporting several others.[22]

We like to associate print with general distribution, but the same popular press that put almanacs in the hands of so many New England farmers was also decentralized and heterogeneous. Widely circulated titles were published by means of loose agreements among a number of printers and booksellers, none of whom alone would have had the kind of commercial network of transportation and marketing that is taken for granted by our more modern notion of a publisher. Because almanacs were produced on a schedule, and because their audience included many people who would not have bought any other book, they represent the peak of the book trade's organization. Uniformity was not at a high premium for other kinds of books. Some of the most widely dispersed titles, for example, were what Hall calls "steady sellers" – books usually of a devotional character that remained in print year after year and can be found in households of very little wealth. But these texts have little stability from edition to edition, since each printing was worked up cheaply by a small-time printer trying to reach a local market and would vary depending on what sources the printer had on hand and what tastes in his customers he anticipated.

The localism of the decentralized book trade meant that many texts circulated in a more or less "popular" fashion, meaning that the book market was capable of articulating a counterpublic print discourse in broadsides and cheap pamphlets. Those in position to represent the order of colonial society – especially ministers – occasionally expressed some anxiety about this counterpublic potential. Cotton Mather wrote in his diary in 1713 that "the Minds and Manners of many People about the Countrey are much corrupted, by foolish Songs and Ballads, which the Hawkers and Peddlars carry into all parts of the Countrey."[23] Unfortunately, we know relatively little about this literature – how much of it there was, what all of it was like, who made it, and how it was perceived and read by those who bought it. The counterpublic literature of broadside ballads, devotional books, and sensational pamphlets never articulated a public threat, depending as it did on an invisible worthlessness for its very existence. Not only did it have to be cheap in order to be hawked in the countryside, but in order to be counterpublic (and thus "corrupting"), it had to be "foolish," that is, without status and without public reference. Yet it was precisely this extraneous relation to claims of public value that Mather found disturbing. Accordingly he spent a considerable part of his writing and publishing career in an effort to match the public discourse of theodicy with the reading tastes of the sensational literature, striving for a seamless representation of the world in printed discourse.

An illustration of just how little status and authority many books had can be found in an anonymous broadside poem of 1731 – a cheap popular artifact, which describes the cheapness of popular artifacts. Titled "Father Abbey's Will," the doggerel broadside lists the possessions that are supposed to have been bequeathed by Matthew Abdy, an aged sweeper and bedmaker employed by Harvard, to his wife. Included are:

A ragged Mat
A Tub of Fat
A Book put out by Bunyan,
Another Book
By Robin Rook,
A Skain or two of Spunyarn.[24]

Here Abdy is an object of comic condescension for his poverty, yet his possession of two books is regarded as not incongruous. A literature without prestige was easily imaginable.

A different kind of cultural authority is visible in this broadside, as well as in the many surviving wills that follow its pattern for listing books. Virtually any New Englander who possessed devotional books such as *Pilgrim's Progress* would also have owned some cheaper kinds of print, such as the ever-present almanacs or broadsides like "Father Abbey's Will." These cheaper artifacts are not mentioned in wills. Their owners almost never went to the expense of having them bound for preservation, as they did for other kinds of works in an age when books were typically purchased in sheets. We consider the cheap artifacts ephemera because they were not considered by New Englanders to be eligible components in the construction of the archive of cultural tradition, any more than they have been considered eligible for the normative archive constructed by literary history.

One of the most important features of the colonists' relation to letters was the ability of certain printed objects to count as wealth. And the close relation between the economic wealth of books and their "cultural" wealth is evident in the ambiguity of the word "heritage." Inheritability was an ambiguous value in books in that it defined cultural tradition and capital at the same time, and was accordingly determined as much by allusion as by bindings and wills. It was and is also a paradoxical value since, in order to count as cultural wealth for the individual, a book must predicate the death of the individual. It is not valued either for its practical use – as, say, a farmer's manual would be for a farmer – or for its exchange, but for the possibility of its surviving the owner. Because of that possibility, because a book owner negates his own life in valuing a book, owning a book symbolically represents a degree of self-consciousness and independence. In the colonies this was markedly less true of manuals, almanacs, newspapers, pamphlets, and broadsides than it was of books in religion, history, and biography. One reason for the difference is that these categories of discourse were able to count as wealth insofar as they were able to thematize the death of the individual.

For New Englanders inheritability was most clearly determined by the sacred reference of a devotional literature, although in the Northern as in the Southern colonies a historical literature had the same potential. Works in the sanctioned discourses of theology and history were by no means all that the colonial presses produced; they are what have survived. Their potential for survival was both a condition of their discourse, which attained self-referentiality by presupposing the death of the individual, and of their material value for the owners whose independence was won by a self-negating investment. Perhaps for the same reason, most of the cheap broadsides that have survived, by far, are funeral elegies. In the main, however, the counterpublic literature of foolish songs and sensational accounts achieved its independence from the centralized forms of cultural authority by abjuring inheritability and, with it, the self-referentiality of a definite tradition.

[. . .]

Transformation

It is not my intention to chronicle the full range of the printing in colonial America. Rather, I have sought to demonstrate that different ways of determining the nature and value of letters were available in different contexts in New England. I have sought not to speak of "print culture," as though to attribute a teleology to print, but to indicate some of the competing symbolic contexts of print. None of them, however, corresponds to Adams' vision of print. We have not yet seen print routinely opposed to authority, identified in its nature with a popular struggle or with emancipatory reflection, or forming the basis of a protonationalist consciousness. The forms of print discourse that have been examined so far have been stable if not homeostatizing. Adams' rhetoric would therefore seem to indicate a new condition for print.

Not until the middle decades of the eighteenth century did the printing trade begin to resemble the scene of circulating information and critical discourse that Adams depicts as natural to it. I have called attention to the regional and contextual differences in ways of determining print in order to suggest, in part, that the development of a public print discourse could not have derived from the nature of print, as is often suggested. The point can be strengthened by noting the lag between the establishment of printing in the colonies and its use for the tasks that Adams describes. The colonial printing trade had been around for a long time by the early eighteenth century; the oldest colonial press had been in operation since 1639. The date is not early in the history of printing (Mexico City had already had a much more active press a century earlier) but it was early for provincial printing in the English world. At the time of the Restoration only three towns in the realm outside of London had presses: Oxford, Cambridge (England), and Cambridge (Massachusetts). In 1662 York was added to the list. Then Boston in 1674, Philadelphia and St. Mary's City (Maryland) in 1685, and New York in 1693. When the restrictions on the press were repealed in England in 1695 the colonies had more towns with printers than England did.[25]

But these colonial presses had also been relatively inactive. Most seventeenth-century colonists were quite content – insofar as we can tell – to do without a press. On several occasions when printing was introduced it was immediately discouraged, sometimes by royal governors, but also by elected assemblies.[26] The early artisans printed no newspapers or magazines. They seldom concentrated their capital or developed broad enough markets to produce big editions or large volumes. In the main they were booksellers or general shopkeepers, retailing not only books imported from London but also stationery and a variety of unrelated goods. In Andrew Bradford's Philadelphia printing shop one could find, in addition to printed goods: molasses by the barrel, whalebone, goose feathers, rum, corks, chocolate, peas, snuff, tea, "very good Pickled Sturgeon," beaver hats, patent medicines, a harpsichord, spectacles, and quadrants.[27] Most printers' income came from a combination of such general sales, a few imprints, and a good deal of job printing, such as blank legal forms and official publications subsidized and controlled by the colonial governments.

By 1765, however, print had come to be seen as indispensable to political life and could appear to men such as Adams to be the primary agent of world emancipation. What makes this transformation of the press particularly remarkable is that, unlike the press explosion of the nineteenth century, it involved virtually no technological improvements in the trade. To the end of the eighteenth century, printers were using a wooden flatbed hand press that had scarcely changed since the German presses of the fifteenth century. The material constraints on the press – such as the scarcity of paper or the lack of the skill to cast type domestically – remained in force until the end of the eighteenth century. Nevertheless, printing changed both in character and in volume, after 1720 growing much faster even than the population.

Number of master printers	1720	1760
Boston	6	14
Philadelphia	1	9
New York	1	5
Elsewhere	1	14
Total	9	42

Source: Stephen Botein, "Meer Mechanics and an Open Press: The Business and Political Strategies of Colonial American Printers," *Perspectives in American History* 9 (1975):127–228.

Thrown into relief by the Stamp Act, figures such as the ones in the accompanying table begin to suggest the resonance of Adams' 1765 historical narrative. Yet the figures would not interest us if they recorded only more printers doing the same job printing. The importance of this expansion is that the trade was now involved in different tasks. The dramatic change had begun at the time of the establishment of newspapers, for only then did colonial printing become a substantial industry, rivaling and communicating with the European book trade. And only then did colonial printing begin to sustain a continuous local discourse. In the decades before Adams and the Stamp Act, the dynamism of the printing trade lay in new contexts of print discourse in commerce and politics. They became the arena in which print would be reconceptualized – and, with it, those dimensions of politics and subjectivity entailed by Adams' vision of republican enlightenment. When Adams politicized the Puritan "Religion of the Closet." his revision articulated the realignment of linguistic technologies and power that integrated print with an emergent republican paradigm as the proper medium of the public.

Notes

1 John Adams, "A Dissertation on the Canon and the Feudal Law," in *Papers of John Adams*, ed. Robert J. Taylor et al. (Cambridge, Mass.: Harvard University Press, 1977–), 1:103–28. Further references to this text will be made parenthetically. The now-familiar title was assigned by the Englishman Thomas Hollis, who reprinted Adams' essay in London in 1768.

2 The relation between letters and the Revolution has been frequently noted. See Daniel Boorstin, *The Americans: The Colonial Experience* (New York: Random House, 1958); Arthur M. Schlesinger, *Prelude to Independence* (New York: Knopf, 1958); Philip Davidson, *Propaganda and*

the *American Revolution, 1763–1783* (1941; repr. New York: Norton, 1973); Bernard Bailyn, *The Ideological Origins of the American Revolution* (Cambridge, Mass.: Harvard University Press, 1967); and Bernard Bailyn and John Hench, eds., *The Press and the American Revolution* (Worcester, Mass.: American Antiquarian Society, 1980).

3 The problem here is virtually the same as that announced in the opening of Max Weber's *The Protestant Ethic and the Spirit of Capitalism* (New York: Counterpoint, 1958). Weber argues that although the development of capitalism involves universalizing values, narratives of technological advance, even the notion of "development," yet it remains culturally specific and local. His book still presents a challenge to theorize the relation between an international phenomenon like capitalism and the local cultural history in which it is constituted. The same challenge arises with the subject of modernity. "Modernity" is most usefully – if controversially – defined by Jürgen Habermas in the first chapter of *The Philosophical Discourse of Modernity*, trans. Thomas McCarthy (Cambridge: MIT Press, 1987).

4 Kenneth Lockridge, *Literacy in Colonial New England* (New York: Norton, 1974). Lockridge is opposed on this point to the more Whiggish narrative of literacy in Cremin, *American Education*. For a similar debunking of the correlation to modernization, but in a nineteenth-century urban setting, see Harvey Graff, *The Literacy Myth: Literacy and Social Structure in the Nineteenth-Century City* (New York: Academic Press, 1979).

5 David Hall, "The Uses of Literacy in New England, 1600–1850," in William Joyce et al., eds., *Printing and Society in Early America* (Worcester: American Antiquarian Society, 1983), 26.

6 Cotton Mather, *Diary of Cotton Mather*, 2 vols. (New York: Ungar, 1957), 2:103 (March 18, 1713).

7 Mather, *Diary*, 2:538 (June 1718).

8 Preface, *The Book of the General Lawes and Libertyes* (Cambridge, Mass., 1660).

9 Samuel Whiting, *Abraham's Humble Intercession for Sodom* (Cambridge, Mass., 1666), v.

10 Mather, *Diary*, 1:65 (June 11, 1683).

11 Julius Tuttle, "The Libraries of the Mathers," *Proceedings of the American Antiquarian Society* 2o (1910): 269–356.

12 The extreme form of this claim is to be found in Harry S. Stout's "Religion, Communications, and the Ideological Origins of the American Revolution," *William and Mary Quarterly* 34 (1977): 519–541. The essay displays an unabashed and uncritical sentimentality, assuming that print was "elitist and hierarchical" (540) and that any form of speech, such as evangelical oratory, must be an egalitarian "opposition to the established social order" (527–528).

13 I refer to the critique of Lévi-Strauss in Jacques Derrida, *Of Grammatology*, trans. Gayatri Spivak (Baltimore: The Johns Hopkins University Press, 1976). Although the subsequent American history of literary deconstruction has obscured the connection, Derrida's deconstructive project arose in the context of an inquiry into the political history in determinations of writing. Indeed, it was to this inquiry that "grammatology" referred.

14 Anon., *Some Few Remarks Upon a Scandalous Book* (Boston, 1701), 11.

15 Cotton Mather, *Utilia* (Boston, 1716), iv.

16 Quoted in Kenneth Silverman, *Life and Times of Cotton Mather* (New York: Columbia University Press, 1985), 198.

17 See Petty Miller, *The New England Mind* (Cambridge, Mass.: Harvard University Press, 1953), 2:245–6. See also Bartholomew Green's *The Printer's Advertisement* (Boston, 1700–1), on Brattle's accusations.

18 Anon., *Some Few Remarks*, 9.

19 Thomas Symmes, *A Discourse Concerning Prejudice in Matters of Religion* (Boston, 1722), i.

20 The point could also be illustrated by the bookplates that Thomas Prince had printed for his library: "This *Book* belongs to *The* New-England-*Library*, Begun to be collected by Thomas Prince, upon his entring *Harvard-College*, July 6, 1703; and was given by said *Prince*, to remain therein forever"; reproduced in Carl Cannon, *American Book Collectors and Collecting* (New York: H. W. Wilson, 1941), 2–3. The durability of the book inspires Prince with the thrill of that closing "forever"; it also contributes to the meaning of his effort to write a history of New England.

21 Symmes, *Discourse Concerning Prejudice*, ii.

22 Hall, "Uses of Literacy," 27–8.

23 Mather, *Diary*, 2:242 (September 27, 1713).

24 Anon., "Father Abbey's Will" (Cambridge, Mass., 1713).

25 Most of the information in this paragraph can be found in Lawrence C. Wroth, *The Colonial Printer*, 2d ed., rev. (New York, 1938). See also Helmut Lehmann-Haupt et al., eds., *The Book in America* (New York, 1951). For the comparative perspective on the spread of printing in the West, see the classic study by Lucien Febvre and Henri Martin, *Coming of the Book*, trans. David Gerard (London: Verso, 1976).

26 The most famous discouragement of printing is that by Governor William Berkeley of Virginia in 1671: "I thank God, there are no free schools nor *printing*, and I hope we shall not have these hundred years; for *learning* has brought disobedience, and heresy, and sects into the world, and *print* has divulged them, and libels against the best government. God keep us from both." Fourteen years later a printer named Buckner published the laws of the state and was forced to post bond under the promise never to print again. The Pennsylvania Council, with Penn in attendance, ordered in 1683 that the colony's laws not be printed. See Leonard Levy, *Emergence of a Free Press* (New York: Oxford University Press, 1985), esp. 16–22.

27 Quoted in Anna DeArmond, *Andrew Bradford, Colonial Journalist* (Newark: University of Delaware Press, 1949), 21.

Likeness as Identity: Reflections on the Daguerrean Mystique

Alan Trachtenberg

As the earliest example of what the "photograph" meant, the daguerreotype continues to haunt the world of the camera. In its day, this peculiarly affecting kind of picture prompted anxious questions regarding what exactly a "photograph" is, how it works, what it is good for, and how it should look. Though now relegated to the prehistory of photography proper, the daguerreotype at one point raised fundamental issues about photographic representation, and about representation as such. With the demise of the metallic "mirror image" these issues lost much of their energy, buried, we might even say repressed, by the massive commercial integration of the paper print into conventional systems of portrayal. To re-encounter the daguerrean portrait as a cultural presence on its own ground is to revive unresolved questions, and restore them to the continuing discourse of criticism regarding the character, the work, and the "good" of the photograph.

The original power of the daguerreotype lay in its physicality. Not only uniquely irreplicable, an image produced without a negative, yet embodying the negative-positive nexus on its face, it is also uniquely physical, a solid, palpable object, an image on a copper sheet polished like a hand-mirror and typically set under a gold-plated mat, contained within a small wooden or leather case adorned with tiny brass clasps. It has weight, and yet behaves like a ghost. No wonder it has inspired a diction of its own, rich in romantic tropes of light and dark. Daguerrean portraits lend themselves to a discourse in which atavistic fascination with images as magical replicas, as fetishes and effigies, mingles with sheer pleasure in undisguised technique, in the rigours of craft.[1] The language of the daguerreotype emerged and flowered in the 1840s and 1850s, especially in America, as a mixed discourse of science, technique, art, and magic.

[. . .]

II

What do we mean by calling the daguerreotype image a "portrait"? There is a literal dictionary sense in which the attributed genre is perfectly sensible – a picture "of" someone, the "of-ness" consisting of a likeness, a correspondence of features between what the image conveys and what the living figure looks like. We can hardly object to the commonplace sense of the term; even posed snapshots are called portraits when they show a person showing herself or himself. At the same time we should hear in the word a compressed history of transference of styles, poses, modes of composition, from the formal painted "portrait" to the mechanically-produced daguerreotype – a history of the formulaic intervention by the photographer into the camera's autotelic act of capturing on a plate whatever falls within the range of its lens. The history of the daguerreotype is a history of such intervention, a history enacted in apprenticeships, informal exchanges of trial-and-error experiences, patented and unpatented technical changes, or "improvements" aimed at producing an image more in accord with formal portraits, and treatises, handbooks, and journals. The portrait styles most commonly assimilated were the head-and-bust likeness in gentle light of the miniature painting, the republican "plain style" of forthright, unadorned limning of face and body, and the more elaborate "grand style" of "heroic" portraitures and "conversation pieces."[2] Countless examples and documents exist for reconstructing the history of the harnessing of the naked power of the daguerreotype into the making of "portraits", and the story has been told fulsomely, mainly as positivist history.[3] To tell that story as cultural history, as many scholars now understand, requires subordinating chronicles of technical detail to the study of patterns of thought, response, and social function.

One way to learn the language of the daguerreotype is to listen to voices speaking it: " 'I don't much like pictures of that sort – they are so hard and stern; beside dodging away from the eye, and trying to escape altogether. They are conscious of looking very unamiable, I suppose, and therefore hate to be seen ... I don't wish to see it any more.' "[4] Phoebe's unease with pictures of the sort produced by daguerreotypes invokes an early moment in the career of photography in America, a moment of shudder, suspicion, and refusal. This particular moment occurs in Nathanial Hawthorne's *The House of the Seven Gables* (1851), an American romance in which the author attempts, as he has his narrator explain in his Preface, "to connect a by-gone time with the very Present that is flitting away from us ... by bringing his fancy-pictures almost into positive contact with the realities of the moment."[5] A present that flits away, fancy-pictures brought "almost" into "positive contact" with "reality", and portraits that dodge the eye and try to escape (to escape detection?): Hawthorne plays teasingly on that apparent trick of the mirrored metallic face of the daguerreotype image, seeming at once here and gone, a positive and a negative, a substance and shadow. What one sees, a shadow or an image, or indeed one's own visage flashed back from the mirrored surface, depends on how one holds the palm-sized image – at what angle of view, and in what light.

Because of its peculiar image-construction, built up, as one recent expert explains, through accumulated surface granules rather than suspended in an emulsion, what is required for the image to seem legible, or as they said at the time, to "come to life", is a specific triangulation of viewer, image, and light.[6] In the face of such contingency and instability of seeing, no wonder that some people, like Phoebe, felt disconcerted by the experience. Others, like Hawthorne in the character of "the Author" in his Preface, spoke warmly of such "fancy-pictures" – while many, presumably, felt both unease and pleasure at once. Indeed Hawthorne's "Author" may also belong

among the undecided in regard to the daguerreotype's truth-value, or perhaps to the aptness of the daguerrean metaphor for his own romance: in any case, the qualifying adverb insinuates prefatory doubt and undecidability. As one critic remarks, the narrative itself might be read as a flickering, apparitional, here-again, gone-again daguerreotype portrait.[7]

Hawthorne's prefatory remarks and Phoebe's near-hysterical outcry, both couched in photographic metaphor already conventional at the time, signal how deeply engaged this narrative is with daguerrean seeing, and its ambiguities of effect and ambivalences of purpose. How are we to understand, for example, the full motives and purposes of the novel's ardent daguerreotypist, Holgrave? Before hearing Phoebe's misgivings when he showed her an example of his work, Holgrave had confessed: "I misuse Heaven's blessed sunshine by tracing out human features, through its agency."[8] We might be tempted to read "misuse" as coyly ironic, merely conventional, for is not his practise of daguerreotypy a sign of Holgrave's most appealing traits, his scientific bent, his rationality, his enthusiasm for truth? Phoebe personifies the sun's purest rays. Her female innocence we are surely meant to take as the novel's least controvertible value; in the end it saves Holgrave from himself. Our smile at "misuse" fades into a deeper, more shadowed concern when we learn of Holgrave's secret purpose of revenge against the Pyncheons, in whose house he resides as a tenant. Is his craft of "seizing the shadow ere the substance fade", as daguerreotypists advertised their magic, a purposeful atavistic regression to the witchcraft of his ancestors, the original Maules from whom Colonel Pyncheon, founder of the family, had stolen the land for his estate and house two hundred years earlier?

In etching his text with ambiguity and dubiety Hawthorne draws widely on figural terms from the popular discourse of the daguerreotype circulating in the print culture of the 1840s and early 1850s. He draws on that heavily-gothicised discourse not for the sake of local colour, but as a vehicle of his deepest purposes in the romance – in the most general sense, an exploration of modernity and the new systems of meaning of which photography serves as an auspicious type. Alternative views of the daguerreotype portrait, of the autoptic process of direct, apparently unmediated seeing and knowing it supposedly represents, and of the physiognomic principles of portraits as such, serve the novel's ulterior purposes. To be sure, it is a narrative more of picture than action, of tableaux than plot.[9] *The House of the Seven Gables* leaves its largest questions unsettled, its complexities and complications aborted by the quick fix of a hastily arranged fairy-tale ending, in which Holgrave seems to abandon daguerreotypy, along with his resentment and radical politics, for pastoral squiredom. This evasive conclusion reflects on the cultural status of the daguerreotype portrait itself, of photography as a representational practice within a culture undergoing unsettling change toward market-centred urban industrial capitalism.

III

The mix of light and shadow by which Hawthorne paints the character of the daguerreotype recapitulates a pattern of ambivalence, an anxious undercurrent within the overt fascination and celebration that greeted the new medium in 1839. He draws on a fund of covert misgivings, the sort of nagging reservation registered, for example, in Philip Hone's otherwise approving remarks in his diary after viewing the first exhibition of French daguerreotypes in America in December, 1839. Hone states that "one may almost be excused for disbelieving it without seeing the very process by which it is created. It appears to me a confusion of the very elements of nature."[10] Among others, Emerson also shared Phoebe's perception of a "hard and stern" look in the earliest daguerrean portraits. "The first Daguerres are grim things," he noted in 1843, "yet show that a great engine has been invented."[11] Are we to take "engine" literally? Indeed, the camera does resemble a machine with moving parts, a polished glass eye, a mysterious chemical procedure. Emerson means, of course, only that photography will prove a great instrument in human culture. But "engine" resonates or rumbles with other senses. By the 1840s, the word had evolved from the simple sense of a product of ingenuity to the more complex modern sense of a self-powered machine, a self-contained mechanical entity requiring no external power. If the trope links photography with other prominent wonders of the first industrial age, the steam-engine, the railway, the telegraph – a linkage Hawthorne also makes in the extraordinary "Flight of the Owls" chapter of *The House of the Seven Gables* – it does so by endowing the photograph with nameless internal powers. The open meaning of engine may suggest no more than a mechanical power, but what can it mean to project upon the daguerreotype an ability to generate its own activity? Similarly Phoebe's language – "They are conscious of looking very unamiable, I suppose, and therefore hate to be seen" – may seem a conventional rhetorical figure, but it implies a will, a

human or extra-human force within the inanimate object. Phoebe's conceit barely restrains an animistic trope common in popular fiction of the 1840s and 1850s: such pictures often possess a life of their own. One might fall in love with them or they with each other, as certain tales imagined.

The *frisson* of an encounter possibly with demons or magicians was often also felt in the experience of sitting before the daguerrean apparatus. T. S. Arthur in an article in *Godey's Lady Book* in 1849 recounts the melancholy tale of a frightened backcountry farmer whose visit to the city brought him into a daguerrean parlour. Once he saw the machinery and the operator's mysterious preparations, he "dashed down the stairs as if a legion of evil spirits were after him". The entire experience of having one's image "taken" exuded a nameless air of possibility, risk, and even erotic temptation. Arthur reports that some clients suffer an "illusion that the instrument exercises a kind of magnetic attraction, and many good ladies actually feel their eyes 'drawn' toward the lens while the operation is in progress!"[12]

How much such responses derive from and rehearse old superstitions and fears about the power of images, especially human likenesses, and how much is triggered locally by the peculiar surface phenomenon of the mirrored daguerreotype, is hard to say. However, surely much of the response is due to the flickering mirror-effect itself, the sense given off by the image of something actually moving, something alive. Both figures, engine and animation, *hum* with wariness about what living energy may lie within the camera-made image, what latent magic the image might perform, and might have already performed. Again, we need to take the power of rhetorical convention itself into account in weighing the cultural valence of such animistic locutions, but their pervasiveness and persistence suggests at least the residue of belief in living pictures. Here is one N. G. Burgess, himself an "operator", writing in one of the early professional journals:

> No enchantress' wand could be more potent to bring back the loved ones we once cherished than could those faithful resemblances wrought out by this almost magic art of Daguerre. For true indeed has this art been termed magic, as it works with such unerring precision and with such wonderful celerity, that it only requires the spells and incantations of the device to complete the task.

The shaman's spells and incantations transposed to the "device", produce a "faithful resemblance" which is both likeness and an identity: this modern avatar of the enchantress, the ancient mother figure, is potent to "bring back", virtually delivering as a new birth, figures from the past or indeed from death. Burgess continues:

> The Daguerreotype possesses the sublime power to transmit the almost living image of our loved ones; to call up their memories vividly to our mind, and to preserve not only the sparkling eye and winning smile, but to catch the living forms and features of those that are so fondly endeared to us, and to hold them indelibly fixed upon the tablet for years after they have passed away.[13]

Burgess and scores of other writers within the newly emerging profession of daguerrean portraitists in the 1850s dipped freely into gothic-tinged diction, but turns of speech like "faithful resemblance" and "almost living image" kept their claims safely this side of blasphemy. David Brewster in 1832 provided a system and rationale for imagining modern science and technology as "natural magic", and daguerrean writers avidly took up the rhetorical trick.[14] They offered magical effects by natural/mechanical means. Daguerrean producers and their publicists fashioned a conceptual frame for their product, a frame which acknowledged simultaneously both the appeal and the threat of the "living image" trope: the threat of demonism (Phoebe's response: not a very deep threat but discomfiting) and the promise of transcendence, of annihilating space and time (a frequent expostulation in the discourse). Commercial portrait-making moved swiftly ahead in the 1840s, and the daguerrean portrait emerged as a habitual commodity, stratified in appearance and cost to match and reinforce the hierarchy of social class consolidating itself in this first industrial era.[15]

IV

The crux of the historical problem of the daguerreotype lies in that process whereby, in rhetoric and in picture-making, the sensation of something *alive* – a talismanic effigy, a breathing icon – gets transmuted into something *crafted*, an unusually vivid likeness, a resemblance whose relation to its subject is expressed by the qualified "*almost* living image" – in short, a portrait. The aim of the profession was to exalt the maker as "artist", for how else might the fashionable studios distinguish themselves from the run-of-the-mill "daguerrean factories" which sprang up in the cities? To claim preternatural power would reduce the maker to a passive (though technically adept)

medium, and the entire event to an autotelic procedure. At the same time, the dominant rhetoric retained a hint of the preternatural, even of divination, partly to distinguish the medium from its predecessors among the hand-crafted methods of portrayal, partly in acknowledgement of the everyday experience of these uncanny images. The problem was of how to preserve the concrete sense of *difference* in this mode of portraiture, and at the same time claim a place for the artefact within the system of formal representation as a "portrait". The solution, the generic seal of "portrait", demystified the image as magic, but remystified it as art.

Daguerreotypes were at first unruly and unregulated experiences. The peculiar link between eye and body at the moment of viewing was one novelty. The character of the flickering image in a mirror was another. And at a deeper level, the way the daguerreotype put into jeopardy conventional expectations about "portrait" as revelation of "self" was another. As in all cases of novelty and invention, the new elicited help from the old for explanation and legitimacy. Likeness and portrait on one hand, living image and apparition on the other: both are familiarising terms, the first from the prevailing system of art, the second from surviving archaic mental and emotional habits. The recurrence of archaic reflexes in response to the daguerreotype traces, I think, the startling, often alarming sense of newness, of rupture within commonplace experience, that the first vivid photographs, those of mirrored metal, provoked. In the vividness of their likeness they seemed like half-forgotten dreams of magic mirrors, simulacra, and virtual identities.

This is to speak only of the apparent *presence* of the images, their astonishing exactness of detail, their seeming, as Edgar Allan Poe put it, not a copy but an "*identity* of aspect with the thing represented" [my emphasis].[16] Resemblance, likeness, verisimilitude: such are misapplied, invading the discourse from adjacent systems of formal representation. Indeed, the camera image can be made to resemble a resemblance, to give an effect of likeness, but only under controls (focus, distance, framing, lighting) derived from the formula of likeness. Logically speaking, in the terms invented by Charles Sanders Peirce, what the camera produces is a *trace* rather than an index or symbol, in the order of a footprint or shadow, a literal *impression* of light delineating form and detail from a palpable surface.[17] Photographic images might function within semiotic systems as symbols (referring to general ideas associated with the depicted referent) or icons (referring to an object by arbitrary convention), but their primary logical status remains that of a direct effect of the physical cause the image replicates. The process itself does not imitate; it reproduces. In this, daguerreotypes are no different from photographs proper; their physical peculiarities only heighten the photographic experience, rendering it in a mode which served as an extraordinary initiation for modern culture into one of its fundamentally new conditions: the instant convertibility of experience into image, the potentiality of endless and continuous doubling of all tangible surfaces, and the reification of the eye as the leading instrument of everyday knowledge.

But the daguerreotype startled for other reasons than the uncanny presence of its images. For just as the polished portraits of the most masterful makers seem a logical (and ideological) outgrowth of the formal portrait tradition – centred heads and bodies within fictive (studio) spaces that are filled with objects signifying possessions, and with lighting and posing arranged to "bring out" bourgeois individuality through "expression" – the camera was also capable of producing images that were strange and estranging. It could decapitate as easily as depict a full head and body, as Samuel F. B. Morse reported about one of Daguerre's own images of a beheaded man having his shoes shined on a Paris street corner:

> Objects moving are not impressed. The Boulevard, so constantly filled with a moving throng of pedestrians and carriages, was perfectly solitary, except for an individual who was having his boots shined. His feet were compelled, of course, to be stationary for some time, one being on the box of the boot-black and the other on the ground. Consequently, his boots and legs are well defined, but he is without body or head because these were in motion.[18]

The camera records motion and duration as blur or absence. Is a "he" depicted without body or head still the same "he?" Is the picture of a person with a blur in place of a head, or the head cropped away, any less a picture "of" that person, no matter how little a *likeness* it projects?

Soon after its appearance photography became a potent source in modern culture for making the conventional idea of the continuous, coherent "self" plausible, but in its most primitive moments, when Daguerre and others doubted that the medium would ever be suited to portraiture, it displayed dangerous tendencies to subvert that same idea.[19] We detect such optical danger in an astonishing likeness the early Philadelphia daguerreotypist Robert Cornelius produced of himself by leaping in front of a camera in his garden. To our taste the image seems wonderfully expressive – not of a "character", but of the medium itself, and of its ability to stop an action in its tracks, yet show it continuing as a blur, or the trace of an event. In the presentness of the moment, in the sense of the figure throwing itself into the lens – hair flying, eyes seeking the lens (seeking, that is, their own mirrored reflection) – the image preserves all the original strangeness and difference of daguerreotypy. Such images defined exactly what had to be overcome.[20]

Pedagogies abounded for operators and sitters, prescribing costume and lighting, studio props and bodily and facial expression. Writers of such guides drew particularly on the popular pseudosciences of physiognomy and phrenology, and laced their texts with citations from Lavater and Sir Charles Bell.[21] The litany was "expression of character", and photographers were urged to learn "the chief power of the old masters in portrait painting", which was "the ability, while watching the changes and expressions of the sitter's countenance when unconscious of the scrutiny, to keep in mind the best, and after the general form was obtained, to paint them in from memory." The lesson for the photographer, who must act at once and cannot rely on memory, was that "outward expression is the revelation of inward feeling, and moods of mind and sentiment are very much under the influence of what affects the senses." The photographer must provide a setting, an ambiance, conducive to the "best" bodily expression of characteristic inward feeling. He must attend particularly to "position" – the expression of inwardness in stillness. "In position he must remember that every organ and every faculty has a special language. A proud man carries his head erect, a little thrown back, and with a stately air. This is the language of self-esteem." Pseudoscience lay behind this advice, based as it was upon the codes of phrenology and physiognomy, with a dash of theatricality thrown in. In fact, the codes imply formulas for the *imitation* of inwardness, and resulted in stereotyped poses and in caricature, the underside of the bourgeois fetish of "character". For the writer whom I am quoting such formulas signify progress in the art of photography: "the days of mystery in photography are nearly gone."[22]

By stilling the sitter and regulating the apparatus, the trade of photography achieved what it sought: a commercially viable and culturally satisfying formal portrait for intimate viewing in galleries, parlours, or private corners. And indeed, the theory of portrait likeness resulted in extraordinary achievements in daguerrean studios and makeshift workshops across the United

States. It permitted something revolutionary to develop within the history of Western portraiture, a new kind of collaboration between sitter and artist. The improved apparatus resulted in images of crystalline clarity and presence, while the imperatives of the apparatus, particularly the duration of exposure, eventually shortened to allow for reasonably relaxed self-presentations, even within the formal portrait frame, and thus gave the sitter considerable control over what the camera saw. Improvisations within the portrait mode changed the entire expectation of portraiture, and had an immediate effect on painting. Cross-fertilisation between painting and photography produced decisive effects in both media; daguerreotype studios employed portrait painters to help pose sitters and arrange lighting, and painters used daguerreotypes (later, paper photographs) as aids in their portraits.[23] No doubt partly as a result of such collaborations, daguerreotype portraits preserve a record of faces and bodies (mainly Euro-American) in an incalculable variety of mood and costume and expressive individuality. (It is a record rivalled in the history of portraits only by late Roman busts.)

If the clarity of the daguerreotype resulted in an unparalleled cultural record, for which the formal codes and conventions of portrait likeness are to be credited, still, the decapitated body and the blurred head never ceased to haunt the high art of this vernacular medium. We detect its power in the increasingly elaborate ornamentation of the daguerreotype case (especially in its depictions of scenes from paintings and statuary in bas-relief), and in the increasingly conspicuous use of colour tints, as if to hold the shadowed image in place. Often the ghost leaps out at us when we remove the plate from its over-mat, and we see the signs of the studio, or extensions of the body cropped by the oval or hectagonal mat. At a stroke that act alone, by disclosing what else lies on the plate, replaces the frame with the edge of the plate, undercuts the aptness of the frame and its ideology, as the boundary of a discrete and coherent space inhabited by a unique "self", whose uniqueness lies as a knowable inscription of manifest inwardness across the body and face. That body, with its pose acting as its expressive vehicle, is assumed to belong to the "self", and is as much its external and material possession as the objects which define the fictive space. The frame designates closure, self-containment, an act which also signifies at the lower levels the alienation of the sitter's appearance from the sitter's being, the reification of pose and look as definitive possession, an apparatus of a piece with other props. The edge designates something quite different

and antagonistic: the contingency of this look and pose upon this event in this place (the studio, not its fictive disguise) and at this time. It designates a relation of image to sitter as that of a radically contingent identity, rather than as an emblematic likeness. The frame encloses and makes utterly still; the edge continues and implies motion, and more accurately expresses the photographic act itself.

For Emerson, in the stillness of the daguerreotype portrait lay deceit:

> Were you ever Daguerreotyped, O immortal man? And did look with all vigor at the lens of the camera or rather by the direction of the operator at the brass peg a little below it to give the picture the full benefit of your expanded & flashing eye? and in your zeal not to blur the image, did you keep every finger in its place with such energy that your hands became clenched as for fight or despair, & in your resolution to keep your face still, did you feel every muscle becoming every moment more rigid: the brows contracted into a Tartarean frown, and the eyes fixed as only they are fixed in a fit, in madness, or in death; and when at last you are relieved of your dismal duties, did you find the curtain drawn perfectly, and the coat perfectly, & the hands true, clenched for combat, and the shape of the face & the head? but unhappily the total expression had escaped from the face and you held the portrait of a mask instead of a man. Could you not by grasping it very tight hold the stream of a river or of a small brook & prevent it from flowing?[24]

The mask is still, the expressive face is in motion, and the mask is separable from the man. Hawthorne wrote after seeing himself in a photographed portrait, "I was really a little startled at recognising myself so apart from myself." And again, "There is no such thing as a true portrait. They are all delusions."[25] Melville simply refused to be photographed by the camera, while Whitman courted it obsessively, each sitting an occasion for another self-making, another emblem of the self's freedom to shift from role to role.[26] In the case of these exceptional sitters (exceptional, at least, in that they left articulate records of their doubts), the daguerreotype even as a portrait likeness seemed to destabilise the idea of self and character which underlay American liberal individualism in the nineteenth century.

That idea and ideology informed the course of the daguerreotype's development in the fifteen years or so it held sway in America before the Civil War. To recognise the tension within that development between likeness and identity helps bring the daguerrean record to life as culture and history. Likeness and identity accrue specific and opposing cultural valences within specific historical occasions, the former serving generally as a conventional token of individuality, the latter as a challenge to convention. The popular ideology of individualism served, at least in part, as a bulwark against the alienating effects of the expanding capitalist marketplace and industrial system. Yet it produced its own estranging effects, of which the reification of likeness as the true representation of character provides one instance. Alexis de Tocqueville understood this cultural paradox. Writing in 1835 about middle-class Americans, he observed that each person, "living apart, is as a stranger to the fate of all the rest; his children and his private friends constitute to him the whole of mankind. As for the rest of his fellow citizens, he is close to them, but does not see them; he exists only in himself and for himself alone; and if his kindred still remain to him, he may be said at any rate to have lost his country."[27]

Tocqueville helps us gloss the American daguerreotype, to parse its visual phrases and translate its passages into our own critical tongue. He describes a plot which may provide a key to the aura of sadness and loss these images often convey. Under the aegis of the theory of likeness, the daguerreotype provided a space and time for inward reflection, and the thoughts (physiognomically expressed) seem rarely happy or satisfied, and often simply blank. When he talks of "that strange melancholy which often haunts the inhabitants of democratic countries in the midst of their abundance, and that disgust at life which sometimes seizes upon them in the midst of calm and easy circumstances", Tocqueville might be speaking of the daguerreotype portrait.[28]

Some admirers discern iconic Americans in these portraits, exuding boundless optimism, pride of character, and an openness to a world spiritual heroism. Any generalisation will stumble over contrary evidence, especially generalisations from the daguerreotype to national traits, if simply because their social profile under-represents whole sections of the nation: the poor, the enslaved, the incarcerated, the unskilled, the excluded and expropriated. It is white middle-class America we see in the main, with marginal figures typically displayed as exotic. And in this limited social panorama, in facial creases and the hump of heavy middle-aged white male bodies, in worry lines etched in the faces of women, and in the solemnity of children, Tocqueville's strange melancholy often seems more present than pride and hope. Do such images portray the costs of individualism, the compulsive boosterism, gamesmanship, and blindness to others

excoriated by leading critics of the time? And also, perhaps, the delusion of selfhood as an unalienable likeness that this ideology of individualism fostered? There are risks in leaping to such conclusions, but it is safe to venture that the daguerreotype confounds the historical tensions between likeness and identity. However, the tensions remain, and all the more vividly bring these images "to life". Likeness *as* identity invariably offers itself as contingent with likeness *and* identity. It is a continuing effect of the daguerrean mystique.

Notes

1 David Freedberg, *The Power of Images* (Chicago, 1989), pp. 231–5, 278–80.

2 Useful sources include *American Portrait Miniatures*, exhibition catalogue by Dale T. Johnson: The Metropolitan Museum of Art (New York, 1990); *American Portraiture in the Grand Manner*, exhibition catalogue by Michael Quick: Los Angeles County Museum of Art (Los Angeles, 1981); Wayne Craven, *Colonial American Portraiture* (Cambridge, 1986); Brandon Frame Fortune, "Charles Wilson Peale's Portrait Gallery: Persuasion and the Plain Style", *Word & Image*, VI (October–November, 1990), pp. 308–24.

3 For example, Floyd and Marion Rinhart, *The American Daguerreotype* (Athens, Georgia, 1981), an invaluable source of information.

4 Nathaniel Hawthorne, *The House of the Seven Gables* (Columbus, Ohio, 1965), p. 91.

5 Ibid., pp. 2–3.

6 Susan M. Barger, "Delicate and Complicated Operations: The Scientific Examination of the Daguerreotype", in *The Daguerreotype*, ed. John Wood (Iowa City, 1989), pp. 97–109.

7 Cathy N. Davidson, "Photographs of the Dead: Sherman, Daguerre, Hawthorne", *South Atlantic Quarterly*, LXXXIX (Fall, 1990), p. 697.

8 Hawthorne, p. 46.

9 Taylor Stoehr, *Hawthorne's Mad Scientists* (Hamden, Connecticut, 1978), p. 90.

10 Quoted in Alan Trachtenberg, *Reading American Photographs: Images as History, Mathew Brady to Walker Evans* (New York, 1989), p. 13.

11 *The Journals and Miscellaneous Notebooks of Ralph Waldo Emerson*, eds. Ralph H. Orth and Alfred R. Ferguson (Cambridge, Mass., 1971), IX, p. 14.

12 T. S. Arthur, "The Daguerreotypist", *Godey's Lady's Book*, XXXVIII (May, 1849), pp. 352–5.

13 *The Photography and Fine Art Journal*, VIII (January, 1855), p. 19. Quoted in Richard Rudisill, *Mirror Image: The Influence of the Daguerreotype on American Society* (Albuquerque, 1971), p. 214.

14 David Brewster, *Letters on Natural Magic* (New York, 1832).

15 See the discussion of this development in Trachtenberg, *Reading American Photographs*, Chapter 1, pp. 21–70.

16 Quoted in ibid., p. 15.

17 Charles Sanders Peirce, "Logic as Semiotic: The Theory of Signs", in *Philosophical Writings of Peirce*, ed. Justus Buchler (New York, 1955), pp. 98–119.

18 Quoted in Trachtenberg, p. 15.

19 See ibid., p. 24.

20 *Robert Cornelius: Portraits from the Dawn of Photography*, exhibition catalogue by William F. Stapp: National Portrait Gallery (Washington, 1983), p. 50.

21 A good example is Marcus Aurelius Root, *The Camera and the Pencil* (Philadelphia, 1864), especially Chapter 7, pp. 84–9.

See Allan Sekula, "The Body and the Archive", *October*, xxxix (Winter, 1966), pp. 30–64.

22 E. K. Hough, "Expressing Character in Photographic Pictures", *The American Journal of Photography*, I (December 15, 1858), pp. 212–13.

23 See Van Deren Coke, *The Painter and the Photograph* (Albuquerque, 1964), Chapter 1, pp. 17–58.

24 *The Journals and Miscellaneous Notebooks of Ralph Waldo Emerson*, eds. William H. Gilman and J. E. Parsons, VIII, pp. 115–16.

25 Quoted in Davidson, pp. 677, 686.

26 On Whitman's subversion of the conventional portrait-self, see Trachtenberg, pp. 60–70.

27 Alexis de Tocqueville, *Democracy in America*, II (New York, 1958), p. 336.

28 Ibid., p. 147.

"I Want to Ride in Geronimo's Cadillac"

Philip Deloria

Geronimo's Cadillac is a historical event. It is a song, an image, a story, a car. It is an idea – or, rather, a cluster of ideas – evocatively represented by Walter Ferguson's 1904 photograph of Geronimo and three companions sitting in an automobile. A short ride in Geronimo's Cadillac can take us through an exploration of the unexpected juxtaposition of Indians and cars. We might start by splitting the person apart from the vehicle. If you had to pick a single person to stand for *Indianness*, you could do worse than Geronimo, the iconic Apache leader who stands in American popular memory for resistant warriors everywhere and the defeated prisoners we imagine they became. (He should also stand for all the Indian cultural actors too easily forgotten and for audiences of indigenous people who might find nothing unexpected about Geronimo's ride in a car.) Likewise, if you had to pick a single car to stand for a world of automobiles, you could do worse than the Cadillac. Its array of rich meanings encompasses not only technical excellence and social aspiration, but also class and race critique and crossing. It meant something when Elvis Presley bought a fleet of Caddies, for example, and it mattered that one of them was pink. Cars make one visible, asserting publicly that driver and riders are certain kinds of people; it would be hard to top the Cadillac in that regard.

To imagine Geronimo riding in a Cadillac, then, is to put two different symbolic systems in dialogue with one another. Indians, we can assert confidently, have been central symbolic elements in American culture for a very long time. Nature and nation, violence and colonial conquest, race and race crossing, nostalgia and guilt – images of Indians have been used to make sense of these things and many more besides. As we have seen, such images have both endangered and imprisoned Indian people and have presented opportunities – in Wild West shows, films, and athletics, for example – to continue waging old struggles on new kinds of cultural terrain. This is not news.

Nor is it news that, in the explosion of mass cultural production that characterized the twentieth century, the automobile has been among our most evocative symbols. Mobility, speed, power, progress: these things matter, and Americans of every race, class, gender, and origin have found ways to express them in automotive terms. Cars serve a utilitarian function of course – and, thus, access to automobility matters critically to those outside the few urban transportation systems in the United States. As important as the moving of people from point A to point B, however, is the fact that automobiles express a driver's sense of self and of the nature of his or her power. The tough guy who needs a military-style sport-utility vehicle, the customized cars emerging out of youth and ethnic cultures, advertisers' gendered invocations of truck-driving manliness and soccer-mom vanliness, the identities, adventures, and nostalgia we invest in the idea of the open road – all these are part and parcel of a culture imaginatively built around automobility.

Things get weird, however, when the symbolic systems built on cars and Indians intersect. Even as today's highways teem with jeep Cherokees, Pontiac Azteks, Dodge Dakotas, and other "Indian cars," there still remains, for many Americans, something disorienting about Geronimo – and his real and metaphoric descendants – cruising around in Cadillacs. On the one hand, there is a palpable disconnection between the high-tech automotive world and the primitivism that so often clings to the figure of the Indian. At the same time, however, those very distinctions are constantly being squashed back together. Take, for example, the Jeep Cherokee. *Jeep* and *Cherokee* overflow in a partnered representation of *nature* – the latter as its human essence, the former as the ironic escape route that gets you away from the city and back to the natural world. The imagined separation of Indians and cars, and the mixing together of meanings, gets even more estranging when you try to juggle the symbolic ambiguities while at the same time admitting that flesh-and-blood Indian people may own, drive, and like cars. How might one think about the uncertainties conjured up, for instance, when the non-Indian world turns to imagine a Cherokee in a Cherokee – or a Geronimo in a Cadillac?

What kinds of expectations cohered among white Americans when their enthusiasm for automotive technological advance intersected with their twentieth-century perceptions of Indians, newly visible in movies, music, and sporting events? How did Indian people deal with the possibilities inherent in the automobile? And how did their actions appear in relation to the expectations being built around the unexpected meeting of technology and Indianness?

[...]

Texas country-folk singer Michael Murphey likely [...] looked back to stories he had heard about Geronimo. Living under house arrest at Fort Sill, Oklahoma, Geronimo had apparently once driven a Cadillac around the grounds. Perhaps Murphey had seen Ferguson's picture showing Geronimo in a top hat seated behind the wheel of a car. Or maybe he'd heard about how, in 1905, Geronimo had ridden in an automobile as it chased a poor bison around a rodeo ring in a Wild West spectacle labeled "The Last Buffalo Hunt."[1] Looking, with a sense of irony and mild outrage, from the vantage point of 1972, Murphey wrote a song, "Geronimo's Cadillac," that suggests the extent to which the lives led by Geronimo, Two John, or slim young Osages would be understood as curiosities of the past, framed by expectations that left little room to imagine Indian people taking the wheel:

Sergeant, sergeant don't you feel, there's something
    wrong with your automobile?
Governor, Governor, don't you think it's strange, to
    see an automobile on the Indian range?

Jesus tells me and I believe it's true; the red man is in
    the sunset too Ripped off his land, won't give it
    back; and they sent Geronimo a Cadillac.[2]

[...]

Michael Murphey's question – isn't it strange to see an automobile "on the Indian range," being driven by an Indian person? – framed a key expectation that emerged in the early-twentieth-century meeting of Indians, Anglos, and automobiles. [...] That strangeness developed historically, in ways that we can trace through these texts, among others.

There are, of course, important social and economic reasons that might help us account for the unexpectedness that Murphey [...] sensed in the idea of an Indian driving a [...] Cadillac. In 1904, it was rare enough to see an automobile anywhere on American roads, let alone on roads in the American west, where most Native people seemed to reside. How much rarer, then, to see an Indian at the wheel?[3] After all, most Native people lacked the material resources that let one acquire an automobile. It was easy to imagine impoverished and primitive Indians along the roadside or beside the tracks, watching as white modernity passed them by. [...]

But there is more to it than that. The sense of estrangement has persisted over the entire life of the automotive century itself, from 1904 through the present. Even as social and economic constraints have eased, the pairing of Indians and automobiles has continued to tweak non-Native anxieties about progress and its costs. Symbolic systems surrounding Indians (nature, violence, primitivism, authenticity, indigeneity) and automobiles (speed, technological advance, independence, identity, progress) continue to evoke powerful points of both intersection and divergence. If the estrangement can be tracked back in time, it can also be broadened beyond the question of cars. Indeed, automotive unexpectedness is part of a long tradition that has tended to separate Indian people from the contemporary world and from a recognition of the possibility of Indian autonomy in that world.

Technology has been a key signifier in that tradition, which has been nurtured since the dawn of Western colonialism and which, of course, reaches far beyond Native America. Every moment of contact in which Europeans sought to impress the natives by firing a gun, demonstrating a watch, predicting an eclipse, or introducing mirrors and steel set expectations about the backwardness of indigenous people and their seemingly genetic inability to understand and use technology. Those European expectations emerged from (and then reproduced) representations of untutored primitives looking on in astonishment at the wonders of the West.[4]

Within any expectation, of course, there is ample room for confusion and contradiction – *unevenness*, to borrow the literary critic Mary Poovey's word. Ideologies develop, mature, and decay historically, and they do so in tension with other ideological formations. In the case of Indian violence, as we have seen, one can trace rough trajectories of expectation, as well as moments of rhetorical overlap, around *outbreak* and *pacification*. Expectations bleed together in any single utterance; it is the mingling that often proves most compelling. Such is the case with the ideas that non-Indians held about automobiles and Indians, which have been more uneven and multiple than a bare-bones colonial vision of indigenous technological backwardness.[5]

Here's one expectation. The NIA missionaries believed in evolution and social development, and they placed Indian people on the familiar progressive trajectory of social Darwinism. Indians, they thought, could and would leave behind their supposed lives as hunters and primitive farmers and evolve into modern people fully capable of using white technology – they just hadn't done so yet. With help, however, Indian people's social development might be accelerated. This evolutionary view underpinned various assimilation programs, which sought to advance and then incorporate Indians, not only into American political and social systems, but also into modernity, American culture, and perhaps even whiteness itself. This transition from radical difference to unremarkable similarity was, in fact, the stated goal of most of the Indian policies of the later nineteenth century.[6]

The NIA and other missionary organizations tended to see the adoption of anything from non-Indian culture as a step forward on this developmental trajectory, and technology proved an evocative indicator. The automobile joined telephones, sewing machines, domestic appliances, and other high-technology items as celebrated markers of Indian progress on the road to civilization. In 1905, for example, a missionary survey of South Dakota's Rosebud and Cheyenne River reservations proudly claimed to have located 28 pianos, 60 organs (signifying the presence of missionary chapels), an astonishing 320 telephones, and 18 automobiles.[7] At least two Rosebud men, Black Cloud and Billy Two Drinks, had acquired automobiles in order to conduct business. Black Cloud spent the summer of 1904 hauling

prospective settlers around the newly opened portion of the South Dakota reservation, while Two Drinks planned to set up a regular stage line through Tripp and Gregory Counties and to underbid horse and wagon teamsters for hauling contracts.[8] Indians launching capitalist enterprises and helping non-Indians settle former reservation lands – this was the sort of anecdotal evidence of social progress that gave missionaries shivers of delight and confirmed the hope that evolutionary development was taking place right before their eyes. The embrace of technology by [...] Two Drinks, and Black Cloud seemed to prove it.

But, if the very idea of Indian cars signified progress to some, to others it evoked a wholly different set of expectations, one frequently announced in terms of "mindless squandering." In a society that had often claimed to link progress, not only with technology, but also with thrift, automobile purchase (for Indians, at least) was irrational waste. Buying a car inverted, in current terms, the selling of Manhattan Island for twenty-four dollars in beads and trinkets – a little tragic, a little humorous, and all too revealing about an essential Indian inability. Unlike those who saw car purchases as evidence of techno-progress, then, critics of the "squandering school" thought that autos demonstrated the utter impossibility of Indian progress. For them, Indian use of technology revealed [...] that Indian difference was not evolving into modern sameness but was, instead, racial, essential, and unchanging. [...] Indians, claimed even nastier critics, couldn't even *see* cars as progressive technology. Rather, they had always been attracted to "bright and shiny trinkets," of which automobiles were simply the latest fashion. Native people were supposed to be incapable of planning for the future or anticipating the consequences of their actions. They were, in a familiar metaphor, "like children" – or worse. "The Indian who purchases a flivver," observed Indian Office Inspector W. J. Endecott, "is held to be a spendthrift or of unsound mind or of dishonest habit."[9]

These rather different expectations – social development as opposed to essential racial difference, progress as opposed to squandering – emerged from the same root, the idea that technology marked a key difference between the West and the globe's indigenous peoples. Not surprisingly, the expectations collided frequently, often within the same utterance. Even as the NIA commentators celebrated evolutionary development and assimilation, for example, they also noted with a nasty chagrin: "Indians have a passion for machines painted in bright colors. Often when they have received $2000 or more for allotted lands the Indians will go to Omaha or Sioux City, see a striking automobile and spend their entire fortune on one like it."[10] Such apparent contradictions within the NIA report suggested the prevalence of powerful assumptions shared by evolutionists and antisquanderers alike. Both expectations – that automobiles signified Indian progress and that they demonstrated its impossibility – insistently proclaimed Indian people to be distant from contemporary technology in both space and time. Whether racially marked or evolutionarily backward, their rural reservations far from the modernity of the cities, Indians (many non-Indians assumed) could not comprehend, much less appreciate, invention, innovation, or technological advance.

Indian country was always to be seen as an anachronistic space. Depending on how one told the story, Billy Two Drinks might be making progress (though perpetually behind whites, with his progressive inclinations always anomalous in relation to the inclinations of Indians as a whole). Or his squandering might demonstrate the problem that racial inability posed for Native social development (and, thus, Two Drinks seemed representative of Indians in general). Such were the key dynamics that structured non-Indian expectations. No white person could fail to have a *general* opinion – a cultural expectation – about Indian people in cars, and no white observer could look at a single automotive Indian person without activating that opinion. As a result, Indian people behind the wheel almost always proved an estranging sight, even for those who thought it worth celebrating.

Imagining Indians as technological primitives empowered an equal and opposite reaction – a celebration of the mechanical advances of a distinct white modernity. Unlike Geronimo, a white American driver of 1904 was pushing the envelope of history. Nor were such self-understandings confined to a story of social evolution, with whites always at the advanced edge of history and Indians and others destined to trail behind. Technological mastery also proved a racial endowment, a further measure of white superiority. And it was, of course, a gendered notion as well. Seeing technology in masculine terms suggested that Indian men – often feminized historically (and, more recently, in the terms of pacification) – were doubly or trebly unsuited to the automobile. Indian women, caught up the mingled terms of race and gender, might be imagined outside the automobile even more easily.

[...]

Non-Indian observers may have claimed that they wished Native people to join them in modernity as soon as possible, but the reality behind the rhetoric was somewhat different. More often, white observers like Eldridge remained hamstrung by notions of proper evolutionary development as something tied to sequence – hunter, then herder, farmer, mercantilist, industrialist, and so on. The expectation was that Indians would make all the regular stops on the trail up from savagery, skipping none. In the early twentieth century, that meant animal-powered agriculture, the supposed next stop. According to Agent C. H. Asbury: "We must insist upon the Indian making his living upon his land even though he may sometimes go a little hungry or have to lay up his automobile for a while for want of gasoline." Leapfrogging over several stages directly into a world of cars and gas seemed like cheating nature and was not to be tolerated.[11]

The cultural labor necessary to set and reinforce such expectations was surely not mobilized simply to account for Two John, Geronimo, and a few slim young Osages – which suggests that Indian people of the early twentieth century may have engaged automobility beyond the expectations of white American observers. Were there other Indian people driving around in forbidden automobiles? What did Indian automobility look like? And from where did it come?

Window of Opportunity

In 1972, Michael Murphey had been struck by the freakishness, the irony, even the tragedy of Geronimo sitting in a car. Geronimo was supposed to be defeated but dignified. In a car, he looked incongruous, like something of a joke. It is possible that he was ordered to sit in the car for Ferguson's photograph, a colonial subject bowing to a command performance. But Geronimo was probably better acquainted with automobiles than most of his non-Indian neighbors. He had conducted a relatively lucrative business in personal appearances and autograph signings at several expositions, events that often displayed the latest in American technological progress.[12] He had been in Omaha for the 1898 Trans-Mississippi and International Exposition. In Buffalo, at the 1901 Pan-American Exposition, he had seen the well-lit Electric Tower, 375 feet tall, not to mention airships and, of course, automobiles. More cars were on hand when he went to work at the 1904 Louisiana Purchase Exposition in Saint Louis. And, along with Quanah Parker, American Horse, Hollow Horn Bear, and others, he had ridden – on horseback – in Theodore Roosevelt's 1905 inaugural parade, which featured one of America's first presidential motorcades.[13] Like the performers who accompanied Buffalo Bill Cody, Geronimo had, in fact, traveled widely and seen American technological innovations firsthand. He'd been painted and photographed countless times. So, when Oklahoma's Miller Brothers 101 Ranch decided to sponsor a "Last Buffalo Hunt" as entertainment for a group of visiting newspaper editors, he apparently had few qualms about riding in the car that chased a bison around the rodeo ring.[14] Nor, we can easily imagine, was he quite so taken aback by the prospect of driving a Cadillac around Fort Sill or of sitting in the front seat to have his photograph taken.

Two John's story would seem to be somewhat different, and, perhaps, more typical, than Geronimo's. After all, Two John did not simply hop into an available car; he took the initiative to purchase one. Such was the case with Black Cloud and Billy Two Drinks, with María Martínez at San Ildefonso pueblo (she invested earnings from "craft performance" at the 1915 San Diego World's Fair in a car), with Marsie Harjo in Oklahoma, with John Bluebird (who got his through a crooked reservation teacher), with Charles Walking Bull (who traded borrowed Indian-issue cattle for his), with William White (who used his as an employee at the Crow reservation school), and with unknown first purchasers on reservations or in towns across the country. What enabled these people to evade the substantial social and economic restraints and use automobiles to imagine and create a new world on their own terms?[15]

[. . .]

An economic window of opportunity and a clear realization of the usefulness of automobiles happened to coincide with sporadic infusions of cash on many reservations in the form of payments from claims cases, land and cattle sales, leasing, allotment sales, and Wild West income. On the Sisseton reservation, for instance, sales of inheritance lands during the first decade of the twentieth century alienated nearly twenty thousand acres and brought over $271,000 into the reservation economy.[16] At Devil's Lake, Dakota people received regular per capita payments from 1904 through 1914, the proceeds from a tribal land sale. A 1924 claims settlement put $130 in the pockets of each Santee Sioux tribal member.[17] And, between 1914 and 1918, agents on many reservations allowed the sale of both tribal and

individual cattle herds in order to take advantage of wartime demand and high prices.[18] At Rosebud, Inspector Charles Davis noted in a 1909 report the infusion of over $2 million in land sales money, amounting to $700 per capita "with more yet to come." "In my judgement," Davis wrote, "it will be advisable to pay a large portion of these funds to the Indians in cash."[19]

By far the most regular source of cash on many reservations came from the sale of individual allotments. Put into place by the Dawes General Allotment Act of 1887, the allotment policy sought to divide Indian land held in common and to force Native people to occupy individual homesteads. Allotment sought to impose forcibly a change in social evolutionary status, from hunter-gatherer (the default position for Indians in American popular thought) to sedentary farmer (or, at worst, semisedentary rancher). From there, Indians would have, in theory, only a few short steps up the ladder to modern industrial capitalism.[20] Originally, the federal government was to hold the title to an individual's allotment in trust for twenty-five years in order to protect the Indian landholder. Changes and amendments to the policy, however, rendered this provision stunningly ineffective.

In 1913, Indian Commissioner Cato Sells dispatched "competency commissions," which issued patents to Indians judged competent regardless of the wishes (or the competency) of the individuals concerned. Often, status was determined by the individual's blood quantum, with a white ancestor taken as evidence of competency. Being judged competent meant that one could sell land. Patents often passed quickly through Indian hands, resulting in the substantial land loss that characterizes the period and the policy. As a standard part of their annual report back to Washington, reservation agents across the country detailed the assignment of fee patents and the resulting flow of money. As early as 1910, for example, the agent to the Kiowas was reporting that 90 percent of patented land had been sold, with half the proceeds "squandered." Judith Boughter's analysis of the Omaha competency commissions reveals a similarly depressing pattern of "forced patents, mortgages, and quick sales." So too does Janet McDonnell's detailed accounting of land loss under the Dawes Act, which shrank Indian landholdings from 138 million acres in 1887 to 52 million at the time of its repeal in 1934.[21]

Allotment, fee patents, and land sales played out in similar ways on many reservations. The exchanges came at the short- and long-term expense of Indian people. Often, Native people never saw money to which they were entitled, and reservation agents, farmers, storekeepers, and ranchers worked innumerable cold-blooded scams to acquire Indian land and capital on the cheap. In many cases, Indian people sold land against their will while government agents watched. People refused their fee patents only to find that they had been issued, mortgaged, and sold, frequently without their knowledge. Nor did it stop there. On western reservations, the mass sale of Indian cattle herds put an end to a short-lived economy, sheltered in part by reservation boundaries and agent oversight, that had made sense to many Native people and functioned as well as any reservation economy ever has. The herds sold off, individual parcels of Indian land were immediately leased to white ranchers, who claimed them as their own. In many cases, then, even when Native people held onto their land, the federal government removed it from Indian control.

The story of early-twentieth-century land loss is without doubt one of the vilest episodes in the long history of American colonialism – rendered even more so by the professed belief of at least some Indian reformers that they had done the right thing. We should not hesitate to mark it, not simply as classically tragic (though it was all that), but as a tragedy marked by a cold viciousness – and by the pain, damage, and distrust left in its wake. Indeed, the linked terms *tragedy* and *squandering* provided cover for those who contemplated the transactions. The rueful comments of one agent on his issuance of fee patents were shared by many: "At least 80 percent have sold their lands and at least 70 percent have squandered the proceeds of the sale and have nothing to show for it." It proved easier to think of sold allotments as squandered than as swindled, for that placed responsibility on Indian people rather than those who cheated them. So too does the sympathetic notion of tragedy efface the fact of vicious greed. At the same time we mark this history, however, it is also reasonable to ask a different question, to think more deeply about what Indian people did with the paltry cash that came their way through land sales, leasing, and per capita payments.[22]

Squandered money often went to automobile dealers. At Yankton, the agent noted: "The Indians found it hard to resist the temptation to own a car when they saw their neighbors riding in one." On the Crow reservation, 80 percent of the proceeds from allotment sales went for "cars and other luxuries." Another agent observed that, when the patents were delivered, Indians were dogged by "land buyers, auto agents and fakes of all kinds." At Cheyenne River, the agent lamented that almost every Indian who received a patent bought a car if the money

was sufficient. The Round Valley, California, agent reported: "Many of the Indians who received patents in fee sold their lands or mortgaged them – bought automobiles and spent their money." And, at Klamath, Agent C. H. Asbury noted "a number of instances where automobiles have been taken in exchange for the land ... whoever gets a second-hand automobile, unless he has a legitimate need for it in his business is cheated." Crow allottee Frank Shane, according to the local agent, "had a very good Overland [car], but a dealer got ahold of him, rang up the bank to know if his check was good for $1300, and when advised that it was, Frank came into possession of a Studebaker seven-passenger car and gave his Overland away." In one bit of agency lore, an Indian judged competent was said to have argued against receiving citizenship and a patent, insisting that he didn't know how to drive a car. And, of course, the homesteaders at Bonesteel, South Dakota, most of whom arrived by train or wagon, admitted to being "amazed to see Sioux Indians whirl into town in family automobiles, squaw in front seat and redskinned youngsters in the rear."[23]

There is no reason to believe that Indian people saw anything valid in the dismissive words of agents and bureaucrats, who insisted that capital – in the form of land or cash disbursements – should be reinvested into individual farms or ranches or perhaps small local stores. As many non-Indian homesteaders in the west would demonstrate, it took far more capital than that possessed by Indian people to succeed at most twentieth-century farming or ranching, particularly on the plains. And, by expanding the distance one could travel in a day, the car itself would, by the late 1920s, spell an end to the small stores that once dotted western reservations and surrounding homesteader areas.[24] Given the disinclination of many tribes to farm, the abundant examples of non-Indian farm and ranch failure, and the uncertain future offered by government policymakers, buying a car seemed wasteful only to white Americans. For Native societies, automobile purchase and travel may have been a more sensible way to make a meaningful life than to take a horse-drawn plow to the soil.

And so many Indian people bought cars. In truth, automobile purchase often fit smoothly into a different logic – long-lived Indian traditions built around the utilization of the most useful technologies that non-Indians had to offer. Just as many plains people had eagerly adopted the horse, transforming their societies in the process, so too did Black Cloud, Billy Two Drinks, and other cultural experimenters of the early twentieth century explore the useful potential of the automobile.

At the founding of the Rosebud and Pine Ridge reservations, for example, the leaders Red Cloud and Spotted Tail had insisted on negotiating freight-hauling contracts for reservation goods and government annuities, and freighting had become a small, culturally resonant industry on those reservations. It made good sense for Billy Two Drinks to consider moving from teams to automobiles, not only in terms of a capitalist service market, but also in terms of the cultural transformations and persistences that allowed horse nomads to become cowboys and freight drivers in the first place. Would Black Cloud or Two Drinks have seen their automobiles as capital investments? Hard to know. It would not be out of line, however, to suggest that their purchases made sense within the social and cultural frameworks in which they lived.

The *auto* and the *mobility* that made up the word *automobile* pointed exactly to the ways in which mobility helped Indian people preserve and reimagine their own *autonomy* in the face of the reservation system. Reservations, we know, functioned as administrative spaces, meant to contain Indian people, fixing them in place through multiple forms of supervision. Despite the assault on Native land bases, many Indian reservations, particularly in the west, remained landscapes characterized by great distances. Automotive mobility helped Indian people evade supervision and take possession of the landscape, helping make reservations into distinctly tribal spaces. Indeed, one might read in the antipathy toward Indian automobility a slight whiff of the nervousness surrounding outbreak and independence. Even as the Crow agent lamented that the "only tangible evidence" of 1910 allottee William White's land sale was an automobile, for example, he also grudgingly admitted that White was gainfully employed as an engineer at the Crow school and seemed to be doing fine. And, even as agents and reformers complained about the lack of progress among Indian actors, Miller Brothers 101 Ranch show performers James Pulliam, Howard and Alexander Bad Bear, Ralph Red Bear, and Charles Wounded pooled their 1929 salaries, bought a new Ford Model A in Pontiac, Michigan, and drove it home to Pine Ridge. Such long-distance travel – and especially such travel between reservations – allowed Native people to imagine an even broader vision of Indian country, one that transcended individual tribes and places and helped create new expressions of the pan-Indian and the intertribal. It is no coincidence that the rise of an intertribal powwow circuit began at the same moment as Indian people were acquiring and using automobiles.[25]

The ways in which automobiles entered Native languages provide some evidence of Indian views of the new technology. Many words reproduced the same meaning carried by the English word *automobile*. In Lakota, *iyéhikiyake* means "it runs by itself." In Pawnee, *ariisit rawari* means the same thing – "goes about by itself." These words are likely independent descriptions, though they may perhaps represent more literal translations of the word *automobile*. Others, however, center on different descriptive characteristics. In Blackfeet, the car is a "skunk wagon." The Pawnee *kiriir aawis tarusta* means "Smoking anus" or "smoke from the anus dragging." Still other words refer to the process of starting or driving a car. In Lakota, *naphópela* describes the sound of a motor being cranked: "it bursts or pops rapidly." The word for wheel – *hugmíya* – means a "round leg." The Blackfeet word for *driving* makes a direct correlation between handling a team and handling a car: the verb for to *drive* is the same as that for to *yell at*, reflecting the practice of yelling at a team of horses in order to start them moving. Finally, some languages may have tried to reproduce the sound of the English word itself. The Kiowas refer to a *caw* and an *aulmobil*, clearly English derivatives. In Arikara, *Kataroopi'Iš* has no clear meaning. The linguist Douglas Parks suggests that it may simply be a pronunciation of *automobile*. These words show Native people working to describe and incorporate automobiles within existing cultural frameworks, even to the point of turning *automobile* itself into a thoroughly Indianized word.

[...]

Automobiles must have seemed particularly useful for the ways they opened up the new while continuing to serve older cultural ideals. The car offered transportation for the frequent visits and gatherings so often part of Native life. On the plains, cars easily served as mobile housing, reprising the older functions of both horse and tipi. Indeed, one of the reasons why Native people seemed more inclined to buy cars than motorcycles may well lie in their ability to serve as both transportation and communal living space. My great-aunt Ella Deloria was known to live in her car while traveling the South Dakota reservations during the 1930s and 1940s, and she was hardly alone. Within their cars, Indian families sometimes replicated the social arrangements of the tipi or other lodging, building blanket partitions in order to maintain the avoidance relations necessary to proper kinship behavior. A son-in-law at the wheel might, thus, avoid looking at his mother-in-law, who occupied her own compartment in the back seat. And, where plains people had once decorated and rubbed their horses with sage, they began to place the plant across the front dashboard.

[...]

Consider the seamless integration of the worlds of the Tlingit photographer, merchant, and trapper George Johnson, who bought a 1928 Chevrolet with beaver skins and had it delivered by paddle wheeler to the Canadian north. Johnson painted the car white and chained the tires, the better to use it for winter hunting on the frozen, ninety-mile-long Teslin Lake. Without access to gasoline, he used naphtha. Lacking antifreeze, he drained the water from his radiator whenever he finished driving and kept a bucket of water on the fire ready to use whenever he spotted game from a lakeside watchtower. He built a three-mile-long road (now part of the Alaska Highway) and, in the summer, charged one dollar per ride in the car, which he had dubbed the "Teslin Taxi."[26]

Rather than succumb to the powerful temptation to imagine Indian automobility as anomalous, we might do better to see it in Indian terms – as a cross-cultural dynamic that ignored, not only racial categories, but also those that would separate out modernity from the Indian primitive so closely linked to it. Automobiles, in this sense, can be seen to stand for a broader history of Native use of technology.

[...]

[M]any texts and images linked symbolic Indians and cars together in ways that spoke primarily to white American anxieties about technology and modernity. Automobility, it turns out, wasn't always a celebration of white social-technical prowess. Antagonism between horse-powered farmers and early motorists, for example, could be angrily expressed and slow to dissipate. Ministers railed against the automobile as a threat to a church-going and moral lifestyle. As late as the 1930s, American critics lamented the impending disappearance of the nation's horse culture and pointed an accusing finger at the automobile.[27]

One of the more significant and worrisome changes under way involved the accelerating shift from an ethic of production to one of consumption.[28] While missionaries and government workers sought to impose thrift on Native people, they might have done better to take a closer look at automobile-inspired squandering among

non-Indians. In 1910, automobile dealers first began selling on credit, and many Americans eagerly embarked on the reckless margin buying that would characterize many forms of consumer finance during the 1920s. Other non-Indian Americans emptied savings accounts in order to purchase cars. And not just a few sober farmers mortgaged their land and homes for a set of wheels.[29] The number of cars on the road quintupled between 1920 and 1930, thanks in large part to an American mania for automobility that displaced older notions of fiscal responsibility. As Paul and Helen Lynd noted in their famous study of "Middletown," Depression-struck Americans were willing to part with everything – clothes, plumbing, even food – in order to hang on to the car.[30]

Even as non-Indian Americans rushed to embrace the convenience of automotive technology, then, many worried about what that embrace really meant. Cars themselves appeared simultaneously as symbols of the promise of the future and symbols of the ways in which progress wreaked havoc on cherished communities and ways of life. They evoked a difficult problem – the inextricability of the car's potential and its threat – and they hinted at a solution (or at least a diversion) in the form of a reassuring, nostalgic past. Automobile adventuring seemed to offer a pleasurable and safe reprise of the classic frontier journey of self-discovery, sans threatening Indians or nature. Cars – and automobile marketing – began to evoke the individualist freedom of the western frontier, its passing so widely lamented at the turn of the twentieth century. The automobile, it was suggested, offered a compensatory freedom – that of the untrammeled road (the physical road and the idea of the road both literally under construction at the time). *Hitting the road, the open road*, and the familiar clusters of ideas we've come to expect in road novels and films – all have endured as particularly automotive expressions of a kind of nostalgic, self-actualizing freedom in the twentieth century.

[...]

As numerous scholars have pointed out, manifestations of modernism and antimodernism in the early twentieth century fed off one another in similarly blurry ways.[31] Indian athletes and supermechanics – and cars themselves – might reflect both modernity and nostalgia. The impulse behind the symbolic vocabulary surrounding Indians tended to focus on those things lost to the transformation. As exemplars of a natural life thought to be pure and unchanging, Indians were among the most important symbols used to critique the modern. Indians, it seemed, possessed the community spirit lacking in the city, the spiritual center desired by those troubled by secular science, the reality so missing in a world of artifice. On silver screen and musical stage, in the summer camps of Camp Fire Girls and Woodcraft Indians, in football stadiums and retreats like Taos and Santa Fe, Indians evoked a nostalgic past more authentic and often more desirable than the anxious present. By imagining such a past, projecting it onto the bodies of Indian people, and then devising means to appropriate that (now-Indian) past for themselves, white Americans sought reassurance: they might enjoy modernity while somehow escaping its destructive consequences. [. . .][32]

To preserve the power of such an Indian antimodernism, of course, imagined Indians had to be protected from the contamination of the modern. That separation has driven expectations – even as it has proved impossible to sustain. As in the case of the Jeep Cherokee, the distinct symbolic vocabularies swirling around Indians and automobiles often meshed together smoothly. The pairing of antimodern Indianness with the primitive freedom and adventure of the open road, for example, proved almost irresistible. In the late 1910s, tourism boosters explicitly linked Indians, frontier, and automobility in their hype for the "Black Hills – Sioux Trail," a route that midwesterners took through Chicago and across the Rosebud and Pine Ridge reservations on their way to Yellowstone National Park.[33] Touring guides and maps made the same kinds of connections. The famous Route 66 wound through Indian country, with a resulting swarm of faux-dobe motels, gift shops, and roadside attractions. Indeed, this simulated return to a better past via an automotive migration west through Indian country proved a favorite of promoters of tourism in general. The well-known Harvey Indian Tours, for example, used motor coaches to shuttle tourists from the Santa Fe railroad to Pueblo dances, offering a bracing dose of primitivism to the traveler.

Not surprisingly, the metaphoric linkages between Indians and nostalgic automobility easily extended to the physical form of the car itself. In 1916, a group of Oklahoma investors sought to encode Indian meanings in a new automobile, gathering together in Enid to found, appropriately enough, the Geronimo Motor Company. In 1926, the Oakland Automobile Company introduced the first Pontiacs. These vehicles – the ancestors of today's Cherokees, Dakotas, and Azteks – should be seen in the light of the exchanges of meaning among Indianness, antimodern primitivism, the individualism and

freedom coded in the open roads of the old west, and the automobile, which allowed one to express these ideas through steel and speed.[34]

[. . .]

Notes

1 Angie Debo, *Geronimo: The Man, His Time, His Place* (Norman: University of Oklahoma Press, 1976), 423–4.

2 Michael Murphey and Charles John Quarto, "Geronimo's Cadillac," *Geronimo's Cadillac* (A&M Records, 1972). See also Jan Reid, *The Improbable Rise of Redneck Rock* (Austin: Heidelberg, 1974), 241–75. At the same time, it is worth noting the powerful Native version of the song offered by Mohican singer Bill Miller on *Reservation Road: Bill Miller Live* (Rosebud Records, 1992).

3 My understanding of automotive history is drawn from Michael L. Berger, *Devil Wagon in God's Country: The Automobile and Social Change in Rural America, 1893–1929* (Hamden, Conn.: Archon, 1979); Christopher Finch, *Highways to Heaven: The Auto Biography of America* (New York: HarperCollins, 1992); James J. Flink, *The Automobile Age* (Cambridge, Mass.: MIT Press, 1988), and *The Cat Culture* (Cambridge, Mass.: MIT Press, 1955); Allan Nevins, *Ford* (New York: Scribners', 1954); Robert Lacey, *Ford: The Men and the Machine* (Boston: Little, Brown, 1986); John B. Rae, *The American Automobile: A Brief History* (Chicago: University of Chicago Press, 1965); and Vincent Curcio, *Chrysler: The Life and Times of an Automotive Genius* (New York: Oxford University Press, 2000), esp. 127–212.

4 For the standard early American studies assessment of the relation between technology and culture, still valuable today, see Leo Marx, *The Machine in the Garden: Technology and the Pastoral Ideal in America* (New York: Oxford University Press, 1964). For more specific treatments considering the colonial dimensions, see Michael Adas, *Machines as the Measure of Men: Science, Technology, and Ideologies of Western Dominance* (Ithaca, NY: Cornell University Press, 1989); and Rudolf Mrázek, *Engineers of Happy Land: Technology and Nationalism in a Colony* (Princeton, NJ: Princeton University Press, 2002).

5 Mary Poovey, *Uneven Developments: The Ideological Work of Gender in Mid-Victorian England* (Chicago: University of Chicago Press, 1988), 1–4; Terry Eagleton, *Ideology* (London: Verso, 1991), 1–31.

6 See, e.g., Frederick Hoxie, *A Final Promise: The Campaign to Assimilate the Indians, 1880–1920* (Lincoln: University of Nebraska Press, 1984).

7 *The Indian's Friend* 17 (September 1905): 7. Luther Standing Bear (*My People the Sioux*, ed. E. A. Brininstool [Boston: Houghton Mifflin, 1928], 282) ("Report of C. L.

Davis on Trader Matters," September 3, 1913, NARA [National Archives and Records Administration, Washington, D.C.], RG-75, 12914, box 45, file "S. A. M. Young").

8 *The Indian's Friend* 17 (September 1905): 7, and 18 (June 1906): 2.

9 "Report of W. J. Endecott on Sac and Fox," April 11, 1921, n.p., NARA, RG-75, E-953, box 58, "Sac and Fox Iowa, 1910–27."

10 *The Indian's Friend* 17 (September 1905): 7.

11 For Asbury, see "Crow Reservation Report," 1918, P. 16, NARA, RG-75, M-1011, Annual Narrative and Statistical Reports, roll 30.

12 See Debo, *Geronimo*, 400–27. For the exposition as a pageant of progress, see Robert W. Rydell, *All the World's a Fair: Visions of Empire at American International Expositions, 1876–1916* (Chicago: University of Chicago Press, 1984), and *World of Fairs: The Century of Progress Expositions* (Chicago: University of Chicago Press, 1993). See also Warren I. Susman, "The People's Fair: Cultural Contradictions of a Consumer Society," in *Culture as History: The Transformation of American Society in the Twentieth Century* (New York: Pantheon, 1984), 211–30. For Indians as spectacles, see Robert A. Trennert, "Fairs, Expositions, and the Changing Image of Southwestern Indians, 1876–1904," *New Mexico Historical Review* 62 (1987): 127–50; and Leah Dilworth, *Imagining Indians in the Southwest: Persistent Visions of a Primitive Past* (Washington, DC: Smithsonian Institution Press, 1996), 47–50.

13 Debo, *Geronimo*, 419.

14 For Geronimo's experiences with glassblowing and other technology, see Debo, *Geronimo*, 415–17. For the buffalo hunt, see ibid., 423–4.

15 On María Martínez, see Alice Marriot, *María: The Potter of San Ildefonso* (Norman: University of Oklahoma Press, 1948), 214. On Marsie Harjo, see Joy Harjo's thoughtful meditation "The Place of Origins," in *Partial Recall: With Essays on Photographs of Native North Americans*, ed. Lucy Lippard (New York: New Press, 1992), 89–93. On Bluebird, see "Report of H. S. Traylor," October 31, 1918, n.p., NARA, RG-75, E-953, box 57, "Rosebud 1909–1917." On Walking Bull, see "Report of C. M. Knight: The Shooting of Charles Walking Bull," January 25, 1917, p. 10, NARA, RG-75, E-953, box 57, "Rosebud 1909–1917." On White, see "Sales," p. 6, NARA, RG-75, M-1011, Annual Narrative and Statistical Reports, Crow, 1912, roll 30. On modernities, see Charles Taylor, "Two Theories of Modernity," 172–96, and Dilip Parameshwar Gaonkar, "On Alternative Modernities," 1–23, both in *Alternative Modernities*, ed. Dilip Parameshwar Gaonkar (Durham, NC: Duke University Press, 2001).

16 For the erosion of restrictions on land sales, see John R. Wunder, *"Retained by the People": A History of American Indians and the Bill of Rights* (New York, Oxford

University Press, 1994), 44–51. For Sisseton, see Roy W. Meyer, *History of the Santee Sioux: United States Indian Policy on Trial* (Lincoln: University of Nebraska Press, 1967), 318.

17 Meyer, *History of the Santee Sioux*, 302.

18 See Peter Iverson, *When Indians Became Cowboys: Native Peoples and Cattle Ranching in the American West* (Norman: University of Oklahoma Press, 1994), 70, 78–9.

19 "Report of Charles Davis," May 18, 1909, n.p., NARA, RG-75, E-953, box 57, "Rosebud, 1909–1917."

20 On allotment policy in general, see Leonard Carlson, *Indians, Bureaucrats, and Land: The Dawes Act and the Decline of Indian Farming* (Westport, Conn.: Greenwood, 1981); and Emily Greenwald, *Reconfiguring the Reservation: The Nez Perces, Jicarilla Apaches, and the Dawes Act* (Albuquerque: University of New Mexico Press, 2002).

21 On allotment and land loss, see Janet McDonnell, *The Dispossession of the American Indian, 1887–1934* (Bloomington: Indiana University Press, 1991); Hoxie, *A Final Promise*; and Donald J. Berthrong, "Legacies of the Dawes Act: Bureaucrats and Land Thieves at the Cheyenne-Arapaho Agencies of Omaha," in *The Plains Indians of the Twentieth Century*, ed. Peter Iverson (Norman: University of Oklahoma Press, 1985), 31–54. For the Kiowa agent's report, see "Sales," n.p., NARA, RG-75, M-1011, Annual Narrative and Statistical Reports, Kiowa, 1910, roll 37. For the Omaha, see Judith A. Boughter, *Betraying the Omaha Nation, 1790–1916* (Norman: University of Oklahoma Press, 1998), 184–204, 186 (quotation).

22 "Section IX, Sales," n.p., NARA, RG-75, M-1011, Annual Narrative and Statistical Reports, Crow Reservation, 1912, roll 30.

23 Howard Echo-Hawk, e.g., bought a Hudson two-seater in 1920 using the proceeds from leases on his allotments (Owen Echo-Hawk Sr., interview with Roger Echo-Hawk, January 2, 1982, near Pawnee, Okla.). My thanks to Roger Echo-Hawk for sharing this material. See McDonnell, *Dispossession of the American Indian*, 101, 106, 113–14. For Round Valley, see "Report of H. G. Wilson," n.p., NARA, RG-75, E-953, box 58, "Round Valley, 1910–1924." For Klamath, see "Report of C. H. Asbury," p. 27, NARA, RG-75, M-1011, Annual Narrative and Statistical Reports, Klamath, 1917, roll 73. For Frank Shane, see "Section VII, Sales," P. 13, NARA, RG-75, M-1011, Annual Narrative and Statistical Reports, Crow Reservation, 1917, roll 30. For Bonesteel, see *The Indian's Friend* 16 (August 1904): 1. For reports on other auto purchases linked to unethical behavior on the part of dealers and local officials, see "Report of C. L. Ellis," November 19, 1920, NARA, RG-75, E-953, Inspection Reports, Rosebud, 1909–1931, box 57, "Rosebud 1909–1917," file "Rosebud, 1919–1931"; and "Report of Frank E. Brandon," March 15, 1921, NARA, RG-75, E-953, Inspection Reports, Rosebud, 1909–1931, box 57, "Rosebud 1909–1917," file "Rosebud, 1919–1931." [...]

Ironically, their practice (opening Indians lands to non-Indians) worked to achieve the exact opposite – the liquidation of Indian capital.

24 See, e.g., historical recollections in *70 Years of Pioneer Life in Bennett County, South Dakota, 1911–1981* (Pierre, SD: Bennett County Historical Society, 1981), 32, 47, 493; Gladys Whitehorn Jorgensen, *Before Homesteads in Tripp County and the Rosebud* (Freeman, SD: Pine Hill, 1974), 47–50, 94–101; and Standing Bear, *My People, the Sioux*, 231–47.

25 On White, see "Sales," p. 6, NARA, RG-75, M-1011, Annual Narrative and Statistical Reports, Crow, 1915, roll 30. On 101 actors, see L. G. Moses, *Wild West Shows and the Images of American Indians, 1883–1933* (Albuquerque: University of New Mexico Press, 1996), 265.

26 Jim Robb, "George Johnston: Trapper, Photographer, Merchant," *The Colorful Five Per Cent Illustrated* (Whitehorse, Yukon Territory) 1, no. 1 (1984): n.p.

27 On conflicts over change, see Flink, *Automobile Age*, 140; and Robert S. Lynd and Helen M. Lynd, *Middletown: A Study in American Culture* (New York: Harcourt, Brace, 1929), 251, 259–60.

28 See, e.g., Warren I. Susman, "Culture Heroes: Ford, Barton, Ruth," in *Culture as History*, 122–49, and "The People's Fair." For a powerful treatment of consumerism in the later twentieth century, see Lizabeth Cohen, *A Consumer's Republic: The Politics of Mass Consumption in Postwar America* (New York: Knopf, 2003).

29 On credit and finance, see Flink, *Automobile Age*, 144–7. Note, however, the class and economic constraints that prevented larger portions of the population from owning automobiles. Almost from the beginning, automobile ownership has been used as a measure of American progress. When one puts the automobile in the context of family, the 1929 statistic "one car for every 4.6 people" sounds impressive (ibid., 140). America's highly unequal distribution of wealth and resources ensured that the actual numbers would be different. In 1927, half of American families had no car (ibid., 142). Indians, of course, figured prominently in the "have-not" half.

30 Lynd and Lynd, *Middletown*, 255–6.

31 For a comprehensive historiographic discussion, see Flannery Burke, "Finding What They Came For: The Mabel Dodge Luhan Circle and the Making of a Modern Place, 1912–1930" (Ph. D. diss., University of Wisconsin–Madison, 2002).

32 Philip Deloria, *Playing Indian* (New Haven, Conn.: Yale University Press, 1998), 95–127.

33 *70 Years of Pioneer Life*, 106.

34 On the Geronimo Motor Company, see Debo, *Geronimo*, ix. On Pontiac, see http://www.pontiac.com/history/index.jsp? brand=home&pagename=home (accessed October 10, 2003). In 1902, the founders of the Indian Motorcycle Company picked that company's name to evoke "a wholly American product in the pioneering tradition." By 1913, Indian controlled 42 percent of the American motorcycle market. On the Indian Motorcycle Company, see http://www.indianmotorcycles.com/company/history/ (accessed October 10, 2003).

Reading the "Book of Life": DNA and the Meanings of Identity

Sarah E. Chinn

What Is Life? DNA as Ontology

As rhetorics of blood, citizenship, and racial identity were shifting ground in the mid-1940s, a new way of looking at genealogy was forming in laboratories around the United States and Europe. Appalled by the results of the research on atomic structure that had been so compelling in the first half of the twentieth century, Western scientists shifted their focus from physics to biochemistry – a field that unpacked the mysteries of life rather than providing the tools for dealing with death. Just as physics had been devoted to discovering the smallest possible entity in the physical world, the biologists created a new field of molecular biology that searched for the most basic constituent element of life.

Erwin Schrödinger's *What Is Life?*, published in 1944, was the bible of the new microbiology (not coincidentally, Schrödinger was already a well-known physicist). Depending on the research of Max Delbrück, Schrödinger speculated that genes were information-carriers that moved hereditary information from parents to children. The existence of something like genes, that is, some system by which visible characteristics could be handed down generationally, had already been theorized by Gregor Mendel in his famous pea-plant experiments, in the mid-nineteenth century. Or rather, Mendel's experiments became famous well after he published them in 1865: not until 1900 were they taken up by the scientific community as meaningful. By the beginning of the twentieth century, though, biology had become a field dominated by the microscope and the desire to see previously invisible elements – microbes, viruses, bacteria – that teemed within living things.

Mendel's study suggested that there was something inside the body that caused inherited traits to be transmitted in a schematic way, and biologists started looking for whatever that thing was. Over the next forty years they discovered chromosomes, the thread-like bodies within the cell on which genes are arranged in a linear order, that were made up of nucleic acid, which was made up of individual nucleotides. Each new discovery led to the finding of a smaller, more basic element: from chromosomes to genes, from the cell nucleus to nucleic acid to nucleotides to the nitrogen, sugar, and phosphorus that formed them (Stent, 1980: xiii–xiv). Schrödinger's suggestion that genes were essentially vehicles for information, telling organisms how to look, grow, and function, inspired the postwar generation of scientists to merge biochemistry and genetics into the new field of molecular biology to find out "what life is" (Watson, 1980: 12).

The molecular biologists of the 1950s created a discourse around genetics whose powerful effects we are still feeling almost half a century later, a discourse that saw genes as the answer to the most basic of ontological questions: "What are we?" and "What does it mean to be human?" At the core of the language of contemporary genetics is the figure of DNA (deoxyribonucleic acid), the material out of which genes are made. In his bestselling account of his and his colleagues' discovery of the structure of DNA, *The Double Helix* (1968/1980), James D. Watson imagined the chemical as "the secret of life," the key to the mysteries of human (and in fact all organic) existence (p. 24). Watson and his colleagues responded to Schrödinger's question, "What is life?" with the answer "DNA."

That such a profound philosophical question can have such a mechanistic answer says a great deal about the ways in which molecular biology has shaped our understanding of the relationships between the interiors of our bodies and how we function in the world. The combined force of DNA testing in judicial contexts and the launch of the Human Genome Project, both established in the late 1980s (and about which I will have more to say below) has transformed the place of genetics in the cultural imaginary of the US in the last two decades of the twentieth century. While the details of molecular biology are out of the reach of most Americans, there is a sense that we know what DNA is, what it can tell us about ourselves, and how central it is to every part of our lives as organisms. Indeed, DNA seems to occupy the space of what Evelyn Fox Keller has called "master molecules": entities that, if we can only correctly isolate them, will provide us with a map of the etiology of human disorders ranging from alcoholism and schizophrenia to reading disabilities and PMS. As Fox Keller argues, "[o]nly partly can this expansion of the category of genetic disease be attributed to the development of scientific know-how. In part it is a result of the ideological and institutional expansion of molecular genetics; in part it is simply a result of the cultural triumph of genetic reductionism" (1994: 89).

At the same time, I do not want to capitulate to the fatalism implicit in Fox Keller's argument. The languages of genetics have osmosed to the very edges of the ways in which we talk about ourselves, from television programs to criminal proceedings to educational theory to medical research, but the "genetic reductionism" that Fox Keller deplores has more than one manifestation. Certainly, some of the discourses of DNA have made room for a genetic determinism that is not so far removed from the eugenics of the beginning of the century, and has forged an even stronger fantasmatic link between the workings of embodied heritability and abstract qualities like intelligence, compassion, and social belonging. But for others, DNA has a utopic quality, bringing people together on the basis of the vast majority of genetic material which all human beings share and looking backward to shared prehistoric ancestors, the originators of the genes we all carry around inside us.

[. . .]

DNA is [often] imagined as the bearer of *true* information. That is, while there is considerable debate about what genetic information can be interpreted to mean and how it links to nonmolecular reality, no one argues that DNA does not show with indubitable accuracy the workings of the human (or any other) body on the molecular level. To all intents and purposes, DNA *is* the truth, incontrovertible. Moreover, the discourse of DNA imagines the body's most basic truth as existing in a realm invisible to the majority of Americans. I want to think, then, about not just how we imagine DNA manifesting itself in everyday life, but also how we fill the immense gap between the strangeness of molecular biology, with its wire models, complex formulae, and geometic diagrams, and the "commonsense" assumptions about genetics that are commonplace in US cultural life.

Finally, I hope to untangle the constructions of DNA as meaning. DNA is envisaged as answering a welter of knotted questions about ontology (Who are we?), etiology (Where did we come from?), taxonomy (Where in nature do we fit?), epistemology (How can we know the world?), teleology (What is our purpose?) and, broadly speaking, eschatology (What will happen to us?). These are heavy burdens for a set of molecules so tiny. While I want to clarify what it is DNA *can* tell us, I also want to examine what it is about the place genes occupy in our cultural (and even personal) imaginations that leads us to believe not simply that DNA research could give meaningful answers, but that these answers are to be found most reliably on the molecular level.

Nowhere has this confidence in DNA as the source of answers been more clearly played out than in reactions to the Human Genome Project (HGP), a $3 billion federally funded, multi-year initiative, among whose goals is to map all the genes within the forty-six human chromosomes (that is, the human genome), working out causal links between genes and organismic processes. Launched by Congress in 1988, the HGP is co-sponsored by the Department of Energy and the National Institutes of Health, an alliance that indicates the broad sweep of the project's goals. This is no easy task: the human genome contains about one hundred thousand genes, many of which serve minimal purpose, and some of which serve several purposes (Deaven, 1994: 13). Through technologies like polymerase chain reproduction, technicians can take segments of DNA and reproduce them in identical copies, making it easier to read and compare genetic material from several different people, working out which genetic structures are specific to individuals, and which are characteristic of human beings overall.

The HGP's goal is to construct two kinds of maps of the genome: genetic and physical. A genetic map would determine where on each chromosome specific genes are located, and in which order. Genes exist in what are called base pairs, linked couplings of complementary nucleotides that connect to sugar phosphate backbones in the shape of a spiral staircase (the phosphates are the skeleton of the staircase, the nucleotides are the steps). The order of the nucleotides determines the function of the genes they comprise. A physical map would represent the distances between the genes in the form of a whole chromosome from end to end.

The HGP's larger goal is to read the human body on the molecular level, and to link genes to traits. A central motivation behind this is the desire to root out the causes of heritable terminal diseases such as Huntington's chorea and cystic fibrosis, as well as to locate which specific genetic mutations cause diseases like breast cancer and Alzheimer's, with a view towards more effective cures and even prevention for such diseases. However, there is hardly a one-to-one relationship between gene and trait. Many genes are "uninformative" – they seem to be just fillers on the chromosome. Moreover, mapping and sequencing genes is not a transparent process; its value depends in large part on "the questions one wants the genome map or sequence to answer" (Primrose, 1998: 9).

Genes do not announce themselves by trait: they don't wear labels that say "breast cancer" or "Parkinson's disease" or "schizophrenia." In fact one doesn't look for a specific gene, but for easily identified marker genes that are linked to the gene for the trait being examined (that is, a gene that reproduces along with the trait-specific gene and is found at the same location within a chromosome as that gene). In addition, the genetic patterns that molecular biologists read look nothing like DNA as it exists within the body. Through a complex process of microfuging, hemolyzation, dissolution, chemical separation, lysation, precipitation, and electrophoresis, scientists extract DNA from blood and render it legible as strips of black, white, and grey squares.

The rhetoric of the HGP is complex, particularly since it has embarked on several projects at once: mapping and sequencing the genome, constructing DNA libraries of cloned genetic material that can be internationally available, linking genes to manifested traits, and (although this goal ranks near the bottom of the list) exploring the ethical, legal, and social implications (ELSI) of genetic research and engineering. A bevy of metaphors surround the human genome as it is: the genome is the "book of life," an "ancient hard disk" (an oddly anachronistic presentism), and a "computer operating system" (Doyle, 1994: 52). Whereas the most common technological metaphor for the body at the turn of the century was the machine or the factory (see Seltzer, 1992), DNA is imagined as part of an enormous computer network that combines both database and operating system.

In part so as to nip in the bud futuristic fears of genetic engineering à la *Brave New World,* or more recently *Gattaca,* the HGP has worked hard to present a positive, even heroic image of its work. The Project sells itself as being about pure science on the one hand and helping people on the other, about the noble quest for knowledge and the selfless desire to prevent and heal disease. Implicitly, the HGP also broadcasts its work as a kind of "ontological research – investigating the mysteries of human life itself," not surprisingly, given that the initial Project Director was James D. Watson (Doyle, 1994: 66).

This revelatory claim dovetails with the belief in DNA as the material of truth: if we can get deep enough inside the body to unlock DNA's codes, we will know without a doubt what it means to be human and what materially differentiates human beings from other organisms and from each other. Being able to sketch the shape and configuration of standard genetic structures, such a belief implies, will lead categorically to an understanding of normality and mutation, of health and disease in body and mind and, by association, the health of society. DNA research offers the promise of reconciling the visible outside and occulted inside of the body. It goes beyond medical care, which in comparison seems at best primitive and at worst barbaric, bypassing the vagaries of treatment and going directly to the origin.

[I]n the discourses of DNA [the] fantasy corporeal transparency approaches its apotheosis. Moreover, DNA materializes the sense that one element of the body can synecdochally speak for and even supplant the whole organism. A sample of DNA from any source within a single body – blood, semen, hair, skin – is the same as any other sample from any other source. Hence we can imagine the body as a collation of millions of copies of the same chunk of information (albeit very complex information) gathered together in the shape of a person. The most basic truth of the human body – what we are – becomes a dizzying prospect in the face of DNA discourse, since the DNA fantasm constructs us as both full of an immense number of meanings (genes full of information), and without a significant, knowing center. Unlike the phrenologists of the nineteenth century, or the hematologists of the mid-twentieth, geneticists posit no anatomical hierarchy. DNA from the brain is no different from DNA from toe-nails, no less packed with genetic information but no more significant as a text to be read.

This fantasy of knowability, however, is less self-evident than it seems. Perhaps the most troubling element of the HGP is the effortlessness with which it constructs categories of "normal" and "diseased" or "mutated" genes. The pathologizing of difference is certainly not a new phenomenon, but it is particularly disturbing to see within a technology whose extravagant truth claims have been so fully digested by both professional and lay audiences. How, after all, do we define normality? How do we determine the standard by which mutation is measured? What is genetic mutation evidence of? How do we distinguish between mutation and disease? As Elisabeth Lloyd poses the question, how do we judge the social as opposed to organismic ill-effects of a putatively genetic difference between people (1994: 106).

Without culturally defined judgments of normal or ab/subnormal outcomes, "genes cannot be labeled as normal or abnormal in any but the most trivial respect – that is, insofar as they differ from the paradigmatic unidimensional causal pathway currently accepted for that gene" (Lloyd, 1994: 107). For example, we see differences in stature within specific parameters as part of the normal variation of height within and between families: the fact that I am 5'3" and my brother is 6'1" does not cause our family concern about possible genetic mutation. However, the fact that I am a lesbian and my brother is straight might lead to quite a different result in some circumstances, given the attempts of research into a "gay gene." The concept of "proper functioning" is enormously elastic. Is a benign tumor a sign of disease as obviously as it is a sign of genetic mutation? As Lloyd asks, what values do we have to attach to genetic mutation in order to classify it as disease? Physical disability of some kind? Or social behaviors that fall outside the cultural norm? Moreover, these questions do not even approach the possibility of "abnormal" phenomena as *not* genetically caused.

It is not, then, that genes do not tell us what we are on the most basic level – the stuff we are made of, and the multiple possibilities housed within our bodies. Clearly, DNA analysis can do just that. A deeper issue is the desire for DNA to tell us *who* we are, our place in the world, our relationships to others, which is beyond the power of nucleotides to communicate. Nonetheless, DNA seems to offer a profound revelation of identity. [. . .] Not only can DNA identify, it can link, forging the connection between past and present through heritable genetic arrangements that take on the shape of a narrative of succession. [. . .] DNA analysis can be both synchronic (he was at a certain place at a certain time), and diachronic (his genetic material stretches back in time to his mother and father and beyond), evidence of who he is and what he has done. It is to these two uses of DNA as ontological evidence that I will now turn.

Traces and Matches: Ontology on Trial

While the Human Genome Project is so immense, technical, and complex that most Americans would have trouble imagining what kind of direct impact it might have on their lives, the deployment of DNA evidence for criminal trials and identification more generally seems as familiar to contemporary US culture as fingerprint technology. From its first US use in 1987, DNA matching of criminal defendants has become if not routine certainly matter-of-fact. The high profile of DNA evidence during the double murder trial of O.J. Simpson in 1994 may have complicated public perception of the impermeability of a case built around genetic matches, but it certainly cemented the role of DNA in criminal investigations, which led to the unquestioned invocation of DNA testing in the impeachment trial of Bill Clinton in 1998.

Developments in the technology of DNA testing have been swift-moving and had enormous impact. The innovation of variable number tandem repeat technology, in which a short nucleotide sequence can be repeated tandemly up to a hundred times, and polymerase chain reaction (PCR) procedures, by which small sections of DNA can be reproduced *ad infinitum* with little to no degradation in genetic material, has had a major effect on the industry of DNA analysis, making available larger volumes of testable genes. Given how recent DNA evidence is – it has been in common usage in courts for little more than a decade – the scientific power it wields is remarkable.

DNA evidence is used in criminal trials for identification purposes, to link an accused person to the scene of a crime, either because the supposed perpetrator left some genetic material at the crime scene (some hair, semen, blood, skin) or because the victim's DNA traveled with the perpetrator (for example, traces of blood on shoes or clothes or hair on clothing). Genetic evidence is not used often, mainly because of the price of laboratory analysis, but it has become at the very least the technology of last resort, implicitly exotic but putatively foolproof. It is what Bruno Latour has called a "quasi-object." DNA evidence mediates between the human and the nonhuman, between the real, the social, and the narrated elements of culture. That is, while we imagine DNA to be an object of fact, we experience it through the story we believe it can tell, and the social meanings it bears. DNA is as much signifier as signified.

[. . .]

Narrative is unpredictable, logy, unquantifiable. And it is in this realm of narration that DNA as incontrovertible evidence faces its most difficult obstacles. The two main forms narration takes in terms of DNA forensics is the translation of human body parts into legible genetic information, and the correspondence between genetic patterns and the frequency with which they occur, particularly in specific ethnic and racial groups. These narrative stumbling-blocks have been the source of much debate both among geneticists and for judicial applications of genetic evidence. [. . .]

The most passionate debate over "genetic fingerprinting" in criminal trials erupted over an issue that DNA evidence was supposed to have erased through its objective display of truth: racial and ethnic difference. Given how similar human beings are to each other in genetic make-up, loci at which genes differ from person to person are crucial for establishing a link between two separate pieces of DNA. But, even with the ability to manufacture long chains of repeating DNA, labs cannot reconstruct the entire genome of each person. They examine several stretches of genes and attempt to match them. The question arises, then: How can one prove that the genetic patterns revealed are uniquely those of the person whom they match?

More complicating was the practice by law enforcement and genetic scientists to compile racially and ethnically specific match likelihoods, defining the chances that another person could have the same genetic arrangement at the same site on the chromosome as a given probability within a certain group, such as one in a million among African Americans or one in 475,000 among whites, or a similar formula. It is this practice of estimating probabilities within racial groups that generated a bitter debate among geneticists in the early 1990s, and that illustrates the problems of the confusions of identity of DNA: as simply a real object and as a real, social, and narrated quasi-object.

In an issue of *Science* (1991) Richard C. Lewontin and Daniel L. Hartl published an article that pointed directly to the ambiguities of the narratibility of DNA as an indicator of sample matching. As Lewontin and Hartl argue, DNA match probability within populations can depend a great deal upon what story one tells about those populations. Imagining, for example, that "Hispanic" is an undifferentiated group creates a very different sense of genetic intermixing from acknowledging the differences (and often continental distances) between Puerto Rican, Chicano, Salvadoran, Ecuadorean, Dominican, and Brazilian (to name a few) populations. Moreover, some Latin American countries like Argentina and Peru experienced major infusions of immigrants from Italy, Eastern Europe, North Africa, and East Asia. The genetic patterns of Guatemalans, many of whom have exclusively or mostly American Indian heritage, can hardly be imagined as lining up with the DNA of Cubans, a large number of whom have predominantly African backgrounds.

Similarly, one story about the ethnic constitution of whites in the United States limns a heterogenous, ethnically intermixed group: the proverbial melting-pot. But, as Lewontin and Hartl argue, most of what might be called white ethnic populations are fairly homogenous in the US. Moreover, even if Jews do not exclusively choose other Jews as partners, or Irish other Irish, or Norwegians other Norwegians, exogamous partnerships are fairly new – often no more than one generation old. In addition, regional shifts within a population group (Lewontin and Hartl give the example of Moorish settlement in southern Spain, and other examples are plentiful, such as the concentration of African-descent people in the Bahia region of Brazil, or the ethnic combinations of any borderland area) mean that there can be major genetic dissimilarities within a single country, let alone a region or race. Finally, Lewontin and Hartl found "one-third more genetic variation among Irish, Spanish, Italians, Slavs, Swedes, and other [so-called 'white'] subpopulations than . . . on the average, between Europeans, Asians, Africans, Amerinds, and Oceanians" (1991: 1747).

Given these differences and similarities, as well as the tendency towards endogamy that was the rule until only a generation or two ago, Lewontin and Hartl argue that a story which constructs meaningful racial categories and then assigns to them genetic probabilities is at best mistaken and at worst "terribly misleading" (1991: 1749). What can "white" or "black" mean, let alone the hugely various categories of "Hispanic" or "Asian" (Korean? Pakistani? Uzbeki? Non-Han Chinese?)?

[. . .]

The image of a black woman [such as Lucy] as a founding mother is as foreign to mainstream US culture as a picture of an African Jesus, or the popular post-Black Power scene of Leonardo's *Last Supper* rendered with black figures, both of which can be found in Afrocentric emporia around the United States. [...] It is not too far [however,] from a version of the founding of the United States that long had *sub rosa* currency and in the past few years has been substantiated by genetic research: the story of a child or children fathered by Thomas Jefferson and borne by his slave Sally Hemings.

Jefferson's biographers have long denied the possibility of a sexual relationship between the President and Hemings, a slave who was decades his junior and was brought into the Jefferson household through Thomas' wife Martha Wayles Jefferson. In fact, Hemings was Martha's half-sister: both shared a father, John Wayles. Hemings accompanied her half-niece Maria Jefferson to join Thomas in Paris in 1786 and remained in France until the Jeffersons returned in 1789, during which time historian Fawn Brodie speculates the relationship between Jefferson and Hemings began (Lander and Ellis, 1998: 13). Although it is not clear when Hemings first became pregnant, since her son Madison claimed she first conceived in Paris but there is no extant record of a child, she definitely conceived and gave birth to a daughter, Harriet, at Monticello in 1795; the baby died in 1796. She bore a son, Beverly, in 1798, and a daughter in 1799, who died in infancy. Over the next nine years, Hemings gave birth to three more children: a second Harriet in 1801, Madison in 1805, and another son, Eston, in 1808. All the children were conceived when Jefferson was at Monticello (Gordon-Reed, 1997: 195–6).

In the two centuries between the birth of Hemings' children and the discovery of probable genetic connections between Jefferson's and Hemings' descendants, a bitter dispute raged over whether Jefferson and Hemings were sexually involved, and whether that involvement produced children. Muddying the controversy was the fact that the first suggestion that such a relationship had existed came from James Callender, a previous Jefferson supporter, who in 1802 spread the story about Jefferson's "nigger children" with his slave "Dusky Sally" in an attempt to smear the then President (Gordon-Reed, 1997: 59). The issue was framed in terms of attacks on Jefferson and defenses of him, in terms of scandal and reputation. Jefferson's "defenders" set the pattern for subsequent biographers, claiming that such a relationship would have been "impossible."

[...]

The Jefferson–Hemings debate remained largely ideological, with the Jeffersonians maintaining the upper hand both in the historical record and as guardians of the Jefferson legacy (no small consideration, since Jefferson descendants have access to free tuition at the University of Virginia and burial in the Jefferson family graveyard at Monticello, among other perks). However, in late 1998, Eugene A. Foster and his colleagues revealed in *Nature* that the Y-chromosome DNA haplotypes (that is, specific sets of genetic arrangements) from male-line descendants of Thomas Jefferson's paternal uncle matched those of descendants of Hemings' youngest son, Eston Hemings Jefferson. Foster and his team took samples from five male-line descendants of Field Jefferson, Thomas Jefferson's uncle, five male-line descendants of the two sons of Thomas Woodson, who was identified as the child Sally Hemings conceived in France, and one male-line descendant of Eston Hemings Jefferson, as well as samples from three male-line descendants of the three sons of John Carr, the grandfather of Jefferson's nephews Samuel and Peter who were also rumored to be the father(s) of Hemings' children. Because a substantial amount of the Y-chromosome is passed relatively unchanged through generations from father to son, it is a reliable indicator of male-line relationship (Foster *et al.*, 1998: 27).

Foster and his colleagues found no haplotype correspondence between the Jeffersons and the Woodson or Carr descendants, but did find significant correspondence between the Jefferson and Hemings descendants. These findings led them to the conclusion that "the simplest and most probable explanations . . . are that Thomas Jefferson, rather than one of the Carr brothers, was the father of Eston Hemings Jefferson" (*ibid.*). Although Foster *et al.* suggested other genetic possibilities for this correspondence, they dismissed such theories as "unlikely" (*ibid.*: 28).

These revelations garnered front-page attention in the US and international press, as well as a fair amount of soul-searching. What is most interesting to me, however, is the ways in which the news generated a series of evaluations from a variety of Americans about the relationship between the biological body, the racial body, and the body politic. Certainly, Foster's research produced evidence for the biological connection between Thomas Jefferson and at the very least one of Sally Hemings' children. But it also highlighted the ironies of the genetic apartheid that had so long been the official policy of the white mainstream, and which had been so early and so often transgressed and denied simultaneously.

Most immediately affected by this news were members of the Monticello Association, an élite organization of the descendants of Jefferson's two daughters. The Association had long excluded the Hemings family, citing the absence of material evidence that they were Jeffersons. However, the Association was hardly extreme; its president Robert Gillespie aligned himself with "the mainstream historians [in their belief] that Jefferson wouldn't have fathered Sally Hemings' children" (Smith and Wade, 1998: 24). The DNA evidence, however, "chang[ed] my attitude" (ibid.).

Indeed, the DNA evidence seemed to render established Jefferson experts disoriented to the point of being tongue-tied, so difficult it was for them to integrate this new information into their image of their subject. Joseph J. Ellis, who had recently published a landmark biography of Jefferson, *American Sphinx: The Character of Thomas Jefferson*, in which he had dismissed the stories about Jefferson and Hemings, focused on the DNA research as evidence, using explicitly legal language to couch his volte-face:

> It's not so much a change of heart, but this is really new evidence. And it – prior to this evidence, I think it was a very difficult case to know. . . . [B]ecause I got it wrong, I think I want to step forward and say this new evidence constitutes, well, evidence beyond any reasonable doubt that Jefferson had a longstanding sexual relationship with Sally Hemings.
>
> (Alexander, 1998: 7)

What is striking about these comments is that they are considered *news*. That is to say, the intermixing of black and white was a reality from the first arrival of Africans in North America in the early seventeenth century. Miscegenation was a common trope of slave narratives and abolitionist tracts, noticed by foreign observers and Americans alike. Indeed, the rumors about Jefferson and Hemings were translated by William Wells Brown into one of the many versions of his novel *Clotelle*, variously subtitled "The Senator's Daughter" and "The President's Daughter." Nonetheless, white Jefferson descendants, and many white observers, "had to be dragged kicking and screaming by the production of DNA evidence into admitting the possibility" that the claims of Eston Hemings Jefferson's progeny were legitimate (Truscott, 1998: 10).

The Jefferson–Hemings story reveals a deep vein of denial within the US imagination about slavery. On the one hand, the impregnation of slave women by their owners

and overseers has become a near-cliché of slavery narratives, with Alex Haley's representation of his ancestor Kizzy's rape by the venal Tom Lea in the book and television versions of *Roots* as an archetype of the genre. On the other hand, the rhetoric of distance disembodies this scenario: with the dissolution of desegregation policies and the widespread belief that racism has been banished to the lunatic fringe, the crime of slavery has been rendered "unimaginable," and hence exempt from actual consideration.

Mainstream press interviews with African Americans about the Jefferson–Hemings relationship reveal a significantly different set of beliefs about the constitution of the United States, and the material effects of the racial mixing that was at the very least a major economic element in the gross domestic product of the US until emancipation. For many black Americans, the evidence of the sexual politics of slavery has lain on the surface of their bodies for centuries. As Fareed Thomas, a high school student in Los Angeles, asked in the days after the Jefferson–Hemings story hit, "[w]hy did 'white society' need DNA evidence to accept what 'ordinary people with common sense like me' had recognized as a fact long ago?" (Terry, 1998: A18).

Thomas' language resituates the rhetoric of common sense and American ordinariness from the white mainstream to the black margins. Black invisibility is recast as white blindness, and white scientific expertise is displaced by black knowingness and clear-sightedness. "Look at the black people in this class," Don Terry quotes history teacher Fahamisha Butler as saying; "we are the color of the rainbow. Our ancestors didn't come over from Africa this way" (Terry, 1998: A18). In the same article titled "DNA Results Confirmed Old News About Jefferson, Blacks Say," African Americans of all classes, from the publisher of the *Chicago Reporter* to a high school teacher to a blue-collar worker invoked the common sense of the visible as preceding and superseding the élite evidence of DNA (not to mention the lower position Jefferson occupied among blacks than whites, given his slave-holding).

Perhaps one of the sharpest ironies of this story is that by the middle of his life Eston Hemings Jefferson was passing for white, at least part of the time. In the 1830 Census, Sally Hemings and her two sons Madison and Eston (all freed after Thomas Jefferson's death in 1826) were listed as white, although from the memoirs of Madison Jefferson it seems clear that both sons' neighbors had heard that they were the children of Jefferson and a slave (Gordon-Reed, 1997: 2). Madison and Eston lived as black in Ohio in the 1860s and 1870s but by 1873 all of Madison's siblings "had left the world of blacks and become part of the white world" (Gordon-Reed, 1997: 18).

Eston Hemings Jefferson's children had been born into whiteness, and their current descendants – at least by Shirlee Taylor Haizlip's definition – *are* white. As one of them, Julia Jefferson Westerinen, described in a letter to the *New York Times* just after Foster and his team published their *Nature* article, the contemporary Hemings descendants were in the odd position of claiming a black heritage which their ancestors had been only too happy to give up. Westerinen was well aware of the chasm between her family and others of similar mixed descent who did not pass:

> We cannot know what it is like to be a modern African American or what it must have been like for Sally Hemings when Jefferson stepped over what should have been a boundary of decency in the master–slave relationship. Our branch of the family passed into white society, and we've never experienced the life that might have been ours had circumstances been different.
>
> (Westerinen, 1998)

Rather than dwelling on racial difference, however, Westerinen used the historical fact of her ancestor's passing to unite the body politic into one family. All Americans, she claimed, "come from a long line of ancestors and cannot say we are from 'unmixed' backgrounds. Our common heritage cannot be denied." Annette Gordon-Reed echoed these sentiments on the public television program *Newshour with Jim Lehrer* in November 1998, citing as "the moral of this story . . . that we're not two separate people, black and white; we are a people who share a common culture, a common land, and it turns out a common blood line" (Alexander, 1998: 7).

The rhetoric of the "American family" as an intertwined racial fiber can fray easily, however. As Drew G. Faust pointed out in a letter to the *New York Times* shortly after Westerinen's letter, the claim that "we're all one American family" is dangerously close to the white male slave-owners' self-image as paterfamilias, talking of their "families white and black." Faust focuses on the disjuncture between biology and mutuality, since "in the context of American slavery, sexual liaisons between masters and slaves were almost certainly not romances [and] were in many cases rapes . . . Proclaiming ourselves family means little if we use the language of our slave-owning

forebears to obscure persisting realities of inequality" (Faust, 1998: A24). Or, in the words of high school student Fareed Thomas, "[w]hat kind of society are we living in when we had a President that even owned slaves?"

[. . .]

This is the paradox of DNA: it divides us, it connects us. Our DNA makes us human, but to focus on genetics is to dehumanize the bodies that are its source and its making. It is minuscule and, some believe, omnipotent. The utopian (and paranoid) promise of the Human Genome Project is that we will be revealed to be the sum of our parts; the message of Shirlee Taylor Haizlip and Sally Hemings is that those parts are more various than we had ever imagined (or wanted to imagine). Perhaps the greatest irony of DNA research is that a tool that has placed unprecedented numbers of African Americans behind bars over the decade since its development is now invoked as the proof that those incarcerated bodies are barely differentiated from the bodies of those who turn the key. Indeed, they could very well be related.

References

Alexander, Daryl Royster (1998) "The content of Jefferson's character is revealed at last. Or is it?" *New York Times*, 8 November, late edn, p. IV.7.

Cranor, Carl F. (ed.) (1994) *Are Genes Us? The Social Consequences of the New Genetics*. New Brunswick, NJ: Rutgers University Press.

Deaven, Larry L. (1994) "Mapping and sequencing the human genome," in Cranor, 12–30.

Doyle, Richard (1994) "Vital language," in Cranor, 52–68.

Faust, Drew G. (1998) "Unhappy Echo," letter to Editor, *New York Times*, 9 November, late edn, p. A24.

Foster, Eugene A., M. A. Jobling, P. G. Taylor, P. Donnelly, P. de Knijff, Rene Mieremet, T. Zergal, and C. Tyler-Smith (1998) "Jefferson fathered slave's last child," *Nature*, 396 (5 November): 27–8.

Gordon-Reed, Annette (1997) *Thomas Jefferson and Sally Hemings: An American Controversy*. Charlottesville: University of Virginia Press.

Keller, Evelyn Fox (1994) "Master molecules," in Cranor, 89–95.

Lander Eric and Joseph J. Ellis (1998) "Founding Father," *Nature*, 396 (5 November): 13–14.

Latour, Bruno (1993) *We Have Never Been Modern*, trans. Catherine Porter. Cambridge MA: Harvard University Press.

Lewontin, R. C. and Daniel L. Hartl (1991) "Population genetics," *Science*, 254 (20 December): 1745–50.

Lloyd, Elisabeth (1994) "Normality and variation: the human genome projects and the ideal human type," in Cranor, 99–117.

Primrose, S. B. (1998) *Principles of Genome Analysis: A Guide to Mapping and Sequencing DNA from Different Organisms*, 2nd edn. London: Blackwell.

Seltzer, Mark (1992) *Bodies and Machines*. New York: Routledge.

Smith, Dinitia and Nicholas Wade (1998) "DNA Test Finds Evidence of Jefferson Child by Slave." *New York Times*, 1 November, late edn, p. 1 +.

Stent, Gunther S. (1980) "The DNA double helix and the rise of molecular biology," in Watson, xi–xxi.

Terry, Don (1998) "DNA Results Confirmed Old News About Jefferson, Blacks Say." *New York Times*, 10 November, late edn, p. A18.

Truscott, Lucian K. (1998) "Time for Monticello to Open the Gate." *New York Times*, 5 November, late edn, p. F1 +.

Watson, James D. (1980) *The Double Helix: A Personal Account of the Discovery of the Structures of DNA* [1968], ed. Gunther S. Stent. New York: Norton.

Westerinen, Julia Jefferson (1998) "In Jefferson-Hemings Tie, a Family's Pride," letter to Editor, *New York Times*, 9 November, late edn, p. A24.

Television and the Politics of Difference

Herman S. Gray

The debate over diversity in American network television is, I contend, the expression of a much longer struggle over the production of a national imaginary and the role of commercial television in the construction of that imaginary.[1] As it concerns governing and order, the integrative function of television is central to this process, as are underlying assumptions about culture and representation. Thus the periodic crisis in television over racial representation is less about the network's loss of markets and audience shares than about governance and order.

[. . .]

The Production and Management of Difference

From its inception, coping with difference has been endemic to commercial network television. From the advertiser's need to differentiate products, to attract desired audiences, to the need to form viewers into distinctive markets, television has always produced and managed some form of difference.[2] A series of smaller but related problems stems from the basic contradiction in what Raymond Williams calls television's cultural form.[3] The prospect that audiences would not view, that they would turn away, that they would get it wrong or that the wrong ones might get it, is a consistent concern of network executives and advertisers.[4]

The networks (as well as journalists and, in some cases, scholars) adopted a discourse in which the power of the medium was thought to lie in its potential to plug each of us into the same events and viewing experience. According to the logic of this discourse, at the very least television would form the basis for a feeling and (electronic) experience of national identification and belonging.[5] But this vision of national belonging and identification depended on the exclusion or, at the very least, domestication of the image of Native Americans, Latinos, blacks, Asians, and the transformation of white working-class ethnics into suburban middle-class consumers. For American television, a crucial moment of discursive production of American national identity was the 1950s postwar period of suburbanization and economic expansion.[6]

Television's role in the production of national identity depended on the careful articulation of social, cultural, political, and economic dimensions. It depended on a construction of Americanness targeted domestically at the transformation of ethnic and gender identities and practices from working-class realities into middle-class aspirations and mobility. On the international level, it depended on America's ability (during the Cold War) to contain communism and make the world safe for democracy.[7] The television industry has, of course, always been concerned with managing uncertainty and reducing the economic risks of market instability through the rationalization of production and through extending control over those markets. Economically, the middle-class ideal of American national identity and belonging was articulated in American network television through advertising.[8]

Socially, the middle-class ideal of Americanness was staged in the theater of domesticity, where social ties and identities based on gender, family, and tradition were its primary targets. Labor and time-saving appliances were aimed at white women, whose work and social domains were increasingly defined in terms of the good mother – a nurturing and unselfish figure who remained at home providing for the husband and kids.[9]

Television programming and advertising encouraged working-class white ethnics to abandon the habits, practices, and identifications based on old ties of neighborhood, family, and community in favor of suburban life filled with consumer goods that announced and confirmed achievement of the mythical American dream. The sphere of domesticity, complete with national brands and new forms of association and community, competed with, transformed, and in some cases displaced social relations formerly defined by clubs, bars, and work.[10] Consumption was the hallmark of what it meant to be an American, and as the latest piece of domestic technology the new medium of television, controlled by advertisers, was the emblem of arrival and the primary means of expressing both modernity and Americanness.[11]

At the semiotic level, the dominant genre that came to define (and dominate) American network television, the situation comedy, was a complementary means to ensure identification with home-centered consumption and entertainment. By combining, hence regulating and managing, images and stories designed to ensure familiarity and sameness, predictability, and consistency, television structured the management of certain kinds of difference into its day-to-day operation and strategies of representation. Through the use of genres such as soap operas, situation comedy, and entertainment variety underwritten by sponsored advertising, network television worked hard to articulate its semiotic and economic dimensions to the rhythms of everyday life in the domestic sphere.[12] Implicit in this articulation was the recognition of social differences such as gender, ethnicity, class, public/private, work/leisure, spatial organization, and generations.

In perhaps its most unsettled (and hence most adventurous and innovative) period, the articulation of the social (domestic) and economic (advertising) with the semiotic was applied to disparate sources of the symbolic materials out of which television would fashion a distinctive identity – film, radio, vaudeville, musicals, entertainment variety, and comedy.[13] Combining these disparate sources of programming was a way to symbolically manage differences in location, identity, tradition, and experience of audiences (largely, but not exclusively, within the domestic sphere), in the process forging them into the constitutive elements necessary for the production of a symbolic national identity. Effectively combining

the social, cultural, and economic dimensions of the industrial and semiotic system in this way was made possible by a conception of commercial television's political function as integrative.

As both Lynn Spigel and George Lipsitz have shown, these strategies produced mixed results at best, since this symbolic construction of what it meant to be American had to contend with the stubborn counter-memories of deeply embedded cultural traditions and social realities of everyday life. In particular, Spigel demonstrates that life in the suburban homes of the newly arrived middle class was anything but ideal.[14] Working-class folks, white ethnics, women, and people of color folded the new media and the consumer dreams they sold into lives lived not just in front of the television screen but also beyond it. Some refused the idealized constructions of and identifications with televisual versions of the dream, others selectively incorporated bits and pieces, while still others harbored suspicions about the world they were being taught to desire.[15]

If this discursive management of difference was to be successful in its use of television, the cultural contradictions of the specifically "American dilemma" could not be kept off television. In the 1950s television's role in the production of the national identity was management through selective incorporation, a kind of incorporation that had to grapple with the root problem of attracting and keeping audiences through differentiation. In order to gain and keep its ideal viewers, consumers, and members of the television nation, the networks had to acknowledge audience differences. From the very beginning, then, television's construction of this idealized America was fraught with contradiction, principally the production and management of a difference that always presented the prospect of rupture and refusal.

[. . .]

The subject of television's 1950s family discourse (and, I would add, the nation's) is white and middle class. This is evident in representations of family situation comedies of the late 1950s and early 1960s. But what about the presence of black people in these domestic spaces – particularly black women – for whom such domestic spaces were not just sites of white male leisure or unrecognized reproductive labor for white women? For black women domestics, suburban households were also the sites of racialized wage labor. For this raced and gendered class of workers, domestic work is best defined in public terms rather than the private spaces of domesticity.

Black women domestic workers were subjected to the discourse of television, except that they had specific and particular gender and racial relations to television and domestic labor, a relationship defined in terms of wages and public labor within the private sphere of domesticity. My point is simply that black female workers in television representations and at work were invisible, and necessarily so, because they represented an intractable expression of difference with which television's discourse of integration (from which the emerging national identity was forged) could not cope.

In the formative years of American network television, it seems that race was too unruly a point of difference in the production of the medium's most cherished subjects – consumers, television viewers, and white suburban members of the imagined nation.[16] Nevertheless, as Sasha Torres argues, the encounter with race offered by the civil rights movement provided both television and the emerging genre of television news documentary some of their most dramatic pictures and stories. At the same time, in its encounter with television the civil rights movement found a potent if momentary ally, capable of circulating the movement's powerful moral message and struggle for recognition to the far reaches of the country and the world. In short, television's role in relationship to black participation in the nation coalesced around questions of television's visual style and authority as a news-gathering and reporting institution and the movement's moral claims on nonviolent resistance as the route to legal enfranchisement.[17] On the question of ethnicity, ties of language, religion, and tradition remained the major social obstacles to making the nation out of differences. But the issue of race presented more deeply structural and intractable obstacles, since the American system of racial subordination was still held in place by the residues of scientific racism, Jim Crow practices of racial terror, and the legal enforcement of the doctrine of separate but equal racial segregation. This related set of factors really enabled the production of the white middle-class suburban consumer as the desired subject of the postwar nation of unlimited abundance, infinite possibility, progress, and homogeneity.

Race, Rupture, and the Management of Difference

In the wake of the civil rights movement and the emergence of black power, the late 1960s provided a formidable challenge to this televisual ideal of national identity, and explicitly raised the question of how to manage a dimension of difference that had heretofore remained repressed through exclusion.

[. . .]

Culturally, race was threatening and disruptive. Threatening, that is, to the logic of a universal, normative, and invisible whiteness on which the national imaginary (as recently as the 1950s and 1960s) depended. This threat required management at the level of television's response (both representational and industrial) and at the level of scholarly and journalist discourse that provided the principal account of how to imagine the nation. Integration did this work. The discourse of integration was deeply rooted in the logic of assimilation, which, in the aftermath of the civil rights movement, was codified into a social project of color blindness, a legal project of equal opportunity, and a moral project of individualism and self-responsibility.

The racial politics of the period, however, proved considerably more intractable and complex. Where many working-class white ethnics aspired to middle-class suburban life, as Lipsitz argues, such aspirations were fashioned out of a historically entrenched structure of racialization that facilitated this aspiration for mobility and its realization. This was the active production of the nation in action. Guaranteed low-interest federal housing loans, massive highway construction, college scholarships, and job training were made available to white service members and other white ethnics to ensure their social and physical mobility.[18] Redlining practices in real estate, together with race-based lending policies of banks and other financial institutions, helped to contain blacks and Latinos in segregated inner-city neighborhoods, entry-level jobs, and limited educational opportunities.[19] Materially, then, the construction of the nation out of white cultural aspirations to realize the American dream was fashioned out of specific historical and material conditions of possibility, in which race-based social practices and legal policies were the order of the day. Culturally, these mobility aspirations were shaped from a desire to move away from the population centers where blacks, Latinos, and Asians were the newly recognized citizens and potential neighbors that many "real" Americans wanted most to avoid. Despite the legally and morally charged language of equal opportunity and color blindness, by the middle decades of the 1960s many whites identified with the dream of segregated suburban middle-class worlds promoted by television representations and, more importantly, they equated these lives with what it meant to be American.[20]

The discourse of color blindness (as distinct from equal opportunity) posed problems for communities of color as well. In the wake of the black power movement and the strong thought of racial and ethnic nationalism, some (black) folk simply rejected the principle of invisibility and the slide toward whiteness as the universal subject of television and the imagined American nation. Blacks wanted cultural membership in the imagined nation constructed by television, but on different terms. At the very least, such terms meant acknowledging significant differences in cultural tradition, experience, and history. Indeed, while many blacks did aspire to the suburban middle-class life promised by the American dream and promoted by television, others insisted on black-generated ideas about the (black) nation that could be programmed within the context of the existing network structure.

These discursive, political, and material circumstances placed the problem of the representation and management of racial difference on a semiotic and economic collision course. Where the racial politics of television's golden era provided a model for managing issues of class, ethnicity, and gender, after the civil rights movement and the onset of racial nationalism, there was little assurance that such a strategy of incorporation and containment within the domestic sphere would result in effective semiotic and political economic management of racial difference. By following the integrationist logic, the gamble was that extending television's national imagination to include racial groups in the sphere of domesticity would sufficiently loosen suspicions about racial and cultural difference. Accordingly, whites would eventually come to feel comfortable with people of color as televisual citizens, friends, neighbors, and family members as WASPs had done with working-class European immigrants. But with the new militancy and nationalism there was little guarantee that communities of color, with their different and particular histories, conflicts, and traditions, would aspire to membership on these terms.

The potential (and actual) rupture occasioned by the problem of race opened complicated debates about the national identity, belonging, and citizenship that have continued to define controversies over network television and racial inclusion. Race is the repressed that returned in the 1970s and 1980s, rupturing the integrationist ideal of the homogeneous middle-class America constructed on network television. So dramatic and far-reaching was this return of the racially repressed that along with the

need to extend network control over an unruly and chaotic market, the confrontation with race forced a modification in the semiotic and political economic order of American commercial network television. In the industry vernacular of the period, the turn to relevant programming included the representations of racial and ethnic difference. Representations of race opened the way for other points of social difference such as class, region, and generation as the basis for distinctive cultural identities with which television (and the nation) had to contend.[21]

The civil rights movement produced blacks, Latinos, and Asians as full political, legal, cultural subjects that television could no longer ignore, marginalize, or blatantly stereotype. At the same time, commercial network television had to figure out how to economically harness and culturally recognize these new legal subjects of the nation. Networks had to figure out how to incorporate the cultural traditions and identities of the new subjects in such a way as to make them profitable and yet not to scare away whites.[22] African Americans did indeed become visible (if contained and limited) subjects in the semiotic landscape of network television, if only as a result of the moral imperative and political pressure on television to meet its responsibility to offer more inclusive and racially diverse programming. The networks still had to avoid alienating whites, and it fell to the discourse of liberal pluralism as a strategy of management and containment to do both – that is, to make blacks visible and to hold the racial center by not alienating whites.

Instead of homogeneity created out of difference through consumption in the suburban domestic sphere, liberal pluralism constructed parallel universes in which different cultural identities based on race were acknowledged but contained (within genres, programming strips, and networks schedules). Rather than one version of domesticity, now there were several – white, black, working-class, middle-class, and so on. Organized into markets based on class and race, consumption and commodities became the currency that held the imagined American national identity together. While the ideal subject of the nation imagined by television remained white, middle-class, and suburban, the discourse of liberal pluralism ensured that television representations would now include blacks (and, to a far less extent, Latinos and Asians) and women. The ideology of equal opportunity could be represented (through consumption and culture) without threatening the political gains of the civil rights movement or the cultural and political hegemony of whiteness. Most of all, this separate but equal universe solved the problem of alienating white viewers and appeasing black ones, all of whom were still connected to the dominant network structure.

This was achieved by the network's organization and structure – its political economy, which was defined by the dominance of the three-network system, and its semiotic economy, which rested on a representational logic that moved between the ideal of racial integration and the reality of a liberal pluralism expressed as racially identifiable programs.[23] Managing black representations through the logic of the three-network structure and explicitly identifiable programming enabled the commercial networks to respond to moral and political pressure (from blacks) and to capitalize on the potentialities of these new audience segments. As the television industry continues to restructure itself, the persistence of this logic produces a periodic crisis around the representation of race. The problem is neither that people of color are absent on television nor that television continues its press toward the representation of the national imaginary as white and homogeneous.[24] Rather, the structural (and representational) logic of difference (e.g., the three network system) around which television structured itself made network television the site least able to construct and hold a coherent view of a national imaginary like the one that network programming presented in its golden age.[25]

[. . .]

Instability and the Necessity of Difference

In the neo-network era, is it possible that we have finally reached the limit of the purported integrative function of commercial network television in the symbolic and imaginary production of the nation?[26] I believe that the answer is yes, owing to structural changes in the organization, production, and circulation of the television industry, to repurposing and recombining of content along a new logic, as well as to conceptions of the nation and struggles over its constitution.[27] In other words, this discursive limit expresses the failure of a liberal pluralist vision of a national imaginary achieved through the management of cultural difference. The three-network structure of commercial television in the United States has proved to be a limited, if not outright ineffective, means of realizing this desire. To the extent that television ever did produce effective national identifications by managing racial difference through exclusion and eventually incorporation, it did so primarily through representation

and consumption. In a three-network system built on relative market stability, the search for the certainty that was guaranteed by increased audience share over competitors was achieved through periodic restructuring that simply divided and redivided a finite market among the three major television networks. From the beginning, network television established its defining cultural identity as a medium of communication located primarily in the domestic sphere. Culturally and socially the home-centered experience of network television produced real access to the symbolic televisual representation of the nation and an imaginary sense of belonging that linked subject, consumer, and citizen within the domestic sphere.[28] This home-centered experience is the basis of the link between citizenship, family, nation, mobility, and consumption that Spigel and Lipsitz saw as so important to the production of the nation and the management of difference from the 1950s through the 1970s.

But American network television is no longer organized simply to manage difference and reduce market uncertainties that threaten the dominance of a limited number of players. The logic of difference and the recognition of unlimited possibilities for new markets have been grafted into the very structure and organization of commercial television, but on a global scale.[29] Conceptions of a finite domestic-centered American market have been replaced with the recognition of the global centrality and possibility of difference.[30] [. . .] The corporate brand name and network logo have become the means of expressing distinction and thus the recognition of the intractability of difference on a global scale. Problems of race and ethnicity have given way to the question of how to link a brand name to specific kinds of difference – culture, nation-states, gender, sexuality, and tradition – in order to establish distinctive brand identifications and loyalty through consumerism.[31]

At the level of political economy, new global entities have been formed through massive restructuring, the emergence of new sites of production, and the introduction of new technologies. Niche marketing, narrowcasting (marketing to a specific demographic segment), repurposing (combining and recombining programs with the purpose of creating new products and attracting new audiences), technological convergence, and alternative forms of service delivery now define the political economic terrain of television and new media.[32] Difference, diversity, and diversification of all sorts are the hallmarks of the industry's political and symbolic economy. Built on diversification, difference, and commodification, the massive restructuring of the global media industries located chiefly, but by no means primarily, in the West is designed precisely to pick up the smallest changes in the market and to respond to them instantaneously.[33]

[. . .]

The proliferation of discourses about difference and the representation of difference also found its way, as might be expected, into the television programming schedules. By the middle of the 1990s, American network television schedules were populated with outward signifiers of all sorts of cultural difference – gays and lesbians, blacks, liberal feminist, even extraterrestrial beings.[34] Program makers and advertisers, in particular, promoted a sensibility that quickly recognized and acknowledged differences of all sorts, especially cultural difference.[35] In the 1960s and 1970s, television played a major role in circulating and translating the civil rights discourse of equality to the level of everyday life and common sense. By the 1990s, television played an equally powerful role in deconstructing and rearticulating that political common sense to a neoconservatism that culturally reinscribed and socially reinstalled white males as the universal subjects.[36] It did so by emphasizing the principle of color blindness and the absence of racism.[37]

Against the backdrop of the cultural politics of difference, the correspondence between market segmentation, service delivery, and identity is no longer just aimed at the incorporation of unruly manifestations of difference that threaten the imagined nation or its ideal racialized subjects. This transformation in the recognition and representation of difference has had a profound impact discursively on the role of television in the making of the imagined nation. That is, television networks, program providers, and viewers are all driven by a logic of difference that ends up (re)structuring the national identity through the recognition and embrace of difference rather than through its elimination, repression, or incorporation.

Differently located and socially constituted active audiences of all sorts seek out, migrate to, and ignore programming now available as a result of the very restructuring forces that were initially designed to reduce the uncertainties of difference. Program scheduling options, though still structured by a few large global players, are no longer confined to three commercial networks, whose operations are defined by the classical monopoly logic of "broadcasting" that dominated the golden era. There is a significant distinction between contemporary active audiences – in their refusals and migrations – and the image of the passive viewer from the 1950s who was

purportedly all too eager to join the imagined television nation. In the neo-network structure of transmodern television, specialized markets, narrow-casting, dispersed production centers, and differentiated profit centers depend on the simultaneous operation of different logics able to recognize and respond to the proliferation of differences of all sorts.[38] It is the centrality of difference and recognition of its multiple logics that make up the terrain on which notions of a collective national imagination is necessarily constructed and represented.

[. . .]

Difference, Illegibility and Instability

I want to [. . .] return [. . .] to the role of television in fashioning national identity through the management of difference structured by specific conceptions of the nation and networks. As I have explained, these discursive investments result in a cultural politics fashioned out of commitments to a liberal pluralist model of society. To my mind, such politics are at best critically impoverished and at worst ineffective because they fail to expose and exploit the discursive gaps and fissures between lingering modernist conceptions of the nation and the shifting logic of television as a transmodern, post-network media (situated in a global information economy).

The signature assumption of liberal pluralist discourses on which idealized conceptions of the national imaginary rest is a notion of stable, orderly, and manageable social order that tries to manage (racial difference) through market choices, electoral politics, and the production of a common cultural identity rooted in consumption. However, [. . .] I want to begin with instability rather than order, where "variation does not come about as a result of the division of a given social entity into a fixed range of meaningful identities," and where "the infinite play of differences . . . make all identities and all meanings precarious and unstable."[39]

In its global reach, the contemporary state of American network television is in just such a condition. The central point here is that nations are limited in their ability to manage and contain difference and to produce homogeneity on the basis of such management. It is the "proliferation of difference that liberal pluralists cannot account for and which the functionalist technology of audience measurement attempts to account for, suppress and tame in the form of ratings or statistical measurement."[40]

Beginning with instability as the basis of a productive theorization of cultural politics suggests, then, that indeterminacy and diversity are the persistent social and cultural realities that structure and economically distinguish contemporary global media. No longer is the primary emphasis just on integrative functions aimed at producing a coherent one-dimensional narrative of homogeneity – the management of difference through incorporation or even its regulation through recognition.

Instead of seeing the network's unwillingness to show more diverse cultural representations as a lack of moral courage, a poor business choice, or a periodic lapse in social judgment, as media activists contend, we can look to the circumstances where such decisions are routine and culturally acceptable in the first place. Furthermore, rather than see audience deficiency when we look at data on viewing patterns by race, what if we reconsider the viewing patterns of (active) audiences of color, regarding their viewing practices as a refusal, an expression of the bankruptcy of the integrative promise of television in the making of the imagined nation.[41] Global media companies, including network television, face a new set of symbolic and managerial challenges. The drive is not just to control the global proliferation of difference, but also to exploit it. This instability and uncertainty are two elements of the new cultural logics of post or neo-network American television.

From the perspective of the infinite possibility of difference we might see the active recognition and structuring of difference by commercial television, where the imagined nation is concerned, as the active production of a kind of illegibility of the nation. [. . .] But from another vantage point, that of audiences and the global movement of programs and images, it may be that many television viewers respond to the loss of meaning and legibility of television's imagined nation by negotiating the television system on different terms. That is, national legibility, social integration, and cultural belonging may no longer be the cultural logic that defines television's relationship to the American nation-state.

[. . .]

I want to claim for the active audiences of color (within limits, of course) a kind of productive potentiality of retreat, withdrawal, and negotiation with television, especially its symbolic production of the nation.[42] Active audiences are both the subjects and objects of modern consumer capitalism. In the United States, the ideology of free access and viewer choice is the primary means by which people are drawn into the system of consumption and reproduction. The choice is, of course, made available within determinations that are by no means infinite and open-ended.

This conception of choice by active audiences within a set of structural limits is important for thinking about audiences of color as active – seeking, retreating, rejecting, and pursuing images and representations they "choose" across the televisual landscape. [. . .] [W]ithin the options available, black audiences, for instance, seek out and follow (black) programming on Fox, Warner Brothers, and United Paramount. This pursuit is also a refusal, the flip side of passively accommodating to programming offerings that they do not find to their liking. Such choosing and refusing follow the systemic logic of the television system, based as it is on measuring audience viewing patterns and deciding from among them which consumers to pursue.

This logic, and the periodic moral panics and the political initiatives they spawn, are rooted in a liberal integrative model of society, governing, nation, and citizenship, one that the current global circumstance renders illegible. It seems to me that political and moral advocates who continue to desire this integrative model of television in the production of the national imaginary implicitly accept a view of the relationship between modernity, broadcasting, and the state born in television's golden era. Despite its moral and cultural rhetoric, in the universe of commercial television, not all viewers are equally desired. Nor is it the case that the consumptive powers of all audiences guarantee a measure of visibility and exchange in the marketplace of consumer choice. Advertisers simply prefer some kinds of consumers, tastes, and desires to others. Liberal journalists, television executives, and activists continue to cling to a liberal model of the power of the market and the state to ensure the integrative management of racial and class difference in the face of this evidence. In doing so, these advocates ignore and reject the forms of popular legibility and cultural practice of active audiences of color whose very moves and negotiation of the television system serve, at the very least, to question and critique discursive constructions of nation rooted in the cultural politics of recognition, representativeness, and integration.

Of course, as a political strategy and galvanizing force of media activism, the integrative promise of network television as an expression of the social and cultural national imaginary continues to have appeal. The logic of this discourse produces politics and moral suasion that periodically pressure the commercial networks to schedule and broadcast programming that includes people of color, women, gays, and lesbians (both in front of and behind the camera). At the level of the industrial organization and media industries, these politics square with the market logic of consumption and commodity choice. This cultural logic also leads to periodic restructuring, which is global in reach, differentiated in structure, and designed to make difference and distinction (rather than incorporation and homogeneity) the basis of profitability.

This cultural logic, which of necessity acknowledges and seeks to exploit difference, appears in expressive forms of popular music, television, cinema, advertising, fashion, and print; it promotes the unstable, fragmentary, and momentary nature of cultural identities made in and through representation.[43] Television makers must increasingly deal with active audiences who register their desire and identities through refusal and retreat, cynicism, inattention, and suspicion. These dispositions now form the basis of critical and active relationships to television representations of the social world and the nation. As such, they can potentially form the critical basis for the realization that nations "are not the natural destiny of pre-given cultures; rather, their existence is based upon the construction of a standardized national culture that is the pre-requisite to the functioning of the modern industrial state."[44]

Notes

1   George Lipsitz, "The Meaning of Memory: Family, Class, and Ethnicity in Early American Network Television," in *Time Passages: Collective Memory and American Popular Culture*, by George Lipsitz (Minneapolis: University of Minnesota Press, 1990), 39–77; Lynn Spigel, "The Suburban Home Companion: Television and the Neighborhood Ideal in Postwar America," in *Welcome to the Dreamhouse: Popular Media and Postwar Suburbs*, by Lynn Spigel (Durham, NC: Duke University Press, 2001), 31–59; Spigel, *Make Room for TV: Television and the Family Ideal in Postwar America* (University of Chicago Press, 1992); William Boddy, *Fifties Television: The Industry and Its Critics* (Urbana: University of Illinois Press, 1990); Michael Curtin, *Redeeming the Wasteland: Television Documentary and Cold War Politics* (New Brunswick, NJ: Rutgers University Press, 1995); Mark Williams, "Entertaining 'Difference': Strains of Orientalism in Early Los Angeles Television," in *Living Color: Race and Television in the United States*, ed. Sasha Torres (Durham, NC: Duke University Press, 1998), 12–34; Pamela Wilson, "Confronting the 'Indian Problem': Media Discourses of Race, Ethnicity, Nation, and Empire in 1950s America," in *Living Color*, ed. Sasha Torres, 35–61; Victoria E. Johnson,

"Citizen Welk: Bubbles, Blue Hair and Middle America," in *The Revolution Wasn't Televised: Sixties Television and Social Conflict*, ed. Lynn Spigel and Michael Curtin (New York: Routledge, 1997), 265–85; Darrell Y. Hamamoto, "White Christian Nation," in *Monitored Peril: Asian Americans and the Politics of TV Representation*, by Darrell Y. Hamamoto (Minneapolis: University of Minnesota Press, 1994), 1–31.

2   Johnson, "Citizen Welk"; Spigel, *Welcome to the Dreamhouse*.

3   Raymond Williams, *Television: Technology and Cultural Form* (New York: Schocken Books, 1974).

4   John Hartley, *The Uses of Television* (New York: Routledge, 1999).

5   The following works examine the way that television's programming content (Newcomb) and industrial structure (Boddy) worked to produce the feeling of national identification and belonging: Boddy, *Fifties Television*; Horace Newcomb, "From Old Frontier to New Frontier," in *The Revolution Wasn't Televised: Sixties Television and Social Conflict*, ed. Lynn Spigel and Michael Curtin (New York: Routledge, 1997), 287–305.

6   Spigel, *Welcome to the Dreamhouse*. In an especially rich line of argument, Sasha Torres suggests that television's news coverage of blacks in this period was far more generous. As she shows, this coverage is less a matter of altruism than the need for television as an emerging medium and genre to establish its legitimacy as a news discourse. Similarly, television provided the movement with the opportunity and the stage to establish its moral claims to social justice and full participation in the nation. In her view, this complex relationship resulted in a television-produced image of a nation struggling with issues of racial difference as the basis of inequality and injustice. See Sasha Torres, *Black, White, and in Color: Television and Black Civil Rights* (Princeton, NJ: Princeton University Press, 2003), 13–36.

7   Curtin, *Redeeming the Wasteland*; See also Michael Curtin, "Dynasty in Drag: Imagining Global TV," in *The Revolution Wasn't Televised: Sixties Television and Social Conflict*, ed. Lynn Spigel and Michael Curtin (New York: Routledge, 1997), 245–65.

8   See Boddy, *Fifties Television*; Mark Alvey, "The Independents: Rethinking the Television Studio System," in *The Revolution Wasn't Televised: Sixties Television and Social Conflict*, ed. Lynn Spigel and Michael Curtin (New York: Routledge, 1997), 139–61.

9   Hartley, *The Uses of Television*; Spigel, *Make Room for TV*; Spigel, "The Suburban Home Companion: Television and the Neighborhood Ideal in Postwar America," in *Welcome to the Dreamhouse*, 31–60.

10 Anna McCarthy, *Ambient Television: Visual Culture and Public Space* (Durham, NC: Duke University Press, 2000).

11 Spigel, *Make Room for TV*.

12 Williams, *Television*.

13 For a fuller discussion of this articulation, see Alvey, "The Independents"; Johnson, "Citizen Welk."

14 Lipsitz, "The Meaning of Memory"; Spigel, *Welcome to the Dreamhouse.*

15 Hartley, *The Uses of Television*; Lipsitz, "The Meaning of Memory"; Spigel, *Make Room for TV*; Spigel, "Outer Space and Inner Cities: African American Responses to NASA," in *Welcome to the Dreamhouse*, 141–85.

16 For a discussion of television's relationship to representations of Native Americans and Asian Americans, see Wilson, "Confronting the 'Indian Problem' "; Hamamoto, "White Christian Nation."

17 Torres, *Black, White, and in Color.*

18 Lipsitz, "The Meaning of Memory"; George Lipsitz, "Law and Order: Civil Rights Laws and White Privilege," in *The Possessive Investment in Whiteness: How White People Profit from Identity Politics*, by George Lipsitz (Philadelphia: Temple University Press, 1998), 24–46.

19 See Melvin L. Oliver and Thomas M. Shapiro, *Black Wealth/White Wealth: A New Perspective on Racial Inequality* (New York: Routledge, 1995); Spigel, "Outer Space and Inner Cities."

20 Marlon T. Riggs, *Color Adjustment*, film (San Francisco: California Newsreel, 1991); Spigel, *Welcome to the Dreamhouse.*

21 For more on the turn to relevance in television, see Todd Gitlin, *Inside Prime Time* (New York: Pantheon Books, 1983).

22 Sarah Binet-Weiser argues that the racial politics of visibility involve making racial difference visible while not disturbing the logic around which the dominant (racial) center holds. See Sarah Binet-Weiser, *The Most Beautiful Girl in the World* (Berkeley: University of California Press, 1999). See also Bambi L. Haggins. "Why 'Beulah' and 'Andy' Still Play Today: Minstrelsy in the New Millennium," in *Globalization, Convergence, Identity: Ethnic Notions and National Identity*, ed. John T. Caldwell and Bambi L. Haggins, special issue, pt. 2, *Emergences: Journal for the Study of Media and Composite Cultures* 11, no. 2 (2001): 189–99.

23 Herman Gray, *Watching Race: Television and the Struggle for Blackness* (Minneapolis: University of Minnesota Press, 1995).

24 See Robert M. Entman and Andrew Rojecki, *The Black Image in the White Mind* (Chicago: University of Chicago Press, 2000).

25 As Lynn Spigel points out, the possible exception to this situation is television news, especially in times of crisis (personal communication, October 1999).

26 On the idea of neo-networks see Curtin, "Dynasty in Drag"; John T. Caldwell, "The Business of New Media," in *The New Media Handbook*, ed. Dan Harries (London: BFI Publishing, 2002); John T. Caldwell, "Convergence Television: Aggregating Form and Re-Purposing Content in the Culture of Conglomeration," in *Television after TV*, ed. Lynn Spigel (Durham, NC: Duke University Press, 2004).

27 Caldwell, "Convergence Television."

28 James Hay, "Unaided Virtues: The Neoliberalization of the Domestic Sphere," *Television and New Media* 1, no. 1 (2000): 53–73.

29 Caldwell, "The Business of New Media" and "Convergence Television."

30 See McCarthy, *Ambient Television.*

31 Caldwell, "Convergence Television."

32 Caldwell, "The Business of New Media" and "Convergence Television"; Anna Everett and John T. Caldwell, eds., *Theories and Practices of Digitextuality* (New York: Routledge, 2003).

33 Curtin, "Feminine Desire in the Age of Satellite Television," and Curtin, "Gatekeeping in the Neo-Network Era," in *Advocacy Groups and the Entertainment Industry*, senior ed. Michael Susman (Westport, Conn.: Praeger, 2000); John T. Caldwell *Televisuality: Style, Crisis, and Authority in American Television* (New Brunswick, NJ: Rutgers University Press, 1995); Caldwell, "Convergence Television."

34 L. S. Kim and Gilberto Moises Blasini, "The Performance of Multicultural Identity in US Network Television: Shiny, Happy Popstars (Holding Hands)," in *Globalization, Convergence, Identity*, ed. Caldwell and Haggins, 287–309.

35 Robert Goldman and Stephen Papson, *Sign Wars: The Cluttered Landscape of Advertising* (New York: Guilford Press, 1999); S. Craig Watkins, *Representing: Hip-Hop Culture and the Production of Black Cinema* (Chicago: University of Chicago Press, 1998).

36 Lipsitz, *The Possessive Investment in Whiteness*; see also Entman and Rojecki, *The Black Image.*

37 Gray, *Watching Race*; Robin D. G. Kelley, *Yo Mama's Disfunktional! Fighting the Culture Wars in Urban America* (Boston: Beacon Press, 1997); Watkins, *Representing.*

38 Caldwell, "Convergence Television."

39 Ien Ang, *Living Room Wars: Rethinking Media Audiences for a Post-modern World* (New York: Routledge, 1996), 172.

40 Ibid., 174.

41 Robin R. Means Coleman, *African American Viewers and the Black Situation Comedy* (New York: Garland Publishing, 2000).

42 Darnell Hunt's empirically based work on race and media is very suggestive in the area of what he calls raced ways of seeing and the assumptions about nation, justice, fairness that are articulated by race. See Darnell Hunt, *Screening the Los Angeles "Riots": Race, Seeing, and Resistance* (Cambridge: Cambridge University Press, 1997), and *O.J.: Fact and Fiction* (Cambridge: Cambridge University Press, 1999). See also Entman and Rojecki, *The Black Image.*

43 Kim and Blasini, "The Performance of Multicultural Identity"; Caldwell and Haggins, *Globalization, Convergence, Identity*, special issue, pt. 2, of *Emergences.*

44 Ang, *Living Room Wars*, 144.

Part VIII

Sites, Space, and Land

The analytic we call Sites, Space, and Land demonstrates an important continuity between traditional and new American Studies. Much of the originality that distinguished traditional American Studies from other forms of literary and cultural history manifested as a claim that the uniqueness of the land itself granted specific qualities to the cultural forms that grew from it. Classic works contextualized canonical and popular literature as encounters between fresh minds and "virgin lands," "gardens," and even "Eden." Newer efforts to situate the place of cultural production have focused on the ways that power is marked on the land, the "legacies of conquest," and the intersection between unequally distributed natural resources and differently distributed cultural resources. Much of the new scholarship that enacts this analytic has been influenced by social science disciplines, particularly the work of cultural geographers. Geography's focus on the specifics of place and the cultural transformations that construct space enables a rethinking of "the garden" in which the machine appears and the absurdity of any concept of "virgin land." The focus on the place of cultural encounters, the space of cultural production, and the legal as well as environmental factors that structure human activity demonstrates that places are and have been peopled and infused with power legacies of overlapping experiences of conquest and multiple contestations.

Scholars have examined the myriad ways in which space, land, and nature are culturally produced, along with exploring the contingent and ongoing specificity of the local. Amy Kaplan challenges images of the purportedly exceptional status of the US Naval Station at Guantánamo that render Guantánamo as a spatial and legal anomaly. For Kaplan, Guantánamo represents the start of the "road to Abu Ghraib" and is "one island in a global penal archipelago." Dismantling the "common sense" that sees the naval station's location in Cuba as "seemingly bizarre," Kaplan reminds us of the US imperial history in Guantánamo Bay and, further, explores the legacy of the *Insular Cases* (1902–22) to understand how 2005 court decisions remapped Guantánamo as an infinite legal borderland between the foreign and domestic. As the Bush administration defined Guantánamo as a space beyond the reach of US domestic law and created the category of "enemy combatants," the courts extended a shadowy hybrid legal system, ambiguous and flexible enough to respond to the shifting needs of US empire. Richard White examines the various and intersecting geographies of energy on the Columbia River and the interaction between the river and human and salmon societies. The energy system of the Columbia River determined where humans could portage, but human labor created the actual route and human social relations determined its form and outcome. White explores the importance of spatial arrangements in human history through examining repeated conflicts over the organization of space at specific locales of rapids and falls along the Columbia that were critical sites in the geography of energy, as well as in the social, cultural, and political geography constructed by humans. Where whites regarded the space as culturally empty and Indians regarded it as culturally full, Indians expected gifts to mediate and smooth passage through the social maze, while whites supplanted gifts with force and the space became uniquely violent.

Scholars have reexamined the specific cultural impact of global capitalist development on local environments, traced the destruction of cities through the pressures of suburbanization and urban renewal, and have reconnected racialized urban and suburban districts to the metropolitan contexts that surround and infuse them. Geographers, in particular, have explored the intersections of space and human practice.

Arguing that white privilege is a form of racism distinct from both institutional racism and overt racism, Laura Pulido argues that white privilege is particularly useful for understanding the urban landscape. Simultaneously spatial and historical, landscapes embody generations of socio-spatial relations; and the study of urban landscapes demand methodological considerations that will account for the historical as well as spatial dimensions. In addition, the concept of the public sphere has been subject to a rigorous interrogation resulting in the reexamination of the ways in which specific populations gain or are refused access to current definitions of legitimate public concerns. Lizabeth Cohen tracks the transformation of the suburban landscape through the development of shopping malls in post-World-War-II Paramus, New Jersey, a model of a new and distinct metropolitan marketplace that emerged in that era. Within the regional shopping center, public space was more commercialized, privatized, and feminized than it had been in older downtown centers. This commercialization of the public and privatization of public space through state transfer of property to the propertied was promoted by developers as an ideal integration of commercial and civic life. But in attempting to filter out the inefficiencies of the city along with the "undesirable people" who lived there, and in fostering dependence on private activities for public activity, the malls threatened government's obligations to its citizens and encouraged the destruction of even a residual ideal of the common. Ruth Gilmore explores the deliberate mobilizations of surplus in the forms of finance capital, land, labor, and state capacity by which California developed the largest prison-building program "in the history of the world." New forms of criminalization and the production of new forms of prisoners were critical to the political transformation of landscape in the siting of prisons.

George Yúdice analyzes the transformation of Miami as the city emerges as the new cultural capital of Latin America, the critical pivot point of a new international networking and partnering of cultural production. As Latin American and Latino artists, entertainers, producers, managers, and executives redefine cultural institutions and production that speak to people throughout the subcontinent, these new cultural industries are trans-territorialized rather than deterritorialized. The problem lies not in the trans-territorialization per se, but in inequities in the means by which the emergent culture industries produce and extract value.

Clyde Woods employs the blues tradition of investigation and interpretation to examine the ways in which Hurricane Katrina revealed the costs of a fragmented, delinked, privatized, and devolved state where no one is in charge. The inability of the state at any level – federal, state, or local – to respond to mass death and human suffering with the collapse of a long-neglected infrastructure, exposed the national abandonment of the poorest black Americans and the demise of the Civil Rights project. While a blues epistemology places human rights at its center, the replacement of Keynesian–Fordist social welfare with a plantation philosophy of governance – with thousands of separate realities governed by increasingly capricious rules – has led to the profound arbitrariness of human rights.

Where is Guantánamo?

Amy Kaplan

I think Guantánamo, everyone agrees, is an animal, there is no other like it.[1]
— Ruth Bader Ginsburg

Strictly speaking, the written accent on the second syllable (Guantánamo) is required to indicate the proper Spanish pronunciation. To Americans this is unnecessary. In the half century of United States occupancy, the accent has disappeared. Guantanamo Bay is in effect a bit of American territory, and so it will probably remain as long as we have a Navy, for we have a lease in perpetuity to this Naval Reservation and it is inconceivable that we would abandon it.[2]
— *The History of Guantanamo Bay*, 1953

In January 2002, the first shackled and hooded men from Afghanistan were incarcerated behind barbed wire at the US Naval Station, Guantánamo Bay, Cuba. In April 2004, when the case challenging the legality of their detention was argued before the US Supreme Court, Guantánamo still appeared to many as a strange aberration, as an "animal," with "no other like it," as Justice Ginsburg stated. Descriptions of Guantánamo as a lawless zone enhanced this image of its exceptional status: a legal black hole, a legal limbo, a prison beyond the law, a "permanent United States penal colony floating in another world."[3] Yet since the revelations of prisoner abuse at Abu Ghraib in Iraq and the leak of the Washington "torture memos," it has become increasingly clear that, more than an anomaly, Guantánamo represents the start of the "road to Abu Ghraib," one island in a global penal archipelago, where the United States indefinitely detains, secretly transports, and tortures uncounted prisoners from all over the world.[4] As a rallying cry against human rights abuses in the US "war on terror," Guantánamo has come to embody what Amnesty International calls a "gulag for our times."[5]

The global dimensions of Guantánamo cannot be understood separately from its seemingly bizarre location in Cuba. Prisoners captured in Afghanistan and around the world were transported here, to a country quite close geographically, yet far politically, from the United States, a country with which the United States has no diplomatic relations. Guantánamo occupies a transitional political space, where a prison housed in a communist nation against whom the US is still fighting the cold war has become an epicenter for the new "war on terror." It also occupies a liminal national space, in, yet not within, Cuba, but at the same time a "bit of American territory," as the 1953 history of the naval base proclaimed. Guantánamo is not clearly under the sovereignty of either nation, nor seemingly subject to national or international law. Where in the world is Guantánamo?

Guantánamo lies at the heart of the American Empire, a dominion at once rooted in specific locales and dispersed unevenly all over the world. The United States first acquired the land around Guantánamo Bay in 1898, when it occupied Cuba in the aftermath of the

Spanish-American War. At a critical historical juncture, the United States reached the limits of its expansion westward and southward into lands violently dispossessed from Indians and Mexicans. During the height of the global "Age of Empire," the year 1898 launched the United States onto the world stage as an imperial force in the Caribbean and the Pacific.[6] Ever since, Guantánamo has played a strategic role in the changing exercise of US power in the region, as a coaling station, a naval base, a cold war outpost, and a detention center for unwanted refugees.[7] The use of Guantánamo as a prison camp today demands to be understood in the context of its historical location. Its legal – or lawless – status has a logic grounded in imperialism, whereby coercive state power has been routinely mobilized beyond the sovereignty of national territory and outside the rule of law. Understanding this history can help us decipher how Guantánamo has become critical to the working of empire today. Thus to ask about the location of Guantánamo is to ask: where in the world is the United States?

Given this history, it is not surprising that Guantánamo has become a subject for international debate at the same time that the idea of the American Empire has gained credence across the US political spectrum.[8] Until recently, the notion of American imperialism was considered a contradiction in terms, an accusation hurled only by left-wing critics. Indeed the denial of imperialism still fuels a vision of America as an exceptional nation, one interested in spreading universal values, not in conquest and domination. Yet, since September 11, 2001, neo-conservative and liberal interventionists have openly embraced the vision of an ascendant American Empire policing and transforming the world around it through military and political might and economic and cultural power.[9] Other commentators of different political perspectives have viewed the United States as an over-stretched empire in chaotic decline.[10] Many have tried to understand the difference between earlier imperial formations based on a nation's territorial conquest and annexation and today's more dispersed forms of globalized power unanchored in particular territorial domains. Some advocates for empire today have in fact turned to the history of US imperialism at the turn of the last century as a model for the present.[11]

The question of empire has rarely entered the important legal debates about the prison camp at Guantánamo, debates about the balance between national security and civil liberties, the rights of the prisoners, the extent of US legal jurisdiction, the domain of international law, and

the thorny question of national sovereignty.[12] While Guantánamo's history occasionally provides background for these deliberations, it has remained largely absent from the discussion of Guantánamo as a legal dilemma. This *American Quarterly* volume on "Legal Borderlands" provides the opportunity to bring together the concerns of legal scholars with civil liberties and human rights and those of American studies scholars with the history and culture of imperialism, precisely because it is a phenomenon that does not simply inform foreign policy abroad but, rather, intimately shapes the contours of US national identity.[13] Guantánamo lies at the intersection of these two inquiries.

In this essay, I argue that the legal space of Guantánamo today has been shaped and remains haunted by its imperial history. This complex history helps to explain how Guantánamo has become an ambiguous space both inside and outside different legal systems. Guantánamo's geographic and historical location provides the legal and political groundwork for the current violent penal regime. The first three sections of the essay show that the political, social, and constitutional legacies of US imperialism inform key contemporary debates about Guantánamo: the question of national sovereignty, the codification of the prisoners as "enemy combatants," and the ambiguity about whether the US Constitution holds sway there.

The essay then turns to the 2004 Supreme Court decision in *Rasul v. Bush*, which seems to answer one question about where Guantánamo is as a juridical space. The Court ruled that the federal courts do have jurisdiction over the US naval base, and that the prisoners therefore should have access to the courts to challenge the legality of their detention. The justices were not only interested in restraining executive power to bring Guantánamo within the rule of domestic law; they also showed concern with the scope of US power in the world and the extent to which the judiciary should accompany or limit US military rule abroad. In a close reading of the Supreme Court's decision and dissent, I argue that the logic and rhetoric of *Rasul v. Bush* rely on and perpetuate the imperial history the Court also elides. In concert with its other recent decisions about civil liberties and national security, the Court, in this decision about Guantánamo, is contributing to the global expansion of US power by reworking the earlier history of imperialism. Its legal decisions respond to the changing demands of empire by creating new categories of persons before the law that extend far beyond Guantánamo Bay, Cuba.

The Imperial Legacy of Limited Sovereignty

The most outrageous claim of the Bush administration about Guantánamo continues to be that the Republic of Cuba has "ultimate sovereignty" over this territory, that therefore neither the Constitution nor US obligations to international treaties apply, and, as a result, that the prisoners at Guantánamo have no rights.[14] Nor, according to this argument, do Cuban laws hold sway there. In other words, because the US *lacks* formal sovereignty, it can do whatever it wants there, and the military can act with impunity to brutally control every aspect of the prisoners' lives. While this legal groundwork was carefully prepared by the Justice Department's legal counsel at the end of 2001, the disavowal of sovereignty over a territory nonetheless controlled by the United States has a long history and was key to US imperial strategy of more than a century ago.

Guantánamo Bay had been a strategic colonial site since the arrival of the Spanish in the fifteenth century. On the southeastern tip of Cuba, it served as a portal for the trade of enslaved Africans, and in the nineteenth century, Caimanera, one of its port cities, became the end point for the railroad that transported sugar and molasses from the plantations of the region to be exported abroad. In 1895, when the Cubans launched their third war for independence against centuries of Spanish rule, the uprising began in the Oriente province, where revolutionary leaders José Marti and General Máximo Gomez landed at a beach near Guantánamo Bay.

In 1898, backed by popular enthusiasm at home, the United States intervened against Spain to aid the anti-colonial struggle of *Cuba Libre*. At the outset of the war, US Marines landed at Guantánamo Bay, where they fought a key battle and remained ensconced after the end of the three-month war. Touted as a war of liberation to rescue the Cubans from a brutal Old World empire, the Spanish-American War secured US control over the remnants of Spanish colonialism in the Caribbean and the Pacific. The swift victory against Spain ended in US reluctance to accept the national independence of Cuba, or that of any of the other territories ceded by Spain. While the United States fought to annex the Philippines in a vicious three-year war against Filipino nationalists and turned Puerto Rico and Guam into territorial possessions, the United States occupied Cuba with the professed goal of ceding to Cuban self-government. Yet after three years of military occupation, Washington agreed to withdraw its troops only after forcing a sweeping amendment it wrote onto the new republic's constitution.

The Platt Amendment reserved to the United States the right to intervene in Cuba militarily and to control its economy and its relations with other countries.[15] It also guaranteed the lease or purchase of coaling and naval stations, a provision that would lead to leasing Guantánamo Bay in 1903. The Platt Amendment legislated US domination of the new republic, as its language perpetuated the paternalistic narrative of rescue. The amendment decreed that "the United States may exercise the right to intervene for the preservation of Cuban independence."[16] This formulation renders the US military intervention, rather than Cuban self-government, as a "right." In this logic of equating intervention with protection, Cuba's independence becomes dependent on the US right to violate its autonomy. Article VII of the amendment guaranteed that the Cuban government would lease or sell lands necessary for coaling or naval stations in order "to enable the United States to maintain the independence of Cuba."[17] In other words, for the United States to protect Cuban independence, the new government of Cuba had no choice but to accept measures that drastically curtailed that liberty. As military governor Leonard Wood wrote to President Theodore Roosevelt, "There is, of course, little or no independence left Cuba under the Platt Amendment."[18]

After the United States intervened militarily several times in the early twentieth century, with Cuba drawn solidly into the economic and political orbit of the United States, the two parties abrogated the Platt Amendment in 1934. At the same time, they extended the lease for Guantánamo in perpetuity, that is, until both parties agreed to cancel it, or "so long as the United States of America shall not abandon the said naval station."[19] The United States could stay as long as it wanted, regardless of the desires of the Cubans. The language of the treaty places the United States in the active position of agent with the prerogative to stay or leave, and Cuba in the passive role of accepting either occupation or abandonment. Indeed, after the revolution of 1959, Fidel Castro tried unsuccessfully to revoke the lease, but he succeeded only in cutting off the water supply and surrounding the base with cactus fields. The US treasury still sends a check each year of $4,085 for "leasing" the land that the Cuban government doesn't cash, because it demands that the United States cease the occupation of its territory. According to the Cuban government, Guantánamo Bay continues to be an illegitimately occupied territory.

Most of today's legal arguments about Guantánamo have hinged on the interpretation of the 1903 lease, which reads: "While on the one hand the United States recognizes the continuance of the ultimate sovereignty of the Republic of Cuba over the above described areas of land and water, on the other hand the Republic of Cuba consents that during the period of the occupation by the United States of said areas under the terms of this agreement the United States shall exercise complete jurisdiction and control over and within said areas."[20] The language of the lease expresses a hierarchy between recognition and consent, rendering Cuban sovereignty over Guantánamo Bay contingent on the acknowledgment of the United States, in exchange for which Cuba agrees to cede sovereignty over part of the territory it never controlled. The Republic of Cuba had no option but to agree to terms that had already been dictated prior to its independence, terms which founded and undermined its sovereignty as a nation.[21] Although the lease refers to the control of territory, the phrase "the continuance of ultimate sovereignty;" key to the government's argument today, implies a strange temporality. "Continuance" is at odds with the fact that Cuba had not yet achieved sovereignty as a nation because it emerged directly from its status as a Spanish colony into the military occupation of the United States. "Ultimate sovereignty" refers to a condition that never quite existed in the past, yet is assured continuity into some unspecified future. Thus as a territory held by the United States in perpetuity, over which sovereignty is indefinitely deferred, the temporal dimensions of Guantánamo's location make it a chillingly appropriate place for the indefinite detention of unnamed enemies in what the administration calls a perpetual war against terror.

The lease and the attribution of limited sovereignty, which the Platt Amendment exemplifies, formed – and continue to form – an effective technology of imperial rule. The United States was following an established practice of other empires at the turn of the twentieth century, as annexation with high administrative costs became less attractive to colonial regimes around the world.[22] In practice, a lease, as opposed to outright annexation, allowed for greater maneuverability of imperial powers, in part because it enhanced their immunity from political and legal accountability to all forms of governance, both in the colony and the metropolis.

The lease of Guantánamo Bay in 1903 also reflected the reigning US imperial strategy and ideology of the "New Empire" as voiced by prominent figures such as Alfred Thayer Mahan and Theodore Roosevelt.[23] Both advocated building a strong navy to support US economic and political expansion around the world, unfettered by the burden of annexing territories with populations to govern. In 1902, Mahan recognized that "it would be difficult to exaggerate the value of Guantanamo, only fifty miles from Santiago de Cuba, to the American fleet off the latter port, which otherwise had to coal in the open, or depend upon a base many hundred miles away."[24] According to Mahan, such stations facilitated the mobility of an empire that would foster economic expansion, through military and political domination. Indeed the key strategic value of Guantánamo Bay for most of the century was not only the control of Cuba, but also its access to the rest of the Caribbean, Central and South America, and the Panama Canal Zone, whose "treaty" was negotiated at gunpoint in the same period.[25] Guantánamo was viewed as a steppingstone to Latin America and across the Pacific, and it was deployed as a launching pad for military interventions in Cuba, the Dominican Republic, Nicaragua, and Guatemala throughout the twentieth century.

Thus the "legal black hole" of Guantánamo did not appear suddenly after September 11, 2001, but is filled with a long imperial history.[26] The government's argument that the United States lacks sovereignty over the territory of Guantánamo has long facilitated rather than limited the actual implementation of sovereign power in the region. In *Rasul v. Bush*, the Court dismissed what Justice Souter called the vague "metaphysics of ultimate sovereignty" in favor of the prisoners' claims that the United States has in practice exercised total control and jurisdiction over the base for a century.[27] Yet the Court's decision still leaves open the question of national sovereignty, and while it supports the prisoners' claim that divorces jurisdiction from sovereignty over territory, this same open-endedness seems to abet a different kind of sovereignty, the executive power to dictate the violent terms of governance over the lives of the prisoners there.

The Racialized Legacy of the Colonial Outpost

In establishing Guantánamo as a space removed from the reach of US domestic law, the administration has concomitantly created the category of "enemy combatants" to deny the prisoners the protections and rights of international law and the Geneva conventions, which they would have as prisoners of war. Secretary of Defense Rumsfeld declared the prisoners to be the "most dangerous, best-trained, vicious killers on the face of the earth."[28] While such statements conjure threatening racist stereotypes of Muslim terrorists as "bad guys" and "evil-doers," the prisoners' presence at the US naval base at Guantánamo has also accrued a history of racialized images from the legacy of US intervention in the Caribbean.

Although Guantánamo was never formally a US colony, the social space of the base has long resembled a colonial outpost. Until the Cuban revolution, the base served as a contact zone of sorts, a site of uneven colonial exchanges between Cubans and Americans, as Cubans entered the base as laborers through a highly regulated passport system, and US sailors used the neighboring towns as an exotic playground for prostitution, drinking, and gambling.[29] In the 1930s through the 1950s, journalists and travelers described the naval station through colonialist discourse as a transplanted Little America and often contrasted its hygienic, well-ordered housing with the reportedly "primitive" and squalid, impoverished conditions of the neighboring Cuban villages. After the revolution, the base became a self-enclosed enclave, where most of the Cuban laborers were replaced with Jamaican and Filipino laborers contracted to work there. The image of the base as small town America, however, continues to circulate today, replete with bowling alleys, video rental shops, golf courses, and McDonald's restaurants. The naval commander has been quoted as referring to the base as "Mayberry RFD with bad neighbors."[30] It is unclear which bad neighbors he was referring to – the Cubans kept out by barbed wire fences and military guards or the prisoners encaged by barbed wire inside the base. With unintended irony, a defense department publication elaborated on the meaning of "Mayberry," the town in television's *Andy Griffith Show* of the 1960s. "Like Mayberry, Guantánamo Bay has virtually no crime."[31]

The current prisoners were not the first to be held in cages in the middle of "Mayberry." In the last decade of the twentieth century, the role of the naval base at Guantánamo changed dramatically: from a way station for the global reach of military might outward, it became a site of detention camps for blocking Haitian and Cuban refugees from entering the United States. Thus, another trajectory that leads to the camps of Guantánamo today is the long history of US imperial relations with Haiti, a nation it occupied from 1915 to 1934. After a military coup ousted Jean-Bertrand Aristide in 1991, tens of thousands of Haitians sought political asylum in the United States, a status the United States had long refused. The coast guard took the unprecedented step of intercepting Haitians on the high seas, and when, under international pressure, the United States stopped repatriating them to the repressive regime at home, they were taken to the base at Guantánamo for "processing," where they were denied any rights to appeal for asylum.

Many were held up to three years in makeshift barbed wire camps, exposed to heat and rain in spaces infested with rats and scorpions, with inadequate water supplies and sanitary facilities.[32] Furthermore, a separate camp was built for those who, through forced testing, were found to carry HIV, where they received inadequate medical care and where medicine was often used coercively; their health rapidly deteriorated.[33] The rationale for detaining the Haitians relied on racist hysteria that imagined Haiti as the source of the AIDS virus and Haitians as the bearers of contaminated blood. Newspaper articles and speeches in Congress envisioned hordes of Haitians invading Florida, as though they themselves were the viruses they were purported to carry. This assumption that Haitian bodies carried disease has a long history as well. From the Haitian Revolution that began in 1791, black Haitian bodies were viewed from the north as bearing the contagion of black rebellion that could "infect" slaves in other countries and colonies.

In 1994, Washington constructed another tent city surrounded by barbed wire to detain almost thirty thousand Cubans who were attempting to reach the United States by sea. "Miserable conditions led some Cuban detainees to attempt suicide. Their numerous uprisings were met by US troops in riot gear with fixed bayonets."[34] The Cubans were trapped in a cold war nightmare. Whereas Cubans fleeing from the communist regime long held privileged status as political refugees, the United States viewed these Cubans, whom Castro had released during an economic crisis, as criminals to repatriate. When the detention camps were shut down in 1995, most of those detained were allowed into the United States, though many were repatriated or sent to third countries. A legacy of Guantánamo's unclear sovereignty, Haitians in the United States who were born in detention there remain "effectively stateless, since the camp authorities would not give them US birth certificates and Haiti has not extended citizenship rights to them either."[35]

It is striking that the current prisoners at Guantánamo, purportedly the most dangerous terrorists in the world, have been brought to the geographic threshold of the United States as though they were aspiring immigrants or would-be refugees who have to be kept out forcibly. If the naval base can still be viewed as a colonial outpost, it is a colony devoid of local inhabitants, and the colonized "others" now comprise a transnational population from forty nations, captured in many places besides Afghanistan, including Pakistan, Bosnia, Turkey, Germany, and Gambia and untold other places around the world. Although the government has lumped them together as terrorists, al Qaeda members, and Islamic extremists, their identities are enormously varied. They speak as many as seventeen different languages; many are immigrants or the children of immigrants to different nations around the world.[36]

The current prisoners not only first literally inhabited the camps built for the Haitian and Cuban refugees, but they also continue to inhabit the racialized images that accrued over the century in the imperial outpost of Guantánamo: images of shackled slaves, infected bodies, revolutionary subjects, and undesirable immigrants. The prisoners fill the vacated space of colonized subjects, in which terrorism is imagined as an infectious disease of racialized bodies in need of quarantine. The category of "enemy combatants" effaces all differences among the detainees and also draws on these older imperial codes. The image of the "enemy combatant" also draws on the conflation increasingly made of immigrants and terrorists, at a time when the Immigration and Naturalization Service (INS) has become part of the Department of Homeland Security, immigrants are detained without legal recourse, and there is an "increased intermingling of immigration law enforcement and criminal law policing."[37] Thus "enemy combatant" is a racialized category, not only because of rampant racism toward Arabs and Muslims, but also because of this history. Stereotypes of the colonized, immigrants, refugees, aliens, criminals, and revolutionaries are intertwined with those of terrorists and identified with racially marked bodies in an imperial system that not only colonizes spaces outside US territories but also regulates the entry of people migrating across the borders of the United States.

The Haitians and Cubans in Guantánamo protested their detention through hunger strikes, riots, and legal suits. While they succeeded in shutting down the camps, the government ultimately refused to concede them any constitutional rights, and the courts never definitely ruled on this issue. In response to litigation brought by Haitian refugees, two circuit courts divided over whether the Bill of Rights applied to noncitizens there.[38] Legally, the justification for detaining Haitians and Cubans without constitutional or international rights at Guantánamo was the same one used by the government today, involving the absence of US sovereignty. In 2001, the government's choice of Guantánamo relied in part on the 1995 decision by the Eleventh Circuit Court of Appeals that "Cuban and Haitian migrants have no First Amendment or Fifth Amendment rights which they can assert."[39] The same decision ruled that international human rights treaties "bind the government only when

refugees are at or within the borders of the United States."[40] Where then is Guantánamo, if not at the border of the United States?

The Ambiguous Legacy of the Insular Cases

The question of whether the US Constitution holds sway in Guantánamo remains unresolved by the Supreme Court in *Rasul v. Bush*. Save for a mention in a footnote, the Court carefully avoided the question of whether noncitizens in Guantánamo Bay have access to constitutional protections and rights. This indeterminacy about the extraterritorial reach of the Constitution has long accompanied the expansion of US rule beyond its national borders.

At the turn of the last century, the legal debate about imperialism revolved around the question of whether the "Constitution follows the flag" into the new territories taken from Spain and the recently annexed territory of Hawai'i.[41] At stake in this question, which resonates today, was whether the nation could remain a republic if it ruled over lands and peoples governed by laws not subject to its Constitution. In a series of decisions that came to be known as the Insular Cases (1902–22), the Court answered that question ambiguously: it decided that parts of the Constitution followed the flag, sometimes, and in certain contexts.[42] In the best-known case, *Downes v. Bidwell*, which concerned whether the uniform clause of the Constitution applied to Puerto Rico, the Court created the new category of "the unincorporated territory," a territory not annexed for the ultimate purpose of statehood. The decision deemed Puerto Rico "foreign to the United States in a domestic sense," a space "belonging to" but "not a part of the United States," whose inhabitants were neither aliens nor citizens.[43] In these liminal spaces, the Insular Cases allowed for a two-tiered, uneven application of the Constitution, claiming that some unspecified fundamental or substantive rights were binding in the unincorporated territories. Yet there were no consistent guarantees of due process or the right to criminal and civil juries or full protection under the Fourteenth Amendment; in other words, there were no clear rights to be protected against unfair procedures.

This differential application of the Constitution created the legal edifice for imperial rule. The designation of territory as neither quite foreign nor domestic was inseparable from a view of its inhabitants as neither capable of self-government nor civilized enough for US citizenship. The Insular Cases legitimated a colonial space, inherently based on racism, to protect US citizens from an acquired population that might belong to a race, "absolutely unfit to receive" the full responsibilities and protections of the Constitution.[44] In *Downes v. Bidwell*, both the territory of Puerto Rico and its inhabitants were not therefore treated as part of an autonomous foreign nation, but they were left in "limbo," according to Chief Justice Melville Weston Fuller's dissent. The "occult meaning" of the "unincorporated territory," he argued, gave Congress the unrestricted power to keep any newly acquired territory "like a disembodied shade in an intermediate state of ambiguous existence for an indefinite period."[45] This language uncannily describes Guantánamo today, and the sense of the occult was echoed in Justice Souter's skepticism about the "metaphysics of ultimate sovereignty." The Insular Cases have never been overruled, even though the international scope of the Constitution has changed greatly in the twentieth century, for the most part expanding the constitutional rights of American citizens abroad rather than those of noncitizens. The imperial origins of these cases, which often remain unacknowledged, continue to haunt their subsequent use as precedent in later cases throughout the twentieth century.

Although Guantánamo Bay, Cuba, was never an "unincorporated territory," the two-tiered legacy of the Insular Cases helped construct the naval base there as an ambiguous legal space where the extent of constitutional rights remains indeterminate. While *Rasul* does not rely directly on the Insular Cases as precedent, it indirectly evokes them in the sole footnote in the decision that addresses the constitutionality of the detentions. *Rasul* ruled that the prisoners at Guantánamo have the right to challenge their detention in the federal courts according to a federal statute (28 US Code Sec. 2241), not according to the Constitution. Yet, in note 15, the Court holds that the detainees might have constitutional rights they could assert in the United States, indicating that the detainees' allegations do provide a basis for a constitutional claim. The Court writes that these allegations, namely, "that, although they have engaged neither in combat nor in acts of terrorism against the United States, they have been held in Executive detention for more than two years in territory subject to the long-term, exclusive jurisdiction and control of the United States, without access to counsel and without being charged with any wrongdoing" do "unquestionably describe 'custody in violation of the Constitution or laws or treaties of the United States.'" By relegating this opinion to a footnote, however, rather than incorporating it into the opinion, the Court leaves open the question of constitutional rights, an openness that has led to diametrically opposing positions on the part of the administration and advocates for the prisoners, and between judges in the federal courts.

To trace the lineage of the Insular Cases in *Rasul*, we have to look further at this footnote. Justice Stevens follows this statement by referring to a comparison with a 1990 case that took the opposite direction of denying constitutional protections abroad. In *United States v. Verdugo-Urquidez*, the Court held that the Fourth Amendment was not available to a suspected drug dealer, whose home was searched without warrant in Mexico, when he was captured by US agents and brought to the United States for criminal indictment.[46] The Court in *Verdugo-Urquidez* drew on the precedent of the Insular Cases to hold that not all constitutional provisions pertain to US governmental activity in foreign territories. As in those cases, Chief Justice William Rehnquist's argument relied not only on the territorial scope of the Constitution but also the extent of its reach to noncitizens. Because the Fourth Amendment used the word "people," instead of "persons," he claimed, it refers to a narrower scope of "a class of persons who are part of a national community or who have otherwise developed sufficient connection with this country to be considered part of that community."[47] He thus read a nationalist hierarchy of rights as already written into the language of the Bill of Rights, only some of which are applicable to the general category of "persons" who are not US citizens.

In *Verdugo-Urquidez*, Justice Anthony Kennedy wrote a concurring opinion, and it is to this opinion that Stevens specifically refers in the *Rasul* note. Kennedy rejected Rehnquist's distinction between "the people" and "persons," but he maintained a boundary between foreign and domestic territory: "The Constitution does not create, nor do general principles of law create, any juridical relation between our country and some undefined, limitless class of noncitizens who are beyond our territory."[48] Even though Kennedy insists on this division, he proceeds to cite precedents that blur these boundaries to argue that the Constitution may still apply abroad in particular circumstances. He quotes Justice Harlan in *Reid v. Covert* (1953), a landmark case that involved the right of US citizens abroad to a trial by jury:

> The Insular Cases do stand for an important proposition, one which seems to me a wise and necessary gloss on our Constitution. The proposition is, of course, not that the Constitution "does not apply" overseas, but that there are provisions in the Constitution which do not necessarily

apply in all circumstances in every foreign place.... There is no rigid and abstract rule.[49]

In 1990, Kennedy concludes from this reasoning that "just as the Constitution in the Insular Cases did not require Congress to implement all constitutional guarantees in its territories because of their 'wholly dissimilar traditions and institutions,' the Constitution does not require US agents to obtain a warrant when searching the foreign home of a nonresident alien." In pursuing this racially inflected differential logic, he argues that "the absence of local judges or magistrates available to issue warrants, the differing and perhaps unascertainable conceptions of reasonableness and privacy that prevail abroad, and the need to cooperate with foreign officials all indicate that the Fourth Amendment's warrant requirement should not apply in Mexico as it does in this country."[50] With this reasoning, Kennedy concurred with the majority in denying that the Fourth Amendment should cross the border to Mexico to accompany the actions of US agents.

The import of this reference in *Rasul* is far from clear. Is the Court suggesting that the prisoners in Guantánamo may indeed have constitutional rights in contrast to the prisoner in *Verdugo-Urquidez*? Or is the Court evoking Kennedy's reasoning in sustaining both limits and flexibility to the extension of constitutional provisions? In *Rasul*, Kennedy concurred with the majority in favor of extending US jurisdiction to the prisoners, but he wrote a separate opinion in order to uphold a dividing line between foreign and domestic territory as he did in *Verdugo-Urquidez*. His reasoning construed Guantánamo in the imperial language of the Insular Cases as "a place that belongs to the United States."[51] By claiming that "Guantánamo Bay is in every practical respect a United States territory," as the basis for extending some rights to the prisoners, he implicitly insists that these rights do not necessarily apply to other locations under US control.

Neither Stevens nor Kennedy answers the question, where is Guantánamo? – whether it is located in foreign or a domestic space as far as the Constitution is concerned. For the legacy of the Insular Cases does not lie primarily in delimiting the extraterritorial scope of the Constitution. It lies more powerfully in legislating an ambiguity that gives the US government great leeway in deciding whether, when, and which provisions of the Constitution may apply overseas, and indeed in determining what territories may be considered "foreign to the United States in a domestic sense."

Because of this historical ambiguity, the Insular Cases have been marshaled both for and against the prisoners. The Justice Department, in its motion to dismiss the prisoners' habeas corpus cases drew on the interpretation of the Insular Cases in *Verdugo-Urquidez* to argue that there is "nothing in the Supreme Court's opinion in *Rasul*" to undermine the conclusion "that aliens, such as petitioners, who are outside the sovereign territory of the United States and lack a sufficient connection to the United States may not assert rights under the Constitution."[52] In January 2005, Federal District Judge Richard J. Leon accepted this argument that no "viable legal theory" accords rights to the prisoners, and he granted the government's motion to dismiss seven of the prisoners' habeas corpus cases.[53]

Two weeks later, however, his counterpart, Federal District Judge Joyce Hens Green, came to the opposite conclusion and relied on the same footnote in *Rasul* to reveal an "implicit, if not express, mandate to uphold the existence of fundamental rights through the application of precedent from the Insular cases."[54] Her decision went farther to declare illegal the Combatant Status Review Tribunals at Guantánamo conducted by the Department of Defense, and she held that the detainees should be treated as prisoners of war. With both decisions still under appeal at the time of this writing, the petitioners remain imprisoned with no change in their status, and the unanswered question may yet return to the Supreme Court to resolve its own ambiguity as to whether the Constitution follows the flag, not only to Guantánamo, but also to other extraterritorial sites under the control of the US military.

The Supreme Court's refusal to squarely rule on the constitutional status of Guantánamo is in part a product of the Insular Cases, which remain doctrinal precedent today. Gerald Neuman, in a brief for the petitioners, wrote that "the *Insular Cases* forged a compromise between the forces of constitutionalism and the forces of empire by guaranteeing that the most fundamental constitutional rights would be honored wherever the US rules as sovereign."[55] Judge Green's decision powerfully endorses this view. Yet history has shown that the Insular Cases resolved that conflict by forging a compromise in favor of empire. In not clearly deciding on whether the prisoners at Guantánamo have constitutional rights, the Supreme Court may have implicitly supported the executive's unrestricted power given to Congress by the Insular Cases, to keep any domain, "like a disembodied shade, in an intermediate state of ambiguous existence for an indefinite period." This ambiguity increases the range and mobility of the exercise of US power abroad, and this uncertainty legitimates a crushing certainty of dominion over the lives of those imprisoned in Guantánamo and other locations around the world.

[...]

Guantánamo Is Everywhere

[...] Though it is too soon to tell, the Court's decision in *Rasul*, in conjunction with their decisions on the same day about citizen enemy combatants in the *Hamdi v. Rumsfeld* and *Rumsfeld v. Padilla* cases, may together facilitate the global reach of US power by creating a shadowy hybrid legal system coextensive with the changing needs of empire.

The Court never fully answers the question of where Guantánamo is. It extends and legitimates the ambiguous legacy of the Insular Cases by ruling that Guantánamo is domestic for some purposes and foreign for others. *Hamdi* blurs the distinctions between aliens and citizens, not by giving them shared rights, but by giving judicial legitimacy to the figure of the "enemy combatant," a designation by executive fiat.[56] Many critics today are outraged that the administration has been ignoring these legal decisions and "treating a historic loss in the Supreme Court as though it were a suggestion slip."[57] But perhaps the administration has not been defeated by these rulings. *Rasul*, read alongside *Hamdi* and *Padilla*, suggests that the Court is not extending the protections of domestic law to the "four corners of the earth," but rather that it is legitimating a second-tier legal structure that can extend the government's penal regime, all the while keeping itself immune from accountability and keeping prisoners from the safeguards of any of these systems. This penal regime cuts a wide swathe across national borders, from Guantánamo to detention centers in Iraq and Afghanistan, to undisclosed military prisons around the world, and to immigrant detention centers and prisons within the United States.[58]

To follow this reasoning, it is necessary to turn briefly to the *Hamdi* decision, the one most heralded by the press as the victory of judicial restraint against unbounded executive power. Yet, in this case, Justice O'Connor, writing for the plurality, accepted Bush's position that the nation is at war and that this open-ended "war on terror" gives the president and the executive branch sweeping powers to jail anyone they accuse of being an "enemy combatant" – citizens and noncitizens alike – without the approval of Congress. The ruling accepted the administration's position that such "enemy combatants" are not entitled to the protections either of the Geneva Conventions on prisoners of war or to full due process rights accorded to criminal defendants in the US courts. This decision thus legitimated an evolving category of persons before the law, who are not defined primarily by citizenship or their relation to national or international law but by their designation by the executive. While the Court upheld Hamdi's right to counsel and to petition for habeas corpus, it also endorsed a legal process skirting both constitutional restrictions and international law, with a weakened adherence to due process, with an assumption of guilt until proven innocent, and with the admission of hearsay as evidence. The Court's decision allows for an unspecified military tribunal in lieu of a civilian trial or a military court-martial, itself a kind of parody of the Geneva Convention provisions for prisoners captured on the battlefield.[59]

In *Rasul*, the Court made clear that it would not specify any procedures or venues for addressing the petitioners' claims. In its response to the Supreme Court's decision, the Justice Department capitalized on this by quickly adopting part of the Court's logic in the *Hamdi* case to argue that aliens in foreign territory (Guantánamo detainees) would certainly not be afforded more constitutional protections than those deemed appropriate for citizens within the United States, such as José Padilla and Yaser Hamdi. To argue for denying due process to the Guantánamo prisoners, the government, in its response, quotes from the Hamdi decision, "that the full protection that accompanies challenges to detentions in other settings may prove unworkable and inappropriate in the enemy combatant setting."[60] Thus, the government relies on *Hamdi* specifically to claim that the Guantánamo detainees have no protections under the Fifth Amendment, and they use the district court's ruling in *Padilla* to claim that the detainees have no constitutional rights to counsel unmonitored by military security.[61]

Although these issues remain unresolved, the Justice Department has been consistent in arguing that the detainees in Guantánamo have no constitutional protections. And it has been aided here by the gaps in the Court's decision. It left mainly unanswered the century-old question of whether the Constitution follows the flag, and the government has called on both the Insular Cases and *Verdugo-Urquidez* to argue that the inmates at Guantánamo have no constitutional protections whatsoever. Although the arguments may sound staggeringly cynical, nothing in the Supreme Court decision really works against them. The Justice Department argues against the Sixth Amendment right for the accused in a criminal proceeding to have "assistance of counsel for his defense" because "petitioners are being detained solely because of their status as enemy combatants, not for any other criminal or punitive purpose."[62] The counsel claims that *Verdugo-Urquidez* established that "aliens receive constitutional protections when they have come within the territory of the U.S. and *developed substantial connections with this country*."[63] Beyond its ongoing insistence that Guantánamo is not "within the territory of the U.S.," the government argues that the detainees do not have "voluntary connections" to the United States, because they were captured involuntarily by the military, and therefore – like slaves – they do not have sufficient connection with the United States to warrant constitutional protection. In other words, the act of imposing arbitrary power – the forced transport to Guantánamo, the lack of criminal charges – tautologically justifies the imposition of arbitrary power immune from constitutional restrictions and international treaties.

Outrage has rightfully been expressed at the government's dismissive response to the Supreme Court's decision, and military and civilian lawyers have persistently challenged these practices and even succeeded in halting them before lower court reviews.[64] Since *Rasul* in June 2004, however, the administration continues its effort to block the access of the prisoners to the lower courts. Despite its many legal defeats, it continues to ignore the courts and to treat the prisoners according to its own rules: by staging farcical administrative hearings to determine the enemy combatant status of prisoners who have already been labeled enemy combatants, by planning military tribunals to judge war crimes run by officers with little training who have the power to condemn the accused to death, by releasing some prisoners at its whim, and by building two maximum security prisons for the indefinite detention of others.[65]

By understanding the long imperial history that fills the black hole of Guantánamo, we can see how the Court decision in *Rasul v. Bush* does not simply rein in executive power or bring Guantánamo inside the rule of law. In perpetuating the differential logic of the Insular Cases, the Court remaps an arena only partially and indiscriminately subject to constitutional restraints, wherein the executive can still exert power with impunity. In creating this ambiguous territory, the Court contributes to reclassifying persons as "enemy combatants," a category that erodes the distinctions among citizens and aliens,

immigrants and criminals, prisoners and detainees, terrorists and refugees. Yet this erosion is not moving toward granting more rights to noncitizens. On the contrary, it moves both citizens and noncitizens further toward the lowest possible rung of diminished liberties. Ultimately, these persons are codified as less than human and less deserving of human, international, or constitutional rights. This dehumanization is shaped by racial, national, and religious typologies and shored up by revamped historical imperial taxonomies, which rebound across national borders. The blurring of legal boundaries between domestic and foreign, and aliens and citizens, does not weaken executive and military authority, as Scalia fears. Instead it creates ever-widening spheres to the "four corners of the earth," where the US administration, abetted by the courts, might manipulate habeas corpus to conceal rather than to "show the bodies" that have been indefinitely detained, sexually humiliated, and medically and psychologically abused and tortured. Haunted by the ghosts of empire, Guantánamo Bay, Cuba, remains an imperial location today. From here the borders of the law are redrawn to create a world in which Guantánamo is everywhere.

Notes

1   Justice Ruth Bader Ginsburg, Oral Arguments, *Rasul v. Bush*, 542 U.S. 466 (2004) (Nos. 03-334, 03-343), 51. Oral arguments (April 20, 2004) are available at http://www.supremecourtus.gov/oral_arguments/argument_transcripts/03-334.pdf (accessed July 11, 2005).

2   Rear Admiral M. E. Murphy, *The History of Guantanamo Bay, 1494–1964*, chap. 1, "Under the Spanish Flag" (U.S. Naval Base, 1953), available at http://www.nsgtmo.navy.mil/gazette/History_98-64/hischp1.htm (accessed July 11, 2005).

3   Many of these phrases have become commonplace. "Legal black hole" was first used in the British Supreme Court in *Abbasi v. Secretary of State for Foreign & Commonwealth Affairs* (2002); see also Joseph Margulies, "A Prison Beyond the Law," *Virginia Quarterly Review* 80.4 (fall 2004): 37–55; for "legal limbo," see Neil A. Lewis, "Red Cross Criticizes Indefinite Detention in Guantánamo Bay," *New York Times*, October 10, 2003, 1; for "penal colony" see Michael Ratner, "The War on Terrorism: The Guantánamo Prisoners, Military Commissions, and Torture," January 14, 2003, http:// www.humanrightsnow.org/guantanamoprisoners.htm. (accessed July 11, 2005).

4   "The Military Archipelago," editorial, *New York Times*, May 7, 2004, A24. Karen J. Greenberg and Joshua L. Dratel, eds., *The Torture Papers: The Road to Abu Ghraib* (New York: Cambridge University Press, 2005).

5 "Amnesty International Report 2005," speech by Irene Khanat, Foreign Press Association, May 25, 2005, at http://web.amnesty.org/library/index/ENGPOL10014200 (accessed July 11, 2005).

6 Eric Hobsbawm, *The Age of Empire, 1875–1914* (New York: Random House, 1987).

7 See Murphy, *The History of Guantanamo Bay.*

8 For a brief review of these changing attitudes toward American imperialism, see Amy Kaplan, "Violent Belongings and the Question of Empire Today – Presidential Address to the American Studies Association, October 17, 2003," *American Quarterly* 56.1 (March 2004): 1–7. For recent books on the subject of diverse political perspectives, see Andrew Bacevich, *American Empire: The Realities and Consequences of U.S. Diplomacy* (Cambridge, Mass.: Harvard University Press, 2002); Bacevich, *The Imperial Tense: Prospects and Problems of American Empire* (Chicago: Ivan R. Dee, 2003); Patrick J. Buchanan, *A Republic, Not an Empire: Reclaiming America's Destiny* (Washington, DC: Regency, 1999/2002); David Harvey, *The New Imperialism* (New York: Oxford University Press, 2003); Chalmers Johnson, *The Sorrows of Empire: Militarism. Secrecy, and the End of the Republic* (New York: Metropolitan Books, 2004); John Newhouse, *Imperial America: The Bush Assault on the World Order* (New York: Knopf, 2003); Joseph S. Nye, *The Paradox of American Power: Why the World's Only Superpower Can't Go It Alone* (New York: Oxford University Press, 2002). One of the major intellectual proponents of American Empire is Niall Fergusson. See, for example, his *Colossus: The Price of America's Empire* (New York: Penguin, 2004).

9 This vision was propounded before 9/11 by the neoconservative Project for the New American Century in their 2000 report "Rebuilding America's Defenses: Strategy, Forces, and Resources for a New Century," available at http://www.newamericancentury.org/RebuildingAmericasDefenses.pdf (accessed July 12, 2005). For a recent essay bringing together US imperialism and universalism, see Michael Ignatieff, "Who Are Americans to Think That Freedom Is Theirs to Spread?" *New York Times Magazine*, June 26, 2005.

10 See Charles A. Kupchan, The *End of the American Era: U.S. Foreign Policy and the Geopolitics of the Twenty-First Century* (New York: Knopf, 2002); Michael Mann, *Incoherent Empire* (London: Verso, 2003); Emmanuel Todd, *After the Empire: The Breakdown of the American Order* (New York: Columbia University Press, 2003); Immanuel Wallerstein, *The Decline of American Power* (New York: New Press, 2003).

11 Max Boot, *The Savage Wars of Peace: Small Wars and the Rise of American Power* (New York: Basic Books, 2002), 341–42. See Robert Kaplan, "Rule No. 7: Remember the Philippines," in "Supremacy by Stealth: Ten Rules for Managing the World," *Atlantic Monthly*, July–August 2003, 80; and Michael Ignatieff, "Why Are We in Iraq? (And Liberia? And Afghanistan?)," *New York Times Magazine*,

September 7, 2003. Imperial sites conquered in 1898, such as the Philippines and Guam, are being retooled by the military to support the current wars. See James Brooke, "Threats and Responses: U.S. Bases: Guam Hurt by Slump, Hopes for Economic Help From Military," *New York Times Magazine*, March 10, 2003, A14.

12 See, for example, Diane Marie Amann, 'Guantánamo," *Columbia Journal of Transnational Law* 42.1 (2004): 263–349; Ronald Dworkin, "What the Court Really Said," *New York Review of Books*, 51.13, August 12, 2004; Neal K. Katyal, "Executive and Judicial Overreaction in the Guantanamo Cases," in *Cato Supreme Court Review*, 2003–2004, at http://www.cato.org/pubs/scr/docs/2004/executiveandjudicial.pdf (accessed July 11, 2005); Gerald L. Neuman, "Closing the Guantánamo Loophole," *Loyola Law Review* 50.1 (spring 2004): 1–66; Kal Raustiala, "The Geography of Justice," *Fordham Law Review*, 73.6 (May 2005): 2501–2560; Michael Ratner and Ellen Ray, *Guantánamo: What the World Should Know* (White River Junction, Vt: Chelsea Green, 2004); Kermit Roosevelt III, "Guatánamo and the Conflict of Laws: *Rasul* and Beyond," *University of Pennsylvania Law Review*, 153 (June 2005): 2017–71. Neuman has long written of Guantánamo in the context of its imperial history, and for my understanding of its legal status, I am indebted to him. Raustiala identifies Guantánamo's imperial history as evidence of an outdated anachronistic attachment to legal spatiality.

13 See, for example, Matthew Jacobson, *Barbarian Virtues: The United States Encounters Foreign Peoples at Home and Abroad, 1876–1917* (New York: Hill and Wang, 2000); Amy Kaplan, *The Anarchy of Empire in the Making of U.S. Culture* (Cambridge, Mass.: Harvard University Press, 2002); Melanie McAlister, *Epic Encounters: Culture, Media, and U.S. Interests in the Middle East, 1945–2000* (Berkeley: University of California Press, 2001); Mary Renda, *Taking Haiti: Military Occupation and the Culture of U.S. Imperialism, 1915–1940* (Chapel Hill: University of North Carolina Press, 2001); Neil Smith, *American Empire: Roosevelt's Geographer and the Prelude to Globalization* (Berkeley: University of California Press, 2003); Penny Von Eschen, *Race Against Empire: Black Americans and Anticolonialism, 1937–1957* (Ithaca, NY: Cornell University Press, 1997).

14 This argument was prepared in "Possible Habeas Jurisdiction over Aliens Held in Guantanamo Bay, Cuba," US Justice Department memo to the Department of Defense concerning the applicability of International Humanitarian Law to the prisoners in the war on terrorism, written by Deputy Assistant Attorney Generals Patrick F. Philbin and John C. Yoo, December 28, 2001, from "The Philbin/Yoo Memo," *Newsweek*, accessible at http://www.yirmeyahureview.com/archive/documents/prisoner_abuse/011228_philbinmemo.pdf (accessed July 11, 2005). See also Brief for the Respondents, *Rasul v. Bush.*

15 The Platt Amendment, 1901, Modern History Sourcebook available at http://www.fordham.edu/halsall/mod/1901platt.html (accessed July 11, 2005).

16 Ibid.

17 Ibid.

18 Philip Sheldon Foner, *The Spanish-Cuban-American War and the Birth of American Imperialism, 1895–1902, vol. 2* (New York: Monthly Review Press, 1972), 632.

19 Treaty Defining Relations with Cuba, May 29, 1934, U.S.–Cuba, Art. III, 48 Stat. 1683, T. S. No. 866 at http://www.nsgtmo.navy.mil/gazette/History_98-64/hisapxd.htm (accessed July 11, 2005).

20 Lease of Lands for Coaling and Naval Stations, February 23, 1903, U.S.–Cuba, Art. III, T. S. No. 418 at http://www.nsgtmo.navy.mil/gazette/History_98-64/hisapxd.htm (accessed July 11, 2005).

21 The Platt Amendment was approved by the US Congress in 1901, two years before its adoption in the Cuban constitution.

22 Thank you to Teemu Ruskola for pointing this out to me in the case, for example, of the Hong Kong lease of 1862. See Martti Koskenniemi, chap. 2, "Sovereignty: A Gift of Civilization: International Lawyers and Imperialism, 1870–1914," in *The Gentle Civilizer of Nations: The Rise and Fall of International Law, 1870–1960* (Cambridge: Cambridge University Press, 2001).

23 Walter LaFeber, *The New Empire: An Interpretation of American Expansion, 1860–1898* (Ithaca, NY: Cornell University Press, 1963).

24 Alfred Thayer Mahan, "Conditions Determining the Naval Expansion of the United Stares," in *Retrospect and Prospect: Studies in International Relations Naval and Political* (Boston: Little, Brown, 1902), 48.

25 The opening epigraph by Justice Ginsburg is followed by: "The closest would be the Canal Zone, I suppose." Although the government counsel rejected this analogy, the reference implicitly evokes another space colonized by the New Empire at the turn of the last century.

26 While the phrase "black hole" evokes its most immediate connotations from astronomy, it also has a prior imperial history. The "black hole of Calcutta" refers to the barracks in Fort William, Calcutta, where in 1756, the Nawab of Bengal allegedly imprisoned more than a hundred Europeans who died overnight, in an incident that became a cause celebre in the idealization of British imperialism in India.

27 Oral Arguments, *Rasul v. Bush*, 52.

28 *Newsweek*, July 8, 2002.

29 Louis A. Perez, *On Becoming Cuban: Identity, Nationality, and Culture* (New York: HarperCollins, 1999), 238–42; Jana Lipman, "Guantanamo: Cubans, Marines, and Migrants, 1955–1965," paper presented at Global Studies Association, Brandeis University, April 2004.

30 "Cuban Base Has American Flavor," *Morning Call Online*, January 2, 2004.

31 Kathleen T. Rhem, "From Mayberry to Metropolis: Guantanamo Bay Changes," *American Forces Press Service*, March 3, 2005, at http://www.dod.mil/news/Mar2005/20050303_77.html (accessed July 11, 2005).

32 Paul Farmer, "Pestilence and Restraint: Guantánamo, AIDS, and the Logic of Quarantine," in *Pathologies of Power: Health, Human Rights, and the New War on the Poor* (Berkeley: University of California Press, 2003), 51–59; Lizzy Ratner, "The Legacy of Guantánamo," *The Nation*, July 16, 2003, at http://www.thenation.com/doc.mhtml?i=20030721&s=ratner (accessed July 11, 2005); Jane Franklin, "How Did Guantánamo Become a Prison?" *History News Network*, April 11, 2005, at http://hnn.us/articles/11000.html (accessed July 11, 2005).

33 Medicine is again being used coercively in Guantánamo. The Red Cross has asserted that currently "some doctors and other medical workers at Guantánamo were participating in planning for interrogations," in what the report called "a flagrant violation of medical ethics." Neil A. Lewis, "Red Cross Finds Detainee Abuse in Guantánamo," *New York Times*, November 30, 2004, 1; Neil A. Lewis, "Interrogators Cite Doctors' Aid at Guantánamo Prison Camp," *New York Times*, June 24, 2005.

34 Franklin, "How Did Guantánamo Become a Prison?"

35 Ratner, "The Legacy of Guantánamo."

36 The administration has not released the names or exact numbers of prisoners at Guantánamo. For the most comprehensive record, see the Web site Cageprisoners.com at http://www.cageprisoners.com/index.php (accessed July 11, 2005).

37 Rogers Smith, "Citizenship Rights, Alien Rights, and the New American Empire," forthcoming in *Radical History Review*. See also Mark Dow, *American Gulag: Inside U.S. Immigration Prisons* (Berkeley: University of California Press, 2004).

38 Neuman, "Closing the Guantánamo Loophole," 42.

39 Ibid.; *Cuban Am. Car Ass'n v. Christopher*, 43 F.3d 1412 (11th Cir. 1995).

40 Ibid.

41 See Brook Thomas, "A Constitution Led by the Flag: The *Insular Cases* and the Metaphor of Incorporation," in *Foreign in a Domestic Sense: Puerto Rico, American Expansion, and the Constitution*, ed. Christina Duffy Burnett and Burke Marshall (Durham, NC: Duke University Press, 2001), 82–103.

42 For the most comprehensive examination of the Insular Cases from different perspectives, see Burnett and Marshall, eds., *Foreign in a Domestic Sense*.

43 *Downers v. Bidwell*, 182 U.S. 244, 341 (1901); Efrén Rivera Ramos, "The Legal Construction of American Colonialism: The Insular Cases, 1902–1922," *Revista Jurídica de la Universidad de Puerto Rico* 65 (1996): 227–328.

44 *Downes*, 306.

45 Ibid., 373.

46 *Rasul*, 564, n. 15.

47 *United States v. Verdugo-Urquidez*, 494 U.S. 259, 265 (1990).

48 Ibid., 275.

49 Ibid., 278.

50 Ibid.

51 *Rasul*, 565 (Kennedy concurring).

52 Response to Complaint in Accordance with the Court's Order of July 25, 2004, *Odah v. United States*, 355 F. Supp. 2d. 482 (D.D.C. 2005) (No. 02-CV-0828).

53 *Khalid v. Bush*, 355 F. Supp. 2d. 311 (D.D.C. 2005).

54 Memorandum Opinion Denying in Part and Granting in Part Respondent's Motion to Dismiss or For Judgment as a Matter of Law, *In re Guantanamo Detainee Cases*, 355 F. Supp. 2d. 443 (D.D.C. 2005) (No. 02-CV0299).

55 Neuman, "Closing the Guantánamo Loophole," 19. The argument of this article is based on his contribution to Brief Amici Curiae of Former Government US Government Officials in Support of Petitioners, *Rasul v. Bush*.

56 On the Department of Defense's definition of "enemy combatant," see William J. Haynes II, General Counsel of the Department of Defense, "Enemy Combatants," presentation to Council on Foreign Relations, at http://www.cfr.org/publicition.php?id=5312 (accessed July 11, 2005). For an analysis of this designation by executive fiat (see Amann, "Guantánamo").

57 Quoted in Adam Liptak, "In First Rulings, Military Tribunals Uphold Detentions of 4," *New York Times*, August 14, 2004, 11.

58 On the relation of the torture of prisoners at Guantánamo and Abu Ghraib to the treatment of prisoners in the US prisons, see Joan Dayan, "Cruel and Unusual: The End of the Eighth Amendment," *Boston Review*, October/November 2004, at http://bostonreview.net/BR29.5/dayan.html (accessed July 11, 2005).

59 *Hamdi v. Rumsfeld*, 542 U.S. 507 (2004) (No. 03-6696).

60 Response to Complaint, July 2004, 19.

61 Ibid., 23.

62 Ibid., 17.

63 Ibid., 13.

64 Prior to Judge Joyce Green's ruling declaring the Combatant Status Review Tribunals unconstitutional and that the prisoners should be treated as prisoners of war, in October 2004 US District Judge Colleen Kollar-Kotelly ordered the Pentagon to stop intelligence eavesdropping on lawyer-client conversations at Guantánamo; Carol D. Leonnig, "U.S. Loses Ruling on Monitoring of Detainees," *Washington Post*, October 21, 2004, 4. In November, US District Judge James Robertson ordered the Pentagon to halt the war crimes trial of a Yemeni who allegedly worked as Osama bin Laden's driver, saying the Military Commissions are flawed, and likewise called the Pentagon's Combatant Status Review Tribunals (CRSTs) an inadequate, nonjudicial alternative to habeas proceedings in federal courts; Warren Richey, "Court Puts off Guantánamo War-Crimes Case," *The Christian Science Monitor*, January 19, 2005, 2. On July 15, 2005, a three-judge panel of the United States Court of Appeals for the District of Columbia Circuit ruled unanimously to reverse Judge Robertson's decision and to resume military tribunals. Neil A. Lewis, "Ruling Lets U.S. Restart Trials at Guantanamo," *New York Times*, July 16, 2005, 1.

65 In the case of *Hamdi*, rather than abide by the Court's decision, the Department of Justice released Yaser Hamdi to return to Saudi Arabia on the condition that he relinquish his US citizenship.

Knowing Nature through Labor: Energy, Salmon Society on the Columbia

Richard White

The world is in motion. Tectonic plates drift across a spinning planet. Mountains are lifted up and eroded to the sea. Glaciers advance and retreat. All natural features move, but few natural features move so obviously as rivers. Our metaphors for rivers are all metaphors of movement: they run and roll and flow.

Like us, rivers work. They absorb and emit energy; they rearrange the world. The Columbia has been working for millennia. During the Miocene, volcanic eruptions deposited layers of basalt across the Columbia Plain. The upper Columbia cut a gutter through which it ran along the margins of the basaltic flow. At Wenatchee the rise of the Horse Heaven anticline caused the river to cut into the basalt; it drained into the Pasco basin, the lowest point on its route east of the Cascades, and emerged from the basin at the Wallula Gap. During the Pleistocene the collapse of an ice dam holding glacial Lake Missoula created the largest known freshwater flood in the earth's history. It was an afternoon's work for one of the Missoula floods to create the Grand Coulee and other rock channels of the Channeled Scablands. In those few hours it accomplished work that it would have taken the Mississippi three hundred years at full flood to duplicate. The flood rushed into the Columbia channel and finally slowed enough to create the "Portland Delta" of the Willamette lowlands. Since then ice dams have blocked the Columbia's bed, temporarily spilling the river into the Grand Coulee; mountains have slid into it, and humans have dammed it. All these changes have left work for the river to do.

For much of human history, work and energy have linked humans and rivers, humans and nature. But today, except when disaster strikes, when a hurricane hits, or earthquakes topple our creations, or when a river unexpectedly rises and sweeps away the results of our effort and labor, we forget the awesome power – the energy – of nature. There is little in our day-to-day life to preserve the connection. Machines do most of our work; we disparage physical labor and laborers. The link between our work and nature's work has weakened. We no longer understand the world through labor. Once the energy of the Columbia River was felt in human bones and sinews; human beings knew the river through the work the river demanded of them.

Early-nineteenth-century accounts of the Columbia can be read in many ways, but they are certainly all accounts of work, sweat, exhaustion, and fear. The men of the early nineteenth century who wrote the Lewis and Clark journals and the accounts of the Astorian trading post, the North West Company and Hudson's Bay Company, knew the energy of the river. They had to expend their own energy to move up, down, and across it. Alexander Ross's marvelous *Adventures of the First Settlers on the Oregon or Columbia River*, a narrative of the arrival of the Astorians and the establishment of the fur-trading outpost of Astoria in 1811, can serve as a primer on the Columbia as an energy system during a time when human beings – Indian and white – had only the wind and the strength of their own muscles to match against the powerful currents of the river.

"The mouth of the Columbia River," Ross wrote, "is remarkable for its sand bars and high surf at all seasons, but more particularly in the spring and fall, during the equinoctial gales." The shoals and sandbars at the

Columbia's mouth are relics of its work and energy. In areas without strong tidal action a river deposits the load it carries to its mouth as a delta, but the Columbia emerges into the Pacific in an area of strong tides and persistent storms.

The river's current and the tides battle at the Columbia's mouth and prevent the formation of a delta. At full flood, Captain Charles Wilkes wrote in 1841, one could "scarcely have an idea of its flow how swollen it is, and to see the huge trunks of thick gigantic forests borne like chips on its bosom astonishes one." During ebb tides the river pushes its freshwater out many miles into the sea. The tides, in turn, are felt as high as 140 miles upriver when the Columbia's water level is at its fall and winter low. This pushing and pulling produces a set of sandbars and islands at the river's mouth. Ocean currents and tides force themselves against the bars with "huge waves and foaming breakers." The result is "a white foaming sheet for many miles, both south and north of the mouth of the river, forming as it were an impracticable barrier to the entrance, and threatening with instant destruction everything that comes near it." To enter the river, ships, powered only by wind and aided by the tide, or boats and canoes powered by human muscle, had to pass through this barrier.

During the Astorians' own terrible entry into the Columbia in 1811, they sent out small boats to find a channel into the river for their ship, the *Tonquin*. In Ross's dramatic telling, the Astorians watched as the *Tonquin*'s first officer, Ebenezer Fox, protested to Captain Jonathan Thorn that the seas were "too high for any boat to live in." In reply Thorn only taunted Fox: "Mr. Fox, if you are afraid of water, you should have remained at Boston." Fox's uncle had died at the mouth of the Columbia. In despair Fox announced that he was "going to lay my bones with his." He shook hands with the Astorians and, getting into the boat, shouted, "Farewell, my friends . . . we will perhaps meet again in the next world." Fox's crew was inexperienced and the sea violent. Not one hundred yards from the ship the boat became unmanageable. The waves hit the craft broadside, whirled it like a top, and "tossing on the crest of a huge wave, [it would] sink again for a time and disappear all together." Fox hoisted a flag to signal his distress, but the *Tonquin* turned about, and they "saw the ill-fated boat no more."

Ross himself took part in a second attempt, and he discovered more immediately the experience of pitting human energy against the energy focused at the mouth of the river. As they first approached the bar with its "terrific chain of breakers," the "fearful suction or current" gripped the boat before they realized what had happened. The second officer, Mr. Mumford, called for them to match their strength against that of the river and sea: "Let us turn back, and pull for your lives. Pull hard, or you are all dead men." They pulled hard and survived, but this attempt to enter the river and two more failed. The *Tonquin* eventually made the passage across the bar, but only after eight men had died.

In their ordeal at the bar the Astorians had confronted storms, sandbars, and currents; men had labored and died. But wave, water, and wind – and human labor – can be represented in ways beyond the immediacy of actual experience. We can abstract them to a single entity: energy. There is a physics to the *Tonquin*'s drama at the river's mouth, and it leads outward beyond the earth to the sun and the moon. Lunar gravitation causes the tides, but virtually all the rest of the energy manifest at the Columbia's mouth originates in the sun. The sun, in effect, provides fuel for a giant atmospheric heat engine which evaporates water from the oceans and produces winds that move the moisture over land. As the clouds cool, the moisture falls as rain. Without solar energy to move the water inland and uphill, rivers would never begin; without gravity to propel the water downhill back toward the ocean, rivers would never flow. In a real sense the Columbia begins everywhere that the rain that eventually enters it falls. The Columbia gathers its water from an area of 258,200 square miles, but not all that water finds its way into the river as it flows 1,214 miles to the sea. Some of it is lost through transpiration and use in plant tissues; some is lost through evaporation.

Physicists define energy as the capacity to do work. Work, in turn, is the product of a force acting on a body and the distance the body is moved in the direction of the force. Push a large rock and you are expending energy and doing work; the amount of each depends on how large the rock and how far you push it. The weight and flow of water produce the energy that allows rivers to do the work of moving rock and soil: the greater the volume of water in the river and the steeper the gradient of its bed, the greater its potential energy.

In fact, however, neither the Columbia nor any other river realizes all of its potential energy as work. Indeed, only about 2 percent of the river's potential energy results in work: the erosion, transportation, and deposition of matter. About 98 percent of the river's kinetic energy is expended in friction as the moving water rubs against itself, its bed, and its bank. This energy is dissipated as heat within the river.

Engineers can measure the potential energy and the kinetic energy of the Columbia with some precision, but early voyagers like Ross recognized the power – the energy – by more immediate if cruder measures. They measured it by the damage it did as it threw ships or boats or bodies against rocks or sandbars. And they measured it by the work they had to perform to counter the river's work. They knew something we have obscured and are only slowly recovering: labor rather than "conquering" nature involves human beings with the world so thoroughly that they can never be disentangled.

During the forty-two days of Ross's first trip upriver from Astoria, the river demonstrated its power again and again. The river upset the Astorians' boat; it dunked the men, drenched them, grounded them, and delayed them. But mostly the river made them work, sweat, and hurt. "On the twenty-third [of the month] . . . we started stemming a strong and almost irresistible current . . ." The "current assumed double force, so that our paddles proved almost ineffectual; and to get on we were obliged to drag ourselves from point to point by laying hold of bushes and the branches of overhanging trees . . ." "The burning sun of yesterday and the difficulty of stemming the rapid current had so reduced our strength that we made but little headway today." "We were again early at work, making the best of our way against a turbulent and still increasing current."

Ross had reached the Cascades, the rapids where the Columbia bursts out of the mountains. Above the Cascades were even worse rapids at the Dalles, and the Dalles commenced with Celilo Falls. Here the current was too strong and travelers had to portage.

Above Celilo Falls, Ross's litany of labor continued. "The current was strong and rapid the whole day." "[We] found the current so powerful that we had to lay our paddles aside and take to the lines." "The wind springing up, we hoisted sail, but found the experiment dangerous, owing to the rapidity of the current." And so they proceeded through Priest Rapids, where the "water rushes with great violence," and through lesser rapids where a whirlpool grabbed a boat, spun it several times, and sent it careening down a chain of cascades. Ross stopped at the Okanogan River. If he had gone farther, more rapids awaited: Kettle Falls, and farther still, the Dalles des Morts. The largest tributaries of the Columbia, the Snake and the Willamette, contributed falls and rapids of their own.

So thoroughly did Ross come to measure the river by the labor he pitted against it, by the feel of his body, by the difficulties it presented, that his return downstream

with the river's energy speeding him back to Astoria from Fort Okanogan could be contained in a sentence. "On the twenty-sixth of February, we began our homeward journey, and spent just twenty-five days on our way back."

With so much energy deployed against them, it was remarkable that voyagers could proceed at all. The first white fur traders built what they called canoes out of cedar planks caulked with gum. Such boats could not stand the rapids. The Astorians longed for another Indian technology – the more familiar birchbark canoes of the eastern rivers. The Northwesters who succeeded the Astorians actually imported the birchbark necessary to make birchbark canoes.

Efficient movement on the river demanded not just muscle power but knowledge and art. The fur traders, fortunately, had examples of both before them. In the Indians' cedar canoes, efficiency and art met and became one. The Indians carved each of their canoes from a single log; Gabriel Franchère, another of the original Astorians, reported that the largest canoes were thirty feet long and five feet wide. And as Robert Stuart, also an Astorian, wrote: "If perfect symmetry, smoothness and proportion constitute beauty, they surpass anything I ever beheld." Some were as "transparent as oiled paper."

The art and knowledge embodied in the canoe demanded an equal knowledge of the river. Lewis and Clark were repeatedly amazed at the conditions Indians ventured out in, and William Clark had thought them "the best canoe navigators I ever saw." Stuart concurred: The Indians were "the most expert paddle men any of us had ever seen." If the river overpowered their canoe, they would spring "into the water (more like amphibious animals than human beings), right and empty her, when with the greatest composure, they again get in and proceed." But the clearest mark of knowledge and skill was when nothing happened, when Indians knew which paths through the river were the most efficient and least demanding of human energy.

The river's lessons that the Astorians learned, the North West Company men would have to relearn. The poverty of the boats and the inability to maneuver them that the governor-in-chief of the Hudson's Bay Company, George Simpson, found on his first voyage of inspection to the Columbia posts in 1824 provoked a spluttering astonishment that still resonates in his journal. "There is not," he wrote, "a Boat at the Establishment [Fort George] fit to cross the River in bad Weather nor a person competent to sail one." Simpson's attempt to cross in a boat with rotten rigging had proceeded only a mile before everyone on board was bailing with hats and buckets. The boat struck a sandbar and drifted off, with the crew rowing madly against an outgoing tide until they "exhausted their strength at the Oars." They were only saved when the tide turned and swept them back into the river, where they made shore, abandoned the boat, and walked back to the fort. Farther upriver, however, where Canadian boatmen were more in their element, the British naturalist David Douglas could in 1826 admire the "indescribable coolness" with which Canadians shot the rapids.

The Canadians showed Douglas that the knowledge of how and where to use the boats was as important as the boats themselves; the complexities of the energy system of the river could be made to work for as well as against travelers. "Our Indians," the American explorer Charles Wilkes wrote in 1841, "cunningly kept close to the shore & thus took advantage of all the eddies." Such knowledge was initially a bodily knowledge felt and mastered through experience and labor. Even when learned from others, the messages sent through nerve and muscle constantly validated or modified acquired knowledge. Knowledge of the river was in large part knowing how its velocity varied and where it was turbulent. With proper experience, traveling against the current on the Columbia demanded less expenditure of human energy than traveling overland. The hydraulics of the river sketched out a map of energy; this geography of energy was also a geography of labor.

[. . .]

As we now understand rivers, they seek the most efficient and uniform expenditure of energy possible. Rivers constantly adjust; they compensate for events that affect them. They are, in this sense, historical: products of their own past history. "The river channel," concluded one geomorphologist, is "a form representing the most efficient – in terms of energy utilization – geometry capable of accommodating the sum total of the means and extremes of variability of flow that have occurred in that channel throughout its history."

Where obstacles slow rivers, rivers try to restore an even velocity; where the gradient increases or the channel constricts, rivers try to widen or build up their bed. The Columbia ceaselessly worked to widen the Dalles and it responded to Celilo Falls by working to downcut the falls and erode the plunge pools until the falls themselves eventually would even out and disappear. When an obstacle such as a beaver dam or a hydraulic dam slows a river's current, for example, its speed and energy decrease. The river drops part of its load – the material it works to move. It gradually builds up its own bed and

increases its gradient, thus increasing its speed and its kinetic energy. Eventually it will remove the obstacle.

In the long run the river's work of eliminating obstructions aids the human work of moving up and down rivers. But in the short run rapids and falls demand greater expenditures of human energy to counter the river's energy. This combination of energies bonded the material and social; the natural and cultural intertwined. The geography of energy intersected quite tightly with a geography of danger and a human geography of labor. Precisely where the river expended its greatest energy, humans had to expend the most labor and confront the greatest danger.

At the falls and rapids travelers had to portage. Indians living at the Cascades had canoes at either end of the portages, but travelers had to carry their cargo and either tow or carry their boats. It was hard and demanding work. Portaging the Cascades brought Lewis and Clark much "difficulty and labour," cost them a pirogue, and left their men "so much fatigued" that they granted them a respite. The missionary Mrs. Elijah White, whose baby drowned at the Cascades, had gladly reembarked two-thirds through the portage because she and David Leslie "with wet feet and fatigue were very uncomfortable." Going upstream, everyone had to portage; going downstream, danger could be substituted for labor.

The Cascades and the Dalles were the most dangerous points on the river and the longest portages. At the Cascades – which one of the literary Astorians described as "that rocky and dangerous portage" – the "laborious task of carrying" made clear the distinction between the work of the river and the work of human beings. In one sense, the expenditure of energy by human workers was as natural as the energy of the river, but human work was socially organized and given cultural meaning. The Cascades and the Dalles, for example, bared class divisions among the Astorians and revealed their relation to work and power. Ross, "not being accustomed myself to carry," instead stood armed as a sentinel against the Indians, but with those subordinate to him "wearied to death," he took up a load. The first ascent left him breathless and able to "proceed no farther." He hired an Indian to carry the load, and the Indian proceeded "full trot" across the portage, only to pitch the pack of tobacco over a two-hundred-foot precipice at the end. He and fifty others laughed uproariously as Ross scrambled to retrieve the load. The joke was about work and power, weakness and dominance, all of which were physical and social.

The river demanded energy to match its energy, and this shaped and revealed the organization of work. The necessity of portages and the limits of human labor caused the Hudson's Bay Company to transport all its goods in ninety-pound packages. The expenditure of labor in carrying these packages involved numerous acts of calculation, conflict, abuse, and cooperation. In these acts a social order became transparent.

If all journeys were downstream, if there had been no rapids or falls, then the human relations on the early-nineteenth-century river would have been different. The labor white men expended in the ascent forced them into close contact with Indians. The knowledge that in passing upstream they had to travel close to shore to take advantage of backcurrents encouraged efforts to accommodate Indians. David Thompson, the remarkable North West Company explorer who descended the Columbia just as the Astorians were arriving at its mouth, succinctly calculated the social result of this mix of river energy and human labor when he explained why he stopped to smoke and exchange gifts with the Sanpoils as he passed downstream.

My reason for putting ashore and smoking with the Natives, is to make friends with them, against my return, for in descending the current of a large River, we might pass on without much attention to them; but in returning against the current, our progress will be slow and close along the shore, and consequently very much in their power; whereas staying a few hours, and smoking with them, while explaining to them the object of my voyage makes them friendly to us.

Passage along the river was, Thompson realized, not just physical; it was social and political. Social and political rituals were as necessary as labor to move against the current. Indians expected gifts and ritual at the portages. The failure of whites to meet such expectations brought conflict from the time of the Lewis and Clark expedition until the 1820s.

In English the words "energy" and "power" have become virtually interchangeable. Horsepower is, for example, a technical measure of energy. But we also speak metaphorically of the power of the state. Thompson spoke of being "in the power" of the Indians. The conflation is partially metaphorical, but it also arises because both meanings involve the ability to do work, to command labor. To be powerful is to be able to accomplish things, to be able to turn the energy and work of nature and humans to your own purposes.

We conflate energy and power, the natural and the cultural, in language, but they are equally mixed as social

fact at the rapids and portages. The energy system of the Columbia determined where humans would portage, but human labor created the actual route of the portage, and human social relations determined its final social form and outcome. The Dalles, per se, did not cause Ross's dilemma. Ross's humiliation was an incident of power. Human labor would later make the Dalles and the Cascades the sites of dams that produced energy – power; they were, however, long before this, sites at which humans contested over social power – the ability to gain advantage from the labor of others.

Spatial arrangements matter a great deal in human history. They reveal the social arrangements that help produce them. The repeated conflicts at the Dalles and the Cascades revolved around a particular organization of space. Whites regarded the space at the Cascades and the Dalles as open, as culturally empty. Indians regarded it as full. In a space that brought together many different peoples, Indians expected gifts to mediate and smooth passages through this social maze. Too often whites replaced gifts with force; they resented what they perceived as theft and pillage. The space became uniquely violent.

II

Examining how humans moved on the river provides one angle of vision on the rapids and falls of the Columbia; examining how salmon moved up and down the river provides a second, equally revealing, perspective. It was, after all, the salmon that brought thousands of Indians to the Cascades, to the Dalles and Celilo Falls, to Priest Rapids and Kettle Falls.

As much as wind, wave, and current, salmon were part of the energy system of the Columbia. Salmon are anadromous fish: they live most of their adult life in the ocean but return to the stream of their birth to spawn since the Columbia does not provide sufficient food to support the salmon born in its tributaries. The precise timing of the movement of young salmon to the sea depends on the species, but eventually all except the kokanee (a form of sockeye which, although nonanadromous, retains the genetic potential to become so) make their way to the ocean. During their time at sea Columbia salmon harvest the far greater solar energy available in the Pacific's food chain and, on their return, make part of that energy available in the river. By intercepting the salmon and eating them, other species, including humans, in effect capture solar energy from the ocean. Salmon thus are a virtually free gift to the energy ledger of the Columbia. They bring energy garnered from outside the river back to the river.

For salmon the rapids and the falls represent obstacles that force them to expend energy, but to the Indians the combination of salmon and rapids and falls seemed providential. In 1811 Gabriel Franchère traveled with one of the sons of Concomly, the leading Chinook chief on the lower Columbia. He told Franchère that in perfecting creation Ekanunum (Coyote) had "caused rocks to fall in the river so as to obstruct it and bring the fish together in one spot in order that they might be caught in sufficient quantities." On the Columbia, where the river was the most turbulent the fishing was best. Rapids and waterfalls forced fish into narrow channels; they forced salmon toward the surface. And as the fish became concentrated and visible, they became more vulnerable to capture.

At the rapids human art and technology altered the river to increase the difficulties for fish. At low water in early May, for example, the Nespelems and Sanpoils built weirs to deflect fish toward artificial channels cleared at certain points in the rapids. The bottoms of the channels were lined with white quartz to make the fish more visible. On smaller tributaries, the Indians built weirs to block the fish until their harvest was complete. At Kettle Falls the Indians fixed timber frames in the rocks of the falls and from them they hung huge willow baskets, ten feet in diameter and twelve feet deep. Leaping salmon would strike the frames and fall into the baskets, where waiting fishermen clubbed and removed them. A single such basket could supposedly yield five thousand pounds of fish a day at the height of the runs.

[. . .]

The internal spacing of activities at the summer fishing sites is also revealing. It is impossible now to re-create in detail the spatial organization of the Dalles or the Cascades. No one mapped them or tapped human memories to demarcate them before they vanished under the waters of the dams. But such maps of memory do remain for Celilo Falls, which was really the beginning of the Dalles. The falls was among the most densely named and intimately known places on the river. The names grew from human labor. Celilo Falls is gone now, buried since 1956 beneath the waters of the Dalles Dam, but once it was thick with specifically known and bounded human spaces. At Celilo, Sahaptin fishers named places where people cast gill nets when the river ran normally; others named places to cast nets when it ran high. At *tayxaytapamá* there was a bed of pale flat stones under clear water which made the fish stand out for spear fishing. Where the river fell at *sapaw-ilalatatpamá*, men could dipnet leaping salmon. At *áwxanaycaš* ("standing place") seven men could stand with their dip nets on twenty-foot poles to dip into the rushing current. Nearly every rock and island in the falls suitable for fishing acquired a name.

Such spatial divisions both made visible and reproduced the social structure of the Chinookans and Sahaptins who fished the rapids. Just below Celilo Falls, at the Wishram villages on the north bank of the Dalles, such fishing stations were owned by groups of relatives who controlled access. Each group seems to have had a station for using dip nets in summer, for spearing in the fall, and for seining.

To watch such fisheries would be to watch an intricate series of convergences among the energy of the river, the work of salmon, and the labor of humans. It would be to see how humans socially and culturally organized this labor and to glimpse how people were connected and ranked. The spatial arrangements created maps of energy, maps of labor, and maps of meaning. Each of these places was unique. They were bounded spaces which, in Michel Foucault's words, were "irreducible to one another and absolutely not superimposable on one another." There was only one *Awxanaycas* at Celilo and which seven men stood there was socially determined.

In this world the human and the natural were tightly linked, but one did not determine the other. The social organization of Indians was not reducible to control of the rapids or access to salmon; there were no recorded "tribal" conflicts over resources or territory. Geography and nature influenced without determining culture.

At the rapids the intersection of labor and nature produced wealth. There is no doubt about that. The abundance was readily apparent to the first whites. Lewis and Clark saw, in Clark's fractured spelling, "emenc quantites of dried fish." They presumed the fish were for trade, but they could not figure out who bought them.

Lewis and Clark presumed a market which reduced everything in the world to an equivalence. Making things equivalent did not mean making everything equal in value, but it did mean that any good could theoretically be traded for any other good. But this was not true on the Columbia. Food normally moved only in exchange for other types of food. The caloric energy of fish was the great wealth of the fishing places, but it could not readily be translated into other forms of wealth with higher prestige value. Food had a different social meaning than did slaves, dentalium shells, or canoes.

Exchanges of food suggested an ongoing relationship rather than a single act in which a person sought advantage. And thus at the Dalles, the great mart of the Columbia, fish occupied only a limited sector of exchange. Those who flocked there to trade came for horses, buffalo robes, beads, cloth, knives, and axes. They traded and gambled while the huge yields of fish supported their numbers. Those who came for fish came because they had the kin connections that allowed them to share the fishery and take their own fish. They created the huge stocks of pounded and dried salmon that Lewis and Clark saw. This salmon would see them through the winter. And because the fish had expended some of their fat in reaching the Dalles, salmon dried there had a lower oil content and would keep better than fish caught lower down. This was prime dried salmon and would be traded, usually for other types of food, up and down the river.

At the Dalles and the Cascades ownership of a particular fishing site did not automatically translate into wealth. The fish belonged to the fishermen who caught them, but old men could freely take the fish they required for their meals. And strangers and relatives both could claim some of the bounty of the catch. Many of the strangers who concentrated at the Dalles during the fishing season never fished, nor did they lay in a supply of fish.

And fish, in any case, had little to do with the competitive social rankings of people and villages apparent in ceremonies such as the potlatch. It was wealth in scarce and valuable goods – in slaves from more distant peoples or dentalium shells or trade goods – that buttressed such rankings. Food, usually abundant and of lesser prestige, could not normally obtain such things. The Dalles and Celilo, the great fisheries and site of this exchange of wealth, thus ranked below the winter towns and villages lower down the Columbia. The winter villages of the lower river where related males lived were the sites of riskier and higher-prestige activities: slave raids, warfare, and religious performances.

The whites partially changed these relations. They offered nonfood valuables for food. And Indians, hesitantly at first, made an exception for them. Ross and Franchère, like Lewis and Clark before them, described the initial difficulty of trading for fish or other food. Fish eventually moved in exchange for the valuables whites offered, but thirty years after the arrival of the Astorians, Charles Wilkes reported that at the Cascades the Indians "refuse to sell any Salmon until after the first run and then always without the heart they have many superstitions in relation to them . . ."

[. . .]

Rethinking Environmental Racism: White Privilege and Urban Development in Southern California

Laura Pulido

The concept of environmental racism – the idea that non-whites are disproportionately exposed to pollution – emerged more than ten years ago with the United Church of Christ's study, *Toxic Waste and Race in the United States* (1987). Given the social, ecological, and health implications of environmental hazards, geographers have explored environmental racism with the goal of contributing to better policymaking. Studies have sought to determine if inequalities exist and the reasons for such disparities, and to make recommendations (Cutter 1995). While these are obviously important research contributions, studying environmental racism is important for an additional reason: it helps us understand racism.

Although the study of racial inequality is not new to geographers (Gilmore 1998; Woods 1998; Jackson and Penrose 1994; Kobayashi and Peake 1994; S. Smith 1993; Anderson 1987), environmental racism offers us new insights into the subject, particularly its spatiality. Unfortunately, scholars of environmental racism have not seriously problematized racism, opting instead for a de facto conception based on malicious, individual acts. There are several problems with this approach. First, by reducing racism to a hostile, discriminatory act, many researchers, with the notable exception of Bullard (1990), miss the role of structural and hegemonic forms of racism in contributing to such inequalities. Indeed, structural racism has been the dominant mode of analysis in other substantive areas of social research, such as residential segregation (Massey and Denton 1993) and employment patterns (Kirschenman and Neckerman 1991), since at least Myrdal's *An American Dilemma* (1944). Not only has the environmental racism literature

become estranged from social science discussions of race, but, in the case of urban-based research, it is divorced from contemporary urban geography. A second and related concern is that racism is not conceptualized as the dynamic sociospatial process that it is. Because racism is understood as a discrete act that *may* be spatially expressed, it is not seen as a sociospatial relation both constitutive of the city and produced by it. As a result, the spatiality of racism is not understood, particularly the relationship *between places*. Yet pollution concentrations are inevitably the product of relationships between distinct places, including industrial zones, affluent suburbs, working-class suburbs, and downtown areas, all of which are racialized. A final problem with a narrow understanding of racism is that it limits claims, thereby reproducing a racist social order. By defining racism so narrowly, racial inequalities that cannot be attributed directly to a hostile, discriminatory act are not acknowledged as such, but perhaps as evidence of individual deficiencies or choices. Yet if we wish to create a more just society, we must acknowledge the breadth and depth of racism.

In this paper, I investigate how racism is conceptualized in the environmental-racism literature. Using Los Angeles as a case study, I apply an alternative concept of racism, white privilege, in addition to more common understandings of discrimination, to explain disparate environmental patterns. I identify three specific issues that contribute to a narrow conception of racism: first, an emphasis on individual facility siting; second, the role of intentionality; and third, an uncritical approach to scale. Typically, a study may acknowledge environmental inequity if nonwhites are disproportionately exposed to pollution, but environmental *racism* is only conceded if malicious intent on the part of decisionmakers can be proven.[1] I argue that the emphasis on siting, while obviously important, must be located in larger urban processes, and thus requires us to "jump scales" in our analysis (N. Smith 1993). This is especially true given recent findings that pollution concentrations are closely associated with industrial land use (Baden and Coursey 1997; Boer et al. 1997; Pulido et al. 1996; Anderton et al. 1994b; Colten 1986). This research recasts issues of intentionality and scale, as it requires us to examine the production of industrial zones, their relation to other parts of the metropolis, and the potentially racist nature of the processes by which these patterns evolved.

Because of the limitations of the prevailing approach to racism, I seek to broaden our understanding through a complementary conception of racism: white privilege. My understanding of racism begins from the premise that race is a material/discursive formation. Because race exists in various realms, racial meanings are embedded in our language, psyche, and social structures. These racial meanings are both constitutive of racial hierarchies and informed by them. Thus, it would be impossible for our social practices and structures *not* to reflect these racial understandings. Given the pervasive nature of race, the belief that racism can be reduced to hostile, discriminatory acts strains logic. For instance, few can dispute that US cities are highly segregated. Can we attribute this simply to discriminatory lenders and landlords? No. Residential segregation results from a diversity of racisms. Moreover, there is growing evidence that racial responses are often unconscious, the result of lifelong inculcation (Devine 1989; Lawrence 1987). Thus, focusing exclusively on discriminatory acts ignores the fact that all places are racialized, and that race informs all places. Clearly, our preoccupation with discrete discriminatory acts ignores vast dimensions of racism.

A focus on white privilege enables us to develop a more structural, less conscious, and more deeply historicized understanding of racism. It differs from a hostile, individual, discriminatory act, in that it refers to the privileges and benefits that accrue to white people by virtue of their whiteness. Because whiteness is rarely problematized by whites, white privilege is scarcely acknowledged. According to George Lipsitz, "As the unmarked category against which difference is constructed, whiteness never has to speak its name, never has to acknowledge its role as an organizing principle in social and cultural relations" (1995:369). White privilege

is thus an attempt to name a social system that works to the benefit of whites. White privilege, together with overt and institutionalized racism, reveals how racism shapes places. Hence, instead of asking if an incinerator was placed in a Latino community because the owner was prejudiced, I ask, why is it that whites are not comparably burdened with pollution (see Szasz and Meuser 1997)? In the case of Los Angeles, industrialization, decentralization, and residential segregation are keys to this puzzle. Because industrial land use is highly correlated with pollution concentrations and people of color, the crucial question becomes, how did whites distance themselves from both industrial pollution and nonwhites?

This study does not attempt to prove that environmental racism exists in Los Angeles, as six studies have already done so (Sadd et al. 1999; Boer et al. 1997; Pulido et al. 1996; Burke 1993; Szasz et al. 1993; UCC 1987). Nor do I suggest that this particular narrative of racism, white privilege, operates in all places in the same way. Rather, my goal is to consider the larger sociospatial processes of inequality that produce environmental racism. In this paper, I first develop the concept of white privilege. Second, I review how racism and space have been conceptualized in the literature and the geography of urban environmental racism. Third, drawing on both primary and secondary sources, I examine the historical processes and their racist underpinnings that have contributed to the environmental racism we see in Los Angeles today. I conclude by summarizing my findings and their implications.

Racism and White Privilege

A clear definition of race and white racism is in order. I employ Omi and Winant's idea of race as "a concept which signifies and symbolizes social conflicts and interests by referring to different types of human bodies" (1994:55). This definition not only recognizes the physical, material, and ideological dimensions of race, but also acknowledges race as contributing to the social formation. Specifically, it allows us to see race as more than colored bodies. It enables us to recognize the pervasive and hegemonic nature of race, its multiscalar nature, and its multiple forms of existence, including ideas, words, actions, and structures. This approach to race serves as a basis for a broader and more fluid definition of white racism. I define white racism as those practices and ideologies, carried out by structures, institutions, and individuals, that reproduce racial inequality and systematically undermine the well-being of racially subordinated populations.

Because there are multiple motives and forms of racism (Goldberg 1993; Cohen 1992; Omi 1992), there are various ways of analyzing racisms. In this paper, I consider only two: scale and intention. In any attempt to understand racism, scale is an important analytical tool in that it is both defined by racism and transcends it. Consider the various scales at which racism exists: the individual, the group, the institution, society, the global. While all are distinct, there is a dialectical relation between these scales. So, for instance, an individual racist act is just that, an act carried out at the level of the individual. Nonetheless, that individual is informed by regional and/or national racial discourses, and his/her act informs and reproduces racial discourses and structures at higher scales. Thus, we can focus on a particular scale, but we must always be cognizant of its relationship to other scales of racism.

A second crucial issue is the question of intent. While most social science scholars acknowledge institutional and structural racism, popular understandings focus heavily on individual malicious intent. Indeed, this trend is reflected in court rulings that have increasingly required proof of intent (e.g., *Washington v. Davis*).[2] For many, a hostile motive is considered necessary for an action or inequality to qualify as racist. While aware of the power of hostile and malicious acts, we cannot allow their reprehensible nature to obscure the *range* of racist motives that exist. For instance, in this society, there are white supremacists, those who avoid people of color, and those who advocate a "color-blind" society. Each of these positions evinces a different motive. And while they may not be morally comparable, they are all racist because they systematically undermine the well-being of people of color (Delgado 1995).

White privilege is a form of racism that both underlies and is distinct from institutional and overt racism. It underlies them in that both are predicated on preserving the privileges of white people (regardless of whether agents recognize this or not). But it is also distinct in terms of intentionality. It refers to the hegemonic structures, practices, and ideologies that reproduce whites' privileged status. In this scenario, whites do not necessarily *intend* to hurt people of color, but because they are unaware of their white-skin privilege, and because they accrue social and economic benefits by maintaining the status quo, they inevitably do. White privilege thrives in highly racialized societies that espouse racial equality, but in which whites will not tolerate either being inconvenienced in order to achieve racial equality (Lipsitz 1998; Delgado 1995; Quadagno 1994; Edsall and Edsall 1991), or denied the

full benefits of their whiteness (Harris 1993). It is precisely because few whites are aware of the benefits they receive simply from being white and that their actions, without malicious intent, may undermine the well-being of people of color, that white privilege is so powerful and pervasive.

White privilege allows us to see how the racial order works to the benefit of whites, whether in the form of economic and political benefits (Ignatiev 1995; Oliver and Shapiro 1995; Almaguer 1994; Harris 1993), or psychological ones (Roediger 1991; Fanon 1967). White privilege is distinct from both white supremacy, a more blatant and acknowledged form of white dominance (Fredrickson 1981:xi), as well as from more individual, discriminatory acts. Rather, it flourishes *in relation* to these other forms. Because most white people do not see themselves as having malicious intentions, and because racism is associated with malicious intent, whites can exonerate themselves of all racist tendencies, all the while ignoring their investment in white privilege. It is this ability to sever intent from outcome that allows whites to acknowledge that racism exists, yet seldom identify themselves as racists.

Evidence of white privilege abounds. It includes the degree to which whites assume ownership of this nation and its opportunities, people of color's efforts to "pass" in order to access whiteness, whites' resistance to attempts to dismantle their privilege, and, conversely, even whites' efforts to shed their privilege.[3] Consider the case of white resistance. White resistance to integrating schools, housing, and the workplace have all been well documented (Quadagno 1994; Almaguer 1994; Massey and Denton 1993; Foner 1974; Saxton 1971). This resistance is hardly surprising and is justified by any number of rationales. What is important is the fact that whites resist because they feel they have something to lose. According to Lipsitz (1998), they have a "possessive investment in whiteness," meaning, whiteness pays off and whites wish to retain those benefits. Legal scholar Cheryl Harris has observed, "The set of assumptions, privileges, and benefits that accompany the status of being white have become a valuable asset that whites sought to protect and that those who passed sought to attain – by fraud if necessary. Whites have come to expect and rely on these benefits, and over time, these expectations have been affirmed, legitimated, and protected by law" (1993:1713). This "pay off" can take the form of higher property values, better schools, or the ability to exclude people of color from the workplace. That whites feel they have the right to exclude others attests to the degree to which they assume ownership of this nation's opportunities.[4] The privileged position of whites is visible in almost every arena, including health, wealth, housing, educational attainment, and environmental quality.[5]

White privilege is particularly useful in the study of urban landscapes because it is simultaneously historical and spatial. Attempts to understand contemporary racial inequality in light of white privilege must be rooted in the past, precisely because of the absence of a hostile motive or single act. Since landscapes are artifacts of past and present racisms, they embody generations of sociospatial relations, what might be called the "sedimentation of racial inequality" (Oliver and Shapiro 1995:5). Similarly, white privilege, as a form of racism, is spatially expressed, indeed it is partially contingent upon a particular set of spatial arrangements. Take the case of neighborhoods. The *full* exploitation of white privilege requires the production of places with a very high proportion of white people. "Too many" people of color might reduce a neighborhood's status, property value, or general level of comfort for white people.

A brief example may demonstrate how white privilege allows us to historicize environmental racism: A polluter locates near a black neighborhood because the land is relatively inexpensive and adjacent to an industrial zone. This is not a malicious, racially motivated, discriminatory act. Instead, many would argue that it is economically rational. Yet it is racist in that it is made possible by the existence of a racial hierarchy, reproduces racial inequality, and undermines the well-being of that community. Moreover, the value of black land cannot be understood outside of the relative value of white land, which is a historical product. White land is more valuable by virtue of its whiteness (Oliver and Shapiro 1995:147–61), and thus it is not as economically feasible for the polluter. Nor is it likely that the black community's proximity to the industrial zone is a chance occurrence. Given the Federal government's role in creating suburbia, whites' opposition to integration, and the fact that black communities have been restricted to areas whites deemed undesirable, can current patterns of environmental racism be understood outside a racist urban history?

The final issue of white privilege is, at whose expense? It is impossible to privilege one group without disadvantaging another. White privilege comes at the expense of nonwhites. Historically speaking, suburbanization can be seen as a form of white privilege, as it allowed whites to live in inexpensive, clean, residential environments (Jackson 1980). It was a privilege denied to most people of color, but one they also bore the cost of, both in terms

of an erosion of central-city quality of life, and in their direct subsidization of white suburbia through their tax dollars (Guhathakurta and Wichert 1998). White privilege is useful in discussing suburbanization and environmental racism because it shifts our understanding of racism beyond discrete siting acts, while also emphasizing the spatiality of racism.

Racism and Space in Environmental Racism Research

Currently, many methodological issues are being debated within the environmental justice literature (Cutter 1995; see Been 1995). Unfortunately, the nature of racism is not one of them. In a review of thirty recent empirical studies, only a handful attempted any substantive discussion of racism itself (Baden and Coursey 1997; Pulido et al. 1996; Hamilton 1995; Krieg 1995; Bullard 1990; UCC 1987),[6] although others have probed the nature of race and racism in general (Szasz and Meuser 1997; Goldman 1996; Pulido 1996; Bullard 1994; Zimmerman 1994). Instead, the literature is largely characterized by "common sense" assumptions that reflect uncritical, popular understandings of racism.[7] A similar pattern exists in terms of spatiality. While space has received considerable attention, spatiality, meaning the relationship between social space and society (Soja 1989), has not. Instead, spatial discussions have centered on issues of distance, location, and scale, eschewing a more theoretical conception of space (see Cutter and Solecki 1996:395 for an exception). An appreciation of spatiality, however, encourages greater attention to race, as it is one of the key social forces shaping our cities (and the US as a whole). In this section, I review how racism and space are expressed in the literature by showing how three practices contribute to an overly restrictive conception of racism and space. First, I discuss the emphasis on facility siting, second, the role of intentionality, and, third, spatial scale. I will address the first two together, as they are closely related.

Siting and Intentionality in Discrete Acts of Racism

Although an earlier generation of scholars explored the relationship between demographics and pollution (Berry 1977), it was not until the 1980s that these issues were framed as environmental justice (McGurty 1995; see Szasz and Meuser 1997 for a complete review). The initial literature on environmental racism documented discriminatory outcomes (Bullard 1990; UCC 1987; US GAO 1984), but did not delve into the processes producing them. Drawing on traditional social science understandings of racism, Bullard (1996) argued that discriminatory outcomes were evidence of racism, regardless of the mechanism (siting, housing discrimination, job blackmail), precisely because of the racist nature of the economy and the larger social formation. He defines environmental racism as "any policy, practice, or directive that differentially affects or disadvantages (whether intended or unintended) individuals, groups, or communities based on race or color" (1996:497). Subsequent scholarship, however, has not only challenged the existence of environmental racism,[8] but has produced an overly restrictive conception of racism. As a result, siting, as a discrete and conscious act, is often analyzed solely with respect to the locations of racially subordinated groups (Bullard 1996:493) without sufficient attention to the larger sociospatial processes that produced such patterns. Likewise, interpretations of environmental racism are considered suspect without "proof" of intentionality.

Historical studies are a good example of how this shift towards a more restrictive conception of racism has occurred. In addition to enhancing our understanding of environmental inequities (Baden and Coursey 1997; Pulido et al. 1996; Yandle and Burton 1996; Krieg 1995; Been 1994),[9] historical research has also problematized racism by asking, what if the people came first? While potentially a fruitful line of inquiry, the narrow conception of racism informing the literature has resulted in challenges to claims of racism: What were the intentions of the responsible parties? For some scholars, if people subsequently moved to polluted locales, and if the motive is unknown, claims of racism cannot be substantiated:

> Which came first? Were the LULUs [locally undesirable land uses] or sources of environmental threats sited in communities because they were poor, contained people of color and/or politically weak? Or, were the LULUs originally placed in communities with little reference to race or economic status, and over time, the racial composition of the area changed as a result of white flight, depressed housing prices, and a host of other social ills? (Cutter 1995:117).

This quote summarizes an oft-stated sequence of events and conception of the problem. I do not dispute its accuracy, but rather its underlying conception of racism, and the absence within the larger literature of alternative explanations. This scenario is predicated on understanding

racism as a discrete and hostile act. In effect, the *siting* of environmental hazards becomes the expression of a potentially racist act. Were polluters or the state consciously targeting nonwhite neighborhoods? Geographers have, understandably, preferred to address a more narrow set of concerns, rather than the more fundamental issues of environmental degradation (Heiman 1990) or racism (Pulido 1996; Goldman 1996):

> An issue as controversial as environmental equity requires research that assesses the spatial coincidence between environmental disamenities and minority or disadvantaged populations, prior to an analysis of causation and the role of racial intent (Bowen et al. 1995:655).

While a laudable position, the resulting research agenda remains theoretically weak and offers only a limited understanding of how racism, environmental quality, and urban processes intersect. The following quotes illustrate not only the emphasis on siting, but also the extent to which siting and the motive accompanying it, versus outcomes, are key to ascertaining if racism exists.

> Clearly, *discriminatory siting is not the primary culprit* behind these cases of "environmental racism." Instead, Houston's disproportionate distribution of landfills can properly be attributed to the dynamics of the housing market (Boerner and Lambert 1994:16, emphasis added).

> There is, therefore, significant evidence of disproportionate siting. The evidence is flawed, however, in several respects. First, the evidence does not establish that the siting process, rather than market forces such as residential mobility, caused the disparity . . . Second, the evidence does not establish that *siting decisions intentionally discriminated against people of color or the poor* (Been 1993:1014, emphasis added).

> A reasonable distinction is that between injustice in outcome and injustice in intent. Injustice in outcome is what most research has investigated, it can be ascertained by examining a point in time and seeing if minorities or the poor are disproportionately represented in areas where waste is. Injustice in intent concerns *siting decisions that are racist in intent – the actual disproportionate siting of waste in poor, minority communities* (Baden and Coursey 1997:4, emphasis added).

There are two points that emerge from these authors' attempts to analytically sever racism from larger social processes (such as housing markets): First, they exhibit

Table 1. Baden and Coursey's Six Sequential Scenarios and Conclusions

Scenario	Event			Description
	1	2	3	
1	Siting	Danger	People	People move into an area known to be dangerous.
2	Siting	People	Danger	People move into an area which is later determined to be dangerous.
3	Danger	Siting	People	A dangerous facility is sited, then people move into the area.
4	Danger	People	Siting	People live in an area, then a facility known to be dangerous is sited near them.
5	People	Siting	Danger	A facility that is not known to be dangerous is sited in a region where people live and is later determined to be dangerous.
6	People	Danger	Siting	A dangerous facility is sited in a community.

Source: Baden and Coursey (1997:14).

the tendency to limit racism to siting, and second, they impose the requirement of intentionality.

Siting. The emphasis on siting is significant for two reasons. First, it reproduces an erroneous understanding of urban dynamics as it separates larger sociospatial processes from explanations of environmental inequity. Second, it is, unfortunately, the primary mechanism considered in terms of discrimination. This can be seen, for instance, in the way that discriminatory siting is carefully distinguished from market forces, which supposedly are nonracist. Baden and Coursey (1997) go even further by making explicit which historical scenarios are potentially racist and which are not (Table 1). They offer six scenarios to explain a community's proximity to dangerous sites. Only scenarios 4 and 6, however, suggest a clear judgment of environmental racism (1997:14). The authors make clear that siting is the only mechanism that can be equated with environmental racism. In referring to scenarios 1, 2, and 3, they note, "if people move into an area known to be dangerous they may be able to claim racism in lending or economic inequality, but the charge of discriminatory waste siting is tenuous" (1997:14). This is not untrue, but it is highly problematic and illustrative of a limited understanding of racism and space. Neither the narrow conception of racism, nor the fetishizing of siting helps us understand the nature of environmental racism in an urban context. In particular, it does not recognize that space is essential to the (re)production of a particular racial formation, nor does it acknowledge the fundamental relationships between racism and the production of industrial zones, pollution, and residential areas (Arnold 1998).

Intentionality. In the quote by Been, above, the author has clearly found evidence of disproportionate

siting. Yet without using the word "racism," she contextualizes her findings so that the reader is alerted that charges of racism cannot be fully substantiated. She does so, first, by suggesting that market dynamics have not been considered, and second, by referring to the question of intentionality. Nor, she writes, does the evidence "establish that siting decisions intentionally discriminated against people of color." In effect, intentionality becomes the litmus test as to whether or not a racist act has been committed. Intentionality not only underlies discussions of racism, but also serves several purposes in defining it, as critical scholars of legal racism have pointed out (Armour 1997; Crenshaw et al. 1995; Delgado 1995). First, the requirement of intentionality reduces the likelihood of viewing collective actions as racist, as it is more difficult to prove group, rather than individual, intent. Second, the emphasis on intentionality allows for a continual contraction in the definition of racism, as seen in recent court rulings (*Washington v. Davis*). Finally, by the requirement of malicious intent, entire dimensions of the social arena are exonerated from contributing to racial inequality, including the unconscious (Devine 1989; Lawrence 1987). The normal functioning of the state and capitalism are thus naturalized, as racism is reduced to an aberration.[10]

A good example of limiting the domain of racism can be seen in conceptions of the market. Instead of viewing the market as both constituted by racism and an active force in (re)producing racism, scholars have treated it as somehow operating outside the bounds of race (for a fuller discussion, see Pulido 1996:146–7; Mohai and Bryant 1992). This is troubling, given the extent to which discrimination and racism have been proven in the "free market," including in employment (Kirschenman and

Neckerman 1991), banking (Dymski and Veitch 1996), and housing (Holloway 1998). Do not these various forces shape a city, and influence where pollution will be concentrated? Such a limited conception of racism prevents us from either grasping the power and spatiality of racism or identifying its underlying effectivity in perpetuating environmental injustice.

Scale and Racism

In addition to siting and intent, spatial scale is also implicated in producing a narrow conception of racism, as it too reflects normative understandings of race and space. Scale is a major methodological issue in the environmental-racism literature (Bowen et al. 1995; Cutter 1995; Perlin et al. 1995; Zimmerman 1993). Not only have researchers examined environmental inequity at different scales, but the question of what is the most appropriate scale has also been contested. Evidence suggests that different units of analysis, such as counties, zip codes, or census tracts, may produce different findings. For instance, county-level data may reveal a pattern of environmental racism, but a census-tract analysis of the same area may not (Bowen et al. 1995; Anderton et al. 1994a). Zimmerman illustrates how spatial scale may confound attempts to "prove" racism.

> How boundaries can affect the outcome of an equity analysis in the judicial context was underscored in the *East Bibb* case. . . . The court used a census tract to define the boundary around an existing landfill, and, on that basis, ruled that a predominantly white community surrounded the landfill; plaintiffs, in contrast, argued that a larger area encompassing both the existing site and a proposed waste site was predominantly black (70%). Another case, *Bean v. Southwestern Waste Management Corporation*, employed statistical analyses both city-wide and for an area more proximate to a solid waste facility (defined at the census tract level). . . . The court, using statistical findings at both geographic levels, ruled that even though no discrimination existed at the tract level, smaller neighborhoods within tracts where the facilities were located are important considerations in determining patterns of discrimination (1993:652–3).[11]

This quote not only demonstrates the problems associated with treating racism as an either/or phenomenon, but also suggests the extent to which a limited understanding of scale is tied to a narrow conception of racism. Both are conceived as discrete objects, rather than as social processes. I do not mean to suggest that

courts should not rely on such findings, or that discrete acts of racism are *not* important, but as geographers, one of our tasks should be to explain patterns and processes. This requires that we critically interrogate our concepts and tools. In this case, not only must we acknowledge structural racism and reconceptualize it as a power relation, but we also need to contextualize scale. As Neil Smith has argued, we need to recognize scale as socially produced, rather than to treat it as a "methodological preference for the researcher" (1993:96). Besides appreciating the fuzzy edges of spatial units, we must recognize that places are the products of a specific set of social relations (Massey 1994; Soja 1989). Moreover, the relevant social relations do not reside solely within the spatial unit under consideration. Rather, places are produced by other places, what Massey (1994) calls "stretched out" social relations. Thus, not only must our analysis operate at several scales simultaneously, but we must also consider the functional role of those places and their interconnections. This has implications for how we use scale in studies of racism. We must bear in mind that our selected scale of analysis may not necessarily coincide with the scale of racist activity. If racism is constitutive of the urban landscape and various types of racisms operate simultaneously, then great care must be taken in our treatment of scale. Racism and its consequences do not necessarily cease at the edges of census tracts or city boundaries.

Accordingly, instead of treating spatial units as if they exist in a vacuum, the study of industrial pollution requires that our focus not be limited to the individual facility, but rather should address the larger industrial zone in which it is located (Arnold 1998). In turn, the industrial zone must be understood in relation to working-class suburbs, affluent suburbs, "inner-cities,"[12] and downtown areas. All of these places represent specific class relations that are functionally linked. At the same time, all these places are racialized, and racism works in particular ways in their formation and evolution.

Collectively, these three practices, the emphasis on siting, intentionality, and a static conception of scale, have a limited ability to explain the geography of urban environmental hazards, particularly their concentration in industrial zones (Baden and Coursey 1997; Sadd et al. 1999; Pulido et al. 1996; Anderton et al. 1994b; Cutter and Tiefenbacher 1991). Anderton et al., in their national study of transfer, storage, and disposal facilities (TSDFs), found "the clearest and most consistent finding across the country is the apparent association between the location of TSDFs and other industrial enterprises" (1994b:239).[13] This finding suggests the need to clarify the relationship between industrial zones, suburbanization, inner cities, and race. As Been has suggested,

> Many factories and other sources of hazardous waste were traditionally located in the center city because of greater access to transportation and markets. In some cities, developers provided cheap housing for workers in the surrounding areas. As *workers moved away*, either because factories closed or because more desirable housing became affordable elsewhere, the cheap housing in the center cities became disproportionately populated by the poor and by people of color (Been 1993:1017, emphasis added).

This process of how "workers moved away" is one key to understanding contemporary patterns of environmental racism. It is my task to unpack this process.

[...]

Notes

1   A word on terminology is in order. In early studies, the term "environmental racism" was used to denote disparate patterns. Over time, the term "environmental equity" became popular as it was more inclusive, encompassing both racial and economic disparities. Many activists, however, also saw it as an effort to depoliticize the antiracist consciousness underlying the movement. Moreover, as Heiman (1990) has pointed out, environmental (in)equity implies the problem is with the allocation of pollution and environmental hazards, rather than with a particular economic system. Activists eventually adopted the term "environmental justice," as it was inclusive and offered a more politicized conception of the problem. While supportive of the environmental justice movement, I use the term environmental racism to highlight racial disparities. At times, I will use "environmental inequities" to refer to allocation issues.

2   *Washington v. Davis* was an employment discrimination suit in which the Court ultimately ruled that a law that produced a racially disparate impact regardless of motive is not unconstitutional.

3   Many thanks to John Paul Jones for this insight.

4   An oft-cited example of this is Senator Jesse Helm's 1992 campaign TV ad featuring a white working-class man denied a job, what should have been *his* job, because of affirmative action (Omi and Winant 1994:182).

5   This is not to deny the vast differences within the categories of "white" and "people of color." Whites are obviously fragmented by class, gender, sexuality, and ethnicity (Brodkin 1998). Likewise, various nonwhite groups are differentially

racialized. For instance, although Asian Americans have the highest incomes of all people of color, they also are frequent targets of hate crimes. The point is that "the color line" remains a central axis of difference and inequality.

6   The following studies included no significant discussion or problematization of racism: Sadd et al. 1999; Boer et al. 1997; Scott et al. 1997; Cutter and Solecki 1996; Yandle and Burton 1996; Bowen et al. 1995; Perlin et al. 1995; US GAO 1995; Adeola 1994; Anderton et al. 1994a, 1994b; Been 1994; Boerner and Lambert 1994; Cutter 1994; Lester et al. 1994; Burke 1993; Hird 1993; Szasz et al. 1993; Zimmerman 1993; Mohai and Bryant 1992; Napton and Day 1992; Cutter and Tiefenbacher 1991; Hurley 1988. But Pollock and Vittas (1995), in a useful discussion, reconsider their findings in light of alternative conceptions of racism.

7   This does not imply that the researchers themselves are not familiar with social scientific understandings of race, but only that these ideas have not found their way into the literature.

8   In most cases, scholars simply want to establish if such inequities exist, but there has also been a move on the part of both corporations and politically conservative institutions to refute such claims (Anderton et al. 1994a, 1994b; Boerner and Lambert 1994; see Goldman 1996). I too, of course, am an ideologically committed scholar, one who would like to reframe the debate from an antiracist perspective.

9   I do not include Hurley's seminal study of Gary, Indiana in this grouping because it appeared at roughly the same time (1988) as the UCC report (1987). Clearly, he was ahead of his time.

10   The notion of racism as an aberration, or as an irrationality is an entrenched part of the liberal discourse on racism. For a critique, see Crenshaw et al. (1995). On the history of racism, see Goldberg (1993).

11   The cases cited are *East Bibb Twigs Neighborhood Association v. Macon-Bibb County Planning and Zoning Commission.* 888 F. 2d 1573 (11th Cir.), affirmed 896 F. 2d (11th Cir. 1989), and *Bean v. Southwestern Waste Management Corporation,* 482 F. Supp. 673 S.D. Tex. 1979. In *Bean,* local residents felt that the siting decision was discriminatory but lost because they could not prove discriminatory purpose under *Washington v. Davis.*

12   I place the term "inner city" in quotes to denote both the fact that it is socially constructed and problematic as a policy and social science concept.

13   The work of Anderton et al. (1994a, 1994b) has been widely criticized on several grounds. The authors' finding of no environmental racism has been challenged on methodological grounds (Been 1995), as has their participation in industry-supported research (Goldman 1996:132–4). Nonetheless, their emphasis on industrial land use has increasingly been corroborated.

References

Adeola, F. 1994. Environmental Hazards, Health, and Racial Inequity in Hazardous Waste Distribution. *Environment & Behavior* 26:99–126.

Almaguer, T. 1994. *Racial Fault Lines: The Historical Origins of White Supremacy in California*. Berkeley: University of California Press.

Anderson, K. 1987. The Idea of Chinatown: The Power of Place and Institutional Practice in the Making of a Racial Category. *Annals of the Association of American Geographers* 77:580–98.

Anderton, D.; Anderson, A.; Rossi, P.; Oakes, J.; Fraser, M.; Weber, E.; and Calabrese, E. 1994a. Hazardous Waste Facilities: "Environmental Equity" Issues in Metropolitan Areas. *Evaluation Review* 18:123–40.

Anderton, D.; Anderson, A.; Oakes, J.; and Fraser, M. 1994b. Environmental Equity: The Demographics of Dumping. *Demography* 31:229–48.

Armour, J. 1997. *Negrophobia and Reasonable Racism*. New York: New York University Press.

Arnold, C. 1998. Planning Milagros: Environmental Justice and Land Use Regulation. *Denver University Law Review* 76(1):1–153.

Baden, B., and Coursey, D. 1997. The Locality of Waste Sites within the City of Chicago: A Demographic, Social and Economic Analysis. Working paper series 97-2. Chicago: Irving B. Harris Graduate School of Public Policy Studies, University of Chicago.

Bean v. Southwestern Waste Management Corporation. 1979. 482 F. Supp. 673. S.D. Tex.

Been, V. 1995. Analyzing Evidence of Environmental Justice. *Journal of Land Use and Environmental Law* 11(1):1–36.

——. 1994. Locally Undesirable Land Uses in Minority Neighborhoods: Disproportionate Siting or Market Dynamics? *Yale Law Journal* 103:1383–1422.

——. 1993. What's Fairness Got to Do with It? Environmental Justice and the Siting of Locally Undesirable Land Uses. *Cornell Law Review* 78:1001–85.

Berry, B., ed. 1977. *The Social Burdens of Environmental Pollution: A Comparative Metropolitan Data Source*. Cambridge, MA: Ballinger Publications.

Boer, J.; Sadd, J.; Pastor, M.; and Snyder, L. 1997. Is There Environmental Racism? The Demographics of Hazardous Waste in Los Angeles County. *Social Science Quarterly* 78:793–810.

Boerner, C., and Lambert, T. 1994. Environmental Justice? Policy Study 21. St. Louis: Center for the Study of American Business.

Bowen, W.; Salling, M.; Haynes, K.; and Cyran, E. 1995. Toward Environmental Justice: Spatial Equity in Ohio and Cleveland. *Annals of the Association of American Geographers* 85:641–63.

Brodkin, K. 1998. *How Jews Became White Folks*. New Brunswick, NJ: Rutgers University Press.

Bullard, R. 1996. Environmental Justice: It's More than Waste Facility Siting. *Social Science Quarterly* 77: 493–99.

——. 1994. Overcoming Racism in Environmental Decision-making. *Environment* 36(4):10–20, 39–44.

——. 1990. *Dumping in Dixie*. Boulder, CO: Westview Press.

Burke, L. 1993. Environmental Equity in Los Angeles. Master's thesis, Department of Geography, University of California, Santa Barbara.

Cohen, P. 1992. "It's Racism What Dunnit": Hidden Narratives in Theories of Racism. In *Race, Culture and Difference*, ed. J. Donald and A. Rattansi, pp. 62–103. Newbury Park, CA: Sage.

Colten, C. 1986. Industrial Wastes in Southeast Chicago: Production and Disposal, 1870–1970. *Environmental Review* 10: 93–106.

Crenshaw, K.; Gotanda, N.; Pellet, G.; and Thomas, K., eds. 1995. *Critical Race Theory*. New York: New Press.

Cutter, S. 1995. Race, Class and Environmental Justice. *Progress in Human Geography* 19:107–18.

——. 1994. The Burdens of Toxic Risks: Are They Fair? *B & E Review* October–December:3–7.

—— and Solecki, W. 1996. Setting Environmental Justice in Space and Place: Acute and Chronic Airborne Toxic Releases in the Southeastern U.S. *Urban Geography* 17:380–99.

—— and Tiefenbacher, M. 1991. Chemical Hazards in Urban America. *Urban Geography* 12:417–30.

Delgado, R. 1995. *The Rodrigo Chronicles*. New York: New York University Press.

Devine, P. 1989. Stereotypes and Prejudice: Their Automatic and Controlled Components. *Personality and Social Psychology* 56:5–18.

Dymski, G. A., and Veitch, J. M. 1996. Financial Transformation and the Metropolis: Booms, Busts, and Banking in Los Angeles. *Environment and Planning A* 28(7), July: 1233–60.

East Bibb Twigs Neighborhood Association. v. Macon-Bibb County Planning and Zoning Commission. 1989. 888 F. 2d 1573 (11th Cir.).

Edsall, T., and Edsall, M. 1991. *Chain Reaction*. New York: W. W. Norton.

Fanon, F. 1967. *Black Skins, White Masks*. New York: Grove Press.

Foner, E. 1974. *Organized Labor and the Black Worker, 1619–1973*. New York: International.

Fredrickson, G. 1981. *White Supremacy: A Comparative Study of Race in American and South African History*. New York: Oxford University Press.

Gilmore, R. 1998. Globalisation and U.S. Prison Growth: From Military Keynesianism to Post-Keynesian Militarism. *Race & Class* 40(2/3):171–88.

Goldberg, T. 1993. *Racist Culture*. Cambridge, MA: Blackwell.

Goldman, B. 1996. What Is the Future of Environmental Justice? *Antipode* 28:122–41.

Guhathakurta, S., and Wichert, M. 1998. Who Pays for Growth in the City of Phoenix: An Equity-Based Perspective on Suburbanization. *Urban Affairs Review* 33:813–38.

Hamilton, J. 1995. Testing for Environmental Racism: Prejudice, Profits, Political Power? *Journal of Policy Analysis and Management* 14:107–32.

Harris, C. 1993. Whiteness as Property. *Harvard Law Review* 106:1709–91.

Heiman, M. 1990. From "Not in My Backyard!" to "Not in Anybody's Backyard!": Grassroots Challenges to Hazardous Waste Facility Siting. *American Planning Association Journal* 56:359–62.

Hird, J. 1993. Environmental Policy and Equity: The Case of Superfund. *Journal of Policy Analysis and Management* 12:323–43.

Holloway, S. R. 1998. Exploring the Neighbourhood Contingency of Race Discrimination in Mortgage Lending in Columbus, Ohio. *Annals of the Association of American Geographers* 88(2): 252–76.

Hurley, A. 1988. The Social Biases of Environmental Change in Gary, Indiana, 1945–1980. *Environmental Review* 12(4):1–19.

Ignatiev, N. 1995. *How the Irish Became White*. New York: Routledge.

Jackson, K. 1980. Race, Ethnicity, and Real Estate Appraisal: The Home Owners Loan Corporation and the Federal Housing Administration. *Journal of Urban History* 4:419–52.

Jackson, P., and Penrose, J., ed. 1994. *Constructions of Race, Place, and Nation*. Minneapolis: University of Minnesota.

Kirschenman, J., and Neckerman, K. 1991. We'd Love to Hire Them, But . . . The Meaning of Race for Employers. In *The Urban Underclass*, ed. C. Jenks and P. Peterson, pp. 203–32. Washington: Brookings Institution.

Kobayashi, A., and Peake, L. 1994. Unnatural Discourse: "Race" and Gender in Geography. *Gender, Place & Culture* 1:225–44.

Krieg, E. 1995. A Socio-Historical Interpretation of Toxic Waste Sites: The Case of Greater Boston. *American Journal of Economics and Sociology* 54:1–14.

Lawrence, C. 1987. The Id, the Ego and Equal Protection: Reckoning with Unconscious Racism. *Stanford Law Review* 39:317–88.

Lester, J.; Allen, D.; Milburn-Lauer, D. 1994. Race, Class, and Environmental Quality: An Examination of Environmental Racism in the American States. Paper presented at the Annual Meeting of the Western Political Science Association, Albuquerque.

Lipsitz, G. 1998. *The Possessive Investment in Whiteness*. Philadelphia: Temple University Press.

——. 1995. The Possessive Investment in Whiteness: Racialized Social Democracy and the "White" Problem in American Studies. *American Quarterly* 47:369–87.

Massey, Doreen. 1994. *Space, Place, and Gender*. Minneapolis: University of Minnesota Press.

Massey, Douglas, and Denton, N. 1993. *American Apartheid: Segregation and the Making of the Underclass*. Cambridge: Harvard University Press.

McGurty, E. 1995. *The Construction of Environmental Justice: Warren County North Carolina*. Ph.D. dissertation. University of Illinois, Urbana-Champaign.

Mohai, P., and Bryant, B. 1992. Environmental Racism: Reviewing the Evidence. In *Race and the Incidence of Environmental Hazards*, ed. B. Bryant and P. Mohai, pp. 163–246. Boulder, CO: Westview Press.

Myrdal, G. 1944. *An American Dilemma: The Negro Problem and Modern Democracy*. New York: Harper and Row.

Napton, M., and Day, F. 1992. Polluted Neighborhoods in Texas, Who Lives There? *Environment & Behavior* 24: 508–26.

Oliver, M., and Shapiro, T. 1995. *Black Wealth, White Wealth*. New York: Routledge.

Omi, M. 1992. Shifting the Blame: Racial Ideology and Politics in the Post-Civil Rights Era. *Critical Sociology* 18:77–98.

—— and Winant, H. 1994. *Racial Formation in the United States*. New York: Routledge.

Perlin, S.; Setzer, R.; Creason, J.; and Sexton, K. 1995. Distribution of Industrial Air Emissions by Income and Race in the United States: An Approach Using the Toxic Release Inventory. *Environmental Science Technology* 29(1): 69–80.

Pollock, P., and Vittas, M. 1995. Who Bears the Burdens of Environmental Pollution? Race, Ethnicity and Environmental Equity in Florida. *Social Science Quarterly* 76:294–310.

Pulido, L. 1996. A Critical Review of the Methodology of Environmental Racism Research. *Antipode* 28(2):142–59.

——; Sidawi, S.; and Vos, R. 1996. An Archaeology of Environmental Racism in Los Angeles. *Urban Geography* 17(5):419–39.

Quadagno, J. 1994. *The Color of Welfare*. New York: Oxford University Press.

Roediger, D. 1991. *The Wages of Whiteness*. New York: Verso.

Sadd, J.; Pastor, M.; Boer, J.; and Snyder, L. 1999. Every Breath You Take . . . The Demographics of Point Source Air Pollution in Southern California. *Economic Development Quarterly* 13(2):107–23.

Saxton, A. 1971. *The Indispensable Enemy*. Berkeley: University of California Press.

Scott, M.; Cutter, S.; Menzel, C.; and Minhe, J. 1997. Spatial Accuracy of the EPA's Environmental Hazards Databases and Their Use in Environmental Equity Analysis. *Applied Geographic Studies* 1(1):45–61.

Smith, N. 1993. Homeless/Global: Scaling Places. In *Mapping the Futures: Local Cultures, Global Change*, ed. J. Bird, B. Curtis, T. Putnam, and G. Robertson, pp. 87–119. London: Routledge.

Smith, S. 1993. Residential Segregation and the Politics of Racialization. In *Racism, the City, and the State*, ed. M. Cross and M. Keith, pp. 128–43. New York: Routledge.

——. 1989. *Postmodern Geographies*. New York: Verso.

Szasz, A., and Meuser, M. 1997. Environmental Inequalities: Literature Review and Proposals for New Directions in Research and Theory. *Current Sociology* 45(3): 99–120.

——; ——; Aronson, H.; and Fukarai, H. 1993. The Demographics of Proximity to Toxic Releases: The Case of Los Angeles County. Paper Presented at the Meetings of the American Sociological Association, Miami.

United Church of Christ, Commission for Racial Justice. 1987. *Toxic Wastes and Race in the United States*. New York: UCC.

US General Accounting Office. 1995. *Hazardous and Non-hazardous Waste: Demographics of People Living Near Waste Facilities*. GAO/RCCD-95-84.

——. 1984. *Siting of Hazardous Waste Landfills and their Correlation with Racial and Economic Status of Surrounding Communities*. Washington: General Accounting Office.

Washington v. Davis. 1976. 426 U.S. 229, 96 S. Ct. 2040.

Woods, C. 1998. *Arrested Development: Regional Planning in the Mississippi Delta*. New York: Verso.

Yandle, T., and Burton, D. 1996. Reexamining Environmental Justice: A Statistical Analysis of Historical Waste Landfill Siting Patterns in Metropolitan Texas. *Social Science Quarterly* 77:477–92.

Zimmerman, R. 1994. Issues of Classification in Environmental Equity: How We Manage Is How We Measure. *Fordham Urban Law Journal* 21(3):633–69.

——. 1993. Social Equity and Environmental Risk. *Risk Analysis* 13:649–66.

Commerce: Reconfiguring Community Marketplaces

Lizabeth Cohen

"By the 1950s the shopping center . . . had become as much a part of suburbia as the rows of ranch houses, split-levels, and Cape Cods," political scientist Robert Wood stated matter-of-factly in his *Suburbia: Its People and Their Politics* of 1959. And indeed, attention within the Consumers' Republic to promoting consumer spending reshaped much more than the character of residential communities in the postwar metropolitan landscape. The physical arrangement of American commercial life became reconfigured as well. As existing suburban town centers proved inadequate to support all the consumption desired by the influx of new residents, as suburbanites more and more attached to their cars increasingly viewed returning to urban downtowns to shop as inconvenient, and as retailers came to realize that suburban residents, with their young families, new homes, and vast consumer appetites, offered a lucrative frontier ripe for conquest, the regional shopping center emerged as a new form of community marketplace. Wood underscored the tremendous increase in suburban share of total metropolitan retail trade from 4 percent in 1939 to 31 percent by 1948; by 1961 it would total almost 60 percent in the ten largest population centers. But as significant as the volume of commerce transacted in suburbia was the setting where that consumption took place.[1]

The development of a new, distinctive kind of metropolitan marketplace suited to mass suburbia lagged behind the construction of residences. New suburbanites who had themselves grown up in urban neighborhoods walking to corner stores and taking public transportation to shop downtown had to contend with inadequate retail options until at least the mid-1950s. Only in the

most ambitious suburban tracts built after the war had developers incorporated stores into their plans. In those cases, developers tended to place the shopping district at the core of the residential community much as it had been in the prewar planned community of Radburn in Fair Lawn, New Jersey, and in the earliest shopping centers such as Kansas City's Country Club Plaza of the 1920s. These precedents, and their descendants in early postwar developments in Park Forest, Illinois, Levittown, New York, and Bergenfield, New Jersey, replicated the structure of the old-style urban community, where shopping was part of the public space at the settlement's core and residences spread outward from there.[2] But most postwar suburban home developers made no effort to provide for residents' commercial needs. Rather, suburbanites were expected to fend for themselves by driving to the existing "market towns," which often offered the only commerce for miles, or by returning to the city to shop. Faced with slim retail offerings nearby, many new suburbanites of the 1940s and 1950s continued to depend on the big city for major purchases, making do with the small, locally owned commercial outlets in neighboring towns for minor needs..

It was not until the late 1950s that a new market structure appropriate to this suburbanized, mass consumption society prevailed. Important precedents existed in the branch department stores and prototypical shopping centers constructed between the 1920s and 1940s in outlying city neighborhoods and in older suburban communities, which began the process of decentralizing retail dollars away from downtown. But the scale required now was much larger. By 1957, 940 shopping centers had already been built. That number more than doubled by 1960, and doubled again by 1963; by 1976 the 17,520 shopping centers in the nation would represent an almost nineteenfold increase over twenty years.[3] With postwar suburbanites finally living the motorized existence that had been predicted for American society since the 1920s, traffic congestion and parking problems discouraged commercial developers from expanding in central business districts of major cities and smaller market towns, already hindered by a short supply of developable space.[4] Rather, retailers preferred catering to suburbanites on the open land where they now lived and drove, deeming it a unique opportunity to reinvent community life with their private projects at its heart.[5]

[. . .]

Although the shift in community marketplace from town center to shopping center was a national phenomenon, Paramus, New Jersey, a postwar suburb seven miles from the George Washington Bridge that became the home of the largest shopping complex in the country by the end of 1957, provides an illuminating case.[6] Within six months, R. H. Macy's Garden State Plaza and Allied Stores Corporation's Bergen Mall opened three-quarters of a mile from each other at the intersection of Routes 4, 17, and the soon-to-be-completed Garden State Parkway. Both department store managements had independently recognized the enormous commercial potential of Bergen and Passaic Counties. Although the George Washington Bridge had connected the area to Manhattan in 1931, the Great Depression and the war had postponed major housing construction until the late 1940s. By 1960 each shopping center had two to three department stores as anchors (distinguishing it from many prewar projects built around a single anchor), surrounded by fifty to seventy smaller stores. Attracting half a million patrons a week, these shopping centers dominated retail trade in the region.[7]

The Paramus malls have special significance because of their location adjacent to the wealthiest and busiest central business district in the nation. If these malls could prosper in the shadow of Manhattan, the success of their counterparts elsewhere should come as no surprise. Furthermore, the Paramus case illuminates three major effects of shifting marketplaces on postwar American community life: in commercializing public space, they brought to community life the market segmentation that increasingly shaped commerce and

residence; in privatizing public space, they privileged the rights of private property owners over citizens' traditional rights of free speech in community forums; and in feminizing public space, they enhanced women's claim on the suburban landscape while circumscribing the power they yielded there.

Commercializing Public Space

Developers, department stores, and big investors such as insurance companies (who leapt at the promise of a huge return on the vast amounts of capital they controlled) built shopping centers to profit from what seemed to be ever rising levels of consumption. As Macy's board chairman, Jack Isidor Straus, who oversaw the development of the Garden State Plaza, confidently explained in 1965, "Our economy keeps growing because our ability to consume is endless. The consumer goes on spending regardless of how many possessions he has. The luxuries of today are the necessities of tomorrow."[8] Why not, then, situate new stores as accessible as possible to the most dynamic sources of demand fueling the thriving economy of postwar America – the new, high-consuming suburbanites? Already a decade earlier, an article in the *New York Times Magazine* marking the growing interest in building shopping centers had concluded, "There is a widely held belief that American households are ready to do more buying than they presently do. . . . They would do it more readily but for the difficulty of getting to the 'downtowns' where the full range of goods is available." The solution proposed: "Bringing the market to the people instead of people to the market."[9]

Focusing on the obvious economic motives developers and investors shared in constructing shopping centers, however, can mask the visionary dimension of their undertaking, which led them to innovate a new retail form. When planners and shopping center developers envisioned this new kind of consumption-oriented community center in the 1950s, they set out to perfect the concept of downtown, not to obliterate it, even though their projects directly challenged the viability of existing commercial centers like Hackensack, the political and commercial seat of Bergen County adjacent to Paramus.[10] They felt that they were participating in a rationalization of consumption and community no less revolutionary than the way highways were transforming transportation or tract developments were delivering mass single-family housing. "Shopping

Centers properly planned by developers and local communities are the rational alternative to haphazard retail development," the International Council of Shopping Centers explained.[11]

The ideal was still the creation of centrally located public space that integrated commerce with civic activity. Victor Gruen, one of the most prominent and articulate shopping center developers, spoke for many others when he argued that shopping centers offered dispersed suburban populations "crystallization points for suburbia's community life." "By affording opportunities for social life and recreation in a protected pedestrian environment, by incorporating civic and educational facilities, shopping centers can fill an existing void."[12] Not only did Gruen and others promote the private construction of community centers in the atomized landscape of suburbia, but their earliest shopping centers idealized – almost romanticized – the physical plan of the traditional downtown shopping street, with stores lining both sides of an open-air pedestrian walkway that was landscaped and equipped with benches. Regional shopping centers would create old-style community with new-style unity and efficiency; statements like "the shopping center is . . . today's village green" and "the fountain in the mall has replaced the downtown department clock as the gathering place for young and old alike," dominated planning for new centers.[13]

Designed to bring many of the best qualities of urban life to the suburbs, these new "shopping towns," as Gruen called them, sought to overcome the "anarchy and ugliness" characteristic of many American cities. A centrally owned and managed Garden State Plaza or Bergen Mall, it was argued, offered an alternative model to the inefficiencies, visual chaos, and provinciality of traditional downtown districts. A centralized administration made possible the perfect mix and "scientific" placement of stores, meeting customers' diverse needs and maximizing store owners' profits. Management kept control visually by standardizing all architectural and graphic design and politically by requiring all tenants to participate in the tenants' association. Common complaints of downtown shoppers were directly addressed: parking was plentiful, safety was ensured by hired security guards, delivery tunnels and loading courts kept truck traffic away from shoppers, canopied walks and air-conditioned stores made shopping comfortable year-round, piped-in background music replaced the cacophony of the street. The preponderance of chains and franchises over local, independent stores, required by big investors such as insurance companies, brought shoppers the latest national trends in products and merchandising techniques.

Garden State Plaza and Bergen Mall provide good models for how shopping centers of the fifties followed Gruen's prescription and became more than miscellaneous collections of stores. B. Earl Puckett, Allied Stores' board chair, went so far as to boast that Paramus's model shopping centers were making it "one of the first preplanned major cities in America," an urban innovation that also maximized profits.[14] As central sites of consumption, they offered the full range of shops and services that would previously have existed downtown. They not only sold the usual clothing and shoes in their specialty and department stores – Stern Brothers and J. J. Newberry at Bergen Mall, Bamberger's (Macy's New Jersey division), JCPenney's, and Gimbel's at Garden State Plaza – but also featured stores specifically devoted to furniture, hardware, appliances, groceries, gifts, drugs, books, toys, records, bakery goods, candy, jewelry, garden supplies, hearing aids, tires, and even religious objects. Services grew to include restaurants, a post office, Laundromat, cleaners, key store, shoe repair, bank, loan company, stock brokerage houses, barbershop, travel agency, real estate office, "slenderizing salon," and Catholic chapel. Recreational facilities ranged from a 550-seat movie theater, bowling alley, and ice-skating rink to a children's gymnasium and playground.

Both shopping centers made meeting rooms and auditoriums available to community organizations and scheduled a full range of cultural and educational activities to legitimize these sites as civic centers, while also attracting customers. Well-attended programs and exhibitions taught shoppers about such "hot" topics of the fifties and sixties as space exploration, color television, modern art, and civics. Evening concerts and plays, ethnic entertainment, dances and classes for teenagers, campaign appearances by political candidates, and community outreach for local charities were some of the ways that Bergen Mall and Garden State Plaza made themselves indispensable to life in Bergen County.

In sum, it was hard to think of consumer items or community events that could not be found at one or the other of these two shopping centers in Bergen County. (In the 1970s a cynical reporter cracked that "the only institution that had not yet invaded" the modern shopping mall was the funeral home.) To a regional planner like New Jersey's Ernest Erber, these postwar shopping centers represented a new kind of urbanism appropriate to the automobile age: the "City of Bergen," he dubbed the area in 1960. Seven years later the New Jersey Federation of Planning Officials was still encouraging its members and their communities to use "appropriate zoning and site development controls to encourage this desirable trend" of making centers "real downtowns for the surrounding area." In time, the *New York Times* would proclaim Paramus's commercial complex the real thing: "It lives a night as well as a day existence, glittering like a city when the sun goes down." In fact, shopping centers prided themselves on their greater "night existence" than most downtowns, as their stores and services were open to patrons from 10 a.m. to 9:30 p.m., at first four nights a week, and by the 1960s six nights.[15]

Making the shopping center a perfection of downtown entailed more than building idealized pedestrian streets, showcasing a full range of goods and services, and staying open long hours. Developers and store owners also set out to exclude from this new public space unwanted urban elements, such as vagrants, prostitutes, disruptive rebels, racial minorities, and poor people. Market segmentation became the guiding principle of this mix of commercial and civic activity, as the shopping center sought, perhaps contradictorily, to legitimize itself as a true community center and to define that community in exclusionary socioeconomic and racial terms.

[...]

Carefully controlled access to suburban shopping centers further supported the class and color line. The operating assumption in planning centers was always that patrons would travel by car. The debate among developers, played out in retailer trade journals and planning conferences, revolved instead around how long that drive could feasibly be; articles like "The Influence of Driving Time Upon Shopping Center Preference" were legion.[16] But not everyone living in metropolitan areas had cars. A survey of consumer expenditures in northern New Jersey in 1960–61 revealed that while 79 percent of all families owned cars, fewer than one-third of those with incomes below $3000 did, and that low-income population included a higher percentage of non-white families than the average for the whole sample.[17] Although bus service was available for non-drivers, only a tiny proportion arrived that way (in 1966 a daily average of only 600 people came to Garden State Plaza by bus compared to 18,000 to 31,000 cars, many carrying more than one passenger). The small number traveling by bus was not surprising, as bus routes were carefully planned to serve non-driving customers, particularly women, from neighboring suburbs, not low-income consumers from cities like Passaic, Paterson, and Newark. Meanwhile, studies of African-American mobility as late as the 1970s documented their great dependence on public transportation to get to work or to stores.[18]

Whereas individual downtown department stores had long targeted particular markets defined by class and race, some selling, for example, to "the carriage trade" at the upper end and others to the bargain hunters at the lower, shopping centers took market segmentation to the scale of a downtown, much the way suburbs converted distinctive urban neighborhoods into homogeneous municipalities. In promoting an idealized downtown, shopping centers like Garden State Plaza and Bergen Mall tried to filter out not only the inefficiencies and inconveniences of the city but also the undesirable people who lived there.

[...]

Privatizing Public Space

Whereas, at first, developers had sought to legitimize the new shopping centers by arguing for their centrality to both commerce and community, over time they discovered that these two commitments could conflict. The rights of free speech and assembly traditionally safeguarded in the public forums of democratic communities were not always good for business, and they could undermine the rights of private property owners – the shopping centers – to control entry to their land. Beginning in the 1960s, American courts all the way up to the United States Supreme Court struggled with the political consequences of having moved public life off the street and into the privately owned shopping center. Shopping centers, in turn, began to reconsider the desirable balance between commerce and community in what had become the major sites where suburbanites congregated.[19]

Once regional shopping centers like the Paramus malls had opened in the 1950s, people began to recognize them as public spaces and to use them to reach out to the community. When the Red Cross organized blood drives, when labor unions picketed stores in organizing campaigns, when political candidates ran for office, when anti-war and anti-nuclear activists gathered signatures for petitions, they all viewed the shopping center as the obvious place to reach masses of people, Although shopping centers varied in their responses – from tolerating political activists to monitoring their actions to prohibiting them outright – in general, they were wary of any activity that might offend customers. A long, complex series of court tests resulted, culminating in several key Supreme Court decisions that sought to sort out the conflict between two basic rights in a free society: free speech and private property. Not surprisingly, the cases hinged on arguments about the extent to which the shopping center had displaced the traditional "town square" as a legitimate public forum.[20]

The first ruling by the Supreme Court was *Amalgamated Food Employees Union Local 590* v. *Logan Valley Plaza, Inc.* (1968), in which Justice Thurgood Marshall, writing for the majority, argued that refusing to let union members picket the Weis Markets in the Logan Valley Plaza in Altoona, Pennsylvania, violated the workers' First Amendment rights, since shopping centers had become the "functional equivalent" of a sidewalk in a public business district. Because peaceful picketing and leaflet distribution on "streets, sidewalks, parks, and other similar public places are so historically associated with the exercise of First Amendment rights," he wrote, they should also be protected in the public thoroughfare of a shopping center, even if privately owned. The *Logan Valley Plaza* decision likened the shopping center to a company town, which had been the subject of a previously important Supreme Court decision in *Marsh* v. *Alabama* (1946), upholding the First Amendment rights of a Jehovah's Witness to proselytize in the company town of Chickasaw, Alabama, despite the fact that the Gulf Shipbuilding Corporation owned all the property in town. The "Marsh Doctrine" affirmed First Amendment rights over private property rights when an owner opened up his or her property for use by the public.[21]

The stance taken in *Logan Valley Plaza* began to unravel, however, as the Supreme Court became more conservative under President Richard Nixon's appointees. In *Lloyd* v. *Tanner* (1972), Justice Lewis F. Powell, Jr., wrote for the majority that allowing anti-war advocates to pass out leaflets at the Lloyd Center in Portland, Oregon, would be an unwarranted infringement of property rights "without significantly enhancing the asserted right of free speech." Anti-war leaflets, he argued, could be effectively distributed elsewhere, without undermining the shopping center's appeal to customers with litter and distraction.[22]

The reigning Supreme Court decision today is *Prune-Yard Shopping Center* v. *Robbins* (1980). The Supreme Court upheld a California State Supreme Court ruling that the state constitution granted a group of high school students the right to gather petitions against the UN resolution "Zionism is Racism." The Court decided that this action did not violate the San Jose mall owner's rights under the US Constitution. But, at the same time, the Court reaffirmed its earlier decisions in *Lloyd* v. *Tanner* and *Scott Hudgens* v. *National Labor Relations Board* (1976) that the First Amendment did not guarantee access to shopping malls, and it let the states decide for themselves whether their own constitutions protected such access.

Since *PruneYard*, state appellate courts have been struggling with the issue, and mall owners have won in many more states than they have lost. Only in six states – California, Colorado, Massachusetts, New Jersey, Oregon, and Washington – have state supreme courts protected citizens' right of free speech in privately owned shopping centers. In New Jersey, the courts have been involved for some time in adjudicating free speech in shopping centers. In 1983, Bergen Mall was the setting of a suit between its owners and a political candidate who wanted to distribute campaign materials there. When a Paramus municipal court judge ruled in favor of the mall, the candidate's attorney successfully appealed on the familiar grounds that "there is no real downtown Paramus. Areas of the mall outside the stores are the town's public sidewalks." He further noted that the mall hosted community events and contained a meeting hall, post office, and Roman Catholic chapel. In this case, and in another one the following year over the right of nuclear-freeze advocates to distribute literature at Bergen Mall, free speech was protected on the grounds that the mall was equivalent to a town center.[23]

In two more recent decisions, in December 1994 and June 2001, the New Jersey Supreme Court reaffirmed that the state constitution guaranteed free speech in shopping malls. In the first case, *New Jersey Coalition Against War in the Middle East* v. *J.M.B. Realty Corp.*, opponents of the Persian Gulf War wanted to distribute leaflets at ten regional malls throughout the state. Writing for the majority, Chief Justice Robert N. Wilentz confirmed how extensively public space had been transformed in postwar New Jersey:

The economic lifeblood once found downtown has moved to suburban shopping centers, which have substantially displaced the downtown business districts as the centers of commercial and social activity.... Found at these malls are most of the uses and activities citizens engage in outside their homes.... This is the new, the improved, the more attractive downtown business district – the new community – and no use is more closely associated with the old downtown than leafletting. Defendants have taken that old downtown away from its former home and moved all of it, except free speech, to the suburbs.

Despite the New Jersey Supreme Court's endorsement of free speech in 1994, it nonetheless put limits on its exercise, reaffirming the regional mall owners' property rights. Its ruling allowed only the distribution of leaflets – no speeches, bullhorns, pickets, parades, demonstrations, or solicitation of funds. Moreover, the court granted owners broad powers to regulate leaflet distribution by specifying days, hours, and areas in or outside the mall permissible for political activity. Mall owners were also allowed to require leafletters to carry million-dollar liability policies, which were often unobtainable or prohibitively expensive.[24]

In 2001 the New Jersey State Supreme Court clarified its position with a ruling in *Green Party of New Jersey* v. *Hartz Mountain Industries*. The Mall at Mill Creek had imposed restrictions on the Green Party of the sort presumably allowed under the court's 1994 decision – such as requiring a $1 million liability policy and limiting access to one day a year – as the party attempted to collect signatures in support of Ralph Nader's presidential run in 1996. In a unanimous decision, the state supreme court reaffirmed the notion of the mall as the "functional equivalent" of the Main Street of yesterday and called for a "balancing test" that more positively weighed the importance of individual liberties like leafletting "in our system of political discourse." Although the judges did not void all restrictions, New Jersey remains a beacon of free speech. In many more states, shopping centers have retained the right to prohibit political action altogether, much as they control the economic and social behavior of shoppers and store owners.[25]

An unintended consequence of the American shift in orientation from public town center to private shopping center, then, has been the narrowing of the ground where constitutionally protected free speech and free assembly can legally take place. As Justice Marshall so prophetically warned in his *Lloyd* v. *Tanner* dissent in 1972, as he watched the Berger Court reverse many of the liberal decisions of the Warren Court:

It would not be surprising in the future to see cities rely more and more on private businesses to perform functions once performed by governmental agencies. . . . As governments rely on private enterprise, public property

decreases in favor of privately owned property. It becomes harder and harder for citizens to communicate with other citizens. Only the wealthy may find effective communication possible unless we adhere to *Marsh* v. *Alabama* and continue to hold that "the more an owner, for his advantage, opens up his property for use by the public in general, the more do his rights become circumscribed by the statutory and constitutional rights of those who use it."[26]

As Marshall's dissent predicted, the privatization of what had de facto become public space in suburban shopping centers had ominous implications for the preservation of democratic freedom in cities as well. For example, the explosion over the quarter century since Marshall's dissent of self-taxing Business Improvement Districts (BIDs) – supported by urban merchants to clean, upgrade, and police their neighborhoods to compensate for what they considered inadequate government attention, but worrisomely free of municipal oversight or public accountability – suggests some of the troubling directions American society may be headed as once-public spaces and services become privatized, in cities and suburbs alike.[27]

[. . .]

Notes

1   Robert C. Wood, *Suburbia: Its People and Their Politics* (Boston: Houghton Mifflin, 1959), p. 63; 1961 statistic from Bert Randolph Sugar, "Suburbia: A Nice Place to Live, but I Wouldn't Want to Define It There," *Media/Scope* 11 (February 1967): 50; for further analysis, see James D. Tarver, "Suburbanization of Retail Trade in the Standard Metropolitan Areas of the United States, 1948–54," in William M. Dobriner, ed., *The Suburban Community* (New York: Putnam's, 1958), pp. 195–205. Estimates of the number of shopping centers before the International Council of Shopping Centers was founded in 1957 vary; Janet L. Wolff, author of *What Makes Women Buy: A Guide to Understanding and Influencing the New Woman of Today* (New York: McGraw-Hill, 1958), p. 223, claims that in 1952 "there were only about 100 organized shopping centers." Historians of suburbanization have paid far less attention to the restructuring of commercial life in the postwar period than to the transformation of residential experience.

2   Ann Durkin Keating and Ruth Eckdish Knack, "Shopping in the Planned Community: Evolution of the Park Forest Town Center," unpublished paper in possession of author; Howard Gillette, Jr., "The Evolution of the Planned

Shopping Center in Suburb and City," *American Planning Association Journal* 51 (Autumn 1985): 449–60; Daniel Prosser, "The New Downtowns: Commercial Architecture in Suburban New Jersey, 1920–1970," in Joel Schwartz and Prosser, eds., *Cities of the Garden State: Essays in the Urban and Suburban History of New Jersey* (Dubuque, IA: Kendall/Hunt, 1977), pp. 113–15; "Park Forest Moves into '52," *House and Home: The Magazine of Building* 1 (March 1952): 115–16; William S. Worley, *J. C. Nichols and the Shaping of Kansas City: Innovation in Planned Residential Communities* (Columbia: University of Missouri Press, 1990); Richard Longstreth, "J. C. Nichols, the Country Club Plaza, and Notions of Modernity," *Harvard Architecture Review*, vol. 5, *Precedent and Invention* (New York: Rizzoli, 1986), pp. 121–32; William H. Whyte, Jr., "The Outgoing Life," *Fortune*, July 1953, p. 85; Michael Birkner, *A Country Place No More: The Transformation of Bergenfield, New Jersey, 1894–1994* (Rutherford, NJ: Fairleigh Dickinson University Press, 1994), pp. 174–77; Special Foster Village Edition, *BR*, Aug. 10, 1949.

3   Statistics compiled by the International Council of Shopping Centers [ICSC], in advertising supplement to the *NYT*, "Shopping Centers Come of Age: International Council of Shopping Centers Observes 20th Anniversary," 1977, GSD, p. 7.

4   Richard Longstreth, "The Mixed Blessings of Success: The Hecht Company and Department Store Branch Development After World War II," Occasional Paper No. 14, January 1995, Center for Washington Area Studies, George Washington University.

5   Kenneth T. Jackson, *Crabgrass Frontier: The Suburbanization of the United States* (New York: Oxford University Press, 1985), pp. 255–61. On precedents in the pre-World War II period, see Richard Longstreth, "Silver Spring: Georgia Avenue, Colesville Road, and the Creation of an Alternative 'Downtown' for Metropolitan Washington," in Zeynep Celik, Diane Favro, and Richard Ingersoll, eds., *Streets: Critical Perspectives on Public Space* (Berkeley: University of California Press, 1994), pp. 247–57; Longstreth, "The Neighborhood Shopping Center in Washington, D.C., 1930–1941," *Journal of the Society of Architectural Historians* 51 (March 1992): 5–33; Longstreth, "The Perils of a Parkless Town," in Martin Wachs and Margaret Crawford, eds., *The Car and the City: The Automobile, the Built Environment, and Daily Urban Life* (Ann Arbor: University of Michigan Press, 1992), pp. 141–53.

6   On the postwar growth of Paramus and Bergen County, New Jersey, see Raymond M. Ralph, *Bergen County, New Jersey History and Heritage*, vol. 6, *Farmland to Suburbia, 1920–1960* (Hackensack, NJ: Bergen County Board of Chosen Freeholders, 1983), pp. 62–71, 76–90; Catherine M. Fogarty, John E. O'Connor, and Charles F. Cummings, *Bergen County: A Pictorial History* (Norfolk, VA: Donning, 1985), pp. 182–93; *Beautiful Bergen: The Story of Bergen County, New Jersey* (Ridgewood, NJ: s.n., 1962); Patricia M.

Ryle, *An Economic Profile of Bergen County, New Jersey* (Trenton, NJ: Office of Economic Research, Division of Planning and Research, New Jersey Department of Labor and Industry, March 1980); League of Women Voters of Bergen County, *Where Can I Live in Bergen County?: Factors Affecting Housing Supply* (Closter, NJ: League of Women Voters, 1972).

7   Samuel Feinberg, "Story of Shopping Centers," *What Makes Shopping Centers Tick*, reprinted from *Women's Wear Daily* (New York: Fairchild, 1960), pp. 2, 94–102; Ralph, *Farmland to Suburbia*, pp. 70–1, 84–5; Mark A. Stuart, *Bergen County, New Jersey History and Heritage*, vol. 7; *Our Era, 1960–Present* (Hackensack, NJ: Bergen County Board of Chosen Freeholders, 1983), pp. 19–22; Prosser, "New Downtowns," pp. 119–20; Edward T. Thompson, "The Suburb That Macy's Built," *Fortune*, February 1960, pp. 195–200; "Garden State Plaza Merchant's Manual," May 1, 1957, and certain pages revised in 1959, 1960, 1962, 1963, 1965, 1969, GSP.

8   "The Economy: The Great Shopping Spree," *Time*, Jan. 8, 1965, pp. 58–62 and cover.

9   C. B. Plamer, "The Shopping Center Goes to the Shopper," *NYT Magazine*, Nov. 29, 1953, p. 40.

10 On the financing of shopping centers, and the great profits involved, see Jerry Jacobs, *The Mall: An Attempted Escape from Everyday Life* (Prospect Heights, IL: Waveland, 1984), p. 52.

11 ICSC, "Shopping Centers Come of Age," p. 2.

12 Victor Gruen, "Introverted Architecture," *Progressive Architecture* 38 (1957): 204–8; Gruen and Larry Smith, *Shopping Towns USA: The Planning of Shopping Centers* (New York: Reinhold, 1960), pp. 22–4; both quoted in Gillette, "Evolution of the Planned Shopping Center." For more on Gruen, see William Severini Kowinski, *The Malling of America: An Inside Look at the Great Consumer Paradise* (New York: Morrow, 1985), pp. 118–20, 210–14; "Exhibit of Shopping Centers," *NYT*, Oct. 19, 1954. For profile of Martin Bucksbaum, another shopping-center builder, see Paul Goldberger, "Selling the Suburban Frontier," *NYT Magazine*, Dec. 31, 1995, pp. 34–5.

13 ICSC, "Shopping Centers Come of Age," pp. 1, 39. One Florida architect whose firm built several shopping centers referred to making the department store the focal point of a center as the "Main Street Plan": Clinton Gamble, "Shopping Centers! A Modern Miracle," *Miami Herald*, Oct. 23, 1955. In a talk to the Urban History Seminar of the Chicago Historical Society, February 17, 1994, Robert Bruegmann made the same point about the way the earliest design of suburban shopping centers resembled downtown shopping streets.

14 Quoted in Feinberg, *What Makes Shopping Centers Tick*, p. 101. In addition to sources already cited on the control possible in a shopping center versus a downtown, see "Shopping Centers Get Personality," *NYT*, June 29, 1958. For a notion of shopping centers as an "integrated

organism," see Howard T. Fisher, "The Impact of New Shopping Centers Upon Established Business Districts," talk at National Citizens' Conference on Planning for City, State and Nation, May 15, 1950, GSD, pp. 3–4. Chains were also favored over independents in shopping centers because they more easily reaped the big bonuses for depreciation of new store upfitting, while small independents had little surplus income to shelter and less specialized tax accounting expertise: e-mail correspondence with Thomas W. Hanchett, Nov. 20, 1996.

Insurance companies made no secret of why they were attracted to investing in shopping centers. John D. W. Wadhams, senior vice president of Aetna, explained that insurance companies saw buying a center "as a way of saying to policy holders that their company is aggressively seeking those equities which will have ever-increasing rates of return and can some day be sold at a good profit, increasing overall yield": ICSC, "Shopping Centers Come of Age," p. 54. Teachers Insurance and Annuity Association–College Retirement Equities Fund (TIAA-CREF) explained why it favored chain stores in centers: 'TIAA normally requires a certain proportion of national tenants in the shopping centers it finances. This means that if a particular center does not turn out well, the leases held by its major tenants will be supported by other stores in that system around the country": William C. Greenough, *It's My Retirement Money, Take Good Care of It: The TIAA-CREF Story* (Homewood, IL: Irwin, 1990), p. 175. In a 1971 publication, TIAA boasted that with shopping center loans accounting for 43 percent of its total conventional mortgage loans, "today [it] is recognized as being one of the leaders among the institutions that finance shopping centers": *TIAA Investment Report for 1971*, pp. 8–9. A year later TIAA would claim investments in 133 shopping centers in 30 states: *The Participant* (Policyholder Newsletter), November 1972, p. 4.

15 Ernest Erber, "Notes on the 'City of Urban,'" Erber, Box B; Dean K. Boorman, "Shopping Centers: Their Planning and Control, Federation Planning Information Report," vol. 2, no. 4 (New Jersey Federation of Planning Officials, September 1967), p. 6, GSD; "Paramus Booms as a Store Center," *NYT*, Feb. 5, 1962; "The Mall the Merrier, or Is It?" *NYT*, Nov. 21, 1976. For details on particular stores and activities at Bergen Mall and Garden State Plaza, see Feinberg, *What Makes Shopping Centers Tick*, pp. 97–100; Fogarty et al., *Bergen County*, p. 189; Prosser, "New Downtowns," p. 119. Almost every issue of the *BR* beginning in 1957 yields valuable material (in articles and advertisements) on mall stores, services, and activities. The discussion here is based particularly on issues from Nov. 8, 13, 19, 1957, Jan. 8, 1958, June 10, 1959, and Mar. 2, 1960. Also see "Shoppers! Mass Today on Level 1," *NYT*, June 14, 1994; press release on Garden State Plaza's opening in GSP, folder "GSP History'"; "It Won't Be Long Now . . . Bamberger's, New Jersey's Greatest Store, Comes

to Paramus Soon," promotional leaflet, stamped Aug. 22, 1956, file "Bergen County Shopping Centers," Hackensack; "The Shopping Center," *NYT*, Feb. 1, 1976.

For data on the allocation of shopping center space in ten regional shopping centers in 1957, see William Applebaum and S. O. Kaylin, *Case Studies in Shopping Center Development and Operation* (New York: ICSC, 1974), p. 101. For evidence of the community orientation of shopping centers nationwide, see Arthur Herzog, "Shops, Culture, Centers – and More," *NYT Magazine*, Nov. 18, 1962, pp. 34–5, 109–10, 112–14; in the *NYT* "A Shopping Mall in Suffolk Offering More Than Goods," June 22, 1970; "Supermarkets Hub of Suburbs," Feb. 7, 1971; "Busy Day in a Busy Mall," Apr. 12, 1972. On the community relations efforts of branch stores, see Clinton L. Oaks, *Managing Suburban Branches of Department Stores*, Business Research Series No. 10 (Stanford, CA: Graduate School of Business, Stanford University, 1957), pp. 81–3.

16 For example, James A. Brunner and John L. Mason, "The Influence of Driving Time Upon Shopping Center Preference," *JM* 32 (April 1968): 57–61; William E. Cox, Jr., and Ernest F. Cooke, "Other Dimensions Involved in Shopping Center Preference," *JM* 34 (October 1970): 12–17; Pierre D. Martineau, "Customers' Shopping Center Habits Change Retailing: Secondary Areas and Scatter Zones Important with Mobility," *Editor and Publisher*, Oct. 26, 1963, p. 16.

17 US Department of Labor, Bureau of Labor Statistics, "Consumer Expenditures and Income, Northern New Jersey, 1960–61," BLS Report No. 237–63, December 1963, Schomburg, clipping file "Consumer Expenses & Income – NJ."

18 "The Wonder on Routes 4 and 17: Garden State Plaza," brochure, file "Bergen County Shopping Centers," Hackensack; "Notes on Discussion Dealing with Regional (Intermunicipal) Planning Program for Passaic Valley Area (Lower Portion of Passaic Co. and South Bergen)," n.d., Erber, Box A, Folder 3; "Memorandum to DAJ and WBS from EE," Nov. 22, 1966, Erber, Box B; National Center for Telephone Research (a division of Louis Harris and Associates), "A Study of Shoppers' Attitudes Toward the Proposed Shopping Mall in the Hudson County Meadowlands Area," conducted for Hartz Mountain Industries, February 1979, Rutgers.

On African-American dependence on public transportation, see Greater Newark Chamber of Commerce, "Survey of Jobs and Unemployment," May 1973, "Q" Files, NPL, "Greater Newark Chamber of Commerce," p. III–2; Donald E. Sexton, "Black Buyer Behavior," *JM* 36 (October 1972): 37. In another New York suburban area, Long Island, highway builder Robert Moses made sure that buses carrying poor and black city residents were unable to reach beaches, parks, and other sites of consumption and recreation by constructing overpasses too low to allow buses underneath: Robert A. Caro, *The Power Broker: Robert Moses and the Fall of New York* (New York: Vintage, 1975), pp. 318–19, 546, 951–2. As recently as 1995, a black teenager was killed crossing a seven-lane highway which had no light or crosswalk because the suburban mall where she worked would not allow her bus from inner-city Buffalo to enter mall property and drop off passengers: "Mall Accused of Racism in a Wrongful Death Trial in Buffalo," *NYT*, Nov. 15, 1999; "Galleria Oks City Bus Access," *Buffalo News*, Jan. 30, 1996; "Mall Bus Policy Called Anti-City," *Buffalo News*, Jan. 28, 1996; I am grateful to Katie Barry for alerting me to this case.

19 Shopping centers retreated from promoting themselves as central squares and street corners not only because of the free speech issue, but also to limit the loitering of young people. From *NYT*: "Supermarkets Hub of Suburbs," Feb. 7, 1971, "Coping with Shopping-Center Crises, Dilemma: How Tough to Get If Young Are Unruly," Mar. 7, 1971; "Shopping Centers Change and Grow," May 23, 1971.

20 For a useful summary of the relevant court cases and legal issues involved, see Curtis J. Berger, "*PruneYard* Revisited: Political Activity on Private Lands," *New York University Law Review* 66 (June 1991): 633–94; also "Shopping Centers Change and Grow," *NYT*, May 23, 1971. The corporate shopping center's antagonism to free political expression and social action is discussed in Herbert I. Schiller, *Culture, Inc.: The Corporate Takeover of Public Expression* (New York: Oxford University Press, 1989), pp. 98–101.

21 On *Amalgamated* v. *Logan Valley Plaza*, see "Property Rights vs. Free Speech," *NYT*, July 9, 1972; *Amalgamated Food Employees Union Local 590* v. *Logan Valley Plaza*, 88 S.Ct. 1601 (1968), *Supreme Court Reporter*, pp. 1601–20; 391 U.S. 308, U.S. Supreme Court Recording Briefs 1967, No. 478, microfiche; "Free Speech: Peaceful Picketing on Quasi-Public Property," *Minnesota Law Review* 53 (March 1969): 873–82. On *Marsh* v. *State of Alabama*, see 66 S.Ct. 276, *Supreme Court Reporter*, pp. 276–84.

Other relevant cases between *Marsh* v. *Alabama* and *Amalgamated* v. *Logan Valley Plaza* are *Nahas* v. *Local 905, Retail Clerks International Assoc.* (1956), *Amalgamated Clothing Workers of America* v. *Wonderland Shopping Center, Inc.* (1963), *Schwartz-Torrance Investment Corp* v. *Bakery and Confectionary Workers' Union, Local No. 31* (1964); with each case the Warren Court was moving closer to a recognition that the shopping center was becoming a new kind of public forum.

22 "4 Nixon Appointees End Court's School Unanimity, Shopping Centers' Right to Ban Pamphleteering Is Upheld, 5 to 4," *NYT*, June 23, 1972; "Shopping-Center Industry Hails Court," *NYT*, July 2, 1972; *Lloyd Corporation, Ltd.* v. *Donald M. Tanner* (1972), 92 S.Ct. 2219 (1972), *Supreme Court Reporter*, pp. 2219–37. The American Civil Liberties Union brief went to great lengths to document the extent to which shopping centers have replaced traditional business districts; see "Brief for Respondents," US Supreme Court Record, microfiche, pp. 20–29. Also, People's Lobby Brief, US Supreme Court Record, microfiche, p. 5.

The Supreme Court majority wanted to make it clear that in finding in favor of the Lloyd Center, it was not reversing the *Logan Valley* decision, arguing for a distinction based on the fact that anti-war leafletting was "unrelated" to the shopping center, while the labor union was picketing an employer. The four dissenting justices, however, were less sure that the distinction was valid and that the *Logan Valley* decision was not seriously weakened by *Lloyd*.

The important court cases between *Amalgamated* v. *Logan Valley Plaza* and *Lloyd* v. *Tanner* included *Blue Ridge Shopping Center* v. *Schleininger* (1968), *Sutherland* v. *Southcenter Shopping Center* (1971), and *Diamond* v. *Bland* (1970, 1974).

23 Berger, "*PruneYard* Revisited"; Kowinski, *The Malling of America*, pp. 196–202, 355–59; "Shopping Malls Protest Intrusion by Protesters," *NYT*, July 19, 1983; "Opening of Malls Fought," *NYT*, May 13, 1984; *Michael Robins* v. *PruneYard Shopping Center* (1979), 592 P.2nd 341, *Pacific Reporter*, pp. 341–51; *PruneYard Shopping Center* v. *Michael Robins*, 100 S.Ct. 2035 (1980), *Supreme Court Reporter*, pp. 2035–51; U.S. Supreme Court Record, *PruneYard Shopping Center* v. *Robins* (1980), microfiche.

The most important Supreme Court case between *Lloyd* v. *Tanner* and *PruneYard* was *Scott Hudgens* v. *National Labor Relations Board* (1976), where the majority decision backed further away from *Logan Valley Plaza* and refused to see the mall as the functional equivalent of downtown: *Scott Hudgens* v. *National Labor Relations Board*, 96 S.Ct. 1029 (1976), *Supreme Court Reporter*, pp. 1029–47.

24 "Court Protects Speech in Malls," *NYT*, Dec. 21, 1994; "Big Malls Ordered to Allow Leafletting," *NSL*, Dec. 21, 1994; "Now, Public Rights in Private Domains," *NYT*, Dec. 25, 1994; "Free Speech in the Mall," *NYT*, Dec. 26, 1994; Frank Askin, "Shopping for Free Speech at the Malls," 1995, unpublished manuscript in possession of the author.

25 "Mall's Limits on Leafletting Struck Down," *NYT*, June 14, 2000; "Staying the Course; Justices Won't 'Mall' Free Speech," *New Jersey Lawyer*, June 19, 2000, p. 3; Michael Booth, "Court Sharpens Fine Print on Malls' Regulation of Leafletters," and "*Green Party of New Jersey* et al. v. *Hartz Mountain Industries, Inc.*, A-59 September Term," *New Jersey Law Journal*, June 19, 2000; "New Jersey Delineates Limits on Leafleting Restrictions at Malls," *State Constitutional Law Bulletin*, July 2000; John D. Cromie and James F. Jacobus, "The N. J. Supreme Court Adopts a Test to Balance Property Rights with Free-Speech Rights in Mall Leafleting Cases, but Fails to Give Guidance as to Which Restrictions Are Permissible," *New Jersey Law Journal*, Oct. 2, 2000.

26 Marshall dissent, *Lloyd* v. *Tanner*, 92 S.Ct 2219 (1972), *Supreme Court Reporter* (1972), p. 2237.

27 From *NYT*: "Business Districts Grow at Price of Accountability," Nov. 20, 1994; "Now, Public Rights in Private Domains," Dec. 25, 1994; "Goon Squads' Prey on the Homeless, Advocates Say," Apr. 14, 1995; "City Council Orders Review of 33 Business Improvement Districts," Apr. 19, 1995; "When Neighborhoods Are Privatized," Nov. 30, 1995; Bruce J. Schulman, *The Seventies* (New York: Free Press, 2001), pp. 249, 314–15; Lawrence O. Houstoun, Jr., *BIDS: Business Improvement Districts* (Washington, DC: Urban Land Institute and the International Downtown Association, 1997).

The Prison Fix

Ruth Wilson Gilmore

The rhetoric of imprisonment and the reality of the cage are often in stark contrast.

Norval Morris and David J. Rothman, *The Oxford History of the Prison* (1995)

You know, in my life I've rarely been amazed. Rarely been amazed. But I'll tell you what amazed me is the last time I was in [prison, in 1992]. I thought, you know, look at all these guys in here. I thought, all these guys were in there for something, you know, that they had done SOME-THING. But then people started telling me what they were in for. More than half the guys, they were in for drugs, for possession. I mean, for NOTHING. That was truly amazing, you know, to me.

40-year-old ex-gangster, personal communication (1994)

How did California go about "the largest prison build-ing program in the history of the world" (Rudman and Berthelsen 1991:1)? California's political economy changed significantly in the 1970s, due both to changes in the location of industrial investment – capital movement – and to "natural" disasters. Those changes, and responses to them, provided the foundation upon which new rounds of capital movement and new natural disasters were played out. These shifts produced surpluses of finance cap-ital, land, labor, and state capacity, not all of which were politically, economically, socially, or regionally absorbed. The new California prison system of the 1980s and 1990s was constructed deliberately – but not conspiratorially – out of surpluses that were not put back to work in other ways. Make no mistake: prison building was not and is not the inevitable outcome of these surpluses. It did, however, put certain state capacities into motion, make use of a lot of idle land, get capital invested via public debt, and take more than 160,000 low-wage workers off the streets.

From Reform to Punishment

Just as the rounds of disinvestment and calamity that occurred in the 1970s political economy set the stage for how the 1980s crises proceeded, so changes in Cali-fornia's prisons in the 1970s formed the basis for the system's expansion. Not once, but twice, the rising power bloc of "tough on crime" and antiurban strategists seized hard-won reforms designed to make the prison-er's lot less desperate and transformed them into their inverse mirror images. Efforts to make the California Department of Corrections (CDC) take rehabilitation seriously wiped rehabilitation from the books. Efforts to free prisoners from crumbling prisons led to the construction program that has never ended.

In 1977, California ended its sixty-year commitment to use the state prison system as the sociospatial means to rehabilitate all but the most intransigent prisoners (Rudman and Berthelsen 1991; Cummins 1994). The

1977 Uniform Determinate Sentencing Act was the legislature's response to a series of executive branch courtroom losses during a twenty-five year struggle with state prisoners. Prisoners had successfully used the federal bench, under the 1867 Habeas Corpus Act, to demand that California treat prisoners equitably, relieve overcrowding, and respect constitutional rights (Cummins 1994). Prisons have never been pleasant places, and overcrowding was not a new phenomenon. Prisoners have always fought both legally and extralegally to secure decent conditions (Cummins 1994; Wicker 1975). However, the post-World War II civil rights movement's courtroom successes encouraged prisoners to use the system against itself; and the growing fraction of Black people in the prison population was cause for identification with struggles in the streets (Jackson 1970; Davis 1971; Wicker 1975; Cummins 1994). The movement also influenced prisoners from behind bars, because the criminalization of political activists brought them into the prison population (Cummins 1994; Davis 1971).

The key issue was sentence length. California's 1917 Progressive rehabilitation scheme had been coupled with indeterminate sentences, on the theory that technically qualified "corrections" professionals would help prisoners become useful and reliable and that the "corrected" prisoners would then persuade local parole boards of their readiness to rejoin society (Norval Morris 1995; Freedman 1996). In practice, parole boards were capricious and racist, representing local elites; prisoners sentenced to one year to life languished in the penitentiary for decades, petitioning at prescribed intervals for a chance to talk their way out of cages (Jackson 1970). California's Progressives had argued that they were devising a new system vastly different from both the exploitative plantation models of Mississippi and Louisiana (Oshinsky 1996; Lichtenstein 1996) and the Golden State's older, punitive system (Bookspan 1991; Rudman and Berthelsen 1991). However, the Progressive movement was generally committed to preserving racial and property hierarchies, while creating institutions that would turn out people who respected authority and knew their own limits (Thelan 1969; Allen 1994; Gordon 1994; see also Mitchell 1996). In practice, California's indeterminate sentences extended to life sentences for Black, Latino, and white prisoners whose failures to be rehabilitated translated as their refusal to learn their proper places in the social order (Irwin 1985; Jackson 1970; cf. Himes [1945] 1986, 1971).

A second class of issues that prisoners litigated centered on conditions of confinement. State, media, and intellectuals of the late 1960s and early 1970s participated in the ideological production of "moral panics" (Hall et al. 1978) to explain the social and political disorder sweeping the United States. At all levels, states worked hard to characterize people agitating for justice as morally wrong rather than politically dissident. The ensuing criminalization of such activists swept what were then record numbers of men and women off the streets and into custody, with California in the vanguard (Miller 1996; Donner 1990; cf. Hall et al. 1978; Bean 1973). The state's prison population grew from about 16,500 to just under 23,000 between 1967 and 1971; the number rose and fell within a fairly narrow band over the next few years, peaking at 24,700 in 1974 and bottoming out at 19,600 in 1977 (CDC 1992; Rudman and Berthelsen 1991; Cummins 1994). In addition to, or as a result of, problems of sheer physical incapacity, the CDC could not or would not respect the rights of inmates to "adequate life safety, health care and recreation, food, decent eating ... and sanitation standards, ... visitation privileges, and access to legal services" (Silver 1983: 118; cf. Cummins 1994). Thus, the hostility, density, and confusion that characterized state prison environments at the time undermined any rehabilitative capacity prisons might have had (Rudman and Berthelsen 1991; Cummins 1994).

Federal courts throughout the United States in the 1970s favorably evaluated many prisoners' writs of habeas corpus and put state corrections departments under federal order to remedy constitutional wrongs (Benton 1983). Courts directed California to relieve overcrowding and also to group prisoners according to a transparent system of classifications in order to enhance the potential for every individual's reform (SPWB 1985; Cummins 1994; Rudman and Berthelsen 1991; see also Bookspan 1991 for earlier attempts at prisoner classification). If the purpose of these federally demanded social and spatial remedies was to carry out the mandates of Progressive-era lawmaking, the legislature responded by voiding the 1917 statute. The 1977 Uniform Determinate Sentencing Act was California's formal abdication of any responsibility to rehabilitate, stating neatly: "[T]he purpose of imprisonment for crime is punishment."

In the 1977 Uniform Determinate Sentencing Act, and again in that year's Budget Act, the legislature directed the CDC to forecast prison bed need (LAO 1986). The CDC's initial attempts to predict shortfall were quite modest and focused on renovating aging facilities and replacing the two eldest prisons – San Quentin (built in 1852) and Folsom (opened in 1880). The department's 1978 Facilities Planning Report proposed renovating 3,000 prison beds around the state. In 1980, the Facilities Requirement Plan expanded the number of new and replacement beds to 5,000, and forecast an increase in the capital needed to carry out the project (LAO 1986).

In the turbulent years of his second and final term (1978–82), Governor Jerry Brown took up the initial CDC analysis and started work on designs for new facilities to replace the tier-and-catwalk-style gothic structures at San Quentin and Folsom (Morain 1994c; LAO 1986). Brown's new prisons were supposed to be used for rehabilitation, in spite of the legislature's 1977 declaration. The 1977 statute did not *forbid* rehabilitation; rather, it excised its central importance (Rudman and Berthelsen 1991). By his own testimony, Brown could have used his power as the state's chief executive to relieve over-crowding by ordering parole for indeterminate-sentence prisoners who had served time equal to the new sentencing requirements and by commuting sentences for others who had been in the system a long time. Instead, he began to investigate the best way to improve plant and modestly expand capacity, intending – or so he claimed – to use state-of-the-art prisons for the benefit of prisoners and society (Morain 1994c).

By 1980, the legislature had already approved replacing San Quentin with two 500-bed, maximum-security units. In the summer of 1982, Brown brought in a premier prison architect-engineer, Paul Rosser, to design small, program- and common-space-oriented prisons that would focus on education and other rehabilitative activities (Morain 1994c; LAO 1986). Brown's planning combined vestiges of the early twentieth-century Progressive sensibility – seeking to produce social peace through old and new institutions and techniques of control – with a late twentieth-century political shrewdness – seeking to convert the moral panic over crime into an opportunity by having a skeptical electorate support the exercise, rather than the restraint, of state expansion (cf. Friedman 1993).

There were so many contradictory processes at work in the 1982 transition year from the lapsed welfare-state Democratic to the supply-side Republican gubernatorial regime that it is sometimes difficult to grasp how they all coincided. The split widened between Brown's commitment to what had become, in law, secondary (rehabilitation), and the primary purpose enshrined in the new penal code. Without opposition from the lame-duck chief executive, the legislature gave the CDC permission to build on a larger scale than Brown had envisioned (Morain 1994d). Brown had financed prison design

studies out of reserve funds appropriated by the legislature and initiated the era of new facilities construction by approving a $25,000,000 expansion at the California Correctional Institution in southern Kern County. But in 1982, new commitments to the CDC started to rise steeply, and the department revised its forecast – for the first time proposing several major *capacity-expanding* facilities instead of concentrating on renovation and replacement (LAO 1986). To meet needs forecast by the CDC, the 1982 legislature approved siting new facilities in Riverside, Los Angeles, and San Diego Counties. That same year, the legislature successfully petitioned voters to approve $495,000,000 in general obligation bonds (GOBs) to build new prisons – based on the argument that more prison cells would enhance public safety and punish wrongdoers (Morain 1994d).

Also in 1982, the legislature reorganized the statutory relationship between itself, the CDC, and the prison expansion project by forming a new entity, the Joint Legislative Committee on Prison Construction and Operations (JLCPCO). Thereafter, the CDC stood apart from all other state agencies in two ways. First, its capital outlays would not be managed by the Office of General Services, which meant that its bidding and budgeting practices varied from long-standing procedures for construction of state physical plant. Indeed, the CDC was explicitly exempted from a competitive bidding process and instead allowed to assign work to outside consultants (BRC 1990; LAO 1986). The explanation for this extreme deviation from normal procedure focused on the CDC's unique new charge to build an unspecified number of similar, expensive, highly specialized facilities in rapid succession (R. Bernard Orozco, interview, 1995; Rudman and Berthelsen 1991; BRC 1990; LAO 1986). Second, the establishment of the JLCPCO kept the CDC's ordinary and extraordinary activities under close scrutiny and direction by elected officials (Rudman and Berthelsen 1991; LAO 1986). The latter appeared to keep the expansion of the prison system in the public eye, insofar as the JLCPCO was required to hold hearings *before* either Department of Finance disbursement of appropriated funds or Public Works Board implementation of CDC plans (BRC 1990).

George Deukmejian's gubernatorial victory in 1982 completed the turn to the right California had begun under Ronald Reagan in the 1960s. Deukmejian used the accumulating illegitimacy exemplified by tax revolts to attack the status quo – starting with the weakest targets, such as persons receiving welfare (cf. Piven 1992). He followed, rather than led, the tax struggle, and at the end of

California's second straight year of well-reported declining crime rates, he proposed budget increases to fight crime, appealing to voters' insecurity. It is more than ironic that he campaigned against big government by arguing how the government should grow. Deukmejian's gubernatorial opponent, Tom Bradley, had as mayor of Los Angeles successfully controlled the rising share of the city budget that the LAPD and the police and fire pension fund had commanded for more than a decade. The police fought back by campaigning – statewide, in uniform – for Deukmejian (Sonenshein 1993). Deukmejian seized the issue and used the Los Angeles dispute to project race, crime, and the need for state-building as a single issue, claiming that the African American mayor's tightening of the LAPD budget could only be the work of a man who was soft on crime.

Once Deukmejian took office in 1983, the administration broadened Jerry Brown's new prison plan but dropped rehabilitation as the reason for new buildings. With punishment, in the form of "incapacitation," now the rationale for prison, the administration, the legislature, and the CDC (all three partially consolidated via the JLCPCO) joined forces to expand the state's built capacity for incarceration. But the state still had two immediate problems: first, how better to guarantee potential prisoners, and second, how to finance the facilities to cage them. Toward solution of the former problem, the legislature changed the classification of certain offenses – such as residential burglary (Rudman and Berthelsen 1991) and domestic assault (Hill 1994) – to felonies requiring prison terms upon conviction. Similarly, new drug laws – to some degree modeled on New York's Rockefeller minimum mandatory sentence laws enacted in the early 1970s (Flateau 1996; Miller 1996) – also enhanced the likelihood of prison time for people not formerly on the prison track (Rudman and Berthelsen 1991). The legislature further authorized a State Task Force on Youth Gang Violence to study what it called "street terrorism" – a topic to which we shall return. The Board of Prison Terms, overseeing parole officers, made common cause with the legislature, and instructed its field staff to be liberal in revoking parole – an option used sparingly before the new prison era; as a result, since 1983 people on parole have had great difficulty remaining out of custody through their supervisory period, with about 70 percent being returned to prison for some portion of that time without having been convicted of new crimes.

With these legal measures in place, the CDC deepened and widened its planning. Beginning with the 1983 Facilities Master Plan, it projected shortfalls in available beds as a crisis (LAO 1986). It is surprising neither that the CDC bed shortage estimates varied considerably nor that they tended to climb. The estimates ranged from 16,100 to 55,000 throughout the 1980s to a 1994 all-time high of 151,641 for 1998, generated by the "three strikes" law (SPWB 1985, 1986a, 1987, 1991; LAO 1986; CDC 1993, 1994, 1996). Under Deputy Director James Gomez, who moved to the CDC from the Department of Social Services Adult and Family Division in 1983, the department expanded its planning staff (from 3 to 118), honed its forecasting, and from 1984 on began to produce five-year master plans that combined technical number-crunching skills with a flair for emphasizing the drama inherent in the "crisis" (LAO 1986). Projected need moved in tandem with the judiciary's legislature-produced capacity to remand persons to CDC custody. With the problem of identifying wrongdoers partially solved, the question was how to pay for all the new beds; and it was the new beds, rather than court commitments, that led the system's growth.

Capital for Construction

Although Sacramento had successfully persuaded taxpayers to vote for the 1982 Prison Construction Bond Act, most elected officials were susceptible to an ongoing fear, inspired by Proposition 13, of asking voters to approve too many general obligation bonds. GOBs pledge the full faith and credit of the state of California, and the state constitution requires that any such debt be approved by the legislature *and* ratified by the electorate (SPWB 1985). GOBs also provide a way to circumvent the constitutional requirement of a balanced budget, because debt service for voter-approved bonds is exempt from the rule (SPWB 1985). The problem became how to expand a politically popular program (prisons) without running up against the politically contradictory limit to taxpayers' willingness to use their own money to defend against their own fears.

Frederic Prager of L. F. Rothschild, Unterberg, Towbin (LFRUT), one of the most creative and well-connected underwriters in the California world of municipal finance, and his new associate Tom Dumphy, came up with a plan approved by a bipartisan power bloc, including Democrats Jess Unruh (treasurer) and Willie Brown (Speaker of the Assembly), the Republican governor, George Deukmejian, and prison-expansion activists in the legislature, led by State Senator Robert Presley (R–Riverside) and Assemblyman Dick

Robinson (R–Orange County). The capitalists and the statesmen crafted a new way to borrow money for prisons from existing debt-raising capacities. The scheme involved using lease revenue bonds (LRBs) to supplement GOB debt.

Prager's savvy and experience had led LFRUT to dominance in California's private college facilities market. The state's independent, not-for-profit postsecondary institutions could borrow in the tax-exempt markets to develop or renovate infrastructure; for California, these debts constitute "off-book" or "no-commitment" loans, because their repayment does not entail any taxing or other fiscal capacity of the state (SPWB 1985; Sbragia 1986). Under Prager, LFRUT put together LRBs for the state's richest and most powerful private universities – Stanford, the University of Southern California, and the California Institute of Technology. The creative firm also devised successful bond issues for schools with more modest debt capacity, such as St. Mary's, Moraga, Cal Lutheran, and the University of the Pacific, so that they, too, could improve their facilities. In 1981–82, Prager worked with the Association of Independent California Colleges and Universities (AICCU) to issue an innovative revenue bond whose proceeds would constitute a forward-funded market for student loans. Thanks to an exposé in the San Jose Mercury News (September 5, 1982), the voters got the incorrect idea that only rich schools (and by inference, rich students) had access to these public funds. Treasurer Unruh, looking to be reelected that fall, demanded that public institutions be included in the deal. The spike in interest rates in the early 1980s made it difficult for middle-income families to borrow for college in the private sector, while at the same time, mounting energy and other costs pushed up tuition (Gilmore 1991). The loan deal was extended to all students in the state; and Unruh used the program during his campaign to reassure the state's 1.5 million students and their parents – presumed members of the voting class – that his office was looking out for their interests. A blunt politician of the old school, Unruh also knew when to reduce flows to the public trough; and in the early 1980s, a bad economy and a transitional gubernatorial regime kept the old power broker's fist tight on the spigot.

Prager brought Dumphy to LFRUT in 1983 to exploit his talents and connections in city government; he had previously been a planner in Los Angeles Mayor Tom Bradley's administration and had also served as a youth probation officer in Massachusetts early in his career. Together, Prager and Dumphy worked hard to develop new California markets for public debt (cf. Sbragia

1986). The private college business was already starting to tighten, because of most institutions' limited capacity to increase tuition – the major source of operating revenue for all expenditures, including student aid and debt service, at all but the wealthiest schools (Gilmore 1991). They were the pivot men between surplus private capital available for investment in the not-for-profit and public sectors and decreasing state-approved outlets where the capital could be put to work. The new prison construction program, in its infancy in 1983, constituted an excellent long-term opportunity for capital investment. Sacramento's old and new guards were ready to unite behind the prison program, but they had to raise much more money than anyone was brave or foolhardy enough to request from voters.

Lease revenue bonds were the solution. LRBs are issued by the Public Works Board of the state of California, established in 1946 to help smooth crisis as California adjusted to the postwar economy (SPWB 1985). Typical LRBs issued by the Public Works Board are for real property loans for veterans and farmers, as well as loans for public college and university facilities and hospital buildings. In all cases, nongovernmental borrower payments or user fees are used to pay back the debt. While in all cases the Public Works Board is forbidden to pledge California's full faith and credit, in the case of public debt for public use, there is an implied *moral* obligation that the state will exercise due diligence to avert defaults (cf. Sbragia 1996). It was a risky but successful political suspension of disbelief to use the state's implied moral obligation to script a scenario in which the Public Works Board and the CDC were characterized as entities buying, selling, and leasing property and rights between them (SPWB 1985). For the prison LRBs, the "revenue" has consisted of general fund appropriations authorized by the legislature to the CDC annual operating budget, designated as "rental payments" to the Public Works Board, which is the actual issuer of the debt (SPWB 1985, 1986a, 1986b, 1987, 1990, 1991, 1993a, 1993b, 1993c, 1993d). Unlike with mortgage, postsecondary, or hospital issues, there is no potential or actual nontax revenue stream at all.

The economics of prison LRBs is almost identical to the economics of prison GOBs; the greatest difference between them is political – the scope of approval needed to borrow huge sums. The economic downside is that LRBs are slightly more expensive than GOBs precisely because they do not pledge the state's taxing power; for any debt, the higher the risk of nonpayment, the higher the interest. However, in order to persuade all members of the prison power bloc to exploit the LRB option, Prager and Dumphy underscored the sole positive economic difference – one that is in large part political as well. LRBs do not have to be placed before the voters in general elections, and on approval by the legislature, they can be relatively quickly organized and issued in order to maximize favorable credit conditions, enabling the CDC to build prisons closer to the time the facilities are bid on, thus theoretically avoiding cost hikes. The capitalists and the statesmen agreed that the trade-off between slightly higher interest costs and quicker cash availability would balance the economic difference and provide an effective political shield from organized antitax activists.

In less than a decade, the amount of state debt for the prison construction project expanded from $763 million to $4.9 billion dollars, a proportional increase of from 3.8 percent to 16.6 percent of the state's total debt for all purposes (SPWB 1985, 1993). During the same period, state debt service (annual expenditure for principal plus interest) increased from 1 percent to 2.8 percent of per capita income (California State Controller 1996: 161).

The new source of capital enabled the CDC to follow the second of two approaches it had proposed. The earlier of these, in the late 1970s, had centered on keeping people convicted of nonviolent offenses in their communities and providing treatment programs for the 70 percent or so of all convicted persons who are addicted to drugs and alcohol (BRC 1990; LAO 1986; PRCC 1996). The state-of-emergency approach, which started to emerge in 1982–83 (in Gomez's first year as deputy director for CDC operations), sought simply to build as many prison cells as possible. The end run around taxpayer-voters in order to raise what turned out to be more than $2.5 billion in LRBs – in addition to nearly $2.5 billion in GOBs – was thus not only a political strategy of economic subterfuge but also one of social policy that set the Golden State in a new direction (SPWB 1985, 1986a, 1986b, 1987, 1990, 1991, 1993a, 1993b, 1993c, 1993d).

[...]

References

Allen, Theodore W. 1994–97. *The Invention of the White Race*. Vol. 1: *Racial Oppression and Social Control*; vol. 2: *The Origin of Racial Oppression in Anglo-America*. New York: Verso.

Bean, Walton E. 1973. *California: An Interpretive History*. 2nd ed. New York: McGraw-Hill.

Benton, F. Warren. 1983. State Prison Expansion: An Explanatory Model. *Journal of Criminal Justice* 11: 121–8.

Bookspan, Shelley. 1991. *A Germ of Goodness: The California State Prison System, 1851–1944*. Lincoln: University of Nebraska Press.

California. Department of Corrections. 1971–2002. *Characteristics of Population in California State Prisons by Institution*. Sacramento: CDC. Published annually.

——. Department of Corrections. 1992. *Historical Trends, 1971–1991*. Sacramento: CDC.

California. State Controller. 1982–2000. *Annual Report*. Sacramento: Office of the Controller of the State of California.

——. 1993c. *Lease Revenue Bonds (Department of Corrections) 1993 Series D (California State Prison – Lassen County, Susanville). Official Statement*. Sacramento: SPWB.

——. 1993d. *Lease Revenue Bonds (Department of Corrections) 1993 Series E (California State Prison – Madera County (II)). Official Statement*. Sacramento: SPWB.

Carlson, Katherine. 1988. Understanding Community Opposition to Prison Siting: More Fear Than Finances. *Corrections Today*, April, 84–90.

——. 1992. Doing Good and Looking Bad: A Case Study of Prison/Community Relations. *Crime and Delinquency* 38 (1): 56–69.

Cummins, Eric. 1994. *The Rise and Fall of California's Radical Prison Movement*. Stanford: Stanford University Press.

Davis, Angela Y., ed. 1971. *If They Come in the Morning: Voices of Resistance*. A Joseph Okpaku Book. New York: Third Press.

Donner, Frank J. 1980. *The Age of Surveillance: The Aims and Methods of America's Political Intelligence System*. New York: Knopf.

Flateau, John. 1996. *The Prison Industrial Complex: Race, Crime & Justice in New York*. New York: Medgar Evers College, CUNY/DuBois Bunche Center.

Freedman, Estelle B. 1996. *Maternal Justice: Miriam van Waters and the Female Reform Tradition*. Chicago: University of Chicago Press.

Friedman, Lawrence M. 1993. *Crime and Punishment in American History*. New York: Basic Books.

Gilmore, Ruth Wilson. 1991. Decorative Beasts: Dogging the Academy in the Late 20th Century. *California Sociologist* 14 (1–2): 113–35.

Gordon, Linda. 1994. *Pitied but Not Entitled: Single Mothers and the History of Welfare*. New York: Free Press.

Hall, Stuart, Chas Cricher, Tony Jefferson, John Clarke, and Brian Roberts. 1978. *Policing the Crisis: Mugging, the State, and Law and Order*. New York: Holmes & Meier.

Hill, Elizabeth G. 1994. *Crime in California*. Sacramento: LAO.

Himes, Chester. [1945] 1986. *If He Hollers Let Him Go*. New York: Thunder's Mouth Press.

Irwin, John. 1985. *The Jail: Managing the Underclass in American Society*. Berkeley: University of California Press.

Jackson, George. 1970. *Soledad Brother: The Prison Letters of George Jackson*. New York: Bantam Books.

———. 1994. Negotiating Local Autonomy. *Professional Geographer* 13 (5): 423–42.

Lichtenstein, Alex. 1996. *Twice the Work of Free Labor: The Political Economy of Convict Labor in the New South.* New York: Verso.

Miller, Jerome G. 1996. *Search and Destroy: African-American Males in the Criminal Justice System.* New York: Cambridge University Press.

Mitchell, Don. 1996. *The Lie of the Land: Migrant Workers and the California Landscape.* Minneapolis: University of Minnesota Press.

Morain, Dan. 1994c. California's Profusion of Prisons. *Los Angeles Times*, October 16, A-1.

———. 1994d. Long-Term Investments: "Three Strikes" Law Will Boost Wall Street Firms That Sell Bonds to Finance Construction.

Morris, Norval. 1995. The Contemporary Prison. In *The Oxford History of the Prison*, ed. Norval Morris and David J. Rothman, 227–62. New York: Oxford University Press.

Oshinsky, David. 1996. *"Worse than Slavery": Parchman Farm and the Ordeal of Jim Crow Justice.* New York: Free Press.

Pardo, Mary. 1998. *Mexican American Women Activists.* Philadelphia: Temple University Press.

Piven, Frances Fox. 1992. Reforming the Welfare State. *Socialist Review* 22 (3): 69–81.

Pulido, Laura. 1995. The Mothers of East Los Angeles. Presentation, annual meetings of the Association of American Geographers, Chicago, Ill. March.

Rudman, Cary J., and John Berthelsen. 1991. *An Analysis of the California Department of Corrections' Planning Process: Strategies to Reduce the Cost of Incarcerating State Prisoners.* Sacramento: California State Assembly Office of Research.

Sbragia, Alberta M. 1996. *Debt Wish: Entrepreneurial Cities, U.S. Federalism, and Economic Development.* Pittsburgh: University of Pittsburgh Press.

Sechrest, Dale K. 1992. Locating Prisons; Open versus Closed Approaches to Siting. *Crime and Delinquency* 38 (1): 88–104.

Silver, Paul. 1983. Crossroads of Correctional Architecture. *Corrections Today*, April, 118–19.

Sonenshein, Raphael J. 1993. *Politics in Black and White: Race and Power in Los Angeles.* Princeton, NJ: Princeton University Press.

Thelan, David. 1969. Social Tensions and the Origins of Progressivism. *Journal of American History* 56: 323–41.

Travis, Kevin, and Francis J. Sheridan. 1983. Community Involvement in Prison Siting. *Corrections Today*, April, 14–15.

Wicker, Tom. [1974] 1994. *A Time to Die: The Attica Prison Revolt.* Lincoln: University of Nebraska Press.

The Globalization of Latin America: Miami

George Yúdice

Globalization and Cities

Miami has been classed as a "minor world city" in the company of Amsterdam, Barcelona, Berlin, Buenos Aires, Caracas, Geneva, Montreal, Shanghai, Taipei, and Washington, DC. World or global cities are generally defined by the concentration of command and control headquarters for transnational corporations and a concomitant critical mass of complementary *advanced* producer services, particularly accounting, advertising, banking, and law. Although these services are found in all cities, only in advanced "postindustrial production sites" do we find the innovations in services that play "a specific role in the current phase of the world economy" (Sassen 1991: 126). New practices like "just in time" production and outsourcing require capitalization, systems analysis and management, and increased telecommunicational capacities, in addition to accountancy and law. These services are concentrated in cities, as Manuel Castells (1996) argues, where innovation results from the synergy of networks of complementary enterprises and from reservoirs of "human talent," much of it composed of intra- and international migrants. To attract such talent, Castells (2000) adds, cities must offer a high quality of life, which means that such cities are also major generators of cultural capital and value. The role of culture in capital accumulation, however, is not limited to this ancillary function; it is central to the processes of globalization, as we will see below, taking Miami as our case study.

Most cities, and Miami is no exception, have experienced globalization according to two logics that have been operative since the 1970s, when a worldwide inflationary crisis brought the Keynesian compromise between capital and labor to an end: the assault on labor via neoliberal policies and the related development of new technologies that have enabled capital to reorganize commensurate with a new world economy in which operations are articulated planetarily in real time. Globalization did not just happen "naturally" but has been the result of policy and conflict.

Falling wages in the developing world, due to US-biased IMF structural adjustment or austerity programs, enabled corporations to relocate manufacturing "overseas." On behalf of transnational corporate reorganization and the new international division of labor, the US government spearheaded the elimination of barriers to trade in goods and services and to portfolio and direct foreign investment. This entailed devaluation, privatization, deregulation, reduction of public programs, and the elimination of protectionist policies that had been used to support national enterprises and that often maintained wage levels. US government and transnational protagonism in this regard has taken place on the stage of GATT and its successor, the WTO.

While labor has certainly felt the stab of these policies, workers have increasingly struggled to maintain the public weal and have disrupted capital at both national and global levels, evident, respectively, in the so-called IMF riots and more recently in the mass demonstrations against the WTO in Seattle, Davos, and Washington, DC. Protestors have yet to target the globalization of culture, including music and the new media, maybe because they are some of their more avid consumers. Perhaps for this reason, technological innovations have provided a more successful opportunity for capital's new regime of accumulation. The telecommunications and Internet technologies that enabled roboticized just-in-time production in both first and third world factories, geographic reorganization of corporations, and decreasing production costs (Cleaver 1995: 166–7), have also made possible the decentralized flow of information on which the anti-WTO protestors rely. Indeed, it has been argued that the Internet is not a technology but an organizational form that fosters network relations (Castells 1996), which characterize the new practices of both the transnational corporate sector and civil society. The rapid development of these technologies has enabled the so-called new information- and knowledge-based economy to supersede the old industrial economy; 80 percent of the US workforce, for example, does not make things but works in offices generating information and providing services (Progressive Policy Institute 2000). A June 2000 US Commerce Department report indicates that the information technology industry is the major engine of economic growth in the country, accounting for one third of that growth (Clausing 2000).

As the price of labor has decreased, largely by relocating it to the developing world, knowledge and information have become the major generators of value. Indeed, "wealth creation" is premised on the production of intellectual property, which requires highly developed and capitalized university systems and the assiduous policing of those who resist capital's regime of appropriation, such as local peoples who have devised herbal medicines or rhythms over many generations, or who poach on it, like unlicensed manufacturers of CDs and video tapes sold by street vendors and software engineers and companies (e.g., Napster) that make it possible to freely exchange music and video with anyone else on the Internet. The United States is far ahead of all other countries in the number of patents registered. Just to give a sense of the importance of knowledge production, the US genomics industry alone is about the size of the entire Argentine economy (Enríquez 2000). As capital accumulation increasingly depends on scientific and technological innovation and as commodity production is further devalued, Latin America and other developing regions will decline even further. Under the current neoliberal consensus among Latin American elites, university research agendas are increasingly driven by market criteria, particularly in the private universities that have sprouted over the past decade or two in every country and even in the increasingly underfunded public universities (Gentili 2000: 13). The result is brain drain from

public to private institutions within Latin America and from Latin America to the United States, where scientifically competent immigrants are needed to fuel the new economy, according to Federal Reserve Chairman Alan Greenspan's depositions before Congress in 2000 and 2001. Indeed, pressed by Internet and high-tech companies, Congress will raise the number of HI-B visas in 2000 ("Ali Asked" 2001). The problem, of course, is not limited to developing countries like those in Latin America or to the United States. Germany, which has "an estimated 75,000 to 100,000 jobs vacant in the booming Internet sector, with few Germans apparently qualified to fill them," is courting high-tech-proficient immigrants from India, a policy that is met with protest and greater appeals for increases and changes in the German university system. According to one observer, "German education with its focus on heavy philosophical concepts does not turn out the people we want" (Cohen 2000). An expression of a new international division of knowledge production is the new Indian policy to produce information technology workers to meet demand in Germany, Japan, Singapore, Britain, and the United States as well as locally ("India Plans" 2000).

Whether the new economy succeeds to the extent of its potential depends on government spending on education, transportation, communications, and, ultimately, technological research. In the past (and indeed in the origins of the Internet) the US government financed the development of new technologies and industries and then put them in the private sector as sources of wealth creation (Madrick 2000). Current policies militate against a direct government intervention, but there are a range of alternatives, among them local public investment and incentives. The creation of Silicon Alleys, Valleys, Parks, and Beaches throughout the world is not solely the product of entrepreneurial genius in the private sector but also of public-private partnerships. Such partnerships have significant transformative effects on the urban fabric, from the renovation of decaying areas (often at the expense of vestigial industrial activity or of poor communities) to the creation of new educational and cultural venues that are being touted as generators of value in their own right. That value, of course, is not distributed evenly, but accrues to those classes that are positioned to gain access. Yet poor populations, often immigrants and minorities, are implicated in the maintenance and reproduction of the digerati: "Alongside technological innovation there has mushroomed an extraordinary urban activity . . . fortifying the social fabric of bars, restaurants, chance encounters on the street, etc. that give life to a place" (Castells 2000). "Giving life" is a matter of policy in many cities, as culture increasingly becomes a part of business and economic development departments, as was recently the case in the City of Miami Beach with the creation of a liaison for the entertainment industry in the Economic Development Division (Dennis Leyva, interview, March 14, 2000; City of South Miami Beach 2000).

Miami: Cultural Capital of Latin America

But it is culture – not raw technology alone – that will determine whether the United States retains its status as the pre-eminent Internet nation.
– Steve Lohr, "Welcome to the Internet, the First Global Colony"

Internet portals will be the engine of development of the entertainment industry and Miami will prosper to the degree that content can be produced there.
– Sergio Rozenblat, interview, March 10, 2002

It has been argued that in the new economy the manufacture and transfer of goods increasingly will take a secondary place with respect to culture. The cultural economy is already defined as the "selling and buying of human experiences" in "themed cities, common-interest developments, entertainment destination centers, shopping malls, global tourism, fashion, cuisine, professional sports and games, film, television, virtual worlds, and [other] simulated experiences." These "represent the new stage of capitalist development" (Rifkin 2000: 29, 265). Such a depiction is sure to induce allergic reactions in those with Adornian proclivities, but neither simulated experiences nor the "elimination" of work are the end-all and be-all of contemporary cultural life. Castells's argument about "giving life" makes it clear that culture encompasses more than the entertainment and tourism industries; it is also a medium in which new intellectual capital is reproduced and maintained in a range of experiences that cut across different classes and social and ethnic groups. This is not fully evident because we are accustomed to thinking of capital in terms of property and commodities. To be sure, the production of the culture industries fits this conception, but there is more to the success of these industries than selling and buying. We might ask what it is about city life, particularly its immigrant populations and their cultures, that can be transformed into value, and what kind of value. I hope to give a sense

of this in my examination of Miami as the "cultural capital of Latin America."

Most studies of Miami, especially from the mid-1980s on, focus on the protagonism of the Cuban exile community and its relations with other ethnic groups, particularly Anglo-Americans, African Americans, and Haitians, in a series of power struggles and compromises (Croucher 1997; Didion 1987; Portes and Stepick 1993; Rieff 1987). This view captures to a great extent the course that the region, south Florida, has taken, but it nevertheless overlooks the most dynamic changes that have been taking place from the early 1990s into the twenty-first century. I am referring to the transformation of Miami and surrounding counties and cities by the fashion, entertainment, communications, and new media industries. They provide the momentum that has already led to characterizations of Miami as a global city based on the numerous multinational articulations that take place in the area (Beaverstock, Smith and Taylor 1999; Beaverstock, Smith, Taylor, Walker, and Lorimer 2000). To be sure, the possibility of making these articulations was facilitated by Cuban exiles with business expertise, hemispheric connections, and cultural talent, as well as two other historical precedents: Miami was chosen as headquarters of the US national security state vis-à-vis Latin America in 1898 and the US government pumped billions of dollars into the Cuban exile community to transform it into a showcase of success vis-à-vis the economically strangled Cubans who remained on their island and vis-à-vis other US minorities at a time when they were attracted to Marxist and anti-imperialist critical frameworks in the 1960s and 1970s. Even in entertainment, which constitutes the backbone of the new industries that are transforming Miami, Cubans have already cleared the way, for example, the Miami Sound Machine, Emilio Estefan Enterprises, El Show de Cristina, and various magazine publishing enterprises. But in the 1990s the impetus of these new industries came from other sources and often chafes against the Cuban exile community. As these new industries give the region a new face, it becomes possible to speak of a post-Cuban and even a post-Caribbean Miami.

[. . .]

Now I would like to make my case for a post-Cuban Miami as a new economy that cannot be separated from culture – let's call it a cultural economy, on the model of political economy – takes root there.

Miami has many attractions for people who are seeking to work in entertainment, new media, and related enterprises that do business in Latin America and/or that cater to US Latino markets. Compared to Latin America, it offers economic stability; the most convenient location in the entire hemisphere for those who travel tri-continentally in Latin America, Europe, and the United States; the lowest cost of living of the major concentrations of Hispanics in the United States (Los Angeles, New York, Miami); excellent communications and mail services; a critical mass of production companies and advanced producer services (accountancy, advertising, banking, law, etc.) and technological production services (studios, laboratories, postproduction, and distribution facilities); high intellectual and artistic capital (composers, arrangers, producers, musicians, scriptwriters, visual, internal, and fashion designers, multilingual translators, universities and specialized training centers); attractive locations for film, video, and photography; tax breaks and other government incentives for production and commerce; and high quality of cultural life (restaurants, bars, nightclubs, galleries, museums, beaches). Moreover, for many people who have relocated there it has the feel of a Latin American city without the crime, grime, and infrastructural dysfunctionality and all the advantages of a first world city (Bruno del Granado, interview, March 13, 2000; Néstor Casonu, interview, March 14, 2000).

People in the entertainment industry list three mid-1980s phenomena as the sources of the new Miami: the Miami Sound Machine, *Miami Vice*, and the renovation of the Art Deco District. It is no doubt an exaggeration to base the genesis of the new Miami on new sound and visual imagery, but entertainment people explain that these attracted film producers and celebrities like Stallone, Madonna, and Cher as well as gave a shot in the arm to a small modeling industry that burgeoned as designers like Giorgio Armani and Calvin Klein established branch offices there and Gianni Versace bought a mansion in the restored Art Deco District. Gay culture also burgeoned, especially in South Beach, and contributed significantly to these industries and consumer lifestyle (e.g., shops, discos, and other entertainment venues). By the early 1990s, the major music multinational corporations like Sony and Warner reestablished offices there, and throughout the 1990s all majors had their regional headquarters (i.e., headquarters for Latin America) in Miami, specifically in South Miami Beach, spurring the renovation of already existing sound studios (e.g., Criteria, active since the 1960s and where artists like Aretha Franklin, Eric Clapton, and Bob Marley recorded) and the construction of others, like Emilio and Gloria Estefan's Crescent Moon Studios, the

Mecca for many Latin American singers like Luis Miguel and Shakira.

Any viewer of Spanish-language television in the United States knows that the dominant network, Univisión, concentrates its production and other operations in Miami, although it maintains its headquarters in LA. Telemundo recently moved its headquarters there from Los Angeles to take advantage of lower production and service costs as well as a more Latin American as opposed to the predominantly Mexican American population of LA. Together, these two networks reach over 100 million viewers in the United States and Latin America. Music and television attracted thousands of celebrities, artists, producers, arrangers, executives, and other entertainment service professionals from Latin America. In addition to the Anglo-American celebrities mentioned above, we can list an ever-growing number of Spanish-speaking artists and professionals, including Julio Iglesias, his son Enrique Iglesias, and the pioneer of the romantic ballad, Raphael; important telenovela actors like the Venezuelans José Luis Rodríguez ("El Puma") and Lucía Méndez, who is also a popular singer; and many television personalities, such as the Dominican comedienne Charytin, the Cuban talk show host Cristina Saralegui, and the Chilean Don Francisco, host of the variety show *Sábado Gigante*; important producers like the Cuban American Rudy Pérez, the Colombian Kike Santander, the Argentine Bebu Silvetti, and the New Yorker Desmond Child; major singers like Ricky Martin and Shakira, and, of course, the staple of Cuban singers and musicians, including Israel "Cachao" López, Arsenio "Chocolate" Rodríguez, and Albita.

The music and entertainment infrastructure has grown to the point that any imaginable service can be found in Miami, from producers, arrangers, backup singers, writers, sound engineers, technicians, and film and video personnel to specialized musicians.... Latin music has enjoyed robust growth unseen in any other segment of the music business, with a 12 percent jump from 1998 to 1999. The US Latin music industry's strong performance is, according to Hilary Rosen, president and CEO of the Recording Industry Association of America, additional to "the Ricky Martin/Jennifer Lopez phenomena, as these artists' recent English language recordings are not classified as Latin" (Cobo-Hanlon 1999). In Miami Beach alone more than 150 entertainment companies have been established in the past five years (Dennis Leyva, interview, March 14, 2000). Almost half of these companies (among them Sony, EMI, Starmedia, MTV Latin America, and WAMI TV) are concentrated in a five-block-long outdoor mall – Lincoln Road – amid stores, restaurants, theaters, and art galleries (Potts 1999). Growth has been so rapid that from September 1990 until March 2000 another twenty-eight companies opened there and it is estimated that another five hundred thousand square feet were to be renovated later that year for office space for the new "dot-coms" and Internet portals that were created in the past couple of years. These new media companies are full-service entertainers providing movies, television, videocassettes, CDs, books, interactive games, theater, and Internet sites (Gabler 2000). Indeed, the building industry has received a potent shot in the arm from all this activity. Even real estate companies have formed partnerships with entertainment concerns. For example, real estate developer Michael Comras has wagered on the continuing prosperity of Miami's entertainment industry by forming a special entertainment division with Miami International Studios that will steer companies from Los Angeles and Latin America to Miami, in particular to Comras's buildings ("Comras" 1998).

The synergy of all of this activity made Miami the most attractive headquarters location for most dot-coms seeking to break into Latin American markets. Although most of these initiatives failed, due to the burst Internet bubble, they did constitute a major site for investment, particularly for portals specializing in entertainment or financial information and counseling. For example, AOL Latin America, Eritmo.com, QuePasa.com, Yupi.com, Elsitio.com, Fiera.com, Aplauso.com, Starmedia.com, Terra.com, and Artistsdirect.com sought to offer music information, download, and services such as Web page creation for musicians; Subasta.com offers an online auction; Sports-Ya.com and Totalsports.com broadcast sports news and ecommerce; R2.com deals strictly with the futures market; and Consejero.com and Patagon.com offer online stock transactions ("Spanish-language Web Sites Specialize" 1999). These new enterprises had wagered that the development of the Internet market in Latin America would grow exponentially, following market studies like International Data Corp.'s, which foresees 19 million subscribers by 2003 (Graser 1999). Brazil alone is expected to have 30 million users in 2005 (DaCosta 2000). Since it was predicted that the Internet would revolutionize the entertainment industry, vast sums of money were invested as part of a Darwinian gambit for survival. The Cisneros Group invested over $200 million in its 50/50 partnership with America Online, and spent $11 million on a media blitz featuring actor Michael Douglas just to launch its Brazil site (Faber and Ewing 1999). Similarly, StarMedia raised $313 million in public offerings in 1999, much of which will be used for marketing and acquisitions, which are estimated to produce a loss of $150 million in 2000 (García 2000). Perhaps the most spectacular merger and acquisition was the deal between Spain's global telecommunications corporation Telefónica and Germany's global media conglomerate Bertelsmann to give Terra, Telefónica's Internet service provider, a boost by acquiring and merging with Lycos (Carvajal 2000). This is the first purchase of a major US Internet company by a European corporation. Terra is expected to make sizable gains in Latin America; nevertheless, it is a global initiative, with significant activity in Europe and the United States as well. Miami, easily accessible to these three regions, is the most convenient site for its headquarters. Together, these companies have carved out a piece of South Miami Beach that is now called "Silicon Beach."

Miami Beach has been particularly active in wooing industry. The Miami Beach Enterprise Zone offers incentives to businesses expanding or relocating there that include property tax credits, tax credits on wages paid to Enterprise Zone residents, and sales tax refunds. The Façade Renovation Grant program provides matching grants to qualifying businesses for the rehabilitation of storefronts and the correction of interior code violations (City of South Miami Beach 2000). As a consequence of this promotional activity, Miami entertainment industries generated about $2 billion in 1997, more than any entertainment capital in Latin America, and boasts a workforce of ten thousand employees (García 1998; Martín 1998). By November 1999 volume had increased to $2.5 billion (Leyva interview 2000). Other Miami counties are also renewing their initiatives to woo the entertainment industries. To counteract the difficulties that producers and film companies encounter in dealing with the complicated bureaucracy of the numerous municipalities in the area that have their own regulations, Jeff Peel, Miami-Dade film commissioner, is leading an initiative that includes his counterparts in other municipalities to change the bureaucracy and draw more film and TV business to South Florida (Jackson 2000). The importance of entertainment in Miami is not only that it supplies most programming for the US Latino market but its attraction of an increasing share of the Latin American market. Miami is the third-largest audiovisual production hub in the United States, after Los Angeles and New York (LeClaire 1998). Currently, Miami entertainment and new media are expanding to global markets ("Boogie Woogie" 1997).

Entertainment and new media have an advantage in relocating to Miami, where the financial sector has established a highly developed infrastructure for business and where transport and communications provide the best connections to Latin America, Europe, and the rest of the United States. Since the 1980s, the location of the largest free trade zone in the United States in the vicinity of Miami airport has attracted more than two hundred corporations specializing in international trade. Some, like Dupont, selected Miami as their regional headquarters over Mexico City, San José, Bogotá, Caracas, São Paulo, Rio de Janeiro, Buenos Aires, and San Juan (Grosfoguel 1994: 366–7). Almost all of the people I interviewed for this study remarked on this convenience. For Néstor Casonu, an Argentine who, in his capacity as regional managing director for EMI Music Publishing, moved from Buenos Aires to Miami, the airport is a much more convenient gateway to all Latin American cities (interview, March 14, 2000). Producer Bruno del Granado, who moved to Miami from Los Angeles in 1994 for the same reasons as Julio Iglesias, recalls the singer's advice: "Julio Iglesias told me that when he came from Spain to the United States he wanted a base. He researched the different cities looking for a convenient central location between Europe, the United States, and Latin America. He was already famous everywhere else, aside from the US. Miami furnished him with a base for launching into the US, while he was only a few hours from Europe and Latin America" (interview, March 13, 2000).

Entertainment and tourism nourish each other. The critical mass of entertainment companies situated in South Beach have transformed it into a major international promenade for the "beautiful people" and those who yearn to walk in their wake. In the early 1900s, following Versace and all the glitz of fashion and entertainment celebrities, "the beautiful people came to town," and, as Neisen Kasdin, mayor of South Miami Beach explains, "people wanted to be around them." Together, these phenomena produced a synergy that increased exponentially the "nonstop creation of new businesses in modeling, new media, broadcasting and electronic commerce" (Kilborn 2000). And of course, this "Hollywood East" or "Hollywood Latin America" has spawned a self-congratulatory hype, embodied in Will Smith's *Miami Mix*, produced by Emilio Estefan at Crescent Moon. Such hype belies the urban conflicts referred to in the beginning of this chapter but also captures the spirit and no doubt part of the reality of what makes Miami so dynamic in the 1990s and early twenty-first century. Let's examine some of this hype.

From the perspective of the financial or entertainment and new media industries, Miami is a gateway or a crossroads. The reason for the location in Miami of the major entertainment conglomerates has more to do with command and control of transnational operations – a major feature of global cities – than with edenic bliss, one that, like every utopia, is ringed by the dystopia of conflict and corruption. As Gabriel Abaroa, executive director of the Latin American Federation of Producers of Phonograms and Videograms, explains, it is much more advantageous to monitor all aspects of the music industry from Miami "since everyone has to go through it" (Abaroa 1998). By "everyone," Abaroa is referring not to the new migrations that are swelling the ranks of the Latino community, but to the critical mass of artists from throughout the Hispanic world who have moved to Miami or who continuously shuttle there from regional capitals. The very logic of capitalizing on Latin culture as a resource is internalized in the discourse of many of the entertainment celebrities in Miami. Miami, in fact, becomes a synecdoche and a metonym of that resource. The variety show host Jaime Bayly refurbishes Simón Bolívar's dream of an integrated Latin America with all the trappings of media glamor: "If what you want is a real Latin American program that will reach an international public, you have to be where all the celebrities are, and that means Miami" (qtd. in Rohter 1996).

This hype and the commercial reality that largely corresponds to it provide the major rationale for business and political leaders' strategies to locate the Center of Hemispheric Integration in Miami. As the rhetoric goes, only in Miami are there significant representatives from each country of the region. Furthermore, Florida sends 48 percent of its exports to Latin America, most of which travel through Miami. According to Luis Lauredo, US ambassador to the Organization of American States, Miami "is a blend of the best of the cultures of the Americas, both North and South" (quoted in Rivera-Lyles 2000). As a center of commerce, technology, and communications whose personnel are at the very least bilingual, it has a comparative advantage. This advantage is expected to increase with the "expansion of its intellectual capital," mostly by way of immigration but also by targeted training programs at institutions like the University of Miami and Florida International University. That FIU graduates more Spanish-speaking students than any other university in the country is not an expression of concern for Latinos as an underprivileged minority but a strategy for reinforcing the business and high-tech sectors. This strategy ensues from the observation that, in the words of FIU's president, the most dynamic "technological and economic urban centers are connected with major research universities" (Rivera-Lyles 2000). As the site of business and trade summits, Miami is touted as a New World Brussels. Should the Free Trade Agreement of the Americas (FTAA; ALCA in Spanish) be sited in Miami, where negotiations have been held over the past couple of years and in whose Intercontinental Hotel its headquarters are temporarily situated, it is likely that the OAS and the Inter-American Development Bank (IADB) would move there. This opportunity will enable Miami to redefine itself when the embargo on Cuba is lifted and tourism, still Miami's largest industry, is siphoned off to that island. The location of a critical mass of communications and Internet companies in Miami is already a step in that direction (Katel 2000).

Magazines in south Florida also have capitalized on the Latin resource. They are having a boom, in great part because advertisers can reach several markets via Miami. The concentration of businesspeople in south Florida makes the area a convenient location for *Latin Trade*, covering the Latin American markets, the US Latino market (with its considerable buying power of $325 billion in 1999, estimated to reach $458 billion in 2000), and readers who enjoy the attractions of South Beach and the rest of South Florida. *Ocean Drive* took its name from the battlefront street on which Gianni Versace bought his mansion in 1992. Similarly, *Channels* features the "beautiful people" and fashions of South Beach; initiated as a regional publication, it went national in 1998. Latin *Girl* and *Generation ñ* are two new magazines for teens and the twenty-something generation, who also flock to Miami Beach (Martínez 1998). *Florida International Magazine* was started in 1998 with a print run of 75,000; by the end of 1999, it had reached a circulation of 100,000. Political and economic instability in Latin America have led to the relocation of publishers and other companies to Miami. For example, the most influential Latin American art journal, *Art Nexus*, relocated there permanently from Bogotá in 2000 (Celia Bibragher, interview, March 15, 2000).

Latin Multiculturalism: Transculturation as Value Added

As suggested earlier, Latin Miami is no longer an exclusively Cuban city. There are hundreds of thousands of immigrants from Nicaragua, the Dominican Republic, Colombia, Venezuela, Argentina, Brazil, and other countries. Some have been in Miami for only a few short years, but they already have national festivals. Argentines' first festival in May 1999 attracted 150,000 people; several hundred thousand Colombians, from Miami, other parts of the United States, and the homeland, swelled Tropical Park on July 17, 1999. Whereas many immigrants have come out of economic necessity or for political reasons, quite a few have come to work in the entertainment and new media industries. Many come for both reasons: telenovela actress Alejandra Borrero and talk show host Fernando González Pacheco both left out of fear of kidnapping by guerrillas and moved to Miami, where they could continue doing television work (Rosenberg 2000).

The new immigrants to Miami fit neither the assimilationist nor the identity politics paradigms familiar to US scholars of race and ethnicity. They maintain ties to their homelands and travel back and forth with frequency, but they have also developed a new spirit of belonging to the city. Daniel Mato's research on the telenovela industry indicates that many new transplants feel comfortable reflecting the reality of Latin American immigrants in the United States (Mato 2000; Yúdice 1999). Some, particularly those in the corporate and entertainment and arts sectors, have developed a new sense of cultural citizenship and seek to reinforce local cultural institutions. Unlike most Latin American immigrants and Latino minorities in other US cities, most of the fifty people I interviewed in March 1999 characterized Miami as an "open city" that accepts new migrants. Not all new transplants are from Latin America; many people have relocated to Miami from other parts of the country and from Europe to take advantage of opportunities. There is a recognition that entertainment, the new media, design, fashion, tourism, and the arts are helping to transform Miami, to give it the cultural sophistication it never had before.

This largely multicultural image of the city was sounded time and again by my mostly middle- and upper-class interviewees. They are cosmopolitans for whom Miami is a convenient hub for their travels throughout the world. Nevertheless, their esprit de corps and will to create a cultural infrastructure for all Miami residents does not emanate only from their role as managers and producers in the center of command and control for Ibero-American culture industries. In the past five years, the new cultural producers, while maintaining a strong Latin flavor, have nevertheless opted for an international image. This is evident in the art world, in which Miami is no longer being promoted as the capital of Latin American art. Although much Latin American art will continue to be shown and bought and sold there, art institutions are focusing increasingly on international trends and on developing local talent. Both of these developments are taking precedence over worn tropicalist stereotypes that have sold well. The new spirit in the art world, as in the entertainment industry, is manifesting itself in the major contributions that Miami artists, Latin or not, are making to contemporary art.

This means that Latinness or Latinoness is undergoing a transformation in Miami; it is less rooted to a specific or minority identity. Perhaps this is because of all US cities (indeed, all cities in the Americas), Miami is the only one from which a generalized international Latin identity is possible. This internationalization is even taking place in the music industry, in which two worlds continue to exist side by side, especially in their administrative aspects: the US Latino (and the aspired-to crossover) market, characterized mostly by Latin pop and salsa (Gloria Estefan, Jon Secada, Albita, and a host of other Latino singers from elsewhere produced in Miami), and the Latin American market, which is largely managed out of Miami. But these two worlds do communicate and thus create an important source of hybridization between the North and the South, between Latinos and Latin Americans. And together they are producing a range of international megastars like Ricky Martin, Shakira, and Enrique Iglesias, in addition to mainstays like Julio Iglesias.

Because Miami has long been held to be a cultural backwater, the fact that it is now a major production hub for the culture industries is providing the impetus to legitimize the city as a cultural capital in the more traditional artistic sense. Latin American and Latino producers, artists, entertainers, managers, and executives are participating in the establishment or redefinition of museums, educational institutions, and philanthropic and training initiatives to produce new cohorts who will feed into the burgeoning entertainment industries. One such initiative is One Community, One Goal, which has targeted specific industries for employment growth. The culture industries are in the forefront of this initiative (Peggy McKinley, interview, March 13, 2000). Among its projects is Arts Related Technology for Entertainment Careers, a program designed to prepare students for technical careers in the arts and entertainment industries.

Composer and producer Rudy Pérez, first president of the Latin American Association of Recording Artists, introduced into Miami various philanthropic programs implemented earlier by the parent NARAS. For example, Pérez is a regular lecturer and performer for the Grammys in the Schools program spearheaded by Quincy Jones for NARAS. Additionally, Pérez has been an outspoken advocate for arts (particularly music) education in the schools. He himself is in the process of opening a school of the arts, with a focus on music and recording/engineering and the music business, and also a children's talent agency. The school is conceived as a complement to the New World School, patterned after the High School of Music and Art in New York, which has stringent requirements in all subjects, making it difficult for musically talented minority youth to gain admission. The school that Pérez has proposed will provide special tutoring to talented black and Latino kids. Like many other people in the arts and entertainment, Pérez finds that although Miami has a high profile it lacks a cultural infrastructure, particularly in performing venues. This problem has been overcome to some degree in the visual arts, where new museums have been built or renovated. And the art scene has gone from one dominated by Cuban and Latin American artists to an international scene that puts a premium on diversity. "Miami is no longer just Cuban or even Latin American. Now there are Italians, Russians, and other Europeans in addition to Brazilians, Colombians, Dominicans, Puerto Ricans, and Central Americans" (Rudy Pérez, interview, March 11, 2000). Despite this cosmopolitanism, Pérez prefers to focus attention on the local communities: "Latins are coming to Miami, having kids here who speak English, and at 16 or 17 they resonate to their Latin cultural background. This is the case with English-language artists like Christina Aguilera, Jaci Velázquez, and Oscar de la Hoya, who have decided to be produced in Miami for their Spanish-language versions. Instead of looking for artists in Latin America, we need to scout for talented kids from the barrios." Some artists, like Aguilera, have turned to producers in Miami to get in touch with roots they have never known. This desire to learn Spanish and make records in that language is no doubt motivated by a desire to further capitalize on sales of over 10 million copies of some of her singles, but also, according to Pérez, because she wants to draw on her heritage for her music. For Pérez, anyone who has not been part of a Latino community in the United States can partake of the transnational Latinness that Miami offers.

Markets and identity evidently go together in Miami's Latin-inflected multiculturalism. The effects of all this Latin cultural production in a US city, no matter how Latinized, is of concern to many Latin Americans, who fear that national and local cultures will be homogenized by this "Miami sound machine." But hybridity and transculturation are the name of the game of pop music in all Latin American entertainment capitals (Yúdice 1999). The results are not a flattening out of music but, on the contrary, its pluralization, observable in the rock of groups like La Ley from Chile and Maná from Mexico, or the "ethnic" musics of Olodum from Salvador and Afro Reggae from Rio de Janeiro. Moreover, there is a constant flow of musics from Latin America into Miami, in the person of the musicians who go there to produce their records, as well as in the influences that arrangers and producers introduce into their work. This emphasis on local taste markets is increasingly reflected in the organizational structure of some entertainment companies, especially the most global ones. Mato points out that some telenovela and serial production companies are selling modular formats that can be tailored to the demographic characteristics of audiences in different localities ("Miami South Florida" 1999: 6). Something similar is taking place in the corporate reorganization of MTV Latin America. Programming and marketing were completely done in the Miami office when MTV Latin America got started with one signal for all of Spanish America in 1993 and another for MTV Brazil. In 1996 it took its first step toward regionalization by doubling the Spanish American signals, centering the northern one in Mexico City and the southern in Buenos Aires. In 1999 it began to produce programming in the regions, following the adage "I want my own MTV." Rather than homogenization, a global corporation like MTV wants local relevance, in every locality. The next step will establish full programming, production, and marketing offices in each of twenty-two countries. Its center of operations will remain in Miami, but direction of content provision will be much more flexible and nomadic as managers and producers move or communicate between Latin American localities and the Miami office (Antoinette Zel, interview March 14, 2000).

Miami is a major center for the fusion of dance and house musics, especially the Latinization of disco, funk, rap, and jungle. The source of this fusion is the DJs and the groups, which hail from all the various ethnicities to be found in Miami. More than in the production side of the entertainment industry or the art scene, dance is the place for the commingling of bodies. As one observer reports, "The cultural mix brings together races, diverse sexual orientations, languages and incomes" (Kilborn 2000). And it is from this commingling that a good part of the creativity that animates the music industry is drawn. Midem, the largest industry showcase for Latin music, showcased dance at its 1998 convention in Miami Beach. Among the local musics featured were the house music of Tito Puente Jr., the Latin-influenced hip-hop acts of 2 Live Crew and DJ Laz, and Afro-Cuban house music by LatinXpress (Cobo-Hanlon 1998). The influence of this music can be found in Gloria Estefan's *gloria!*, which overlays salsa onto disco, and Ricky Martin's dance-mix version of "The Cup of Life." According to recording star Alegra, "This music is a breeding ground for experimentation" (qtd. in Cobo-Hanlon 1998).

Experimentation in dance, house, salsa, hip-hop, and other musics is regular fare in the lively nightclub life of Miami. From there it moves up the industrial stream to those stars who make records for the majors: Jaci Velazquez, Shakira, Albita, Ricky Martin, and Gloria Estefan. The Chirino sisters have recorded a Spanish-language record with "Latin/rock/pop/gypsy rhythms, produced by the Colombian Juan Vicente Zambrano of Estefan Enterprises" (Pérez 2000). As Latinized music makes its way beyond the clubs and Latin artists, it serves up the promise of the crossover.

This mainstreaming is also being pursued on television, which is not limited to the production of telenovelas. Producers Mo Walker and Robert Fitzgibbon have teamed up with Francisco García in the design of a Latinized *American Bandstand*-like music show for network television. Its pilot show features a block party in South Miami Beach where youth of all ethnicities engage in transculturating Latinness through rhythm, movement, and language (Mo Fitzgibbon, interview, March 10, 2000).

These musical and bodily fusions reflect the dynamism of Miami's dance clubs, where very diverse groups come together, yet there are considerable ethnic conflicts over access to jobs and (un)fairness in immigration policy. The tendency of culture, particularly Latin culture, and economy to merge, embodied in the entertainment industry itself, provides greater opportunities for the bicultural and bilingual professional class in Miami than in any other US city. This transformation is likely to exacerbate the subordination of certain immigrant populations, such as Haitians and other non-Spanish-speaking groups, particularly if they are black. Of the Cubans and Haitians who, if lucky, arrive intact on Miami shores, only the former get to stay. The Elián González affair only heightened this difference, leading Haitians and many other observers to suspect racism at work (Putney 2000; Ramírez 2000; Simmons-Lewis 2000). The multiculturalism that is being showcased is not that of the poor and working classes, but of the professionals and middle classes that have given Miami an economic boost. It has been argued that Miami is adopting a typical Latin American discourse of racial democracy, whereby Latinness is inclusive of all races and classes except for blacks (Grosfoguel 2000). Contrary to Cubans' and Cuban Americans' denials that they harbor any racism or color prejudice, many scholars of race relations readily point to the fact that dark-skinned Cubans have always been on and continue to occupy the lower rungs of the socioeconomic ladder in Cuba and Miami (Casal 1980; Croucher 1997; Helg 1990; Zeitlin 1970). A report on two recent immigrant friends from Cuba, one black and one white, part of a *New York Times* series on race in the United States, detailed how they were each incorporated into separate communities based on their color. The report brings home the point that racial differentiation is greater in Miami than in Cuba, perhaps because of accommodation to the US model of ethnic competition and identity politics (Ojito 2000). The report belies the claims to color-blindness that abound among Latin Americans.

Latin American claims to color-blindness are founded on the myth of the racial melting pot or mestizaje. National identity in many Latin American countries since the late 1930s and early 1940s was premised on a cultural citizenship identified with a racially hybrid subject. Fernando Ortiz ([1940] 1995), Cuba's best-known scholar of Afro-Cuban culture, advocated the abandonment of the concept of race in favor of the notion of *transculturation*. In those countries in which this transculturated, mestizo identity was accepted by whites and most racially mixed people, blacks found it difficult to make claims for equal treatment on the basis of race and were often accused of racism for even raising the issue. A Latin American equivalent of normative whiteness in the United States, mestizaje presumably included everyone as a member of the nation, but not necessarily as a beneficiary of the privileges of citizenship.

It is beyond the scope of this chapter to elaborate on the precedents of this issue in Cuba and Latin America. Suffice it to say that music and dance are two privileged areas of appropriation whereby a national cultural style is fashioned from the practices of subordinated groups. This observation makes it important to take into consideration the racial repercussions of Latin entertainment industries in the United States.

It is this very appropriation of the vernacular cultures, of what happens in the dance clubs, to get back to Miami, that ultimately produces value for the entertainment industry. It is here that another aspect of immigrant cultures – the meeting places of different classes – is productive of value, adds value to a cultural commodity. Latin culture industries in the United States derive a double value. On the one hand, they have a growing *market* value in Latin America, the United States, and elsewhere; on the other hand, they gain an extra *political* value as they are embraced by US discourses of diversity and multiculturalism. Latin culture in Miami can even claim, as we have seen, to provide a solution to the social and racial problems that rack US cities. As such, it has a comparative advantage over the cultures of other groups.

The value added by transnational, transcultural immigrant cultures to the entertainment industries in Miami is an excellent example of a new international division of cultural labor. Toby Miller (1996) proposes using this term to capture the split in production of cultural commodities across continents, taking as his model the imbrication of transnational industrial production across first, second, and third worlds. Mental and physical labor hail from varying locations, disrupting the mercantilist model whereby raw materials from the third world were transferred to the first for the manufacture of commodities. In the post-Fordist era, culture, like the clothes we wear, may be designed in one country, processed in several other countries, marketed in several locations, and consumed globally. Nation of provenance is increasingly an insignificant notion, although the post-Fordist model retains the basic insight that surplus value accrues to power elites, in this case transnational corporations, despite the disseminated structure of leadership, production, and consumption.

Hollywood, maintaining control over all operations despite geographically fragmented territories, exemplifies the new international division of cultural labor for Miller. Latin entertainment industries in Miami, though not exactly counterhegemonic, do present some significant manifestations of production and distribution that are not fully and maybe not even significantly in the hands of US corporations. This last statement requires an analysis of just what the status of corporations like Sony and the Cisneros Group, to mention two global corporations, is when sited in the United States. According to Carlos Cisneros, CEO of Cisneros Television Group, a subsidiary of the Cisneros Group of Corporations (CGC) that moved to Miami from Caracas in 2000, "Miami is becoming a world production city . . . no longer limited by region" (qtd. in Moncrieff Arrarte 1998). That is, relocation to the United States, especially Miami in the case of Latin entertainment, enables corporations from other places to use the United States as a springboard to increase their global reach. That CGC is (or was) a Latin American corporation, that it has divested itself of all commodity production and distribution to concentrate on the media enhances the possibility that it can, at least in its executives' eyes, penetrate the United States. Indeed, it aims to do so *culturally*. Gustavo Cisneros, CEO of CGC, claims that "Latin American culture has truly invaded the United States . . . Our local content is going to make it to the United States. We planned it that way. So I wonder who is invading whom?" (qtd. in Faber and Ewing 1999: 52).

Is this a delusion or the manifestation of something else? It seems to me that as a complement to the new international division of cultural labor proposed by Miller, we need also to focus on a new international networking and partnering of cultural production, which, though headquartered in places like Miami, is also structured like an archipelago of enclaves that cut across the developed and developing world. Does it make any difference, especially to the poor consumers of this cultural production, whether it is Hollywood or Latin CEOs who reap the profits? Yes, for two reasons. In the first place, relocation to the United States means that these companies and the immigrant intellectual and cultural labor they hire pay fewer taxes in their country of origin. Why shouldn't Buenos Aires or Bogotá increase its tax base as Miami does? In the second place, it does seem to make a difference that Latin American executives, producers, and arrangers can and indeed do produce culture that speaks to people throughout the subcontinent, even if that production takes place in Miami. The culture industries, as Mato writes, are not deterritorialized as much as they are transterritorial (2000: 4, 6).

Perhaps the problem is less this transterritorialization than the various means by which these industries produce, or better yet, extract value. To get an idea of how this takes place, we need to follow the network economy of which Castells writes, to all of its connections. Some of those connections, the advanced producer services, are characterized by more or less equitable contractual relations. Others, often involving independent producers and content providers, are less than equitable. But there are still others that are almost invisible. Network relations imply some kind of collaboration. I underscore the root "labor" in the word "col*labor*ation" to emphasize that two or more parties who undertake a task or contribute to it are doing work. As Miller and Leger (forthcoming) note, culture industries are among the most labor intensive. Many tasks are socially constructed in such a

way that only some of the parties engaged in the activity are to be remunerated financially. The other col*labor*ators, who contribute value added to the activity, presumably derive a nonmaterial return for their participation. As I explain in greater detail in chapter 9, this differential distribution of value for labor is similar to that of "women's work," especially their col*labor*ation within the family unit, where the satisfaction of motherhood was considered proper remuneration. Cultural work often goes unremunerated financially because it is assumed that those engaged in it derive spiritual or aesthetic value from it. In a cultural economy like that of the Latin entertainment and new media industries in Miami, there are many col*labor*ators, especially those immigrants and other groups that provide the rhythms, fusions, and hybridities that drive "content" or, in Castell's words, "give life" through new musics or situations for a telenovela.

References

Abaroa, Gabriel. 1998. "Q & A with Gabriel Abaroa." *Latin Music Quarterly* 24 January 1998.

"Ali Asked to Film Public Announcement." 2001. *New York Times*, 23 December (online edition).

Beaverstock, J. V., R. G. Smith, and P. J. Taylor. 1999. "A Roster of World Cities." *Cities* 16.6: 445–458. http://info.lboro.ac.uk/departments/gy/research/gawc/rb/rb5.html

Beaverstock, J. V., R. G. Smith, P. J. Taylor, D. R. F. Walker, and H. Lorimer. 2000. "Globalization and World Cities: Some Measurement Methodologies." *Applied Geography* 20.1: 43–63. http://lboro.ac.uk/departments/gy/research/gawc/rb/rb2.html

"Boogie Woogie." 1997. *Latin Trade* (July): http://www.latintrade.com/archives/july97/tradetalk.html

Carvajal, Doreen, with Andrew Ross Sorkin. 2000. "Lycos to Combine with Terra Networks in a $12 Billion Deal." *New York Times*, 16 May (online edition).

Casal, Lourdes. 1980. "Revolution and Race: Blacks in Contemporary Cuba." *Working Papers of the Woodrow Wilson International Center for Scholars*. Washington, DC.

Castells, Manuel. 1996. *The Rise of the Network Society*. Oxford: Blackwell.

———. 2000. "La ciudad de la nueva economía." *La factoría* 12 (July–August). http://www.lafactoriaweb.com/articulos/castells12.htm

City of South Miami Beach. 2000. "Economic Development Division." http://www.ci.miami-beach.fl.us/

Cleaver, Harry. 1995. "The Subversion of Money-as-command in the Current Crisis." In *Global Capital, National State and the Politics of Money*, ed. Werner Bonefeld and John Holloway. London: St. Martin's.

Cobo-Hanlon, Leila. 1998. "Dance Music Gets Latin Flavor: Mix of Trendy and Traditional Taps Pulse of Nightclub Culture." *Miami Herald*, 23 August (online edition).

——. 1999. "Midem Will Be Here in 2000, If Anywhere." *Miami Herald*, 6 October (online edition).

Cohen, Roger. 1993a. "Once Dull, GATT Enters Realm of Pop Culture." *New York Times*, 7 December: D1, D6.

——. 2000. "Germans Seek Foreign Labor for New Era of Computers." *New York Times*, 9 April (online edition).

"Comras Betting on Entertainment Industry." 1998. *Miami Herald*, 11 August (online edition).

Croucher, Sheila L. 1997. *Imagining Miami: Ethnic Politics in a Postmodern World*. Charlottesville: University of Virginia Press.

DaCosta, Carolina. 2000. "Behind Brazil's Internet Boom." *InfoBrazil.com* 2.55 (28 July–3 August). http://www.InfoBrazil.com

Didion, Joan. 1987. *Miami*. New York: Vintage.

Enríquez, Juan. 2000. "Technology and the Future of the Nation State." Paper presented at the symposium "Recentering the Periphery: Latin-American Intellectuals in the New Millennium." New School for Social Research, New York, 7 April.

Faber, Elio, and Reese Ewing. 1999. "Cisneros Goes Online." *Latin CEO* (December): 46–53.

Gabler, Neal. 2000. "Win Now, or Lose Forever." *New York Times*, 3 May (online edition).

García, Beatrice E. 1998. "Entertainment Industry Survey Is Off the Mark." *Miami Herald*, 5 December (online edition): 1C.

——. 2000. "StarMedia: The Next Generation: Latin Internet's First Born Fights Growing Competition." *Miami Herald*, 4 June (online edition).

Gentili, Pablo. 2000. "The Permanent Crisis of the Public University." *NACLA Report on the Americas* 23.4 (January–February): 12–18.

Graser, Graser. 1999. "'Silicon Barrio' Getting Latin America Online." *Variety*, 1–7 November: M32–M33.

Grosfoguel, Ramón. 1994. "World Cities in the Caribbean: The Rise of Miami and San Juan." *Review* 17.3 (summer): 351–81.

——. 2000. "Multiple Colonialities in a Symbolic World-City: Miami in the World-Economy." Paper presented at the 23d International Congress of the Latin American Studies Association, Miami, 17 March.

Helg, Aline. 1990. "Race in Argentina and Cuba, 1880–1930." In *The Idea of Race in Latin America*, ed. Richard Graham. Austin: University of Texas Press.

"India Plans to Double IT Workers to Meet Global Demand." 2000. *New York Times*, 5 August (online edition).

Jackson, Terry. 2000. "Lights, Camera. Where Is the Action?" *Miami Herald*, 5 March (online edition): 1M.

Katel, Peter. 2000. "El futuro de Miami mira hacia el sur." *El Nuevo Herald*, 1 January (online edition): 1A.

Kilborn, Peter T. 2000. "Miami Beach Clubgoers Creating New, Unwanted Image." *New York Times*, 27 February (online edition).

LeClaire, Jennifer. 1998. "Latin America Makes Miami Major Entertainment Player: 'Hollywood East' Is Now Third-largest Production Hub." *Christian Science Monitor*, 17 August (online edition).

Lohr, Steve. 2000. "Welcome to the Internet, the First Global Colony." *New York Times*, 9 January 2000 (online edition).

Madrick, Jeff. 2000. "Government's Role in the New Economy Is Not a Cheap or Easy One." *New York Times*, 11 May (online edition).

Martín, Martín. 1998. "Studio Miami: How Does an Entertainment Capital Rise from the Ground Up? Cash, Connections and Cool." *Miami Herald*, 13 December (online edition): 1I.

Martínez, Draeger. 1998. "Magazines Target Hispanic Readers." *Miami Herald*, 10 November (online edition).

Mato, Daniel. 2000. "Miami en la transnacionalización de la industria de la telenovela: Sobre la territorialidad de los procesos de globalización." Paper presented at the panel "Global Cities and Cultural Capitals I: Media and Culture Industries," 22d Congress of the Latin American Studies Association, Miami, 16–18 March.

"Miami South Florida." 1999. Special section of *Variety*, 1–7 November: M1–M33.

Miller, Toby. 1996. "The Crime of Monsieur Lang: GATT, the Screen and the New International Division of Cultural Labour." In *Film Policy: International, National and Regional Perspectives*, ed. Albert Moran. London: Routledge.

Moncrieff Arrarte, Anne. 1998. "Region Emerges as Entertainment Capital." *Miami Herald*, 25 June: 1A.

Ojito, Mirta. 2000. "Best of Friends, Worlds Apart: Joel Ruiz Is Black. Achmed Valdés Is White." *New York Times*, 5 June (online edition).

Ortiz, Fernando. [1940] 1995. *Contrapunteo cubano del tabaco y el azúcar*. Havana: Jesús Montero.

Pérez, Edwin. 2000. "Memo: Etc." *El Nuevo Herald*, 18 February (online edition): 5C.

Portes, Alejandro, and Alex Stepick. 1993. *City on the Edge: The Transformation of Miami*. Berkeley: University of California Press.

Potts, Jackie. 1999. "Lincoln Road Revitalized." *Variety*, 1–7 November: M25–M26.

The Progressive Policy Institute. 2000. "What's New about the New Economy?" http://www.neweconomyindex.org/

Putney, Michael. 2000. "Sea Escape: As Most Non-Cuban Refugees Discover, There's Just One Thing Missing from Our Immigration Policy: Fairness." *Miami Metro Magazine* (March): 33–5.

Ramírez, Adam. 2000. "Some in Broward See Elian Matter as a Dade Problem." *Miami Herald*, 24 April (online edition).

Rieff, David. 1987. *Going to Miami: Exiles, Tourists, and Refugees in the New America*. Boston: Little, Brown.

Rifkin, Jeremy. 2000. *The Age of Access: The New Culture of Hypercapitalism, Where All of Life Is a Paid-for Experience*. New York: Jeremy P. Tarcher/Putnam.

Rivera-Lyles, Jeannette. 2000. "FIU hacia la elite universitaria de EU." *El Nuevo Herald*, 4 January (online edition).

Rohter, Larry. 1996. "Miami, the Hollywood of Latin America." *New York Times*, 18 August (online edition).

Rosenberg, Carol. 2000. "Miami Attracting Celebrity Exiles: Famous Flee Colombia for Life in Quieter, Safer South Florida." *Miami Herald*, 3 April (online edition).

Sassen, Saskia. 1991. *The Global City: New York, London, Tokyo.* Princeton: Princeton University Press.

Simmons-Lewis, Suzanne. 2000. "Outrage over Refugee Plight: Haitians Slam U.S. Decision to Send Boat People Home." *Village Voice*, 10 January: 15.

"Spanish-language Web Sites Specialize." 1999. *Miami Herald*, 14 September (online edition): 2C.

Yúdice, George. 1999. "La industria de la música en el marco de la integración América Latina-Estados Unidos." In *Integración económica e industrias culturales en América Latina*, ed. Nestor García Canclini and Carlos Moneta. Mexico City: Grijalbo.

Zeitlin, Maurice. 1970. *Revolutionary Politics and the Cuban Working Class.* New York: Harper and Row.

Do You Know What it Means to Miss New Orleans? Katrina, Trap Economics, and the Rebirth of the Blues

Clyde Woods

I hear the Blues everywhere/I feel the Blues all in the air . . . /Now you may not believe in reincarnation/But I know the Blues will live again/With all this hatred, of nation against nation/That put the Blues right in its tread./I want to tell you, people if I can/That the Blues and trouble both run hand in hand/And at a time like this, I know the Blues is in command.

Memphis Slim[1]

The Katrina tragedy was a blues moment. The legitimacy of the United States is dependent upon multiethnic and multiracial cooperation at home and abroad, yet it affirms its status as the architect of a new world order by denying the existence of racism. Katrina has exposed both the absence of social justice and the futility of this "plausible deniability" dance. The blues tradition of explanation and development provides both a way out of the inner workings of inequity and a way into the Third Reconstruction.

The picture of twenty thousand slowly dying African Americans chanting "we want help" outside of New Orleans's Convention Center was a blues moment. It disrupted the molecular structure of a wide array of carefully constructed social relations and narratives on race, class, progress, competency, and humanity. In the blink of an eye, African Americans, an identity fraught with ambiguity, were transformed back into *black people*, a highly politicized identity. Mass suffering simultaneously killed the dream and "learnt" the blues to the hip-hop generation. Katrina's message was unmistakable. For example, on September 9, in an essay written for *The Monitor* of Kampala, Uganda, Vukoni Lupa-Lasaga summarizes the message sent to the African diaspora and the world at large:

This wasn't the way America was supposed to be . . . Many people in the United States genuinely believe – with a fervor that puts religious fanatics to shame – that nobody else in the world can do anything better than America. But the failure of government at all levels in responding to the hurricane disaster rehashes a much older story about the United States, one that has been steadily and deliberately noisily drowned or whited out of mainstream discourse. It is the story of race, class, poverty, and studied incompetence . . . for the rest of us, blacks in the United States serve as the proverbial canary in a coal mine. Those images on TV should, therefore, be a lesson for Africans and other people of African ancestry all over the world. Whether you are in peril in Darfur, Sudan, Ruhengeri, Rwanda, or New Orleans, saving your black behind isn't a priority for the American government, founded on a doctrine of white supremacy.[2]

The victims of Katrina were victimized once again by an army assembled to deny what they experienced, from administration officials such as Secretary of State Condoleezza Rice to leaders of the African American community who cautioned restraint. In this moment of crisis, many other black leaders, intellectuals, and professionals lost the gift of voice.[3]

Prior to the Katrina tragedy, there existed a raging global debate over the Bush administration's views on racial justice. Several incidents were ongoing sources of tension: the 2000 presidential election and black disenfranchisement, the undermining of the United Nation's Conference on Racism in 2001, opposition to affirmative action in 2003, Texas redistricting, the rise of racial profiling, and crises in the Middle East and along the Mexican border. In June 2004, NAACP chairman Julian Bond accused Bush and the Republican Party of appealing to the "dark underside of American culture . . . They preach racial equality but practice racial division . . . Their idea of equal rights is the American flag and Confederate swastika flying side-by-side."[4]

The 2004 election's themes of war, social intolerance, and disenfranchisement further poisoned the well. After Katrina, this debate began to converge on the federal indifference to the crisis's victims. On a September 2 nationally televised benefit for the victims, hip-hop artist Kanye West expressed the sentiments of the majority of African Americans who saw racism in the federal response. His comment revived the debate over the Bush presidency. By September 26, the crisis was deepening. At the Congressional Black Caucus's Town Hall meeting, Congressman Charles Rangel of Harlem proclaimed President Bush "our Bull Connor."[5] By this time, West's humorous and bitter song on sexual politics, "Gold Digger," had been remixed into a political manifesto by the Legendary K. O. hip-hop group from Houston:

I ain't saying he's a gold digger, but he ain't messing with no broke niggas (2x)/George Bush don't like black people (4x)/Five damn days, five long days/And at the end of the fifth he walking in like "Hey!"/Chilling on his vacation sitting patiently/Them black folks gotta hope, gotta wait and see/If FEMA really comes through in an emergency/But nobody seem to have a sense of urgency/Now the mayor's been reduced to crying/I guess Bush said, "Niggas been used to dying!"/He said, "I know it looks bad, just have to wait"/Forgetting folks who too broke to evacuate/Niggas starving and they dying of thirst/I bet he had to go and check on them refineries first/Making a killing off the price of gas/He would have been up in Connecticut twice as fast/After all that we've been through nothing's changed/You can call Red Cross but the fact remains that [chorus][6]

In his introduction to Frantz Fanon's *Wretched of the Earth*, French philosopher Jean Paul Sartre discussed the role of the anticolonial wars of the 1950s and 1960s in undermining Europe's claims of superiority. To paraphrase

Sartre, Katrina has replaced the celebration of American civilization with a striptease of American humanism. "There you can see it, quite naked, and it's not a pretty sight."[7] We must look at this disaster from the eyes of working-class African Americans, blacks, from the eyes of the impoverished, and, more important, through the eyes of impoverished black children for whom this is a defining moment. This new blues generation is being constructed out of the same disaster-induced social ruins that were created after the biblical Mississippi flood of 1927. To keep African American families in Arkansas, Louisiana, and Mississippi, Red Cross camps were turned into concentration camps. After free Red Cross supplies such as food, clothing, and seeds were distributed to displaced whites and planters, the remaining supplies were then sold to penniless blacks to create new debts. These events deeply radicalized several generations already suffering from racial pogroms throughout the South. After serving on the federal Colored Advisory Commission established by President Herbert Hoover to investigate the disaster, Langston Hughes crafted a still pertinent four-line dissertation on poverty, abandonment, and state blindness titled "Justice":

That justice is a blind goddess
Is a thing to which we poor are wise
Her bandage hides two festering sores
That once, perhaps, were eyes.[8]

The Blues Grid and Trap Economics

Captain, Captain/What make you treat me so mean?/Captain, Captain/What make you treat me so mean?/You know I asked you for water/And you brought me gasoline.

Muddy Waters[9]

Katrina not only revealed ongoing racial projects and practices; it revealed them at the pinnacle of a long half-century march against the New Deal, the Freedom Movement, the War on Poverty, and the Poor People's Campaign. It transformed a relatively peaceful burial of the welfare state by setting the stage for ugly racial conflicts from one end of the country to the other. The arrival of desperate African Americans in large towns and small cities has often been accompanied by both an outpouring of sympathy and surging gun sales. To systematically understand the origins, form, and direction of this atavistic upsurge, it is necessary to choose an ontological and epistemological approach to this crisis that does not further marginalize working-class African American voices or blind their boundless social vision.

The blues tradition of investigation and interpretation is one of the central institutions of African American life. It is a newly indigenous knowledge system that has been used repeatedly by multiple generations of working-class African Americans to organize communities of consciousness. The blues began as a unique intellectual movement that emerged among desperate African American communities in the midst of the ashes of the Civil War, Emancipation, and the overthrow of Reconstruction. It was used to confront the daily efforts of plantation powers to erase African American leadership and the memory of social progress. It produced a new type of African American intellectual through a system of teachers, professors, apprentices, and schools. The blues and its extensions are actively engaged in providing intellectually brutal confrontations with the "truths" of working-class African American life. It draws on African American musical practices, folklore, and spirituality to reorganize and give a new voice to working-class communities facing severe fragmentation. This tradition has been engaged in the production and teaching of African American history from its inception. Many of the subsequent African American cultural traditions can be viewed as movements designed to revitalize the blues ethic of social justice. For Willie Dixon, the blues is also a form of social realism upon which African American survival is predicated: "Had it not been for the blues, the black man wouldn't have been able to survive through all the humiliations and all the various things going on in America . . . he had nothing to fight with but the blues . . . the blues is the facts of life."[10]

In New Orleans, experimentation by the organic intellectual, community leader, and trumpet player Buddy Bolden with the blues became known as jazz. The essential relationship between the blues, jazz, and African American dignity was expressed by Rev. Dr. Martin Luther King Jr. in his address to the 1964 Berlin Jazz Festival:

> Jazz speaks for life. The Blues tell the story of life's difficulties, and if you think for a moment, you will realize that they take the hardest realities of life and put them into music, only to come out with some new hope or sense of triumph. This is triumphant music. And now, Jazz is exported to the world. For in the particular struggle of the Negro in America there is something akin

to the universal struggle of modern man. Everybody has the Blues. Everybody longs for meaning. Everybody needs to love and be loved. Everybody needs to clap hands and be happy. Everybody longs for faith. In music, especially this broad category called Jazz, there is a stepping stone towards all of these.[11]

The growing power of the blues tradition results from its evolution as the antithesis of the neoplantation development tradition as the latter has grown to become the dominant national and international regime. Among the central concerns of the blues tradition of social investigation is the breaking of the bonds of dependency in all of their economic, political, social, cultural, gender, class, and racial manifestations. In the US context, these bonds have a number of forms, including racialized impoverishment, enclosure and displacement, neoplantation politics, the arbitrariness of daily life, the denial of human rights, cultural imposition, the manufacture of savages, regionally distinct traps, and the desecration of sacred places. I would like to explore the question of racism within the Katrina tragedy through these nine blues lenses.

The Misery of Daily Life

Imagine this, imagine that/Everything you want in life, you will never get/From the ghetto cause it's crazy/Most niggas want roses but they get daisies/Imagine this, little kids with no shoes on/And every homeless person I see I'm willing to take them home/But I can't cause my life is pure misery/Every dollar I make, ten go back to Bill and Hillary/I guess life is real but I know deep inside I was dealt a bad deal/ . . . We was born dreaming/ . . . Imagine this, David Duke as our President/ . . . I'll keep holding on (These little kids ain't got a chance!)

Master P[12]

A central question in the blues tradition is: What happened to African American communities in the Louisiana and Mississippi Deltas after the passage of the Voting Rights Act in 1965? When you visit these regions, you will see a swath of human devastation and permanent crisis that has been pejoratively called "Third World on the Mississippi" and "America's Ethiopia." The decision of white leaders, black leaders, and scholars to accept this situation in silence is a racist project. Mississippi and Louisiana are the two poorest states in the nation. They have been, and are, the sites of intense racial schism. Sadly, many Americans are unable to connect these dots and an entire poverty studies industry has arisen to make sure that this understanding does not occur. Therefore, in many regions, poverty in America is a white supremacist social construction in that its roots lie in the effort to deny the historic claims of African Americans for the redistribution of political power and economic resources. As biological and religious forms of explanation were being roundly condemned in the 1930s, social science was charged with rendering invisible both these historic demands and increasing monopolization with a cloak sewn from reinvigorated plantation theories of culture and behavior. This new discourse protected southern planters engaged in the expulsion of millions of African Americans on the eve of the restoration of their civil and voting rights. It was also used by northern blocs who welcomed southern refugees with extreme forms of residential and occupational segregation. In 1940, President Franklin Roosevelt's liberal secretary of agriculture, Henry Wallace, identified the central innovative tenet of this new social science paradigm. "It must be recognized that the problem of sustaining indigent populations is not the problem of agriculture . . . The problem itself is a sociological one and must be treated as such."[13]

After prolonged attacks, the neoplantation social philosophy reemerged in the 1980s with its psychological, sociological, cultural, and journalistic descriptions of African American inferiority intact. With a perfect eugenics-informed pedigree, "underclass" models of deviancy, family dysfunction, criminality, and nihilism were once again deployed. This time the social scientists were charged with masking the expulsion of millions of African Americans from historic urban communities, the mass incarceration of African Americans, and mass disenfranchisement with categories such as renewal, gentrification, revitalization, new urbanism, and "smart growth."[14]

In 2004, Mississippi and Louisiana had the first and second highest rates of poverty in the nation and the second and fifth lowest rates of median household income; they were among the bottom three states in unemployment benefits. Approximately 36.6 percent of black Louisianans and 34.9 percent of black Mississippians are considered impoverished. The destruction of public housing, neighborhood displacement, and the manufacture of the homeless were raging full tilt in New Orleans in 2005. On the eve of Katrina, the city's impoverished residents had already been abandoned.[15] Past and present racial schisms in the region have devastated its family, social service, educational, and physical infrastructure. A central question for the blues tradition would be: What is the relationship between historic and deepening poverty and the fabulous fortunes amassed by the region's sugar, rice, cotton, oil, gas, chemical, tourism, and gaming empires? These heavily subsidized and lightly taxed sectors were protected by Governor Barbour of Mississippi and former Governor Foster of Louisiana, even as they savaged health care and other antipoverty programs.

This regional movement has been replicated at the national level to make new forms of dependency-creating institutions or traps. The overthrow of the right to social welfare benefits, Aid to Families with Dependent Children, by President Clinton and the congressional neoplantation bloc was cynically titled the Personal Responsibility and Work Opportunity Act of 1996. Their reversal of the right to public housing was even more cynically titled Hope VI. All of these projects were manufacturing destitution in New Orleans and Mississippi before the Katrina tragedy. Now, hundreds of thousands have been thrown upon a social safety net consisting of several frayed threads. This man-made disaster has been compounded by Bush's FY2006 budget, which contains massive program cuts: food stamps, elementary and secondary education, education for the disadvantaged, special education, school improvement, vocational and adult education, the Women, Infants, and Children (AC) nutrition program, Head Start, rental assistance, child-care assistance, low-income energy assistance, the Ryan White HIV/AIDS program, community block grants, and aid to localities. To pay for the costs of Katrina, more cuts from these programs, including Medicaid and Medicare, have been proposed by movement leaders within Congress. This feeding frenzy on the poor calls to mind the title of an 1857 book written by George Fitzhugh, the first plantation social scientist, *Cannibals All!*[16]

Neoplantation Politics: That Ol' Black Magic

When compared to the triumphalism often associated with civil rights historiography, the blues tradition provides one of the few epistemologies capable of grasping the origins, meaning, and scope of neoplantation movement that has come to dominate national politics. It has never stopped asking what happened to the White Citizens Council's massive resistance movement, launched out of the Mississippi, Arkansas, and Louisiana Deltas in 1954 to defeat *Brown v. Board of Education* and the civil rights movement as a whole. It led southerners opposed to civil rights into the Republican Party. A 1962 article in the *Louisville Courier Journal* heralded the birth of "Racial Republicanism." "The truth is that this Republican upsurge, if that is the word, owes much of its momentum to the very thing that has kept the South in one-party bondage for nearly a century – an unreasoning passion to maintain 'white supremacy.'" The Southern Strategy of the Nixon and Reagan campaigns crafted a southern, western, and northern national compact based on white economic and racial fears. In 1981, Lee Atwater explained the movement's rhetorical evolution as a series of "black magic" spells:

> You start out in 1954 by saying, "Nigger, nigger, nigger." By 1968, you can't say "nigger," that hurts you. Backfires. So you say stuff like forced bussing, states' rights and all that stuff. You're getting so abstract now [that] you're talking about cutting taxes, and all these things you're taking about are totally economic things and a byproduct of them is [that] blacks get hurt worse than whites . . . [It] is getting that abstract that coded that we are doing away with the racial problem one way or another. You follow me.[17]

Before becoming the Republican National Committee chair, Atwater provoked a national racial panic to secure the election of George H. W. Bush as president in 1988. The reborn White Citizens Council, the Council of Conservative Citizens, counts among its allies leading Mississippi politicians: US Senator Trent Lott, former Governor Kirk Fordice, and current governor Harley Barbour. The organization also noted that Louisiana "ultra-conservative David Vitter won 50% of the vote to win the US Senate seat held by retiring Democrat John Breaux. Vitter advanced to the senate from a congressional seat representing the suburban New Orleans district that once elected David Duke to the statehouse."[18] Suburban New Orleans has also given the world David Duke, a national Ku Klux Klan leader, who became a Republican state legislator. He then went on to receive 60 percent of the white vote in his losing bid for the US Senate in 1990 and 55 percent of the white vote in his unsuccessful bid for governor in 1991. After having received an honorary

doctorate from a university in Ukraine, Dr. Duke now spreads his message of white anxiety and African American depravity globally.[19] It is within these confines that decisions about relief and the survival of black communities in New Orleans and Mississippi are being made.

Arbitrariness and Human Rights

The ascendance of the states rights movement to federal power led to the replacement of the Keynesian and Fordist social welfare philosophy with a reborn plantation philosophy of governance. One reality became thousands of separate realities – every plantation has its own regulations. Increasingly, access to subsistence, services, health care, social justice, and even safe roads varies widely. This combination of weak federal authority and local authoritarianism has hobbled the Delta states for generations. Katrina revealed the present and future human costs of a fragmented, de-linked, privatized, and devolved state; no one is in charge. Other markers of this neoplantation system include runaway factories, technological displacement, ethnic rotation, subminimum wages, multiple levels of citizenship, educational disaster zones, and a justice system that creates instability and demographic collapse in black and Latino neighborhoods. The embodiment of arbitrariness was Robert Davis's night in the French Quarter on October 9. One minute the retired school teacher was asking for directions, and the next minute he was lying on the sidewalk with blood gushing from his head and a jackboot on his back. For Mbembe, the chaos of daily life, this "contingent, dispersed, and powerless" existence, reveals itself in the form of arbitrariness. A growing feature of this new world is the multiplication of forces, official and unofficial, in society possessing the "absolute power to give death any time, anywhere, by any means, and for any reason." This is not "just any arbitrariness, but arbitrariness in its comedy and stark horror, a real shadow that, while totally devoid of beauty, does not lack clarity."[20]

At the same time there are growing certainties, such as the practices of residential segregation, which kept the black community of New Orleans in a floodplain surrounded by a faulty levee system further devastated by recent Bush administration budget cuts. Black Louisianans have also been systematically subjected to some of the worst instances of environmental racism in the world. In 1990, Louisiana legislator Avery Alexander described an environment that had been turned against the African American community. "Should we celebrate or mourn the fact that among African American women, near Saint James . . . that vaginal cancers are 36 times the national average . . . here in Louisiana . . . we have found the job promises empty and the risk of poisoning inevitable."[21]

Attaining human rights is a fundamental category in the blues epistemology, particularly the fate of the incarcerated and the abused, since upon these pillars African American identity was born. Lawyers for New Orleans inmates moved to a facility in Jena, Louisiana, requested US Department of Justice investigation. The 450 prisoners interviewed complained that "guards had been beating them, stripping them naked and hitting them with belts, shaving their heads, threatening them with dogs, shocking them with stun guns, and assaulting them after they attempted to report the abuse." On August 7, 2005, a rally to oppose "police terrorism" was held in the Treme neighborhood of New Orleans. Remembered was Chief Tootie Montana, who died on the steps of city hall in June 2005 at a press conference. He was demanding that Mayor Nagin stop his campaign of police harassment, brutality, and the destruction of African American housing and culture. The organizers reminded participants that the New Orleans Police Department killed twenty-five people in 2005 and fifty in 2004. They also reminded them to listen to the Families Against Police Brutality Radio Show.

> The Heart Ache Brass Band joined the rally to mourn a member "gunned down by the police." They led us in a second line . . . We also danced, laughed, sang, screamed, while we moved around the Treme streets with Heartache expressing that throughout our heartaches, the losses from police terrorism and police brutality, our collective action still comes from the spaces within us that are joy-filled, hopeful, and resilient.[22]

Cultural Imposition: On Becoming Savage and Postsavage New Orleans

In her study of the Acâgchemem and Mission San Juan Capistrano, Lisbeth Haas refers to the tendency of the Spanish to build their institutions on sacred sites central to Native American identity and autonomy as superimposition:

> The missionary's selection of this site illustrates a deliberate strategy used by the Spaniards in their conquest

of the Americas, one that had served them well already for three centuries prior to the conquest of this area of California. By choosing such locally meaningful places for their own rituals of appropriation, the missionaries attempted to replace indigenous structures of authority, power, and memory with their own.[23]

From their very conception, the blues, jazz, rock and roll, and hip-hop have had to battle two forms of cultural imposition. On the one hand, it was said that they were prima facie evidence of black savagery. On the other hand, it was said that they don't belong to blacks; they're universal. This bit of surrealism gave rise to the observation that "your blues ain't like mine." The black community of New Orleans is now engaged in a somewhat similar superimposition battle, a battle for its very survival.

First, there are those who attempted to define this community as savage with now discredited stories of rape, mutilation, beheading, cannibalism, and white genocide. Then the intellectuals weighed in with their genocidal musings. Columnist George F. Will attacked men, women, and children. It "is a safe surmise that more than 80 percent of African American births in inner-city New Orleans . . . were to women without husbands. That translates into a large and constantly renewed cohort of lightly parented adolescent males, and that translates into chaos in neighborhoods and schools, come rain or come shine." Out of the blue, the former US secretary of education Bill Bennett decided it was a good time to attack black babies. "But I do know that it's true that if you wanted to reduce crime, you could – if that were your sole purpose – you could abort every black baby in this country, and your crime rate would go down." Others viewed the disaster as a gift from God. Republican congressman of Louisiana, Richard Baker, was quoted as saying, "We finally cleaned up public housing in New Orleans. We couldn't do it, but God did." Evangelist Franklin Graham declared that the city had a "dark spiritual cloud" hovering above it because of Mardi Gras, gays and lesbians, and the presence of African traditional religions. "There's been satanic worship. There's been sexual perversion. God is going to use that storm to bring revival. God has a plan. God has a purpose."[24]

Others simply lusted for blood. Governor Kathleen Blanco decided it was time to shoot to kill while Brigadier General Gary Jones stated that New Orleans "is going to look like Little Somalia. We're going to go out and take this city back. This will be a combat operation" against "the insurgency." In an article titled "New Orleans Descends into Africa-like Savagery," Dr. David Duke asks, "Is this a story about tribal brutality in Uganda?" In "White Genocide in New Orleans," he concludes that not "all of the people of New Orleans are acting like savages, but unfortunately there are significant numbers of the African American community behaving that way."[25] Once the savagery discourse was imposed, then justifications for denying water to dying babies and refusing to let hundreds of people cross the Gretna Bridge for days are made to sound reasonable instead of what they are: racism, criminal activity, and gross human rights violations.

Gumbo Philosophy and the Third Reconstruction

Distinctive regional identities and relations are constructed, and reproduced, through movements and countermovements. With one thousand persons dead and with hundreds of thousands either unemployed, homeless, evicted, and scattered among forty-four states, New Orleans stands at the crossroads. The now dominant social philosophy has been used to wage an attack on the very programs needed to bring the city back to what it once was. Yet, there is no going back. The "Bring New Orleans Back" Committee formed by Mayor Nagin is top heavy with corporate leaders who are driven to build a city reflective of their desires. They and others in Congress view the disaster as an opportunity to remake the city without its black majority. Excluded from this new disaster in the making are working-class African American voices, visions, and movements.

Why should anyone want to live in, or return to, a place of great suffering? This question has haunted the millions of African Americans who migrated out of, and then back to, the South during the twentieth century in search of refuge. It was addressed by Louisiana's State Poet Laureate at the American Studies Association's Annual Meeting in November 2005. New Orleans native Brenda Marie Osbey insisted that residents should return to their homes; it was the government, not the city, which treated them poorly. To paraphrase several of her poems, she told the audience that New Orleans is both a city where "the Saints walk in Congo time" and where "death is a road upon which walks those we loved and those we loved not long enough." It is a place where the "slaves of the city" still ask "who will betray us today." Through Osbey's works, we understand that New

Orleans is a city whose people and their ancestors will call forth the dawn of a new world.[26]

In many regions of Africa, religious ceremonies were held in sacred groves and forests. This practice was carried across the Atlantic to sacred bush arbors, woods, and rivers of North America. With urbanization, churches emerged in massive edifices and on street corners. Both became sacred. Several places became so important to the meaning of blackness that they became churches and cathedrals themselves. Then there are the Mecca and Jerusalem of African American culture, the Sea Islands and the Mississippi Delta, which receive humble pilgrims generation after generation. New Orleans is the Black Vatican. The Ado Bambara, Chamba, Canga, Congo/Angola, Fon, Ibo Maninga, Mina, Wolof, and Yoruba reconstituted in Louisiana were known for their resistance to all forms of bondage and defeatism. With the assistance of Native American allies they fought numerous wars against the French, the Spanish, and the American plantocracy. Many became maroons in the swamps, forests, and cities. The center of their survival was the communal gumbo pot. This stew came to symbolize the sacred struggle for dignity and the ability to make something out of nothing, to make freedom out of slavery. After the Civil War, these communities pushed the blues agenda, the Reconstruction agenda, and its endless definitions of freedom. Tragedy befell New Orleans, the blood of a heroic people flowed through its streets. What emerged next was a sound known throughout the world as the very sound of freedom itself. The Queens, Big Chiefs, Professors, Tribes, Whoadies, Saints, and Mothers of the city guarded its culture, knowing that without it, future generations could not stand.[27]

Today the People's Hurricane Relief Fund, among others, carries the flag of the future. This grand coalition does what the governments have refused to do: honor African American sacrifice and courage. Thousands of New Orleans musicians have gone out to spread this lesson; in the words of the Stooges Brass Band, we "Can't Be Faded" or as the Mardi Gras Indians chant "Big Chief Won't Bow Down."[28] The first cornerstone laid in the new New Orleans must be named social justice. Can American studies, the United States, and the global community possibly understand the cosmic significance of missing New Orleans? Perhaps. If so, they must work to defend this indigenous culture and ensure its return by removing the mask of the neoplantation regime and its social philosophy. They could learn a great deal from another iconic symbol of black dignity and determination.

John Henry said to his captain
You know a man ain't nothin' but a man
Before I let anyone beat me down
I'll die with my hammer in my hand
I'll die with my hammer in my hand[29]

Notes

1 Memphis Slim, "Blues Everywhere," ACT: Lost Blues Tapes/More America Folk Blues Festival, 1963–1965, ACT Music, ACT 6000-2.

2 Vukoni Lupa-Lasaga, "Katrina Unmasks the Real America," *The Monitor* (Kampala, Uganda), September 9, 2005.

3 Laura Jakes Jordan, "Rice Defends Bush Against Racism Charges," *Associated Press*, September 4, 2005; Earl Ofari Hutchinson, "Playing the Katrina Race Card," available at http://www.blacknews.com/pr/racecard101 (accessed October 6, 2005).

4 Quoted in William Douglas and Amy Worden, "Bush: NAACP Hostile to Me," *Miami Herald*, July 10, 2004.

5 Quoted in Meghan Clyne, "Rangel's Jibe at President Draws Support from Democrats," *New York Sun*, September 27, 2005.

6 The Legendary K. O., "George Bush Doesn't Care about Black People," available at http://www.k-otix.com (accessed September 25, 2005).

7 Jean-Paul Sartre, Preface, in Frantz Fanon, *The Wretched of the Earth* (New York: Grove Press, 1963), 24–25.

8 Clyde Woods, *Development Arrested: Race, Power, and the Blues in the Mississippi Delta* (London: Verso, 1998), 119; Langston Hughes, "Justice," *New Masses* 7 (August 1931): 15.

9 Muddy Waters, "Captain Captain," *ACT: Lost Blues Tapes/More America Folk Blues Festival 1963–1965*, ACT Music ACT 6000-2.

10 Willie Dixon, "Willie Dixon: A Tribute," *Living Blues* 103 (May–June 1992): 47.

11 Rev. Dr. Martin Luther King Jr., "Opening Speech at the 1964 Berlin Jazz Festival: Humanity and the Importance of Jazz," *HR-57: Center for the Preservation of Jazz and Blues,* available at http://www.hr57.org/pages/903831/ (accessed October 18, 2005).

12 Master P, "The Ghetto Won't Change," *Ice Cream Man*, Priority Records 53978.

13 *Delta Council News* (Stoneville, Miss.: Delta Council), September 1940; Woods, *Development Arrested*; Lee D. Baker, *From Savage to Negro: Anthropology and the Construction of Race, 1896–1954* (Berkeley: University of California Press, 1998); Daryl Scott, *Contempt and Pity: Social Policy and the Image of the Damaged Black Psyche, 1880–1996* (Chapel Hill: University of North Carolina Press, 1997).

14 John T. Metzger, "Planned Abandonment: The Neighborhood Life-Cycle Theory and National Urban Policy," *Housing Policy Debate* 11, no. 1 (2000); Jerome G. Miller, *Search and Destroy: African-American Males in the Criminal Justice System* (New York: Cambridge University Press, 1997); Brett Williams, "Poverty Among African Americans in the Urban United States," *Human Organization* 51, no. 2 (1992).

15 Arloc Sherman and Isaac Shapiro, "Essential Facts about the Victims of Hurricane Katrina," Center on Budget and Policy Priorities, September 19, 2005; Isaac Shapiro, "Benefit Levels for Unemployed Hurricane Victims Are Too Low," Center on Budget and Policy Priorities, September 27, 2005. Both articles are available at www.cbpp.org/pubs/katrina.htm (accessed October 5, 2005).

16 Peter Edelman, "The Worst Thing Bill Clinton Has Done," *Atlantic Monthly* 279, no. 3 (March 1997): 43–58; George Fitzhugh, *Cannibals All! Or Slaves Without Masters* (1857; Cambridge, Mass.: Harvard University Press, 2004).

17 J. Earl Williams, *Plantation Politics: The Southern Economic Heritage* (Austin: Futura Press, 1972), 46–56; Bob Herbert, "Impossible, Ridiculous, Repugnant," *New York Times*, October 6, 2005, A35. See also Alexander P. Lamis, *Southern Politics in the 1990s* (Baton Rogue: Louisiana State University Press, 1999).

18 Council of Conservative Citizens, available at http://www.cofcc.org/news.htm (accessed October 5, 2005).

19 Numan V. Bartley, *The Rise of Massive Resistance: Race and Politics in the South during the 1950s* (Baton Rogue: Louisiana State University Press, 1999); Joan Vennochi, "Can GOP 'Unplay' the Race Card?" *Boston Globe*, July 19, 2005.

20 Achille Mbembe, *On the Postcolony* (Berkeley: University of California Press, 2001), 13.

21 United States Lower Mississippi Delta Development Commission, *Louisiana Public Hearing*, January 23, 1990 (Memphis: LMDDC, 1990).

22 David Rohde and Christopher Drew, "Evacuated after Hurricanes Allege Abuse," *New York Times*, October 2, 2005; Elizabeth Cook, "Goodbye Chief Tootie Montana," available at http://neworleans.indymedia.org/news/2005/06/3523 (accessed October 16, 2005). Letter to author from Johonna McCants, Blackout Arts Collective, October 2, 2005.

23 Lisbeth Hass, *Conquest and Historical Identities in California, 1769–1936* (Berkeley: University of California Press, 1995), 13.

24 George F. Will, "A Poverty of Thought," *Washington Post*, September 13, 2005; "Washington Wire," *Wall Street Journal*, September 9, 2005; Michael A. Fletcher and Brian Faler, "Bennett Defends Radio Remarks, *Washington Post*, October 1, 2005; Steve Szkotak, "Graham Sees 'Revival' for New Orleans," *Washington Post*, October 4, 2005.

25 Joseph R. Chenelly, "Troops Begin Combat Operations in New Orleans," *Army Times*, September 2, 2005; David Duke, "New Orleans Descends into Africa-like Savagery," *David Duke's European American Homepage* available at http://www.davidduke.com/index (accessed September 29, 2005).

26 Brenda Marie Osbey, *Ceremony for Minneconjoux* (Lexington: Callaloo Poetry Series, 1983); *In These Houses* (Connecticut: Wesleyan University, 1988); *Desperate Circumstance, Dangerous Woman* (Brownsville, Oregon: Story Line Press, 1991); and *All Saints: New and Selected Poems* (Baton Rouge: Louisiana University Press, 1997).

27 Gwendolyn Mildo Hall, *Africans in Colonial Louisiana: The Development of Afro-Creole Culture in the Eighteenth Century* (Baton Rouge: Louisiana State University, 1992); The "tribes" of the Mardi Gras Indian Nation include the following: Seventh Ward Hunters, Ninth Ward Hunters, Black Eagles, Black Hawk Hunters, Black Feathers, Black Seminoles, Blackfoot Hunters, Carrollton Hunters, Cheyenne Hunters, Comanche Hunters, Congo Nation, Creole Osceola, Creole Wild West, Fi-Yi-Yi, Flaming Arrows, Geronimo Hunters, Golden Arrows, Golden Blades, Golden Comanche, Golden Eagles, Golden Star Hunters, Guardians of Flames, Mohawk Hunters, Morning Star Hunters, Red Hawk Hunters, Seminole Hunters, Seminole, Skull & Bones, White Cloud Hunters, White Eagles, Wild Apache, Wild Bogacheeta, Wild Tchoupitoulas, Wild Magnolias, Yellow Pocahontas, Young Navaho, Young Brave Hunters, Young Monogram Hunters, Young Cheyenne, and the Seventh Ward Hard Head Hunters.

28 Stooges Brass Band, *It's About Time*, Gruve Music Gr1006.

29 Memphis Slim and Willie Dixon, "John Henry;" *ACT: Lost Blues Tapes/More America Folk Blues Festival 1963–1965*, ACT Music ACT 6000-2.

Part IX

Memory and Re-Memory

The emphasis on memory as an object of scholarly inquiry has gone hand in hand with critiques of what we now call "the archive," a discursive system dictating what is and is not worth remembering. Studies of memory are studies of the processes of exclusion or inclusion in the archive, setting the terms and conditions for what is considered valid historical knowledge. By no means limited to Americanist scholarship, memory has been a particularly fruitful analytic for innovative work from the margins that has challenged traditional, dominant knowledge and formulations of American nationhood. The approach to memory in these articles as an integral force in the contest over the American nation and its history relies on the identification of new archives through the recovery of marginalized histories by scholars and writers long excluded from the mainstream US academy. Scholars working in what was known as "Negro history" during the 1930s and 1940s took up the subject of slave revolts and documented the testimony of former slaves, waging a challenge to reigning antiblack accounts of slavery and Reconstruction. The paternalism and overt racism of US scholarship on slavery was contested by work placing black peoples at the center of historical narratives. The instructively titled landmarks from the 1930s, W. E. B. Du Bois's *Black Reconstruction*, and C. L. R. James's study of Toussaint L'Ouverture and the Haitian Revolution, *Black Jacobins*, influenced subsequent generations of US historiography on race, democracy, and labor in post-emancipation societies, and democracy. Such work from the margins exposed an archive defined by the selective memory of American nationalism. Moreover, its expanded horizons resituated America within a black

Atlantic frame, and could be seen, additionally, as important harbingers of what we know as postcolonial studies. This scholarship recast the image of America and its history by the recovery of aspects of the past we were never taught; counternarratives of the middle passage, enslavement, resistance, and slave rebellions, and Reconstruction as a democratic experiment. Such acts of scholarly rebellion against US historiographies marked by white supremacy gained momentum with the decolonization of Africa and the Civil Rights movement.

Yet the recovery of silenced, oppositional histories is contested, and itself subject to the political stakes inherent in memory and the archive. Insofar as the impact of revisionist US histories of race, labor, slavery, resistance, and Reconstruction was mitigated by a reassertion of the white nationalism of Reagan-era corporate and religious conservatism and patriotism, a growing body of American studies scholarship has examined the salience of memory for determining what counts as history. These articles remind us that power, legitimation, and consent to dominant US nationalism are the stakes of the practice of history. History, and the power to narrate it, marks the struggle between oppositional and dominant narratives of American nationhood. History, these articles suggest, is at once an act of narration and silencing: history was complicit in the silenced voices and vanished inner lives of enslaved peoples of African descent; history was the product of the epistemic power that defined which events, perspectives, and sources were considered valid, thus dictating the very possibilities of historical imagination.

Michel Rolph-Trouillot engages the crucial matter of the archive, recounting the extent to which the Haitian revolution, the only successful slave revolt in human history, was relegated to silence by historians as an unthinkable event. Such historians, says Trouillot, echoed contemporaries blinded by enlightenment racial hierarchies and the pervasive view that black resistance was anomalous and pathological. Little wonder that many historians, writing of "The Age of Revolutions," have cast into oblivion the slaves' military defeat of France, leading to the establishment of the independent black republic of Haiti in 1804.

Avery Gordon's article on Toni Morrison's *Beloved* engages the ways in which we, as Americans, remain haunted by the unresolved past of racial slavery, the history of the middle passage, and stories too painful to pass on, such as the murderous act of resistance at the center of the novel, a fictionalized retelling of historical events surrounding Margaret Garner, "the slave mother who killed her child rather than see it taken back into slavery" when confronted by slavecatchers empowered by the Fugitive Slave Act.

David Blight's history of the Southern myth of the Lost Cause illuminates the stakes of collective memory, in this case, that of Confederate political leaders, officers, and other advocates in crafting a partisan history that, at various moments, served to vindicate the South's involvement with racial slavery, provided an ideological basis for postbellum reconciliation between North and South, and lent sanction to white supremacy during the era of Jim Crow segregation.

Marita Sturken's article on the national Vietnam Veterans Memorial in Washington, DC highlights the power of that site as an icon of memory, providing veterans with a site for identity construction, and the basis for finding meaning in their combat experience in the face of the incommunicable, disorienting experience of modern warfare. The memorial has countered for many veterans the alienation of the war, compounded by their struggles upon their return to an American society unable to welcome them as heroes. Noting the magnetic appeal of the memorial for veterans, Sturken sees the memorial as an important site for the contestation over the war's legacy, and even for commentary on wars and issues of national importance since Vietnam. But the memorial's significance as a site of memory is ambiguous. While veterans and their loved ones participate in history-making by leaving personalized objects at the wall, constituting an archive of their own making against the silencing of their experience, Sturken points out that discussions of the memorial never mention the Vietnamese people as casualties of the war, suggesting that remembrance and forgetting are simultaneous effects.

In "*The Patriot* Acts," Donald Pease is concerned with the contemporary uses of memory in popular culture, and how ideological treatments of the past in film must be read in the immediate context of their political moment. Pease's provocative and wide-ranging analysis of the 2000 Mel Gibson film *The Patriot* views that film as an allegory for the complex distortions of memory; the ways in which the construction of the American nation and its legal and patriotic ideals seek to repress the memory of the lawless violence of state-making to which the nation owes its very existence. Pease powerfully links the film's anachronistic deployment of the South's Lost Cause ideology in the context of the American Revolution as a reinscription of the American nation that was serviceable for the Patriot Act's expansion of the emergency powers of the national security state.

Taken together, these articles invite us to ponder the extent to which we remain haunted by the past. The work done in these articles represents the effort of scholars of the new American studies to remember, in their writing, that which those in the corridors of power would have the rest of us forget.

Not only the Footprints but the Water Too and What is Down There

Avery Gordon

The Palimpsest

"They 'forgot' many things" (Morrison in Clemons 1987: 74). The slave narratives, that is. The slave narrative was the principal form by which the experience of slavery was conveyed to the nineteenth-century primarily white and female reading public. The slave narrative was an authenticated testimony, written by slaves or former slaves in an autobiographical address, that sought to reverse for the author and for the society the conditions of bondage it described. The slave narrative was thus an autobiography and a sociology of slavery and freedom. Like much sociology, it combined the autobiographical (it contained the traces of the one who scripted it), the ethnographic (it spoke in the third person for/of someone else), the historical (its present tense was never on its own), the literary (it was created within an available grammatology of voice and convention), and the political (it produced interested accounts of power). The slave writers' purpose, as an instance of the sociological imagination, was to describe the "intricate connection between the patterns of their own lives and the course of world history . . . [and] what this connection means for the kinds of men [and women] they are becoming and for the kinds of history-making in which they might take part" (Mills 1959: 4). In its most general outlines, the slave narrative tried to connect its audience to the foundationally divisive social relations that underwrote the slave experience, an experience most of its readers were able to keep at a distance from themselves. It tried to make the agony and moral illegitimacy of slavery palpably present and to create a relationship between reader and slave so that, in the best of

narratives (e.g., Jacobs [1861] 1987), the nexus of force, desire, belief, and practice that made slavery possible could be exposed and abolished. It accomplished its task of laying bare slavery by producing a morality of verisimilitude, by forging a congruence between realism and sympathy. It told the bare, real truth of slavery, from the point of view of the one who was or had been in it, so that the reader would be moved to comprehend, empathize, and seek salvation for the slave and the nation.

But the slave narrative was also produced, distributed, received, "conscripted," in John Sekora's words, into the "loose but elaborate network of abolitionist clergymen, politicians, merchants, writers, editors, printers, and advocates . . . transatlantic in scope and resources" (1988: 106, 108). Well above and beyond the usual "vagaries of American printing and bookselling" (ibid.: 106), the slave narrative, whatever else it attempted to and did accomplish, was greatly constrained by the demands placed on it by the abolition movement, its primary sponsor and its largest consumer. Sekora asks:

Does it matter who controls the shape of the story – author or sponsor? Does it matter that the facticity demanded by sponsors may preclude individual personality? . . . Does it matter that a slave's story is sandwiched between white abolitionist documents, suggesting that the slave has precious little control over his or her life – even to its writing? Does it matter that several people . . . alleged that most black agents – including the great Douglass – had no stories until abolitionists gave them one? Does it matter that the very sponsors of slave narratives attempt to muffle the slave voice? (ibid.: 109)

And, we might add, does it matter that Margaret Garner never even wrote her own biography, which was written for her first by the newspapers and then by the prominent Cincinnati abolitionist Levi Coffin, being passed on thus at an even greater remove? The answers to these questions is undoubtedly yes.

For the majority of lay abolitionist readers, the slave narrative was popular sociology. It possessed a distinctive factual value because it told you what life was really like for the slave striving to be free. And it possessed a distinctive factual-moral value because it provided the believable proof that the slave, legally property, was a potential citizen, a human being. The slave narrative was expected to bear witness to the institution and experience of slavery simply in plain speech and thus, by implication, sincerely. It was not to display any literary self-consciousness because "nothing that might prompt the reader to suspect that he or she was reading fiction could be allowed" (Andrews 1988: 90). This was arguably a challenge for the writer, and as William Andrews notes, "in the two decades before Emancipation, black autobiography served as a kind of sociocultural crucible in which some of the era's most interesting . . . experiments were conducted in how to tell the truth about experience. . . . By the mid-nineteenth century, black autobiographers had recognized that their great challenge was much more than just telling the truth; they had to *sound* truthful doing it" to those, including a "noted leader of the American Anti-Slavery Society," who, in his own words, " 'thought that the slave, as a general thing, is a liar' " (ibid.: 89–90). How could known liars sound truthful? They would have to display, with the utmost genuineness (which often meant acknowledging the reader's suspicions about veracity), just those qualities that we associate with a conventional sociological realism: a plain unembellished style of writing that conveyed only the *believable* facts, a balanced assessment with no "exaggeration" and "nothing that smacked of 'the imagination' " (ibid.: 90). (The need for understatement was no doubt tied to the desire to distance the slave narrative, a serious, genuine, political work by and for the legally and "materially" oppressed, from sentimentality and the sentimental novel, a woman's genre, with all its emotional melodrama and claim on the reader's feelings.) To be sure, to produce such a realism this popular sociology required an astute calculation of the entirety of the ideological parameters of American life itself. It required apprehending just what aspects of slavery and the slave experience would, indeed, be believable, that is, consumable by an audience who may or may not have believed in slavery, but whose parameters of knowing were certainly established within the larger confines of the existence of racial slavery itself. Sounding truthful, acquiring the condition of believability, then, was as important to the slave narrative's success as a political document as any truth about slavery it would remit.

If this sociological realism was already a very complicated venture, bound heart to hand by what it could *not* say, it was further elaborated by the additional burden of attesting not simply to the slave as a reliable reporter, but also to her or his basic humanity. "The slave's texts . . . could not be taken as specimens of a black 'literary culture.' Rather, these texts could only be read as testimony of defilement: the slave's *representation* of the master's attempts to transform a human being into a commodity, and the slave's simultaneous verbal witness of the possession of a 'humanity' shared in common with Europeans" (Gates 1988b: 52). The complex articulation of this double bind – I testify to my transformation into a Slave while I testify to the existence of my shared humanity with you – is what the slave narrative was asked to express. In this scheme, where the law forbade reading and writing (literacy), but the "human community" required them as tokens of membership, slaves not only had to "steal" some learning as evidence of the criminal system that prevented them from acquiring it rightfully, they also had to become author(ized) as evidence of an already extant humanity. Literacy became, then, as Henry Louis Gates Jr. has argued, a key trope in the slave narrative itself, as the writers displayed, referred to, and commented on the possession *and* illegality of it. The resourceful and often quite ingenious play on literacy in the slave narrative does not alter the fact that the slave narrative, by the very nature of its being a believable written document, constituted proof that the slave possessed the recognizable "*visible* sign of reason" that the European American demanded (ibid.: 53).

Beloved is not a simulated slave narrative. It is avowedly fiction; it is not written in the traditional autobiographical voice; it is not sponsored by nor is its testimony vouchsafed by a white authority; and it begins in 1873, well after Emancipation. (We will return to the significance of the opening date later.) But it does retell the story of Margaret Garner, *the slave mother who killed her child rather than see it taken back to slavery*, claiming its continuous relation to the history (slavery) and form (narrative) of the origins, in the most general sense, of African-American writing in the United States. As it retells one story and in this way summons another, it remembers some of what the slave narrative forgot, creating a palimpsest, a document that has been inscribed several times, where the remnants of earlier, imperfectly erased scripting is still detectable.

A palimpsest certainly, but is *Beloved* to be read as popular sociology today? A good deal of the exceptional scholarship on the slave narrative has amply demonstrated that the slave narrative was a literature produced by writers drawing on a range of particular conventions, styles, creative designs, and tropes that place it more accurately in the history of African-American autobiography and literature. There are several reasons for this interpretive application, notwithstanding the obvious desire to study a notable part of African-American culture and one only relatively recently addressed by scholars since its virtual disappearance in American culture after the Civil War. But an important motivation concerns the troubling implications of treating black literature as *unquestioned* sociology, a concern, in part, about the sanctioned use of black literature as a teaching tool of tolerance (Morrison 1989: Morrison in Angelo 1989, 121). (Indeed, *Beloved* contains a carefully considered disquisition on tolerance that, as is Morrison's special talent, captures the lived caliber of what enables someone's magnanimity, what precludes its forbearance, and what registers its limitations.) The variegated history of the use and abuse of black literature is well beyond the scope of my pursuit here. Suffice to say that part of that history takes its cue from the conjunction of verisimilitude and sympathy the abolitionist movement (and later the discipline of ethnology/anthropology) established as the valid, legitimate, and sensible condition of knowledge and consensual political persuasion (see Cruz 1999; Dent forthcoming). But what other kind of popular sociology might be warranted or invented on the basis of *Beloved*'s revisions and way of seeing? The elaboration or the evocation of this other sociology is what I hope this chapter, by the end of it, will have announced.

This other sociology that *Beloved* might entitle revises the slave narrative in at least two ways germane to the discussion here. First, Morrison rejects literacy as the supreme measure of humanity, but more significantly, she refuses the task of having to prove the slave's (and by implication her descendants') humanity. Second, Morrison will proffer a different type of sociological realism, one that encompasses haunting and the complexity of power and personhood that inheres in its work.

According to Davis and Gates:

Almost all of the [slave] narratives refer to literacy in three ways: they recount vividly scenes of instruction in which

the narrator learned to read and then to write; they underscore polemical admonishments against statutes forbidding literacy training among black slaves; and they are prefaced by [an] ironic apologia ... which ... transforms the convention of the author's confession of the faults of his tale ... [into a] denunciation of that system that limited the development of his capacities. (1985: xxviii)

In *Beloved*, these features take an interesting turn.

The political message of the scene of instruction was, in Ishmael Reed's terms, to show that "the slave who was the first to read and ... write was the first ... to run" (Gates 1987: 108). In *Beloved*, however, the decision to run is made collectively when schoolteacher, a professional reader and writer who "was teaching us things we couldn't learn" (B 191), becomes intolerable. Although the threshold of tolerance for schoolteacher is broken down in its own way for each person at Sweet Home, Sethe's reason for running is most apt here. Sethe runs not when she learns to read and write, but when she learns how she will be read and written, when she learns how she will be represented in a book, literacy's most prized artifact. When she hears schoolteacher's directions to his pupil that he should put her animal characteristics on the right and her human characteristics on the left, she does not know what the word *characteristics* means and has to ask, but she nonetheless understands the conjuncture of power and epistemology that is the very stakes of her representability. Sethe may not be "literate," but she can read the situation perfectly well (perhaps too well), and her reading and writing skills are explicitly located in relation to her refusal to be any part of schoolteacher's book or part of the larger economy in which this particular literate learning has value. Here, all too audaciously, literacy literally measures humanity, savagely, as only a culture schooled in racial science could dream up.

Just as *Beloved*'s scene of instruction points to the contradictory valence of the slave narrative's maxim "In literacy was power" (Gates 1987: 108), so too do the "polemical admonishments against statutes forbidding literacy training among slaves" find another connotation. For the most part, in *Beloved* the exhortations are quietly reinscribed, set not in the context of polemic but in the context of everyday talk and activity. Sethe is taught "the alphabet" by members of the black community during her "twenty-eight days ... of healing, ease and realtalk" (B 95). Baby Suggs "always wished she could read the Bible like real preachers" (B 208). Denver discusses her father's philosophy of reading and writing – "But my daddy said, If you can't count they can cheat you. If you can't read they can beat you" – and decides that "it was good for me to learn how, and I did until it got quiet and all I could hear was my own breathing and one other who knocked over the milk jug while it was sitting on the table" (B 208).

But loudly resounding off the page is the painful irony of Sethe's making ink:

> "He [schoolteacher] liked the ink I made. It was her [Mrs. Garner's] recipe, but he preferred how I mixed it and it was important to him because at night he sat down to write in his book. It was a book about us but we didn't know that right away. We just thought it was his manner to ask us questions. He commenced to carry round a notebook and write down what we said. I still think it was them questions that tore Sixo up. Tore him up for all time." She stopped. (B 37)

When she begins again, she halts, still deciding whether or not she has the energy to beat back her tiredness. *I made the ink, Paul D. He couldn't have done it if I hadn't made the ink* (B 271). Within the violence of an economy in which Sethe made the ink used to write her into a book that would literally measure her alterity, the equation literacy equals power unmasks its sinister shadow. A terrifying recognition, from inside its embrace, of the mode of production that underwrote the laws against slave literacy and a harbinger of a continuing problem.

Beloved begins "124 was spiteful" and ends with the refrain "This is not a story to pass on." There are no apologies for the spite, although some are asked for, and there are no apologies for passing on a story that was not to be passed on. And yet, through an elaborate tapestry of oral-become-written storytelling, stitching the movements between past and present, between victimhood and agency, between limits and possibilities, a system is denounced, with perhaps less irony than the older narratives and with a great deal of studied passion. A system is denounced, but gently so too is the need to keep refuting, in the late twentieth century, that "*Blacks became slaves*, finally" (Robinson 1983: 176); that slavery created so total a condition of subjection that all trace of humanity vanished; that slavery became these African-Americans as the totality of their ontology. As Cedric Robinson and Morrison both suggest, it is indisputable that "slavery altered the conditions of their being" but also indisputable that slavery "could not negate their being" (ibid.: 177). Robinson's remarks about certifying or sanctifying this point over and over again are significant and worth quoting at length:

> The American revisionists . . . have transformed this African people into *human beings*, capable of judgment, injury, accommodation and heroism. In short, a people possessing, as Blassingame put it, 'the same range. . . .' To this point, their project has been successfully executed. . . . Still this 'political' triumph is but a partial one, for the defence of the slaves addresses its antagonists in their terms. Expectedly, in a post-slave society where the historical victory of the enslaved stratum was incomplete, the question of the humanity of the enslaved people would linger. It would . . . have to be spoken to. We now 'know' what the master class certainly knew but for so long publicly denied only to be confronted with the truth in its nightmares, its sexual fantasies and rotting social consciousness: the enslaved were human beings. But the more authentic question was not whether the slaves (and the ex-slaves and their descendants) were human. It was, rather, just what *sort* of people they were . . . and could be. (ibid.: 176–7)

And thus all the liberal abolitionist pressure to get the slave writer to display his or her humanity, hoping against hope to convince themselves of what was always a fragile truth, or in any event a limited one entirely compatible with a belief in the basic inequality of men, is left waiting in the wings as Morrison goes to the heart of Robinson's "more authentic question." What sort of people were the slaves and the former slaves and their descendants? What sort of people could they be? To be sure, these questions still participate in a "collective and individual reinvention of the discourse of 'slavery,'" but the perhaps unavoidable effort "attempt[s] to restore to a spatio-temporal object its eminent historicity, to evoke *person/persona* in the place of a 'shady' ideal" (Spillers 1989: 29).

If the slave narrative was expected to speak for those who had no audible public voice and who had no legal access to writing or to personhood, then *Beloved* will not only retell the story of Margaret Garner, but will also imagine the life world of those with no names we remember, with no "visible reason" for being in the archive. Morrison does not speak for them. She imagines them speaking their complex personhood as it negotiates the always coercive and subtle complexities of the hands of power. The slave narrative was supposed to corroborate the vitality of American ideologies of individualism. It said, "I have transcended absolutely impossible circumstances in order for this story to reach you." But it also had to disclaim its exceptionality in order to legitimately represent those who had no publicly sanctioned right to write, but were in the same circumstances. If the slave narrative had to struggle to manage such a crisis of representation, *Beloved*, by contrast, gives individual voices and faces to those who lacked public ones, but does so within a decentered structure of storytelling that deploys the sounds and rhythms of call and response.

But *Beloved* also problematizes the retrieval of lost or missing subjects by transforming those who do not speak into what is unspeakable, so that in that marvelous power of negative dialectics it can be conjured, imagined, worked out. What gestures the unspeakable? In this other sociology, which is willy-nilly another politics, the ghost gesticulates, signals, and sometimes mimics the unspeakable as it shines for both the remembered and the forgotten. This other sociology stretches at the limit of our imagination and at the limit of what is representable in the time of the now, to us, as the social world we inhabit. Stretching to bend, the close of *Beloved* summons the challenge: "Everybody knew what she was called, but nobody anywhere knew her name. Disremembered and unaccounted for, she cannot be lost because no one is looking for her, and even if they were, how can they call her if they don't know her name? Although she has claim, she is not claimed" (B 274).

Finally, then, if the slave narrative could not display a literary consciousness, because nothing that might prompt readers to suspect that they were reading fiction was permissible, in *Beloved* we are forced to contend with what might be the exemplar of "fictional pretenders to the real thing" (Andrews 1988: 91), that is, ghosts. Whatever can be said definitively about the long and varied traditions of African-American thought, writing, and radicalism, the social reality of haunting and the presence of ghosts are prominent features. The capacity not only to live with specters, in order to determine what sort of people they were and could be, but also to engage the ghost, heterogenously but cooperatively, as metaphor, as weapon, as salve, as a fundamental epistemology for living in the vortex of North America. The significance of ghosts and particularly spirit work in African-American culture and letters no doubt owes some of its origin to their respected place in African life and thought, "a consciousness implicated," as Robinson puts it, "in what Amos Tutuola so many generations later would name the 'bush of the ghosts'" (1983: 245; see also Christian 1993). But above and beyond the African inheritance, it is not so difficult to see that any people who are not graciously permitted to amend the past, or control the often barely visible structuring forces of everyday life, or who do not even secure the

moderate gains from the routine amnesia, that state of temporary memory loss that feels permanent and that we all need in order to get through the days, is bound to develop a sophisticated consciousness of ghostly haunts and is bound to call for an "official inquiry" into them.

[...]

A Long Way

Denver looked at her shoes. "At times. At times I think she was — more."
                              TONI MORRISON, *Beloved*

A woman walked out of the water thirsty and breathing hard having traveled a long distance looking for a face. Nobody counted on her walking out of the water. Especially the ones who counted. The others were more generous and took her for one of their own, even though she had not made the first passage, but arrived late, speaking in a language they recognized, but had needed to forget. They made her language their own and fell in love with her, but she was thirsty and breathing hard having traveled a long distance looking for a face. She remembered a ship men without skin iron waters angry limbs protruding wild sea beasts and the smell and look of the color red. They all had reasons to avoid remembering red and they all had reasons they never spoke to avoid remembering why the woman arrived late. *How bad is the scar?* But the woman saw a face in the waters she was desperate to find and so she walked out of the water thirsty and breathing hard having traveled a long distance looking for that face. She found one but it was not the one she saw in the waters, even though the face she found was also looking for a face she had lost. The woman drank the stories belonging to the face she found, trying to satisfy a hunger the other only fed. She was bound to be unforgiving. After all, she'd traveled a long distance, holding a memory the waters did not drown. *How bad is the scar?* But she was also bound to be forgotten again because her hunger was insatiable and the living could not afford to feed her. A woman walked out of the water thirsty and breathing hard having traveled a long distance looking for a face. Nobody counted on her walking out of the water, but when she did, she reminded them of things they had forgotten or hadn't even got around to remembering yet. *How bad is the scar?* A woman walked out of the water thirsty and breathing hard having traveled a long distance looking for a face. Nobody counted on her walking out of the water. Nobody counted her until she forced an accounting. But even then, she had come too far and they had their own memories that were looking for a story. *How bad is the scar?*

The ghost's desires? It is already a lot to deal with what keeps jarring and jamming the reconstructive efforts demanded by 1873, a bad and depressing year all around.

> She shook her head from side to side, resigned to her rebellious brain. Why was there nothing it refused? No misery, no regret, no hateful picture too rotten to accept? Like a greedy child it snatched up everything. Just once, could it say, No thank you? I just ate and can't hold another bite? . . . No thank you. I don't want to know or have to remember that. I have other things to do. (B 70)

The other things Sethe has to do involve refashioning her life and becoming a different somebody than she was before, hardly minor tasks; the whole project exacerbated by, if not doubly motivated by, the ghost in the haunted house. In this very personal process of reconstruction, which is intimately linked to the Reconstruction the date 1873 signs yet at a certain daily remove from it, the pressing problem of the present is the disjunction between a historical rupture (Emancipation) and the remaking of subjects. In a context in which History is said to be in the making all the exhilarating and troubling "choices and passions" that define an individual's life world – the things I have to do – converge on just that point where "determinism" or a collective logic of history spirals around them (Jameson 1991: 328). The relationship between subjection and subjectivity is an old problem, but not any less prevalent for being so persistent.

The year 1873 forms a crossroads in post–Civil War history. In the summer, the War Department and the Department of the Interior sponsored "competitive surveying expeditions" in South Dakota's Black Hills (Slotkin 1985: 329). These expeditions marked a turning point in the ongoing continuation of the Civil War as a Western war on Indian tribes. They consolidated the military's control of Indian policy and initiated extermination raids against the Sioux. The government surveys were the first step in opening Sioux lands to economic development, and 1873 advanced the alliance of white supremacism, industrial expansion, and permanent war. The year also brought industrial expansion to a halt in a collapse so protracted and severe that it was

known until the 1930s as the Great Depression. Recent advances in wages and working conditions were swept away by an increasingly Darwinian business environment that starved or crushed tens of thousands of small businesses and accelerated the concentration of ownership and economic control (Foner 1988: 513). Finally, the opposition to these fusions of racism, poverty, coercion, and violence known as Radical Reconstruction had entirely exhausted itself. Racial violence had pushed the Republican Congress to pass the rather strong Enforcement Acts and Ku Klux Klan Act in 1870 and 1871, but the rise of the Liberal Republicans prior to the election of 1872 had further weakened Republican support of Reconstruction. When the voice of reform itself spoke to the former slaves, as embodied in Liberal presidential candidate Horace Greeley, it said, "Root, Hog, or Die!" Radical Reconstruction had tried to combine the formal, legal freedom of Emancipation with the political self-rule and social resources that would make freedom secure and powerful. By 1873, these efforts were dead.

Morrison's oblique focus on the period in American history we call Reconstruction is instructive here. While only the crudest of structuralists (or the laziest of ideologues) reads a pronouncement as experiential reality, for many it has not been as obvious as it may seem that freedom is not secured when the state proclaims it thus. The pronouncement only inaugurates the lengthy walk into the discriminating contradictions of the newly heralded modernity. And indeed, no one in the novel (or, we can surely say, in real life) gained freedom from the pure fact of the Emancipation Proclamation. They either ran, were bought out of slavery by a relative, or were freeborn and actively assisted fugitives as they dealt with the Northern version of free racism in the post-Emancipation United States. Twenty years after the Emancipation Proclamation, the characters in *Beloved* are struggling with the knowledge that "freeing yourself was one thing; claiming ownership of that freed self was another" (B 95).

The novel takes on this crucial task of shifting the historical and analytic burden away from the Civil War and the Emancipation Proclamation as the decisive moment when America solved the problem, eliminated enslaving conditions, affirmed a new morality of the state, and made everyone free to Reconstruction. The "twenty awful years" (Du Bois [1935] 1992) from 1854 to 1877 enfold Morrison's story, a story about ordinary black people, now free and living in Ohio, trying to remake their lives in the shadow of a Reconstruction that turned out to be expansionist, militaristic, and subjugating. In this regard, the presence of Sixo, an Indian and slave at Sweet Home who "stopped speaking English because there was no future in it" (B 25), and the sick and dying fugitive Cherokee Paul D meets escaping from prison in Alfred, Georgia, who refused to walk to Oklahoma on the "trail of tears" when the discovery of gold in the Appalachians forced their removal in 1838, links east and west in the story of the regenerative violence (Slotkin 1973) that founds the United States in the crucible of the Civil War and the Emancipation Proclamation. Between 1860 and 1890, the West was finally "won" from the remaining free tribes in a series of wars that were absolutely essential to yet remain ideologically unassimilable to the Civil War, which constructed a nation freed from the tyranny and political-economic limitations of a slave economy. The Civil War and the appropriation of Indian Territory – a liminal category in which *Indian* is the foreign possessive name for a category, territory, which is the white man's future: a state to be – were the joint imperatives of a manifest destiny that enabled the official Reconstruction of the United States as a modern racial capitalist enterprise. This manifest destiny was already prophesied, and even the Sioux's Ghost Dance in 1890, a ceremonial hope for a "new land" where only Indians and the ghosts of their ancestors would live among "sweet grass," "running water and trees," and "great herds of buffalo and wild horses," could not prevent it (see Brown 1970: 389–412).

Reconstruction ratified a prevailing but limited notion of freedom as the freedom to own property, to sell one's labor, and to not be owned as property. From slave labor to wage labor, what kind of freedom did capitalist freedom produce? Although Baby Suggs is surprised and excited by the prospect of money – "Money? Money? They would pay her every single day? Money?" (B 144) – by the time Stamp Paid is tired enough to understand why, when they came into her yard, Baby Suggs got weary and just had to go to bed, he is already smelling "skin, skin and hot blood" (B 180). Smelling the lynchings and the long march of those now possessing "free" status into the twentieth century. Reconstruction was a failure politically, socially, and economically, and we still live today with the consequences of the great divide between legal right and substantive freedom.

Reconstruction is American History, but it also must perforce be fashioned by people who unavoidably make their long or short way – who remember and forget – in the vortex of those spiraling determinations. The inevitable but intrusive presence of spiraling determinations creates the haunting effect but also sets limits on what can be remembered and what needs to be reckoned with now in the very charged present. At the start of the novel, some seventeen years after she has murdered her baby, Sethe is immobilized. She cannot move forward and she is holding fast to her steely determination to keep the past at bay, hoping against hope that repressing it will bring the peaceful comfort she longs for. But Paul D lovingly touches (enlivens) the tree of scars on her back, which Sethe knows is there but cannot see or feel; Beloved arrives, the fleshy talking return of the repressed; and despite the fact that Paul D has run the specters out of the house, it is haunted again. In 1873 what haunts revolves around what can be remembered right then and there in Sethe's contemporaneity as she negotiates the complex and dangerous transferential relations that Beloved's arrival has generated. What can be remembered in 1873 is broadly contained in the statement passed down to us, *Margaret Garner, the slave mother . . . killed her child rather than see it taken back to slavery.* Yet we know there is more. Sethe cannot remember the more of Beloved's story, even though she believes that remembering and telling her own will explain Beloved's and reconcile the damage. There is a limit, the nature of which is lived history, to what Sethe and the community can remember or confront. *No thank you. I just ate and can't hold another bite.* This limit restricts our ability to rest secure in history as determinate context. (Indeed, it sets us the challenge of always taking the so-called answer, the determinate context, as the contentious soliciting question.) But such a limit also harbors the ineluctable promise of making contact with the ghostly haunt. *For taking the dead or the past back to a symbolic place is connected to the labor aimed at creating in the present a place (a past or future), a something that must be done.* Almost at the end of the Reconstruction that will be a failure, excited about new prospects but also tired, the memories and nightmares of Sweet Home all too vivid, the baby ghost living in the house, what could Sethe and Paul D and the rest possibly remember if not that which would create a hospitality for the present?

Yet we know there is more. We know that it is Beloved's *how can I say things that are pictures* (B 210) that marks the other side of the limit of what Sethe's rebellious brain refuses to accept. And we also know that a conflict is readied between Sethe and Beloved because despite the seeming saturation of having remembered it all – of thinking that everything repressed has returned made patently clear to Sethe by the ghost's very live manifestation – there is more. Unfortunately (for it would be simpler), it is not a question of assuming that if Sethe could only remember the more of Beloved's story she would have the whole story. The whole story is always a working fiction that satisfies the need to deliver what cannot possibly be available. You might recall that Beloved had two dreams, *exploding and being swallowed*, and these are monitory premonitions for us all. Morrison makes us aware here of the problem of exploding or being swallowed as she operationalizes her haunting theory of rememory. As we approach Beloved from Sethe's point of view, we can see how she acts as a screen for the memory of Sethe's dead child (Freud [1899] 1953–74). As Sethe grapples with the memory of the child and why she killed her, Beloved as ghost is a haunting reminder of what Sethe and not Beloved must contend with. And in a sense she couldn't be otherwise because Beloved's return and the repetition and displacement of memory the whole text stages must remain partial to the living, to 1873. *When the living take the dead or the past back to a symbolic place, it is connected to the labor aimed at creating in the present a something that must be done.* But we also approach Beloved now in the late twentieth century under different conditions, and when we do we are reminded of what Morrison's characters cannot remember or digest in 1873: the more of Beloved's story as a slave-to-be who never arrived, a history of barely legible traces imagined or conjured up out of *Documents Illustrative of the Slave Trade*. *They never knew where or why she crouched* or quite understood that the ghost haunting them could be haunted too. *We* can admit the haunted ghost into evidence and she gives notice, paradoxically, to the unspeakability of her story and to her yearnings:

"Ain't you got no brothers or sisters?"
… "I don't have nobody."
"What was you looking for when you came here?"
… "This place. I was looking for this place I could be in."
"Somebody tell you about this house?"
"She told me. When I was at the bridge, she told me."
… "How'd you come? Who brought you?" … "I asked you who brought you here?"
"I walked here…. A long, long, long, long way. Nobody bring me. Nobody help me." (B 65)

And if we shift perspective, begin to approach the ghost's desires, what will we find?

An Engraving

The clearest memory she had, the one she repeated, was the bridge – standing on the bridge looking down.

TONI MORRISON, *Beloved*

how can I say things that are pictures. Beloved is trying desperately to remind them, to tell them something about a passage they have mostly forgotten, but "the repressed is not easily discerned; its language is a graphic presence of bodies conjured up from visions or memories of other worlds" (Conley 1988: xix). She has pictures of another world she is trying to conjure up for them so that she may find calmer waters. *the man on my face the men without skin small rats crouching standing the little hill of dead people the circle around her neck the bridge flowers a face song is gone* (B 210–13). A ghostly presence, she has come a long way alone to haunt their present, to quench her thirst, to listen to their stories, to ask them questions, to find the face she lost. She is looking for them. She is looking for a place to be in. Somebody told her to look there. *The clearest memory she had … was the bridge – standing on the bridge looking down.*

I look for her in the archive, and among the charters, ship logs, and cash receipts I find an engraving. The engraving of the plan and cross section of the slaver *Brookes*, "officially sponsored by the Abolitionist Society," was "sent 'to the Members of both Houses of Parliament & to such other persons as may be thought expedient by the Committee of Distribution'" on the occasion of "William Wilberforce's speech in the House of Commons on 12 May [1789] proposing a resolution for the abolition of the slave trade" (Honour 1989: 64–5). The purpose of the engraving is to create an impression of the violence of the slave trade so that we – who were not on the ship – can apprehend its essence. The engraving does create an impression of the dehumanization of the slave trade, but it does so unwittingly, by being able to represent only the plan of the ship and the space for its cargo. The invisibility and the insignificance of the men, women, and children who inhabited the 6 *feet by 1 foot 4 inches* (men), *5 feet 10 in. by 1 foot 4 in.* (women), *5 feet by 1 foot* (boys), and *4 feet 6 in. by 1 foot* (girls) allotted them is an offense that cannot be avowed in the representation itself. Were it to be allowed, the "historical and social consciousness of these Africans," what *they* carried in their nakedness on the ship with them, the ship that supposedly carried only cargo and not culture, would have to be present in some form.

> These cargoes . . . did not consist of intellectual isolates or deculturated blanks – men, women and children separated from their previous universe. African labour brought the past with it, a past which had produced it and settled on it the first elements of consciousness and comprehension. . . . It would be through the historical and social consciousness of these Africans that the trade in slaves and the system of slave labour was infected with its contradiction. (Robinson 1983: 173; emphasis in the original)

And so the signs of this consciousness, the cultural "seeds" of contradiction and "opposition" (Cabral in Robinson 1983: 174), were removed from the Description, an example if there ever was one of that civilizing document that is at the same time a document of barbarism. Our ghost – and she is our ghost because we do see her *how can I say things that are pictures* there where these things have been removed – is buried alive in this scriptural tomb of a Description although her "absence [is] so stressed, so ornate, so planned [it] call[s] attention to [itself]" (Morrison 1989: 11). The call to attention is our inheritance of the history of an exchange of people whose official history leaves only the Description of a Slave Ship, a description that forces us to imagine what it only gestures toward; that forces us to call again for an "official inquiry," this time into the condition of the haunting remainder of the ship, its ghosts.

To perfons unacquainted with the mode of carrying on this fyftem of trading in human flefh, thefe Plans and Sections will appear rather a fiction, than a real reprefentation of a flave-fhip. A recognition that real representations are fictions too enables us to find the "imaginary zone . . . every culture has . . . for what it excludes," for what is personally, historically, and sociologically unspeakable (Cixous and Clément 1986: 6). A recognition that real representations are fictive too disrupts the illusion that we could find the real woman precisely where she will not be, in the "Description" that is the real representation. Lost on the way from there – Africa – to here – America – Beloved is a sign without a referent for those to whom her return is addressed. *Everybody knew what she was called, but nobody anywhere knew her name. Disremembered and unaccounted for, she cannot be lost because no one is looking for her, and even if they were, how can they call her if they don't know her name? Although she has claim, she is not claimed* (B 274). Claimed or not, "somewhere every

culture has an imaginary zone for what it excludes and it is that zone we must try to remember today." We must try to remember today if for no other reason than that a ghost is haunting the living, forcing us in that uncanny way hauntings have to "track the image" or the apparition "back to a *point of density*" – the engraving – and toward a "*potentiality* induced from a *dispersion* of gestures" (Spillers 1989: 51). And in this sense, haunting is essential to this laborious work. After all, we need to know that something is missing in order to even begin to look for it or its dispersion of gestures anywhere, in the archive or in the imaginary zone. The ghostly haunt gives precisely this notification. *The clearest memory she had . . . was the bridge – standing on the bridge looking down.* The ghostly haunt says, Something is happening you hadn't expected. It says, Something is making an appearance to you that had been kept from view. It says, Do something about the wavering present the haunting is creating.

If we make a leap I realize is not easy and try to grasp the ghost's standpoint, its voice only ever fragmentary fantastic pictures, we are led to conclude that the ghost is a living force. It may reside elsewhere in an otherworldly domain but it is never intrinsically Other. It has a life world, in the strongest sense of the term, of its own. And it carries this life world with all its sweet things, its nastiness, and its yearnings into ours as it makes its haunting entry, making itself a phenomenological reality. There is no question that when a ghost haunts, that haunting is real. The ghost has an agency on the people it is haunting and we can call that agency desire, motivation, or standpoint. And so its desires must be broached and we have to talk to it. *The ghosts desire*, even if it is nothing more than a potent and conjectural fiction, must be recognized (and we may be able to do no more than simply feel its haunting impact) if we are to admit that the ghost, particularly as it functions as a figure for that which is invisible but not necessarily not there, is capable "of strategy towards us" (Spivak 1989: 273). *Sethe's is the face that left me . . . her smiling face is the place for me* (B 213).

But the modus operandi of a ghost is haunting, and haunting makes its only social meaning in contact with the living's time of the now. As Barbara Christian (1993) suggests, the need of the dead to be remembered and accommodated, and these are two of Beloved's cravings, is inseparable from the needs of the living. In other words, the ghost is nothing without you. In this sense, the ghost figures what systematically continues to work on the here and now. When a ship, a bridge, a face, an inert object, an ordinary building, a familiar workplace, a patch of grass, a photograph, a house becomes animated, becomes haunted, it is the complexities of its social relations that the ghostly figures. This sociality, the wavering present, forces a something that must be done that structures the domain of the present and the prerogatives of the future.

[…]

We are asked, then, to consider two counterintuitive features of haunting. The first is that the ghost cannot be simply tracked back to an individual loss or trauma. The ghost has its own desires, so to speak, which figure the whole complicated sociality of a determining formation that seems inoperative (like slavery) or invisible (like racially gendered capitalism) but that is nonetheless alive and enforced. But the force of the ghost's desire is not just negative, not just the haunting and staged words, marks, or gestures of domination and injury. The ghost is not other or alterity as such, ever. It is (like Beloved) pregnant with unfulfilled possibility, with the something to be done that the wavering present is demanding. This something to be done is not a return to the past but a reckoning with its repression in the present, a reckoning with that which we have lost, but never had. The ghost always also figures this utopian dimension of haunting, encapsulated in the very first lines of Jacques Derrida's book on specters: "Someone, you or me, comes forward and says: *I would like to learn to live finally*" (1994: xvii).

The second feature of haunting we are asked to consider involves this wavering yet determinate social structure, or what we could call history. History, Morrison suggests, is that ghostly (abstract in the Marxist sense) totality that articulates and disarticulates itself and the subjects who inhabit it. It is, in contrast to sociology and other modern retrieval enterprises, never available as a final solution for the difficulties haunting creates for the living. It is always a site of struggle and contradiction between the living and the ghostly, a struggle whose resolution has to remain partial to the living, even when the living can only partially grasp the source of the ghost's power. What is not so counterintuitive is Morrison's broadest claim that we should beware forgetting the enslavement or domination that persists and that often masquerades as emancipation or freedom.

A woman walked out of the water breathing hard, and we are reminded that when ghosts haunt, that haunting is material. A woman walked out of the water breathing

hard having traveled a long distance looking for a face, and we are reminded that her desires will make all the difference to those she meets. A woman walked out of the water thirsty and breathing hard having traveled a long distance looking for a face, and we are reminded that she returned to a place and a time she never was. A place and a time where her arrival could only be understood within the memoryscape her haunting both produced and interrupted. A woman walked out of the water thirsty and breathing hard and within the gap between more memories than seem tolerable and there being still more, we are reminded of haunting's affliction and its yearning for a something that must be done.

Reference

Andrews, William L. 1988. "Dialogue in Antebellum Afro-American Autobiography." In *Studies in Autobiography*, ed. James Olney, 89–98. New York: Oxford University Press.

Angelo, Bonnie. 1989. "'The Pain of Being Black': An Interview with Toni Morrison." *Time*, May 22, 120–2.

Brown, Dee. 1970. *Bury My Heart at Wounded Knee*. New York: Washington Square.

Christian, Barbara. 1993. "Fixing Methodologies: *Beloved.*" *Cultural Critique* 24 (Spring):5–15.

Cixous, Hélène, and Catherine Clément. 1986. *The Newly Born Woman*. Trans. Betsy Wing. Minneapolis: University of Minnesota Press.

Clemons, Walter. 1987. "A Gravestone of Memories." *Newsweek*, September 28, 74–75.

Conley, Tom. 1988. "Translator's Introduction: *For a Literary Historiography.*" In Michel de Certeau, *The Writing of History*, trans. Tom Conley, vii–xxviii. New York: Columbia University Press.

Cruz, Jon. 1999. *Culture on the Margins*. Princeton, NJ: Princeton University Press.

Davis, Charles T., and Henry Louis Gates Jr., eds. 1985. *The Slave's Narrative*. New York: Oxford University Press.

Dent, Gina. "Developing Africa into America: The Role of Anthropology in the Literary History of Blackness." Forthcoming Ph.D. dissertation, Columbia University.

Derrida, Jacques. 1994. *Specters of Marx: The State of the Debt, the Work of Mourning, and the New International*. Trans. Peggy Kamuf. New York: Routledge.

Du Bois, W. E. B. [1935] 1992. *Black Reconstruction in America*. New York: Atheneum.

Foner, Eric. 1988. *Reconstruction: America's Unfinished Revolution 1863–1877*. New York: Harper & Row.

Freud, Sigmund [1899] 1953–74. "Screen Memories." Trans. James Stratchey. *The Standard Edition of the Complete Works of Sigmund Freud (SE)*, vol. 3. London: Hogarth Press and the Institute of Psycho-Analysis.

Gates, Henry Louis Jr. 1987. *Figures in Black: Words, Signs, and the "Racial" Self*. New York: Oxford University Press.

———. 1988b. "James Gronniosaw and the Trope of the Talking Book." In *Studies in Autobiography*, ed. James Olney, 51–72. New York: Oxford University Press.

Honour, Hugh. 1989. *The Image of the Black in Western Art*, Vol. 4, Part 1: *Slaves and Liberators*. Cambridge, Mass.: Harvard University Press.

Jameson, Fredric. 1991. *Postmodernism: or, The Cultural Logic of Late Capitalism*. Durham, NC: Duke University Press.

Morrison, Toni. 1987a. *Beloved*. New York: Knopf.

———. 1989. "Unspeakable Things Unspoken: The Afro-American Presence in American Literature." *Michigan Quarterly Review* 28, 1:1–34.

Robinson, Cedric J. 1983. *Black Marxism: The Making of the Black Radical Tradition*. London: Zed Books.

Sekora, John. 1988. "Is the Slave Narrative a Species of Autobiography?" In *Studies in Autobiography*, ed. James Olney, 99–111. New York: Oxford University Press.

Slotkin, Richard. 1973. *Regeneration through Violence: The Mythology of the American Frontier, 1600–1860*. Middletown, Conn.: Wesleyan University Press.

———. 1985. *The Fatal Environment: The Myth of the Frontier in the Age of Industrialization, 1800–1890*. New York: Atheneum.

Spillers, Hortense J. 1989. "Changing the Letter: The Yokes, the Jokes of Discourse, or, Mrs. Stowe, Mr. Reed." In *Slavery and the Literary Imagination*, ed. Deborah E. McDowell and Arnold Rampersad, 25–61. Baltimore: Johns Hopkins University Press.

Spivak, Gayatri Chakravorty. 1989. "Who Claims Alterity?" In *Remaking History*, ed. Barbara Kruger and Phil Mariani, 269–92. Seattle: Bay Press.

The Lost Cause and Causes Not Lost

David Blight

The lost cause took root in a Southern culture awash in an admixture of physical destruction, the psychological trauma of defeat, a Democratic Party resisting Reconstruction, racial violence, and with time, an abiding sentimentalism. On the broadest level, it came to represent a mood, or an attitude toward the past. It took hold in specific arguments, organizations, and rituals, and for many Southerners it became a natural extension of evangelical piety, a civil religion that helped them link their sense of loss to a Christian conception of history. Like all great mythologies, the Lost Cause changed with succeeding generations and shifting political circumstances.[1]

From the late 1860s to the late 1880s, diehards, especially though not exclusively in Virginia, tended to shape the Confederate memory. They made Robert E. Lee into the God-like embodiment of a leader whose cause could be defeated only by overpowering odds. Thus ennobled in a revolution crushed by industrial might, and newly emboldened by a sense of righteousness born of successful resistance to radical Reconstruction, the Lost Cause emerged by the 1890s as that oft-told explanation of history that O'Ferrall and Johnson had represented at the dedication of the Confederate Museum. But by the 1890s, and until at least World War I, the Confederate memorial movement came under the control of new leadership and organizations, especially the United Daughters of the Confederacy (UDC) and the United Confederate Veterans (UCV). The mass of rank-and-file former Confederates (the majority of whom now lived in states west of the eastern seaboard) formed the grassroots of Lost Cause ritual activity. During this surge of Lost Cause sentiment Southerners succeeded, by and large, in

helping shape a national reunion on their own terms. By the turn of the century, the Lost Cause (as cultural practice and as a set of arguments) served two aims – reconciliation and Southern partisanship. For natural reasons, some Lost Cause traditions began to wane in the wake of the Spanish-American War of 1898, and through the patriotic upheavals of World War I. But many of the assumptions of Confederate memory forged over fifty years endured to haunt America into the 1920s and beyond.[2] Especially in racial terms, the cause that was *not* lost, as Johnson had insisted in 1896, reverberated as part of the very heartbeat of the Jim Crow South.

Throughout the spread of the Lost Cause, at least three elements attained overriding significance: the movement's effort to write and control the *history* of the war and its aftermath; its use of *white supremacy* as both means and ends; and the place of *women* in its development. From the earliest days of memorial activity, the diehards were determined to collect and write a Confederate version of the history of the war. Frequently disclaiming partisanship, and eager to establish what they so frequently called the "truth of history," diehard Lost Cause advocates, many of them high-ranking officers and political leaders of the Confederacy, forged one of the most highly orchestrated grassroots partisan histories ever conceived.

From his prison release in 1867 to his death in 1889, Jefferson Davis set the tone for the diehards' historical interpretation. In private and public utterances, Davis's fierce defense of state rights doctrine and secession, his incessant pleas for "Southern honor," and his mystical conception of the Confederacy gave ideological fuel to diehards. It was forever a "misnomer to apply the term 'Rebellion'" to the Confederacy, Davis wrote in 1874. "Sovereigns cannot rebel." Diehards could look to Davis for endless expressions of solemn faith. "We may not hope to see the rebuilding of the temple as our Fathers designed it," Davis counseled a friend in 1877, "but we can live on praying for that event and die with eyes fixed on the promised land."[3]

In his two-volume, 1,279-page memoir, *The Rise and Fall of the Confederate Government*, Davis wrote what may be the longest and most self-righteous legal brief on behalf of a failed political movement ever done by an American. He placed responsibility for secession and the war entirely at the feet of the North. The South's action was merely to protect its natural rights against the "tremendous and sweeping usurpation," the "unlimited, despotic power" of the federal government. Every war measure enacted by the Lincoln administration or by Congress, from confiscation to emancipation, was a further step in the "serpent seeking its prey." In his defense of the Confederacy, Davis developed a case for what James McPherson has called the "virgin-birth theory of secession: the Confederacy was not conceived by any worldly cause, but by divine principle."[4]

In language that became almost omnipresent in Lost Cause rhetoric, Davis insisted that slavery "was in no wise the cause of the conflict, but only an incident." Moreover, he contributed a defense of slavery itself that was as direct as any written in the postwar South. "Generally," Davis claimed, African Americans' ancestors "were born the slaves of barbarian masters, untaught in all the useful arts and occupations, reared in heathen darkness, and, sold by heathen masters, they were transferred to shores enlightened by the rays of Christianity." In this benevolent environment now crushed by Yankee armies and politicians, blacks had been

put to servitude . . . trained in the gentle arts of peace and order and civilization; they increased from a few unprofitable savages to millions of efficient Christian laborers. Their servile instincts rendered them contented with their lot, and their patient toil blessed the land of their abode with unmeasured riches. Their strong local and personal attachment secured faithful service . . . Never was there happier dependence of labor and capital on each other. The tempter came, like the serpent of Eden, and decoyed them with the magic word of "freedom" . . . He put arms in their hands, and trained their humble but emotional natures to deeds of violence and bloodshed, and sent them out to devastate their benefactors.[5]

Davis helped give the Lost Cause its lifeblood. Here again were the faithful slaves, the natural-born laborers in the idyll of the Old South performing a new service – they were the broken symbols of lost glory and Yankee idiocy. It is telling to observe that virtually all major spokespersons for the Lost Cause could not develop their story of a heroic, victimized South without the images of faithful slaves and benevolent masters – the "sovereigns" of a state had to be protecting something besides principles on parchment. And so, in such reasoning, was the Civil War about and not about slavery.

Davis had many predecessors upon whose work he built his mystical defense of the Confederacy. The diehard era (1860–late 1880s) of the Lost Cause emerged in several polemical books in the immediate postwar years, and especially in new magazines founded as the vehicles of Southern vindication. In his book *The Lost Cause* (1866), Edward Pollard warned that what the South had lost on battlefields it would carry on in a "war of ideas." Only two years later, with his militancy under more control and no longer urging Southerners to still take up arms, Pollard wrote a campaign tract, *The Lost Cause Regained* (1868), in which he counseled reconciliation with conservative Northerners on Southern terms. Those terms coalesced in a central idea. "To the extent of securing the supremacy of the white man," wrote Pollard, "and the traditional liberties of the country . . . she [the South] really triumphs in the true cause of the war." Alfred Taylor Bledsoe, a former professor of mathematics at the University of Virginia and undersecretary of war in the Confederacy, led the diehards in the defense of secession. His *Is Davis a Traitor, or Was Secession a Constitutional Right before 1861?* (1866) and *A Constitutional View of the Late War between the States* (1868–70) laid out a vehement justification of state rights doctrine. Most importantly, Bledsoe created a polemical magazine, the *Southern Review*, in Baltimore in 1867. Along with D. H. Hill's *The Land We Love*, founded in 1866 in Charlotte, North Carolina, the *Southern Review* kept up an intensive defense of the Confederate legacy until the end of Reconstruction. Indeed, the political and racial struggles over Reconstruction policy itself became central themes of these magazines, most of which faded away with the steady growth of political reconciliation in the late 1870s.[6] In organizations, however, the Lost Cause found new and more permanent footing.

The earliest Confederate veterans' groups formed around two aims: charity to members and families, and as the Charleston, South Carolina, Survivors'

Association put it, to create "a Southern history." In these first years after the war, Confederate veteran activists devoted themselves to the most basic duty of memorialization, tabulating elaborate rolls of honor of both the living and the dead. But with meager resources at the local levels, they sought to carry on the battle for historical memory as well. In 1869, the leader of the New Orleans Survivors' Association invited his counterpart in Charleston to share in this historical enterprise. "We wish to collect," wrote Reverend B. M. Palmer to Edward McGrady, "everything that can illustrate the history of our Southern country . . . to publish volumes of transactions, spreading before our people and before the world the very documents from which all true history is to be drawn." Within the South Carolina association, a Rock Hill veteran wrote to the leadership, endorsing as its central objective "the necessity of transmitting the *truth* to posterity."[7] In its earliest manifestations, therefore, the Lost Cause was born out of grief, but just as importantly, it formed in the desire to contend for control of the nation's memory. Whatever the extent of Union victory on the battlefield, the verdicts to be rendered in history and memory were not settled at Appomattox.

From its beginnings in New Orleans in 1869, in its original circular letter, the Southern Historical Society (SHS) declared its object to be the "collection, classification, preservation, and final publication" of the Confederate story. The founders of the SHS announced that their society would not represent "purely sectional" interests, "nor that its labors shall be of a partisan character." But in all its work the organization sought to "vindicate the truth of history."[8] Many ex-Confederates put enormous faith in history as their source of justification. While the history they had lived ruined them, the history they would help write might redeem them.

The editor of the *SHS Papers*, J. William Jones, and the society's members who wrote so vigorously, labored as though they were under a literary siege. Like all polemicists, in the sheer repetition of the word "truth" they claimed credibility and sought justification. The SHS's fifth annual report acknowledged contributors of "material for a true history of the war," offered its aid to writers "elucidating the truth of Confederate history," and praised supporters for choosing the "cause of truth" over money with their donations of personal collections. For all to see, the official seal of the SHS, blazoned on the cover of every volume, contained the slogan: "Truth Is the Proper Antagonist of Error." The SHS worked from the assumption that the war's victors would never do them

justice in the history books or in the emerging memoir literature. Based on the collection they had assembled in the offices reserved for them in the Virginia state capitol, the SHS leadership put their faith in the power of documentation.[9] These ex-soldiers demanded respect and would try to argue their way to righteousness before the bar of history.

In the early years of forging Lost Cause ideology, diehards fashioned a historical creed, demanded discipleship, and worked with urgency to counter Northern histories. "Our adversaries leave no stone unturned to defeat us through the South," wrote former general John B. Gordon in 1872 as vice president of a publishing firm. "Their offensive books" demanded answers, Gordon maintained. "We must meet their attacks when it seems wise to do so." To the charge from Jubal Early that he had become too infected with "progressive ideas to care for the preservation of history," the former presidential candidate and Confederate general John C. Breckinridge assured Early that he "would know better some day. I seek no man's society who speaks of us as 'traitors,' nor will I associate with our former adversaries upon the basis of mere sufferance." Early told a fellow diehard in 1871 that he kept very active fighting Northerners' false history. "Every now and then," he wrote to D. H. Hill, "I manage to land a bomb against the enemy, in the way of exploding some of their lies, and that affords me some consolation." In his windy way, P. G. T. Beauregard rejoiced over the creation of the SHS. "After having taken an active part in *making* history," he wrote to Early, the job of the generals was to "see that it is correctly *written*." Robert S. Dabney, a chaplain and chief of staff for Stonewall Jackson during the early part of the war and one of the most unreconcilable of the diehards, saw the Lost Cause as a sacred trust that required theological devotion and a strong sense of denial. In his *A Defense of Virginia and through Her of the South* (1867), Dabney was obsessed with historical judgments about the war and Southern slaveholding. He believed the South had "been condemned unheard," and that the "pens" of its "statesmen" had been too silent. In the tradition of the older proslavery writers, Dabney praised the South as an "organic" society, the bulwark against all the disorder now championed by radical Republicanism. In one of the most desperate expressions of the diehard spirit, Dabney called on Southerners to wield the pen and count on God. Yankees would ultimately meet their just fate, Dabney believed, "in the day of their calamity, in the pages of impartial history, and in the Day of Judgment."[10]

Until his death in 1894, Dabney was never at home in the world the war had made. Almost as much as he hated Yankee rule, he eventually condemned the New South movement for its materialism and anti-agrarianism. Dabney believed Southerners needed major literary works that would do for them what John Foxe's *Book of Martyrs* had done for seventeenth-century English Protestants. "The South needs a book of 'Acts and Monuments of Confederate Martyrs,'" he told D. H. Hill in 1873. Dabney argued that Southern writers should model the pathos of *Uncle Tom's Cabin*, but in reverse. "Paint the picture skillfully," he urged, "of Southern martyrdom under ruthless abolition outrages." He called for "helpless sufferings of *weakness* under the brute hand of merciless *power*."[11] This was not quite the kind of Lost Cause that Thomas Nelson Page would give the nation, but it did eventually find its author in Thomas Dixon's *The Clansman* (1905) and its immortal place in motion pictures in D. W. Griffith's *Birth of a Nation* (1915).

As in most lost causes, ex-Confederates had scores to settle with each other as well as with their former enemies. In their canonization of Lee, Virginians in particular sought to make James Longstreet the scapegoat for the Southern loss at Gettysburg. In a speech at the dedication of the Lee Chapel in Lexington, Virginia, in January 1873, William Nelson Pendleton, Lee's chief of artillery, attacked Longstreet. Longstreet was a Georgian and scorned by the diehards for renouncing Lost Cause sentiments and urging his fellow Southerners to get on with rebuilding their economy as early as 1867. He was especially vilified for being "so slow" in his attacks on the second and third days of the battle of Gettysburg. A bitter controversy raged until the end of the century over these charges against Longstreet and lasted even longer in the enduring Lee legend. In spite of ample evidence to demonstrate that Lee himself had deeply respected Longstreet, this dispute had a long life in the pages of the *SHS Papers* and elsewhere because essential tenets of the Lost Cause were at stake – the military and moral infallibility of Lee, and the myth of Confederate invincibility.[12]

By the late 1870s, diehards were no longer merely explaining defeats; they had a victory to bequeath to history as well. From the beginning, Lost Cause diehards attacked Reconstruction policy nearly as much as they appealed for history true to the Confederate cause. After acknowledging Ulysses Grant's appeal for "peace," Jubal Early ended an article on federal numerical superiority during the war with a diatribe against the current situation in the South in 1870. The elections of 1870, claimed Early, were "superintended by armed agents of the United States Government . . . for the purpose of perpetuating the power of the ruling faction, through the instrumentality of the ballot in the hands of an inferior race." When John T. Morgan addressed the 1877 annual meeting of the SHS, he portrayed the period 1868–77 as the "nine years war of Reconstruction" and the era of "dishonorable oppression for an unworthy cause." Reconstruction, Morgan maintained, had been the "second war." "If we have now met in peace and reconciliation upon the broad concessions, mutually accepted, that the war was not a crime," he said, "we need not inquire who was right or who was wrong." In such language, Lost Cause advocates found a victory narrative. They had won the second war over Reconstruction; they had thrown off "Negro rule" and redeemed their states. In a speech to a group of veterans of the Army of the Tennessee in July 1878, Jefferson Davis made the victory over Reconstruction an explicit element of Lost Cause ideology. The normally morose Davis described a cause reflowering in a new season. "Well may we rejoice in the regained possession of local self-government," Davis said, "in the power of people to . . . legislate uncontrolled by bayonets. This is the great victory . . . a total non-interference by the Federal Government with the domestic affairs of the States."[13] By regaining home rule, defeating black equality, and throwing off all vestiges of Reconstruction, the South had found a new cause: a story of redemption and victory that could serve the ends of both diehards and reconciliationists.

During the 1890s, three entities took control of the Lost Cause: the United Confederate Veterans (UCV), founded in 1889; a new magazine, the *Confederate Veteran*, founded in 1893 and edited in Nashville by Sumner A. Cunningham; and the United Daughters of the Confederacy (UDC), founded in 1894. Both the UCV and the UDC grew rapidly as organizations that complemented one another. The UCV was born in New Orleans in June 1889, out of a growing impulse among local veteran organizations to amalgamate into larger groups. Survivors' associations and associations of particular armies had long engaged in fraternal support and local remembrance. But as the national reunion took hold, so too did ex-Confederates seek more national forms of expression. The UCV's first commander-in-chief was former US Senator and then governor of Georgia, John B. Gordon. Gordon was a New South politician with heroic credentials, and he provided an eloquent voice for both Confederate memory and reconciliation on Southern economic and political terms. By 1896, the UCV had 850 local camps, and by 1904, they had 1,565. The geographical distribution of UCV camps included at least one in 75 percent of the counties of the eleven former Confederate states. The best estimate of membership in the UCV seems to be 80,000 to 85,000 in 1903, a peak year.[14] Appealing to the interests of the ordinary veteran, especially against the fears and trials of 1890s economic collapse and political turmoil, the UCV became a safe haven of comradeship and celebration for the full range of Lost Cause attitudes and rituals.

For its part, the UDC spread across the South and also established some chapters in the North. By 1900, the UDC boasted 412 chapters and 17,000 members in twenty states and territories. By World War I it may have had as many as 100,000 members engaged in a wide variety of memorial activities. The generally well-heeled UDC women were strikingly successful at raising money to build Confederate monuments, lobbying legislatures and Congress for the reburial of Confederate dead, and working to shape the content of history textbooks. They distributed tens of thousands of dollars in college scholarships to granddaughters and grandsons of Confederate veterans. The UDC ran essay contests to raise historical consciousness among white Southern youth, and by the turn of the century they had launched an ongoing campaign to designate "War between the States" as the official name for the conflict. In all their efforts, the UDC planted a white supremacist vision of the Lost Cause deeper into the nation's historical imagination than perhaps any other association. Working largely from women's sphere as guardians of piety, education, and culture, many UDC members nonetheless led public-activist lives; although most opposed women's suffrage, many of their leaders were intensely political people. Behind, and often at the center of, every Confederate reunion (their pictures adorning the pages of nearly every issue of the *Confederate Veteran*) were UDC women, old and young, the "auxiliaries," "sponsors," and "maids of honor" without which the Lost Cause could not have dominated Southern public culture as it did.[15]

The UDC served its patrician class interest, but its activists both eroded and hardened the bonds of Southern womanhood. UDC women included advocates of women's suffrage as well as those who opposed it. Women such as Lila Meade Valentine of Richmond might grow up ensconced in the planter class and weighted down with the full burden of the Lost Cause as well as the expectations of a Southern "Lady." But some, as in Valentine's case, became gradualist, progressive reformers and persistent crusaders for women's rights.

Valentine embraced most tenets of the Lost Cause, but also became president of the Equal Suffrage League in Virginia. Within women's sphere, and while preserving a genteel white supremacy, women like Valentine believed the "New South Lady" could be the agent by which the whole South could transcend the legacies of defeat and Reconstruction.[16]

At a proliferating array of veterans' reunions that Southern cities competed to host, and in oratory and writings, Confederate memory transformed into a set of arguments for a cause not lost. Ex-Confederates still had much to mourn, but the Lost Cause now appeared more as chapters in a victory narrative. This new ideology still nurtured dogmatism and mysticism, but it took hold in five potent arguments. First, veterans and the Daughters continued to glorify the valor of Southern soldiers and to defend their honor as defensive warriors who were never truly beaten in battle. Second, Lost Cause advocates of the 1890s especially promoted the Confederate past as a bulwark against all the social and political disorder of that tumultuous decade. Third, the UCV and the UDC established history committees that guarded the Confederate past against all its real and imagined enemies. Fourth, contrary to the norm in Blue-Gray fraternalism, many Lost Cause writers and activists during the reconciliationist era were not at all shy of arguing about the *causes* of the war. Fifth, and most strikingly, a nostalgic Lost Cause reinvigorated white supremacy by borrowing heavily from the plantation school of literature in promoting reminiscences of the *faithful slave* as a central figure in the Confederate war. Together, these arguments reinforced Southern pride, nationalized the Lost Cause, and racialized Civil War memory for the postwar generations.

Sentimental journeys into Civil War memory had become a national pastime. In *The Mind of the South*, Wilbur Cash observed that "the growth of the Southern legend was even more sentimental than it was grandiloquent." It was both. Under the influence of Thomas Nelson Page and others, the Lost Cause spread by pathos and pompousness. In his fictional stories, Page touched every chord of Lost Cause emotion. "The Gray Jacket of 'No. 4'" (1892) ends with a Confederate veterans' parade where, in a crowd rising as a "tempest" at the sight of the old soldiers,

Men wept; children shrilled; women sobbed aloud. What was it! Only a thousand or two of old or aging men riding or tramping along through the dust of the street, under some old flags, dirty and ragged and stained. But they represented the spirit of the South; they represented the spirit which when honor was in question never counted the cost; the spirit that had stood up . . . against overwhelming odds . . .; the spirit that is the strongest guaranty to us today what the Union is and is to be; the spirit . . . glorious in victory . . . yet greater in defeat.

And in his nonfiction such as *The Old South* (1892), Page gave Lost Cause ideology full voice. The heroism of the South almost surpassed understanding, according to Page. The North had arrayed the "world against her . . . its force was as the gravitation of the earth – imperceptible, yet irresistible."[17] The South had lost, but only by gloriously resisting the engines of nature itself.

Here was the South as America's fallen man, the source of sacrificial blood for the remission of national sins – "greater in defeat." Hence the reunion was dependent upon a New South still draped in images of the Old. As with soldiers' reminiscence, such sentimentalism met with a warm welcome among powerful Northern publishers. In 1890, Richard Watson Gilder imperiously rejoiced at "how much more national" Northern periodicals had become because of the presence of Southern writers. "It is well for the North, it is well for the nation," said Gilder, "to hear in poem and story all that the South burns to tell of her romance, her heroes, her landscapes; yes, of her lost cause."[18] Thus did Gilder and other Northern editors nurture the rise of the Confederate Lost Cause as a national heritage.

In 1896 a Southerner, Albert Morton, attended a UCV reunion in Richmond and a GAR reunion in Saint Paul, Minnesota. He found a "marked contrast" between the two events. Both involved enormous crowds and festooned streets. In Richmond, Morton found "tumultuous" enthusiasm, the singing of Confederate songs by "thousands of throats," and tears everywhere as women kissed old flags and people cheered wildly for the marching veterans. In the more staid Saint Paul, Morton was disappointed at a parade where "the heart was lacking." He found himself "astounded at the apathy, the woodenness of the onlookers." Hardly anyone cheered the Union veterans as they marched by; Morton saw even a "cripple who hobbled along on his crutches amidst profound silence." Judging by the character of these reunions, Morton concluded: "I felt, as I watched the blue coated veterans pass, that I would rather have been a soldier under the Southern cross."[19] When it came to commemorating the war, Southerners seemed to have more passion and more fun.

Moreover, in 1894, the *Confederate Veteran* reported a story of a Southern mother and her son attending a production in Brooklyn, New York, of the play *Held by the Enemy*. The boy asks his mother, "What did the Yankees fight for?" As the orchestra strikes up "Marching through Georgia," the woman answers: "For the Union, darling." "Painful memories" bring sadness to the mother's face as she hears the Yankee victory song. Then, earnestly, the boy asks, "What did the Confederates fight for, mother?" Before the mother can answer, the music changes to "Home Sweet Home," which fills the theater with "its depth of untold melody and pathos." The mother whispers her answer: "Do you hear what they are playing? *That* is what the *Confederates* fought for, darling." "Did they fight for their *homes*?" the boy counters. With the parent's assurance, the boy burst into tears, and with the "intuition of right," hugs his mother and announces: "Oh mother, I will be a Confederate!"[20] Apocryphal or not, this tale represents a place that the Confederate veterans and their cause had reached in American popular culture. They had lost the war in 1865, but were winning the hearts of millions and providing a healing balm for the worried and disruptive society of the 1890s. Their conservative rebellion now seemed an antidote to the new ethnic invasion of America's shores, and especially to farmers' and workers' revolts. In the bewildering technological and industrial society, and amidst resurgent racism, a white boy growing up in America in the 1890s might find safe havens in the past and present by just *being a Confederate.*

Many Confederate Memorial Day speakers embraced memories of the Old South as a way of denouncing the New. At an 1895 gathering in Savannah, Georgia, the orator, Pope Barrow, rejected all "prating of a 'N—South.'" He set the Lost Cause off as the protector of the real America now under threat. "The Southern people are the Americans of Americans," proclaimed Barrow, "and ex-Confederates of today are representatives of an American army – not an army made up largely of foreigners and blacks fighting for pay . . . I believe in the Old South." These code phrases for racial supremacy and nativism often spilled into more explicit expressions. At Memorial Day ceremonies in Nashville in 1894, a US district judge, G. R. Sage, embraced reconciliation by warning of impending threats to the American political order. "How soon the crisis may be upon us . . . we do not know," offered Sage. But he called on North and South to "stand shoulder to shoulder and present a united . . . front against the vicious and revolutionary and communistic elements which threaten the public safety." At a reunion in Waco, Texas, another judge, George Clark, told assembled veterans that their cause was "not lost" and "could not be lost" in the nation's new hour of peril. Pointing to a Confederate flag, Clark declared that it stood for "the right of the enjoyment of our liberty and that equal dignity of right to enjoy the fruits of our labor." Clark made the new enemy clear. He called on his comrades to join ranks "against the aggressions of government, against the aggressions of anarchy, against the aggressions of communism in every shape."[21] In the 1890s the Lost Cause emerged as a useful weapon against radicalism and a bulwark against social diversity and disorder. Indeed, many of our controversies at the turn of the twenty-first century over the continuing presence of Confederate symbols, especially the battle flag, can be traced to this era when the Lost Cause changed its skin and became both a force of reunion and reaction.

During this second era of Lost Cause discourse, its advocates accelerated the fight to control historical interpretation of the Civil War. UCV and UDC history committees, in conjunction with a proliferation of state history associations, engaged in what one historian has called "a grand crusade to secure in the hearts and minds of the region's young" what it had lost on battlefields, and to "immunize southern children against democratic reforms then threatening the South's ruling class." "Thought is power," declared Mary Singleton Slack at a Louisville, Kentucky, meeting in 1904. She called on the Daughters to build the "greatest of all monuments, a thought monument" for the "pulsing hearts and active brains" of Southern youth.[22] Slack captured much of what was at stake in the struggle to control Civil War memory in turn-of-the-century America.

Since the 1860s every organ of Lost Cause thought had declared itself a bulwark against prejudiced Yankee history. In 1893, as S. A. Cunningham launched his *Confederate Veteran*, he announced a "fraternal" mission of peace. "Bitterness," he said, would not be his stock in trade. Above all else, though, Cunningham declared that his magazine would "vindicate the truth of history at all hazards." The *Confederate Veteran* became the voice of the UCV, the clearinghouse for Lost Cause thought, and the vehicle by which ex-Confederates built a powerful memory community that lasted into the 1930s. Many veterans wrote to Cunningham expressing their love for the journal, which with "every succeeding year," wrote a Tennessean, "adds luster to the Lost Cause." Similar to the role that *Century* played with its war series in the 1880s, the *Confederate Veteran* attracted hundreds of poems, copies of war records, and reminiscences from old soldiers and their wives and families. New South recon-ciliationists, as well as the most unreconstructed rebels,

seemed to find their interests met in Cunningham's popular repository of Confederate heritage.[23]

Cunningham himself was no towering intellect, but he was a dogged defender of the South and a tireless organizer of veterans' activities. He was often at odds with the UCV leaders, who practiced too much Blue-Gray fraternalism for his taste. Cunningham made white supremacy central to the magazine's vision, welcoming to its pages frequent tributes to "faithful slaves" and denouncing the racial equality attempted during Reconstruction. Eventually Cunningham all but banished the terms "Lost Cause" and "New South" from the journal because they did not sufficiently vindicate the Confederacy's wartime goals. His brand of reconciliation folded easily into the South's new victory narrative. "No! No! Our cause was not lost because it was wrong," he announced in 1909. "No! No! Our cause was not lost for the reason that it was not wrong." Cunningham reprinted or endorsed hundreds of speeches from reunions and dedications, none more forcefully than Bradley T. Johnson's tribute to Confederate triumphalism and white supremacy at the opening of the Confederate Museum (quoted near the beginning of this chapter), which he contended "should become a part of the education of every child in the South."[24] In endless refrains about true history and non-partisanship, the preservers of the Confederate tradition built one of the most enduring and partisan mythologies in American experience.

As early as 1899, UDC chapters endorsed a pro-Southern textbook and began their decades-long crusade to fight what many perceived as a Yankee conspiracy to miseducate Southerners.[25] When UDC women took up the cause of history they did so as cultural guardians of their tribe, defenders of a sacred past against Yankee-imposed ignorance and the forces of modernism. They built moats around their white tribe's castles to save the children from false history and impure knowledge. But they did so by manning the parapets and by constant incursions into enemy territory. Many UDC leaders were anything but pious, quietistic women adorning irrelevant parlors with approved books. They were activists eager to fight to control America's memory of slavery, the Civil War, and Reconstruction. They delivered public speeches, wrote in the popular press, and lobbied Congressmen. On a popular level, they may have accomplished more than professional historians in laying down for decades (within families and schools) a conception of a victimized South, fighting nobly for high Constitutional principles, and defending a civilization of benevolent white masters and contented African slaves. If the Lost

Cause now marched to a victory song, the UDC provided much of its spirit and its righteous indignation.

Many UDC activists harbored abiding memories of wartime loss and suffering. Janet Weaver Randolph, the founder and spirit of the Richmond UDC chapter, was seventeen when the war ended in 1865. She spent the entire war on her family's 179-acre farm near Warrenton, in northern Virginia. Her thirty-eight-year-old father had died of typhoid as a Confederate private, and her mother had been captured and detained as an alleged Confederate spy while trying to reach relatives in Philadelphia for financial help. The Weavers boarded and cared for wounded men on both sides, and young Janet's memorial work began even before the war ended with Sunday rituals of placing flowers at gravesites of dead soldiers. In 1880, Janet Weaver married Norman V. Randolph, a Confederate veteran active in the Lee Camp in Richmond. She was a founding member of the women's group that converted the White House of the Confederacy into a museum, and with time she became the UDC's most effective lobbyist with politicians. Her long efforts to get the Congress, War Department, and two Presidents to reinter the Confederate dead from Northern cemeteries to their various Southern homes, as well as to erect monuments to the prison dead at Northern sites, resulted in an extensive reburial of Southern soldiers in Arlington National Cemetery in 1903. Fiercely loyal to the Lost Cause, Janet Randolph nevertheless used her memorial work to struggle against some of the barriers encircling women's sphere. In an interview in 1916, she called herself an "uneducated woman" who had grown up with the hardships of the war. "The women who spend their all to get the advantage of even a few months at the University," she complained, "are not accorded the degrees that will rank them with the men. Do you call this chivalry to women? Is it placing them on that lofty pedestal our opponents so delight to talk of?" Randolph reflected on the obstacles in her own life and seemed to recognize that she lived on the cusp of a new age. "I am not a suffragist," she said, "but it is just such injustice that will cause the women of Virginia to become suffragists."[26]

The UDC woman who may have had the greatest influence on Southern historical consciousness was Mildred Lewis Rutherford of Athens, Georgia. Serving as historian general of the UDC from 1911 to 1916, Rutherford gave new meaning to the term "diehard." A prolific lecturer, writer, and organizer, Rutherford was the most conspicuous woman among many who prompted local chapters to conduct essay contests and to solicit reminiscences – the collection of which, along with similar efforts by the *Confederate Veteran* and some libraries, produced an extensive oral history of the Lost Cause. From the late 1890s onward, Rutherford was active in historical work, and for twenty-seven years she was principal of the Lucy Cobb Institute, a school for girls in Athens. She considered the Confederacy "acquitted as blameless" at the bar of history, and sought its vindication with a political fervor that would rival the ministry of propaganda in any twentieth-century dictatorship. She assembled dozens of scrapbooks, documenting every conceivable aspect of the Lost Cause and white supremacy. Rutherford traveled the country in period gowns with hoop skirts and delivered speeches entitled "Wrongs of History Righted" or "Historical Sins of Omission and Commission." Her conception of Southern history included large doses of romantic plantation imagery. "How restful the old life was!" went a typical expression. "What a picture of contentment, peace and happiness it presented! It was something like our grandmother's garden." She seemed to borrow directly from Page's stories. "The Negroes under the institution of slavery were well-fed, well-clothed, and well-housed," she claimed. "How hard it was for us to make the North understand this!" Rutherford's absolutism flowed in endless recitals of the "horrors" of Reconstruction. She peddled the theory of black racial decline since emancipation. Had blacks "benefitted by freedom"? she asked in speeches. "As a race," she answered, "unhesitatingly no!" Slave health had been exemplary, she claimed. "I never saw a case of consumption . . . and now negroes are dying by the hundreds yearly. I never heard of but one crazy negro before the war. Now asylums cannot be built fast enough to contain those who lose their minds."[27]

For all who would listen, Rutherford fashioned Confederate memory into a revival crusade and the Old South into a lost racial utopia. In an era when patriotism and history instruction were thoroughly conflated in the public schools, Rutherford insisted that the Confederacy be ranked in glory with the American Revolution. She lectured teachers to display and teach about the Confederate battle flag, and urged that pictures of Confederate heroes be hung in every school. She provided to instructors lists of Civil War causes (five primary and ten "aggravating"), all of which placed responsibility at the feet of abolitionists. And Rutherford spoke with utter certainty that the American reunion was a victory for Southern righteousness. "While we are trying to right the wrongs of history and literature," she declared in 1915, "let us be very careful to do it in the spirit of truth and peace. Surely the South can best stand gracefully for peace, for she has the most to forgive."[28]

The UCV entered this history crusade earlier than the UDC, and the fervor of its efforts no doubt inspired the women. Under the leadership of former general Stephen D. Lee, the UCV Historical Committee issued a remarkable report at its 1895 reunion in Houston, Texas. The committee portrayed itself as a political force engaged in a moral struggle for the soul of the South. They urged a social and educational awakening that would demand "vindication of the Southern people, and a refutation of the slanders, the misrepresentations, and the imputations which they have so long and patiently borne." The committee defended the right of secession and rejected slavery as the cause of the war. "Slavery," said the UCV committee, "was the South's misfortune, the whole country's fault." "The true cause of the war between the states," it further argued, "was the dignified withdrawal of the Southern states from the Union . . . and not the high moral purpose of the North to destroy slavery, which followed incidentally as a war measure." The target of the report was "New England historians" who had foisted upon the country histories full of "prejudice" and "passion." In the need to organize themselves into an "influential agency" of a proper historical memory, the UCV committee demonstrated above all else its embrace of a particular conception of history.[29] The implicit assumption at work in its report was that history, especially for those who judge themselves aggrieved, is at heart a form of political advocacy. Historical memory, therefore, was a weapon with which to engage in the struggle over political policy and a means to sustain the social and racial order.

The UCV's attempt to produce a "deeper, surer . . . permanent mode of vindicating the South" was nothing less than a political movement, a quest for thought control aimed at shaping regional and national memory of the war. The Historical Committee ranked school histories of the United States in three categories: first, Northern books that were "pronouncedly unfair to the South"; second, Northern-authored works that were "apparently fair" but still judged "objectionable"; and third, "Southern histories," those that passed all of some nine tests, including whether a book had properly represented the "unparalleled patriotism manifested by the Southern people in accepting" the war's "results." Eight books, all written by Southerners, made the recommended list. Mildred Rutherford and the UDC produced similar approved lists and condemnations of Northern histories. "We are absolutely powerless if we permit ourselves to be dominated by the book trust," she charged, "and allow Northern publishing houses to place books unfair to us in our schools." Everywhere she went, Rutherford urged that "no library should be without" approved Southern histories and "all of Thomas Nelson Page's books."[30] In such constant appeals for "truthful history," Lost Cause ideology, especially the notions that slavery really did not cause the war and that Reconstruction was the vicious oppression of an innocent South and the exploitation of ignorant blacks, sunk deeper with each passing year into the South's and the nation's memory.

No argument in the Lost Cause formula became more an article of faith than the disclaimer against slavery as the cause of the war. In reunion speeches, committee reports, and memoirs, it is remarkable to note the energy Southerners spent denying slavery's centrality to the war. Some, like John B. Gordon in his *Reminiscences* (1903), allowed that slavery was the "immediate fomenting cause" of conflict, "the tallest pine in the political forest around whose top the fiercest lightnings were to blaze." But "responsibility" for slavery, he contended, could not be "laid at her [the South's] door." So familiar and ubiquitous were these arguments that they flowed effortlessly from Southern pens. "It was not the desire to hold others in bondage," contended a Richmond Memorial Day orator in 1894, "but the desire to maintain their own rights that actuated the Southern people throughout the conflict." At a Franklin, Tennessee, Memorial Day in 1901, an orator carried the argument about responsibility to its utopian conclusion. "In 1861," declared Judge H. H. Cook, "the southern people were the best informed, most energetic, the most religious, and the most democratic people on earth." They had "no classes" and "perfect equality" among whites. As for the slaves, who had been imposed on them by Northern traders, they had nobly "civilized and Christianized 4,000,000 of this unfortunate race."[31] The Lost Cause imagined millions of willing and contented slaves in its nostalgic remembrance, with slaveholders in the role of providers and mentors for African bondsmen.

So eager were ex-Confederates to deny responsibility for slavery's existence, as well as their role in causing it, that it would have been impossible to grow up in the South from 1890 to World War I and not have heard or read such arguments many times over as the common sense of white Southern self-understanding. Many Confederate veterans wrote of their refusal to "be handed down to the coming generation as a race of slave-drivers and traitors." The stock Confederate Memorial Day speech contained four obligatory tributes: to soldiers' valor, women's bravery, slave fidelity, and Southern innocence regarding slavery. Robert E. Lee, grandson of the famous general, hit all of these chords at an Atlanta gathering of five thousand people in April 1911, but with an assertion of Southern innocence he twisted history inside out. "If the South had been heeded," said Colonel Lee, "slavery would have been eliminated years before it was. It was the votes of the southern states which finally freed the slaves."[32] In such strange logic, the Lost Cause not only absolved Southerners of responsibility for slavery, but made them the truest abolitionists. Protected by such mists of sentiment, the past could be anything people wished.

With time, women's organizations and state departments of education took over much of the responsibility for historical work, publishing elaborate guides containing defenses of secession and condemnations of the antislavery movement.[33] From this combination of Lost Cause voices a reunited America arose pure, guiltless, and assured that the deep conflicts in its past had been imposed upon it by otherworldly forces. The side that lost was especially assured that its cause was true and good. One of the ideas the reconciliationist Lost Cause instilled deeply into the national culture is that even when Americans lose, they win. Such was the message, the indomitable spirit, that Margaret Mitchell infused into her character Scarlett O'Hara in *Gone with the Wind* (1936), and such, perhaps, is the basis of the enduring legend of Robert E. Lee – through noble *character*, he won by losing.

Notes

1 Definitions of the Lost Cause abound. Some scholars have employed the term "myth" to describe the character and meaning of the Lost Cause. See especially Rollin G. Osterweis, *The Myth of the Lost Cause, 1865–1900* (Hamden, Conn.: Archon Books, 1973), esp. 3–15; and Paul M. Gaston, *The New South Creed: A Study in Southern Mythmaking* (New York: Knopf, 1970), 1–42, 215–46. Thomas L. Connelly and Barbara L. Bellows, *God and General Longstreet: The Lost Cause and the Southern Mind* (Baton Rouge: Louisiana State University Press, 1995), 1–5, 107–148.

2 On periodization of the Lost Cause, see especially Foster, *Ghosts of the Confederacy*. Foster argues that the Lost Cause traditions declined significantly as cultural practice after 1900 (163–79). See also Connelly and Bellows, *God and General Longstreet*, 107–48. On the literary dimensions of the Lost Cause and its changes over time, see Fred Hobson, *Tell About the South: The Southern Rage to Explain* (Baton Rouge: Louisiana State University Press,

1983), 85–128; and Osterweis, *Myth of the Lost Cause,* 42–91.

3 Jefferson Davis to Frank Heath Alfriend, August 17, 1867, Montreal, Canada; Davis to unknown, July 6, 1874, Memphis; Davis to General C. J. Wright, December 8, 1877, GLC, ML.

4 Jefferson Davis, *The Rise and Fall of the Confederate Government,* 2 vols. (1881; rpr. New York: Da Capo Press, 1990), vol. 2, foreword by James M. McPherson, iii–iv.

5 Ibid., vol. 2, iv, 161–2.

6 Edward A. Pollard, *The Lost Cause* (New York: Gramercy, 1989), 750; Edward Pollard, *The Lost Cause Regained* (New York: G. W. Carleton, 1868), 14. On Pollard, Bledsoe, Hill, and the magazines, see Hobson, *Tell About the South,* 88–92; Foster, *Ghosts of the Confederacy,* 49–50; and Charles R. Wilson, *Baptized in Blood: The Religion of the Lost Cause, 1865–1920* (Athens, University of Georgia Press, 1983), 84.

7 Edward McGrady to Rev. B. M. Palmer, May 20, 1869, Palmer to McGrady, July 7, 1869, Iredell Jones to McGrady, December 19, 1869, Papers of the Survivors' Association of Charleston, South Carolina, SCHS.

8 Copy of "Official Circular," 1869, Papers of the Survivors' Association of Charleston, SCHS; reprinted in *SHS Papers* 1 (January 1876), 39–43.

9 *SHS Papers* 5 (January–February 1877), 1, 34. At annual meetings, the SHS often passed resolutions reconfirming its pursuit of "truth" in the history of the war. See *SHS Papers* 7 (January–December 1879), 589.

10 John B. Gordon to P. G. T. Beauregard, May 10, 1872, New York, John B. Gordon Papers, PL, DU. Gordon's publishing firm, which specialized in schoolbooks, was University Publishing Co. of New York and Baltimore. John C. Breckinridge to Early, August 10, 1873, P. G. T. Beauregard to Early, July 17, 1873, Jubal Early Papers, LC; Jubal Early to D. H. Hill, February 27, 1871, D. H. Hill Papers, SHC, UNC; Dabney, quoted in Hobson, *Tell About the South,* 97–9.

11 Robert S. Dabney to D. H. Hill, Dec. 1, 1873, Hill Papers, SHC, UNC.

12 Published in *Southern Magazine* 15 (December 1874). Pendleton delivered his Lexington speech about Longstreet many times elsewhere in the South. Early, Fitzhugh Lee, Richard Taylor, and others also wrote similar anti-Longstreet articles and speeches. See *SHS Papers* 5 (January–February 1877), 138–9, 162–94. On the Longstreet controversy, see William Garret Piston, *Lee's Tarnished Lieutenant: James Longstreet and His Place in Southern History* (Athens: University of Georgia Press, 1987); Gary Gallagher, "Scapegoat in Victory: James Longstreet and the Battle of Second Manassas," in Gallagher, *Lee and His Generals in War and Memory* (Baton Rouge: Louisiana State University Press, 1998), 140–2; and Connelly and Bellows, *God and General Longstreet,* 30–8. The first six volumes of the *SHS Papers*

are replete with articles about Gettysburg; volumes 4–6 are especially devoted to the creation of the image of Lee as invincible. For an example of Early's quest to demonstrate the North's "superior numbers," see letter, November 19, 1870, in "The Relative Strength of the Armies of Generals Lee and Grant," *SHS Papers* 2 (July–December 1876), 6–21.

13 Early, in *SHS Papers*, vol. 2, 21; Morgan, in *SHS Papers*, vol. 5, 10–11, 21–2; Davis, address to Louisiana Division of the Association of the Army of the Tennessee, a ceremony in Mississippi City, Mississippi, where the veterans presented Davis with a badge and certificate of membership, in *SHS Papers* 6 (January–February 1878), 169.

14 Herman Hattaway, "The United Confederate Veterans in Louisiana," *Louisiana History* 16 (Winter 1975), 5–37; Foster, *Ghosts of the Confederacy* 106–7.

15 Mrs. Roy Weeks McKinney, "Origins," in Mary B. Poppenheim, et al., eds., *The History of the United Daughters of the Confederacy* (Raleigh, NC: Edwards & Broughton, 1956), vol. 1, 2–10; Coski and Feely, "A Monument to Southern Womanhood," 137–8; Karen Lynne Cox, "Women, the Lost Cause, and the New South: The United Daughters of the Confederacy and the Transmission of Confederate Culture, 1894–1919" (Ph.D. diss., University of Southern Mississippi, 1998), 1–76.

16 Vanessa Harris, "Three Southern Women and the Weight of the Past: Race, Gender, and Memory, 1890–1920s" (senior thesis, Amherst College, 1999), chs. 1–2; Marjorie Spruill Wheeler, *New Women of the New South – The Leaders of the Women's Suffrage Movement in the Southern States* (New York: Oxford University Press, 1993), 39.

17 W. J. Cash, *The Mind of the South* (New York: Knopf, 1991), 136; Thomas Nelson Page, "Gray Jacket of 'No. 4,'" in Page, *The Burial of the Guns: The Novels, Stories, Sketches and Poems of Thomas Nelson Page* (1892; rpr. New York: Scribners, 1912), 235–236; Thomas N. Page, *The Old South: Essays Social and Political* (Whitefish, MT, 2005), 50.

18 Richard Watson Gilder, "The Nationalizing of Southern Literature: Part II – After the War," *The Christian Advocate* 10 (July 1890), 442. Also see Michael Kreyling, "Nationalizing the Southern Hero: Adams and James," *Mississippi Quarterly* 34 (Fall 1981), 383–385.

19 "Two Great Reunions," and "Why He Would Be a Confederate," *CV* 4 (October 1896), 333–335. The two reunions attended by Morton were in Richmond, July 2, and St. Paul, September 2, 1896.

20 *CV* 2 (June 1894), 182.

21 *CV* 2 (April, June, 1894), 122–123, 166; and *CV* 3 (May 1895), 130–131. S. A. Cunningham, editor of the *Confederate Veteran*, also adopted the occasional use of "N—— South" as a derogatory term.

22 Fred Arthur Bailey, "Free Speech and the Lost Cause in the Old Dominion," *Virginia Magazine of History* 103 (April 1995), 237; *CV* 1 (April 1893), 112; Mrs. Mary Singleton

Slack, "Causes That Led to the War between the States in 1860," paper read before the Albert Sidney Johnston chapter, UDC, Louisville, Ky., March 16, 1904, Historical Records of the United Daughters of the Confederacy, comp. Mildred Lewis Rutherford, Athens, Ga., MOC.

23 J. H. Brunner to Cunningham, October 13, 1899, Hiawassee College, Tenn., S. A. Cunningham Papers, SHC, UNC.

24 *CV* 17 (July 1909), 313; *CV* 6 (August 1898), 357. See also John A. Simpson, *S. A. Cunningham and the Confederate Heritage* (Athens: University of Georgia Press, 1994), 90–116.

25 *Minutes of the Sixth Annual Meeting of the United Daughters of the Confederacy*, 1899 (Nashville, Tenn., 1900), 72–74, MOC; Coski and Feely, "A Monument to Southern Womanhood," 138.

26 Coski and Feely, "A Monument to Southern Womanhood," 142–3; interview with the *Fauquier Democrat* (Warrenton, Va.), April 8, 1916, Mrs. Norman V. Randolph Papers, MOC. For Janet Randolph's lobbying, see Randolph to Sen. J. B. Foraker, April 15, 1903; Randolph to President William McKinley, July 24, August 8, 1900; Franklin H. Mackey to Randolph, February 16, 1898; Randolph to "Honorable Sec. of War," early Fall 1900; W. T. Patten, Quartermaster of U.S., to Randolph, October 10, 1900; Congressman J. Wheeler to Randolph, March 2, 1899; Congressman John Lamb to Randolph, February 28, 1899, December 11, 24, 1900; and Senator Thomas Martin to Randolph, October 18, 1900, Randolph Papers, MOC, box 8A. On the reinterment in Arlington Cemetery, see Foster, *Ghosts of the Confederacy*, 153–4. See chapter on Lila Valentine, leader of the Women's Suffrage League in Virginia, in Harris, "Three Southern Women and the Weight of the Past," ch. 2.

27 See clippings, Mildred Rutherford Scrapbooks 6, 60, MOC. Also see "Wrongs of History Righted" and "Historical Sins of Omission and Commission," 7, 35, in UDC Addresses, MOC; Coski and Feely, "A Monument to Southern Womanhood," 188; and Cox, "Women, the Lost Cause, and the New South," 143.

28 "Word to School Teachers," Rutherford Scrapbooks 9, MOC; "Address," June 1, 1915, and "Causes That Led to the War between the States," Historical Records of the UDC 6, 60, MOC; "Historian General's Page," *CV* 23 (October 1915), 443–445. Rutherford's list of "the five causes" were (1) the Missouri Compromise, (2) the unjust tariff acts, (3) the unjust distribution of money in the treasury, (4) the "personal liberty-bills" in violation of the Fugitive Slave Law, and (5) the election of Abraham Lincoln by a sectional party on a sectional platform. The "other aggravating causes" included: "Dred Scott case; John Brown's raid; Beecher's Bibles; Wilmot Proviso; Kansas and Nebraska bill; Uncle Tom's Cabin; vituperations from the press; falsehoods from the pulpits; the slave trade in violation of the Constitution [which she blamed on the North!]; and the Underground Railroad."

29 "Report of the Historical Committee," *CV* 3 (June 1895), 163–167. On the establishment, membership, and work of the UCV Historical Committee, see Herman Hattaway, "Clio's Southern Soldiers: The United Confederate Veterans and History," *Louisiana History* 12 (Summer 1871), 217–242.

30 *CV* 3 (June 1895), 167–170; Rutherford, "Address," delivered to group of Sons of Confederate Veterans, Richmond, June 1, 1915, Historical Records of the UDC 6, MOC. The irony in the political character of this movement to control history textbooks stems from the UCV's origins and principles. In an 1894 statement, UCV commander General John B. Gordon declared that "neither discussion of political or religious subjects, nor any political action, will be permitted in the organization." Gordon ended, however, with a seemingly contradictory reminder to the membership: "But you realize that a people without the memories of heroic suffering or sacrifice are a people without a history." See *CV* 2 (April 1894), cover page. On the issue of school and state histories in the 1890s, also see "In the Interest of School Histories," *CV* 3 (October 1895), 316; "Southern Social Relations," *CV* 4 (December 1896), 447–443; "Telling the Truth to Children" and "Correct History of Missouri," *CV* 6 (January 1898), 29. For an account of the Southern crusade to control history, especially through state histories, see Fred Arthur Bailey, "The Textbooks of the 'Lost Cause': Censorship and the Creation of Southern State Histories," *Georgia Historical Quarterly* 75 (Fall 1991), 507–533. A comparative account of textbooks is Daniel E. Boxer, "Dueling Memories: The Retelling of the Civil War in Textbooks of Boston and Richmond," (senior thesis, Amherst College, 2000).

31 John B. Gordon, *Reminiscences of the Civil War* (1903; rpr. Baton Rouge: Louisiana State University Press, 1993), 18–19; oration by Rev. R. C. Cave, Richmond, May 30, 1894, *CV* 2 (June 1894), 162; "Judge Cook's Tribute to Confederate Dead," *Nashville Banner*, May 27, 1901, HCF, fiche 271.

32 "The Causes of the War," address by Richard Henry Lee, Old Chapel, Va., at dedication of Confederate monument, *CV* 1 (July 1893), 201; Arthur Marshall, Springfield, Mo., letter to editor, *CV* 1 (November 1893), 323; "Gray Warriors Extolled by Grandson of Leader," *AC*, April 27, 1911.

33 *Memorial Day Annual, 1912: The Causes and Outbreak of the War between the States, 1861–1865* (Richmond: Department of Public Instruction and Confederate Memorial Literary Society, 1912), in Rutherford Scrapbooks 60, MOC.

The Wall and the Screen Memory: The Vietnam Veterans Memorial

Marita Sturken

The forms remembrance takes indicate the status of memory within a given culture. In acts of public commemoration, the shifting discourses of history, personal memory, and cultural memory converge. Public commemoration is a form of history-making, yet it can also be a contested form of remembrance in which cultural memories slide through and into each other, creating a narrative tangle. With the Vietnam War, public commemoration is inextricably tied to the question of how war is brought to closure in American society. How does a society commemorate a war whose central narrative is one of division and dissent, a war whose history is still formative and highly contested? The Vietnam War, with its lack of a singular, historical narrative defining a clear-cut purpose and outcome, has led to a unique form of commemoration.

Questions of public remembrance of the Vietnam War can be examined through the concept of the screen. A screen is a surface that is projected upon; it is also an object that hides something from view, that shelters or protects. The Vietnam Veterans Memorial in Washington, DC, both shields and is projected upon; the black walls of the memorial act as screens for innumerable projections of memory and history – of the United States' participation in the Vietnam War and of the experiences of Vietnam veterans since the war.

A singular, sanctioned history of the Vietnam War has not yet coalesced, in part because of the disruption of the standard narratives of American imperialism, technology, and masculinity that the war's loss represented. The history of the Vietnam War is still being composed from many conflicting histories, yet two particular elements within the often opposing narratives are uncontested –

the divisive effect of the war on American society and the marginalization of Vietnam veterans. In this chapter I analyze how narratives of the war have been constructed out of and within the cultural memory of the Vietnam Veterans Memorial. I examine how the walls of the memorial act to eclipse – to screen out – personal and collective memories of the Vietnam War in the design of history and how the textures of cultural memory are nevertheless woven throughout, perhaps over and under, these screens.

The 1980s and 1990s have witnessed a repackaging of the 1960s and the Vietnam War – a phenomenon steeped in the language of nostalgia, healing, and forgiveness. Within this rescripting of history, the Vietnam Veterans Memorial has become a central icon in the process of healing, of confronting difficult past experiences. When it was constructed in 1982, the memorial was the center of a debate over how wars should be remembered and who should be remembered (those who died, those who participated in it, those who engineered it, those who opposed it). The memorial has received an extraordinary amount of attention: it has been the subject of innumerable coffee-table books, several exhibitions, and a television movie, among other things. Virtually all texts written today concerning Vietnam veterans make reference to it. It has played a significant role in the rehistoricization of the Vietnam War.

The Status of a Memorial

Although now administered by the National Park Service of the federal government, the impetus for the creation of the Vietnam Veterans Memorial came from a group of Vietnam veterans who raised the funds and negotiated for a site on the Washington Mall. Situated on the grassy slope of the Constitutional Gardens near the Lincoln Memorial, the Vietnam Veterans Memorial, which was designed by Maya Lin, consists of a V shape of two walls of black granite set into the earth at an angle of 125 degrees. Together, the walls extend almost five hundred feet, with a maximum height of approximately ten feet at the central hinge. These walls are inscribed with the names of the 58,196 men and women who died in the war, listed chronologically by date of death, with opening and closing inscriptions. The listing of names begins on the right-hand side of the hinge and continues to the end of the right wall; it then begins again at the far end of the left wall and ends at the center again. Thus, the name of the first American soldier killed in Vietnam, in 1959, is on a panel adjacent to that containing the name of the last killed there, in 1975. The framing dates of 1959 and 1975 are the only dates listed on the wall; the names are listed alphabetically within each "casualty day," although those dates are not noted. Each name is preceded by a diamond shape; names of the approximately 1,300 MIAs (those missing in action) are preceded by a small cross, which, in the event that the remains of that person are identified, is changed to a diamond. If an MIA should return alive, this symbol would be changed to a circle (but, as one volunteer at the memorial told me, "We don't have any circles yet"). Eight of the names on the wall represent women who died in the war. Since 1984 the memorial has been accompanied by a figurative sculpture of three soldiers, which faces the memorial from a group of trees south of the wall. In 1993 a statue commemorating the women who served in Vietnam was added three hundred feet from the wall.

The memorial functions in opposition to the codes of remembrance evidenced on the Washington Mall. Virtually all the national memorials and monuments in Washington are made of white stone and designed to be visible from a distance. In contrast, the Vietnam Veterans Memorial cuts into the sloping earth: it is not visible until one is almost upon it; if approached from behind, it seems to disappear into the landscape. Although the polished black granite walls of the memorial reflect the Washington Monument and face the Lincoln Memorial, they are not visible from the base of either structure. The black stone creates a reflective surface, one that echoes the reflecting pool of the Lincoln Memorial and allows viewers to participate in the memorial; seeing their own image reflected in the

names, they are implicated in the listing of the dead. The etched surface of the memorial has a tactile quality, and viewers are compelled to touch the names and make rubbings of them.

Its status as a memorial, rather than a monument, situates the Vietnam Veterans Memorial within a particular code of remembrance. Monuments and memorials can often be used as interchangeable forms, but there are distinctions in intent between them. Arthur Danto writes:

> We erect monuments so that we shall always remember, and build memorials so that we shall never forget. Thus we have the Washington Monument but the Lincoln Memorial. Monuments commemorate the memorable and embody the myths of beginnings. Memorials ritualize remembrance and mark the reality of ends. . . . The memorial is a special precinct, extruded from life, a segregated enclave where we honor the dead. With monuments we honor ourselves.[1]

Monuments are not generally built to commemorate defeats; the defeated dead are remembered in memorials. Whereas a monument most often signifies victory, a memorial refers to the life or lives sacrificed for a particular set of values. Whatever triumph a memorial may refer to, its depiction of victory is always tempered by a foregrounding of the lives lost.

Memorials are, according to Charles Griswold, "a species of pedagogy" that "seeks to instruct posterity about the past and, in so doing, necessarily reaches a decision about what is worth recovering."[2] The Lincoln Memorial, for example, is a funereal structure that gains its force from its implicit reference to Lincoln's untimely death. It embodies the man and his philosophy, with his words inscribed on its walls. The Washington Monument, by contrast, operates purely as a symbol, making no reference beyond its name to the mythic political figure. This distinction between the two outlines one of the fundamental differences between memorials and monuments: Memorials tend to emphasize specific texts or lists of the dead, whereas monuments offer less explanation; a memorial seems to demand the naming of those lost, whereas monuments are usually anonymous. Danto states, "The paradox of the Vietnam Veterans Memorial in Washington is that the men and women killed and missing would not have been memorialized had we won the war and erected a monument instead."[3]

The traditional Western monument glorifies not only its subject but the history of classical architecture as well. The obelisk of the Washington Monument, which was erected between 1848 and 1885, has its roots in Roman architecture; long before Napoleon pilfered them from Egypt to take to Paris, obelisks carried connotations of the imperial trophy. The Lincoln Memorial, which was built in 1922, is modeled on the classic Greek temple, specifically referring to the Parthenon. The Vietnam Veterans Memorial, however, makes no direct reference to the history of classical art or architecture. It does not chart a lineage from the accomplishments of past civilizations.

[. . .]

Modernist sculpture has been defined by a kind of sitelessness.[4] Yet the Vietnam Veterans Memorial is a site-specific work that establishes its position within the symbolic history embodied in the national monuments on and around the Washington Mall. Pointing from its axis to both the Washington Monument and Lincoln Memorial, the Vietnam Veterans Memorial references, absorbs, and reflects these classical forms. Its black walls mirror not only the faces of its viewers and passing clouds but also the obelisk of the Washington Monument, thus forming a kind of pastiche of monuments. The memorial's relationship to the earth shifts between context and decontextualization, between an effacement and an embracement of the earth; approached from above, it appears to cut into the earth; from below, it seems to rise from it. The site-specificity of the Vietnam Veterans Memorial is crucial to its position as both subversive of and continuous with the nationalist discourse of the Mall.

It is as a war memorial that the Vietnam Veterans Memorial most distinguishes itself from modernist sculpture. As the first national war memorial built in the United States since those commemorating World War II, it makes a statement on war that diverges sharply from the declarations of prior war memorials. The Vietnam Veterans Memorial Fund (VVMF), which organized the construction of the memorial, stipulated only two things – that it contain the names of all of those who died or are missing in action and that it be apolitical and harmonious with the site. The veterans' initial instructions stated: "The memorial will make no political statement regarding the war or its conduct. It will transcend those issues. The hope is that the creation of the memorial will begin a healing process."[5] Implicit within these guidelines was the desire that the memorial offer some kind of closure to the debates on the war. Yet, with these stipulations, the veterans set the stage for the dramatic disparity between the message of this memorial and that of its antecedents. The stipulation that the work not espouse a political stand in regard to the war – a stipulation that, in the ensuing controversy, would appear naive – ensured that the memorial would not glorify war.

The traditional war memorial achieves its status by enacting closure on a specific conflict. This closure contains the war within particular master narratives either of victory or of the bitter price of victory, a theme dominant in the "never again" texts of World War I memorials. In declaring the end of a conflict, this closure can by its very nature serve to sanctify future wars by offering a complete narrative with cause and effect intact. In rejecting the architectural lineage of monuments and the aesthetic codes of previous war memorials, the Vietnam Veterans Memorial refuses to sanction the closure and implied tradition of those structures. It can be said both to condemn and to justify future memorials.

[. . .]

The Names

There is little doubt that the memorial's power is due to the 58,196 names inscribed on its walls in a form that engages visitors. The design of the memorial draws spectators inward and down toward its center, so that one has the sensation both of descending below the ground and the Washington Mall and of being pulled inward toward the walls. Hence, the design creates spaces in which the names surround visitors and invite them to touch and to see themselves within the listings.

These names, by virtue of their multiplicity, situate the Vietnam Veterans Memorial within the multiple strands of cultural memory. The memorial does not validate the collective over the value of the individual. In response to the memorial, visitors commonly think of the widening circle of pain emanating from each name, imagining for each the grieving parents, sisters, brothers, girlfriends, wives, husbands, friends, and children – imagining, in effect, the multitude of people who were directly affected by the war.

This listing of names creates an expanse of cultural memory, one that could be seen as alternately subverting, rescripting, and contributing to the history of the Vietnam War as it is being written. The histories these names evoke and the responses they generate are necessarily multiple and replete with complex personal stakes. These narratives concern the effect of the war on the Americans who survived it and whose lives were irrevocably altered by it. The listing of names is steeped in the irony of the war – an irony afforded by retrospect, of lives lost for no discernible reason. All accounts of the war are tinged with the knowledge that this country did not accept its memory and that the veterans were stigmatized by the nation's defeat.

Although these names are now marked within an official history, that history cannot contain the ever-widening circles that expand outward from each. The names on the walls of the memorial constitute a chant; they were read out loud at the dedication ceremony and at the tenth anniversary as a roll call of the dead. They are etched into stone. The men and women who died in the war thus achieve a historical presence through their absence. These names are listed without elaboration, with no place or date of death, no rank, no place of origin. The lack of military rank allows the names to transcend a military context and to represent the names of a society. It has often been noted that these names display the diversity of America: Fredes Mendez-Ortiz, Stephen Boryszewski, Bobby Joe Yewell, Leroy Wright. Veteran William Broyles, Jr., writes:

> These are names which reach deep into the heart of America, each testimony to a family's decision, sometime in the past, to wrench itself from home and culture to test our country's promise of new opportunities and a better life. They are names drawn from the farthest corners of the world and then, in this generation, sent to another distant corner in a war America has done its best to forget.[6]

Broyles is not atypical in portraying the diversity of names as indicative of America as the promised land (what of those who came here not by choice, for instance?) or in positioning the United States at the center, from which these places of cultural origins and foreign wars are seen as "distant corners." His reading of the ethnicity of the names on the walls does not consider the imbalances of that diversity – that this war was fought by a disproportionately high number of blacks and Hispanics, that the soldiers predominantly came from working- and middle-class backgrounds. Proper names in our culture have complex legal and patriarchal implications, identifying individuals specifically as members of society. On this memorial, these names are coded as American – not as Asian, black, or white. The ethnic derivations of these names are subsumed into a narrative of the American melting pot – into which, ironically, Maya Lin, as an agent of commemoration, will not fit.

The names act as surrogates for the bodies of the Vietnam War dead. It is now a ritual at the memorial for visitors to make rubbings of the names to take away with them, to hold with them the name marked in history. These names thus take on significant symbolic value as representations of the absent one. Yet what exactly do they evoke? Clearly they mark the dead irrevocably as a part of the history of the United States's involvement in the Vietnam War; but what sense of the individual can a name in stone portray? Judith Butler asks; "But do names really 'open' us to an intersubjective ground, or are they simply so many ruins which designate a history irrevocably lost? Do these names really signify for us the fullness of the lives that were lost, or are they so many tokens of what we cannot know, enigmas inscrutable and silent?"[7] The name evokes both everything and nothing as a marker of the absent one. This may be why, with both the AIDS Quilt and the Vietnam Veterans Memorial, visitors have felt compelled to add photographs, letters, and other memorabilia in attempts to fill the names with individual significance.

It is crucial to their effect that the names are listed not alphabetically but in chronological order. This was Lin's original intent, so that the wall would read "like an epic Greek poem" and "return the vets to the time frame of the war." The veterans were originally opposed to this idea; because they conceived the memorial specifically in terms of the needs of the veterans and family members who would visit it; they were worried that people would be unable to locate a name and simply leave in frustration. They changed their opinion, however, when they examined the Defense Department listing of casualties. Listed alphabetically, the names presented not individuals but cultural entities. There were over six hundred people named Smith, sixteen named James Jones. Read alphabetically, the names became anonymous, not individuals but statistics.

Read chronologically, however, the names on the Vietnam Veterans Memorial create a narrative framework; they chart the story of the conflict. By walking along the wall, one figuratively walks through the history of the war. As the number of names listed alphabetically within a casualty day swells, the escalation of the fighting is conveyed. In addition, the fact that visitors must look up a name in the index and then find it on the wall places them in an active role; Lin and others have referred to it as a "journey." For veterans, the chronological listing provides a spatial reference for their experience of the war, a kind of memory map. They can see in certain clumps of names the scene of a particular ambush, the casualties of a doomed night patrol, or the night they were wounded.

This is not a linear narrative framework. Rather, the names form a loop, beginning as they do at the central hinge of the memorial and circling back to the center. This refusal of linearity is appropriate to a conflict that has had no narrative closure. The hinge between the two walls thus becomes a pivotal space, the narrow interval between the end of one war and the beginning of another; it connotes a temporary peace within the cycle of war.

The question of who is named and not named on the wall is crucial to the intersection of cultural memory and history in the memorial. Veterans of the VVMF intended the memorial as a tribute not only to those who died but also to those who survived the war, hence the opening and closing inscriptions that read, in part: "In honor of the men and women of the Armed Forces who served in the Vietnam War. The names of those who gave their lives and of those who remain missing are inscribed in the order they were taken from us." There is little doubt that the memorial has become a powerful symbol for all Vietnam veterans, yet only the names of the war dead and the MIAs are inscribed on the wall, and thus within history. The distinction between the named and unnamed will determine how this memorial constructs the history of the Vietnam War after the generation of Vietnam veterans has died.

One could also argue that the listing of names limits the narrative of the memorial because of who remains unnamed. In the nationalist context of the Washington Mall, the Vietnamese become unmentionable; they are conspicuously absent in their roles as collaborators, victims, enemies, or simply the people on whose land and over whom (supposedly) this war was fought. Those whose lives were irrevocably altered or who were killed because of their opposition to the war are also absent from the discourse surrounding the memorial, except insofar as antiwar protesters are referred to by the more conservative participants in the debate as the people who would not let the war be won.

As a practical matter, the inscription of names on the memorial has posed many taxonomic problems. Though the VVMF spent months cross-checking and verifying statistics, errors have occurred. There are at least fourteen and possibly as many as thirty-eight men who are still alive whose names are inscribed in the wall.[8] More than two hundred names have been added to the memorial since it was first built (the initial number inscribed on the walls was 57,939), names that were held up previously for "technicalities" (such as, for example, a dispute over whether or not someone was killed within the "presidentially designated" war zone). Such problems signify the war's lack of closure. The impossibility of managing 58,196 sets of statistics, of knowing every detail (who died, when, and where) in a war in which human remains were often unidentifiable, has prevented any kind of closure. It has been barely noted in the media, for instance, that the Tomb of the Unknown Soldier for the Vietnam War, which was approved by Congress in 1974, was left empty and uninscribed until 1984, when some publicity drew attention to the situation.[9] The reason for this delay, according to the Army, was the absence of any unidentifiable remains (although the Army did have unidentified remains in its possession). Technology's ability to decipher the individual identity of a body and hence to achieve a kind of closure is thus at stake here.

Names will continue to be added to the Vietnam Veterans Memorial; there is no definitive limit to the addition of names. It has been noted that the names of veterans who have died since the war from causes stemming from it are not included on the memorial – veterans who committed suicide, for instance, or who died from complications from their exposure to Agent Orange. Are they not casualties of the war? The battles still being fought by the veterans foreclose a simple narrative of the Vietnam War.

Yet the memorial, like all memorials, is essentially a "forgetful monument," to use James Young's term. He writes, "A nation's monuments efface as much history from memory as they inscribe in it."[10] Framed within the nationalist context of the Washington Mall, the Vietnam Veterans Memorial must necessarily "forget" the Vietnamese and cast the Vietnam veterans as the primary victims of the war.

[. . .]

The Healing Wound

The "healing wound" metaphor that has prevailed in descriptions of the Vietnam Veterans Memorial is a bodily metaphor. It evokes many different bodies – the bodies of the Vietnam War dead, the bodies of the veterans, and the body of the American public. This wound is seen to heal through the process of remembering and commemorating the war. To dismember is to fragment a body and its memory; to remember is to make a body complete.

Where are the bodies of the memorial? The chronology of names represents bodies destroyed and inscribed permanently with the identity of war dead. Families seek out names as they would visit a grave, as the receptacle of the body; indeed, the names act as surrogates for the bodies. Many people imagine that the bodies of the dead lie behind the walls, where Lin envisioned them. The status of these bodies has been transformed by the context of technological warfare. Some families of the war dead claim they did not receive the correct remains – that the remains weighed too much, for instance.[11] In addition, the unpublicized controversy over the Tomb of the Unknown Soldier was a dispute over the status of bodily remains. The belief that technology has rendered all remains identifiable ironically conflicted with the destructive capacity of modern warfare; some men's remains amounted to less than 30 percent of their bodies. This destructive power, which dates from World War I, renders the status of the bodies of the war dead highly problematic. Many of the most horrific descriptions of combat in Vietnam deal with the total annihilation of whole bodies. In *Dispatches*, Michael Herr wrote:

> Far up the road that skirted the TOC was a dump where they burned the gear and uniforms that nobody needed anymore. . . . A jeep pulled up to the dump and a Marine jumped out carrying a bunched-up fatigue jacket held out away from him. He looked very serious and scared. Some guy in his company, some guy he didn't even know, had been blown away right next to him, all over him. He held the fatigues up and I believed him. "I guess you couldn't wash them, could you?" I said. He really looked like he was going to cry as he threw them into the dump. "Man," he said, "you could take and scrub them fatigues for a million years, and it would never happen."[12]

In war, the "tiny, fragile, human body" becomes subject to dismemberment, relegated to the "dump," to a kind of antimemory. The absence of these bodies – obliterated, interred – is both eclipsed and invoked by the names on the memorial's walls. Yet the bodies of the living Vietnam veterans have not been erased of memory. As the bodies of survivors, they have complicated the history of the war. Indeed, history operates more efficiently when its agents are no longer alive. These veteran bodies, dressed in fatigues, scarred and disabled, contaminated by toxins, refuse to let certain narratives of completion stand. Memories of war have been deeply encoded in these bodies, marked literally and figuratively in their flesh – one of the most tragic aftermaths of the war is the widespread genetic deformity caused by Agent Orange among veterans' children and the Vietnamese.

The bodies of the surviving veterans resist the closure of history and provide a perceptible site for a continual remembering of the war's effects. In *The Body in Pain*, Elaine Scarry describes how the war wounded serve as vehicles for memorialization. She notes that "injuries memorialize without specifying winner or loser" and have "no relation to the contested issues." The act of injuring, according to Scarry, has two functions: as "the activity by means of which a winner and a loser are arrived at" and as a means of providing "a record of its own activity."[13] The wound functions as a testament to the act of injuring. Thus, the body of the veteran itself is a tangible record, a kind of war memorial.

The veterans' healing process requires an individual and collective closure on certain narratives of the war. But when that healing process is ascribed to a nation, the effect is to erase the individual bodies involved; the wounds of individuals become subsumed into the nation's healing. Similarly, Scarry writes, the traditional perception of an army as a single body tends to negate the body of the individual soldier:

> We respond to the injury as an imaginary wound in an imaginary body, despite the fact that that imaginary body is itself made up of thousands of real human bodies, and thus composed of actual (hence woundable) human tissue. . . . A colossal severed artery, if anything, works to deflect attention away from rather than call attention to what almost certainly lies only a very short distance behind the surface of that image, a terrifying number of bodies with actually severed arteries.[14]

Yet the body Scarry describes is the wounded body of the conventional army – the army of fronts, rears, flanks, and arteries. In the Vietnam War the army was not, from the beginning, a whole body but rather a body of confused signals, infiltrated bases, mistaken identities, fragging (the killing of incompetent or unpopular officers by their own troops), and a confusion of allies and enemy. In this already fragmented body, remembering (restoring the wholeness of the body) is highly problematic. What happens when the body to be restored is the nation? Does healing mean a foreclosing or an expansion of the discourse of the war? Is it a coming to terms or a desire to put the war behind us? The healing process of the veterans has been couched in terms of atonement and asking forgiveness; when applied to the nation, this process connotes not remembrance but forgetting, an erasure of problematic events in order to smooth the transition of difficult narratives into the present.

The Memorial as Shrine

The Vietnam Veterans Memorial has been the subject of an extraordinary outpouring of emotion since it was built. More than 150,000 people attended its dedication ceremony, and some days as many as 20,000 people walk by its walls. It is the most heavily visited site on the Washington Mall, with an estimated total of 22 to 30 million visitors. The memorial has taken on all of the trappings of a religious shrine; it has been compared to Lourdes and the Wailing Wall in Jerusalem. People bring personal artifacts to leave at the wall as offerings, and coffee-table photography books document and interpret these experiences as a collective recovery from the war. The wall has also spawned the design of at least 150 other memorials, including the Korean War Veterans Memorial, which was dedicated in July 1995. That sculpture, a group of nineteen gray, larger-than-life figures walking across a field, stands on the opposite side of the reflecting pool from the Vietnam memorial.

The rush to embrace the memorial as a cultural symbol reveals not only the relief of telling a history that has been taboo but also a desire to reinscribe that history. The black granite walls of the memorial act as a screen for myriad cultural projections; it is easily appropriated for a variety of interpretations of the war and of the experience of those who died in it. To the veterans, the memorial makes amends for their treatment since the war; to the families and friends of those who died, it officially recognizes their sorrow and validates a grief that was not previously sanctioned; to others, it is either a profound antiwar statement or an opportunity to recast the narrative of the war in terms of honor and sacrifice.

The memorial's popularity must thus be seen within the context of a very active scripting and rescripting of the war and as an integral component in the recently emerged Vietnam War nostalgia industry. This sentiment is not confined to those who wish to return to the intensity of wartime; it is also felt by the news media, which long to recapture their moment of moral power – the Vietnam War made very good television. Michael Clark writes:

> Vietnam was recollected by the cultural apparatus that had constituted our memory of the war all along . . . [it] summoned a cast of thousands to the streets of New York, and edited out information that was out of step. It healed over the wounds that had refused to close for ten years with a balm of nostalgia, and transformed guilt and doubt into duty and pride. And with a triumphant

flourish it offered us the spectacle of its most successful creation, the veterans who will fight the next war.[15]

As the healing process is transformed into spectacle and commodity, a complex industry of nostalgia has grown. The veterans are not simply actors in this nostalgia; some are actively involved in orchestrating it. Numerous magazines that reexamine and recount Vietnam War experiences have emerged; the merchandising of Frederick Hart's statue (posters, T-shirts, a Franklin Mint miniature, and a plastic model kit) generates about $50,000 a year, half of which goes to the VVMF and half to Hart;[16] and travel agencies market tours to Indochina for veterans. In the hawkish *Vietnam* magazine, advertisements display a variety of war-related products: the Vietnam War Commemorative Combat Shotgun, the Vietnam Veterans Trivia Game, Vietnam War medallions, posters, T-shirts, and calendars. Needless to say, the Vietnam War is also now big business in both television drama and Hollywood movies.

As a kind of "history without guilt," according to Michael Kammen, nostalgia is not a singular activity pursued by former participants. Nostalgia about the Vietnam War takes many forms. Those who fought and experienced the war – the veterans, the war reporters, the support staff – look back on the highly charged experience of combat, the intensified relationships they formed, and the feeling of purpose that many of them, however ironically, felt (this latter response is most notable in the accounts of women nurses). The media have become nostalgic for their own moment of purposefulness in covering and exposing the "real" stories of the war, which the military and political establishment attempted to hide. Finally, those who were too young to experience the Vietnam War or the antiwar movement are fascinated by this particular time. As I will discuss in chapter 3, this generation has flocked to see films about the war, their concepts of it shaped by *Apocalypse Now* (1979) and *Platoon* (1986). This nostalgia represents a desire to experience war.

Though the design of Maya Lin's memorial does not lend itself to marketable reproductions, the work has functioned as a catalyst for much of this nostalgia. The Vietnam Veterans Memorial is the subject of no fewer than twelve books, many of them photography collections that focus on the interaction of visitors with the names.[17] The memorial has tapped into a reservoir of need to express in public the pain of this war, a desire to transfer private memories into a collective experience. Many personal artifacts have been left at the memorial: photographs, letters, poems, teddy bears, dog tags, combat boots and helmets, MIA/POW bracelets, clothes, medals of honor, headbands, beer cans, plaques, crosses, playing cards. At this site the objects are transposed from personal to cultural artifacts, items bearing witness to pain suffered.

Thus, a very rich and vibrant dialogue of deliberate, if sometimes very private, remembrance takes place at the memorial. Of the approximately 40,000 objects left at the wall, the vast majority have been left anonymously. Relinquished before the wall, the letters tell many stories:

– Dear Michael: Your name is here but you are not. I made a rubbing of it, thinking that if I rubbed hard enough I would rub your name off the wall and you would come back to me. I miss you so.

– We did what we could but it was not enough because I found you here. You are not just a name on this wall. You are alive. You are blood on my hands. You are screams in my ears. You are eyes in my soul. I told you you'd be all right, but I lied, and please forgive me. I see your face in my son, I can't bear the thought. You told me about your wife, your kids, your girl, your mother. And then you died. Your pain is mine. I'll never forget your face. I can't. You are still alive.

– Dear Sir, For twenty-two years I have carried your picture in my wallet. I was only eighteen years old that day that we faced one another on that trail in Chu Lai, Vietnam. Why you didn't take my life I'll never know. You stared at me for so long, armed with your AK-47, and yet you did not fire. Forgive me for taking your life, I was reacting just the way I was trained, to kill V.C. . . .

The memorial is perceived by visitors as a site where they can speak to the dead (where, by implication, the dead are present) and to a particular audience – seen variously as the American public and the community of veterans. It is because of this process that the wall is termed by many a "living memorial." It is the only site in the Washington, DC, area that appears to be conducive to this kind of artifact ritual.

Many of these letters are addressed not to visitors but to the dead. They are messages for the dead that are intended to be shared as cultural memory. Often they reflect on the lives the dead were unable to live: one offers symbols of traditional life passages, such as a wedding bouquet, baby shoes, Christmas tree ornaments, and champagne

glasses to "celebrate your 25th wedding anniversary"; another is placed in a gold frame with the sonogram image of a prospective grandchild. The voices of the Vietnam War dead are also heard through their own words, as many families leave copies of letters written by GIs, letters tinged with irony because they represent lives cut short.

For many, leaving artifacts at the memorial is an act of catharsis, a release of long-held objects to memory. A well-worn watch, for instance, was accompanied by a note explaining that it was being left for a friend who was always asking what time it was and who died wearing it. A Vietcong wedding ring was accompanied by a note reading, "I have carried this ring for 18 years and it's time for me to lay it down. This boy is not my enemy any longer." Other objects include a can of C-rations, a "short stick" (on which GIs would mark how much longer they were "in country"), a rifle marked with eighteen notches (possibly signifying either kills or months spent in country), Vietnamese sandals, and a grenade pin, each imbued with memory and carried for many years. For those who left these objects, the memorial represents a final destination and a relinquishing of their memory.

The artifacts left at the memorial are talismans of redemption, guilt, loss, and anger. Many offer apologies to the war dead, and many are addressed to "those who died for us." Some appear to be ironically humorous – a shot of whiskey or a TV set – whereas others display deep-set anger (a "Hanoi Jane Urinal Sticker"). A few are simply startling: someone left a Harley-Davidson motorcycle. The dominant tone, though, is one of asking forgiveness for the suffering, the loss, for having lived.

The National Park Service, which is now in charge of maintaining the memorial, operates an archive of the materials left there. Originally the Park Service classified these objects as "lost and found." Later, Park Service officials realized the artifacts had been left intentionally and began to save them. The objects thus moved from the cultural status of being "lost" (without category) to being historical artifacts. They have now even turned into artistic artifacts; the manager of the archive writes:

These are no longer objects at the Wall, they are communications, icons possessing a substructure of underpinning emotion. They are the products of culture, in all its complexities. They are the products of individual selection. With each object we are in the presence of a work of art of individual contemplation. The thing itself does not overwhelm our attention since these are objects that are common and expendable. At the Wall they have become unique and irreplaceable, and, yes, mysterious.[18]

Labeled "mysterious" and thus coded as original works of art, these objects are given value and authorship. Some of the people who left them have since been traced. To write *Shrapnel in the Heart*, Laura Palmer sought out and eventually interviewed the authors of various letters (although some declined), and several television shows concerning the memorial have attempted to assign authorship to the artifacts.[19] The attempt to tie these objects and letters to their creators reveals again the shifting realms of personal and cultural memory. Assigned authorship and placed in a historical archive, the objects are pulled from cultural memory, a realm in which they are meant to be shared and to participate in the memories of others.

That the majority of objects are left anonymously testifies to the memorial's power as a site of cultural remembrance. Initially, many of the items left at the memorial indicated a certain spontaneity: letters scribbled on hotel stationery, for instance. Now more letters are computer printed, and some are personally addressed to Duery Felton, Jr., curator of the collection. It would seem that people now leave things at the memorial precisely because they know that they will be preserved and thus attain the status of historical artifacts. This cataloguing affects the capacity of visitors at the memorial to experience the artifacts. Many of them are placed in plastic bags by volunteers, which makes people reluctant to touch them, and they are all removed at the end of the day they are left.

The memorial has become not only the primary site of remembrance for the Vietnam War but also a site where people pay homage to current conflicts and charged public events. Artifacts concerning the abortion debate, the AIDS epidemic, gay rights, and the Persian Gulf War have been left at the memorial. Hence, the memorial's collection inscribes a history not only of the American participation in the Vietnam War but also of national issues and events since the war. It is testimony to the memorial's malleability as an icon that both prowar and antiwar artifacts were left there during the Persian Gulf War.

The ritual of leaving something behind can be seen as an active participation in the accrual of many histories; the archiving of these artifacts also subsumes these artifacts within history. Michel Foucault has written:

> The archive is first the law of what can be said, the system that governs the appearance of statements as unique events. But the archive is also that which determines that all these things said do not accumulate endlessly in an amorphous mass . . . they are grouped together in distinct figures, composed together in accordance of specific

regularities . . . it is that which . . . defines at the outset *the system of enunciability*.[20]

The traditional archive serves a narrative function, prescribing the limits of history and defining what will and will not be preserved. The archive determines what will speak for history. However, the archive of the Vietnam Veterans Memorial is less restrictive than many archives. It contains all artifacts left at the memorial that have been personalized in some way (flowers are not saved, and flags are only saved if they have writing on them).[21] Objects are collected daily and marked with the date and location. The criteria of inclusion in the archive are thus decided by the public, whose leaving of artifacts increasingly reflects a conscious participation in history-making.

Because the collection of artifacts has received significant attention, including a book, *Offerings at the Wall*, Felton has been concerned with increasing public access to it. In 1992 an exhibition of artifacts opened at the Smithsonian Museum of American History. Though it was only intended to remain on display for six months, the public response was so huge that the show has been extended indefinitely. Since that time several other exhibits have been held throughout the country, and the collection is being photographed and assembled on CD-ROM. However, public exhibition and publication of the artifacts raise issues of copyright and ownership. To whom do the artifacts actually belong? Felton has created standards to protect the privacy of the living (he will not exhibit objects that display the name and address of a living person). He also feels issues of religious belief must be observed. For this reason, he invited several Native American shamans to conduct a blessing ceremony at the archive before the artifacts were placed on exhibit.[22]

One of the most compelling features of the Vietnam Veterans Memorial collection is its anonymity, mystery, and ambiguity. Felton, himself a combat veteran, has established a network of veterans throughout the country who help him to identify obscure insignia and the meanings of some objects. Through this network, a very specific history is being compiled, one informed by the particular codes of the participants of the war. According to Felton, those who have left artifacts range from those who want to tell only him the story behind it, to those who don't want to talk about it all, to those who seek press attention. However, it appears that the stories behind a substantial number of artifacts may never be known and that the telling of these stories to history was never the purpose of their being placed at the memorial. Though couched within an official history and held by a government institution, these letters and offerings to the dead will continue to assert individual narratives, strands of cultural memory, that disrupt historical narratives. They resist history precisely through their obscurity, their refusal to yield specific meanings.

[...]

Notes

1 Arthur Danto, "The Vietnam Veterans Memorial," *The Nation* (August 31, 1985), p. 152.

2 Charles Griswold, "The Vietnam Veterans Memorial and the Washington Mall," *Critical Inquiry* 12 (Summer 1986), p. 689.

3 Danto, "The Vietnam Veterans Memorial," p. 153.

4 Rosalind Krauss, "Sculpture in the Expanded Field," in Hal Foster, ed., *The Anti-Aesthetic* (Port Townsend, WA: Bay Press, 1983), pp. 31–42.

5 Jan Scruggs and Joel Swerdlow, *To Heal a Nation* (New York: Harper & Row, 1985), p. 53.

6 William Broyles, Jr., "Remembering a War We Want to Forget," *Newsweek* (November 22, 1982), p. 82.

7 Judith Butler, "Review Essay: Spirit in Ashes," *History and Theory* 27, no. 1 (1988), p. 69.

8 See Associated Press, "38 Living Veterans May Be on Memorial," *San Jose Mercury News*, February 15, 1991.

9 Peter Ehrenhaus, "Commemorating the Unwon War," *Journal of Communication* 39, no. 1 (Winter 1989), p. 105.

10 James Young, "Memory and Monument," in Geoffrey Hartman, ed., *Bitburg in Moral and Political Perspective* (Bloomington: Indiana University Press, 1986), p. 105.

11 Duncan Spencer, *Facing the Wall* (New York: Macmillan, 1986), p. 51.

12 Michael Herr, *Dispatches* (New York: Avon, 1978), p. 111.

13 Elaine Scarry, *The Body in Pain* (New York: Oxford University Press, 1985), pp. 115–16.

14 Ibid., p. 71.

15 Michael Clark, "Remembering Vietnam," *Cultural Critique* 3 (Spring 1986), p. 49.

16 See William Welch, "$85, 000 in Royalties for Memorial Sculptor," *Washington Post*, November 11, 1987, D1, D6.

17 In addition to Scruggs's book, these books are *The Wall: Images and Offerings from the Vietnam Veterans Memorial*, by Sal Lopes; *The Last Firebase: A Guide to the Vietnam Veterans Memorial*, by Lydia Fish; *The Vietnam Veterans Memorial*, by Michael Katakis; *Facing the Wall: Americans at the Vietnam Veterans Memorial*, by Duncan Spencer; *Shrapnel in the Heart: Letters and Remembrances from the Vietnam Veterans Memorial*, by Laura Palmer; *Always to Remember: The Story of the Vietnam Veterans Memorial*, by Brent Ashabranner; *Reflections on the Wall: The Vietnam Veterans Memorial*, by Edward Ezell; *Let Us Remember: The Vietnam Veterans Memorial*, by Louise Graves; *The Wall: A Day at the Veterans Memorial*, edited by Peter Meyer and the editors of *Life*; a children's book, *The Wall*, by Eve Bunting; and *Offerings at the Wall: Artifacts from the Vietnam Veterans Memorial Collection*, by Thomas Allen.

18 Quoted in Lydia Fish, *The Last Firebase* (Shippensburg, PA: White Mane, 1987), p. 54.

19 Laura Palmer, *Shrapnel in the Heart: Letters and Remembrances from the Vietnam Veterans Memorial* (New York: Vintage, 1988), p. 227.

20 Michel Foucault, *The Archaeology of Knowledge* (New York: Pantheon, 1972), p. 129.

21 From an interview by author with Duery Felton, Jr., in Lanham, Maryland, August 22, 1991.

22 From a telephone interview with author, June 1, 1995.

55

The Patriot Acts

Donald E. Pease

The cooperation between the society-transforming initiatives of governmental policymakers and the film scenarios through which they are naturalized has been frequently observed. Film's narrative emplotments and the characterization and stylized behavior of its heroes have been formalized into a system of visual representation that has acquired the power to dramatize fundamental shifts in the society's ideology. Because these collaborations produce the imaginary spaces through which alternative sociopolitical outcomes become imaginable, film scenarios have substituted for more politically elaborated rationalizations of policy. The screen's versions of the past have thereby been made to undergird the history of the present.

Throughout the cold war era, the cowboy western and the combat platoon film proved especially effective in their power to absorb political and social crises into the terms of an older consensus. Core metaphors and symbols such as the western frontier and the patriotic soldier that were embedded within these film genres supplied the interpretive grid through which to come to terms with contemporary political crises and to manage the public's response to them. But *The Patriot*, a Roland Emmerich film that was released during the southern phase of the 2000 presidential primaries, replaced these foundational metaphors with a series of substitutes – the revolutionary South for the cowboy West, the lost cause for the frontier, and paramilitary terrorism for British (or Soviet) tyranny – which signaled a major reconfiguration of the sociopolitical order as well as the cinematic formulas through which that reconfiguration was naturalized. The afterlife the film has enjoyed as a feature presentation on Home Box Office television and through its wide distribution at first as a video cassette and more recently a DVD has extended its popularity into the juridico-political domain organized out of the emergency measures spelled out in John Ashcroft's USA PATRIOT Act.

The time in which the film takes place mirrors the moment in which it was released – a historical moment when the political landscape was rapidly changing and the nature of domination was itself in ferment. This film appeared in the aftermath of the cold war, when US nationalism no longer needed to be endowed with ideological substance out of opposition to a common enemy, when the private sector had become a replica of the market, and when the state had been reduced to its policing function. *The Patriot*'s reconfiguration of central themes and agents organizing the national mythology is also indicative of a fundamental shift in governmental policy, which the film at once reflects and represents.

The proximate context for *The Patriot*'s reception was shaped by an ongoing debate over the appropriate attitude to assume with regard to the nation's history – specifically whether discussion of shameful political events should overshadow pride in the nation's achievements. The film deals with the crisis of values raised during this debate by resituating the conflict between shame and pride within the mythic terrain of the nation's founding. The film's stance toward these primordial national sentiments weirdly echoes Richard Rorty's admonition in *Achieving Our Country: Leftist Thought in Twentieth-Century America* that "as long as the American Left remains incapable of national pride, our country will only have a cultural left and not a political one."[1]

When Rorty criticizes the "antipatriotic" legacy of the New Left for being too concerned with culture, he intends to contrast it with the Old Left, which he characterizes as primarily concerned with real or electoral politics. We have a "spectatorial, disguised, mocking Left rather than a Left which dreams of achieving our country" (35), as Rorty elaborates on this insight. After explaining that an unpatriotic Left has never achieved anything, Rorty concludes that a Left that fails to take pride in our country cannot expect to have an impact on its politics, because it will soon become an object of contempt rather than a beacon of hope.

Rorty's cautionary remarks draw on the common-sense belief that just as too little self-respect makes it difficult for a person to display moral courage, so insufficient national pride makes energetic participation in and effective debate about national policy unlikely. "Emotional involvement with one's country – feelings of intense shame or glowing pride aroused by various parts of its history, and by various present-day national policies – is necessary if political deliberation is to be imaginative and productive. Such deliberation will probably not occur unless pride outweighs shame" (3).

Throughout this meditation, Rorty seems to believe that the distinction between shame and pride can be firmly ascertained, and that shame should finally give way to pride in the nation if our politics are not to be spectatorial but actual. Released two years after the publication of Rorty's *Achieving Our Country*, *The Patriot* would appear to have elevated Rorty's formulation into its organizing coda. The film tracks the ordeal of Benjamin Martin, a South Carolinian veteran of the French and Indian War, as he confronts the difficult task of discovering how to transform his shame over the war crimes he committed during that campaign into the grounding motives for the acts of patriotism required for the successful execution of the Southern phase of the Revolutionary War.

But the film is the more astonishing for the spectacular turn it gives Rorty's admonition. For, after corroborating Rorty's assessment of shame as an unpatriotic affective economy, *The Patriot* turned Rorty's analysis on its head and recast patriotic pride as the effect of the restaging of historically shameful events as heroic deeds. After the disembodied voice with which the film opens confesses that "I have long feared that my sins would return to visit me, and the cost is more than I can bear," Ben Martin, the subject of that confession, designates the atrocious actions he committed during the French and Indian War as the referents for the "sins," whose revenance he fears. But the affective intensity of the shame that accompanies Martin's testimony ceases after a certain point to remain connected solely with the crimes against humanity he committed at Fort Wilderness eighteen years earlier. His shame encompasses, as well, the entirety of the South's discredited history of civic violence.

In *The Patriot*, the Revolutionary War that had not yet facilitated the founding of the United States of America became a screen memory for Ben Martin's traumatic experiences during the French and Indian War eighteen years earlier, and for the Civil War that would not take place for another fourscore and five years. Its geographical setting is haunted by Martin's past actions during the French and Indian War as well as the South's future history of disgrace, which the film renders more or less equivalent manifestations of shameful behavior. Indeed, the film's ideological work is discernible in the equivalence it produces between two otherwise incompatible temporal registers: Martin's efforts during the Revolutionary War era to overcome Colonel Tavington's Green Dragoons, on the one hand, and, on the other, the New South's efforts to dissever itself from the history of civic violence that had resulted in its discrediting. I intend to offer a brief explanation of the way in which the film inextricably intertwines these registers at the conclusion of these remarks. But the rationale for that operation requires that I analyze each of these dimensions of *The Patriot* separately.

The Force of Patriotism

Screenwriter Robert Rodat constructed the character of Ben Martin out of an amalgam of three legendary figures from the Revolutionary War era: Thomas Sumter, whose exploits on the battlefield won him the nickname the "Carolina Gamecock"; Daniel Morgan, the rifleman who stated that he would risk everything for the American cause; and Francis Marion, who was popularly known as the "Swamp Fox" because of his ability to slip unnoticed into the Carolina swamps and gather together his hapless band of militia who mounted from there a series of successful guerrilla raids against the British.[2] The film specifies the difference between Ben Martin and the historical personages on which his character was loosely based with a scene in which Colonel Tavington, Martin's antagonist, proposes the sobriquet the "Ghost" to index Martin's ability to elude capture and to strike without warning.

The "Ghost" also indicates that the figure who moved in between the positions of the family and the militia is neither the father nor the colonel but an affective intensity that supports yet threatens both of these socially mandated roles. While Ben Martin may have provisionally identified with each of these roles, the figure that is mobilized into action under the name of the "Ghost" is reducible to neither. The "Ghost" embodies instead the nameless violence that could not expend itself in the name of any cause other than the return of violence for violence.

It is this economy of reciprocal violence to which Martin's sentence "I have long feared that my sins would return to visit me, and the cost is more than I can bear" has reference. The "cost" of Martin's unregulatable violence is unbearable in that it is expended outside the restricted economy of calculable loss and gain and by way of an agency of reversibility that remains external to the subjectivity through which it is borne. It is because violence can neither be lost nor gained that Martin describes the enactments of its expenditure as "sins," and to the "return" he has "long feared" as the agent responsible for the visitations.

Acts of reciprocal violence cannot be stably attached to the name of the subject through whom they are exercised. The subject through whom reciprocal violence takes place is perforce displaced by the violence that passes through this outlet – as it is projected onto the force facilitating its return. When violence appears, the subject through whom it is expended disappears into the enactments through which violence executes itself.

One of the film's organizing paradoxes turns on the fact that, although he is the father of two devoutly patriotic sons, Ben Martin never construes any of the activities he performed during combat to have been motivated by patriotism. Before he marries and fathers seven children, Martin participates in the ritual dismemberment and mass extermination of the French soldiers and the Cherokee warriors responsible for the murder of women and children at Fort Charles. After he marries, Martin becomes a slaveholding member of the Southern plantocracy and a potential secessionist who harbors serious questions about the political validity of the "causes" for which his sons Gabriel and Thomas are willing to risk their lives.

But it is precisely Ben Martin's paradoxical relationship with patriotism that enables *The Patriot* to correlate the nation-founding violence of the colonists' struggle for independence from the British Empire with the state-preserving violence Colonel Ben Martin's "Irregulars" expended against British terrorists. The military formation against which Martin's South Carolina militia is mounted in opposition is not General Cornwallis, who is rendered ineffectual out of his strict adherence to the rules of war, but Colonel Tavington, the commander of a paramilitary battalion known as the Green Dragoons, who does violence to those rules. Tavington's character is based on that of Lieutenant Colonel Banastre Tarleton. "Bloody Ban," who was also called "the Butcher" by members of the Continental Army, was notorious for his administration of the "Tarleton Quarters" – a euphemism for Tarleton's practice of killing all the members of the oppositional forces no matter whether they surrendered or they did not.[3]

Colonel Tavington adds the following items to the "Butcher's" list of war crimes: the targeting of civilian populations; the mass conflagration of the inhabitants of Pembroke, South Carolina; and the hanging of envoys carrying marked parcels. Ben Martin regards Tavington as an unlawful combatant after he murders Thomas, Martin's second-oldest son, and then orders that Martin's house and property be destroyed and that Martin's first son, Gabriel, be hanged as a spy. I have described Martin's violence as state-preserving because his band of militia exercises the force necessary to sustain the survivability of the Continental Army, which was the security state apparatus of the not yet emergent nation. *The Patriot* represents the Southern militia rather than the Continental Army as the military agency responsible for the successful overthrow of General Cornwallis's troops at the battle of Cowpens. If the act of signing the Declaration of Independence had retroactively produced "We the people," the film suggests that it was the "Ghost's" irregulars who supplied the force necessary to guarantee the accomplishment of that activity.

Martin's state-preserving violence is unlike the nation-founding violence of Colonel Burwell, who led the Carolina contingent of the Continental Army, in that Martin's counter-terrorism cannot depend on soldiers who are willing to give up their fives for the "national cause." The state's counterterrorism arm preferred figures like the "Ghost," whose violence is regulated solely by the antagonist, which he must mirror in order to oppose. But insofar as the members of Martin's militia are haunted by the unsanctioned violence they oppose, their counterviolence must perforce operate outside the canons of war.

However, before his forces can overpower Colonel Tavington, Ben Martin must not merely mirror Tavington's violations of the rules of war; he must additionally enact a violence that would preserve the laws of war against Colonel Tavington's efforts to violate them. In order to protect the law against its destruction by Tavington's alien legality, that is to say, Martin must proceed to occupy a space within the law that is exempt from the law's regulations. For it is only by exercising powers that are not subject to the regulations of already existing laws that he can protect the entire order of law.

Martin's acts of law-preserving violence differ from Tavington's violations insofar as his transgressions of law's individual rules take place at a space internal to the law where the law might be imagined as having arrogated to itself the power to declare the legitimacy of the law as such – in its totality. But since the law can declare its own legitimacy only from a position that perforce lacks legitimacy, the position from which Ben Martin would preserve the law might also be described as transgressive of the legal system as such, and transgressive as well of every particular law he would preserve.

In his important meditation on what he calls the mystical foundations of the law, Jacques Derrida has described the paradoxical relation to the law of war that Ben Martin occupies with exceptional lucidity: "There is a law of war, a right to war. . . . Apparently subjects of law declare war in order to sanction violence, the ends of which appear natural (the other wants to lay hold of territory, goods, women; he wants my death, I kill him). But this warlike violence that resembles 'predatory violence' outside the law is always deployed *within* the sphere of the law. It is an anomaly *within* the legal system with which it seems to break. Here the rupture of the relation is the relation. The transgression is before the law."[4]

It is precisely because Martin enacts his law-preserving violence at the limit point which is internal to the otherwise limitless reach of the law that it must remain exempt from the rules it would (transgressively) enforce. But since this space from within which he would preserve already existing laws itself lacks any legal warrant, it would be more accurate to describe this space as one in which Martin's violence founds the law he claims to preserve. Because the law Martin founds is as yet lacking a nation over which it can exercise its jurisdiction, however, Martin's violence might also be described as having preemptively founded the emergency state (in the restricted form of the militia and the extensive form of the Continental Army) as the precondition for the emergence of the nation. Whereas the state normally requires that the subjects under its protection cede their right to violence as the precondition for the state's monopoly over the legitimate use of violence, it is Ben Martin's very refusal to surrender his violence that empowers him to personify the state's monopoly.

Martin demonstrated his preparedness to personify the state's monopoly at Fort Wilderness eighteen years earlier. Before decapitating them, he, along with the soldiers he led to victory within that encampment, first tore out the tongues of the French and Cherokee survivors. Then they gouged out their eyes, cut off their fingers, and flayed the skin from their faces. Next, Martin ordered that these accumulated body parts be sorted into two piles and addressed to separate destinations: The decapitated heads were to be placed on pallets and sent to the French military headquarters; the tongues, fingers, and eyes were to be arrayed on rafts and set adrift in the river that passed through Cherokee territory. After Fort Wilderness, the Cherokees broke their treaty with the French. "That's how they (the British settlers) justified it," as Martin explains this matter to his son Gabriel.

Martin offers this account of the mass extermination in which he had collaborated after Gabriel interrogates his father as to the rationale for the heroic standing that his fellow Carolinians attributed to him in the wake of the Wilderness campaign. Throughout this recollection of the events that took place there, Martin appears to struggle against this former version of himself that has accompanied these ghastly memories. But as he recounts these "sins" to his oldest son, Martin is also discovered to be engaged in a practice of ritualized violence that is continuous with that earlier compulsive behavior. Throughout Martin's confession, the camera meticulously tracks the weird ceremony of violence in which Martin places one of Thomas's toy soldiers on a spoon, then he carefully inserts the spoon into the campfire to melt the metal out of which the soldier was composed into a liquid substance that Martin reshapes into the bullet with which he intends to kill the man who killed his son.

Because he places his family's security above the country's honor, the reach of Martin's affective attachments is restricted to familial loyalties. Martin joins the Continental Army only after his home is destroyed by Colonel Tavington's Green Dragoons. But the bloody acts of aggression that he performs in an effort to protect his family members have rendered him unrecognizable to them. Martin's neighbors and the Carolinian legislators retroactively assign patriotic motives to the unregulated violence he displayed at Fort Wilderness, but, as he indicates in the confession with which *The Patriot* opens, Martin understands his actions there to be part of a vicious cycle of violence. Martin's sons may have believed in the political ideals of liberty and representative government as the cause for which they would gladly sacrifice their lives, but Martin's former experience of war places in crisis these justifications of violence.

Rather than the principles that would appear to have motivated his sons, who have lost their lives in the name of the new nation, Ben Martin is motivated instead by imperatives of revenge and rage. Martin never fights for the country in the name of nationalist principles; he fights to avenge Tavington's violations of the rules of war. As the agent of the law's revenge, Martin gives expression to an excessive violence that his patriotic sons must disown as the precondition for their allegiance to the cause.

Martin's work of mourning entails the transformation of relics of the dead sons from whom he cannot part into the instruments for the absolute destruction of the persons he holds responsible for their deaths. As he transmutes the remnants of his dead sons – Thomas's toy soldiers, but also the cloth flag Gabriel has been repairing throughout the course of the film – into raw materials for the weaponry with which he will avenge their loss, Martin has converted these signs of his son's patriotism into expressions of his unappeasable violence, which is to say the "sins" that never stop returning to visit him.

Martin's motives for military action – rage over the deaths of his sons and despair over the loss of his household – embroil the principle of patriotism itself in an irresolvable contradiction. The affective intensities of rage and despair that traverse his "patriotism" at first arouse the desire belatedly to designate that principle as the motive for actions which have left him at once ashamed and afraid of retribution. But these intensities also subsequently annul that desire. As its "Ghost," Ben Martin haunts patriotism with an uncanny violence that patriotism can neither justify nor regulate.

Patriotism's Lost Cause

At a crucial moment in *The Patriot*, the film produces a tacit correlation between the colonists' struggle for independence and the lost cause of the Southern confederacy. In the scene to which I refer, a wounded soldier watches Gabriel Martin pick up a tattered piece of cloth from the ground on which it had been trampled. After noticing that the cloth bears the imprint of the Stars and Stripes, the veteran announces to his interlocutor that both he and Gabriel are caught up in a "lost cause" for which there exists no hope for success. In associating the flag under whose authority the revolutionists sought to overthrow British rule with the "Lost Cause," the scene encrypts the ideology of Confederate nationalism onto a

historical scene in which nationalism had not yet been achieved.[5]

But when *The Patriot* rendered the "cause" for which Gabriel and Tom Martin sacrificed their lives equivalent to the Southerners' "Lost Cause," it encouraged its viewers to imagine the new American nation as having emerged at a site within which the "Lost Cause" was also redeemed. The film's anachronistic strategies did not merely assimilate the South within an encompassing national geography; they also ostensibly restaged the emergence of the American nation within a geographical region that had formerly been all but excluded from the national symbolic order.

The political imperatives of the secessionist South and revolutionary America become mirror images at the South Carolina Congressional Assembly in Charleston, where Ben Martin becomes engaged in a debate with Colonel Burwell, the head of the Southern wing of the Continental Army, over whether he should join the Revolution. In the course of their debate, Martin declares his autonomy from the demands of the cause by declaring his need to protect and defend his family as the basis for a more primordial loyalty. He refuses to vote in favor of the Revolution, and he invokes his need to protect his family as the grounds for his refusal. But Colonel Burwell does not recognize a father's moral obligation to protect his family as a rationale that takes moral precedence over the needs of the state.

After becoming ashamed at his father's declaration that his need to protect his family takes precedence over his desire to liberate the colony from British rule, his oldest son, Gabriel, volunteers. Gabriel quite literally joins the army in order to fill up the space his father had symbolically evacuated during the Congressional Assembly when he abstained from casting a vote in favor of (or against) the Revolution. In choosing to sign up for the revolutionary cause, Martin's son thereby remakes himself in the image of the principles – of loyalty, freedom, and honor – that his father has repudiated. These nation-making principles repress and supplant the father's violence, which is thereby rendered less important than the patriotic cause to which Gabriel has pledged his allegiance.

When Gabriel Martin repudiates his father's wishes in order to become a citizen-soldier, the state absorbs Martin's desire for his son yet disavows it as the father's desire. Because the family alone can produce the male warriors that it requires to advance its purposes, the state has claimed the son Martin's family has produced – but for the purpose of engendering the nation. The son becomes a patriotic soldier at the very instant in which the father states that he cannot afford the principles of the patriot. As a realm of blood kinship rather than arms, the family occupies the space whose violent disruption the state has presupposed as the basis for its affiliations. Indeed, the social basis for the successful inauguration of a state might be understood to transpire through the forcible supplanting of local kinship bonds with patriotic affiliations.

Martin's placing his loyalty to the family above his allegiance to the nation-state preenacts a crime against the state that will subsequently assume the form of the South's secession. But in *The Patriot*, the South's threat to secede does not merely precede the founding of the nation. The threat of secession also opens up the space within the law in which the distinction between state-making violence and nation-preserving violence can be founded.

As the force whose exercise produces the distinction between the state and the nation, Ben Martin holds the place of the transposition of the state's founding violence into the symbolic order. Because the state does not require an ideological justification for the exercise of the force required to protect and defend the symbolic order, Martin enacts the terrible power whose enforcement of the domestic order is presupposed by the socially symbolic roles of the father and patriot.

The film thereafter elaborates this tacit analogy between the acts of violence that Ben Martin enacted during the Southern phase of the Revolutionary War and the nation-preserving violence of the Civil War into the organizing matrix for its plot. The plot resituates the historical events – lynchings, slavery, civic violence – for which US history had discredited the South within the period of the nation's emergence. Then it reassigns the historical agency responsible for their commission to the Tavington unlawful supplement to the British occupying force. The national shames that took place after the Civil War are thereby reinscribed as the terrible events that the nation-making war was represented as having overcome.

This temporal displacement and transference of the South's discredited history literally unstitch the South from the ideological shames to which it has been sutured and recharacterize the South as the site for the birth of the nation. The substitutions through which the film replaces the South's history of disgraces with its representations of British terrorism generates a series that renders homologous the South's liberation from Britain and the slave's emancipation from slavery, the murderous

fraternal battles that took place during the Civil War and Colonel Tavington's slaughter of the brothers Thomas and Gabriel Martin, the South's history of civic violence and Colonel Tavington's targeting of civilian populations. This last substitution effects a slippage between the actual violence Southern slaveholders performed against black victims and the symbolic violence that the South reputedly suffered in its segregation from national history. The film's inclusion of the South within the consecrated ground of the nation's founding might be understood as an imaginary restitution for this imagined wrong.

The composite result of these serial substitutions and that symbolic restitution is the obliteration of the entire history of Southern civic violence from popular memory. But if the film affirms the history of Southern civic violence through the repetition of its denial, it must also be said that these repeated denegations provide the only "cause" for US patriotism that *The Patriot* acknowledges. After it obliterates the history that had connected the South to these ideological significations, *The Patriot* proceeds to designate the South's state-founding violence as the occult foundation of the national order. More specifically, the film proposes that the South's actual effort to secede from the Union be imagined as having opened up the aforementioned space in which Ben Martin's violence founded the emergency state that preserved the law in its entirety.

It was the South's very failure to accomplish this secession that rendered its transgression of the US Constitution a ruptural event that took place within the law. Rather than founding an alternative order of legality, the South's unsuccessful effort to found an alternative American nation enabled the emergency state to reoccupy the space hollowed out by the South's attempt to secede. The state of emergency designated the place from which the law exempted itself from its own rules so as to overcome the secessionist threat to the legal order as if it were an event formative of the law-preserving transgression internal to the legal order itself. When the state suspended Southerners' civil rights in the aftermath of the Civil War, it turned the South's former violation of the law into the authority for this suspension. For in attempting to found a new nation, the South had also perforce transformed the North's law-preserving violence into the grounds on which the emergency state was founded. When the emergency state declared the South's effort to secede illegitimate, the law grounded its own legitimacy on and by way of the emergency state's declaration of the illegitimacy of Southern secession. The law, that is to say, turned the War of Secession into the occasion to prove that it was the state of emergency rather than the nation (or the people) that exercised a monopoly over power.

Now, when I propose that the law derived the power to legitimate itself from the South's attempt to secede, I do not mean that the law identified with the substantive cause of the secessionists. I mean to propose instead that the law reentered the position that the secessionists had opened up when they posited alternatives to the articles of the constitution, and with the obliteration of each and every individual alternative, the law produced an external legal authority that operated within the law as the law's power to regulate itself.

As the representative of a (lost) cause that the state was required to disown, the secessionist South became the ideal space in which to restage the origins of the United States – as the birth of the emergency state. Unlike the American nation, the emergency state does not require an ideological cause to justify its pronouncements. By deriving the legitimacy of Ben Martin's state-founding violence from the disavowed civic violence of the secessionist South, *The Patriot* has emptied the South's lost causism of its ideological substance so that it might serve as the object cause of US patriotism under a state of emergency.

The Emergency State's Family Values

I'm a parent. I don't have the luxury of principles.
                                        – Ben Martin, in *The Patriot*

Because I have mentioned John Ashcroft's USA PATRIOT Act as one of the contemporary contexts for the film's reception, before concluding these remarks, I should also observe that *The Patriot* has already supplied a representation of the space within which Attorney General Ashcroft has enunciated the state's emergency measures. But the film associates this space with the place of internal transgression formerly occupied by the Southern secessionists. When the measures enumerated within the Ashcroft act legally violate the civil liberties specified within the Constitution, they enable the USA PATRIOT Act to demonstrate the emergency state's power to protect the Constitution as a whole from the threat it understands to have been posed by an alien system of legality. It is in order to protect the Constitution as a whole that Ashcroft declares his suspension (or attenuation) of civil rights and liberties to lie beyond the regulative reach of any of the particular articles of the

Constitution. But in legally violating the civil rights that the Constitution was designed to guarantee, Ashcroft's USA PATRIOT Act might also be understood to have reenacted the civic violence of the secessionist South but to have voided its (lost) cause of the secessionist rationale.

To turn now to that conclusion, throughout this discussion, I have proposed that Ben Martin personifies the emergency state's monopoly of violence. I have also argued that, as the conduit through which the state effected the transposition of a settler colony into an emergent nation, Martin is not motivated by patriotism. But I have also claimed that, insofar as the family replaces the nation as the value system in whose name he fights, Martin places family loyalties above his allegiance to the nation. Having suggested that Martin's family values comprise for him a "cause" that would appear to substitute for patriotic pride, however, I am obliged to explain the relationship between Martin's devotion to family and his personification of state violence.

As the ghostly embodiment of the unregulatable violence through which the state secures the survivability of the nation, Martin does not require the mediation of a nationalist ideology. And his motives for action cannot be reduced to a "cause." If Martin experiences his relation to the state through his need to protect and defend his family (rather than his country), he experiences his relation to the state as the need to introduce Martin family values into the state military apparatus.

His oscillation between state violence and family security transforms Martin into the meeting point through which these otherwise incomparable value systems become inextricably intertwined. The violence with which Martin achieves his family's security results in the transformation of his home into a militarized zone. His original motives for entering the military, moreover, involve the extension of his zone of domestic protection to the defense of his son Gabriel, who, unlike his father, signs up for the cause of liberty. Because he believes that Gabriel's adherence to the rules of war have rendered him vulnerable to Tavington's illegal violence, Martin founds a paramilitary organization within the Continental Army through which he would insure Gabriel's safety. The core family value of domestic security, which Martin forms the militia to propagate, has thereby rendered the domestication of the military sphere virtually indistinguishable from the militarization of the domestic sphere. Which is to say that *The Patriot* has represented the Martin family's values (rather than, say, patriotism) as the means necessary for the national security state to reproduce itself. In rendering family security and national security interchangeable (state/family), *The Patriot* has bypassed national principles either as a mediator or as justification for the exercise of (patriotic) violence.

Notes

1 Richard Rorty, *Achieving Our Country: Leftist Thought in Twentieth-Century America* (Cambridge: Harvard University Press, 1998), 38. Subsequent references to this work are cited parenthetically.

2 Rachel Aberly and Suzanne Fritz, *"The Patriot": The Official Companion* (London: A Carlton Book, 2000), 28.

3 Ibid., 34.

4 Jacques Derrida, *Acts of Religion*, ed. and with an introduction by Gil Anidjar (London and New York: Routledge Press, 2002), 273; my emphasis.

5 For an illuminating analysis of the religion of the lost cause with great relevance to this discussion, see Charles Reagan Wilson, "The Religion of the Lost Cause," in *Myth and Southern History*, ed. Patrick Gerster and Nicholas Cords (Urbana: University of Illinois Press, 1989), 169–90.

56

Silencing the Past: Power and the Production of History

Michel-Rolph Trouillot

[...]

Debates about the Alamo, the Holocaust, or the significance of US slavery involve not only professional historians but ethnic and religious leaders, political appointees, journalists, and various associations within civil society as well as independent citizens, not all of whom are activist. This variety of narrators is one of many indications that theories of history have a rather limited view of the field of historical production. They grossly underestimate the size, the relevance, and the complexity of the overlapping sites where history is produced, notably outside of academia.

The strength of the historical guild varies from one society to the next. Even in highly complex societies where the weight of the guild is significant, never does the historians' production constitute a closed corpus. Rather, that production interacts not only with the work of other academics, but importantly also with the history produced outside of the universities. Thus, the thematic awareness of history is not activated only by recognized academics. We are all amateur historians with various degrees of awareness about our production. We also learn history from similar amateurs.

[...]

Theorizing Ambiguity and Tracking Power

History is always produced in a specific historical context. Historical actors are also narrators, and vice versa.

The affirmation that narratives are always produced in history leads me to propose two choices. First, I contend that a theory of the historical narrative must acknowledge both the distinction and the overlap between process and narrative. Thus, although this book is primarily about history as knowledge and narrative, it fully embraces the ambiguity inherent in the two sides of historicity.

History, as social process, involves peoples in three distinct capacities: 1) as *agents*, or occupants of structural positions; 2) as *actors* in constant interface with a context; and 3) as *subjects,* that is, as voices aware of their vocality. Classical examples of what I call agents are the strata and sets to which people belong, such as class and status, or the roles associated with these. Workers, slaves, mothers are agents. An analysis of slavery can explore the sociocultural, political, economic, and ideological structures that define such positions as slaves and masters.

By actors, I mean the bundle of capacities that are specific in time and space in ways that both their existence and their understanding rest fundamentally on historical particulars. A comparison of African-American slavery in Brazil and the United States that goes beyond a statistical table must deal with the historical particulars that define the situations being compared. Historical narratives address particular situations and, in that sense, they must deal with human beings as actors.

[...]

Workers work, much more often than they strike, but the capacity to strike is never fully removed from the condition of workers. In other words, peoples are not always subjects constantly confronting history as some academics would wish, but the capacity upon which they act to become subjects is always part of their condition. This subjective capacity ensures confusion because it makes human beings doubly historical or, more properly, fully historical. It engages them simultaneously in the sociohistorical process and in narrative constructions about that process.

[My approach entails] a concrete focus on the process of historical production rather than an abstract concern for the nature of history. The search for the nature of history has led us to deny ambiguity and either to demarcate precisely and at all times the dividing line between historical process and historical knowledge or to conflate at all times historical process and historical narrative. Thus between the mechanically "realist" and naively "constructivist" extremes, there is the more serious task of determining not what history is – a hopeless goal if phrased in essentialist terms – but how history works. For what history is changes with time and place or, better said, history reveals itself only through the production of specific narratives. What matters most are the process and conditions of production of such narratives. Only a focus on that process can uncover the ways in which the two sides of historicity intertwine in a particular context. Only through that overlap can we discover the differential exercise of power that makes some narratives possible and silences others.

Tracking power requires a richer view of historical production than most theorists acknowledge. We cannot exclude in advance any of the actors who participate in the production of history or any of the sites where that production may occur. Next to professional historians we discover artisans of different kinds, unpaid or unrecognized field laborers who augment, deflect, or reorganize the work of the professionals as politicians, students, fiction writers, filmmakers, and participating members of the public. In so doing, we gain a more complex view of academic history itself, since we do not consider professional historians the sole participants in its production.

This more comprehensive view expands the chronological boundaries of the production process. We can see that process as both starting earlier and going on later than most theorists admit. The process does not stop with the last sentence of a professional historian since the public is quite likely to contribute to history if only by adding its own readings to – and about – the scholarly productions. More important, perhaps, since the overlap between history as social process and history as knowledge is fluid, participants in any event may enter into the production of a narrative about that event before the historian as such reaches the scene. In fact, the historical narrative within which an actual event fits could precede that event itself, at least in theory, but perhaps also in practice. Marshall Sahlins suggests that the Hawaiians read their encounter with Captain Cook as the chronicle of a death foretold. But such exercises are not limited to the peoples without historians. How much do narratives of the end of the cold war fit into a prepackaged history of capitalism in knightly armor? William Lewis suggests that one of Ronald Reagan's political strengths was his capacity to inscribe his presidency into a prepackaged narrative about the United States. And an overall sketch of world historical production through time suggests that professional historians alone do not set the narrative framework into which their stories fit. Most often, someone else has already entered the scene and set the cycle of silences.

[. . .]

Silences enter the process of historical production at four crucial moments: the moment of fact creation (the making of *sources*); the moment of fact assembly (the making of *archives*); the moment of fact retrieval (the making of *narratives*); and the moment of retrospective significance (the making of *history* in the final instance).

These moments are conceptual tools, second-level abstractions of processes that feed on each other. As such, they are not meant to provide a realistic description of the making of any individual narrative. Rather, they help us understand why not all silences are equal and why they cannot be addressed – or redressed – in the same manner. To put it differently, any historical narrative is a particular bundle of silences, the result of a unique process, and the operation required to deconstruct these silences will vary accordingly.

[. . .]

The production of a historical narrative cannot be studied, therefore, through a mere chronology of its silences. The moments I distinguish here overlap in real time. As heuristic devices, they only crystallize aspects of historical production that best expose when and where power gets into the story.

But even this phrasing is misleading if it suggests that power exists outside the story and can therefore be blocked or excised. Power is constitutive of the story. Tracking power through various "moments" simply helps emphasize the fundamentally processual character of historical production, to insist that what history is matters less than how history works; that power itself works together with history; and that the historians' claimed political preferences have little influence on most of the actual practices of power. A warning from Foucault is helpful: "I don't believe that the question of 'who exercises power?' can be resolved unless that other question 'how does it happen?' is resolved at the same time."

Power does not enter the story once and for all, but at different times and from different angles. It precedes the narrative proper, contributes to its creation and to its interpretation. Thus, it remains pertinent even if we can imagine a totally scientific history, even if we relegate the historians' preferences and stakes to a separate, post-descriptive phase. In history, power begins at the source.

The play of power in the production of alternative narratives begins with the joint creation of facts and sources for at least two reasons. First, facts are never meaningless: indeed, they become facts only because they matter in some sense, however minimal. Second, facts are not created equal: the production of traces is always also the creation of silences. Some occurrences are noted from the start; others are not. Some are engraved in individual or collective bodies; others are not. Some leave physical markers; others do not. What happened leaves traces, some of which are quite concrete – buildings, dead bodies, censuses, monuments, diaries, political boundaries – that limit the range and significance of any historical narrative. This is one of many reasons why not any fiction can pass for history: the materiality of the sociohistorical process (historicity 1) sets the stage for future historical narratives (historicity 2).

The materiality of this first moment is so obvious that some of us take it for granted. It does not imply that facts are meaningless objects waiting to be discovered under some timeless seal but rather, more modestly, that history begins with bodies and artifacts: living brains, fossils, texts, buildings.

The bigger the material mass, the more easily it entraps us: mass graves and pyramids bring history closer while they make us feel small. A castle, a fort, a battlefield, a church, all these things bigger than we that we infuse with the reality of past lives, seem to speak of an immensity of which we know little except that we are part of it. Too solid to be unmarked, too conspicuous to be candid, they embody the ambiguities of history. They give us the power to touch it, but not that to hold it firmly in our hands – hence the mystery of their battered walls.

We suspect that their concreteness hides secrets so deep that no revelation may fully dissipate their silences. We imagine the lives under the mortar, but how do we recognize the end of a bottomless silence?

[. . .]

The seventeenth century saw the increased involvement of England, France, and the Netherlands in the Americas and in the slave trade. The eighteenth century followed the same path with a touch of perversity: the more European merchants and mercenaries bought and conquered other men and women, the more European philosophers wrote and talked about Man. Viewed from outside the West, with its extraordinary increase in both philosophical musings and concrete attention to colonial practice, the century of the Enlightenment was also a century of confusion. There is no single view of blacks – or of any non-white group, for that matter – even within discrete European populations. Rather, non-European groups were forced to enter into various philosophical, ideological, and practical schemes. Most important for our purposes is that all these schemes recognized degrees of humanity. Whether these connecting ladders ranked chunks of humanity on ontological, ethical, political, scientific, cultural, or simply pragmatic grounds, the fact is that all assumed and reasserted that, ultimately, some humans were more so than others.

For indeed, in the horizon of the West at the end of the century, Man (with a capital M) was primarily European and male. On this single point everyone who mattered agreed. Men were also, to a lesser degree, females of European origins, like the French "citoyennes," or ambiguous whites, such as European Jews. Further down were peoples tied to strong state structures: Chinese, Persians, Egyptians, who exerted a different fascination on some Europeans for being at the same time more "advanced" and yet potentially more evil than other Westerners. On reflection, and only for a timid minority, Man could also be westernized man, the complacent colonized. The benefit of doubt did not extend very far: westernized (or more properly, "westernizable") humans, natives of Africa or of the Americas, were at the lowest level of this nomenclature.

[. . .]

Colonization provided the most potent impetus for the transformation of European ethnocentrism into scientific racism. In the early 1700s, the ideological rationalization of Afro-American slavery relied increasingly on explicit formulations of the ontological order inherited from the Renaissance. But in so doing, it also transformed the Renaissance worldview by bringing its purported inequalities much closer to the very practices that confirmed them. Blacks were inferior and therefore enslaved; black slaves behaved badly and were therefore inferior. In short, the practice of slavery in the Americas secured the blacks' position at the bottom of the human world.

With the place of blacks now guaranteed at the bottom of the Western nomenclature, anti-black racism soon became the central element of planter ideology in the Caribbean. By the middle of the eighteenth century, the arguments justifying slavery in the Antilles and North America relocated in Europe where they blended with the racist strain inherent in eighteenth-century rationalist thought. The literature in French is telling, though by no means unique. Buffon fervently supported a monogenist viewpoint: blacks were not, in his view, of a different species. Still, they were different enough to be destined to slavery. Voltaire disagreed, but only in part. Negroes belonged to a different species, one culturally destined to be slaves. That the material well-being of many of these thinkers was often indirectly and, sometimes, quite directly linked to the exploitation of African slave labor may not have been irrelevant to their learned opinions. By the time of the American Revolution, scientific racism, whose rise many historians wrongly attribute to the nineteenth century, was already a feature of the ideological landscape of the Enlightenment on both sides of the Atlantic.

Thus the Enlightenment exacerbated the fundamental ambiguity that dominated the encounter between ontological discourse and colonial practice. If the philosophers did reformulate some of the answers inherited from the Renaissance, the question "What is Man?" kept stumbling against the practices of domination and of merchant accumulation. The gap between abstraction and practice grew or, better said, the handling of the contradictions between the two became much more sophisticated, in part because philosophy provided as many answers as colonial practice itself. The Age of the Enlightenment was an age in which the slave drivers of Nantes bought titles of nobility to better parade with philosophers, an age in which a freedom fighter such as Thomas Jefferson owned slaves without bursting under the weight of his intellectual and moral contradictions.

[...]

The Enlightenment, nevertheless, brought a change of perspective. The idea of progress, now confirmed, suggested that men were perfectible. Therefore, subhumans could be, theoretically at least, perfectible. More important, the slave trade was running its course, and the economics of slavery would be questioned increasingly as the century neared its end. Perfectibility became an argument in the practical debate: the westernized other looked increasingly more profitable to the West, especially if he could become a free laborer. A French memoir of 1790 summarized the issue: "It is perhaps not impossible to civilize the Negro, to bring him to principles and *make a man out of him*: there would be more to gain than to buy and sell him." Finally, we should nor underestimate the loud anti-colonialist stance of a small, elitist but vocal group of philosophers and politicians.

The reservations expressed in the metropolis had little impact within the Caribbean or in Africa. Indeed, the slave trade increased in the years 1789–1791 while French politicians and philosophers were debating more vehemently than ever on the rights of humanity. Further, few politicians or philosophers attacked racism, colonialism, and slavery in a single blow and with equal vehemence. In France as in England colonialism, pro-slavery rhetoric, and racism intermingled and supported one another without ever becoming totally onfused. So did their opposites. That allowed much room for multiple positions.

Such multiplicity notwithstanding, there was no doubt about Western superiority, only about its proper use and effect. *L'Histoire des deux Indes*, signed by Abbé Raynal with philosopher and encyclopedist Denis Diderot acting as ghost – and, some would say, premier – contributor to the anti-colonialist passages, was perhaps the most radical critique of colonialism from the France of the Enlightenment. Yet the book never fully questioned the ontological principles behind the colonialist enterprise, namely that the differences between forms of humanity were not only of degree but of kind, not historical but primordial. The polyphony of the book further limited its anti-slavery impact. Bonnet rightly points that the *Histoire* is a book that reveres at once the immobile vision of the noble savage and the benefits of industry and human activity.

Behind the radicalism of Diderot and Raynal stood, ultimately, a project of colonial management. It did indeed include the abolition of slavery, but only in the long term, and as part of a process that aimed at the better control of the colonies. Access to human status did not lead *ipso facto* to self-determination. In short, here again, as in Condorcet, as in Mirabeau, as in Jefferson, when all is said and done, there are degrees of humanity.

The vocabulary of the times reveals that gradation. When one talked of the biological product of black and of white intercourse, one spoke of "man of color" as if the two terms do not necessarily go together: unmarked humanity is white. The captain of a slave boat bluntly emphasized this implicit opposition between white "Men" and the rest of humankind. After French supporters of the free coloreds in Paris created the *Société des Amis des Noirs*, the pro-slavery captain proudly labelled himself "l'Ami des Hommes." The Friends of the Blacks were not necessarily Friends of Man. The lexical opposition Man-versus-Native (or Man-versus-Negro) tinted the European literature on the Americas from 1492 to the Haitian Revolution and beyond. Even the radical duo Diderot-Raynal did not escape it. Recounting an early Spanish exploration, they write: "Was not this handful of *men* surrounded by an innumerable multitude of *natives* . . . seized with alarm and terror, well or ill founded?"

One will not castigate long-dead writers for using the words of their time or for not sharing ideological views that we now take for granted. Lest accusations of political correctness trivialize the issue, let me emphasize that I am not suggesting that eighteenth-century men and women *should* have thought about the fundamental equality of humankind in the same way some of us do today. On the contrary, I am arguing that they *could not* have done so. But I am also drawing a lesson from the understanding of this historical impossibility. The Haitian Revolution did challenge the ontological and political assumptions of the most radical writers of the Enlightenment. *The events that shook up Saint-Domingue from 1791 to 1804 constituted a sequence for which not even the extreme political left in France or in England had a conceptual frame of reference.* They were "unthinkable" facts in the framework of Western thought.

[. . .] The unthinkable is that which one cannot conceive within the range of possible alternatives, that which perverts all answers because it defies the terms under which the questions were phrased. In that sense, the Haitian Revolution was unthinkable in its time: it challenged the very framework within which proponents and opponents had examined race, colonialism, and slavery in the Americas.

[. . .]

To sum up, in spite of the philosophical debates, in spite of the rise of abolitionism, the Haitian Revolution was

unthinkable in the West not only because it challenged slavery and racism but because of the way it did so. When the insurrection first broke in northern Saint-Domingue, a number of radical writers in Europe and very few in the Americas had been willing to acknowledge, with varying reservations – both practical and philosophical – the humanity of the enslaved. Almost none drew from this acknowledgment the necessity to abolish slavery immediately. Similarly, a handful of writers had evoked intermittently and, most often, metaphorically the possibility of mass resistance among the slaves. Almost none had actually conceded that the slaves could – let alone should – indeed revolt. Louis Sala-Molins claims that slavery was the ultimate test of the Enlightenment. We can go one step further: The Haitian Revolution was the ultimate test to the universalist pretensions of both the French and the American revolutions. And they both failed. *In 1791, there is no public debate on the record, in France, in England, or in the United States on the right of black slaves to achieve self-determination, and the right to do so by way of armed resistance.*

Not only was the Revolution unthinkable and, therefore, unannounced in the West, it was also – to a large extent – unspoken among the slaves themselves. By this I mean that the Revolution was not preceded or even accompanied by an explicit intellectual discourse. One reason is that most slaves were illiterate and the printed word was not a realistic means of propaganda in the context of a slave colony. But another reason is that the claims of the revolution were indeed too radical to be formulated in advance of its deeds. Victorious practice could assert them only after the fact. In that sense, the revolution was indeed at the limits of the thinkable, even in Saint-Domingue, even among the slaves, even among its own leaders.

We need to recall that the key tenets of the political philosophy that became explicit in Saint-Domingue/Haiti between 1791 and 1804 were not accepted by world public opinion until after World War II. When the Haitian Revolution broke out, only five percent of a world population estimated at nearly 800 million would have been considered "free" by modern standards. The British campaign for abolition of the slave *trade* was in its infancy; the abolition of slavery was even further behind. Claims about the fundamental uniqueness of humankind, claims about the ethical irrelevance of racial categories or of geographical situation to matters of governance and, certainly, claims about the right of *all* peoples to self-determination went against received wisdom in the Atlantic world and beyond. Each could reveal itself in Saint-Domingue only through practice. By necessity, the Haitian Revolution thought itself out politically and philosophically as it was taking place. Its project, increasingly radicalized throughout thirteen years of combat, was revealed in successive spurts. Between and within its unforeseen stages, discourse always lagged behind practice.

The Haitian Revolution expressed itself mainly through its deeds, and it is through political practice that it challenged Western philosophy and colonialism. It did produce a few texts whose philosophical import is explicit, from Louverture's declaration of Camp Turel to the Haitian Act of Independence and the Constitution of 1805. But its intellectual and ideological newness appeared most clearly with each and every political threshold crossed, from the mass insurrection (1791) to the crumbling of the colonial apparatus (1793), from general liberty (1794) to the conquest of the state machinery (1797–98), from Louverture's taming of that machinery (1801) to the proclamation of Haitian independence with Dessalines (1804). Each and every one of these steps – leading up to and culminating in the emergence of a modern "black state," still largely part of the unthinkable until the twentieth century – challenged further the ontological order of the West and the global order of colonialism.

This also meant that the Haitian revolutionaries were not overly restricted by previous ideological limits set by professional intellectuals in the colony or elsewhere, that they could break new ground – and, indeed, they did so repeatedly. But it further meant that philosophical and political debate in the West, when it occurred, could only be reactive. It dealt with the impossible only after that impossible had become fact; and even then, the facts were not always accepted as such.

[...]

Erasure and Trivialization: Silences in World History

I have fleshed out two major points so far. First, the chain of events that constitute the Haitian Revolution was unthinkable before these events happened. Second, as they happened, the successive events within that chain were systematically recast by many participants and observers to fit a world of possibilities. That is, they were made to enter into narratives that made sense to a majority of Western observers and readers. I will now show how the

revolution that was thought impossible by its contemporaries has also been silenced by historians. Amazing in this story is the extent to which historians have treated the events of Saint-Domingue in ways quite similar to the reactions of its Western contemporaries. That is, the narratives they build around these facts are strikingly similar to the narratives produced by individuals who thought that such a revolution was impossible.

The treatment of the Haitian Revolution in written history outside of Haiti reveals two families of tropes that are identical, in formal (rhetorical) terms, to figures of discourse of the late eighteenth century. The first kind of tropes are formulas that tend to erase directly the fact of a revolution. I call them, for short, formulas of erasure. The second kind tends to empty a number of singular events of their revolutionary content so that the entire string of facts, gnawed from all sides, becomes trivialized. I call them formulas of banalization. The first kind of tropes characterizes mainly the generalists and the popularizers – textbook authors, for example. The second are the favorite tropes of the specialists. The first type recalls the general silence on resistance in eighteenth-century Europe and North America. The second recalls the explanations of the specialists of the times, overseers and administrators in Saint-Domingue, or politicians in Paris. Both are formulas of silence.

The literature on slavery in the Americas and on the Holocaust suggests that there may be structural similarities in global silences or, at the very least, that erasure and banalization are not unique to the Haitian Revolution. At the level of generalities, some narratives cancel what happened through direct erasure of facts or their relevance. "It" did not *really* happen; it was not that bad, or that important. Frontal challenges to the fact of the Holocaust or to the relevance of Afro-American slavery belong to this type: The Germans did not really build gas chambers; slavery also happened to non-blacks. On a seemingly different plane, other narratives sweeten the horror or banalize the uniqueness of a situation by focusing on details: each convoy to Auschwitz can be explained on its own terms; some US slaves were better fed than British workers; some Jews did survive. The joint effect of these two types of formulas is a powerful silencing: whatever has not been cancelled out in the generalities dies in the cumulative irrelevance of a heap of details. This is certainly the case for the Haitian Revolution.

The general silence that Western historiography has produced around the Haitian Revolution originally stemmed from the incapacity to express the unthinkable, but it was ironically reinforced by the significance of the revolution for its contemporaries and for the generation immediately following. From 1791–1804 to the middle of the century, many Europeans and North Americans came to see that revolution as a litmus test for the black race, certainly for the capacities of all Afro-Americans. [...] Haitians did likewise. Christophe's forts and palaces, the military efficiency of the former slaves, the impact of yellow fever on the French troops, and the relative weight of external factors on revolutionary dynamics figured highly in these debates. But if the revolution was significant for Haitians – and especially for the emerging Haitian elites as its self-proclaimed inheritors – to most foreigners it was primarily a lucky argument in a larger issue. Thus apologists and detractors alike, abolitionists and avowed racists, liberal intellectuals, economists, and slave owners used the events of Saint-Domingue to make their case, without regard to Haitian history as such. Haiti mattered to all of them, but only as pretext to talk about something else.

With time, the silencing of the revolution was strengthened by the fate of Haiti itself. Ostracized for the better part of the nineteenth century, the country deteriorated both economically and politically – in part as a result of this ostracism. As Haiti declined, the reality of the revolution seemed increasingly distant, an improbability which took place in an awkward past and for which no one had a rational explanation. The revolution that was unthinkable became a non-event.

Finally, the silencing of the Haitian Revolution also fit the relegation to an historical backburner of the three themes to which it was linked: racism, slavery, and colonialism. In spite of their importance in the formation of what we now call the West, in spite of sudden outbursts of interest as in the United States in the early 1970s, none of these themes has ever become a central concern of the historiographic tradition in a Western country. In fact, each of them, in turn, experienced repeated periods of silence of unequal duration and intensity in Spain, France, Britain, Portugal, The Netherlands, and the United States. The less colonialism and racism seem important in world history, the less important also the Haitian Revolution.

Thus not surprisingly, as Western historiographies remain heavily guided by national – if not always nationalist – interests, the silencing of Saint-Domingue/ Haiti continues in historical writings otherwise considered as models of the genre. The silence is also reproduced in the textbooks and popular writings that are the prime sources on global history for the literate masses

in Europe, in the Americas, and in large chunks of the Third World. This corpus has taught generations of readers that the period from 1776 to 1843 should properly be called "The Age of Revolutions." At the very same time, this corpus has remained silent on the most radical political revolution of that age.

In the United States, for example, with the notable exceptions of Henry Adams and W. E. B. Du Bois, few major writers conceded any significance to the Haitian Revolution in their historical writings up to the 1970s. Very few textbooks even mentioned it. When they did, they made of it a "revolt," a "rebellion." The ongoing silence of most Latin-American textbooks is still more tragic. Likewise, historians of Poland have paid little attention to the five thousand Poles involved in the Saint-Domingue campaigns. The silence also persists in England in spite of the fact that the British lost upward of sixty thousand men in eight years in an anti-French Caribbean campaign of which Saint-Domingue was the most coveted prize. The Haitian Revolution appears obliquely as part of *medical* history. The victor is disease, not the Haitians. The Penguin *Dictionary of Modern History,* a mass circulation pocket encyclopedia that covers the period from 1789 to 1945, has neither Saint-Domingue nor Haiti in its entries. Likewise, historian Eric Hobsbawm, one of the best analysts of this era, managed to write a book entitled *The Age of Revolutions, 1789–1843,* in which the Haitian Revolution scarcely appears. That Hobsbawm and the editors of the *Dictionary* would probably locate themselves quite differently within England's political spectrum is one indication that historical silences do not simply reproduce the overt political positions of the historians involved. What we are observing here is archival power at its strongest, the power to define what is and what is not a serious object of research and, therefore, of mention.

The secondary role of conscious ideology and the power of the historical guild to decide relevance become obvious when we consider the case of France. France was the Western country most directly involved in the Haitian Revolution. France fought hard to keep Saint-Domingue and paid a heavy price for it. Napoleon lost nineteen French generals in Saint-Domingue, including his brother-in-law. France lost more men in Saint-Domingue than at Waterloo – as did England. And although France recovered economically from the loss of Saint-Domingue, it had indeed surrendered the control of its most valuable colony to a black army and that loss had ended the dream of a French empire on the American mainland. The Haitian Revolution prompted the Louisiana Purchase. One would expect such "facts," none of which is controversial, to generate a chain of mentions, even if negative. Yet a perusal of French historical writings reveals multiple layers of silences.

The silencing starts with revolutionary France itself and is linked to a more general silencing of French colonialism. Although by the 1780s France was less involved than Britain in the slave trade, both slavery and colonialism were crucial to the French economy in the second half of the eighteenth century. Historians debate only the extent – rather than the fact – of France's dependence on its Caribbean slave territories. All concur that Saint-Domingue was, at the time of its Revolution, the most valuable colony of the Western world and France's most important possession. Many contemporaries would have agreed. Whenever the colonial issue was evoked, for instance in the assemblies, it was almost always mingled with Afro-American slavery and both were presented – most often, but not only, by the colonists – as a matter of vital importance for the future of France.

[. . .]

The list of writers guilty of this silencing includes names attached to various eras, historical schools, and ideological positions, from Mme. de Staël, Alexis de Tocqueville, Adolphe Thiers, Alphonse de Lamartine, Jules Michelet, Albert Mathiez, and André Guérin, to Albert Soboul. Besides minor – and debatable – exceptions in the writings of Ernest Lavisse and, most especially Jean Jaurès, the silencing continues. Larousse's glossy compilation of *The Great Events of World History,* meant to duplicate – and, one supposes, fashion – "the memory of humankind" produces a more polished silence than the Penguin pocket dictionary. It not only skips the Haitian Revolution; it attributes very little space to either slavery or colonialism. Even the centennial celebrations of French slave emancipation in 1948 did not stimulate a substantial literature on the subject. More surprising, neither the translation in French of C. L. R. James's *Black Jacobins* nor the publication of Aimé Césaire's *Toussaint Louverture,* which both place colonialism and the Haitian Revolution as a central question of the French Revolution, activated French scholarship.

The public celebrations and the flood of publications that accompanied the Bicentennial of the French Revolution in 1989–1991 actively renewed the silence. Massive compilations of five hundred to a thousand pages on revolutionary France, published in the 1980s and

directed by France's most prominent historians, show near total neglect both for colonial issues and the colonial revolution that forcibly brought them to the French estates. Sala-Molins describes and decries the near total erasure of Haiti, slavery, and colonization by French officials and the general public during ceremonies surrounding the Bicentennial.

As this general silencing goes on, increased specialization within the historical guild leads to a second trend. Saint-Domingue/Haiti emerges at the intersection of various interests: colonial history, Caribbean or Afro-American history, the history of slavery, the history of New World peasantries. In any one of these subfields, it has now become impossible to silence the fact that a revolution took place. Indeed, the revolution itself, or even series of facts within it, have become legitimate topics for serious research within any of these subfields.

How interesting then, that many of the rhetorical figures used to interpret the mass of evidence accumulated by modern historians recall tropes honed by planters, politicians, and administrators both before and during the revolutionary struggle. Examples are plentiful, and I will only cite a few. Many analyses of marronage ("desertion" some still would say) come quite close to the biophysiological explanations preferred by plantation managers. I have already sketched the pattern: slave A escaped because she was hungry, slave B because she was mistreated. . . . Similarly, conspiracy theories still provide many historians with a deus ex machina for the events of 1791 and beyond, just as in the rhetoric of the assemblymen of the times. The uprising must have been "prompted," "provoked," or "suggested" by some higher being than the slaves themselves: royalists, mulattoes, or other external agents.

The search for external influences on the Haitian Revolution provides a fascinating example of archival power at work, not because such influences are impossible but because of the way the same historians treat contrary evidence that displays the internal dynamics of the revolution. Thus, many historians are more willing to accept the idea that slaves could have been influenced by whites or free mulattoes, with whom we know they had limited contacts, than they are willing to accept the idea that slaves could have convinced other slaves that they had the right to revolt. The existence of extended communication networks among slaves, of which we have only a glimpse, has not been a "serious" subject of historical research.

Similarly, historians otherwise eager to find evidence of "external" participation in the 1791 uprising skip the unmistakable evidence that the rebellious slaves had their own program. In one of their earliest negotiations with representatives of the French government, the leaders of the rebellion did not ask for an abstractly couched "freedom." Rather, their most sweeping demands included three days a week to work on their own gardens and the elimination of the whip. These were not Jacobinist demands adapted to the tropics, nor royalist claims twice creolized. These were slave demands with the strong peasant touch that would characterize independent Haiti. But such evidence of an internal drive, although known to most historians, is not debated – not even to be rejected or interpreted otherwise. It is simply ignored, and this ignorance produces a silence of trivialization.

In that same vein, historian Robert Stein places most of the credit for the 1793 liberation of the slaves on Sonthonax. The commissar was a zealous Jacobin, a revolutionary in his own right, indeed perhaps the only white man to have evoked concretely and with sympathy the possibility of an armed insurrection among Caribbean slaves both *before the fact* and in a public forum. We have no way to estimate the probable course of the Revolution without his invaluable contribution to the cause of freedom. But the point is not empirical. The point is that Stein's rhetoric echoes the very rhetoric first laid out in Sonthonax's trial. Implicit in that rhetoric is the assumption that the French connection is both sufficient and necessary to the Haitian Revolution. That assumption trivializes the slaves' independent sense of their

right to freedom and the right to achieve this freedom by force of arms. Other writers tend to stay prudently away from the word "revolution," more often using such words as "insurgents," "rebels," "bands," and "insurrection." Behind this terminological fuzziness, these empirical blanks and these preferences in interpretation is the lingering impossibility, which goes back to the eighteenth century, of considering the former slaves as the main actors in the chain of events described.

Yet since at least the first publication of C. L. R. James's classic, *The Black Jacobins* (but note the title), the demonstration has been well made to the guild that the Haitian Revolution is indeed a "revolution" in its own right by any definition of the word, and not an appendix of Bastille Day. But only with the popular reedition of James's book in 1962 and the civil rights movement in the United States did an international counter-discourse emerge, which fed on the historiography produced in Haiti since the nineteenth century. That counter-discourse was revitalized in the 1980s with the contributions of historians whose specialty was neither Haiti nor the Caribbean. Then, Eugene Genovese and – later – Robin Blackburn, echoing Henry Adams and W. E. B. Du Bois, insisted on the central role of the Haitian Revolution in the collapse of the entire system of slavery. The impact of this counter-discourse remains limited, however, especially since Haitian researchers are increasingly distant from these international debates.

[. . .]

Part X

Internationalization and Knowledge Production about American Studies

The internationalization of knowledge production about the United States is not a new phenomenon. From the nineteenth century on, writers visiting from Europe wrote widely distributed descriptions and analyses of life in the United States. Alexis de Tocqueville, Charles Dickens, Frances Trollope, and others contributed trenchant and less than flattering portraits of the young nation. Scholars from Africa, the Caribbean and Latin America, like José Martí, C. L. R. James, Frantz Fanon, and Eduardo Galeano produced immanent critiques of the United States' imperial projects, along with its apparent inability to live up to its ideals of inclusion and equality. US-based scholars began rereading these critiques in the final decades of the twentieth century and found their arguments more compelling than ever. To a certain extent, these analyses became part of the American Studies canon; they were incorporated into the knowledge base of the field. But in the process of this incorporation, the specific local context and specific crises out of which these critiques had grown often faded into the background.

In the current century, new claims are being made for the importance of non-US-based scholarship about the United States. Although such claims were articulated before the events of 9/11 and taken account of by many American Studies scholars working in the United States, they have intensified recently and circulated more widely in the wake of the US invasion and occupation of Iraq. These latter events have exacerbated ongoing transformations in global geopolitics and together produced a fundamental requirement that the specific local contexts of these non-US-based studies be acknowledged.

Not quite twenty years ago, with the end of the Cold War, it seemed to many that a unipolar global hegemony would belong to the United States for decades to come. This hegemony was driven by military might, certainly, but also by the power of a global capitalism that found its most forthright articulation and legitimation in mainstream American culture. Like all hegemonies, however, this US dominance soon produced multiple counter-hegemonic struggles, only the most spectacular of which is Wahabist fundamentalism. In the wake of these multiple, often globalized struggles, the specificity of position has become ever more important. Even as many American Studies practitioners within the United States have eschewed claims to a privileged epistemological position, radical post-9/11 shifts in US policy have made pursuing international dialogue at once more difficult and urgent. As massive restrictions in visas and travel were imposed in the wake of 9/11, the implications were felt immediately – by the American Studies Association as scheduled speakers from the Middle East were denied visas or entry into the country to attend the annual ASA meeting – and by US universities and colleges as faculty and students who did not hold US passports experienced disruptions including detentions, interrogations, and denied entry. Long-standing practices and institutions of American studies around the world, with their own histories of and struggles about allegiance to and distance from US policy, find themselves transformed by the need to establish their specific difference from the policies and practices that shape current global antagonisms.

In the current state of flux, we cannot possibly do justice to the contingent and unique developments in

American Studies in various nations and regions of the globe. We do want to note, however, the issues of translation and the epistemological limits of the field of US-based American Studies that prevent us from engaging fully some of the fundamental questions about the transformation of American Studies globally. For example, in conversation with internationally based colleagues from around the world, we have been told of an apparent decline in interest and enrollment in American Studies in different locations. This might be a result of declining US power; it might also be the result of increasing economic and cultural interest in other aspects of global politics. But pursuing these questions can only happen through an engagement with scholars with proficiency in different languages and with different histories and situations around the globe. Indeed, a host of new research questions might emerge that can only be addressed in a far more internationally engaged American Studies than has existed in the past.

The articles in this part raise multiple questions about the conditions of knowledge production about the United States. Liam Kennedy explores the opportunities for strategic critiques of US empire in the current crisis and warns of the limits of the European Americanist self-positioning as a marginalized academic perspective. Above all, Kennedy rejects any totalizing view of American Studies. Insisting that critics must avoid the hubris of the view "from nowhere," Kennedy cautions all Americanists to rethink our relation to empire – from the open-ended histories of European imperialism to the current American imperium. Robyn Wiegman calls for critical attention to the cultural imperatives – the wish – that the project of internationalization represents. Probing the citational networks, translation projects and collaborations necessarily entailed in the internationalizing project, Wiegman differentiates between critiques of the US imperial state, the institutional and organization hegemony of US-based American Studies, and the related differential power of the "American Americanist." Employing the concept of "refused identification" to explore the power and limits of various strategies among American studies practitioners, Wiegman examines numerous positionalities that explicitly and implicitly respond to the affective dilemmas presented by an inside/outside model of American Studies, and reads these strategies as "transferential idealism to new objects of study" neglected by dominant models.

Examining field formation in Italian American Studies, Donatella Izzo insists on attention to "the different temporalities operating in American Studies in different cultural contexts." Challenging the teleologies implied in current invocations of post-, inter, and trans-nationalisms, Izzo insists that Americanists not conflate the disclaimers and critical stances that we produce as intellectuals with performative acts that would have the power to transform the relations we criticize. Izzo challenges us to examine the irony of promoting a post-hegemonic American studies "at exactly the historical juncture when the USA is deploying its world hegemony on an unequalled and unprecedented scale." For Izzo, Americanists must reject the impulse toward panoptic global views in favor of a more modest historical specificity.

Spectres of Comparison: American Studies and the United States of the West

Liam Kennedy

. . . one should say to detractors of the new US imperialism: those who do not want to engage critically with Europe should also keep silent about the US.

(Žižek, 2004: 7)

In March 2002 the French writer Regis Debray published a satirical novel entitled *L'Edit de Caracalla ou Plaidoyer Pour des Etats-Unis d'Occident par Xavier de C**** (The Edict of Caracalla, or a Plea for the United States of the West by Xavier C***). The novel takes the form of a long letter in which Xavier explains to Debray why he has become an American citizen and argues that all Europeans should identify themselves with the United States in the wake of 9/11. Xavier proposes the creation of a 'United States of the West', a federation that would permit Europeans to move 'from the status of second-class Americans to that of full Americans' (Debray, 2004: 30). He offers some 'history lessons' to support his proposal. 'To become American in the 21st century will be like becoming Roman in the 1st century', he writes, when to become a Roman was 'to graduate from the status of Syrian, Spaniard, Gaul or slave, to that of a man'. Xavier goes on to argue the particular merits of Caracalla, the Roman emperor who granted 'full Roman citizenship to all free men in all the provinces' in AD 212, and thereby 'rejuvenated an exhausted Roman polis' (Debray, 2004: 33–5). Xavier does not live to see his vision realized. Due to his language skills the Pentagon despatches him to Afghanistan where '[I]n the twilight of a freezing day in November 2001, Xavier C*** was killed by friendly fire' (Debray, 2004: 130). His vision survives him, though, in the posthumous letter, a cunningly drafted modest proposal that Debray addresses to a French (and more

broadly a European) public still uncertain about the meanings of the growing estrangement between 'Old Europe' and the global hyperpower of the USA. Debray's book certainly offers some insight into European disenchantment with American power and also illustrates the deep ambivalence that underlies this, the admixture of desire and repulsion in European responses to American culture. A key ingredient of the uncertainty surrounding transatlantic alliances, Debray recognizes, is the paradoxical force of an anti-Americanism that shadows so much critical thinking about America in Europe. Xavier neatly articulates this when he argues to Debray: 'Your passport is from the European Union . . . but your libido is made in the US' (Debray, 2004: 72).

This is or should be a position many Europeans recognize, including those who identify as European Americanists. I will comment here on some of the paradoxes of such a position as they show up in critical discourses on American relations with Europe. I will also speculate on some possible frames and points of focus for European Americanists if they are to engage critically (as I think they should) the immanence of American empire and address their local and regional roles in relation to the new internationalist agendas that are currently being projected for American studies.[1]

European critiques of American culture and foreign policy have a long history, embedded in distinctive national concerns but also reflecting on a broader European imaginary. In the 20th century, spurred by the growing international evidence that the USA was the driving force of modernity, European intellectuals and media began to focus their critique on what came to be termed 'Americanization'. To be sure, much of this commentary was focused on the perceived crudities of American media or popular culture, but also more engaged, intellectual debates about European traditions and identities have been tied to ideas of 'America'; particularly at times of significant historical rupture – the aftermaths of both World Wars and again after September 11 – we find great intellectual confusion and ambivalence about support for American brands of 'internationalism'.[2] A notable feature of many of these critiques of American culture and foreign policy is a dialectical impetus that projects 'America' as a screen for analysis of more localized concerns, whether national or supranational – the issues of European integration or union being a common example. In other words, America became 'a tertium comparationis' in culture and political struggles in Europe, centring on the control of the discourses of national and transnational European identities (Kroes, 1999a).[3] Not only the debates on Americanization but also discourses of anti-Americanism across the 20th century activate this dialectic.

Debray is clearly very aware of the dialectic; in a sense his satirical structure works off it as he repeatedly asks his interlocutor to acknowledge the logic of joining a United States of the West, which only confirms the dominance of the European imagination by the American empire. In Xavier's words: 'While transatlantic citizenship remains a right to be acquired, Americanness is an established fact' (Debray, 2004: 103). It may be that he plays off this dialectic in ways that more pointedly satirize European than American targets and he has admitted to wanting to make the French confront their nation's growing irrelevance in European and international affairs. At any rate, such dialectical treatments of the meanings of America are part of a more complex framework of reflections (some more conscious than others) on national and intranational identities in Europe, and on Europe's borders with its 'outside'.

What makes this debate particularly complex and enlivened today is that the context for this dialectic is one of great historical uncertainty under the growing shadow of the American empire, as the borders of European identity are destabilized on so many fronts. The end of the Cold War began a process of recognition by Europeans that American power was now unbalanced and that a period of unipolarity was emerging, in which the role of Europe was by no means certain. In the wake

of 9/11, the wars in Afghanistan and Iraq not only hardened this recognition but also ignited a latent anti-Americanism throughout much of Europe and especially in what Donald Rumsfeld has termed 'Old Europe'. At the same time, there is an ongoing debate about European unity and enlargement, and 10 new states were integrated into the European Union in 2004. While this was an occasion for public celebration in many of these states, such a large expansion has not been a smooth process and debates about borders, security and immigration are running at a heightened, tabloid-sensationalized pitch in Europe. Issues of citizenship have moved explosively to the fore of European politics and the agreement struck to move towards a referendum on a European constitution promises political division across Europe for some time to come.

In such a volatile political context European efforts to critique or interpret American empire take on an especially potent dialectical charge, reflecting back on the uncertainties in European futures. Debray is far from alone in perceiving America as a constituent part of European reflections on Europe; I want to comment briefly on the views of two other well-known European intellectuals before moving on to the field of American studies in Europe.

Passions for the Real

The events of September 11 stimulated a great deal of European commentary on American culture and foreign policy. A notable intellectual intervention in this respect was the publication by Verso of three short books by Jean Baudrillard, Paul Virilio, and Slavoj Žižek in September 2002, describing them on the book jackets as 'analyses of the United States, the media, and the events surrounding September 11 by Europe's most stimulating and provocative philosophers'. In each book we find these theorists testing their theory against the 'event' of September 11; in doing so they make more explicit the political animus of their work and either mimic or address the fascinations that bind America to the European intellectual imagination. All three theorists show striking unity of thought in their articulations of globalization as the driving force behind fundamentalist violence of different stripes, time and again claiming that the attacks of September 11 find their hidden causes within American imperialism. Their treatment of these causes, though, and their theoretical contextualizations of the 'event' of September 11 differ in distinctive ways. Of the three, it is Žižek's text, *Welcome to the Desert of the Real*, that I want to comment on here as it is more challenging to intellectual audiences, advancing provocative ideas in a nuanced theoretical fashion – using his own inimitable brand of Lacanian psychoanalysis. This is not to say he provides a focused argument: Žižek ranges widely across popular and high cultures, turning out propositions that annoy and amuse in about equal measure, but rarely entail an expository theory. What he hangs many of his ideas on is a central, repeated proposition (following Alain Badiou) that 'the key feature of the twentieth century' was 'the passion for the Real' (Žižek, 2002: 5). For Žižek, 'the Real' is not everyday social reality, but that which structures its deceptions and is only revealed as a violence of transgressive defamiliarization. The Real culminates not in verisimilitude but in spectacle – whilst the postmodern twist is that a passion for the semblance of the spectacle 'ends up in a violent return to the passion for the real' (Žižek, 2002: 10).

More fulsomely than either Virilio or Baudrillard, Žižek addresses the question of the role of fantasy in the attacks of September 11 and responses to them. With references to popular film (the title of his book is taken from the film *The Matrix*) he argues that Americans, 'immobilized in their well-being', are haunted by dreams of catastrophe (Žižek, 2002: 17). As fantasy, these dreams sustain the Real through its fictionalization, 'as a fantasmatic spectre whose presence guarantees the consistency of our symbolic edifice' (Žižek 2002: 32). The challenge for Americans following September 11, Žižek argues, is to recognize that the 'war on terror' is an extension of such fantasizing and a mirror of the dialectics of American exceptionalism: 'America's "holiday from history" was a fake: America's peace was bought by the catastrophes going on elsewhere' (Žižek, 2002: 56). It is with this in mind that Žižek goes on to argue that the 'state of emergency' instituted in the wake of September 11 is 'part of a desperate strategy to *avoid* the true emergency and return to the "normal course of things"' (p. 67; emphasis in original). Yet he also sees the opportunism of the state in the way it articulates this emergency and thereby legitimates suspending or redrafting legal and citizenship rights. In this he divines (following Giorgio Agamben) the advent of *homo sacer*, a category of identity for those denied full citizenship and political subjectivity in the global emergencies of 21st century societies.

While *Welcome to the Desert of the Real* allows Žižek to revisit and extend many of his theoretical concerns, it is also marked by his particular European location and reflects back on broad issues of European identity. Large parts of the closing chapters of the book are given over to a convoluted defence of the role of his native Slovenia in the break-up of Yugoslavia. At the same time he advocates a unified Europe as a counterweight to American hegemony and asks:

> Is not the 'war on terrorism' the abominable conclusion, the 'dotting of the I', of a long, gradual process of American ideological, political and economic colonization of Europe? Was not Europe again kidnapped by the West – by American civilization, which is now setting global standards and, de facto, treating Europe as its province? (Žižek, 2002: 143)

Arguing that Europe needs 'to distance itself clearly from the American hegemony', he goes on to assert that

> the real politico-ideological catastrophe of September 11 was that of Europe. . . . In the name of the 'war on terrorism', a certain positive vision of global political relations is silently imposed on us Europeans. And if the emancipatory legacy of Europe is to survive, we should take the September 11 fiasco as the last warning that time is running out, that Europe should move quickly to assert itself as an autonomous ideological, political and economic force, with its own priorities. It is a unified Europe, not Third World resistance to American imperialism, that is the only feasible counterpoint to the USA. (Žižek, 2002: 144–6)

Žižek may be sceptical about the possibilities of creating 'an autonomous European political initiative', yet he apparently sees little other option than to promote European modernity as a counter to American hegemony – a perhaps surprising outcome to this particular example of dialectical reflection on Europe through the discursive mediation of America.

A more fulsome promotion of European modernity has recently been advanced by other leading European intellectuals addressing the emergence of the American hegemon and its global role as a European matter. To date, the 'intellectual' intervention that has received most public attention is the joint statement by Jurgen Habermas and Jacques Derrida titled 'February 15, or What Binds Europeans Together'.[4] In it Habermas urges Europe's intellectuals to add their voices to the massive demonstrations against the war in Iraq that took place across Europe in February 2003. To Habermas the demonstrations were 'a sign of the birth of a European public sphere' (Habermas and Derrida, 2003: 291). Habermas argues that 'Europe has to throw its weight on the scale to counterbalance the hegemonic unilateralism of the United States' (p. 293). He calls for European intellectuals to contribute to the articulation of a European identity beyond the legacies of Eurocentrism and the logic of nation-states and to 'promote a cosmopolitan order on the basis of international law against competing visions' (p. 294). In Habermas' view, European secularization has been the basis of a painful process of learning to acknowledge difference and European history has created 'sensitivity to the paradoxes of progress' (p. 296). He adds that the experience of the loss of empire has made European nations sensitive about the violence of modernization: 'With the growing distance of imperial domination and the history of colonialism, the European powers also got the chance to assume a reflexive distance from themselves' (p. 297). Habermas' plea is very much in line with his intellectual work over many decades as he nurtures the legacy of the critique of the 'dialectic of enlightenment' and projects European modernity as an unfinished project.

In Habermas' text, as with Žižek's, there is a personal intellectual trajectory, a politics of intellectual location, underwriting his transatlantic theorizing and shaping the dialectical thrust of the arguments. Despite (or perhaps because of) this, both writers' theorizing shows signs of strain in the efforts to envision Europe as a political bloc countering the US hegemon. The strain is not so much in the idealism of the projection – Habermas is certainly self-conscious about the idea of the public sphere as a political ideal – rather it is what their European imaginaries repress or only allude to that produces a strain in their thinking: the spectres or spectral effects within their texts of the violent claims to belonging and citizenship that recur in European history and that are presently apparent in the geo-political borders of European identity. Žižek makes reference to this in his comments on the deformation of the former Yugoslavia. His commentary is heated, accusatory and contradictory, on the one hand positing Slobodan Milosevic's ascendance to power as evidence of neofascist fundamentalism that mirrors a 'New World Order', while on the other decrying NATO intervention as a punishment of sovereign states. In Habermas' text the projection of Europe as counterweight to US hegemony is uneasily staged, in that it relies on a rhetorical confidence that Europe's loss of its empires is a completed history; he thus creates a curious moral plateau from which to proffer rational and corrective vision on the doings of the American

empire. We should note that this is an idea repeated by many liberal-left commentators in Europe and the USA in the last few years. Richard Rorty, for example, endorses Habermas' statement and argues that 'the European Union is the only likely sponsor of an alternative to Washington's project of a permanent pax Americana ... Europe has, in the second half of the twentieth century, found a solution to the problem of how to transcend the nation state' (Rorty, 2003). Of course, the conservative caricature of such a perspective is that made famous by Robert Kagan (2003), who charges that Europeans perceive themselves in a posthistorical paradise and then mockingly suggests 'Americans are from Mars and Europeans are from Venus'.

Habermas' idea of an emergent European public sphere and a concomitant cosmopolitanism deserves fuller attention in relation to a growing international debate about globalization and cosmopolitanism. Here, I only want to note further that it defines the relation between Europe and America as one of Western discourse and ideas – most obviously when he argues that 'the nations of Europe share [a] mental habitus, characterized by individualism, rationalism, and activism, with the United States, Canada, and Australia. The "West" encompasses more than just Europe' (Habermas and Derrida, 2003: 294). Of course, Habermas does not envisage a 'United States of the West', pace Regis Debray's satirical perspective, but his sense of the transatlantic relationship is clearly circumscribed by his perception of modernity. Moreover, the dialectics of that relationship in his writing conceal the spectres of European history – what is repressed and displaced in his theorizing are the spectres of European empires and their fallout – of (de)colonizations, sectarian divisions, wars and genocides. These spectres haunt his – and many other – efforts to formulate an effective political expression for the historical and moral identity of Europe and generate an alternative to US imperial power. Again and again, these projects are linked together in the dialectics of Atlantic debate. In other words, the challenge of and to American hegemony energizes discourses of and on European identity and the efforts to distinguish this identity signify the borders and spectres that traverse its symbolic presence in the discourses.[5]

Empty Castles

What do these debates about the identity and role of Europe as counter to American empire and hegemony mean for the work of European Americanists? American studies in Europe has its own complex history in relation to 'America', though European Americanists are, I suggest, much less haunted by the Cold War origins of their field than Americanists in the USA; in Europe, there has not been the same sense of intellectual or disciplinary agony in relation to this history. That said, I want to comment on a point of origin from which we may yet have much to learn, that of the Salzburg seminars of the immediate post-war years.

The first Salzburg seminar was held in the summer of 1947 at Schloss Leopoldskron, a rococo 18th-century castle just outside Salzburg in Austria. It was organized by several Harvard students and faculty with a view to introducing 'American civilization to the young generation of post-war Europe', or as one of the founders put it, 'a Marshall Plan of the mind' (Ryback, n.d.). Over a hundred young Europeans gathered to take classes from American faculty who gave their services for free – indeed, the strong voluntary ethic was important to many involved as a way of distancing any association with propaganda. Some famous scholars met together at Salzburg that summer, among them F. O. Matthiesen, Alfred Kazin and Margaret Mead. The purpose of the seminar was given clearest articulation by Matthiesen in the opening session, when he remarked they were assembled there 'to enact the chief function of culture and humanitarianism, to bring man again into communication with his fellow man' (quoted in Smith, 1949). It was felt by most concerned that a focus on American civilization – with literature and history as central subject areas – was best suited to this purpose.

Margaret Mead wrote a report on the seminar, a remarkable document in its allusions to European and American civilizations at this historical moment and in its anthropological treatment of the event, as much of it focused on group behaviour and organization. Mead presented a very suggestive picture of the setting in which the students came together. In the spacious castle they

> were able to meet in a mood which combined a sense of distance from real life, and a sense of the importance of the traditions of civilization. From a Europe where no-one will ever live again the kind of life for which the Leopoldskron is an appropriate setting, the European students walked, as it were, upon a stage where some of the more insistent difficulties of their real life situation could be forgotten. (Mead, 1947)

But this somewhat idealized intellectual space does have an outside, a 'real' no less symbolic than the castle's airy interiors. Mead names and describes it:

> Salzburg with its bombed areas, its American MP's, in large bright tin helmets, its DP camps and its Jewish refugees, its population among whom there was not a single plump child . . . pulling the seminar members back to the real world and assuring them that Leopoldskron was not an escape but merely a setting within which it was possible to meet each other and breathe in new air for the months to come. (Mead, 1947)

This is an evocative spectacle of the interiorization and exteriorization of the seminar's symbolic work. The rarefied space of the castle and of the intellectual communications that took place inside it echoes the semi-autonomy of a post-war intellectual life in retreat from the Second World War's aftermath, devoted to the life of the mind, to 'a world elsewhere'. But its condition is also represented in the material effects of the war on the urban landscape. What Mead conjures is an imaginary moment of juncture of competing but related modernities, the aftermath of a clash of civilizations, one in decline and another rising, the *mise en scène* of their juncture apparent in the spectacle of stateless peoples and armies of occupation in a landscape of ruin.

At a point when East/West relations were growing extremely tense and the Iron Curtain was being drawn, Salzburg as a 'setting' for the study of American civilization takes on further historical connotations – located in Austria, the gateway to Central Europe, it is sited both in the centre of (Old) Europe and at the border of the (New) West. The significance of this position is indicated in the final paragraphs of Mead's report, where she suggests that the seminar has

> demonstrated that one of the major contributions that Americans can make to Europe, is to give the members of the different European nationalities a wider identification, a sense of their Europeanness. At the present time, Europe, as a civilization – rather than as a geographical area – seems more real to Americans than to Europeans. This means that Americans can do a great deal to shape an emerging sense of European civilization. (Mead, 1947)

In conclusion, Mead proposes that with the Salzburg seminar as an example, 'a rich variety of new centres of Euro-American study should be developed all over

Europe, where many empty castles stand waiting' (Mead, 1947).

Mead's proposal has not quite been fulfilled as she would seem to have intended. European castles have indeed become sites of Atlantic connections, filled as they often now are by American hotel chains, multinational businesses and so on. In another way, what Mead refers to as 'centres of Euro-American study' did take shape, as sites of American studies teaching and research began to surface across Europe in the 1950s and 1960s. The practice and scope of American studies varied greatly from country to country in Europe. In the early stages it tended to focus on literature and history as core disciplinary threads and it rarely questioned the American exceptionalism apparent in US American studies. In this it very much presented itself as what Mead called 'Euro-American study'. (Henry Nash Smith (1949), who participated in the Salzburg seminar in 1948, observed that the seminar 'restated the potential unity . . . of Occidental culture'.) In time the field of American studies in Europe became more highly diversified in disciplinary and methodological ingredients, becoming more cultural in the 1970s and 1980s and more comparative in the 1990s. It has also become more questioning of American exceptionalism in recent years, enjoining some of the academic discourses that seek to dislocate the nation as axis of focus: the transnational, the post-national, the transatlantic, the Black Atlantic, the circumatlantic – all offer frames that European Americanists are becoming keen to discuss, and I believe these more comparative frames offer promising grounds for the critical enquiries about American empire that are needed to make European American studies critically commensurate to the current international crises.

However, the legacies of 'Euro-American' studies still linger and require comment. For much of the last 50 years, European Americanists have tended to write as though part of a transatlantic intellectual class and in so doing have not questioned but lent support to the authority of US-centred knowledge based in American institutions and publishers. Until recent years they have been generally disinclined to engage home-grown theoretical movements until after they had been digested by US American studies and fed back to Europe. The German Americanist Heinz Ickstadt makes the point:

Although European theories (structuralism and post-structuralism, or the sophisticated socialism of the Frankfurt School) had a considerable impact in the United States, they influenced American studies in Europe only after they had been absorbed and recycled as deconstructionism, or new historicism, or feminist theory. (Ickstadt, 1996)

The relation of American studies in Europe to American and European circuits of knowledge-production are of course much more complex than Ickstadt summarizes, but his point has force in reminding us of the spell of intellectual authority cast by American academia.

European Americanists may be said to have found themselves in the paradoxical position Regis Debray satirizes and that every thinking European feels acutely: our passports are from the European Union . . . but our libidos are made in the USA. For the European Americanist the bind is particularly acute: after all, 'America' is our purported object of study, the raison d'etre of our professionalization, and the privileged medium for our passions for the Real. By this last comment I do not mean to suggest that European Americanists are bound to false consciousness; rather, there is a tendency within European-based American studies (differentially located and articulated) to study the sign of America as a locus of otherness or difference, without pursuing what I think is the necessary concomitant of such study: asking how this passion for the Real structures their intellectual frames of enquiry (not to mention their cultural fantasies) – here I am thinking, for example, of the romance or fetishization of the trope of race in European studies of American culture.[6]

I intend no summary judgement; rather, I want to draw attention to this aspect of European American studies as further evidence of the uncanny dialectic that haunts Atlantic theorizing. For many years American studies has functioned as a marginal or alternative academic space throughout Europe, attracting scholars, teachers and students who wanted to work beyond the boundaries of what had come to seem traditional disciplines. This sense of marginal or alternative academic perspective that American studies can lend in many institutional settings outside the USA should not be underestimated as a very valuable impetus for (critical) study of the USA, but it can also function as a prison house of representation, reproducing an American exceptionalism through the valorization of American culture as sites of marginality, of dissent, of the new and subversive. In short, the field imaginary of American studies in Europe has all too often coalesced with the marginalized self-image of faculty and displaced more local, non-academic concerns onto the phantasm called 'America'.[7]

For Europeans who purport to write as Americanists a more careful attention to their frames and grounds of interpretation is required. This means that European Americanists should be wary of the Atlantic divide as a device of disengagement. Writing in *American Quarterly*, Heinz Ickstadt suggested that European scholars 'can look at the United States as an object of political, social, and cultural analysis without running the risk of being considered chauvinistic or parochial' (2002: 555), a privileged 'outside-position' – but this is the privilege of a view from nowhere, and I do not think European Americanists should endorse it as a way to frame 'America'.

So, what more can European Americanists do to 'contest the universalism of American exceptionalism' and critique the rise and perpetuation of American empire? First, they can rethink the dialectics of Americanization as a way to study relations between Europe and America. A great deal of fine work has been done by European Americanists in studies of Americanization but a great deal of this is fixated on it as a mode of cultural hegemony or exchange. What needs further thought is the role and parameters of the American state in the manifestations of America in Europe and beyond, so that critical frames and commentaries would focus more clearly and more strategically on the state as the condition and the tool of imperial power. This is also to say that American studies, under the shadow of empire, should work to focus on the state rather than the nation as its object of knowledge and critical enquiry.[8] As the transatlantic alliance stutters there are opportunities for strategic American studies critiques. I mean strategic in the sense that the 'war on terrorism' teaches us that all information is strategic and that we need to rethink the relation of our formations and productions of knowledge to the shifting meanings of America in Europe – as information, culture, propaganda – and be attentive to the ways in which the meanings of America hit the ground across Europe.

Second, if we are to do this intellectual and cultural work in and through Europe, then we also need to rethink our relation to empire – not just to the American empire of the present but also the European empires of the past and their haunting legacies in the present, legacies that are intimately tied up with the American imperium we behold today. Contrary to Habermas, we should not work from a closed history of empire but rather from the open-ended histories of European imperialisms. We can proceed to do this by reconfiguring temporal and spatial scales of historical study and by constituting strategic alliances with other fields of critical and area studies. For example, a strong case has been made by Brian Edwards for asserting the inseparability of the Cold War and postcolonial periods (in 'Western' history), so that we 'link the US-Soviet contest with the political struggle for and within Europe's former colonial holdings and the cultural formations that emerge in the wake of that contest' (Edwards, 2003: 71). More particularly, this can mean study of the violence of belonging within the European super-state – Northern Ireland and the former Yugoslavia are obvious examples, and the recent histories of both have been marked by American interventions – and the violence at its borders – in the Middle East, in North Africa, in the Soviet Union. In each of these border areas we can locate legacies of European empires being played out in relation to new interventions by the American empire, whether these be the hard power of military operations or the soft power of cultural, educational and commercial diplomacy. European Americanists are well placed geographically and culturally to critically chart these intersections of imperial legacies and power, including their presence in metropolitan centres as well as at the geopolitical borders of Europe, for the presence of the postcolonial is of course inscribed in the migrant and immigrant communities of urban Europe, where its real everyday existence haunts the debates on unity, citizenship and a European constitution.[9]

In this recasting of European American studies under the sign of empire we should be attentive to the territorialization of history and culture in claims to 'European' identity. Etienne Balibar provides a useful clue to doing this in his recent writings on the borders of Europe. He comments:

> Undoubtedly Europe and America are not separate spaces, any more than Europe and Eurasia, or Europe and the Middle East. . . . No European 'identity' can be opposed to others in the world because there are no absolute borderlines between the historical and cultural territory of Europe and the surrounding spaces. And there are no absolute borderlines because Europe as such is a 'borderline' . . . More precisely, it is a palimpsest of borderlines – a superimposition of heterogeneous relations to other histories and cultures, which are reproduced within its own history and culture. (Balibar, 2003: 322)

In Balibar's view, Europe is fundamentally a space of translation and transition – a somewhat idealized view, to be sure, but one articulated with a shrewd sense that this idea of Europe as a borderline keeps it open to comparative interpretations. An understanding of this spatial dislocation of Europe is crucial to a reconceived field of (comparative) American studies in Europe that can trace the contours of European and American empires in these borderlines. Post-war Salzburg was one such borderline, a complex site of modernity's creative destruction and a primal scene of European American studies' inauguration; its legacies haunt us still, a disturbing but necessary spectre of our intellectual belonging, and a prefiguration of the scenes on Europe's borders today.

And finally, reconstellating European American studies under the sign of empire means developing a new self-consciousness about the politics of intellectual place-making and the spatial scales of disciplinary enquiry. There are signs of new geographies of American studies scholarship emerging, and while such an emergence remains fraught with questions of power and knowledge it also promises new spaces for conducting research, new opportunities for transdisciplinary work, and new possibilities of intellectual affiliation and alliance. If it is to take a critical hold on the future it should not be conceived as totalizing but rather as taking account of the 'intellectual regionalism' that already exists, recognizing the need to collaborate with related disciplines (likely experiencing their own paradigm dramas) and working to put local, national and global dimensions of American studies into dialogue with each other (Rowe, 1998: 20). Of course this means that Americanists everywhere need to work to resist the spectatorial role into which the power of the American empire casts us. Such resistance is no simple matter – as Debray's satirical commentator reminds us, we should take neither our passports nor our libidos for granted.

Notes

1   A prominent example is Amy Kaplan's call for Americanists to 'contest the universalism of American exceptionalism' and critique American empire (see Kaplan, 2003: 10).

2   There is a voluminous literature on 'Americanization' by European writers and scholars, covering cultural, political and economic influences (see Berghahn, 2001; Campbell et al., 2005; Ellwood, 1992; Kroes, 1996; Kuisel, 1993; Nolan, 1994).

3   As Rob Kroes has observed, there are discernible deep structures and enduring repertoires of cultural and metaphoric contrast in the projections of 'Europe' and 'America' by each other. Kroes' own work has gone some way to critically sketching what he calls 'a canon of European reflection on America as a counterweight to an imagined Europe' (see Kroes, 1999b).

4   First published in *Frankfurt Allgemeine Zeitung* on 31 May 2003, the statement was composed by Habermas; Derrida was a co-signatory.

5   There is further clear evidence of this if we look to the response of intellectuals in Central and Eastern Europe to the war in Iraq and the advent of American empire. (In this respect, Žižek is *not* representative.) Many intellectuals in Central and Eastern Europe have been dismayed or angered by what they see as the self-aggrandizing anti-Americanism of Western European intellectuals. Dissident intellectuals such as Vaclav Havel, Gyorgy Konrad and Adam Michnik do not readily identify with Habermas' model of European modernity nor with the ideal of cosmopolitanism that underlies his vision of a postnational European democracy (see Auer, 2005: 16–22). These differing understandings and responses to European history and modernity are significant markers in the intellectual perspectives on European relations with the USA and how these reflect back upon European identity. In other words, the dialectics of Atlantic theorizing in Central and Eastern Europe suggest not so much an Atlanticist disposition as a propensity towards an anti-anti-Americanism that says as much about intellectual differences with Western Europe as it does about relations with the USA – once again, the USA functions as a floating signifier of more localized concerns.

6   This is a question that could and should be asked of other European intellectual formations, for 'America' has long worked to hone European theorizing – as with Roland Barthes' early work on mythologies, or Jacques Lacan's critique of American ego psychology. Surprisingly, there has been little academic study of these theoretical projections of America in the machinery of European critical and cultural theory.

7   To recognize how this works we need to grasp Žižek's notion (following Lacan) of 'traversing the fantasy' – this would not liberate us from the hold of American hegemonies; we do not get our libidos back so easily. Rather it entails more fully identifying ourselves with the fantasy that structures our sense of the 'real' (see Žižek, 2002: 17).

8   On the need to focus critical attention on the state, see Bove (2002), Berube (2003), Kaplan (2003), and Kennedy and Lucas (2005).

9   Many countries in Europe now have large Muslim minorities and globalization has accelerated a process of multiculturalization of European educational systems and public spheres. With the emergent debates on Islam and European identity there are opportunities for new forms of comparative discussion and study that would foreground the histories of alternative modernities, including alternative histories of human rights and conflict resolution, and of the role of religion in international affairs. Such comparison might usefully challenge the lazy thinking on the 'transatlantic rift' post 9/11, which posits a secular Europe in contrast to a religious America.

References

Auer, S. (2005) 'Whose Europe Is It Anyway? Derrida, Habermas, Havel and Rumsfeld Debate the Meaning of European Identity', unpublished paper.

Balibar, E. (2003) 'Europe: Vanishing Mediator', *Constellations* 10(3): 312–38.

Berghahn, V. R. (2001) *America and the Intellectual Cold Wars in Europe*. Princeton, NJ: Princeton University Press.

Berube, M. (2003) 'American Studies without Exception', *Publications of the Modern Language Association (PMLA)* 118(1): 103–13.

Bove, P. (2002) 'Can American Studies Be Area Studies?', in M. Miyoshi and H. Harootunian (eds) *Learning Places: The Afterlives of Area Studies*, pp. 204–25. Durham: Duke University Press.

Campbell, N., Davies, J. and McKay, G., eds (2005) *Issues in Americanization and Culture*. Edinburgh: Edinburgh University Press.

Debray, R. (2004) *Empire 2.0: A Modest Proposal for a United States of the West by Xavier de C****. Berkeley: North Atlantic Books.

Edwards, B. (2003) 'Preposterous Encounters: Interrupting American Studies with the (Post)Colonial, or *Casablanca* in the American Century', *Comparative Studies of South Asia, Africa and the Middle East* 23(1&2): 70–86.

Ellwood, D. (1992) *Rebuilding Europe: Western Europe, America, and Postwar Reconstruction*. London: Longman.

Habermas, Jurgen and Derrida, Jacques (2003) 'February 15, or What Binds Europeans Together: A Plea for a Common Foreign Policy, Beginning in the Core of Europe', *Constellations* 10(3): 291–97.

Ickstadt, Heinz (1996) 'Teaching American Studies Abroad: The European Experience', *U.S. Society and Values* (USIA Electronic Journals), 1(15), http://usinfo.state.gov/journals/itsv/1096/ijse/icks.htm (accessed 10 December 2005).

Ickstadt, Heinz (2002) 'American Studies in an Age of Globalization', *American Quarterly* 54(4): 543–62.

Kagan, R. (2003) *Of Paradise and Power: America and Europe in the New World Order*. New York: Knopf.

Kaplan, Amy (2003) 'Violent Belongings and the Question of Empire Today: Presidential Address to the American Studies Association, October 17, 2003', *American Quarterly* 56(1): 1–18.

Kennedy, Liam and Lucas, Scott (2005) 'Enduring Freedom: Public Diplomacy and US Foreign Policy', *American Quarterly* 57(2): 309–33.

Kroes, Rob (1996) *If You've Seen One, You've Seen the Mall: Europeans and American Mass Culture*. Urbana: University of Illinois Press.

Kroes, Rob (1999a) 'American Empire and Cultural Imperialism: A View from the Receiving End', www.ghi-dc.org/conpotweb/westernpapers/kroes.pdf (accessed 10 December 2005).

Kroes, Rob (1999b) 'World Wars and Watersheds: The Problem of Continuity in the Process of Americanization', *Diplomatic History* 23(1): 71–7.

Kuisel, R. (1993) *Seducing the French: The Dilemma of Americanization*. Berkeley: University of California Press.

Mead, Margaret (1947) 'The Salzburg Seminar in American Civilization', URL (accessed May 2004): www.salzburgseminar.org/reports/1947_MeadArticle.pdf.

Nolan, M. (1994) *Visions of Modernity: American Business and the Modernization of Germany*. Oxford: Oxford University Press.

Rorty, Richard (2003) 'Humiliation or Solidarity: The Hope for a Common European Foreign Policy', URL (accessed May 2004): www.dissentmagazine.org/menutest/articles/fa03/rorty2.htm.

Rowe, John Carlos (1998) 'Post-Nationalism, Globalism, and the New American Studies', *Cultural Critique* 40: 11–27.

Ryback, T. W. (n.d.) 'The Salzburg Seminar: A Community of Fellows', URL (accessed September 2004): www.salzburgseminar.org/2005History.cfm.

Smith, Henry Nash (1949) 'The Salzburg Seminar', URL (accessed September 2004): www.salzburgseminar.org/2005History.cfm?goto=overview.

Žižek, S. (2002) *Welcome to the Desert of the Real*. London: Verso.

Žižek, S. (2004) 'What Lies Beneath?', *The Guardian* (1 May): 7.

58

Romancing the Future:
Internationalization as Symptom and Wish

Robyn Wiegman

Points of Departure

This essay began as an address to the Australian and New Zealand American Studies Association in 2004 and explores the critical challenges that attend the ongoing demand to internationalize the field of American Studies.[1] It makes its appearance in this Blackwell volume by invitation and offers a commentary on the ways that internationalization currently operates as both a designation for critical practices variously focused on the transnational, diasporic, postnational, and postcolonial, *and* as a discourse about the US university and the political economy of knowledge production on a global scale. By forging what I take to be a necessary distinction between the critical analytics that animate the field and the practices of knowledge production that comprise it, my essay hopes to map the incommensurate and at times contradictory efforts that currently aim to transform the field's geopolitical formation. In the end, my contribution does not seek to provide a new formula for completing the project that internationalization engages, nor does it determine which critical framework will solve the vexing conundrums that American Studies as a global entity raises. Instead, I am interested in tracking how efforts to internationalize the field reveal and compound the complexities they seek to address. This is the case in part because the central problem that internationalization raises is not the geographical "fact" or the "imaginary" formation or the epistemological "privilege" or even the daunting "exceptionalism" of "America" so much as what stands in the way of coming to terms with all of this at once.

Such a sweeping claim requires a good bit of careful explication, especially if my destination is ultimately to demonstrate the ways in which the renewed conversation about internationalization participates in what I have come to call, with affection, the symptom and wish school of American Studies. As wish, the discourse of internationalization speaks to the urgency of transcending the critical horizons of the nation in order to track the transnational circulations of the US as an object of study. It calls for new citation networks, translation projects, and scholarly collaborations, and seeks to recognize the fundamental interconnections of a world system of social, economic, and conceptual relationships. But the wish it promotes never travels far without the symptoms that generate it, in part because so much of what is at stake in internationalizing American Studies arises from a political struggle over and against the geopolitical weight of the object of study itself. Americanists, whether in Pakistan or Croatia, Argentina or Canada, the US or one of its unacknowledged colonies, want not to be implicated in its imperializing historical present, nor to extend, by reproducing, the US's self-centered self-reflection and mono referentiality as the moral and intellectual leader of both modern political history and the contemporary globalized world. But getting out from under the power of the US is no simple task, and not just because of the enormous military, economic, and cultural dominance of the American state. "America," after all, is the object of all kinds of attachments; it has an affective life, and that life is made and remade, refracted and critiqued, not in the US alone, but in the complicated ways that national identities, symbolic systems, cultural forms, languages, discourses, governments, capital, commodities, and people interact and transform one another.

The reconfiguration of the field that internationalization wishes for is thus two pronged, at the very least: it requires a critique of the dominance of the object as a self made entity, such that the emergence of "America," as both fact and fiction, is resituated in a larger sphere of action, beyond national narratives that confer on it the myth of its own autonomous beginning. It is in this context that "American American Studies" has been defined and challenged as a specific (and specifically invested) iteration of the field.[2] At the same time, internationalization requires attention to the content, form, and meaning of "America" in its transnational production, and to the forms of relationality its circulation entails. Taken together, these two trajectories can be vexing, even contradictory, as when scholars committed to the critique of the dominance of the US must consider the various attachments, identifications, and symbolic redeployments of the global travels of "America," such that the object of study is made incommensurate with the nation-state that claims it as its own.[3] People – scholars among them – can love something about the idea of "America" and yet hate the violent realities of its state operations. To be sure, they can hate both, but that tends, ironically, to usher them into kinship with the contemporary American Americanist, whose identificatory refusal with her object of study has become her most characteristic mark. This is a point of no small importance, as you will see.

To speak in the language of love and hate is incommensurate, of course, with the critical habits of American Studies in any contemporary frame, but I invoke this affective sphere deliberately. After all, the two trajectories that internationalization cultivates – the critique of the object on one hand and its differential deployment in transnational practice on the other – are overwritten by affective investments of all kinds. While it might be too much to say that internationalization is most interesting for the affect it reflects, I venture the suggestion anyway, in order to situate the transcendent desire of the wish and the symptoms that provoke and animate it in a different trajectory altogether, one that prioritizes the inner logics and affective attachments of the field imaginary of which internationalization is a generative and generated part. I characterize this field imaginary as one governed and sustained by "refused identification," which is a concept I use to capture the affective investments that have motivated Americanists everywhere to find a means for transcending complicity

with their object of study. In what follows, I track the use of refused identification across the geopolitical and epistemological divide that internationalization repeatedly evokes, between the seeming "inside" of American Studies in its domestic formation to its international "outside." My aim in doing so is to foreground the various scales of analysis that attend internationalization and to deliberate on the incommensurabilities that are thereby exposed between critical practices that are organized by importantly different targets of critique, including most prominently the US imperial state, the organizational hegemony of US American Studies, and the American Americanist herself. By reading the discourse of internationalization as collectively organized by refused identification but as internally disaggregated through the targets and scales of its critique, I pursue in the following pages what is persistent, not new: the structure of a field imaginary in which object relations (between practitioners and the field of study and among practitioners) are invested with, if not repeatedly read *as*, the very relations of geopolitical material life that internationalization sets out to chart.[4] Let me explain what I mean.

Implication

Throughout the US university today, the humanities and interpretative social sciences rely, in various ways and to differing degrees, on what I am calling *refused identification* as a primary mode of meaning making for politically engaged scholarship.[5] It might be true to say that it was first deployed as a tactic for revisionary work in disciplines that had long occluded the specificity of the human subject in gendered, racial, sexual, and economic terms.[6] It is certainly true to say that whole generations of scholars have now been trained to practice refused identification as the means by which they approach the normative assumptions of their disciplines, undoing canons, transforming methodologies, and resisting not simply particular histories, but the privileges such histories ascribed to specific critical vocabularies and habits of thought.[7] In US American Studies, refused identification, aimed against the consensus model of a homogenous US culture, has been the primary response to the exceptionalism of the Cold War object of study, opening investigations to a range of people, practices, and critical questions seemingly excluded by the discourses of American Studies pursued in the post-war period. The controversy surrounding Janice Radway's 1998 Presidential address to the US American Studies Association – on the extent to which empire was inescapably embedded in the organization's name – took its heat, in part, from her claim that the field imaginary had already been transformed by work in feminist, ethnic, queer, and postcolonial studies such that a name change would reflect what had already transpired.[8] As Radway and others have told it, what I am calling refused identification made its way into US American Studies through inquiries into power and difference born from the perspectives launched by social movements, thus delivering scholars from the analytic and political constrictions of a field formation that seemed too committed to synthesis, singularity, and commonality, and too reiterative of the hegemonic practices and ideological norms of the social world in which its objects of study had formed.

This did not mean – nor does it now – that American Americanists refused identification with their objects of study altogether. Indeed, part of what refused identification performs, in US American Studies and elsewhere, is a transferential idealism to new objects of study, most often to the dispossessed identities and categories of analysis that the dominant model is taken implicitly or explicitly to abject.[9] These transferences not only transform the field by making both legible and legitimate new objects of studies, methodological priorities, analytic practices, and critical questions, but they establish an oppositional political imaginary through which practitioners understand their scholarship as socially significant and productively ethical. In this way, the field imaginary of American Studies and its political project have been – and are – intimately connected in both a historical and genealogical sense, if not mutually generative, and it has been the critical force of this intimacy that first brought the Cold War exceptionalist model into focus, such that scholars roundly refused identification with it by shifting the terrain of their critical investments away from it. Hence the New American Studies, as we now call the work amassed to critique Cold War American Studies, has prioritized ethnic and gendered differences over homogeneous national identity, dissensus over consensus, theories of everyday resistance over seamless interpellation, and interrogations of culture over the official narratives of the state. Refused identification has thus served the political function of disarticulating American American Studies from its prior analytic attachments, which were coded and ceded as complicit with the state projects of economic and social domination of various kinds.

But the transformation of a field is never a fully conscious formulation; it arises from historical forces, institutional impulses, and political ir/rationalities quite separate from the subjects who practice what it teaches, which is why any articulation of a field's inner workings becomes most legible in its critical aftermath, not in the inchoate moments in which it is most challenged. This is just one way of saying that critical intention is never an adequate explanation for historical or political effect, nor a measure of the affect that generates it. It also means, more importantly, that any refusal of identification with a field's prior analytic attachments must make legible the demand for identification it sets itself against. In this, it is not simply in opposition to but productive of the analytic attachments it rejects. I take this to be part of what Leo Marx means when he writes about the Great Divide in American American Studies that now stands between the Cold War project and the New American Studies.[10] To Marx, this binary alignment misrecognizes the plurality of positions that have animated American Studies in the US since its very beginnings, *and* the continuities that exist across the divide, including the ways in which New Americanist disidentifications, while borne from the social experiences of Vietnam, segregation, and xenophobia, might be said to nurture the founding democratic expectation, if only in negative critical guise.[11] New Americanist critique, in other words, invests – and invests heavily – in consolidating the monolithic power of the Cold War apparatus in order to produce itself as the comprehensive political project that can transcend it.

While there is much to contest in Marx's essay, including his own tendency to dismiss theory altogether, I want to let his most provocative suggestion – that the New American Studies cannot possibly be wholly distinct from the Cold War project it rejects – hover, as I return to the pressing question of internationalization and the field imaginary that generates it. As I hope to demonstrate in the following section, all of the most prominent scholarly models that have sought, overtly, to respond to the internationalizing imperative are devoutly attached to identificatory refusal as their signal critical practice. Some strategies turn Cold War American Studies inside out by taking internationalization as a demand to trace the routes of labor, politics, and culture that proceed from the imperial core, thereby refusing the mythic "America" for more materialist accounts of its historical formation at the complex intersections of colonialism and capitalism. Others situate "America" from the generative space of an epistemological and increasingly territorial outside, thereby invoking a post-nationalist future in which American Studies will no longer originate in America itself.

Still others argue for comparative analytics and new geographical imaginaries that disorient inside/out logics and offer new ways to think about proximity and location, often as a means of refusing identification with the global authority of American American Studies and its practitioners. Regardless of their analytic aim or the target of their refusal, however, all of these strategies reiterate as a consolidated identity the formation of the field they simultaneously reject, in a powerful and contradictory structure of affective investment and strategic disavowal. This makes them neither critically inadequate nor politically useless – indeed, I find them all important ways of thinking through and about "America" as historical entity, geopolitical sign, cultural form, imperial power, and emblem of social struggle. My point is rather to demonstrate how analytically attached and symptomatically productive they are of the field imaginary they mutually share, no matter how much the debates between them might seek to situate their differences otherwise.

It is, then, the explication of the field imaginary that refused identification offers that most interests me, and the ways in which practitioners invest in the belief that the field can be disarticulated in some complete and final way from its implication in its object of study. As I hope is already clear, my point is not to belittle this belief, nor to lament its consequences for the field of American Studies, nor even to show that all acts of analysis are modes of implication (if for no other reason than that a full accounting of our own historicity is never available to us). Indeed, I take very seriously the motivations and investments that generate the critical habit of establishing an object of study as a project of political refusal – whether through its symbolic ideation, its materialization in state practices, its history of analysis, or in the figure of its homegrown practitioner. But my goal here is more modest, in that I want to provide a framework, first, for understanding the essays collected in this Blackwell volume, which demonstrate the widespread commitment of US American Studies to discourses of internationalization through analytic attachments to transnational, diasporic, and postcolonial critical frameworks; and second, for measuring the absolute difficulty of leveraging internationalization to extricate American Studies from its analytic and historical implication in the entity it studies.

Inside and Out

An early, but by no means the first, formulation of internationalization, established by Amy Kaplan and Donald

E. Pease and elaborated more recently by Laura Briggs, Shelley Streeby, Laura Wexler, and others, turns Cold War American Studies on its head by explicating the project of empire in US nation-state formation.[12] This work pays attention to how distinctions between the domestic interior and foreign exterior, along with citizen and alien, have been built. Its rendering of internationalization extends the New American Studies emphasis on racialization to colonized and annexed geopolitical sites, identifies forgotten wars (with Mexico, the Philippines, and Korea) as a new archive for historical study, and establishes the critique of imperialism as the generative force and critical destination of the field. Its mechanism of refusal operates against both the exceptionalist state and its formalization of American Studies in the US university in the mid twentieth century. A second strategy, best exemplified by the work of Lisa Lowe, tracks "the international within the national" in order to disrupt the persistence of inside/outside logics and to open the field to transnational critical practices.[13] It finds itself less interested in the explicitly imperial practices of a militarized state than in rethinking identity formation as a material effect of the transnational history of US empire. Lowe's specific case is Asian American Studies which is understood not as a project of proto nationalism on the part of a minoritized population, but as a response to the political economy of US imperialism and the migrations of people which the routes of empire beget. Other scholarship in this vein includes Amy Kaplan's "Manifest Domesticity," which links white women's nation building practices in the home to the export of US empire transnationally, and Inderpal Grewal's *Transnational America*, revealing how the concepts of inside and outside are riven with transactions, both material and symbolic, that mire the domestic, in all senses of the term, in international exchange.[14] This model continues the critique of the Cold War knowledge apparatus by not only engaging resistant cultural formations that are brought into being by US international economic and military strategy, but also, as in the case of Grewal, looking at the complex histories of capitalism and coloniality.

A third response to the internationalizing imperative, articulated most prominently by José David Saldívar and often referred to as border studies, likewise refutes notions of inside and outside that make nation formation distinct from the transnational circulations of people, goods, labor, culture, and knowledge.[15] This work establishes its internationalism to challenge the conflation of the United States with the American hemisphere by drawing heavily on scholarship in Latin American

Studies and by refusing to limit its understanding of culture to a mono-linguistic one: all in order to think about transcultural and transnational identities and cultural practices irreducible to national territories or the imaginaries they beget. It allies itself to the New American Studies in its emphasis on dispossession, including the dispossession of Latino culture and its critical studies from the most prominent histories of US social struggle and educational reform. Its signatory refusal collates around geographical imaginaries that suture state formations to cultural practices by delineating histories of competitive imperialism in the hemisphere, turning back to contestations between England, Spain, and France for "new world" sovereignty. A fourth and compellingly related mode, diaspora studies, draws most heavily from the intersection of African American and African Studies, and proceeds from new projects on modernity, the Black Atlantic, Black Europe, and other configurations of black intellectual traditions from Fanon and CLR James to Paul Gilroy, Carole Boyce Davies, and, in her most recent work on black global cities, Hortense Spillers.[16] Internationalism is here historically linked to pan-African politics and offers the possibility of revising standard representations of civil rights struggle to utilize some of its most challenging post-national implications. Its work is multi-sited and has come to grapple increasingly with the minoritized status of Africa in studies of globalization and in the discourse on diaspora as well. Diaspora studies in this vein privileges displacement as an axis of interrogation and has the difficult task of attending to the symbolic weight of the US in global histories of black identity formation. Its identificatory refusals take shape against nation-state organizations of knowledge and culture. In its analytic practice, the generic story of nation formation is less a history of emancipatory anti-colonialism than a critical grappling with the toxic accumulation of human life as property.[17]

A fifth strategy calls for a comparative national perspective to de-center the US from its universal representation as the quintessential national form, thereby locating operations of culture in cross-national formulations that are multi-national in scope. This work, established by Günter Lenz, Klaus Milich, John Carlos Rowe, Paul Giles, and others, situates itself within reconfigurations of the knowledge industry on a global scale as it encounters and seeks to rethink area studies models with more fluid and flexible ideas about nations as imaginary formations with deeply material effects.[18] Its identificatory refusals are aimed at the provincializing enclosures

of US based American Studies and at the high cultural focus of much of the scholarship in the field as enunciated in the Cold War era. A sixth and one of the most internationally prominent formulations of internationalization builds on much of the preceding work to explore the relationship between the national and the international in the modes of knowledge production at work in American Studies as a global scholarly enterprise. Elaborated by Jane Desmond, Virginia Dominguez, Rob Kroes, and others, it pays attention to the uneven distribution of power – in resources, cultural capital, and critical authority – that accompanies the production and circulation of American Studies across national university systems, and calls attention, as Desmond writes, "to the different goals, stakes, and histories of US-based, and non-US based scholarly communities."[19] Expressing an aversion to glib celebrations of transnationalism or globality, she emphasizes the importance of mapping the specificity of each scholarly exchange, thereby addressing in concrete practices the limitations that cross-national collaborative work by its very nature will encounter.[20] By focusing on issues of knowledge production in the national university systems in which scholars work, Desmond's model seeks to attend to the material history of the nation itself. As she says, the "collaborative cognitive mapping [of American Studies] must recognize the continuing importance of nationalism and national contexts in shaping knowledge."[21] Under this framework, a great deal of work is currently being done to map the political economy of American Studies in the local, national, and regional contents in which it is embedded, and it is from this kind of endeavor that the force of the particularity of what is now called "American American Studies" has largely emerged.

A seventh model of internationalization has grown from the work of the sixth, emphasizing both collaboration and comparative analysis, but in a context of even stronger identificatory refusal with American American Studies itself. Captured most succinctly by Djelal Kadir in his presidential address, "Defending America Against Its Devotees," delivered at the inaugural International American Studies Association meeting in 2003, this model calls for a transcendence of the "tautological Americanness of American Studies" through perspectives that do not "originate in America itself."[22] Such perspectives are internationalist both in their refusal to limit the study of America to a national scale and in their refusal to rely on the disciplinary priorities – "literary studies, popular culture, and ethnic studies" – that have dominated the field in its convergence with "U.S. cultural politics" (137). Instead, Kadir favors the rise of "political science and international relations, economics, demographic analysis, and information technologies and media assessments" – fields that will enable the break from the "nationalist cocoon" through which practitioners in US American Studies have served "as unwitting instruments of nationalist unilateralism, exceptionalism, and incomparability" (137, 147).[23] In an earlier essay, "America and Its Studies," Kadir defines the international perspective as one born in the refusal to identify with American American Studies, which would enable the field "to arrive," as he puts it, "at a discriminating and self-critical position by and on America."[24] This position entails confronting how "America is something other than what it deems identical to itself," which means turning the study of the object "out of itself' through a "comparative and relational refocusing of America in the larger world context" (21, 20, 22). "The best hope for American Studies," he writes, "is for it to cease to be American" (11).

This list, of course, is not comprehensive, but it is extensive enough, I hope, to demonstrate the various ways in which internationalization has been deployed to contest contemporary formulations of American Studies. Those that prioritize internationalization as a critique of the imperial state tend to follow the route of empire from the *inside out*, precisely to refuse the Cold War narrative of an embattled domestic space unimplicated in the threat posed by its foreign outside. Their refusal of identification is deeply, profoundly, staked to Cold War ideologies and modes of critical address. When the destination of critique extends to the configurations of people and cultures that are displaced by the brutality of nation building, as in both border and diaspora studies and in the incorporative modality that Lowe calls "the international in the national," internationalization follows, rather literally, the cross-national routes of travel that empire has generated, the imaginary delineations it has drawn between people, and the modes of affiliation and collective life it has engendered, through resistance, in the process. At this scale of analysis, Cold War models of cultural and national homogeneity are rejected, and the New American Studies names itself by making culture and nation both antagonistic and distinct. This distinction between cultural formation and the apparatus of the nation-state grows increasingly less discernible in the latter formulations of internationalization, as the study of the US is resituated from the critical standpoint of a geographical outside. These projects are deeply invested in de-centering the US by thinking at a comparative

scale of analysis about nation and region, and by establishing new international venues for the collaborative production of the field. They also forward the assumption that exceptionalism cannot be resolved from within the auspices of US democratic struggle, no matter how crucial that struggle is for articulating histories of exclusion and for thinking about the deep discontinuities between democratic governmentality and capitalism. This is the case, Desmond and others argue, because the New American Studies has not fundamentally unseated the hegemony of American American Studies as the primary voice in the global articulation of the field. It is for this reason that scholars have cast debates about race, gender, and sexuality as nationalist, even parochial matters, entrenched in a set of internal domestic references.[25]

But what, we must ask, is internal? After all, if the New American Studies is formulated by multiple discourses of internationalization, as it surely is, what precisely domesticates these discourses so completely that only from outside the geopolitical locus of their academic production can one have epistemological purchase on the situation of the US in the world? This, of course, is a vexing question for a field that seeks to account for relationality on a global scale, not simply because relationality always requires attention to the different scales of analysis that are used to account for it (otherwise we have only universalisms), but also because of the enormous transference at work here, such that critical practice becomes the privileged frame for examining global power relations and resisting them at once. To say, as we are now bound to say, that there are always power relations embedded in the critical act and in the relationship between practitioners does not mean that critical practice can resolve the power relations it reveals, no matter how much we may wish it to be otherwise. What must be acknowledged instead is how reliant are the strategies of internationalization on refused identification as the means for establishing both their critical differences from one another and their political intentions. Each invests in establishing a critical strategy – whether epistemological, collaborative, identitarian, or geopolitical – to disentangle itself from implication in either the historical power and everyday force of its object of study, "America," or in the field formation, American American Studies, that has been cast repeatedly as overly invested in, if not analogous with the object itself. It is for this reason that I want to claim that the outside to Cold War or New Americanist American Studies that internationalization variously promises is well inside the field imaginary that governs it. To put this more succinctly and no doubt with just a touch of aggression, let me say this: that being outside American American Studies today is one of the most intriguing and paradoxical ways to make one's home within it. This paper has explicated the persistence of refused identification to explain why.

The Object Which is Not One

It is no doubt strange for me to ascribe so much seeming agency to a critical operation, as though internationalization actually *is* something. But in what sense is this not true? Left critique in many parts of the world has long been convinced that ideas have material effects (think ideology), but there is no agreed upon understanding of precisely how they take on a life of their own, which is why at this late date there is still the standoff between theory and the real. (I won't take you down that road again, other than to say that no critical conceptualization is adequate to what it hopes to name – and for reasons that don't belong to theory alone.) The more salient point is that conceptual entities, such as internationalization, may lack definitive ontological and phenomenological dimensions, but they do *do* something, if "only" because they cultivate the possibility of inhabiting a symbolically different kind of world. To call this a romance, as my title puts it, is not to render it insignificant or fantastical in the negative sense. Political optimism is not possible without fantasy, and actions are not always traceable to distinctly material incitements. No, the most difficult issue here is not about ascribing false agency to internationalization. It has to do instead with what lurks beneath internationalization's aspiration to craft a set of critical practices and priorities that relieve American Studies of being implicated in the power or history of what generates it. This is the belief, as I have suggested above, that the relationships both between practitioners and their objects of study *and* among practitioners themselves are not only indices but inscriptions of the social relations of US global hegemony.

Generally speaking, this belief is not unique to American Studies, as many fields of study, in the US and elsewhere, put their faith – I use that word purposely – in the making and remaking of their knowledge apparatus, investing in new objects of study, critical questions, and specific methods of inquiry to mark significant and field-claiming departures from prior critical habits and their generational heirs. I think of this less in oedipal terms than as part of the legitimizing structures of modern

state institutions, where traditional and emergent practices and orientations butt heads in a competition for authority. Surely, from this perspective, it is no accident that many of the contestations within universities between traditional knowledges and new formations can be traced quite directly to transformations in national and regional forms of political struggle over identities and identifications of various kinds. American Studies in the US, along with sociology, have their roots here, in a populist emphasis on class and culture. British Cultural Studies emerges from the routes of reclamation engendered by both postcolonial critique and the vestiges of working class analysis within popular British politics as a whole. South Asian Subaltern Studies takes shape as the critical counter to historical effacements produced by colonial education. Indeed, twentieth century social movements as a whole – often collectively called decolonization movements – have been armed to the teeth, so to speak, with knowledge projects, and many have taken both education as an institution and the knowledge practices they engage as primary targets for intervention. In this context, it is certainly possible to say that there are definitive linkages, borne of various colonial inheritances, within the modern nation state form between education, social struggle, and academic field formation, and further that these linkages are not exceptional ones – they do not arise from the specific discourse of self creation within one nation as opposed to another.

What does it mean, then, to read American American Studies, not simply as the homogeneous and hegemonic entity that provokes the need for internationalization but as formative to the field imaginary that inaugurates the wish that internationalization now stands for? Is this reading simply a defense of American American Studies produced by an American Americanist unable to relinquish her authority in the field or to see past the narcissism of her own national critical investments? Or is there a way to parse the global relationality not simply of one Americanist to another, but of both knowledge projects and the objects of study that they generate in different institutional and historical economies of material and cultural life? Is there a way, in other words, for an internationalized American Studies to apprehend how internationalization functions as a critical imperative *within* American American Studies, without eliding the necessity of specifying it or succumbing to the desire to refuse it? These questions are not intended to forge an alibi for American American Studies, but rather to *situate* it within the critical project that American

Studies in its internationalist idiom currently pursues. After all, internationalization promises to account for relationality on a global scale, but relationality so scaled is never sufficient to understanding the ways that location and scale work to organize struggles of all kinds, from environment to institutional access to various kinds of subject construction and knowledge production. Nor does the global as privileged scale do much to interrupt long standing gender discourses that cast, in an effort to ignore, whole domains of social life as "domesticated." The confounding problem, then, for an internationalized American Studies is how to produce an analysis of the located frameworks of interpretation, meaning, and political attachments that circulate and construct the object of study and its attending discourses wherever it goes, including when it purportedly stays at "home."

Notes

1   It is true that there are other terms that have circulated in American Studies to name similar goals, including the postnational and the transnational. I characterize the entire discourse about global relationality as "international" because of its generative and nominative use in new organizational bodies (The International Association of American Studies) and its general usage in conversations about American Studies across world regions.

2   The origin of this naming is not clear, but while it now circulates as an entity in conversations about internationalization in a way that gives the category a near ontological status, it is worth noting that Ron Clifton in 1979 talked about "American Americanists" in his essay, "The Outer Limits of American Studies: A View From the Remaining Frontier." *American Quarterly* 31.1 (1979): 365. For Clifton, the remaining frontier was American Studies abroad where, he strikingly noted, the field could continue to innovate, locating new "virgin lands," and producing new interdisciplinary projects with a whole new generation of "founding fathers."

3   Two of the most influential essays for my thinking on issues of incommensurability in the production and circulation of the object of study in American Studies are Donatella Izzo, "Outside Where? Comparing Notes on Comparative American Studies and American Comparative Studies," *The State(s) of American Studies*, eds. Elizabeth Dillon and Donald E. Pease (forthcoming), and Liam Kennedy, "Spectres of Comparison: American Studies and the United States of the West," *Comparative American Studies* 4 (2006): 135–50.

4   This investment is not new, as my work on *The Futures of American Studies*, edited with Donald E. Pease, would suggest. But while that volume sought to provide a taxonomy of the temporal tactics of the field and to sketch emergent paradigm shifts, this paper, arising in part from critiques of *Futures*'s insufficient attention to internationalization, is interested in the multiple identificatory refusals that produce *every* romance with the field's own transcendence, including those articulated by those of us long identified with the New Americanists. See Sheila Hones and Julia Leyda, "Geographies of American Studies," *American Quarterly* 57.4 (December 2005): 1019–32.

5   Let me offer a few comments on my intentions for "refused identification." At first, I called the critical practice I am delineating here "failed identification" which risked the implication that scholars *ought* to identify with their objects of study. This is not the case, as my interest was rather in discerning the now ubiquitous critical practice through which an object of study is chosen precisely to stage disidentification with it. In a very different context, Judith Butler uses the concept of refused identification to consider the production of heterosexuality in psychic terms. See "Melancholy Gender/ Refused Identification." *The Psychic Life of Power: Theories of Subjection* (Stanford University Press, 1997): 132–50.

6   It might also be true to say that refused identification has been the critical habit of American Studies in the US since its earliest articulation in the 1930s, in its resistance to the educational hegemony of British culture as the focus of humanities education. My narrative here stresses the use of refused identification in the rhetorical and analytic practices of left critique that became hegemonic in some fields in the dismantling of the Cold War organization of the university. I worry however that this narrative risks installing a monolithic understanding of American Studies in its US formation in the heyday of its institutionalization as wholly complicit with the exceptionalist state – a familiar narrative, to be sure, but one that has not sufficiently articulated the internationalism of that era of American American Studies!

7   Joel Pfister has referred to these critical practices as "complicity critiques," in an essay so titled (*American Literary History* 12.3 (Autumn 2000): 610–32). His point is that American literary and cultural studies scholars need to consider the importance of affirmative renderings of culture; hence, he turns to earlier work in race studies that focused on the positive workings of culture, such that scholarship can emphasize the dynamic, even brilliant ways that people transform cultures of domination to survive. But returning to liberation/agential models to escape the negative affect of critique is, in my view, to simply flip the coin to the other side. The complicity-affirmation dyad is symptomatic of the larger problematic of identity objects of study.

8   See Janice Radway, "What's in a Name? Presidential Address to the American Studies Association, 20 November 1998." *American Quarterly* 51.1 (1999): 1–32.

9　This is why within the fields that Radway names –
Women's Studies, Ethnic Studies, and Gay and Lesbian
Studies – identification with the object holds critical sway,
even as certain poststructuralist hesitations have seemed to
undermine what I think of as the inaugural value forms of
these domains in which knower is also the object to be
known. A longer discussion is needed to extrapolate the way
that these identificatory practices have been inverted in
American Studies as each set of inquiries into race, gender,
and sexuality take their aim against the dominant ideology
and economy of the US by refusing identification with
"America" as symbolic sign, discourse, or geopolitical
entity.

10　Leo Marx has talked about the refusal endemic to the
New American Studies in his essay, "On Recovering the
'Ur' Theory of American Studies," *American Literary
History* 17.1 (Spring 2005): 118–134. Numerous scholars
have responded, including George Lipsitz, "Our America,"
American Literary History 17.1 (Spring 2005): 135–40;
Amy Kaplan, "A Call for a Truce," *American Literary
History* 17.1 (Spring 2005): 141–7; and Donald E. Pease,
"9/11: When Was American Studies After the New
Americanists?" *boundary 2* 33.3 (2006): 73–101.

11　In a different vein of discussion altogether, Eva Cherniavsky
productively revisits the New American Studies to consider
other kinds of continuity, no matter how adamant are
some of its practitioners about their own definitive break
from the critical effects of the Cold War apparatus. See
"Subaltern Studies in a U.S. Frame," *boundary 2* 23.2
(Summer 1996): 85–110.

12　See Amy Kaplan and Donald. E. Pease, Jr., *Cultures of
United States Imperialism* (Durham: Duke University
Press, 1993); Laura Briggs, *Reproducing Empire: Race, Sex,
Science and U.S. Imperialism in Puerto Rico* (Berkeley:
University of California Press, 2002); Shelley Streeby,
*American Sensations: Class, Empire, and the Production of
Popular Culture* (Berkeley: University of California Press,
2002); Laura Wexler, *Tender Violence: Domestic Visions in
an Age of U.S. Imperialism* (Chapel Hill: University of
North Carolina Press, 2000).

13　See Lisa Lowe, "The International in the National,"
Cultural Critique 40 (Fall 1998): 29–47.

14　See Amy Kaplan, "Manifest Domesticity." *American Literature* 70.3 (1998): 581–606; and Inderpal Grewal, *Transnational America: Feminisms, Diasporas, Neoliberalisms*
(Durham, North Carolina: Duke University Press, 2005).

15　José David Saldívar, *Border Matters: Remapping American
Cultural Studies* (Berkeley: University of California Press,
1997) and *The Dialectics of Our America: Genealogy,
Cultural Critique, and Literary History* (Durham: Duke
University Press, 1991).

16　See especially C. L. R. James, *Beyond a Boundary*
(Durham: Duke University Press, 1993, 2nd edition);
Paul Gilroy, *The Black Atlantic: Modernity and Double
Consciousness* (Boston: Harvard University Press, 1993);

Carole Boyce Davies, *Moving Beyond Boundaries: Black
Women's Diasporas* (New York: New York University
Press, 1995); and Carole Boyce Davies, Meredith Gadsby,
Charles Peterson, Henrietta Williams, *Decolonizing the
Academy: African Diaspora Studies* (Lawrenceville, New
Jersey: Africa World Press, 2003).

17　An important new work in this vein is Saidiya Hartman's
Lose Your Mother: A Journey Along the Atlantic Slave Route
(New York: Farrar, Straus and Giroux, 2007).

18　See Günter Lenz, "Toward a Dialogics of International
American Culture Studies," *The Futures of American
Studies*, eds. Donald E. Pease Jr and Robyn Wiegman
(Durham: Duke University Press, 2002): 461–85, and with
Klaus Milich, eds., *American Studies in Germany: European
Contexts and Intercultural Relations* (New York: St.
Martin's Press, 1995); John Carlos Rowe, "A Future
for American Studies: Comparative U.S. Cultures Model,"
in *American Studies in Germany*, 262–78, "The New
American Studies," *The Futures of American Studies*, eds.
Donald E. Pease Jr and Robyn Wiegman (Durham: Duke
University Press, 2002): 167–82, *The New American
Studies* (Minneapolis: University of Minnesota Press,
2002), and his edited collection, *Post-National American
Studies* (Berkeley: University of California Press, 2000);
and Paul Giles, "Virtual Americas: The Internation-
alization of American Studies and the Ideology of
Exchange." *American Quarterly* 50.3 (1998): 523–47.

While some scholars interpret the comparative model
as a post-national American Studies, this should not be
confused with the ongoing elaboration of the postnation-
alist developed by Pease. In his first talks and essays on
the concept, Pease used postnational to refer to the kinds
of transformations via social movements in the exceptionalist model of Cold War American Studies that Radway
cites. See especially "New Americanists: Revisionist Interventions into the Canon," *boundary 2* 17.1 (1990): 1–37,
"National Identities, Postmodern Artifacts, and Postnational Narratives." *boundary 2* 19.1 (1992): 1–13. His more
recent conceptualizations use the postnational to position
the field and the scholar "outside" democratic nationalism
and in the contradictions and conflicts between state
formation and national culture. See especially "C. L. R.
James, Moby-Dick, and the Emergence of Transnational
American Studies," *The Futures of American Studies*, eds.
Pease and Wiegman (Durham: Duke University Press,
2002), 135–63.

19　See Jane Desmond and Virginia Dominguez, "Resituating
American Studies in a Critical Internationalism." *American
Quarterly* 48.3 (1996): 475–90; Jane Desmond, "Transna-
tional American Studies and the Limits of Collaboration:
Implications Drawn from the Russian-U.S. Relationship,"
American Studies International XLI: 1–2 (Feb 2003):
17–27; and Rob Kroes, "National American Studies in
Europe, Transnational American Studies in America," in
American Studies in Germany: European Contexts and

Intercultural Relations, eds. Günter Lenz and Klaus Milich (New York: Martin's, 1995): 147–58. Citation is from Desmond, "Transnational American Studies," 18–19.

20 According to Desmond, these limitations include 1- the differing "use values" attached to American Studies knowledge in its production and consumption in different global regions and national contexts, along with 2- the different methodologies and epistemological values that legitimate scholarly work and 3- the different educational systems and publishing conventions that govern the field, including 4- the language of publication and 5- such practical issues as differences in the availability of translation, the costs of travel and joint research, and scholarly access to research materials, all of which must be situated within 6- the nature of the shared geopolitical history that governs the exchange (18).

21 Ibid.

22 Djelal Kadir, "Defending America Against Its Devotees," *Comparative American Studies* 2.2 (2004): 137, 136, 137.

23 In her response to Kadir's presidential speech, Amy Kaplan, then President of the US American Studies Association, points to the difficulty of the differentiation that Kadir's rendition of internationalization seeks to make, given its insistence that internationalization must wholly displace the nation and nationalisms of every kind to escape complicity with the object of study that organizes the field. While agreeing with Kadir that the field must "remap the terrain of the object of study," Kaplan nonetheless warned of the "danger that geographical location could become reified . . . and that the politics of location could turn into the politics of identity . . . The production of knowledge circulates too globally, unevenly, and circuitously to fit neatly into this inside/outside model. . . . Furthermore, if one posits the possibility of viewing the United States from a purely external vantage, one risks recuperating a vision of the nation as a monolithic, cohesive, and unitary whole, even from a critical perspective. See Kaplan, "The Tenacious Grasp of American Exceptionalism: A Response to Djelal Kadir, 'Defending America Against Its Devotees.'" *Comparative American Studies* 2.2 (2004): 154–5.

24 Kadir, "America and Its Studies," *PMLA* 118.1 (2003): 21.

25 In line with this analysis, Kadir has characterized Janice Radway's emphasis on difference and diversity in "What's in a Name?" as a "national soliloquy" of "nation-centered and nationalist discourse" ("America and Its Studies," 22 note 3).

59

Outside Where? Comparing Notes on Comparative American Studies and American Comparative Studies

Donatella Izzo

In their introduction to the 2002 volume on *The Futures of American Studies*, Donald Pease and Robyn Wiegman usefully bring to bear on American Studies Foucault's concept of "heterotopia."[1] Heterotopias, as Foucault explains, are real places "which are something like counter-sites, a kind of effectively enacted utopia in which the real sites, all the other real sites that can be found within the culture, are simultaneously represented, contested, and inverted."[2] Foucault offers the mirror as his first instance of this "other" place: a utopia, in so far as it is "a place-less place" that enables me to "see myself there where I am not"; but also, "a heterotopia in so far as the mirror does exist in reality, where it exerts a sort of counter-action on the position that I occupy." Foucault then adds something that I find very interesting and very useful for the kind of argument that I will be trying to unfold here: "From the standpoint of the mirror I discover my absence from the place where I am since I see myself over there. Starting from this gaze that is, as it were, directed toward me, from the ground of this virtual space that is on the other side of the glass, I come back toward myself; I begin again to direct my eyes toward myself and to reconstitute myself there where I am" (24).

What I find so instructive and fascinating in this example is not just the contestatory power of heterotopias in relation to the ordinary spaces of social experience and organization – a contestatory power that is of course the main focus of Pease and Wiegman's use of the notion – but the way it connects the question of alternative spatial configurations with the question of the gaze, its localization and de-localization, and its capacity to effect estranging and self-reflexive moves. What I will try to offer here is exactly one such estranging and self-reflexive move based in a set of heterotopias of my own. Unlike Pease and Wiegman, who called for a radical American Studies as *itself* the heterotopia capable of reconfiguring the field in new and unpredictable ways by opening it to different temporalities, I will be taking American Studies in the United States as an institutional and culturally sanctioned space, and I will juxtapose to it two alternative spaces or "counter-sites," in Foucault's term, which I hope will act as "mirrors" producing self-alienation and consequently self-perception. These counter-sites share the paradoxical spatial situation that is typical of hetero-topias: they are both "outside American Studies," as the title of this Institute prescribes – one geographically, as being outside the boundaries of America; the other intellectually, as being outside the boundaries of American Studies as a disciplinary formation. At the same time, though, they are also both in different ways sufficiently connected to American Studies to be capable of acting as mirrors that simultaneously re-present the mirrored subject as "absolutely real, connected with all the space that surrounds it" and de-realizes it by framing it in the utopian space where "it is not" (Foucault 24). Therefore, they are ideally situated, it seems to me, to weave a dialogue with US American Studies that will, I hope, complicate the opposition between the inside and the outside of American Studies and "counteract," as Foucault would have it, the position that American Studies occupies. Finally, by suspending the self-image of American Studies in the mirror of its "counter-sites," I hope to be able to do what interests me most, that is, as Foucault promises, foreground and redirect the observer's gaze.

My first heterotopia – or "mirror site," as I am tempted to call it with reference to that other heterotopia, cyberspace – is Italian American Studies, whose model of development I will compare to the prevalent models whereby the history of American Studies has been described in the United States. In doing so I will be giving a self-aware twist to the notion of "Comparative American Studies" that figures prominently in my title. Ever since Paul Lauter called for a comparative model for the study of American literary traditions in their ethnic, gender, and class multiplicity, Comparative American Studies has been mostly defined in terms of the *inner* diversity of American culture and of the consequent need for a comparative model for its study and description.[3] What I propose to do here is temporarily take the notion of comparative American Studies in a more literal acceptation, one closer to the traditional notion of comparativism as going on *between* rather than *within* cultures – a difference that I mean to go back to later in this paper, when discussing my second heterotopia, that is, comparative literature in some of its most recent definitions and debates. The former, Italian American Studies, may be provisionally described as a localized, highly specific, but also in many ways representative instance of the international grafting of a national discipline. It takes place "inside" American Studies in as much as it *is* American Studies, but simultaneously "outside" it in as much as it goes on from outside the national culture it refers to; later in this essay I will try to explore the implications and contradictions of this twofold positionality. The latter, comparative literature, is (or defines itself as) a de-territorialized, wide-ranging, world-wide intellectual enterprise, and therefore is "outside" American Studies both in object and in origin, although, as I will try to show, increasingly "inside" it in point of view. I shall briefly illustrate each before going on to discuss their possible relevance to a critical outlook on American Studies as an intellectual *and* an institutional pursuit.

Heterotopia #1: Parallel Worlds

American Studies in Italy is a hot subject: it is, and has always been, a politically charged field, from its inception during the Second World War to one of its latest episodes – the accusations of anti-Americanism that a right-wing Italian Americanist levelled at the then President of the American Studies Association, Amy Kaplan, for a lecture she had delivered at the 2003 annual meeting of the Italian American Studies Association, critical of the recent international policies of the United States and of the current Iraq war.[4] This highly political connotation of the field has no equivalent in, say, Italian English Studies or French Studies. To better account for it, let me go back to the beginning and briefly outline its history.

Although the interest of Italian intellectuals in the culture and institutions of the United States dates back to the Risorgimento, the first large-scale discovery of American culture in Italy was made in the 1930s and 1940s by Cesare Pavese and Elio Vittorini, two militantly anti-Fascist writers who would become public intellectuals in the post-war years.[5] Their generation shared a veritable "myth of America," as some critics have called it, as a counterweight and antidote to the narrowly provincial and intellectually stifling cultural atmosphere created by Italian Fascism.[6] Militantly committed to the cause of political democracy, these writers read and intensively translated from American literature as the thematic and stylistic analogue of a free world – a politically free, but also a socially mobile and culturally authentic world, as opposed to the layers of hypocrisy, tradition, and elitism that seemed to envelop contemporary Italian society. In one way or another, those left-wing writers who were then "discovering America," as Pavese would later put it in a memorable retrospective piece,[7] all drew from D. H. Lawrence's well known idea of an America "tense with latent violence and resistance," whose essential soul is "hard, isolate, stoic, and a killer"; but they reversed the potentially more troubling implications of Lawrence's vision into a powerful myth of cultural regeneration. "Thoughtful and barbarous, happy and quarrelsome, wanton, fertile, burdened with the whole past of the world and yet young and innocent": such was America to Cesare Pavese.[8] Its literary tradition, therefore, was envisaged as vital insofar as it had given expression to the ordinary life of the ordinary individual, evading the strictures of a European world by now perceived as oppressively bourgeois and of its related literary diction; what it offered to Italian writers and readers was "a language so identified with things as to pull down all barriers between the ordinary reader and the most abysmal symbolic and mythical reality"[9] – a style "under which the earthly matter is still fresh, and whose fullness springs from the presence of new objects: new machines and new houses, new relations between men."[10] In other words, they produced what might well be termed an exceptionalist view of America before even US institutional American Studies did;[11] using their understanding of culture as an active social force, they independently shaped their own democratic American Studies along the same lines and with the same aims as, according to Michael Denning, the Popular front in the States during the 1930s.[12] Interestingly enough, none of the creators of this cultural image was ever able to travel to the United States: as can easily be seen, America for these intellectuals was first and foremost a utopia – or rather, a heterotopia, a real place that took on a radically subversive function when seen as a political alternative to the reality they experienced, and capable of acting, quite literally, as a self-reflexive mirror: "During those years – Pavese would later write – American culture allowed us to watch our own drama unfolding as if on a giant screen" (movie theatres being of course, as Foucault reminds us, heterotopias *par excellence*).[13] Unsurprisingly, Cesare Pavese was a passionate translator of Melville, and a competent and appreciative critic of Sinclair Lewis, Sherwood Anderson, Edgar Lee Masters, John Dos Passos, Walt Whitman, William Faulkner, and Richard Wright, but never even mentioned, say, Henry James: his America was robustly democratic, physical, committed to the celebration of the language and experience of the man in the street – everything that Italy under Fascism was not.

An extremely telling episode of early American Studies in Italy as a politically conflicted field is the publication of Elio Vittorini's *Americana* – a monumental anthology of American narrative prose, the first of its kind to be published in Italy, and a veritable epitome of his generation's view of American culture and of the political tensions and contradictions that produced it. Let me underscore the fact that at the time Italy was governed by Fascism and was *at war* with the United States, which makes Vittorini's initiative unbelievably daring. Vittorini originally prefaced the anthology with a set of introductory notes, amounting to a short history of American literature that unmistakably embodied his preoccupation with art as an instrument of cultural renewal and social progress for Italy, with a strong emphasis on class issues, and his view of America as the land of democracy and civil rights. As a result, *Americana* – published in 1941 by Bompiani, the Milan publishing house where Vittorini had been working since 1938 – was immediately censored by Fascist authorities, and was only reissued in 1942, with Vittorini's prefatory notes replaced by an introduction by Emilio Cecchi, a conservative writer and critic politically close to Fascism.[14] Vittorini's choice of texts, however, was kept, and it clearly mirrors his cultural priorities, as witness the fact that works by twentieth-century writers – from Willa Cather to John Fante – comprise more than half of the whole. A prominent role is allotted to the writers gathered under the headings "Contemporary History" (three stories by Faulkner, three by Hemingway, one each by Thornton Wilder, James Cain, John Steinbeck, and Thomas Wolfe) and "The New Legend" (two stories each by Caldwell and Saroyan, one by Fante). Even among late nineteenth-century writers most of the space is devoted to realist, naturalist and regionalist writers such as Mark Twain, Bret Harte, Ambrose Bierce, Stephen Crane, O. Henry, Frank Norris, Jack London, and Theodore Dreiser (11 stories in all), representative of Vittorini's preference for America's robustly democratic "roaring voice."[15] Henry James is featured, along with W. D. Howells, under the rubric "The Literature of the Bourgeoisie" – a damning enough category in Vittorini's literary lexicon – where each writer is represented by one story. In other words, the criterion for Vittorini's choice was less canonical representativeness than a strong personal, projective investment into an American culture that could be put to use for the political and cultural renewal of Italy.[16]

In striking contrast to Vittorini's political and cultural agenda, and consequently to his reading of American literature and to the rationale of the whole cultural project of *Americana*, Emilio Cecchi's introduction is tuned to a distinctly traditional and conservative view of both literature and society. One of the first Italian critics, along with Mario Praz, to discover the literature of the United States (where, unlike Pavese and Vittorini, he had also repeatedly traveled) and a subtle reader of Poe, Melville, Dickinson, and Whitman, as well as of his contemporaries, Cecchi was nevertheless sympathetic to Fascism; to him, the intellectual was the aristocratic keeper of the aesthetic and spiritual values attesting to the superiority of European civilization, which America could not possibly embody and indeed threatened, and literature was the business of an elite of men of letters educated in the high European tradition. American literature, insofar as it was not molded by the legacy of that tradition, and hence derivative, was the epic product of a country of barbarians – occasionally powerful but inevitably unpolished. His reservations are evident from the very outset of his introduction, where he defines the current vogue of American literature in Italy as "the symptom of a fashion, or indeed of an infatuation, rather than as the fruit of intellect and taste," the outcome of "the confusion of consciences, the exasperation of feelings, the anguishing perspectives for the future" created by the war, encouraging "ravenous and unsystematic readings done on frequently artless translations" (IX).[17] The rest of Cecchi's introduction is also rich in remarks describing American literature as "a literature rushing unleashed and without banks" (X), "as if demented and shaken by St. Vitus's dance" (XVIII), "full to the brim with shameless and repulsive situations" (XIX). While criticizing his contemporaries – both American writers and Italian translators – for their lack of taste and discrimination, however, Cecchi also offered a corrective to what he rightly identified as the latter's "delusion of having at last met with a literature that would have nothing to do with literature, that would not be spoiled or enfeebled by literature: a 'barbarous,' or as it were primitive literature" (XVI). In an effort to counterbalance Vittorini's penchant for what was new, violent, and raw in American literature, Cecchi called for a comparative approach that would reclaim the European tradition as both an origin and a standard for American literature, highlighting the European literary roots of such authors as O. Henry, Hemingway, and Faulkner and redeeming them from the "millennialist emphasis" (XVII) of their celebrators.

A monument to contradictory critical impulses, *Americana* thus figures as the battleground between two highly political views both of America and of the role of culture and of the intellectual: on the one hand, Vittorini's social and political standard for literary value and his view of America as the democratic antidote to current totalitarianism; on the other hand, Cecchi's preoccupation with a correct assessment of aesthetic value and his view of American literature as expressing the "bloodshed . . . folly . . . and despair secretly poisoning the proud euphoria" of a materialistic country "led astray by a false ideal of prosperity and groping for its ethnic and ethical wholeness" (XXIII).

American Studies in Italy, then, started as a politically progressive pursuit committed to change in both society and literary taste, and was resisted by those who were more steeped in nationalistic notions of the superiority of European civilization. The culture of the United States was seen by those progressive intellectuals as the bearer of internationally viable humanistic and political values, much in the tradition of F. O. Matthiessen's Christian Socialism, but with a stronger emphasis on class issues. However paradoxical this may seem today viewing the story in retrospect, the United States were then disparaged and culturally patronized by those very social and political constituencies that would later become their strategic political allies, whereas those who upheld America as a political and cultural model were mostly close to or actual members of the Communist party (in whose local branches, incidentally, Jack London and John

Steinbeck would long continue to be read side by side with Marx, Gramsci, and the classics of Marxist thought).

This pattern, where America becomes a contested field and political alignments seldom coincide with cultural ones, has been repeated throughout the history of Italian American Studies. McCarthyism, the hearings of the Un-American Activities Committee, the Rosenbergs' trial and their execution in 1953, all dealt a hard blow to the image of the United States formerly cherished by progressive Italian intellectuals. "The times when we were discovering America are over," wrote Pavese bitterly in the essay I quoted above, dated 1947. "Without a Fascism to oppose, that is, without a historically progressive thought to embody, even America, for all the skyscrapers and automobiles and soldiers it may produce, will not be the vanguard of any possible culture. Without a progressive thought and struggle, indeed, it will risk becoming itself a prey to fascism, though in the name of its best traditions."[18] Still, Pavese's essay, even while it denounced the political and cultural risks inherent in the repressive turn in American life and proclaimed the end of the Italian fascination with things American, was devoted to yet another American author – namely, an *African* American author, Richard Wright.

This contradiction announced an emblematic split within American Studies in Italy, which would become fully visible in the following decades. At a time when a New Critical view of the canon had already congealed as a shared consensus at universities throughout the United States, and when American Studies was being established in Italy as an academic discipline strongly influenced by such classics as *American Renaissance*, *The American Adam*, and *Virgin Land*, Italian Americanists, progressive by tradition and committed to modernity, went about reclaiming their view of American culture even in the middle of the bipolar world of Cold War, and even when America was no longer in their eyes the beacon of democracy it had seemed during Fascism.[19] The second myth of America was developed by the generation of readers and scholars coming of age in the 1960s, and it was grounded in the idea of the "two Americas" – the official one of the administration, of political repression at home and abroad, of the imperialist wars in Korea and then Vietnam; and the "other America" of Civil Rights movements, of feminism and Free Speech, of African Americans and Native Americans, of Woody Guthrie and the United Mine Workers, all of which were being discovered and passionately studied – once again, a heterotopia in the strict sense, a real place that was nevertheless also a site of radical utopian contestation of the existing order. This accounts for another striking characteristic of Italian American Studies, its early and sustained attention to the ethnic and class diversity of US culture. If, as may safely be assumed, the revisionary impulse of the New Americanists in the United States has been a matter of acknowledging plurality beyond the assumed coherence of the established canon and of restoring the historical and social contexts of literary and cultural production to their reading and interpretation, then it can be argued that Italian American Studies have been revisionary from the very outset. Due to the strong influence of a well established historicist, materialist, and Marxist critical tradition, acting as a corrective to the transcendent aestheticism of the high modernist critical paradigm, and due to a strong leftist tradition of commitment to forms of political struggle and resistance, Italian American Studies on the whole has displayed a very early attention to the issues of class, race, and gender, as witness a sizable number of studies in African American literature and culture, the Native American renaissance, women writers, social history, and the like, starting from the 1960s.[20] All in all, many Italian Americanists have constantly envisaged their scholarly work as a means of promoting an awareness of that "other America" that lay beyond, and within, literary texts. This early adoption of an anthropological, cultural, and political approach as opposed to the belletristic tradition still prevalent in Italian academia has contributed to render American Studies in Italy a conflicted field not only politically but also intellectually, as witness the fact that it is still being resisted as culturally "inferior" and not formative enough by many powers that be within university faculties as well as the Italian Department of Education.[21]

The strong politicization of American Studies in Italy and the relative disconnection of its ways of reading the United States from the more predictable political assessments engendered by the country's international alignment – or rather, the chiasmatic disposition of the field, where the political critics of the United States are its cultural defenders and vice versa – both point to the fact that Italian American Studies as a discursive formation has never really bought into the exceptionalist self-image conveyed by consensus American Studies in the United States. If anything, it has created an exceptionalism of its own, tuned to the ideological demands of each successive generation, and hence ready to question the nationalistic formation undergirding the field in the US from its very inception. Far from being merely imported and/or acquired through Fulbright programs and the United States Information Service, its version of

American Studies has been a highly idiosyncratic and, so to speak, customized one, strongly localized to meet the needs of local intellectuals. Grafted onto a different cultural situation and obeying a different logic, it has from the very beginning highlighted conflict and diversity rather than consensus and homogeneity as an integral part of its representation of the United States – indeed, it has made conflict and diversity into the very roots of its interest in American culture, thus forerunning those developments that would decisively alter the self-representation of American Studies in the US during the 1980s.[22]

Chronopolitics

I am offering this short history of Italian American Studies as a term of comparison to US American Studies not in a competitive spirit – like, "we got there before you" – but as a reminder of the different temporalities operating in the discourse of American Studies in different cultural contexts.[23] In other words, I am offering it as a counter-site mirroring the history of American Studies from outside and with a difference. By insisting on Italian American Studies as throughout dissensual and connected from the beginning to projects of social emancipation both in the US and in Italy, I am trying to disturb the received wisdom on American studies that has dominated the field over the last decade or so and to disrupt its frequently complacent linearity, in an effort to counteract what seems to me the emergent teleological narrative of American Studies in the United States. Increasingly, American Studies tends to be represented according to a from-to model: from exceptionalism to critical internationalism, from monoculturalism to multi-culturalism, from consensus to dissensus, from nationalism to post- and trans-nationalism, from hegemonic to post-hegemonic, from aesthetically- to socially and historically-minded . . . Of course I am not referring to the truly wonderful work that has been done by all those individual studies that have explored formerly submerged voices or undervalued issues, traditions, and connections, but to the meta-narratives embodying the self-perception and self-representation of the discipline and of its significance and directions – what Donald Pease has rightly called its field imaginary. The present master narrative of American Studies as it emerges from countless volumes, anthologies, introductions, presidential addresses, and occasional essays, tends to be a linear one, retrospectively assessing the consensus American

Studies of the *past* from the vantage point of a *present* awareness of internal diversity and global interaction, intent on producing the radical and cutting-edge post-nationalist American Studies of the *future*.[24] In other words, it seems to me that what American Studies is presently intent on construing is once again very much a "usable past," even though the past tends to be depicted in self-deprecatory rather than self-celebratory accents and its uses have dramatically changed from the times of Van Wyck Brooks. By envisaging an American Studies capable of fully meeting the challenge both of multiculturalism and of globalization, both of inner diversity and of continental, Atlantic, and world trans-actions – what Janice Radway has called its "intricate inter-dependencies"[25] –, the discipline seems to be effectively recontaining, through an "optative mood," the critical impulses that have threatened to disrupt it.[26] This is evidenced not just – as Radway has noted in her much quoted Presidential Address – in the choice of its institutional professional organization to keep its time hon-ored name referring to "American" as a pseudo-national entity, but more subtly, in its tellings and retellings of its story as a unitary narrative.[27] It is this narrative *as such*, I would argue, that, even while it unsparingly attempts to disarticulate it from within and to "provincialize" it from without, incessantly re-produces the discourse of the discipline, producing the present "American Studies" as a more capacious disciplinary field reconceptualized as virtually boundless as regards the tasks, competences, and objects of its practitioners. These range from a global pedagogy of the oppressed to a full-scale confrontation of gender, ethnic, and class issues in their transnational reach, to an overall reconsideration of US history in the worldwide context of "collaborative comparative studies of empires and their legacies."[28] Even the plural inscribed in the title of the Dartmouth Summer Institute – "The Futures of American Studies" – does not wholly escape this tendency, underwritten as it is by the inevitable teleology of chronological representation, which, while not foreclosing history as *one* future, still implicitly outlines it as a kind of developmental narrative leading from past entrenchment to future plurality and openness.

Openness becomes the operative word here, effecting the transition from a discourse of time to a discourse of space. My question here is: who does the opening? This way of representing the history of American Studies in the US as a "progressive" narrative of unfolding radical potentialities, I would argue, crucially depends on its being seen as a self-enclosed and self-sufficient process. Its opening is effected *from the inside* and in its exclusive

interest, obeying the inner logic of its internal develop-ment, and intersecting the trajectories of other and outer histories at exactly the moment, and to the extent, that is right within that inner logic. Let me quote a small, but significant, linguistic index among many: at one point in her admirable "What's in a Name?," Janice Radway talks about the need to "reconceptualize the American as always relationally defined and therefore as intricately dependent upon 'others' that *are used* both materially and conceptually to mark its boundaries" (17, my emphasis). Who is the subject thus making use of the useful others, I wonder? is it just "the American" as a material and ideological formation, or is it also the American Studies scholar that is reconceptualizing it while belonging within its precinct?

I take this question as a telling symptom of a real prob-lem that persists, in spite of the political good will and theoretical sophistication of those who are addressing it. Does the present insistence of American Studies on post-, inter-, and trans- prefixes qualify as a recognition of otherness – the outer spaces whose different tempor-alities "would usher in future organizations of the field" (Pease and Wiegman, 11) – or isn't it rather another way of playing out the discipline's field imaginary on a larger scale and in a wider field, appropriating the different temporalities of other discourses or cultures and reduc-ing them to one's own, rather than confronting them in their historical and geographical difference? What my own "look from the outside" as an Italian Americanist tells me is that to the extent that I wish to interact with US American Studies, I have to play by the rules of US American Studies, publish my books with US publishers according to the standards of US university presses, write them in English and circulate them in US journals, and participate in US-based international Institutes and conferences. While entering a dialogue as an equal partner and of my own free will, I am in fact simultane-ously responding to a sort of Althusserian interpellation, hailing me from within the disciplinary field that my presence would open and attracting me into its ideo-logical orbit. In other words, as you begin to hear my voice, I am no longer an "other": my difference has virtually dis-appeared – only the smallest and most superficial trace of it is left, be it in the form of a jet-lagged slowness of reaction, a foreignness of accent, or a slightly unfamiliar turn of phrase. All that is left of my "otherness" may be, indeed, exactly my status as a foreigner and a scholar from a different country, a husk that makes me "useful" as a token of internationalization, marking the new and enlarged boundaries of the discipline.[29]

What this all comes to, I think, is the question of hegemony. In introducing some of the contributions collected in *The Futures of American Studies*, Pease and Wiegman present them as "post-hegemonic in that they presuppose the end of U.S. hegemony but that they do not propose counterhegemonies" (26). Such a phrase definitely arrests one's attention. In the editors' use of the expression, Radway's questioning of the name of the American Studies Association is an instance of the post-hegemonic, since by questioning its name, it radically questions the hegemonic self-representation of the association, thus opening liberatory alternative possibilities engendered by disallowing pre-existing norms. The question of hegemony, though, is a tricky one. We can certainly use the notion "post-hegemonic" within the context of US American Studies in referring to the demise of a historically specific disciplinary formation undergirded by a historically specific, exceptionalist representation of the US as nation. The more generalized and current use of the notion of hegemony, however, is the one referring to the political sphere and describing relations of economic and political domination between states (in the sense that dates back to the word's Greek etymology), or relations of political and cultural predominance between classes, aimed at naturalizing and maintaining the economic primacy of one class over another, as first theorized by Antonio Gramsci. As soon as we step *outside* the precinct of American Studies, in other words, the phrase "U.S. hegemony" no longer alludes exclusively to the field imaginary manufactured by consensus US American Studies, or even to the predominance of US American Studies in setting the agenda of the field on a worldwide scale. Read from *outside* the United States, "the end of U.S. hegemony" inevitably echoes the internationalist, anti-imperialist slogans and battle cries of countless marches, rallies and demonstrations from the 1960s onwards. But in that sense, "post-hegemonic American Studies" could only be the American Studies of a United States that were no longer a hegemonic world super-power. And even though, as political scientists keep telling us, that may very well be the case in what announces itself as the Chinese century, at present the utopian thrust towards superseding the hegemonic function of the United States (as expressed also, but *not only*, in its subsumption of America as coterminous with itself) seems at the very least premature if framed as a statement of fact. The symbolic gestures of self-awareness and the disclaimers we produce in our critical stance as intellectuals should not be confused with performative acts having the power to *transform* the material power

relations that we would criticize. Adopting the notion of hegemony, as American Studies is increasingly in the habit of doing, while limiting its scope to the relations of dominance *within* the cultural field, can paradoxically result in exactly the opposite of the original implication of the term and the original intentions of its users, that is, in *disconnecting* that very link between history and social movements, on the one hand, and the literary, cultural, and critical domain, on the other, that all innovative trends and approaches to American Studies have attempted to reinstate in one way or another over the last two decades. Hence the paradox of the emergence of a *post-hegemonic* American Studies in the United States at exactly the historical juncture when the USA is deploying its world hegemony on an unequalled and unprecedented scale.

The need to dismiss exceptionalism as an ideological formation and as an object of nationalist identification, in other words, should not make us blind to the fact that in today's world the United States are indeed exceptional – not as a God-given country, but certainly in terms of their present power differential with any other country in the world. Treading the thin line between exceptionality and exceptionalism is undoubtedly a difficult exercise, but collapsing distinctions is not without its pitfalls: the effort of framing the United States as "a nation like any other nation," while on the one hand effective in counteracting what Kaplan has termed its "imperial insularity," on the other hand can lead to mystify anew its actual role in those very worldwide relations and power struggles that a focus on the imperial cultures of the United States had helped unearth.

As a way of drawing attention to the material – economic, political, military – underpinnings of the ascendancy of the United States in the creation and circulation of its own cultural self-representations (even, as it increasingly happens, its self-critical ones), a focus on the operation of hegemony in its wider field of application can provide useful conceptual tools for the study and understanding not just of national cultures, but also of their transnational implications. The recent emphasis on transnational American Studies has given increasing currency within the discipline to an expression whose former field of application had been economic, prevalently applied to multinational corporations. American Studies seems to have picked up this expression with a fair dose of (possibly artless) candor, infusing it with radical, progressive, innovative potentialities. These, however, do not wholly manage to erase the involvement of the word in the logic of capital in the age of its global circulation.

"Can we even imagine a transnational community that is not wholly given over to the dominant rationality of capital?" ask Rob Wilson and Wimal Dissanayake in introducing a collection of essays on the global/local; "Are the intellectuals of the world willing to participate in transnational corporatism and be its apologists?" echoes Masao Miyoshi.[30] While these questions may be cast in slightly apocalyptic terms, in their implicit suggestion of the all-pervasive power of global capital, they certainly capture, to my mind, one of the paradoxes of the present transnational turn in American Studies. If, as George Lipsitz has argued, the isomorphism between place, nation, and culture can no longer be taken for granted in present-day American Studies (as well as in contemporary culture at large), then it seems to me that this disconnection should also be investigated in its specific modes of operation in different places, for different nations, and under different circumstances.[31] In the networks of interdependency created by globalization, some actors undoubtedly get the better part of the deal: even assuming the global nature of the forces shaping national life at any given site, it is still a fact that the United States as a nation-state formation has a unique capacity to act as a global force, shaping the destiny of other statal and national formations to a much larger extent and much more effectively than they shape its own. Betraying my soft spot for detective fictions, I will intentionally ask a naïve and theoretically crude question: who stands to profit from the transnational turn in American Studies? Transnational corporations, as is well known, are accountable to their own executive councils rather than to the constituencies of individual nation-states; they require of their workers that they be loyal to the corporate identity rather than to their own nationality; and they create homogeneity among the members of the globalized upper social strata, through generalized consumption of those brand name commodities that are the "cultural products of the transnational class" (Miyoshi, 94). Could it be that American Studies is turning into a US-based transnational enterprise, displaying a remarkable capacity of homogenizing both its products and its practitioners within a globalized flow of cultural capital? And in that case, wouldn't the corporate interest of transnational American Studies accrue to the United States as its main stockholder?

An unusually forthright answer to my queries comes from John Carlos Rowe, who, in discussing the relevance of postnationalism and globalism to the new American Studies, calls for new "ways in which the new American studies should begin to reconstitute its fields of study,

especially as the United States (along with other first-world nations) claims an ever greater responsibility for global economics, politics, language, and identity."[32] The various suggested moves towards internationalism, transnationalism, and the opening of "contact zones" are here frankly acknowledged as *functional* to the reconfiguring of a field that is framed as *immediately* related to the United States and as an *emanation* of its new global "responsibilities" (with the latter expression – in spite of its mitigating involvement of other first-world nations, or perhaps exactly because of that – unintentionally recalling another well known euphemism, "the white man's burden"). Rowe's call for the creation of "intellectual and cultural contact zones" is also revealing in this sense, since he defines the contact zone as "a semiotic site where exchanges may occur from both (or more) sides, even when the configurations of power are inequitable (as they usually are)" (173), but effectively elides the colonial scenario underlying Mary Louise Pratt's model and hardly interrogates the significance, consequences, and directions of such unequal power relations. Rowe's discussion, coming as it does from an engaged, innovative, and progressive critic, provides another striking instance of the unintentional split between the intellectual and the socio-historical dimension, effected by way of the very categories that would grant a firmer historical grounding and a keener political edge to literary studies. Transnational American Studies thus figures as what might be termed a *technology of transnationalization*, effecting the translation of the new worldwide horizon of the economy into culture and transferring the old nationalistic version of American identity onto a globalized stage.

Whose transnationalism, then? American Studies, I suspect, is no less American for having turned transnational. Indeed, quite beyond the intentions and beliefs of its proponents, its new, looser, and less geographically defined configuration may well be a new form of isomorphism, whose protean shape is no longer rigidly modelled on the legal borders of the state, but flexibly follows it in its deterritorialized interests and extraterritorial ventures.[33]

Heterotopia #2: Panoptical Worldviews

Where is the outside, then, when the opening is effected unilaterally from within obeying the logic of enlarging and complicating the inside – or rather, can there possibly *be* an outside? In order to explore this question I will now turn to my second heterotopia, comparative literature.

Over the last few years, comparative literature has been trying to redefine its field, methods, and objects, in order to overcome the limits dictated by its original grounding in the self-enclosed and allegedly self-sufficient world of the European literary cultures that emerged in the Renaissance – a world that until the inception of decolonization and globalization had seemed to include everything anybody ever needed to know about Literature (with a capital L). This process has appeared particularly urgent in the English-speaking countries, more affected than others by the impact of post-colonialism and by the role of English as an international medium, and has produced an insistent return of the notion of *Weltliteratur*, or World Literature, first defined by Johann Wolfgang von Goethe in the framework of an Enlightenment representation of modernity as universally affording equal opportunities for poetry and intellectual conversation to each and all countries in the world, and later taken up by Karl Marx in his *Manifesto*.[34] Interestingly, this notion, which once circulated in German, now tends to enter the debate in its English version even in non-English-speaking countries – a tribute to the success of English in replacing German in its former role as the language universally expressing philosophical categories of thought.

One of the most stimulating and controversial interventions in the debate over world literature has been Franco Moretti's "Conjectures on World Literature," published in 2000.[35] I shall briefly summarize its argument, before proceeding to underline the ways in which its ways of addressing comparative literature seem to me to throw light on the present predicament of American Studies. Moretti's starting point is that "the literature around us is now unmistakably a planetary system" (54) which cannot be understood inductively, "[r]eading 'more'" (55) and requires instead to be understood systematically by "taking an explanatory matrix from social history and applying it to literary history" (56). The explanatory matrix he chooses is Immanuel Wallerstein's theory of globalization and world-systems, which enables him to represent the literary world as "one and unequal" in its interconnections and flows from center to periphery, along with Darwin's theory of natural selection, which accounts for the way some literary genres survive and thrive while others disappear. Moretti's test case for the operation of his "law of literary evolution" (58) is the history of the European novel in its spread from its original core to the whole world, where it engenders local forms that are "a compromise between a western formal influence . . . and

local materials" (58). "World literature" is thus conceptualized as "a system of variations" of literary forms "struggl[ing] for symbolic hegemony across the world" (64) and its study is seen as a "comparative morphology" (64) investigating the regularity of those variations in order to produce an overall theory of the literary world system. In order to do so, the comparative scholar will have to give up close reading (rejected as typical of the United States [57]) and embrace the practice of "distant reading": "literary history . . . will become 'second hand': a patchwork of other people's research, *without a single direct textual reading*. . . . the more ambitious the project, the greater must the distance be. . . . If we want to understand the system in its entirety, we must accept losing something" (57; emphasis in the original). Scholars will then be divided into those who specialize in the study of national literatures and world literature scholars, "in a sort of cosmic and inevitable division of labour" (66) dictated both by practical needs and by the difference of the respective theoretical projects: "national literature, for people who see trees," that is, the branching out of unity into diversity; "world literature, for people who see waves," that is, uniformity engulfing diversity (66).

Moretti's theory of world literature has been attacked by many, who have criticized his mechanical and partial use of economic models; his restrictive notion of literature as exclusively written and identified with the novel; his ambition to provide a *single*, universal model for describing literary interactions; his representation of world peripheries as inevitably the passive receivers rather than active producers of literary forms; his rejection of close reading and simultaneous reliance on it to validate his deductive system; and so on.[36] Jonathan Arac, in particular, has raised the twofold question of his systematic evasion of the issue of language in the uncritical acceptance of English monolingualism, and of the doubtful political implications of the comparativist's role as the "global synthesizer" and – quoting Dante – "*il maestro di color che sanno*," the master of those who know, who thereby become no longer their own masters (45). Of special interest to me is, finally, the critique of Gayatri Spivak, who addresses Moretti in a long endnote to her *Death of a Discipline* – a book entirely devoted to the perspectives of comparative literature faced with the need to reconfigure its paradigms by integrating the "skill of reading closely in the original" typical of old comparative philology with the historical awareness and interdisciplinary approach of Area Studies.[37] Spivak is uncompromising in her critique, which I will quote at some length. Defining Moretti's essay as a "training for new global encyclopedias, although it claims to describe the entire burden of a global comparative literature," she asks a series of trenchant questions: "Should our only ambition be to create authoritative totalizing patterns depending on untested statements by small groups of people treated as native informants? . . . The others provide information while we know the whole world. . . . How can "close reading" be the hallmark of the United States . . . when the new Moretti-style comparativist must rely on close reading from the periphery? Should one point out that now may be the exactly wrong moment to follow the youngish Marx at his most totalizing?" (107–8). Spivak then concludes her critique of Moretti with two remarks that lead me back to the question of American Studies: "And indeed, this *is* nationalism, U.S. nationalism masquerading as globalism. . . . The real problem is the claim to scopic vision" (108).

This charge of US nationalism is a striking one, since as is well known, Moretti is Italian by origin, education, and citizenship, although he has been working at US universities for several years. It is exactly this circumstance, however, that makes Spivak's remark illuminating. "US nationalism" is not a matter of nationality, it is a matter of *positionality* – a position inside the boundaries of US academia, the privileged vantage point that enables the "scopic vision," as Spivak has it. The need to overcome the limits of a Eurocentric conception of comparative literature becomes for Moretti a claim to a Hegelian, totalizing synthesis of multiplicity into a unitary system, logocentrically seen as the only possible guarantee of scientific knowledge, and implicitly defined as a normative, regulatory, and closed structure, rather than as a non-hierarchical network of interrelated parts. From his undemonstrated premise – the *need* for understanding world literature as a system and for understanding the system in its entirety – depend all the most questionable points in his essay: the mechanical equation of *literature* with *literary market*, and the drastic rejection of the diversity of languages, literatures, genres, texts, and traditions as an *obstacle* to the system's formalization rather than its very substance and *raison d'être*. Underlying this postulate of the need for a system, however, is the unacknowledged role of the systematizer and above all, the elision of his presence *within* the field of observation: the claim to scopic vision that Spivak underscores, strategically depends on the presence of a transcendent subject from whose "central" panoptical vantage point the whole field can be seen and controlled, embracing the multiplicity of local, peripheral, and relative visions and changing them into true knowledge, that is, totality. The

enabling condition for occupying such a role is itself predicated, however implicitly, on the center-periphery model: like the literary world system, the comparative critical world system will inevitably function along the lines of economic globalization, and the global synthesizer will ideally be based in an English-speaking country, complete with research facilities, well-funded private institutions, and well-provided libraries crammed with English translations of foreign texts marketed on a global scale. Conditions that can hardly be fulfilled in, say, West Africa, North Cambodia, or Ukraine (or even Italy, for that matter); indeed, there is only *one* country in today's world that can offer those conditions for intellectual work, and that country is the United States – and even there, those conditions are only available to a very small percentage of its intellectual workers.[38] Contextualized within its own material and institutional conditions, Moretti's phrase on the inevitable "cosmic division of labor" takes on truly troubling overtones, positioning the world literature scholar – in a striking, but by no means coincidental convergence with the economic implications of the "transnational" that I recalled above – as the stock holder of a multinational corporation, reaping benefits from the work of local laborers who, in turn, can only have access to the global market through the former's mediation and never on their own.[39]

As I argued quoting Foucault at the beginning of this paper, the function of the mirror is to provide the standpoint whereby as observers we can discover our own gaze, direct our eyes toward ourselves, and reconstitute ourselves there where we are. If taking comparative literature as a heterotopia to American Studies has anything to teach, I think this teaching lies in the foregrounding of the observer's gaze and in the framing of the observer's position as viewed from a de-centered virtual site. The self-erasure of the perceiving subject from the picture, that is, the elusion of the situatedness of knowledge – which, incidentally, brackets two decades of feminist theory[40] – seems to me what the debate over world literature can teach us to recognize in American Studies. Herein lies the deep congruence between the global ambitions of the new comparative literature and the de-territorialization of American Studies as a virtually boundless field spanning the whole world in its effort to account for US culture in a non-nationalistic, non-exceptionalist, non-isolationist fashion. In both, the opening of national frontiers and the erasure of national labels often seem to operate as a unilateral assumption theorized as a universal intellectual need from the vantage point of a privileged position within a strong institutional apparatus. This apparatus, I would argue, is the unexamined and unacknowledged premise authorizing (and indeed, enforcing) the reduction of multiplicity to unity – be it the unity of the world literary system or of American Studies as an internally diversified but institutionally unitary and ever more engulfing disciplinary field. To that extent, the much questioned "American" in "American Studies" retains all its descriptive power: when taken literally, it expresses the deep unity not so much of the *object* of its own efforts, as of the vantage point from which those efforts are framed and conceptualized. The "territorial imaginary" (Pease and Wiegman, 20) that American Studies has long been in the process of successfully deconstructing as regards its object still very much prevails as regards the *locus* of its production.

Needless to say, no Americanist in the US can be held accountable for the institutional conditions in which she or he operates, nor would the Third World scholar be in any way empowered by their demise: quite the reverse, the existence of such spaces for critical thinking in the humanities as still exist in the First World is enabling for all. But we should not delude ourselves as to the actual existence of an "outside" of American Studies that is not always already coextensive with the inside, at the very moment that it is co-opted into its disciplinary field, drawn into its apparatus, and geared to its institutional mode of operation. However much we may intellectually and politically foster a recognition of cultural diversity inside the US and an awareness of its manifold world transactions, we'll be still tautologically differentiating and enlarging *the same* field. Like Derrida's "il n'y a pas de hors texte," American Studies has no outside.

Sallies

Is there no way "out," then? I want to conclude on a different note than the Foucauldian pessimism of American studies as a self-regulating, homeostatic apparatus ready to contain what would resist it. To the ambiguities of transnational American Studies as an engulfing project intent on unintentionally reconfiguring the whole world as a "contact zone" of unequal colonial encounters, I would tentatively oppose some alternative paths. They may well sound like too old-fashioned recipes, and in fact, as I have tried to show, "recipes" – in the sense of totalizing metadiscourses offering instructions based on simplified representations of complex intellectual and material issues – are exactly what we do *not* need. Indeed, as I hope to have made clear, I envisage the

predicament of American Studies as a major intellectual aporia – one of the *nec tecum nec sine te* kind, such as only a rigorous application of the philosophical weapons of deconstruction might elucidate in all its intractability.[41] Hence the intentionally low-key quality of my proposals, which I advance (at the risk of incurring a whole gamut of accusations, from regressive nostalgia to facile eclecticism to indulgent self-contradiction) in a self-aware tactical fashion – as paths inviting guerrilla incursions (or possibly, sallies) rather than full-scale confrontations.

The first is the nation, not as an essentialistic entity or a rallying cry for nationalistic identification, but as a historical and political category, and therefore a fitting object of analysis for any discourse that defines itself as critical and oppositional. The discourse of the nation is not just the "gravitational tug" of an old literary and cultural model, reproduced through pedagogical institutions and conditioning us through our education and socialization.[42] It is also the cultural and ideological interface of the state, the material locus where our institutional practices are grounded and empowered (or disempowered). And finally, but all-importantly, it is a lasting agglomeration of economic, political, and military power, whose systems of hegemony – institutions, modes of thought, and ideological apparatuses (including scholarly associations and critical trends) – still deserve to be investigated rather than hurriedly disposed of for fear of being complicitous with them.[43] As Teresa de Lauretis wrote of gender some years ago, the construction of an ideological category "is also effected by its deconstruction; that is to say, by any discourse . . . that would discard it as ideological misrepresentation."[44] This is also true of the nation, whose discursive deconstruction in no way affects – and may even paradoxically serve to mystify – the material conditions of inequality that it is its function to contain inside and to produce and perpetuate outside itself. And in that sense, the superseding of the nation in contemporary culture might well be another ruse of power, revamping the nationalistic ideology in new and more globally functional terms: after all, as Althusser reminds us, "what thus seems to take place outside ideology . . . , in reality takes place in ideology. . . . That is why those who are in ideology believe themselves by definition outside ideology: one of the effects of ideology is the practical *denegation* of the ideological character of ideology by ideology: ideology never says, 'I am ideological.'"[45]

The second and connected one is comparative literature – another controversial field, as my previous discussion has shown, and one that has been as loosely and as diversely defined as any field in the humanities, partly because of the diverse methodological and theoretical assumptions of its practitioners, partly because of its very lack of a strong and "self-evident" disciplinary grounding, such as the nation has long provided for literary studies. Let me then offer my own definition of the kind of comparative literature that I envisage as a potentially fruitful approach to an American Studies that is still, to my mind, very much a "national" field. The comparative literature I have in mind is not a metadisciplinary project subsuming all possible objects of inquiry into the enlarged ken of its planetary ambitions; rather, it is a "delocalized" investigation of the *heterogeneity* of its different objects seen both in their particular linguistic and historical existence and in their manifold theoretical, cultural and historical relations. In other words, it is not a panoptical space open to totalizing appropriation and ruled by one-way influence, but a field crisscrossed by multiple, non-hierarchical relations: a *differential* formation where individual linguistic, literary, and cultural traditions mutually elucidate and unsettle each other through their very coexistence and through their intractable difference as well as relatedness, enforcing on the onlooker the kind of "double view" that comes from being simultaneously within and without the field being observed. As a pursuit that de-centers each national culture from its position as its own only possibile standard of reference and questions its self-contained, self-engendered, and self-legislated status, comparative literature may operate as the contestatory occasion that pries open the field of American Studies *from without* rather than *from within*.[46]

My third tactical path is philology. Philology has not enjoyed a very good reputation over the last few decades – it is commonly seen as a pedantic, irrelevant, even reactionary discipline dedicated to minute details of textual editorship rather than to an intellectual understanding or interpretative grasp of the text itself in its deeper or wider significance. Details, though, may be exactly what we need as an antidote to the sweeping, world-wide panoptical points of view. In her intelligent critical response to Franco Moretti's essay, Emily Apter contrasts Moretti's "distant reading" with the linguistic engagement of texts and the "staged cacophony of multilingual encounters" (256) practiced by one of the founders of modern philology, Leo Spitzer, whose "policy of *nontranslation* adopted without apology" (277) she sees as the sign of an "explicit desire to disturb monolingual complacency" (278).[47] In that sense, I take philology not as a self-sufficient discipline whose horizon does not exceed the

boundaries of textual reconstruction, but as complementary to the kind of comparative literature I have sketched above. As a methodological reminder of the need to confront the historically specific "otherness" of each individual other in its resistant linguistic texture and minute materiality, philology may effectively counter the increasing tendency (a tendency that goes well beyond American Studies) to produce reductionist travesties of "the other" in the guise of sweeping generalization, reified essentialization, or assimilated self-extension. In other words, I am taking my lead from Edward Said in characterizing philology as a form of the *secular* in criticism, and in defining it as that "care" and "scrupulosity," typical of traditional humanism, that still deserves to be carried over to different areas of inquiry inspired by ideologically critical and politically oppositional projects.[48] In its power to situate its objects in their linguistic and historical particularity, and thereby to make them physically present in their separate existence and "untamed complexity," in Hans Gumbrecht's phrase, philology can function as a kind of *micropolitical* intervention allied to what resists incorporation (be it by the flows of global capital or by the overriding logic of a disciplinary field).[49]

These tactical interventions, as well as such others as might be advanced, are in no way meant as a full-fledged theoretical and methodological proposal for a New-New American Studies, nor could they be: if anything, they are offered as that "space of illusion that exposes every real space . . . as still more illusory" (Foucault 27), as heterotopian stimuli towards possible ways of rethinking American Studies from an outside that is not just geographical but conceptual. While they obviously do not measure up to the major constitutive dead-end of the field, collectively they can function as the spadework needed to restore some margin to the discipline – that *outside* that American Studies needs if it is not to implode for its very lack of boundaries.

Notes

1 Donald E. Pease and Robyn Wiegman, "Futures," in Donald E. Pease and Robyn Wiegman, eds., *The Futures of American Studies* (Durham and London: Duke University Press, 2002).

2 Michel Foucault, "Of Other Spaces," tr. Jay Miskowiec, *Diacritics* 16: 1 (Spring 1986): 22–7, here 24.

3 Paul Lauter, "The Literatures of America: A Comparative Discipline" [1985], in *Redefining American Literary History*, ed. A. LaVonne Brown Ruoff and Jerry W. Ward,

Jr. (New York: MLA, 1990); now in *Canons and Contexts* (New York: Oxford University Press, 1991).

4   See the message from Luca Codignola, posted on the electronic forum "Studiamericani," 18 November 2003. Codignola attacked Kaplan's views as illiberal and her choice to express them on the occasion of an invited scholarly lecture as professionally unethical and a sign of intellectual imperialism; Sergio Perosa supported his arguments in a post sent on November 19. Several other members of the list responded both on the same day and in the days that followed, all defending both the actual political positions upheld in Amy Kaplan's speech and, more generally, her right to express them in her lecture.

5   Cesare Pavese (1908–50) graduated with a dissertation on Walt Whitman and worked as a teacher and translator; from 1933 he collaborated with anti-Fascist publisher Giulio Einaudi, and was convicted and sentenced to confinement for political reasons. Among his books are *Il carcere, Verrà la morte e avrà i tuoi occhi, Il compagno, La casa in collina, La bella estate, La luna e i falò, Dialoghi con Leucò* (all published between 1936 and 1950 to great critical acclaim). He committed suicide in 1950. Elio Vittorini (1908–1966), after being an anarchist and then a left-wing Fascist, became a communist, was arrested in 1943 as an anti-Fascist, and then participated in the Resistenza. He worked as proof-reader and translator, and began writing in the 1930s; *Conversazione in Sicilia* is of 1938–9 (published in book form in 1941), *Uomini e no* was written during the Resistenza and published in 1945. After the war he briefly directed *L'Unità* (the daily newspaper of the Italian Communist Party), founded *Il Politecnico* (where he famously polemicized with Mario Alicata and Palmiro Togliatti over the freedom of the intellectual from party directives), and directed an innovative series for Einaudi ("I Gettoni"), acting as talent scout for many important writers and exerting a decisive influence over post-war Italian literature. In 1959 he founded *Il Menabò* with Italo Calvino, and in 1960 began directing Mondadori's series "la Medusa," where several important American and European writers were first published, as well as other innovative series with both Mondadori ("Nuovi Scrittori Stranieri") and Einaudi ("Nuovo Politecnico").

6   On the American myth in Italian culture, among many other studies see Vito Amoruso, "Cecchi, Vittorini, Pavese e la letteratura americana," *Studi Americani* 6 (1960): 9–71; Dominique Fernandez, *Il mito dell'America negli intellettuali italiani dal 1930 al 1950* (Caltanissetta and Rome: Sciascia, 1969); Claudio Gorlier, "La situazione del romanzo americano in Italia" and Agostino Lombardo, "L'America e la cultura letteraria italiana," both in Alfredo Rizzardi, ed., *L'America e la cultura letteraria italiana* (Bologna: CLUEB, 1981).

7   Cesare Pavese, "Richard Wright. Sono finiti i tempi in cui scoprivamo l'America" [1947], in *La letteratura americana e altri saggi* (Milan: Il Saggiatore, 1971; original ed.,

Torino: Einaudi, 1962), 183. Here as elsewhere, translations from Italian are mine.

8   C. Pavese, "Ieri e oggi" [1947], in *La letteratura americana e altri saggi*, 187.

9   C. Pavese, "Maturità americana" [1946], in *La letteratura americana e altri saggi*, 174.

10   Giaime Pintor, "Americana," in *Il sangue dell'Europa (1939–1943)*, ed. Valentino Gerratana (Turin: Einaudi, 1950), 213. A less internationally renowned figure than Pavese and Vittorini, due to his premature death in 1943 (at the age of 24, while organizing partisan resistance), Pintor was an extraordinarily perceptive critic and translator of German literature, as well as a committed intellectual contributing to the creation of Einaudi, the anti-Fascist publishing house where both Pavese and Vittorini would work as editors, translators, and cultural organizers. As his enthusiastic endorsement of Vittorini's *Americana* shows, he shared a view of America as a symbolic place of moral regeneration for the decadent and corrupt Europe that had produced Nazism and Fascism.

11   The American Studies Association was established in 1951; *American Quarterly* had begun its publications in 1949. Although, as Gene Wise argued, as a "movement" American Studies had come into existence in the late 1920s with Parrington's *Main Currents in American Thought* (1927), the institutional foundations of the field were not secure until the early 1940s. See Gene Wise, "'Paradigm Dramas' in American Studies: A Cultural and Institutional History of the Movement," *American Quarterly* 31:3 (1979); now in Lucy Maddox, ed., *Locating American Studies. The Evolution of a Discipline* (Baltimore and London: The Johns Hopkins University Press, 1999).

12   Michael Denning, *The Cultural Front* (New York and London: Verso, 1996).

13   C. Pavese, "Ieri e oggi" [1947], in *La letteratura americana e altri saggi*, 189.

14   Emilio Cecchi (1884–1966) was one of the most prominent men of letters and essay writers in Italian culture between the two World Wars. On his attitude to American literature see the essays by Amoruso and by Lombardo cited above, as well as Agostino Lombardo, "Cecchi e gli scrittori angloamericani," in Roberto Fedi, ed., *Emilio Cecchi oggi. Atti del convegno Firenze 28–29 aprile 1979* (Florence: Vallecchi, 1981): 86–134.

15   Elio Vittorini, *Diario in pubblico (1929–1956)* (Milan: Bompiani, 1957), 116.

16   Elio Vittorini, ed., *Americana. Raccolta di narratori. Dalle origini ai nostri giorni*, with an introduction by Emilio Cecchi (Milan: Bompiani, 1942). Excerpts from Vittorini's "Breve storia della letteratura americana" (A short history of American literature) are included in the volume as short introductions to the individual sections, along with excerpts from other authors. Vittorini's original introduction to the volume can be found in its entirety in *Diario in pubblico (1929–1956)*.

17 Emilio Cecchi, Introduzione, in *Americana*.

18 C. Pavese, "Richard Wright. Sono finiti i tempi in cui scoprivamo l'America," 183, 190.

19 Less canonical but extremely influential on Italian American Studies and more generally on Italian counterculture was Leslie Fiedler's *Love and Death in the American Novel* (1960), whose timely Italian translation is dated 1963. Fiedler was a regular visitor in Rome starting from 1952.

20 To name but a few examples: as early as 1966 Alessandro Portelli (who had graduated in American literature from Rome university with a dissertation on Woody Guthrie, later published in book form) started editing and translating collections of folk songs and Black Power songs, and starting from the early 1970s he published several important essays and books on African American literature and culture as well as on popular music and other noncanonical subjects. Bruno Cartosio started his investigations into the social history of African American and working class movements in the 1960s. Beniamino Placido published his parallel analysis of *Benito Cereno* and *Uncle Tom's Cabin* in the context of an investigation of the treatment of slavery and of the literary power and political impact of sentimental literature in 1973, that is, eight years before Jane Tompkins's "Sentimental Power." Paola Ludovici and Giorgio Mariani studied, translated, and collected Native American texts, both literary and political, through the 1970s; and the list might go on. A group of scholars and critics recently went over the experience of those years in micro-historical forms, that is, using their own intellectual autobiographies as fragments of a collective history, at a meeting organized by Mario Corona and held at Università di Bergamo (April 16, 2003), tellingly titled "Gli anni della svolta: dal vecchio al nuovo canone negli studi nordamericani" [The years of the turning point: from the old to the new canon in North-American studies].

21 As I write, December 2004, the Ministry of Education has not yet found its way to settling an age-long dispute over whether graduates in American literature are entitled to teach English in schools, or whether this should be a privilege reserved for those who have studied the Queen's variety of the language. The dispute has been going on for over a decade in spite of repeated official requests from the Italian American Studies Association and from the US Department of State, as well as op-eds and articles in newspapers. The Ministry's position would be ludicrous in its evident untenability on linguistic, cultural, sociological, and historical grounds alike, were it not a symptomatic manifestation not just of the academic entrenchment and enduring domination of the corporation of English literature scholars – bent on keeping for their field whatever privileges in terms of posts and funding the dwindling resources allotted to the Italian university system still afford – but of a lasting prejudice against American culture as less aesthetically valid, less uplifting, less formative than its British counterpart.

22 The story, of course, might go on. American Studies in Italy has certainly not disappeared after the oppositional wave of the 1960s and 1970s; quite the reverse, it has gained an indisputable academic standing in spite of all opposition, and it has grown in depth, scope, and number of practitioners, creating an increasing number of international connections as the younger generations of scholars tend to become more internationalized, to spend more time studying and doing research at US universities, and to address an international audience in their scholarly work. A phenomenon that is not without its drawbacks and shadowy implications, as I will try to argue.

23 John Carlos Rowe raises this question in "Postnationalism, Globalism, and the New American Studies," *Cultural Critique* 40 (Fall 1998); now in Pease and Wiegman, eds., *The Futures of American Studies*.

24 This is of course to some extent an oversimplification, which takes no account of the efforts of those scholars from within the US, like Michael Denning or George Lipsitz, that have complicated this pattern by referring the successive developments in American Studies to coeval social movements. It is no accident, as I will try to show, that such sobering moves come from scholars whose explicit effort is to connect American Studies with what is "outside" it.

25 Janice Radway, "What's in a Name? Presidential Address to the American Studies Association, 20 November, 1998," *American Quarterly* 51:1 (1999): 1–32, here 10.

26 See the impressive frequence of expressions such as "should," "must," "might," etc. referring to the present and future tasks of the discipline in all discussions of its perspectives.

27 That the search for a unified national narrative lies at the very foundation of American exceptionalism is of course David W. Noble's thesis in *The End of American History* (Minneapolis: University of Minnesota Press, 1985).

28 Such are only a few of the tasks advocated by some of the most prominent and vocal Americanists over the last decade, at least since the forum on "American Literary History: The Next Century" at the 1994 MLA Convention (published in *American Literature* 67:4 [December 1995]) and the publication, in the same year, of such landmarks in the debate as the two volumes edited by Donald E. Pease, *National Identities and Post-Americanist Narratives* and *Revisionary Interventions into the Americanist Canon* (Durham and London: Duke University Press), and the thoughtful review essay by Carolyn Porter, "What We Know That We Don't Know: Remapping American Literary Studies," *American Literary History* 6:3 (Fall 1994): 467–526. Such calls have variously echoed in the American Studies debate, with different emphases depending on the individual positions and interests of individual scholars. The quotation is from Amy Kaplan, "The tenacious grasp of American exceptionalism. A response to Djelal Kadir, 'Defending America against its devotees'," *Comparative American Studies* 2:2 (2004): 153–9, here 158.

29 Let me note in passing that the very definition of "American Studies" for scholarly work done outside the United States is to a remarkable extent misleading: like most literary scholars studying American literature in Europe, I specialize in the sort of critical pursuits that in the States would prevalently belong in English Departments rather than in American Studies ones, and only become an "American Studies" scholar in translation, for lack of a better definition, since to us, "English" unequivocally denotes *British*. In spite of the disciplinary history which, as I recalled above, has made us all more or less attentive to the social and political implications of literature and criticism, Italian (as well as most European) scholars studying the literature, history, and culture of the United States seldom adopt the kind of concern with culture as an integrated manifestation of national identity that is typical of the ideology and practice of American Studies in the sense prevalent in the United States.

30 Rob Wilson and Wimal Dissanayake, "Introduction: Tracking the Global/Local," in Rob Wilson and Wimal Dissanayake, eds., *Global/Local. Cultural Production and the Transnational Imaginary* (Durham and London: Duke University Press, 1996): 6; Masao Miyoshi, "A Borderless World? From Colonialism to Transnationalism and the Decline of the Nation-State," in Wilson and Dissanayake, eds., *Global/Local*, 91. Miyoshi's essay, originally published in *Critical Inquiry* 19 (Summer 1993), is quite uncompromising in diagnosing some of the current academic preoccupations as "suspiciously like another alibi to conceal the actuality of global politics" and strikingly prophetic – in view of the present state of international politics – in its contention that "colonialism is even more active now in the form of transnational corporatism" (79).

31 George Lipsitz, *American Studies in a Moment of Danger* (Minneapolis and London: University of Minnesota Press, 2001): XVI.

32 John Carlos Rowe, "Postnationalism, Globalism, and the New American Studies," in Pease and Wiegman, eds., *The Futures of American Studies*, 173 (originally published in *Cultural Critique* 40 [Fall 1998]).

33 According to George Lipsitz's dialectical argument, each successive stage of American Studies from the 1940s onwards has been marked both by its link to coeval social movements and by the legacy of the social and political contradictions the previous movements had left unsolved, which exploded at a later stage. Following in his steps, one might perhaps suggest that the deconstruction of American identity as unified, static and homogeneous that served progressive functions in the 1970s and 1980s, by its prevalent focus on internal policies rather than international power relations and transnational dynamics of exploitation, opened the way to its later potential to obfuscate the actual role of the United States *qua* nation-state at home and abroad. This, however, is a point that would need to

be explored in detail, expanded, and historically supported before being advanced as an argument.

34 A significant outcome of this perceived need to re-establish comparative literature on new foundations is the Bernheimer Report, commissioned by the American Comparative Literature Association in 1992 to establish the new objects and methods of comparative literature for the decade. The report was the fruit of the joint work of a committee including, along with Bernheimer, Jonathan Arac, Marianne Hirsch, Ann Rosalind Jones, Arnold Krupat, Ronald Judy, Dominick LaCapra, Sylvia Molloy, Steve Nichols, and Sara Suleri. See Charles Bernheimer, "Introduction. The Anxieties of Comparison," in Charles Bernheimer, ed., *Comparative Literature in the Age of Multiculturalism* (Baltimore and London: The Johns Hopkins University Press, 1995). Other recent interventions in this debate are Emory Elliott, Louis Freitas Caton, and Jeffrey Rhyne, eds., *Aesthetics in a Multicultural Age* (New York: Oxford University Press, 2002) and David Damrosch, *What Is World Literature?* (Princeton and Oxford: Princeton University Press, 2003). The 2004 report of the American Comparative Literature Association is now in the process of being produced by a committee headed by Haun Saussy and including Emily Apter, Djelal Kadir, Steven Ungar, Christopher Braider, David Damrosch, David Ferris, Gail Finney, Caroline Eckhardt, Fedwa Malti-Douglas, Françoise Lionnet, and Roland Greene. Its drafts may be consulted on the ACLA website, and show a significant presence of some of the concerns I have discussed so far.

35 Franco Moretti, "Conjectures on World Literature," *New Left Review*, 1 (January–February 2000): 54–68; now in Christopher Prendergast, ed., *Debating World Literature* (London: Verso, 2004), a volume that collects many responses to Moretti's essay, including the ones I will quote below.

36 See Christopher Prendergast, "Negotiating World Literature," *New Left Review* 8 (March–April 2001), 100–21; Efraín Kristal, "Considering Coldly . . . ," *New Left Review* 15 (May–June 2002), 61–74; Jonathan Arac, "Anglo-Globalism?," *New Left Review* 16 (July–August 2002), 35–45, all in the volume cited above. Moretti's response to his critics has been published as "More Conjectures," *New Left Review*, 20 (March–April 2003), 73–81.

37 Gayatri Chakravorty Spivak, *Death of a Discipline* (New York: Columbia University Press, 2003), 6.

38 Another likely candidate might of course be the United Kingdom: in a much-quoted study by the Chinese Academy of Sciences, Cambridge (UK) ranks fifth in the list of the best research universities in the world, after Harvard, Stanford, Caltech, and Berkeley. The diminishing resources allocated on research and education throughout the European Union, however, make me doubt that any European scholar can easily fulfill the structural conditions

required for Moretti's world scholar from an institutional position within most European countries, however "First-World" these may be in other respects.

39 In his enthusiasm over the potentialities opened by the world literary system, Moretti seems to have forgotten that the other nineteenth-century prophet of world literature, Karl Marx, even while echoing Goethe and extolling at his most optimistic the great progressive achievements of the bourgeoisie, never forgot to point out that these were made possible by "its exploitation of the world market": "The bourgeoisie has through its exploitation of the world market given a cosmopolitan character to production and consumption in every country. To the great chagrin of Reactionists, it has drawn from under the feet of industry the national ground on which it stood. All old-established national industries have been destroyed or are daily being destroyed. They are dislodged by new industries, whose introduction becomes a life and death question for all civilised nations, by industries that no longer work up indigenous raw material, but raw material drawn from the remotest zones; industries whose products are consumed, not only at home, but in every quarter of the globe. In place of the old wants, satisfied by the productions of the country, we find new wants, requiring for their satisfaction the products of distant lands and climes. In place of the old local and national seclusion and self-sufficiency, we have intercourse in every direction, universal inter-dependence of nations. And as in material, so also in intellectual production. The intellectual creations of individual nations become common property. National one-sidedness and narrow-mindedness become more and more impossible, and from the numerous national and local literatures, there arises a world literature." Karl Marx, *Manifesto of the Communist Party* (1848), part I.

40 See Donna J. Haraway, "Situated Knowledges: The Science Question in Feminism and the Privilege of Partial Perspective," in *Simians, Cyborgs, and Women. The Reinvention of Nature* (London: Free Association Books, 1991); originally published in *Feminist Studies*, 14:3 (1988). Even though Moretti's essay displays no marks gendering the world system critic as male, his whole argument is a fine example of the patriarchal philosophical tradition of the West as described by Susan Bordo in "Feminism, Postmodernism, and Gender-Scepticism," in Linda J. Nicholson, ed., *Feminism/Postmodernism* (New York and London: Routledge, 1990).

41 As my previous discussion should have made clear, I believe that theory, with its relentless interrogation of the foundations of all literary, cultural and critical discourses, still has much to teach American Studies. While theory has undoubtedly been one of the main impulses behind the renewal of the field, I would contend that its intellectual potential has been left partly unexplored, its contribution too hurriedly conflated with the more urgent political needs that have driven the reconfiguring of American Studies over the last two decades. This point, however, would need a far more exhaustive treatment than the scope of this essay possibly allows.

42 Stephen Greenblatt, "Racial Memory and Literary History," *PMLA* 116:1 (January 2001): 48–63, here 49.

43 Let me quote again Miyoshi's remark in its entirety: "Are the intellectuals of the world willing to participate in transnational corporatism and be its apologists? How to situate oneself in this neo-Daniel Bell configuration of transnational power and culture without being trapped by a dead-end nativism seems to be the most important question that faces every critic and theorist the world over at this moment" (91).

44 Teresa de Lauretis, "The Technology of Gender," in *Technologies of Gender. Essays on Theory, Film, and Fiction* (Bloomington: Indiana University Press), 1987, 3.

45 Louis Althusser, *Lenin and Philosophy and Other Essays*, tr. Ben Brewster (New York: Monthly Review Press, 2001), 118.

46 At least, this is for me the teaching of my experience as American Literature professor in the Comparative Studies program of Università di Napoli "L'Orientale," a program that is atypical in more than one sense: as a comparative program uncharacteristically based not on European languages and literatures but on two mandatory majors in languages, literatures and cultures from two different areas of the world (one from the West and one from either Asia or Africa); as a program involving Western languages launched within a university traditionally specializing in the study of Asian and African cultures; and as a rather popular and successful pedagogical venture managing to flourish within a conservative national academe that still tends to envisage everything that is not western-European in terms of exoticism, orientalism, or extreme scholarly specialization. This combination of multiple positionings, all in some ways "against the grain," makes for a slightly edgy but extremely stimulating environment, where graduates do not just reproduce the specialized competence in an individual field possessed by each of their teachers, but acquire through their twofold education a kind of cross-cultural critical outlook that goes beyond anything they have been separately taught. Judging from its average results, this kind of "bipolarity" (quoting the apt self-definition offered by one of my students) has been intellectually fruitful; it certainly has helped effect a (more or less willing) decentering of each discipline's pretensions.

47 Emily Apter, "Global *Translatio*: The 'Invention' of Comparative Literature, Istanbul, 1933," *Critical Inquiry*, 29 (Winter 2003), 253–81.

48 As Said synthetically put it in an interview with Jennifer Wicke and Michael Sprinker, his attempt as regards Eric Auerbach and the other philologists to whom he devoted his attention throughout his work was to "expose the lapses and the ethnocentric soft spots" but also "to extend

their work into areas that interest me. In other words, I'm not exactly answering them, but I'm extending their work into areas they avoid by adopting some of their modes of examination, their attention to texts, their *care*, which I think is the central factor here. It's a kind of scrupulosity, which I suppose you could call humanism. If you pare down that label and relieve it of the unpleasantly triumphalistic freight that is carried with it, you are left with something that I think is very much worth saving." Edward W. Said, "Criticism and the Art of Politics," in Michael Sprinker, ed., *Edward Said: A Critical Reader* (Oxford: Blackwell, 1992); now in Gauri Viswanathan, ed., *Power, Politics, and Culture. Interviews with Edward W. Said* (New York: Vintage Books, 2001), 127–8. On the question of Said's "secular criticism" and its relation to philology, to progressive politics, and to the theory and practice of exile and minority status, see Tim Brennan, "Places of Mind, Occupied Lands: Edward Said and Philology," in Michael Sprinker, ed., *Edward Said: A Critical Reader*; Bruce Robbins, "Secularism, Elitism, Progress, and Other Transgressions: On Edward Said's 'Voyage In,'" in Keith Ansell-Pearson, Benita Parry, and Judith Squires, eds., *Cultural Readings of Imperialism: Edward Said and the Gravity of History* (New York: St. Martin's, 1997); Aamir R. Mufti, "Auerbach in Istanbul: Edward Said, Secular Criticism, and the Question of Minority Culture," *Critical Inquiry* 25:1 (Autumn 1998): 95–125.

49   Hans Ulrich Gumbrecht, *The Powers of Philology. Dynamics of Textual Scholarship* (Urbana and Chicago: University of Illinois Press, 2003), 7.

Index

CPSIA information can be obtained
at www.ICGtesting.com
Printed in the USA
FSHW022206060821
83703FS